The Thirty Years War

PETER H. WILSON

The Thirty Years War
Europe's Tragedy

The Belknap Press of
Harvard University Press
Cambridge, Massachusetts

Printed in the United States of America

First Published 2009 by the Penguin Group
Penguin Books Ltd, 80 Strand, London wc2r orl, England

First Harvard University Press paperback edition, 2011

Library of Congress Cataloging-in-Publication Data

Wilson, Peter H. (Peter Hamish)
The Thirty Years War : Europe's tragedy / Peter H. Wilson.
p.   cm.
Includes bibliographical references and index.
ISBN 978-0-674-03634-5 (cloth : alk. paper)
ISBN 978-0-674-06231-3 (pbk.)
1. Thirty Years' War, 1918–1648.   2. Europe—History, Military—1492–1648.   I. Title
D258.W55   2009
940.2'4–dc22
2009011266

For my family

Contents

PART THREE

Aftermath

List of Illustrations

Photographic acknowledgements are given in parentheses. Every effort has been made to contact all copyright holders. The Publishers will be happy to make good in future editions of this book any errors or omissions brought to their attention.

List of Maps and Battle Plans

Maps

Battle Plans

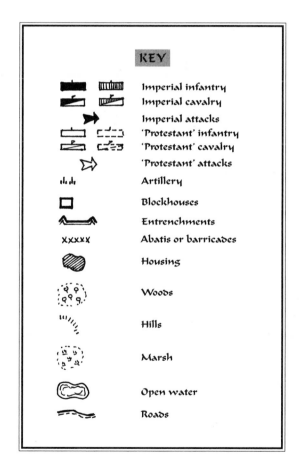

List of Tables

Note on Form

Place names are given in the form most commonly used in English-language writing. For east Central European locations, this tends to be the German version. The current name is given in parenthesis at the first mention. Individuals are identified in the text using their first name and the title by which they are best known. Full names and titles, along with dates of birth and death (where known) are given for each person in the index. Emperor Ferdinand II's general has become known as Wallenstein since Schiller's drama trilogy at the end of the eighteenth century. This version has entrenched itself in English writing and will be used here rather than the Czech original, Waldstein. In contemporary documents, he generally appears as 'the Friedländer' after his duchy of Friedland. Though anachronistic, the term 'Britain' will be used for the lands of the Stuart monarchy in preference to the still more misleading 'England', unless it is intended to refer to the individual kingdoms or principalities. All dates are given in the New Style according to the Gregorian calendar introduced into the Catholic parts of Europe and the Holy Roman Empire around 1582. This was ten days ahead of the Julian calendar retained by Protestant Germans generally until 1700.

The Habsburg Family Tree 1500–1665

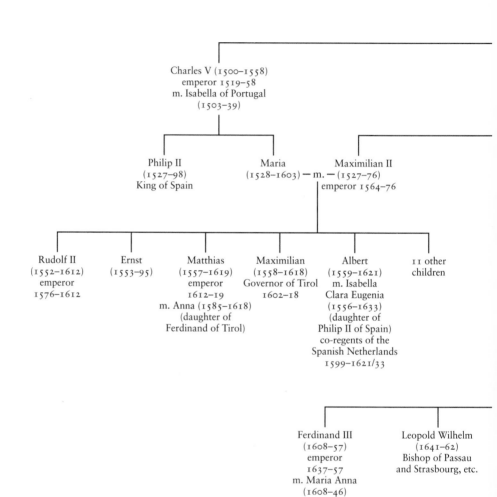

Charles V (1500–1558)
emperor 1519–58
m. Isabella of Portugal
(1503–39)

Philip II
(1527–98)
King of Spain

Maria
(1528–1603) — m. — (1527–76)

Maximilian II
emperor 1564–76

Rudolf II
(1552–1612)
emperor
1576–1612

Ernst
(1553–95)

Matthias
(1557–1619)
emperor
1612–19
m. Anna (1585–1618)
(daughter of
Ferdinand of Tirol)

Maximilian
(1558–1618)
Governor of Tirol
1602–18

Albert
(1559–1621)
m. Isabella
Clara Eugenia
(1556–1633)
(daughter of
Philip II of Spain)
co-regents of the
Spanish Netherlands
1599–1621/33

11 other
children

Ferdinand III
(1608–57)
emperor
1637–57
m. Maria Anna
(1608–46)

Leopold Wilhelm
(1641–62)
Bishop of Passau
and Strasbourg, etc.

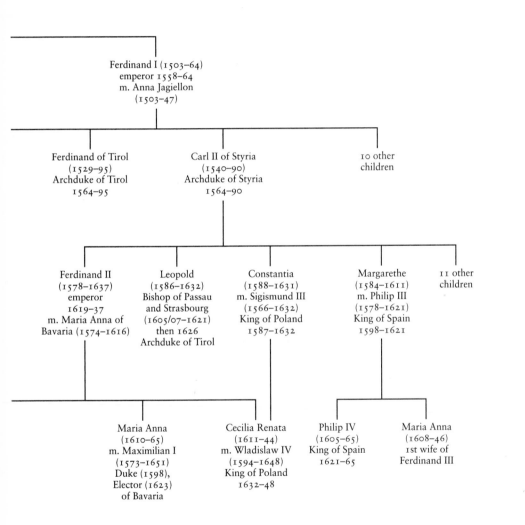

Ferdinand I (1503–64)
emperor 1558–64
m. Anna Jagiellon
(1503–47)

Ferdinand of Tirol
(1529–95)
Archduke of Tirol
1564–95

Carl II of Styria
(1540–90)
Archduke of Styria
1564–90

10 other
children

Ferdinand II
(1578–1637)
emperor
1619–37
m. Maria Anna of
Bavaria (1574–1616)

Leopold
(1586–1632)
Bishop of Passau
and Strasbourg
(1605/07–1621)
then 1626
Archduke of Tirol

Constantia
(1588–1631)
m. Sigismund III
(1566–1632)
King of Poland
1587–1632

Margarethe
(1584–1611)
m. Philip III
(1578–1621)
King of Spain
1598–1621

11 other
children

Maria Anna
(1610–65)
m. Maximilian I
(1573–1651)
Duke (1598),
Elector (1623)
of Bavaria

Cecilia Renata
(1611–44)
m. Wladislaw IV
(1594–1648)
King of Poland
1632–48

Philip IV
(1605–65)
King of Spain
1621–65

Maria Anna
(1608–46)
1st wife of
Ferdinand III

CENTRAL EUROPE, 1618

Boundary of the Holy Roman Empire
Boundaries between empires, kingdoms, etc., outside the Holy Roman Empire
Approximate boundaries of some territories within the Holy Roman Empire

North Sea

ENGLAND

DENMARK

Kiel

HOLSTEIN

Segeberg

Lübeck

Glückstadt

Hamburg

R. Elbe

EAST FRIESLAND

Bremen

Lüneberg

Dömin

R. Ems

Amsterdam

The Hague

HOLLAND

UNITED PROVINCES

Osnabrück

Minden

Hannover

BRUNSWICK

Hildesheim

Wolfenbüttel

Münster

Stadtlohn

Hameln

Lutter

Verden

ZEELAND

Breda

Bergen-op-Zoom

Wesel

Paderborn

WESTPHALIA

R. Leine

Göttingen

Calais

Dunkirk

Antwerp

Venloo

Roermond

Mühlhausen

FLANDERS

Brussels

Maestricht

Jülich

Cologne

R. Meuse

Erfurt

Lens

SPANISH NETHER-LANDS

BRABANT

Liège

Aachen

HESSE

Arnstadt

Cambrai

Fleurus

Ehrenbreitstein

NASSAU

THURINGIA

Corbie

Rocroy

Bacharach

Hochst

Frankfort-on-the-Main

Hanau

Compiègne

R. Oise

R. Meuse

Treves

R. Mosel

Zimmern

Kreuznach

Mainz

Aschaffenburg

Würzburg

R. Seine

Senlis

Luxembourg

Oppenheim

Worms

Darmstadt

FRANCONIA

Paris

R. Marne

Thionville

Frankenthal

Mannheim

Mergentheim

Verdun

Metz

Zweibrücken

RHENISH PALATINATE

Heidelberg

Rothenburg

Fürth

Speier

Germersheim

Wimpfen

Nuremberg

R. Seine

Toul

Moyenvic

Landau

Phillipsburg

Heilbronn

Nancy

Hagenau

ALSACE

Stuttgart

Nördlingen

Strasbourg

WÜRTTEMBERG

Allerheim

Donauwörth

Rain

LORRAINE

Benfeld

Tübingen

Zusmarshausen

Wittenweier

Ulm

Augsburg

Rottweil

SWABIA

Breisach

Tuttlingen

FRANCE

Belfort

Sennheim

Hohentweil

Überlingen

Kempten

Basel

Rheinfelden

L. Constance

FRANCHE-COMTÉ

Laufenburg

Lindau

R. Rhine

Besançon

Säckingen

Bregenz

Bern

SWISS CONFEDERATION

Chur

LES GRISONS

TYR

R. Saône

L. Geneva

Val Telline

L. Como

REPUBLIC VE

SAVOY

MILAN

R. Rhône

Susa

Casale

MANTUA

R. Po

Turin

Note on Currencies

Currency	Equivalent
Escudo (Spain)	1.1 ducats (Spain, from 1620), or 2.5 fl. (Dutch)
Ducat (Spain)	2.35 fl. (Dutch), or 1.4 fl. (German)
Ducat (Naples)	0.7 ducat (Spain)
Florin (German)	1.7 fl. (Dutch)
Livre (French)	initially 0.7 fl. (German); 0.5 fl. after 1640
Pound sterling	4.2–4.8 talers
Riksdaler (Denmark/Sweden)	1–1.5 fl. (German)
Taler (Empire)	1.5 fl. (German), or 2.5 fl. (Dutch)

It is difficult to give modern equivalents to seventeenth-century currency. As a guide to value, 7.5–10 florins would buy enough grain to feed a person for a whole year in 1618.

Preface

The history of the Thirty Years War is rich in specialist studies, but poor in general accounts. Few authors provide more than short overviews intended for students. It is easy to see why. To cover all aspects would require knowledge of at least fourteen European languages, while there are sufficient archival records to occupy many lifetimes of research. Even the printed material runs to millions of pages; there are over 4,000 titles just on the Peace of Westphalia that concluded the conflict. The sheer volume of evidence has affected how previous histories have been written. Some cut through the detail by fitting the war into broader explanations of Europe's transition to modernity. Others give more scope to personalities and events but often signs of fatigue set in as the author approaches the mid-1630s. By then the heroes and villains giving life to the opening phases were largely dead, replaced by other figures ignored by posterity. There is a rush to wrap up the story and the last thirteen years are compressed into a quarter or less of the text, much of which is devoted to discussing the peace and aftermath.

The present work seeks to redress this through a more even coverage across the entire time span. Some of the distinctive features of this approach are set out in the introductory chapter. The most important is to view the war on its own terms as a struggle over the political and religious order of Central Europe, rather than submerging it within a general account of European conflict throughout the first half of the seventeenth century. While this simplifies some aspects, it also directs attention to the war's origins in the complex situation in the Holy Roman Empire during the later sixteenth century. The task of the first part of the book is to explain this and place it in the wider European context. The second part follows the unfolding tragedy roughly chronologically, paying particular regard to why peace-making efforts failed before the mid-1640s. The final part examines the war's political, economic, social and cultural impact and longer-term significance. Throughout, structural explanations have been combined with an emphasis on agency and contingency, giving more space than customary to minor as well as more prominent participants. Referencing is selective, excluding much of the older material used in favour of recent works that are more accessible for most readers and provide a useful guide to the specialist literature.

It is a great pleasure to acknowledge the support of the Arts and Humanities Research Council for a Research Leave Award in 2007–8 that enabled this book to be completed. I have also benefited from a supportive research environment during my time at the University of Sunderland, as well as a warm welcome by the History Department at Hull where the final sections were written. Leopold Auer and the staff of the Haus-, Hof- und Staatsarchiv Vienna provided valuable assistance during my all-too-brief visit in 2006. I am grateful to Scott Dixon, Robert Evans, Ralph Morrison and Neil Rennoldson for their help in locating obscure works, and especially to Kacper Rekawek for assisting with Polish-language material. Clarissa Campbell Orr, Tryntje Helfferich, Michael Kaiser, Maureen Meikle, Géza Pálffy and Ciro Paoletti all generously shared their knowledge on numerous points of detail. I am particularly indebted to Trevor Johnson for providing a pre-publication version of his book on Bavarian policy. Sadly, his sudden death in 2007 means I am no longer able to reciprocate.

Simon Winder's encouragement sustained my faith that the book would eventually be completed, while his editorial advice greatly improved its clarity. Charlotte Ridings' careful copyediting rooted out inconsistency and error, and Cecilia Mackay transformed my wish-list of illustrations into reality.

Eliane, Alec, Tom and Nina patiently tolerated my immersion in the past and, as usual, have provided the greatest assistance and inspiration. This book is dedicated to them with love.

PART ONE

Beginnings

I

Introduction

THREE MEN AND A WINDOW

Shortly after 9 a.m. on Wednesday 23 May 1618, Vilém Slavata found himself hanging from a window of the Hradschin castle in Prague. This was not a predicament the 46-year-old aristocrat had encountered before. As president of the Bohemian treasury and a supreme court judge, he was a senior figure in the royal government with a distinguished career in the service of the ruling Habsburg dynasty. Thanks to his marriage to the heiress Lucia Ottilia, he was also one of the richest men in the entire kingdom.

Moments before, his equally distinguished colleague, Jaroslav Borita von Martinitz, had been seized by five armed men. Martinitz's pleas to be allowed a confessor had merely enraged his assailants who flung him unceremoniously headfirst from the same window from which Slavata now clung, dangling precariously above the seventeen-metre drop to the ditch below. Angry voices in the room indicated no prospect of human help. At that moment, Slavata felt the sharp cut of metal as someone smacked a sword hilt against his fingers. The pain became too much; his grip loosened and he plummeted downward, cracking the back of his head open on the sill of a lower window. As he disappeared into the void, his attackers noticed his secretary, Philipp Fabricius, his arms clutched around one of the less intimidating members of the gang. Ignoring his pleas for mercy, he was summarily despatched out of the window to share his master's fate.

That, however, turned out other than intended. While Slavata landed squarely at the bottom of the ditch, Martinitz had fallen further up. He now slithered down to help his friend, injuring himself on the way down with his own sword that his attackers had neglected to unbuckle. Shots rang out from the window above, but Martinitz managed to help the dazed Slavata to his feet and together they escaped to the nearby Lobkowitz palace, home of the Bohemian chancellor who had been absent from their disrupted meeting. Two men were sent to finish them off, but Lobkowitz's wife, Polyxena, bolted the door and eventually persuaded them to go away. Martinitz fled across the frontier to Bavaria the next day, but Slavata's injuries prevented him from leaving immediately and he was forced to hide. Fabricius, who, amazingly, had landed on his feet, meanwhile raced to Vienna, heart of the Habsburg monarchy and political centre of the Holy Roman Empire, to alert the emperor.[1]

This event has entered history as the Defenestration of Prague that triggered the Bohemian Revolt, the commonly accepted start of the Thirty Years War that claimed eight million lives and transformed the political and religious map of Europe. The war occupies a place in German and Czech history similar to that of the civil wars in Britain, Spain and the United States of America, or the revolutions in France and Russia: a defining moment of national trauma that shaped how a country regards itself and its place in the world. The difficulty for later generations in coming to terms with the scale of the devastation has been compared to the problem of historicizing the Holocaust.[2] For most Germans, the war came to symbolize national humiliation, retarding political, economic and social development and condemning their country to two centuries of internal division and international impotence.

INTERPRETATIONS

This interpretation originated in a much later defeat that both revived interest in the Thirty Years War and transformed how it was regarded. For those who lived through it, and their children, the war retained the immediacy of contemporary events. From the outset, the conflict attracted wide interest across Europe, accelerating the early seventeenth-century 'media revolution' that saw the birth of the modern newspaper (see Chapter 23). The concluding Peace of Westphalia was an international bestseller, running through at least thirty editions within a year. Interest gradually dissipated towards the end of the seventeenth century as Central Europe entered another thirty years of war, mainly against France and the Ottoman Turks. The memory of the earlier conflict continued to be kept alive, however, in annual festivities celebrating the Peace of Westphalia, as well as through a relatively small number of books intended for a popular market. Like the public ceremonies, these works presented a broadly positive interpretation of the war's outcome in preserving the liberties of Protestant Germans and strengthening the imperial constitution.[3]

The view darkened dramatically in the wake of the French Revolution and Napoleon's dismemberment of the Holy Roman Empire. The Austro-Prussian counter-attack against Revolutionary France in 1792 dragged Germans into another cycle of invasion, defeat, political upheaval and devastation. These experiences coincided with new intellectual and cultural currents associated with Romanticism and the literary 'Storm and Stress' movement. Lurid tales of mass death, rape and torture from the Thirty Years War had an immediate resonance, while the dramatic lives of individuals like the imperial general Wallenstein, or Sweden's King Gustavus Adolphus, assumed new meaning through comparison with Napoleon and other contemporary figures. Friedrich Schiller, the leading Storm and Stress writer, found an eager audience when he published his history of the war in 1791, followed by his *Wallenstein* trilogy in 1797–9 which remains the equivalent of Shakespeare's history plays for the German-speaking world.

The Romantic reinterpretation of the war established three elements that still shape writing today. One is a Gothic preoccupation with death, decline and destruction, with Germany usually presented as the helpless victim of foreign aggression. Atrocity stories were culled from folk tales and contemporary fiction, notably *The Adventures of Simplicius Simplicissimus* by Grimmelshausen, which was rediscovered by the Romantic poets as the first authentic German novel and reissued in numerous 'improved' editions in the early nineteenth century.[4]

The reappearance of these tales in historical novels and paintings, as well as school history lessons, reinforced folk memory and family tradition, not only in Germany but in other countries affected by the fighting. The Thirty Years War became the benchmark to measure all later wars. The inhabitants of eastern France interpreted each subsequent invasion in the light of stories told about the Swedes and Croats who devastated their region in the 1630s. Soldiers fighting in the trenches along the eastern front of the First World War believed they were experiencing horrors not seen in three centuries. In his radio broadcast on 4 May 1945, Hitler's architect and armaments minister, Albert Speer, announced 'the destruction that has been inflicted on Germany can only be compared to that of the Thirty Years War. The decimation of our people through hunger and deprivation must not be allowed to reach the proportion of that epoch.' For this reason, he went on, Hitler's successor, Admiral Dönitz, had given the order to lay down arms. Public opinion surveys carried out in the 1960s revealed that Germans placed the Thirty Years War as their country's greatest disaster ahead of both world wars, the Holocaust and the Black Death.[5]

The impact of TV undoubtedly shifted this perception in the later twentieth century, especially through the dissemination of photographic images of more recent carnage. Nonetheless, even in the twenty-first century, German authors could assert that 'never before and also never since, not even during the horrors of the bombing during the Second World War, was the land so devastated and the people so tortured' as between 1618 and 1648.[6]

The second feature established by nineteenth-century historiography is the air of tragic inevitability. This is already apparent in Schiller's *Wallenstein*, which presents its central figure as an idealistic hero seeking peace but doomed to be murdered by his closest subordinates. The sense of unstoppable descent into chaos became general in writing after the Napoleonic Wars. The earlier positive reception for the Peace of Westphalia seemed inappropriate given the Empire's demise in 1806. Far from strengthening the imperial constitution, the war now seemed to have started its unravelling. More recent work reinforces this impression by shifting attention from personalities and constitutional failure to the long-term transition of the European economy from feudalism to capitalism that allegedly triggered the 'General Crisis of the Seventeenth Century'.[7] Others see the crisis as primarily political, environmental, or a combination of two or more factors. All versions, however, claim that underlying structural change stoked tensions that exploded into violent revolts and international conflict across Europe after 1600.[8]

Disagreements over the interpretation of these events in the Empire produced the third and probably most influential element in nineteenth-century German writing. The history of the Thirty Years War became enmeshed in the controversy surrounding German development after 1815. Two competing narratives emerged, each associated with one of the possible future Germanies. The 'Greater German' solution envisaged a loose federation that included Habsburg Austria as well as Hohenzollern Prussia and the 'third Germany' of the smaller states like Bavaria, Nassau and Württemberg. The 'Lesser German' alternative excluded Austria, largely because of the complications of incorporating the Habsburgs' other subjects in Italy and the Balkans. The Lesser German solution triumphed with Prussia's victory over Austria in 1866 and was consolidated with the defeat of France in 1870–1, establishing the Second Reich. Both visions for Germany's future had clear religious associations that were transposed onto the dispute over the country's past. The assumption that the Thirty Years War had been a religious conflict seemed so self-evident it was scarcely questioned.

It proved highly significant that the conflict over German statehood coincided with the birth of modern historical scholarship. Leopold von Ranke, the founder of the German empirical school, chose Wallenstein as the subject of the only full biography among his extensive publications. Ranke and his contemporaries made a real effort to study the surviving archival material, and much of their writing remains of great value. They profoundly influenced how historians in other countries interpreted the war, though each country also fitted the conflict into its own national narrative. French historians generally saw it through the lens of Richelieu and Mazarin, whose policies reputedly laid the foundations for the era of 'French preponderance' over the continent from the mid-seventeenth century to Napoleon. For Spanish writers, the theme was one of national decline as their country appeared to have overreached itself after 1618. The Swiss, Dutch and Portuguese associated the conflict with national independence, in each case from the Habsburg monarchy, while Danes and Swedes placed it in the context of their mutual rivalry over the Baltic. British interpretations remained closest to the German view, partly because the Stuart dynasty was associated with the elector Palatine's fateful decision to support the Bohemian rebels after the Defenestration. Many contemporaries saw this dynastic link in religious terms as the 'Protestant Cause', something that was echoed in the confessionalized writing of nineteenth-century Germans whose works provided the main sources for historians working in Britain.[9]

The idea of a religious war also fitted the broader Protestant narrative behind much nineteenth- and early twentieth-century historical writing that viewed events following the Reformation as liberation from the Catholic yoke. The same progressive trajectory could also be presented without a confessional bias as one of secularization and modernization. In one recent account, the war becomes the 'developmental and modernisation crisis' of European civilization; an 'inferno' that produced the modern world.[10]

It is a commonplace in historical writing and political science that the Westphalian settlement initiated the system of sovereign states that came to structure international relations around the globe. Military historians routinely credit key figures like Gustavus Adolphus as the 'fathers' of modern warfare. Politically, the war is believed to have fostered an era of absolute monarchy that dominated much of the continent until the French Revolution. The Europeans exported their quarrels to the Caribbean, Brazil, western Africa, Mozambique, Sri Lanka, Indonesia and the Atlantic and Pacific Oceans. The silver that paid the soldiers of Catholic Europe was mined in appalling conditions by Mexicans, Peruvians and Bolivians, many thousands of whom can be numbered among the war's victims. African slaves toiled in Brazil for Dutch sugar planters whose profits helped finance their republic's struggle with Spain, along with money from the Baltic grain trade and North Sea fisheries.

Interest in this wider dimension has come to dominate writing in English on the war that presents events in the Empire as part of a wider struggle of France, Sweden and English, Dutch and German Protestants against Spanish-Habsburg hegemony. The war in the Empire was either an adjunct of this larger conflict, or became part of it once Sweden and France intervened in Germany in the 1630s. Though one leading exponent dismisses the older German interpretation as 'parochial', this international war school remains strongly influenced by nineteenth-century historiography, presenting the outbreak as inevitable, and the conduct characterized by escalating violence and religious animosity.[11]

THE ARGUMENT

The Thirty Years War was an extremely complex event. The problems of interpretation derive from attempts to simplify it by overemphasizing one facet to the detriment of others. The present book seeks to reconnect the different elements through their common relationship to the imperial constitution. The war in the Empire was related to other conflicts, but nonetheless remained distinct. Observers even outside the Empire believed the struggle that began with the Bohemian Revolt continued until the Peace of Westphalia. They began talking of a five or six years war in the early 1620s and continued counting until its conclusion in 1648.[12]

Nonetheless, all Europe was affected and the course of the continent's history would have been very different had the war been avoided, or had another outcome. Of the major states, only Russia remained uninvolved. Poland and the Ottoman empire exercised a significant influence without engaging directly. The Dutch just managed to keep their own conflict with Spain separate, while trying to shape events in the Empire with limited indirect assistance. British engagement was more substantial, without that state ever becoming a formal belligerent. France and Spain intervened, but kept their participation separate from their own mutual struggle that had separate origins and continued another eleven years beyond 1648. Denmark and Sweden were full belligerents, though their intervention had little to do with the war's origins. Likewise, other neighbouring principalities like Savoy and Lorraine were drawn in, without losing sight of their own agendas and regional squabbles.

The second major distinction of the present argument is that it was not primarily a religious war.[13] Religion certainly provided a powerful focus for identity, but it had to compete with political, social, linguistic, gender and other distinctions. Most contemporary observers spoke of imperial, Bavarian, Swedish, or Bohemian troops, not Catholic or Protestant, which are anachronistic labels used for convenience since the nineteenth century to simplify accounts. The war was religious only to the extent that faith guided all early modern public policy and private behaviour. To understand the conflict's true relationship to the disputes within Christianity, we need to distinguish between militant and moderate believers. All were religious and we should not see moderates as necessarily more rational, reasonable or secular. The difference lay not in their religious zeal, but how they related faith and action. All were convinced their version of Christianity offered the only true path to salvation and the sole correct guide to justice, politics and daily life. Moderates, however, were more pragmatic, regarding the desired reunification of all Christians within a single church as a general, rather distant objective. Militants saw this goal as within their grasp and were not only prepared to use force rather than persuasion but also felt personally summoned by God to do so. They interpreted the Bible in providential, apocalyptical terms, relating current events directly to the text. For them, the conflict was a holy war; a cosmic showdown between good and evil in which the ends justified almost any means.

As we shall see, militants remained the minority, largely experiencing the war as observers or victims of defeat and displacement. Nonetheless, then as now, militancy proves especially dangerous when combined with political power. It creates a delusional sense in those who rule of being chosen by God for a divine purpose and reward. It encourages the conviction that their norms alone are absolute, their form of government is automatically superior to all others and their faith is the only really true religion. Such fundamentalists demonize 'the other' as evil in the psychological equivalent of declaring war, cutting off all possibility of dialogue or compromise. They no longer feel obliged to treat opponents as human beings. Problems to which they might have contributed are blamed entirely on the enemy. But such self-confidence is inherently dangerous to themselves as well as their enemies. The belief in divine assistance encourages fundamentalists to take risks, convinced that mounting odds are merely part of God's plan to test their faith. They remain convinced that ultimate victory is theirs by right. This can stiffen resolve and motivate stubborn resistance, but it is poorly suited to achieving military success. Fundamentalists have no real knowledge of their opponents, whom they make no effort to understand. These beliefs certainly shaped key decisions, including the Defenestration and the elector Palatine's decision to join the Revolt. Militants' influence was at times disproportionate to their numbers, but this does not mean we should interpret the conflict through their eyes.

The third key distinction of the present argument is that the war was not inevitable. The link between seventeenth-century European strife with wider environmental and economic problems is circumstantial at best. The entire continent was not convulsed by a general wave of violence. Despite sharing similar underlying problems with the war zone, much of the Empire remained at peace after 1618, until the conflict escalated in 1631–2. Nor did conflict inevitably follow the Religious Peace of Augsburg (1555) that addressed the tensions stoked by the Reformation. There were a few violent incidents within the Empire (see Chapter 7), but no general conflict until after 1618. This is the longest period of peace in modern German history, not matched until 2008 by the 63 years following the Second World War. The significance of this becomes even clearer when the Empire's relative tranquillity is contrasted with the brutal civil wars in France and the Netherlands after the 1560s.

Given the success of the 1555 settlement, the subsequent outbreak of general war after 1618 requires some explanation. This is the task of the first eight chapters, which also set out the general situation in Europe and introduce the key issues and many of the main characters. The next twelve chapters follow events broadly chronologically, paying particular attention to the period after 1635 that has been unduly neglected, yet is essential for understanding why peace proved so elusive. The final three chapters examine the political consequences, as well as the human and material cost, and assess what the war meant to those who experienced it and for subsequent generations.

2

Trouble in the Heart of Christendom

THE EMPIRE

Events in the Holy Roman Empire before 1618 were not without drama, but it was that of the courtroom rather than the battlefield. Sixteenth-century Central Europeans were embroiled in long-running – and often long-winded – legal disputes that later generations have dismissed as tedious and irrelevant, compressing the decades prior to the Thirty Years War into a short narrative of confessional and political polarization towards inevitable war. This is understandable, since the Empire can be exceedingly difficult to explain.

The indefatigable Johann Jakob Moser, who found time outside his legal career to compose six hundred Protestant hymns and raise eight children, gave up trying to describe the imperial constitution after publishing over a hundred volumes in the later eighteenth century. The only way to approach the problem, as T.C.W. Blanning has aptly remarked, is to love anomaly, since the Empire did not fit any recognized pattern.[1] This is the reason behind the famous seventeenth-century depiction of the Empire as a 'monstrosity' by the philosopher Samuel Pufendorf, who pointed out that it was neither a 'regular kingdom', nor a republic. Another contemporary metaphor offers a better starting point. Natural philosophers like Descartes were beginning to explain the world in mechanical terms, interpreting living organisms and planetary motion as complex mechanisms. In this context, the Empire appears a slow, cumbersome juggernaut, operated by an intricate, elaborate yet surprisingly robust internal system of weights and balances. The kings of France, Sweden and Denmark might smash at this machine with their swords, while the sultan battered it with his mace, denting the exterior and disrupting some of the more delicate parts, but this did little to alter its lumbering progress.

Communities

What propelled this juggernaut was the labour of millions of peasants and common folk living in the 2,200 towns, at least 150,000 villages, and numerous monasteries, convents and other communities across the Empire. It was at the level of these communities that things got done: people married, children were born, work was organized, crops harvested, goods made and exchanged. It is these communities that dominate Matthäus Merian's *Topographia Germaniae*, a monumental publishing venture that was begun while the war was still at its height in the 1630s and not completed until forty years later.[2] The work contains scarcely any description of the natural environment, instead grouping by region all the settlements that Merian and his collaborators had visited or heard of, and then describing them in alphabetical order. The numerous accompanying engravings perfectly illustrate the three elements of these communities and how they related to the structures of power within the Empire.

Each settlement is shown clearly against the countryside, delineating the community as a distinct social space. Most were located on rivers, essential for communications with the wider world, as well as for carrying away rubbish and providing some barrier against intruders. Unlike modern rivers, those of the seventeenth century still followed their natural course, swelling with heavy rain or melted snow and spreading out wherever there were meadows or low-lying land. Larger streams changed course over time, leaving islands and inlets that ingenious bridge-builders incorporated in their structures to span the water. Medieval walls surrounded towns and larger villages, often using rivers or streams to provide a wet ditch around the settlement. These high, but relatively thin walls, with their prominent towers and gatehouses, were being supplemented by additional, more modern outer defences to protect against artillery bombardment. Some cities had acquired these defences already, in the sixteenth century, but most built them, or modernized existing structures, in the 1620s as the dangers of war became more pressing. The thick, low-lying walls, with their massive, stone-fronted bastions, spread outwards round the medieval core, sometimes encompassing newer suburbs, other times brutally sweeping these away to clear fields of fire. Only those with an experienced eye could make out the elaborate geometrical patterns they cut into the ground, since the systems of walls, outworks and ditches were largely hidden from view on the ground by additional banks of earth pushed further into the countryside. The few buildings that remained outside the walls were either those used for industrial purposes, like sawmills or brick kilns, or were ecclesiastical foundations, like monasteries or convents that constituted separate communities themselves.

Even small villages and hamlets were fenced in to keep out wild animals and mark their inhabitants' sense of place. Gates would be closed at dusk, and were guarded even in relatively tranquil times. Those passing through would be asked their business and often obliged to pay a toll on their goods. The walls, and more particularly the expense and trouble of expanding them, kept housing crammed close together, building upwards to a third storey or more in larger cities, and using every possible space beneath the roof and in the cellar. Stone or brick was often used only on the ground floor, with the rest being built around a timber frame. Fire was an ever-present danger, often doing far more damage than military action. Proximity encouraged inquisitiveness. A habitually drunken neighbour was not only a reprobate; he was a fire hazard. Likewise, communities were rarely sufficiently large to be anonymous. Society remained face-to-face and outsiders immediately attracted comment and frequently suspicion. The approach of war would bring large numbers of armed strangers across the rolling hills, or through the woods towards the settlement. They would speak different dialects or even foreign tongues. There would be many mouths to feed; often more than the community itself. If the intrusion was contested, there was the risk that familiar landmarks would be damaged or obliterated. A breach in the walls violated the community's protected space and signalled an assault that was almost invariably followed by plunder, pillage and often worse.

The church spires that rose prominently above the walls and rooftops pointed to a second, theological dimension to each settlement as a community of believers. Churches were generally built of stone and were among the largest structures in each settlement. They are carefully identified in Merian's engravings, each one being labelled and the more important sometimes given a separate plate of their own. Even relatively small towns would have four or more churches, each serving as the focal point of its parish. Larger villages with a church would provide for the spiritual needs of the surrounding hamlets. Monasteries and convents offered additional places of worship. The number and size of these buildings testifies not only to the significance attached to faith, but also to the economic muscle of organized religion that was present in all important communities.

The other buildings a traveller would see from afar were those associated with political authority. The town hall, palace or bailiff's house were the largest buildings alongside churches, generally far more substantial and certainly more ornate and imposing than any industrial structures. Like the churches, they symbolized the inhabitants both as a distinct group and as members of a wider community. Towns and most villages enjoyed considerable autonomy over their internal affairs, managing these through representatives elected from the enfranchised inhabitants, generally male property owners who were married heads of families. Arrangements varied considerably, but generally included jurisdiction over lesser offences, limited powers to raise resources and labour for common tasks, and the management of land and economic assets held communally. Crucially, these powers usually included the right to decide who could reside in the community and sanctions that could be imposed on those who transgressed its norms. Yet no community was completely independent. Anyone entering its principal government building would see a carved or painted coat of arms, identifying a higher authority to which the community would answer.

It was the imperial constitution that linked these thousands of settlements by binding them in a series of hierarchically ordered, overlapping jurisdictions. Though 'Germany' appeared in the title of Merian's work, it actually covered the Empire, an area that still stretched for over 680,000km^2, including not only all of modern Germany, Austria, Luxembourg and the Czech Republic, but also much of western Poland, and Alsace and Lorraine that are now in France. While missing in Merian, most of the modern Netherlands and Belgium were also still associated with the Empire in 1600, as was a further 65,000km^2 of northern Italy, even if these regions were not represented in imperial institutions.[3]

Emperor and Princes

As a whole, the Empire symbolized the late medieval universal ideal of a single Christendom. Its ruler was the only Christian monarch with an imperial title, elevating him above all other crowned heads. His pretensions to be the secular head of Europe rested on the idea of the Empire as the direct continuation of that of ancient Rome and so the last of the four great world monarchies prophesied in the Book of Daniel. The universal ideal was very distant from the arena of practical politics in the localities, ensuring that the emperor did not rule the numerous communities directly. Instead, his authority was mediated through the Empire's hierarchy of jurisdictions that in turn related to its medieval, feudal origins. The emperor was the superior lord over a host of lesser authorities bound in chains of vassalage. The distinctions between these lords had grown sharper, particularly as the Empire had to deal with a variety of internal and external problems since 1480. A fundamental division had emerged between those lords who were immediately under the emperor's jurisdiction (*Reichsunmittelbar*), and those 'mediate' authorities who were subordinate to intervening jurisdictions.

Immediate lords possessed full imperial fiefs (*Reichslehen*) held directly from the emperor in his capacity as their feudal overlord. These fiefs were generally composed of other, lesser fiefs held by mediate lords, or other jurisdictions exercised by subordinate communities. Thus, the towns, villages and other settlements were bound together within a complex legal and political web of rights, prerogatives and jurisdictions. These rights gave whoever possessed them a claim on the respect, subservience and resources of those bound by them. A lord exercising jurisdiction over a village could expect the deference of its inhabitants, a share of their produce and some of their time and labour for certain tasks. In return, he or she was expected to protect their interests against malevolent outsiders, uphold their communal distinctiveness within the wider imperial framework, and to intervene in the management of their internal affairs to resolve serious problems.

The strength of the community as social and political space meant that these rights were rooted in the land, so that whoever held them, held authority over that area. However, those holding one type of authority were not necessarily barred from possessing another; thus the lord of an immediate imperial fief might also hold other land that bound him in vassalage to one of his peers. Similarly, the presence of the church, with its vast material resources, created a host of ecclesiastical lords that had traditionally had a close relationship with the emperor and who considered themselves collectively as the 'imperial church' (*Reichskirche*). The material basis of the imperial church rested on the settlements and assets it controlled through its possession of imperial fiefs and other jurisdictions. However, these territorial jurisdictions did not match spiritual jurisdictions that extended to the churches in the settlements held by secular lords. Finally, jurisdictions could be shared by more than one lord, while different lords could hold separate rights in the same community.

Most rights were acquired by inheritance and were held by the 50–60,000 noble families living in the Empire. The vast majority of these were 'territorial nobles' (*Landadel*), possessing only lesser rights subject to the superior jurisdiction of the exclusive group of lords with imperial fiefs. There were around 180 lay and 130 spiritual fiefs that collectively constituted the territories of the Empire. They varied considerably in size, and there was no direct correlation between geographical extent and political weight. The Empire had taken shape when its population had been concentrated in the south and west. The density of settlement in these parts enabled them to sustain a higher concentration of lordships than the more sparsely populated north and east that were not fully incorporated in the imperial constitution until the beginning of the sixteenth century.

Consolidation of the constitution forged the lay and spiritual lords into three groups by 1521. The smallest, but most senior, were the seven electors who held the fiefs associated in the Golden Bull of 1356 with the exclusive right to chose each emperor. The prevailing social distinctions gave precedence to the clergy as 'first Estate' over the nobility, on account of their societal function of praying for the entire community's salvation. The premier electorate was thus that of the archbishop of Mainz, followed by his colleagues in Cologne and Trier, none of whom had many more than 100,000 subjects. The secular electorates were headed by the kingdom of Bohemia, the only land with a distinct royal title in the Empire (see Chapter 3). Bohemia was also the largest electorate, covering 50,000km^2 and with 1.4 million inhabitants living in 102 towns, 308 market centres, 258 castles and 30,363 villages and hamlets with 2,033 parish churches. Brandenburg was the next in size, but the most junior in status, covering 36,000km^2 but with only 350,000 people. Saxony was smaller, but more densely populated with around 1.2 million subjects. The Palatinate ranked second after Bohemia, covered about 11,000km^2 in two parts, one (Lower) on the Rhine, the other (Upper) north of Bavaria, with a combined population of about 600,000. Together, the electors held around a fifth of the Empire, and over a sixth of its population.

The other imperial fiefs fell broadly into one of two types. Fifty spiritual and thirty-three lay fiefs were held by lords of princely rank, though their actual titles ranged from archbishop and bishop, through duke, landgrave and margrave (marquis). All lay fiefs were formally acquired by inheritance or purchase; in both cases the transfer was subject to the emperor's approval. Spiritual rulers, including the three electors, were chosen by the cathedral or abbey canons of the principal church in their land, again subject formally to the emperor's and, in this case, pope's agreement. The number of princes was always less than the total of fiefs, since it was possible for electors to acquire princely fiefs, while existing princes could hold more than one and prince-bishops might seek election in another see. The Habsburg dynasty was the most successful of all princely families in accumulating influence this way, having acquired not only the eleven Austrian provinces but also Bohemia and its associated lands, together with the seventeen Netherlands provinces, giving them 303,000km^2 of territory, or over two-fifths of the entire Empire. With the parts of Hungary that also fell to the dynasty in 1526, the Habsburgs governed over 7 million subjects by 1600, compared with around 17 million people in the rest of the Empire. This territorial base ensured the dynasty's virtual monopoly of the imperial title between 1438 and the end of the Empire in 1806. They stood head and shoulders above the other princes, few of whom had more than 100,000 subjects.

The second group of around 220 fiefs were smaller still and lacked full princely status, ruled by a count, lord or prelate, most of whom had only a few thousand subjects. A further 400 baronial and knightly families held a further 1,500 fiefs directly from the emperor as 'imperial knights' (*Reichsritter*). Individually, their holdings were no larger than those of the far more numerous territorial nobility who lacked the status of imperial immediacy, and they had ceased to play a significant role in imperial politics by the mid-sixteenth century.

Cities

The vast majority of communities fell under one or more of these jurisdictions, but some remained outside lordly control. The most important were the eighty or so 'free and imperial cities' that lay mainly in Swabia and Franconia, the old imperial heartlands of the south and west. They included most of the Empire's largest settlements, notably Augsburg, which was the biggest with 48,000 inhabitants, or four times the size of Berlin. It headed a small group of Nuremberg, Hamburg, Cologne, Lübeck and Strasbourg, each with around 40,000 people. They were followed by places like Frankfurt, Bremen, Ulm and Aachen, with about 20,000 inhabitants apiece, and by a far larger number of towns like Nordhausen, Heilbronn, Rothenburg and Regensburg, with less than half that. Most had fewer than 4,000 inhabitants, though some, like Schwäbisch-Hall, controlled a significant number of surrounding villages. The cities' influence rested in part on their direct relationship to the emperor that preserved them from incorporation within neighbouring principalities. Anyone doing business with the bailiff of Eriskirch village by Lake Constance in 1619 would see the arms of the city of Buchhorn above the door – the city's symbols of a tree and a hunting horn, identifying it as lord of Eriskirch, which it had acquired in 1472, while the city's allegiance to the emperor and the Empire was shown by the imperial arms above its own. The black double-headed eagle symbolized the fusion of the Empire with the former kingdom of Germany. Surrounding the eagle was the Order of the Golden Fleece, badge of a chivalric order founded in 1429 to defend the church. This was the highest distinction awarded by the Habsburgs, directly linking their family to the emperor's traditional role as Christendom's protector. The red-white-red Habsburg colours were reproduced at the centre of the eagle, further underscoring the dynasty's association with the imperial title, and the city's membership of the Empire under their authority.[4]

The Imperial Constitution

Direction of the Empire was shared between the emperor and his vassals, but given the hierarchical character of the constitution, rights and responsibilities were divided unequally. The emperor was overlord and sovereign, holding considerable reserve powers that derived directly from his title rather than possession of any fief. These imperial prerogatives were deliberately left vague, because fixing them in law would imply limits to the emperor's universal pretensions. However, the need to deal with pressing problems forced the emperor and his vassals to define their relationship more precisely and created additional powers at various intermediary levels between the emperor and the Empire's component communities. Though the Habsburgs monopolized the imperial title, they did not hold it by right, but had to negotiate with the electors to secure acceptance. It was possible to persuade the electors to accept an emperor designate, known as the king of the Romans, who could assume power on his father's death. Otherwise, there would be an interregnum regulated by the Golden Bull. This handed imperial prerogatives to the elector of Saxony in the north and the elector Palatine in the south, while fixing a deadline within which all seven electors were to convene and select a successor under the direction of the elector of Mainz as arch-chancellor of the Empire. Candidacy was not open to all, since the emperor was not a kind of life president but a sovereign majesty, which presupposed that whoever was chosen would already possess certain 'royal' qualities.

The growth of Habsburg resources made the dynasty the obvious choice, since imperial prerogatives conferred executive authority but supplied few means to put decisions into effect. The electors expected the emperor to use his own lands to fund not only his personal court and imperial institutions, but also much of the defence against the Ottomans and other, Christian enemies. However, they recognized that changes in warfare made this impossible without some assistance from the rest of the Empire. The princes and cities accepted this as well, as the willingness to contribute imperial taxes became the criterion for imperial immediacy, marking them out from all the other lords and towns that merely paid into territorial treasuries. These imperial contributions became known as 'Roman months' after the cost of the escort intended to take Charles V to his coronation in Rome. Each territory was assessed according to a scale fixing its share of a single month's pay for 24,000 soldiers. Taxes could be raised as fractions or multiples of this basic quota, and levied either as a one-off payment, or spread across several months or even years.

Matriculation in the tax register by 1521 became the deciding factor in whether a particular territory secured representation in the imperial diet, or Reichstag, and so secured recognition as an imperial Estate (*Reichsstand*). The Reichstag was not a parliament in the modern sense, but embodied the early modern principle of representation through the monarch's obligation to consult his leading subjects on matters of common concern. True to the Empire's hierarchical nature, such consultation took place in three separate colleges of electors, princes and cities. The composition of the princely college was still in flux at this stage, since the existing princes were reluctant to accord full participation to the more numerous counts and prelates who were forced to share a handful of votes between them. The emperor held the initiative through his right to propose subjects for debate. Each college took a decision by majority vote, with each member or their representative speaking in turn according to a strict order of precedence. The colleges then conferred in pairs, the electors generally talking to the princes, before consulting the cities. Once a mutually acceptable wording had been hammered out, the collective decision was presented as a 'recommendation' to the emperor, who was free to accept or reject it. If he accepted it, it was incorporated into the concluding document, called an imperial Recess, issued when the Reichstag finished. The Reichstag had emerged relatively rapidly from about 1480 in response to new problems and its legislation created precedents that were incorporated into the imperial constitution. While not formally obliged to consult it, it became the only way the emperor could secure binding agreements on all territories, and it was a useful forum to test opinion and lend greater legitimacy to his policies. Though cumbersome, the Reichstag met fairly regularly at the emperor's request throughout the sixteenth century, passing a considerable body of legislation, as well as voting increasingly regular taxes to sustain a permanent defence against the Turks (see Chapter 4).

Additional taxes were raised to discharge the other principal constitutional task of preserving internal order and resolving disputes between the different lords and cities. The Reichstag of 1495 agreed a perpetual public peace, obliging the emperor and all his vassals to submit their disagreements to independent arbitration through a new supreme court, the *Reichskammergericht*, which was soon set up in the imperial city of Speyer. The emperor could name only the presiding judge and a few of his assistants. The territories proposed other candidates who were then

selected by the sitting judges and swore an oath to the court that superseded any obligation they might have to a territorial master. The imperial
legal system has received a very bad press from later generations, not
least for failing to resolve the problems leading to the Thirty Years War.
However, its development enabled the Empire to make the transition
from violent self-help through feuds to peaceful arbitration in the court,
where the aim was not so much to establish absolute truth or guilt,
but to secure mutually acceptable, and hence workable, solutions. The
system was expanded in the 1520s to deal with unrest within territories,
as well as conflicts between them. The electorates and larger territories
created their own judiciaries that were partially outside the supreme
court's jurisdiction, but possibilities of both appeal and intervention
remained. The emperor accepted the court's independence not least
because he was able to establish another court based in Vienna. This
Reichshofrat dealt with matters relating directly to imperial prerogatives, but since these were ill-defined, they provided a legal basis to
intervene in areas originally intended for the Reichskammergericht.
Though creating potentially conflicting jurisdictions, this also gave the
Empire a second legal heart that could beat faster if the case load
paralysed the Reichskammergericht.

Court verdicts were enforced through regional institutions interposed
between the territories and the Empire. Territories were assigned to one
of ten *Kreise*, or 'circles', to select candidates for the Reichskammergericht, and to raise the regular subscription to maintain it, as well as
special imperial taxes and troop contingents to enforce internal peace,
or defend the Empire. Imperial law evolved by 1570 to give considerable
scope for autonomous action at this level. Each Kreis had its own
assembly where, unlike at the Reichstag, each member had a single vote
in a common chamber, thus giving the minor ones greater weight. The
Kreis assemblies were summoned by the emperor, or through an imperial
Recess, or on a local initiative by their convening princes, generally one
lay and one ecclesiastical lord for each region. The assemblies offered
additional fora to resolve disputes, debate policy and coordinate action.
Their development varied, depending on how much they were needed
by their members. The Habsburg lands were grouped into separate
Burgundian and Austrian Kreise that they alone dominated, while the
Bohemian lands were omitted from the structure entirely. The four
Rhenish electors banded together to form one Kreis, despite the fact that

much of their territory was scattered in other regions. The smaller western and southern territories were grouped into more compact Lower Rhenish (or Westphalian), Upper Rhenish, Swabian, Franconian and Bavarian Kreise. The latter was dominated by the duchy of Bavaria, which, with over 800,000 inhabitants, was the largest principality and richer than the electorates. The presence of thirteen other members, notably the archbishop of Salzburg, prevented the duke from completely dominating the Bavarian Kreis. The northern lands were divided into the Upper (eastern) and Lower (western) Saxon Kreise. The former was dominated by Brandenburg and Saxony, while the latter was more evenly balanced between a number of bishoprics and duchies.

Political Culture

Thus, most of the imperial fiefs were both imperial Estates and Kreis Estates, represented in the Reichstag and their regional assembly. The emperor could approach them either in his capacity as their personal overlord, or through his representatives in the Reichstag, imperial courts or Kreis assemblies. Except in his own dynastic lands, he had no direct claim on the vast majority of the Empire's inhabitants that lived under the authority of one or more of the territorial lords. Representation in imperial institutions made these lords advocates of 'German Freedom', the language of liberty in seventeenth-century imperial politics. This did not equate liberty with equality or fraternity, but with 'liberties', or the privileges, immunities and rights accruing to individuals as members of a legally recognized corporate group. As imperial Estate-members, the territorial lords enjoyed their own special set of liberties, marking them out from their subjects and vassals. Their liberties gave them the privilege of being consulted by the emperor and a share in the collective governance of the Empire. But they also brought the responsibility of defending the autonomy and rights of their own territories and the peoples and communities that composed them. It is here that the checks and balances of the imperial juggernaut become most apparent. Each lord or prince sought to maintain his or her particular place within the imperial hierarchy. No one thought of independence. Even the largest electorates lacked the resources for an independent political existence, while all rulers derived their authority and status from their membership of the Empire, setting themselves apart from aristocrats in other countries who were the subjects of mere kings. As imperial Estate-members, they distinguished between the emperor and the Empire. They were loyal to both, but their ties to the emperor were personal, whereas that to the Empire was collective and corporate.

In the sixteenth century, political systems, both in the Empire and elsewhere in Europe, were shifting from personal dealings with an over-lord to subordination to an impersonal state that transcended the lives of its rulers. The coronation of Emperor Maximilian II in 1562 was the last to be attended by all electors in person. While minor counts and prelates seeking full recognition as imperial Estate-members continued to participate in person in the Reichstag, other rulers generally sent trained lawyers to represent their interests. Ever conscious of the expense, many imperial cities entrusted their votes to a single deputy. Yet personal meetings retained great significance at a time when it could take two weeks for a letter from Berlin to Heidelberg. Face to face, lords could discover common interests in hunting or art that bridged years of political and even confessional tension. Even if sharing a religious service or copious quantities of alcohol failed to foster good feeling, the complex imperial constitution offered numerous fora to continue a dialogue.

Rather than force an issue, most preferred temporizing, waiting until passions cooled, or shifting negotiations to a different level in the imperial constitution where there might be more allies or better chances of success. The long process of consultation offered the chance to dodge unwelcome burdens by citing new circumstances that had arisen after talks began, or by delaying agreement by the excuse of needing to consult other parties. Imperial politics was thus a series of formal meetings of rulers and their representatives at irregular intervals, supplemented by lesser assemblies to discuss specific issues, such as currency regulation, or tax quotas. Contact was maintained in between by couriers or informal personal meetings. The large number of relatively weak elements made it difficult for anyone to act alone, discouraging extremism and diluting any agenda to a minimum that all could agree.

This cumbersome process certainly made it difficult for the Empire to act decisively, but it gave it a particular strength that ensured it survived the most prolonged and bloody civil war in its history. The modern democratic state assumes responsibility for implementing decisions once they have been taken by majority vote. The dissenting minority now confront the full power of the state and, if they choose to resist, the situation can descend into violence as there is no legal basis for their failure to comply. No such separation existed in the Empire, because law-making and law enforcement remained common matters for the emperor and the imperial Estates. The minority continued to confront the majority, not the Empire itself. It was as if the process of decision-making was not yet complete and the majority view remained provisional until accepted by the minority. This situation was clearly problematic, as the dissenters could still hope to reverse unwelcome decisions completely, while the majority could grow frustrated if their opinion remained ignored. Constant postponement of controversial issues might render definitive arrangements impossible. However, the chances of violence were greatly reduced as long as a compromise remained possible. Moreover, neither side rejected the Empire that remained the accepted forum in which to reach a decision. Dissenters opposed the interpretation of laws, not the institutions that made or enforced them. Thus, while the Empire's inhabitants fought over the interpretation of the imperial constitution, they did not dispute its existence and it provided the framework within which they eventually made their peace.

CONFESSIONALIZATION

Religious tension impaired the working of the imperial constitution and contributed to the outbreak of the war in 1618. However, the link was far from straightforward. The sixteenth century was far less violent than much of the Middle Ages that had seen numerous feuds and even emperors deposed by their vassals. To understand the role of religion, we need to know how matters of faith became entwined with disputes over earthly authority, and for this we need to examine the process of forming distinct confessional identities following the Reformation.

All Christian confessions sprang from common roots, but developed a momentum of their own due to vested material interests, social concerns for status and prestige, and the psychological need to belong and to define that belonging by distancing oneself from those holding different views. The theological controversy forced believers to take a stand, leading each principal denomination to stress particular aspects as distinctive. Catholicism emphasized the primacy of organization, with the Roman church as the only competent authority to interpret the word of God for all Christians. Lutherans stressed the primacy of doctrine, claiming to free the Word of God from being misinterpreted by a church that had lost its way. Calvinism stood for the primacy of practice, calling for Luther's 'reformation of doctrine' to be followed by a second 'reformation of life', to bring behaviour in line with faith.[5]

Catholicism

Martin Luther's initial challenge sprang from wider attempts to renew Catholicism, but his break with Rome forced the papacy to respond politically as well as theologically. The council of cardinals convened at Trent in 1545–63 was intended to heal the rift, but ended by passing judgment on the evangelicals as heretics. Its final decrees concentrated on defining Catholicism and outlining a programme to exterminate heresy by renewing Catholic life. One issue was the Eucharist dispute over Christ's reference to the bread and the wine at the Last Supper. This assumed such significance because of the centrality of the mass as a collective act of worship, bringing priest and community together. The Council's decrees affirmed the primacy of the church by stating that the intervention of the priest consecrated the wafers, transforming them into the body of Christ who was then present at the service. Acceptance of this 'Tridentine mass' signalled subordination to the pope's other rulings on doctrine. It was accompanied by a revival of the medieval Eucharist cult, manifest through Corpus Christi processions of the faithful who walked behind religious banners and images on the Thursday after Trinity Sunday to celebrate mass together under the auspices of a cleric.

The Council issued a wide range of decrees to silence Luther's criticism that the clergy were not up to their role as mediators between God and believers. Education was expanded so that priests understood official doctrine and did not mislead their flocks. Bishops were to serve their dioceses, not exploit them. Carlo Borromeo (1538–84) became the model to follow. He was the first archbishop of Milan for eighty years to reside in the city, regularly visiting his churches and sponsoring religious orders to go out into the community and encourage a more active Christian life. The modern confessional box was his invention, greatly increasing the attraction of confession, which became no longer an act of public shame but an opportunity for individual spiritual guidance.

He spearheaded the counter-attack against heresy in Switzerland and soon became the focus of his own cult, leading first to his elevation as cardinal, and then to papal recognition of his sainthood in 1610. The veneration of saints itself became a mark of Tridentine Catholicism, celebrating pious figures not only as role models, but as direct intercessors with God.

Local saints further reinforced religious identity and assisted in Catholicism's response to evangelical collectivism. Though the liturgy remained in Latin, other aspects of worship were held in the vernacular and were accompanied by music, singing and activities intended to strengthen solidarity. Pilgrimages were revived, especially to the two bleeding heart shrines at Weingarten and Walldürn that survived the Reformation. Their protection, by the duke of Bavaria and elector of Mainz respectively, allowed these princes to demonstrate their Catholic credentials. The number of visitors already reached 10,000 a year in the 1590s, rising to two or three times that by the 1620s and both continued to do good business throughout the war, apart from the three years of Swedish occupation. The Holy Family also assumed greater prominence. The saintly character of Joseph was emphasized, presenting him as the devoted defender and guardian of all Christian families, while the cult of the Madonna reached new heights, particularly with the development of pilgrimage sites at Altötting and Passau along the Danube. Marian confraternities were expanded to admit lay members alongside clergy, furthering the integration of the Catholic church within a community. Membership of that in Cologne grew to 2,000 out of a population of around 45,000 by 1650.

Tridentine reform extended to the very heart of the Catholic church, with reform of the papal curia and expansion of its diplomatic network as the pope responded not simply to Protestantism but to shifts in the European balance of power.[6] Spain's victory over France gave it control of Italian territory either side of the Papal States by 1559, tightening the Habsburg grip on the pontiff who had not forgotten that it had been the emperor's soldiers, not the Protestant hordes, that had sacked his capital in 1527. The pope recognized that Catholicism needed the Habsburgs as rulers of both Spain and Austria, together with their new overseas empire in the Americas and Indies. He saw himself as *padre commune*, using his influence to broker reconciliation within the Christian community. But the political situation forced him to work through

Catholic rulers, many of whom he suspected of placing dynastic advantage above confession. He looked to France and to the remaining independent Italian rulers as counterweights to Habsburg predominance, and was forced to surrender the initiative to other rulers to advance local Catholic interests.

Protestant propaganda presented the Thirty Years War as a papal crusade, with the Jesuits as the pontiff's storm troopers. Officially called the Society of Jesus, the Jesuit order had been established by papal decree in 1540 following the initiative of Ignatius Loyola.[7] The Jesuits had a clear mission to extirpate Protestantism, which their founder called 'an epidemic of the soul'. They would first remove the causes of the 'infection' by displacing Protestants, and those Catholics who would not cooperate, from positions of influence, and then restore 'health' by promoting the vitality of Catholic life and doctrine. These tactics were overtly political and set the Jesuits apart from other Catholic orders, such as the Capuchins who continued the Franciscan tradition of working among ordinary people. Cardinal Borromeo sent them into the Alpine villages, where they worked to restore Catholicism among the Swiss and the Habsburg subjects in the Tirol from the 1580s. By contrast, the Jesuits started at the very top of the political hierarchy, believing that if they won over a territory's ruler and its elite, gradually the rest of society would follow. Acting on Loyola's orders, a Jesuit accepted the post of confessor to the king of Portugal in 1552, commencing a policy of actively seeking such positions. Protestants saw this as a papal conspiracy, quickly fitting the confessors into the role of evil advisers exercising disproportionate influence.

Even among Catholics the order aroused hostility. The more traditional orders resented the pushy Jesuits who acquired churches, schools and other assets through their political connections. Many were alarmed by their apparent radicalism. A deranged former Jesuit tried to assassinate Henri IV of France in 1594, while another member defended tyrannicide in a book published five years later, and it was easy to believe they were behind other conspiracies, such as the English Gunpowder Plot of 1605. However, Jesuits had to reconcile their Counter-Reformation mission with their hierarchical world view, and evolved a distinct approach to their role as confessors. They believed that the devil tempted princes to grant concessions to the heretics. If this had occurred, they would reassure the prince that God would forgive him provided such concessions had been politically necessary, and if they were revoked at the first opportunity. Such arguments opened the door to pragmatism where compromise could cloud militancy. It also fitted the varied personalities of the different confessors who were, after all, engaged in a very personal relationship with their prince. The flexible, pragmatic Martin Becan served Emperor Ferdinand II from 1620, but was followed by the militant hardliner William Lamormaini, who remained his confessor until the emperor's death in 1637. Ferdinand's son and successor chose Johannes Gans, known for his love of good dinners and more secular lifestyle. Moreover, this unbroken line of confessors was not matched elsewhere in Europe where the order had considerably less influence than in the porous political structure of the Empire.

The order expanded rapidly in the Empire, growing from 50 members out of a total of 1,000 at Loyola's death in 1556, to 1,600 out of 13,100 worldwide by 1615. Their main task was not that of confessor, but of teacher, since the order's primary influence stemmed from its role as educator of the lay and clerical elite. There were 22 Jesuit colleges in the Rhineland by the outbreak of the Thirty Years War, as well as another 20 in south Germany and 23 more in Austria and Bohemia by 1630. Enrolment rose dramatically too, with that at Trier leaping from 135 students at its foundation in 1561, to 1,000 by 1577. Colleges provided the basis for an expansion into higher education as the Jesuits persuaded rulers to confer university status, enabling them to recruit students from more prosperous and elevated social backgrounds. Their success attracted attention and they were invited to take over struggling institutions. For example, the humanist colleges of Ingolstadt and Dillingen were both entrusted to them in the mid-sixteenth century, while their activities in Vienna allowed them to take over the university there. This expansion was due to a range of teaching methods that seem obvious today, but were cutting-edge at the time. All Jesuits were university graduates and applied a common curriculum throughout the colleges, combining the existing humanist model of the grammar school with the deeper, systematic study of theology and philosophy. Schooling was open to anyone who could pass the entrance examination, and there were no tuition fees. Pupils were streamed into classes according to ability, enabling progression, while the presence of more than one teacher at each establishment allowed for specialist instruction with regular lesson plans. The educational programme had broad appeal across German society, but those destined for a higher clerical career were often sent on to the order's *Collegium Germanicum*, founded in Rome in 1552 and funded by the papacy. Though enrolment declined during the Thirty Years War, the Collegium made a profound impact on the imperial church, providing around a seventh of all cathedral canons during the first half of the seventeenth century. As with the confessors, Jesuit influence through education needs to be set in context. There were other Catholic universities; eight universities were founded in Protestant territories in the century after 1527; and total student numbers across the Empire rose from 2,700 in 1500 to 8,000 by 1618; a figure that was not reached again until the nineteenth century.[8]

Jesuit influence was also blunted by other traditions within German Catholicism. Secular Catholic rulers were keen to combat heresy, since religious dissent was widely seen as the first step to sedition, but the spread of the Reformation largely confined Catholicism to the imperial church territories. Apart from the Habsburg lands, only Bavaria and Lorraine remained as large Catholic secular principalities by the mid-sixteenth century. Bavaria and the Habsburgs became the order's principal sponsors within the Empire, since many ecclesiastical princes viewed the Jesuits with suspicion. Though numerous, the ecclesiastical territories were relatively small, and their political institutions were under-developed. Government in each territory was largely in the hands of the cathedral or abbey chapter that elected the bishop or abbot. Jurisdiction was fragmented by the presence of other collegiate churches and religious foundations. For example, five collegiate churches in Speyer controlled a quarter of all parishes, while half of the archbishopric of Trier was incorporated in foundations and monasteries beyond the elector's direct control.[9] The Tridentine decrees enhanced bishops' powers to supervise autonomous foundations and parish clergy, who frequently opposed interference in their affairs. Most of the middle and senior clergy in the Empire associated faith with lifestyle and local interest. This Catholic establishment was closely tied to the noble and patrician elite in their area and shared their worldly, Renaissance humanist outlook. There were long-standing patterns of placing younger sons and unmarried daughters in the imperial church, which provided suitable social status and a comfortable income. As institutions of the Empire, religious foundations and cathedral chapters were woven into the imperial constitution, with their own rights and prerogatives. They exercised political jurisdictions that were local and particular, and clashed with the Jesuits' allegiance to Rome. Election to an abbey or bishopric depended on membership of the relevant chapter, and the canons preferred candidates who shared their views. Even the model Tridentine bishop Cardinal Borromeo had been ambivalent towards the papacy's universalist pretensions, and had represented the conciliar tradition of a church governed by its senior clerics that had been smothered by the assertion of papal supremacy at Trent. The political influence associated with the imperial church encouraged its leading clerics to continue the pattern of absenteeism by accumulating benefices and sees wherever possible. Tridentine reforms were implemented only slowly and selectively, making their main impact only in the later seventeenth century, long after the Thirty Years War.

Reforming militancy also met strong opposition on the ground where priests lived as members of the community and were conscious that their position there depended largely on how they were accepted by parishioners. They saw the human face of everyday life that was frequently ignored or misunderstood by militants urging confessional conformity. Doctrine was bent to fit local practices, pragmatic and material interests, contributing to the diversity, as well as the strength of Catholicism within the Empire.

Lutheranism

It was precisely such heterodoxy that the Lutheran Reformation sought to eliminate. Luther wanted to reform the existing church, not create a new one, and only contested papal authority when the pope refused to agree with his interpretation of doctrine. It was the centrality of doctrine to Lutheranism that set it apart from the Roman church and sustained what became a distinct community of believers. Regarding the Bible as the source of all truth, Luther translated it into German to free it from papal misinterpretation. Luther's followers considered themselves an evangelical movement, only gradually adopting the label 'Protestant' that derived from the formal protest by Lutheran princes at the decision of the Catholic majority in the 1529 Reichstag at Speyer to take action against heresy. The dispute forced the Lutherans to define their beliefs in a series of written statements, beginning with the Confession of Augsburg that was delivered to the emperor at the Reichstag meeting in that city in 1530.

The stress on the Word of God direct from the Bible lessened the role of the priest as intermediary, and prompted Luther to reduce the sacraments to only baptism and the Eucharist. On the latter he broadly accepted the Catholic doctrine of real presence, but increased lay participation in the service. Other doctrines were developed in new directions, notably the concept of justification by faith. This separated justification (salvation) from sanctification (good works), arguing that entry to heaven came as a gift from God and could not be earned. An individual was not trapped in a cycle of sin, confession, contrition and penance, since God alone decided who would be saved. The faithful should concentrate on living a good, Christian life, rather than constant preparation for a 'good death' through confession, good works or indulgences. These ideas had implications that Luther had not intended. The concept of a priesthood of all believers implicitly challenged the political as well as clerical hierarchy, providing a theological basis for popular radicalism that culminated in the German Peasants War of 1524–6. This attempt to settle a host of local grievances contained a powerful political vision of an Empire without any lords between the emperor and the 'common man'. Though crushed with considerable brutality by both Protestant and Catholic princes, the rebellion left a lasting impact on the Empire. Rulers agreed to allow ordinary folk to take their grievances to court, thus binding the territories further within the imperial judicial system and strengthening the hierarchical imperial constitution. The experience also fundamentally changed Lutheranism, shifting it in a more conservative direction. Theologians reaffirmed the role of secular authority in supervising both laity and clergy, while enhancing the latter as the guardians of true doctrine.[10]

Given the fragmentation of political authority within the Empire, this resulted in separate Lutheran church structures in each territory adopting the new faith. The territory's ruler broke with Rome and assumed the supervisory role previously held by the bishop or archbishop in whose diocese his lands lay. Given the Lutheran distinction between worldly and spiritual matters, these episcopal powers were delegated to two new institutions. Responsibility for spiritual management was entrusted to a consistory staffed by theologians who vetted parish priests according to their conformity with approved doctrine. Each priest was expected to deliver at least two hundred sermons a year, including two each Sunday. Drafts had to be sent to the consistory

for approval and hour glasses were set up in churches to ensure parishioners were not short changed. Regular sermons reinforced the community of believers and provided a convenient opportunity for the
secular authorities to disseminate their decrees. The confessionalizing
drive of Lutheranism could thus dovetail with state social disciplining,
each authority seeking obedience, thrift and morality. The new clergy
were maintained by confiscating the material assets of the Catholic
church that lay within the ruler's political jurisdiction. This process has
been labelled secularization, a rather misleading term, since it did not
follow the route taken in the English Reformation where Henry VIII
sold monastic land to subsidize state expenditure. Some money was
diverted to pay for the princely household or music at court, but
otherwise the assets were consolidated as Lutheran 'church property'
(*Kirchengut*) and entrusted to a church council that used them to support
the territorial church.[11] Spiritual practices that had no foundation in
Lutheran doctrine were discontinued, such as the ritual of masses for
the dead in Catholic convents and monasteries, but other activities that
were similar to those undertaken by Catholic foundations, such as poor
relief, the provision of hospitals and education, were expanded.

Political leadership from the princes was also necessary to defend
Lutheranism within the Empire. Emperor Charles V tried to settle the
doctrinal controversy by sponsoring meetings of theologians. Their failure to agree forced him to invoke the public peace legislation since
Catholics accused the Protestants of stealing their church's property and
fomenting sedition among their subjects. Charles summoned Luther
before the Reichstag at Worms in 1521 to answer the charges brought
by the papacy. The emperor's final judgment was based on his traditional
role as defender of the faith; Luther was found guilty of heresy and
placed under the imperial ban, the Empire's highest secular sanction,
making him an outlaw and subject to pursuit and punishment under the
framework of the public peace.

The spread of Lutheranism among the princes and imperial cities
entrenched the schism, shattering the unity of law and religion on which
the emperor's verdict had been based. The Protestants denied the pope's
right to judge doctrine, and claimed their subordination to God superseded the loyalty they owed the emperor. The political story of the
Reformation is essentially that of a series of Protestant attempts to
postpone or annul Charles's Edict of Worms from 1521 by mobilizing

through the imperial constitution. Though their territories were larger and more populous, Protestants remained outnumbered in imperial institutions by the smaller but more numerous Catholic Estates. Threat of prosecution through the Reichskammergericht forced the elector of Saxony, the landgrave of Hessen and other Lutheran princes and cities to form the Schmalkaldic League in 1531, setting a significant precedent of a Protestant defence association outside the constitution. Problems with France and the Ottomans kept the emperor busy until 1546 when he returned to Germany with a large army, defeating the elector of Saxony at the battle of Mühlberg in April 1547. The victory cleared the way for Charles to impose his solution to the Empire's problems.

The doctrinal dispute was silenced by a compromise statement of faith, known as the Interim since it was considered provisional pending papal approval. Though containing some concessions to Protestantism, the Interim broadly endorsed Catholic interpretation on most points. Meanwhile, the Empire was reorganized to make it easier for the Habsburgs to manage. Burgundy and the Habsburg possessions in Italy were assigned to Spain, where Charles's son Philip had been designated heir. Austria, Bohemia and Hungary were entrusted to Charles's brother Ferdinand, while the remaining non-Habsburg imperial Estates were to be brought within a special alliance with the emperor. The Saxon electoral title was taken from the senior Ernestine branch of the Wettin family that had opposed Charles and given to Duke Moritz of the junior Albertine branch who had backed the emperor in the Schmalkaldic War.[12]

Such a sweeping demonstration of imperial authority was alarming, even to its beneficiaries. Prompted by a mixture of personal and political motives – Charles had refused to release the duke's father-in-law, the landgrave of Hessen – Moritz conspired to reverse parts of the 1548 settlement. French support was bought by permitting the occupation of the bishoprics of Metz, Toul and Verdun on the Empire's western frontier in February 1552. Charles retreated to Innsbruck as his support in the Empire fell away, leaving his brother Ferdinand to negotiate with the rebels. Ferdinand granted Moritz's demands in the Peace of Passau in June 1552: confirmation of his electoral title, release of his father-in-law, suspension of the Interim and the assembly of another Reichstag to reach a definitive settlement. Increasingly disillusioned, Charles handed the initiative to his more moderate and pragmatic brother who concluded the Religious Peace of Augsburg in 1555 (see below, p.41). The emperor transferred the imperial government to Ferdinand the following year and retired to Spain. His death two years later split the Habsburgs into Austrian and Spanish branches, with Ferdinand recognized by the electors as the new emperor.

These events represented a deep crisis for German Lutheranism. The controversial role of figures like Moritz of Saxony threatened to discredit the princely leadership of the religious movement. Armed opposition to the emperor threw religious and political loyalties into conflict. The loss of three territories to France was never recognized by the emperor and suggested the dangers of seeking external help to defend religious liberty. More fundamentally, inability to agree political action fuelled disagreements over doctrine. Luther's death in 1546 coincided with the moment of crisis as his followers faced the stark choice of compromising their core beliefs, or defying the emperor and plunging the Empire into civil war. Pragmatists followed Philipp Melanchthon, who represented the Erasmian humanist strand of Lutheranism that was already prepared to accept peripheral elements of traditional worship in return for recognition within the imperial constitution. Their opponents styled themselves Gnesio Lutherans, after the Greek for 'real thing'. They insisted on the original 1530 Confession of Augsburg, rejecting the revised 'Variata' version prepared ten years later by Melanchthon with Luther's tacit approval. To them, the Interim represented the first step towards eradication and they inclined to an apocalyptic vision of a final struggle between true Christians and the Antichrist. Their symbol was the city of Magdeburg that defied the Interim until finally taken by imperial troops in November 1552.

These conflicts fragmented both factions. The Gnesio Lutherans purged their more extreme members, generally known as Flacians after the Croatian Matthias Flacius, who was convinced by such things as deformed babies that mankind was physically degrading, portending the end of the world. More orthodox recruits were drawn from younger men who had grown up since the Reformation and were making their careers in the new Lutheran church establishment. They rejected the Philippists' hope of eventual reconciliation with Catholics, trying instead to convert them. Uncertainty led some Lutherans to drift back to Catholicism, or to embrace more extreme evangelical beliefs. As leader of the evangelical princes, Saxony tried to broker a compromise after 1573. The Saxon court preachers compiled the Book of Concord between

1577 and 1580, which endorsed the Gnesio Lutheran interpretation of their faith, rejecting Flacianism and most of Philippism. Saxony led the drive to sign up the Protestant imperial Estates, securing acceptance of the new statement from twenty princes, thirty other lords and forty cities by 1583.[13]

Calvinism

Dissenters criticized this imposition of orthodoxy as the 'Book of Discord', claiming it sacrificed the Reformation's potential to truly transform Christian life. Those seeking this 'second Reformation' became associated with the theology of the French reformer Jean Calvin, whose ideas spread into Germany after the Religious Peace of Augsburg. The conversion of the elector Palatine around 1560 gave the new movement a considerable boost and helped ensure that, unlike Calvinism elsewhere in Europe, Calvinism in the Empire was led by princes rather than more humble folk. Around twenty counts and minor princes followed the elector's example by 1618, but the landgrave of Hessen (1603) and the elector of Brandenburg (1613) were the only other important rulers to openly embrace the new faith.

They called themselves the Reformed, since the term Calvinist had connotations of an illegal sect. Their aim was the completion of Luther's Reformation by eradicating the remnants of 'papist superstition' in both ritual and doctrine. The high altar and clerical vestments were banished from churches, while paintings and sculptures were smashed to demonstrate that these cultic objects were powerless. Ministers adopted sober academic dress, appearing as professionals qualified to preach and teach. Long-standing elements of doctrine were rejected, such as exorcism at infant baptism and the concept of real presence during mass – Calvinists abhorred the notion that Christ was physically present since this entailed his body being turned into excrement as the wine and wafers passed through the digestive systems of the congregation. Communion was transformed into a commemorative ceremony, where the parishioners shared a meal round a table, the East Frisians even drinking beer instead of wine.

However, like Luther, Calvin also developed some Catholic ideas in new directions. The most important politically was his emphasis on predestination. This gave his religion its dynamic self-confidence, while fostering seeds of doubt and indecision among some of his followers at the same time. The early Christian church had condemned the view that people could earn eternal reward simply through their own merit and following Christian tenets. St Augustine argued God alone decided salvation and, since this decision occurred prior to birth, some people were predestined as the 'elect' to be saved. Calvin rejected this Catholic interpretation, because it implied that God was not powerful enough to save the reprobate, and developed his own doctrine of double predestination where God selected both the elect and the reprobate. He discouraged individual speculation on fate, arguing that believers simply had to trust God since faith would lead them away from sin and towards a life lived according to the Commandments. Yet doubt would not go away, inducing a brittle confidence in many Calvinists that crumbled in the face of adversity as they interpreted personal reverses as signs they were not among the elect.

A new doctrine of living was to accompany these beliefs. Calvin's reorganization of the Genevan church provided a model that was copied to a varying extent by his followers elsewhere. The princely character of the 'second Reformation' in the Empire meant that German Calvinists generally already had a Protestant church structure, because the new faith made its converts from among the Lutherans, rather than the Catholics. Having only recently established a Lutheran church, most converts to Calvinism simply entrusted it with new tasks. A system of mutual monitoring was established, where parishioners and ministers were encouraged to report on each other's doctrinal conformity and moral standards. This social disciplining element appealed to princes and urban magistrates in the later sixteenth century as they struggled to master problems stemming from inflation, population growth, rising underemployment and poverty. Lutherans and Catholics also intended doctrinal purity to be matched by moral renewal, but the combination of the disciplinary drive with other aspects of Calvinist theology convinced its followers that they were the true inheritors of the early church.

Fundamentalism was reinforced by Calvinism's international character that saw its followers scattered widely across Europe, nowhere in a majority. Lutherans could draw on the humanist national tradition that associated truth and honesty as true German (*Teutsch*) characteristics, in contrast with the deviousness of foreigners (*Welsch*), especially those south of the Alps. The Danes and Swedes shared much of this cultural tradition, and like their German co-religionists, could relate their new Lutheran churches with national defiance of Rome. By contrast, Calvinism took root in individual cities and princely homes, denying it an obvious centre. Each new community looked to established ones elsewhere for guidance and support. As a leading imperial Estate-member, the elector Palatine was the obvious choice for German Calvinists and the Heidelberg Catechism of 1563 became the main model within the Empire, displacing the influence of Geneva from the 1580s. Over two hundred Hungarian and five hundred French students attended Heidelberg University between 1560 and 1610, strengthening the Palatinate's standing among believers elsewhere. The elector also founded the new town of Frankenthal to welcome French Huguenot and Dutch Calvinist refugees fleeing their religious civil wars that broke out in 1562 and 1566 respectively. Accustomed to interpreting contemporary events through biblical examples, Calvinists identified with the Israelites. The common experience of a hard life on the road and finding a home in a new community forged bonds between students and refugees, establishing ties that lasted if individuals returned home or moved elsewhere. Believers saw their own local struggles as part of a wider battle between good and evil, especially as Spanish involvement in the French and Dutch civil wars reinforced the impression that they were confronted by an equally international Catholic conspiracy to thwart the righteous at every turn.

Limits to Confessionalization

The emergence of competing varieties of Christianity by the later sixteenth century suggests a society that was becoming deeply divided by religion. Many aspects of everyday life were becoming confessionalized, erecting invisible barriers between and even within communities. A person's faith could be discerned from his or her name, with Joseph becoming increasingly popular alongside Maria among Catholics, while Calvinists rejected saints' names, selecting instead Abraham, Daniel, Zacharias, Rachel, Sarah and others from the Old Testament. Luther's translation of the Bible spread his Saxon dialect throughout central and parts of northern Germany as the correct written form, while the Jesuit standardization of High German entrenched this in the south. When a territory changed its confessional allegiance, its written language followed suit, and the same has been detected for individual converts, such as the novelist Grimmelshausen, who was raised a Lutheran but adopted Catholicism during the Thirty Years War. Other artistic activity was also partly confessionalized. Calvinists rejected all theatre, while Lutherans used it in schools and the Jesuits in their colleges. Catholic sermons concentrated on the Madonna and the saints, while Lutherans and Calvinists focused on morality.[14]

Nowhere were the differences more obvious than in time-keeping. Pope Gregory XIII decreed that the date should be set back ten days on 15 October 1582, and henceforth the new year was to start on 1 January, not 25 March, in order to bring the calendar in line with scientific calculations. The Habsburgs and German Catholics adopted the new Gregorian calendar by 1584, but while Protestant scientists like Johannes Kepler favoured reform, their clergy rejected anything from Rome and the credulous believed the papists were trying to steal ten days of their lives. The discrepancy became obvious in the Empire where Lutherans and Catholics lived together officially since the Peace of Augsburg. Nine-tenths of the Augsburg population were Lutherans, but the Peace had made the city formally bi-confessional. After difficult negotiations, the magistrates imposed the new calendar in 1586, but the Protestants continued to observe 'their' Sunday and went to services in churches across the frontier.

However, there is considerable evidence that society was not as confessionalized as it was by the early eighteenth century. Mixed marriages and social contact remained fairly common in Augsburg prior to the Swedish occupation in the 1630s. Protestants and Catholics drank together in the same taverns without the court records recording sectarian brawls. Craft hostels became segregated only following the Peace of Westphalia when the magistrates took bi-confessionalism to legal extremes. Evidence from other territories suggests that the citizens of Augsburg were far from alone in their pragmatic approach.[15] Some people outwardly conformed while inwardly dissenting. Others selected the beliefs and practices they found most meaningful and useful in their daily lives, regardless of orthodoxy. Traders sought profit over piety and sold to whoever would buy their wares. While it was not possible to escape censorship entirely, political fragmentation in the Empire offered opportunities to disseminate and receive a variety of views.

Perhaps most importantly, fundamentalists of all creeds struggled to stamp distinctive patterns of thought and behaviour on a society that carried a rich pre-Reformation heritage. The humanist educational ideal that spread in the fifteenth century continued to shape schools, universities and literary societies regardless of confession. Though the content of lessons may have varied, the form of instruction at least provided some common ground. Moreover, the wealthy and fortunate continued the tradition of attending several institutions during their studies, often irrespective of their confession. The common veneration of classical forms helped elevate the exchange of ideas above sectarian strife, and even during the war the emperor chose Protestants as imperial poets laureate.[16] Humanism also offered the example of Erasmus who pursued a more private faith, free of clerical supervision. Both Emperor Ferdinand I and his successor Maximilian II sponsored humanist scholars who sought common elements among the confessions as a basis for reuniting Christians. The descent of France and the Netherlands into sectarian violence at a time when the Empire was enjoying peace provided further pause for thought, notably after the Massacre of St Bartholomew in 1572 when Catholics slaughtered an aristocratic Huguenot wedding party in Paris. The emperor's key military adviser, Lazarus von Schwendi, wrote that such violence would impair the Empire's ability to fight the Ottomans who represented a threat to *all* Christians. His proposals for toleration suggest an approach similar to the *politique* position in France that sought peace by placing loyalty to a strong monarchy above confessional interest. However, there were others who went further. The imperial treasurer, Zacharias Geizkofler, readily identifiable as a Protestant from his forename, argued that secular authority had no right to dictate matters of conscience and that toleration should stem from mutual understanding, not political expediency.

While Geizkofler was in a minority, it is clear that sixteenth-century Europeans inhabited multiple mental worlds simultaneously, accepting different ideas without trying to reconcile them. Things that might appear illogical and incompatible today did not necessarily seem so at the time. Militancy was certainly growing, particularly as those who had only known a confessionally divided world reached maturity and positions of influence around 1580. But it is impossible to ascribe the outbreak of war in 1618 directly to such sentiment. In order to appreciate the connection between religion and the war, we need to review the Religious Peace of Augsburg and investigate how confessional differences became intertwined with constitutional disputes.

RELIGION AND IMPERIAL LAW

The Peace of Augsburg 1555

The agreement of 1555 has entered Anglophone historical writing as the Religious Peace, but in fact the section on confessional differences formed only a small part of a wide-ranging reform package agreed by the Reichstag.[17] The religious settlement was thus brought within wider constitutional reforms adjusting the public peace, revising imperial tax quotas, and providing new regulations on currency, policing and the operation of the Reichskammergericht. Article 29 obliged the emperor to accept the religious terms as part of the Empire's fundamental laws and Ferdinand confirmed this when he became emperor in 1558.

Unlike 1548, pacification of the Empire was not linked to a statement on doctrine. None of the so-called religious articles actually defined faith. Instead, they sought to bring adherents of two opposing confessions within the same legal framework. The difficulties this entailed were to be a root cause of major war after 1618, but responsibility for the outbreak of that conflict cannot be laid upon those who drafted the peace of 1555. They were faced with piecing together the shattered medieval unity of law and faith. The two were considered indivisible because religion provided the guide for all human endeavour: since there could be only one truth, there could be only one law. But now Catholics and Lutherans both claimed to be right. The public peace obliged all imperial Estates to forswear violence and the inconclusive fighting of 1546–52 indicated the impossibility of re-establishing unity by force of arms.

A fully secular *Pax Civilis* was not an option for the Empire as a whole. This solution was advocated two decades later by the French lawyer Jean Bodin in response to his own country's civil war; the state was still envisaged as broadly Christian, but disassociated from any particular confession, using its power to preserve religious plurality and domestic order. Such a powerful secular monarchy was incompatible with both German Freedom and the emperor's Holy Roman credentials.

Instead, the peace-makers of 1555 deliberately blurred the religious distinctions to maintain an element of the old universal ideal of a single Christendom. Lutherans were referred to as 'adherents of the Confession of Augsburg', without defining what that meant, while use of words like 'peace', 'religious belief' and 'reformation' were a deliberate attempt to incorporate values that all still shared, yet understood differently. For Lutherans, 'reformation' meant the right of legally constituted authorities to change religious practice in line with their founder's teachings. To Catholics, it confirmed their church's role in spiritual guidance.

These ambiguities were carried over into the confessional element of the settlement. While France, Spain and the Dutch were still fighting to achieve victory for a single confession in their domains, the Empire agreed to recognize both Catholicism and Lutheranism at its territorial level. Contrary to the later impression, this did not leave the princes entirely free to choose between the two faiths. The formula 'he who rules, decides the religion' (*cuius regio, eius religio*) was not included in the text and emerged in debates about the treaty only after 1586. Rather than allowing perpetual change, the intention was to fix matters as they were mid-century. Various articles were interpreted collectively as the right of reformation (*jus reformandi*), but this was meant to acknowledge territorial rulers' duties as secular guardians of religion in their own lands, rather than unilateral powers to change things on a whim. Other articles placed severe restrictions on the right of reformation, notably Article 19 that fixed the Peace of Passau and 1552 as the normative year (*anno normali*). Duke Moritz had secured Ferdinand's recognition that the Lutherans could retain those Catholic assets they had incorporated into their territorial churches by that date, and this was now accepted in the general peace. To reconcile Catholics, Ferdinand inserted Article 18 against Lutheran protests, stipulating that rulers of the remaining Catholic ecclesiastical territories that embraced the new faith after 1555 had to stand down. Known as the 'ecclesiastical reservation', this article safeguarded the Catholic character of the imperial church and with it the in-built Catholic majority in imperial institutions, thus preserving the Holy Roman element of the Empire. Similarly, the imperial knights were denied the right of reformation, since they were not full imperial Estate-members, while the faith of the imperial cities was fixed permanently, including eight that were to remain bi-confessional.

Other articles were concerned to minimize friction between the two confessions, such as suspending the jurisdiction of Catholic bishops over Lutheran territories, forbidding the use of heresy laws against them and obliging both parties to submit any disputes to arbitration through the Reichskammergericht. The latter provision embedded the religious settlement within the secular framework of the imperial public peace. The inclusion of the right to emigrate (*jus emigrandi*) represented a further secular intrusion that curbed the princes' powers of reformation. Subjects who dissented were free to leave without being fined or losing their property. This innovation pointed towards the later philosophy that individual freedoms should take precedence over collective, corporate rights. It suggested a freedom of conscience for which the Protestants had lobbied in the hope of protecting their followers living in Catholic territories. Catholic objections reduced this to the right to emigrate, but Ferdinand nonetheless issued a separate declaration, dated 24 September like the Peace, conceding limited freedom of conscience to existing Lutheran nobles and burghers in the ecclesiastical territories.

The Peace was clearly ambiguous and contradictory, but it would be wrong to conclude with Geoffrey Parker that it merely 'put a temporary end to open confessional warfare in Germany'.[18] No major war occurred for another 63 years and even where Central Europeans did come to blows after 1583, their disputes remained localized and largely free of the brutality that accompanied the prolonged violence in France and the Netherlands. Schwendi's fear of the Ottomans points to one reason preserving the peace, though the Turkish menace spilled over into major war only after 1593 at a time when confessional tensions were growing, rather than receding. The primary factor behind the Peace's longevity was its comparatively satisfactory settlement of the religious and political difficulties. Its strength can be seen by the fact that it provided the basis for the internal settlement of the Empire at the Peace of Westphalia that modified rather than replaced it.

The Three Dubia

The real cause of later troubles is to be found in the diverging interpretation of three key terms. The first and most important of these *Dubia* or uncertainties concerned the fate of the immediate ecclesiastical lands of the imperial church. As recognized imperial Estates, the territories of the archbishops, bishops and prelates had largely escaped incorporation into Lutheran territorial church property prior to 1552. The electors of Brandenburg and Saxony were on their way to incorporating three bishoprics apiece, but this stemmed from long-term territorial ambitions pre-dating the Reformation. The more immediate threat had come from the Catholics. Charles V himself annexed Utrecht and asserted protectorates over other bishoprics close to his existing territory, while France had seized Metz, Toul and Verdun. Overall losses were relatively small, considering that the imperial church still encompassed three electorates, around forty prince-archbishoprics and bishoprics, as well as about eighty abbeys and convents. The Catholic character of these lands was protected by the ecclesiastical reservation, but Ferdinand's separate declaration permitted nobles in such territories to practise Lutheranism. Protestant penetration of the cathedral chapters thus continued, especially since Lutheran princes and nobles were not prepared to abandon the social and political advantages to be gained through service in the imperial church. The fact that Luther had been prepared to accept the idea of Protestant bishops by the 1540s provided theological underpinning for these ambitions.[19] Lutherans argued that the ecclesiastical reservation was not part of the Peace, since they had objected to it, and did not preclude a cathedral chapter electing a Protestant bishop.

The emperor dodged the issue by recognizing Protestants as administrators rather than bishops. The territories remained parts of the imperial church and their rulers exercised their rights as princes, rather than clerics. This prevented complete secularization and preserved the possibility that the next election would secure a return to Catholicism. It also suited the Protestants who had no desire to annex these lands outright, because that could extinguish their distinct representation in imperial institutions, as indeed occurred with the three bishoprics that Brandenburg incorporated during the sixteenth century. Matters only became pressing after 1582 because the number of ecclesiastical territories falling under Protestant administration began to threaten the Catholic majority in the Reichstag and other institutions (see Chapter 7).

The second area of uncertainty concerned the mediate ecclesiastical property that lay within the jurisdiction of a Lutheran ruler, but had not been incorporated into his territorial church property by 1552. The status of such foundations had often been disputed prior to the Reformation as secular rulers claimed the right to protect particular religious houses, or shared rights and revenues with them. It was sometimes unclear whether a particular monastery was mediate, or in fact an imperial Estate – a status that some abbots in southern Germany claimed when threatened with incorporation in Württemberg and other Lutheran lands. Rulers who converted after 1555 faced even greater difficulties, but could still point to the terms of the Peace suspending the jurisdiction of Catholic bishops across Lutheran lands as a basis to supervise ecclesiastical property in their territories.

Subjects' religious freedoms constituted the third contentious issue. There were more Catholic territories with Lutheran minorities than the reverse. Unsurprisingly, Catholics claimed the terms as an exclusive prerogative of rulers to expel dissenters, whereas Lutherans interpreted them as voluntary freedoms, allowing their co-religionists to continue their worship or emigrate as they chose. The question grew more pressing after the 1570s as Catholic rulers sought to stem the spread of Lutheranism in their territories by making religious conformity a benchmark of political loyalty (see Chapter 3, pp.64–75).

Discussion of the Dubia filled imperial politics from the 1560s, with Catholics and Lutherans presenting each Reichstag with lengthy *Gravamina*, or legal arguments defending their interpretation of the Peace. All three Dubia touched material and personal interests, but the complex arguments obscured the fundamental underlying problem: the Peace had given Lutherans legal equality, but left Catholics with a political majority. This was crucial, because the imperial judicial system could neither be disentangled from the political structure nor was it able to fulfil the expectation of 1555 and resolve all religious disputes. The supreme court's inability to do this raised the constitutional question as to where ultimate authority lay. No one wanted matters referred to the pope, since even the Catholics contested his legal and political jurisdiction over the Empire. The concept of German Freedom made any approach to the emperor difficult. He was regarded as an adjudicator, rather than lawgiver. The most contested parts of the 1555 Peace – the ecclesiastical reservation and Ferdinand's declaration – were attacked by their opponents as arbitrary imperial fiats rather than binding agreements freely negotiated by all parties in the Reichstag. The emperor's ability to smooth over such disagreements depended largely on his standing among the princes. Both Ferdinand I and Maximilian II worked hard to foster a moderate common ground, but the erratic Rudolf II allowed this to be eroded after his accession in 1576.[20]

Distinct Protestant and Catholic positions on all disputed points emerged fairly early on and people were already well aware of the ambiguities when the Peace was first concluded. There is little basis then for the standard interpretation of the period 1559–1618 of steadily polarizing opinion. Instead, moderate and militant perspectives co-existed on both sides, with one or other current growing stronger depending on the particular interplay of personalities and wider circumstances. The chronology of these shifts will be picked up in a later chapter; the remainder of this one outlines the opposing views.

Catholic Opinion

The Catholic position on the Dubia was set out in 1566 by Pope Pius V who interpreted the Peace as a tactical concession; the lesser evil of toleration, to avoid a greater evil of religious civil war at a time when the Ottomans were baying outside Christendom's eastern bulwark. This perspective was repeated by Catholic commentators, including Pope Pius XII on the anniversary of the Peace in 1955. However, this position was open to both moderate and militant interpretations. The former saw the Peace as a fixed concession that left the Lutherans as a dissenting minority within a common legal framework with their Catholic neighbours. They were to be tolerated for the greater good, but were not fully equal and so could not be given additional political rights. Many moderates went further in asserting that 1555 simply set limits to Lutheranism, while allowing those who saw the error of their ways to return to the true faith. Change was possible, but only in one direction. Militants drew on the Jesuit interpretation of the doctrine of the lesser evil to argue that 1555 had merely suspended the original ban on Luther and his followers pronounced in 1521. They derived some support for this interpretation from Article 25 that stated the Peace was to last only until the theologians could resolve their differences. To Catholics, these matters had already been settled by the Tridentine Decrees of 1564, casting doubt on the continued legality of the 1555 treaty. Thus, both moderates and militants found support in imperial law for their claims that they were simply stating the 'clear letter' (*klare Buchstabe*) of the Peace.

Protestant Resistance Theories

Protestants also based their position on the Peace and likewise clung to the hope that Christendom would be preserved and the schism would be only temporary. However, to them 1555 represented the start, not the limit of the project to convince all Christians to embrace Luther's reform. Calvinists believed they should be included too, since their faith had sprung from the Confession of Augsburg. Opinion divided when confronted with Catholic refusals to countenance what they regarded as infringements of 1555, with militants being far more likely than moderates to consider constitutional change and even resistance.

The idea of resistance existed in Catholic thought, but assumed greater significance for Protestants since they were the political minority in both the Empire as a whole and in the Habsburg lands, where Lutheran nobles and towns opposed a dynasty solidly behind the old church. As in the case of confessional tension, it is important not to interpret the discussion of resistance as a process of radicalization, nor to see Calvinists as necessarily more ready to rebel than Lutherans. The history of political ideas is often distorted by teleology that implies the originators of key ideas were far more influential at the time than their more mainstream contemporaries.[21] French and Dutch resistance theories were partially discredited by the violence of their civil wars in the later sixteenth century, prompting Germans to draw mainly on their own experience in the first half of the century, as well as ideas from Hungary and Poland where the nobility had a strong tradition of opposing tyranny.

Any theory of resistance encountered the same three questions that were posed by the use of force in the international arena. War or rebellion had to be considered just if those shedding blood were to reconcile their actions with Christian commandments and so avoid damnation. A just war could be waged only by a recognized authority, but it was unclear who this was when it came to rebellion. Likewise, what constituted a just cause for resistance, and did it extend to defence of temporal as well as religious rights? Finally, it was unclear whether resistance should simply combat injustice or overthrow its perpetrators.

All theologians stressed obedience, arguing that secular authority was divinely ordained and tyrannical rule should be endured as a test of faith. Calvin even urged Christians in the Ottoman empire to obey the sultan. Blanket approval of authority crumbled when the fate of the true church appeared at stake. Already in 1524, some Protestants borrowed the classical model of the lesser magistrates, such as the Spartan ephores and the Roman tribunes, who safeguarded subjects' liberties against a potentially tyrannical sovereign. Luther reluctantly accepted the princes as the Empire's ephores when called upon to endorse the Schmalkaldic League. This was particularly welcome for the League's founders, conscious that the theological claim that duty to God superseded temporal loyalty was dangerously close to the arguments advanced by the rebellious peasants they had crushed in 1524–6. Since the princes were hereditary rulers, Luther accepted them as divinely ordained, whereas the emperor was merely elected by them. People must obey the princes, but the princes could oppose the emperor if he disregarded the true faith. Such arguments chimed with the language of German Freedom that saw the electors and princes as collectively responsible for the Empire's welfare, thus reconciling opposition to an individual emperor with continued loyalty to the imperial constitution.

Most Lutherans rapidly distanced themselves from these views after the experience of 1546–52, while the acceptance of their faith in the Peace of 1555 made resistance less pressing. The spread of Calvinism also lessened hostility to the emperor, since the new faith made most of its converts at the Lutherans' expense. Loyalty was strengthened by the emperor's refusal to assist Spain and the Catholic parties in the French and Dutch civil wars. Lutherans rejected the Calvinists' claim that the Massacre of St Bartholomew represented an attack on all Protestants, arguing the French Huguenots had brought it upon themselves by taking up arms against their king. As the religious minority within a political minority, Calvinists were more inclined to consider extra-constitutional means to defend their interests. Growing Catholic militancy and doubts about Rudolf II's leadership forced some Lutherans to do the same. Real radicalization followed only because the Habsburgs' opposition to Protestantism among their own subjects convinced some that the right of resistance also extended to nobles and even burghers facing persecution.

3

Casa d'Austria

LANDS AND DYNASTY

The House of Austria has generally been cast as the villain in our story. C.V. Wedgwood's widely read history was published in 1938, the year of appeasement, and portrays a weak British ruler, James I, conciliating impending Habsburg dictatorship. The Czech historian Josef Polisensky experienced the Nazi occupation first hand, and explicitly compared the failure of the western powers to assist the Bohemian rebels in 1618 with the Munich crisis over three centuries later. Günter Barudio's popular German-language account presents Gustavus Adolphus as a champion of peace and justice fighting for German Freedom against Habsburg hegemony. The older, German perspective was even more overtly partisan, associating the emperor with Catholic tyranny, seeking to extinguish the forces of light and historical progress. It is also unfortunate that the best writing in English on this period concentrates on Spain, neglecting the Austrian branch whose problems were central to the causes, course and conclusion of the conflict.

The dynasty's fortunes had been a long time in the making. For much of the later Middle Ages they had trailed behind more powerful competitors in the struggle for influence within the Empire. Acquisition of the imperial title in 1438 had thrust them onto centre stage, but their real power derived from the rapid accumulation of additional provinces and kingdoms between 1477 and 1526. Chief among these was Spain, inherited in 1516 as it was on the cusp of conquering a new world empire. Government remained a family business. Not only did the Habsburgs lack the technical expertise and resources to establish a uniform system of rule, such centralization was not even on their agenda. Each acquisition or conquest added a new title to the family's growing list, magnifying their power and prestige among Europe's crowned heads. Of these, the imperial title was unquestionably the most important, but it was linked to Spain through the person of Charles V only between 1519 and 1558. His vast domains touched every problem facing the early modern world: religious schism, rapid demographic and economic change, encounters with new lands and peoples, international conflict. The challenge was met by creating new branches in the family firm; a process that, as we have seen in Chapter 2, was well under way in the 1540s and led to the formal partition of the dynasty on the emperor's death.

Charles's brother, Emperor Ferdinand I, continued the Austrian branch, which remained formally the most senior through its retention of the imperial title, as well as the Bohemian and Hungarian crowns. Charles's son, Philip II, was given Spain and its overseas empire, together with the Netherlands, which as the Burgundian Kreis were nominally still part of the Empire, and the Habsburg possessions in Italy, many of which also fell under imperial jurisdiction. Inferiority in status was amply compensated by superior resources, given the economic might of the Netherlands, and the American silver now reaching Europe (see Chapter 5). By contrast, Ferdinand I faced the complex problems of the Empire, most of which he ruled only indirectly and which contributed comparatively little against the Turks who had overrun much of Hungary. The Austrian state debt rose fivefold over Ferdinand's reign to reach 10 million florins by his death in 1564, equivalent to nearly five years' revenue. The cost of servicing this sum consumed 1.5 million fl. a year, while the defence of the eastern frontier required another million. The emperor left a further 1.5 million in personal debts, as well as owing his soldiers a million in pay arrears.[1] Ferdinand's posthumous solution was further devolution; in his will he entrusted the imperial title to a senior line, while establishing two junior branches for his younger sons. In the short term, this allowed the dynasty to intensify its rule by sharing the burden of government between three archdukes. However, economies of scale were lost as the debts were split between the branches, forcing each to raise taxes to pay off its share. The centrifugal forces, already present in provincial autonomy, gained momentum as each line concentrated on local problems and evolved its own identity.

As the youngest son, Archduke Carl received the poorest share, consisting of five provinces collectively known as Inner Austria, but often named after Styria, the most populous, that had around 460,000 inhabitants by 1600.² The combined total for the others (Carinthia, Krain, Görz and Gradisca) came to around 600,000, giving the archduke more subjects than most electors. However, his lands were located at the Empire's south-eastern corner, placing them immediately behind the front line against the Ottomans. Though the Styrian economy expanded, thanks to copper and iron mining, its taxes were increasingly diverted to subsidize Croatian and Hungarian border defence. Nonetheless, the Styrian branch assumed second place within the Austrian hierarchy since its relative growth outstripped that of the Tirol line, founded by the middle son, Archduke Ferdinand. The silver mines that had once made the Tirol the family's richest province were in terminal decline, and though salt production provided alternative revenue, the entire area had just 460,000 inhabitants scattered in Alpine valleys and across the region known as Further Austria, a string of small enclaves along the Upper Rhine stretching west into Alsace. Only a third of Alsace belonged directly to the Habsburgs, and their influence over the rest of it and elsewhere in Further Austria depended largely on jurisdictions associated with the imperial title that was reserved for the senior branch.

As eldest son, Maximilian received Austria, together with the Bohemian and Hungarian crowns, and was accepted by the electors as the new emperor. However, only the two provinces of Upper and Lower Austria were directly inherited, and though they had a combined population of 900,000, they produced less revenue than the more populous kingdom of Bohemia.³ The Habsburgs succeeded to Bohemia after the death of their relations, the Jagiellon dynasty, in 1526. The new rulers regarded their crown as hereditary, but had been unable to persuade the local nobility to formally renounce their theories of elective monarchy. Bohemia was a patchwork of five distinct provinces, each with its own laws and government. As a kingdom, Bohemia itself claimed precedence, including denying the other four from participating in choosing their monarch. With around 650,000 inhabitants, the margraviate of Moravia was around half the size of Bohemia, but shared more with it than the other provinces, including the predominance of the Czech language and the legacy of the Hussites. The latter were theological precursors to Luther who related religious freedoms to a campaign for political autonomy and had been crushed only with difficulty by their ruler with assistance from the German nobility in the 1430s. The experience sharpened distinctions with the other, predominantly German-speaking provinces of Silesia and Upper and Lower Lusatia that lay beyond mountain ranges to the north and east.

Habsburg authority was shakiest in Hungary that had also been acquired in 1526 when the last representative of another branch of the Jagiellons died, along with three-quarters of his army at the battle of Mohács against the Turks. The surviving Hungarian nobles divided sharply over whether to accept Habsburg claims to their crumbling kingdom. The majority opposed a foreign ruler, preferring instead one of their own, János Zápolyai, whom they proclaimed king in accordance with their theory of elective monarchy. The others accepted the Habsburgs, who granted wide concessions to buy support. United resistance against the Turks collapsed and the Ottomans captured over 120,000km^2 of the country, acquiring 900,000 new subjects by 1541. Zápolyai retreated north east, creating his own state by amalgamating the largely autonomous principality of Transylvania with Ruthenia, a region that is now part of the Ukraine but was then known as the Partium and consisted of eight Hungarian counties east of the Tisza river. This gave him around 80,000km^2 of territory, with perhaps three-quarters of a million subjects. He secured Habsburg recognition as prince on the condition that Transylvania would pass to them on his death. However, the local nobility had no intention of losing their rights and instead elected István Báthori as their new ruler, who secured Ottoman protection in 1571. Transylvania thus emerged as an autonomous axis between Ottoman Hungary governed from Buda and the rump Habsburg kingdom based at Pressburg (Bratislava). The influx of refugees fleeing the Islamic advance gave the Habsburgs marginally more subjects than either of the other two parts, but the split deprived them of over two-thirds of the former kingdom.[4] Only the Croatians fully accepted the dynasty as their new rulers, using this opportunity to enhance their own autonomy from the Hungarians. The latter remained royalists, accepting Habsburg possession of the ancient crown of St Stephen but steadfastly insisting on their rights not only to elect each king but to oppose him if he broke their constitution. As in Bohemia, these political differences were not a clash between monarchism and republicanism, but represented diverging conceptions of mixed monarchy, alternatively stressing the rights of the ruler or his Estates.

ESTATES AND CONFESSION

Estates Representation

The Estates were early modern representative institutions that were found in all the Habsburg provinces and many of the German territories in the Empire. Just as the lay and ecclesiastical princes, lords and free cities considered themselves the imperial Estate-members sharing powers with the emperor, so the principal nobles, clergy and burghers constituted the Estates of their territory. The Estates' social composition and political role has been open to widely different interpretations. Much writing in the nineteenth and early twentieth centuries echoed complaints from seventeenth-century rulers in presenting the Estates as obstacles to good government and bastions of petty interests. Conversely, liberals championed them as precursors to modern parliaments, struggling valiantly against selfish and reckless rulers who risked their subjects' lives and property in the pursuit of their personal ambitions. Czech and Hungarian writers gave this a distinctive twist by claiming their Estates as guardians of national traditions that were extinguished by Germanic Habsburg aggression. Marxists minimized these conflicts of interest, regarding rulers and the largely aristocratic Estates as part of the same feudal class, united in their exploitation of the peasantry.[5]

Lurking behind all these interpretations is the question whether monarchy or Estates offered the better route to integrate the diverse Habsburg lands into a modern state. This preoccupation with 'modernization' is unhelpful, since such ideas were far from the minds of seventeenth-century Europeans. The Estates certainly contributed positively to the development of the Habsburg monarchy by providing fora for the dynasty to meet their most important subjects. Their development helped dampen the violence that had characterized the later fifteenth century, especially in Austria where the local nobles had even besieged their ruler in the family's Hofburg palace in Vienna in 1461. As with the 'juridification' of imperial politics through the development of the Reichstag, politics in the Habsburg provinces shifted from armed confrontation to legalistic debates about the precise meaning of a growing body of charters and other constitutional documents.

Estates represented corporate groups, not individuals, reflecting the tripartite hierarchical division of early modern society along functional lines into three social 'estates'. The clergy, whose function was to pray for everyone's salvation, were ranked first as the closest to God, followed by the noble estate of warriors and the third, or commons, that provided for society's material welfare. Representation was generally indirect. Bishops, abbots and the heads of religious houses generally represented the bulk of the clergy, who together numbered no more than 2 per cent of the population. Noble representation was through the possession of qualifying manorial estates associated with a seat in the Estates' assembly, or diet (*Landtag*). Nobles comprised around 1 per cent of all Austrians, slightly more of Bohemians and around 5 per cent of Hungarians, but collectively acted as 'the country', speaking for their dependent tenants and serfs who were denied any direct participation. The commons were thus restricted to the urban population living in 'crown' towns directly under Habsburg authority, and excluded those settlements under the jurisdiction of a lay or ecclesiastical lord. Only in the Tirol did the wider population gain access through the communal representation of numerous villages entitled to send their mayors elected by the propertied, male householders.

Of all the Habsburg Estates, only those of the county of Görz conformed to the classic tri-cameral model of clergy-nobles-commons. Elsewhere, the nobles were divided into lords (*Herren*) and knights (*Ritter*). These sat together in a single house in the Inner Austrian provinces, but separately in Upper and Lower Austria, as well as Hungary and the Bohemian lands. Around 200 lords and 1,000 knights were entitled to sit in the Bohemian diet, compared to 90 and 189 respectively in Moravia in 1618. Eighty-seven lordly and 128 knightly families were represented in Lower Austria, but there were always additional nobles without qualifying land who were disenfranchised. Around 300 noble families remained unrepresented in Upper Austria, outnumbering the 43 lords and 114 knights who were. The situation was complicated in Silesia by the presence of the princes of Jägerndorf, Troppau, Liegnitz and elsewhere who together ruled about a third of the duchy. They claimed precedence over all Bohemian lords and had pretensions, thanks to dynastic marriages, to join the ranks of the imperial princes with representation in the Reichstag. Their presence kept most of the lesser nobles and towns disenfranchised, restricting the Silesian Estates to only forty members, including the bishop of Breslau.

Peasant communes existed as a fourth estate alongside the towns and a relatively weak clergy and nobility in the Tirol. The latter two were absent entirely in the small Voralberg Estates, composed only of burghers and peasants. The commons were strong in the other lands of the Tirolean Habsburgs, reinforcing the introspective character of their diets that wanted little to do with grand affairs beyond their valleys. Separate clerical and urban estates existed everywhere else, except in Bohemia where the clergy lost their franchise during the Hussite emergency, but the clergy lacked cohesion, given the absence of powerful bishops outside Vienna, Prague, Breslau, Olmütz and Gran. The Habsburgs acquired wide powers over the Austrian clergy through a papal concordat in the fifteenth century and established a bureau to manage the monasteries and convents in 1568. The clergy were thus caught between Habsburg political supervision and the spiritual jurisdiction of bishops who were generally members of the imperial church beyond the frontier in Passau, Freising, Bamberg, Regensburg and Salzburg. The urban estate was weaker still, since the exclusion of patrimonial towns on land owned by lay and spiritual lords reduced representation to those on the crown domains (*Kammergut*). One hundred towns were excluded for this reason in Moravia, reducing urban representation to six royal towns. Towns still played a role in Bohemia, where there were 32 represented in the Estates, including the 4 that together composed the city of Prague. Only in Hungary did the royal and mining towns sit together with the gentry, facing an upper house of aristocrats and senior clergy reminiscent of the bi-cameral English Parliament. Everywhere, however, townsmen were considered inferior by the nobles, not merely on grounds of social status, but distrusted politically due to their close relationship with the ruling dynasty.

Habsburg Administration

Like those in the German lands, the Habsburg Estates emerged in the fifteenth century to advise their ruler. As representatives of propertied and corporate groups, they spoke for the country on matters of common concern, claiming to offer more impartial advice than servile courtiers or foreign-born councillors. The Habsburgs soon tired of being told unpleasant truths, and developed their own advisory bodies better suited to coordinating policy across their many domains. The basic administrative framework was created by Ferdinand I who had already been entrusted with governing Austria in 1522 by his absentee elder brother Charles V. Ferdinand formed a new privy council in 1527, appointing men by ability as well as status, and created separate Bohemian and Austrian chancelleries to deal with the correspondence and paperwork between Vienna and the various provinces. Other specialist departments emerged, notably the treasury (*Hofkammer*) and court war council (*Hofkriegsrat*), to handle particular business and provide expert advice to assist the privy council. We should not make too much of this. Habsburg administration remained extremely sloppy. Gundacker von Liechtenstein was appointed president of the treasury by Ferdinand II in August 1620, but was surprised to receive post a few days later addressed to Seifrid Christoph von Breuner, while his subordinates all thought Gundacker von Polheim was in charge.[6] Despite their imperial prestige, the Habsburgs found it difficult to attract skilled and experienced staff. Considering their appalling record as employers, this is not surprising: Rudolf II died in 1612 owing two and half million florins in back pay to his officials and servants.

The ability of the central agencies to reach into the localities was severely restricted. The Habsburgs could appoint a governor (*Statthalter*) in those provinces without a resident archduke, but had to consult the Estates when naming the lord lieutenant (*Landmarschall*) and his deputy who commanded the local militia. They could also appoint bailiffs in the crown towns and stewards to manage the economic assets of their domains, but these rarely constituted more than 5 per cent of each province. Virtually all other local administration was in the hands of the nobility. In Bohemia, for example, the nobles ran the provincial court that resolved disputes between them, passed laws and exercised jurisdiction over the entire rural population. The situation was even more extreme in Hungary where half the villages were owned by 50 aristocratic families, and most of the rest belonged to the 5,000 gentry families. Only the royal towns fell under Habsburg jurisdiction, but even the largest of these, Debrecen, had fewer than 20,000 inhabitants. The king could not even name a governor, known here as the palatine, but simply proposed candidates to the diet that chose who was to exercise royal prerogatives when the monarch was out of the country.

With the majority of subjects living outside the crown lands, the Estates became a vital link between the dynasty and the bulk of the population. It was difficult to achieve anything without their assistance, or at least acquiescence. In particular, their help was essential to raise taxes, since domains' income covered only a fraction of Habsburg expenditure. Medieval monarchs had been expected to 'live off their own', only drawing on their subjects' resources in critical situations, such as facing invasion or natural disaster. Estates emerged in Central Europe to facilitate such extraordinary grants at a time when rulers were assuming wider responsibilities during the fifteenth century. The growing permanence of royal government and the complexity of the problems it faced led to more frequent assemblies, gradually transforming intermittent taxation into regular, annual levies. Estates were compelled to create their own institutions, forming standing committees to liaise with the ruler when the diet was not in session, as well as a secretariat to maintain records and a treasury to administer the taxes. The Habsburg treasury received taxes from the Estates as well as revenue remitted by the stewards on the domains. The size and regularity of the Estates' taxes improved their credit rating, enabling them to borrow additional sums and to assume responsibility for some of the dynasty's debts, in return for permission to levy further taxes to pay these off.

A parallel governmental structure thus emerged alongside that of the dynasty, but the Estates had little desire to usurp political power. Their theory of mixed monarchy left the initiative in the ruler's hands, particularly in dealings with outsiders and in times of crisis. They saw their role as guardians of the established order, to preserve the common good by preventing their ruler embarking on reckless or illegitimate policies. Rights and liberties had been established through several centuries of bargaining with the ruler. The Estates saw it as their duty to defend and enhance these, objecting to new laws that transgressed old charters and resisting measures that lacked their consent. Yet, this did not amount to modern parliamentarianism, since the Estates were vehicles for sectional and even individual interests. Nowhere can this be more clearly seen than in the campaign for religious liberties that accompanied the spread of the Reformation to the Habsburg lands, since Protestantism became associated with corporate privileges, not individual freedoms.

The Spread of Protestantism

Despite Protestant hopes that this or that archduke might convert, the Habsburgs remained uniformly Catholic. Protestantism thus lacked the political support that produced the territorial churches elsewhere in the Empire. Converts in the Habsburg lands were forced to build their organization from the bottom up, making the nobility, not the dynasty, the key players. Nobles exercised local jurisdiction that often extended to patronage over the appointment of parish priests and school teachers for their tenants. Spiritual jurisdiction still rested with the bishop, but he was usually far away and relied on the landlords to pay the priests. The church's weakness was replicated in the Estates, where it deferred to the nobles. Given the Estates' role in passing laws on moral and social behaviour, the nobles were well-placed to promote the second Reformation of life, as well as that of the Word. Whatever their personal convictions, Protestantism also suited the intensification of lordship by uniting the right of patronage with other proprietorial rights. As one prominent Lower Austrian put it, nobles were 'at the same time lords and bishops on our property, we hire and fire clerics and they have to obey us'.[7] The presence of Lutheran noblemen within a province soon created the phenomenon known as 'exodus' (*Auslauf*), as peasants and burghers left neighbouring Catholic manors and towns to attend Protestant services. The nobles' pivotal role is demonstrated by the case of the Tirol, where the new faith remained tainted by the experience of early sixteenth-century radicalism while Catholicism grew more attractive thanks to Capuchin missionaries sent by Cardinal Borromeo. The Tirolean nobles remained solidly Catholic and the Estates backed the archduke in ordering Protestants to convert or leave in 1585.

By then, Catholicism was under severe pressure in the other provinces. Nine in ten Lower Austrian nobles had embraced Lutheranism, as had 85 per cent of those in Upper Austria, where three-quarters of the urban population and half the peasants were Protestants. Around 70 per cent of the Inner Austrian population had also abandoned Rome, and only 5 out of the 135 Styrian nobles remained Catholic. Though the largely Slovene peasantry rejected what they saw as a German religion, 16 of the 22 Styrian crown towns had accepted Lutheranism by 1572.[8] As nobles converted they began lobbying through the Estates to secure formal recognition from the Habsburgs. With Catholic membership dwindling, the dynasty had no choice but to compromise with the Protestants to secure continued assistance with its mounting debts. The tripartite division of the dynasty in 1564 forced each branch to negotiate separately with its own Estates. Those of Upper and Lower Austria obtained the Religious Assurance (*Assecuration*) in 1568 and 1571 respectively, granting freedom to accept Lutheranism for the lords, knights and their tenants, in return for the Estates paying off 2.5 million fl. of Habsburg debts. The privileges were extended in 1574 to allow nobles to worship in their town houses that now became de facto churches in crown cities, notably Vienna. The Inner Austrian Estates assumed responsibility for another 1 million fl. of debt in 1572 in return for similar privileges. These were consolidated six years later in the Pacification of Bruck (*Brucker Libell*) in return for regular taxes to maintain border defences against the Turks. Debt amortization had cost the Inner Austrians 1.7 million fl. by 1600, while subsidies for the frontier accounted for a further 2.93 million between 1588 and 1608.[9] The population paid dearly, buying the Austrian nobles their own version of the religious freedoms granted the German princes in the Peace of Augsburg.

The situation was different in Bohemia where agreements from 1436 and 1485 already recognized Utraquism alongside Catholicism. Utraquism was a moderate development of the Hussite faith, so-called because it insisted the faithful receive the Eucharist in both bread and wine (*sub utraque specie*), rather than the latter being exclusively reserved for the clergy. Services were in Czech and the church lay outside episcopal jurisdiction, though the Utraquists compromised with Rome by sending their priests to Venice for ordination. The Habsburgs confirmed these privileges when they acquired Bohemia in 1526, not least because Utraquism was losing its momentum and most Catholics hoped its followers would soon rejoin them, although a radical minority of Utraquists split to become the Unity of Brethren, refusing to submit to Rome or abandon the Hussites' social programme. Utraquism's close ties to Czech culture restricted the spread of Lutheranism to the German-speaking urban population and some of the nobles. When the Czech nobility refused to back the Habsburgs in the Schmalkaldic War in 1547, Ferdinand cracked down on the radical Brethren and initiated a programme to revitalize the Catholic church. A Jesuit college was founded in Prague in 1556 and an archbishop appointed there five years later, after a vacancy of a century and a half.

The Catholic revival caused the other faiths to draw closer together. The Bohemian Estates brokered the *Confessio Bohemica* in 1575 that attempted to establish a broadly Protestant church by glossing over the theological differences between Lutheranism, Utraquism and the Brethren. However, no deal comparable to those in Austria followed. Maximilian II saw no reason to extend recognition beyond the Utraquists and consequently the Estates rejected his successor's request to amortize the Bohemian crown's debts of 5 million fl. The Brethren split, many defecting back to Utraquism to receive official protection, while others embraced Calvinism that was brought into Bohemia by Palatine immigrants and by nobles returning from German universities in the 1580s. Lutheranism took hold only in Silesia and Lusatia, though the Silesian princes and educated burghers also adopted Calvinism in the early 1600s.

The religious spectrum in the kingdom had become more diverse than in Austria. Catholics were reduced to less than 15 per cent of Bohemians and around 35 per cent of Moravians, the others being mainly Utraquists, Brethren or Lutherans. Calvinists composed only 3 per cent of the total population but they had disproportionate political influence thanks to their numbers among the elite of society. The situation remained fluid as the Estates continued to regard religion as a gift from God that could not be determined by mere mortals. Relations with the ruler were based on mutual respect for each party's interests, with negotiations intended to secure lasting compromise. This tradition penetrated deeply into the fabric of society where it was not uncommon for the same family to have adherents of different churches. Understandably, most nobles refused to acknowledge their faith publicly, particularly in Moravia where the local Brethren continued to make converts and even Anabaptist communities persisted. Many noblemen had books from a variety of confessions in their libraries, and most seem to have favoured a non-denominational Erasmian personal faith. There were tensions, but no sense of imminent crisis.

Calvinism was stronger in Hungary where Lutheranism had long been distrusted as too 'Germanic'. Less than a fifth of the Magyar population embraced Lutheranism, and then mainly those in mountain villages away from aristocratic domination. Luther's faith also found some acceptance among the Slovaks of Upper Hungary in the north-east, as well as among the southern Slavs of Croatia and Slovenia. However, nearly half the nobility embraced Calvinism, as did many of the Magyar peasantry. Only one in ten Magyar nobles stayed loyal to Rome and there were only 300 Catholic priests left in Habsburg Hungary by 1606, mainly concentrated around the episcopal seats of Gran, Raab and Neutra. Croatia and the three Slovene counties remained predominantly Catholic, mainly because the local nobility depended on employment on the Military Frontier and faced competition for appointments from Lutheran Inner Austrians.

Social Tensions

The spread of the competing faiths had depended everywhere on the attitudes of the nobility. Though Catholics were in a minority outside Croatia and the Tirol, none of the varieties of Protestantism succeeded in securing complete acceptance. Their legality rested on rights extorted from the Habsburgs through the Estates' power of the purse. Such rights had not yet been hallowed by time and their preservation depended on how far those who benefited from them convinced others of their necessity. Protestant nobles not only faced internal opposition from their remaining Catholic peers, but wider economic developments made it hard to sustain the support of other corporate groups.

Noble wealth derived from the largely agrarian economy that produced rye, oats, wheat and barley. Mining assumed some significance in the Tirol and part of Inner Austria, but the Habsburgs retained control of much of this. Textile production was growing in Upper Austria, Bohemia and western Moravia, while horse breeding was important in other parts of Moravia and in Hungary. All these activities required land and labour and these in turn were controlled through feudal jurisdictions. Like the Habsburgs, most lords managed only a small part of their property directly as domains, leasing the rest to tenant farmers in return for fixed rents. Rising inflation made this less attractive in the later sixteenth century, but it was difficult to force tenants to pay more since they often owed obligations to multiple landlords and could play one master against another. The Habsburgs were also extending the right of appeal to peasants as a means of inserting themselves as arbiters of the rural world between landlords and peasants, except in Hungary where the diet prevented this in 1556. The rising urban population of north-western Europe stimulated the demand for grain, creating new opportunities for eastern and Central European landlords in the six-teenth century. They expanded their domains by purchase, foreclosing or simple eviction, while intensifying feudal jurisdiction to compel dependent peasants to work for them.

This process has been labelled 'second serfdom' since it emerged around 1500 just as medieval serfdom declined elsewhere in Europe. It was pronounced in Poland, Hungary, Bohemia, parts of Austria and north-eastern Germany, but was far from uniform, nor necessarily the dominant form of lordly exploitation even in regions where it was practised.[10] Nonetheless, when combined with inflation, demographic and environmental change, the spread of this 'manorial economy' grew increasingly oppressive and symbolized a wider commercialization of the rural world. Lords began exploiting forests and other assets in new ways, for example charging peasants for collecting firewood or letting their pigs root for food. The changes also fuelled tensions within the elite, as some lords were better placed to seize opportunities than others. The situation was most extreme in Hungary where around fifty magnate families accumulated 41 per cent of the entire country, creating econo-mies of scale and winning clients among the gentry and peasants through their ability to pay private armies to combat banditry and oppose the Turks. The decline of the Hungarian gentry was paralleled in Bohemia where the number of knights fell by nearly a third in the five decades before 1618. Wealth became increasingly concentrated to the point where a quarter of the country was held by only eleven aristocratic families.

Peasant resentment exploded first in Upper Austria in 1595, and spread to the western parts of Lower Austria the following year. Heavy-handed attempts to reimpose Catholic priests in some Protestant parishes provided a trigger, but the underlying causes ran deeper and protests were soon directed against the Lutheran nobles who dominated the Estates. Peasants called for 'Swiss Freedom', demanding representation in the Estates as well as the abolition of recent dues and taxes. As the current head of the dynasty and archduke in Austria, Emperor Rudolf II tried to broker a compromise, but he antagonized both sides by linking his mediation to clumsy moves to restore Catholicism. Faced with a resurgence of violence in the autumn of 1596, Rudolf handed the initiat-ive to his younger brother Matthias, whom he had already appointed governor of Austria the year before. Matthias combined more effective military counter-measures with an investigation of peasant grievances. It was the policy that had worked so well in the wake of the 1525 German Peasant War. Around a hundred alleged ringleaders were executed and several thousand others were mutilated by cutting off their noses and ears to underscore the illegitimacy of rebellion. Protest through the 'proper' legal channels was meanwhile rewarded by decrees in June 1598, restricting peasant labour service on landlords' fields to two weeks a year.

The emergency exposed the nobility's continued dependency on the ruling dynasty, not least because the provincial militia proved useless against the peasants. It also revealed the difficulties of forging a broad alliance across the corporate divisions in society. Even where they shared the same faith, nobles, burghers and peasants remained bitterly divided. Burghers despised peasants and were often involved in their exploitation, extending expensive credit to indebted tenants, or paying their families miserable wages for piecework in the nascent textile industry. They had little interest in the peasants' calls to extend Estates representation to the villages. More fundamentally, all communities were split by deep inequalities that generally overrode the neighbourliness of living in close proximity and left them divided, especially when it came to responding to demands from landlords and other outsiders. Though communities largely managed their own affairs, only a minority of propertied inhabitants were enfranchised. The poorer, disenfranchised majority frequently lacked firm rights of residence, especially in the towns, and relied on common assets, such as meadows for grazing their few animals, to supplement irregular or casual employment. Richer peasants tried to shift the burden of additional taxes or labour demands onto their unrepresented poorer neighbours, while restricting access to valuable communal assets in danger of erosion through over-usage. Far from bringing people together, religion added new fissures through confessional antagonisms that cut across social and economic divisions. The question of how best to achieve common goals prompted bitter disputes as some placed their faith in official promises to address grievances through the courts, while others felt violent protest was the only option. Nobles showed some respect for peasants' religious convictions, provided these coincided with their own. However the rebellion demonstrated the difficulty of linking religious to political liberty, as Lutheran lords joined their Catholic counterparts to hire mercenaries to assist Archduke Matthias in 1596.

THE CATHOLIC REVIVAL

The leading members of the Habsburg family became convinced that the future of their dynasty depended on restoring Catholicism as the basis of political loyalty. This goal was not unrealistic, given the continued presence of a Catholic minority in the Estates and the deep divisions among the Protestants, the majority of whom remained loyal subjects despite the confessional differences. The religious freedoms extorted in the 1570s had been granted as special privileges to the nobles and towns of individual provinces, and had yet to be accepted by all members of each Estate as integral parts of their corporate rights. The Estates lacked a platform to coordinate a response to the dynasty since they had failed to develop a viable general assembly. Here, the partition of 1564 actually worked to the dynasty's advantage since it reinforced the practice of negotiating with each province separately and ensured that the general Austrian diet never reassembled after the early sixteenth century. Bohemia's refusal to recognize the kingdom's other four provinces as equals ensured that its general diet did not meet for nearly a century after 1518. The initiative thus lay in Habsburg hands, with fair chances of success provided the different branches could work together and present a united front.

Rudolf II

As head of the main line, it fell to Rudolf II to provide leadership once he became emperor on his father Maximilian's death in 1576.[11] At the age of eleven Rudolf had been sent in 1563 to Madrid with his younger brother Ernst to keep him away from Protestant contagion and to curry favour with the powerful Spanish Habsburgs. The austere, emotionally detached environment of the Spanish court left a lasting impression on both boys who witnessed the harsh realities of power firsthand. Don Carlos, Philip II's son by his first marriage, became mentally unstable and was imprisoned after developing a pathological hatred of his father. Carlos's already delicate health was undermined by his hunger strikes and the intrusive remedial measures of his gaolers. His death in 1568 immediately sparked rumours that he had been poisoned to remove him as a political liability and the Dutch rebels later openly accused Philip of this. Though the charge is certainly false, there was nonetheless something awful about the king's conduct, remaining at his desk busy with the affairs of state while his son died in agony. The affair may have convinced Rudolf of the impossibility of matching his uncle's strict devotion to duty. Contemporaries certainly noted a change in his behaviour upon his return to Vienna in 1571. Though he had adopted the stiff Spanish formality, it was clear he had no love for his uncle's kingdom. Despite considerable pressure from his relations to ensure a legitimate heir, he refused to marry Philip's favourite daughter, Isabella, preferring instead his long-term mistress, Katharina Strada, with whom he had at least six children. This close relationship was an exception, as Rudolf found it increasingly difficult to deal with the living, retreating into an exaggerated veneration for his ancestors. Those who did get to meet him, often after waiting literally months at a time, were struck by his intelligence, curiosity and wide knowledge. He became an avid art collector and patron of astronomers, alchemists and poets. His Spanish experience left him with an inflated sense of majesty that prevented him from delegating responsibility to those who wanted to help him. While not afraid of hard work, his mind was crowded by too many thoughts, leading to indecision, especially as he was likely to get discouraged if his initial efforts failed to meet immediate success.

This became apparent at the very start of his reign when he decided to set an example in promoting Catholicism in his capital. Local clerics and laity had revived the Corpus Christi brotherhood in 1577 and planned a procession through Vienna the following May. Rudolf placed himself at its head, flanked by his brothers Ernst and Maximilian, as well as Duke Ferdinand of Bavaria and other dignitaries. It was an explicit challenge to the largely Protestant population in the manner of the Orange Order marches in modern Belfast. Lutheran stallholders who refused to move out of the way were roughly handled by the imperial bodyguards, knocking over a jug of milk for sale in the process. The ensuing Milk War riot startled the emperor, precipitating a serious illness in 1579–80 that left him permanently altered. It is doubtful if he was ever clinically insane, though at least one of his illegitimate children also exhibited schizoid tendencies. Rather, he suffered from what contemporaries diagnosed as melancholia, or severe depression.[12] His own intelligence probably contributed to this by making him acutely aware of the yawning gap between his sense of majesty and the stark realities of limited power. Though he had never been on good terms with his mother, her departure for Spain in 1581 deprived him of one of his few remaining confidantes. He grew still more isolated by moving his court to Prague two years later, shutting himself away in the Hradschin palace, high above the city, refusing to see anyone for days and leaving important documents unsigned. In September 1591 one of his chemical experiments went wrong, burning his cheek and beard and killing his master of horse who had the misfortune of being beside him. The accident plunged him deeper into despair and he now shut himself away for months at a time. His persistent refusal to marry caused mounting disquiet among his relations, driving Philip II to arrange the betrothal of Isabella to another of the emperor's brothers, Archduke Albert, in 1597. Their marriage two years later deepened Rudolf's suspicions towards Spain and finally forced him to confront the frustrations of his own personal life. His obsession with astrology encouraged growing paranoia as the new century dawned, especially as Rudolf interpreted Tycho Brahe's predictions for September 1600 to mean there was a plot to assassinate him. His mood swings became more violent and he lashed out at his courtiers, even injuring one of them.

Melchior Klesl

Rudolf's move to Prague and subsequent nervous breakdown heightened the centrifugal forces within the dynasty, as Austrian government was devolved to Ernst. Neither he, nor his successor Matthias after 1595, was able to devote much time to Catholic renewal, which now fell to the son of a Lutheran baker from Vienna, Melchior Klesl. Klesl had converted to Catholicism while a student at Vienna University and rose, thanks to Jesuit and Habsburg patronage, to become chancellor of his former alma mater by 1580, then bishop of Wiener Neustadt in 1588 and of Vienna itself a decade later. Extremely shrewd, with a tongue as sharp as his mind, Klesl made enemies easily, especially as he came to regard himself as the only one competent to advise the Habsburgs, ignored formal structures and made policy on his own. As familiar with Machiavelli as with the Bible, he has often been depicted as a secular politician in clerical robes. He was certainly worlds apart from Cardinal Borromeo, spending more time at Rudolf's court than either of his two bishoprics after 1590. His absence itself speaks for the slow pace of Catholic renewal. Religion nonetheless remained central to his world view as the underpinning of proper order, rather than any sentimental, mystical or spiritual attachment.[13]

Klesl targeted Vienna where Protestantism was spreading rapidly thanks to the presence of the Lower Austrian Estates' assembly hall, numerous Lutheran aristocratic town houses, and the practice of exodus that saw thousands of Viennese leave the city each Sunday to worship at surrounding Lutheran manors. The Milk War riot was used as a pretext to install a Catholic city council and withdraw permission to use the assembly hall for Lutheran services, while those worshipping outside the city were fined. A year after becoming chancellor, Klesl ruled that only Catholics could graduate from the university. He then worked with new councillors to transfer to the church around 90 of the 1,200 houses within the city walls for use as places of worship or education.[14] The Catholic presence in the city was further boosted by the return of the court after Rudolf's death in 1612. Courtiers, nobles and their servants squeezed the burghers from the more desirable properties around the Hofburg, especially in the inflationary years of the early 1620s when rich Catholics bought houses with debased coin. The number of Catholics had already quadrupled from the time of Rudolf's accession to reach 8,000 by 1594.

The collapse of peasant protest by 1598 encouraged Klesl to extend his activities deeper into the countryside. The Upper Austrian lord lieutenant was sent with an armed escort to install Catholic parish priests and to close the Protestant Estates' school in Linz. The following year, Klesl led 23,000 Lower Austrian pilgrims to Mariazell in Styria, initiating what had become an annual event by 1617. Other pilgrimage sites were developed, especially those associated with Austrian history and the dynasty to reinforce the links between piety and loyalty. These developments did not go unopposed. When the Corpus Christi procession was introduced to Linz in 1600, the citizens seized the priest and drowned him in the river. As with the Milk War, this merely offered a pretext to remove more Protestant privileges, in this case expelling all school teachers from Upper Austria. When the salt miners downed tools in the Salzkammergut in further protest, Archduke Matthias sent 1,200 troops and militia to force them back to work in February 1602. However, impressive though it seemed, the Catholic revival in Austria lacked firm foundations and even as late as 1600 three-quarters of the 50,000 Viennese still dissented from the official faith.

Catholic Strategy

Greater success was achieved in Inner Austria, where the combination of religious and political loyalty was developed more systematically after inauspicious beginnings. Archduke Carl was staunchly Catholic, but was driven by debts and the cost of border defence to concede the Pacification of Bruck in 1578. He had hoped to keep this secret, but to his horror the jubilant Protestant members of his Estates published an unauthorized version of the concessions and he was promptly excommunicated by an unsympathetic Pope Gregory XIII. Chastised, he went to meet his brother, Ferdinand of the Tirol, and brother-in-law, Duke Wilhelm V of Bavaria, in Munich in October 1579. His relations accepted his explanation that the published text misrepresented his intentions, but felt that it was too dangerous to revoke it. Only three months before, 5,000 Viennese had demonstrated before the Hofburg to protest against the Catholic policies there. None of the archdukes had more than a handful of troops and they had to avoid anything that might unite opposition against them. A less confrontational policy was required and the Munich meeting provided it in the form of a programme that became the blueprint for all subsequent measures up to 1618.

It was agreed that the present concessions represented the limit of what could be granted. Rather than revoking existing privileges, the archdukes would insist on a strictly Catholic interpretation of them, banning all Protestant activities that were not expressly sanctioned under the law. They had no desire to crush the Estates, since it was impossible to govern without them. Instead, the Protestant members were to be isolated by denying them any further favours, while loyal Catholics were to be rewarded and promoted. Here the Habsburgs could draw on their uncontested archducal, royal and imperial prerogatives to ennoble, legitimize children and confer degrees and other honours. These powers extended their influence throughout the Empire, since most princes could not create new nobles but merely recommend individuals to the emperor for special favour. As self-regulating corporations, the Estates could chose who to admit as members, but they depended on the Habsburgs to ennoble people in the first place, while the dynasty alone elected lords from the existing knights and exercised further influence over the church and crown towns. A significant number of Austrian noble families died out during the sixteenth century, creating further opportunities to increase the proportion of loyal Catholics. For example, forty new families joined the Inner Austrian nobility between 1560 and 1620, mainly from Italy, and sixteen of these acquired Estates membership.

Further efforts were made to make Catholicism more attractive, by ensuring a better-educated, disciplined and more numerous clergy that paid greater attention to the spiritual needs of ordinary folk. Pope Gregory was persuaded to support the plan and began to encourage other rulers to participate. Germanico Malaspina, a veteran of the Council of Trent, was appointed as a new nuncio for Inner Austria to persuade lay and ecclesiastical rulers to stop bickering over jurisdiction. Able though he was, Malaspina could not resolve all the disputes, not least because most bishops were also at loggerheads with their cathedral canons. Nonetheless, Salzburg reached a concordat with Bavaria in 1583, followed by an Austrian agreement with Passau nine years later, which ushered in an era of better relations. The new archbishop of Salzburg, Wolf Dietrich von Raitenau, was inspired to travel to Rome in 1588 and returned fired with Counter-Reformation fervour, while his suffragan dioceses also passed into the hands of more reform-minded clerics, notably Martin Brenner who became bishop of Seckau in 1585.

However, the Munich programme required time to take effect and the new unity soon shattered when Carl's precipitous attempt to ban Protestant worship in his crown towns stirred resistance in December 1580. Fearing an imminent revolt, his allies got cold feet and refused to send assistance. Lack of qualified personnel prevented any headway on the ground, and the archduke was forced to restrict his policies to his capital at Graz where he recruited a group of loyal advisers and raised the status of the Jesuit college there to a university to train more priests and officials. By 1587 he felt sufficiently strong to start again, targeting the smaller provincial towns that were expected to offer less resistance. Invoking the right of reformation accorded him as an imperial prince under the Peace of Augsburg of 1555, he established a 'reform commission' under Bishop Brenner, protected by a military escort, to tour the country installing new priests, closing Protestant schools and transferring each town council to Catholic hands. The measures were presented as moderate and reasonable, with the archduke simply wanting peace and reconciliation between his subjects, taking action only to defend Catholic faith and property against Protestant vandalism. Anxious to avoid the commission being extended to their manors, the nobles did little to help their burgher allies who were picked off, one by one. Brenner met only passive resistance until Carl fell ill in May 1590. A serious riot in Graz then forced the authorities to release an imprisoned Protestant student. Sensing weakness, disorder soon spread to other towns, especially after Carl died in July leaving his twelve-year-old son, Ferdinand, as the new archduke. The Estates asserted their traditional right to step in during the regency, rejecting the boy's Bavarian relations as unsuitable and placing government in the hands of Archduke Ernst, who had no stomach for further confrontation.

Archduke Ferdinand

When Ferdinand was declared of age in 1595, it seemed highly unlikely that he would be able to recover the ground lost to the Estates, let alone become one of the most powerful men of his age. The future emperor has received a mixed reception, particularly among Anglophone historians who echo contemporary Protestant opinion that he was 'but a silly Jesuited soule'. His mother, Maria of Bavaria, sent him to the Jesuit college in Ingolstadt to escape Protestant influence in March 1590, but his father's death forced him to cut short his studies and return to Graz. He was a short youth, something that probably accounted for his shyness, and his family grew concerned at his poor health, especially because his elder brother had already died. Such fears were unfounded, as Ferdinand grew up physically fit, becoming an accomplished horseman and passionate hunter. Unlike his cousin Rudolf, Ferdinand was friendly and well-disposed to those around him, an impression enhanced by his red complexion and later corpulence. He grew fond of food, especially game and other rich meats that made him put on weight and develop asthma. Unlike most of his contemporaries among the German princes, he refrained from heavy drinking and his confessor proudly reported that he never received women alone in his room. Allegedly, to quell carnal urges he wore a hair shirt prior to his marriage and subsequently as a widower. The papal nuncio, Carlo Carafa, later reported that

he goes to bed around ten in the evening as is the German custom; he is already up around four in the morning or earlier ... Once he has got up, His Majesty goes to the chapel to hear two masses, one for the soul of his first wife, who, though of shaky health, was tenderly loved by the emperor. If it is a feast day, the emperor then takes holy communion, for which purpose he goes to the church and hears a German sermon. This is usually given by a Jesuit and lasts an hour. After the sermon he remains at the high altar, usually for an hour and a half accompanied by specially selected music . . . On those days that are not feast days, the emperor, after attending two masses (something from which he never deviates), spends the rest of the morning and often much of the afternoon in council meetings.[15]

He continued this routine of heavy meals, work, hunting and long hours of prayer in draughty churches throughout his life; after his autopsy, his doctors were amazed he had lived so long.

While he chose three successive Jesuit confessors after 1595, Ferdinand was devout rather than a fanatic. His desire to advance Catholicism was tempered by a deep legalism that prevented him from deviating from what he understood as the constitution. While he told the Inner Austrian Estates that he was an 'absolute prince', he rejected Machiavellian reasons of state, believing that political success depended on adhering to Christian principles. Faith in divine providence was reinforced by his own experience during the Graz riots of 1590 when a thunderstorm dispersed the protesters and averted what the Catholics feared was an impending massacre.[16] The success of his later reform efforts strengthened his convictions, because most of his advisers had predicted they would end in revolt. Yet, doubts persisted that God might abandon him if he made a mistake, encouraging caution and the desire to consult widely before taking action.

Ferdinand immediately signalled his intent by reverting to the old princely oath on his accession, rather than the version from 1564 modified to be less offensive to the Protestants. He also refused to acknowledge the Pacification of Bruck as part of the territorial laws. None of the Estates wanted a confrontation and took his silence for assent, accepting him as their ruler by 1597. To Ferdinand, their submission left his conscience clear to revoke the 1578 privileges as soon as he was strong enough. His political advisers urged caution, conscious of Archduke Carl's earlier failures, but bishops Brenner and Georg Stobaeus of Levant urged him to follow his conscience. Having travelled to Rome to consult the pope, and after long discussions to ensure all his 'team' were on board, Ferdinand finally revived the reform commission in April 1598. Careful preparations were made to avoid a repetition of the protests of 1580 and 1590. All three Inner Austrian Estates were summoned simultaneously but separately to keep them busy and prevent combined opposition. Each was forced to accept a Catholic cleric on its executive committee who them promptly blocked any anti-government measure. Ferdinand did not shy away from naked force. Two Estates officials were seized and tortured until they agreed to surrender control of the principal school in Graz. The entire regular garrison of 800 men were deployed to protect the commission and troops were billeted on any burghers who protested. Operations entered full swing in 1599 as Brenner visited each Styrian town in turn, expelling Protestant teachers and pastors to break the back of any resistance and installing a Catholic priest. Once passions subsided, the commission would return for more provocative actions, closing the Protestant school, destroying the cemetery and demolishing the church, sometimes spectacularly as at Eisenerz where it was blown up. Brenner soon earned the sobriquet of *Ketzenhammer* – hammer of heretics – as he went out of his way to humiliate and denigrate his foes, trampling on everything they held dear:

The bodies of the faithfull digged up, and given to be devoured by Dogs and Hogs; as also the Coffins taken and set by the highway side, some burnt with fire; a worke both barbarous and inhumane. Also upon the burial-places of the faithfull, were erected Gibets and places for execution of malefactors. Also upon those places where Protestant Churches stood, or where the Pulpit stood, or the Font-stone, were erected alwaies most filthy spectacles most ugly to behold.[17]

Events climaxed as Brenner returned in triumph to Graz in 1600 to preside over a bonfire of 10,000 Protestant books. Ferdinand celebrated by marrying Maria Anna, the pious and dutiful daughter of Wilhelm V of Bavaria, in an eight-day festival that April. All remaining Protestant pastors and teachers were then expelled, as were those burghers who refused to convert. In all, around 11,000 left the Inner Austrian provinces between 1598 and 1605, either by expulsion or by choosing exile. Many went to Protestant territories in the Empire, like Württemberg where the duke founded Freudenstadt (literally 'Joy Town') to welcome them.

Throughout, Ferdinand had remained within his albeit narrow interpretation of the law. The commission officially targeted 'heresy', not Lutheranism, and it was not until 1609 that Catholicism was made a formal prerequisite for office-holders. Brenner also hit Lutheran church structures that lacked explicit privileges, leaving private belief un-touched. Special concessions were made to the miners to forestall disruption to the economy and revenue. The Estates had already retaliated by withholding taxes in 1599 and appealing to the emperor. When Ferdinand prohibited further appeals, 238 nobles signed a petition threatening to emigrate unless he restored free worship. He simply called their bluff; most stayed at home and a second tax strike collapsed in 1604.

Bohemia

The sea change around 1600 was even felt in Bohemia where Rudolf remained aloof in his palace. As in the Austrian provinces, re-Catholicization targeted the crown towns as the weak link in the Estates. Catholic sympathizers won a majority on the Utraquist consistory by portraying the more radical Brethren as a Calvinist fifth column. Supported by the official Catholic and Utraquist church establishments, the Habsburg government began appointing loyalists as bailiffs of the royal towns, securing control of their councils even though only Pilsen and Budweis had predominantly Catholic populations. The Corpus Christi procession was revived in Prague after 1592 and soon extended to other towns where local dignitaries were obliged to participate. The crown also benefited from the extinction of many Bohemian noble families, sequestrating or purchasing their properties to increase its share of the kingdom from 1 per cent to over 10 per cent by 1603. The proportion belonging to the church and the royal towns rose to 9 per cent, giving the crown control of around a fifth of the country. The proportion was larger still in Moravia where the church had retained more land. Catholic wealth was influential given the undercapitalized state of the Bohemian economy.

The character of Bohemian Catholicism was also changing. Seven major landowning families died out between 1597 and 1611, and their wealth passed largely to those who were more militantly inclined. Vilém Slavata, whom we last met hanging from a window in the Hradschin, inherited the Neuhaus (Hradec) estate in 1596, while Karl Liechtenstein acquired the Boskowitz fortune in Moravia a year later. Many of the new generation were converts and included the men who were to hold power at the outbreak of the revolt. Liechtenstein, who later became governor of Bohemia, was raised as one of the Bohemian Brethren, as was his younger brother Gundacker, who converted in 1602 and subsequently became treasury chief in 1620. Michael Adolf von Althann from Lower Austria was converted by Klesl in 1598 and was made governor of Gran in 1606 and an imperial count in 1610. Another Lower Austrian, Franz Christoph von Khevenhüller converted and was made ambassador to Spain, later returning to write the *Annales Ferdinadei*, an extended biography of Ferdinand II. The Styrian Lutheran Johann Ulrich von Eggenberg likewise became a Catholic in the 1590s and had become Ferdinand's closest adviser by 1597. Maximilian von Trauttmannsdorff, another Styrian who became the Habsburg monarchy's leading statesman, was also raised a Lutheran, but followed his parents in adopting Catholicism during Brenner's reform commission. Slavata converted from personal conviction while studying as a young adult in Siena, but others were persuaded at an earlier age, such as Peter Pázmány who embraced Rome under Jesuit influence at the age of twelve. Pázmány succeeded Ferenc Forgach (another convert!) as cardinal and archbishop of Gran in 1616 to spearhead Catholic reform in Hungary. Conversions helped raise the Catholic proportion among the nobility to one in ten in Upper Austria, one in five in Bohemia and one in four in Lower Austria by 1610.

The accumulation of wealth and office emboldened the militants to exclude Protestants from government. The papal nuncio in Prague persuaded the unstable Rudolf to make Zdenko Lobkowitz Bohemian chancellor on 24 August 1599, the anniversary of the Massacre of St Bartholomew. Inspired by his reading of Spanish political theorists, Lobkowitz then pressed the emperor to dismiss his Protestant advisers in 1600 and reissue the mandate outlawing the Bohemian Brethren. Clerical vacancies were filled by new men of vigour. The position of bishop of Olmütz, head of the Moravian church, went to Franz Dietrichstein in 1598, a graduate of the Jesuit Collegium Germanicum who owned a thirteenth of the entire province. The aggressive Wolfgang Setender was appointed abbot in Braunau, while Klostergrab (Hrob) with its associated monasteries at Tepl and Strahov was entrusted to Archbishop Johann Lohelius, who held a synod in Prague to promote Tridentine reform. Whereas all key government posts in Moravia had been occupied by Protestants in 1594, the administration was uniformly Catholic a decade later.

On the surface, the situation looked promising for the militants as the new century dawned. The Munich programme had proved quite successful in Inner Austria, moderately so in Upper and Lower Austria and was beginning to bear fruit in Bohemia and Moravia. But the policies were alienating many previously loyal Protestants at a time when Catholics remained outnumbered at least three to one outside Croatia and the Tirol. Continued momentum depended on unity within the ruling family and there were clear signs this was approaching imminent collapse. Rudolf was incapable of providing the necessary leadership. While he favoured Catholic renewal, intellectually he belonged to the moderate climate of the 1570s, rather than the polarized, confessional environment of 1600. Having been cajoled into backing militant measures, he then welcomed the astronomer Johannes Kepler, a Lutheran whom Archduke Ferdinand had just expelled from Styria. As the pressures mounted, he became engrossed in trivia, spending months designing a new imperial crown, even though there was already a perfectly good one kept safely in Nuremberg.[18] Meanwhile, relations between his younger brothers and cousins cooled rapidly as the monarchy became mired in a long war against the Turks that finally precipitated a major crisis after 1606.

4

The Turkish War and its Consequences

THE TURKISH MENACE

Rudolf confidently took up a challenge to his lands from the Ottomans in 1593, embarking on what became the Long Turkish War that proved a fiasco for both sides. The thirteen-year struggle contributed to a chain of problems that kept the Ottoman empire out of the Thirty Years War and ensured a period of relative tranquillity for Hungary. With hindsight, this was of undoubted benefit for the Habsburgs, since it enabled them to concentrate on the problems of the Empire and their western and northern European enemies. However, this was not clear at the time and the Turkish menace remained a constant source of anxiety. Worse, the Turkish War left the Habsburgs financially and politically bankrupt, in turn contributing to the outbreak of renewed conflict in 1618.

The Scourge of God

These events and their consequences have not received the attention they deserve, leaving the Ottomans as a shadowy presence in most accounts of the Thirty Years War. Their empire was the superpower of the early modern world, stretching for 2.3 million square kilometres across three continents with at least 22 million inhabitants, well over three times the number in the Habsburg monarchy.[1] Much of the original dynamism was lost after the death of Süleyman the Magnificent in 1566, but it would be wrong to categorize the Ottomans as in decline. They remained the terror of Europe, associated by Protestants and Catholics alike with the scourge of God sent to punish a sinful mankind and viewed with a mixture of awe and revulsion.[2] Their empire continued to expand, particularly in the east where they seized Georgia and Azerbaijan from the Shiite Persian empire between 1576 and 1590. The Habsburgs were sufficiently alarmed by this that they accepted humiliating terms in November 1590 to obtain an eight-year extension to the truce agreed at the end of the previous Turkish war in 1568. Despite the expense, the emperor maintained a permanent embassy in Constantinople, whereas the sultan disdained to deal with the infidel and rarely sent ambassadors to Christian courts. The Austrian diplomats struggled to secure accurate intelligence at a court that was truly the successor to medieval Byzantium. They were kept waiting for weeks before being received by officials who gave evasive or contradictory answers. The presence of Dutch, English, French, Venetian and other Christian embassies was a further source of concern as these were all powers considered hostile to the emperor.

The difficulty in obtaining a clear picture prevented outsiders from perceiving the Ottomans' mounting internal difficulties. The absence of accepted rules of succession bred bitter family feuds and forced each new sultan to command his deaf mutes to strangle his immediate brothers and sisters. The internal intrigues weakened the sultanate that lost direction at a time when their most dangerous foes to the east were entering a period of renewed vigour under the Safavid dynasty in Persia. The new conquests failed to bring sufficient rewards to satisfy the groups essential to the running of the Ottoman empire – notably the army, which had once been a pillar of strength and which now entered politics with disastrous results. Accustomed to rich bonuses from new sultans, the regular Janissary infantry began extorting rewards in return for continued loyalty, leading to the assassination of Osman II in 1622, setting a precedent that was repeated in 1648 and again later in the seventeenth century.[3]

The internal problems of their empire made the Ottomans more unpredictable in their actions, adding to an already unstable situation in south-east Europe at the point where their empire met that of the Habsburgs to the west and the lands of the Poles to the north. The war that broke out in 1593 was essentially a struggle between two of these powers to extend influence over the intervening region while denying access to their rivals. Hungary to the west was already split into Habsburg and Ottoman spheres, with the emperor controlling the north and south-west, along with Croatia, while the sultan commanded the central area and south-east. Neither side had a clear position in the region further east that was split into four principalities, all nominally under Turkish suzerainty, but pursuing varying degrees of autonomy. The area along the northern shores of the Black Sea belonged to the Crimean Tartars, the descendants of Ghengis Khan who had paid tribute to the sultan since the later fifteenth century. They provided useful auxiliaries for his armies, but were largely left alone since they served as a buffer between Ottoman territory and that of the Russian tsar further to the north-east. The three Christian principalities of Moldavia, Wallachia and Transylvania lay to the north and west of the Tartars. They likewise paid tribute, but were more open to influence from Poland and Austria. The Poles sought access to the Black Sea by pushing into Podolia, between Moldavia and the Crimea. Polish influence grew pronounced in Moldavia during the 1590s and they also intrigued in Transylvanian and Wallachian politics.

Translyvania

Of the three, Transylvania is the most significant to our story, and an examination of its internal politics reveals much that was typical for Moldavia and Wallachia as well. Formed from the wreckage of old Hungary in the 1540s, Transylvania was a patchwork of four major and several minor communities. In addition to pockets of Turkish peasants and Eastern Slavs, there were Orthodox Romanians, Calvinist Magyars, Lutheran German immigrants, called Saxons, and finally the self-governing Szekler people, living in the forested east, who remained Catholic.[4] The prince maintained power by brokering agreements between these groups, particularly the three 'nations' of Magyar nobles, Saxon towns and Szekler villages entitled to sit in the diet. The balance was enshrined in the Torda agreement from 1568 that extended equal rights to Catholics, Lutherans, Calvinists and the radical Unitarians (who rejected the doctrine of the Holy Trinity and refused to believe that Christ had been human in any way). Separate princely decrees extended toleration to Jews and the substantial Romanian population.

It was an arrangement that worked surprisingly well at a time when people elsewhere in Europe were murdering each other in God's name. All parties recognized Transylvania's vulnerability and wanted to deny predatory outsiders a chance to intervene. Over time, toleration became embedded in society and political culture, enhancing princely power since he could pose as the defender of all faiths and their liberties against Habsburg confessionalization and absolutism. However, it created confusion for external relations, particularly once the prince converted to Calvinism in 1604. While nine-tenths of his nobles now shared his faith, the peasantry were mainly Catholic or Orthodox, while the burghers were Lutheran. Christian powers looking to Transylvania only saw its leadership and mistook the principality as a Protestant champion ready to save them in their hour of need. While it might serve his purpose to present himself as such to outsiders, the prince remained conscious that his rule depended on preserving the balance between the ethnic and confessional groups.

There were also significant material obstacles that inhibited Transylvania from playing a major role in European affairs. Over half its territory was covered by forest and barely a fifth lay under cultivation. The population was concentrated in isolated pockets largely cut off from each other by trees and mountains. It was impossible to maintain a western-style regular army, and in any case, such an army would be ill-suited to operating in such conditions. Like its immediate neighbours, Transylvania relied on lightly armed cavalry able to cover 35km a day, supported by smaller numbers of irregular musketeers to hold outposts on the border. Such forces lacked staying power in a formal battle, which they generally avoided, preferring to break their opponent's will to resist by rounding up livestock and civilians. These tactics were thwarted if the enemy took refuge in walled towns or fortresses, since the Transylvanians lacked artillery and the disciplined infantry needed for a siege. They were also unable to sustain operations for more than a few months, waiting until the grass grew in the spring for their horses before setting out, and returning home with their booty before the high summer scorched the ground.

Strategy and Logistics

These logistical problems were found elsewhere in the Danube valley and across the Hungarian plains (*puszta*) where temperatures soared in the summer and plummeted below freezing in winter, and hampered all combatants. The surrounding mountains were blocked by snow from the autumn until the spring thaws that swelled the rivers and flooded a third of the plains for much of the year, providing a rich breeding ground for malarial mosquitoes. Hungary lay at the north-west periphery of the Ottomans' world empire, 1,100km from their European base at Adrianople (Edirne). A field army of 40,000 infantry and 20,000 cavalry required 300 tonnes of bread and fodder a day.[5] Crop yields in eastern Europe were half those of Flanders and other western agricultural regions that could support ten times more non-producers. Even Poland, rapidly becoming the bread basket of western European cities, exported only about 10 per cent of its net crop in the later sixteenth century. It was often impossible to requisition supplies locally in the Danube area, especially as the population tended to be concentrated in isolated pockets, as in Transylvania. The Turks were forced to follow the line of the river during hostilities, reducing their advance to 15km a day. If they set out in April, they could not reach Vienna before July. Not surprisingly, Ottoman armies relied on Belgrade once war broke out, since this was already two-thirds of the way to the front and was the first major city on the Danube west of the Iron Gates (Orsova) pass between the Transylvanian Alps and the northern reaches of the Balkan mountains of modern Bulgaria. These strategic and logistical factors imposed a certain routine on the Turks' campaigns. Operations began slowly with the collection of troops from across the empire at Adrianople or Belgrade. The main army reached the front in July, leaving only a few months to achieve success before the autumn rains set in during September, while the sultan traditionally suspended campaigns on 30 November with the onset of winter.

Major operations were the exception and most fighting involved cross-border raiding that remained endemic due to political, ideological and social factors. The region lay at the extremity of both the Ottoman empire and the kingdom of Poland, and while physically closer to the heart of Habsburg power, it was still politically distant. All the major powers were forced to rely on local landowners and their private armies who commanded the resources, loyalty and respect of the scattered population. Though wealthy, the magnates in Hungary and Transylvania were adopting expensive new lifestyles, with decorated country houses, foreign university education and grand European tours for sons and heirs. They could not afford large permanent forces to defend the frontier and also needed to satisfy poorer clients who relied on banditry to supplement their incomes from livestock, horse breeding or farming. Those at the centre tolerated the situation as the only way to retain the loyalty of the unruly border lords, and as a convenient means to put pressure on their international opponents. As the secular representatives of opposing world religions, neither the emperor nor the sultan could accept permanent peace without implying recognition of an alternative civilization. The lack of clear frontiers allowed a policy of gradual expansion by encroachment, whereby whichever side was currently stronger exploited weakness in the other to assert the right to collect tribute from border villages. Frontiers shifted back and forth like sand with the tide, while major fortified towns remained immovable rocks that required open war to crack.

Such fortresses began to be built during the 1530s as both the Ottomans and Habsburgs entrenched their hold over Hungary. The Turks had the advantage of shorter interior lines of defence, with a compact position along the middle Danube and in Bosnia to the south-west. They relied on around 65 relatively large castles held by 18,000 regular soldiers, with 22,000 militia recruited from their predominantly Christian subjects to patrol the gaps. The Habsburgs were forced to defend an 850km-long arc to the west and north, partly detached from Austria and Bohemia by chains of mountains. Lateral movement was restricted, since all the rivers drained eastwards into the Ottoman-held Hungarian plain. Each Austrian and Bohemian province had its own militia, but mobilization depended on the Estates who wanted them mainly for local defence. The Ottoman siege of Vienna in 1529 proved a shock and prompted the construction there of new bastioned fortifications in the Italian manner between 1531 and 1567. Plans to modernize these had to be shelved in 1596 due to the peasant unrest and a lack of funds, leaving the capital weakly defended when the Bohemians and Transylvanians attacked in 1619. The civic militia was converted into a regular garrison in 1582, but they numbered only five hundred men.[6]

The Military Frontier

To keep the Turks at bay, the Habsburgs revived and expanded existing Hungarian defence measures to create what became known as the 'military frontier'.[7] This militarized zone around 50km deep ran the entire length of the frontier and rested on 12 major and around 130 minor fortified posts held by over 22,000 men by the 1570s. Its development and upkeep was heavily subsidized by the Reichstag, which voted eight grants with a nominal value of around 12 million fl. between 1530 and 1582, plus well over another million towards fortress construction. At least four-fifths of this amount was actually paid, despite the confessional tension in the Empire, since the Ottomans were considered a common menace to all Christians.[8] Indeed, the largest two grants had been made in 1576 and 1582 at a time when many historians think confessional tension was growing worse. However, disagreements did ensure there was no immediate renewal when the last grant expired in 1587, increasing the dynasty's dependency on taxes voted by its Estates to maintain particular sectors. Only about half the border troops could be spared from their garrisons, limiting the scope for offensive operations. A major army of 55,000 men was reckoned to cost at least 7.4 million fl. for a single campaign, a figure way in excess of the monarchy's entire revenue.

Financial considerations forced the Habsburgs to place large sections of the frontier in local hands. The southern or maritime border, based around Senj on the Adriatic, was held by a people known as the Uskoks, after the Serbian for 'refugee'. This mountainous region could not support the growing number of refugees who were supposed to be paid by the government to defend the frontier with Ottoman Bosnia. Chronic indebtedness forced the Habsburgs to tolerate Uskok raiding and piracy instead. The next sector to the north was the Croatian border around the castle of Karlstadt that had been built in 1579 with funds granted by the Inner Austrian Estates in return for the Pacification of Bruck, and which protected the upper reaches of the Save river, blocking an invasion of Carniola. The Slavonian border around Warasdin on the upper Drava was also subsidized by Inner Austria since it protected Styria. Around half of all the minor posts were concentrated in these two sectors and were manned by colonists settled on crown land in return for militia duty. They received little help from central coffers and were expected to supplement their meagre existence from farming by raiding villages across the frontier.

The Hungarian border was split into three sections, with that in the south stretching from the Drava to the southern end of Lake Balaton and containing the important fortress of Kanizsa. The middle section ran north from Lake Balaton to the Danube, before curving east around the Ottoman salient at Gran where the river makes a right-angled turn from due east to flow south past Buda and Pest. This was the most heavily contested sector, because the Danube valley gave the best access for both sides. The Ottomans were concerned to protect Buda as the seat of their Hungarian government and as a forward base for an attack against Vienna. To forestall this, the Habsburgs built Komorn at the east end of Schütt Island, a large area that stretched west to Pressburg which was formed by two branches of the river and often flooded. Another fortress was constructed at Raab, approximately 40km south west of Komorn, to guard the only practicable route south of Schütt Island into Lower Austria. The lesser fortress of Neuhäusel covered Komorn's northern flank by blocking the Neutra river. The final Hungarian section stretched eastwards from there to the Tisza river and Transylvania. Its main fortress was Erlau, which blocked the road north over the Matra mountains into Upper Hungary and so safeguarded communications between Austria and Transylvania. Central funds covered only the principal garrisons, leaving the intervening sections in the hands of Hungarian magnates who maintained private armies of *haiduk* infantry. The haiduks were originally nomadic oxen drovers who had been forced by the partition of Hungary to accept a semi-settled existence as border guards, living in their own villages under elected headmen and relying on banditry between wars to supplement their irregular pay.

THE WAYS OF WAR

The Military Significance of the Turkish War

The Long Turkish War saw the largest mobilization of troops in the Empire and Habsburg lands since 1568 and was the opportunity for many soldiers to gain experience of major operations prior to 1618. The list of Rudolf's officers reads like a roll-call of the senior generals of the first half of the Thirty Years War. Wallenstein began his career as an ensign in the imperial infantry in 1604 and was wounded in the left hand during the final stages of the conflict. Both Schlick and Rudolf von Tieffenbach made early reputations against the Turks, while Trauttmannsdorff, the monarchy's greatest diplomat, performed his only military service in this war. Charles de Nevers, the man at the centre of the Mantuan War of 1628–31, reputedly saved Wallenstein's life at the siege of Kassa where he was himself serving as one of the many French Catholic volunteers. A significant number of the Italians who later rose to prominence also participated, including Count Collalto who became president of the Imperial War Council, Rodolfo de Colloredo who became a field marshal, and Ernesto Montecuccoli who subsequently commanded in Alsace. Some Italians were drawn to the Austrian forces by established patterns of serving the emperor; others arrived with the men sent to reinforce the Imperialists by Spain and the papacy, including Marradas and Dampierre, as well as Tilly from the Netherlands. Franz von Mercy, the Bavarian commander in the later stages of the Thirty Years War, also began his career against the Turks. The same was true for many of those who were later to oppose the emperor, including all three principal commanders of the Bohemian rebels: counts Thurn, Hohenlohe and Mansfeld.[9]

The presence of these figures has largely been overlooked by military historians who concentrate on warfare in western Europe and underestimate the impact of the Turkish campaigns on subsequent developments. The western focus is embedded in the concept of a 'military revolution' that has become the accepted way of viewing early modern warfare.[10] The proponents of this approach variously stress Spain, the Dutch and Sweden as the progenitors of new ways of fighting during the sixteenth century that relied on gunpowder weaponry wielded by large, disciplined units. Innovations in tactics and strategy allegedly made warfare more decisive, as well as increasing its scale and impact on state and society. Developments are fitted into a sequence with one power replacing another as the most efficient war-maker. Initial Spanish predominance is shaken first by the Dutch who are regarded as developing a more flexible military system that Sweden later improved upon and finally France perfected during the later seventeenth century. Scant attention has been paid to the imperial forces during the Thirty Years War, because they are perceived to have clung to an increasingly obsolete Spanish system that is associated with the pedantic positional warfare of the Dutch Revolt. In fact, Spanish ways of fighting often proved successful and were in constant evolution. Methods that were developed from the 1570s to deal with the Dutch were also effective against the Turks who likewise frequently evaded battle and sheltered behind fortifications. However, the Hungarian theatre encouraged its own practices that influenced how armies fought later in Germany, so it is more appropriate to see imperial ways of war as an amalgam of different experiences and ideas.

Military Technology

The Spanish system developed following the 'real' military revolution, in the sense of the largely technologically driven changes in warfare between 1470 and 1520 that saw the widespread adoption of hand-held firearms by both horse and foot, and their combination with new shock tactics by large, disciplined bodies of troops.[11] These developments in turn sprang from changes in metallurgy and gunpowder milling that made firearms truly effective for the first time in Europe. Relatively rapid improvements followed in both handguns and cannon that forced commanders to rethink their use of these weapons. Guns and artillery were deployed on a larger scale in battle and were combined with existing weapons in new offensive and defensive tactics. The pace of technological change slowed from the mid-sixteenth century, by which time all the basic weapons had appeared while further developments were restricted by manufacturing problems. For example, cannon production lagged considerably behind ballistic theory because gun founders were unable to deliver pieces that matched the potential that mathematicians had calculated. It proved difficult boring straight tubes in solid barrels before the mid-seventeenth century. Instead, cannon were cast using an iron rod coated with clay, horse hair and manure as the bore that was covered with a mixture of molten copper, tin, lead and brass in a mould to form the bronze barrel. The core was then removed and a drill used to finish the bore to the required calibre in a method that was both time-consuming and not entirely reliable.

The bewildering variety of heavy guns essentially fell into two types. Cannon proper (*Kartaunen*) were short-barrelled, thin-walled pieces firing solid round shot of between 24 and 75 pounds each and were used primarily to batter fortifications. Such guns were very heavy and required ten or more horses to shift them. Culverins (*Schlangen*) were longer-barrelled, thicker tubes that were safer to use, and had greater range and accuracy. Their stronger barrels required more metal, making them generally twice as heavy as cannons firing shots of equivalent weight. They tended to be used for six- or twelve-pound shot, and were often produced in smaller, two to four pounder versions called falconets (*Falkone*) that could be pulled in battle by two to eight horses. These guns were supplemented for siege work by mortars, short stubby guns that lobbed round shot or primitive shells over walls and obstacles.

The full range of equipment and projectiles already existed by the 1590s, including poison gas shells (used in the Netherlands and which contained various noxious substances intended to asphyxiate or blind their targets). Firebombs, or heated round shot, could be used to create firestorms in towns by igniting the tightly packed flammable buildings. There were also shells with flint and steel detonators, and those that exploded using a fuse ignited by the propellant charge in the barrel. Attacking troops could be mowed down with canister and other anti-personnel rounds that burst on exiting the barrel, turning it into a large shotgun. In short, there was little left to invent by the later sixteenth century, and future developments were largely refinements of what already existed by improving manufacture to make weapons more reliable and less hazardous to use.

The same applied to handguns that also existed in great variety but were increasingly called muskets for foot soldiers and pistols for horse-men. The former were between 125 and 144cm long, weighing 4–10kg and firing a lead ball of 40g around 300 metres, with an effective range of less than half that. The heavier versions required a rest to steady the barrel as the musketeer fired. The lighter version was still called an arquebus and was largely restricted to infantry trained to fight in looser formations, and by cavalry relying on firepower rather than cold steel. Improved manufacture enabled the lighter muskets to withstand a larger charge, and led to the disappearance of both the arquebus and the musket rest from around 1630. Most cavalry, including those trained to attack with lances and swords, carried long-barrelled pistols in hol-sters either side of their saddles. Pistols were rarely effective beyond 25 metres, but their metal-weighted handles could be used as a club in close combat. The technological advances associated with later centuries were already in existence, including rifled barrels, breach loading and a wide variety of mechanisms to ignite the propellant charge. There were mechanical wheel locks for pistols and the snaphance, or flintlock, for muskets, that used a flint to spark the powder. The flintlock became the principal infantry weapon between 1680 and 1840, because it was more reliable in wet weather and less susceptible to accidental discharge than the matchlock. This relied on pulling a lever to depress a metal claw holding a slow-burning match onto loose powder in a pan that sent flame through the vent to ignite the main charge in the barrel. There was a one in five chance that the flame failed to pass through the vent, providing the origins of the expression 'flash in the pan'. This was double the chance of a misfire with a flintlock, but both these and wheel locks were still expensive, delicate weapons that often broke. Manufacturing problems restricted flintlocks' use to hunting, while matchlocks remained cheap, sturdy and easy to use.

Infantry

Contemporary drill books convey a false impression that an elaborate sequence of hand, arm and body movements was necessary to load and fire. In fact, the carefully itemized movements reflected the prevailing scientific concern to fix and understand human movement, rather than actual practice. The most complicated manoeuvre was the counter-march, intended to provide continuous fire during an advance or retreat. Each rank fired in turn; those who had just discharged their weapons remained stationary to reload while the next line stepped through the gaps between each man to take its turn. By the time the last line had fired, those who had shot first would have reloaded and could move forward. This was modified around 1595 so that men stood in blocks of five, peeling off as a group right or left once they had fired so as to reduce the number of gaps required in the line. Arquebuses and lighter muskets took around a minute to load, requiring fewer ranks to maintain continuous fire than heavier muskets that needed up to three minutes to reload. The Dutch practised the retiring counter-march, enabling them to fire while avoiding contact with an approaching foe. Well-trained, motivated troops could cover up to forty metres a minute with an advancing counter-march and about half that if retiring. The system could also be used while stationary, with each man peeling off to the rear once he had fired and the soldier behind stepping into his place to fire. The Dutch deployed in only ten ranks, accepting lighter firearms as a consequence, and so kept their evolutions relatively simple. The Spanish preferred deeper formations of 15 to 25 ranks, and appear to have let their men fire in their own time, simply grouping those with lighter, quicker-firing weapons nearer the front.

Musketeers carried short swords for personal protection, either a 'tuck' for stabbing, or a heavier 'hanger' for cutting. Most were of poor quality that bent or blunted, so mêlées were fought largely by inverting the muskets and using the heavy, angled stock as a club. Such weapons were of limited use against opposing cavalry who could close rapidly before musketeers could reload. Already in the late fifteenth century it had become customary to combine 'shot', or firearm troops, with pike-men, each armed with a long pole of around five metres tipped with a steel spike. Pikes could be used offensively by soldiers in a compact block advancing with levelled weapons towards the enemy in the manner of an ancient Greek phalanx. When acting defensively, each man in the front rank would stretch back his right leg, plant the pike butt against his foot and bend his left leg forward to hold his weapon at a low angle. The next few ranks held their pikes level at shoulder height so the formation presented a forest of points in the enemy's face.

Given their defensive role, pikemen initially wore at least a steel helmet, vaguely resembling that of modern American firefighters, and a breastplate. Some wore a full corselet that also included a backplate and additional sheets protecting the thighs. Armour continued in use because the trend towards lighter-calibre muskets reduced their penetrative power and meant that the steel sheets retained their protective value. It was impossible to thicken them, since a man could not be expected to carry more than around eighteen kilos of equipment in battle without becoming prematurely exhausted. For this reason, as well as expense, no more than half of pikemen wore a full corselet around 1600, relying instead on a leather 'buff' coat, and increasingly many lacked even a helmet. Musketeers had a helmet at the most, because they needed greater freedom of movement, both to operate their weapons and to act in looser formations. They frequently wore a cloak to protect their powder horns from getting wet. They needed two horns, one for coarse-grain barrel powder for the main charge, the other for finer, priming powder. Both hung on cords over the right shoulder to be carried on the left hip where they were fastened with iron hooks to a waist belt to stop them swinging. Musketeers also carried single round charges in wooden containers hung on cords from a bandolier over their left shoulder, resting on their right hip where a leather bag for the shot was also attached, along with other items needed to clean and repair their match-lock. The bandolier arrangement was known as the 'twelve apostles' after the number of charges. It was gradually replaced around 1630 by prepared paper cartridges, each with a ball and powder that were carried in a hip satchel, or 'cartouche'. Finally, a musketeer had to carry four to six metres of coiled match around his neck and shoulder, or attached to his bandolier while on the march. Since it burned relatively quickly at the rate of ten to fifteen centimetres an hour, only one in ten men would keep it lit on the march to light those of his comrades if the unit came into action. Musketry was a dangerous business, since the burning match could easily ignite the apostles or loose powder that spilled onto the men's clothes. For this reason soldiers deployed two to four paces apart, only closing files when attacking.

The question of uniforms has attracted considerable attention from military historians, with many crediting the Swedes as being the first to introduce them. However, it is clear that many German units already wore uniform coloured coats prior to 1618, because they were territorial levies issued with clothing in bulk by their prince. Red and blue appear the preferred colours but needed expensive dyes, and white, or rather undyed cloth, was more common. Bodyguards frequently had more lavish costumes, sometimes with decorated armour. The widespread use of short, leather trousers fastened at the knee, as worn by peasants and artisans, would have also contributed to uniformity. The scale and duration of the conflict after 1618 and its associated cost interrupted this earlier trend towards purpose-made uniforms, and led to a more ragged, dull appearance with a mix of greys, browns, greens and other dark colours. However, the practice of paying troops partly in cloth ensured some continued uniformity, at least in the imperial army where most of the infantry wore light 'pearl' grey coats by the 1640s.

The optimum combination of pike and shot, both as a numerical ratio and as a form of deployment, remained hotly debated in military treatises. Setting aside the numerous theoretical models, essentially only two formations were used in the field. Those adopting the Dutch-style counter-march needed thinner lines and more shot than pike, deploying a ratio of two to one in a ten-rank line by the 1590s, with the pikemen in the centre, flanked by equal numbers of musketeers. The Spanish and imperial infantry favoured the larger, deeper formations that had been the norm earlier in the sixteenth century. Their pike were grouped as a central block with always twice the number of men in each line as there were ranks deep, because each man needed twice the amount of space in depth as in width to wield his weapon. The effect was to produce a square block that would be flanked by 'sleeves' of musketeers. An additional three to five ranks of light arquebusiers generally lined the entire front to maximize firepower. If caught by a cavalry attack, the musketeers could shelter under the pikes that would stretch over their heads. When attacking enemy foot, the arquebusiers would retire round the flanks once they had fired, leaving the pike free to charge. Spanish and imperial commanders sometimes grouped additional blocks of musketeers on the four corners, which can be seen in many battle engravings from the early seventeenth century. This was simply a formation for deploying and advancing, and the additional shot would fan out towards the enemy to fire, falling back to a less exposed side of the square if the formation came under attack.

The large square formation has become known as the tercio after the term used by the Spanish for their infantry regiments, while the thinner, longer Dutch formation is called a battalion. It has become a historical convention to see the latter as inherently superior to the former, not least because of its association with firearms that have appeared to later generations as obviously more advanced than pikes, weapons first used by the ancient Greeks. This distinction is not accurate, nor does it correspond to sixteenth-century military thinking that drew directly on the ancient world for its inspiration. The deeper block formations offered better all-round fighting ability than the thinner Dutch lines, where each unit relied on its neighbours standing firm or its vulnerable flanks would be exposed if the enemy broke through. Though only the first five ranks of the tercio could fire at any one time, the presence of another ten or more behind stiffened the resolve of those in front, or at least made it harder for them to run away. The unit assumed a more imposing presence on the battlefield; something that was a considerable advantage as it bore down on a wavering foe. In an age of black powder, the battlefield soon filled with smoke, making it extremely difficult for commanders to see what was happening. It was easier to lose control of long thin lines, composed of smaller, but more numerous battalions, than a deployment of fewer, larger tercios. These could be positioned *en échelon*, or diagonally staggered in chequerboard fashion about 200 metres apart. If one became detached or separated, it was generally large enough to fight on alone until rescued.

There was a trend towards increasing the ratio of shot to pike and to stretch formations into thinner lines that became pronounced in the 1630s, as we shall see later. It was partly related to minor technological advances producing the lighter muskets, and possibly also to pressure from soldiers themselves. Recruits generally preferred becoming musketeers rather than pikemen, who often had to stand under fire without personally being able to retaliate. Pikemen had originally received higher pay and were still seen by officers as more honourable than musketeers. Men who rose from the ranks did so 'from the pike up' (*von der Pike auf*), and not from the musket. Pikemen killed using cold steel, like the traditional knight's lance, whereas musketeers relied on the devilish invention of gunpowder producing thick clouds of acrid smoke, striking their foes from a distance, rather than looking them in the eye. Pikemen also accused their more lightly equipped colleagues of being more prone to plunder, whereas they could not enter houses with their long weapons – something that clearly had a ring of jealousy to it. Certainly, pikemen were more likely to throw away their weapons if their formation broke, thus becoming defenceless, whereas musketeers could flee still fully armed.

The trend towards more shot around 1590 was also due to the deployment of musketeers in smaller, looser formations to open a battle or to delay an enemy while the rest of the army assembled. Parties of 50 or more musketeers would be pushed out in front of the main line, covered by groups of 250 pikemen as a reserve and rallying point. Such methods anticipated those of 200 years later, but generally disappeared around 1630 with the growing emphasis on massed, disciplined firing by ranks developed by the Dutch and copied by the Swedes. Given the inaccuracy of individual shots, commanders emphasized the volume of fire, and later also its rapidity, culminating in the disciplined firing by platoons adopted around 1700.

Cavalry

Cavalry had evolved into five distinct types by 1590 in an attempt to address the different tactical roles of shock, firepower and reconnaissance. Shock tactics exploited the physical and psychological impact of a charge by heavily armed and armoured horsemen riding large horses. Cavalry mounts were around 16 hands high, weighing 500kg and could gallop at over 40kmh, though the weight of the rider meant that most attacks were delivered at considerably less than this. Horses were conditioned by being exercised in fields full of blazing straw and heaps of carrion to get them used to the sights and smells of the battlefield. They were also trained to kick and to manoeuvre in formation at various gaits.

Two types of 'heavy' cavalry evolved to use these tactics. Lancers were favoured by the Spanish and French as 'gensdarmes' and wore a full helmet that closed with a visor, as well as armour covering the entire torso, upper arms and upper legs. High leather boots protected the lower legs and feet, while leather or steel gauntlets covered the hands and forearms. They carried steel-tipped wooden lances around three metres long, enabling them to strike crouching foot soldiers as well as unseat opposing horsemen. The spread of firearms reduced the number of lancers in western and Central European armies to a small proportion by 1610, but Hungarian and Polish nobles still fought in this manner as 'hussars', wearing mail coats or armour made from layered metal sheets. These eastern lancers fastened pennons to their weapons and often wore 'wings' of bird feathers fixed to a wooden frame on their backs that created a rushing sound as they charged, adding to their fearsome appearance.[12] Elsewhere, lancers joined the second group of heavy cavalry called cuirassiers, who wore the same armour but relied on long, straight swords for thrusting. These were easier to use in close combat than lances that were largely useless if the initial shock failed to break the opponent.

Both types of cavalrymen also carried a brace of pistols that were used both to shoot at stationary targets and in close combat. Pistols were carried in the saddle holsters with the triggers facing outwards, because their long barrels meant they had to be drawn with the hand turned towards the back. They could be fired only one at a time, as the rider needed a hand free to hold the reins. Ideally, each rider turned his horse to the left and fired with his right arm outstretched at right angles to avoid startling his horse or burning its ears if he fired directly over its head. As most men were right-handed, they had to hold the reins in their left hand and reach over to draw their left-hand side pistol or their sword. The latter was also difficult to extract while mounted, since there was no hand free to hold the scabbard. Firing a carbine was harder still, because this required both hands. Such difficulties persisted till the end of cavalry in the early twentieth century. While later technological developments made firearms easier to use on horseback they did little to resolve the basic problems of fighting while mounted.

Shock tactics were of limited use against disciplined infantry. Experienced commanders became skilled in judging whether opposing foot were likely to run by seeing how steadily they held their pikes. However, a charge could still falter if the infantry remained together, since the horses would not throw themselves on the pikes. Even those horsemen who did break through often found that their mounts simply bolted through the gaps between the enemy ranks, carrying them right through the formation. Swords were often blunt and failed to do much damage, even against the woollen cloaks of the musketeers.

Such problems encouraged the use of firearms instead, based on the caracole, a tactic similar to the counter-march that had been developed earlier by German pistoleers in the 1530s. Successive ranks would trot within range, fire and ride back to reload, sacrificing the psychological impact of shock tactics to the accumulative effect of firepower. The caracole was less tiring on the horses and required less resolve from soldiers than a charge, since the men did not need to close with their opponents. Even men trained to charge home with cold steel would often panic and break off their attack around ten metres from their target, 'bouncing' back to their start positions. This explains why contemporary accounts speak of repeated 'charges' by the same unit in battle.

The desire to improve mounted firepower led to a third type of 'medium' cavalryman called the arquebusier or carabineer, equipped with a light arquebus or carbine with greater range and penetrating power than a pistol. They generally wore less armour, usually no more than a helmet, breastplate, buff coat, boots and gauntlets, and so rode smaller horses and were cheaper to raise. Since they carried two pistols and a sword as well, they could be used for shock tactics and consequently gradually replaced the more expensive cuirassiers and lancers around 1630. Many regiments were composed of a mix of cuirassiers and arquebusiers into the 1620s, with the former deployed in the front ranks if the unit made a charge.

The fourth type of cavalry was a form of mounted infantry, called dragoons, who rode lighter horses or ponies and generally lacked any armour, including the high boots that were difficult to walk in. Dragoons were a mix of pike and shot, using their mounts for rapid movement to stiffen scouting parties, support infantry skirmishers sent forward to secure key positions, or turn an enemy flank. The last type was often employed on similar tasks, but remained mounted to fight. These 'light' cavalry were most numerous in Hungarian, Polish and Transylvanian armies and were a major feature of 'eastern' warfare that was integrated into the imperial forces. Around a fifth to a quarter of the imperial light cavalry carried lances and were generally called Cossacks or Poles, regardless of their actual origins, while the rest were Croats, distinctive in their red cloaks and fur hats, each armed with a carbine and a pair of pistols. They were grouped in regiments of generally less than five hundred men and attacked rapidly in a zigzag, first firing their right-hand pistol, then their left and finally their carbine again on their right, before racing away to reload.

Organization

The regiment was the primary administrative unit for both horse and foot, subdivided into companies, still called 'banners' (*Fähnlein*) in the Empire. This organization derived from the way soldiers were recruited, whereby a prince contracted a colonel to raise a regiment who then subcontracted the task of recruiting individual companies to captains. Influenced by the classical model of the Roman legion, most colonels strove to have regiments of ten companies, but actual numbers varied from four or five up to twenty companies in some foot units. Captains who received commissions direct from their paymaster raised 'free companies' unattached to any larger unit. Such companies were recruited to garrison fortresses or were raised by ambitious individuals hoping to rise through the ranks by proving their value as recruiting officers.

The military hierarchy of ranks still used in the twenty-first century was already in place by 1600.[13] A colonel was assisted by a lieutenant-colonel who commanded in his absence. A major supervised training and administration and could command part of the regiment if it became detached from the rest of it. These three 'staff' officers were supplemented by secretaries, chaplains, doctors and a provost in charge of punishment. The same pattern was repeated in each company, with the captain assisted by one or two lieutenants, together with an ensign (called a cornet in the cavalry) responsible for the flag. There was generally also a company scribe, a barber surgeon and a number of non-commissioned officers (NCOs). Together, these senior ranks were known as the *prima plana*, or 'first page', on account of their names being listed before all the others in the muster register. The overall size of foot companies fell from three to four hundred, to two to three hundred over the sixteenth century, with cavalry companies averaging around half these sizes. The number of officers remained the same throughout, reflecting the growing emphasis on hierarchical order and enabling more complicated manoeuvres to be carried out. Officers and NCOs had 'staff' weapons in addition to swords, with the former carrying a partisan, or half-pike, that resembled a broad-bladed spear, while the latter held a halberd, or spear with an axe-head attached. Both these weapons symbolized rank, and had a practical purpose since they could be used for dressing the ranks by grasping the shaft in both hands and pushing it against several men simultaneously. They could also be used to push pikes or muskets up or down, especially to stop overexcited musketeers from firing prematurely.

The officer-to-men ratio remained relatively static after 1590, because of the technical limitations of the available weapons that required them to be used en masse. Around one officer or NCO could supervise about fifteen soldiers, but captains found it hard to command more than three hundred, as the smoke and noise of battle limited their ability to see what was happening and to shout instructions. This was another reason why infantrymen were packed close together in large formations, since it kept them within the sight of their mounted colonel. The flags and drums would be grouped in the centre and used to signal commands to the rest of the unit. Command problems also placed a premium on experienced men and it was reckoned at least a third of the strength had to be veterans to provide cohesion and sufficient old soldiers to teach new recruits the rudiments of drill and how to survive the rigours of campaign. However, personnel policy remained decentralized and in the hands of individual colonels who were reluctant to part with experienced men to assist the formation of new regiments. Regiment size also dictated prestige, as large formations commanded greater respect and resources than smaller ones that were more likely to be disbanded or amalgamated.

These factors encouraged Spanish and imperial colonels to recruit foot regiments of two to three thousand men, and mounted ones of around a thousand. The latter would be split into two to five squadrons, each of two companies, as tactical units formed into six to ten ranks. These squadrons were interspersed between the battalions in Dutch deployment, or massed on the flanks of the tercios in the Spanish system. Cavalry formed between a fifth and a third of western and Central European field armies, though the total proportion of infantry was higher since additional foot soldiers would garrison fortresses. Large infantry regiments could deploy as a single tercio, but weak ones had to be brigaded together to achieve the right numbers. Dutch-style battalions numbered between four and seven hundred men, so a large regiment might form two.

Artillery lacked formal organization as gunners still regarded themselves a separate guild under St Barbara, the patron saint of miners. Serving the guns was considered a special art with its own tradition and rituals. Catholic gun crew made the sign of the cross before firing and all faiths gave their pieces individual names. German theorists reckoned two to four pieces were required for every thousand soldiers, but usually only the lighter culverins and falconets accompanied the infantry and cavalry in battle. Large guns were expensive to produce and difficult to move, making them both valuable and vulnerable prizes for a victorious enemy.

Battle Tactics

Battle tactics sought the optimum combination of the three main military arms. Battles generally opened with a cannonade at under a thousand paces, while skirmishers went forward to probe and reconnoitre the enemy position. These moves bought time for the rest of the troops to assemble, and could be used simply to delay an enemy while the army made good its escape. The preference for large infantry formations kept deployment relatively varied, since these could be interspersed with artillery and cavalry in different patterns according to the terrain and the commander's intentions. As Dutch-style firing tactics became more influential, the infantry tended to be massed in the centre in one or more continuous lines with only narrow gaps between each battalion to prevent enemy cavalry striking their vulnerable flanks. Second and subsequent lines were kept between a hundred and three hundred metres behind the first: any closer and they risked shooting their comrades in the back; any further and they would be too far away to assist in a crisis. This linear tactic encouraged commanders to place their cavalry on either side of the infantry lines in the manner that became standard in the later seventeenth and eighteenth centuries. Full adoption of linear tactics was inhibited by doubts about the relative merits of firepower over shock, and by the conditions in eastern Europe where the Turks and others employed more flexible enveloping tactics using larger numbers of light troops. Imperial generals operating in Hungary relied on earthworks or wagons and other movable defences to protect their foot.

Generally, each of the three arms fought it out with their counterparts. The artillery sought to silence the enemy guns before its own troops moved forward and obscured the field of fire. The cavalry engaged the opposing horse, trying to drive them from the field and expose the flanks of the enemy foot. Each side hoped it would have sufficient artillery and cavalry left to tip the balance by the time the slower-moving foot soldiers had closed to within musket range, since the combination of two or more arms was generally superior to only one. Infantry could be pinned down by the threat of a cavalry attack, forcing them to remain in defensive formation while the enemy pounded them with artillery and musketry. Firepower could also be used to crack opposing formations, encouraging them to make a premature attack, or lose cohesion and so open them to a charge. Generalship and tactical innovation relied on variations in this standard pattern to achieve the effective combination of the three arms at an earlier stage in the engagement, thereby securing an easier and less costly victory.

THE LONG TURKISH WAR

A New Crusade

There were few opportunities to test these tactics in large battles during the Turkish War of 1593–1606, which mainly consisted of sieges and skirmishes like the Spanish operations in Flanders against the Dutch. Hostilities arose from the systemic problem of endemic banditry and unstable frontiers. The Habsburgs could do little for the Uskoks who were facing overpopulation and were forced to intensify their piratical activities in the Adriatic. Venice, the chief target of their seaborne attacks, encouraged them to redirect their attention to Ottoman Bosnia and Hungary after 1591. The pasha of Bosnia retaliated by besieging a Croatian border fort and was captured and executed by its defenders. Sinan Pasha, the energetic grand vizier, persuaded a reluctant Sultan Murad III to agree general war in 1593. As an opening move, Sinan seized the Habsburg embassy and enslaved its staff: an occupational hazard for those posted to Constantinople.

Rudolf's advisers believed the war offered a golden opportunity to expand Habsburg influence in the region and extend control over Transylvania. The Croats' minor victory convinced them the Ottomans were in decline and they thought war against the Turks would rally Christians within the Empire and so reduce problems there. Certainly Rudolf was roused from his depression, and readily embraced what he saw as his traditional role as defender of the true faith. The Reichstag reconvened in 1594 and voted another substantial tax grant, renewing this four years later and again in 1603. At least four-fifths of the 20 million florins promised actually reached the imperial treasury, along with a further 7 to 8 million paid when Rudolf appealed to the Kreis assemblies as well. The Habsburg lands raised around 20 million, and another 7.1 million flowed in from the pope, Spain and Italy. Even the maverick Henri IV of France promised assistance, and many Catholics, recently defeated in that country's civil war, now flocked to the imperial standard. Others came from further afield, including Captain John Smith, the later founder of Virginia. The princes of the three subject principalities of Transylvania, Wallachia and Moldavia followed suit, and although the Poles refused to help directly, their Ukrainian Cossacks attacked the Crimean Tartars and so prevented these from aiding the sultan. The imperial field army doubled to around 20,000 men, supplemented by about 10,000 Hungarians and about twice that number of Transylvanians and other auxiliaries.[14]

After all the effort, the result was a crushing disappointment. Some of the assistance proved rather meagre in practice, as in the case of the Russian tsar who sent a huge consignment of furs that flooded the market and brought little return. Worse, imperial planning was unrealistic. Talks were opened with Morocco and Persia to open additional fronts, but an embassy from Shah Abbas did not arrive until 1600, by which time it was unlikely the emperor could win. The sultan managed to keep 60–100,000 men in the field and so generally held the initiative.

The war opened in the south, where the main Ottoman offensive made some gains at Croatian expense in 1593 before the onset of winter forced Sinan to suspend operations. Thereafter, the Croatian, Slovenian and Senj border defenders held their own. Other Ottoman assaults against both ends of Lake Balaton were driven off, and from November 1593 the Habsburgs made periodic counter-attacks from this sector, trying to seize the Turkish fortress of Stuhlweißenburg that guarded the

south-western approaches to Buda. The next Ottoman offensive hit the
crucial central Hungarian sector, scoring a major success with the capture of Raab in September 1594, thus outflanking Komorn and opening
the way to Vienna. Habsburg efforts concentrated on reversing, or at
least offsetting, this blow and Archduke Matthias managed to puncture
the Ottoman salient by taking Gran and Visegrad the following year.
The sultan retaliated by shifting the war north-eastwards, leading his
army in person to take Erlau in 1596, and defeating a relief army
at Mezőkeresztes, the war's only major field battle, that October. All
attention now focused on the three principalities of Transylvania,
Wallachia and Moldavia that had defied the sultan and entered the war
on the emperor's side.

Intervention in Transylvania

Habsburg planners saw the new Transylvanian alliance as a means of
extending Habsburg suzerainty, and even forcing that country back
under royal Hungarian control. The moment seemed opportune, since
the current prince, Sigismund Báthory, appeared to welcome a Habsburg
takeover. Polish influence had been strong under his predecessor but
was now on the wane due to that country's new preoccupation with
Sweden (see Chapter 6, pp.179–81). Imperial troops retook Raab in
1598, stabilizing the main front, while mounting difficulties in the Ottoman empire sparked widespread revolts there from 1599. The apparent
success of Catholic reform in Austria contributed to the growing sense
of confidence among the emperor's advisers, and led to the fateful
decision to invade Transylvania in conjunction with Prince Michael of
Wallachia, who hoped to get Moldavia out of the bargain. A period of
confused fighting ended with the Habsburgs' complete defeat thanks to
unofficial Polish intervention that restored Sigismund and installed
Polish puppet-rulers in the other two principalities.

Rather than cutting their losses, the Habsburgs stepped up operations
in the region, entrusting new, larger forces to Giorgio Basta whose
subsequent conduct earned him the reputation of a cruel tyrant among
Hungarian and Romanian historians. Basta was one of the many Italians
in Habsburg service and had risen from drummer boy to commander of
a company of mounted arquebusiers in Spanish service in Flanders. He
came to Hungary with a Spanish contingent in 1597 and soon acquired

a general's rank. Schlick, Marradas, Collalto and Ernesto Montecuccoli all served under him, but his influence spread further thanks to his numerous theoretical writings and military commentaries, many of which heavily criticized his employers for failing to pay their soldiers properly. The subsequent campaign presaged much that later followed in the Empire after 1618. As the man on the spot, Basta was forced to act quickly in rapidly changing circumstances. It was often impossible to refer back to the imperial government in Prague where Rudolf's intentions were, in any case, far from clear. Having successfully conquered Transylvania again with Prince Michael's help in August 1600, Basta had his ally murdered the following year, because he considered him a liability. As the Poles refused to rescue him a second time, Sigismund abdicated in return for a Habsburg pension in June 1602, leaving the Transylvanian diet no choice but to pay homage to Rudolf in return for confirmation of its privileges.

It was a pyrrhic victory. The diversion of manpower to Transylvania weakened the defence of the other sectors, and the Turks advanced up the Save in the summer of 1600, taking Kanizsa and opening the way to Styria. Though Archduke Matthias captured Stuhlweißenburg in 1601, this was lost the following year to one Turkish army, while another broke into Styria. Worsening financial problems prevented a coordinated defence as parts of the imperial army were paralysed by mutinies, with some of the French and Walloons even defecting to the Turks.[15] Matthias retrieved the situation by capturing Pest in October 1602, precipitating a crisis for the Ottomans who now faced revolts in five provinces. Sultan Mehmet died of a heart attack and was succeeded by his thirteen-year-old son Ahmet I. Shah Abbas seized his chance and attacked from Persia, recapturing Azerbaijan and Georgia by 1604. Faced with a war on two fronts, Ahmet opened peace talks with the emperor in February 1604.

By making excessive demands, Rudolf squandered this last chance to end the war before his own position collapsed. Prolonged warfare had devastated Transylvania to the extent that it could no longer support the Habsburg garrisons. With no prospect of help from Prague, Basta resorted to seizing the property of any nobles who opposed his government. Matters spiralled rapidly out of control once the general received secret instructions from the emperor to implement the Austrian policies of Catholic renewal. As in Austria, this began with the towns, with the intention to repopulate the country with Catholic settlers and discharged soldiers after the war. Other measures targeted Upper Hungary where General Jacopo Belgiojoso began evicting Lutheran pastors from the strategic town of Kassa in January 1604, while the garrisons of 90 border posts were rotated to replace the Hungarians with 12,000 German troops. The policy of confiscations was extended to Hungary where Matthias even seized the manors of István Illésházy, a Protestant magnate who was stripped of his post as Hungarian palatine. This proved too much and the disaffected Magyars now made common cause with the oppressed Transylvanians.

The Bocskai Revolt 1604–6

Opposition coalesced around István Bocskai, a Calvinist landowner from Wardein in Upper Hungary. Bocskai's journey from loyal servant to rebel leader encapsulates how Habsburg policies were alienating many of their most influential subjects. He had led the Transylvanian auxiliaries during the initial campaigns but was distrusted on account of his religion by Rudolf, who deprived him of his command and had him brought to Prague in 1598. He escaped execution, and retired to his estates that became a centre for malcontents.[16] Though hailed by the local Calvinist clergy as a Hungarian Moses, Bocskai avoided inflaming religious passions for fear of alienating potential supporters, drawing instead on widespread popular discontent at the seemingly endless Turkish war. Having intercepted letters from the conspirators, Belgiojoso advanced from Kassa with his 3,500 men to arrest Bocskai, but Bocskai escaped and rallied 5,000 haiduks by granting them noble status and distributing abandoned land. Belgiojoso retired on Kassa, but the disgruntled citizens opened the gates to Bocskai who entered in triumph on 12 December 1604. The fall of Kassa severed the communications between Belgiojoso in Upper Hungary and the 5,000 Habsburg troops holding down Transylvania. As more haiduks rallied to his standard, Bocskai was able to leave a blocking force against Belgiojoso and invade Transylvania with 4,000 light cavalry in January 1605. Though the Habsburgs had the backing of the Szekler people, their troops were scattered in isolated garrisons which had all fallen to Bocskai by September. The Transylvanian diet had already proclaimed Bocskai as their new prince in February, while he was welcomed as the 'illustrious prince of all Hungary' when he returned westwards with the rest of his army in April.

By now, the Habsburg position was on the verge of collapse. Basta had been recalled to the main Hungarian sector in July 1604, but despite having 36,000 men, he had been unable to relieve Pest, which fell to the Ottoman besiegers. The imperial army disintegrated as it retreated northwards, allowing the Ottomans to recover both Gran and Visegrad. Bocskai captured Neuhäusel and met the new grand vizier, Lala Mehmed Pasha, outside Pressburg on 11 November 1605 where he was crowned king of Hungary with a special crown made in Constantinople.

Bowing to pressure from his relations, Rudolf reluctantly replaced Basta with Archduke Matthias who was empowered to open negotiations with Bocskai in May. The Bohemian Estates mobilized 17,000 militia, including units commanded by Wallenstein and Count Thurn, to stem the rebels' advance into Moravia during that summer. Many of Bocskai's aristocratic supporters were growing concerned that he was simply exchanging Habsburg rule for that of the Turks. They also doubted his ability to control the haiduks, to whom he had promised so much, and felt that the rebellion had achieved its original objectives of halting re-Catholicization and liberating Transylvania. Following a ceasefire in January 1606, the Hungarian and Transylvanian nobility concluded the Treaty of Vienna with Matthias on 23 June at the expense of both Rudolf and their own supporters. Lutheran and Calvinist Hungarian nobles received formal toleration that was extended to the royal towns and Military Frontier, but denied to peasants. Hungarian political autonomy was strengthened by restoring the post of palatine, removing financial control from Vienna, reserving administrative posts for natives, and replacing the German troops with Hungarians in the frontier fortresses. Transylvanian autonomy was also enhanced. Bocskai renounced his new Hungarian crown but kept the courtesy title of king and was recognized as prince of Transylvania by the Habsburgs, who ceded the territory another five Upper Hungarian counties east of Kassa.

While Bocskai did not live long to enjoy his success, his revolt set an important precedent. Militant Catholicism had been reversed, not by the passive resistance that had failed so miserably in Inner Austria, but by armed force. Whereas the Austrian Protestants had used their influence in the provincial Estates to bargain local concessions in the 1570s, the Hungarians and Transylvanians established a viable alliance between their countries. It was an example the Bohemians were to follow in 1618.

Habsburg–Ottoman Relations after 1606

More immediately, the Peace of Vienna cleared the way for Matthias to end the debilitating conflict with the sultan by concluding the Treaty of Zsitva Török on 11 November 1606. This fell short of a permanent peace that neither side was willing to accept. Nonetheless, both the sultan and the emperor were obliged to recognize each other as equals, and the humiliating annual tribute of 30,000 florins paid by the Habsburgs since 1547 was to be replaced by a final 'free gift' of 200,000. The sultan retained Kanizsa and Erlau, but had to permit the emperor to construct new fortresses opposite them. The arrangement was to last twenty years, during which cross-border raiding would be tolerated, provided no regular troops were involved.

It was the Habsburgs' good fortune that the Ottomans were unable to renew the war after 1606. The sultan managed to suppress his own revolts by 1608, but was forced to accept peace with Persia by 1618, confirming the loss of Azerbaijan and Georgia. The Persians exploited ongoing unrest within the Ottoman empire to renew the war in 1623, capturing Baghdad and slaughtering all the Sunni inhabitants who failed to escape. The loss of Iraq triggered convulsions throughout the Ottoman empire, including major revolts in Syria and Yemen which disrupted revenue collection and the routes to the holy sites. The sultan meanwhile lost control over the Crimean Tartars who provoked an undeclared war with Poland that lasted, intermittently, until 1621. Faced with these problems, he was only too happy to confirm Zsitva Török in 1615, accepting minor boundary adjustments that improved Habsburg defences around the Gran salient. The Bohemian Revolt coincided with Persia's victory, and the sultan went out of his way to conciliate the emperor, even offering him a few thousand Bulgarian or Albanian auxiliaries in the summer of 1618. Though these were politely declined, Osman II sent a special ambassador to congratulate Ferdinand II on his election as emperor the following year. Ottoman benevolence was doubly welcome, because the Reichstag did not renew the last frontier subsidy when this expired in 1615. The Bohemian crisis forced the Austrians to denude the frontier of troops, raising 6,000 cavalry from Croatia and Hungary in 1619. Around 4,000 frontier troops served with the imperial army thereafter until 1624, largely under the command of Giovanni Isolano, a Cypriot with property in Croatia who established his reputation during the Long Turkish War. There was little money left to pay the remaining garrisons on the frontier, prompting mutinies in the Slavonian and Croatian sectors in July 1623. Though the Transylvanians sided with the Bohemians, the sultan refrained from exploiting the opportunity, and without his help their intervention soon collapsed.[17]

With their respective governments distracted by war elsewhere, cross-border relations devolved to the Hungarian palatine and the Ottoman pasha in Buda. The former position was held by Miklós Esterházy between 1625 and 1645. He fostered the humanist vision of Hungary as Christendom's bulwark and encouraged the Magyar nobility to place their faith in the Habsburgs as the best guarantors for immediate defence and the eventual recovery of the lands lost to the Turks.[18] His negotiations at Szöny with the pasha of Buda in 1627 secured a fifteen-year extension to Zsitva Török, buying more time for the emperor to confront his Christian enemies. The Ottomans did exploit the Mantuan War to plunder fourteen villages in the upper Mur valley in 1631, but they rejected a Venetian suggestion to extend their attacks. Though Sultan Murad IV finally restored order in the Ottoman empire around 1632, suppressing the provincial revolts, he preferred to turn against the Persians, hoping to defeat them while the Habsburgs were preoccupied in Germany. Ottoman armies recovered Azerbaijan, Georgia and Iraq, retaking Baghdad in 1638 and forcing Persia to accept these losses the following year.

The relative quiet allowed the emperor to draw more soldiers from the frontier as the war in Germany intensified from 1625. An initial Croat regiment was raised that year, followed by two more by 1630. Swedish intervention that year prompted a dramatic expansion to fourteen regiments by 1633, as well as 1,500 Kapelletten, or light cavalry recruited in Friuli and Dalmatia. The number of Croat regiments peaked at 25 in 1636, falling to 10 three years later and 6 by the end of the war. Constant recruiting nonetheless depleted the frontier garrisons, leaving only 15,000 effectives by 1641, around 7,000 below official establishment.[19] This was still a large force, equivalent to the numbers deployed in a major battle during the latter stages of the war. It represented a major commitment in men, money and materials at a time when the emperor was increasingly hard-pressed, a factor that has been mostly overlooked when assessing the imperial performance during the conflict.

The continued military presence along the frontier indicated how deeply the Habsburgs still feared the Ottoman menace. Their concerns seemed justified when the Turks followed their peace with Persia in 1639 by launching major raids intended to consolidate their hold on Kanisza. Things might have got much worse if the Persian war had not resumed, prompting the sultan to renew Zsitva Török again in 1642, this time for twenty years. The sultan's problems weakened his hold over Transylvania, which had remained nominally under his suzerainty after 1606. As Transylvania grew more independent, its prince felt emboldened to intervene again in the Thirty Years War in 1644–5 (see Chapter 19). Thus, while Ottoman weakness kept the sultan out of the war, it paradoxically enabled Transylvania to join it. Still, it was always preferable to face the Transylvanians rather than the more powerful Ottomans. Fears that the pasha of Buda would back the prince with infantry and artillery never materialized, which rendered Transylvanian intervention in the war largely ineffective. Just as Transylvania made peace, the sultan became preoccupied with a new conflict against Venice that dragged on until 1669. Demobilization following the Peace of Westphalia obliged the emperor to withdraw his troops from the Empire, and he moved them into Hungary where they deterred further Ottoman raids until 1655. It was not until the late 1650s that the Ottomans were strong enough to pose an active threat and their attempts to reassert influence over Transylvania prompted another war with the emperor after 1662 that ended with a further renewal of Zsitva Török in modified form two years later. The stalemate only broke with the failure of the Ottoman siege of Vienna that opened the Great Turkish War of 1683–99. International assistance enabled the Habsburgs to drive the Turks from Hungary, which was converted to an hereditary kingdom in 1687, followed by the annexation of Transylvania four years later. The victory transformed Austria into a great power in its own right, lessening the significance of the Holy Roman title.[20]

These glories would have appeared an impossible dream to the Habsburgs surveying the wreckage of Rudolf's policies by 1606. The frontier had been weakened by the loss of two of its greatest fortresses, the dynasty had lost ground in Hungarian politics, and all influence in Transylvania had been extinguished. However, the repercussions went well beyond the Habsburgs' eastern kingdom to shake the very foundations of their monarchy. Despite receiving over 55 million fl. in subsidies and taxes during the war, Rudolf's debts had climbed to 12 million. Key sources of revenue, such as the Hungarian copper mines, had been pawned to raise further loans. The border troops were already owed 1 million fl. in back pay by 1601, while the field army had arrears of twice this by the end of the war. Six thousand soldiers loitered in Vienna demanding at least a million florins to disperse. Habsburg inability to keep order in their own capital underlined their failure. Disappointment and disillusionment spread to the Empire where the princes found it hard to believe that their money had not bought victory. The imperial treasurer, Geizkofler, was formally charged with embezzling half a million florins, and though he was acquitted in 1617, many princes failed to pay their share of the last border subsidy, voted in 1613, which was still 5.28 million fl. in arrears by 1619.

THE BROTHERS' QUARREL

The Feuding Archdukes

The search for scapegoats extended to the Habsburgs themselves. Having executed Field Marshal Rußwurm – a Calvinist like Bocskai – for the loss of Gran in 1605, the archdukes turned on each other once peace was finally concluded. The ensuing 'Brothers' Quarrel' compounded the damage done by the war, further weakening the dynasty and emboldening radicals within the Estates to believe that violent confrontation could advance their confessional and political goals. Crucially, the family feud distracted the emperor's attention from the Empire at a critical time, undermining the remaining goodwill and frustrating the efforts of those who sought a peaceful resolution of tensions there. Interpretations of the Brothers' Quarrel have been influenced by Franz Grillparzer's play of the same name. One of the great works of nineteenth-century Austrian literature, this casts Matthias in the role of the reckless, power-hungry usurper against Rudolf who appears, despite all his faults, as the peace-loving monarch. Matthias's position was altogether more complex, while the other archdukes had more than mere bit-parts in the unfolding drama.

Recriminations over the war forced the family to confront the deeper, unresolved problem of the succession. Rudolf agreed with his five brothers in April 1578 not to repeat their grandfather's partition of 1564 that had fragmented the Austrian lands. As the eldest representative of the main branch, he would retain Austria, Bohemia and Hungary, giving his brothers allowances and roles as provincial governors, pending more suitable accommodation elsewhere. Unfortunately, the spread of Protestantism throughout the Empire reduced the number of opportunities within the imperial church as bishoprics fell under Lutheran administration in the 1580s. Archduke Wenzel's early death in September 1578 left four brothers to be provided for. Ernst, the next eldest, seemed content with his post as governor of Austria and Hungary after 1578 and his death removed him from the reckoning in 1595. Albert, the youngest surviving brother, remained in Spain after 1571, and was eventually chosen by Philip II as the husband for his daughter Isabella, whom Rudolf had earlier refused to marry. Though his name was invoked by various parties, Albert's Spanish associations prevented him from becoming a serious contender for the succession in Austria and the Empire.

A childhood illness had kept Maximilian, the middle brother, from the customary trip to Spain. He had been groomed by his mother for a career in the imperial church, but showed more military ambitions. A compromise was found by engineering his appointment as grand master of the crusading Teutonic Order in 1585. Elected minority candidate in the disputed Polish royal election of 1586–7, he failed to assert himself over the favourite, Sigismund of Sweden, who captured him in battle. Though ransomed by Rudolf in 1589, Maximilian blamed his defeat on his brother's lack of support. The outbreak of the Turkish War gave him a new outlet for his energies and he was considered by observers as the best of the archdukes to try his hand at command. The indiscipline of his troops cost him victory at Mezőkeresztes and brief involvement in the Transylvanian quagmire added to his disillusionment. Rudolf's breakdown in 1600 appears to have galvanized Maximilian back into action. Of all the archdukes, he had the widest contacts among the German princes, thanks especially to his position as Teutonic grand master. The Order remained pan-Christian, rather than narrowly confessional, matching Maximilian's own pragmatic attitude to faith and concern for peace. Discouraged by his earlier failures from putting himself forward as Rudolf's successor, Maximilian now emerged as honest broker between the princes and archdukes, and he concentrated on consolidating Habsburg authority in the Tirol where he became governor in 1602.[21]

This left Matthias, the next eldest brother after Ernst and the main contender for the succession after 1595.[22] Matthias escaped the Spanish education and so lacked his two elder brothers' stiff formality. At first glance, he appears the least sympathetic of all the archdukes, living the life of a playboy prince, self-indulgent and increasingly lazy. Nonetheless, he possessed a certain charm and in a family noted for its dour, gloomy disposition, he had an uncharacteristic sense of fun. He also retained something of the moderate spirit of his father, Emperor Maximilian II, and believed he could resolve confessional strife. One night in 1577 he dashed off without a word to anyone and appeared suddenly in the Netherlands at the height of the crisis there, accepting the rebels' offer to become their governor. He was completely out of his depth. The rebel leadership simply used him as a face-saving device while they gathered their forces and they expelled him in 1581. It proved a sobering experience, but one that left him kicking his heels, since none of his relations trusted him. Still, he was the only available archduke to replace Ernst as governor of Austria in 1595, while the Turkish War provided opportunities for field command. There were clear signs he was maturing by 1600, thanks partly to the influence of Bishop Klesl with whom he worked closely in Austria to revive Catholicism and pacify the peasant revolt.

Archduke Ferdinand and his brother Leopold of the junior Styrian line had their own claims to the Austrian inheritance. As young men of the Counter-Reformation generation, they represented a more attractive alternative to Spain and Bavaria than the elder archdukes who clung to their father's hopes of transcending confessional strife. Ferdinand was linked by marriage to Bavaria and had impressed Spain and the papacy with his personal piety and commitment to Catholic renewal. As a younger brother, Leopold had been destined for the church, a calling for which he was entirely unsuited. Despite becoming bishop of Passau (in 1605) and Strasbourg (in 1607), he never took higher clerical vows, and remained the wild card in the Habsburg pack, more interested in war and political ambitions than his benefices.

The Opening Round

Rudolf's increasingly erratic behaviour convinced the archdukes that they had to act. The Spanish ambassador had already raised the possibility of deposing the emperor in 1603, but the pope was reluctant to condone such a step when it was far from clear whether Rudolf was actually mad. The outbreak of Bocskai's revolt dispelled such scruples and the archdukes convened in Linz in April 1605, agreeing that they would compel Rudolf to hand over Hungary as a preliminary step. Bishop Klesl carefully steered Matthias, restraining him from doing anything rash – such as accepting the crown of St Stephen from the Hungarian rebels – and working hard to mollify the Spanish who still blamed Matthias for exacerbating the Dutch Revolt. A master of public relations, Klesl appreciated the value of presenting Matthias as a man who understood his subjects' concerns, whereas Rudolf clung to the older, more reclusive style of monarchy.[23] Klesl gathered the archdukes again in Vienna on 25 April 1606, and won their agreement to back Matthias as sole successor. Rudolf was to be declared mentally unfit, clearing the way for his lands to pass to Matthias who could then negotiate from a position of strength with the electors to be named king of the Romans, thus securing the imperial title as well.

Spain backed the plan and allowed Albert to sign it in November, but Ferdinand played a double game, appearing to go along with Matthias, but secretly hoping Rudolf would name him heir instead. When Matthias learned about this, he published the April 1606 pact, ruining his rival's credit with Rudolf and temporarily removing him from the running. However, Rudolf's determined opposition unsettled the imperial electors who were reluctant to discuss a successor while he was still alive – and in any case the elector Palatine and the Protestant princes preferred Archduke Maximilian to Matthias as a successor. Matters were brought to a head by the haiduks who rebelled in October 1607, protesting at being abandoned after the Bocskai revolt. The Hungarian magnates suspected Rudolf of deliberately encouraging them in order to sabotage the Peace of Vienna. The crisis ended Klesl's hopes of settling the succession without recourse to further concessions to the Estates, and he now embarked on the high-risk strategy of enlisting Hungarian support to force Rudolf to agree. Having finally secured his appointment as governor of Hungary in June 1607, Matthias defied Rudolf and summoned the diet to Pressburg the following January. Representatives arrived from Upper and Lower Austria, joining the Hungarians in an alliance with Matthias agreed in February. Ostensibly, this was to uphold the settlement ending Bocskai's revolt and ensure that Rudolf did not disturb the truce with the Turks. In practice, it transferred the Hungarian crown to Matthias in return for further guarantees for Hungarian Protestants and concessions to the nobility at the expense of the peasants.

Rudolf still had backing from the Hungarian Catholic minority that refused to join the alliance, but his policies were alienating his dwindling supporters. Clumsy intervention in Moravia's internal affairs prompted the Estates there to close ranks and join Matthias's alliance in April. Matthias now deliberately escalated the situation, hoping to trigger a crisis that would rally Bohemia to his standard as well and leave Rudolf completely isolated. Backed by the Protestant majority in the Estates, Matthias collected 20,000 Austrian and Moravian troops at Znaim, just across the Moravian frontier from Vienna. A further 15,000 Hungarians assembled on the March river further east. Matthias planned to appear in strength at a general assembly of all Habsburg Estates he had summoned for Cáslav, half-way between his camp and Prague, and he issued a manifesto to the German princes justifying his actions as restoring stability within the monarchy and Empire.

The Bohemians now held the trump card. If they defected, the Silesians and Lusatians would follow, leaving Rudolf alone. Encouraged by religious militants in Germany, the Bohemian Protestant leadership seized the opportunity to extort formal recognition for their faith denied them by the Habsburgs' refusal to acknowledge the Bohemian Confession of 1575 (see Chapter 3, p.60 above). Rudolf had only 5,000 unpaid men under Colonel Tilly who were in full retreat on his capital. He had lost the confidence of the Spanish ambassador, who advised him to cut a deal before it was too late. Rudolf tacitly allowed the Bohemian Estates to assemble in Prague and begin their own military preparations in May. Seeing that Matthias had also run out of money, the Bohemians showed their hand by refusing his summons to attend at Cáslav and declaring for Rudolf instead. Both men were outmanoeuvred by their respective backers, who secured their own objectives under the cloak of Habsburg reconciliation in the Treaty of Lieben, signed on 25 June 1608. Rudolf was compelled to abandon plans to renew the war against the Ottomans, surrender the crown of St Stephen to his brother and recognize him as ruler of Moravia and Upper and Lower Austria. The Moravians received greater autonomy from Bohemia and established a new government under Karel Zierotin, an intelligent adherent of the Bohemian Brethren who sincerely desired peace.

The Austrians, Moravians and Hungarians used the opportunity of their meeting at Matthias's camp to forge their own alliance on 29 June, agreeing to cooperate to extract further concessions from the dynasty. Matthias and Klesl had expected this and tried to negotiate with each province in turn, hoping to limit the damage. Matthias received the Moravians' homage in August 1608 in return for promising that no one would be persecuted on the grounds of faith. This fell far short of the full legal rights desired by the Protestant radicals, but Zierotin held them in check, happy simply that his country had secured greater political autonomy. The situation was very different in Austria where the Estates' leadership was passing into the hands of men like Baron Tschernembl, who had entered the Upper Austrian house of lords in 1598. A former student of the radical Altdorf University, he had toured Protestant Europe in the 1580s meeting the leading intellectuals and discussing their opposition to tyranny. Though he opposed the peasants' revolt of 1595–7, he was more prepared than his fellow lords to concede the right of resistance to ordinary folk. Because of this, he has attracted considerable attention from later historians, often distorting his actual significance.[24] As a Calvinist, he was in a minority among the Austrian Protestants, but the Habsburgs' feuding gave him a chance to push himself forward and seize the Estates' leadership. However, he never succeeded in rallying all the Lutherans, while his extremism eroded the scant remaining common ground with the moderate Catholics.

Tschernembl argued that Rudolf's renunciation of Austria created an interregnum, leaving power in the Estates' hands until they agreed to accept Matthias as successor. This technicality convinced 166 Upper and Lower Austrian Protestant lords and knights to gather in the radicals' stronghold of Horn in Tschernembl's home province. Here they swore a solemn confederation on 3 October 1608, effectively declaring their secession from the moderates and Catholics and establishing an alternative government in both provinces. They voted money (to be paid by their tenants!) for troops and sent emissaries to Hungary and to the Calvinist leadership in the Palatinate. Matthias went to Pressburg to head them off by meeting the Hungarians himself. He agreed to implement the treaty of Vienna, and had to watch while the diet restored the Protestant Illésházy as palatine. Having confirmed Hungarian and Transylvanian autonomy, the diet finally recognized Matthias as the new king of Hungary on 19 November.

With the Austrians still defiant and his brother plotting in Prague, Matthias's position was far from secure. Unable to sleep at night, he is reported to have cried out, 'My God, what should I do! If I don't give them what they want, I'll lose my lands and subjects. If I agree, I'll be damned!'[25] On 19 March 1609, he conceded most of Tschernembl's demands, halting Catholic reform, restoring the Religious Assurance of 1571, and extending this by a verbal promise of free worship for the crown towns. The painstaking efforts to combine Habsburg authority and Catholic conformity over the previous thirty years were swept away. Though the Austrians now accepted him as archduke, Matthias alienated the Catholic minority who felt abandoned. The wily Klesl remained discreetly in the background, remaining in Vienna when his master embarked on his rebellious invasion of Bohemia in 1608. He publicly refused Matthias the sacraments during Easter 1609, while secretly advising the concessions as a tactical expedient. Under pressure from Tschernembl to banish Klesl as an arch-schemer, Matthias considered persuading the pope to make him a cardinal in a face-saving device to send him to Rome. But as relations became strained with his adviser, Matthias was unable to recover any ground against the Estates.

The Letter of Majesty 1609

The Bohemians, meanwhile, lost no time in holding the emperor to his Faustian bargain. The struggle with his brother had exhausted Rudolf's remaining credit and he had no one else to turn to to prop up his crumbling imperial dignity. Having been dismissed in 1608, the Protestant members of the Estates unilaterally reassembled in April 1609 and forced their way into the emperor's inner sanctum in the Hradschin, in defiance of an express order to leave him in peace. As in Austria, the heady atmosphere allowed the radicals to elbow their way to the front. Some shouted 'This king is no good, we need another!', while Count Thurn was applauded when he called for military preparations, this time against the emperor.[26] The count's family had originally hailed from north Italy as the della Torre, but like many of their compatriots, they had acquired land in Austria and Bohemia. He has received an almost universal bad press and certainly proved a singularly inept political leader and poor strategist. Though a Lutheran, his actions suggest he was driven more by personal ambition than religious conviction, with his radicalism of 1609 motivated by his dissatisfaction with Rudolf's failure to reward his services during the Turkish War.

Thurn orchestrated a relentless barrage of demands until the fragile Rudolf capitulated on the evening of 9 July, signing the infamous Letter of Majesty that granted the Bohemian Protestants religious and political freedoms exceeding those won by their Austrian and Hungarian counterparts. Henceforth, the lords, knights and royal towns were free to choose which Christian confession to follow, and each group could elect ten 'Defensors' to safeguard their rights. This effectively created a parallel government under the presidency of Vaclav Budovec von Budov, alongside the formal Habsburg administration under Chancellor Lobkowitz. Thurn and Colonna von Fels, another military nonentity of Italian descent, were named as commanders of the Protestant militia. Other Protestants took over Prague University and the Utraquist consistory, thus acquiring the institutional framework to construct their own provincial church.[27] The Silesians extracted a similar Letter of Majesty on 20 August, giving Lutheranism equal status to Catholicism.

The Bohemian Catholics, who had been in the ascendant since 1599, were cast adrift by the dynasty on which their fortunes depended. Slavata lost his post of Castellan of Karlstein, associated with guardianship of the crown jewels, which Rudolf transferred to Count Thurn. Lobkowitz led the Catholics in refusing to sign the Letter of Majesty, leaving the emperor still more isolated. Habsburg prestige plummeted to new depths, convincing Tschernembl and his radical allies in Germany that the dynasty was on the verge of total collapse. Their hopes seemed justified when Rudolf offered the Austrians their own Letter of Majesty provided they defected to him.

The crisis coincided with the formation of hostile Protestant and Catholic princely alliances in the Empire and with international tension surrounding the Jülich-Cleves inheritance dispute (for which, see Chapter 7). Yet, no major war followed and the immediate threat to the Habsburgs receded. This requires some explanation, before we turn to events elsewhere in Europe.

The radicals were victims of their own success. The concessions of

1608–9 represented the achievement of long-cherished dreams that left most Protestants satisfied and dampened desires to forge closer links with co-religionists in the Empire and further afield. Since the gains had been won at sword point, few Germans wanted anything to do with the Habsburg malcontents who were widely regarded as disloyal subjects of the imperial dynasty. Blinded by their apparent success, the radical minority failed to see their support slipping away. An envoy to the Protestant princes to solicit a loan returned empty-handed late in 1608 and by February 1610 the Bohemians decided to disband their expensive militia.[28] While Zierotin still held the Protestants and Catholics together in Moravia, the two parties no longer met together in the other provinces. The radical Protestants' boycott of the formal diets opened the way for the Catholic minority to seize control of the Estates while their opponents met in separate sectarian assemblies that lacked a firm constitutional basis.

The outbreak of the Turkish War in 1593 had brought dangers and opportunities. Rudolf rediscovered a personal sense of purpose, while militants of all hues were marginalized as the German princes and Habsburg Estates closed ranks behind him and voted substantial support for the glorious crusade. The inability to make any headway in Hungary bred mounting frustration among Rudolf's relations and subjects. The situation became increasingly precarious as first Ferdinand of Styria and then Matthias and Rudolf intensified Catholic renewal in their parts of the monarchy. The Catholic revival was explicitly linked to the dynasty's attempt to reassert political authority, representing a shift from the era before 1576 when Ferdinand I and Maximilian II pinned their influence on reconciling the competing faiths. Habsburg policy became increasingly inflexible as its dynastic and confessional interests became closely intertwined making it impossible to grant concessions in one area without undermining the family's position in another. The difficulties became clear when Rudolf extended this policy to Upper Hungary and Transylvania after 1600. With the Turkish War still raging, this was sheer folly and provoked Bocskai's revolt, forcing Matthias to intervene and conclude an unsatisfactory peace with the Ottomans. The Habsburgs were rescued from a worse disaster by the sultan's own problems after 1606, but their monarchy now lurched from international conflict to civil war as the Brothers' Quarrel spiralled out of control. The rival archdukes gambled away much of their family's remaining credit in a game they both lost. While Matthias emerged with tangible gains in Austria, Moravia and Hungary by 1609, these were only at the cost of strengthening the Protestant faction in the Estates. Rudolf granted still more damaging concessions to the Bohemians and Silesians in his Letters of Majesty. The Tirol escaped, thanks to its lack of an hereditary arch-duke after 1595, while Ferdinand's temporary exit from the family feud kept Inner Austria out of this stage of the dispute. Nonetheless, the overall impact of sixteen years of unbroken international and civil war left the Austrian monarchy severely weakened, and overshadowed by its richer Spanish cousins.

5

Pax Hispanica

THE SPANISH MONARCHY

Spain's Many Dominions

The period between 1516 and 1659 is regarded as Spain's Golden Age and era of European predominance. The international perspective on the Thirty Years War subsumes it within a broader series of struggles by other European countries against perceived Spanish hegemony. Certainly, it was largely through Spain and its overseas empire that the repercussions of the Central European struggle after 1618 were felt across the globe. Spain's presence was a constant factor throughout, even if, as we shall see, its own problems were distinct from those of Habsburg Austria.

In one important respect, however, the difficulties were similar. Like their Austrian cousins, the Spanish Habsburgs ruled a large empire that proved difficult to manage and sustain. This empire had recently grown considerably bigger with the Union of Crowns forced on the Portuguese by Philip II in 1580. The young Dom Sebastiao had died with the flower of the Portuguese nobility in the disaster of al-Qasr el-Kabir in Morocco in 1578, extinguishing the House of Avis that had ruled since 1385. It was a shotgun marriage forced by an invading Spanish army, but one which many Portuguese came to appreciate for the access it gave to Spanish wealth and trading opportunities. Portugal itself only brought another 1.1 million new subjects to the union, but it had staked claims to Brazil, Africa and Asia. These possessions were thinly held, with perhaps no more than 30,000 Europeans and 15,000 slaves in Brazil by 1600, facing around 2.4 million indigenous inhabitants scattered across the vast, largely unexplored hinterland. A few thousand Portuguese manned forts in Angola and Mozambique, while around 10,000 more were posted across the *Estado da India*, or the possessions east of the Cape that were governed from Goa in western India.[1]

Spain itself had around 8.75 million inhabitants in Castile and the associated lands of Catalonia, Aragon, Valencia and the Basque provinces. Contrary to the trend elsewhere in Europe, Castilian population growth stalled around 1580 with the onset of poor harvests, plague, emigration to the colonies and, above all, the burden of war and taxation. By 1631, there were only 4 million Castilians, about 1 million fewer than forty years earlier. Spain's overseas colonies were likewise affected by population decline, but in this case it was a direct consequence of the conquest itself, which brought disease and overwork for the indigenous population, reducing it from over 34 million to around 1.5 million by 1620. At that point, there were around 175,000 colonists and a roughly similar number of African slaves and peoples of mixed descent scattered across Mexico, the Caribbean, the western and northern coasts of South America and around Manila in the Philippines.[2] The statistics help put Spain's colonial empire into perspective when compared to its European dominions that had 1.5 million subjects in the southern Netherlands, over a million apiece in Milan and Sicily, and 3 million more in Naples.

The importance of Spain's dominions and colonies was magnified by the stagnant state of its own economy. Apart from the re-export of American silver, Spain's main contributions to European trade were raw materials and some foodstuffs. Growth was inhibited by the country's system of cartels with monopolies over particular products, a practice that extended to colonial trade with the crown's collaboration with Seville making it the sole gateway to the Americas. Harvest failure and the onerous fiscal burden resulted in land flight as people migrated to the towns or colonies, weakening the survivors' resistance to aristocratic and clerical encroachment on their remaining common lands. Private investors and merchants relied on silver receipts to fund consumption, since the country failed to feed its own population and had to import much of its food. The inability to produce useful goods in sufficient quantities prevented Spaniards from benefiting from the growth in colonial trade that expanded in line with the rising white population in the Americas. Dutch and other foreign merchants crowded into the market, obtaining special concessions to use Spain's Atlantic ports around 1600.

Fifty years later there were over 120,000 foreigners in Spain, notably in Seville where they formed a tenth of the city's population.

Silver: The Lifeblood of Empire

Though the colonial economy did diversify over time, silver remained Spain's primary interest. The New World produced 50,000 tonnes of silver between 1540 and 1700, doubling the existing stock in Europe. Exports only really got under way after the discovery of rich seams at Potosí in Bolivia (in 1545) and Zacatecas in Mexico (1548) and the introduction of German mining techniques in 1555 that used mercury to separate silver from waste. Zacatecas drew its mercury imports from Almadén in Spain, but Potosí's production soared after the development of mercury mines at Huancavelia in Peru.[3] Potosí relied on forced labour through the *mita* system, whereby native Indians were compelled to work four months every seven years. Labourers died at the rate of forty a day, working six-day shifts at an altitude of 6,000m. Increasingly, Indian villages bought exemption by paying tribute to hire labourers who constituted over half the workforce by 1600, but the system was still controlled by a corrupt local elite that was not above murdering a government inspector with a cup of poisoned hot chocolate. The silver was carried on the backs of thousands of llamas and mules down the mountains to Arica on the Pacific coast where mercury and food were collected for the return journey. Meanwhile, the precious cargo was shipped north to Panama and then carried across the isthmus for transhipment to Seville. Attempts by the local viceroy to improve the atrocious conditions at the mercury mine in Huancavelia contributed to fluctuating production in Potosí from 1591, and then a steady decline after 1605 from a peak of 7.7 million pesos in 1592 to 2.95 million by 1650. The shortfall was made good by Zacatecas where output increased from 1615 thanks to more plentiful labour, but Mexican production depended on Spanish mercury, leaving it vulnerable if the sea lanes were interrupted.

The lifeline rested on a convoy system established by 1564 that saw two fleets sail across the Atlantic most years. The *galeones* left Seville in August, headed south-west towards the African coast and then passed the Canaries to pick up the Trade Winds that took them due west to the Leeward Islands. From there, they steered south-west to Cartagena in modern Colombia, or Portobello in Panama, a journey of 6,880km taking eight weeks. The normal escort was a squadron of eight warships crewed by 2,000 sailors and marines, though the large merchantmen were also armed. Having collected the Potosí silver, along with cochineal, hides and other colonial products, the fleet wintered in Havana, before heading back to Seville. The other fleet, called the *flota*, set out from Cadiz in April or May with two warships. It followed the same route as far as the Leeward Islands, before turning north-west to Hispaniola, Cuba and then Vera Cruz in Mexico, to deliver the Almadén mercury and collect the Zacatecas silver. Both fleets had to return via Cuba through the Bahama Channel that posed the most dangerous section of the entire voyage due to hurricanes and reefs. The *galeones* sailed 29 times during the first half of the seventeenth century, but only two silver convoys were lost to enemy action (in 1628 and 1656). Spanish trade with the Americas was worth about 10 million ducats a year by 1600, roughly twice that of Portugal with the East Indies.

The Portuguese also used a convoy system, called the *cafila*, to protect their share of the valuable spice trade across the Indian Ocean and back round Africa. In addition, they were developing a presence at Axim and Elmina on the Gold Coast (modern Ghana) to secure the gold and slave trades, establishing further forts around the mouth of the Congo and at Benguela on the Angolan coast south of Luanda in 1617. Communications with Portugal were secured through possession of the islands of Cape Verde and São Tomé. As elsewhere, Portuguese influence depended on good relations with local rulers, particularly the king of Ndongo east of Luanda. Access to the hinterland was provided by the Imbangala, called Jagas by the Portuguese, who raided slaves to sell on the coast. The Portuguese were already importing African slaves at the rate of over seven hundred a year in the mid-fifteenth century and began shipping them to Brazil after 1535. Slaves cost around 400 pesos, equivalent to eight months' wages for an Indian labourer, and it was not until the 1570s that they began to be transported in large numbers to replace the dwindling local population. Expansion into the Congo and Angola enabled the Portuguese to ship 4,000 slaves a year by the 1620s, by which time Africans had entirely replaced Indian labour on the Brazilian sugar plantations. Eventually, at least 3.65 million people were transported to Brazil by the time the trade was formally suspended in 1850. Slaves became essential to the Brazilian economy that only took off with the sugar boom around 1600. Already by 1628 three hundred ships were needed to transport a crop worth 4 million cruzados to Portugal each year. Average annual exports tripled thereafter to reach almost 40,000 tonnes by 1650, accounting for nine-tenths of Brazilian export earnings, a situation that did not change until the development of rival Caribbean production in the eighteenth century. The colony expanded from its main base at Salvador in Bahia, northwards along the coast to Pernambuco where two-thirds of the sugar industry was established.

Impressive though these colonial developments were, Spain and its European dominions remained the real fiscal basis of the empire. Despite a stagnating economy and inefficient administration, Spain managed to send 218 million ducats to sustain the war in Flanders between 1566 and 1654, whereas American silver receipts totalled 121 million across the same period.[4] Direct and indirect taxes agreed with the Castilian *Cortes* or parliament produced 6.2 million ducats a year around 1600. The most important of these was the *millones* tax, introduced in 1590, that raised 90 million ducats between 1621 and 1639, or three times the amount arriving from America across the same period. By contrast, Catalonia, Valencia and Aragon paid virtually nothing, since their local assemblies refused to grant regular taxes to the crown. The church did pay three levies – known as the 'three graces' – worth about 1.6 million ducats annually. The Spanish Netherlands provided 3.6 million, Milan around 2 million and Naples twice that, but most of these sums were consumed by local defence. By contrast, silver imports provided only 2 million ducats each year to the crown at the turn of the century, since the monarch only received the surplus from the colonial treasuries, as well as a percentage of the much larger private shipments landed in Seville. American silver's real value was as a source of credit, since lenders retained faith in the crown's ability to pay its spiralling debts with future imports. Creditors were given *consignaciones*, or claims on specific revenues, or *juros* that were government bonds paying fixed interest. The latter developed into a form of funded debt as they became traded on the international money market through Genoese bankers who handled most of Spain's external credit until 1670.

The basic pattern was already firmly established by the mid-sixteenth century. Only a small proportion of current expenditure could be met from ordinary revenue, with a growing share set against debt using silver imports to sustain credit. Politics supplanted economics as finance became a matter of sustaining public confidence in the monarchy's ability to repay its burgeoning debt. Bankruptcies occurred each time this confidence was shaken, such as in 1559 when the debt totalled 25 million ducats, or at Philip II's death in 1598 when it had climbed to 85 million, or ten times ordinary revenue. The difficulty in sustaining credit forced the crown into a series of expedients to bridge blockages in cash flow. Offices and titles were sold in Iberia and the colonies, especially certificates of ordinary nobility, while 169 new lordships were created between 1625 and 1668, doubling the size of the aristocracy. Royal rights over 3,600 Castilian towns and villages were pawned, while large parts of the customs service were privatized throughout the monarchy. In addition to providing desperately needed ready cash, these expedients created a new elite with a vested interest in the silver system, since most of the purchasers of royal rights and titles were those who had got rich from the Atlantic trade. It thus became difficult to reform the system without alienating the crown's chief creditors. Moreover, the expedients reduced long-term revenue, for instance by increasing the number of tax-exempt nobles to 10 per cent of the Castilian population. The crown had created a monster that consumed thousands of Indian and African lives, bore heavily on the backs of its European subjects, and from which it could not escape.

Imperial Defence

All this economic activity was directed towards perpetuating Spanish imperialism. Military expenditure rose from 7 million ducats in 1574 to 9 million by the early 1590s. Between 1596 and 1600 Spain sent 3 million ducats a year just to sustain the Army of Flanders, while the Dutch War consumed a total of 40 million between Philip II's death and the 1609 truce. Spanish forces numbered around 100,000 men worldwide in 1600, with the 60,000 in the Army of Flanders representing the largest operational army in Europe. Spain also became Europe's leading naval power during the last two decades of the sixteenth century. It played the major part in the victory of Lepanto over the Ottomans in the Mediterranean in 1571, allowing it to scale down its galley fleet there to around twenty vessels, supported by smaller squadrons operating from Sicily, Naples and Genoa. Resources were redirected to developing the high seas *Armada del Mar Océano* after the failure of the attempted invasion of England in 1588 demonstrated Spain's lack of modern warships. The new *millones* tax funded 56,000 tonnes of new construction, much of it at La Coruña on the northern coast, between 1588 and 1609, creating a fleet of sixty large warships by 1600.[5] This was divided into three roughly equal squadrons, with that at Lisbon patrolling the Atlantic to provide additional security for the two silver convoys. A second squadron patrolled the Straits securing access to the Mediterranean, while the third was based at La Coruña for operations against France and the Protestant powers. A small Pacific squadron of six ships was formed in 1580 to protect the silver shipments between Arica and Panama, but attempts to form an additional Caribbean squadron were frustrated by the continual detachment of its ships to assist the Atlantic convoys.

Naval expansion pushed personnel requirements up to 27,000 by 1590 at a time when the army also needed more recruits and the Castilian population stopped growing. As the supply of volunteers dwindled, it became harder to rely on the established system of issuing commissions to officers to recruit units. The state diversified its approach, retaining direct management of the army and navy, but contracting out key aspects of recruitment, logistics and weapons procurement. Philip II co-opted local nobles and magistrates to recruit men and tried to revive the defunct militia to provide a measure of security in the hinterlands of the outlying provinces like Catalonia, Levante, Andalusia and Galicia. Meanwhile, the state monopoly over weapons production, created in 1562, was progressively dismantled after 1598, placing all works in private hands by 1632 except the Cartagena powder mill.[6] Privatization did not necessarily mean weakness. For example, private shipyards could build a warship for 31 ducats a tonne in the 1630s, 4 ducats a tonne less than the state yards, saving an average of 2,000 ducats a ship. However, such measures were clearly unplanned and unwanted, forced upon the monarchy by its inability to master its burgeoning debt.

Only 5.1 million ducats of Spain's revenue in 1598 was directly available for the crown to spend, because the other 4.1 million was mortgaged to creditors or needed to pay interest on the *juros*. Revenue anticipation increased, reducing the 'free' proportion to only 1.6 million by 1618. Meanwhile, annual expenditure climbed to 12 million, set against a total revenue that fell from 12.9 million at Philip II's death to 10 million or less by 1621. Philip III broke the long tradition of Spanish probity by issuing debased coin a year after his accession in 1598. Though he agreed to stop issuing this copper *vellón* currency in 1608 in return for increased tax grants, he resorted to it again in 1617 and 1621, driving good coin from circulation. The crown lost in the long run, because Spaniards paid their taxes in *vellón* but the soldiers would accept only good silver. The funded *juro* debt rose from 92 to 112 million ducats across Philip III's reign, driving annual interest payments up to 5.6 million, equivalent to half of ordinary revenue.

These problems led many Spaniards to believe that 'the ship is going down' (*se va todo a fondo*) and later historians have echoed this sense of decline. Writers in the 1590s drew on classical thought that suggested a natural life cycle of states from rise, through maturity to eventual decline, and many were afraid their country was entering the final stage. However, while all were convinced that only God could reverse this process, there was wide disagreement on how far human intervention could slow it. The government was certainly not short of ideas, as its subjects wrote numerous proposals, identifying possible weaknesses and suggesting remedies.[7] All were concerned with the monarchy's reputation (*reputación*), which was correctly identified as essential to sustaining the system of credit. They were less concerned with the underlying problems of depopulation, de-industrialization, agrarian depression and stagnant trade that later historians have concentrated upon. Whereas the historical concept of 'Spanish decline' assumes that a loss of political influence automatically followed economic setbacks, early seventeenth-century Spaniards were not unduly pessimistic. They recognized that periodic bankruptcy induced setbacks such as the 1609 truce with the Dutch, but they had no sense of imminent collapse. Spain remained a wealthy country where life was very good, at least for the fortunate few at the top of the social scale: the 115 grandees collectively enjoyed an annual income of 5 million ducats, equivalent to half the state's revenue. Spain still had numerous experienced soldiers, sailors, administrators and diplomats with extensive contacts throughout Europe. It remained strong relative to its main rival, France, which continued to be racked by crises into the mid-seventeenth century. Above all, Spain had built up sufficient political and military momentum by 1621 that its imperial juggernaut carried on for two decades after it had run out of fuel.

Concern for *reputación* places the monarchy at the heart of any discussion of Spanish power. The Spanish concept of majesty stressed the exalted nature of kingship where the monarch was specially selected by God to rule, in charge of his own destiny and that of his subjects. The Estates, councils and other advisers that featured so prominently in older ideas of mixed monarchy, still played a role, but they were firmly subordinated to the king who took decisions alone.[8] As ever, practice lagged considerably behind theory. Philip II had tried to force his advisers to work together by refusing to single anyone out for particular favour, but this merely drove personal rivalries under the surface. The situation was compounded by the king's refusal to acknowledge constitutional checks on his power, circumventing established institutions by the creation of ad hoc committees, or *juntas*, for particular tasks. This could introduce new flexibility but generally just added new layers of bureaucracy, creating confusion and demarcation disputes. The Council of State (*Consejo de Estado*) offered the main forum to debate general matters and formulate policy. It spawned a large number of specialist *juntas*, many of which evolved into permanent councils, such as that for war, finance, the crusade (for Catholic renewal) and the different parts of the monarchy: the Indies, Portugal, Castile, Aragon, Italy and Flanders. The presence of the latter indicates how the empire remained a composite state, with wide powers entrusted to viceroys and governors in the Netherlands, Milan, Naples, Sicily, Sardinia and the colonies. Portugal also retained its own government in Lisbon to satisfy local pride. All governors faced advisory councils of notables and had to pay attention to provincial interests, as well as orders from Madrid, particularly since their salaries, together with those of their government and garrison, depended on local taxes.

Not surprisingly, imperial defence assumed first place in Spanish grand strategy.[9] The very extent of the empire increased the potential enemies, while the spread of heresy raised the spectre of internal unrest that manifested itself most clearly in the Dutch Revolt after 1566. Defence of the trade monopoly with the Indies also expanded with the acquisition of Portugal, whose colonies now required protection. However, what gave Spain its sense of mission was a defence of Catholicism that became fused with national identity. The completion of the *Reconquista* in 1492 saw the defeat of the last Moorish kingdom in Iberia and earned the monarch the title of His Most Catholic Majesty from the papacy. Overseas conquests added a new missionary role as Spaniards saw themselves as civilizing the New World. Defence of the Mediterranean against the

Ottomans maintained the ideal of the crusade that broadened with the fight against heresy throughout Europe.

The Catholic mission extended to the incorporation of Rome itself into Spain's 'informal empire', or imperial influence extending beyond its formal possessions.[10] This began with the accession of the Borga Pope Alexander VI in 1492, who divided the New World between Spain and Portugal by the Treaty of Tordesillas two years later. It evolved into a symbiotic relationship whereby each drew benefit from the other, but Spain was the dominant partner. In an age where other monarchs were renouncing Rome, Spain remained respectful. Papal feudal jurisdiction over Naples was formally acknowledged by payment of an annual tribute of 7,000 ducats and a magnificent white horse, while fees from vacant sees across the monarchy were still remitted to the pontiff's treasury. Rome relied increasingly on grain imported from Sicily and other Spanish possessions, and Spanish charity funded poor relief, hospitals and churches. The Spanish community grew to a quarter of the city's population by the late sixteenth century and assumed a central role in its political and ceremonial life. The Spanish ambassador arranged for the presentation of the white horse from Naples to be made part of the feast of St Peter after 1560, symbolically placing Spain at the heart of papal politics. Payments of up to 70,000 ducats a year ensured a favourable majority in the College of Cardinals. Though the Spanish presence aroused considerable popular resentment, the papacy generally appreciated the benefits. Protected by Spain, defence spending could be slashed from over half to under a fifth of the papal budget. While money flowed from Spain to Rome, even more went directly into the Spanish treasury thanks to papal sanction, and the 'three graces' and other ecclesiastical levies were worth 3.68 million ducats a year by 1621, accounting for a third of ordinary revenue.

The close ties to the universal church reinforced Spain's imperial mission. Though Charles V's imperial title passed to his brother, not his son Philip, his legacy enhanced Spain's own sense of empire and Spanish warships and troops continued to carry flags with the imperial black double eagle into the seventeenth century. While the Austrian branch of the Habsburgs retained the Holy Roman imperial title, Spanish writers claimed their own monarchy pre-dated even ancient Rome, identifying a son of Noah as the first king of Spain.[11] To its critics, however, Spanish imperialism was a spectre stalking Europe, using religion as a cloak to impose universal monarchy. Spain's enemies had little knowledge of its many problems, believing that its American riches meant it could fight war on a scale that would soon exhaust their own resources. This was acutely felt in France where many felt encircled – by Spain to the south, Spanish-ruled Milan and the Franche-Comté to the east, Luxembourg and Flanders to the north, with the Armada closing the Atlantic to the west. For Protestant Europe, the Armada of 1588 encapsulated the twin threat of tyranny and persecution and this image of an aggressive Spain has often been repeated by later historians.

Spain and the Empire

In fact, Spain generally did not intervene in other countries unless it perceived threats to its core interests and there was usually a strong body of opinion in the Council of State urging caution and disengagement. This can be seen clearly by examining Spanish attitudes to the Empire which were to shape involvement there during the Thirty Years War.[12] Philip II spent 1548–51 in Germany and knew many princes personally, as well as Rudolf and his brothers Ernst and Albert from their stay in Spain. These personal contacts provided a firm basis for Spanish diplomacy after the Habsburg partition of 1558 when each branch developed distinct interests. Philip's concern for Catholicism did not prevent good working relationships with conservative Lutheran princes, such as the Saxon elector and Duke Heinrich Julius of Brunswick-Wolfenbüttel, as well as the duke of Bavaria and other leading Catholics. Philip had no interest in establishing a permanent presence within the Empire. Rather, as with the papacy, he sought to smooth the way for more effective government and rally local opinion behind an allied ruler by offering pensions and other rewards. In particular, he concentrated on building a pro-Spanish party around Bavaria and Cologne that could be mobilized to block the emperor if he embraced any policies contrary to Spanish interests. He also had some success in cultivating courtiers around Rudolf in Prague. Chancellor Lobkowitz was related to Hurtado de Mendoza, one-time Spanish ambassador to the Empire, while Cardinal Dietrichstein had been born in Spain and was related to the influential Cardona family. As we have seen (Chapter 3, pp.73–5), such connections proved instrumental in shifting Rudolf in favour of the militant Catholics in Bohemia and Hungary after 1598.

Protestants suspected a malevolent Spanish–papal conspiracy, but most of those who were labelled members of the 'Spanish party' were simply concerned to consolidate Austrian influence and cooperated with Madrid only so far as it suited their own interests. Spanish influence declined when the imperial court moved from Prague back to Vienna on Rudolf's death in 1612. Zúñiga, the new ambassador, established ties to Archduke Ferdinand of Styria, but the Inner Austrian branch of the dynasty remained more closely allied to Munich than to Madrid. Ferdinand's mother and first wife were Bavarian princesses, while nearby Italy exerted a stronger influence on the culture of the Graz court. This continued once the Styrian branch acquired the imperial title in 1619, and though Ferdinand III's Spanish wife stimulated some interest in Iberian culture, Italy still set the tone in Vienna throughout the seventeenth century.[13] The situation was matched by the declining Austrian presence in Spain. Whereas Maximilian II sent three of his sons to be raised in Madrid, only Albert remained and he was paradoxically regarded as more Spanish than Austrian. Neither Rudolf nor Matthias had children to send and both resented Spanish interference in the Empire. Austria maintained an ambassador in Madrid, but unlike the embassy in Constantinople, this was not permanent. Ferdinand of Styria's sister, Margaret of Austria, married Philip III in 1599. She used her eight pregnancies to keep her husband attentive, but after her death in 1611, the Austrian presence in Spain was reduced to Margaret of the Cross, Matthias's youngest sister, who lived in the Descalzes convent in Madrid and acted as a surrogate mother for Margaret's children.

Ironically, Spanish interest in the Empire declined because Philip thought Rudolf was a reliable Catholic who would manage affairs more soundly than his father, Maximilian II. Bavaria and Styria appeared dependable allies, while a treaty with the Catholic Swiss cantons in 1587 reduced the strategic significance of the Tirol by providing Spain an alternative route over the Alps, communications between different regions in Spain's empire always being a source of anxiety (see below, p.151). The advice prepared for Philip III on his accession in 1598 gave Germany a low priority and represents a complete contrast to later historians' assessment of the situation there. The Protestant princes were considered too disunited to pose a threat, while the Austrians were incapable of independent action. Despite their imperial title, they had slipped to junior partners within the Casa d'Austria. Provided the king of Spain left them alone, the Germans would not cause trouble. National prejudice reinforced the reluctance to meddle in German affairs. Spanish ambassadors' reports presented a country in moral decline. The Catholic German princes were flirting with heterodoxy and failing to pay their full share of taxes for the Turkish War, while the Germans as a whole were regarded as backward and boorish, too busy gorging themselves on fatty foods and guzzling barrels of beer to achieve the heights of Castilian civilization. They lived in a rain-soaked land of dreary forests, muddy roads and expensive, uncomfortable inns.

Unlike his father, Philip III had no personal experience of the Empire and it assumed even less significance in his political calculations. The new monarch has been described as 'the laziest ruler Spain has had', echoing Philip II's own assessment that 'God, who has given me so many kingdoms, had denied me a son capable of ruling them'.[14] After an initial brief interest, he is widely supposed to have left government in the hands of his favourite, the count, later duke, of Lerma, and retired into a private world of self-glorification. As a result, according to one modern historian, 'nobody ruled in Madrid; a world empire was run on an automatic pilot'.[15] Such criticism is not only unjust, it creates a false division between a supposedly dynamic Spain under Philip II and one that was in decline under his son. Philip III attended the Council of State almost daily from the age of fifteen and was already signing documents for his increasingly frail father by 1597. He inherited his father's exalted sense of majesty and retained the final decision on all important matters. The real difference lay in the more realistic attempt to put this form of absolutism into practice. The king concentrated on the symbolic representation of power through intensifying his father's already remote, inaccessible, lofty majesty by physically removing the monarch from government. Practical business was devolved to the duke of Lerma who now dealt directly with the different ministers and *juntas*.

Lerma had risen by one of the classic routes to power by attaching himself to the heir apparent's suite and making himself indispensable. His career demonstrates the vulnerability of the court favourite, a person who had clients but rarely friends. He stressed his own grandeur to distance himself from rivals and emphasize his allegedly unique qualifications to be Philip III's right-hand man. It was a fine line to tread, since his haughty demeanour led his enemies to claim he was seeking to eclipse the monarch. His influence was already shaken between 1606 and 1608 when his main allies died, retired, or were arrested, like the count of Villalonga who became a scapegoat for the 1607 bankruptcy. Friar Aliaga, who had been Lerma's own confessor, turned against him when he became royal confessor in 1608. Criticism mounted when Lerma concluded the Twelve Years Truce with the Dutch in 1609, temporarily suspending attempts to crush their revolt.

THE DUTCH REVOLT 1568–1609

The Dutch Ulcer

The revolt of the Netherlands became Spain's most pressing problem during the later sixteenth century and continued to shape its policy in the first half of the seventeenth. It dictated how Madrid reacted to problems elsewhere, since these could not be tackled fully until the Dutch had been dealt with. While it did not cause the Thirty Years War, the Revolt heightened international tension and militants of all hues were quick to draw parallels between it and their own struggles in Central Europe. It is important to understand the political, strategic, religious and economic situation in the Netherlands in order to comprehend how Spain responded to Austria's difficulties after 1618.

Attempts to impose greater control over the Low Countries from Madrid stirred opposition among the Protestant nobility, particularly the House of Orange. Orange also owned the principality of that name in southern France and was related to the counts of Nassau in the Rhineland. Resentment deepened with Spanish demands to continue with high levels of taxation despite concluding peace with France in 1559. Philip II's insistence on a more active persecution of heresy added confessional motives to the mix, and popular rioting widened into an ill-coordinated revolt after 1566. Philip poured oil onto the flames in April 1567 by sending the duke of Alba and 10,000 troops north along what would become known as the Spanish Road. Alba occupied Antwerp and other major towns, building new citadels to overawe their inhabitants and instituting a repressive tribunal to root out heresy and treason. Though the numbers executed fell far short of the 100,000 claimed in Protestant propaganda, the situation was sufficiently appalling for 60,000 refugees to flee to north-west Germany and England by 1572.[16]

Spanish repression triggered a renewed rising after 1571. Alba launched a major counter-offensive in April 1572 against Flanders and the other southern provinces to cut the rebels off from the French Huguenots. The survivors retreated into Holland and Zeeland. These formed a natural redoubt, surrounded by the sea, rivers and low-lying land that could be flooded. The decentralized political structure assisted the rebels, since each province had its own States, or assembly, composed of knights from the rural areas and representatives of the Regents, or magistrates, who ran the towns.[17] The revolt spread from town to town, enabling the rebels to dominate the States of Holland and elect William the Silent, prince of Orange, as *stadholder*, or provincial captain in charge of the militia. As the process was repeated in other northern provinces, the rebels soon controlled the key institutions, shutting out Spanish sympathizers.

The Revolt shook Spain's *reputación*, forcing the government to declare another bankruptcy and prompting the 'Spanish Fury' when unpaid troops sacked Antwerp in 1576.[18] The disorder dislocated military operations and seemingly confirmed the 'Black Legend' spread by Protestants describing Spain as a brutal, tyrannical power. Spain had to agree a truce in February 1577, withdrawing into Luxembourg and Flanders to regroup. In the army's absence, the rebels enlarged their inner redoubt to include Utrecht and western Gelderland. They were now protected to the east by the river Ijssel with its crossing at Zutphen, to the south by the Rhine and Maas, and to the west by the Zeeland islands that now fell into their hands. The south-eastern approaches to the rebel-held territories were largely blocked by the neutral bishopric of Liège and the barren Kempen heath, and the capture of Antwerp secured the Scheldt estuary and the south-western approaches. Only the route from Germany to the east remained vulnerable and this was barred by the emperor who tried in vain to mediate a peaceful solution. Having secured all seven northern provinces of the Low Countries, the rebels formed the Union of Utrecht in January 1579, which agreed the Act of Abjuration in 1581, repudiating Philip II's authority as a preliminary step towards full independence.

Though neither side realized it, these moves essentially partitioned the Netherlands, since the Spanish were unable to reconquer the northern Dutch, while the rebels could not liberate the remaining five southern provinces. The conflict continued because Spain refused to renounce the lost provinces, while the Dutch needed a clear victory to secure their precarious international position. Both sides began building institutions to sustain what was to be a further seven decades of violence. Victory over the Turks at Lepanto and the sultan's difficulties with Persia reduced the Ottoman threat in the Mediterranean, enabling Spain to switch resources northwards at a time when silver imports were also increasing. Alessandro Farnese, duke of Parma, was appointed to govern the Spanish Netherlands and take charge of the army. Both a tactful diplomat and a skilful strategist, he was responsible for developing the Flanders school of warfare that became a central feature of the Spanish military system we encountered in the discussion of the Turkish War in the previous chapter.

The Flanders School

The Flanders school took a careful, methodical approach to warfare. Parma opened each campaign by sending his cavalry in all directions to confuse the enemy, while shifting his main body of troops from town to town, reducing Dutch strongholds, especially those along the numerous waterways that were vital to move troops and supplies. The Dutch had strengthened their urban defences with concentric rings of fortifications in the Italian manner, intended to keep the enemy at a distance and prevent him from bombarding their houses. Their expertise as dyke-builders enabled them to flood the surrounding countryside, as well as the usual system of ditches around their positions, while further out-works extended the garrison's field of fire. Such fortresses required significant numbers of men to attack them. Besiegers had to dig trenches parallel to the enemy's works to protect themselves from the defenders' fire. Once they had entrenched their own artillery to provide covering fire, they would begin the laborious process of digging towards the selected point of attack, stretching out a second and possibly a third 'parallel' as they approached the enemy works. Each time, they would bring their guns forward, until at last these were entrenched at point-blank range to batter a hole in the main wall. An energetic garrison commander would organize sorties, especially at night, to harass the besiegers, destroy their trenches and spike their guns. Moreover, the besiegers themselves often had to dig an entire outer circle of entrenchments to protect against attack by a relief army.

Given this dangerous and lengthy process, it became customary to summon the garrison to surrender at various points. Sometimes, the defenders would agree to capitulate if not relieved within a certain time. Garrisons that surrendered at an earlier stage were more likely to be granted the honours of war, entitling them to march out with their families, possessions and symbols such as flags and one or two cannon, and make their way to the nearest friendly town. Those that surrendered later often had to do so as prisoners of war, though only the officers would actually be interned since no government could afford the cost of keeping ordinary soldiers incarcerated. Rank and file who were captured were generally pressed into their captor's unit, accepting this as the only way to ensure their survival. Their last opportunity came once the inner wall had been breached. If they refused to surrender now, they would face an assault and their town would be given over for plunder and sometimes massacre if the enemy managed to break in.[19]

Spain's determination to crack the Dutch defences led it to create Europe's largest army, once Parma persuaded the remaining five loyal provinces to readmit Spanish troops after 1582. Already by October of that year, the Army of Flanders totalled over 61,000 men, while the monarchy maintained a further 15,000 in Italy and over 20,000 in Spain and its other possessions.[20] There were only around 2,000 cavalry in Flanders, while over a quarter of the troops elsewhere were mounted. The downgrading of the principal shock arm of battle has been regarded as a retrograde step, condemning the Spanish to fight a war of attrition rather than decisive battles. Yet, Parma's strategy was well-suited to the circumstances where the numerically inferior Dutch avoided battle after 1579. Moreover, the Spanish system remained tactically flexible, since siege warfare and outpost duty provided experience of operating in small groups.

Only a small proportion of this huge army was actually Spanish. Castilians were regarded as the elite of the troops, with Italians second, followed by the Burgundians from Franche-Comté and Luxembourg and the Catholic Irish. The Walloons from Flanders were considered unreliable when serving at home, but steady in Germany and elsewhere and they made up the bulk of the cavalry in the Army of Flanders. Germans had been preferred earlier in the sixteenth century, but were slipping in Spanish estimation and were often poorly regarded while serving in Flanders. Many of those who were to play important roles in the Thirty Years War served with the Army of Flanders. The most prominent was Jean Tserclaes Tilly whose early life exemplifies the often difficult relationship between the Netherlands and Spain. Tilly's father was implicated in the initial revolt and fled to escape Alba's tribunal. Tilly himself was placed in the care of the Jesuits, possibly as a hostage for his father's good behaviour. He entered Spanish service in 1576, two years after his father's properties had been returned, and served in Flanders and the operations around Cologne and Strasbourg, before entering imperial service in 1594.[21] Other noted commanders from the southern Netherlands included Count Anholt who became Tilly's subordinate during the Thirty Years War, and Count Bucquoy who made his name at the battle of Nieuport and siege of Ostend, before becoming the imperial commander-in-chief from 1618 to 1621. His successor, Hieronymus Girolamo de Carafa from Italy, had served in the Army of Flanders since 1587, before transferring to the Spanish forces in his homeland in 1607. Spanish influence was not restricted to Catholic Germany, since Protestant princes also joined the Army of Flanders. Georg of Brunswick, the future duke of Calenberg, decided to complete his military education after serving the Dutch by switching sides in 1604 to see out the rest of the war in the Spanish forces.

While the officer corps remained dominated by the nobility, it was becoming more professional and it was possible for men of talent to rise from the ranks. Johann Aldringen, the son of a Luxembourg town clerk, joined the Army of Flanders in 1606 and rose to become Bavarian commander-in-chief after Tilly's death in 1632. Johann Beck, a messenger's son, started his career as a private at the age of thirteen, eventually transferring as a general to the imperial army in 1634, before returning to command the Spanish six years later. Jan Werth, a peasant from electoral Cologne, joined the Spanish army around 1610 as an ordinary soldier, and ended his career as commander of the imperial cavalry. Parma's renown and the prestige of his methods attracted men seeking to complete their military education. For example, Count Schlick joined the Army of Flanders as an officer in 1604, having fought previously against the Turks. Such men helped to disseminate Spanish military thinking throughout the Empire where it was interpreted in the light of previous German experience and the lessons of the Turkish wars.

The Dutch Republic

Parma's strategy was vindicated by the success of his operations after 1579, which recovered Maastricht, Tournai, Oudenarde, Bruges, Ghent, Brussels and finally, after a long siege, Antwerp in August 1585. The conquests secured the southern provinces and encouraged the still Catholic rural population in the north to rebel against the Calvinist rebel leadership, returning another three provinces temporarily to Spanish control. Coinciding with the assassination of Stadholder William the Silent, these developments prompted the Dutch to offer sovereignty to Elizabeth of England. She was reluctant to accept anything from rebels, but was nonetheless sufficiently alarmed by the Spanish victories to become the first major power to ally with the Dutch. A small army was despatched in 1585 under the earl of Leicester, whom the Dutch accepted as their political and military leader. It was not a happy arrangement. The unpaid English troops failed to defend the Dutch, while Leicester conspired with Calvinist militants to seize greater authority. The failure of his attempted coup in 1587 decisively shifted the Dutch towards republican government under the influence of Johan van Oldenbarnevelt, the moderate leader of the Holland States. Opposing narrow confessional militancy, Oldenbarnevelt favoured a broad coalition to defeat Spain and enlisted the support of the House of Orange by persuading the provinces of Holland and Zeeland to elect William's seventeen-year-old son, Maurice of Nassau, as their new stadholder. The move cemented a powerful alliance between Holland, which generally favoured the moderates, and the House of Orange that usually served as a focal point for militants. Dutch republicanism gradually took shape, especially through the writings of the political philosopher Hugo Grotius. Republican ideals rested on the myth of Batavian freedom – Batavia being the Roman name for the Netherlands – and combined a utopian vision of biblical Judaea with that of ancient Athens to claim that liberty, stability, virtue and prosperity were best guaranteed by a consultative government of wealthy, educated men with time to dedicate themselves to the public good.[22]

These ideals found practical expression in a formal confederation between the rebel provinces in 1588 that retained each province's autonomy but delegated powers to a States General in which each province had one vote. The States General met daily in The Hague after 1593 but remained a debating forum, since all important decisions required ratification by the seven provincial States. It was balanced by the stadholderate headed by Maurice, whose influence rested on social prestige rather than formal authority, and was emphasized through his connections to European royalty and his own personal court. Outside finance and military affairs, central institutions remained minimal, with most of the administration decentralized to provincial and local level. Though cumbersome, the Republic functioned because it integrated the localities within a common framework. Having rejected Philip II's interference in their affairs, the local oligarchs needed the Republic to prevent Spain regaining control.

Holland's phenomenal demographic and economic growth sustained the fledgling state during its protracted struggle for independence. The northern provinces' population doubled between 1520 and 1650, already reaching 1.5 million by 1600, with numbers boosted by the influx of a further 150,000 refugees fleeing the south between 1572 and 1621.[23] With 760,000 inhabitants by 1650, Holland's population far outnumbered that of the next largest province, Friesland with 160,000, while Drenthe, the smallest, had only 22,000. Holland was also the most heavily urbanized province, with 175,000 people living in Amsterdam and another 365,000 in 22 other cities. The concentration of people, wealth and talent fuelled economic growth, securing Dutch primacy in world trade by 1590. This rested primarily on shipping, in terms of both construction and transport for European and world goods. The colonial trade caught the contemporary imagination, but the Baltic and North Sea remained the most important areas of activity. The Dutch fishing fleet totalled 2,250 boats in 1634, while 1,750 ships were employed in the Baltic and Mediterranean trade, compared to only 300 in colonial traffic. Ships in the European trade could make up to four trips a year, but a voyage to the Indies took two years. Much of the colonial trade was linked to European industry, such as the 800 boats that visited the Caribbean between 1599 and 1605 to collect Venezuelan salt to preserve the North Sea fishing catch. Nonetheless, the spice trade was extremely valuable, with the 2,710 tonnes landed annually at the turn of the century worth 137 tonnes of silver, compared to the 125,000 tonnes of grain shipped from the Baltic, worth only 88 tonnes of silver.[24]

The Dutch prominence in the carrying trade made their Republic the entrepôt for European and colonial goods, and encouraged demand for their own products, such as textiles, salted fish and other processed food. The flow of goods gave Dutch merchants a commanding share of the European market, since people turned to them for products they could not find at home. As the Dutch responded to shortages elsewhere, they attracted investment and credit, enabling Amsterdam to supplant the traditional financial centres in Antwerp and Genoa. The exchange bank (*Wisselbank*) founded in 1609 thrived unlike so many attempts elsewhere because it had access to the considerable local resources of private investors and municipalities. The Dutch were able to fund cheaper, long-term loans, reducing the rate paid by their government to 10 per cent by 1600 and half that forty years later.[25] This gave Dutch finance a stability their opponents lacked. Each year, the States General approved a central budget for the next twelve months, apportioning the burden according to a fixed ratio among the provinces. There was no central treasury; rather each province was assigned specific items of expenditure to meet from its own taxes. It was here that Holland's influence was felt, since it was responsible for 60 per cent of expenditure, whereas the others contributed the rest, with Overijssel paying a mere 4 per cent. Despite economic growth and rising revenue, the burden remained very heavy and the Dutch undoubtedly paid far more tax in fighting for their liberty than they had ever paid to their former Spanish rulers.

Dealers in Death

In addition to cash, the Dutch economy turned out valuable war material, since the Low Countries were the centre of Europe's arms industry. The Spanish hold on the southern provinces gave them control of the Mechelen cannon foundry, the Maastricht small arms works and the armour and musket workshops in Namur. The bishopric of Liège was the most important centre in the south, producing a full range of equipment, and especially firearms, armour and edged weapons, and selling to both sides as a way of preserving its neutrality. The nearby imperial cities of Aachen and Essen also produced firearms and the entire region was vital for the rest of the Empire where production was limited. The famous Steyr arms factory in Styria was not established until 1639 and then had a capacity of only around 3,000 muskets a year. The main German centre was Suhl in Thuringia where the 4,000 inhabitants turned out at least 70,000 muskets and 13,000 pistols, mainly for the imperial army, between 1620 and 1655. The metal-workers of Solingen and Nuremberg remained an important source of edged weapons, but altogether Central European production was overshadowed by that in the northern Netherlands. Amsterdam produced small arms, cannon, gunpowder and armour, while other centres were more specialized, with Delft and Dordrecht concentrating on small arms, Gouda supplying match, Utrecht making armour and grenades and The Hague producing bronze cannon. However, it was their wider trading networks that made Dutch arms dealers so significant. They procured saltpetre from Asia and the Baltic, sulphur from Sicily and Elba, as well as parts from other suppliers that were assembled into finished weapons in the Republic.

The combination of a dense population, weapons production and good communications made both the southern and northern Netherlands attractive to potential combatants. Both the Spanish authorities in Brussels and the Dutch in The Hague often released surplus weapons to help dealers complete contracts with friendly powers. The Dutch armaments were in such demand that they never gave discounts, but their government sometimes sold part of its own stockpile to allies at reduced prices. Dutch access to credit and stores enabled them to offer package deals, for example supplying Christian of Brunswick's army with a full set of arms, armour, belts, powder, match, shot, picks and shovels in 1622. Heavy spending by the state and the two colonial India companies sustained dealers. The East India Company (VOC), for example, regularly spent 1.5 million fl. each year, guaranteeing stable demand. Political considerations did influence exports. The last major consignment sold to the emperor was in 1624, ostensibly to fight the Turks but in reality for use against the Transylvanians. Exports to Protestant German states ceased around 1625, partly because these had largely been eliminated as distinct belligerents, but also because the Republic wished to avoid becoming entangled in the war there. Exports continued to France, England, Denmark, Sweden and Venice who were all friendly towards the Republic, and Portugal was added to the customer list once it had rebelled against Spain in 1640. The Dutch bore no grudge against Spain when it came to business, supplying weapons as soon as peace was concluded in 1648, even though these were clearly going to be used against France, the Republic's former ally.

Exports during the first half of the seventeenth century totalled at least 200,000 small arms worth 1.2 million fl. A further 100,000 suits of armour, worth half a million, were sold abroad, along with 2.7 million kilos of match and over 2.2 million kilos of gunpowder worth over 25 million fl. The trade earned at least 50 million fl., representing 5 per cent of the total economy, equivalent to the VOC's contribution to the Republic's Gross National Product (GNP). To this must be added a similar amount earned from the sale of ships' stores, copper, lead, tin, saltpetre and other war materials. Some fortunes were made, such as those of the Trip family who started as riverboat captains, or the De Geers who arrived in Amsterdam as refugees from Liège. However, it is notable that both families owed their success to diversified, if integrated, business interests. Elias Trip and Louis de Geer secured the monopoly on the Swedish copper industry by loaning money to Gustavus Adolphus, operating a consortium whose working capital was equivalent to more than a third of that of the VOC. The Trip family mansion in Amsterdam, built in 1660–2 and decorated with chimneys shaped like cannon barrels, cost a quarter of a million florins and now houses the Dutch Academy of Sciences, while Louis de Geer died worth 1.7 million fl.[26]

The connection between war and trade was clearest when it came to the navy. This was funded from customs duties and fees paid by merchants in return for its protection. Naval administration was decentralized, befitting the general republican structure, with five admiralties, three of which were in Holland and the others in Zeeland and Friesland. Though this created scope for personal rivalries, it did facilitate interaction with the local mercantile communities that remained a vital source of additional ships and manpower. The navy developed to provide close support for the army in the crucial inland waterways but expanded to blockade the Flemish coast, cruise the North Sea and English Channel and convoy merchant ships. The latter task was paid for by the merchants, while the fishing fleet equipped its own guard boats and the two colonial trading companies created their own squadrons to protect trade with the East and West Indies respectively. Larger, more heavily armed ships were collected from 1596, giving the navy the capacity to attack the Spanish coast and the Azores.[27]

Home defence was maintained by the urban militia (*Schutters*), which were reorganized in the 1570s and recruited from burghers and other richer residents. Though it was possible to buy exemption, service became a matter of pride, associated with republican values, masculine sociability and solidarity. Militia companies commissioned leading artists to paint their portraits, of which Rembrandt's *The Militia Company of Captain Frans Banning Cocq* (better known as *Night Watch*) became the most famous example. In the front line the militia were replaced by merging the regular troops of the different provinces into a common army under the prince of Orange as captain general.

The Dutch Military Reforms and their Influence

Though the amalgamation of the provinces' troops took place in November 1576, it was not until a decade later that this army really took shape under the command of Maurice of Nassau.[28] The young prince came to power unexpectedly after the assassination of his father, because his elder brother, Philip William, was in the hands of the Spanish and unable to take his place. He also lacked the title of captain general, since Friesland, Utrecht and Gelderland all chose other stadholders, breaking the unity of command. Nonetheless, thanks to Oldenbarnevelt's support, Maurice had Holland's political backing and emerged as the dominant military figure, as well as leading representative of the House of Orange in Dutch politics. His name is associated with a series of military reforms that not only underpinned the Dutch way of war, but exerted considerable influence on German and Swedish military organization. These measures addressed a problem common throughout Europe, but because they achieved success earlier than similar efforts elsewhere, they became the model to follow and the one that has attracted subsequent historical attention.[29]

Maurice sought to harness the cohesion of professional mercenaries while firmly subordinating them to political control. His measures were a practical attempt to apply insights from philosophy, science and medicine to solve contemporary problems. Late sixteenth-century thinkers were fascinated by the belief that patterns could be detected in the natural world that would unlock the divine secrets of the universe. This early rationality was combined with the late humanist rereading of classical texts, looking for other answers in the world of the ancient Greeks and Romans. The clearest expression of these approaches was found in the work of Justus Lipsius who taught at the university of Leiden where Maurice had studied and who presented his *Politicorum sive civilis doctrinae libri sex* to the prince in 1589.[30] Like many of his generation, Lipsius was horrified by sectarian violence and searched classical literature for a remedy, reworking ancient Greek philosophy as Neo-Stoicism. He argued that passions blinded humans to their collective best interests, leading to irrational violence. Accordingly, emotions should be suppressed, ideally by iron self-discipline, or failing that, by external coercion. Through a reading of Roman history in its later, imperial phase, Lipsius broadened his philosophy into a plea for firm yet responsible government, where rulers had a duty to protect their subjects from harming themselves, as well as against external threats. These ideas gained such force because they were combined with a strong dose of the Christian morality so desired by Protestant and Catholic reformers of life.

From this basis, Lipsius articulated a four-fold concept of discipline. Drill had made the ancient Roman army invincible and should now be applied, not only for weapons training, but to condition soldiers to accept subordination within a disciplined unit. Such thinking affected other spheres of life. For example, dance styles were changing away from formations in straight lines that allowed partners to interact swiftly with one another, and towards circular, geometrical movements enabling individuals to make better use of the space around them. Unnecessary movement was to be avoided, with the dancer – or soldier – only moving parts of his or her body from a stable equilibrium; for example, thrusting a pike forward while keeping the head strictly aligned and facing forward. Order provided a second element, because a hierarchical command structure was required to direct individual movement and ensure all the cogs functioned smoothly in the military machine. Crucially, order was extended to the higher ranks, who could no longer treat their subordinates as they pleased. Thirdly, regular drill was part of a wider strategy of coercion, to break the autonomous mercenary culture and encourage internalized self-discipline. The final element stressed rewards and punishments. Articles of war ceased to be an expression of soldiers' collective organization and became a means of institutionalizing the new military culture. Drafted by trained lawyers and linked to new mustering and oath ceremonies, they were intended to break collective pay bargaining by standardizing service contracts and including all personnel within a common legal framework.

These proto-absolutist ideas chimed with the social disciplining agenda of church and state, but were intended by Lipsius to render war less violent and destructive. His ideas made Maurice's reforms intellectually respectable and they were widely disseminated, because the Netherlands was already a centre for printing and publishing. Jacob de Gheyn's famous illustrated manual of arms published in 1607 appeared in Danish later that year and in German in the next. Numerous other practical handbooks followed, such as the three by Johann Jacob von Wallhausen in 1615–16 that were frequently reprinted or rehashed throughout the seventeenth century.[31] Still more influential were the numerous volunteers who flocked to learn the military art under Maurice, now that the English alliance and the foundation of the Republic removed the stigma of rebellion and made Dutch service more attractive. As in the case of the Army of Flanders, these personal connections were to exert a powerful influence on the conduct of the Thirty Years War. A few rose through the ranks, like Peter Eppelmann, a Calvinist peasant from Hademar in Nassau, who had enjoyed a university education thanks to good family connections and changed his name to the more elevated 'Melander', the Greek version of 'Apple man'. Melander served as Maurice's secretary before becoming an ensign in his army, later transferring to Venetian and then Hessen-Kassel service, finally ending his career as an imperial commander and ennobled under German translation as 'von Holzapfel'. Many German Protestant nobles joined Dutch service, including Johann von Geyso, another ennobled commoner who replaced Melander as Hessen-Kassel commander in 1640, and Baron Knyphausen who was made a Dutch captain in 1603 and later a Swedish general. Others took their experience elsewhere, like the Welshman Charles Morgan who later commanded a British expeditionary force to northern Germany, or the Scot Alexander Leslie, who served under Maurice as captain between 1602 and 1608, before transferring to Sweden and then rising as the earl of Leven to command first the Covenanters and then the Royalists in the British Civil Wars. Meanwhile, Gaspard de Coligny, marquis de Châtillon, commanded two Huguenot regiments in Dutch service, helping to transmit Maurice's reforms to France.

Political ties provided a third route for Dutch influence, particularly through Count Johann VII of Nassau-Siegen, a nephew of William of Orange who served under Maurice and implemented the reforms in his own territories. It was Johann's drill book that de Gheyn illustrated, while Wallhausen was director of the military academy the count ran in his capital at Siegen between 1616 and 1623. Johann combined the Dutch ideas with past German practice, so making the new methods more applicable to the situation within the Empire. The duke of Alba's march north along their borders in 1567 greatly alarmed the Rhenish princes, particularly the Nassau counts as relations of the rebel leadership. Fearing that the regular Spanish reinforcements following Alba might be redirected into their own lands, the Nassau counts forged an alliance with their neighbours in the Wetterau region. All ruled small, sparsely populated territories unable to maintain large numbers of regular soldiers. Johann recognized that militiamen could not replace professionals for offensive operations, but believed they would be motivated to defend their homeland. Subjects were already obliged to turn out in emergencies, but they appeared with an odd assortment of rusty swords, farm implements and cudgels. What they needed, thought Johann, was a good dose of Dutch discipline to stiffen their resolve and enable them to make the best use of modern weapons.

Local officials were charged with registering the male population, dividing it into groups according to age, marital status and fitness, and then selecting unmarried young men for regular instruction by professional drill sergeants. Men were grouped into companies of a standard size with large communities providing complete units and smaller parishes combining to field one. The select portion (*Auswahl*) would drill each Sunday on the village green, periodically assembling in camps to practise manoeuvring in larger formations. Summoned by the church bells in emergencies, they would collect their weapons from the bailiff's house and muster under their drill sergeants and those members of the local gentry with military experience. All elements of this 'territorial defence system' (*Landesdefensionswesen*) were in place in Nassau by 1595 and were disseminated through Johann's written advice among Protestant princes who adopted the new militias around 1600.[32]

The reforms were an important part of the changing relationship between rulers and subjects. The German princes and other territorial rulers could already summon their subjects to perform *Landfolge*, or assistance against invasion and natural disaster, as well as *Gerichtsfolge* against lawbreakers. The development of the imperial public peace (see Chapter 2, pp.21–2) strengthened these powers by 1570, since rulers could now call on their subjects to uphold imperial law and defend the

Empire, although the territorial Estates disputed whether these powers extended to conscripting subjects to fight offensive wars and generally refused to vote taxes for these.[33] Princes saw the new militias as a way of extending their authority over their subjects and believed that regular drill would spearhead social change in line with the disciplinary and moral drives present in confessionalization. Like these measures, implementation of the territorial defence system relied on the same network of parish priests, village headmen and princely bailiffs. However, princes encountered resistance from their territorial nobility who refused to allow their own tenants to be incorporated. The result was a compromise, since the reforms depended on the Estates' agreement to pay the drill sergeants, buy the new weapons and provide beer and other inducements to encourage men to turn up for training. Militia enrolment was restricted to electoral towns in Brandenburg, while in Saxony 9,664 men were selected from the elector's 93,000 able-bodied tenants, and the 47,000 fit men under the imperial knights' jurisdiction were obliged to field only 1,500 pioneers. Nobles were unable to dodge the system entirely, since their fiefs were associated with the obligation to perform military service. These long-standing personal ties were incorporated within the territorial defence system by forming cavalry from the feudal levy. The Saxon knights were obliged to raise two regiments totalling 1,593 men, while those elsewhere generally provided a tenth of the total militia. Overall, around one in ten able-bodied males were incorporated into the militias, or about 2.5 per cent of the total population.[34]

The militias were not intended to replace regular troops in the field as some later historians have believed. Instead, they were to provide immediate local defence against incursions and marauders, as well as garrisoning strategic fortresses. The latter formed the most expensive element of the system as princes built new works in the Dutch manner, or modernized existing installations. The Palatinate, because of its dispersed territory and vulnerability, embarked on the most ambitious programme, constructing Mannheim between 1606 and 1622 around an older village, complete with a seven-bastion citadel (the Friedrichsburg), as well as walls around the rest of the city with another six full and two half bastions. Another fortress was built at Frankenthal in 1608 and strengthened in 1620–1, while the existing Heidelberg castle was expanded. In all cases, princes maintained small cadres of professionals as bodyguards and garrisons. The combination of militia, fortresses and small professional bodyguards formed the basis of military organization across the German territories by 1600.

It is easy to understand why the Estates doubted their rulers' assurances that the measures were purely defensive, since the professionals could be used to stiffen mobilized militia for operations in the field. Subjects regarded drilling as another chore on top of mounting labour service demands, and the heavy drinking that often accompanied the training sessions disproved the theorists' predictions that drill would foster Christian morality. The Brandenburg towns persuaded their elector to abandon the militia in 1610 and return to the previous practice of hiring men when he summoned them to assist him. Such setbacks slowed the introduction of the reforms; plans in the Palatinate from 1577 were not fully implemented until 1600, while the Estates delayed the organization of the Saxon militia until 1613.

Assessment of these measures and of the Dutch reforms generally has suffered from anachronistic back-projection of later concerns. Conservative Germans took the militias to be a milestone in the development of universal military service as a patriotic duty that was frustrated by the Empire's political fragmentation, forcing the princes to fall back on mercenary recruitment after 1618. Others interpreted militias as potential people's armies, noting how peasants used the system to organize their revolts. Neither perspective is entirely apt. Both the Dutch *Schutters* and the German militias incorporated distinctly early modern visions: the former as privileged burghers of a decentralized republic, the latter as obedient subjects of a territorial prince. Dutch influence was, in any case, only one inspiration behind the German measures. Fabian von Dohna, who led the Prussian reforms in 1602, had served under Maurice and helped organize the Palatine militia. Yet, the Prussian system was called Wibranzen, after the Polish word *Wybrancy* for 'selected', while reforms elsewhere were stimulated by the Turkish menace after 1593. Moreover, Catholic territories were also reorganizing their traditional militias along similar lines, notably in Bavaria where measures implemented in 1593–1600 formed 22,000 men into 39 rural and 5 urban regiments.

Many of the Dutch ideas and those associated with the German militia reforms were highly theoretical, preoccupied with devising geometrical formations of little utility. Even those more concerned with practical advice often opposed technological change, such as Wallhausen who bemoaned the decline of the lance as the cavalryman's main weapon. Dutch methods were often not dissimilar to those of their opponents, for example in their reduction of cavalry to a small proportion of the army. Their preference for thinner lines was not solely driven to maximize firepower; it was also an expedient since they were generally outnumbered. Above all, Dutch success did not depend on new weaponry or military theory, but on financial stability and a specific business mentality. Spain, despite its vast wealth, still relied on fidelity and loyalty to social superiors to keep men in the ranks even when the money ran out. Such thinking was anathema to the Dutch for whom a contract was a binding agreement: it could not be otherwise in a commercializing economy where continued growth depended on sustaining faith in credit. Soldiers were employees and, as such, were entitled to regular payment.

Since the spread of mercenary recruitment around 1500, it had been customary to pay soldiers monthly, giving them one or more additional month's pay as a recruitment bounty and as a bonus upon discharge. Soldiers' pay rose between 50 and 100 per cent in the fifty years before 1530 when rulers began fixing upper limits for each rank. By threatening mutinies, soldiers had forced the authorities to pay them in growing quantities of silver coin thereafter, though the official monthly rate remained around 4 gold florins for an infantryman. As Spain and the Dutch formed regular armies, their costs rose still further since they had to pay these all year round, and not just during the campaign season, as was still customary at the beginning of the sixteenth century. The so-called 'Dutch month' was introduced in 1576 as an economy measure, dividing the year into eight blocks of 42 days, plus one of 29, thereby reducing the number of pay instalments the government owed each year. Others tried this, with the Austrians, for example, reducing the year to nine months by 1607, the pay for two of which would be given in cloth to make uniforms. The Austrian measures merely prompted further mutinies, since the imperial soldiers already had huge pay arrears. By contrast, the Dutch made it work, because they at least honoured their promise to pay the reduced rates. Regular pay underpinned cohesion in an army where over half the men came from outside the Republic and sustained loyalty despite periodic defeats, especially as the government's credit remained unshaken. The Bohemians and Protestant Germans were unable to replicate this financial stability and so their attempts to copy Dutch tactics and organization after 1618 rested on very shaky foundations.

Defence of the Republic 1590–1609

While the Dutch forces enjoyed a sounder financial footing, they remained outnumbered, with Maurice mustering around 20,500 troops in 1588, about a third of the number in the Spanish forces. However, he benefited from Philip II's diversion of resources, first to the Enterprise of England in 1588, and then to fruitless intervention in the French Wars of Religion after 1590. Parma accepted these orders from Madrid with reluctance, and Archduke Albert, who followed him as governor in 1593, was obliged to continue the campaigns in Artois in support of the French Catholic League. This enabled Maurice to go on to the offensive with a series of strikes to strengthen the Republic's southern frontier by seizing strategic towns. The capture of Breda in March 1590 enlarged the Dutch salient into Brabant in the south-west, securing a launch pad for possible thrusts deeper into the Spanish Netherlands. The captured territory was not incorporated into the Republic on an equal basis with the other provinces, but governed in common as the Generality. It would become the most hotly contested area from the 1620s onwards. A three-pronged offensive enlarged the salient in the following year by taking Hulst, only 16km from Antwerp, as well as recapturing Zutphen and Deventer, thus securing the line of the Ijssel, while the seizure of Nijmegen on the Waal rounded off the frontier to the southeast. With the entire southern front secure, Maurice turned north in 1592 to crush the Catholic rebellion in the northern provinces that had broken out seven years before. The capture of Groningen in 1594 completed this campaign and restored all seven provinces to republican control.

Having regrouped in 1595–6, Maurice struck east into the remaining Spanish territory across the Ijssel in August 1597 in a move that was to have fateful consequences for the Empire, since it shifted the war towards the imperial frontier. The Dutch swiftly captured another seven fortified towns, extending their territory up to the edge of the Westphalian Kreis, as well as capturing the vital crossing over the Lower Rhine at Rheinberg, a town belonging to electoral Cologne.[35] The northern Catholic population in the Republic was now completely cut off from the Spanish, unless Madrid was prepared to breach imperial neutrality and outflank the Dutch by going further east through Westphalia. The Spanish belatedly responded by sending 24,000 troops into Münster, Recklinghausen and the four Lower Rhenish duchies of Jülich, Cleves, Mark and Berg in September 1598 to secure these before the Dutch got there. The decentralized structure of the public peace allowed local rulers to activate imperial defence, even though Emperor Rudolf failed to respond. The five western Kreise eventually mobilized 16,000 troops, but these did not assemble until July 1599, three months after the Spanish had departed, leaving only a few garrisons just inside the German border. An attempt to retake one of these towns failed miserably, and the Kreise army disintegrated in September when its pay ran out.[36] Known as the 'Spanish Winter', this episode reinforced the Germans' desire to stay out of the Spanish-Dutch quarrel, and Cologne, Münster and other territories in the vicinity opened talks with both sides to persuade them to limit their incursions.

The Spanish move into Germany was a consequence of the Peace of Vervins, agreed with France in May 1598, which ended Spain's two-front war and enabled Albert to redeploy the entire Army of Flanders against Maurice. He switched the focus back to the west and renewed the assault against the Republic's heavily defended frontier around the Scheldt estuary. Operations soon stalled in front of the Dutch defences and then collapsed as the army mutinied over its mounting arrears. Maurice struck south from the Brabant salient down the Flanders coast, intending to eliminate the naval base the Spanish had developed at Dunkirk. Albert's attempt to intercept him led to the battle of Nieuport on 2 July 1600, the first major engagement since the mid 1570s. The action demonstrated the constraints of the Flanders school of positional warfare. Though the Army of Flanders then totalled 4,000 cavalry and 60,000 infantry, Albert had difficulty in finding 1,500 horse and 8,000 foot for the battle because the rest were required to garrison the fortified towns, or were still defying orders because of the mutiny.[37] Equally, the action underlined the limits of a more aggressive strategy of seeking battle. Despite defeating the Spanish army, Maurice was unable to take Dunkirk and ended the campaign back in his starting positions.

Albert decided to block any further attempts on Dunkirk by attacking the Anglo-Dutch garrison in Ostend in July 1601. Ostend became the seventeenth-century equivalent of the First World War battle of Verdun. Both sides poured men and materials into the contest as possession of the port assumed symbolic significance out of all proportion to its strategic importance. The Dutch were forced to enlarge their army from

35,000 in 1599 to 51,000 by 1607, not least because Maurice's earlier successes had given the Republic a longer frontier to defend.

Nonetheless, Spanish preoccupation with Ostend gave Maurice another chance to extend his positions eastwards, this time concentrating on protecting the north-eastern frontier to secure the newly reconquered areas around Groningen. This was one of the many porous border regions in Europe where territorial jurisdictions had yet to establish firm frontiers. The entire North Sea coast shared a similar topography, social organization and political culture, despite the eastern part lying within the Empire, while the west now belonged to the Republic. People on both sides of the frontier cherished their peasant communal autonomy, expressed as 'Frisian Freedom'. Those at the eastern extremity lost this when the Danish king forcibly incorporated their villages in what is now Holstein in modern Germany into his dominions in the mid-sixteenth century. Those in the west tried to preserve it as a province of the new Dutch Republic. In between lay the county of East Frisia that had been incorporated into the Empire only in 1464 and was governed by the Cirksena family, itself descended from village headmen who still lived relatively modestly. East Frisia was troubled by an internal dispute, like so many other German territories in the later sixteenth century, notably Jülich-Cleves, Hessen, Baden, Cologne and Strasbourg (see Chapter 7). While none ever led to major war, all involved issues that concerned foreign powers to whom one or more of the factions appealed for assistance. Their stories have been told by local historians, and by those examining the wider panorama of European relations who tend to see them as potential flashpoints for great-power conflicts. These two perspectives need to be integrated, since the real significance of these disputes lies in their proclivity to suck external powers incrementally deeper into imperial affairs. Foreign intervention was always intended to be temporary and directed at preventing hostile parties from interfering. Little thought was given to an 'exit strategy', and once involved it often became difficult to withdraw without creating a vacuum that might be filled by opposing forces.

East Frisia illustrates these general points, as well as serving as background for important events in north-west Germany during the 1620s (for which see Chapter 10). Like many secular north German rulers, the Cirksena family embraced Lutheranism during the early sixteenth century. This remained the faith of their subjects living in the poorest third of the county, a region of heath and moorland under the count's direct jurisdiction. The other two-thirds was marshland that was more prosperous, because the fertile soil supported more market-orientated agriculture. The marsh peasants secured representation in the territorial Estates and forced the count to ban further rent increases. They, and the few local nobles, converted to Calvinism and forged an alliance with the burghers of Emden, the only large town. Strategically situated at the mouth of the Ems, Emden was the westernmost North Sea port and serviced the trade of much of Westphalia. The town experienced a boom following the outbreak of the Dutch Revolt as merchants sought a safer place to do business, while refugees headed there for a new life. Gradually, Calvinism became associated with the opposition of Emden and their richer peasant allies against attempts by the Lutheran Cirksena to assert greater authority.

The Dutch grew concerned with the accession of Count Enno III in 1599, because he seemed more determined to impose his will than his predecessors, and had relations in Spanish service. Maurice's failure to take Dunkirk raised the spectre of a new Spanish naval strategy to disrupt the trade upon which republican independence rested. Dunkirk privateers were already intercepting Dutch ships in the English Channel and it was feared they would be able to attack the Baltic trade as well if they were allowed to use Emden. The Republic persuaded the Emden burghers to admit a Dutch garrison in 1602, and then to extend this by allowing troops into Leerort, a fort further up the Ems by the little town of Leer that blocked the only route into East Frisia from the south-west across the marsh and heath. Emden now became a radical political and religious centre, one of the few places in Germany where the Calvinists adopted the decentralized presbyterian organization used by their co-religionists elsewhere. The town hired Johannes Althusius as its advocate in 1604, expressly because of his book *Politica* which had attracted wide notoriety for its suggestion that magistrates were entitled to resist tyrannical princes.[38]

War of Attrition

The Spanish remained stuck in their trenches before Ostend. The war had cost them 1,500 dead every year since 1582, in addition to further losses among their Walloon, Italian and German troops. Another 40,000 fell in the four years of the siege that was finally brought to a successful conclusion by Ambroglio di Spinola in September 1604. Spinola's appointment as commander the year before was symptomatic of Spain's financial and military problems. He hailed from Genoa, the hub of Spain's credit and logistical system. His younger brother played a major role in establishing the Armada of Flanders after the capture of Dunkirk in 1583, but Ambroglio stayed at home to marry and run the family bank. Like many bankers, he owed his success to diversifying his business, securing a cardinal's hat for one of his sons by financing military recruitment, as well as becoming heavily involved in Spain's Mediterranean trade. The bank amassed a working capital of 2 million ducats, enabling Spinola to raise and equip 13,000 soldiers for Spain by 1602. His interests had become entwined with those of the monarchy; the king needed him for the war effort, while Spinola needed victory to sustain his bank's credit. His capture of Ostend validated the decision to make him a general and he officially replaced Archduke Albert as commander of the Army of Flanders in 1605. What could have been a disaster became an effective partnership. Both were reasonable men, while Spinola's tact and skill soon won him the respect of his more seasoned subordinates.

He now renewed the policy of outflanking the Dutch to the east, striking with 15,000 men at the Ijssel sector to retake many of the towns lost there in 1597, including Rheinberg by 1606. However, Spinola failed to penetrate the Republic's inner defences, while the Dutch responded to a Spanish embargo on their trade since November 1598 by declaring unrestricted commerce raiding. The move was equivalent to the German submarine campaign of the First World War and just as controversial. Small vessels were licensed as privateers to intercept enemy trade, disguising themselves as harmless fishing boats, or friends in distress to deceive merchantmen. There was a thin line between this and piracy, which was bad enough that Barbary Corsairs from Algiers regularly raided the Channel, and even enslaved Cornish villagers. The Dutch assuaged their pious burgher consciences by issuing regulations to distinguish patriotic privateers from godless pirates, but turned a blind eye to their frequent infringement of these. Privateering was not only a lucrative weapon of war but was also deeply embedded in Dutch culture. A land of seafarers, the Dutch celebrated the free-booting 'Sea Beggars' who had sustained their cause between Alba's repression and the capture of the Holland-Zeeland redoubt in 1572. As with the German U-boat campaign, the naval war dragged into a conflict of attrition in which the Dutch in turn suffered heavily from the depredations of the Dunkirkers.[39] Dutch defence spending had doubled over ten years to reach 10 million florins by 1604. There were clear signs that despite its efficiency, the Republic's fiscal-military system was cracking up. The central debt climbed to 10 million fl., while the inland provinces were falling into arrears and by 1607 the army was 11,000 men short of its official establishment of 62,000.

With both sides locked into a protracted struggle on land and at sea, logistics became a vital factor. The growth of the Dutch sailing navy, together with the privateering campaign, made it difficult to supply the Army of Flanders by sea. Though the Spanish had recaptured Antwerp in 1585, the Dutch hold on the Zeeland islands effectively blocked the Scheldt, while the numerous sandbanks that protected Dunkirk and made it an excellent privateering base rendered it unsuitable for large vessels. These problems had been graphically exposed during the Armada campaign of 1588 when the Spanish fleet had been unable to find a safe port to escape the English attacks and collect Parma's troops.[40] The difficulties of supply by sea heightened the strategic significance of the route taken by duke of Alba in 1567 that had become known as the 'Spanish Road'.

THE SPANISH ROAD

Though called a 'road', this vital artery in fact still involved a journey by sea from Spain's Mediterranean coast to Genoa that, like Rome, was part of Spain's informal empire. Troops, money and supplies were convoyed by the Genoese galley squadron that formed an unofficial part of Spain's Mediterranean fleet. From Genoa, the men marched north to Milan, centre of Spanish power in northern Italy, where they were refreshed and often joined by recruits from Spain's Italian possessions. The main route ran from the fortress of Alessandria in the south-west Milanese lands across to Asti in Piedmont, a territory belonging to the duke of Savoy who was an ally until 1610. The road forked here, with one branch running north-west via Pinerolo which gave access to the Alpine pass of Mont Cenis and thence to Savoy proper and the upper

Rhône, from where the soldiers could march north into the Franche-Comté. A subsidiary track ran along the Val de Susa west of Turin and over the Mont Genèvre. Alternatively, the men could head directly from Milan north up the Ivrea valley and cross by the Great or Little St Bernard passes through Aosta, down the Arve valley in Upper Savoy to Geneva, and then north-east along the Jura into the Franche-Comté. The three routes converged there and then headed north across the duchy of Lorraine into Luxembourg and the front. Sea transport from La Coruña covered about 200km a day, compared to the 23km a day average soldiers took to march the 1,000km from Milan to Flanders, but the overland route was safer and Spain sent over 123,000 men this way between 1567 and 1620, compared with 17,600 by sea.[41]

The French Wars of Religion

Concern for the Road drew Spain deeper into French and Savoyard internal affairs during the 1580s, rather in the manner that the Dutch and other powers were sucked into German quarrels. In Spain's case, however, involvement did escalate into major war, because France posed a much greater potential threat than any German territory.

France had entered a dynamic period of expansion following its victory over England in the Hundred Years War. The Valois kings consolidated royal control over the central provinces, while subduing previously autonomous border regions: Normandy in 1450, Provence in 1481, Brittany (1491), Bourbonnais and Auvergne (1523) and Saluzzo (1548). Attempts to seize Burgundy after the death of its last duke in 1477 sparked a long-running war with the Habsburgs that widened with Charles VIII's invasion of Italy in 1494. Though this conflict ended with eventual French defeat by 1559, the country's population had doubled across the previous century and continued to grow, reaching 19 million by 1600. The ability of the French crown to exploit this potential was hamstrung by its weakness following Henri II's accidental death in a tournament in 1559. Government passed to his widow, Catherine de Medici, who acted as regent for a succession of the late king's young sons: Francis II (1559–60), Charles IX (1560–74) and Henri III (1574–89). Aristocrats and others who had lost out during the previous century of growing royal power now sought to reassert their influence, under the leadership of the princes of the blood. These grandees were related by intermarriage with the royal family but excluded from rule by the principle of hereditary succession and the crown's desire for more exclusive authority. Religion complicated matters since many princes and their provincial clients became Huguenots around 1560, embracing the French version of Calvinism, while their rivals remained Catholic. A series of bitter feuds, known as the French Wars of Religion, developed after 1562 and eroded royal authority by exposing the Valois' inability to guarantee the peace.[42]

International peace was no longer threatened by French aggression but by the danger that the kingdom's implosion would suck neighbouring countries into its civil war. This was a particular problem for the Empire where princes claimed the right to recruit soldiers to assist friendly Christian powers as one of their German Freedoms. While recruitment was regulated by imperial legislation forbidding it against the emperor or the public peace, territorial fragmentation made it hard to prevent princes collecting troops for their relations or friends across the frontier.[43] The Huguenot leaders had already appealed to the German Protestant princes in April 1562 for assistance, receiving 4,000 cavalry in the first of seven German military expeditions totalling over 70,000 men. Other soldiers were provided by the Protestant princes for the Dutch rebels, but the Catholics were equally active, supplying Spain with 57,200 men between 1567 and 1575 alone, while a further 25,000 Germans served Sweden and Denmark during their war of 1563–70. These figures illustrate the Empire's importance, because it provided more troops than any of the other unofficial participants in the French and Dutch wars. Around 20,000 Britons served in the Huguenot and Dutch forces between 1562 and 1591, while 50,000 Swiss fought for the French crown and 20,000 for the Huguenot rebels over roughly the same period. The Palatinate was the prime mover behind German recruitment for the Huguenots, since its elector converted to Calvinism in 1560 and part of its territory lay close to the terminus of the Spanish Road. Germany's rising population ensured that the princes had the men, but they relied on the Huguenots and their international sponsors to pay for them. The money invariably arrived late and never covered the full cost. Consequently, German intervention was intermittent and short-lived, with most expeditions lasting only a few months and ending in a shambles.

Lorraine and Savoy

Recruitment also exposed the princes to retaliation from the French Catholics who formed the League (*Ligue*), or 'Holy Union' as they preferred, in 1584 when it became obvious that the only plausible heir to Henri III, the last Valois, was Henri de Bourbon, king of Navarre and Huguenot leader. The League was a vehicle for the powerful Guise family, who were related to the Valois and controlled north-eastern France around Champagne, as well as the largely French-speaking duchy of Lorraine which was formally part of the Empire. The Guise considered themselves to be the guardians of French Catholicism and were keen to prevent anyone occupying the French throne who might want to curb their political autonomy. Their territories made them a major factor in Habsburg strategic thinking, since their cooperation was essential to secure the last stretch of the Spanish Road, as well as blocking any hostile French moves towards Alsace and the Rhine. Philip II's decision to subsidize the League from December 1584 transformed what had been a series of seven fierce but brief civil wars into a protracted international struggle lasting until 1598. The situation within France simplified as the different factions polarized into two opposing camps, each with powerful foreign backers. England complemented its involvement in the Dutch Revolt by allying with Henri de Navarre in 1585 and funding the largest German expedition to date that lasted five months from August 1587. The League retaliated by invading the Protestant territories west of the Rhine, burning 62 villages in Mömpelgard alone.

Lorraine's involvement was matched by that of Savoy, another territory maintaining a precarious autonomy on the Empire's western periphery.[44] Savoy narrowly escaped being another victim of French expansion during the early sixteenth century, thanks to Habsburg intervention that forced France to return its territory in 1559 after 23 years of occupation. Duke Emanuele Filiberto saw France's subsequent troubles as a chance to escape the tutelage of foreign kings. He moved his capital from Chambéry in Savoy across the Alps to the relative safety of Turin in Piedmont in 1560, and began fostering a more distinct identity. Italian was declared the official language, the prized Holy Shroud was moved to Turin in 1578, and writers were paid to elaborate the myth that the new capital had been founded by a wandering Egyptian prince and so pre-dated Rome and Troy. These moves were given a nationalist gloss by nineteenth-century writers, especially once the House of Savoy became kings of the newly united Italy in 1860. The family had no such grandiose plans in the sixteenth century, concentrating instead on securing recognition as the equals of other European royalty and capturing enough new territory to sustain its independence. It became a matter of pride to recover Geneva, which had been lost during the French invasion of 1536 and subsequently became an independent Calvinist republic, while its hinterland in the Vaud joined the Swiss Confederation. The duke also planned to move south over the Ligurian Apennines to seize Genoa and gain access to the sea. There were also hopes of pushing westwards into Provence and the Dauphiné, as well as east into Milan. Such ambitions could not be achieved alone, and Savoyard policy relied on capitalizing on its strategic position as 'gatekeeper of the Alps'. In addition to controlling the Tenda Pass between Nice and Piedmont south of Turin, all three routes of the southern section of the Spanish Road ran across its territory.

The accession of Carlo Emanuele I in 1580 saw the start of a more aggressive policy. The new duke has been dismissed as an opportunist, darting in and out of Europe's wars over the next forty years. However, his frequent shifts of international alignment were forced upon him since he could not afford to pin his fragile independence too closely to any one power, and his goals of dynastic aggrandizement remained constant underneath. The failure to retake Geneva in 1582 convinced him of the need for a powerful ally and he married Philip II's daughter, Catalina Michaela, in 1585, agreeing to back his father-in-law's intervention in France. In 1588 he recaptured Saluzzo in the upper Po valley just east of the Alps that had been lost to France forty years earlier. He retook the Vaud the following year, but another attempt on Geneva ended in failure, prompting him to redirect his efforts against Provence and the Dauphiné, thinking they would be easier pickings.

Supported by the Savoyard invasion of the south, the Catholic League was able to take Paris in May 1588 in defiance of Henri III's orders. The king's assassination by a Catholic militant on 2 August 1589 removed the last constraints on the League, which began a vicious persecution of the Huguenots. The League's apparent success was its undoing, since it lacked its own candidate for the vacant throne. Most moderate Catholics regarded Henri de Navarre as their legitimate sovereign, but the prospect of him being recognized as king was a major challenge to Spain's reputation. Not only was he a heretic, but he was locked in his own dispute with Spain, which had annexed half of Navarre in 1512. Having used the League and Savoy to fight the war by proxy, Philip II now intervened directly by ordering Parma's invasion of Artois in 1590 – the act which had such a serious impact on the conduct of the Dutch War. The Palatinate and Saxony organized the seventh and last German expedition in 1591–2 to assist Henri, but the king gained his crown largely through his conversion to Catholicism in July 1593, reportedly saying 'Paris was worth a mass'. Though his conversion alienated the more militant Huguenots it allowed the far more numerous moderate Catholics to join him, and his formal coronation as Henri IV in February 1594 was followed by his entry into Paris a month later. Philip II's health was failing and in the face of mounting setbacks he was unable to prevent Pope Clement VIII from welcoming Henri back into the Catholic church in August 1595. The new king copied Spain's methods with regards to the papacy, relaxing opposition to papal jurisdiction over the French church and swiftly building up a faction of around twenty cardinals. Though Spain remained the dominant factor in Rome, it was no longer the only player in town, especially as France's rising influence allowed the pope to increase his own freedom by playing one power against the other.

With Henri IV accepted as king, the League looked increasingly like a Spanish puppet and its leaders defected one after another, leaving Spain to fight alone. Henri formally declared war on Spain in January 1595, invading the Franche-Comté and cutting the Spanish Road. Spain had to re-route this section further east into the Empire via Saarbrücken. Two years later, Field Marshal Lesdiguières drove the Savoyards from the Dauphiné and captured the Maurienne and Tarantaise valleys, cutting the southern end of the Road. Spain launched a counter-attack from the Netherlands, capturing Amiens after bitter fighting, but it was clear its intervention in France had proved counterproductive. Both sides accepted papal mediation, leading to the Peace of Vervins in May 1598, whereby Spain recognized Henri IV, returned Amiens and Calais, and compelled Lorraine to surrender occupied Metz, Toul and Verdun. The French evacuated Savoy and put the question of Saluzzo to papal arbitration.[45]

Savoy offered to surrender its French-speaking possessions between the Rhône and Saône if it could keep Saluzzo – a possession that completed its hold on the western Alps. The proposal alarmed Spain, because it would expose the Road as it left the Alpine valleys and skirted Calvinist Geneva. Carlo Emanuele was secretly encouraged to hold out for better terms by the offer of Spanish military assistance. Henri lost patience and sent 20,000 men back into Savoy before any Spanish help could arrive, and Carlo Emanuele cut his deal with France with the Treaty of Lyons on 17 January 1601, ceding his French-speaking subjects in return for Saluzzo. The Road narrowed to the Chezery valley between Mont Cenis and the two-span bridge at Grésin over the Rhône, west of Geneva, and its vulnerability was demonstrated when France temporarily closed it in July 1602. Spain tried to reopen the Geneva route deeper in the mountains by sponsoring Carlo Emanuele's assault that December: the famous 'escalade' that failed to retake the city and led to rapidly deteriorating relations between Spain and Savoy. Keen to maintain good relations with a resurgent France, Savoy placed growing restrictions on Spain's use of the Grésin route, finally expelling the soldiers guarding it in 1609. The political reorientation was completed in a formal alliance with France the following year. Spain needed another way over the mountains.

The Swiss Passes

Concern for the western route had already prompted Spain to sign a treaty with five of the seven Catholic Swiss cantons in May 1587 to use the St Gotthard pass. This was the only practical way across central Switzerland and ran through the Catholic cantons east of lakes Luzern and Zug, and then down the Reuss valley to the Rhine. From here, soldiers could march through the friendly Austrian possessions of the Breisgau and Upper Alsace and rejoin the original Road north via Lorraine to Luxembourg. The only alternative way through central Switzerland via the Simplon Pass to the upper Rhône was long and could be blocked by the powerful Protestant canton of Bern. The governor of Milan managed to renew the 1587 treaty in 1604, but the Catholic Swiss were growing nervous over the revival of French influence, and one of the original signatories refused to sign. Though the Catholic cantons had formed a holy alliance in 1586, they had no desire to fight their Protestant neighbours. Swiss politics were a tangle of local relationships, like those in the Empire, where conflicting interests inhibited

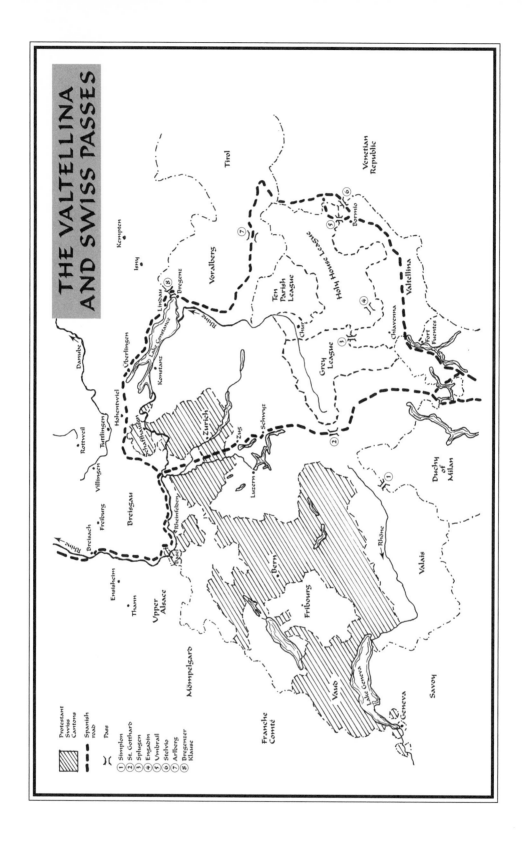

THE VALTELLINA
AND SWISS PASSES

Tirol

Venetian
Republic

Kempten

Isny

Vorarlberg

⑦

Bregenz

⑥

Bormio

⑤

Ten
Parish
League

Holy House League

Valtellina

Lindau

Überlingen

Danube

Lake Constance

Konstanz

Rhine

Chur

⑧

④ Chiavenna

Grey
League

③

Fort
Fuentes

Hohentwiel

Rottweil

Villingen

Tuttlingen

Schaffhausen

Zürich

Zug

Schwyz

Luzern

②

Duchy
of
Milan

Basel

Rheinfelden

Breisgau

Freiburg

Breisach

Rhine

Ensisheim

Thann

Upper
Alsace

Mömpelgard

Franche
Comté

Bern

Fribourg

Rhône

Valais

①

Savoy

Vaud

Lake Geneva

Geneva

Protestant
Swiss Cantons

Spanish
road

Pass

① Simplon
② St. Gotthard
③ Splügen
④ Engadin
⑤ Umbrail
⑥ Stelvio
⑦ Arlberg
⑧ Bregenzer
Klause

polarization into sectarian violence. The renewed treaty obliged Spain to march its troops in detachments of two hundred men at two-day intervals, with their weapons loaded separately in wagons. Spain used the St Gotthard route six times between 1604 and 1619, but the Catholics of Uri and Schwyz closed it temporarily in 1613, preventing the governor of Milan from drawing on German recruits during the war with Savoy. These were not conditions that a great power could tolerate for long.[46]

It was possible to send men by sea through the Adriatic to Trieste and then across Inner Austria and the Tirol to the Rhine. However, this was not only very long but liable to disruption by Venice, a power that frequently opposed Spanish policy in Italy. Venice also controlled the Brenner Pass, which offered the best access to the Tirol from Italy. Only three routes remained between these eastern routes and the central Swiss passes. One road ran north from Milan over the Splügen Pass, east of the St Gotthard, and down the Upper Rhine past Chur and Lake Constance to the Breisgau. East of the Splügen lay the Engadin valley that exited through the upper reaches of the Inn into the Tirol. Finally, there was the 120km corridor of the Valtellina that ran north-east from Lake Como to enter the Tirol either through the Stelvio Pass, open between June and September, or the slightly lower Umbrail, generally passable throughout the year. Though further east, the Valtellina offered a faster route, taking roughly four days to cross, compared to ten days over the St Gotthard.

All three routes were in the hands of the Rhetian free states, more commonly known as the Grisons, or Grey Leagues. Rhetia was a federation of three alliances loosely associated with the Swiss Confederation, but also nominally allied to the Austrian Habsburgs. Like the Swiss, Rhetia had emerged from a network of alliances among the Alpine communities that rejected Habsburg rule during the fourteenth and fifteenth centuries. The actual Grey League controlled the far upper reaches of the Rhine, including the city of Chur, whose bishop refused to join. The Holy House League held the Engadin valley of the upper Inn, while the smaller Ten Parish League bordered on the Tirol in the north-west. All three were composed of self-governing communes that sent representatives to a council to coordinate external relations. The Grey League held a majority, but agreement of at least two of the three alliances was necessary for binding decisions. Rhetia's strategic significance derived from conquests it made from Milan in 1500–32. The mountaineers had not only taken the Valtellina but also the county of Chiavenna at its southern end: this controlled access both southwards into Milan and northwards along the Splügen and Engadin routes.

Like Switzerland, Rhetian government was not democratic in the modern sense. A significant part of the population was disenfranchised, and while the inhabitants of Chiavenna and the Valtellina had been left with self-government, they were treated as conquered territories and denied any representation in the Rhetian council. Social tensions grew more pronounced as population growth placed increasing pressure on the relatively meagre local resources by the 1570s. Communal government fell into the hands of the 'Big Johns' (*Grosse Hansen*), networks of families who secured a controlling stake in the village councils and increasingly assumed noble titles and lifestyles. As in Switzerland, the decentralized political structure ensured that local control translated into greater opportunities for wealth and influence at a higher level. Foreign powers were prepared to pay handsomely for favourable decisions in the Rhetian council to open the passes or permit military recruitment among the overpopulated villages. External influence encouraged factions aligned to different powers, heightening existing tensions. Conflicts in the council passed back to village level as the Big Johns used their influence in the local law courts to pursue personal vendettas. This struck at the heart of the communal ideal upon which Rhetian (and Swiss) society was based, since the primary purpose of all early modern association was to preserve the public peace and the courts were intended to uphold this. The spread of Lutheranism complicated this from the 1520s, as many families converted, while others remained Catholic. Protestants regarded their faith as an expression of independence from Habsburg jurisdiction and that of the bishop of Chur. Their disenfranchised southern subjects (the *Sudditi*) in the Valtellina clung to Catholicism as an expression of their own identity. Linguistic differences reinforced these divisions, since the northerners spoke German, while the southerners spoke Italian.

Matters worsened as the Rhetian church fell under Calvinist influence and began insisting on greater supervision at parish level to enforce the reformation of life just as the Capuchins and other missionaries sent by Cardinal Borromeo and the bishop of Chur arrived to promote Catholic renewal. The Rhetian leadership felt increasingly beleaguered, not least because their three alliances were outnumbered by their subject populations in Chiavenna and the Valtellina. These grew increasingly restless, revolting in 1572 and 1607. Matters were further complicated by the fact that the majority of the inhabitants of the actual Grey League also remained Catholic, while the 4,000 Protestants living in the Valtellina felt very insecure. It is scarcely surprising that the Calvinist political leadership equated Catholicism with subversion and used its influence in the local courts to instigate a campaign of persecution from 1617.

Fuentes, the governor of Milan, induced the Rhetians to permit small detachments of Spanish soldiers to transit the Valtellina after 1592, but the council then promised exclusive access to the French in December 1601 and signed a similar agreement with Venice two years later. The governor retaliated, building Fort Fuentes at the top of Lake Como to block the entrance into Chiavenna in 1603 and imposing a grain embargo. The Rhetians remained unmoved, so that by 1610, Spain was without a satisfactory route across the Alps. Fortunately, this was now less pressing since the conclusion of the Twelve Years Truce with the Dutch.

SPANISH PEACE-MAKING

Spain's association in French and Protestant historiography with aggressive policies has overshadowed its attempts to find peaceful solutions to many of its problems around 1600. Spain was not alone in doing this, and indeed its relative success in bringing some of its wars to an end was due in part to the desire of other European powers to make peace. Peace-making was not altruistic, but linked instead to competing visions of European security whereby one dominant power could safeguard its own interests by arbitrating disputes between its rivals. James I of England and Henri IV of France both saw their own power and posthumous reputations as depending on their ability to resolve European conflicts. The papacy also hoped to break free from Spanish and French influence by assuming this arbiter role.[47] Such attempts also responded to the deeper underlying shift in European relations away from medieval Christendom and towards an international order based on sovereign states. At this stage, economic and political connections were binding states more clearly within a common system, but the exact nature of their interaction had yet to be resolved. Order was associated with hierarchy, not equality, implying the presence of a pre-eminent power to guarantee peace for all, equivalent to the king within a kingdom, or the magistrate within a city.

The Spanish vision of Pax Hispanica was central to its monarchy's imperial mission. Like the peace-making efforts of other European monarchs, Spain intended to resolve conflict from a position of strength, but was often forced to do so through its own weakness. Given these mixed motives and the fragility of the resulting settlements it is easy to dismiss peace-making as mere tactical withdrawals in longer-running struggles. This is certainly how Spain's efforts have been interpreted for the period between Philip II's death and the outbreak of the Thirty Years War by those who subsume the entire period within a protracted anti-Habsburg struggle. Yet, peace-making was neither naïve nor cynical, and an examination of negotiations to end hostilities reveals how contemporaries saw themselves engaged in a series of distinct, if related, conflicts.

Pax Hispanica had its origins in the 1559 peace with France that ended the struggles of the first half of the sixteenth century and guaranteed the 'tranquillity of Italy' for fifty years. Renewed bankruptcy in November 1596 and the failure of the 1597 Armada convinced Philip of the impossibility of defeating France, England and the Dutch simultaneously and led to the negotiations that concluded in the Peace of Vervins in 1598 (see p.156 above). In one sense, Vervins was a tactic in the further struggle against the Dutch, since it broke the Triple Alliance of Greenwich of May 1596 by which Spain's three enemies swore not to make any separate treaties of peace with her. However, it was also a product of a broader desire to end European conflict, since it was brokered by both the pope and Elizabeth of England. Moreover, Spain clearly wanted it to last. The duke of Lerma resisted calls to exploit France's troubles following Henri IV's assassination in 1610 and stuck to the policy of fostering closer relations. Henri's widow agreed in April 1611 to Lerma's plan for a double dynastic marriage that took place four years later.[48]

Belgian Autonomy

Lerma also continued Spain's serious efforts to end the Dutch Revolt that began when the dying Philip II devolved greater autonomy to the Spanish Netherlands in May 1598 by entrusting them to his daughter

Isabella. This arrangement stemmed partly from the king's concern to provide for his favourite daughter now that it was obvious Emperor Rudolf would never marry her. The alternative match with Archduke Albert was celebrated in 1599 but it had been planned by Philip, who stipulated that Belgian autonomy would continue if the couple had a son. Meanwhile, the couple would rule jointly as 'the Archdukes' from Brussels. The hope was that an autonomous Netherlands would prove more acceptable to the Dutch who might be induced to abandon their struggle with Spain and accept union with Brussels instead.[49] This was undoubtedly too little too late, coming a full decade after the foundation of the Dutch Republic, while the entire project was compromised by the continued presence of the Army of Flanders in the south, still reporting directly to Madrid. Yet, the plan should not be dismissed too hastily. Albert and Isabella were determined to assert their autonomy and matters might have turned out differently had they had a son. Isabella was one of the most attractive personalities to emerge from the gloomy Spanish court. Her portraits show her taller than her husband, and she was certainly a feisty character, scoring a bull's eye with her first shot at the Brussels shooting club tournament in 1615. The event led to her being fêted as an Amazon queen in text, image and ritual in what was clearly an orchestrated attempt to raise the couple's regal status.

Practical measures underlined these efforts and were intended both to secure local loyalty and to foster sympathy within the rebel provinces. Though they asserted their authority over Brussels and other towns, the couple generally respected local privileges. Their revival of Catholic life included the usual sponsorship of the Jesuits, but was more generally directed at renewing the older Erasmian tradition to make Catholicism more attractive to potential northern converts. Albert already had experience of government from his time as viceroy of Portugal (1583–93). He managed to cooperate with General Spinola without compromising Belgian autonomy, sending his own envoys to England, France and Rome, and he opened direct talks with the Dutch in 1600. He played a major part in persuading the Madrid government to secure peace with England by recognizing James VI of Scotland as successor to Elizabeth of England who had died in 1603. Belgian mediation helped secure the Treaty of London in 1604 which ended the nineteen-year-long war with England and initiated a gradual Anglo-Spanish rapprochement that lasted, despite serious moments of tension, into the mid-seventeenth century.

The Twelve Years Truce

The Archdukes recognized that their autonomy ultimately rested on achieving peace with the Dutch. Military operations increasingly focused on forcing the Dutch to accept reasonable terms, and Albert negotiated an armistice in March 1607 to give more time to conclude the talks. The Dutch refusal to grant toleration to northern Catholics caused considerable disquiet in Madrid, since any truce would sacrifice spiritual concerns to pragmatic pressures, such as renewed bankruptcy in November 1607. Some also feared it would give time for the Dutch to regroup and so make it even harder to defeat them in the future. The Scheldt had to be kept closed to trade and many feared the Dutch would now penetrate the vulnerable Indies trade, despite promising to postpone the foundation of their proposed new West India Company (WIC). They refused to disband the existing East India Company that was already stealing markets from the Portuguese and the final terms effectively restricted the truce to Europe. Philip III and Lerma overruled objections to the truce, arguing that continuing the war risked inflicting even greater damage, and agreed the Twelve Years Truce with the Dutch on 9 April 1609.

Spain had thus successfully extricated itself from all three western wars by its agreements with France, England and the Dutch between 1598 and 1609. As a military strategy, diplomacy clearly worked; it shattered the hostile Triple Alliance, and allowed tensions to grow within the Dutch Republic that left it weaker in some respects by the time the Truce expired in 1621. However, just because Philip III presented peace-making as an expedient doesn't mean that we should 'take him at his word'.[50] Given the controversy surrounding the settlements, especially that with the heretical Dutch, the king could scarcely present them otherwise in public without harming his prestige.

Lerma swiftly became the target of all those who regarded peace-making as a sell-out of Spain's core interests. Even the duke of Uceda, Lerma's own son, joined the growing ranks of his critics. To deflect attention, Lerma ordered the expulsion of the Moriscos on the day the Truce was signed. The Moriscos were converts from Islam living in Spain since the defeat of the Moors in 1492 and they formed around 4 per cent of the country's population. Coinciding with demographic and economic stagnation, the policy was certainly misguided, reducing

Valencia to subsistence farming and swelling the numbers of corsairs who intercepted supplies for Spain's North African garrisons in Ceuta and Tangiers. Spain was obliged to devote growing resources to defend its own south coast. The ensuing fruitless campaign against the Barbary pirates at least enabled Spain to make common cause with England and France, who also suffered their depredations, as well as offering a chance to polish its traditional image of Christian crusader.

Savoy and Mantua

It was also part of Lerma's wider reorientation of Spanish policy towards the Mediterranean, which he saw as the country's proper arena in Europe. He sought to punish Savoy for its defection to France and so restore Spanish prestige and reopen the Spanish Road to the Netherlands. The marquis of Hinojosa, a relative and political ally, was made governor of Milan after Fuentes' death and directed to step up pressure on Savoy. Events intervened to precipitate an unwanted war that was to be the first of a series of struggles over the duchy of Mantua. The disputed Mantuan succession requires our attention, because it forms the Italian dimension to the Thirty Years War and also illustrates the importance of dynasticism as a cause of war.

When Duke Francesco IV died in 1612 after a reign of less than a year, his brother Ferdinando seized power and sent his bereaved sister-in-law, Margherita, packing on the grounds she had failed to produce a son. She was the eldest daughter of Carlo Emanuele of Savoy who saw an opportunity to consolidate his eastern borders by claiming the marquisate of Monferrato as compensation. Unlike Mantua itself which was a male fief, Monferrato could be inherited by women, enabling Carlo Emanuele to demand it on his daughter's behalf. The matter should have been adjudicated by the emperor, since Mantua, like Savoy, was part of imperial Italy and so fell under his jurisdiction. However, the Brothers' Quarrel left little time for the emperor to look to Italian affairs, prompting Savoy to invade Monferrato in April 1613, starting the first major war in Italy since 1559. Hinojoso had been instructed to avoid war, but felt obliged to respond since the disputed territory lay sandwiched between Milan and Savoy. Madrid presented its actions as a defence of Ferdinando's inheritance and, after much prodding, Hinojoso counter-attacked in 1614, ejecting the Savoyards from Monferrato and invading Piedmont. Lerma had no desire for a major conflict and was pessimistic about Hinojoso's chances of fully defeating Savoy. Hinojoso accepted French mediation, agreeing to a provisional peace at Asti in June 1615 that obliged him to withdraw from Piedmont and left Monferrato's fate open.

The war increased the pressure on Lerma at the Spanish court, particularly as the duke of Uceda copied his father's strategy and cultivated the friendship of the crown prince and those hoping for a changing of the guard in Madrid. Personal rivalries intermingled with principled disagreements on what was best for Spain. As criticism of Lerma mounted, Philip III rejected the peace deal of Asti and Lerma was forced to dismiss Hinojoso as a scapegoat to save his own position.

Carlo Emanuele's position grew stronger thanks to foreign assistance. While not seeking war, France was quite happy to exploit Spain's predicament to enhance its own international standing, despatching up to 10,000 auxiliaries to reinforce the Savoyard army.[51] Venice also regarded Savoy as a foil to the Habsburgs, and paid one-third of its military expenses in 1616 and 1617, and Carlo Emanuele was able to recruit 4,000 German mercenaries under Ernst von Mansfeld who arrived in time for the 1617 campaign. Savoy reopened the war in 1616 by reconquering Monferrato, but the majority of the French had failed to arrive, while Venice had become embroiled in its own war with Archduke Ferdinand (see Chapter 8), and refused to open a second front against Milan. Moreover, Carlo Emanuele's rhetoric of Italian liberty failed to impress the other rulers in the area, who continued to regard Spain as the best guarantor for regional peace. The marquis of Villafranca arrived as the new governor of Milan and reorganized Spanish forces. The Catholic Swiss temporarily suspended objections to Spain's use of the St Gotthard route over the Alps, enabling reinforcements to arrive from the Army of Flanders, as well as German recruits. Villafranca took Vercelli after a six-month siege, breaching Piedmontese frontier defences. With the war turning in its favour, Spain renewed efforts to secure a satisfactory peace through Franco-papal mediation. A double peace was concluded in the autumn of 1617, with the Treaty of Pavia ending the Mantuan dispute and that of Paris settling Venice's war with Inner Austria. Spain returned Vercelli in exchange for a Savoyard withdrawal from Monferrato, which was now left for Duke Ferdinando of Mantua.

Neither of these settlements was particularly satisfactory and Savoy was to challenge that over Monferrato again in 1627. However, relations between European rulers were always subject to a degree of friction. What is more important is that there was nothing to suggest a major war was inevitable. The Dutch truce still had a third of its time to run, and the Brussels government, as well as a significant section of that in Spain, felt that it should be renewed, at least if the Dutch agreed to modified terms. Above all, there was nothing in western or southern Europe which seemed to point to conflict erupting in Central Europe within a year.

6

Dominium Maris Baltici

DENMARK

The Baltic and European Conflict

Scandinavian involvement in the Thirty Years War linked Central European problems with a struggle for Baltic dominance. Like Spanish and French intervention, Swedish and Danish participation helped prolong and widen the conflict, rather than contributing directly to its causes. Scandinavian concerns remained distinct, with the Baltic struggle beginning well before the Central European strife, and rumbling on beyond the Peace of Westphalia. However, unlike the western powers, Denmark and Sweden were more closely involved with the constitutional issues at the heart of the Empire's problems. In Denmark's case, this was because its king was already an imperial Estate-holder and was deeply involved in the religious politics of northern Germany. Sweden was relatively distant at this stage, and indeed was regarded by most Germans as barely part of the civilized world. However, its intervention in 1630 seriously complicated imperial politics and resulted in Sweden becoming tied to the imperial constitution, both through its guarantee for the peace settlement and its acquisition of territory that remained part of the Empire.

Sweden and Denmark were joined in the Baltic struggle by Poland after 1599. Polish involvement linked Baltic affairs with those further east, notably the civil war in Muscovy, as well as with the troubles along its own southern borders with Transylvania, Wallachia and Moldavia. All three Baltic rivals were related by marriage and political alliances with German princely houses, including in the Danish and Polish cases with the Habsburgs. Trading interests added further connections to western countries like the Netherlands, and the Stuart monarchy in the British Isles. The latter were bound by the marriage of King James VI to Anne of Denmark in 1590.

Of the three rivals, Denmark was initially the most important as it had been at the heart of the Scandinavian Union of Kalmar since 1397. This had been a purely personal union, since Denmark, Sweden and Norway retained their own royal councils composed of leading nobles to safeguard their laws and interests.[1] Denmark was also more closely linked to imperial politics, being governed since 1448 by a branch of the Oldenburg dynasty whose court spoke German. Other relations ruled the small principality of Oldenburg itself, while a further branch in Gottorp shared the duchies of Schleswig and Holstein with the Danish king. Schleswig lay entirely under Danish jurisdiction, but Holstein was part of the Lower Saxon Kreis and possession of it made both the king and his Gottorp cousin imperial Estate-members with representation in the Reichstag.

Danish pre-eminence within the Union of Kalmar was sustained by the subordination of Norway since 1387. The royal branch of the Oldenburgs governed around 1.18 million subjects by 1620, of whom two-thirds were in Denmark and the rest in Norway. There were another 185,000 in Holstein, while the Gottorps had 50,000 in their part of the principality, and twice that in Schleswig. Possession of the Faeroe Islands and Iceland added a few thousand more, but the combined total was still relatively small in European terms, being roughly comparable to that of the kingdom of Bohemia. Sweden and Finland had a combined population of 1.2 million in 1620, with a further 250,000 scattered in provinces along the southern Baltic (of which more shortly). Like the Danes and Norwegians, the Swedes and Finns were concentrated primarily in the southern portions of their respective countries, with the vast hinterland remaining virtually uninhabited.

The struggle for dominance of the Baltic followed the collapse of the Union of Kalmar in 1520–3 when the Swedish nobility rejected the Danish king and chose their own monarch. The two fragments of the former union, Denmark-Norway and Sweden-Finland, quarrelled over their bilateral relations while fighting internally over their forms of government. Both kings claimed the united legacy of the three crowns of Sweden, Denmark and Norway, and Denmark contested Sweden's secession from the union, harbouring hopes of subordinating it again, or at least maintaining its own position as the dominant Baltic power. The dispute focused on the western Baltic, especially the Sound that gave the sole access to the North Sea. The practical issues were expressed symbolically in the contest for the exclusive right to the old coat of arms bearing the three crowns on a common shield. Rivalry did not preclude periods of relative quiet, even of cooperation, but nonetheless it led to six so-called 'Northern Wars' (in 1563–70, 1611–13, 1643–5, 1657–8, 1658–60 and 1675–9), before being settled in the last, Great Northern War (1700–21) that exhausted both rivals and allowed Russia to seize the eastern end of the Baltic.[2]

The early stages of the conflict saw Denmark retaining Scania in southern Sweden, restricting its rival's access to the Sound to a narrow strip of land along the Göte river that drained Lake Vänern into the North Sea. This strategic corridor was secured by the coastal fortress of Alvsborg, next to the modern city of Gothenburg. It would remain a bone of contention until Sweden captured the entire western and southern coasts of the Sound in 1658. Sweden sought to secure its independence, and then to displace Denmark from pole position, both by driving it from the northern side of the Sound and by acquiring a more prominent European profile for the Swedish royal house.

Danish Wealth and Power

Neither monarch had the full support of his people for these wars. International rivalry required resources that the thinly populated Baltic found difficult to produce, heightening tensions between the kings and their subjects who had enjoyed a large degree of autonomy within the decentralized medieval union. Christian III emerged victorious from a civil war in Denmark to impose greater royal authority after 1536.[3] Norway and Iceland lost their autonomy and were placed under direct royal rule, while Lutheranism was consolidated with a state church on the German model. The Danish Catholic bishops were imprisoned, at a stroke reducing the once-powerful council (*Riksråd*) to around twenty secular advisers who were obliged to swear an oath to an abstract concept of a crown transcending the life of an individual monarch. The king confiscated the Catholic church lands, amounting to a third of the cultivated area, giving him direct control of half of the country. The 2,000 nobles remained powerful through their possession of a further

44 per cent of the cultivated land. They were reconciled to the new order by being given greater authority over their tenants, who now slipped to the status of serfs. The elective character of the monarchy formally remained intact, however, and the Riksråd's consent was still necessary to raise taxes or declare war.

The Danish settlement established a balance between a greatly strengthened monarchy and a still-powerful nobility. The king enjoyed autonomy beyond the Danish constitution through his persona as duke of Holstein, enabling him to circumvent the Riksråd. For example, Christian IV forced the councillors to back his war against Sweden in 1611 by threatening to start it anyway in his capacity as duke. The crown also intervened in landlord–peasant relations, imposing rent controls to retain residual loyalty from the rural population. Economic growth kept most nobles happy, as they profited from the booming grain trade. More subtly, the crown influenced the composition of the nobility by manipulating its feudal jurisdiction to award vacant fiefs to sympathetic families. By 1625 one-third of the nobility had accumulated three-quarters of the crown fiefs, creating an aristocracy closely allied to the monarchy. As their wealth allowed them to send their sons to foreign universities and on European tours, the aristocracy came to share the crown's wider horizons, as well as its desire to defend Lutheranism and its pretensions to Baltic dominance.

Above all, the Danish king became immensely wealthy, largely freeing him from the fiscal constraints that emasculated his peers.[4] The Sound tolls were the most obvious and strategically sensitive source of royal bounty. Denmark controlled all three passages between the North Sea and the Baltic: the two minor routes passed the islands off the Jutland coast, and the Oresund, or great channel between the islands and Scania that was the only practical route for large ships. Baltic trade was booming, fuelled by the symbiotic development of the western European population and the eastern European manorial economy. In addition to grain, the region produced timber, tar, hemp, copper and other vital 'naval stores' essential for all maritime nations. Nearly 5,400 ships passed through the Sound in 1583, three times the number which made the journey fifty years before. An increasingly sophisticated toll system combining weight and cargo value was developed at Elsinore, while additional toll points were established in northern Norway to tap the alternative route to Russia through Murmansk. Annual toll revenue surged tenfold between 1560 and 1608 to reach 241,000 riksdalers. Its real value was as an independent source of income that flowed directly into the king's private account rather than the national treasury.[5] The tolls also enhanced the king's international influence, because he could reward allies with preferential rates that were vital in the highly competitive bulk transport market.

Rather like Spain's silver, Denmark's tolls obscured underlying economic and fiscal weaknesses that were only exposed once the country became involved in the Thirty Years War. Though it collected the tolls, it did not control the trade. Over half the ships passing through the Sound were Dutch, with the remainder mainly English and German. Denmark's trading participation was restricted to producing some of the grain and timber for transport, as well as Norwegian deep-sea fishing. The Danish monarchy thus remained what is termed a 'domain state', heavily reliant on income derived from the crown lands that accounted for 67 per cent of royal revenue in 1608. The domain economy relied on barter, with the monarchy extracting produce directly from its tenants in lieu of rent. A large part was consumed directly by the royal court, or transferred as payment to officials who were only just beginning to receive salaries in coin. The remainder was sold on the market for cash.

The crown's concern to emancipate itself from the nobility led it to avoid asking the Riksråd for regular funds. Taxes were used only as a temporary expedient during the 1563–70 Northern War and continued in its aftermath until 1590 to clear the remaining debts. The same procedure was adopted for the 1611–13 war with apparent success, creating a sense of optimism that was sustained by the economic boom that continued in Denmark until 1640, well beyond that elsewhere in Europe. Revenue from the crown lands continued to rise, producing annual surpluses of over 200,000 rd. after 1615. Despite spending vast sums on military preparations, Christian IV accumulated cash reserves worth at least 1 million rd., making him the third richest person in Europe after Duke Maximilian of Bavaria, reputedly worth 10 million florins, and his own mother, Sophia of Mecklenburg, who was worth 2.8 million rd. on her death in 1631. The Danish monarchy was in the unusual position of being a creditor rather than debtor. The king invested 432,000 rd. in his own East India Company that established a small colony at Tranquebar on the Coromandel coast. He also subsidized the whaling industry to undercut Dutch and British competitors, as well as promoting trade with Iceland, starting a silk factory in Copenhagen and other ventures intended to boost prestige and promote real economic development. By 1605 he had become banker to his nobility, and he extended further loans to help them weather temporary disruption in the manorial economy in 1618–23. This paid off politically by discouraging criticism of royal policies, while international loans complemented toll manipulation in winning foreign allies. However, the apparent wealth was deceptive. It gave the crown the means and confidence to embark on foreign adventures while obscuring the state's shaky fiscal base. The tolls and grain exports would suffer if war failed to meet immediate success, especially as Sweden, the most likely enemy, was well-placed to disrupt both. And once the reserves had been spent, the crown had only the relatively inflexible domestic economy to fall back on, and lacked a sophisticated fiscal structure to tap even this.

Military expenditure consumed the lion's share of royal wealth. The cash reserves gave the king an impressive first-strike capacity, enabling him to start major wars relatively rapidly. German mercenaries numbered no less than 24,000 in an army of 28,000 men when Denmark fought its first war with Sweden in 1563.[6] Christian IV shifted the emphasis after 1596, concentrating on enhancing the country's permanent defensive capability, while still relying on cash reserves to mobilize a strike force if needed. At least 1 million riksdalers were spent modernizing and expanding fortresses between 1596 and 1621. Eight major installations were completed to secure Scania and the other provinces in southern and western Sweden, while Christiana (modern Oslo) was built to protect Norway. Another two fortresses were developed on Själland, the largest of the islands, to cover Copenhagen. Three more were built to guard access into western Holstein: at Stade in the archbishopric of Bremen, Glückstadt on the north bank of the Elbe and Krempe just to its north-east. Other works were constructed to protect eastern Holstein, Schleswig and Jutland.

The militia was reorganized between 1599 and 1602 to provide trained manpower to garrison the fortresses and defend the country without the expense of maintaining a large army. Cavalry were formed from the feudal knights' service (*rostjeneste*) owed by the nobles holding crown fiefs, while infantry were raised from the freeholders and crown tenants. The militia was consolidated into a national system in 1609 and reorganized in two stages, in 1614 and 1620–1, following the second war with Sweden. It now totalled 5,400 peasant conscripts serving for three years, drawn through quotas imposed on each district and paid by the crown directly from its domains' revenue, while the nobles maintained twelve permanent cavalry companies. The crown accepted certain constraints as the price for the nobles' cooperation, and agreed the militia would only be used for national defence. The conscripts defined this rather more narrowly than the crown, and those sent to build Glückstadt after 1617 quickly deserted. Christian's reforms had distinct Danish roots, but he was certainly influenced by the Nassau militia and it is no surprise that he had Count Johann's drill book printed in Danish. Like Johann, the king also believed a cadre of professional troops was vital to stiffen the conscripts and began maintaining around 4,000 regulars, many of them recruited in northern Germany. These formed the basis of the Danish strike force in 1611 and 1625, in both cases being supplemented by further mercenaries hired with the cash reserve, while the militia was mobilized to garrison the fortresses.

Christian also invested heavily in the navy, fully appreciating its significance in Baltic warfare. The Danish fleet in 1588 was already the same size as that of the English who defeated the Armada. Naval expenditure in 1618 was six times that consumed by the fortress programme, enabling total tonnage to be increased from 11,000 in 1600 to 16,000 by 1625. More importantly, the king invested heavily in new designs, building larger, more heavily armed warships, including the 44-gun *Victor*, launched in 1599, which was replaced by the 54-gun *Store Sophia* as flagship in 1627.[7]

Denmark and the Empire

Contemporaries and later generations speculated on the purpose of these armaments that are strikingly at odds with subsequent Danish history as a pacific minor power. Some have projected this later image back into the seventeenth century, arguing that the Riksråd represented true Danish interests of pacific non-alignment against Christian IV's reckless personal ambitions. More recent research suggests that the king was also concerned for his country's security and it was this that prompted his involvement in European affairs. The real reason behind the Riksråd's objections was the nobles' realization that royal adventures would affect their incomes and domestic political influence. Baltic interests remain paramount in Danish accounts of what followed, but the Oldenburg dynasty retained German roots and continued interest in the Empire. King Frederick II's elder sister married the elector of Saxony in 1548, establishing firm ties to the premier Lutheran territory and so associating Denmark with the Saxon concern to preserve the 1555 religious and political settlement.[8]

Danish policy became more aggressive when Frederick's son, Christian IV, achieved his majority in 1596. Having succeeded his father at the age of eleven, Christian spent eight years guided by a regency of four aristocratic councillors. The experience gave him a good insight into the mentality of his nobility and he learned how to manipulate their sensibilities. Denmark was the most powerful Protestant monarchy alongside England and both Frederick and his son regarded themselves as guardians of Lutheran interests throughout Europe; however, while outwardly orthodox, Christian remained a moderate who was driven more by his sense of duty to his kingdom than by religious goals. He was a man of restless energy, likely to plunge enthusiastically into projects, only to fall into despair at the first setback, before bouncing back with renewed confidence. A good organizer, he often wrecked his plans through impatience and a reluctance to delegate. Despite significant defeats, he passed into Danish consciousness as the country's best-loved king, not least for his lively character, great appetite and energetic love life. A loveless first marriage to Anna Catherina of Brandenburg was followed by a succession of mistresses, culminating in a second, morganatic marriage to Kirsten Munk, a well-connected young Danish noblewoman who failed to return her husband's devotion and later tried to murder him. A lack of passion did not preclude three sons from the first marriage. The eldest prince shared his father's first name and passion for drink, but none of his intellect or vigour and predeceased him in 1647. Ulrik, the youngest, died at 22 in 1633, leaving only Frederick, the middle son, to succeed their father in 1648. The two early deaths could not have been predicted, of course, and for much of his reign, Christian was driven by his strongly Lutheran sense of family responsibility to provide for two princes who could not inherit the kingdom.

The search for suitable accommodation for the younger princes was one factor behind Christian's intrusion into the politics of the north German imperial church. It would be wrong to reduce Danish strategy to a stark choice between 'Baltic' or 'German' options, since Christian's policies served a number of complementary aims. Baltic domination was not simply a Scandinavian matter but involved Denmark's standing in Europe, and this in turn related to the dynasty's involvement in the Empire as the heart of Christendom. The Oldenburgs were related to most of the Protestant German princely families. Though Holstein lacked electoral status, the dukes' own royal pedigree inclined them to act as if they were second only to the emperor in terms of rank and influence. Influence in the Empire reflected positively on Denmark's standing elsewhere and would deter the upstart Swedes from interfering in what Christian considered his own backyard. The installation of his sons as Protestant administrators in north German bishoprics would not only give them status and incomes but would advance Denmark's Lutheran credentials by safeguarding these lands for the German Protestants. The archbishopric of Bremen and the other prime targets of Danish ambitions lay in a ring from the North Sea round to the south of Holstein and up north-eastwards to the Baltic. Danish national security would be enhanced if these lands were in friendly hands, and Denmark would assume the dominant place in Lower Saxon politics. Finally, the church lands straddled the Weser, Elbe and other rivers draining north Germany into the two seas. Their possession would enable Denmark to extend its toll system into Germany and to assert supremacy over the powerful Hanseatic League.

The Hanseatic League began in 1160 and grew to encompass seventy German towns, as well as another hundred associate members from Flanders to Finland. It was the most successful of a number of medieval civic leagues, whose principal role had been to force European rulers to grant extensive trading concessions to their members. However, it failed to match the military potential of large monarchies and was in a slow, terminal decline. Many members saw inclusion within the Empire as imperial cities as a better guarantee for economic and political autonomy. Lübeck, the founding city, had already secured this, and others, like Magdeburg and Brunswick, saw Hanseatic membership as a means of escaping the jurisdiction of their own territorial ruler. The status of the Hanseatic towns was thus unclear; major cities like Bremen and Hamburg regarded themselves as autonomous yet they did not have full recognition as imperial cities.

The situation enabled Denmark to forge close ties with other north

German princes who were also seeking to suppress civic autonomy and acquire bishoprics for their relations. Christian's most important ally was Duke Heinrich Julius of Brunswick-Wolfenbüttel, who sought to subjugate the city of Brunswick and had already become administrator of Halberstadt in 1566. He married Christian's sister Elisabeth, thus tying Denmark to the Guelph family who had long played a major role in imperial politics and were the most prominent secular princes in north-western Germany. Heinrich Julius favoured other Guelphs to follow him, notably his youngest son, Christian, who became administrator of Halberstadt in 1616. However, his widow promoted the career of Christian IV's middle son Frederick, who was admitted to the Halberstadt chapter in April 1623 and groomed as successor. Heinrich Julius's brother, Philipp Sigismund, was Protestant administrator in Verden and Osnabrück and also furthered Frederick's career, ensuring his succession in Verden in 1623. Meanwhile, Prince Ulrik became administrator of the small bishopric of Schwerin, extending Danish influence to the east.

Bremen was the big prize. It was both the largest church land in the region and, as an archbishopric, the most prestigious. Its acquisition would give Denmark possession of both the Weser estuary and the southern side of the Elbe. Holstein already gave Christian part of the northern bank and he used this to assert claims to Hamburg, the largest, most vibrant and successful of all the Hanseatic towns. Arguing that the city belonged to Holstein, he deployed troops to force it to swear allegiance in October 1603. However, the burghers successfully took him to court and the Reichskammergericht ruled in their favour in July 1618. Christian retaliated by developing Glückstadt on Holstein land below the city from where he could levy tolls on ships passing between Hamburg and the North Sea. However, attempts to get Bremen were bitterly resisted by his Gottorp relations who had been administrators there and in the small bishopric of Lübeck since 1585. Relentless pressure forced them to accept Prince Frederick as coadjutor in November 1621, leading to his accession as archbishop of Bremen thirteen years later. Denmark now surrounded both Hamburg and the city of Bremen.[9]

THE DIVIDED HOUSE OF VASA

Sweden's Brothers' Quarrel

The growth of Danish influence in northern Germany was offset by that of its rival at the opposite end of the Baltic. Sweden's rise as a European great power is one of the most remarkable stories of seventeenth-century international relations. Though the material basis of Swedish imperialism lay earlier in the conquest of the Livonian and Estonian ports, it was only Gustavus Adolphus's victories in Germany in 1630–2 that brought international recognition of the country's new status. Rapid expansion was accompanied by equally dramatic developments in religious and cultural life as the country's elite sought European acceptance, while foreigners arrived bringing ideas and influences from across Europe.

Sweden's internal development broadly followed that of Denmark. The monarchy emerged from a civil war after the collapse of the Union of Kalmar. Gustavus Vasa suppressed aristocratic opposition to hereditary rule and expanded the crown's economic base by pushing its share of the 100,000 peasant farms to over 21 per cent, while reducing the proportion under the nobles' control to 16 per cent. The rest were freeholders, in contrast to the situation in Denmark where their counterparts held only 6 per cent of all farms. These statistics underscore the relative weakness of the Swedish nobility who numbered only around four hundred families in 1600. A mere fifteen aristocrats held 60 per cent of all seigneurial land, leaving the rest mostly with fewer than ten peasant tenancies apiece. Nine out every ten Swedes were peasants, and virtually all economic activity was organized at household level because there were no manorial estates like those in Denmark or Poland. Social stratification was less extreme, and though life was relatively hard for all the inhabitants, the poor were not as impoverished as they were elsewhere. Peasants had thick black woollen coats, hats and gloves, and wore sturdy leather boots in place of the wooden clogs of most western Europeans. Nobles lived modestly, and though they were beginning to send their sons on grand educational tours by 1600, they had not yet adopted the more lavish lifestyles already popular in Denmark and Poland based around fine clothes, rich food and sumptuous country houses.[10]

The monarchy's more immediate problems came not from recalcitrant nobles, but from feuds within the ruling dynasty in a situation broadly similar to that among the Austrian Habsburgs where rival brothers struggled for supremacy. Erik XIV, Gustavus Vasa's eldest son, was initially accepted as king and began a policy of expansion in the eastern Baltic. He exploited the collapse of the Teutonic Order that had conquered the entire Baltic coast from Prussia through modern Lithuania and Latvia to Estonia but fell apart after its defeat by Poland at Tannenberg in 1410. The Poles captured western (royal) Prussia containing the Vistula delta, immediately east of Pomerania and the imperial frontier. They also seized the bishopric of Semgallia immediately north east of the rest of Prussia, thus cutting the Order state in two. Eastern Prussia escaped annexation solely because the grand master, Albrecht von Hohenzollern, converted to Lutheranism and secularized it as a duchy under Polish overlordship in 1525. His line died out after a long history of mental illness, and ducal Prussia passed to the Brandenburg Hohenzollerns in 1618. The remaining Teutonic knights struggled on as a separate Livonian Order in the area north beyond Semgallia, but came under growing Russian pressure in the mid-sixteenth century. They appealed to the emperor for assistance, but most German princes doubted whether the region belonged to the Empire, forcing the knights to follow the Prussian example and convert to Lutheranism, accepting Polish protection. Only those knights in the southernmost area were successful in this, joining the Polish-Lithuanian Commonwealth in 1561 as the duchy of Courland (now western Latvia).[11] Erik saw his chance to seize the rest of what was then known as Livonia and landed an expeditionary force that captured Reval (Tallinn) in June 1561, bringing Sweden and Poland to the verge of war.

In the event, it was the Danes who drew their swords in 1563, believing they had to strike before their rivals became established in Livonia. Since Erik's actions had stirred both Polish and Russian hostility, Denmark also saw a chance to reconquer Sweden itself. One Danish force attacked Livonia, while another captured the strategic fortress of Alvsborg, triggering a crisis within Sweden. Duke Johan, Gustavus Vasa's second son, had close ties to the Polish royal family, having married Katarzyna Jagiellonka in 1562, the sister of the last Jagiellon king of Poland. He conspired with his relatives and the small Swedish aristocracy to depose Erik, declaring him insane on the grounds of his marriage to a peasant girl and imprisoning him in 1568. Johan extricated his country from the war, agreeing to pay a large ransom to recover Alvsborg, but clinging on to Estonia, the most northerly part of the old Order state, at the cost of a protracted struggle with Russia that dragged on until 1595. The real beneficiary of this Danish-Swedish war was Poland, which annexed the rest of Livonia, thus securing much of the south-eastern Baltic coast.

Though Johan was recognized as the Swedish king in 1569, he was obliged to share power with a council of the realm dominated by the aristocracy. Relations became strained when his Polish ambitions led him to reverse the slow progress of the Reformation in Sweden and favour Catholicism. His son Sigismund was raised a Catholic, as were many Swedes at this time, and groomed to succeed the Jagiellon dynasty that died out in 1572. These efforts met with success when the Polish nobles accepted the Swedish prince as King Sigismund III in 1587. However, the situation grew more difficult with Johan's death in 1592, leaving the absent Sigismund as his heir. Actual government passed to Karl, Gustavus Vasa's third son, who had been made duke of Söderman-land by Johan to stop him claiming the throne. In many ways the least attractive of the three brothers, Karl conspired to prevent his nephew displacing him, and so formally declared Sweden a Lutheran country in 1593. Sigismund was obliged to accept this when he finally arrived in Sweden, and also to leave government to Karl when Polish affairs forced him to return there. Religious, provincial and personal factors fuelled the formation of two factions around the uncle and his nephew. Matters came to a head when Sigismund returned at the head of a small Polish army in 1598. Karl rallied the burghers and peasants under the Lutheran banner and drove his nephew from Sweden in 1600, instigating the infamous Linköping Bloodbath to execute those aristocrats who failed to escape or change sides. The survivors accepted him as King Charles IX in 1604. This did not end the wider war, however, and the Poles evicted the Swedes from Livonia after the battle of Kirkholm in 1605, while the conflict dragged on to 1611. The Vasa dynasty was permanently split into hostile Catholic-Polish and Lutheran-Swedish branches, entrench-ing enmity between the two countries lasting into the eighteenth century.

The civil war left Sweden isolated. Protestant rulers continued to look to Denmark for leadership, regarding Charles IX as a usurper, despite his Lutheran credentials. Moreover, Charles overreached himself in an attempt to seize control of trade in the eastern Baltic. The conquest of

Estonia and its port of Narva in 1581 closed Muscovy's access to the Baltic and forced it to redirect trade through the Arctic, founding the port of Archangel in 1583. Charles now tried to intercept this trade by claiming Lapland and the north Norwegian coast (Finnmark). These regions were largely uninhabited but essential if Sweden was going to levy tolls on trade through the White Sea. The attempt precipitated the second Northern War in 1611. This essentially repeated the first. Denmark again demonstrated military superiority by taking Alvsborg and other strategic points, but its margin of victory was less convincing and it ended the war with the Peace of Knäred in 1613. Sweden renounced its claims to northern Norway and to Ösel Island in the Baltic, and again ransomed Alvsborg, paying 1 million riksdalers in 1616–19.[12]

Gustavus Adolphus and Oxenstierna

Sweden accepted these terms because Charles's death in October 1611 left government in the hands of his seventeen-year-old son, Gustavus Adolphus, who, under Swedish law, could not be king until his twenty-first birthday. The aristocracy saw a chance to recover their influence lost by backing the wrong Vasa in the civil war. Many still sympathized with Sigismund and they used the Polish threat to force concessions. Coming against the backdrop of defeat by Denmark, the crisis could easily have led to renewed civil war, and there were already rural revolts against taxation levied for the war and the subsequent Alvsborg ransom. However, a deal was brokered by the 28-year-old nobleman Axel Oxenstierna who drafted the Charter of Accession in 1611 that the new king had to agree to before being accepted. The nobles' domination of the council was confirmed and they were also left with the great offices of state, including the chancellorship that went to Oxenstierna. The council's knowledge, advice and consent were required for declaring war, levying taxation and conscription. The crown also had to negotiate with the diet (*Riksdag*) composed of the country's four Estates (nobles, clergy, burghers and freeholders) and which could set limits to taxes.

The small size of Sweden's elite contributed to the success of this arrangement. There were no more than six hundred adult male nobles at this point, and only a few were active in central or provincial politics. Government was a series of personal relationships and it was Sweden's good fortune that the two leading figures were not only exceptionally talented, but good friends. Gustavus Adolphus was one of the most remarkable figures of the seventeenth century and already attracted almost mythological status in his own lifetime.[13] He clearly made a distinct impression on those who met him, certainly qualifying to be what later generations would label 'charismatic'. In an age where personal impressions were central to political relations, he possessed the key ability to speak to people regardless of status without compromising his own standing or losing their respect. Such a gift was essential in a country where the king regularly came into contact with ordinary subjects, through his travels or dealings with peasants in the Riksdag and provincial assemblies. Swedish peasants were less likely to address their superiors in the submissive terms expected elsewhere: one told Gustavus that 'if my wife were as well dressed as yours, King Gustav, she would look as lovely and attractive as the queen'.[14] Though they did not dispute the general direction of royal policy, ordinary Swedes still needed to be convinced that it was necessary to dig deep into their pockets to pay for it or, more urgently, to see thousands of native sons drafted each year. Gustavus's ability to present his objectives in persuasive language to different groups was a vital element in winning support for his far-flung plans.

His character also exerted an influence on events. Many contemporaries noted an impulsive streak. He was liable to violent outbursts which, though they usually remained verbal rather than physical, were soon regretted. Despite efforts to master his emotions, he remained acerbic and peremptory, but his restless enthusiasm could be infectious. Though he liked to weigh options and take advice, his quick temper often cut in and prompted a sudden change of direction. While he did plan methodically, he remained above all a man of action who personally drilled soldiers, tested new cannon and sailed warships. He kept his countrymen's modest habits, living frugally while on campaign and self-consciously sharing his soldiers' hardships, even to the point of drinking unboiled water – a highly dangerous habit that led to at least one serious illness. Exposure to the richer German diet after 1630 made him stout during his last two years. He had little time for pomp or ceremony, but appreciated their political utility to sustain his regal status. He also enjoyed the social occasions central to aristocratic and courtly life. When he discovered that there were not enough female partners at a ball in Frankfurt in 1631, he ordered reinforcements drafted in from the city.

His fame was magnified by his apparently charmed life. On several occasions his horse was shot from under him, or crashed through the thin ice of a frozen river. Friends were smashed to pieces beside him, yet each time he miraculously survived. It was said that a cannon ball entered the side of his tent and swerved to miss his head at the siege of Riga in 1621. Certainly, he was hit in the neck at Dirschau in August 1627 and though the bullet lodged permanently, he recovered, albeit with lifelong stiffness. Such episodes reinforced his faith in divine providence and belief that he was doing God's will. Later writers, like the philosopher Hegel, took the king at his word and interpreted him as an instrument of world spirit, destined to unfold history. Gustavus grew up with his father's propaganda that linked the Vasas' dynastic struggle to the Protestant cause. He appears to have sincerely believed that these two interests were genuinely the same. While on a visit to Germany in 1620, he bribed a priest in Erfurt to let him secretly observe mass, an experience that confirmed all his prejudices about Catholicism. However, his own faith remained broadly evangelical rather than narrowly confessional, and he rejected the Swedish clergy's demand to endorse the conservative Book of Concord in the 1611 Charter. He was also prepared to manipulate religious sensitivities for political ends. His father had well-known Calvinist inclinations and while Gustavus personally remained closer to Lutheranism, he did little to disabuse Calvinist German princes from their belief that he was one of their church.

Oxenstierna was the other figure in the partnership. Gustavus famously remarked of their relationship that 'if my ardour did not put some life into your phlegm, we should never get anything done at all'.[15] In some respects, the new chancellor was indeed the opposite of the king. Oxenstierna had travelled with his brothers to Rostock, Wittenberg and Jena to receive a good Protestant university education. He was the model undergraduate, growing accustomed to working late into the night and retaining this habit when he entered the Swedish administration in 1605. The elector of Saxony dismissed him as a 'scribbler', and he certainly voiced regrets that official business kept him away from his library and own intellectual interests. His formidable memory and attention to detail ensured his rapid rise as much as his aristocratic connections to Sweden's leading families. Nonetheless, his privileged upbringing inclined him to arrogance and he could be blunt with colleagues, feeling that he alone knew best. Unlike the king, he lacked all sense of humour, but was at least blessed with good sleep, able to remain calm, cool and calculating under extreme pressure.

The Basis of Swedish Power

The partnership between Gustavus and Oxenstierna can be divided into five phases. The first six years were spent extricating the country from conflicts begun by Charles IX. Then followed a brief period of domestic reform that greatly strengthened Sweden's ability to fight major wars. This was first put to the test after 1621 when Gustavus embarked on a protracted struggle with Poland lasting until 1629 (see Chapter 13). Intervention in Germany followed in 1630, before Gustavus's death in battle two years later left Oxenstierna alone as guide for the king's young daughter, Queen Christina.

Conclusion of the Danish and Russian wars by 1617 permitted the king and his chancellor to stabilize the Swedish monarchy by staging the long postponed coronation. They suppressed the autonomous duchies previously granted to members of the royal family to stop these becoming focal points for the intrigues of Catholic Swedish émigrés in Poland. Government was also reorganized, though here we should be careful not to make too much of the reforms. It is true that they became models for other countries, notably Brandenburg-Prussia, and the Russia of Peter the Great, but this did not happen until later in the seventeenth century following the widespread admiration for Sweden's victories from the 1630s to the 1650s. The reforms were gradual, and did not represent a clear blueprint for rational change. The royal council (Råd) slowly detached itself from the noble Estate in the Riksdag and evolved into a professional body representing the government rather than a social group. This was related to the division of business along functional lines into specialist departments, or 'colleges', around the five great offices of state: justice, treasury, chancellory, admiralty, army. The colleges had emerged in practice by 1630 and were formally recognized in further reforms four years later. None of these changes was particularly remarkable. Indeed, most German territories were already well on the way to similar administrative developments a century before. But once

Sweden started, it soon forged ahead in terms of efficiency, providing a platform for further fiscal and military reforms.

The imperative of paying the Alvsborg ransom forced Sweden to revise its finances, introducing new taxes based on a population census conducted with the clergy's assistance. The new tax registers permitted permanent taxes from 1620 that no longer needed to be negotiated with the Riksdag. The nobles accepted them, because they enjoyed personal exemption, while their tenants paid only half the rate collected from those on crown farms. Sweden modernized its domain economy faster than its Danish rival, moving over to payment in cash rather than kind and intensifying efforts to produce goods that could be sold on international markets. Dutch experts helped introduce an urban excise tax in 1623, as well as double-entry bookkeeping into the treasury the following year that soon gave Sweden the most advanced accounting system in Europe. Others were hired to develop natural resources, notably the Dutch Trip and Geer consortium that effectively started Swedish industry in the 1620s. Under its guidance, annual copper production rose fivefold over the next thirty years to reach 3,000 tonnes, and iron and copper already accounted for 67 per cent of exports by 1637.[16] Participation in international trade was a vital prerequisite for military expansion since it gave access to foreign credit. Sweden developed a network of agents in key commercial centres, like Johan Adler Salvius in Hamburg, who negotiated with foreign political and financial backers. The profits from the copper trade, together with more reliable domains' revenues, were used as security for loans that the agents used to buy war materials and recruit mercenaries.

Large sums were spent on the navy, which was expanded to 31 sailing warships and 5,000 personnel by 1630. The navy served as both a bridge and a bulwark for the Swedish empire.[17] Its offensive capacity lay in the ability to transport the army to the southern Baltic shore, or to the Danish islands, and then provide coastal support. It also offered the first line of defence to prevent an enemy reaching Sweden. Two different types of warship were required to deal with the varied character of the Baltic and its coasts. The waters off the eastern Swedish and southern Finnish coasts were shallow with narrow passages between numerous islands. The German coast from Mecklenburg to the Oder estuary was also generally shallow and covered by sandbanks, as were many of the ports further east. The Swedes developed small, oared vessels to support the army by operating close inshore and up the major rivers that drained into the Baltic. These galleys could also be used to defend Sweden's own coasts, but larger, sail-powered ships were required for the main battle fleet to intercept the more powerful Danish warships at sea. The two ship types were combined for operations in the deeper waters off the western Swedish and Norwegian coasts where there were also numerous islands. Sweden could not afford two separate fleets and was forced to balance the need for deep-water battleships with shallow draught galleys for amphibious operations and coastal defence.

Sweden's military reforms have attracted more attention than the naval developments. The country was divided into recruiting districts in 1617–18, using registers that had been compiled since 1544. Each district was to provide one regiment (later more) by regular conscription from all able-bodied males aged between 18 and 40. Some towns were exempt, as were the properties of the senior aristocrats and the iron- and copper-mining communities. As with the administrative changes, the Swedish military system took several decades to develop and was not formalized until 1634, when the army was fixed at 13 Swedish and 10 Finnish infantry regiments, and 5 Swedish and 3 Finnish cavalry regiments. Each regiment bore the name of the province that provided its recruits in a system that lasted until 1925. Conscripts from coastal areas were sent to the navy, though few were experienced sailors before they were drafted. Administration was improved by requiring each regiment to send regular muster returns to the College of War, while new disciplinary codes were issued in 1621 and 1632.[18] Conscription was tightened in 1642–4 by the administrative grouping of farms into files (*rotar*), each group being obliged to pay for one soldier. This provided the basis for the final stage that came in 1682 with the *Indelningsverket* system that lasted until 1901. One farm in each group was now set aside in peacetime to support the soldier, whose neighbours cultivated the plot when the army mobilized.

Later writers have read much into these measures, especially in the United States thanks to the reception of Gustavus Adolphus's legacy through the syllabus of the West Point military academy. The king is praised as 'one of the outstanding soldiers of world history, who was perhaps also the greatest military architect and innovator of all time' who developed 'a completely original military doctrine'.[19] Britain's leading military theorist of the twentieth century proclaimed the king as the 'founder of modern war', because he was allegedly the first to appreciate the full implications of firearms and the first to plan a campaign with a clear objective.[20] The Swedish military reforms created the 'first modern army', thanks to its apparent reliance on national conscription, a professional officer corps and its ability to fight both offensively and defensively.[21]

Such praise is the product of the teleological nature of most military history that searches the past for lessons and precedents for contemporary doctrine. Similar comments have also been made about Frederick the Great, the Prussian king who defeated Austria in the mid-eighteenth century using an army that was also raised partially by limited conscription. Both monarchs have been presented as warrior kings who won spectacular victories against seemingly impossible odds. Eighteenth-century Prussian successes, like those of seventeenth-century Sweden, have been ascribed to the allegedly national character of both armies, supposedly more motivated than their heterogeneous opponents. Yet, more than half of both forces were composed of paid professionals, many of whom came from other countries.[22] Like Prussian conscription, Gustavus's system was the expedient of a poor state with an under-commercialized agrarian economy on the fringe of Europe's market networks. Conscription was a blood tax in a state that lacked enough cash to pay for more professionals. Contemporaries recognized this; draft quotas were debated along with ordinary taxes in the Riksdag. The quotas fell heaviest on the poor, since those without visible means of support were automatically drafted, while the other men in each parish drew lots. Furthermore, the preoccupation with Gustavus as 'great captain' obscures why the system actually worked. The largely pastoral economy of Sweden and Finland left production decentralized in peasant households where many tasks could be taken over by women in their menfolk's absence. A far higher proportion of the male population could be conscripted than in the cereal economies of Central and eastern Europe, where men were required to work on their landlords' fields.

Imperial Ambitions

The true significance of the reforms after 1617 lies in their transformation of Sweden from a defeated and humiliated minor power to one with the capacity to dominate the Baltic by the mid-seventeenth century.

However, the development of a fiscal-military infrastructure only explains how the Swedes built an empire, not why they wanted one. This is a legitimate question, since there were many reasons for Sweden to avoid war: it was on the periphery of Europe, with few resources and no significant allies. Explanations for Swedish imperialism fall into two camps.[23] The so-called 'old school' is represented by Gustavus Adolphus's principal biographers, who argue that Swedish expansion was a defensive response to thwart Danish and Polish encirclement. While these writers do point to structural factors, such as Sweden's geographical location and the European balance of power, their main emphasis is on human agency through the person of the king and his immediate circle. It was clear after 1600 that Sigismund was determined to recover the Swedish throne and was only constrained by the Poles' unwillingness to back him. The dynastic division deepened with confessional antagonism, while Swedes were inspired by their national mythology as the successors to the Goths who had sacked ancient Rome.

The opposing 'new school' identifies the need to distinguish between motive and justification, claiming that defence was a propagandist device to mask commercial motives. Swedes wanted to control the lucrative Baltic trade, especially targeting Russian grain, furs and other goods. Tolls produced only 6.7 per cent of net state revenue in 1623, indicating both the lack of indigenous commerce and the reality of Danish control of the Sound. Just over 23 per cent came from the profits of the copper trade, but this was an extractive industry simply exporting raw materials, while nearly 45 per cent of revenue still came directly from royal domains. Such an economy promised neither great-power status, nor aristocratic riches. However, if Sweden conquered the eastern Baltic shore, it could tax Russian and Polish produce nearer source and so pre-empt the Danish tolls. Some have elaborated this strand of the argument to claim that the Swedish monarchy made war deliberately to enrich itself and its aristocratic allies. Certainly, involvement in war provided new opportunities, particularly for the nobility who emerged as a wealthier and more socially distinct group in this period. In 1633 nobles secured partial exemption for their tenants from the taxes introduced in the 1620s, whereas crown tenants still paid in full. Conscription also fell heavier on the crown lands and freeholders, one in ten of whom was drafted, compared to one in twenty noble tenants. Essentially wealth was being redistributed into the nobles' pockets, since the lighter state burdens permitted nobles to take a larger share of peasant produce. They also profited more directly from war, since the crown was compelled to transfer royal rights in lieu of payment, in a manner similar to that occurring in Castile between Spanish nobles and the monarch since the 1590s.

While we should indeed distinguish between justification and motive, the new school remains, on balance, less convincing. Wealth accumulation remained a means to a variety of other ends. Most recently, Swedish imperialism has been explained by the desire of the country's elite to prove itself on an international stage and gain recognition for themselves and their kingdom.[24] A craving for recognition afflicted all European monarchs and aristocrats, but it is difficult to see why this motive should necessarily take precedence over confessional, dynastic and strategic interests. Rather, it is simply another facet of a more complex mix of motives that also varied according to the situation. We must remember that Gustavus, Oxenstierna and other key figures could not take decisions in a void, but were forced to react to circumstances beyond their control. Once Sweden's imperialism was set in motion, developments assumed a certain internal logic from which it was difficult to escape. Since the country lacked resources for a protracted war, it had to borrow in order to mobilize and so gambled on a swift victory to capture the means to sustain solvency. However, the initial victories were never enough to provide either the necessary resources or adequate security for existing possessions. Further operations became necessary to sustain an empire that could not afford to stand still. Such structural factors only surfaced consciously when the king and his advisers talked about defence and their concern at the hostile intent of other powers. Defence was legitimate, in their eyes, because they were God's servants on earth, defending the true faith and the king's rights as divinely ordained sovereign.

Sweden and the Empire

Dynasticism provided the initial stimulus. Both Gustavus and the aristocrats who accepted him as king stood to lose if Sigismund reconquered Sweden. Gustavus's concern at the plots of Swedish Catholic émigrés may seem fanciful, but it represented the seventeenth-century equivalent of the modern belief in coherent international terror networks. The Poles were thought to be plotting with the Habsburgs and French nobles to create a new Catholic crusading order dedicated to overthrowing the

Lutheran Vasas. The Örebro Statute of 1617 ordered all Catholics to leave Sweden within three months, on pain of death. Catholicism was equated with treasonable contact with Sigismund, yet despite intensive surveillance, the authorities only managed to bring three Swedes to trial for assisting a German Jesuit to distribute Catholic literature.

International plots had to be confronted by an equally broad alliance of the righteous. Gustavus was already related to several important German Protestant families. His mother (Charles IX's second wife) was Christina of Holstein-Gottorp, granddaughter of Philip of Hessen, one of the heroes of the Reformation. Gustavus was also related to the leading German Calvinist family through Charles IX's first wife, Maria, the daughter of the elector Palatine Ludwig VI. Their daughter Katarina, Gustavus's elder half-sister, married Johann Casimir, a representative of the Zweibrücken branch of the Palatines. The question of Gustavus's own marriage began to loom large, since it was imperative that he produce a legitimate heir to forestall a Polish restoration. His family grew concerned at his relationship with Margaretha Slots, the Dutch wife of an army officer, who bore him an illegitimate son (Gustav Gustavsson) in 1616.

Negotiations were opened in 1615 for Gustavus to marry Maria Eleonora, eldest daughter of Elector Johann Sigismund of Brandenburg. The proposed match would link Sweden to a second Protestant electorate and promised distinct strategic advantages. Brandenburg was due to inherit ducal Prussia (as occurred in 1618), a territory that lay south of Livonia. With this in friendly hands, Polish Livonia could be outflanked, since Sweden already controlled Estonia to the north. There was also the possibility of neutralizing Danish influence in Brandenburg following Christian IV's marriage to Johann Sigismund's sister, Anna Catherina. However, the proposal placed the elector in a dilemma. A Swedish alliance might increase his leverage with Poland over Prussia, but equally could incur King Sigismund's long-term enmity. The elector's wife was Anna of Prussia, who feared the Poles would sequestrate her homeland if the marriage went ahead, and so declared she would rather see her daughter in the grave than in Sweden. Alternative proposals of marriage arrived from Denmark and Poland, intensifying the pressure. All suitors clearly overestimated Brandenburg's potential, since it was the weakest of the four secular electorates. The attention went to Maria Eleonora's head and she developed a passion for Gustavus, whom she was not allowed to meet privately until her fate had been decided.

Gustavus lost patience and, ignoring the advice of relations and councillors, appeared in Berlin in April 1620. He could scarcely have picked a worse moment. The elector had just died, and his son and heir, Georg Wilhelm, was away in Königsberg seeking Polish confirmation of his Prussian inheritance. After a frosty reception by the dowager electress, Gustavus gave in to his brother-in-law, Johann Casimir, and dashed off to Heidelberg to meet a much-praised Palatine princess instead. No sooner had he gone than Anna had a change of heart, fearing a Polish match for her daughter would have even worse repercussions. Gustavus returned and worked his magic at a private meeting with Maria on 18 June. The betrothal was announced the following day and his future wife and mother-in-law travelled to Stockholm for the wedding in November. Georg Wilhelm wisely stayed in Königsberg throughout, loudly protesting that he had nothing to do with the business.

The match was a disaster for all concerned. Gustavus had married for political reasons and described his intelligent, sentimental wife as 'a weak woman'. She hated her new home that contained nothing more than 'rocks and mountains, the freezing air, and all the rest of it'.[25] She had wanted a husband, but married a king. He found her jealous possessiveness irritating. Worse, she failed to produce the longed-for son, bearing two daughters of whom only the second, Christina, survived as the sole legitimate heir. Swedish law permitted female succession, but the bulk of the population found the idea very strange. Gustavus's nephew, Charles Gustav, son of Johann Casimir, was deliberately raised with Christina as a possible replacement, and indeed followed her on to the Swedish throne as Charles X after her abdication in 1654. The political advantages also failed to materialize. Georg Wilhelm studiously avoided antagonizing Poland and was duly enfeoffed with Prussia. Gustavus Adolphus regarded his brother-in-law with mounting exasperation and finally little more than contempt once Sweden entered the Thirty Years War.

Though the marriage brought little personal or political reward, it is important in two respects. It illustrates the general significance of dynasticism in European relations, indicating not merely the importance of male family members, but also the roles of their female relations. More specifically, it indicates how limited Sweden's horizons were at this stage. Gustavus had rejected the option of wider ties with the Palatinate in favour of a less important German family closer to the

Baltic coast. Sweden was in no position to assume the mantle of Protestant champion, a role that still very much belonged to Denmark.

POLAND-LITHUANIA

A Noble Commonwealth

The Polish-Lithuanian Commonwealth (*Rzeczpospolita*) was the largest, and potentially most powerful, of the three contenders for Baltic domination. By 1618 it covered 900,000km^2, twice the size of France, and encompassed the area of not only modern Poland and Lithuania, but also Latvia, Belarus and the western half of the Ukraine. Even though it was thinly populated, it still mustered 11 million inhabitants, or around three times the number of Denmark and Sweden combined. Like its two rivals, the Commonwealth was a composite state, but one in which the various parts retained greater autonomy and where the monarchy remained considerably weaker.[26]

The kingdom of Poland and grand duchy of Lithuania remained distinct after their Union of Lublin in 1569, but accepted a common monarch who was elected by the *Sejm*, or parliament that met in a field outside Warsaw every two years. As in the Empire, the elective principle did not preclude de facto hereditary monarchy. The Jagiellon dynasty ruled Poland from 1386 until 1572, and was followed after a brief interval by the Vasas between 1587 and 1668. However, politics developed differently from Central Europe where the leading nobles acquired constitutional rights through the possession of hereditary lands and titles. The Polish nobles (*szlachta*) considered themselves the descendants of an ancient race of conquerors who collectively ran the country as equals. Apart from a few Lithuanians, none of them had titles, and their status rested on the hereditary possession of the royal offices of palatine responsible for a province, governor of a district, or castellan of a castle. While other posts remained in the royal gift, some of the most important – like that of grand hetman commanding the army – were retained for life by the successful candidate. The nobles thus acquired a stake in government largely beyond the monarch's influence. However, they varied greatly in wealth, with a few like the Radziwills possessing vast estates, and the majority being comparatively poor, sometimes little better off than peasants. Regardless of wealth, the nobles considered themselves as 'the nation' and saw the constitution as an expression of their liberties. Ambitious nobles used landownership to support a national political role through the Sejm and in regional alliances, or 'confederations' (*rokosz*), permitted by the constitution against royal tyranny.

The Commonwealth's internal conflicts were primarily political rather than religious. Its decentralized structure and consensual political culture encouraged a more relaxed approach to religious pluralism than that of Central or western Europe. Like the Transylvanians, the Commonwealth's leaders sought to avoid sectarian violence through agreements recognizing parity and demarcating jurisdictions and rights. Political consensus was accompanied by irenicist or peace-making efforts to bridge the theological divide by finding common ground between the confessions. For example, the Greek Orthodox community acquired full parity with Catholics in Lithuania after 1563, and the two faiths merged into the Uniate or Greek Catholic church in 1596, which retained Orthodox ritual but submitted to papal authority. Lutheranism spread especially in the German-speaking towns of royal Prussia, but these communities deliberately distanced themselves from their co-religionists in the Empire by rejecting the Book of Concord and forging closer ties to Polish Protestants instead. The latter included Calvinists and Bohemian Brethren, as well as Lutherans. Their representatives negotiated the Sandomierz Consensus in 1570, a supra-confessional statement intended to avoid doctrinal disputes. It received royal approval, despite objections from Catholic bishops, thus including Protestants within the Commonwealth's constitution.[27]

Royal power depended greatly on the king's ability to win the trust of his leading nobles through the slow process of building support through the representative institutions. The regional assemblies of nobles (*Sejmiki*) sent delegates to the Sejm where full agreement of all envoys was necessary for decisions to be binding. This arrangement effectively gave individual nobles a veto on all legislation, and the Sejm broke up six times between 1576 and 1606 without deciding anything. Unable to persuade the nobles to back his efforts to recover the Swedish crown, Sigismund III became increasingly secretive, but unlike Christian IV in Denmark he had no independent income to finance his schemes. He resorted to measures similar to those employed by the Austrian

Habsburgs to foster a loyal clientele within their Estates by favouring Catholics in royal appointments. Having ejected the Swedes from Livonia in 1605, Sigismund planned wider reforms, including the adoption of majority voting in the Sejm and permanent taxation. The result was a noble rebellion in 1606, coinciding with Bocskai's revolt in Habsburg Hungary, both involving the defence of aristocratic liberties. However, unlike in Hungary, the revolt lacked a strong confessional character, because the Polish Protestants were too few to rebel without Catholic support. They were forced to mute their confessional grievances to forge the Confederation of Sandomierz on the basis of political resentment at Sigismund's plans. This was not as widespread as they hoped, because the great landowners remained loyal to the king who, despite all his faults, had respected their role. The confederates' support was reduced largely to the disaffected nobles who resented the magnates' growing wealth, and the rebellion collapsed in 1607.

Polish Resilience and Strength

This violent episode seems to confirm the standard picture of Polish politics as anarchic. Like the Empire, the Commonwealth has often been dismissed as ineffective and out of step with the general European trend towards stronger, more centralized states. Ultimately, the nobles paid the price for their liberties when their country was partitioned out of existence by the three absolute monarchies of Austria, Prussia and Russia between 1772 and 1795. The later conditions should not be transposed to the seventeenth century, however, when the Commonwealth was one of Europe's most powerful and successful states. Once Sigismund re-established trust among his nobles after 1613, the Sejm voted substantial and sustained increases in taxation, with only one meeting (1615) failing to reach agreement. Unlike other countries, the Commonwealth managed to wage warfare without accumulating a large debt. Moreover, it generally defeated every enemy it faced, until the Cossack Rebellion of 1648–54 precipitated a period known as the Deluge, when the country was invaded by the Swedes, Russians, Transylvanians and Brandenburgers. Even this crisis was weathered and the Commonwealth demonstrated its resilience by making a major contribution to the defeat of the Ottomans before Vienna in 1683.[28]

Polish military potential has been underestimated because its forces were not organized along western lines. There was a small permanent force of 3–5,000 light cavalry, called the Quarter Army (*Kwarciani*) after the proportion of royal revenue designated to sustain it. This was used to patrol the south-eastern frontier against Tartar raids, and could be increased only if the Sejm voted additional taxes. However, the king had his own royal guard and could conscript around 2,000 peasant militia (*Wybranieka*) from the crown lands. He could also call upon the private armies of the great nobles that could be summoned as a feudal levy for national defence. The levies generally took months to assemble and often became opportunities for nobles to voice grievances rather than fight. However, the eastern-style of raiding warfare provided ample chance for booty and so attracted volunteers willing to serve as light cavalrymen. The Commonwealth also began registering Ukrainian Cossacks from 1578 as a border militia, similar to that of the Habsburg Military Frontier, and had 10,900 men on the books by 1619. The Poles relied on their hussars, or armoured lancers, supported by medium cavalry (*Pancerni*), together forming half or more of a typical field force. Such troops could be very effective even against soldiers trained in the modern Dutch manner. The Swedes deployed 10,900 men at the battle of Kirkholm, including a large number of Germans and other mercenary infantry, but were virtually annihilated by 2,600 Polish cavalry backed by only 1,000 foot soldiers.[29] The Commonwealth also responded to developments elsewhere, raising so-called 'German' infantry and cavalry trained to use disciplined fire tactics. Many of these were indeed Germans and other foreigners, but the onset of war in Central Europe, together with the Polish nobles' suspicion of outsiders in their king's army, prompted such formations to be recruited largely from their own people by the 1630s. The Commonwealth forces thus combined eastern and western tactics, as they needed to do given that they faced enemies from both directions.

Wars with Russia and Sweden

The Polish-Swedish struggle was put on hold after 1605 by the implosion of Muscovy, where a succession of pretenders claimed to be Dimitrii the last Riúrik prince, who had in fact died in 1591. The ensuing 'Time of Troubles' offered both Sweden and Poland the opportunity to seize Russian territory. Sigismund intervened in 1609, intending to make his son Wladyslaw the new tsar. The quarrelling Russian factions eventually accepted Michael Fedorovich Romanov instead in 1613, founding a dynasty that lasted until the 1917 Revolution. Sigismund abandoned his intervention by the Peace of Deulino in December 1618, retaining Smolensk, which had been captured in 1611 and brought the Commonwealth frontier well east of the Dnieper. The gain was offset by Sweden's Russian conquests after 1613 when peace with Denmark enabled Gustavus to exploit Russia's difficulties. The new tsar ceded Ingria and Karelia by the Peace of Stolbova in March 1617, giving Sweden control of the entire Gulf of Finland and shutting Russia out of the Baltic until the early eighteenth century. However, Sweden failed to monopolize access to Russian trade, because Denmark still held the northern route past Norway to Archangel. Though expectations remained high, Sweden never derived great wealth from Russia and already after 1617 Gustavus shifted his target westward along the southern Baltic shore towards Poland.[30]

Gustavus was overconfident after Stolbova and tried to exploit the Commonwealth's ongoing struggle with Tsar Michael by invading Livonia from Estonia in 1617. Hetman Kristof Radziwill and a large army relieved Riga the following spring, obliging the Swedes to accept a two-year truce. Permanent peace was impossible, because Sigismund refused to renounce his claims to Sweden. The wars with Lutheran Sweden and Orthodox Russia enhanced Sigismund's Catholic credentials, and attracted expressions of goodwill from Spain and the papacy. Sigismund reciprocated, improving ties with the Austrian Habsburgs who had opposed his election in Poland in 1587. Relations had remained strained over conflicting interests in Transylvania, Wallachia and Moldavia, but Sigismund nonetheless established a close connection with the Inner Austrian branch of the Habsburgs after 1592.[31] Dynastic marriages led to a formal alliance in March 1613 that promised mutual assistance against rebels, a term that implied the Swedish Vasas, but took a very different meaning with the outbreak of the Bohemian Revolt five years later.

7

From Rudolf to Matthias 1582–1612

RELIGION AND THE
GERMAN PRINCES

The problems inherent in the Religious Peace of Augsburg became more apparent from 1582, six years into Emperor Rudolf's reign, and grew pronounced as the seventeenth century commenced, leaving a difficult legacy for Matthias on his imperial accession in 1612. While tensions mounted in the Empire, there was no inexorable slide towards war, however. The problems were certainly serious, but not insurmountable, particularly if the emperor was prepared to act more forcefully and consistently to provide the impartial guidance most princes desired. As the following will show, there were formidable barriers to polarization along confessional lines. Two hostile alliances did coalesce after 1608, but both remained expressions of disparate and partially contradictory princely interests. These interests need to be teased out and examined in some detail, because they reveal why some were prepared to take up arms against the emperor in 1618, while others backed him and the majority sought peace.

Potential Catholic Leaders

The Empire's hierarchical structure encouraged disaffected princes to expect leadership from above. The emperor was the Catholics' natural choice of leader, but he was extremely reluctant to favour them openly. By brokering the Augsburg settlement, the Austrian Habsburgs associated their imperial role with cross-confessional politics. There were good reasons for them to continue this when many of their subjects were

Lutherans and broad support was required to maintain defence against the Ottomans. Emperor Ferdinand I founded the Landsberg Alliance in 1556 that was expressly dedicated to upholding the Augsburg settlement and renounced religion as a ground for violence. Bavaria, Salzburg and other leading Catholics joined, as did important Protestant territories, such as the imperial cities of Nuremberg and Augsburg. The duke of Alba's application to join was rejected by Maximilian II in order to preserve the alliance's bi-partisan character.[1]

The Habsburgs' stance deterred other Catholics from stepping out of their shadow to form a separate confessional party. The elector of Mainz was the next potential leader, as senior Catholic prince and arch-chancellor of the Empire, but he followed the emperor in favouring dialogue with moderate Lutherans in the interests of the public peace. Like the other two ecclesiastical electorates, he lacked the resources for an independent role and witnessed with dismay the sectarian violence just across the frontier in France and the Netherlands. The lack of hereditary rule within the imperial church lands also focused attention on more immediate concerns of nepotism or promoting internal Catholic renewal. Personal ambitions intersected with competing visions of Catholicism to create further rifts within and between the numerous bishoprics, priories and other foundations. What has been taken by some historians as evidence of a united Counter-Reformation front crumbles upon closer inspection into a series of local struggles for influence that inhibited any coherent common action against Protestantism.

A good example is the ambitious Bishop Julius Echter von Mespelbrunn, who was elected to Würzburg by a small majority in 1573. At first sight, he appears an archetypal Counter-Reformer who reversed the spread of Protestantism into the Franconian church lands. He swiftly secured financial independence from his cathedral chapter by blurring the distinction between local and imperial taxes, extracting more from his subjects than the territory actually owed as assistance against the Turks. This enabled him to undercut the influence of the Franconian imperial knights, who dominated the chapter and were defecting to Lutheranism, and to finance measures to revive Catholic life. He founded a new hospital and a university in 1582, and reorganized the bishopric into 24 parishes, each staffed by a more qualified priest.[2] Six hundred Lutherans were expelled from the diocese in 1586, followed by the formal promulgation of the Tridentine decrees in the bishopric three years later.

With his own diocese secure, Echter turned his attention to his neighbours, starting with Fulda where he engineered the removal of Abbot Dernbach in 1576. Though Dernbach had been raised a Protestant, he had converted and had begun his own programme of Catholic reform in 1571. Echter's intervention led to cases in the imperial courts that restored Dernbach in 1602. By then, most of the local nobles had secured legal immunities for their Lutheran faith, eventually escaping the abbot's jurisdiction altogether as imperial knights in 1652. Reform was delayed, because Dernbach now concentrated on seeking episcopal status to preserve Fulda's autonomy. Similar problems followed in Bamberg where Echter tried to get himself elected bishop, even though the current incumbent was promoting his own reforms. The presence of Echter's supporters split the Tridentine vote when a vacancy occurred in 1599, giving the election to Johann Philipp von Gebsattel, a representative of more traditional Renaissance Catholicism who tolerated a resurgence of Lutheranism. In return for large loans to Bavaria, Echter won political backing for his protégé Aschhausen who eventually became bishop in 1609 and belatedly began a reform programme. Elsewhere, ecclesiastical princes squabbled over precedence in imperial institutions, or jurisdiction over individual foundations. None was able to offer clear leadership and the idea of a coordinated, coherent Counter-Reformation was a figment of Protestant paranoia.

Though there were far more Catholic than Protestant princes, the majority were ecclesiastics, because few secular rulers remained loyal to Rome. The duke of Lorraine was too heavily involved in French politics to serve as a Catholic leader in Germany, leaving Bavaria as the only possible alternative to the Habsburgs.[3] Bavaria had already consolidated political authority on the basis of Catholic conformity before the Habsburg archdukes attempted this in their own lands. Admittedly, Bavarian Protestantism had been far weaker, allowing the duke to outmanoeuvre the few senior nobles who dabbled with Lutheranism and forge an alliance with the lesser nobility who remained overwhelmingly Catholic. By 1600 Bavaria was the best-governed German territory, with a relatively comprehensive administrative network reaching into local communities to extract regular taxes. Certain factors did suggest that Bavarian militancy might translate into political activism. The long-standing rivalry with their Palatinate relations deepened as these embraced Calvinism in the 1560s, and the duke was heir to a proud heritage that included his ancestor Ludwig IV, who had been emperor between 1314 and 1347.

However, a more prominent role for the duchy would inevitably strain relations with the Habsburgs, who had been happy to help Bavaria provided the duke remembered his place as junior partner. Duke Albrecht IV had married Kunigunde, sister of Emperor Maximilian I who backed Bavaria in its violent inheritance dispute with the Palatinate in 1503–5. Albrecht V, who became duke in 1550, and his grandson Maximilian I, who ruled from 1598, both married Habsburg princesses, while Albrecht's daughter Maria married an archduke and Maximilian's sister, Maria Anna, married the future emperor Ferdinand II. However, Austrian territory enclosed Bavaria to the south and east and the Habsburgs had helped themselves to Kuefstein and other areas on the Tirolean border in 1505. Austria contested Bavarian influence in the large but sparsely populated archbishopric of Salzburg that lay between them, and both were rivals in the salt trade that constituted their principal export.

Bavaria needed to tread carefully, generally supporting the Habsburgs, but expecting rewards intended to lift the duke into the princely premier league. Promotion was eventually to be secured through the transfer of the Palatine electoral title in 1623, mirroring the elevation of the Albertine Saxons at the Ernestines' expense in 1547, after the Schmalkaldic War. However, there was no opportunity to press such a demand before the seventeenth century, and none of the dukes showed any inclination to do so prior to the accession of Maximilian I. Albrecht V solidly backed Habsburg cross-confessionalism, even vetoing the application of the bishop of Augsburg to join the Landsberg Alliance because he was too militant. His successor from 1579, Wilhelm V, showed more interest in extending Bavarian influence within the imperial church, but otherwise restricted his activity to his own lands by embarking on a major building programme in Munich.

Perhaps the most significant barrier to a Catholic alliance was Catholicism itself. To most Catholics, the empire was still a single *respublica Christiana* within a unitary Christendom. Since their own faith represented the only 'true' religion, they had no need to separate themselves from existing institutions as a distinct confessional block. To do so would suggest the established order was somehow defective and imply that the Protestants were justified in criticizing it.

1. The Defenestration of Prague: Martinitz disappears head-first out of one window, while Slavata is bundled out of the other. The terrified Fabricius, seized in the centre of the room, will be next.

HISPANISSCHE INQVISITION.

2. The 'Persecution of Christians'. This Protestant German broadsheet from 1622 links hostility towards Catholics with xenophobia through its depiction of the 'Spanish Inquisition'.

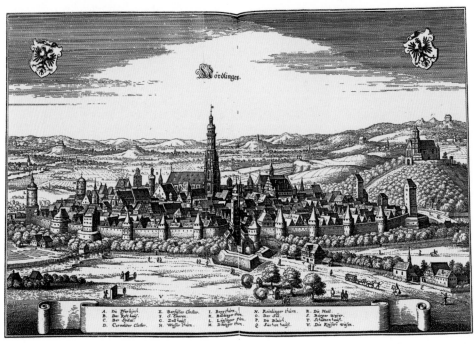

3. The imperial city of Nördlingen, a typical example from Merian's Topographia Germaniae.

4. The village of Friedenswunsch in the duchy of Wolfenbüttel. The manor house (*right*), church (*centre*) and boundary fence are clearly visible.

5. The coat of arms of the imperial city of Buchhorn over the door of its district office at Eriskirch (*see p. 19*).

6. Rudolf II as he wished to appear: detail from his imperial crown of 1602.

7. Ferdinand II. A good likeness despite the idealized engraving which shows him wearing the Order of the Golden Fleece.

8. Matthias and his wife Anna in an early example of Habsburg baroque piety.

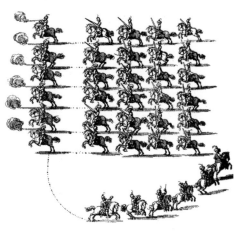

9. Musketeers from a Swiss drill manual of 1644. Most soldiers during the second half of the war would have looked like these.

10. Mounted arquebusiers perform a caracole from a Spanish drill book of 1630.

11. Archduchess Isabella with her country retreat of Mariemont in the background.

12. Gustavus Adolphus sketched during his invasion of Germany.

14. Maximilian of Bavaria strikes a martial pose.

13. Axel Oxenstierna, Sweden's great chancellor.

15. Frederick V painted as king of
Bohemia, 1619.

16. Christian I of Anhalt, a key figure in
widening the war.

17. Probably the
most accurate portrait
of Tilly, painted by
an anonymous artist
around the time
of his victory at
White Mountain.

Eigentliche Abbildung deß Procefs der Pragerischen Execution.

Welcher gestalt auff der Röm: Käy: Mayrt. gnädigisten Befelch vnnd Verordnung die Böhemilchen gewesenen Directores, von Grafen Herren, Ritter vnd Burgerstands Persohnen, Sambstag den 9. (19.) Junij, dieses 1621 Jahrs / uff dem Königlichen Schloß zu Prag vervrtheilt, vnd Montags den 11 (21) Junij hernach uff dem Altstädter Ring Iustificirt vnd hingericht worden sindt

Diese Figur gibt eigentlich zu erkennen, wie die 24 Persohnen, einer nach dem andern enthauptet, vnd hernach noch 3 andere mit dem Strang gerichtet worden

18. Execution of the Bohemian rebels by the Prague Blood Court, 1621. Note the regiment of infantry drawn up to overawe the onlookers.

19. The 'Mad Halberstädter', Christian of Brunswick, wearing armour blackened to prevent rust.

Potential Protestant Leaders

Protestant princes displayed even less cohesion than the Catholics, because they disagreed over doctrine, as well as all the usual conflicts about status and dynastic interest. Two distinct groups emerged gradually as the issues became more sharply defined. Most backed a moderate, Lutheran group led by Saxony which favoured working within the constitution to preserve the gains of 1555. A more radical, Calvinist group led by the Palatinate sought constitutional change through confrontation, and won only modest support from minor counts and territorial nobles. The division was neither clear nor final. Calvinist Brandenburg and Hessen-Kassel oscillated between the two factions, while important Lutheran princes like Württemberg and Ansbach sided with the Palatinate for considerable periods. Moreover, while the divisions came to be expressed confessionally, the differences over tactics pre-dated the emergence of Calvinism as a political force within the Empire.

As the birthplace of the Reformation, Saxony was the obvious choice as Protestant leader. Historians have generally shown little sympathy for Saxony, the least understood of all the protagonists during the Thirty Years War. Given that most have thought the war inevitable and the Empire in terminal decline, Saxon attempts to sustain the Augsburg settlement naturally appear naïve and doomed to failure.[4] Yet the 1555 peace largely satisfied Saxon objectives by stabilizing a religious and political balance within the Empire. Since it adhered strictly to Lutheran orthodoxy, it had nothing to gain from the radicals' campaign to include Calvinism within the peace. Though it did not assume formal control of the bishoprics of Zeitz-Naumburg, Meissen and Merseburg until 1561–81, it claimed these had already been secularized in 1542 and so were covered by the terms agreed in Augsburg. The elector was interested in placing relations as administrators in neighbouring Magdeburg and Halberstadt, but the main obstacle here was competition from rival Protestants, not Catholic resistance. Above all, the elector never forgot that he owed his title to Habsburg favour in 1547. Duke Moritz's leadership of the princes' revolt in 1551–2 had been an aberration in otherwise continued Albertine-Habsburg cooperation dating from 1487, and he reverted to backing the imperial dynasty immediately after Ferdinand agreed terms at Passau. His brother and successor, August, continued this during his reign, from 1553 to 1586, because this seemed the best guarantee for Saxony's new status. It also inclined August to remain aloof from his Ernestine relations and other established princely families, preferring instead the company of his fellow electors within their exclusive college at the Reichstag. Saxony's determination to preserve the status quo did not mean its policy was inflexible. On the contrary, August developed a standard tactic that his successors continued into the war after 1618. Each new problem was to be isolated diplomatically to prevent it from disturbing the constitutional balance, and then shifted to imperial institutions where it could be resolved through peaceful compromise.

The Palatinate's development prompted its rulers to reject such tactics in favour of constitutional change. The Palatinate had been very powerful in the later Middle Ages, especially when Elector Ruprecht I had ruled as German king between 1400 and 1410. In addition to territory, its electors had acquired the quasi-sovereign rights associated with the Palatine title, including powers to ennoble and feudal jurisdiction over numerous weaker territories on the middle Rhine. The end of the powerful Luxembourg dynasty, the kings of Bohemia, in 1437 left the Palatine Wittelsbachs as the Habsburg's principal rivals in the Empire, a factor behind Emperor Maximilian's alliance with Bavaria that led to the Palatinate's defeat in 1505. The consolidation of Habsburg imperial rule under Charles V shifted political gravity eastwards away from the middle Rhine where it had rested throughout the later Middle Ages. The adoption of the Reformation in the 1540s further distanced the Palatinate from the ecclesiastical electors and its other former allies within the imperial church.

The elector assumed the mantle of Protestant militancy that had been discreetly dropped by Saxony after 1547. This began at the Reichstag of 1556–7, the first session after the Augsburg settlement, where the Palatinate presented a series of demands that became the political programme it carried into the war after 1618. It sought to overcome the in-built Catholic majority by splitting the Reichstag along confessional lines, at least when religious issues were discussed. Catholics and Protestants would debate the matter separately, regardless of princely or electoral status, and then confer to reach a common agreement. This mechanism became known as *itio in partes* and was enshrined in the Peace of Westphalia in 1648, but had no previous foundation in imperial law and was bitterly opposed by Saxony and others who feared it would undermine the Empire's hierarchical constitution. The second demand was for the Protestant grievances (*Gravamina*) to be settled by accepting their interpretation of the disputed points in the Augsburg settlement. While Saxony broadly supported the abolition of the ecclesiastical reservation and other specific points, it vehemently opposed Palatine tactics to achieve these goals. The Palatinate proposed withholding imperial taxes against the Turks and blocking the election of a king of the Romans. This would effectively engineer an interregnum and so allow the Palatinate and Saxony, as imperial vicars, to exercise imperial authority at least long enough to effect the proposed changes. Saxony had advocated these tactics itself in the 1530s, but had no interest in such confrontational methods now.

The Palatine programme pinpointed the central problem with the Augsburg settlement that Saxony chose to ignore. The 1555 Peace tried to defuse tension by taking doctrine out of politics, but had done nothing to integrate the confessional groups into the Reichstag or other imperial institutions. As long as the Protestants regarded themselves as a party with specific interests, they would feel threatened by the in-built Catholic majority. The Palatine programme addressed this by attempting to reconfigure politics along confessional lines. The Catholics were not prepared to make such sweeping concessions, leaving the Palatinate little choice but to go outside the constitution and seek a separate confessional alliance, as Saxony had done in the 1530s.

It took over thirty years for the disagreement over tactics to produce two distinct Protestant parties. Neither Saxony nor the Palatinate wanted to allow their differences to be exploited by the Catholics. Saxony restrained Württemberg which had called for the Palatinate's isolation after Elector Friedrich III converted to Calvinism in 1560. The next elector, Ludwig VI, reversed course after 1576 and re-embraced Lutheranism, largely removing the confessional rift until his death in 1583. Political interests also hindered confessional polarization. Both electors worked with their Catholic colleagues to consolidate their collective pre-eminence over the princes, notably in brokering the transition to Ferdinand I after Charles V's abdication. In return, they were permitted to maintain a permanent 'electoral alliance' (*Kurverein*), entitling them to meet and discuss imperial affairs.

Protestant Disunity

More fundamentally, the Protestant princely dynasties were divided among themselves by a range of conflicting interests that inhibited any stable grouping based exclusively on confession. Though they controlled all the larger principalities other than Austria and Bavaria, the Protestant princes weakened their potential power through frequent dynastic partition. The Reformation stopped the general trend towards accepting primogeniture, prompting Protestant princes to retain or even reintroduce partible inheritance in order to provide equally for their children.[5] Unfortunately this coincided with changes in imperial law that fixed political rights in existing imperial fiefs by 1583. Rulers were no longer able to create additional votes in imperial institutions by partitioning their territories, but now had to decide either to share princely rights among their heirs, or give juniors appanages created from the main territory.

The latter route reduced the chances of making an equitable marriage since the junior princes no longer held land associated with constitutional rights. In some respects this contributed to Protestant activism. Younger sons sought alternative careers, raising mercenaries for the Dutch and Huguenots, or seeking posts as Protestant administrators in the imperial church. The Ernestine Wettins provide a good example. Dynastic partitions created four branches in Altenburg, Coburg, Eisenach and Weimar after 1572. Weakness encouraged reconciliation with electoral Saxony, which also wanted better relations. However, none of the branches could sustain further partitions. Johann Ernst was faced with seven brothers to provide for after he became duke of Weimar in 1615, and it is little surprise that he and his relations were among the most active of the lesser princes in the Protestant armies of the Thirty Years War.

More generally, partitions emasculated Protestant territories by dissipating their resources or creating debilitating inheritance disputes. The first of these problems was experienced by Brandenburg, contributing to its position as the weakest electorate and condemning its rulers to a minor role in imperial affairs. The main electorate had been split by partition in 1535, and though reunited under Johann Georg after 1571, further problems were created by the adoption of primogeniture on his death in 1598. The new elector, Joachim Friedrich, was 52 and preoccupied with his Lutheran duty to provide for his relations who could now no longer inherit the electorate. The incorporation of the secularized bishoprics of Havelberg, Brandenburg and Lebus into the electorate in 1598 removed them as alternative accommodation. Joachim Friedrich had been administrator of Magdeburg since 1566 and managed to pass this to his youngest son, Christian Wilhelm, on his accession, but only at the cost of friction with Saxony. Rather than keeping Ansbach and Bayreuth, which belonged to his Franconian relations, when he inherited them in 1603, the elector handed them to his half-brothers and his second son.[6]

Other territories suffered serious inheritance disputes, of which the most important affected Hessen, the territory that had, along with Saxony, been Protestant leader during the Reformation. Four lines were created in 1567, of which those in Marburg, Kassel and Darmstadt survived after 1583.[7] The original partition stipulated a common Lutheran church, but when the Hessians were asked to endorse the Book of Concord in 1576, Wilhelm of Hessen-Kassel refused. His lands became the target of Calvinist evangelizing, leading to the formal conversion of his successor, Landgrave Moritz, in 1603. Confessional differences sharpened the inheritance dispute that developed with the extinction of the Marburg line in October 1604. Not only did Landgrave Ludwig V in Darmstadt remain Lutheran, but he was no longer content with representing a junior branch and wanted to grab all of Marburg, the cultural centre and the seat of the common Hessian consistory. Moritz compromised his own claim by introducing Calvinism into the northern part of Marburg in 1605. Ludwig used this as a pretext to open a case at the Reichshofrat, beginning a process that placed Darmstadt in the imperial camp throughout the Thirty Years War.

The Hessen case illustrates a second general factor undermining Protestant unity. It was not only princes who disagreed over doctrine, but also their subjects who sometimes embraced a different variety of Protestantism from their rulers. Landgrave Moritz encountered serious difficulties when he began his 'second Reformation' in Kassel and Marburg. His neighbour, Count Simon VI of Lippe, faced an open revolt when he attempted the same in 1607, forcing him to relocate his capital from Detmold to Lemgo. Serious unrest also broke out in Brandenburg following Elector Johann Sigismund's public commitment to Calvinism at Christmas in 1613. The elector found little support outside the court and the university of Frankfurt on the Oder. Even his wife, Anna of Prussia, openly criticized him and rallied Lutheran opposition.[8]

The Protestant states were also divided by two further forms of rivalry. Large territories often tried to assert jurisdiction over their weaker neighbours, often using religion to supplement older feudal claims. For example, the Palatinate expected the smaller counts and imperial knights in its vicinity to follow its lead in embracing Calvinism, while Landgrave Moritz wanted Lutheran Waldeck to copy his second Reformation.[9] Protestants also clashed over competing claims to Catholic lands that often pre-dated the Reformation. Darmstadt and Kassel disputed possession of the large imperial abbey of Hersfeld that had been a Hessian protectorate since 1432. Hessen-Kassel, Cleves and the Guelph dukes all claimed rights over Paderborn and had factions in its cathedral chapter. Kassel's influence caused many Paderborn nobles to become Calvinists, adding a further confessional dimension to the dispute. As a result, Protestant influence cancelled itself out there, ending eight years of Lutheran administration by permitting the election of Dietrich von Fürstenberg as Catholic bishop in 1585 – the Protestant Hessian canons even voted for him to prevent the Guelph candidate obtaining a majority! Similar Guelph-Hessian rivalry permitted a resurgence of Catholic influence in the strategic abbey of Corvey.[10]

Political interests could take precedence over confessional solidarity. Darmstadt's hopes for a favourable verdict in its inheritance dispute led it to back the emperor. Württemberg hesitated to antagonize the Habsburgs who had sequestrated the duchy when its duke broke the public peace in 1517. Though the emperor restored it in 1534, he delayed confirmation of Württemberg's status as an imperial fief until 1599 and then inserted its revision to the Habsburgs if the ducal family died out. The powerful Guelph family also had good reasons to abstain from radical Protestant politics. Like the Wittelsbachs, they had a long and proud history, having once ruled all of Saxony before being defeated by Emperor Friedrich Barbarossa in 1180. The long process of rebuilding their regional power was threatened by the absence of primogeniture, which they only adopted in 1592 when there were two main branches of the dynasty. The weaker Lüneburg line governed part of Brunswick from Celle, while the senior Dannenberg branch held Wolfenbüttel, Calenberg, Grubenhagen and Göttingen. Both branches claimed a protectorate over the city of Brunswick with its 20,000 inhabitants and role as a major economic centre. The adoption of Lutheranism by the citizens and both the dukes failed to produce harmony as the city sought to emancipate itself through membership of the Hanseatic League. Heinrich Julius of Brunswick-Wolfenbüttel was one of the ablest and most learned princes of his day, sharing much in common with Rudolf II in terms of artistic and intellectual interests. He went to Prague in 1602 to press his case against the city, but was opposed by his Lüneburg relations despite their common interest in asserting dynastic authority over the Brunswickers. Having twice failed to take the city by force, Heinrich Julius bowed to a Reichskammergericht injunction to halt operations in 1606. He remained in Prague where his presence in the emperor's privy council encouraged many moderate Lutherans to remain loyal to the Habsburgs. Meanwhile, his attacks on Brunswick alienated the Protestant imperial cities who remained suspicious of any princely alliance, fearing it would be used against them rather than to defend religion. Competition over the church lands even encouraged Heinrich Julius to raise three of his sons as Catholics, giving them the tonsure in 1578 so that they might stand for election in the neighbouring bishoprics.[11]

CONFESSION AND IMPERIAL POLITICS TO 1608

The Cologne Dispute 1583–90

The Guelphs had already been thwarted in their earlier attempts to secure the entire bishopric of Hildesheim, having acquired 21 of its 24 districts in 1523, reducing the bishop to the remaining three districts around the town itself. The town converted to Lutheranism in 1542 and accepted a Guelph protectorate. Facing complete extinction, the remaining Catholic canons elected Ernst of Bavaria bishop in 1573.[12] The new bishop was the seventh son of Duke Albrecht V of Bavaria. Unlike the Protestants, the Catholic rulers still enjoyed access to the imperial church to offset the problems of primogeniture. Ernst himself was far removed from Cardinal Borromeo's model of a post-Tridentine bishop, but the papacy had been impressed by Bavarian dedication to Catholic renewal, and considered its ruling dynasty better sons of the church than the Austrian Habsburgs who had accepted the Augsburg settlement. The pope and Spain swung behind Ernst as their man to secure German bishoprics in danger of falling under Protestant administration. Hildesheim was Ernst's second see; he had already become bishop of Freising at the age of twelve in 1566. It was followed by election to Liège in 1581, but the main target was Cologne, where a disputed election led to the first significant sectarian violence in the Empire since the Schmalkaldic War.

The same kind of rivalry between Catholics that delayed reform in Franconia had facilitated Protestant penetration of the electorate of Cologne. Ernst's candidacy there in 1577 had been opposed by Johann von Manderscheid who was already bishop of Strasbourg, allowing Gebhard Truchsess von Waldburg to win by a narrow margin. Spain was not overly concerned, because Truchsess appeared a good Catholic with close links to the Jesuits, whereas Ernst had not even been ordained. However, the new archbishop fell in love with a nun, Agnes von Mansfeld, and married her in February 1582, dividing the local population. Renaissance Catholicism tolerated concubinage, but this was more than it could stomach. The controversy radicalized Truchsess who raised troops, seized the capital at Bonn and then announced his conversion to Calvinism on 19 December. He declared that he would not pass the territory on to his heirs, clearly expecting the emperor to accept him as another Protestant administrator, but Cologne's prominence as an electorate, and the decision to embrace Calvinism rather than Lutheranism forced the issue. Germans were compelled to confront the ambiguities of the Augsburg settlement, but rather than representing a step towards inevitable war, the Cologne dispute revealed how the complexity of the issues prevented polarization into two clear sides.

The pope's deposition of Truchsess on 1 April 1583 immediately alarmed the remaining Catholic electors, who joined their Protestant colleagues in doubting whether anyone had the power to remove one of the highest princes of the Empire.[13] Meanwhile, Truchsess's choice of Calvinism alienated the Lutherans who rightly feared that it would render the emperor's tacit toleration of Protestant administrators untenable. They rejected the Palatine interpretation of the situation in confessional terms, even though Truchsess's conversion gave them a majority in the electoral college. The elector Palatine raised 7,000 troops, sending 1,000 to reinforce Truchsess in Bonn, while the Calvinist Wetterau counts and the Dutch also promised support. However, Saxon and Brandenburg opposition deterred others like Hessen-Kassel from joining in, and even most Palatine officers refused to cross into Cologne territory, because of an imperial order to disband.

Bavaria seized its opportunity, demanding not only Truchsess's removal, but his replacement with Ernst. Spain realized its mistake and now feared for the security of the Spanish Road running close to Cologne. It despatched 3,000 infantry (including Tilly as a young ensign), while the cathedral chapter convened to elect a new archbishop. Such enthusiasm was far from universal among Catholics. Most bishops and abbots were slow to respond to Ernst's calls for contributions to his war chest, while Emperor Rudolf opposed both Spanish intervention and Bavaria's blatant dynasticism. However, the Habsburg candidate stood no chance,[14] forcing the reluctant emperor to endorse Ernst who was elected on 23 May 1583. Having collected his forces, Ernst struck in December, taking Bonn with the help of local Catholic nobles the following month and forcing Truchsess to flee to Holland. The Palatinate had been paralysed at this critical juncture by the death of Elector Ludwig in November 1583, leaving government to his seven-year-old son. The other electors fell into line and acknowledged Ernst by January 1585, and he secured his fifth diocese by being elected to Münster with Spanish and papal support in May 1585.

Nuremberg and the Tirol resigned from the bi-partisan Landsberg Alliance in protest in 1584. Though it remained formally in being until 1598, the organization effectively collapsed, indicating the erosion of the moderate middle ground in the Empire. However, its demise was more a product of disillusionment with Rudolf's handling of the affair than confessional polarization. Matters had been settled by force of arms, casting doubt on the ability of imperial institutions to solve complex problems. Spanish intervention widened the foreign involvement in imperial politics. Spain left troops in the electorate, because Truchsess's supporters and Dutch auxiliaries held out in a few towns. Ernst's acquisition of Münster deepened Spanish involvement, because he now controlled a large block of territory straddling the Lower Rhine around the Republic's eastern flank. The Dutch considered Ernst a Spanish ally and treated his lands as enemy territory. Spain felt obliged to protect him, while the Spanish soldiers, who had not been paid properly for years, saw a chance to seize supplies in the rich ecclesiastical lands. Fighting was limited to minor cross-border raids until December 1587, when 600

Protestants captured Bonn where the Spanish had left only 140 men. The duke of Parma despatched a large force that retook the city the following September after a six-month siege. He then moved north to capture Rheinberg in February 1590, a Cologne enclave that provided access across the Rhine and facilitated the subsequent campaigns to outflank the Dutch Republic from the east. The Empire's territorial integrity had been compromised, but only at its north-western corner. The damage was limited, because neither Spain nor the Dutch wanted to become embroiled in German politics. Spain even bowed to Protestant protests and refrained from turning Bonn into a major fortified base.[15]

The Strasbourg Bishops' War 1592–1604

The problems in Cologne were followed by similar difficulties in the bishopric of Strasbourg that inflicted more damage to Rudolf's prestige. Strasbourg lay further up the Rhine and surrounded the Protestant imperial city of that name that contained the most northerly permanent bridge over the river. Like Cologne, its location beside the Spanish Road attracted international interest, but, as so often with imperial politics, the actual dispute began with personal animosities far removed from the concerns of great powers.

Truchsess was deacon of the Strasbourg cathedral chapter and three of the canons who backed him in Cologne were also members, along with eleven other Protestants and seven Catholics. Matters came to a head with the death of Bishop Manderscheid in 1592. The Protestant majority were concerned at the presence of Duke Charles of Lorraine, who had been accepted as a canon by the Catholic minority and so was entitled to stand for election. As a cardinal and bishop of Metz, Charles was already a powerful figure with wide connections (he was a grandson of Catherine de Medici, and was related by marriage to Duke Wilhelm V of Bavaria). The Protestants feared they would fall victims to a Spanish-Lorraine-Bavarian plot, and be driven from their benefices like their colleagues in Cologne. They collected a few supporters and stormed the episcopal offices that were inside the city of Strasbourg. Safe behind the city's defences, they elected Johann Georg, a fifteen-year-old student at the local Protestant college, as the new bishop. As grandson of the current Brandenburg elector, the choice was intended to rally Lutheran support within the Empire. They also counted on help from

Württemberg, which held small enclaves in Alsace and bitterly opposed Lorraine after the French Catholic League's devastation of Mömpelgard in 1587–8. Dynastic interests lurked behind a thin skin of Protestant solidarity. Duke Friedrich I of Württemberg exploited the young bishop's precarious position by loaning him 330,000 fl. in return for a controlling stake in the bishopric. Württemberg was given the district of Oberkirch that established a land bridge between it and its Alsatian enclaves, while Friedrich's six-year-old son was made a canon and named as Johann Georg's successor.[16] Meanwhile, the Catholic canons fled to the strong episcopal town of Saverne and duly elected Duke Charles as rival bishop.

Rather than a straightforward contest between Protestants and Catholics, the ensuing dispute saw a three-cornered struggle between Lorraine, Johann Georg and Württemberg, while outsiders sought a peaceful settlement. Christian of Anhalt took command of the few troops Johann Georg had recruited locally and managed to stop Lorraine from overrunning the entire bishopric in 1592. With Rudolf incapable of mediating, Henri IV of France brokered a temporary partition the following year, giving Saverne and six other districts to Lorraine, and leaving the remaining six, including Oberkirch, to Johann Georg. Württemberg then used its financial muscle to revise this arrangement through further negotiations, leading to two agreements in 1604. Johann Georg surrendered his entire position to Württemberg in return for an annual pension and payment of his debts. Württemberg then handed the bishopric over to Lorraine, which let it keep Oberkirch for thirty years.

The so-called 'Bishops' War' saw even less fighting than the Cologne dispute. All parties remained willing to negotiate and let material and dynastic interests dictate the final outcome. Nonetheless, the public peace had been breached a second time and further damage done to Rudolf's standing in the Empire. Worse, coming after the 'Spanish Winter' of 1598–9, the Catholic victory in Strasbourg raised the spectre of a concerted Counter-Reformation against German Protestants.

Dreams of a Protestant Alliance

The Spanish intervention along the Rhine after 1583 suggested that the French and Dutch wars were spreading to Germany. Denmark and England viewed events with alarm. Fears of Spanish or Jesuit activity in their own countries naturally inclined the Danish and English leaderships to see Catholic plots extending to Germany as well. England forged its alliance with the Dutch rebels in 1585 and supplied money and volunteers to the French Huguenots. Denmark channelled money for the Huguenots through the Palatinate, and both countries desired closer ties to German princes who assumed a significance in Protestant calculations far in excess of what they might actually contribute to any alliance.[17] A central tenet of the militant outlook was the belief that the pope intended to strike at Germany first as the birthplace of the Reformation. The German princes also enjoyed a higher international standing at this point than they would do after 1648. Though clearly inferior to sovereign monarchs, they remained part of the international community of rulers and regularly travelled abroad. Their territories were centrally located with access to Scandinavia, the Netherlands and France, making them an ideal base for operations against perceived Catholic threats, while their military reputation was sustained by the presence of German volunteers and mercenaries in all Protestant armies.

In reality, the prospect of an international Protestant alliance was an illusion. The different national trajectories of the Danish and Anglican churches and the diverging political ambitions of their monarchs prevented any firm agreement between the two potential foreign backers. As one grew more militant, the other's ardour waned, inhibiting synchronization of interests. The controversy surrounding the conservative Lutheran Book of Concord added a further stumbling block that assumed greater proportions after 1582, despite the apparent urgency of the Cologne and Strasbourg disputes. The viability of any alliance among German Protestants depended on attracting external sponsorship, but neither England nor Denmark would bankroll a group unless both Saxony and the Palatinate were included. Yet the rift between the two leading German Protestant princes grew following Palatine resentment at Saxony's failure to back it over Cologne. Matters worsened as Palatine government passed into the hands of Johann Casimir, from the junior branch of Pfalz-Lautern, who acted as regent between 1583 and 1592. He surrounded himself with exiles and veterans from the western religious wars, rather than the men who had run the Palatinate until then. Viewing the world from the militant perspective, he had no time for the traditional consensual politics of the Empire and vigorously reversed the reintroduction of Lutheranism under the previous elector, even provoking a revolt in the Upper Palatinate in 1592. This lurch towards extremism pulled the Palatinate further away from potential allies in the Empire and was also fuelled by personal disappointments. The marriages of the Saxon elector's niece and daughter to Calvinists William of Orange and Johann Casimir had both failed by 1583.

Unable to work with Saxony in the electoral college, the Palatinate resumed its policy of building a distinct Protestant party (*corpus evangelicorum*) outside the formal constitutional framework of the Empire. Protestants now had a clear choice to advance confessional goals. They could follow Saxony and work through imperial institutions to safeguard the status quo, or they could join the Palatinate's new group, based entirely on common faith, which held its congresses separately from the Reichstag and Kreis assemblies. As the 1580s progressed, it became increasingly obvious that most princes preferred the Saxon model above the confrontational Palatine option. Saxony renewed its old alliance with Hessen-Kassel in 1587, thus bringing the other leader of the defunct Schmalkaldic group into its party. Württemberg, Pomerania, Mecklenburg and the Ernestines all backed Saxony, which extended its alliance to include Brandenburg in 1614.

Much now depended on the attitude of the Saxon elector and there were signs of a possible rapprochement with the Palatinate with the accession of Christian I in 1586. The new elector rejected his father's orthodoxy in favour of the Philippist variety of Lutheranism, but since he never openly declared a conversion to Calvinism, his ultimate intentions remain unclear. Already an alcoholic and gambling addict prior to his accession, he was unable to master the personal rivalries at his court, allowing other figures to exert greater influence. His chancellor, Nikolaus Crell, also favoured Philippism, and introduced a new Bible against mounting popular opposition from 1589. The internal reorientation was accompanied by a change of direction in imperial politics as Saxony opened negotiations with the Palatinate in February 1590, leading to the Union of Torgau the following January. The move has been interpreted as a radical departure, presaging a powerful, united Protestant front.[18] Christian was more prepared to cooperate with the Palatinate than his father, but rather than representing a conversion to Palatine radicalism, his agreement at Torgau was intended to steer his new partner towards a more moderate course. Though the allies sent a military expedition to France, this was no longer such a radical step now that Henri IV was king. Moreover, their cooperation in the Empire was restricted to sending a joint protest to Rudolf seeking redress for Protestant grievances through constitutional means. Of the other Protestant rulers, only Hessen-Kassel backed the Union, which collapsed with Christian's death in September 1591.

The Union's fragility was revealed when Christian's unexpected death immediately sparked rumours that he had been poisoned by the Saxon Lutheran establishment to forestall a Calvinist second Reformation. Had he lived longer, it is unlikely that the Union would have presented a serious challenge to imperial authority, because the outbreak of the Turkish War in 1593 rallied broad support behind Rudolf. Christian died leaving three sons, of whom the eldest, Christian II, was only eight. A regency was established under Friedrich Wilhelm of Weimar and the boy's maternal grandfather, Elector Johann Georg of Brandenburg. His mother, Sophie of Brandenburg, orchestrated a purge of Philippists and crypto-Calvinists in 1591–3, imprisoning Crell. All pastors were obliged to swear allegiance to the Book of Concord and the measures found broad popular approval in anti-Calvinist riots. Saxony not only returned to its previous stance in imperial politics, but also drifted into political passivity, since the regents were reluctant to take any risks. Christian II continued the family tradition of alcoholism and was even less able to assert himself than his father, allowing his mother to maintain Saxon support for Rudolf. As a Saxon privy councillor noted in 1610, 'politically we're papists'.[19] The only tangible reward was the Reichshofrat's confirmation of a death sentence for Crell, despite the lack of any evidence for a conspiracy and in defiance of pleas for mercy from Elizabeth I of England and Henri IV. Convinced that Crell had corrupted her husband, Sophie took the seat of honour at his public execution in Dresden's main square on 9 October 1601. This piece of personal revenge was widely interpreted as Saxony's determination to oppose Calvinism.

The Saxon preoccupation with settling scores left the political stage open for the Palatinate to resume its efforts to recruit its alternative confessional alliance. Protestant politics diverged again as Saxon conservatism contrasted with growing Palatine militancy. The new elector Palatine, Friedrich IV, was not an obvious radical. Raised a Lutheran, he converted to Calvinism under the influence of Johann Casimir whose regency only ended in 1592. However, he never embraced the Calvinist work ethic, and was moody and often ill, especially from 1602. Friedrich's love of pomp led to serious overspending on the court, creating debts of 1.8 million fl. by 1613.[20] The expansion of the court also allowed the aristocratic element, already present during the regency, to gain the upper hand, significantly changing the character of Palatine politics. Previously, government was in the hands of a privy, or 'upper', council (*Oberrat*), created in 1557 and staffed largely by commoners who had been educated at humanist universities. Their collegiate decision-making induced caution, whereas Friedrich IV's growing reliance on aristocratic courtiers and military men increased scope for individual influence. The situation was exacerbated by the elector's declining health which reawakened his religious fervour and inclined him to see matters more in confessional terms.

One man particularly attracted his attention and favour: Christian of Anhalt, one of the most important figures in the outbreak of the Thirty Years War. Usually dismissed as a reckless schemer, there can be no doubt he would have been considered a far-sighted strategist had the Bohemian adventure been crowned with success. His presence in the Palatinate is a further example of the problems facing the numerous Protestant princely families. Though he served the elector, he was himself a prince from the Askanier family which claimed a 1,000-year-long ancestry and had once been one of the most powerful dynasties in the Empire. By the late sixteenth century it was reduced to ruling Anhalt, a principality sandwiched between Brandenburg and Saxony. Lack of primogeniture fragmented even this small holding, splitting it five ways between Christian and his brothers after 1586. Christian's share at Bernburg was too cramped for a man of his ambition, and he sought a more prestigious court that would give him a wider role.

He went first to Saxony in 1586 where he converted to Calvinism, embracing his new faith with particular fervour and immersing himself in its eclectic belief in a magical system of universal knowledge. Like many ardent Calvinists, he was convinced it was possible to discern divine will by correctly interpreting events according to the Bible. He was given command of the joint Saxon-Palatine force sent to assist Henri IV in 1591. Like the previous German expeditions, none of the backers came through with the money and Anhalt was left to pay the 1.3 million talers expenses himself – a debt his descendants were still claiming from France in 1818.[21] Still, the eleven-month campaign brought him into contact with the key players of the Calvinist international, notably Count Johann of Nassau-Siegen. Having commanded the Protestant forces in the brief Strasbourg Bishops' War, he was ready to accept an offer from Rudolf to take command against the Turks in 1593. Count Johann persuaded him this would be contrary to the Protestant cause, and facilitated an alternative appointment as governor of the Upper Palatinate in 1595.

The post enabled Christian to display his many undoubted talents. The Upper Palatinate lay considerably to the east of the electorate that acquired it in 1329. It was administered separately by its own government in Amberg, whereas the Lower, or electoral, Palatinate was ruled from Heidelberg. Its religious traditions were also distinct, and while Lutheranism had been a court phenomenon on the Rhine, it was genuinely popular among the Upper Palatines who resisted the re-imposition of Calvinism by Johann Casimir. Anhalt regained their loyalty by a mixture of tact and cunning and was so successful that the local Estates gave strong support to the later Bohemian adventure.[22] His success as governor raised Anhalt's profile at the Heidelberg court, where his influence grew with the appointment of his protégés and other figures associated with international Calvinism.

The Four Monasteries Dispute 1598–1601

By the late 1590s Anhalt was in a position to revive Johann Casimir's activist policy and take it to its logical conclusion by forming a Palatine-led Protestant alliance. To persuade the other princes to abandon Saxon constitutionalism, Anhalt sought to demonstrate that existing institutions no longer safeguarded Protestant interests. He deliberately chose imperial justice as his battleground, because the Augsburg settlement rested on the Empire's ability to resolve disputes through peaceful arbitration in the courts. It is quite likely that he, or at least others in the Palatine administration, genuinely believed that the existing institutions were not only inherently biased against Protestants, but had been captured by the Jesuits as agencies of Counter-Reformation. Nonetheless, by politicizing imperial justice, Anhalt greatly escalated the tensions within the Empire.

The impact of the Palatine programme can be seen by comparing the situation after 1598 with the preceding forty years. The Augsburg settlement entrusted the Reichskammergericht with resolving cases involving religious issues. The court was largely staffed by Catholics, because it was up to the territories of each Kreis to propose new judges to fill vacancies. As territories chose their co-religionists, only a third of the judges were Protestants in the three decades prior to the Thirty Years War, roughly reflecting the Protestant proportion among the princes. Despite this, Protestant territories continued to pay their regular contributions to maintain the court. Moreover, they did not protest as a succession of Catholics were chosen as presiding judges between 1559 and 1570. It was not until 1576 that the Palatinate had seriously suggested introducing religious parity, by demanding that the presidency alternate between Catholics and Protestants.[23] The emperor rejected this not only as an attack on his prerogative, but also as unnecessary, because religiously sensitive cases were already judged by a senate, or review panel of three Protestant and three Catholic judges. If one senate failed to agree a verdict, they had to refer the matter to another panel, also composed of equal numbers from both confessions. This procedure had worked so successfully that there were only seven formal complaints against court verdicts between 1559 and 1589.

None of the cases in the so-called 'four monasteries dispute' (*Vierklösterstreit*) that the Palatinate singled out in 1598 differed substantially from those that had been successfully resolved in the past. The first, from January 1597, involved a verdict in favour of the Carthusian order against the count of Öttingen, ordering him to return their monastery, which he had secularized in 1556, thus falling after the normative year specified at Augsburg. The court made a similar judgment in a second case against the Hirschhorn imperial knights who had appropriated a Carmelite convent in 1568. The third verdict instructed the city of Strasbourg to refrain from meddling in the internal affairs of the Maria Magdalena nunnery within its walls. Finally, the court required the margrave of Baden and count of Eberstein to release the abbess of Frauenalb whom they had arrested for having allegedly led a disorderly life. All the decisions had been reached by majority vote in bi-confessional review panels, indicating that some Protestant judges had sided with their Catholic colleagues.

The Palatinate politicized these cases by raising confessional, rather than legal objections. The court had judged each case according to property rights and jurisdictions, yet all involved fundamental disagreements over the purpose and use of church property. Moreover, the verdicts lacked solidity, because the appeals procedure had collapsed. Known as the Visitation, this had been established in 1532 and confirmed by the Peace of Augsburg, and involved an annual review of the Reichskammergericht cases by a special committee with rotating membership drawn from all imperial Estates. In the wake of the Cologne dispute, Rudolf had blocked the Lutheran administrator of Magdeburg from taking his seat when his turn came in 1588, stalling the review process. The Catholics wanted a functioning court as much as the Protestants and used the 1594 Reichstag to propose entrusting the Visitation to the imperial Deputation. This was another committee formed by members drawn from all Estates and charged with dealing with special matters when the Reichstag was not in session. Given that Protestants currently had even fewer members on the Deputation than the Visitation panel, they rejected this as another Catholic plot against them.

However, the problem was not simply confessional; it also revealed a serious deficiency in the imperial constitution. The Reichskammergericht was not a modern constitutional supreme court empowered to deal with legal loopholes or new problems by offering its own interpretation of the law. Instead, it was charged with implementing existing legislation passed by the Reichstag, leaving final judgment as the emperor's prerogative. Since the melancholic Rudolf refused to become involved, the matter passed back to the Reichstag, opening relatively minor cases to heated political debate. The Protestant litigants in the four cases simply requested that parity be introduced into the Deputation to ensure a fair appeal, but their pleas were ignored by the Palatinate which rallied Brandenburg and Brunswick to dispute even this body's authority to review cases. The move paralysed the Deputation by 1601, allowing the Palatinate to take the matter to the next Reichstag that met between March and July 1603.

The Palatine leadership hoped the four monasteries dispute would finally convince the doubters to abandon Saxony and join a distinct Protestant party. Since the 1594 Reichstag, the Palatinate had chaired six Protestant congresses to debate tactics to be employed in the formal imperial institutions. While delegates obediently affirmed the Palatine policy of withholding assistance against the Turks, Saxony's boycott of these congresses rendered their decision largely meaningless. Spanish encroachment in the Lower Rhine did prompt Ansbach and Hessen-Kassel to open talks in 1596 for a new Protestant union, but again, without Saxon participation neither Denmark nor England would back the project. The militants' lack of support was exposed once the 1603 Reichstag opened. James VI of Scotland, who had just become king of England, politely declined Anhalt's invitation to lead a new union. France rejected similar offers, because Anhalt had sheltered the duc de Bouillon, a Huguenot grandee with his own sovereign duchy at Sedan on the Meuse, who had led a conspiracy against Henri IV. Fearing they would be left exposed, Ansbach and Hessen-Kassel backtracked at the last minute and refused to join the Palatinate in opposing renewed assistance against the Turks. The atmosphere became so poisoned that when someone shot at Elector Christian II while he was out riding in April 1603, the Saxons immediately accused Anhalt of planning an assassination.[24] Saxony was assisted by the numerous moderate Catholics who had been alarmed by the collapse of the Deputation and avoided giving the Palatine representative an excuse to orchestrate a walkout.

Bavaria

Though the Reichstag closed with its customary imperial Recess listing its decisions endorsed by all participants, there were clear signs that the old consensual political culture was under great strain. Palatine behaviour fuelled Catholic suspicions that all Protestants were inherently unreasonable, contributing to a growing reluctance to tolerate perceived infringements of the Augsburg settlement. Catholic intransigence grew as Wilhelm V brought his 24-year-old son Maximilian into the Bavarian government in 1594, and then handed over completely four years later in order to retreat into a life of pious contemplation.[25] Unlike other principal figures around the turn of the century, Duke Maximilian saw out the entire Thirty Years War and was the most influential and dynamic German Catholic prince. There is some debate on his character. While all agree he was determined and ambitious, his principal biographer, Dieter Albrecht, rather overstresses his natural caution and circumspection.

A convinced Catholic like his brother-in-law Ferdinand of Styria, Maximilian put himself through a punishing routine of personal devotion, spending hours daily in prayer or at mass. He developed a particular attachment to the Virgin, proclaiming her patron of Bavaria in 1616 and dedicating himself to her in a vow written in his own blood and deposited in a silver tabernacle at the Altötting shrine in 1645. Her intercession was sought before key decisions with, for example, the intervention in Donauwörth (1607) and the invasion of the Upper Palatinate (1621) timed to coincide with important dates in her calendar. However, like Ferdinand, Maximilian's personal piety did not preclude dialogue with those not sharing his faith. In 1601 he restaged the famous disputation between Luther and Catholic theologians by inviting leading thinkers from both faiths to Regensburg to seek common ground. Albrecht is certainly correct in presenting Maximilian as sharing Ferdinand's legalistic outlook on political action, inclining him to a deference towards the emperor that was both psychological and practical. Like his Saxon contemporaries, Maximilian still thought of the Empire as a divinely ordained hierarchy and naturally looked to the emperor to provide guidance. He was reluctant to act without prior imperial approval, seeking explicit sanction from the emperor before taking action, as well as negotiating safeguards in case of failure.

Such attitudes conditioned Bavaria to remain discreetly in the background, and it is unlikely that its dukes harboured long-standing plans to create a separate Catholic party. But is clear that, like the Saxon and Palatine electors, Maximilian was convinced that his own confessional and dynastic goals were in the broader interests of his church, and of the Empire as a whole. The duke felt that Catholics had given too much ground already since 1555 and that it was high time for them to take a firm stand to prevent the Empire sliding into chaos. The stance was influenced by a book, *Autonomia*, published in Munich in 1586 by Andreas Erstenberger, a secretary at the Reichshofrat, who criticized the toleration extended by the Catholic *politique* faction in France in an attempt to pacify the Huguenots. For Erstenberger, there could be no 'autonomy', since freedom of conscience was simply a licence to serve the devil. Bavaria led the other Catholics at the 1593–4 Reichstag in threatening to walk out if the Magdeburg administrator was allowed to take up his seat. The action implied a concerted rejection of all administrators as a precursor to bringing their bishoprics back into Catholic hands. Maximilian continued this line at the next Reichstag in 1597–8 when he insisted on the validity of majority voting to contest Palatine calls for parity along the lines of *itio in partes*.

Donauwörth

The Catholic position was stiffened by a string of imperial verdicts between 1604 and 1608 that attempted to restore the Catholic interpretation of the Augsburg settlement in the imperial cities. While the Protestants argued the terms permitted freedom of conscience, Catholics pointed to other clauses suggesting the cities' religion had to remain as it had been in 1555. Lutheranism had always been attractive to urban burghers who had been among its first adherents. It spread after 1555 into Aalen, Colmar, Essen, Hagenau and elsewhere, eroding their formal Catholic character. For example, there were only 30 Catholics left in Dortmund by 1602, while 80 Catholics faced 700 Protestants in Kaufbeuren and a mere 16 households remained true to Rome of the 4,000 people living in Donauwörth. While each case had its local colour, all involved similar problems. The Catholic minority faced growing intimidation from armed gangs, particularly during council elections, so that civic government passed into Protestant hands, for example in Aachen in 1581. Once in power, the new councillors enacted legislation in favour of their faith, for example blocking the introduction of the Gregorian calendar, or denying citizenship to new Catholics, as in Donauwörth despite its being formally bi-confessional. The dwindling Catholic population left their institutions vulnerable, allowing Protestants to take control of hospitals, schools, churches and other valuable real estate. Such actions had wider repercussions through the overlapping web of jurisdictions in the Empire. For example, the sole remaining Catholic church in Donauwörth by 1605 belonged to the Benedictine monastery of the Holy Cross which claimed exemption from the city's jurisdiction and enjoyed the protection of the bishop of Augsburg.

The paralysis of the Reichskammergericht left the Reichshofrat as the only fully functioning imperial court. Based in Vienna, this was staffed entirely by Habsburg appointees who acted as both judges and the emperor's political advisers. It was not only faster than the Reichskammergericht, but its decisions enjoyed the emperor's direct backing. For this reason, its case load rose from 250 a year prior to the mid-1580s to twice that by 1590, before levelling off slightly; within this the number of politically sensitive cases rose from around 25 before 1585 to 60 a year by the early seventeenth century. Though they accepted its competence in feudal law, the Protestants did not trust the Reichshofrat completely and always referred religious cases to the Reichskammergericht as it enjoyed greater judicial independence.[26] However, the cities were directly subject to Rudolf's authority as overlord, and previous emperors had intervened to rewrite civic constitutions and restore order. Thus, Rudolf was widely believed to be acting within his powers when the Reichshofrat issued a series of mandates against the Protestant councils in Aachen, Dortmund, Esslingen, Hamburg and Kaufbeuren after 1604.

Like the four monasteries dispute, the individual cases were not particularly serious, but became so because they were politicized by the Palatinate to mobilize support for its plans for a confessional alliance. The Donauwörth case proved so controversial because it came after Catholic restorations in a number of other cities, and because Rudolf's mishandling of the affair opened him to charges of arbitrary justice. The incident was sparked by a religious procession that, like those in Austria, symbolized a struggle to control the community. Bishop Knöringen of Augsburg and the Jesuits at his university in Dillingen encouraged the abbot of the Holy Cross monastery to reintroduce the St Mark's Day procession. The city council ruled in May 1605 that the monks could only march with their banners furled. Backed by Augsburg, the abbot appealed to the Reichshofrat, which invited the council to present its case while ordering it not to disrupt the procession in the meantime. The local Catholics took this for tacit approval of their position and marched in April 1606 with their flags unfurled. The ensuing 'battle of the flags' saw Protestant burghers rip up the banners and chase the monks back to the abbey. The Reichshofrat ruled on 3 September that their actions constituted a clear breach of the peace, rejecting the council's argument that it had been powerless to restrain the mob.

Rudolf's intervention at this point transformed an unexceptional local case into a high political drama. Maximilian of Bavaria had already executed the mandate against Kaufbeuren in 1604 and on 17 March 1607 the emperor empowered him to do the same in Donauwörth. Maximilian appeared a loyal Catholic and Rudolf wanted to win Bavarian favour given the Brothers' Quarrel. However, his choice breached the custom of entrusting such imperial commissions to the leading princes of the Kreis where the verdict was to be enforced. Since the city was in Swabia, not Bavaria, Duke Friedrich of Württemberg took it as a deliberate slight and tried to mobilize the south German Protestants to complain. Rudolf hesitated, losing face in the process, while Maximilian would not move without an explicit order. Meanwhile, Donauwörth militants, angry at their council's apparent timidity, instigated a riot in April 1607 and expelled some Bavarian representatives who had been sent to investigate the previous disturbance. Maximilian now had the excuse he needed, but still waited until Rudolf reluctantly placed the city under the imperial ban and then finally ordered Bavaria to act on 1 December. Maximilian now had to move quickly, because the Reichstag had been summoned and he feared the matter would be referred there instead. Within a week of Rudolf's decision, 6,500 Bavarian troops were on the march. The agitators fled at their approach and they entered the city unopposed on 17 December.

The incident compromised the Reichshofrat's reputation, enabling the Palatinate to widen its charge of corrupt institutions. Though Rudolf had genuinely wanted a peaceful settlement, he had seriously mishandled the affair. He refused to follow Saxon advice and issue a statement denying his judgment was sectarian. His inflated sense of majesty prevented him from seeing the need to explain his actions. It fell to Bavaria to do this, undermining the emperor's credibility and raising the spectre of arbitrary rule.

Though the incident is widely taken as leading directly to the formation of confessional alliances,[27] Swabian Protestants showed little enthusiasm for Württemberg's protest and convened with their Catholic colleagues in the Kreis assembly again in 1609. Maximilian also tried to avoid inflaming the situation. He restored parish churches to Catholic control in Donauwörth, but refrained from suppressing Lutheranism until 1609 and only then in relation to his wider goal of annexing the city. Rudolf placed Donauwörth under Bavarian administration until it paid Maximilian's expenses. The arrangement was integral to imperial justice as it relied on territories recouping the cost of serving the courts from the guilty party. However, Maximilian's deliberately excessive punitive expedition cost over 300,000 fl., which the city, with an annual revenue of 15,000 fl., stood no chance of repaying. The duke was there to stay and had already removed the city's imperial title from all official documents after 1609. As he now regarded the citizens as his own subjects, he felt no compunction to respect their faith.

The 1608 Reichstag

Even now, Anhalt found it hard to drum up support for a confessional alliance. An agreement with Brandenburg and the Dutch from 1605 was still-born, because the Brandenburgers placed their dynastic interests above the Protestant international and paid the money earmarked for the Dutch to Poland instead to guarantee their succession to ducal Prussia. Württemberg and Baden-Durlach preferred a local arrangement with Pfalz-Neuburg, leaving the Palatinate to conclude a pact with Ansbach, Bayreuth and Nuremberg in 1607, restricted to the defence of the Upper Palatinate against possible Bavarian attack.

Nonetheless, the coincidence of the Donauwörth incident with the Brothers' Quarrel convinced Saxony that something had to be done to safeguard Protestant interests. Rudolf's choice of Archduke Ferdinand of Styria to represent him at the planned Reichstag suggested little could be expected from the imperial proposals. Saxony now accepted the Palatinate's argument that majority voting should not apply to issues where religion was at stake. As with the Torgau Union, this was not a clear shift towards militancy, because Saxon prestige meant it was now the spokesman for the Palatine programme, and of course expressed it in more moderate language. The Palatinate fell into line and even held talks with the ecclesiastical elector of Mainz to smooth over controversial issues.

The Reichstag opened in February 1608 with Archduke Ferdinand's response to the Protestant demand for formal confirmation of the Peace of Augsburg. Ferdinand offered to confirm it, provided the Protestants restored all Catholic church property taken since 1552. The proposal represented a significant hardening of the Catholic position, suggesting restitution should come from a definitive interpretation of the 1555 peace, rather than by individual case through the imperial courts. It has been rightly identified as the origins of the Restitution Edict, issued by Ferdinand as emperor in 1629 at the height of his political and military power.[28] Saxon moderation was rendered untenable in the face of this proposal, passing the initiative back to the Palatinate that countered with a series of demands, including that Rudolf should extend toleration to Hungarian Protestants, even though this lay well outside the Reichstag's jurisdiction. Saxon and Mainz efforts to preserve sanity were drowned out amid rising passions, culminating in a Palatine walkout, followed by Hessen-Kassel, Baden-Durlach and others. Many moderate Catholics were exasperated and now backed Bavaria and militants like the bishop of Augsburg.

UNION AND LIGA 1608–9

The Protestant Union

The 1608 Reichstag was the first to end without the customary final Recess. Its collapse, coming after the failure of the Reichskammergericht Visitation and the Deputation, suggested constitutional paralysis and the futility of the elector of Saxony's faith that established institutions provided adequate safeguards. Anhalt moved quickly, skilfully using the emotive occasion of Friedrich of Württemberg's funeral in February 1608 to make his proposals directly to the Protestant princes. A group reconvened in the symbolic setting of Auhausen, a monastery that had been secularized by Ansbach, and agreed a new Protestant Union on 14 May, just eleven days after the unsatisfactory conclusion of the Reichstag.[29]

The Union essentially merged the existing Palatine defence group from 1607 with the south-west German alliance of Pfalz-Neuburg, Baden-Durlach and Württemberg from 1605. Only four other princes had joined by the spring of 1609, but the Jülich-Cleves crisis (see below) added Brandenburg, Hessen-Kassel, Zweibrücken, Anhalt's brothers and the count of Öttingen, as well as sixteen imperial cities, including Nuremberg, Ulm and Strasbourg. Once these had joined by January 1610, the Union still only encompassed around half the Protestant territories. Hessen-Kassel's membership ensured Darmstadt's abstention, while the Guelph dukes refrained because they hoped for Rudolf's support in their dispute with Brunswick. Suspicion of princely intentions also deterred many important imperial cities, including Augsburg, but the most obvious empty seat belonged to the Saxon elector, whose refusal to join kept all the north-eastern dukes and counts away.

With its membership only half full, the Union remained a south German regional alliance based on the Palatinate's existing dynastic and political network. The cities joined primarily because the Union made Donauwörth's full restoration one of its main demands. Though they outnumbered the princes, revisions to the Union's charter in 1610 reduced the cities to second-class members by ensuring that the princes always had two more votes. The initial charter was for ten years, under Palatine directorship for the first three, but the entire organization remained provisional, because it was envisaged that a second, north German directorate would be created when Saxony joined. All members forswore violence among themselves, and agreed to coordinate their participation in imperial institutions. The Union held 25 plenary congresses throughout its 13-year existence, but failed to develop its own institutions. Though conceived as a vehicle for the radical Palatine programme, the Union was compelled through its own weakness to rely heavily on the existing imperial constitution for its fiscal and military arrangements. Members used the quotas assigned them by the imperial tax register to determine how much they paid the Union if it decided to mobilize an army. Reliance on the imperial constitution was also a political expedient, since the Union had to present itself as an adjunct of the formal public peace framework to avoid condemnation as an illegal organization. Consequently, it failed to institute its own judiciary or mechanisms that would have allowed ordinary members to hold the director to account. All correspondence was routed through Heidelberg, because the Palatinate was the only territory with sufficient bureaucratic development capable of handling the business.

The Catholic Liga

Catholic rulers formed a rival organization fourteen months later. This has entered history as the Catholic League, or *Liga*, thanks to Protestant propaganda that sought to brand the group as the German equivalent of the notorious French Catholic *Ligue*. Like the Union, the new organization emerged from a combination of two earlier groups. The three ecclesiastical electors had been disappointed by the outcome of the 1603 Reichstag and had already considered forming a confessional alliance dedicated to defending the Catholic interpretation of the Augsburg settlement. However, the new elector of Mainz from 1604, Johann Schweikhard von Kronberg, preferred to continue negotiations with Saxony for an amicable compromise. Rudolf's passivity also deterred the electors of Trier and Cologne, because they felt the emperor had to be included for any alliance to be legitimate. It was also hard to conceive of a group without Bavaria, but at this point Maximilian opposed any confessional alliance, particularly one that included the Habsburgs, for fear of being sucked into the Austrian Brothers' Quarrel. The political fallout from the Donauwörth incident forced Maximilian to change his mind and he now worked to form an alliance to enhance Bavarian security. He was careful to remain discreetly in the background, though, using Bishop Knöringen of Augsburg as a front man to recruit the Swabian, Franconian and Bavarian bishops.

The core of the future Liga came together at a personal meeting with Maximilian in July 1609 that concluded an alliance between Bavaria and the bishops of Augsburg, Konstanz, Kempten, Passau, Regensburg, Ellwangen and Würzburg. They agreed a mutual defence pact for nine years dedicated in vague terms to defending Catholicism. The organizational details were left sketchy, because no agreement had been reached with the three ecclesiastical electors. Maximilian then used Augsburg and Konstanz to recruit additional south German members, while encouraging his uncle Ernst of Cologne to promote a Rhenish group. The Jülich-Cleves crisis prompted Schweikhard of Mainz to drop his objections to a confessional alliance, and both parties came together at a secret convention in Würzburg in February 1610 that represented the Liga's real foundation. Bavaria was to lead a southern directory which included the original 8 members from 1609, together with Bamberg and 19 Swabian prelates who had been recruited. These 28 territories were grouped into 3 subdivisions based on their membership of the Bavarian, Swabian and Franconian Kreise. A second, Rhenish directory was led by Mainz and included Cologne, Trier and the bishops of Speyer and Worms.[30]

The Liga shared many of the Union's defects. It likewise presented itself as an auxiliary of the imperial constitution, intended only to become active should existing institutions fail to resolve problems or provide security. The Liga's more detailed and explicit structure embraced the imperial constitution more readily than the Union had done, because Bavarian aims were more conservative. Like in the Union, Liga members were to use their imperial quotas if summoned to provide men or money. There was a clearer, more centralized command structure, but also more accountability to plenary congresses that were necessary to ratify the directors' decisions.

Common Problems

Both Bavaria and the Palatinate were determined that their new alliances were to support their own dynastic and confessional goals. By associating themselves with other territories, they hoped to increase their respective influence within imperial institutions. The alliances also served as platforms to attract external sponsors who could provide money and security, especially if tensions in the Empire led to open violence. Though intended for security, the alliances made adventurous policies more likely, because both Bavaria and the Palatinate could spread the costs among their allies. Other territories joined for similarly selfish motives, notably the Protestant princes who hoped the Union would assist their dynastic objectives as well. The overriding concern, however, was for security with all members regarding their participation as insurance should the imperial institutions fail them.

The tension between dynastic ambition and security concerns quickly became obvious as opinions diverged between directors and members over three key issues. The Palatinate and other Union radicals saw the Habsburgs as irredeemably compromised as impartial leaders through their suppression of Protestant liberties in their own lands and through Rudolf's apparently arbitrary justice. The others simply hoped the emperor would see sense and resume an active, but impartial role. Bavaria was also wary of the imperial dynasty and resisted pressure from Mainz, Spain and the papacy to admit the Austrian archdukes. Habsburg membership would force Bavaria to surrender control of the Liga, which would then lose its utility as a vehicle for Maximilian's dynastic goals. Since he could not refuse a formal application from them, he devised other strategies to keep the Habsburgs out. He won the confidence of the Spanish ambassador, Balthasar de Zúñiga, securing Spanish and papal support for the Liga in August 1610 in return for acknowledging King Philip III and Archduke Ferdinand as its 'protectors'. Spain failed to pay anything, and the pope delivered only a fraction of the subsidy he promised, but political recognition of Bavarian leadership was far more valuable. Spain accepted that Austria's low standing in the Empire meant it had to cooperate with Bavaria. Maximilian's insistence on the Liga's confessional character added a further barrier to Austrian membership, because even Rudolf recognized he could not join an openly Catholic alliance. Maximilian also blocked Schweikhard's calls to admit

Saxony, Hessen-Darmstadt and other moderate Lutherans, since their membership would remove the stigma of sectarianism and thus allow Rudolf to join.

Both organizations were also divided about their primary purpose. The Palatinate and Union radicals believed religious war was inevitable and urged preparations, to be ready to strike at the best moment. The others simply saw the Union as a device to pressure the Catholics into becoming more reasonable in the ongoing negotiations. Maximilian was less belligerent than his Palatinate counterpart, but nonetheless regarded the Liga as a framework for spreading the cost of Bavarian defence among his neighbours and allies, whereas they saw it as an insurance policy and hoped its mere existence would be sufficient to deter the Protestants from doing anything foolish.

External relations provided a third area of disagreement. Anhalt and other Palatine leaders were convinced Catholics throughout Europe were conspiring to extirpate the true Protestant faith, and argued for a similarly broad war on the Catholic threat. The refusal of the others to countenance such action forced them to become increasingly secretive and pursue their own foreign policy in the Union's name without consulting the membership. The roles were reversed in the Liga where the director opposed calls to include Spain formally, fearing it would lead to Rudolf's joining and the organization becoming drawn into the Habsburg struggle against the Dutch.

THE JÜLICH-CLEVES CRISIS 1609–10

These tensions strained both alliances as they faced their first test with the contested Jülich-Cleves inheritance. The crisis represented the third outbreak of violence on the Rhine following the Cologne and Strasbourg disputes. It is generally fitted into the narrative of mounting confessional tension in the Empire, because fighting between rival Catholic and Protestant claimants threatened to draw in foreign powers. Some have even seen 1609 as the true start of the Thirty Years War, or argued that a general conflict was only postponed because it was not then in the interests of Spain and the Dutch.[31] However, the inhabitants of the Empire were perfectly capable of fighting each other when they wanted to, and did not need to wait for the approval or assistance of other powers, as 1618 was to prove. The lack of major conflict in 1609–10 stemmed from widespread opposition to violence and a general desire to negotiate a peaceful solution.

The Jülich-Cleves Inheritance

Serious issues were at stake. The disputed territories were substantial, totalling around 14,000km², and strategically situated at the end of the Spanish Road and across the south-eastern approaches to the Dutch Republic. The duchy of Cleves straddled both sides of the Rhine as it entered the Netherlands, thus separating the electorate of Cologne from Dutch territory. The duchies of Berg and Jülich lay further south, either side of Cologne, with Jülich controlling the routes between the Rhine and Meuse. The large county of Mark lay separately to the east of Berg, with the smaller county of Ravensberg around Bielefeld further north-east. The relatively insignificant county of Ravenstein was an enclave in Dutch territory. All were indisputably part of the Empire, belonging to the Westphalian Kreis, but they were at its exposed north-western corner where it met Spanish, Dutch and French territory. They were also important economically. Jülich alone had 180,000 inhabitants, making it one of the most densely populated parts of the Empire. Commerce and industry had been stimulated by exiles from both the northern and southern Netherlands, contributing to the growth of cloth-dying in Jülich, mining and metallurgy in the more forested Berg and Mark, and agriculture in Cleves.

The inhabitants shared many of the political traditions of the Netherlanders, with whom they had close confessional, cultural and economic ties. Each territory had its own Estates that together formed a union in 1496, before the lands passed into the hands of a common dynasty in 1521. Other local customs forged bonds between Jülich and Berg, as well as between Cleves and Mark, while the uneven spread of Protestantism created further ties cutting across territorial boundaries. Berg and Ravensberg were mainly Protestant by 1609, but Catholics formed half the population of Cleves and Mark and most of that in Jülich. Calvinism spread with refugees from the Netherlands in the 1570s, especially in the town of Wesel in Cleves where they almost doubled the local population of around 7,000.[32]

Duke Johann Wilhelm was already mentally ill before he succeeded his father in 1592 and, with no children to succeed him, his relations waited eagerly for his death.[33] The Habsburgs had claims stemming from intermarriage and Charles V's attempts in the 1540s to incorporate Cleves into the Netherlands. Rudolf, however, could not afford to press his case openly without compromising his standing as impartial judge, and instead sought the succession of a friendly dynasty, with imperial sequestration only to be considered should that not be possible. Saxony also had rights, and there were at least seven other parties, although only Brandenburg and Pfalz-Neuburg had credible claims through recent marriages to Johann Wilhelm's aunts. Typically, Rudolf could not make up his mind, and tried to postpone a decision so as not to alienate any of the claimants and their potential foreign sponsors. Indecision created a vacuum in Jülich-Cleves where different parties manoeuvred to secure their position should Johann Wilhelm die. As in Cologne and Strasbourg, the factions did not divide clearly along confessional lines. Duchess Jakobe von Baden-Hochberg, a devout Catholic, collaborated with the predominantly Protestant Estates to escape the influence of her husband's Catholic advisers who curried favour with Rudolf in the hope of guaranteeing their positions. The councillors persuaded Rudolf to arrest the duchess shortly before her death in 1597 on charges of imprisoning her husband, corruption and adultery. Meanwhile, the government steered a middle course between Spain and the Dutch in the hope of preserving neutrality. All the major claimants were Lutherans who grew alarmed, not at Jülich's irenicist culture, but because Rudolf's interference suggested the emperor was planning to pre-empt them by sequestrating the territories.

The conflicting dynastic, confessional and strategic interests inhibited polarization and the prospects of a peaceful settlement remained good when Johann Wilhelm died on 25 March 1609. Though the Protestant Union was then ten months old, the Liga had not yet formed and Spain and the Dutch were on the verge of concluding their Twelve Years Truce (9 April 1609). France was also not overly interested, provided neither Spain nor Austria acquired the duchies, and all the other claimants favoured an amicable settlement. Unfortunately, Rudolf was embroiled in his quarrel with Archduke Matthias and looked for a way to delay a decision without compromising his authority. A regency was established on 2 April consisting of the duke's second wife, Antoinette of Lorraine, the privy councillors and an imperial commissioner. Rudolf then

announced on 24 May that the Reichshofrat would pronounce a definitive verdict within four weeks. Both Pfalz-Neuburg and Brandenburg
interpreted these steps as intended to cut them out of their inheritance.
They closed ranks in the Treaty of Dortmund (10 June), agreeing to
reject all other claimants and establish a provisional government in
collaboration with the local Estates. They also agreed to settle their
conflicting claims within twelve months, or pass the matter to a commission of impartial princes. The implicit rejection of both Rudolf and
the Reichshofrat reflected their disillusionment with imperial justice in
the wake of the Donauwörth incident. Elector Johann Sigismund of
Brandenburg sent his brother, Margrave Ernst, as his representative to
the duchies, while Philipp Ludwig of Pfalz-Neuburg appointed his son
and heir, Wolfgang Wilhelm, to safeguard his interests. Accompanied
by a few troops, the two established themselves as the 'Possessors'
(*Possidierenden*), in defiance of both the regency government in Jülich
and Emperor Rudolf.

It is unlikely that the emperor would have done much about it if his
cousin Archduke Leopold had not intervened. Though only 23 and not
yet a cleric, Leopold had been elected as bishop of Passau and Strasbourg
as part of a Habsburg strategy to counter Bavarian influence in the
imperial church. Leopold was overconfident and believed that firm
action in Jülich would restore imperial prestige generally and raise his
own profile in the Brothers' Quarrel. Having been convinced by Leopold,
Rudolf annulled the Treaty of Dortmund on his own authority and,
without consulting the Reichshofrat, made the young archduke imperial
commissioner on 14 July. Leopold dashed to Jülich, but once in the
town he was quickly surrounded by the Possessors who raised three
times as many troops as he had.[34] Jülich had been strongly fortified in
1547–9, but Leopold lacked the men to venture beyond the walls.
Having repelled a raid to Aachen and captured Düren, the Possessors
tightened the noose, and his position looked increasingly hopeless.

Coinciding with unrest in the Habsburg lands and the formation
of the confessional alliances, the Jülich-Cleves crisis was profoundly
unsettling. The majority of princes favoured mediation and Rudolf was
obliged to accept a meeting that convened in Prague on 1 May 1610
to broker a general settlement. Archdukes Ferdinand and Maximilian
attended in person, while Archduke Albert sent an envoy. German
moderate opinion was represented by the electors of Mainz, Cologne

and Saxony, as well as Duke Heinrich Julius of Brunswick and Land-grave Ludwig of Hessen-Darmstadt. The princes pushed Rudolf to replace Leopold with a more impartial imperial commissioner, as a preliminary step to an amicable settlement. Fearing for his prestige, Rudolf made one of his snap, arbitrary decisions and enfeoffed Saxony with the entire Jülich-Cleves inheritance on 7 July. Though not unwelcome for Saxony, there was little chance of it benefiting, given that Brandenburg and Pfalz-Neuburg had now overrun all the territories, apart from the city of Jülich where Leopold still held out. The princes maintained their pressure, forcing Rudolf to reverse course and convene another peace conference that opened in Cologne in August.

French Intervention

Each delay increased the likelihood of unwelcome foreign intervention. France had already opened parallel negotiations with the Protestant Union and Savoy, leading to a marriage alliance with the latter in December 1609 and a draft military pact with the former in January 1610. The move suggested a two-pronged assault on either end of the Spanish Road, something that appeared to get under way when Savoy expelled the Spanish regiment that had been guarding the Grésin bridge since 1602. Meanwhile, Henri IV more than doubled the size of his army and assembled 22,000 men under Field Marshal de la Châtre in north-east France.[35] Nineteenth-century writers read these events through the lens of the French Revolution and Napoleon III's support of the House of Savoy against Austria in 1859, presenting Henri IV as having a Grand Design to help nations struggling to free themselves from the Spanish yoke. French preparations in fact were mere sabre-rattling intended to intimidate Spain and assert Henri's role as arbiter and peace-bringer. Having carefully fostered the king's image as guaranteeing domestic tranquillity after the Wars of Religion, the French monarchy sought now to project this on an international stage. It was an implicit challenge to Rudolf, as Henri was attempting to appropriate the positive elements of the traditional imperial role and leave the emperor with its negative associations of Habsburg oppression. France had little intention of coming to blows, particularly now that Spain had agreed its truce with the Dutch. Henri was already frustrated at the Possessors' inability to agree a division of the inheritance, and he remained suspicious of the Union because of Anhalt's attitude over the renegade duc de Bouillon. The massive military preparations were intended to overawe all other parties and render actual fighting unnecessary.

Rumours of impending intervention caused anxiety among French Catholics, who feared their king might fight Spain and the emperor. To bolster his regime and provide an excuse to delay joining the army, Henri attended the coronation of his wife, Marie de Medici, on 13 May 1610. He went to Paris the next day to prepare for her formal entry into the city, scheduled two days later. His coach was stuck in the morning traffic in the rue de la Ferronerie when François Ravaillac reached in and stabbed him. He had survived 23 previous assassination attempts, but this one proved fatal. Though the king's sudden death means we can never know his ultimate intentions, it is significant that French military preparations continued without interruption. Fearing they would be tarred as the assassin's accomplices, the Catholic zealots dropped their criticism of royal policy and joined the regency under his widow in a chorus of praise for the dead king's virtues as a peace-maker. All agreed that French foreign policy should be directed at recovering the country's former influence and accepted the crown's presentation of the military preparations as intended to induce all parties in the Jülich-Cleves dispute to reach an amicable agreement.

The inheritance dispute assumed long-term significance in this respect, because subsequent French intervention in Germany was related to this earlier episode and Henri's hallowed memory. Later, both Richelieu and Mazarin had to deal with the inherent contradictions of Henri's policy. French prestige rested on its claims to be seeking European peace, yet its arbiter role required military strength. Intervention to preserve the European balance of power necessarily involved contesting Spain and the Habsburgs as Europe's predominant powers, yet this threatened to put Catholic France on the side of heretics like the Dutch and German Protestants.

Actual intervention, when it finally came, was relatively restricted and further underlines the fact that France was not actively seeking war. Only 9,000 men were sent in August 1610 and each had signed up for only four months. They advanced slowly from Metz down the Meuse through the middle of the bishopric of Liège, having previously been granted free passage by Archduke Albert on 13 May. The situation looked tense, because other powers also mobilized. Prince Maurice of Nassau concentrated 14,000 Dutch infantry and 8,000 cavalry at Schenkenschans close to Cleves in mid July, but the statesman Oldenbarnevelt had no desire to provoke a rupture with Spain and the presence was intended mainly to demonstrate republican strength.[36] Philip III authorized Albert to support Leopold, but only if France and the Dutch actually joined the siege of Jülich. Albert did reinforce his garrisons along the frontier, but simultaneously sent a representative to the Prague congress to seek a negotiated settlement. Spain, like the Dutch, was mainly concerned with saving face. The duke of Lerma's prime preoccupation was Italy, not the Rhine, and he had no intention of letting the situation get out of hand. Albert was in constant touch with Maurice and allowed him to advance up the Rhine from Schenkenschans and to cross the river at Rheinberg.

German Intervention

The troop movements heightened anxiety in the Empire where there was little firm information about what the foreign powers actually intended. The Palatine leadership initially regarded the dispute as a private matter for Brandenburg and Pfalz-Neuburg and refused assistance. Anhalt was also reluctant to become involved until a firm alliance could be concluded with a friendly power, while the other members opposed seeking an ally precisely because they feared this would suck them into a war. Anhalt was forced to conduct his negotiations with France, England and the Dutch in secret, not revealing them until the congress that convened in Schwäbisch-Hall in January–February 1610. The Union now agreed to mobilize 5,000 men, provided the Possessors would foot the bill.

Leopold naturally appealed to the Liga for assistance, but while Mainz was prepared to offer subsidies, Maximilian of Bavaria kept the issue firmly off the agenda, because he wanted to avoid all entanglements with the Habsburgs. Leopold faced considerable difficulties collecting an army to relieve Jülich. He could not use Passau, because any men raised there would have to run the gauntlet of the Franconian and Swabian Protestants to reach the Rhine. Archduke Maximilian of the Tirol refused permission to recruit in his lands, blaming Rudolf for creating the crisis. This left only the bishopric of Strasbourg where Leopold's officers collected 1,000 cavalry and 3,000 infantry, dispersing them in the villages to conceal them from the Palatine forces nearby.

The Liga members also began collecting troops, but only for their own protection. News of these preparations alongside rumours of Leopold's activities heightened anxiety among the Protestants. The elector Palatine met the duke of Württemberg and margrave of Baden-Durlach in Heidelberg on 13 March 1610 and agreed a counterstroke without consulting the rest of the Union. Count Otto von Solms-Braunfels led 2,000 men, mainly from the territorial militia, into Strasbourg territory.[37] Leopold's commander simply repeated the Catholic tactics during the Strasbourg Bishops' War and retreated into Saverne and the other walled towns. The invaders ran out of money and their ill-disciplined troops went home after a few weeks, exposing the Union's weakness.

Nonetheless, the operation prevented Leopold's forces moving north to relieve Jülich where the situation was increasingly desperate, particularly after Maurice intercepted other men who had been raised in Liège in May. The three Protestant princes rallied the Union for a second attempt, assembling 7,300 infantry and 2,500 cavalry in their territories and billeting some on Würzburg and Bamberg, partly to intimidate the Catholics but also simply to save money. Meanwhile, the margraves of Ansbach and Baden-Durlach led a second army across the Strasbourg bridge to attack Leopold's men.[38] These retreated into the towns again, but this time the Unionists had brought artillery with them, and soon captured Dachstein, Molsheim and Mutzig. However, Leopold's cavalry still remained at large in the countryside, while the remaining infantry held out in Saverne. Though larger and better equipped than the first invasion force, the Union army was also more expensive. The Strasbourg burghers resented the princes' conspiratorial politics and stopped supplying food to the troops, whose operations ground to a halt. A local truce was agreed on 10 August to allow time for the duke of Lorraine and the Alsatian nobles to broker a mutual withdrawal.

By then, Jülich's fate was sealed. Leopold had managed to escape in May, leaving the 1,500-strong garrison inside. The arrival of Union reinforcements brought the Possessors' blockading force up to 2,200 horse and 8,000 foot by 28 July, at last large enough for a proper siege. The arrival of Maurice and Châtre added a further 23,000 troops, and the garrison surrendered on 1 September after four weeks in return for free passage to join the rest of Leopold's men in Upper Alsace.

The French and Dutch presence was a matter of saving face, because the siege had progressed beyond the point where they could remain on the sidelines. Had Leopold's garrison been less diligent and surrendered sooner, neither Maurice nor Châtre would have intervened. As it was, the latter's painfully slow progress down the Meuse raised suspicions among the Protestants of French betrayal. Châtre did not arrive until 19 August after the city's outworks had already fallen, and could scarcely wait to leave once the garrison marched out. The Dutch were gone a week later, leaving only a small detachment in Jülich under Captain Pithan. They were joined the following year by another garrison in Wesel, the strategic crossing-point over the Rhine in Cleves. Dutch influence there matched that in Emden, with similar intentions and effects. The town formally converted to Calvinism in 1612, while its garrison threatened Spanish communications with the places taken by Spinola east of the Ijssel in 1605–6. Other than this, all parties moved swiftly to disengage. The Union and Liga agreed mutual withdrawals on 24 October 1610 and had disbanded their forces by the new year, while Leopold retreated across Swabia to Passau in December.

Consequences

This first 'Jülich War' was not a dress rehearsal for the Thirty Years War, but it offered some military lessons that the later belligerents failed to learn. Operations had been relatively brief and were largely restricted to Alsace and parts of the Lower Rhine. Leopold probably never mustered more than 7,000 men at any one time, while his opponents fielded 30,000 at the climax in August 1610, plus 23,000 French and Dutch auxiliaries. The Liga mobilized up to 19,000 men by September, but had not been engaged. This effort completely exhausted all parties. Two of the remaining three Pfalz-Neuburg companies in Jülich had to be disbanded in 1611 after mutinying over their pay arrears, while Brandenburg retained just 100 men there and another 400 in Aachen. Leopold claimed his involvement cost him 2.6 million fl., while the damage in the Austrian part of Alsace alone was estimated at 1.14 million. Leopold had only managed to travel to Jülich in the first place because the Spanish ambassador had loaned him the money. Spanish passivity was imposed partly through fear that the Army of Flanders would demand its back pay if ordered to the front. French involvement cost 5.38 million fl., or one-third of the war chest Henri had built up since 1598. Even neutral territories suffered, like the Tirol, which was forced to raise its wine tax in January 1612, triggering peasant unrest that lasted until September 1614.[39]

The financial consequences deepened the political damage to both confessional alliances where arguments over policy were now complicated by disputes over who would foot the bill. The crisis broke before either group was fully formed, and both experienced an influx of new members seeking security but who were swiftly disillusioned by what they found. Leopold was frustrated by Bavaria's refusal to see the dispute as a Liga matter. Though the Liga congress agreed defensive mobilization in August 1610, most members regretted this because of the expense and the fact that recruitment made them targets for Unionist billeting. They resented Bavaria's continued opposition to Habsburg membership, fearing they would not be safe until the Austrian archdukes could join. They vented their feelings by failing to pay their contributions in full, leaving Bavaria to make good the shortfall.

The impact was deeper still on the Union because this had been directly involved. Neither of the Possessors paid for the assistance they received, while the Palatinate was unable to find the 300,000 fl. it needed for the 1610 campaign. Though the Union relied heavily on militiamen, its operations went way over budget, with the expenses swollen by the hordes of camp followers accompanying the army. The margrave of Ansbach marched the 18,000 men, women and children with their 4,000 wagons out of Alsace in October 1610 to Ulm to demand payment. With the troops on their doorstep, the Swabian and Franconian members had no choice but to dig deep into their pockets. The shambles dispelled any rejoicing at Jülich's capture, and deepened the suspicions surrounding Anhalt's conspiratorial leadership, especially as the original inheritance dispute remained unresolved.

8

On the Brink?

EMPEROR MATTHIAS

The Jülich-Cleves dispute inflicted crippling damage on Rudolf and was swiftly followed by a resumption of the Brothers' Quarrel. Yet, Rudolf's death and Archduke Matthias's succession in 1612 saw many problems being tackled with considerable success. The Liga was dissolved, while the Protestant Union was marginalized and on the point of collapse by 1618. Imperial institutions revived, as the Reichstag met again in 1613, this time concluding a Recess, and the imperial courts resumed their activity. Some confidence had been restored in the Habsburgs and there was little to suggest that the Empire was on the brink of catastrophe. However, the period of recovery was too short to make up the ground that had been lost since the 1570s. Crucially, the imperial dynasty remained relatively weak and therefore vulnerable if its opponents were prepared to take the risk and attack. This weakness was personal, as well as structural. Though more dynamic than his brother, Matthias, now 55, was worn out by the long struggle to gain the throne and had little energy to rule once he became emperor.

The Final Act in the Brothers' Quarrel

The transition from Rudolf to Matthias came in two stages. Matthias first stripped his brother of his remaining power, and then persuaded the electors to accept him as successor. The first round of their quarrel had left both brothers exhausted and at the mercy of their Estates after 1608 (see Chapter 4, pp.106–15). The deadlock was broken by Archduke Leopold who, though thwarted at Jülich, still had his army, which regrouped in Passau in December 1610. Led by Colonel Ramée,

this was increased to 4,000 horse and 8,000 foot by recruiting unemployed veterans from the Turkish War with the covert assistance of
the Austrian War Council. Undaunted by his recent setbacks, Leopold
saw a new chance now that the Bohemian Estates had disbanded their
militia, in February 1610. He believed Rudolf would name him his
successor if he delivered the emperor from his semi-imprisonment by
the Protestants in the Hradschin palace since 1609. It was a high-risk
strategy, because Leopold had not even paid for the Jülich War and
could start a new operation only by promising the men Rudolf would
reward them once they reached Prague.

The assembly of what became known as the 'Passauers' raised fears
of a resumption of violence. The moderate princes pressed Rudolf to
negotiate. Heinrich Julius of Brunswick managed to convene a meeting
with the emperor, but Rudolf merely used this as an opportunity to
rail against his feckless relations. Eventually, Archdukes Ferdinand and
Maximilian and the representatives of Matthias and Albert apologized
to Rudolf, handing him the ripped shreds of their pact against him from
April 1606. In return, the emperor promised to pay Leopold to disband
his army. Bishop Klesl, Matthias's adviser, rightly regarded this as
worthless, since Rudolf lacked the motive and the means to keep his
side of the bargain. Colonel Ramée led his unpaid and increasingly
desperate men into Upper Austria on 21 December 1610 where they
stayed for five weeks, doing 2 million fl. worth of damage, before
crossing into Bohemia with 269 wagons full of booty. Another detachment, still in the bishopric of Strasbourg, meanwhile plundered Archduke Maximilian's territories in Upper Alsace.

Having got their fingers burnt in 1606–9, neither Rudolf nor Matthias
did anything, recognizing that countermeasures would entail further
concessions to their Estates who alone had money. Only Heinrich Julius
dashed about trying to find funds to bribe Ramée to disband. Leopold,
increasingly embarrassed by his army's behaviour, joined it to enter
Prague from the west on 15 February 1611. The Estates had recalled
their militia and blocked the Charles Bridge, denying access to the larger
part of the city across the Moldau. The Passau cavalry stole the money
Heinrich Julius had collected and took off, leaving the infantry, who
threatened to defect to the Estates in the hope of being paid. Leopold's
bluff had been called, and Rudolf refused to speak to him. The young
archduke scuttled out of the city at night on 10 March.

Matthias seized his chance, and having scraped together 2,500 soldiers, he set out from Vienna, gathering Austrian and Moravian levies in the name of restoring order. He had 18,000 men by the time he entered Prague two weeks later and could now negotiate from a position of strength. A face-saving deal was struck with Leopold, blaming the entire episode on Ramée who was condemned to death (although he managed to escape). The remaining Passau troops were paid off. Matthias was credited by the German and Bohemian Protestants with having saved them from the murderous Passauers. Written confirmation of the Bohemian Protestant privileges also went down well. Meanwhile, Spain dropped Leopold as a liability, backed Matthias as Rudolf's successor, and gave him a welcome present of 200,000 ducats. The Estates of the Bohemian lands met in a general diet that April and accepted Matthias as their king. The new monarch threatened to cut off food supplies to the Hradschin, until Rudolf surrendered the crown in May 1611. The emperor was confined to his apartments and placed on a strict budget. Matthias now had Austria, Hungary and all Bohemia, while Ferdinand remained ruler of Inner Austria, Archduke Maximilian retained the Tirol and Leopold was still bishop of Strasbourg and Passau.

The Imperial Election of 1612

The electors met in Nuremberg from September to November 1611 to debate the imperial succession. Regardless of confession, they wanted an orderly transition of power to quell the civil war in the Habsburg lands and resolve tension in the Empire. The pushy Leopold was completely unacceptable to them. The ecclesiastical electors favoured the mature, capable Albert who was still in Brussels, but Saxony blocked him as too closely associated with Spain, while Maximilian was reluctant to put himself forward. Matthias was still distrusted as a schemer and considered by the Catholics as too soft towards the Protestants. The delay in accepting him prompted Rudolf to fill his last days with feverish plots to recover his lands. Rumours spread that the elderly emperor would marry the elector Palatine's widowed mother, join the Protestant Union and create a new army under the margrave of Ansbach.[1]

Fearing trouble, the electors agreed to reconvene on 21 May 1612 to elect a king of the Romans. Having been present in Nuremberg as electoral Bohemian representative, Klesl fully appreciated the obstacles facing his master's election. He made careful preparations, persuading Spain and the other archdukes in December 1611 to make Matthias their only candidate, thus removing Albert from the running. Matthias married his cousin Anna of Tirol on 4 December, raising the prospect of children and an orderly succession from his line. His election motto – 'concord is stronger than light' – clearly signalled his determination to foster unity between the confessional parties. The ground was ready when Rudolf's death on 20 January 1612 made the forthcoming meeting a full imperial election.

The moment was opportune, given Protestant weakness. Elector Johann Georg had only just succeeded his elder brother, Christian II, in Saxony and was eager to get the whole business resolved as rapidly as possible. Palatine policy was hamstrung by Friedrich IV's death on 8 October 1610 at the height of the Jülich-Cleves crisis and, as in 1583, leaving another under-aged successor. Frederick V was just fourteen and the Calvinist Heidelberg court selected the mature and able Johann II of Zweibrücken as regent. However, Lutheran relations in Pfalz-Neuburg challenged the arrangement, and the rivalry consumed all Johann's energies and frustrated Anhalt's plans to use the imperial interregnum to effect constitutional changes.[2] The electors met in Frankfurt as scheduled and after a discussion in which the Palatine representative was accused of deliberately trying to delay matters, Matthias was elected unanimously on 13 June.

Klesl

The new emperor was already exhausted. While personally inclined towards peace and genuinely wanting to settle the Empire's problems, he never had a head for detail. He was content simply to enjoy life with his new wife half his age amid the splendour of the imperial court. Policy was left to Bishop Klesl who now emerged fully to the fore as the dominant figure in imperial politics. Klesl's role remains controversial and was already subject to bitter criticism at the time, enemies casting doubt on his sincerity and accusing him of deliberately leaving problems unresolved to make himself indispensable. Others have been more generous regarding his motives, but still interpret his efforts as a futile struggle against the surge towards war.[3]

Klesl was unable to do much about the decline in the emperor's international standing. The growth of Spanish power had overshadowed the Austrian Habsburgs despite their retention of the imperial title. The Empire's formal neutrality throughout all the major wars in western Europe after 1562 further reduced it as a factor in international relations. Nonetheless, the imperial court had remained an important centre for diplomacy, not least because the emperor had tried to mediate peaceful settlements in those conflicts. The preoccupation with the Turks and Rudolf's growing aloofness reduced the emperor's presence in the west from the 1580s. Permanent envoys were no longer maintained in western capitals, leaving the imperial government to rely on the Fugger news-letters (an early equivalent of Reuters) and information supplied by Brussels and Madrid that often gave a misleading impression of events. The failure of the Turkish War further dented imperial prestige; James I of England took a particularly dim view, having believed the initial claims for a new crusade.[4]

Klesl retained the eastern orientation of the Empire, partly because it was initially far from clear that the Turkish truce of 1606 would last and also because the Ottoman menace was a useful device to rally support behind Matthias. This was also used in domestic politics to head off the Estates' attempt to exploit the transition of power in 1612 to extort further concessions. The Protestants pushed Matthias to convene a general assembly of all Habsburg Estates, intending to use the meeting to forge a closer confederation along the lines of the Upper and Lower Austrian alliance from 1608 (Chapter 4, pp.110–12). Klesl lanced this with a demand for new taxes to repair the Military Frontier. This was backed by the Hungarians who, in any case, were largely satisfied with the autonomy they had obtained in 1608 and abstained from the pro-posed assembly. Klesl was able to negotiate with each province in turn, securing their agreement to amortize 21 million florins of Rudolf's 30 million fl. debts in 1615–16. Though the Reichstag voted additional taxes in 1613, there was little enthusiasm for renewed war against the Ottomans and Klesl wisely accepted confirmation and extension of the truce in 1615.

'Composition' or Succession?

Any attempts to rebuild international standing had to follow resolution of the Empire's internal problems. The most urgent task was to dissolve the two confessional alliances, and pave the way for a more general pacification. In addition to the unresolved question of the Jülich-Cleves inheritance, the Empire needed to settle the Guelphs' dispute with Brunswick and the religious cases in the cities. Not only was the Union still demanding the full restoration of Donauwörth, but Protestants had used the interregnum to seize power from the Catholic council in Aachen. The unrest symbolized the emperor's declining authority: Aachen was the traditional venue for imperial coronations, but Matthias had been forced to use Frankfurt instead. Klesl was determined to restore imperial prestige and recognized that reviving faith in imperial justice was an essential prerequisite of this. However, his plans went further, to tackle the deeper, underlying problems as well. He intended nothing short of a resolution of confessional tension through a policy known as 'composition'. This derived from the contemporary concept of *amicabilis compositio*, or friendly compromise over religion which was to be negotiated outside the formal imperial framework. The idea had been first proposed by the Palatinate at the 1603 Reichstag, when it pressed for Protestants and Catholics to meet in two separate groups, rather than the customary three hierarchical colleges. Whereas the Palatine proposal aimed to fuse religion and politics, Klesl hoped to detach both through a bi-partisan committee of equal numbers of Protestants and Catholics to resolve the contentious issues separately, so as not to disrupt the smooth running of imperial institutions. The plan was encouraged by the imperial treasurer, Geizkofler, a Lutheran who had long favoured an amicable settlement and maintained a long correspondence with Klesl discussing the idea.

The strategy appears strange at first glance. Like many converts, Klesl pursued his new Catholic faith with greater vigour than those born into it, and he had played a major part in stemming the Lutheran advance into Lower Austria. Protestant princes regarded his sudden apparent readiness to compromise with suspicion, while the Catholics grew alarmed, and doubted the wisdom of giving him the cardinal's hat that he received in December 1615. The new strategy was in fact a continuation of Klesl's previous policy but applied with greater vigour and coherence now that his master was emperor, and no longer merely archduke. The consolidation of Catholicism within the Habsburg lands was to continue, but it was to be coupled with a more pragmatic approach in the rest of the Empire. He is reported as often telling Protestant princes that he did not believe Catholicism would ever fully recover, and he appears to have accepted the erosion of the imperial church as irreversible, at least in the medium term. It is noticeable that he dropped Rudolf's earlier opposition to the administrator of Magdeburg taking his seat when the Reichstag reconvened in 1613, arguing that this was a political rather than spiritual office. In short, the intention of composition was to bring Catholics and Protestants sufficiently close together again to make the Empire manageable, and through this, allow them to find common spiritual ground as the tensions ebbed away.

The Catholics were immediately suspicious because of the policy's similarity with the Palatine political programme and the lack of any constitutional precedent for the proposed bi-partisan committee. They felt Klesl was putting the cart before the horse, given the unresolved question of the imperial succession. The electors had given Matthias and his new wife an elaborately decorated crib as a wedding present in a clear message to produce an heir and end the doubt over the Habsburgs' future. Anna was only 27, so there was still plenty of ground for hope, but despite rumours of pregnancies, the couple remained childless and it rapidly became obvious that the 1612 election had merely postponed the dominant question from Rudolf's reign. The matter became pressing, given Matthias's ill-health and his wife's growing obesity, which contributed to her death on 15 December 1618. Her loss plunged the gouty, but previously jovial emperor into terminal depression.

Beer George

Klesl was determined to postpone the question of the succession until his composition policy bore fruit, not only to prolong his political influence, but also to negotiate with the rival candidates from a position of strength. He won some support from moderate Catholics like Schweikhard of Mainz, who had long urged compromise. His programme also appealed to Johann Georg of Saxony, because it was intended to stabilize the 1555 settlement. Like Matthias, the new Saxon elector belonged in character to an earlier political era, sharing the emperor's love of Renaissance display, hunting, good humour and heavy drinking. The latter trait was so pronounced in Johann Georg that it earned him the sobriquets of 'Beer George' (*Bierjörg*) and the 'Merseberg Beer King'. As the younger brother, he had gone on a fourteen-month educational trip to Italy in 1601, returning with little prospect of inheriting power. His elder brother, Elector Christian II, already sported the characteristic Saxon 'beer belly' at the age of 28. Having taken part in a tournament in full armour on 23 July 1611, he climbed off his horse, gulped beer to cool down and was felled by a heart attack.

There seemed little to suggest that Johann Georg would fare better, but he was to reign 45 years, seeing out the entire Thirty Years War. Unlike the industrious Maximilian of Bavaria, Beer George was lazy, spending his time drinking and hunting (he notched up a tally of 113,629 kills between 1611 and 1653), and has entered history as an incompetent who squandered Saxony's political capital by allowing others to displace him as leader of the German Protestants.[5] Certainly, the new elector devolved much decision-making to his privy council, but this was in line with his predecessors and the councillors stuck to the existing policy of defending the Augsburg settlement. Saxon government involved lengthy consultations with advisers who offered their opinions orally, making it difficult to reconstruct Johann Georg's role. He seems to have rarely intervened and generally to have followed their advice that was always presented as a unanimous memorandum masking what must have often been heated preliminary discussions. He certainly loathed papists and Calvinists in roughly equal measure but, like Klesl, distinguished between his personal feelings and pragmatic politics. He greatly enjoyed meeting visiting dignitaries who generally departed favourably impressed. A visit from Matthias was a great success, but Johann Georg even managed to get on well with Catholic hardliners like Ferdinand of Styria who shared his passion for hunting. However, he found it hard to stick to his verbal promises once the bonhomie of the moment faded and harsh political realities intruded once more.

Frederick V

Whereas Johann Georg's beer culture looked back to the Empire's past as a network of personal relationships, the wine-drinkers of the Rhenish Palatinate embraced a very different ethos. The regent handed over government to the young Frederick V in July 1614. The new elector was more serious and, in some respects, more talented than his father, but he was also more ambitious and obstinate.[6] He fully believed in the existence of a Catholic plot to extirpate German Protestantism and convert the Empire into a Habsburg hereditary monarchy. For him, the defence of Protestantism could not be detached from the princes' German Freedom. His firm Calvinism convinced him of the righteousness of his cause and induced an unshakeable faith in ultimate victory. Certain that God was on his side, his motto was 'Rule me, Lord, according to your word'. In social and political terms, however, his faith was far from the spartan Puritanism that was then taking root among the inhabitants of English and Dutch towns. He had been chosen for a divine purpose because of his dignity as senior secular elector and his family's honourable heritage in imperial politics. His lofty outlook was greatly inflated by his marriage to Elizabeth, daughter of James I, negotiated by the regent Johann II in 1611, and intended to link the Protestant Union to the powerful Stuart kingdom. James I agreed a six-year alliance with the Union in April 1612, and was followed by the Dutch who concluded a treaty for fifteen years in May 1613.

Frederick travelled to England to fetch his bride and was entertained at a wedding banquet that cost his father-in-law £53,294. The festivities were presided over by George Abbot, the Puritan archbishop of Canterbury, who remained in correspondence with Elizabeth once she departed for her new home in April 1613. Abbot and Christian of Anhalt saw the world as they wanted, believing James to be firmly committed to an international alliance ready to battle the Antichrist. James was in fact one of the few entirely sensible European monarchs, and much preferred peace to war. For him, the marriage was intended as part of a wider strategy to balance the hostile forces in Europe. Having placed his daughter in the Protestant camp, the king planned to find a Spanish bride for his son, the future Charles I.[7]

The newly-weds travelled in style, accompanied by an entourage of 4,000 in 34 decorated barges up the Rhine to reach Heidelberg on

7 June. Their arrival provided an excuse for more celebrations, including a tournament that had become a feature of Protestant princely gatherings since the wedding of Duke Johann Friedrich of Württemberg to the elector of Brandenburg's daughter in 1609.[8] Frederick liked to attend tournaments dressed as figures from classical myth and history chosen to accentuate his challenge to the Habsburgs. He appeared as Jason the Argonaut, the man who stole the golden fleece, the symbol adopted as the Habsburg's highest chivalric order. He also dressed as Scipio, conqueror of Carthage, a veiled threat to Spain where the modern city of Carthagena lay. The choice of Arminius was more blatant, since he was the first-century German chieftain who trounced the Roman legions. The 1613 celebrations included a theatrical performance in which figures representing Germania, surrounded by nymphs (a.k.a. the Kreise), commented in verse on the recent Reichstag, blaming its unsatisfactory outcome on Spain, the Jesuits and the Capuchins. The message was clear: the Protestant princes stood solidly for German unity and liberty that were threatened by malevolent foreign forces. Lavishly illustrated books depicting the festivities ensured that others further afield got the point, including James who was sent a copy in English translation.

The Heidelberg court now assumed a more regal atmosphere, befitting the new royal relations. French language and culture were already becoming fashionable before 1613, thanks to the young elector's upbringing at the Huguenot court of the duc de Bouillon in Sedan. It helped set the Palatinate further apart from the bulk of German princes who remained embedded in the late humanist world of Latin and German, and had received their education in German universities teaching the traditions of imperial law. They were more likely to distinguish between person and power than the proto-absolutist French courtly ethos that brooked no criticism of the monarch.[9]

Christian of Anhalt's influence flourished in the new environment. He had already acquired a freer hand during the regency after 1610 when he began to pursue foreign policy as he saw fit. The increasingly aged group of privy councillors were already too overworked to interfere in his running of the Union. The Dutch Nassau and Wetterau counts who had assumed a prominent place in Palatine government since the 1580s, lost interest when the Twelve Years Truce removed the threat to their region after 1609. Johann VI and Johann VII of Nassau both left Palatine service, leaving Count Johann Albrecht of Solms-Braunfels as court chamberlain and nominal head of government. Their departure created a void that was filled by men without any formal appointment in the administration, like the Dohna brothers from ducal Prussia who played a significant role in Frederick's education after 1606 and were soon employed as Anhalt's secret envoys.

Henri IV's murder convinced Anhalt that God had selected Frederick to smash the Catholic conspiracy. It became increasingly difficult for both of them to see beyond the fantasy bubble of the Heidelberg court, especially after the publication of a series of tracts allegedly by a 'Christian Rosenkreuz' in 1614–21. These purported to contain the work of the Rosicrucians, a (fictitious) secret society of wise and benevolent philosophers who had unlocked the mystical keys of divine understanding and were now emerging to guide mankind to a new enlightened age. The entire thing had been fabricated by Johann Valentin Andreae, the son of the orthodox Lutheran superintendent who had organized the Württemberg territorial church. Already deeply involved in cabalistic texts, Anhalt readily believed this nonsense and it reinforced his conviction that the Union had been chosen by God to forge a new age.

The 1613 Reichstag

Frederick and Anhalt searched for an opportunity to recover the initiative lost in the wake of the Jülich-Cleves crisis. Their opportunity came when Matthias summoned his first Reichstag for 1613. This was the first meeting since the disaster of 1608 and offered the chance to rally the Protestants solidly behind the Union by engineering another crisis. It was also the first test of Klesl's composition policy and he prepared the session by proposing a wide range of concessions intended to isolate the Palatinate by convincing the moderates of his sincerity. He ordered an investigation into all the complaints about imperial justice, including the four monasteries dispute, and suspended the imperial ban against Aachen. The readmission of the Magdeburg administrator in the Reichstag represented a serious attempt to restore faith, since his exclusion had triggered the collapse of the Reichskammergericht Visitation in 1588 and had led to a backlog of 300 outstanding appeals. To ensure no misunderstanding, Klesl wrote personally to many Protestants, including Anhalt, before the meeting opened to stress his desire for an amicable settlement.

These proposals naturally alarmed the Catholics and were opposed by some of his colleagues within the Habsburg administrations. Johann Ludwig von Ulm vehemently rejected what he regarded as appeasement. His criticism was significant, because his office as imperial vice-chancellor made him the link between the Habsburg agencies in Vienna and the imperial chancellery in Mainz that formally oversaw institutions like the Reichstag. Duke Maximilian of Bavaria rightly suspected Klesl's suggestions as an attempt to isolate the Catholic Liga. He was already struggling to assert his authority over the alliance. In late October 1611 he had sent 10,000 troops into Salzburg and imprisoned Archbishop Raitenau, who had long opposed the Liga and Bavarian influence in general. Maximilian disarmed papal protests that Raitenau was a good Catholic by revealing that the archbishop had ten children by a long-term mistress, Salome Alt. Raitenau remained locked away in his own palace until his death six years later, but the Salzburg canons refused to bow to Bavaria and elected a successor equally determined to avoid joining a confessional alliance.[10] The duke had greater success on the Rhine where, following the death of their uncle Ernst in 1612, he assisted his younger brother Ferdinand to obtain Cologne and Ernst's other bishoprics. Ferdinand had been educated by the Jesuits from the age of nine and became one of the order's greatest patrons. His religious views were closer to his post-Tridentine brother than their uncle who remained a Renaissance Catholic. He was also relatively young and inexperienced, and quite prepared to defer to his older brother, provided Maximilian handled him sensitively.[11] However, this failed to prevent Schweikhard of Mainz from pushing for Saxony to be admitted as a third Liga director, to end the alliance's confessional character and open the door to Habsburg membership. Klesl took up this demand from 1612 as a way of either subordinating the Liga or rendering it innocuous. Maximilian was hard-pressed to persuade the members to resist when the Liga convened in Frankfurt in March 1613 to prepare for the coming Reichstag. As soon as he left, Mainz persuaded the others in a separate session to embrace Klesl's plans.

The Unionists met simultaneously in the Protestant imperial city of Rothenburg in Franconia, where they were cajoled by Anhalt to endorse the radical Palatine programme. They refused to disband as long as the Liga existed, and reiterated the by-now customary demands for religious parity, freedom of conscience and Donauwörth's restoration. When they reassembled in Regensburg for the Reichstag that opened on 13 August, the members mostly remembered their lines and joined the Palatine representative in another walkout when their demands were not immediately met in full. This time, however, the duke of Pfalz-Neuburg broke ranks by remaining behind, along with Saxony and other moderates who joined the Catholics in agreeing a Recess by the customary majority vote on 22 October. This granted limited aid for Habsburg frontier defence and agreed that the Reichstag would reconvene in May 1614 to resume talks for a compromise. Though meagre, this result at least preserved a semblance of unity and avoided the affront to imperial dignity of the 1608 session. Yet, it was also clear to Klesl that he would achieve nothing so long as the rival alliances existed and he found excuses to delay the Reichstag indefinitely (it did not reconvene until 1640).

The Habsburgs and the Liga

Klesl now tried to undermine the alliances more directly. He already had a foot in the Liga's door thanks to Schweikhard of Mainz, so he concentrated his efforts in this direction first, to remove the Palatinate's excuse for prolonging the Union. Schweikhard led the weaker members in rewriting the Liga's charter when it reconvened in Regensburg after the end of the Reichstag. The Swabians were detached from Bavarian supervision and entrusted to Archduke Maximilian of the Tirol as a third director, while the organization was formally named 'Christian Defence' to disassociate it from sectarianism. The new organization was endorsed at a further congress at Augsburg in March 1614 when its charter was renewed for nine years.

The new director favoured irenicist reconciliation between the confessions and had long opposed the Liga. Pushed by his relation Karl, margrave of Burgau, and other Swabian Catholics, the archduke eventually assumed his directorship in April 1615. The hard-line bishops of Augsburg and Ellwangen opted to remain in the Bavarian directory, while the other Swabians failed to pay their contributions. The Tirol government could not fund the organization alone and plans for a new regional militia had to be scrapped. Nonetheless, the Habsburg presence rendered the Liga useless as a separate platform for Bavarian interests. Recognizing that he had been outmanoeuvred, Duke Maximilian formed a shadow alliance with his more immediate neighbours in March 1614 that remained in being when he formally resigned his own directorship on 14 February 1616.[12] Klesl moved swiftly to wind up the remnants of the Liga, which was ordered by Matthias to disband on 3 April 1617. The Liga's demise indicated the strength of the imperial recovery under Matthias, as well as the impossibility of a separate Bavarian-led Catholic group without Habsburg approval. It also prevented the Catholic princes from becoming involved again in the Jülich inheritance.

Renewed Crisis in Jülich-Cleves, 1614

The Jülich-Cleves inheritance question had remained open since 1610, because Brandenburg and Pfalz-Neuburg possession rested on military victory, not recognized rights, and their administration was not fully accepted by the various Estates. The uncertainty allowed Saxony and other claimants to renew their own demands. The Union was unable to broker agreement because the conflicting claims became entwined in the dispute between Zweibrücken and Pfalz-Neuburg over the Palatine regency in 1610–14. Matthias confirmed Rudolf's enfeoffment of Saxony with the inheritance in February 1613, but was not in a position to uphold this.

Whereas the first dispute saw two Protestant claimants jointly opposing imperial sequestration, the second was characterized more clearly by confessional polarization. The Brandenburg governor of the duchy, Margrave Ernst, converted to Calvinism in 1610 and actively promoted it in the areas garrisoned by his troops. The public conversion of his brother in Brandenburg three years later stemmed from personal conviction, since the electorate's association with Calvinism undermined support for its claims to Jülich among the Lutheran princes. Meanwhile, the Pfalz-Neuburg governor, Wolfgang Wilhelm, had grown impatient and already opened secret talks with Archduke Leopold in 1609. Encouraged by Zúñiga, the Spanish ambassador, he turned to his Wittelsbach relations in Munich, converting to Catholicism on 19 July 1613, without telling his father. His marriage to Duke Maximilian's daughter Magdalena four months later completed his reorientation before his father's death in 1614 gave him control of Pfalz-Neuburg.[13]

Brandenburg and Pfalz-Neuburg officials were no longer speaking to each other by the beginning of 1614. Wolfgang Wilhelm became convinced the Brandenburgers were plotting a coup with Dutch assistance:

300 Dutch troops reinforced Captain Pithan in Jülich in May, ejecting the Pfalz-Neuburg company, while others stood ready in nearby Moers. Wolfgang Wilhelm retaliated, expelling the Brandenburg administration from Düsseldorf and raising another 900 troops. It was an unfortunate misunderstanding. The new Brandenburg governor, Electoral Prince Georg Wilhelm, was indeed plotting a coup, but the Dutch had no intention of assisting – indeed Oldenbarnevelt had tried to reconcile the two claimants and the reinforcements were intended to enable Pithan to prevent them coming to blows. The Dutch sent another 2,000 men to Jülich in July to stabilize the situation, while using their financial muscle to restrain Brandenburg which had raised 3,900 men it could not afford. Peter Hoefyser, the receiver of the Dutch Admiralty, brokered a 100,000 fl. loan at 8 per cent. Since Brandenburg could not pay even the interest, it was obliged to follow Dutch wishes in the region.[14]

Further misunderstandings followed, since Spain interpreted the Dutch military build-up as a challenge to its influence on the Lower Rhine. Archduke Albert and Spinola decided that a show of force was needed to induce the Dutch to stick to the Twelve Years Truce. With Lerma preoccupied with Italy, they mobilized 13,300 infantry and 1,300 cavalry from the Army of Flanders on their own initiative. By the time the men were ready it had become clear that Oldenbarnevelt actually wanted to avoid war, but it was too late to return meekly to barracks without losing face. Spinola set out from Maastricht on 22 August 1614, reaching Aachen two days later where he used the convenient excuse of enforcing a renewed mandate against the Protestant council to justify his presence. He then pressed on to Düren, joining Wolfgang Wilhelm's men in occupying the duchies of Jülich and Berg. There was little bloodshed, because all parties studiously avoided contact. Spinola did attack the strategic crossing point of Wesel, under Dutch occupation since 1611, but the garrison surrendered after only 36 shots on 5 September. Maurice and a roughly equivalent number of Dutch troops meanwhile secured the rest of Cleves, occupied Mark and reinforced the Jülich garrison.

Talks opened in Xanten (in Cleves) on 13 October, leading to a draft partition treaty under French and English mediation on 12 November. The inheritance was split according to the historic associations of Jülich-Berg and Cleves-Mark. Since the latter were smaller states, Ravensberg and Ravenstein were assigned to them, even though Ravensberg had formally been associated with Jülich. Brandenburg and Pfalz-Neuburg were to draw lots to see who got which half. Since the proposed partition roughly reflected the situation on the ground, it effectively sanctioned the result of the Spanish and Dutch intervention. Brandenburg disbanded its troops by 1616, while those of Pfalz-Neuburg were drastically reduced. Spain and the Republic agreed to withdraw and though they removed most of their men, they left garrisons in the towns they had seized. These were adjusted by further minor operations in 1615–16, while the two claimants negotiated for guarantees against renewed military intervention.

Spanish intervention significantly enhanced its strategic position in north-west Europe, securing 10 Cleves towns, 28 in Jülich and 24 in Berg and Mark. The capture of Wesel along with Rheinberg and Orsoy gave Spain three major Rhine crossings, reopening communications with the other garrisons east of the Ijssel that had been cut by Dutch intervention in 1610. Though reinforced, the Dutch garrison in Jülich was now isolated and the Republic's gains were less significant. Maurice had taken the Rhine crossing of Emmerich in Cleves, as well as most of the towns in Mark. He went on to build a new fort between Bonn and the city of Cologne, satirically called *Pfaffenmütze* (Priest's Cap) to overawe the elector. Nonetheless, his positions were outflanked by Spanish troops to either side. Both Spain and the Dutch had become involved in the Jülich crisis against their will, and though they extracted rewards, they showed little desire to fight. The rival garrisons avoided confrontation until after the Truce expired in April 1621.

The Imperial Recovery

The crisis worked in Klesl's favour by undermining the Protestant Union for him. Not only did Pfalz-Neuburg defect to the Liga, but other members stopped paying their contributions. Brandenburg alone owed 160,000 fl. by December 1613, refusing to pay, on the ground that its actions in Jülich were for the common cause. Renewed action by the duke of Wolfenbüttel to seize the city of Brunswick in 1615 wrecked any chance of widening the membership to the northern Protestants. The Palatinate was also losing the political argument after the second walkout from the Reichstag isolated the Unionists within the Empire. A Protestant judge took the unprecedented step of resigning from the

Reichskammergericht in 1614 when the presiding Catholic judge breached the hallowed procedure of entrusting religious cases to a confessionally balanced review panel.[15] Yet the Palatinate was unable to extract any advantage from this, because Klesl's efforts had reconciled most Protestants to imperial justice.

The number of complaints about breaches of the religious peace dropped dramatically after 1612, while the Reichshofrat's caseload soared from under 200 disputes a year to 440 by 1618. The increased business was not so much a sign of mounting tension than one of the princes' greater willingness to submit their perennial family and feudal disputes to imperial arbitration. Disputes over inheritance, such as those in Jülich, Hessen or Baden, were no longer seen in stark confessional terms, and even the Palatine government dropped its objections to the court's jurisdiction and let it resolve a border dispute with the bishop of Speyer in 1615. Much of this was due to Matthias's more relaxed style of rule. Unlike Rudolf, he accepted Saxon advice and ensured that the Reichshofrat consulted the electors in controversial cases before issuing a verdict.

THE USKOK WAR AND THE HABSBURG SUCCESSION 1615–17

The Uskok War 1615–17

The main threat to peace was not confessional tension in the Empire, but the continued uncertainty surrounding the Habsburg succession. Matters were brought to a head by renewed trouble on the Ottoman–Habsburg frontier that led to far more serious fighting than that around Jülich.[16] The unsatisfactory outcome of the Turkish War saw large numbers of refugees joining the already overcrowded Uskok community at Senj in the Adriatic. Ferdinand, as archduke of Styria, was responsible for this sector of the Military Frontier, but was unable to abandon Senj given the loss of nearby Bihač to the Turks in 1592. The renewal of the truce with the sultan in 1615 made it imperative to avoid provoking the Ottomans with cross-border raids, prompting local Habsburg officials to redirect Uskok banditry into Adriatic piracy. The Uskoks were soon a major threat to Venetian and other merchants.

The Venetian Republic already resented the Habsburg presence to its north and east that constrained its landward expansion. The Habsburg acquisition of the county of Görz also gave them the Istrian ports and access to the Adriatic, impinging on Venetian claims to an exclusive *dominium culfi*. Venice used the excuse of Uskok piracy to impose high tolls on Trieste merchants, hoping to end their irritating commercial rivalry. Ferdinand was keen to settle matters peacefully, but lacked the means to shut down Senj, and so the Venetians tightened their naval blockade and resolved on war. As a trading republic, Venice took a pragmatic attitude to faith, at least when dealing with foreign governments. It signed alliances with the English and Dutch whose ships were also suffering from the Uskok's piracy, and secured the Union's agreement to supply soldiers, and that of the Protestant Swiss to block the Alpine passes to Habsburg reinforcements. With Spain distracted with Savoy over Mantua, and Matthias busy in the Empire, Venice felt confident that gunboat diplomacy would bring swift success.

Sabre-rattling escalated into open war on 20 December 1615 when Venetian troops captured the narrow strip of Austrian territory west of the Isonzo river, before being blocked by the small garrison in Gradisca. The offensive had stalled where the front would be exactly 300 years later in the great battles of the First World War between Italy and Austria-Hungary. By February the Venetians had massed 12,000 men and were able to subject Gradisca to a regular siege. They also enjoyed the covert support of the inhabitants of Ottoman Bosnia who were equally tired of the Uskoks. Ottoman raids increased tenfold, tying down the Croatian-Slovenian border militia and preventing Ferdinand redeploying them on the Isonzo. With only 600 Germans and a similar number of Uskoks at the front, the archduke was forced to remain on the defensive. His Estates provided some cash and sent small detachments of militia, but otherwise refused involvement, accusing Ferdinand of bringing the matter upon himself. The situation was critical, since a defeat could open the door for the Estates to challenge Ferdinand's hard-fought Catholic renewal.

The Gradisca garrison clung on, however, as the Venetians wasted away through disease, relaxing their siege with the onset of winter. The Republic redoubled its efforts for 1617, appointing a new commander and rebuilding its forces with the arrival of 3,000 Dutch mercenaries under Johann Ernst of Nassau-Siegen, to give the Venetians 16,000 men by May 1617. A further 2,000 Dutch arrived, with additional English troops in November, while a powerful Anglo-Dutch squadron joined the 86-ship strong Venetian fleet.

Strong Anglo-Dutch support has been interpreted as bringing 'a general European conflict perceptibly nearer' by consolidating mutually hostile international alliances along largely confessional lines.[17] This was certainly how militants of all hues viewed it at the time, yet neither England nor the Dutch wanted an open breach with Spain, while the conflict remained largely an Austro-Venetian affair, despite their presence. The 22 English and Dutch ships were sailing under Venetian flags, having been hired, like the soldiers, rather than sent freely as allies. The troops had come by sea because the Spanish governor of Milan blocked the southern exits from the Alpine passes in line with his government's official policy of neutrality. Spanish participation was restricted to the viceroy of Naples, Pedro Duke of Osuna, who acted without authorization from Madrid. The Neapolitans resented Venetian mercantile predominance and had already sent privateers to harass the Republic's shipping in the Adriatic in 1616. The arrival of the Anglo-Dutch squadron forced the privateers to return to port, prompting Osuna to send his regular fleet instead. This fought an inconclusive engagement with the Venetians on 20 November 1617, before retiring.[18] Philip III refused to condone Osuna's actions, because he had no desire to fight another war in Italy after the struggle over Monferrato.

Spain and the Austrian Succession

Philip's main interest in the Uskok War was not the presence of the Dutch and English, but the repercussions for the Habsburg succession. Ambassador Zúñiga had raised the question of the succession in the wake of Leopold's failure at Jülich in 1610. Discussions in Madrid focused on the extent to which Spain itself had claims and which candidate it should back for whatever was left over. Philip III's advisers believed he had good claims to the Hungarian and Bohemian crowns on the ground that his mother, Anna of Austria, had never renounced her rights.[19] Convinced his *reputación* would suffer if he relinquished his claims, Philip wanted his Austrian relations to formally recognize him as head of the family.

Spanish ministers were divided over how to achieve this. A few clung to the legacy of Charles V's pan-European empire, suggesting Philip should claim the entire inheritance and even put himself or his son forward as next emperor. Others were more realistic, advocating trading Spain's formal claims in return for strategic concessions from Austria. The archdukes should be compelled to honour their obligations according to the Spanish interpretation of the Burgundian Treaty from 1548, which implied the Dutch still belonged to the Empire and should be punished for breaking its public peace. Though less pressing given the Twelve Years Truce, this remained the main legal argument used to demand Austrian assistance against the Dutch during the Thirty Years War. More immediately, the ministers thought Austria should surrender some land to enhance Spanish imperial security, but differed widely on what this should be. One faction doubted whether the archdukes would ever hand over part of their hereditary lands and advocated demanding the imperial jurisdictions over parts of the Ligurian coast to consolidate Spain's position in Italy. The other, led by Spinola, argued for the cession of Alsace and the Tirol to give control of the middle section of the Spanish Road.

Neither party wanted anything to do with the Empire that was felt to lie outside Spain's main sphere of interest. Nonetheless, Spain still had to agree a candidate to back as Matthias's successor to ensure that Central European issues did not trouble either Flanders or Italy. Archduke Leopold's wild behaviour removed him from the running, while Maximilian surrendered his rights in favour of Ferdinand in October 1612. With the only viable candidate embroiled in war, Spain decided to force Matthias to recognize him as his successor before the electors chose a less congenial alternative.

Spanish intervention frustrated Klesl's plans to delay consideration of the succession until his composition policy had succeeded. He resorted to dirty tricks to undermine not just Ferdinand but also Albert, who still enjoyed considerable sympathy among German Catholics. In 1616 he leaked details to Anhalt of a plan hatched two years before by the Reichshofrat president that Albert should lead an army into Germany and join the Liga in restoring imperial authority. This left only Ferdinand, whose war effort Klesl covertly undermined by delaying the despatch of aid from Austria. It is possible that he was driven by personal animosity, but more likely by the conviction that open support for Ferdinand would wreck any chance of composition with the Protestants.

It is certainly suspicious that the Venetian senate voted him a gift of 8,000 scudi in 1616.

Meanwhile, matters were complicated by the phantom candidacy of Maximilian of Bavaria whose name was already circulated in the 1590s as a possible future emperor. Anhalt misinterpreted Maximilian's resignation from the Liga directory as a step towards collaboration against the Habsburgs. He approached the duke in May 1616 with a proposal to merge the Union and Liga to block a Habsburg succession. Despite Maximilian's polite but consistent refusals, Anhalt persisted with this hare-brained scheme, to the point of sending the elector Palatine Frederick V to visit Munich in February 1618. By then, Maximilian was playing along to put pressure on the Habsburgs to make concessions in Bavaria's favour in various regional disagreements. Frederick left Munich not only under the entirely false impression that Maximilian would stand for election, but even convinced the duke would embrace Protestantism![20]

The Oñate Treaty 1617

Klesl's refusal to cede Austrian territory forced Spain to drop demands for the Tirol and concentrate on seeking the Further Austrian lands of Alsace and the Breisgau that were currently governed by Archduke Maximilian, a man with no direct heirs. Ferdinand's counter-offer of the Adriatic ports and a large slice of Inner Austria was rejected as remote from Spanish interests. Matthias's failing health and the Uskok crisis forced Ferdinand to concede a series of agreements collectively known as the Oñate Treaty after the Spanish negotiator.[21] The public documents from 6 June 1617 contained Philip III's formal renunciation of his claims to Bohemia and Hungary, but gave his sons precedence in future claims over Ferdinand's daughters. It was also arranged that Spain would be compensated with an unspecified Austrian province at a later date. Matthias agreed to this when it was shown to him, but neither he nor the other archdukes knew of a further, secret undertaking from March of that year that Ferdinand ratified on 29 July. This specified that Ferdinand would surrender the Austrian parts of Alsace to Spain, together with the Ortenau enclave on the Upper Rhine, once he had inherited them from Archduke Maximilian. In addition, Ferdinand's eldest son was to marry Philip III's daughter and vague references were made to Spain being enfeoffed with imperial rights in Italy.

Only Ferdinand and his adviser Eggenberg knew of these terms before February 1619, but they were vital to his bid to secure Matthias's entire inheritance. Free from the fear that Spain might object, Ferdinand opened talks with the Catholic faction in Bohemia to secure its crown. Chancellor Lobkowitz persuaded the Bohemian Protestants to drop their objections in return for Ferdinand's apparent confirmation of the Letter of Majesty. Having received permission from Matthias, Ferdinand was crowned Bohemian king on 29 June 1617.

End of the Uskok War

Ferdinand's concessions to Oñate coincided with the start of the long-awaited Venetian offensive along the Isonzo. As the defenders of Gradisca clung on, Ferdinand frantically appealed for aid. His Bavarian brother-in-law sent some money and gunpowder, while the Inner Austrian Estates finally opened their purse strings and Klesl dropped his opposition to troop recruitment in Matthias's lands. The Bohemian coronation greatly improved Ferdinand's credit, and enabled him to collect 4,000 men by the end of the year. As the money became available, Ferdinand called on his contacts from the Turkish War – Marradas, Dampierre and Colloredo. Wallenstein seized the chance to further his career, arriving with 260 men who had plundered their way from Moravia, literally stealing the clothes from the peasants' backs. Aldringen was also present as an ensign of foot, as were others who would later rise to prominence in the Thirty Years War, like Torquato Conti and Otto Heinrich von Fugger. Many of the same men were to answer Ferdinand's call again, barely a year later when he faced the Bohemian Revolt.

Despite having a numerical superiority of four to one, the Venetians were not able to crack the Austrian defences along the Isonzo. Ferdinand was keen to end the futile struggle and turn his full attention to the impending succession. He accepted French and Spanish mediation that led to the Treaty of Madrid on 26 September 1617. The Venetians agreed to withdraw in return for the Habsburgs resettling the Uskoks further inland. The Republic reduced its forces, including discharging the now mutinous Dutch and English, while Ferdinand cut his to 1,000, which were used to force the Uskoks to move further north-east along the Military Frontier by June 1618.

Venice was now free to deal with the troublesome Neapolitans who had been plotting to overthrow the Republic. Naval operations were stepped up until Philip III had the duke of Osuna arrested in 1620 and imprisoned on charges of conspiring to make himself independent prince of Naples.

PALATINE BRINKMANSHIP

The Approach of the Apocalypse

While the Habsburg succession was slowly resolving itself in Ferdinand's favour, Anhalt had been struggling to sustain Protestant militancy in the Empire. The imperial cities rebelled at the Union's congress in Heilbronn in April 1617, demanding major concessions before agreeing to extend the organization in defiance of an imperial order to disband. In return for a veto over future military action and a prohibition of assistance to princes who were not members, the cities agreed to a three-year extension of the Union from 1618 when the original charter was due to end. Brandenburg resigned in disgust at these concessions, while Landgrave Moritz of Hessen-Kassel refused to attend at all, because the Union appeared to offer him nothing.

The outcome simply drove Anhalt to deeper deception, and though the Union convened another eleven times before 1621, far more frequently than before, these were no longer plenary congresses but personal meetings of the core group of Anhalt, the Palatinate, Württemberg, Ansbach and Baden-Durlach. Anhalt had already widened his secret contacts in 1616 by sending Christoph von Dohna to Prague to talk to the Bohemian radicals, while other emissaries went to Baron Tschernembl in Upper Austria, and to Savoy and Venice.[22]

These actions only make sense when viewed from the increasingly fevered perspective of a Palatine court that had become gripped by millenarianism as the new century dawned. Apocalyptic beliefs had a long heritage within Christianity, but the papacy had distanced itself from these traditions in the Tridentine decrees, as had the Lutheran Book of Concord. The Calvinist establishment in Geneva also condemned the belief in a golden age on earth in 1566, but the ideas nonetheless gained ground from the 1580s. They were expressed by ordinary Calvinists, like Christoph Kotter, a tanner from Sprottau who claimed to see visions from 1616. More influential among the Palatine aristocrats were the writings of Johann Heinrich Alsted and Johann Amos Comenius, who were associated with the Calvinist academy Johann VI of Nassau-Dillenburg had founded at Herborn in 1584. Alsted became the academy's most prominent teacher and Comenius took his ideas back to Bohemia having studied under him. Both believed that their close reading of the Bible identified the Habsburgs with the forces of darkness described in the Revelation of St John. This provided an alternative to the positive ideology of the imperial translation that maintained the Empire was a direct continuation of the last Christian phase of ancient Rome. Alsted transformed the Empire from the benevolent Fourth Monarchy in the Book of Daniel to the nameless fourth beast of Revelation. He was convinced its end was nigh in the battle of the kings (also prophesied in the Book of Daniel) in which the king of the south overruns the sanctuary and forces its people to renounce their faith. The king of the north then intervenes, defeating his rival and delivering the people.

Support from intellectuals like Alsted and Comenius made apocalypticism respectable and chimed with the fluid boundaries between science and the occult. The increased frequency of hailstorms and other natural phenomena caused by climate change during this period, known now as the Little Ice Age, encouraged the view that the world was approaching its end. Witch- and demon-crazes appeared further manifestations of this. It was clear to those that believed that the sanctuary was Protestant Germany, while the Habsburgs and Spain represented the king of the south. Alsted predicted the king of the north would arrive in 1625 (the year Denmark did indeed intervene in the war) and this would lead to a thousand-year reign of the Righteous from 1694 up to the last Judgment in 2694. The use of the lion, the animal associated with the king of the north, in the heraldic devices of the Palatinate, Hessen-Kassel, Bohemia, England and Sweden appeared further corroboration that Alsted had unlocked the divine significance of the holy text.

Millenarianism peaked with the arrival of Halley's Comet in November 1618. This was followed within a few weeks by 120 pamphlets prophesying disaster, a not unusual consequence of comets. A previous sighting in 1577 led the Danish astronomer Tycho Brahe to predict trouble for Spain and the Empire, a pretty safe bet in view of the Dutch Revolt.[23] What made the current bout so dangerous was its grip on the minds of the radical Protestant leaders who commanded the resources to initiate Armageddon.

Protestant Discord

Convinced that a major struggle was approaching, Anhalt intensified efforts to rally the more numerous moderate Protestants into the radicals' camp. He realized that the Palatinate's recent setbacks and its Frenchified culture had damaged its standing and set it apart from the hard-drinking camaraderie of Dresden and the other Protestant courts. He sought ways of making Palatine radicalism more attractive by bringing influential Lutherans and Calvinists together in congenial surroundings. He established an aristocratic Order of the Golden Palm at the Upper Palatine capital of Amberg in 1617, and collaborated with his brother Ludwig, who was related by marriage to the Weimar court, to found the influential Fruitful Society (*Fruchtbringende Gesellschaft*) that year. The Fruitful Society became the most important of a number of contemporary literary societies and rapidly attracted a large membership.[24]

The Society has generally been interpreted in nationalist terms, given its ostensible aim of the purifying the German language through the exclusion of foreign expressions and the development of new poetic forms. In fact, its membership was international and included Swedes and even six Scots. Though it went on to embrace Bavarian and imperial generals, its initial purpose was to twist the humanist irenicist programme to assist Anhalt's political agenda of bridging the divide between Lutherans and Calvinists. It was paralleled by attempts by Calvinist theologians to open a dialogue with their Lutheran colleagues. David Pareus published a book in 1614 arguing they had more to unite than divide them. He attracted wide support from Hessian and Brandenburg clergy, as well as from the remaining Philippists who thrived at Weimar and its university of Jena.

The overture fell on deaf ears in Dresden where the orthodox rebuttal was orchestrated by the Saxon court preacher, Matthias Hoë von Hoënegg.[25] Like his near contemporary Klesl, Hoë was born in Vienna, though he was from a rather more prosperous background, and attended the local university. Whereas Klesl had converted, Catholic pressure on Hoë had the opposite effect of reinforcing his Lutheran convictions. He left to complete his studies in Speyer and Wittenberg where the orthodox Lutheran atmosphere fostered an abiding hatred of all those who deviated from Luther's original beliefs. He had published seven books by 1613, mainly attacking the papacy. The Pfalz-Neuburg court chaplain was so impressed he converted to Lutheranism after reading one, and they were reprinted in nineteenth-century Germany during Bismarck's repression of Catholic culture. However, Calvinists became Hoë's main target after he assumed the post of senior Saxon preacher in 1613. He viciously rooted them out in Dresden, forcing his deputy out of office by disrupting his sermons and hurling insults. Calvinists retorted by using his Austrian parentage to cast doubt on his integrity, dubbing him the 'Saxon Pope' and the 'New Judas' who was selling out to the papist Habsburgs.

The mud-slinging reached new depths during the centenary jubilee of the Reformation, celebrated in October 1617. Saxony was determined to use the occasion to assert theological supremacy over German Protestantism from a traditional Lutheran position of defying the pope. The mere act of celebrating was a challenge to Rome, because the papacy claimed a monopoly over jubilees since 1300 and naturally condemned any commemoration of Luther. The great hero was celebrated as the 'German Moses' in state decrees, school plays, fireworks, processions, sermons, woodcuts and medals throughout Saxony.[26] Elector Johann Georg saw no contradiction between this and his political support for Matthias, because Saxony had always distinguished between honest German Catholics who abided by the Augsburg settlement, and vicious papists elsewhere who conspired to destabilize the Empire. The political distinction was theologically sound, because Luther had only challenged the pope's misrepresentation of the truth, not the church itself to which his followers felt they still belonged.

Concern for German Catholic sensitivities merely redoubled Saxon bile directed at the Calvinists. Frederick V had used the Union congress at Heilbronn in April 1617 to call for common celebrations, and his court preacher presented the Calvinists as continuing Luther's tradition of reform. Hoë roundly condemned the Calvinists as cynically trying to pass themselves off as Lutherans in order to enjoy the benefits of the Peace of Augsburg. Anhalt's cultural initiatives were attacked as a surreptitious drive to suborn Lutherans from their true faith. The Saxon government expressly based its celebrations around texts from the Book of Concord and it became a test of loyalty whether other territories followed suit. Württemberg distanced itself from the Union by following the Saxon format for its commemoration of 1517, condemning Calvinists along with 'false teachers and bloodthirsty tyrants, Turks and pope, Jesuits, Zwinglians . . . and other sectarians' bent on suppressing the true faith.[27]

The Failure of Composition

Paradoxically, Protestant infighting undermined Klesl's composition project by reviving Catholic fears that Lutheran and Calvinist disagreement meant neither could be trusted. Having abandoned the Reichstag after 1613, Klesl had pushed for his proposed bi-partisan committee to meet. Lack of any precedent opened numerous questions that ultimately derailed the entire project. There was no agreement on whether it should be an electoral congress, or a wider meeting of an equal number of Protestant and Catholic princes. Klesl wanted Archduke Maximilian to chair it to deflect any blame from Matthias should it fail, but Maximilian was reluctant for that very reason, while others objected to involving any Habsburgs. Above all, the leading Catholics wanted to resolve the succession issue first, whereas the Palatine and Brandenburg electors insisted on prior talks over religion. Klesl seized on their demand as a further excuse to delay the dreaded succession, and it is likely that Anhalt's promotion of Maximilian of Bavaria's imperial candidacy was another device to sow dissension among the Catholics and buy more time to rally the ephemeral Protestant international.

Matthias also threw obstacles in Ferdinand's path, insisting he could not transfer Hungary to Ferdinand without going there in person, and then claiming he was too ill to travel. Ferdinand forced his hand by pointing out that the Hungarian diet could assemble without royal permission, obliging Matthias to call it to save face. The Hungarian magnates insisted on confirmation of their monarchy's elective character before accepting Ferdinand. Klesl hoodwinked them by recording in the minutes that they had exercised their 'traditional rights' after Matthias had recommended Ferdinand as his successor, a move that allowed the Habsburgs to claim later that Ferdinand acceded by hereditary right. Klesl's role probably reflected his concern at Matthias's failing health and the consequent urgency of mending fences with Ferdinand. The

Estates duly proclaimed Ferdinand as their new sovereign on 16 May 1618, also accepting the Catholic Sigismund Forgách to fill the vacant post of palatine. Ferdinand was still in Hungary having lunch with the archbishop of Gran on 27 May when news arrived that his representatives in Bohemia had been hurled from a window.

PART TWO

Conflict

9

The Bohemian Revolt 1618–20

FOR LIBERTY AND PRIVILEGE

The Bohemian Revolt was the first serious clash over the political and religious issues facing the Empire. Unlike the Jülich crisis, or the Donauwörth incident, it proved impossible to contain the violence which kept drawing in outsiders. The rapid internationalization of the conflict is deceptive. Europe was not poised for war in 1618, as all the major powers remained afflicted by their own problems. Therein lay the danger. With their rivals apparently preoccupied, each power felt safe to intervene in the Empire. Few intended their involvement to lead to a major war, and no one thought of a conflict lasting thirty years. The revolt is generally considered a discrete phase of the war, ending with the Bohemians' defeat in 1620 and the shift of the conflict to the Rhine until 1624. There is some merit in this standard periodization that highlights what made each stage distinct, but the approach is also a product of German and Czech national perspectives. Events unfolded together, as the revolt exposed the emperor's weakness and emboldened the elector Palatine to join the Bohemians.

An Aristocratic Conspiracy

Only with hindsight does the revolt seem obvious. Contemporaries were caught unprepared. To explain this, we need to return briefly to the situation in Bohemia after Rudolf II's death in 1612. The revolt was not a popular uprising, but an aristocratic coup led by a minority of desperate militant Protestants. Though Matthias had confirmed the Bohemian and Silesian Letters of Majesty, Protestant institutions rested on insecure foundations. Their leaders sought to anchor these more firmly on the kingdom's constitution by widening their share in foreign policy and control of the armed forces. Matthias and Klesl had countered by giving greater coherence to Rudolf's existing policy of preferring Catholics in crown appointments, isolating the Protestants in their parallel institutions. Chief among these institutions was the committee of thirty 'Defensors' established in 1609 to uphold the constitution. This body lacked executive authority which remained in the hands of the ten Regents appointed by the Habsburgs. Elected by the Estates, the Defensors claimed to speak for the country, yet the Estates were split between a Catholic minority that regarded the Defensors with suspicion and a Protestant majority itself divided by confession and political opinion. Since the Catholic crown appointees were also Bohemians, 'they were immune from the allegation of being alien stooges of the dynasty'.[1] Politics polarized along confessional lines, since religion was the only ground on which to attack royal policy.

Matthias believed the Bohemian Letter of Majesty had been unfairly extorted from his brother and felt obliged to respect only its formal provisions. Some crown land was transferred to the Catholic church to reduce the area covered by the grant of toleration. Crown peasants were prevented from attending church services on neighbouring private estates, and in 1614 Protestant worship was banned in two German-speaking towns in north-east Bohemia on the grounds that Braunau (Broumov) fell under the jurisdiction of the Catholic Brevnov abbey, while Klostergrab (Hroby) was under that of the archbishop of Prague. Ferdinand confirmed these measures when he became king of Bohemia three years later. They suited his legalistic approach and were technically correct, but their implementation by Archbishop Lohelius was deliberately provocative. Ferdinand compounded the mistake by arresting petitioners complaining that the archbishop's agents had demolished Klostergrab church, and then ordering royal judges to supervise public funds in an effort to cut financial support to Protestant parishes.

These measures featured prominently in the rebels' *Apologia* published after the Defenestration to justify their violent action.[2] The rebels no doubt saw them as the thin end of the wedge, yet they were no worse than the usual Habsburg chicanery and, on their own, not sufficient to spark a full revolt. That lay in the Habsburgs' failure to appreciate the level of dissatisfaction among the Protestant Bohemian aristocracy. This is unsurprising, given that the dynasty had got its way with minimal opposition: only two delegates at the 1617 diet opposed the accession of Ferdinand as king. Ferdinand had confirmed Protestant privileges and, in his mind, was still respecting these. The Habsburg court returned to Vienna, adding further distance at this critical juncture. Despite Rudolf's aloofness, the Bohemians had grown used to having their king in their midst. Though the ten Regents included three Protestants, the others were known Catholic hardliners like Chancellor Lobkowitz, Jaroslav Martinitz and Vilém Slavata.

The opposition was led by Count Thurn, one of the two dissenting voices in 1617, who had subsequently been deprived of his post as castellan of Karlstadt and replaced by Martinitz. This simply reversed Rudolf's act six years earlier when the job had been taken from Slavata to win Protestant support. Yet it was highly symbolic, because the castellan was in charge of the royal regalia and Ferdinand wanted to ensure these were not removed to crown a rival. Thurn was compensated with the post of senior feudal judge that paid considerably less and necessitated his resignation from the Defensors committee. The move was interpreted as a deliberate attempt to undermine the Protestant leadership that now rarely spoke to their Catholic counterparts in the kingdom's formal administration.

The division deepened as Thurn's allies among the Defensors summoned a special Protestant assembly in March 1618 to press their grievances over the perceived infringements of their rights. Many of the towns did not send representatives, but the leadership remained determined. In the absence of dissenting voices, it proved easy to convince those present that the entire Letter of Majesty was under threat. A petition was despatched to Emperor Matthias and the assembly agreed to reconvene on 21 May to discuss his reply. Klesl saw Thurn's relative isolation as a chance to demonstrate royal resolve, writing a sharp reply forbidding the assembly from reconvening. While Klesl wielded the stick, Matthias offered the carrot, promising to return to Bohemia to discuss the situation. Klesl's letter was delivered through the Regents as the crown's local representatives.

Thurn seized on this to rally wider support, since it was easier to attack the Regents as 'evil advisers' than to openly defy either Ferdinand or Matthias. He persuaded the Defensors that Klesl's prohibition breached the Letter of Majesty, and ensured pastors used the Sunday sermon to announce that the delegates would reconvene to debate the

Catholics' 'secret tricks and practices' that were undermining the unity of the kingdom. The assembly duly met on 21 May and though attendance by the nobles had improved, many burghers still stayed away. Undaunted, Thurn and his associates defied another, more conciliatory order from the Regents to disband, and whipped up passions by claiming the Regents intended to arrest them. It was time, Thurn declared on 22 May, to 'throw them out of the window, as is customary'.[3] This was a clear reference to the defenestration of 30 July 1419, when the Prague mayor and councillors had been murdered at the start of the Hussite insurrection. He met his closest supporters that evening in Albrecht Jan Smiřický's house near the castle to coordinate the plot for the next day. It seems likely he planned to repeat the action of April 1609 when the Protestants had forced their way into the Hradschin and compelled Rudolf to grant the Letter of Majesty. This time, however, the conspirators were fully prepared to use violence to cut through the slow pace of negotiations and radicalize their supporters.

Summoned by Thurn, the city councillors joined the conspirators and other delegates early on 23 May and sang hymns to bolster their spirits. They were let into the Hradschin by pre-arrangement with the Catholic (!) captain, and went up the narrow staircase to the room where the Regents were meeting, but found only four of them, together with their secretary. The conspirators wanted to prove the Regents had been responsible for Klesl's inflammatory letter and demanded they admit their guilt. Pinned against the wall, the first two denied responsibility and were bundled out of the room, leaving Slavata and Martinitz who had been the intended victims all along. Both thought they were simply going to be arrested. As it dawned on them that death was to be their fate, it was already too late, because Thurn's seconds had whipped the meeker Defensors into a frenzy; however, it is likely that many in the room were still oblivious to what was planned. Certainly, Count Andreas Schlick had objected to Thurn's plan, but it was difficult to see what was going on by the window. Once the two victims had disappeared headfirst, there was no going back and poor Fabricius was despatched after his masters.

Thurn had achieved his objective of radicalizing the situation, but the failure to kill the intended victims was an inauspicious beginning for the revolt. Protestant propagandists sought to mask the debacle by reporting the victims had landed in rubbish piled in the castle ditch – an interpretation that gained wide currency after its incorporation by Schiller into his history of the war.[4] Martinitz had called on the Madonna's protection as he fell. Seeing him stagger to his feet, Ulrich Kinsky, a leading Defenestrator at the window above, exclaimed 'By God! His Maria has helped him!'[5] This gave rise to the myth that the Virgin had unfurled her cloak under the falling men, encouraging the Catholic identification with her in battle-cries and columns to celebrate their victories. Cloaks probably played a part, but they were the victims'. It had been a cool morning and with typical Habsburg parsimony the room had been unheated, obliging the Regents to retain their thick cloaks and hats. With rather greater generosity, the dynasty ennobled Fabricius as 'von Hohenfall' (of the high fall).

The Rebel Leadership

The conspirators moved swiftly to convert their parallel institutions into an interim government. The Protestant assembly declared itself a diet on 25 May and elected twelve Directors from each of the three Estates of lords, knights and towns to replace the Regents and the functions of the Bohemian Chancellery. Otherwise royal administration was left intact, though Habsburg loyalists were replaced. For the moment the rebels refrained from deposing Ferdinand. Instead they simply ignored him by addressing their demands directly to Matthias, to whom they maintained a show of deference. The situation resembled the opening stage of the Dutch Revolt when the rebels had presented themselves as loyal patriots opposing a corrupt local government, not the king himself. The result was a lack of direction as moderates sought to steer the movement away from a clear breach with the Habsburgs.

No one of the stature of William of Orange emerged to provide inspiring leadership. The Directory was headed by Vilém Ruppa, a compromise candidate who was unable to reconcile the factions. Rivalry within the Bohemian barons prompted Thurn, the real leader, to spurn a directorship in favour of army command, with his friend Colonna von Fels as deputy. Concerned to prevent Thurn becoming too powerful, the Directors appointed Count Georg Friedrich of Hohenlohe as a kind of defence minister. Though Hohenlohe had been well-rewarded by the Habsburgs for his service in the Turkish War, his religion and kinship ties placed his family in the radical Protestant camp: his mother was a relation of Maurice of Nassau and his wife, Eva, came from the extensive Bohemian Waldstein family. Hohenlohe soon criticized Thurn and the other senior officers, and insisted on a share of the command in the field.[6]

Indecision was reflected in policy. The rebels' manifesto hinted darkly at Jesuit plots against the Letter of Majesty. Thurn ordered their expulsion from Prague, but they were a very soft target as they were widely resented even by Catholics. A Catholic was appointed to the Directory, which initially refrained from confiscating church property. Indeed, it now proved impossible to push faith to the fore without opening a Pandora's box concerning what constituted true religion in a country of many faiths. Constitutional issues played better to more moderate outsiders, most of whom believed the Defenestrators had broken the law. The Directory called up every tenth peasant and eighth burgher at the beginning of June, and diverted existing taxes away from the Habsburg treasury to fund a professional army. However, Thurn mustered only 4,000 mercenaries in June, a total that eventually rose to 12,000 by September, while the militia call-out proved a failure. These numbers were scarcely adequate to defend an area of nearly 50,000km^2, let alone take the war to Vienna. Thurn opened offensive operations in late June, but talks continued, partly to gain time, but also to convince potential supporters that the fault lay with the Habsburgs.

The Habsburg Response

With Spanish support for his succession secured in the Oñate Treaty, Ferdinand had been biding his time until the sickly Matthias died. As the Bohemian crisis deepened, however, it appeared the entire monarchy might disintegrate before he could inherit it. Ferdinand became increasingly impatient with Klesl who had conceded virtually all the rebels' earlier demands in the hope of defusing the situation quickly. But Thurn and his supporters had gone too far to accept these generous terms now and used Klesl's condition that they lay down their arms as an excuse to reject his offer. Klesl had already resolved on using force by the middle of June, but it would take time to assemble a sufficient army.[7]

Ferdinand saw the cardinal rather than the lack of soldiers as the primary obstacle to decisive action. Even some moderates now felt Klesl was so discredited among the Protestants that his continued presence was inhibiting a compromise. A succession of plots since 1616 had failed to unseat him, and a bullet narrowly missed his head during the banquet celebrating Ferdinand's coronation as king of Hungary on 1 July 1618. Fearing for the church's reputation, the papal nuncio persuaded Archduke Maximilian to ensure he was removed by less dramatic means. Maximilian invited the cardinal to meet him, Ferdinand and Oñate at the Hofburg on 20 July. When Klesl arrived, he found the three already locked in discussion and was ushered into an antechamber by the archduke's servant. There, he was seized by Colonel Dampierre and whisked away to Innsbruck. His cash and jewels worth 300,000 florins disappeared into the virtually empty imperial war chest. Bedridden, Matthias could do nothing. His loyal wife rounded on Ferdinand: 'I see clearly that my husband is living too long for you: is this the thanks he gets for having given you two crowns?'[8] Klesl was eventually put on trial in June 1619 and made the scapegoat for Habsburg failures, including the Letter of Majesty and the Uskok War. After the College of Cardinals ratified the guilty verdict, he was moved to Rome in 1622 under house arrest, until Ferdinand allowed him to return to Vienna three years later where he lived out his life in comfortable retirement.

Archduke Maximilian's death on 2 November 1618 left just Matthias between Ferdinand and the imperial succession. The initiative nominally remained with Matthias, whose condition worsened notably after his wife's death on 15 December, and he spent the last three months of his life worrying about astrology and looking at Rudolf's vast collection of curios.

Within days of the Defenestration, the local Habsburg commander rushed all available men to Budweis and Krumau, securing the Linz–Prague road. Together with Pilsen, Krumau and Budweis remained the only loyal towns in the kingdom. Some men were withdrawn from the Military Frontier to reinforce the 1,000 soldiers retained by Ferdinand after the Uskok War, but even with additional recruits, there were only 14,200 available by 21 July in Lower Austria. Count Bucquoy, kept on retainer since 1614 after he had served with distinction in the Army of Flanders, arrived a month later to assume command, but Thurn had already repulsed Dampierre's attempt to break through to the three towns from Lower Austria.[9]

The Scramble for Support

Both sides appealed for assistance. The Bohemians employed confessional and constitutional arguments, depending on their audience. This inconsistency also reflected deep divisions over objectives. Many saw military preparations as a means to force the Habsburgs to confirm the concessions already granted in 1608–9. Others wanted to go further, though few at this stage contemplated rejecting the dynasty entirely. The Habsburgs presented themselves as patient patriarchs confronted by wilful, rebellious children. As military operations began, the dynasty stressed their opponents' radicalism, claiming they intended to establish a Swiss- or Dutch-style republic.[10] There was no rush to back either side. Pope Paul V's response in July was lukewarm and the first instalment of his subsidy did not reach Vienna until September. Paul remained convinced the Habsburgs were exaggerating the danger and that it would all be over by Christmas.

Spain was preoccupied with other matters and had not expected trouble in the Empire. The question of intervention became entangled in moves to oust the duke of Lerma, fracturing opinion. Lerma had recently been made a cardinal and wished to retire from court. He urged caution and even some of his critics believed involvement would distract Spain from the Mediterranean and allow Venice and Savoy to make more trouble. Others felt the country's proper role was fighting the Ottomans, not heretics. Zúñiga was almost alone in arguing for intervention in June and July, but he managed to convince the Council of State that Spain's deepest humiliations had been inflicted by Christians, not Muslims, and that the country should address these first to restore prestige. His argument was that if Austria lost Bohemia, and with it their vote in the imperial election, the electors might chose a member of another German dynasty as Matthias's successor, to the detriment of the entire Habsburg family. Yet, Zúñiga had no desire to widen the war and rejected a call from Philipp von Sötern, bishop of Speyer, to revive Charles V's Catholic front of 1546 and extinguish Protestantism in Germany. Intervention was simply to nip trouble in the bud, stabilize the Empire and stop its troubles complicating Spain's position elsewhere. Spain sent money from July onwards, but much of this had already been promised to Ferdinand to disband his army after the Uskok War. Instead of paying the soldiers off, it was now used to rebuild his forces and by

October Spain was maintaining around 3,000 soldiers, largely German.[11]

The Habsburgs also appealed to Protestants for support. Johann Georg of Saxony immediately summoned his militia to seal off the frontier with Bohemia. Having watched developments and listened to envoys from both sides, he concluded in August that the Bohemians were misrepresenting events as a religious struggle. Saxon policy remained one of defusing tension on the basis of the existing constitution and the elector invited all interested parties to join him in the Bohemian town of Eger for talks.[12] The Union's response was similarly disappointing for the Bohemians. News of the Defenestration caught its leadership completely unprepared. Frederick V and Anhalt were busy provoking a dispute with Bishop Sötern on the ground that his construction of a modern fortress at Udenheim on the Rhine represented an unacceptable threat. The Union leadership hoped the crisis would rally flagging support to renew the organization's charter. Backed by Württemberg and Baden-Durlach, the Palatinate sent 5,200 militia and peasant pioneers to demolish Udenheim on 15 June. The coup backfired by alarming the other members of the Union, who now trusted the leadership even less.[13] In an effort to retrieve the situation, Frederick sent his own offer to mediate that Matthias politely declined.[14] The Union congress convened in October to discuss the situation. All bar three imperial cities accepted Anhalt's argument that it was a religious issue, but undermined this by failing to vote for positive action. Anhalt continued to work behind the scenes to promote intervention, but realized England and other powers were unlikely to help unless the Bohemians could persuade the kingdom's other provinces to join them.[15]

Moravia occupied a pivotal position. Though only around half the size of Bohemia, it lay between it and Lower Austria, Silesia and Hungary with relatively good access through Znaim over the mountains to Vienna. Lack of Moravian support had contributed to the defeat of the 1547 Bohemian rebellion. The senior figure in the Moravian Estates was Cardinal Dietrichstein, bishop of Olmütz, a Counter-Reformer whose loyalty to the Habsburgs was unsurprising. Less expected was the support of Karel Zierotin whose tireless efforts for peace had continued despite Habsburg ingratitude. As an adherent of the Bohemian Brethren, Zierotin enjoyed wide respect among the local Protestants, most of whom wanted to retain the existing balance between the crown and the Estates. Rebel sympathizers persuaded the Moravian diet to mobilize

3,000 men in August, but Zierotin and Dietrichstein ensured they remained in the province to maintain neutrality, while also granting transit to Habsburg forces. Protestants elsewhere hesitated to join the rebellion without the Moravians, while the Hungarians remained aloof.

The War Begins

Bucquoy decided to bypass Thurn's army and head for Prague through Moravia, collecting Dampierre's detachment on the way. Thurn abandoned his fruitless sieges of the three remaining Habsburg strongholds and entrenched at Cáslav to block Bucquoy's way into the Elbe valley. Peasant guerrillas cut the Habsburg supply lines. Having destroyed 24 villages around Cáslav looking for food, Bucquoy retired south-west to be closer to Budweis in September. The military situation moved in Thurn's favour as Count Mansfeld arrived to besiege Pilsen with over 2,000 Swiss mercenaries, retained after the fighting in Italy, who had been waiting in Ansbach. They were joined by 3,000 Silesians under the margrave of Jägerndorf, despatched in October after the radicals finally gained the upper hand in that province's diet. Pilsen surrendered on 25 November and became Mansfeld's primary base. Bucquoy and Dampierre fell back separately to Budweis and Krems respectively, having lost half their men to disease and desertion.

The relatively easy success encouraged Thurn to split his forces. Hohenlohe was left to besiege Bucquoy, while Thurn headed east to bully the Moravians, and Heinrich Schlick marched on Vienna. The division rendered these moves largely ineffective. Schlick reached Zwettl in Lower Austria on 25 November, but had only 4,000 men and they lacked winter clothing and could march no further. Numbers fell again over the winter, and by February 1619, only 8,000 remained in total in all three detachments. The Imperialists used the lull to regroup. Though the Upper Austrian Protestants barred access through their province, Mansfeld had failed to block the Golden Track across the southern Bohemian mountains from the Danube at Passau. The route was swiftly secured by the Habsburgs with blockhouses and used to feed reinforcements as they arrived along the river. A new cuirassier regiment of 1,300 Walloons, raised by Lieutenant-Colonel La Motte for Colonel Wallenstein, crossed to break through Hohenlohe's crumbling blockade and reinforce Bucquoy.

With neither side able to gain a clear advantage, both consented to the Saxon-sponsored talks. Just as the envoys were assembling, news arrived of Matthias's death on 20 March 1619. Habsburg Austria now passed to Ferdinand who was already king of Bohemia and Hungary. His position remained uncertain, however, until he had been accepted by his subjects through the formal homage of his Estates. The Upper Austrian radicals clung to the fiction that Matthais's brother Archduke Albert, not his cousin Ferdinand, was their ruler, while they waited for the situation to improve. Ferdinand moved swiftly to seek his subjects' approval, reluctantly confirming Bohemian privileges and offering an amnesty if the rebels laid down their arms. By rejecting this, the rebels committed themselves to open defiance, as they could no longer maintain the pretence they were opposing merely Ferdinand, not the entire dynasty.

There was no turning back. On 18 April the Directors authorized Thurn to invade Moravia. Having added 5,000 new militia to his 4,000 mercenaries, he crossed the frontier five days later, advancing on Znaim where the province's Estates were still in session. Dampierre had only 2,000 men in Krems. He raced north, but was too late as Moravian neutrality was torn apart. One of the three Moravian regiments defected to the invaders. The foot regiment under Wallenstein also mutinied. Wallenstein killed their major, and marched with the reliable soldiers to Olmütz where he seized the Estates' treasury, and then escaped south over the frontier.[16] Ferdinand's response seems surprising, but illustrates his legalistic view of politics. Arguing that Wallenstein had acted without orders from his employers, Ferdinand sent the troops home with the cash in the hopes of bolstering the loyalists under Cardinal Dietrichstein who were now negotiating with Thurn in Brünn. Thurn used Wallenstein's action to discredit the cardinal, marching into his house and pointing to the window, suggesting that a similar fate to that of the unfortunate Prague Regents awaited him. Dietrichstein resigned his Estates' functions, but Zierotin refused to endorse an alliance with the Bohemians. His opposition undermined Protestant unity and Thurn secured only a four-month truce. Dietrichstein took the opportunity to escape, disheartened at the Estates' army that drank the contents of his wine cellar, worth 30,000 fl. His bodyguard held out in the episcopal castle of Nikolsburg until 3 February 1620.[17]

The 'Stormy Petition'

Thurn gambled on attacking Vienna to persuade the Moravians and others to commit themselves, crossing the frontier at Znaim with 10,000 men at the end of May. The last remaining Protestant on the Vienna city council was poised with a group of conspirators to seize control once Thurn breached the city's defences. A local noble had collected boats at Fischermend east of the city, enabling Thurn to cross the Danube and drive off the few Hungarian light cavalry screening the capital. The inhabitants fled the suburbs as Thurn reached the village of St Marx, just outside the city to the south on 5 June, where he waited for a signal from the conspirators inside.[18]

Thurn's advance forced the Lower Austrians to take sides. The Protestants had stormed out of a diet summoned by Ferdinand the previous month, but had reconvened on 4 June. They were emboldened to walk out again at 10 a.m. the next morning and march into the Hofburg palace to see Ferdinand himself. Legend has it that one grabbed Ferdinand in an attempt to force him to grant their demands. He took shelter in the castle chapel where, clutching a crucifix, he prayed for deliverance. At that moment, five companies of Dampierre's new arquebusier regiment clattered into the courtyard dispersing the protesters. In fact, Ferdinand had summoned the Protestant deputies himself to facilitate reconciliation with their Catholic colleagues. They indeed left after Dampierre's arrival, but returned that afternoon for further talks when Ferdinand apologized for the cavalry's sudden appearance. The arrival of the 400 horsemen nonetheless boosted Ferdinand's morale. The unit, surviving until 1918 as dragoon regiment number 8, received the unique privilege of being allowed to enter the Hofburg with its own band playing, while the crucifix Ferdinand had held is still preserved in the chapel.

Other reinforcements, together with mobilized students, brought the defenders up to 5,000. Some held the Prater islands, while four gunboats crewed by haiduks threatened Thurn's communications across the river. Without siege artillery, and with no signal from the city's fifth column, Thurn retreated northwards on 12 June. As soon as he had gone, Archduke Leopold supervised a house-to-house search, rounding up subversives and seizing weapons. The episode convinced the Lower Austrian Catholics to ignore their doubts about Ferdinand and accept him as ruler. The Protestant nobles had been exposed as conspirators and fled to the small fortified town of Horn, where they established their own Directory and began levying troops on their estates.

The rebels' failure before Vienna was compounded by a reverse in Bohemia in the war's first pitched battle. Receiving word that Mansfeld had abandoned his attempt to cut the Golden Track and was moving with 3,000 troops to join Hohenlohe, Bucquoy led a sortie of about 5,000 men to intercept him. Mansfeld blundered into the trap at Netolitz on 10 June, and fell back to Záblati where he barricaded himself in the outskirts of the town and appealed for Hohenlohe to join him. Having sealed off the possible escape routes to the north, and driven in Mansfeld's outposts, Bucquoy set fire to the town which largely consisted of wooden houses with thatched roofs. The fire spread rapidly, igniting an ammunition dump. Most of Mansfeld's troops were cut down by the imperial cavalry as they tried to escape. As an outlaw since February 1619, Mansfeld could not afford to be taken, and managed to cut his way through with fifteen followers. With his typical bad luck, the Bohemian garrison of Moldautein mistook him for an imperial officer and opened fire, before finally letting him in. Around half his forces were cornered in a wood by Bucquoy's men. Unpaid, they changed sides in return for a month's pay. Though only 7km away, Hohenlohe failed to intervene and had to lift his blockade and rejoin Thurn as he retreated from Vienna. The feuding Bohemian commanders regrouped, still out-numbering Bucquoy whose troops now overran southern Bohemia. The war continued, but Bucquoy's victory provided a timely boost as Ferdinand presented himself in Frankfurt for election as Matthias's successor.

A KING FOR A CROWN

The Imperial Crown

Unlike the Brothers' Quarrel, the dispute over the Habsburg succession was no longer confined to the dynasty. For Ferdinand, the Bohemian Revolt was a distraction from his primary goal of securing the imperial crown. He had written to the imperial Estates on 12 April 1619, stressing how the rebels had rejected his efforts to resolve matters peacefully.[19] The improving military situation allowed him to set out for Frankfurt on 10 July where the electors were gathering. The election revealed the bankruptcy of Palatine policy. Frederick V's failure to win Saxon support frustrated his hopes of using the election to bargain for concessions. Unable to find a viable alternative to Ferdinand, he was forced into the paradoxical position of proposing Duke Maximilian of Bavaria as a candidate. Plans to use Union troops to seize Frankfurt were aborted when the landgrave of Hessen-Kassel refused to cooperate. Rumours of a Protestant coup merely added to an already tense situation. The Frankfurt civic guard mistook the elector of Mainz's bodyguard for an invasion force and opened fire. The Mainz troops retreated to avoid provocation, but the guards still killed the elector of Cologne's courier as he tried to leave the city.[20]

Ferdinand was eventually able to enter to join the electors of Mainz, Cologne and Trier, while Saxony, Brandenburg and the Palatinate sent representatives. The Bohemians were not admitted, but the electors also ruled that Ferdinand could not exercise the Bohemian vote. Ferdinand did himself no favours, accidentally shooting the elector of Cologne's page while out hunting during a break in the deliberations.[21] Nonetheless he was the only candidate, and any discussion of alternatives was purely for form's sake. As it became obvious he would be chosen, the Palatine representative gave his assent as well, fearing an objection would merely isolate his master still further.

The Bohemian Confederation

Ferdinand's unanimous election as emperor on 28 August was offset by his opponents' moves to deprive him of his existing Bohemian and Hungarian crowns. The five Bohemian provinces agreed a Confederation on 31 July 1619, a week after their representatives met in Prague. The Upper and Lower Austrian Protestant radicals joined as allies on 16 August in a special ceremony in the Hradschin.[22] The 100 articles of confederation replaced government through the republican Directory with a mixed monarchy based on the Protestant institutions created under the Letter of Majesty. The Defensors were re-established as constitutional guardians and now extended to all provinces along with the religious privileges they were to uphold. Catholic spiritual jurisdiction over Protestants was abolished, and though Catholics could hold junior offices in the administration, they were expected to swear loyalty to the articles of confederation. The monarchy was confirmed as elective, but in a more significant move Bohemia accepted the right of the other four provinces of Moravia, Silesia, and Upper and Lower Lusatia to participate, merely retaining the deciding vote in the event of a tie. The Confederation represented an attempt to organize a state along aristocratic principles, similar to those guiding the Venetian Republic or the Polish-Lithuanian Commonwealth. Its true potential can never be known because it was born and destroyed in battle, but it is significant that, unlike the Dutch and Swiss systems, it failed to defeat the Habsburgs.

The Protestant Austrians remained allies, rather than full partners, because Tschernembl opposed membership, seeing cooperation simply as a means to force Ferdinand to grant local concessions. Since the majority of the Estates in both Austrian provinces refused to back even an alliance, support for the Bohemians ran solely through the radicals' own ad hoc institutions.[23] Many of the actual members felt coerced into the Confederation, notably the Moravians. The Silesians joined in return for special concessions intended to enhance their administrative autonomy, while Moravia was also given its own consistory and university. Some effort was made to establish central coordination, but each province retained its own diet and distinct laws.

The establishment of the Confederation prior to settling the matter of the Bohemian crown indicated the rebels' determination to assert control over the monarchy. The assembled delegates formally 'rejected' Ferdinand as king on 19 August, claiming that the 1617 procedure had been unconstitutional and that he was never officially their monarch. Most hoped Johann Georg of Saxony would present himself as candidate, but he only entertained the idea to keep the Bohemians interested in his peace proposals.[24] The second favourite was Bethlen Gábor who had emerged as prince of Transylvania after renewed unrest there in 1613.[25] From the poor Calvinist Magyar nobility, Bethlen had been raised by his Szekler mother and well educated. Some have accepted his claims that he sought a federation of east Central European provinces, but it is more likely he just aimed to demonstrate Transylvanian independence from both the Habsburgs and Ottomans. Habsburg diplomats convinced the sultan that Bethlen could not be trusted, removing the possibility he could attack Hungary with Ottoman support and weakening his influence in Prague. Carlo Emanuele of Savoy's candidacy was even more improbable. Like Bethlen, he saw a royal title as a means of underpinning his country's precarious independence, but he was even less choosy where he found it, having already offered to liberate Albania from the sultan if its inhabitants made him king. Though a Catholic, he had already demonstrated his anti-Habsburg credentials in the fighting in Italy and was believed to be very rich. He had helped fund Mansfeld's expedition, but was compromised when this was discovered when Bucquoy captured documents at Záblati that incriminated him. Carlo Emanuele quickly back-pedalled, and by 1620 was offering Ferdinand 12,000 men if he was given a royal title. This left Frederick V as the only viable option and he was duly elected king of Bohemia by 144 votes on 26 August, his twenty-third birthday, though six delegates voted for Johann Georg despite his refusal to stand.[26]

A Fateful Decision

Naturally indecisive, Frederick was sufficiently intelligent to realize the enormity of the consequences of accepting this offer. His advisers spent the next month arguing what he should do. His mother and the native Palatine officials urged rejection since it would obviously lead to war; Anhalt and Camerarius, another influential outsider, advocated acceptance. There seems little reason to accept the old tale of a hen-pecked elector bullied by his ambitious English wife eager to be queen, but Elizabeth certainly encouraged false expectations that James I would provide support. James had renewed his alliance with the Union in January 1619, while the Dutch promised a modest subsidy for Bohemia the following month. Frederick found it hard to distinguish between the possible and the probable, mistaking vague expressions of goodwill for firm commitments. Another suggestion has been that Anhalt urged Frederick on because he had invested heavily in the Upper Palatine sheet-metal industry that was increasingly dependent on Bohemia for imports.[27] It is, however, very unlikely this weighed heavily in the final decision, which combined a heady mix of long-standing dynastic ambitions with a conviction that God had summoned Frederick as his instrument on earth. Militants across the Palatinate, Silesia and Lusatia prophesied a golden age with Frederick as the 'last emperor' before the Day of Judgment. A truer guide to Palatine ambitions was the elector's decision to name his fourth child, born in Prague on 17 December, Ruprecht. Better known in later British history as Prince Rupert of the Rhine, his name referred to the only emperor from the Palatine dynasty, who had ruled in the early fifteenth century. Dynastic ambitions were confirmed when the Palatinate Estates accepted his first son, Friedrich Heinrich, as his successor designate in April 1620. Frederick's public explanation naturally omitted these objectives, and merely restated the complaints raised in the Defenestrators' *Apologia*, along with the standard reference to the need to stabilize the Empire in view of the Ottoman menace.[28]

Entrusting Palatine government to Johann Casimir of Zweibrücken, Frederick left Heidelberg on Monday 7 October 1619 with the more gung-ho of his officials and a cavalcade of 153 wagons that included boxes of toys for his eldest son, as well as a coach with his heavily pregnant wife. A landslide en route almost removed the future Prince Rupert from history as a rock landed on Elizabeth's lap. Anhalt joined them with 1,000 troops in the Upper Palatinate and, with no imperial troops able to bar their way, they entered Prague at the end of the month. The cheering crowds included 400 citizens dressed as Hussite revolutionaries. Just in case Frederick had not got the point, the commemorative medal struck for his coronation bore the inscription 'King by the Grace of God and the Estates'.[29]

The Bohemian War Effort

The Bohemians expected their king to bring solid international support. They were bitterly disappointed. The Union congress met in September but, as the Strasbourg representative put it, could not decide whether 'God means to punish us or reward us' by Frederick's election.[30] They reconvened in November once it became obvious he had accepted, but were fearful of the experience of 1546-7 when the Schmalkaldic League had been crushed at the same time as a Bohemian rebellion. Only Ansbach and Baden backed Frederick, while Hessen-Kassel resigned in protest. The Union assembled troops but these were intended to deter Catholic reprisals. The Dutch allowed two regiments to be recruited from Britons and Germans serving in their army, but refused to become involved and in August 1620 even stopped their subsidy, which they had never delivered in full in any case. Protestant disunity was crassly revealed when Lutheran fundamentalists in Berlin provoked riots by claiming the British troops marching to assist the Bohemians were really intended to impose Calvinism on the Brandenburgers.

Worse, James declared himself 'most afflicted' that his son-in-law had failed to wait for his advice before accepting the crown. 'England mystified contemporaries and, after them, the historians.'[31] Matters are not helped by the controversy surrounding James himself. Complacent, pompous and escapist, James often contradicted himself, and yet sincerely sought peace by navigating the rival factions at home and abroad. The central plank of this policy was to find a suitable Catholic bride for his son Charles to counterbalance his own marriage to a Danish princess and his daughter's match with Frederick V. Most Britons saw continental affairs in simplified, confessionalized terms and could not understand why their monarch was not rushing to help the oppressed Protestants in the Habsburg lands. They looked back nostalgically to the Elizabethan golden age, when Britons had vanquished the Armada and seemingly saved the Dutch and French Huguenots. Whereas disputes had then been about the means, not ends, there were now serious disagreements over national objectives. A small, but influential faction shared their king's belief that their country's proper role was as European arbiter, above the individual factions.

British mediation stood very little chance, however. The principal mission led by the earl of Doncaster exposed the basic problems that would frustrate all Stuart efforts to shape the war. The British were poorly informed and their ambassadors arrived too late. Doncaster's departure was delayed by James falling ill and he did not set out until May 1619. The practice of lavish, old-style embassies – he travelled with 150 companions in an expedition costing £30,000 – further impeded progress. Above all, Britain had nothing to offer. The Habsburgs were interested only if James could restrain his son-in-law, which he obviously could not. They only entertained future embassies so as not to give fuel to the faction in London demanding full-scale military support for the 'Protestant Cause'. Meanwhile, Frederick wanted men and money, not more advice, and could not understand why his father-in-law was not honouring his renewed commitment to the Protestant Union. James even refused a loan, though the Palatine envoy raised £64,000 in public subscriptions to recruit Sir Andrew Grey's regiment of 2,500 Britons.[32] James's Danish in-laws remained aloof, while Gustavus Adolphus's wife-hunting trip to Heidelberg in the spring of 1620 reinforced his convictions of German Protestant disunity (see Chapter 6, p.191). Europe joked that Frederick would be saved by the Danes who would send

1,000 pickled herrings, the Dutch would supply 10,000 boxes of butter, while James would despatch 100,000 ambassadors.[33]

With Palatine resources fully committed to defend its own exposed territory, Frederick looked to his new Bohemian subjects when he returned from the disappointing Union congress at the end of 1619. He set out on a royal progress through his new domains until this was cut short by military events in March 1620. His noble bearing and powers of public speaking ensured a warm reception, but his subjects were less impressed with his wife thanks to her daring French fashions and failure to learn German. Frederick's view of Catholic rights was as narrow as Ferdinand's of Protestant rights. Frederick claimed he would accept Catholics provided they remained loyal, but did little to stop local harassment. Chronic shortage of cash soon forced the seizure of Catholic estates and church property.[34] Such actions did not worry the Bohemian rebels, but Frederick's policy towards local Protestants soon caused concern. The new king and his entourage showed little understanding for the complexities of Bohemian Protestantism. The Calvinist court preacher, Abraham Scultetus, regarded the Utraquists as crypto-Catholic subversives. Ignoring his own failure during Brandenburg's second Reformation, he launched an assault on all he held in contempt. His efforts to remove the religious statues from Prague's Charles Bridge were thwarted by popular opposition, but Palatine Calvinists vented their iconoclastic fury on St Vitus Cathedral at Christmas 1619, removing or destroying priceless medieval art works, tearing down the great crucifix above the altar, poking through paintings, and breaking open saints' tombs. The Bohemians were deeply offended, not so much for confessional reasons but because the Cathedral symbolized their distinct identity.

Such action reduced the general willingness to make sacrifices on Frederick's behalf. The Bohemian Confederation relied on methods of military recruitment used during the Brothers' Quarrel, with each province raising its own regiments and sending some or all to join the common army. The soldiers are often described in secondary accounts as militia, but were mainly mercenaries recruited by officers commissioned by the Estates. The Bohemians summoned a general levy of 30,000 subjects in September 1618, but only 10,500 assembled and they were sent home a month later. The experiment was repeated in March 1619, summoning 12,000 in the hope that by being more selective, the force would be more willing and effective. Feudal obligations were invoked to call out the nobility, even though the rebels lacked a king at that point. These militia soon dispersed, or were absorbed into the regular units. Moravia and Silesia later mobilized militia for their own defence, but otherwise also relied on professionals. Numbers fluctuated considerably, but Bohemia itself generally fielded around 12,000 men, Moravia and Silesia around 3,000 each, while Lusatia paid cash in lieu. The Upper and Lower Austrian Protestants only began mobilizing during 1619 and never completed their preparations, sending only a few thousand to the Confederate army. Foreign assistance was concentrated in Mansfeld's army that operated separately in western Bohemia and was easier to reach from outside the country. This included the two British regiments and at least seven German, one Dutch and four Walloon units, together totalling around 7,000 soldiers.[35]

The Confederates failed to match the Dutch, or later English and Scottish parliamentarians, who organized potent 'new model' armies to defeat their royalist opponents. Thurn and the other Bohemian commanders relied on their previous experience against the Turks, copying the organization and tactics of the imperial army. Dutch methods were advocated by the growing number of Protestant Germans and other volunteers and were eventually implemented when Anhalt assumed command in the spring of 1620.[36] However, many Bohemians opposed the changes and disagreements over organization added to those over command. The problems were partly structural, stemming from the system of separate contingents, each under its own general, answerable to the Estates that raised and paid for them. Major operations required extensive consultation, but the likelihood of agreement was also frustrated by the clash of personalities, notably among the Bohemians and between them and Anhalt and Mansfeld. Thurn was unable to balance his political and military roles, and favoured operations most obviously linked to furthering the rebellion. This necessitated relinquishing command in one area and travelling considerable distances to assume responsibility elsewhere, as at the end of 1618, when he left Hohenlohe in south-western Bohemia and went to deal with the Moravians. He repeated this in October 1619, again allowing Bucquoy to escape and regroup. In addition, operations were delayed for two months from March 1620 while the Confederates waited for Anhalt to arrive.

Paltry foreign support, combined with the leadership's reluctance to abandon established practices, ensured the Confederation remained chronically underfunded. The Bohemians eventually agreed taxes twice the level of the previous (1615) grant, while the other provinces also added new levies, but even the official amounts were considerably short of what was required. Those of Moravia covered only 60 per cent of actual costs, even assuming it had been possible to collect all that was owed. The war, along with growing popular discontent, ensured substantial arrears. The Directors and individual nobles made substantial loans, or sold their estates to raise regiments, while Prague's Jewish community was coerced into providing additional money and more came from property confiscated from Habsburg loyalists who had fled. However, the Directors decided against selling Rudolf's art collection, because they did not think they could find a buyer, and it even proved difficult to sell the confiscated land, some of which was simply given away to settle some of the Confederation's mounting debts. The poor response, together with the reluctance of creditors to advance loans, indicates widespread scepticism over the Confederation's future.

The Hungarian Crown

The Bohemians increasingly looked to Bethlen Gábor to save them. The Transylvanian prince had his eyes set on the Hungarian crown, always a more realistic prospect than the Bohemian one. He wrote to the Bohemians on 18 August 1619, announcing he would soon join them in Moravia. This was a ploy to win their support, which would improve his position in negotiations with the Hungarians who were meeting in Pressburg. A wave of re-conversions among the leading Magyar nobles of the western and north-western counties since 1608 had given the Catholics a majority in the diet again. However, neither they nor the Protestants wanted to be drawn into the Bohemian conflict. Bethlen posed as mediator, winning backing from disaffected Upper Hungarian Protestant magnates, like György Rákóczi and Counts Szaniszló and Imre Thurzó. His envoy persuaded the Ottoman grand vizier, Mehmed Pasha, to sanction war against the Habsburgs and promise Turkish infantry as auxiliaries.

Bethlen's intervention betrayed the problems that would bedevil all Transylvanian involvement in the war. He was convinced Frederick and the Bohemians were rich and would provide the subsidies he needed to keep his largely irregular cavalry army in the field and pay for the infantry and artillery required to take the Habsburg fortresses. For their part, Frederick and his advisers saw what they wanted: a man who claimed to have read the Bible 26 times had to be a crusader of the righteous against Habsburg Catholic tyranny. Bethlen had already demanded 400,000 talers and all of Inner Austria in June, but decided to start operations before Frederick agreed, since he needed a tangible success to convince the Bohemians and the sultan to back him. He left Cluj (Klausenburg) on 26 August with 35,000 men, while Rákóczi entered Kassa unopposed with 5,000 Upper Hungarians a week later. György Széchy and other Upper Hungarian supporters threatened Pressburg to disrupt the efforts of the loyalist Hungarian palatine, Sigismund Forgách, to organize resistance. The Upper Hungarian mining towns declared for Bethlen, but he delayed his own advance to convene a special assembly of supporters at Kassa who declared him 'Protector of Hungary' on 21 September, effectively deposing Forgách. Ferenc Rhédey was sent with over 12,000 horsemen across the Little Carpathians into Moravia, while Bethlen resumed his advance with the rest of his army towards Pressburg, destroying a Habsburg detachment sent to save it.

The situation looked dire for the Habsburgs. Garrisons along the Military Frontier declared for Bethlen, leaving only Komorn, Raab and Neutra loyal. Forgách could muster only 2,500 men in the field, while a mere 2,650 under Archduke Leopold held Vienna with a further 560 in Krems and the other Danube towns. Bucquoy and the main army of 17,770 was away around Tabor and Pisek in south-west Bohemia, with Dampierre and 8,600 along the Moravian frontier.[37] The timing was significant. Ferdinand was still on his way back from his coronation in Frankfurt, while the Bohemians had just declared their Confederation and elected Frederick. Bucquoy was obliged to abandon his advance against Prague, leave 5,000 men to hold his current positions and race with the rest to save Vienna.

Panic again gripped the Lower Austrian population as Bethlen's light cavalry crossed the Danube at Pressburg and swarmed across the area to the south during late October. Refugees crowded into the city, while the rich fled over the Alps. Bucquoy had joined Dampierre, but decided not to risk the emperor's only army as it was outnumbered three to two by Hohenlohe, Thurn and Rhédey approaching from Moravia. He retreated across the Danube at Vienna, burning the bridge on

25 October. Though they controlled the entire north bank, the Confederates could not reach the city on the other side, and were obliged to march east to cross downstream at Pressburg. Bethlen used the lull to consolidate his position in Hungary. Having captured Forgách at Pressburg, he forced him to convene a diet on 18 November to start the process of deposing Ferdinand as king. The Confederates finally crossed the river on 21 November, and moved west again on the south side, defeating Bucquoy's attempt to delay them at Bruck five days later. The Lower Austrian Protestants moved 3,000 men east towards Krems, cutting the Habsburg forces off from the other side.

For a third time within a year, the enemy was at the gates of Ferdinand's capital. Undaunted, the emperor dodged snow, refugees and Transylvanian marauders to re-enter the city. Leopold had made careful preparations since the last attack, stockpiling enough food to feed the 20,000 soldiers and 75,000 civilians who were now inside the city. The besiegers again appeared without heavy artillery and Bucquoy had torched the surrounding countryside so that it could not now sustain the 42,000 troops ringing Vienna. Heavy rain worsened their plight, especially among the Bohemians who had gone months without pay. The promised Turkish auxiliaries had yet to appear. The mutual disillusionment between Bethlen and his allies added to tensions in the Confederate camp where disease halved their effective strength. The final straw was news on 27 November that Transylvania had been attacked. The siege was abandoned a week later, with all the contingents hurrying home except the Bohemians, who remained in Lower Austria.

Polish Intervention

The attack on Transylvania followed long Habsburg efforts to enlist Polish support. Poland was potentially a more important ally than Spain, and Sigismund III was as devout a Catholic as Philip III. Poland's military power was to be demonstrated in 1621 when it was to raise an army of 45,000 backed by 40,000 Cossacks.[38] More significantly, Poland bordered on Silesia and Hungary, placing it in a direct position to help, and it had signed a mutual assistance pact in 1613 promising aid against rebellions. As Emperor Ferdinand's sister, the Polish queen naturally championed intervention, but the king remained undecided. His own ambitions remained firmly fixed on the Baltic and he was disappointed at his in-law's lack of assistance when Sweden invaded Livonia in 1617–18. (Ferdinand would again fail to help against a second invasion in 1621.) Sigismund also had to consider his nobles who preferred raiding against their traditional targets, the Turks and Muscovites. However, the Russians had made peace in December 1618, widening Sigismund's options.

Many Polish clergy were receptive to Habsburg arguments that the Protestant Bohemians posed a common threat. Sigismund had instructed his son Wladyslaw to decline a Bohemian invitation to stand in their royal election.[39] As the situation worsened during 1619, Ferdinand held out inducements, including an offer to relinquish the bishopric of Breslau to Poland. Many Polish historians regard the Thirty Years War as a lost opportunity, arguing that Sigismund should have accepted this offer, or grabbed Silesia by playing the role later adopted by Sweden and joining the German Protestants.[40] Sigismund had no such plans. Instead, he sought a way of satisfying the Polish pro-Habsburg lobby without committing himself to a long war that would distract from his primary objective of recovering Sweden. The leaders of the Sejm agreed, because limited intervention provided a way of removing the 30,000 unpaid Cossacks. These troops had been discharged after the recent war with Russia and their raiding across the southern frontier risked provoking a new conflict with the sultan. The Cossacks have entered history as the Lisowski, after their original commander, Aleksander Lisowski, a Lithuanian veteran who commanded a regiment in the Russian war. The Lisowski were the kind of cavalry that 'God would not want and the Devil was afraid of'.[41] Unlike the traditional Polish cavalry, they wore no body armour, relying on speed and fake retreats to lure opponents into traps. They were happy to be paid, but also fought for booty, deliberately terrorizing civilians into submission.

The Habsburg ambassador intended to recruit the Cossacks to reinforce the imperial army, but they were reluctant to serve too far from home in a land they considered full of impregnable fortresses where plunder would be hard to take. Plans were changed so that 4,000 Lisowski joined 3,000 other Cossacks recruited by György Homonnai, an Upper Hungarian magnate who was also a member of the Transylvanian Estates and a personal enemy of Bethlen, who he believed had cheated him in that country's election of 1613. Having been driven into exile, Homonnai had already fostered two failed rebellions. He now struck across from his estates in Podolia at the end of October 1619. Bethlen had left Rákóczi with only 4,000 men in Transylvania, refusing to believe Homonnai posed a threat. The two armies met near Ztropka (Stropkow in modern Slovakia) on 22 November, where Rákóczi's men were routed after they mistook the classic feigned retreat for the real thing.[42]

Homonnai's attack fuelled an already volatile situation in east Central Europe. Despite the grand vizier's promise, the Ottomans had hesitated to break their truce with the Habsburgs. Nonetheless, they regarded Bethlen as their client and did not want him driven from Transylvania, especially by the Poles who were already interfering in neighbouring Moldavia. Peace had just been concluded with Persia, allowing the sultan to send the Tartars, backed by Ottoman regulars, into Moldavia where they routed a Polish relief force at Cecora in October 1620. Sigismund sent a huge army the following year that entrenched at Chocim (Hotim) on the Dneister and managed to repel almost twice its number of Tartars and Turks. Fresh problems with Sweden forced Sigismund to agree peace later in 1621, restoring the pre-1619 situation, though Poland had to accept the sultan's candidate as prince of Moldavia. This conflict was separate from the Thirty Years War, but nonetheless proved significant for the Empire in preventing Poland and the Ottomans from intervening.

The threat to Bethlen was already receding before he left his camp outside Vienna. He had arrested most of Homonnai's supporters after the earlier rebellions. Finding few willing to support him, Homonnai was already in retreat by 2 December. With the wider situation remaining unclear, Bethlen was nonetheless forced to accept the mediation of the Hungarian diet, agreeing an eight-month truce with Ferdinand on 16 January 1620. Bethlen remained a threat to Ferdinand, but the immediate danger had passed.

Sigismund refused to allow the Lisowski back into Poland, and redirected them along the mountains into Silesia to join the imperial army. Five detachments totalling 19,000 fighters set out between January and July 1620, though some were intercepted by the Silesian militia. The steady reinforcement enabled Bucquoy to resume the offensive, launching three attacks from Krems in March, April and early June against Thurn's Bohemians and Austrians entrenched around Langenlois to the north. The Silesians and Moravians returned, bringing the Confederate army up to 25,000 by May when Anhalt arrived to take command.[43] They were joined by 8,000 Hungarian and Transylvanian cavalry sent by Bethlen who, despite Ferdinand's generous terms, still distrusted the emperor and decided to re-enter the war. Bethlen and Frederick had already sent a joint delegation to Constantinople in March 1620 to seek Ottoman assistance for the revolt. Mehmed Aga reached Prague in July to deliver the sultan's belated congratulations on Frederick's coronation. He asked to see where the Defenestration had taken place and enthusiastically promised 60,000 Ottoman auxiliaries for Bohemia. Many in Prague were deeply uncomfortable with courting the Ottomans, yet the leadership was seduced by the fantastical scheme of a grand alliance smashing both Poland and the Habsburgs. Scultetus did a theological somersault to stress common ground between Calvinism and Islam, while Baron Tschernembl argued any means were justified provided they saved the true cause from the papists. Despite misgivings, Frederick wrote to the sultan on 12 July, making Bohemia a tributary state of the Ottoman empire in return for assistance.[44] A delegation of a hundred Bohemians, Hungarians and Transylvanians set out for Constantinople with 70,000 fl. in bribes to seal the deal. Meanwhile, Frederick promised 300,000 fl. to Bethlen, even pawning his jewels to raise the first instalment.

With support growing, and having easily repulsed another attack by Homonnai in August 1620, Bethlen seized control of the diet at Neusohl in Upper Hungary. This had convened in May at Ferdinand's request to broker peace among all Hungarians. Bethlen's supporters declared the abolition of the clerical Estate and the confiscation of the property of all who opposed them. Ferdinand ordered the diet to disband on 13 August. Twelve days later, Bethlen's supporters elected him king of Hungary. Throughout, the solidly Catholic Croatian diet (*Sabor*) rejected the Hungarians' overtures and aligned itself with its Inner Austrian neighbours, still loyal to the Habsburgs.

FERDINAND GATHERS HIS FORCES

The deteriorating situation throughout 1619 at least encouraged Ferdinand's potential supporters to accept his appeals as serious. The Habsburg monarchy was at breaking point. Ferdinand found himself with 20 million florins of debts on his accession. Crown revenue was only 2.4 million, but much of this was now controlled by the rebel Estates whose taxes, worth 3 million fl. annually, he was also denied. The imperial army consumed 5 million fl. in pay, provisions and munitions in the ten months to June 1619, whereas revenue, forced loans and Spanish and papal subsidies provided just 3 million. When pay arrears and other liabilities were included, the military deficit reached 4.3 million fl., in addition to the monarchy's existing debt.[45]

Ferdinand might struggle on with further expedients, while the Poles might yet eliminate Bethlen, but he could never defeat all his opponents without substantial additional help. From his imperial coronation he launched a concerted effort to secure this. Spain, France and the papacy were approached for cash and diplomatic assistance in deterring the Protestant Union from intervening, while Bavaria and Saxony were asked to provide direct military support.

Bavaria

Duke Maximilian saw his chance to achieve his long-cherished ambitions. He ignored Habsburg appeals for help throughout 1618 while quietly preparing to re-establish the Liga they had forced him to disband. Frightened by the Bohemian crisis, the former members welcomed the chance to strengthen their security. Maximilian was careful not to show his hand, allowing Mainz to take the lead in reviving the organization that was essentially active again from August 1619.[46] Ferdinand's visit to Munich in October on his way back from Frankfurt and his election enabled Maximilian to move to stage two, seeking not merely confirmation for the Liga but the promise of concessions at the Palatinate's expense. The growing crisis at Vienna forced Ferdinand to accept 'the Bavarian devil to drive out the Bohemian beelzebub'.[47] In the Treaty of Munich of 8 October 1619, Ferdinand recognized the Liga and requested its assistance, thereby establishing the legal basis for all future Bavarian action. As the emperor's auxiliary assisting to restore the imperial public peace, Maximilian was entitled to proper compensation. Though the entire Liga would assist, only Bavaria's expenses were covered, in a separate arrangement that promised the duchy part of Austria until Ferdinand could repay Maximilian.[48]

The Liga met in Würzburg in December, its first congress since 1613, and agreed to raise an army of 25,000 funded by members' contributions. The previous organization was re-established, with south

German and Rhenish Directories under Bavaria and Mainz respectively. Membership was exclusively Catholic and predominantly ecclesiastical, as the smaller imperial counties and cities abstained or only participated intermittently. Salzburg learned from Raitenau's fate in 1611 and cooperated, but still refused formal membership.[49] Maximilian secured exclusive direction of the Liga's military affairs, underpinned by his efficient bureaucracy and Jean Tserclaes Tilly as an experienced field commander. Mainz declined to replace Bavaria when Maximilian's term of office expired at the end of 1621, leaving the duke in charge of the general direction of the Liga throughout its remaining existence. Ferdinand of Cologne, Maximilian's brother, refused to join, but nonetheless cooperated with the Liga and became the real head of the Rhenish members.

For Maximilian, war was a demonstration of power (*potestas*), not violence (*violentia*). He had himself painted as a warrior prince in full armour, but had little interest in personal glory. He dutifully accompanied his army in 1620, but left actual command to Tilly in whom he had complete trust. Operations were to be the legally sanctioned, controlled application of force for precise objectives.[50] He refused to move until the emperor took the necessary steps to sanction Bavarian intervention and provide cast-iron guarantees that Maximilian would receive his reward. Ferdinand had already annulled Frederick's election as Bohemian king on 19 January 1620. At Maximilian's insistence, he issued an ultimatum to surrender the crown by 1 June or face the imperial ban. This would make Frederick an outlaw, entitling the emperor to confiscate his possessions and reassign them to whoever he chose. Five days after the deadline expired, Ferdinand authorized Maximilian to intervene in Bohemia, which he followed by a similar mandate on 23 July against the Upper Austrian rebels.

With typical caution, Maximilian sought additional confirmation from Spain and the papacy. Frederick's acceptance of the Bohemian crown finally convinced the pontiff that the situation was serious and he doubled his existing subsidy to the emperor. In all, Pope Paul V sent 380,000 florins between 1618 and 1621, equivalent to a mere single month's pay for the imperial army.[51] He proved more generous towards Maximilian, because the Liga's existence allowed him to prove his Catholic credentials without directly assisting the Habsburgs. However, he refrained from digging into his own pockets, imposing instead a special levy on the German and Italian clergy that raised 1.24 million fl. across 1620–4. Contributions from the Liga's other members in the same period totalled 4.83 million, while Paul spent more than six times as much on building projects and nepotism. For him, this clearly was not a religious war.

The approach to Spain had rather more significant consequences. Maximilian generally opposed Spanish involvement, but needed it now. He could not move against the Austrian and Bohemian Confederates without exposing the Liga territories to potential reprisals from the Protestant Union forces. Spanish intervention on the Rhine would pin these down and free the Liga army under Tilly to turn eastwards. Spain had been slow to respond to the situation after Emperor Matthias's death because this coincided with a long-planned state visit to Portugal intended to bolster the monarchy. Absent since April 1619, Philip III fell ill on his return in September and never fully recovered. Many still opposed intervention in Germany, but Frederick's acceptance of the Bohemian crown was considered such an affront to the Casa d'Austria that it could not go unpunished.[52]

The complex nature of Spanish involvement takes some unravelling. Just over 2 million florins were sent in 1619–21 to subsidize the maintenance of the imperial army and help pay the Polish Cossacks. Imperial officers were allowed to recruit new units in Spanish possessions, chiefly 6,000 Walloons raised after January 1619. Some additional help came from Spain's Italian allies, notably the grand duke of Tuscany who financed Dampierre's regiment of Germans and Walloons whose arrival in the Hofburg so startled the Lower Austrians. Other units were sent directly under Spanish command and pay, though many of these were newly recruited since the monarchy had only about 58,000 soldiers at this point.[53] Like Bavaria, Spain presented its involvement as upholding the imperial constitution. The first column of 6,000 foot and 1,000 horse under Marradas and Johann VIII von Nassau marched from the Netherlands as 'Burgundian Kreis troops', ostensibly fulfilling the region's obligations under the public peace legislation. They deliberately avoided Union territories as they crossed from Alsace to Passau and thence to join Bucquoy in Upper Austria in July 1619. A second column of 7,000 Italians crossed the St Gotthard pass and moved down the Etsch valley to reach Innsbruck on 15 November 1619. Four thousand continued down the Rhine to bring the Army of Flanders back up to strength, leaving only 3,000 under Verdugo and Spinelli to march north over the Golden Track into Bohemia in January. A third column of 9,000 Spanish and Italians marched north from Italy later in 1620, but were sent along the Chérzery valley to reinforce the Army of Flanders. This was the last use of the western stretch of the Spanish Road that had become too exposed through Savoy's defection to France. It was part of a wider strategy to rebuild Spain's offensive capacity as the Twelve Year Truce with the Dutch neared its end, and by June 1620 the Army of Flanders mustered 44,200 foot and 7,000 horse.[54]

The Final Pieces

Failure of Saxon mediation forced Johann Georg to change tack and join Ferdinand in the hope his participation would keep the crisis contained to Bohemia. He used his influence in the Upper and Lower Saxon Kreise to frustrate efforts by Union activists to recruit troops, though he was unable to prevent his Ernestine relations in Thuringia from sending several units to Bohemia. The elector of Mainz and Maximilian refused to drop demands that the Protestants return church land taken since 1552, but they did compromise with Saxony and Hessen-Darmstadt at a meeting in Mühlhausen in March 1620. Johann Georg accepted Bavaria's interpretation that Frederick had broken the public peace. In return, Bavaria and Mainz promised not to use force to recover the former bishoprics, provided their current Lutheran administrators remained loyal to the emperor.[55]

Maximilian pressed Ferdinand to complete the process and place Frederick under the imperial ban in March, but backed away once he realized this was blatantly exposing his ambitions to supplant his cousin as elector. It was agreed to wait until a clear victory established a more suitable opportunity. Ferdinand also addressed Johann Georg's concerns over the legitimacy of Saxon intervention by specifically commissioning him in April 1620 to restore order in Lusatia. The commission was revised in June at his request to include special safeguards for the Lutheran inhabitants, while a month later Ferdinand agreed Saxony could retain both parts of Lusatia until he could refund its expenses.

Neutralization of the Union removed the final obstacle to action. Another Union congress in June 1619 had authorized the mobilization of 11,000 men for home defence. The activists agreed privately to raise more but had still only mustered 13,000 under the margrave of Ansbach at Ulm in May 1620, having failed to intercept the Spanish reinforcements. They had been completely out-recruited by the Liga, now massing 30,000 troops opposite them at Lauingen and Günzburg.[56] Nonetheless, Maximilian wanted to be sure the Union would not attack once Tilly headed east into Bohemia. Talks opened on 18 June with the intention of avoiding violence altogether in Germany, and France finally intervened as Louis XIII sent the duc d'Angoulême to mediate. Ferdinand had sought French support, claiming that, like the Huguenots, the Bohemians represented a religious and political threat to Catholic monarchy; however, Louis rejected the call for solidarity in favour of asserting what he regarded as his country's proper role as European arbiter (see Chapter 11). With Angoulême's assistance, the Liga and Union agreed a truce on 3 July, promising not to fight each other in Germany but leaving Maximilian free to intervene in Bohemia, while the Union activists could oppose Spain if they wished. Angoulême hoped to extend this into a general peace, but Ferdinand seized the opportunity to attack.

WHITE MOUNTAIN

The Habsburg Offensive

Ferdinand's offensive involved six separate armies. Bucquoy left Dampierre to hold Vienna with over 5,000 men against Bethlen, and advanced from Krems with 21,500 to eject Anhalt from his foothold in Lower Austria. Maximilian placed 8,600 men to guard his frontier with the Upper Palatinate, and accompanied the main army of 21,400 drawn from the troops that had blocked the Unionists at Ulm to enter Upper Austria on 24 July. Spain joined in by invading the Lower Palatinate, leaving Johann Georg no choice but to start operations against Lusatia in September. These moves were the necessary preparatory steps to the final assault on Bohemia itself.

The Confederates' lacklustre campaign during the first half of 1620 disillusioned the Lower Austrians whose homes were being wrecked in the fighting. Ferdinand split the opposition by giving the verbal assurance he would respect the religious privileges of individual nobles provided they paid homage: 86 Lutheran lords and knights joined 81 Catholics and the representatives of 18 crown towns in accepting

Ferdinand as the legitimate ruler of Lower Austria on 13 July. The remaining 62 Protestant nobles fled to Retz on the Moravian frontier from where they issued a declaration of defiance. The peasant militias offered only minimal resistance in the Upper Austrian mountains as the Bavarians poured in, capturing Linz on 3 August. Tschernembl and the radicals fled, leaving the moderates to surrender on 20 August, placing their 3,500 regular troops at the Liga's disposal. Ferdinand now declared 33 of the Retz signatories outlaws. A couple of Austrian regiments remained with Anhalt's army, but effectively both provinces had been lost to the Confederate cause. Adam von Herberstorff was left to hold Upper Austria with 5,000 men, while Maximilian and Tilly headed east along the Austrian–Bohemian frontier to join Bucquoy. Despite the Protestant majority among their inhabitants, both Austrian provinces had been recovered permanently for the Catholic Habsburgs without a single battle.

The situation grew even more serious for Frederick along the Rhine where his supporters were collecting to oppose Spain. After leaving Ulm, Ansbach marched north-west to Oppenheim, between Mainz and Worms, to cover the right half of the Lower Palatinate that protruded west of the Rhine. Together with 5,700 local militia, he now mustered 21,800 troops, and was joined by a further 2,000 English volunteers under Sir Horace de Vere in October, convoyed south by 2,000 Dutch cavalry under Prince Frederick Henry, Maurice's younger brother. Sir Horace was one of the 'Fighting Veres' family with long experience of the Dutch wars, including the siege of Jülich. His regiment was the second British contingent, arriving five months after Grey's regiment.[57] Despite his numerical superiority, Ansbach was reluctant to fight, pinning his hopes of British mediation.

Luis de Velasco and 18,000 men were concentrated in Flanders to deter the Dutch, while Spinola left Brussels on 18 August with another 19,000, heading east through the electorate of Trier. Having secured Koblenz, Spinola rapidly overran Palatine territory west of the Rhine, taking Kreuznach and Alzey. Apart from brief skirmishes between the cavalry, Ansbach avoided contact. Nonetheless, Spinola remained concerned at the possibility of more substantial Dutch intervention with only a few months remaining until the end of the Truce, while his Italians refused to undertake another siege given the lateness of the season and the worsening weather. Ansbach retained the principal fortresses of

Oppenheim, Heidelberg, Mannheim and Frankenthal as both sides retired into winter quarters in December. The Dutch went home, disgusted with the lacklustre Union leadership.

These operations dispelled Johann Georg's hopes of a mediated settlement and he began his own advance, despite the obvious lack of enthusiasm among his officers. Count Wolfgang von Mansfeld, a distant relation of Frederick's general, concentrated 8,300 soldiers and 3,000 militia at Dresden, prompting the Bohemians to halt grain sales to Saxony. Having summoned the Lusatian Estates to meet him, Johann Georg finally invaded on 3 September 1620, overrunning the western half of the two provinces. The margrave of Jägerndorf still held the east and had put 2,000 men into Bautzen. A Saxon defeat would destroy Johann Georg's remaining credit in Protestant Germany and give the Bohemians a much needed boost. Despite obstruction from his subordinates, Wolfgang Mansfeld pressed on, forcing Bautzen to surrender on 5 October after a short bombardment that destroyed most of the town. Most of the Lusatian nobles and towns now accepted the Saxon guarantee for their privileges in return for renouncing the Confederation, but Jägerndorf still held out in Görlitz in the south-eastern corner of the province and it was now too late in the season to begin operations against Silesia further east.[58]

The main Confederate army had been paralysed by three pay mutinies from the end of June, which finally ended on 2 August when the government extorted more money from the Prague Jews. This denied Anhalt the last opportunity to crush Bucquoy before Maximilian joined him. Abandoning his positions in Lower Austria, he retreated north into Moravia, thinking his opponents were heading in that direction. This had been Bucquoy's intention but Ferdinand overruled his own general, placing him under the command of Maximilian who followed Tilly's advice to march directly on Prague. Maximilian had received 5,000 additional Liga troops, but his army already had 500 sick before it left Bavaria and was now gripped by 'Hungarian fever', a form of typhus or cholera depending on the contemporary diagnosis, that would kill 12,000 Catholic troops before the year was out.[59]

The epidemic is an indication that the full horrors of war were present from the outset, and were not a product of escalating barbarity. The irregular forces on both sides were already infamous for their cruelty. The first group of Cossacks crossing Moravia in January 1620 had disrupted a wedding, kidnapping the bride after murdering the groom. Ferdinand informed the Saxon elector after the siege of Vienna that

> the Hungarians had devastated, plundered and burned everything where they had stayed, and (it is said), stripped the people to their last threads, ruined, cut them down and dragged a large number of them as prisoners, subjected them to unheard of torture to find money and property, dragged away numerous lads of twelve to sixteen years old, and so ill-treated pregnant women and others, that many of them were found dead everywhere on the roads. They pulled ropes around the men's necks so tight that their eyes popped out of their heads.

Ferdinand concluded with a remark that became the standard refrain throughout the war: 'Indeed, the enemy has behaved so terribly every-where, that one can almost not remember whether such tyranny was ever heard of from the Turks.'[60]

The Liga troops behaved terribly during their invasion of Upper Austria, despite being well-supplied. The violence may partly have been revenge for the peasant resistance along the frontier, but there was already disorder on the march through Bavaria and the targets were indiscriminate, the men plundering Catholic monasteries and convents as well as Protestant homes. Catholic diarists depict such breaches of discipline as divine punishment for the heretical rebels, and clearly many senior figures used this as an excuse, ignoring the duke's efforts to maintain order, like his courtiers who helped ransack Schloss Greilenstein in Lower Austria.[61] Religious hatred was fanned by a large crowd of priests accompanying the combined imperial-Bavarian army, including the superior general of the barefoot Carmelite order, Domenico à Jesu Maria. Born Domingo Ruzzola in Aragon, he already had a reputation for prophesy and had won Maximilian's confidence after curing an eye infection and other 'miraculous' acts.[62]

Realizing his mistake, Anhalt hurried west to block the invasion from a position at Tabor as the imperial-Bavarian army reached Budweis. Thurn was still sulking at being replaced by Anhalt, while Count Mansfeld resented Hohenlohe's promotion to field marshal and refused to cooperate, marching south-west in a futile attempt to distract Maximilian by threatening Bavaria. The duke bypassed Tabor to the west, storming Prachatice on 27 September, and moving through Pisek to reach Pilsen on 5 October. Mansfeld raced back, arriving just in time, while Anhalt followed to Rokycany a short distance to the east.

Mansfeld opened the first of what would prove an almost continuous series of secret talks over possible defection (see Chapter 10, p.326). Maximilian and Bucquoy thought it was a ploy to gain time – supplies were running short and the duke was allegedly reduced to eating black bread while Tilly snatched an apple from a passing Dominican friar. It grew so cold that some soldiers froze to death at night.[63]

Determined to maintain momentum, Tilly had no intention of being stuck outside Pilsen all winter and, backed by Maximilian, overruled Bucquoy to march north towards Prague. Marradas was left to blockade Pilsen, while Wallenstein was sent with a small imperial detachment into north-west Bohemia to establish contact with the Saxons still beyond the mountains. Anhalt dashed north to block the way to Prague, to an important road junction at Rakovnic. Possibly influenced by Maximilian's example, Frederick now joined his troops, confirming Anhalt's authority and temporarily boosting morale. The soldiers agreed to suspend another pay protest and dig into a wooded ridge behind a marsh. Maximilian was stuck in front of this position from 27 October. Bucquoy was badly injured in a skirmish on 3 November, but a supply train arrived the following day, reviving morale. Maximilian and Tilly knew they had only a short time to force a battle before winter suspended operations and gave Frederick a reprieve. Covered by morning mist and some noisy musketeers left to distract the Confederates, the army slipped round the ridge on 5 November and raced towards Prague. Anhalt only realized the danger later that evening, but force-marched his men to overtake his opponents and reach the White Mountain, about 8km west of the city, at midnight on 7 November.

The Battle of White Mountain

The coming battle was the first major action of the war and proved to be the most decisive.[64] Anhalt's position was relatively strong. The White Mountain ridge, taking its name from chalk and gravel pits, ran north-east to south-west for about 2km, rising about 60 metres from the surrounding area. It was strongest at the northern (right) end where the incline was steepest. This end of the ridge was covered by a walled, wooded game park containing the Star Palace, a small pavilion where Frederick and his wife had stayed prior to their triumphal entry to Prague a year earlier. The marshy Scharka stream lay about 2km in front of his position, but was deemed too far from the hill to be defended.

Anhalt had 11,000 foot, 5,000 cavalry and 5,000 Hungarian and Transylvanian light cavalry. He wanted to entrench the entire length of the ridge, but his mutinous soldiers were exhausted and said digging was only for peasants. Frederick went on to Prague, persuading the Estates to find 600 talers to buy spades, but it was too late and the soldiers managed to make only five small sconces. Most of the artillery had not caught up, and the ten cannon with the army were distributed along the line. Johann Ernst of Weimar held the Star Palace with his infantry regiment, while the rest of the Confederate army drew up along the ridge in two lines in the Dutch manner, interspersing cavalry squadrons in close support between the infantry battalions. The light cavalry were dispirited, having been surprised earlier that night and most were positioned fairly uselessly as a third line in the rear, while some covered the extreme right. Despite obvious shortcomings, Anhalt remained optimistic, believing the enemy would simply stall in front of his position as at Rakovnic, and Frederick remained in Prague to eat breakfast.

Thick fog obscured the imperial-Bavarian approach on the morning of Sunday 8 November. The advance guard secured the two crossings over the stream, followed by the rest of the army that deployed from 8 a.m. The Liga regiments drew up on the left opposite the northern end of the ridge, while Bucquoy's Imperialists took station on the right. Together, they had 2,000 more men and two more cannon than their opponents, and they were in better spirits. Both halves of the army deployed in the Spanish fashion, grouping the 17,000 foot into ten large blocks, accompanied by small cavalry squadrons.

The commanders conferred while their men took up their positions and heard mass. Bucquoy wanted to repeat the earlier trick and slip past to Prague, but Maximilian and Tilly were convinced it was time for the decisive blow. The dispute was allegedly resolved by Domenico bursting in and brandishing an image of the Madonna whose eyes had been poked out by Calvinist iconoclasts. If this is true, it was a calculated act, because the Carmelite had found the icon in a ruined house over three weeks before. The Catholic troops were elated when they received the order to attack; they were tired of chasing the Confederates across Bohemia and savoured the prospect of plundering Prague.

The artillery had been firing for some time to little effect. At about

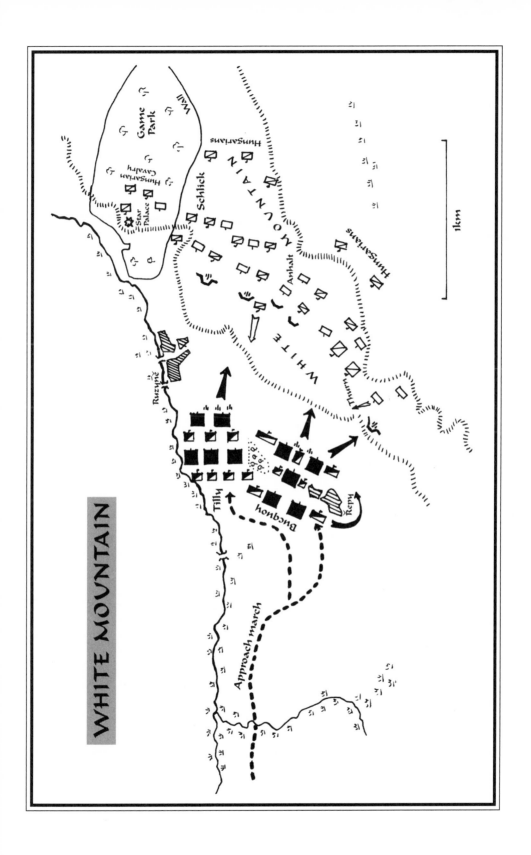

WHITE MOUNTAIN

Game Park

Wall

Hungarians

Star Palace

Hungarian Cavalry

Schlick

MOUNTAIN

Anhalt

Hungarians

WHITE

Ruzyné

Tilly

Buquoy

Repy

Approach march

1km

fifteen minutes after midday all twelve guns fired simultaneously to signal the advance. The Imperialists had less ground to cover to reach the ridge than the Bavarians who also faced a steeper climb. Anhalt decided on an active defence, sending two cavalry regiments down the slope to drive off the imperial cavalry screening the flanks of the Italian and Walloon infantry spearheading the assault. Thurn's own infantry regiment then moved down to engage the enemy foot as they laboured up the slope. Seeing their own horsemen retiring, the Thurn regiment fired a general salvo at extreme range and fled. Anhalt's son tried to retrieve the situation with his own cavalry regiment from the Confederate second line, his men using their pistols to blast their way into one of the imperial tercios. For a brief moment it looked as if the Confederates might yet snatch victory, but more imperial horse came up, and even Bucquoy arrived, despite his earlier wound, to rally the infantry. Anhalt junior was captured and within an hour of the main action starting the Confederate horse were in full retreat, many units pulling out of the line without even engaging the enemy. The Bohemian foot followed soon after, while the Hungarians fled, some dismounting in order to escape through the vineyards covering the way to Prague. Despite claims of their being spooked by Domenico's sudden appearance through the smoke, the panic stemmed from reports that Bucquoy's Polish Cossacks had ridden round the south-west end of the ridge and were already at the rear. Schlick's Moravians on the right lasted longer, largely because of the time it took Tilly to reach them, but they too gave way around 1.30 p.m. A few survivors resisted for another half hour in the Star Palace before surrendering.

Frederick stayed in Prague all day and was tucking into lunch when the first fugitives arrived. Many drowned in the Moldau in their desperation to escape. The imperial-Bavarian army lost 650 killed and wounded, mostly to young Anhalt's brave attack. The Confederates left 600 dead on the field, with a further 1,000 strewn on the way to Prague, as well as 1,200 wounded. The losses were severe, but most had escaped. Prague was a large, fortified city and it was unlikely the enemy could besiege it with winter approaching. It was here that Tilly's strategy of relentless pressure paid dividends, transforming a respectable battlefield success into a decisive victory. Already weakened by Tilly's vigorous campaign, Confederate morale collapsed. Even Maximilian was surprised at the extent of the enemy's demoralization, expecting defiance when he summoned Prague to surrender. Confederate leadership was utterly pathetic. Tschernembl and Thurn's son, Franz, tried to organize a defence on the Charles Bridge to stop the Bavarians crossing the river. Frederick hesitated, but Anhalt and the elder Thurn thought the situation hopeless. Queen Elizabeth, heavily pregnant with her fifth child, left early the next morning. Her husband feared angry citizens might prevent him escaping if he took the crown with him, so he left it behind, along with his other insignia and numerous confidential documents, and joined the refugees streaming eastwards out of the city.

Collapse of the Confederation

Imperialists were already entering the western side of the city, catching the tail of the royal baggage train. Many Confederates were still loitering, demanding their back pay, but they dispersed once Maximilian granted them amnesty on 10 November. Those foolish enough to remain were murdered over the next few days. The city was stuffed full of valuables, cattle and other property brought there for safekeeping prior to the battle and now abandoned in the precipitous retreat. Along with empty mansions and houses, it was too tempting for the victorious troops who began seizing what they found in the streets, then breaking into homes, and finally robbing with violence. 'Those who have nothing, fear for their necks, and all regret not taking up arms and fighting to the last man.'[65]

Under these conditions, further pursuit was impossible. The winter was also exceptionally cold, with even the Bosporus said to have frozen over. Mansfeld still held most of western Bohemia, while Jägerndorf was in Silesia and Bethlen in Hungary. Yet nothing could slow the collapse of Frederick's regime as moderates distanced themselves from the revolt. The Moravian Estates already paid homage to Ferdinand at the end of December. Frederick fled east over the mountains into Silesia in the middle of November, but was given a frosty welcome by a population angry at his perceived Calvinist extremism. Fearing the Saxons would block his escape to the north, Frederick hurried on down the Oder into Brandenburg in December, leaving the Lusatians and Silesians to surrender to Johann Georg after prolonged negotiations completed in March 1621.

Bethlen had finally renounced his truce with the emperor on 1 September, advancing again with 30,000 horsemen to overrun Upper

Hungary and retake Pressburg, where he intended to hold his coronation with the St Stephen's crown he had captured the year before. Most of the Polish Cossacks arriving during 1620 had been attached to Dampierre's command and deployed to cover the harvest against Transylvanian raiders. A Liga regiment arrived at the end of September 1620, as well as Croats and the private retainers of Magyar magnates tired of Bethlen's depredations. The Inner Austrian Estates mobilized 2,500 men, while their Lower Austrian counterparts sent a Protestant regiment that had not joined the Confederate army. Dampierre advanced to disrupt Bethlen's coronation, and though he was to be killed on 9 October he had managed to burn the Pressburg bridge, denying access to the south side of the Danube. Bethlen sent another 9,000 troops to help Frederick, but these arrived too late for White Mountain and retreated rapidly through Moravia in November.

Though the grand vizier ratified the alliance agreed with Frederick in July, it became clear that the sultan was only using this to pressure Ferdinand to adjust the 1606 truce. News of White Mountain reached Constantinople in January, removing any doubts about the wisdom of avoiding a breach with the emperor. Meanwhile, the Ottoman pasha of Buda seized the Hungarian border town of Waitzen long claimed by his master. This alarmed the Magyar nobility, exposing the consequences of their internecine struggle and Bethlen's inability to protect them from the Ottomans. The leading families either declared for Ferdinand or at least joined the French ambassador in pressing Bethlen to reopen talks at Hainburg in January 1621.

ACCOUNTING FOR FAILURE

The Confederate commanders sought to exonerate themselves in letters sent to Frederick.[66] Thurn echoed the views of Calvinist propagandists, blaming the defeat on the sins of the Bohemian people, comparing their situation to God's punishment of the Israelites – an argument implying there was still hope since God later delivered them from Egypt. Anhalt was more forthcoming. He cited points raised by others, such as the reluctance of some units to engage, but emphasized the general declining cohesion and growing insubordination. These he blamed on lack of foreign support and the wilful failure of the civil administration to meet the army's pay arrears, which had climbed to 5.5 million fl. by the time of the battle.

Confederate organization was certainly deficient, and it was not until August 1620 that a war council was established to oversee pay, supplies and fortifications. Poor accounting inflated the total arrears, because few checks were carried out to verify the amounts claimed by the soldiers. However, the defeat was not due to lack of resources. Mansfeld's men had not been paid for six months when they were defeated at Záblati, yet Bucquoy found 100,000 fl. in gold, along with their general's own plate worth another 50,000 talers. Bucquoy went on to take castles in south Bohemia, finding further hoards, including 300,000 talers in Frauenberg (Hluboká) alone.[67]

The aspects highlighted by the commanders were symptoms, not causes of the defeat. Failure to mobilize resources indicated the leadership's incapacity to develop the revolt's potential. This lay in a common political culture, not religion, language or ethnicity, all of which divided supporters. Protestants formed the majority across Bohemia, Moravia, Silesia, Lusatia and Austria, but lacked a common creed. Even where there were strong theological similarities, as between Palatine Calvinists and the Bohemian Brethren, cultural factors could override this as Frederick discovered with his iconoclastic programme in Prague. The Bohemians were largely Czechs, but many of their nobles spoke German. Some families with German names conversely spoke Czech, while the Moravians spoke Czech or Slovak, the Silesians either German or Polish, and the Lusatians either German or Wendish. Leading Habsburg loyalists like Lobkowitz, Martinitz and Slavata were Czech speakers, while other families such as the Waldsteins, Dietrichsteins, Kinskys, Kaunitz, Czernin and Tiefenbachs had members on both sides. There were common myths of origin, with one presenting Poles and Czechs as descendants of two brothers, Lech and Cech. Yet, Pavel Stránsky, who supported the revolt, denied the Czechs of Bohemia and Moravia were of the same nation. In short, there was no match between confession, language and political loyalty, and attempts to portray events as a national movement against German oppression are anachronistic.[68]

What united the Bohemian rebels was their cultural and political identification with the crown of St Wenceslas and what this symbolized. Stránsky and other writers linked nation to Estates' rights, not language or religion, and it was through this political culture that the Confederates forged alliances with the Austrians, Transylvanians and Upper Hungarians.[69] The Bohemian magnate Vilém Rozemberk considered it entirely appropriate to present himself as a 'native' candidate in the Polish royal election of 1573. Though Stránsky was a burgher and while there were also educational and commercial links across the provinces, the common political culture was primarily restricted to the nobility, and therein lay much of the problem.

The Confederates' slogan of Estates' rights represented a form of monarchy, not a rejection of kingship.[70] They objected to exclusion from the exercise of royal power, not the presence of a king. The Confederation's founding diet explicitly rejected Dutch republicanism in 1619, legitimating itself according to existing laws, not new, abstract ideals of liberty or sovereignty of the people. Unlike the Dutch rebels or the English and Scottish parliamentarians, Central European nobles were unable to broaden their movement's social base. Tschernembl was prepared to abolish serfdom in return for peasant support by 1620, but his colleagues rejected this, preferring an alliance with the sultan instead. Peasant attacks on the invaders were largely self-defence, and they also struck at Confederate troops who, for instance, demolished entire villages in their frantic search for firewood on the eve of White Mountain. The urban burghers were predominantly Utraquists, closer theologically to Catholicism but culturally and politically aligned with the Lutherans and Bohemian Brethren. Already alarmed by the Defenestration, they rapidly lost sympathy with the revolt as the nobles sought to shift the burden of military taxation onto them.[71] The aristocrats also marginalized the poorer knights, many of whom were excusing themselves from the Confederate army by 1619, claiming ill-health.

Personal rivalries undermined solidarity even among the aristocrats, as we have seen. However, the personal character of early modern politics exposed a further weakness. The individual character of vassalage offered people the chance to change sides, seeking a pardon in return for an appropriately humble submission. Ferdinand played on this, carefully selecting those he declared outlaws, leaving the majority free to seek his forgiveness.

Far from being the faith of historical progress, Bohemian Protestantism symbolized a fading version of aristocratic corporatism threatened by the growth of a more centralized state. The Habsburgs' decision to make Catholicism the touchstone of political loyalty gave centralization a confessional character, though there was nothing specifically 'Catholic' about it, as indicated by the reverse pairing of Protestantism with the political establishment in countries like England. The limited opportunities for military and political appointments encouraged Protestants to identify with a romanticized world of paternalist landlords, something that found direct expression through their patronage of parish appointments. They remained linked to territorial and provincial politics through their possession of estates entitling them to seats in the diet. However, power was shifting to the centre with the growth of regular taxation that improved the crown's ability to reward service with salaries, rather than land grants. These relationships were still *early* modern, since they were mediated through the ruler's court rather than an impersonal state; and because they remained personal, cultural capital assumed considerable importance. Like other princes, the Habsburgs stressed emotive concepts like trust, fidelity, prestige and honour, rewarding those who displayed these virtues in their service. This social capital was necessary to take full advantage of economic resources, as exemplified by the numerous landless nobles who remained respected ahead of richer burghers.

The underdeveloped nature of communication heightened the court's significance as the venue to acquire social and cultural capital. It was the place to meet influential people, and gain experience and the skills required to succeed as a noble.[72] Patronage was inherently unstable, depending on the patron's continued ability to meet competing aspirations among his clients from limited resources. The Habsburg court grew from six hundred people under Ferdinand I to eight hundred under Rudolf, while the junior branches added perhaps six hundred more places. These were still relatively few compared to the establishment of Elizabeth I in England who had more courtiers than Rudolf, or even Cardinal Richelieu who maintained an entourage of 480. As emperors, the Habsburgs had to cater to additional clientele from the Empire, leaving too few posts for their own nobles. Patronage also represented only a 'soft' form of control. It entailed a reciprocity that was not legally enforceable. The patron had no sanction for disloyalty beyond public disgrace and dismissal. Moreover, by shifting bargaining from the constitutional arena of the Estates to the informal world of the court, patronage arguably retarded political development. It proved divisive, as favouritism concentrated rewards for some, fuelling resentment among others.

The situation was exacerbated by the two relatively close imperial successions. Officials still served a monarch, not an impersonal state. There was no job security, as a new ruler was free to dismiss his predecessor's advisers and appoint his own favourites. This proved particularly divisive in 1619 as Ferdinand brought his existing, exclusively Catholic Inner Austrian clientele into the Habsburg and imperial government, displacing many of the Protestants still in service.

Nobles faced growing competition for land, which led to falling incomes in some cases, and cultural pressures (partly influenced by the court) entailing expensive grand tours for their sons and elaborate new mansions and country houses. The number of Protestant nobles without land in Lower Austria rose from 61 to 117 across 1580–1620. Only 43 of the 334 Protestant nobles had crown appointments by 1620, compared to 72 of the 123 Catholics. Crown appointments employed over half the landless Catholic nobility, giving them a source of income denied their Protestant counterparts. Moreover, state service rather than wealth increasingly determined admission into the nobility, as the Habsburgs ennobled their servants. This, in turn, gave recipients access to more land, as salaries could be invested in land sold by indebted families. From being predominantly smallholders in the later sixteenth century, Catholics emerged as the major Lower Austrian landowners by 1620.[73] Protestants responded by sending their sons to Germany to acquire the university education increasingly required for state employment, but many returned radicalized by the confessional militancy on campus, effectively excluding themselves from the jobs they were seeking.

Confessional differences merely sharpened existing tensions between the horizontal solidarity of kinship and corporate ties among nobles and the vertical relationship between patron and clients. Despite constituting the majority of the nobility in the Habsburg provinces, Protestants failed to form a united front against the dynasty. Of the Lower Austrian Protestants, 77 paid homage to Ferdinand in April 1619, while 121 remained uncommitted and 102 joined the revolt, of whom only 50 actually fought against the crown. The splits across many families may have been due to a deliberate policy of hedging bets, sending sons to serve on both sides while the father or an uncle remained neutral and looked after the property. Nonetheless, the relatively small number of active supporters indicates a high level of distaste for the rebel cause. It was not so much a failure of aristocratic corporatism to defeat monarchical absolutism. Rather, the idealized Protestant version proved less attractive than the alternative, equally corporate identity of a nobility united and rewarded by royal favour.

Other factors played their part. Unlike the Dutch, the Bohemians lacked a natural redoubt into which they could retreat. Failure to take Budweis and Krumau gave the Habsburgs bases across the southern frontier, and once Saxony joined the emperor, the rebels were effectively surrounded. The Bohemians' failure to achieve any real victories early on deterred others from joining. Nonetheless, England had backed the Dutch in 1585 before it was clear they would defeat Spain. The fact that no foreign power, other than Bethlen, openly supported Frederick indicates attitudes were hardening towards rebels across Europe as a whole.[74] This explains the prominence given to religion in pro-Bohemian propaganda, since it was easier to appeal on this basis than champion them as an alternative, federal system of government.

10

Ferdinand Triumphant 1621–4

THE PALATINE CAUSE

The Winter King

Within a few weeks of White Mountain, placards appeared in Brussels and Vienna offering a reward for news of 'a king, run away a few days past – age, adolescent, colour sanguine, height medium; a cast in one eye, no beard or moustache worth mention; disposition, not bad so long as a stolen kingdom does not lie in his way – name of Frederick'.[1] The fugitive was soon mocked as the 'winter king' after the brevity of his reign. His entire world seemed to collapse as he sped north from Silesia. His remaining supporters were demoralized and untrustworthy. He sought shelter in Berlin, but the elector sent him packing after receiving an imperial reprimand in January. Bethlen had opened talks with the Imperialists in Hainburg , while the Silesians surrendered in February. That month, the Protestant Union began negotiations to evacuate the Lower Palatinate and Mansfeld agreed a six-week truce with Tilly. Saxony, Denmark and Britain all advised Frederick to make peace as it was clear Ferdinand had recovered Bohemia. The Twelve Years Truce was due to expire in April, but many still hoped it might be extended. The prospect of peace, at least in the Empire, was not unrealistic, the emergency appeared to be over and the Liga congress at Augsburg voted in March to reduce its army to 15,000.[2]

Peace foundered on Frederick's refusal to compromise. His defiance encouraged others to remain in the field, while the renewal in the spring of the Spanish-Dutch war suggested foreign assistance would be forthcoming. Talks did open with Saxon mediation in January, and Frederick declared he was prepared to renounce Bohemia and accept Ferdinand as king, but he attached conditions that even Johann Georg thought unreasonable: Ferdinand was to confirm the Confederation, grant full religious liberty, assume all of Frederick's Bohemian debts and refund Palatine military expenses![3] Ferdinand responded by placing Frederick, Anhalt, Hohenlohe and Jägerndorf under the imperial ban on 29 January 1621, paving the way for the confiscation of their lands and titles. Frederick simply became more inflexible. With only his dignity left, he felt he could not break his promises to his supporters, most of whom were now also exiles. Their only hope was to fight on.

There seemed little prospect of this when Frederick and Elizabeth reached The Hague in the middle of April. Their first accommodation was a house rented by the States General that belonged to van der Mijle, a man the Republic had driven into exile in its own internal power struggle two years before (see p.318 below). The Dutch later provided the Wassenaer palace that became Elizabeth's home for the next forty years. Dutch and English handouts were initially comparatively generous, but soon dwindled, especially once the British Civil Wars began in 1639, and in the end visitors to the Wassenaer reported seeing rats scuttling under Elizabeth's skirts.[4]

Anhalt had already left the Palatinate, ostensibly to represent Frederick in northern Germany. He was worn out and depressed by White Mountain where his son had been captured. Christian IV of Denmark eventually granted him asylum on the condition he abstained from intrigue. Concerned for his son's release and to prevent the imperial sequestration of Bernburg, Anhalt went to Vienna in 1624 and secured a pardon. He spent the remaining six years of his life battling to spare his lands the consequences of a war he had done much to unleash. Hohenlohe fled to Emden until his relations secured a pardon for him in 1623, after which he devoted himself to trying to pass on the stigma of defeat to Colonel Stubenvoll. Many younger, middle-ranking officials also left, seeking better prospects and job security elsewhere. Others were obliged to compromise with the Bavarian and Spanish forces that soon overran the electorate. The burden of work fell on the remaining elderly loyalists, assisted by some rapidly promoted juniors who often lacked adequate training or experience.[5] Those like Camerarius, who actively promoted the Bohemian adventure, temporarily fell from grace, creating a vacuum filled partly by Elizabeth's English secretaries, reflecting the court's dependency on her father's assistance. Continued defeats discouraged many of those who remained, like Achaz von Dohna who retired to his East Prussian estates in 1624.

The change of personnel contributed to the general lack of direction and Frederick's inability to assert his authority. The next two years saw a struggle between those, like Chief Justice Pawell, who pushed a maximalist agenda aimed at recovering everything, including Bohemia, and others, like the young rising star Rusdorf, who favoured the more realistic option of accepting British mediation to secure at least a partial restoration of Frederick as elector. Palatine propagandists responded to the Habsburg presentation of Frederick as a usurper by propagating the myth of a just king unrightfully forced into miserable exile. Comparisons were drawn with David and Goliath, as Frederick struggled to recover his home occupied by the mighty Habsburgs. Elizabeth had lost her kingdom, but was still 'queen of hearts' to her supporters, in a deliberate effort to counter the Habsburg depiction of her as the 'Helen of Germany' who had led the country to a destructive conflict. The romantic sense of adventure, defending the underdog, appealed to English diplomats and nobles who composed sonnets and, rather more practically, joined Frederick's remaining forces as volunteers.[6]

The End of the Protestant Union

Frederick remained leader of the Union, but the organization was already collapsing. Württemberg, previously one of the activist members, backed away once Frederick committed himself to Bohemia and fell back on cooperation with its Catholic neighbours through the official Kreis structure.[7] Many others also doubted the utility of their extra-constitutional confessional alliance. Emperor Ferdinand timed the announcement of the imperial ban perfectly, bringing home the consequences of opposing him just as the Union congress met to discuss the renewal of its charter. The majority seized the offer of mediation from Mainz and Hessen-Darmstadt which, as the Palatinate's neighbours, had no wish to see the war arrive in their vicinity. Spinola, conscious of the imminent expiry of the Dutch Twelve Years Truce, was happy to agree to the Treaty of Mainz on 12 April. The Union evacuated its positions in the Lower Palatinate, in return for Spinola suspending further operations and promising to halt them permanently if James I could persuade his son-in-law to accept Ferdinand's terms.

The Union congress dissolved on 14 May 1621 without having renewed its charter, effectively disbanding the organization. Though it had enhanced the Palatinate's profile and attracted the Stuart marriage, the Union never matched the cohesion of its Catholic Liga rival. Whereas Maximilian pursued dynastic goals within a confessional context, some Palatine leaders had tried to reverse this relationship, widening the gap between themselves and the wider Union membership that only ever sought local security.

The Resumption of the Spanish-Dutch War, 1621

The Union's collapse coincided with the end of the Twelve Years Truce. The decision to let the Truce expire had little to do with the situation in the Empire. Factions in both Spain and the Republic saw war as the means to assert control over their own governments and promote what they regarded as their country's best interests.

The Truce had opened deep divisions in Dutch society, just as its Spanish advocates had hoped. The end of Spain's trade embargo benefited some Dutch, while hurting others. Those who had invested in militarized ventures like the East India Company lost heavily, as did the textile industry that faced renewed Flemish competition.[8] However, the most serious division proved to be that within Calvinism. The Republic's leadership was solidly Calvinist, but the proportion of adherents in the rest of society climbed slowly to only about a fifth by 1609. Calvinists found it hard to progress from a clandestine movement to an organized church. Their insistence on tough moral standards and a detailed grasp of theology deterred new members. Much of the rural population clung to the old religion, either to hedge their bets in case Spain recovered the northern provinces or because they preferred the still vital pre-Tridentine Catholicism; the influx of Lutheran economic migrants from northern Germany into Dutch towns also provided an alternative faith. Local and even provincial government was frequently still in Catholic hands. Calvinists remained isolated in their own homes, 'haunted by a deep sense of their own insecurity'.[9]

Their response was to turn inwards in a bitter dispute over their true doctrine that swiftly became aligned with wider disagreements over the Truce. Many shared the Lutherans' unease about Calvin's doctrine of predestination. A group known as the Remonstrants, or Arminians after their leading theologian, Jacobus Arminius, sought to soften Calvin's harsh view that individuals had no influence over their own salvation. They won support among merchants keen for a more tolerant faith that would widen their trading contacts, as well as those favouring an extension of the Truce. The latter included Johan van Oldenbarnevelt, who had been the effective head of the Republic's civil government since 1586, who argued the Truce had already brought most of the benefits of independence and was preferable to the uncertainty of war. The hardline Calvinist position was espoused by the Counter-Remonstrants led by Franciscus Gomarus, who championed the civil independence of the Calvinist church and wanted faith to guide politics. They won support from those suffering economically from the Truce, as well as southern Netherlands refugees hoping renewed war would recover their homes, and the Republic's captain general, Maurice of Nassau.[10]

The situation grew ugly as Maurice refused to provide soldiers to help Oldenbarnevelt maintain order against mounting Gomarist agitation. Arminian councillors were swept from office by Gomarist mobs, changing the political balance in the States General after 1617. The crisis peaked when Maurice openly declared his hand in July 1618 by disarming militia hastily assembled by the remaining Arminians. Hoping to head off trouble, Oldenbarnevelt convened a national synod at Dordrecht (Dordt) to resolve the theological controversy. By now, however, he had lost control of the States General which passed a secret motion on 28 August authorizing Maurice to arrest him and other Arminian leaders, including Hugo Grotius, later famous as the theorist of modern international law. Assured of support, the Gomarists easily defeated their rivals when the synod finally opened in November. After a show trial, Oldenbarnevelt was executed on 13 May 1619. Grotius was imprisoned, but managed to escape to Paris. The coup appeared to confirm the Gomarist view of predestination – that God's elect would triumph regardless of the odds. Oldenbarnevelt's death broke the opposition of the powerful Holland States to Maurice's political influence, but three provinces still opposed a resumption of war with Spain. The Gomarists faced a backlash of rioting as republicans rallied behind Arminianism to oppose the House of Orange's monarchical tendency.

The unfolding chaos determined the Republic's response to the Bohemian Revolt. Maurice refused to be drawn on the question of renewing the Truce while he still faced opposition at home. Although

Frederick never appeared a credible ally, Maurice provided just enough assistance to stoke the Central European fires and draw away the Spanish firemen. Despite his domestic alliance with the Gomarists, Maurice did not subscribe to international Calvinism and was determined to keep his options open. The Republic did not even maintain a permanent envoy in the Empire until 1646 and remained careful never to commit itself formally to war there. Meanwhile, Maurice continued talks with Archduke Albert, fostering false hopes that he would renew the Truce.[11]

The defeat of the Dutch doves coincided with a victory for the Spanish hawks. The duke of Lerma was forced to resign in 1618, while his key supporter, Calderón, was arrested and later executed on trumped-up charges of witchcraft. Power was shifting to Zúñiga and his nephew, Count Olivares, whom he had placed strategically in the household of the future Philip IV. Zúñiga argued that Spain had already spent too much treasure trying to conquer the Dutch to give up now, allegedly exclaiming 'a monarchy that has lost its *reputación*, even if it has lost no territory, is a sky without light, a sun without rays, a body without a soul'.[12] Renewal of the treaty was still advocated by Albert and Isabella who could see the benefits the Truce brought to the southern Netherlands' economy. They favoured a solution similar to that granted by Austria to the Swiss in 1499: to give the Dutch independence in return for a permanent alliance. The demand that the Republic grant religious freedom to its Catholic subjects was put on the agenda to satisfy religious sensibilities in Madrid, and the Dutch Catholics could not be abandoned without damage to Spanish prestige. Freedom of conscience was already incorporated as Article 13 of the Republic's founding charter from 1579, but it was restricted in practice by the Calvinist establishment. More serious were Spain's demands that the Dutch stop interfering in the East and West Indies, as well as lift the blockade of the Scheldt which continued to strangle Antwerp's economy. Maurice could not grant these terms without alienating his supporters. As it became obvious Albert could not persuade Madrid to moderate its demands, Maurice gambled on the talks collapsing to force his remaining opponents in the States General to hand the political and military initiative to him.

Like the Republic, Spain had no intention of becoming involved in Germany and increasingly regarded the war there as a serious distraction. A significant portion of the Army of Flanders remained in the Lower Palatinate and would continue operations with imperial and

Liga troops until 1623, but both Madrid and Brussels sought rapid disengagement in order to concentrate on the struggle against the Dutch. Operations along the Lower Rhine allowed Spain to eject the Dutch from many of the areas they had occupied since 1614, but the object was to contain them, not to spread the war to north-west Germany. Limited assistance was provided to Tilly and the imperial army to help them defeat Frederick's remaining German supporters in line with Spain's general goal of pacifying the Empire. This remained the Spanish objective throughout the rest of the Thirty Years War since it was clear no assistance could be expected in return from Austria until this was achieved.

The Protestant Crowns

The Protestant monarchies were equally reluctant to help Frederick. Denmark was unquestionably the most powerful Protestant kingdom at this point and enjoyed cordial relations with Frederick's Stuart in-laws. (By contrast, Gustavus Adolphus of Sweden dangled the prospect of massive intervention in Germany simply to attract interest in his own plans to conquer Poland's Baltic coast.) Unfortunately for Frederick, Christian IV of Denmark took a dim view of his actions, demanding 'who advised you to drive out kings and seize kingdoms?'[13]

Nonetheless, the Danish king felt obliged to act. Like Johann Georg of Saxony, he feared Frederick's rash action had jeopardized German Lutherans and that Ferdinand, possibly under the influence of Jesuits and other 'evil advisers', might deprive them of their constitutional rights, just like Charles V after his victory of Mühlberg in 1547. Christian combined a display of Lutheran resolve with pressure on Frederick to appease Ferdinand through a humble submission. He convened a conference in March 1621 at Segeberg in Holstein, attended by Frederick and representatives of the Lower Saxon Kreis, the Protestant Union, Brandenburg, James I and the Dutch. Denmark deployed 5,000 men in its German possessions, while the Lower Saxons agreed at their own congress in April to mobilize. This rather feeble attempt at Protestant solidarity failed because none of the participants had any intention of actually forcing Ferdinand to concede their request to revoke the imperial ban against Frederick. Many questioned the legitimacy of their own mobilization, which was presented as upholding the public peace. More fundamentally, the key players were at cross-purposes. Sweden refused to participate at all, while Christian used the deployment to intimidate the Hanseatic towns into conceding Danish jurisdiction and toll rights over the north German rivers. This not only alarmed the Lower Saxons but alienated the Dutch too, who already resented the high Sound tolls and were major trading partners of the Hanseatic League.[14] Christian could not oppose Ferdinand openly without jeopardizing the positions of his sons, who were Lutheran administrators in Schwerin and Verden, and he accepted the emperor's confirmation of the Mühlhausen declaration from March 1620 that left these bishoprics in Protestant hands.

British policy continued to swerve indecisively, responding to events with piecemeal, often ill-judged interventions. Neither James, nor his son Charles I after 1625, managed to reconcile the tension between confessional aspirations and political realities. The former suggested intervention on Frederick's behalf, the latter necessitated negotiation with the Habsburgs who soon held the entire Palatinate. Intervention was fraught with risk, while negotiation continued to stall on Britain's lack of leverage over the wayward elector. Yet the crown felt it had to act, if only to satisfy popular pressure and to maintain its prestige. Periodic expeditions were sent, initially as volunteers to support Frederick, later as official forces to put pressure on Spain or France. Throughout, foreign powers were allowed to recruit Britons directly into their own armies with varying degrees of royal support (see Table 1). Recruitment represented a heavy burden. Elizabethan levies totalled 106,000 men while the country was at war between 1586 and 1602, equivalent to 2 per cent of the total population. Stuart recruitment was at least 25 per cent higher, and its impact was magnified by the virtual absence of any military effort between 1603 and 1620. It fell heavily on south-east England, because it was convenient to recruit here for expeditions to the continent, as well as Scotland, where around 10 per cent of adult males enlisted. It was also expensive: the monarchy spent £1.44 million to maintain the Palatine court in exile and recruit for it and for Mansfeld between 1620 and 1632, whereas crown debts already topped £1 million by 1625.[15] To put things into perspective, approximately the same number of men left the Stuart kingdoms to fight on the continent as were conscripted in Sweden and Finland between 1621 and 1648, yet, by comparison, the effort had negligible diplomatic impact and brought no strategic gains.

Table 1: British military involvement

Expedition	Date	Total Enlisted	Serving	Composition
A) *For the 'Protestant Cause'*				
Sir Andrew Grey	Jan. 1620	2,500	Bohemia	Anglo-Scots
Sir John Seton	1620	1,200	Bohemia	Scots
Sir Horace de Vere	1620–2	2,250	Palatinate	English
Other volunteers	1620–2	2,000	Bohemia-Palatinate	Anglo-Scots
Anglo-Dutch Brigade*	1621	8,000	Dutch	Anglo-Scots
Anglo-Dutch Brigade*	1624–6	6,000	Dutch	Anglo-Scots
Mansfeld	Jan. 1625	13,300	Mansfeld**	Anglo-Scots
Cadiz	Sept. 1625	10,000	Charles I	English
Sir Charles Morgan	1627–9	18,700	Denmark	75% Scots, rest English & Welsh***
Ile de Ré	1627	6,000	Charles I	Anglo-Welsh
Marquis of Hamilton	1631	6,000	Sweden	80% Scots
Swedish army	1632–9	24,000	Sweden	80% Scots
Lord Craven	1638	3,000	Palatinate	English
French army	1624–44	25,000	France	Scots-Irish
		127,950		
B) *For the Habsburgs*				
Jerzy Ossolinski	Mar. 1621	5,000	Poland	British
Army of Flanders	1621–3	2,300	Spain	Irish
Army of Flanders	1631–3	1,800	Spain	Irish
Army of Flanders	1635	7,000	Spain	Irish
Army of Flanders	1640	150	Spain	Irish
Direct to Spain	1641–53	4,337	Spain	Irish
Army of Flanders	1642	2,000	Spain	Irish
Army of Flanders	1649–53	20,000	Spain	Irish
		42,587		
		170,537		

Notes:

The table indicates the numbers sent, not the total serving at any one time

* Augmentation to those already serving who numbered 5,000 in 1621

** The survivors joined the Danes in 1626

*** Survivors transferred to Sweden 1629

Sources: S. Murdoch, *Britain, Denmark-Norway and the House of Stuart, 1603–1660* (East Linton, 2003), pp.49–51, 56, 62, 227–8; M.C. Fissel, *English Warfare 1511–1642* (London, 2001), pp.105–10, 271; R.B. Manning, *An Apprenticeship in Arms. The origins of the British army 1585–1702* (Oxford, 2006), pp.62–93, 98, 101; M. Glozier, *Scottish Soldiers in France in the Reign of the Sun King* (Leiden, 2004); F.G.J. Ten Raa et al., *Het staatsche Leger 1568–1795* (8 vols., The Hague, 1911–59), III, pp.167–70, 178–82; R.A. Stradling, *The Spanish Monarchy and Irish Mercenaries: the Wild Geese in Spain 1618–68* (Blackrock, 1994); R.I. Frost, 'Scottish soldiers, Poland-Lithuania and the Thirty Years War', in S. Murdoch (ed.), *Scotland and the Thirty Years War* (Leiden, 2001), pp.191–213.

Bethlen and Jägerndorf

Only in the east did Frederick's old supporters renew the struggle. The margrave of Jägerndorf still held Görlitz in Upper Lusatia, as well as Glatz, which blocked the main pass between Bohemia and Silesia. He was joined by those Bohemians and Moravians who refused to submit to Ferdinand, including the younger Count Thurn. His position nonetheless became untenable once the Upper Lusatian and Silesian Estates submitted to the elector of Saxony and agreed to assist the imperial army in return for Ferdinand's confirmation of the religious guarantees issued by Johann Georg. He abandoned Görlitz on 3 March 1621, but decided to fight on since he had been declared an outlaw, and was encouraged by Bethlen's decision to break off the Hainburg talks on 22 April.

Ferdinand was prepared to grant the extensive territorial concessions already offered Bethlen in January 1620, but insisted on remaining king of Hungary. Like Frederick, Bethlen felt he could not abandon the Bohemians without compromising his honour, and demanded they be included in the proposed peace, as well as insisting on remaining king himself. Both sides had harassed each other's positions throughout the talks, using the lull to collect their forces. The Moravian Estates swung behind their colleagues in Lower and Inner Austria by funding regiments in the imperial army, while the Hungarian magnates provided hussars and haiduks, and the Croats sent irregulars. The emperor had retained 2,000 Cossacks and had additional German infantry, giving Bucquoy a respectable 20,000 men north of the Danube, while Collalto guarded the southern bank with another 5,000. Bethlen could muster only 17,000 light horse and 4,000 foot.[16] These numbers indicate the scale of the fighting in east Central Europe, equivalent to the much-better publicized operations along the Rhine at this point (see below).

Bucquoy moved as soon as the talks broke up, seizing Pressburg after a short bombardment on 5 May, while Collalto captured minor posts south of the river against minimal opposition. Bucquoy then took Tyrnau and Neutra to secure Moravia and Lower Austria against further Transylvanian raiding, before besieging Neuhäusel on the Neutra river, an important fortress along the Military Frontier that had defected to Bethlen in 1619 and was now held by Szanisló Thurzó. Bethlen retreated east to Kassa, appealing to Jägerndorf to join him. The margrave had regrouped at Schweidnitz and Jauer, but the advance of 8,000 Saxons through Silesia left him no choice and he retreated southwards along the mountains into Upper Hungary in July.

Bethlen meanwhile sent 6,000 light cavalry ahead of his main force to relieve Neuhäusel, which had already been under siege for seven weeks. The cavalry drove in the imperial outposts and soon the besiegers were themselves besieged. Bucquoy was killed as he led some cavalry out to find food. His death was considered a major blow and the emperor did not find another general of similar stature until 1625.[17] Command devolved to Colonel Maximilian Liechtenstein whose situation grew desperate as Bethlen arrived with the rest of his men, raising Transylvanian numbers to 15,000. Abandoning his siege train, Liechtenstein tried to escape across the Neutra at night on 11 July 1621, but was caught in the marshy ground. Only 8,000 men made it onto Schütt Island where they were essentially trapped, dependent on supplies sent from the imperial garrisons at Raab, Komorn and Pressburg.

Bethlen ignored them, heading west to retake Tyrnau on 30 July and was joined by Jägerndorf with over 8,000 men, mainly infantry with artillery – just the troops he needed. Pressburg was besieged from 18 August and the Transylvanians raided into Moravia, while Bethlen's western Hungarian supporters resumed their attacks into Lower and Inner Austria south of the Danube. Yet, the underlying trend was against him. His army was only half as large as it had been the previous year. He had no money to pay Jägerndorf's infantry, while the Hungarians were tired of fighting and contingents from eleven counties went home. The inability to take Pressburg further depressed morale. Wallenstein collected 4,000 men in Moravia for the emperor, while the main army was brought back up to 12,000. Ferdinand wanted a quick settlement and improved the terms offered at Hainburg.

Following his usual practice, Bethlen had already opened negotiations during his advance in July. Operations were suspended in October as Szanisló Thurzó negotiated with Cardinal Dietrichstein and Miklós Esterházy at Nikolsburg in Moravia, agreeing terms at the end of 1621 that were ratified on 6 January. Bethlen was allowed to keep the 7 Upper Hungarian counties (modern Slovakia) offered in January 1620, including Kassa, leaving Ferdinand with just 24 counties across Hungary. His supporters were given amnesties and Hungarian religious privileges were confirmed. He was also enfeoffed with the vacant Silesian duchies of Oppeln and Ratibor, while Ferdinand effectively recognized Transylvanian independence. In return, Bethlen surrendered the St Stephen's crown and renounced the royal title he had assumed in August 1620. The deal was sealed by Thurzó's defection. Ferdinand included him as the only Protestant of the four candidates proposed to the Hungarian diet to replace palatine Forgách who had died earlier that year. Thurzó was duly elected governor, but converted to Catholicism in August 1622 as agreed secretly with the emperor.[18]

Abandoned, Jägerndorf retreated northwards towards Glatz, his only surviving garrison, but without land, and thus without money, his army disintegrated. By March 1622, Saxon, imperial and Silesian troops had surrounded Glatz. The town finally surrendered on 25 October. The Saxons evacuated Silesia, but the emperor left 10,000 men to occupy Moravia and suppress the Slovak peasants whom the Bohemian exiles had stirred to rebellion.

PROTESTANT PALADINS

New Champions

The void was filled by new champions for whom the Palatine cause became an honourable cloak for a variety of more personal ambitions. These paladins operated without secure bases. Their deference to Frederick was largely conditional on how far he could deliver British support. They were prepared to take extraordinary risks, sometimes simply to avoid imminent disaster, but also in the hope that a stunning victory would enhance their reputation and attract more solid political and financial backing.

At their head was Count Ernst von Mansfeld, one of the war's most controversial figures. His motives remain unclear and his actions duplicitous. To most, he appears the archetypal mercenary who has come to characterize soldiers generally for this period.[19] Whereas the controversy surrounding Wallenstein centres on his political ambitions, only baser motives are attributed to Mansfeld. Perhaps the key to understanding this complex man is his illegitimate birth as the thirteenth, natural son of Peter Ernst, count of a small territory in Upper Saxony and a Spanish field marshal. With no prospect of inheriting the county that, in any case, his father had to share with numerous relations, Mansfeld chose a military career, hoping to secure both legitimacy and reward. His lack of status made him quick to take offence and won him little sympathy. Along with plain bad luck, this frustrated hopes of rapid advancement and left him with a sense of grievance against the Habsburgs, heightened both by their failure to reimburse his expenses and because they twice removed him from command for his own mistakes. Rudolf II eventually declared him legitimate after the Turkish War, but he sought recognition from others, for example being ennobled by the duke of Savoy in 1613. He defected to the Union during the first Jülich crisis in 1610, but only after he had been captured. Though he tolerated Protestantism, he had been raised a Catholic and there is no clear evidence he converted. Certainly, he was disliked by those with genuine faith and it seems his allegiance to his new employers was determined by better prospects and lingering animosity towards the Habsburgs.

Mansfeld's subsequent prominence derives from his abilities as an organizer that in turn rested on a network of experienced recruiting officers. Some of these contacts dated from his service in Savoy in 1613–18, like Joachim Karpzow who served in the Protestant Swiss regiment Mansfeld took to Bohemia in 1618. Karpzow later attracted notoriety for having his wife beheaded without a trial. Association with such characters did nothing to enhance Mansfeld's own reputation, despite his published *Apologie* (1621) presenting himself as a chivalrous knight defending the Winter Queen's honour. He possessed considerable strategic and tactical ability, combined with ruthlessness and a willingness to risk his men's lives. As a result, he often compounded his defeats by rapid retreats during which his forces disintegrated, making him expensive to employ.

The count was also a victim of his employers' own failure to pay properly, forcing him to extort money and supplies from the areas where he operated. His position was already precarious by February 1619 when he was placed under the imperial ban, well before Frederick's other supporters. Even before White Mountain, Mansfeld was acting independently, consolidating his hold over western Bohemia to trade for a pardon and compensation. He offered to surrender Pilsen in October 1620 in return for 400,000 florins to pay off his troops. Similar proposals followed, generally coupled after November 1621 with demands for territorial compensation and a military command, preferably in the archdukes' service.[20] It was never clear whether he was genuine or just playing for time. His health was also failing by the early 1620s when he suffered heart trouble and asthma, forcing him to travel in a coach. His territorial demands were opportunistic, mainly centred on Lower (northern) Alsace and parts of the bishopric of Speyer that he overran in November 1621, and later East Frisia when he occupied it in 1622.

Mansfeld's close association with Frederick ensured he received cash and militia from the Palatinate, as well as the bulk of the foreign support. These assets gave him an operational strength of 15–20,000 men, higher than the other paladins, but his strategic difficulties were greater given the dispersal of Palatine territory. He began 1621 with his forces concentrated in the heavily forested, hilly Upper Palatinate, coupled with isolated garrisons in north-west Bohemia. These positions were 175km from the better fortified Lower Palatinate, which itself suffered from the strategic problem of being cut in two by the Rhine. The right half was covered by rich maize and wheat fields near the river, but became more hilly and forested further east around Heidelberg. Its key was Mannheim, a fortified new town at the confluence of the Neckar and Rhine. The latter river could also be crossed downstream at Oppenheim and upstream at Germersheim. The area west of the river was crossed by a series of wooded ridges separating it from Mainz to the north and Trier to the west. The route west across Trier to Spanish Luxembourg was guarded by Kreuznach, but the real stronghold was Frankenthal, built just west from the Rhine flood plain opposite Mannheim. After the Union's dissolution, these positions were defended by 7,000 men under the Englishman Colonel de Vere.[21]

By contrast, Frederick's other supporters were all ruling princes or their legitimate offspring. Landgrave Moritz and Margrave Georg Friedrich were his neighbours in Hessen-Kassel and Baden-Durlach respectively. Both were Union members, but whereas Georg Friedrich supported the Bohemian adventure, Moritz had resigned in protest. Their common bond was the fear that Frederick's defeat would expose them to unsympathetic imperial justice. Moritz had good reason to believe Ferdinand would deprive him of Marburg, which he had seized from his Darmstadt relations in 1604. Though Lutheran, Landgrave Ludwig V of Darmstadt spent 1618–19 travelling to France, Spain, Rome and Munich rallying support for the emperor, and helped the elector of Mainz broker the truce with Spinola that triggered the Union's collapse in May 1621. With a large, well-administered territory, Moritz had the most substantial indigenous resources of all the paladins and mustered 2,950 regular soldiers and 9,350 militiamen at the end of 1620. His land was also strategically located just north of the Main, placing him between Westphalia and Lower Saxony to the north and the Palatinate and Franconia to the south.[22]

Full of ingenious ideas to benefit his subjects, the landgrave was opposed by his nobles who largely remained Lutheran and refused to support military adventures. His isolation increased with growing reliance on Calvinist outsiders, like Dr Wolfgang Günther who headed the civil administration by 1623.[23] Together, they completely misread the situation in 1621, seizing the opportunity for action but, with typical Protestant disunity, attacking the neighbouring Lutheran county of Waldeck. With good connections to the Nassau dynasty, Waldeck appeared a natural ally, but Moritz disputed its status as an imperial fief and claimed overlordship. The count was a member of the Wetterau Union that coordinated security among the patchwork of Calvinist, Lutheran and a few Catholic micro territories sandwiched between the Rhine, Main and Hessen. These territories mobilized their connections; the Dutch accused Moritz of betraying Protestantism, while the Catholics condemned him as a second winter king. The Hessian Estates negotiated behind his back with Darmstadt and the emperor, and the landgrave abandoned Waldeck following a Reichshofrat judgment against him in March 1622. The episode ruined Moritz's reputation and left him exposed as the war swept in his direction.

Georg Friedrich of Baden-Durlach was more vulnerable still, having used his relations' bankruptcy as an excuse to seize their territory, Baden-Baden, in 1594. Inability to obtain imperial approval, as well as the desire to escape the influence of his more powerful Lutheran neighbour, Württemberg, encouraged Georg Friedrich to embrace Calvinism and then join the Protestant Union. He claimed to have read the Bible 58 times, twice as many as Bethlen, yet his Lutheran subjects resisted the change of faith. Militias formed half his 11,500-strong army, but his territory was too small and poor to pay for professionals. Apart from his own bodyguard, the rest of his force comprised regiments loaned by Mansfeld, as well as two provided by Magnus of Württemberg, most likely recruited from the duchy's Union contingent discharged in March 1621.[24] Magnus was the much younger brother of the reigning duke, Johann Friedrich. With little prospect of ruling, he seized an opportunity for glory that would cost him his life at the battle of Wimpfen. Johann Friedrich's refusal to back the adventure denied Georg Friedrich access to Württemberg's more potent resources.

The remaining paladins resembled young Magnus: scions of princely or noble families without sufficient means to sustain their status or activities to satisfy their ambitions. The most important was Duke Christian of Brunswick-Wolfenbüttel, a younger son of Duke Heinrich Julius.[25] Christian had antagonized his elder brother, the considerably less able reigning duke, Friedrich Ulrich, by tactlessly revealing that the latter's Brandenburg wife was having an affair. Christian owed his own position as Lutheran administrator of Halberstadt partly to the influence of his mother, Christian IV of Denmark's sister. As administrator, his status was by no means secure, but this alone cannot account for his rash decision to declare for Frederick – typical of the general behaviour that earned him the sobriquet 'the Mad Halberstädter'. As part of Lower Saxony, Halberstadt was covered by the Mühlhausen guarantee that satisfied both Saxony and Denmark. And given his Danish kinship, his powerful Guelph relations and his own moderate Lutheranism, he could be relatively confident that Ferdinand would not depose him.

The slogan 'God's friend – papists' foe' on one of his banners suggests conventional confessional motives, but another, 'For God and her', meaning the Winter Queen, indicates how Christian was stirred by the chivalric dimension of the Palatine cause. He undoubtedly had territorial ambitions, probably intended to be at the current bishop of Paderborn's expense, but the brevity and inconstancy of Christian's involvement make them difficult to determine. He operated at the greatest disadvantage, since Halberstadt offered an inadequate base to raise a major army. Apart from some money sent by his mother, he was completely without additional resources prior to his temporary entry into Dutch service in August 1622. Consequently, his force rarely topped 10,000 men and contained a high proportion of cavalry. Though nominally more expensive than infantry, they were relatively easy to recruit in the horse-breeding region of Lower Saxony and, being mounted, could live off the land better than foot soldiers.

The Weimar brothers' involvement was broadly similar, though they were already deeply committed to Frederick's cause, having supplied units to Bohemia in 1620. Duke Johann Ernst, the eldest brother, remained aloof to preserve the family property, while his younger siblings

backed a cause from which, if successful, he too would benefit. Friedrich
and Wilhelm went to Bohemia and were joined in 1621 by Bernhard,
the youngest and subsequently most famous, who became an officer in
Wilhelm's regiment. Like Anhalt, the Weimars lacked adequate
resources, but also had a political and confessional agenda. They had
been educated at Jena, one of the more radical Lutheran universities
which taught arguments similar to the Calvinist theory of resistance. In
addition to the prospect of conquering Catholic land, there was the hope
of recovering the electoral title from their relation Johann Georg of
Saxony, whose loyalty to Ferdinand made him a potential target.[26] Their
Altenburg relation, Duke Friedrich, was more opportunistic: having
contemplated converting to Catholicism he joined Duke Christian in
January 1623 after Spain failed to pay the troops he had raised.[27]

There were also structural factors behind the burst of Protestant
activism. Bavaria and the Liga recruited at least 50,000 men in 1619–20,
half of whom died of disease, deserted or were killed in action. There
were still many willing to enlist. Underemployment remained high, given
a rapid growth in population since the 1530s that had yet to level off or
be reversed by the war. Food prices outstripped wages and the situation
was especially acute due to hyperinflation in 1621–3. The 'trade of
war' appeared to offer easy money, since recruiters promised enlistment
bounties, good wages and a bonus upon discharge. The prospect of
plunder was an added attraction, alongside all the customary pressures
encouraging enlistment, like the desire to escape unpleasant personal
circumstances. Moreover, German recruiters lacked competition from
other powers. Though both the Army of Flanders and that of the Dutch
Republic roughly doubled their establishment in 1618–22, much of their
manpower was found locally, while France, Denmark and Sweden had
yet to recruit substantial numbers of Germans.

There were also many experienced soldiers to draw upon, including
those who had served during the Turkish War, the Jülich crises, and the
recent fighting in Italy. They provided the cadres needed to stiffen
inexperienced units and were consequently in high demand. It was
fortuitous that several friendly governments disbanded their armies precisely when the paladins were recruiting. Mansfeld was able to enlist the
bulk of the former Unionists, while Duke Christian enlisted around
2,500 men discharged by Hamburg after its crisis with Denmark (see
pp.320–1). The latter included Baron Knyphausen who had also pre-

viously served the Dutch and now raised one of the better regiments in Christian's rather disorderly army.

The Emperor's Countermeasures

The paladins' dispersal across western and northern Germany shifted the war to these regions, away from the Habsburg lands where the fighting was drawing to a close. The Saxons returned Silesia to Habsburg control in May 1622 and disbanded their army. The emperor still had 15–20,000 men, but these were fully occupied against Bethlen. Archduke Leopold had another 6,000 in Alsace, where he was reinforced by 9,000 Cossacks for the summer of 1622.[28]

The Spanish contingent remained with the main imperial army until June 1622 when it totalled 7,500 men under General Caracciolo and joined the operations in the Lower Palatinate, before departing to Flanders the following year. The resumption of the Dutch War had already prompted Spinola to send about 10,000 men under Count van den Bergh to Jülich, leaving only 11,000 under General Córdoba in the Lower Palatinate in 1621. Spain followed its own objectives. Apart from Caracciolo's corps, its forces lay outside imperial command, and Córdoba's task was to secure the area west of the Rhine, rather than to be drawn into Germany. While Bergh contested possession of the Lower Rhine against the local Dutch garrisons, the two claimants of the Jülich inheritance pursued their own feud.

The main operation was Bergh's siege of the Dutch in Jülich from September 1621. Since the Spanish drew straw and oats from Duke Wolfgang Wilhelm of Pfalz-Neuburg's territories, the Dutch began 'catching and stretching' (*Fangen und Spannen*) hostages in reprisals that continued in a vicious cycle throughout the war.[29] Wolfgang Wilhelm raised his own forces, eventually numbering 2,500, to assist Bergh take Jülich in July 1622, and then Pfaffenmütze in January 1623, removing a threat to Bonn. Fearing its own possessions would be next, Brandenburg transferred its 1,300 troops in the area to Dutch service at its own expense in an effort to retain influence without unduly exposing itself. Unwilling to fight, Brandenburg surrendered Ravenstein to Wolfgang Wilhelm in May 1624 in return for his recognition of their mutual possessions.[30] Spain had gained the upper hand by then, having ejected the Dutch and Brandenburgers from Jülich, most of Mark and

Ravensberg. It now had 11,000 men holding fifty outposts across Jülich, Cleves and into the western part of Münster. However, its strategy was to isolate the Dutch Republic, not assist the emperor.

Spain's disinterest in imperial affairs and the weakness of his own forces left Ferdinand dependent on the Catholic Liga. Duke Maximilian had a direct interest in conquering the Palatinate as his reward for saving the emperor in Bohemia. Ferdinand did retain some influence, because Maximilian needed his approval to act. Bavaria delayed invading the Upper Palatinate until Ferdinand gave permission on 9 July 1621, while Tilly's march to the Rhine was legitimized by a commission in November to apprehend the outlaw Mansfeld. Several thousand Bavarians remained holding down Upper Austria, and Tilly left most of the rest behind in the Upper Palatinate when he pursued Mansfeld, taking instead the contingents of the other Liga members. Maximilian remained Liga commander, because the elector of Mainz declined his rights under the Liga charter to take over once the army reached the area of his Rhenish Directory. Nonetheless, the new situation fundamentally changed the organization. The associated Westphalian members felt exposed with the resumption of the Dutch War and Duke Christian of Brunswick-Wolfenbüttel's raiding into Paderborn. Ferdinand of Cologne raised his own contingent in 1621, which was soon reinforced by other units to create a separate Liga corps of about 12,000 men under Tilly's second-in-command, Count Anholt. This became the nucleus of an autonomous Westphalian army directed by Cologne that remained an important factor throughout the war.[31]

Tilly against Mansfeld

Mansfeld proved a resourceful and tenacious opponent. Having failed to break through north-west Bohemia and join Jägerndorf in May 1621, he entrenched 13,000 men at Waidhaus on the Nuremberg–Pilsen road just inside the Upper Palatinate. The remaining 2,000 were posted in Amberg and Cham to cover his rear against the Bavarians while he faced Tilly and Marradas, who had collected over 18,000 Liga and imperial troops opposite him at Roshaupt (Rozuadov) across the pass. The two armies spent the next four months alternately assaulting and shelling each other's encampments in the first of a series of protracted struggles that characterized the war as much as the better-known pitched battles.

Tilly remained weak, despite his superior numbers, because Maximilian had withdrawn his best regiments to form a second Bavarian army at Straubing totalling 14,500 men. The soldiers were replaced by fewer numbers of militia, who performed badly in the prolonged positional warfare.[32]

Maximilian's preparations at Straubing were finally complete by mid-September 1621. Within a week he had taken Cham and was closing against Amberg, intending to trap Mansfeld against the mountains. With his customary negotiations going nowhere, Mansfeld broke out one stormy night and dashed to Neumarkt. Once Tilly had crossed the pass to join Maximilian, Mansfeld's position became untenable and he raced westwards on 9 October, through Nuremberg to Mannheim, abandoning stragglers to arrive two weeks later with 7,000 unruly, unpaid troops.

His escape was embarrassing for Tilly, but an opportunity for Maximilian. The Upper Palatinate submitted without further resistance, freeing Tilly to pursue Mansfeld. Maximilian was concerned the Spanish might seize the entire Lower Palatinate and wanted to capture at least its capital Heidelberg as it was associated with the electoral title. Mansfeld escaped across the Rhine to ravage Lower Alsace, abandoning the area to the east to Tilly. Sickness and detachments had reduced the main Liga army strength to fewer than 12,000, and it was unable to take either Heidelberg or Mannheim, while Córdoba and the Spanish similarly failed to dislodge the British defenders in Frankenthal.

The resistance of his fortresses revived Frederick's hopes and he travelled incognito through France to join Mansfeld at Germersheim on 22 April 1622. Georg Friedrich of Baden-Durlach declared his hand, handing over government to his eldest son and mustering his own troops at Knielingen, near modern Karlsruhe. Duke Christian had been unable to break through Anholt's cordon at the end of 1621, but did eject Wolfgang Wilhelm's garrison from Lippstadt in the County of Mark in January. Dutch engineers helped transform the town into a major fortress, while Christian's cavalry ransacked nearby Paderborn. The contents of the episcopal treasury were sold to buy arms and build the army to around 10,000 men.

Tilly faced the formidable task of defeating the three paladins before they could combine. New recruits had given him 20,000 men ready to besiege Heidelberg. Frederick and Mansfeld crossed the Rhine at

Germersheim, plundering their way across the bishopric of Speyer, but found Tilly's position at Wiesloch too strong. They fell back, hoping Georg Friedrich would join them. Tilly pounced at dawn on 27 April, catching them as they crossed the swollen Kleinbach stream at Mingols-heim 10km south of Wiesloch.[33] Tilly had about 15,000 men with him, 3,000 less than Mansfeld. The Liga advance guard threw Mansfeld's cavalry into confusion as they tried to cover the crossing of the rest of the army. Cohesion was lost as men raced for the bridge and the road became clogged with abandoned wagons. Tilly's Croats set the village on fire, but a Protestant Swiss regiment held it long enough for the fugitives to regroup on a hill to the south. Mansfeld and Frederick had gone on ahead, but now returned and rode along the lines exhorting the men to redeem the honour lost at White Mountain. Tilly attacked over the bridge as his infantry arrived that afternoon, but Mansfeld counter-attacked with his cavalry from behind the hill and chased Tilly's troops back through Mingolsheim until they were halted by the Schmidt infantry regiment of Liga veterans. Mansfeld's rearguard remained on the hill until dusk, before following the rest of the army that had already retreated having lost 400 killed. Discipline was collapsing. Many of Mansfeld's men had lost their shoes scrambling across the marshy stream and spent the afternoon stripping the dead. Tilly's losses were greater, possibly 2,000, and he retired east to Wimpfen.

The first round had been a draw, but the advantage of numbers still lay with the paladins as Georg Friedrich joined Frederick and Mansfeld at Sinsheim on 29 April to give them a total force of 30,000. They wasted time besieging the small town of Eppingen, failing to crush Tilly before he was joined by Córdoba who had crossed the Rhine with 5,300 men. Short of supplies, Mansfeld marched to attack the Spanish garrison in Ladenburg that cut the road between Mannheim and Heidelberg, leaving a few regiments to give Georg Friedrich 12,700 men.[34] Tilly dissuaded Córdoba from departing to save Ladenburg and persuaded him instead to attack the margrave, who was overconfident and unaware of the Spaniards' arrival. They spent the night of 5 May 1622 deploying on a wooded hill south of Wimpfen. As he served a king, Córdoba took the place of honour on the right, while Tilly's 12,900 Liga troops occupied the left. The overnight rain had cleared, leaving hot and sunny weather the following morning. The men rested in the shade, fortifying themselves with breakfast and a wine ration, while their artillery shelled the Baden army deployed to the south. Georg Friedrich had chosen a bad position in the right-angle formed by the Neckar and the marshy Bölliger stream that was to his rear, with a wood on his left and his right flank next to Ober Eisesheim village, just west of the Neckar. The entire front was covered by 70 wagons, some mounting small cannon, protecting 2,000 musketeers, with the remaining infantry drawn up behind. It appeared strong, but left little chance for retreat if things went wrong.

Tilly and Córdoba began a general advance at 11 a.m., but were forced back by heavy fire and retired to the shade of the trees. Georg Friedrich also broke for lunch, recalling his outposts, including those in the wood to his left. Córdoba immediately occupied this with Spanish musketeers. The battle resumed as Georg Friedrich sent infantry to retake the wood, while launching most of his cavalry in a surprise attack from Ober Eisesheim. Their advance was screened by the thick clouds of smoke from the ineffectual cannonade and dust thrown up by skirmishers riding about the plain between the two armies. Several Liga units broke and the entire left began to give way as Georg Friedrich's riders fanned out along the hill, capturing the artillery. Men of the Schmidt regiment saw one of their comrades, who had left the ranks to relieve himself, suddenly 'come running, holding his trousers in his hand and shouting: The enemy! The enemy!'[35] The regiment quickly formed a defensive hedgehog, pikes pointing in all directions, while some of its musketeers rushed to man four cannon to their left that the gunners had just abandoned.

Georg Friedrich's cavalry lost cohesion as some swirled around the immovable Schmidt regiment, while others dashed after the units that had broken earlier. His infantry were still stuck behind their wagons, too far away to assist. Meanwhile, Córdoba's musketeers had worked their way round the far end of the line and were threatening its rear. Numbers and experience eventually prevailed as the Liga and Spanish cavalry regrouped and pushed their opponents off the field by the late afternoon. The infantry launched a final assault around 7 p.m. on the wagon line. At that moment, some powder wagons to the rear exploded, sending more smoke into the evening sky and creating the myth of the white-robed woman urging the Catholics to victory. Despite being mainly militia, the Baden infantry resisted stoutly, the final detachment surrendering at 9 p.m. The assault cost Tilly and Córdoba 1,800 casualties, but Georg Friedrich's army had ceased to exist. A quarter were

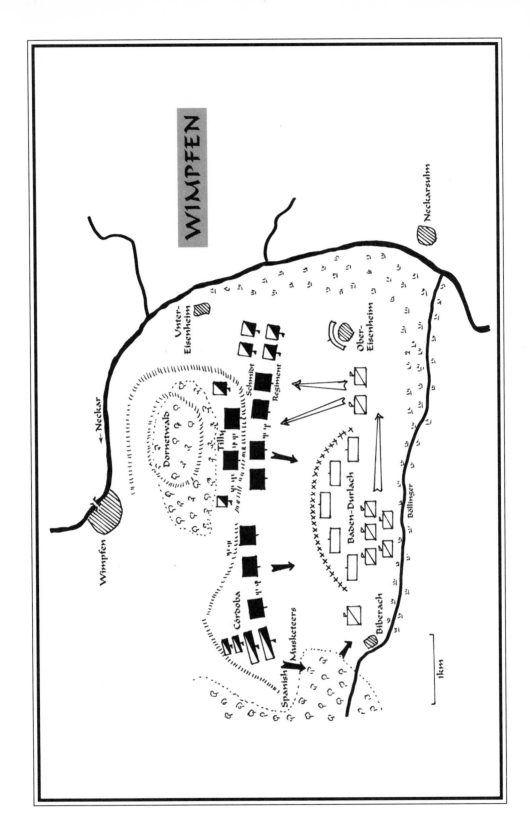

WIMPFEN

Neckarsulm

Unter-Eisenheim

Ober-Eisenheim

Neckar

Dornetwald

Wimpfen

Tilly

Schmidt Regiment

Córdoba

Spanish Musketeers

Baden-Durlach

Böllinger

Biberach

1km

killed or captured, and around half dispersed, leaving barely 3,000 to join Mansfeld, who finally captured Ladenburg on 8 May.

Mansfeld temporarily re-crossed the Rhine to chase away Archduke Leopold who was threatening his new base of Hagenau in Alsace. Duke Christian's army at last approached the Main, but its route south to join Mansfeld lay through the lands of the ostensibly neutral, but secretly pro-imperial landgrave of Hessen-Darmstadt. Mansfeld returned from Alsace in early June and seized the landgrave to force him to give Christian passage. Córdoba re-crossed the Rhine with most of his men in the other direction, but Tilly was more than compensated by the arrival of General Caracciolo's other Spanish corps from Bohemia, as well as Anholt who had been shadowing Christian's march from Westphalia. This gave him 30,000 men, the largest force he had yet commanded. Having blocked Mansfeld's march north at Lorsch on 10 June, Tilly boldly abandoned the area south of the Main to cross at Aschaffenburg and move past Frankfurt to catch Christian as he was crossing at Höchst, just west of the city on 20 June.

Mansfeld had managed to reinforce Christian with 5,000 men, but he was still outnumbered two-to-one. This time there was no repeat of the mistakes at Mingolsheim. Tilly methodically isolated the 2,000 infantry Christian had left at Sossenheim to delay him, relying on panic to do its work. The Höchst bridge became clogged with wagons and collapsed after only 3,000 had crossed. Christian ordered his cavalry to swim across, but many drowned. Disorder increased with the appearance of a Liga cavalry regiment sent just for that purpose. Höchst castle held out until 10 p.m., but Christian lost a third of his army, while many of the survivors were without weapons. Tilly repaired the bridge and continued the pursuit southwards the next day. Christian joined Mansfeld, who lost another 2,000 men covering their combined retreat to Mannheim. The rest of the baggage was captured, while Christian's cavalry regretted the fine Westphalian hams they lost as they ditched their saddle-bags to get away.[36]

The battle sealed the Palatinate's fate. Georg Friedrich had already opened negotiations for a pardon, disbanding his remaining troops on 22 June, abdicating in favour of his son and returning the land taken from his relations. Mansfeld and Christian retreated to Hagenau. Under pressure from King James to placate the emperor, Frederick cancelled Mansfeld's contract on 13 July 1622. Sending Anholt in pursuit of

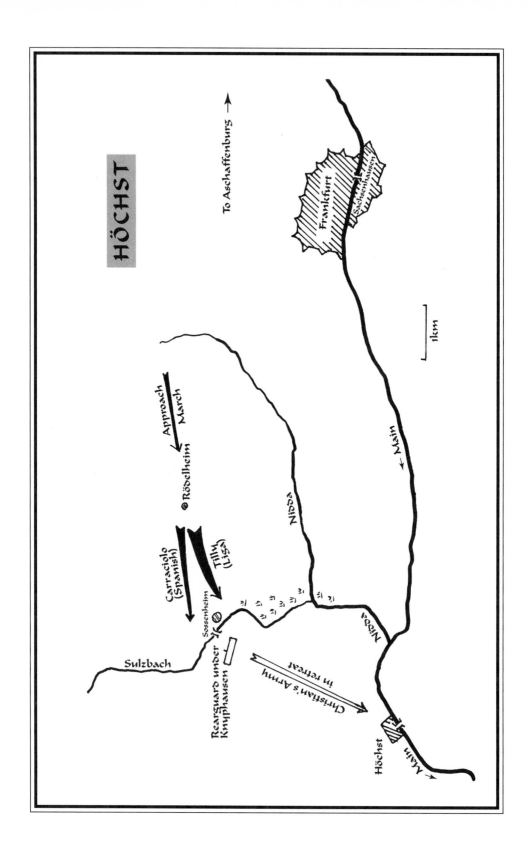

HÖCHST

To Aschaffenburg →

1km

Frankfurt

Sachsenhausen

Main

Approach March

● Rödelheim

Carraciolo (Spanish)

Tilly (Liga)

Sossenheim

Nidda

Nidda

Sulzbach

Rearguard under Knyphausen

Christian's Army in retreat

Höchst

Main

Mansfeld, Tilly remained east of the river, retaking Ladenburg and finally capturing Heidelberg (on 15 September) and Mannheim (on 2 November) after long sieges. Duke Maximilian now held the entire eastern half of the Lower Palatinate and installed Heinrich von Metternich as governor.[37]

Harried by Anholt, Leopold and the 9,000 Cossacks who had just arrived, Mansfeld evacuated his loot from Hagenau and retreated with Christian through neutral Lorraine to Sedan. Relations between the two commanders were tense and they came close to fighting a duel. Renewed negotiations with all parties resulted in their gaining a contract to enter Dutch service for three months on 24 August. Spinola had concentrated 20,600 men to besiege Bergen-op-Zoom, the fortress that secured the Dutch salient south of the Rhine and supported the crippling blockade of Antwerp. The two paladins were supposed to assist in its relief, but this necessitated their dashing across Spanish territory. They had already lost 11,000 deserters since leaving Alsace and were down to 6,000 cavalry and 8,000 infantry, most of whom were mutinous and barely under orders. Córdoba had marched after them. He now overtook their columns and blocked the way at Fleurus, west of Namur, with 9,000 foot and 2,000 horse on 29 August. After repeated attacks, the Spanish right gave way and all who could sped past. The paladins lost all their baggage and artillery, and most of their infantry, but many of the cavalry reached Breda the next day. Wounded, Christian had his lower left arm amputated to the accompaniment of martial music, and he issued a commemorative medal inscribed *Altera restat*: I've still got the other one! Like Mingolsheim, the battle was hailed as a great Protestant victory, but it made little difference to the siege of Bergen, which was finally abandoned by Spinola on 4 October when it became obvious the Dutch could resupply the garrison by sea.[38]

The War Enters North-west Germany

With the Germans' contract due to expire, the Dutch were keen to get rid of the unruly troops. They had no desire to intervene in Germany, but Bergh's operations in Jülich threatened the security of their eastern frontier. It was agreed to send Mansfeld into East Frisia, where he could live at the locals' expense and prevent the Lutheran Count Enno III from conspiring with Bergh to oust the Dutch garrison from Emden. Having been paid and re-equipped by the Dutch, Mansfeld marched from Schen-kenschans along the western edge of Münster, down the Ems into East Frisia with 6,000 men at the end of October 1622. Emden's inhabitants sabotaged Enno's attempt to flood the frontier and, once inside, Mansfeld was secure behind East Frisia's natural defences. The west was protected by the Dutch frontier, the north by the sea, while most of the south and east comprised barren heath and marsh. Mansfeld closed the door by garrisoning Meppen and Leer on the Ems in the south west. The only other route in ran through the duchy of Oldenburg to the north east and that was protected by Denmark.

Emden had wanted help, but not like this. Mansfeld's invasion brought disaster. Using the tax registers, he set about systematic plunder. Emden's trade boom was abruptly halted as the town was swamped with refugees fleeing the countryside.[39] Christian arrived in January having bought Dutch arms for 7,000 men. Mansfeld named him cavalry commander, but the two had fallen out and Christian continued east over the Weser into Lower Saxony with his few followers.

Both paladins became the focus of intense diplomacy. Maximilian and the Habsburgs were keen to wind matters up. Peace talks with British intermediaries led to Frankenthal's surrender on 20 March on James's orders. Two of Sir Thomas Fairfax's sons had died defending the place and many of the defenders were furious, but its situation was hopeless and James hoped its surrender would encourage Ferdinand to offer better terms to Frederick, now back in his Dutch exile. The emperor declared a truce throughout the Empire to give time for Archduchess Isabella of the Spanish Netherlands to organize a conference to settle the Palatine question. It was clear, however, that the emperor intended to resolve matters to his satisfaction, arguing that Mansfeld's continued presence in the Empire removed any obligation to be conciliatory towards Frederick.[40] A princes' congress (*Fürstentag*) convened in Regensburg in February 1623 to advise measures against Mansfeld and receive lavish rewards from the emperor. The Liga congress met in parallel session, and agreed to maintain Tilly's army at 15,000.

The Protestant powers remained at cross-purposes both with each other and with France, which was currently seeking allies to oppose Spain in Italy (see Chapter 11). France agreed to sponsor Mansfeld to launch a diversion against Spain, sending him money and 6,000 recruits by sea in June. Their arrival brought his army to over 20,000, equivalent to a third of the local population and far more than East Frisia could support. Meanwhile, Duke Christian's presence in Lower Saxony embarrassed his Guelph relations who feared it would provide an excuse for Ferdinand to break the Mühlhausen guarantee. Christian IV felt the same and sent Danish troops to keep Christian away from Bremen and Mansfeld out of Oldenburg. Christian was saved by his brother, Friedrich Ulrich, who used his influence in the Lower Saxon Kreis to hire him in March to uphold the region's neutrality for three months. The money and respite allowed him to collect 21,000 men in Halberstadt and Wolfenbüttel by June. Elector Johann Georg mobilized the Upper Saxons that April to stop him moving east.[41]

Ferdinand had already authorized Tilly to protect Westphalia in February 1623, but Tilly remained to the south, partly to reorganize but also to allow time for the emperor's envoys to defuse the situation. Ferdinand offered to let Christian keep Halberstadt and pardon both him and Mansfeld, provided they disbanded their forces. These were generous terms, but they were rejected as dishonourable. Christian insisted the emperor extend the pardon to his officers, including those who were Bohemian exiles. In the meantime, Count Thurn was writing encouragingly from Constantinople that Bethlen would rejoin the fight.

Anholt moved 12,000 men to cover the southern half of Westphalia, while Tilly collected 17,000 in the Wetterau to enforce a new Reichshofrat verdict against Landgrave Moritz of Hessen-Kassel in April. This awarded Marburg to Darmstadt in clear recognition of the latter's loyalty and as compensation for the 3 million fl. worth of damage inflicted by Mansfeld's troops on its territory. Collalto reinforced Tilly with 8,000 Imperialists from Bohemia in May, and together they moved to Eschwege on the Lower Saxon frontier at the end of June. At Maximilian's request, Ferdinand issued an ultimatum to the Lower Saxons to assist Tilly if Christian refused to submit. Christian's cavalry already skirmished with Imperialists as he moved west from Halberstadt to block the frontier at Göttingen. Tilly advanced and Christian finally broke off negotiations on 16 July.

The Battle of Stadtlohn

Christian's prospects looked bleak. Fearing his relations would help Tilly, he sped west hoping the Dutch would employ him again. He resigned his bishopric on 28 July in favour of Denmark, but this won him no favours. Mansfeld refused to leave East Frisia, despite Christian heading north into Osnabrück to shorten the distance between them. This allowed Tilly to catch up as he took the more direct route west, reaching Greven on the Ems just half an hour after Christian had left on 4 August. Anholt now joined him, but detachments and the usual campaign wastage meant they mustered only slightly over 5,000 cavalry, 15,000 infantry and 14 guns, including Collalto's imperial detachment.[42]

Christian still had over 50km to go to reach the Dutch garrison of Bredevoort, across relatively flat country cut by small rivers and boundary ditches. He adopted the tactics used at Höchst, leaving a strong rearguard to cover his retreat from one 'defile', or choke point, to another. He managed to get over the Steinfurter Aa on the evening of Saturday 5 August. Tilly's Croats caught up at Bergsteinfurt, forcing Christian to retreat precipitously past Horstmar to camp at Strönfeld just across the Vechta. Leaving instructions that the baggage was to set out at 11 p.m., to be followed by the rest of the army in stages, he fell asleep. He awoke at 3 a.m. to find his exhausted soldiers still slumbering. His rearguard finally abandoned the Vechta crossing at Metelen at 8 a.m., without destroying the bridge, falling back past Nienborg where Colonel Styrum was left with a fresh detachment of 500 cavalry to hold the Dinkel crossing at Heek village.

Tilly's force was already in hot pursuit, crossing the Vechta past the smoking embers of Christian's camp fires. Anholt attacked Colonel Styrum's men at 9 a.m., forcing Christian to send 500 musketeers to extricate them and fall back across the Ahauser Aa where Baron Knyphausen was posted with a more substantial rearguard of 2,000 musketeers and 2 guns between Wessum and Wüllen, west of the river. Christian deployed the rest of the army south of Wüllen on the Quantwicker hill, holding this position for three hours to give time for his baggage to cross the Berkel, the last obstacle before Bredevoort, about 9km further south-west. Though the hot weather reduced the water level, the banks remained wet, making it impassable to wagons that had to cross either by the Stadtlohn bridge or another immediately to the east. His army was down to 15,000 with 16 guns. Around half were raw recruits, many without arms, who were already showing signs of panic.

Knyphausen's men gave way, forcing Christian to make a final stand behind the Wüllener Landwehr, a parish boundary ditch half way between the village and Stadtlohn. The most reliable units, chiefly those of the Weimar brothers, were placed in the centre. His left deployed on the Lohner Bruch, a marshy heath largely dried by the heat. The right rested on the Liesner wood and the deep cut of the Lepping stream. The heath and stream narrowed to the south-west like a funnel, cramping Christian's forces crowding by the Berkel, whilst allowing Tilly greater space to deploy to the north.

It was now 2 p.m. on 6 August, the Feast of the Transfiguration, deemed auspicious by the Catholics. While Anholt deployed, the Liga artillery began to unsettle Christian's infantry. Two counter-attacks failed, allowing Tilly to advance about ninety minutes later. His veteran infantry closed to musket range, while the cavalry swept round the enemy's right flank. Christian's army disintegrated as it was herded towards Stadtlohn. The recruits fell on their knees begging for mercy, but the Croats and Cossacks cut down fugitives until the following dawn.

Tilly lost 1,000 men killed and wounded, the latter including his nephew Werner who commanded one of the cavalry regiments. Most reports put the Protestant dead at 6,000 with a further 4,000 captured along with a large quantity of munitions and the entire baggage train except two wagons loaded with cash that escaped with Christian just in time. All the artillery was taken and put on display at Coesfeld market-place. Around 1,000 prisoners enlisted with Tilly, but soon deserted after discovering he insisted on better discipline than they were used to. The rest were taken to Münster where they were kept under such appalling conditions that the inhabitants and clergy organized relief for them. Having promised not to take up arms against the emperor again, they were released. Over sixty senior officers, including six princes and counts, were handed over to the emperor. Wilhelm of Weimar was held until December 1625. His brother Bernhard was wounded, but managed to escape. The loss of so many officers made it very difficult for Christian to recruit a new army. Accompanied by 5,500 survivors, he entered Dutch pay for ten weeks, unfairly blaming Knyphausen for the disaster.

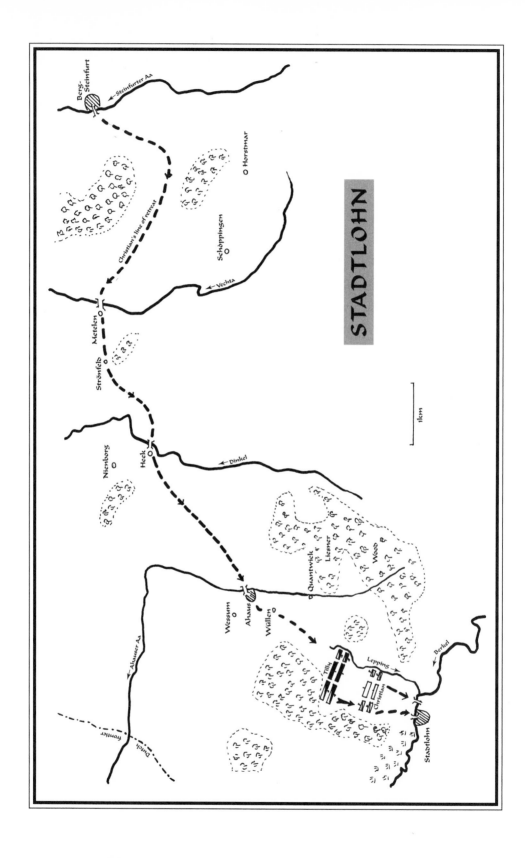

STADTLOHN

Bergs-Steinfurt
←Steinfurter Aa

○ Horstmar

Schöppingen ○

←Vechta

Christian's line of retreat

Metelen

Strönfeld ○

Niemborg ○

Heek ○

←Dinkel

Wood

Liesner

Quantwick

Wessum

Ahaus

Wüllen ○

Tilly

Lepping →

Christian

Berkel

Stadtlohn

Dutch frontier

Ahauser Aa

1km

Mopping Up

Spain hoped that the Dutch decision to again shelter a fugitive army would prompt Maximilian and Ferdinand to join them against the Republic. Maximilian refused, consistently regarding the two conflicts as separate.[43] Besides, Tilly's army was in no condition to undertake further major operations. In the meantime, Anholt's arrival in Westphalia in November 1622 triggered the first popular opposition to the war in Germany. The towns of the bishopric of Münster were predominantly Protestant, but their resistance was driven by a general desire to avoid violence. Fearing Dutch reprisals, they refused to let Anholt's troops through their gates for the winter. Unpaid and starving, his corps roamed the countryside, while the peasants fled to the marshes. The damage in the duchy of Westphalia alone was put at six times the usual annual tax bill. Elector Ferdinand of Cologne was already ill-disposed towards the towns and considered their defiance an act of rebellion. Anholt spent the spring of 1623 besieging them while he waited for Christian and Tilly to move west. Stadtlohn cleared the way for more thorough action. Assisted by Liga troops, a commission toured the towns into 1624, rewriting their charters and imposing new Catholic councils. Only Münster itself escaped with its privileges intact, because it had already agreed not to grant citizenship to any more Protestants and to supply food to the army. However, the arrival of Tilly's forces in its vicinity exhausted its resources, leading to a week of plundering as his ravenous troops broke into monasteries and houses in September 1623.[44]

Tilly still had to deal with Mansfeld who had enhanced East Frisia's natural defences by burning the border villages and flooding the remaining tracks across the heath. He tried to break in using the route Mansfeld had taken the previous October, capturing Meppen in August, but got no further. A march east to Oldenburg proved equally futile as this way was blocked as well. With winter approaching, Tilly dispersed his men into billets along the frontier, hoping to starve Mansfeld out.

The growing crisis brought the feuding population together. Emden collaborated with the count to intercept supplies sent by the Dutch. The situation worsened as Christian's small army returned to East Frisia after its second Dutch contract expired. Mansfeld found that foraging parties sent to raid across the frontier simply deserted. The duke of Oldenburg scraped together 90,000 talers that Christian accepted to disband his remaining 2,000 men in January 1624. As Mansfeld held out for more, the Dutch loaned the East Frisian Estates the equivalent of three years' taxes which he accepted on behalf of the 4,500 men that remained with his colours; most promptly enlisted in the Dutch army after pocketing their share at the end of the month.

Meanwhile, Tilly had sent a detachment south into Hessen-Kassel to force Duke Moritz to disarm in October 1623. Like Georg Friedrich the year before, Moritz fled, eventually abdicating in favour of his son, Wilhelm V, to save the territory from sequestration. Tilly's troops stayed until 1625, extracting over 5 million fl. in contributions. Wilhelm bowed to local pressure and had Wolfgang Günther executed as a scapegoat for his father's policies.[45]

Back in Upper Hungary, encouraged by the indefatigable Thurn, Bethlen had conspired throughout 1623, believing Christian was marching east to join him. He resurrected the grand scheme of 1620, receiving the sultan's promise of a force of 30,000 Turks and Tartars in return for agreeing to make Hungary and Bohemia tributary states once they had been conquered. The auxiliaries began assembling in June 1623, while the Croatian and Slavonian border militia mutinied the following month in protest at being paid in debased coin. The need to bring in the harvest delayed Bethlen's advance until mid August. The Imperialists had already been alerted in May as the Hungarian malcontents intensified their raiding. Caraffa and Wallenstein collected 7,500 troops on the March river to block the way into Moravia and Lower Austria, assisted by 10,000 Cossacks. A further 9,000 men were redirected from Germany and Austria as reinforcements. Bethlen temporarily suspended operations when he learned of Christian's defeat, but resumed in September, trapping the Imperialists in Göding (Hodonin) on the March and enslaving 15,000 of the local population. Vienna was again thrown into panic. Ferdinand considered fleeing to Innsbruck, while things were so bad inside Göding that Wallenstein's men were reduced to eating their own horses.

As in 1622, the underlying trend was clearly against Bethlen. The Silesian militia mobilized to block his advance northwards, while more Cossacks arrived to contain the raiding. Unaware of his enemy's panic and only conscious of his own isolation, Bethlen accepted another truce in November, which was converted into peace in May 1624. Ferdinand granted Bethlen lenient terms, essentially confirming the Nikolsburg treaty. He could afford to be magnanimous. It had been a narrow victory but a decisive one. Bethlen's credibility was shattered. The Dutch had refused aid, while the sultan was persuaded not to risk his own truce with the Habsburgs. Bethlen sent a Catholic noble to Vienna with an offer to change sides, marry Ferdinand's daughter and bequeath Transylvania to the emperor. Ferdinand did not take this seriously. He consolidated his hold over his part of Hungary, arriving at the next Pressburg diet in October 1625 accompanied by a large escort. Assisted by Cardinal Pazmany, he obtained majority agreement to his demands. The diet elected the Catholic Miklós Esterházy the new palatine to replace the deceased Thurzó, as well as accepting the emperor's seventeen-year-old son, Archduke Ferdinand, as king in December. Though Ferdinand confirmed the religious concessions of 1606, it was clear that the growth of Catholic influence in the diet offered the prospect of revoking these in the future.[46] The paladins had been routed and the war in the Empire appeared to be over. Ferdinand and his supporters could concentrate on exploiting their victory.

THE CATHOLIC ASCENDANCY 1621–9

Change and Continuity

The battle of White Mountain was long regarded as a turning point. Those favourably inclined to the Habsburgs argued it was a victory for progress, ending feudal anarchy and preventing Bohemia from slipping into 'a Polish future'.[47] For most Czechs, however, it was a national disaster, starting an 'age of darkness' and cultural decline under alien rule. On 3 November 1918, a week after the Czechs broke from the Austro-Hungarian Empire, a large crowd gathered on the White Mountain battlefield to hear speeches trumpeting independence as a triumph over the shame of 1620. The people then marched to Prague Old Town Square and pulled down the column of the Virgin, regarded as a symbol of Habsburg absolutism. This view persists today and the title of a recent popular account of the battle translates as 'Black Day on White Mountain'.[48]

It was not until the 1950s that this interpretation met a challenge from social and economic historians who pointed to long-term continuities across the 1618–20 political divide. The association of this alternative interpretation with state-sponsored Marxist history between 1948 and 1990 did much to discredit it. Certainly, the events cannot be reduced to a struggle within a single ruling class over economic assets. Nonetheless, there were important continuities, while analyses of the nobility provide important clues as to what changed.

In order to understand the impact of the military events, the consequences for Bohemia must be viewed in common with those in the rest of the Empire. The situation in Bohemia was distinct only because the kingdom was part of the Habsburg hereditary lands, allowing Ferdinand greater freedom to act there than in the defeated German territories. National distinctions based on language or alleged cultural differences mattered nowhere but in the propaganda of the defeated rebels and the later writings of those desiring Czech independence.

The significance of the victories of 1620–3 lay not in sweeping constitutional or institutional changes, but in the redistribution of power and wealth to the emperor's supporters. These, in turn, were identified most clearly by their Catholicism, the propagation of which was merely part of a broader programme to stabilize the Habsburg dynasty after its decline under Rudolf. Ferdinand's attitude towards his opponents remained the same, regardless of whether they spoke Czech or German. Those that took up arms were rebels who had forfeited their rights. His victories made him a conqueror, entitled to dispose of their property as he pleased. Nonetheless, his actions remained guided by what he regarded as the correct interpretation of the imperial constitution and his duties as emperor. His mandates and ultimatums were considered fair warning. Those failing to take advantage of his clemency placed themselves demonstrably in the wrong. Further punishment depended on formally branding them outlaws. The appropriate penalties were then decided through consultation with electors and princes, or by legal tribunals in the case of the hereditary lands. The distinction lay in the different character of Ferdinand's dual status. In Bohemia and Austria he regarded himself as hereditary ruler facing his own subjects who were liable to lose their lives as well as property. Elsewhere, he acted as emperor towards disobedient vassals. The concept of 'notorious rebels' made a formal hearing unnecessary, but it was also unwise to expose imperial prerogatives to criticism by seeking unduly harsh sentences. In any case, Ferdinand was not seeking death but the expropriation of his opponents' lands and titles. This could be achieved through consultation with his supporters and, ideally, the accused whom Ferdinand was quite willing to pardon provided they accepted their 'guilt' and acquiesced in a reduction of their territory.

Stabilizing the Dynasty

Ferdinand's adherence to established norms is most apparent in the political changes he made. The general tendency was, predictably, to enhance his authority in a move towards what is labelled 'absolutism'. We should not, however, overemphasize centralization or moderniz-ation. No new institutions were created. Instead, existing arrangements were modified to reduce the potential for formal opposition.

Ferdinand addressed the legacy of the Brothers' Quarrel by adding a codicil to his will on 10 May 1621, introducing primogeniture to ensure his son, Archduke Ferdinand, would succeed to all his lands. Even here, however, older practices persisted, as the emperor ceded the Tirolean lands in two stages (in 1623 and 1630) to his brother Leopold, who had been made governor there after Archduke Maximilian's death in 1618. Ferdinand also dropped plans to raise Austria to a kingdom in 1623 because Leopold feared this would diminish his status within the com-posite Habsburg monarchy.[49]

Despite their role in the rebellion, no attempt was made to abolish the Estates. The Saxon occupation of Lusatia and intervention in Silesia meant the institutions there escaped with their privileges intact, thanks to the elector's guarantees. Elsewhere, Ferdinand could act more force-fully, but eventually only promulgated 'renewed constitutions' for Upper Austria (1625, revised 1627), Bohemia (1627) and Moravia (1628) that remained in force until the 1848 revolution. The monarchy was declared hereditary, eliminating Bohemian claims to elect their king. The Estates retained the right to vote on taxation, but lost that of free assembly, as well as control of the formally hereditary great offices of state. Rudolf's Letter of Majesty was revoked, leaving Catholicism the sole official faith, though special dispensations remained for Jews. Estates' powers now rested on dynastic grace, not inalienable corporate rights. Diets lost their significance as real influence shifted to permanent, salaried committees. Even in the Tirol, a region that remained loyal and escaped changes, peasants increasingly selected lawyers to represent them in the diet as government became more bureaucratic and technical.[50]

Regardless of the fighting, the Estates' role was changing in this period from corporate representation to administration. Their participation in deciding taxation was to help the crown find the amount of money the country could reasonably bear, and to assist in collecting it. The monarch alone now represented the country in external relations. This central element of Ferdinand's programme revived Charles V's project from 1548 to make the Empire easier to manage by securing full autonomy for the hereditary lands. Already in 1620, Ferdinand separated the Austrian and imperial chancelleries that had merged in 1559. The Austrian chancellery now handled Ferdinand's business as hereditary ruler, including diplomatic correspondence, whereas the imperial chancellery dealt with relations with the imperial Estates. Formally, the elector of Mainz remained head of the imperial chancellery, but Habsburg policy in the Empire ran through the vice-chancellor, who was the emperor's appointee. The Bohemian chancellery remained, but moved to Vienna in 1624. Both it and its Austrian counterpart began issuing patents of nobility, widening the Habsburgs' patronage independently of the imperial title that was traditionally associated with ennoblement. Coordination was provided by the privy council. This had emerged in the 1520s but now became more important under its chairman, Baron Eggenberg, Ferdinand's trusted adviser.

The institutional adjustments were less significant than the changes in personnel. The rebellion had shown that the problem lay not with the Estates as such, but in their use by the regime's opponents. The actual Estates had split, with a substantial proportion of their membership remaining loyal or at least neutral after 1618. It is here that the significance of religion can be gauged since Catholicism remained the most obvious mark of loyalty. The victories after 1620 enabled Ferdinand to extend his existing patronage to the rest of the Empire. By redistributing conquered land, he undermined the opposition's economic base while strengthening his supporters'. By sparing the land of moderates or those showing contrition, he could win them over and enlarge the pool of talent at his disposal.

It is important not to overestimate the coherence of this strategy. Its implementation was improvised and clearly driven in part by fiscal expediency. The full impact worked through only after several generations. The immediate beneficiaries owed status and wealth to backing the winning side. Rewarded with land and high office, they provided the glue holding the monarchy together through the war. Their fortunes were immediately entwined with that of the dynasty, just as the fate of the Bohemian exiles and other victims depended on the success of the emperor's remaining enemies like Sweden. The post-war generation were largely the children of these beneficiaries. Unlike those rising in revolt in 1618, they harboured no ambitions to alter political arrangements, but rather to improve their place in the Habsburg court and administration. The dynasty met their aspirations thanks to the continued growth of its army and bureaucracy, as well as by creating new titles and honours. Representation of local and provincial interests now largely ran through these informal channels, as the prominent aristocratic families promoted their own clients within the system.

The Blood Court

The first stage of this process began with the summer offensive of 1620 and involved identifying the victims. Three mandates issued after August 1620 named 65 Lower and 51 Upper Austrians as rebels who had forfeited their property. The others were targeted in January and February 1621 when Frederick and his principal German supporters were placed under the imperial ban, while a special commission began work in Prague headed by Karl Liechtenstein and Cardinal Dietrichstein. Vienna sent a list of 82 men to be arrested, including the Bohemian Directors as well as the Defenestrators. Some, like Colonna von Fels, were already dead, or had fled. Many naïvely remained in Prague, ignoring Tilly's hints in November 1620 to escape. The trial lasted two months. Johann Georg ignored Protestant pleas and handed over the Defenestrator Joachim Andreas Schlick who had sought shelter in Saxony. Thirty-two were sentenced to death on the ground that their crimes constituted treason. Along with another eleven whose lives were spared, all lost their property, thereby punishing their families as well. The form of execution was deliberately barbaric: most were to have their tongue pulled out, or right hand chopped off, prior to being killed.

Ferdinand wrestled with his conscience on receiving the verdicts, consulting his advisers and travelling to the Mariazell shrine for divine guidance. The Bohemian chancellor Lobkowitz, and the future imperial vice-chancellor Stralendorf, urged the emperor to commute the sentences to galley service. Slavata and Martinitz also had no desire for revenge and opposed the death sentences on their Defenestrators. Ferdinand pardoned five, and alleviated the form of execution for some others, but he signed 28 death warrants on 23 May 1621, the third anniversary of the Defenestration. Liechtenstein was told to hurry to carry out the sentences because the emperor did not want his triumphal entrance into Prague to coincide with the executions. The garrison was augmented and the city gates closed. Twenty-seven men were led to the Old Town Square on 21 June along with the corpse of the other condemned man who had committed suicide in prison. The victims were three lords, seven knights and seventeen citizens, including the university rector who remained the only one to have his tongue pulled out to punish his speech praising Frederick. They included one Catholic: Dionys Czernin, the captain who had let the Defenestrators into the Hradschin.

The executioner, Jan Mydllar, required four axes for his grisly task, though three of the commoners were hanged. Twelve heads, two hands and the rector's tongue were stuck over the town gates where they remained until the Saxons removed them in 1631. Another 29 fugitives were condemned to death *in absentia*. The event has entered Czech history as the Blood Court. It was the logical consequence of Ferdinand's interpretation of the events as rebellion. The number of victims was comparatively small compared to the duke of Alba's Council of Blood at the start of the Dutch Revolt, or the repression following failed rebellions in seventeenth- and eighteenth-century Britain. Yet, it was undoubtedly unnecessary and a mistake. The mood changed in Prague. Whereas the rebel leadership had been blamed for the disaster, they now attracted sympathy.[51]

The Saxons handed over three Lusatians to Ferdinand, and fined eleven others. Of the Moravians, only Colonel Friedrich von Tieffenbach was executed, in Innsbruck on 27 May 1621. Dietrichstein and Slavata held a second tribunal that condemned twelve Moravians to death, but none of them was executed. Some had fled, while Dietrichstein and Karel Zierotin interceded on the others' behalf. Ferdinand apparently learned from his mistake in Prague and commuted the sentences to life imprisonment – all were released before the decade was out.

The Land Transfers

The executions intensified the exiles' bitter hatred of the emperor, but the land confiscation was historically more important. The Liechtenstein commission began expropriating rebel property after the Blood Court using lists prepared since November 1620. It was the largest transfer of property in Europe before the seizures during the Communist takeover after 1945 in which, among others, the descendants of those benefiting in the 1620s lost their estates. Protests obliged the commission to stop seizing land from nobles in October 1623, by which time it had already confiscated the possessions of those who had supported the revolt. Property continued to be taken from burghers, but this was obviously on a much smaller scale. The action affected 680 Bohemian noble families, of whom 166 lost everything, as well as 135 Prague burghers and others in 50 towns. Around 150 Moravian estates were seized from 250 families. Since the process involved the transfer of the former owners' feudal jurisdiction over their tenants, its scale can be gauged from the fact that half the Moravian population changed landlord. Few properties were taken in Upper Silesia, but the chief beneficiaries of the redistribution in Bohemia and Moravia also acquired land there.

The whole episode proved even more emotive for later generations than the executions. Czech historians labelled it 'deliberate robbery'.[52] The Slavata were the only senior Czech family to expand their possessions in Bohemia, where they had over 2,000 dependent peasant households. Another 16 Czech families controlled 10,000 more households, or 18 per cent of the total. While Czech remained the predominant language among Bohemian nobles, it was displaced by German in Moravia where the members of the Zierotin family who backed the revolt lost nearly three-quarters of their 10,000 households.

Land confiscation was the standard punishment for rebellion. None of those protesting questioned the basic legality, instead they sought mercy by claiming mitigating circumstances. The process entailed a massive expansion of the state without altering the fundamental legal and property arrangements. The crown did not expropriate the land itself, keeping only 1.6 per cent of the total. It also avoided punishing relations who had not participated in the rebellion, leaving entailed land untouched, and taking only that owned directly by rebels. Confiscation often resembled a forced sale as compensation was sometimes paid, though in debased coin. The growth of state power thus flowed through the reordering of personal relationships as Ferdinand restructured and expanded his clientele, rewarding loyalists regardless of family origin or the location of the property. The monarchy acquired a universal reach without having to destroy provincial privileges. More families now held land in several provinces simultaneously, while newcomers were integrated into the Habsburg elite. Germans, Spaniards, Italians and Belgians comprised 281 of the 417 families entering the Bohemian nobility between 1621 and 1656. The majority were imperial army officers, or Catholics from other parts of the monarchy.

Wealth became heavily concentrated in the hands of a few leading families, largely those who had already backed Ferdinand prior to 1618. The Liechtensteins and Lobkowitzs held huge estates in Bohemia, Moravia and Silesia, while the Slavata held land in Bohemia and Moravia. Together with the Dietrichsteins, the Liechtenstein family controlled a quarter of Moravia, while Baron Eggenberg emerged as the principal Bohemian landowner. Confiscation, exile and the influx of outsiders broke the social cohesion of the old Bohemian nobility. The marriage market widened. Language and involvement in local politics ceased to be defining criteria. Many nobles became absentee landlords as participation in the court and central government assumed greater significance.

The Palatine Lands and Titles

The policy was extended beyond the Habsburg hereditary lands even before Tilly's year of victories in 1622 made implementation a realistic option. A Hamburg paper speculated as early as September 1619 that Ferdinand would transfer the Palatine title if Frederick accepted the Bohemian crown.[53] The obvious recipient was Maximilian of Bavaria who was in a strong position to demand compensation on the basis of the Treaty of Munich from October 1619, as well as holding imperial commissions for Bohemia and Upper Austria in August 1620. Maximilian recognized the difficulty of assuming responsibility for Bohemia, and renounced his function there on 13 January, retaining only Upper Austria, formally transferred to him by Ferdinand on 15 February until he was able to repay Bavaria's war costs.[54] This gave Maximilian leverage over the emperor, since it was highly unlikely the Habsburg treasury would ever find the money to redeem the province. The legal preparations for reassigning the electoral title were completed when Ferdinand bowed to Bavarian pressure and declared Frederick an outlaw on 29 January 1621.

However, Ferdinand was in no hurry to go further, recognizing that Frederick would become irreconcilable if deprived of his electoral, as well as royal Bohemian, title. He also foresaw that sequestrating the Palatinate would provide an excuse for other powers to take up Frederick's cause. There was the additional problem of Spain, whose intervention in the capacity of its membership of the Burgundian Kreis entitled it to compensation too. Few Habsburg advisers favoured transferring the Palatine title to Bavaria, but Frederick's intransigence at Segeberg in March convinced Ferdinand there was no point in being lenient. He extended Maximilian's commission in June 1621 to include the Upper Palatinate and then secretly transferred the electoral title to him on 22 September. The award would only take effect once Ferdinand acknowledged it publicly, but Maximilian hesitated to press him until both were sure of Spain's support, and Spain did not want to relinquish the western Lower Palatinate, a valuable asset in negotiations with James I. Unlike his predecessor, the new pope, Gregory XV, saw the conflict as a holy war and convinced Spain of the advantage in transferring the title of this Calvinist stronghold to the Catholic Maximilian.

Tilly's victories secured the ground, especially with the capture of Heidelberg and Mannheim by November 1622. An imperial deputation convened in Regensburg in December, and expanded into a princes' congress that, as we have seen, ran parallel to a meeting of the Liga and peace talks sponsored by James and Isabella. Ferdinand wished to restore unity and was prepared to be magnanimous. Anhalt, Hohenlohe and others were pardoned. Negotiations continued with Mansfeld and Duke Christian, offering them clemency if they laid down their arms. Unlike in Bohemia, there were no plans to execute opponents. Nor did Ferdinand intend to break the Mühlhausen guarantee for the north German bishoprics. There were already calls from some ecclesiastical princes for a full restitution of former church land, but these were not incorporated into the emperor's programme. All restitution involved secular principalities – Baden-Baden, Marburg, Waldeck.

This just left the Palatinate, a territory sufficiently large to satisfy more than Maximilian. Frederick's share of three districts in northern

Bavaria was given to his Pfalz-Neuburg relations to reconcile them to Maximilian's new status. The Forest Road (*Bergstrasse*) which Mainz had lost to the Palatinate in the fifteenth century was returned to it, while Sinsheim went to Speyer as compensation for Frederick's destruction of Udenheim in 1618. Darmstadt received two districts in lieu of the damage done in 1622, as well as some properties belonging to the counts of Löwenstein, Solms-Braunfels and Isenburg who had served as colonels in Mansfeld's army.[55] These transfers were relatively minor: the two districts given to Darmstadt had only 850 inhabitants. The real beneficiary remained Maximilian who received the entire Upper Palatinate and the remainder of the eastern Lower Palatinate on 25 February 1623.

The electoral title was also publicly transferred on the same day, significantly the seventy-fifth anniversary of the switch of the Saxon title between the Ernestine and Albertine Wettins by Charles V. The event was boycotted by Pfalz-Neuburg, Saxony, Brandenburg and the Spanish ambassador, Oñate, while Isabella sent a protest. It retained a sense of impermanence, since the land transfers were attached to Maximilian's temporary possession of Upper Austria and together set against Ferdinand's obligation to refund his war expenses, agreed at 12 million florins. Maximilian remained bound to Ferdinand whose help he needed to secure wider recognition of his new status. Mainz's mediation persuaded Johann Georg in July 1624 after the emperor handed Lusatia to Saxony on similar terms as the pledges to Bavaria over Upper Austria, this time in lieu of expenses set at 3.93 million florins.[56]

Important though these decisions were, they have overshadowed another strand of Ferdinand's programme. Starting in Regensburg, the emperor had by August 1624 created eleven new princes, in contrast to only four elevations over the preceding seventy years. They included three members of the Catholic branch of the Hohenzollerns, as well as their relation Field Marshal Count Salm. The others came from the Habsburgs' own territorial nobility and included the three Liechtenstein brothers, Cardinal Dietrichstein and General Wallenstein. The electors were lukewarm at this attempt to pack a future Reichstag with Habsburg supporters and insisted the new princes acquire appropriate fiefs before they could exercise their votes. The requirement intensified the integration of the Habsburg and imperial nobility: not only did imperial counts and knights serving in the emperor's army acquire property confiscated from rebels in the Habsburg hereditary lands, but Habsburg aristocrats now assumed a more significant share of the Empire's lands and titles. Ferdinand also made full use of his prerogative to raise over a hundred families to the status of imperial baron and another seventy to that of imperial count, including Tilly in September 1622.[57] Those counts that purchased or married into appropriate land acquired a voice in Kreis assemblies. Again, there was a close association with the Habsburg elite: ten of the emperor's privy councillors joined the Swabian counts between 1627 and 1654.

As in the Habsburg lands, Ferdinand's programme worked by changing people, not institutions, bringing loyalists to the fore and marginalizing opponents. The scale of the changes was already significant, but not more than could be accommodated within the imperial constitution. The real problems only began after 1627 when the defeat of Denmark and its north German allies provided opportunities for a more fundamental redistribution of lands and titles (see Chapter 12, pp.420–1).

Re-Catholicization

Ferdinand's measures were nonetheless controversial, not least because they were associated with the promotion of Catholicism. This process has been labelled 're-Catholicization', though many of those affected had lived their entire lives as Protestants. The Catholicism that was imposed was the post-Tridentine version, not that which had existed before. This created tensions among those implementing the policy, some of whom preferred the less austere pre-Reformation Catholicism. Though Catholicism was the primary test for political loyalty, the secular imperative sometimes contradicted the policy's spiritual dimension.[58]

The primary purpose was to form a solidly Catholic political and social elite, and neither Maximilian nor Ferdinand's principal advisers showed a great desire to extend the measures to the rest of the population. Maximilian and the leading Habsburg officials favoured continuing the pre-war gradualist approach of avoiding direct attacks on legally recognized Protestant populations, while encouraging them to convert. Persuasion remained a major element of re-Catholicization into the post-war era and was preferred by many clerics. The pope, Jesuits and some others advocated a more robust approach, however. The Jesuits pressed ahead without local support in the small principality of Sulzbach and failed miserably.[59] Success clearly depended on political backing and the papal nuncio pressed Ferdinand to sanction the use of force. While the emperor wished to remain within his version of the law, he was nonetheless susceptible to militant arguments. His belief that his opponents were rebels convinced him they had forfeited their religious as well as political rights and property. Maximilian was more cautious, partly because his possession of the Palatinate remained insecure until recognized by the other electors in 1628. The delay allowed him to observe the problems Ferdinand encountered in his hereditary lands, as well as Duke Wolfgang Wilhelm of Pfalz-Neuburg's difficulties in persuading his Jülich and Berg subjects to embrace Catholicism.

Despite these differences, the programme followed the pattern devised in 1579 to promote Catholicism in Austria and Bavaria discussed in Chapter 3. The Protestant infrastructure was targeted first, as pastors and teachers were expelled, turning churches and schools over to Catholics. This began in December 1621 in Bohemia, though Liechtenstein initially tried to exempt Lutherans, who were not ordered to leave until October 1622. The measures were delayed in Lower Austria until 1626, while Maximilian did not apply the policy to Calvinists in the Upper Palatinate until three years after his conquest. The Habsburgs then targeted Protestant towns. Catholicism had already become a criterion for Viennese citizenship in 1623 and this was extended to Bohemian and then Upper and Lower Austrian towns. The 'renewed constitutions' destroyed the legal basis for the remaining Protestant rights, clearing the way for a series of 'general mandates' in Bohemia, Upper and Lower Austria (all in 1627), and then Moravia and Inner Austria (both in 1628), giving the population six months to convert or emigrate.

Maximilian implemented the measures in reverse order, issuing a general mandate in the Upper Palatinate in April 1628 before going further than Ferdinand and completely abolishing the local Estates in 1629. He obtained Ferdinand's permission for this step that removed an institution with much weaker roots than those in the Habsburg monarchy. Bavarian measures also attacked Calvinism, a faith widely resented by the largely Lutheran Upper Palatines and even unpopular in much of the Lower Palatinate. Re-Catholicism there only began in 1628 and was much less systematic since Maximilian controlled only a third of the territory, a half being in Spanish hands and the rest divided between Mainz, Speyer and Darmstadt. The Spanish left religion alone, just as they did in their Lower Rhenish garrisons. Darmstadt was

Lutheran, while Mainz and Speyer failed to coordinate with Bavaria owing to disputes over jurisdiction. Lutheran towns that had surrendered to Tilly were left alone, while the occupying Bavarian authorities were too busy raising war taxes to press on religious issues.

The Bavarians introduced the other elements of re-Catholicization, including the Gregorian calendar and confession certificates to prove observance. Those failing to attend mass or who ate meat at forbidden times were liable for fines, but the Bavarians were less vigorous in expelling dissenters than the Habsburgs. The Upper Palatinate mandate only applied to Maximilian's prime target, the nobility. Ninety families converted by 1630 and though another 93 left, they were not required to sell their property and simply became absentee landlords. Other social groups were not affected until July 1660 and even then heads of households were exempt. There was no need for these measures in Bavaria where few people had embraced Protestantism. Maximilian also left the Bavarian Estates intact, relying on economic pressures that made court, administrative and military appointments increasingly attractive to the local nobles. As these appointments were open to Catholics alone, Protestant nobles were thus given a compelling incentive to convert.[60]

A significant proportion of the Habsburg nobility also converted. The revolt intensified the association between Protestantism and subversion, making the faith both dangerous and morally suspect. The battle of White Mountain appeared to indicate that God favoured Catholics. Some converted to avoid punishment, or to share in the spoils. A notable example of opportunism was Johann Ludwig of Nassau-Hadamar who renounced Calvinism in 1629 to win Ferdinand's support over a disputed inheritance. He became the first of the Nassau dynasty to be made an imperial prince (in 1639) and represented the emperor at the Westphalian peace congress. For others, conversion was simply an extension of their existing loyalty to the dynasty. The Styrian Lutheran Rudolf von Tieffenbach had commanded the artillery at White Mountain and converted in 1623, despite the execution of his brother who was caught on the other side. Twenty-one Hungarian magnates and their sons converted between 1613 and 1637, further reducing the Protestant proportion in the diet. Even in Lower Austria, where the Lutheran nobility retained freedom of conscience, only a third of the 420 nobles remained Protestant by 1650.

Major factors in Catholicism's success were the punitive measures that drove most of the Protestants into exile. A significant number had fled in the wake of White Mountain and the confiscations. Others, mainly more humble folk, followed after the general mandates. It is likely that 100,000 people left Inner and Lower Austria to avoid persecution between 1598 and 1660. A similar number fled Silesia, despite Saxon intervention to secure Lutheran rights, while around 150,000 left Bohemia and Moravia across the same period. The majority went in the 1620s. Though forming a minority of the emigrants, the nobility suffered disproportionately. The 1628 Inner Austrian mandate prompted 750 Styrian and 160 Carinthian nobles to leave, while over 300 of the 1,400 Bohemian and Moravian noble families departed. The exodus fuelled the reconstruction of the Habsburg elite, because the emigrants sold their land. The political gain to the Habsburgs came at a high price, reducing the population by at least 7 per cent and depleting its wealth. Those leaving were often the ones that could: the 150 citizens departing Vienna after 1623 took property worth 300,000 fl.[61] These losses compounded the damage inflicted by the war, pushing the burden onto those who remained, including the devout Catholics. There were also too few of the latter qualified to fill the vacancies left in the church and administration: two-thirds of Bohemian parishes lacked a priest in 1640.

These problems slowed the acceptance of Catholicism. Considerable effort was expended to make the official faith more attractive. Wallenstein's brother-in-law, Cardinal Ernst Albrecht von Harrach, was indefatigable in promoting Catholicism as a focus for loyal Czech identity, fostering the existing cult of the Bohemian cleric John of Nepomuk, who was eventually canonized in 1729 and became a symbol of Habsburg piety.[62] The Jesuits burned 10,000 Protestant books in the Upper Palatinate, but distributed their own free devotional literature and developed a sophisticated cultural outreach programme based on community theatre. Once the nobles had left or converted, the authorities accepted the need for patience. Maximilian effectively gave up on converting the Lutheran adults in the Upper Palatinate, leaving the Jesuits to concentrate on indoctrinating their children.

The vibrancy of Austrian, Bavarian and Czech Catholic culture testifies to the long-term impact of these measures, even if Protestant minorities survived to benefit from Emperor Joseph II's toleration patent of 1781.[63] Re-Catholicization nonetheless brought misery to the generation pressured to abandon beliefs and rituals that had given meaning to their lives. Czech Utraquism, the faith of the poor, was largely eliminated. The exiles suffered additional hardship and were often cruelly treated by their hosts for whom they were either an embarrassment or a convenient political pawn. The Inner Austrians largely fled into western Hungary, or trekked west to Württemberg, Franconia and the south German imperial cities. Upper and Lower Austrians went up the Danube to Protestant cities like Regensburg. Many Moravians went to north-west Hungary, but at least half the Bohemians fled to Saxony where they received a frosty reception. The Saxon government cooperated with the emperor in seizing property and even extraditing leading figures for trial. Not until Ferdinand's general mandates of 1627-8 did Johann Georg ask his advisers whether the refugees should be granted asylum on religious grounds. The conservative consistory favoured asylum for orthodox Lutherans, though many senior clergy remained sceptical. The growth of Czech-speaking minorities in Pirna and other border towns raised fears of Calvinist infiltration, because the local Saxon officials could not understand what was being said in the exiles' churches. The exiles were regarded as poor persecuted Christians worthy of sympathy, but who were nonetheless expected to wait – gratefully of course – tolerated by the elector until the situation allowed them to go home. The degree of welcome declined with social status, and peasants and poorer burghers were not granted asylum until the second wave of refugees in the early 1630s. Restrictions on the exiles were only relaxed in the 1650s to repopulate the devastated electorate, and were reimposed by 1680.[64]

Embittered, the exiles pinned their hopes on continuing the war, like the South Netherlands refugees who lobbied for the Dutch not to renew the Twelve Years Truce. Frederick V, the most prominent exile, became the focus of those powers hostile to the Habsburgs. The Palatine and Bohemian causes, both defeated, lived on as justification for Danish and Swedish intervention.

I I

Olivares and Richelieu

The revival of Catholicism in the Empire was received with mixed feelings by France and Spain. Their response to the Empire's crisis underscores the distinction between their own rivalry and the imperial civil war, as well as illustrating the weakness of confessional solidarity. France viewed Ferdinand's triumphs as a threat to its own interests, while Spain resented them as diverting energy and resources that might otherwise have been used against the Dutch.

OLIVARES

The Count-Duke

Renewal of the Dutch War coincided with a change in the Spanish government. Philip III died on 31 March 1621 after two years of failing health. The new king, Philip IV, was to reign for 44 years without a single day on which his country was at peace. He matured as a cultured man, with some sympathy for his subjects' plight, but nonetheless easily distracted by personal pleasures and especially by pretty women. Only sixteen years old on his accession, Philip was heavily reliant on Zúñiga and, increasingly, Zúñiga's ambitious nephew Don Gaspar, Count Olivares. Like Zúñiga, Olivares came from the Guzmán clan, a junior branch of the great Medina Sedonia dynasty. After succeeding to his father's lands and title in 1607, he devoted his considerable energies to breaking into the court, finally gaining a place in Prince Philip's entourage. He skilfully overcame the future king's initial hostility and won his confidence by remaining deferential, yet prepared to offer frank advice and convey unpleasant truths.

On hearing of Philip IV's accession, Olivares remarked 'now every-thing is mine'.[1] He collaborated with his uncle in eliminating the remain-ing clients of the previous favourite, Cardinal Lerma. His determination to distance himself from the former regime grew more pronounced after Zúñiga's death in October 1622 and within two years Olivares had made himself the undisputed master of the court and government. He was quick to secure rewards, enlarging his estates in Andalusia and joining the ranks of the grandees in 1625 as duke of Sanlucar la Mayor, henceforth becoming known as the count-duke. He also promoted his clan, many of whom received high office or made personal fortunes. In his mid-thirties, dark and heavy in appearance, Olivares was an im-patient man, convinced he alone knew best, and was prepared to work late into the night to prove it. He deliberately avoided the ostentatious display of both Lerma and Cardinal Richelieu, his French counterpart, cultivating instead the new image of the dedicated bureaucrat. He assumed places on the existing councils, rather than create a new pos-ition for himself, and he remained personally austere, concealing his wealth and leaving the limelight to the king.

There could hardly have been a more striking contrast than between the cardinal [Richelieu], looking every inch a prince of the church as he swept into a room with his impressive entourage, and the count-duke bustling around the palace with state papers stuck into his hatband and dangling from his waist, reminding those who saw him of nothing more than a scarecrow.[2]

The style signalled his programme as he swept to power on a wave of revulsion at the perceived corruption, waste and failure of the Lerma era. The language of austerity suited the sombre mood after the resump-tion of the Dutch War, which culminated in an eclectic mix of financial, administrative and moral reforms in February 1623. The attempt at better government was contradicted by a renewal of war that wrecked any chance of balancing the budget. Olivares was unable to escape the circumstances that propelled Spain to fight. Unlike Lerma and Isabella, he could not see how to reconcile Spanish prestige and peace with the Dutch. The principal change lay in the greater energy, coherence and flexibility he brought to Spanish strategy. Nonetheless, the world had moved on since the days of Philip II, and Olivares accepted that total victory was no longer possible. Operations were intended to force the Dutch to concede a *buen concierto*, or agreement acceptable to Spain, chiefly by abandoning their colonial ambitions, restoring freedom of worship to their Catholic subjects and accepting some nominal subordination to Spanish majesty. Like his uncle, Olivares saw a greater role for naval power in achieving this by protecting Spanish colonies and strangling Dutch trade. Land operations were incorporated into a strategy that crystallized by 1625 into an ambitious attempt to surround the Republic.[3]

From the Spanish Match to Breda

Spain sought good relations with Britain, despite religious differences and latent colonial rivalry. Relations over the past decade had been relatively cordial, encouraging Olivares' hopes that James I might provide naval support against the Dutch who had recently attacked English merchants in Indonesia. Conscious that Spanish forces held much of the Lower Palatinate, James also sought a rapprochement but chose the wholly unsuitable method of proposing that his son Charles should marry the devoutly Catholic Infanta. Madrid had already decided against this by 1621, but James persisted and Charles set off to fetch his bride in the romantic Scottish tradition, arriving unannounced in March 1623 with his friend George Villiers, later duke of Buckingham, posing implausibly as John and Tom Smith. Olivares was obliged to open serious negotiations and, to his surprise, Charles offered to convert to Catholicism. Olivares doubted his sincerity, while Charles grew impatient and went home to an overtly Protestant welcome. To mask its humiliation, the British government blamed the failure on allegedly irreconcilable differences over the Palatinate.[4]

Whereas James saw military preparations as a means to force Spain to make concessions in the Palatinate, Charles and Buckingham planned war. Buckingham was convinced that Spanish 'arrogance' made further marriage talks pointless. He engineered an alternative French match with Charles's betrothal to Louis XIII's youngest sister, Henrietta Maria, in December 1624. Britain was drawn into a complex web of negotiations that the pious interpreted as an evangelical alliance but were, in practice, just a sordid attempt to get others to do the fighting. Since neither Denmark nor Sweden was prepared to commit itself to restoring Frederick V, the western powers continued their existing policy of financing the Protestant paladins instead.

As the only commander left in the field by the end of 1624, all attention now focused on Count Mansfeld. Various projects were concocted to help him form a new army on the Lower Rhine to advance upstream and liberate the Palatinate. Britain's interest was primarily dynastic, while France and the Dutch saw it as a chance to distract Spain and wanted Mansfeld to go on to cut the Spanish Road by invading the Franche-Comté. Mansfeld saw a chance to resurrect his own principality that fleetingly had existed in Alsace at the turn of 1622. James promised to pay Mansfeld to raise 13,000 Englishmen in the Treaty of London on 4 May 1624. Duke Christian arrived in England, hoping to command the cavalry, while Georg Friedrich of Baden-Durlach wrote from his refuge on the Upper Rhine that he would join once they landed.

Recruitment was slow, and James resorted to impressment to fill the ranks. Louis XIII failed to join the alliance and refused Mansfeld permission to land in France. The men were kept on transport ships to stop them deserting or plundering Dover. It grew bitterly cold and many fell ill after being reduced to drinking sea water. Both Britain and France were distracted by their own problems by the time Mansfeld sailed to Zeeland in February 1625. A Huguenot rising that winter diverted French attention and turned British opinion against Charles's new wife. Reduced by disease to 7,000 men and with no prospect of French support, Mansfeld ignored James's instructions and cooperated with the Dutch instead.[5]

The latter were hard-pressed by General Spinola who had deployed a third of his 70,000-strong Army of Flanders to avenge his defeat at Bergen by besieging nearby Breda from August 1624. The Dutch army totalled only 48,000, including 9,000 in the fortress. Spinola built a vast line of entrenchments around Breda to starve it into submission. Mansfeld's arrival made little difference. Dutch relief efforts were hampered by Maurice of Nassau's death on 23 April 1625. Command passed to his younger brother, Frederick Henry, but his attack in May failed to pierce Spinola's entrenchments and the town surrendered on 5 June after 13,000 defenders and civilians had died. Breda was compared with Caesar's epic siege of Alesia (52 BC) and celebrated by the Spanish as a great victory in poems, plays and Velázquez's famous painting.[6]

The War at Sea

Breda was the first of four triumphs in what would prove to be Spain's year of victories. The others were won at sea where Olivares' new strategy coincided with a period of rapid transformation. The general trend was away from large, bulky, high-sided ships that fought by individual duels in which one crew tried to board and capture another. In their place sailed longer, narrower vessels designed to carry improved naval artillery, fighting in more disciplined formations that evolved into the classic line ahead to maximize broadside fire. It was not yet obvious which design or tactic would prove superior and much depended on the skill and courage of individual crews.

The Dutch were gradually increasing the size of their ships, from 80 to 160 tonnes by 1590 to 300 or 400 tonnes thirty years later, but by then the Dutch East India Company (VOC) already had 1,000-tonne ships for its long voyages of armed trade.[7] Large warships could carry up to a hundred guns and were prestige objects. Gustavus Adolphus ordered his Dutch naval architect to oversee the construction of four great ships in Stockholm. The principal one, dignified by the name *Vasa*, displaced 1,400 tonnes, and carried 64 bronze guns and 430 sailors and marines. The desire to load it with ordnance meant the gun ports were too close to the waterline and it capsized and sank in a light breeze on its maiden voyage in August 1628.[8] The episode illustrates the risks and costs of experimenting with new technology and assembling naval power.

Spain had previously relied on large galleons in the Atlantic and galleys in the Mediterranean. Construction consumed huge quantities of timber: an ocean-going warship of 560 tonnes required 900 oak trees, a galley needed over 200 pines. Spain benefited from the large oak forests of Galicia, Asturias and the rest of its northern coast, while the Catalonian pine woods served the galley fleet. It managed its resources better than its rivals, notably the Stuarts who had deforested much of England by the 1640s and become dependent on imports from Scotland, Ireland and America. Richelieu's naval programme stripped Brittany of its fine trees and forced France to import timber from the Rhineland. The Dutch Republic was largely treeless and relied on imports from the outset, while all powers depended on imports of pine, tar and hemp from the Baltic. Superior yard management enabled the Dutch to build between five hundred and a thousand ocean-going ships a year during this period, strengthening their hold over maritime trade and creating a fleet large enough to blockade the Flanders coast.

Spain struck back with a new squadron of twenty purpose-built, government-owned commerce raiders at Dunkirk in 1620, supplemented by around sixty privately operated boats that paid the crown 10 per cent of their profit and split the rest between the captain, crew and owners. These ships, prototypes of the later frigates, were smaller than conventional warships and relatively lightly armed. They relied on speed, hunting individually or in packs with their names reflecting their tactics: Cat, Fox, Hare, Black Mole, Savage, Chopper.[9] Led by daring captains like Jan Jacobsen, the Dunkirkers began raiding as soon as the Twelve Years Truce expired in 1621. Dutch freight charges doubled within a few months, while maritime insurance costs soared, cutting profits. Only 52 Dutch ships risked the Channel route between the Mediterranean and the Baltic in 1621–7, compared to 1,005 between 1614 and 1620. Other sectors of the economy also experienced a serious decline, triggering a slump that persisted through the decade. The Dunkirkers intercepted ships of other nations bound for the Republic, or just caught in the wrong place. The English lost 390 vessels between 1624 and 1628, equivalent to a fifth of their mercantile marine, and 35 of the 58 Dover-registered ships were laid up by 1626.

Dutch merchants called for immediate reprisals against this new 'Algiers of the North'. Half the Dutch fleet was stationed off Dunkirk, eventually catching Jacobsen's ship as he tried to run the blockade late in 1622. Jacobsen earned himself martyr status by blowing himself up rather than be taken. The Dutch hanged his surviving crew, but failed to deter the other privateers.

The Dunkirkers' greatest triumph came in the autumn of 1625 when the Dutch decision to cooperate with the English fleet against Spain forced them to weaken their blockade of the port. A storm dispersed the rest of the blockading ships, enabling the privateers to sortie in force into the North Sea and attack the Dutch fishing fleet off the Shetlands in October. Within two weeks, they had destroyed 150 boats, including 20 fishery protection vessels, and captured 1,400 sailors. Later successes were more modest, but nonetheless forced the VOC to institute convoys for its ships in European waters. Dutch losses of ships and merchandise totalled at least 23.3 million fl. after 1626, while the French lost

2.35 million after they became targets in 1635 until Dunkirk was captured in 1646. Spain inflicted more damage than it suffered. The Dunkirkers were destroying 250 ships a year in the 1630s, whereas in the entire century after 1546 the Seville fleet sailing the Atlantic lost only 62 vessels to enemy action.

The Global Dimension

Unable to defeat the Spanish in European waters, the Dutch took the war to the Americas. Spain's Caribbean bases proved too strong, while a large expedition sent round Cape Horn to the Pacific in 1623 was repulsed and finally limped home three years later. Spain's distraction did enable the British and French to gain American footholds, however. The British settled in Virginia in 1607, followed by a presence in Guyana (1609) and the Amazon (1619). Spain had already abandoned the smaller Caribbean islands due to piracy, and the duke of Buckingham sponsored efforts to colonize these, notably St Kitts and Barbados. The French meanwhile overran Hispaniola, renamed Haiti, and occupied other islands, including Martinique and Guadeloupe. The Caribbean's economic and strategic importance to both the British and French outweighed that of their outposts in Canada, but the region was yet to assume the significance it acquired in the eighteenth century.

The main Dutch effort was directed at the Portuguese possessions in Indonesia and Brazil. The States General had already declared the Truce over in the East Indies in 1614, and the VOC established itself in Batavia five years later. Pressure on the Portuguese increased as the rival English East India Company drove them from Ormuz at the entrance to the Persian Gulf, a fortress that had previously been considered impregnable. The VOC launched an offensive in 1621 that saw it conquer most of Portugal's Indonesian possessions within two years to give it the commanding position in the spice trade.

A new Dutch West India Company (WIC) was formed in June 1621 to muscle in on the Brazilian sugar boom that had flourished during the Truce. The Portuguese lacked the capacity to exploit Brazil's economic potential and the WIC soon controlled over half of the sugar trade into Europe. Pressed by its Calvinist investors to produce better returns, the company organized major expeditions to seize the other two points on the 'Atlantic triangle' by capturing the vulnerable Portuguese settlements along the Brazilian coast, as well as the slaving posts at Luanda (Angola) and Elmina on the Gold Coast (modern Ghana). The African expedition was repulsed, but Piet Hein with 26 ships and 3,300 men captured the principal Brazilian port of Bahia against minimal opposition in May 1624. The Portuguese responded with the 'Voyage of the Vassals' as the country's nobility mounted the largest campaign since their ill-fated crusade of 1577, sending 52 ships and 12,566 men who not only retook Bahia in May 1625, but cleared the Dutch from the Caribbean and returned in time to chase the English from Cadiz.[10]

Cadiz

James I's death on 27 March 1625 removed the last constraint on Charles and Buckingham. They were still resolved to punish their humiliation in Madrid. A combined Anglo-Dutch assault was agreed at the Treaty of Southampton on 18 September and a Dutch squadron joined the English fleet to make up a force of 33 warships, 70 transports and 10,000 soldiers. The fleet attacked Cadiz only to find the Spanish had removed their ships to safety and were waiting for them behind formidable defences. The English troops eventually landed, got drunk on plundered wine and started shooting each other in the confusion. They were re-embarked and the expedition limped home in November. Charles and Buckingham were castigated for their abject failure to live up to the glories of the Elizabethan age. Yet the standard picture of Caroline decline has been modified by recent research indicating that England's weakness was relative rather than absolute. Buckingham had enlarged the navy from 23 ships on his appointment as Lord Admiral in 1619, to 34 by 1625. However, other powers were more systematically creating state navies of purpose-built warships. From only 3 ships in 1620, France had 17 by 1625 and 53 in 1640.[11] Britain still relied on merchantmen to supplement its forces as in the Elizabethan age. However, the long peace with Spain since 1604 had convinced English merchants that profit lay in trade, not privateering, and they had little interest in joining the crown's plundering expeditions.

The defeat damaged Britain's standing in Europe and reduced Charles I's credibility as an ally. France distanced itself by signing an agreement with Spain in March 1626. Charles continued the war into 1626, sending Captain Sir John Pennington to cruise the Channel and intercept Spanish shipping. Pennington netted prizes worth £50,000, but since he also seized French ships, the operation merely increased Britain's isolation.

The Union of Arms

Spain's successes on land and at sea encouraged Olivares to redouble efforts to defeat the Dutch. His famous 'Union of Arms' derived from his earlier reforms and has been interpreted as an attempt to centralize and unify Spain.[12] The programme was actually more limited and improvised. Each province was intended to maintain a fixed number of men for its own defence, as well as contribute tax for the main army and navy, thus adding a reserve of 140,000 men to the existing forces. The plan threatened cherished provincial autonomy and Olivares encountered considerable opposition as he negotiated with each province in turn from November 1625. Implementation was undermined by a lack of accurate information about the country's resources. For example, Catalonia with only 400,000 inhabitants was asked to provide the same number of men as Portugal and Naples, each of which possessed over three times that population. The Union's importance was as an expression of Olivares' vision of empire, and as a means to establish a basis for additional taxes in lieu of mustering the reservists. Implementation was patchy, with Catalonia refusing to participate altogether, Valencia paying additional money, and Aragon eventually sending extra men after 1641.[13]

Philip IV's widely cited boast of 1626 that he had 800,000 men under arms is an exaggeration, exceeding even the theoretical limits of the Union of Arms.[14] The real total was more like 130–150,000, of whom about 17,000 were in Iberia, Naples and the Atlantic outposts, with the rest in Flanders and Lombardy. The fleet was also less than the 108 warships the king claimed, but it was still impressive. New construction had doubled the sailing navy to about fifty major ships by 1630, or the equivalent to the peak in 1600, while the galley fleet was only slightly below the earlier total of around forty vessels. Olivares remained optimistic and Philip was regarded by his subjects as the 'planet king', because his enemies and their satellites all appeared cowed by his brilliance.

Breda had indicated the cost of land operations, prompting Olivares to develop the trade embargo imposed since April 1621 into a comprehensive strategy to strangle the Dutch economy. The navy would cut the seaways while the army seized the Rhine, Ems, Weser, Maas and Scheldt using its cordon of garrisons. Work was begun on the Fosse Eugeniana canal in 1625 to divert trade from the Rhine just south of Wesel and reroute it to Venlo on the Maas in Spanish territory. Meanwhile, a system of licences was developed from late 1624 to monopolize northern European trade. Known as the 'Admiralty of the North' (*Almirantazago de los Países Septentrionales*), the system used a network of agents overseen by a court based in Seville to certify the place of origin for merchandise transported to and from Spanish ports. It was intended to stamp out the smuggling of Dutch goods that were passed off as German or other nations' products. Spanish experts considered northern European waters to be more important to the Dutch than the Indies.[15] Attempts to create a rival trading company failed, but the licence system was pursued with vigour. Denmark and the Hansa were offered incentives to replace the Dutch in carrying naval stores and textiles, and the British were included in the system once they made peace in November 1630. Spain refused to admit cargoes in Dutch-built vessels, triggering a boom in the Norwegian and north German shipyards. The system was never completely enforced but it seriously affected the Dutch, until the Portuguese revolt reopened some Iberian ports. 'Together, the total package of Spanish mercantilist measures in the 1620s and 1630s represents one of the most fundamental and decisive factors shaping the development of the world economy in the seventeenth century.'[16]

RICHELIEU

Divisions in the French Monarchy

Spanish armaments were directed against the Dutch, but they alarmed France as it continued to fear its southern neighbour more than the trouble east of the Rhine. France's ability to respond was severely restricted by its own instability. Though he was four years older than Philip IV, Louis XIII became king at the even younger age of eight when his father was assassinated. Government passed to the queen mother, Marie de Medici, who remained regent until 1614. The situation bore an uncanny resemblance to that of 1559 when another Medici queen, Catherine, wielded power for a succession of young kings. This time, France stepped back from civil war. Though Henri IV had been killed by a Catholic fanatic, he had enjoyed broad support throughout the country. After his murder, even the Jesuits joined the near universal chorus of praise that swiftly established the myth of a benevolent and successful monarch who wanted to put a chicken in every peasant's pot.[17]

Unlike 1559 when the monarchy had been bankrupt, Marie enjoyed revenues of 24 million livres and a cash reserve of 12 million. However, many of the problems that had destabilized France after 1559 remained after 1610 and would restrict the king's ability to intervene in European conflicts. Foremost were the divisions within the ruling family and its close relations among the 'princes of the blood', who held grand titles and vast estates, and regarded senior public offices, like provincial governorships and army commands, as theirs by right. Some of these aristocrats were Catholic, like the Guise family, including the dukes of Lorraine who were related by marriage to the previous Valois dynasty. Others were, at least until recently, Huguenots and related to the current Bourbon dynasty. The most senior, Henri II de Bourbon, duc de Condé, grandson of the Huguenot leader in 1562, led a revolt in 1614 demanding a greater role in the regency. Much of Marie's cash reserve was wasted defeating this challenge. The underlying problem persisted, however, because the French monarchy lacked the means to integrate its proud, rich aristocrats and their numerous provincial clients into the political system.

The traditional method to deal with this had been for the monarch to assert himself by force of personality, balancing the competing aristocrats by the careful distribution of offices and rewards. Louis XIII was prematurely declared of age in 1614, largely with this in mind. Marie, however, was not prepared to relinquish power and continued to treat her son as a child: the new king had to formally petition his mother to stop beating him for his mistakes. Louis is generally assumed to have been a weak figure, exchanging his mother's tutelage for that of Richelieu after 1624. Certainly, he lacked his father's good humour and charm. He grew up warped by the well-intentioned but misguided interference of his parents, physicians and governess. His father reputedly put a gun in his hands straight after his birth. His playroom resembled an arsenal. He already owned 55 arquebuses by the time he was 13 and took his gun cabinet with him wherever he went. When told that Ravaillac had murdered his father, he exclaimed, 'Ha! If I had been there with my sword, I would have killed him.' This bravado was not matched by any skill as a commander and he found it much harder to lead real men than he did his toy soldiers. Nonetheless, he was not bereft of ideas and a more recent biographer suggests he worked well with Richelieu because both men essentially held similar views.[18] Richelieu's influence derived from his ability to channel Louis' angry passions into more constructive activity. Louis trusted him, but also needed Richelieu as a shield to deflect criticism of his own personality and mistakes.

The division between mother and son lasted until her death in 1642 and was soon supplemented after 1614 by the added rivalry between Louis and his younger brother Gaston d'Orleans, known simply as 'Monsieur'.[19] Though a valuable asset when royal mortality was a political liability – Louis outlived his mother by only a year and died when his own son was just four and a half – the role of brother to the king was ill-defined and hard to play. Gaston clearly resented his subordinate part. The personal differences combined with deep disagreements on how the country should be governed and how to respond to events abroad. Individuals within the royal family and the aristocracy emerged periodically as the focus for competing political and religious aspirations, but the situation remained fluid as rival factions coalesced and fragmented rapidly.

The Huguenots

The basic consensus was for the monarch to act as arbiter at home and abroad. The notion of arbiter had been strengthened by Bodin's theory of alliances – that any group of three or more required a leader to provide direction and ensure disagreements did not threaten the union. This could be applied internally through the role of the monarch, and internationally with one powerful country ensuring European peace.[20] There was some support for the king to exercise a firmer hand and prevent a reoccurrence of civil war. However, royal authority remained limited, especially in the outlying provinces only incorporated into France over the previous century. Even in the core provinces, royal decisions became law only when registered by the relevant *parlements*, or senior law courts. Religious division reinforced provincialism in the areas covered by the Edict of Nantes that brought the earlier cycle of civil wars to a close in 1598.

This was a very different kind of settlement to the Peace of Augsburg. The Peace had been an integral part of the imperial constitution and gave Lutherans rights in formal institutions. The French *parlements*, however, had registered only the half of the Edict that confirmed Catholicism as the majority faith while giving restricted freedom of conscience to the Huguenot minority. This numbered 904,000 people living in a swathe of territory in a diagonal from La Rochelle on the Atlantic coast, across the Dordogne, Lot and Tarn rivers to Montauban and the Languedoc on the Mediterranean. Another 120,000 lived in Béarn in the extreme south-west, the rump of the old kingdom of Navarre which had only recently been incorporated within the French monarchy. Though numerous, the Huguenots represented a much smaller proportion of France's 20 million inhabitants than the Protestants in the Empire. They remained scattered in aristocratic manors and the two hundred towns that received special privileges under the rest of the Edict, but issued solely on royal authority. This permitted them to maintain their own troops in half of the towns at royal expense and garrison the other half with their militia. Though resented by French Catholics, these privileges fell far short of those enjoyed by German Protestants. Crucially, the Huguenots lacked a political platform equivalent to representation in the Reichstag: the Edict only sanctioned consistories and synods.

Initially, the Huguenots relied on the influence of their lords at the royal court. However, a gulf opened between the rich aristocrats and the poorer provincial nobles, many of whom inclined to religious militancy and represented a pool of supporters for those *grandes* who fell from royal favour. An important example was Henri, viscount Turenne, who had acquired the tiny sovereign duchy of Bouillon around Sedan between the Meuse and Spanish Luxembourg. His wife was Frederick V's aunt, linking him to the Calvinist international and fuelling delusions of grandeur. Forced to flee after plotting against Henri IV in 1602, his presence in the Palatinate had been a major reason why France failed to assist the Protestant Union.

The Huguenots sought a more stable platform for their interests by converting their religious assemblies into political meetings, electing Henri de Rohan as leader in 1611. From the relatively humble provincial nobility, Rohan travelled widely and fought for both Maurice of Nassau and Henri IV who made him a duke in 1603. Rohan was convinced the Huguenots held the political balance within France and refused to back Condé's rebellion in 1614.[21]

The Huguenots' presence considerably complicated French politics. Protestant powers viewed France as a potential partner, given that the ruling Bourbon dynasty converted to Catholicism only in 1593 and Louis XIII had confirmed the Edict of Nantes on his accession. France's concern at potential Spanish encirclement provided additional common ground. The French crown also sought ties with Protestant states, including the German princes. However, divisions within the monarchy and senior aristocracy prevented the king from monopolizing external relations. Both Louis XIII's mother and brother, as royalty, offered respectable alternative potential partners for foreign powers, while Bouillon, Rohan and other Huguenot grandees maintained their own contacts through the Calvinist network.

Like the Bohemian rebels, the Huguenots felt the anxiety of an ambitious minority without a firm place in the established political order. The monarchy was now firmly Catholic and while it did not follow the Austrian Habsburgs in making confession a test for loyalty, it clearly resented the Huguenots' privileged place in French society, if only because it made it harder for the king to satisfy competing demands for status and resources. The crown's association with the Edict also complicated its relationship with Catholic powers.

Richelieu

Opinions diverged on how to master this situation. One group, calling themselves *Les Bons Catholiques*, took up the spiritual and political legacy of the Catholic Ligue from the Wars of Religion. They were inspired by St François de Sales whose views that human acts should display Catholic devotion were set out in his *Introduction à la vie dévote* (1609), the book that gave the group its other name of the *dévots*. Politics should be guided by religion since divine will took precedence over reasons of state. France could exercise its proper role as arbiter of Europe only by winning the respect of other Catholic powers like Spain. This could not be achieved while heretics were tolerated at home, or alliances made with Protestants abroad.[22] Richelieu later portrayed them as naïve, but dévots like Michel de Marillac, superintendant of finance after 1624, also advanced sound practical reasons for their strategy. Marillac argued that alliance with Spain would spare France the expense of a major war. Money could be diverted to alleviate suffering and eliminate the dangers of a popular insurrection that appeared ever-present in an age of crop failure and gross social inequality. The dévots hoped Richelieu, as a man of the church, would represent their interests once he entered government. They were bitterly disappointed.

Richelieu had been destined for a military career, but switched to take a brother's place as bishop of Luçon to safeguard his family's clerical interests in 1607. He won papal approval for his diligent enforcement of the Tridentine decrees. His political career began in 1614 and he spent the next ten years navigating the treacherous waters of court politics, managing to stay on good terms both with Louis and Marie, as well as with the pope who made him a cardinal in 1622. Marie had him appointed to the 'council upstairs' in April 1624, the key decision-making body that met on the palace's first floor. Within four months, he became the council's head and effectively first minister in France.[23]

In reaching this position, Richelieu had overcome repeated political setbacks that would have broken a weaker man. He acquired an iron resolve and ruthless determination, underpinned by his embracement of Neo-Stoicism, the philosophy behind the Dutch army reforms. He was certainly avaricious, amassing a fortune of around 20 million livres, but he adopted ostentation as a political tactic to outshine rivals, while remaining personally austere. It is clear he wanted to leave his mark on history, building a new town around his ancestral home at Richelieu on the Poitou–Touraine border and having this raised to a duchy in 1631. His oft-quoted memoirs were another attempt to shape the opinion of posterity, along with skilful propaganda directed at contemporaries, coordinated by his friend the Capuchin Father Joseph, who entered history as the 'grey eminence' behind the 'red eminence' of the cardinal.[24]

Discrepancies between the carefully cultivated image, actual policy and contemporary aspirations and criticism have caused later opinion to diverge radically on all important points. Richelieu is variously cruel or magnanimous, a war-monger or peace-maker, the architect of modern France or the man who plunged it into a protracted and costly war. Critics accuse Richelieu of Machiavellianism, and even those favourably disposed stress his cool, calculating strategy. He was an opportunist only in that he sought to turn circumstances to his advantage. Politics was like a game of chess, already a contemporary metaphor, with Richelieu thinking several moves ahead, but knowing there were many more to go before checkmate.

Growing up during the last and most destructive phase of the Wars of Religion, Richelieu endorsed Bodin's belief in a strong monarchy as the bulwark against both tyranny and anarchy. He also embraced the Gallic tradition of recognizing the pope's spiritual role while asserting the administrative autonomy of the French church. 'The interests of a state and the interests of religion are two entirely different things,' he declared in 1616.[25] The state must serve Christian goals, but it was a political collective without an immortal soul and so could afford measures not permissible to individual Christians. This placed him closer to the dévots' opponents, *Les Bons Français*, who were prepared to compromise with the Huguenots for the greater good of France. The Huguenots were still considered a threat to both the monarchy and the true faith, but it would be wrong to risk renewed civil war, especially given dangers abroad. The growth of Spanish power was seen as threatening France's 'traditional' role as arbiter, and thus posed a greater threat to Christendom than the presence of heretics at home. Richelieu's goal was 'a good peace for Christendom', a concept he deliberately left undefined. He did, however, employ the metaphor of the sun, presenting Louis XIII as the benign centre of a harmonious universe, radiating order beyond France. Just how far Richelieu believed this himself remains disputed. Nonetheless, it became the chief justification for both domestic and foreign policy.

The Huguenot Rebellions

At home Richelieu sought to consolidate royal power by gradually curbing the autonomy of the grandees and the Huguenots. Louis XIII had already embarked on this, imposing his authority on Béarn in 1618. This bloodless campaign, along with two brief clashes with his mother when she resorted to arms to regain influence, helps to explain France's relatively low-key policy during the Bohemian Revolt. Renewed struggles against the Huguenots from 1621 inhibited intervention in the Empire's troubles thereafter.

The coincidence of renewed civil war in France with the resumption of the Spanish-Dutch conflict and the fighting in the Empire gives the impression of a general conflagration. This is certainly how it appeared to many Huguenots and to the dévots. Like the Bohemian leadership, Huguenot militants believed there was a Catholic conspiracy to extirpate their faith and eliminate their political influence. The Huguenot assembly convened in La Rochelle in December 1620 without royal permission. The city had grown rich on international trade and was well-integrated into the Protestant commercial network. Almost entirely surrounded by sea and salt marshes, it supplemented its natural defences with modern fortifications built between 1596 and 1611. Radical congregationalists seized control of the city and appealed to Britain for protection. Many were dissatisfied with Rohan and the aristocratic leadership, whom they believed were placing careers at court above religious duty. La Rochelle assumed the character of a secessionist government defying royal authority, and acquired growing significance as Huguenot influence elsewhere contracted.[26]

Like the resumed Dutch War, the Huguenot risings followed their own trajectory, distinct from strife elsewhere on the continent. Their origins lay in Catholic resentment of the Edict of Nantes and Huguenot anxiety at their lack of political integration. The conflict flared in three bursts: April 1621–October 1622, January 1625–February 1626 and July 1627–June 1629. The fighting was intermittent, because neither side was willing or able to press matters to a conclusion. The crown could rarely assemble over 20,000 men for more than a few months at a time and used these to secure temporary dominance in particular regions. Operations were concentrated in the south and east before 1627. Fighting was often savage as the conflict reopened local feuds from the earlier Wars of Religion. The crown tempered its repression with displays of benevolence intended to sustain royal prestige and foster acceptance for the progressive dismantling of Huguenot autonomy. Each peace in 1622 and 1626 confirmed freedom of worship and pardoned those who had taken up arms, but captured strongholds were not returned. By 1627, the Huguenots were essentially restricted to Montauban and La Rochelle. Access to the latter was constricted by the royalist capture of the islands of Oleron and Ré commanding the mouth of the Charente river. These were fortified, along with the town of Brouage to the south, as bases for Richelieu's new navy.[27]

The Huguenots still posed a threat, and Richelieu feared that any reverse would be exploited by Marie, Gaston d'Orleans, or other grandees jealous of his influence. Rumours of plots, real or false, swirled around him, attracting Spanish interest as Olivares increasingly saw him as a dangerous opponent. Alleged Spanish involvement in these plots merely added to Richelieu's conviction that all European conflicts were related, not by religion, but by Habsburg malevolence. He believed Philip IV wanted to make Ferdinand absolute ruler and marshal German resources to conquer the Dutch.

The feeling was mutual. Philip IV fumed at Louis' shabby treatment of his sister Anne, who had married the French king in 1615 as part of Lerma's and Marie's policy of rapprochement. Since her arrival, Anne had been shut out from politics and the king's affections, actions that perverted what Spain saw as natural Catholic solidarity. France seemed in league with the devil, tolerating heretics at home and subsidizing the Dutch abroad. Spanish propaganda contrasted French belligerence with Spanish claims to be the oldest monarchy and first Christian people.[28]

Richelieu's Strategy

Richelieu developed four methods to counter the Spanish threat, pursuing each option with varying intensity depending on the circumstances.[29] His preferred policy was a network of alliances to enable France to overcome Spanish hegemony and effect the desired general pacification of Europe. This explains his involvement in long negotiations with the more powerful European states for a grand anti-Habsburg front after 1624. He was well aware of the obstacles to this, and so pursued parallel talks for separate German and Italian leagues. The latter embraced the slogan of the 'liberty of Italy' from Spanish domination and entailed efforts to combine Venice, Savoy, Parma, the papacy and other states in a defensive alliance to isolate the Spanish garrisons in Milan and Naples. Negotiations in the Empire trumpeted 'German liberty' as a means of emasculating the emperor. Richelieu's preferred plan was an understanding with Bavaria to convert the Catholic Liga into a pro-French neutral party that could stop Ferdinand sending troops against the Dutch. However, he was also prepared to talk to Protestant princes like Johann Georg of Saxony, if they were willing to cooperate with this objective.

Bilateral alliances with individual states were a second strategy to substitute for the failure to persuade others to join a more general alliance. Such alliances were deliberately distant to avoid compromising France's Catholic credentials or committing it to objectives in which it had little interest. Richelieu's preferred method was to offer subsidies, and less often recruits, to assist an ally without openly supporting it. This characterized his support for the Dutch and Swedes until 1635 whom he hoped would keep both Habsburg branches occupied.

The third option was to offer protection to weaker territories that might assist France by allowing passage for French troops.[30] France had already asserted a protectorate over the bishoprics and associated cities of Metz, Toul and Verdun in 1552 which provided access into Lorraine and threatened the Spanish Road (see Chapter 5, p.154).The system was extended around 1600 when France offered protection to Sedan and Geneva, as well as approaching minor Alsatian and Italian rulers for similar arrangements. France's revival after the Wars of Religion had made such offers attractive. Rudolf II's incapacity weakened the value of imperial protection (*Reichsschütz*), especially to vulnerable territories on the Empire's periphery. Swiss neutrality was very restricted, since the Confederation was reluctant to admit new associates or become involved in affairs beyond the Alps. However, French strength also made its protection a potential first step to annexation. For it to be effective, France had to establish a military presence that was both burdensome for the protectorate and alarming to its neighbours. Protection thus became an option of last resort for the weak once it was clear others would not respect their neutrality.

Protection could also cause problems for France, pulling Richelieu towards his fourth and least desired strategy of military action. Armed force was intended to lend weight to diplomacy, especially in conjunction with alliances. Conquests were limited and closely connected to protection. Both were means of obtaining gateways across the French frontier to block foreign invasion and allow France to intervene elsewhere. Richelieu did not invent this strategy. French involvement in Italy since 1600 was already directed at securing Susa, Pinerolo, Saluzzo and Casale as a safe route over the Alps. Ostensibly defensive, this policy was inherently aggressive and tended to suck France into conflicts just beyond its frontiers. The long-standing desire to annex Metz, Toul and Verdun encouraged interference in Lorraine's internal affairs to eliminate the duke's influence in the three bishoprics. Intervention in Lorraine in turn drew France into the neighbouring German territories and was, as we shall see later in Chapter 16, a major cause of war with Spain in 1635.

Like Olivares', Richelieu's strategy was fundamentally flawed. Both men viewed war in Clausewitz's sense as the continuation of diplomacy by other means. Neither wanted a major conflict. The application of force was intended to make the other side be more reasonable. Unfortunately, neither possessed accurate information regarding the other's strength or interests. Once started, it became difficult to break the cycle as pressure from one side prompted the other to escalate matters elsewhere. The incidents remained individually relatively minor, but negotiations over them became progressively more difficult as the points of contention accumulated and mistrust mounted.

THE VALTELLINA

The Holy Slaughter

These difficulties are best illustrated by the tension over the Valtellina, a dispute that pre-dated Richelieu's coming to power. Here the Bohemian Revolt had disturbed the stand-off between the Spanish governor of Milan and the Rhetian Free State occupying the Alpine valley. The radical Calvinists who had taken control of the Rhetian council welcomed Frederick's election as Bohemian king and later supplied him with troops.[31] Madrid instructed the duke of Feria, appointed governor in August 1618, to reopen the pass provided he could restrict military action to the Valtellina. Feria exceeded his instructions. Without telling Madrid, he conspired with the Valtellina Catholics who had appealed for help against their Protestant masters. Capuchin monks acted as couriers in precisely the kind of plot Protestant militants suspected everywhere. Seeing Spanish troops massing at Fort Fuentes at the southern end of the valley, the Rhetians began countermeasures. Fearing they would be discovered, however, the Catholics struck before Feria was ready, initiating fifteen days of 'holy slaughter' that left at least four hundred Protestants dead in July 1620. The survivors fled west and north into Switzerland and Rhetia.[32]

Rhetian troops counter-attacked, backed by 1,500 Protestant Swiss, and routed the locals, destroying their churches. A thousand Spaniards then advanced from Fort Fuentes, capturing Chiavenna and the southern half of the valley by September. The Catholic rebels established their own government behind new Spanish forts at Morbegnio, Sondrio, Nova and Riva. Pressure on the Rhetians mounted as Archduke Leopold saw an opportunity to reassert Austrian jurisdiction and called in military assistance from the archbishop of Salzburg. The Habsburgs' initial advance was repulsed at the northern end of the valley in March 1621, but by the following January the Rhetians had capitulated, surrendering authority over eight members of the Ten Parish League, as well as the Lower Engadin valley belonging to the Holy House League. This reduced Rhetia by nearly a third and threatened its hold over the northern Valtellina. Catholicism was imposed by force in the southern half where pastors were given a year to leave. A Protestant rising temporarily ejected the Austrians in April 1622, but was crushed by fresh troops who annexed the Lower Engadin and Davos for the Tirol in September. Hunger caused widespread suffering that winter.

Though Madrid had retrospectively sanctioned Feria's action, it proved highly embarrassing. Intervention had not resolved the stalemate that left no one able to use the valley, and had caused alarm in Italy, where Venice and the papacy opened talks for a French alliance in 1621. French involvement was the last thing Spain wanted and it sought a diplomatic solution. Distracted by its own problems, France also wanted to avoid a fight, but needed to act to preserve its influence in Italy. Louis' representatives began a series of deliberately well-publicized talks with Savoy and Venice, culminating in the Treaty of Lyons in February 1623 that envisaged an army of 40,000, possibly under Mansfeld, to eject the Spanish.

Spain was not prepared to risk war and accepted the face-saving device of papal mediation. Both parties agreed a week after the Treaty of Lyons that papal troops should replace the Spanish in the valley. Though Spain managed to send 7,000 reinforcements along the Spanish Road through the valley to Germany in October 1623, the situation remained unsatisfactory. Moreover, the election of the Francophile Urban VIII as the new pontiff that August signalled a shift against the Habsburgs. Urban was convinced the religious crisis had passed and stopped his predecessor's subsidies to the emperor and the Catholic Liga. The anti-Habsburg trend continued following Richelieu's assumption of power in 1624, as he saw the Valtellina dispute as a chance to ratchet pressure onto Spain without unduly exposing France.

War 1625

Richelieu received eager assistance from Carlo Emanuele of Savoy, who wanted to settle his long-standing dispute with Genoa over the fief of Zuccarello and signed a secret pact with France in November 1624.[33] An attack on Genoa would cut the southern end of the Spanish Road and knock out Spain's banker. The time seemed opportune, with the apparent convergence of Protestant hostility to the Habsburgs, and explains French participation in the London talks with Mansfeld. Richelieu hoped Britain and the Dutch would send a fleet to assist his own squadron in cutting the seaway between Spain and Genoa, while Venice attacked Milan. D'Estrees and 3,500 French troops crossed Protestant Swiss territory to join a similar number of Rhetians levied with French money. More subsidies and troops poured into Savoy, where the French formed a third of the 30,000-strong army that began operations against Genoa in February 1625.

The attack caught the Spanish and Genoese unprepared. Most of Genoa was overrun, while 4,000 reinforcements from Spain were intercepted by French warships in March. D'Estrees quickly conquered the Valtellina, because the papal garrisons offered no resistance except at Riva and Chiavenna. Richelieu's elaborate plan then began to unravel. The Valtellina operation placed France in direct opposition to an essentially Francophile papacy, incensing the dévots. The duke of Feria sent 6,000 men to reinforce the city of Genoa itself, which continued to resist the Franco-Savoyard siege. Venice abstained from the fighting, while British and Dutch support failed to materialize, enabling Spain to break through the relatively weak French fleet and relieve Genoa in August. A fresh Huguenot rising in 1625 meanwhile distracted Richelieu at home: it was typical of the tortuous politics of the Calvinist international that the French Protestants contributed to their government's inability to assist their Alpine brethren.

The rebellion at least gave Richelieu an excuse to open talks to escape an increasingly dangerous situation. Papal mediation culminated in the Treaty of Monzón on 5 March 1626, which restored the pre-1617 situation with important qualifications. Rhetian jurisdiction was nominally restored over the Valtellina; this was now recognized as Catholic, which strengthened its autonomy and introduced doubt as to who could decide on transit through the valley. Papal troops replaced the French, though the forts were supposed to be destroyed.[34] Monzón represented a serious reverse for Richelieu who blamed his envoy for the terms and feigned illness to avoid seeing the furious Savoyard ambassador. Abandoned, Savoy was obliged to make its own peace and now sought a Spanish alliance and intrigued with French malcontents against Richelieu, including possible involvement in the Chalais plot to murder the cardinal in 1626. Spain had won the first round.

12

Denmark's War against the Emperor 1625–9

TROUBLE IN LOWER SAXONY

The North German Bishoprics

Mansfeld's evacuation of East Frisia in January 1624 essentially ended the war in the Empire. Danish intervention in June 1625 began what the Danes called the *Kejserkrig*, or war against the emperor. Fighting was largely concentrated in Lower Saxony, a region that had escaped conflict until now. Though a distinct phase in the conflict, most people regarded it as the continuation of the earlier trouble. The Palatine question represented one element of continuity, particularly for the British, who hoped Denmark would succeed where Mansfeld had failed. Far more significant, however, were the hopes and fears stirred by the shift of power in the Empire since 1618 surrounding the restitution of church land taken by Protestants since 1552.

At stake were seven Lower Saxon and five Westphalian bishoprics, each group constituting over a quarter of their respective regions (see Table 2).[1] Catholic influence in the region was restricted to south-western Westphalia, where it depended entirely on Elector Ferdinand of Cologne. The Protestant presence was magnified by the fact that virtually all the secular land was also in their hands, but their influence was lessened by rivalry among local dynasties and between them and the Danish king. Divisions led to the loss of Osnabrück, where Cardinal Hohenzollern was elected as the first Catholic bishop for 49 years in 1623. Though Emperor Ferdinand still respected the Mühlhausen guarantee, he was clearly exasperated at the Lower Saxons' failure to prevent Duke Christian raising armies in 1621 and 1622–3. For their part, the Lower Saxons suspected the emperor's repeated calls for money to repel

Bethlen and the Turks were a ruse to amass resources for a strike against them. Tilly's continued presence across the Weser in Westphalia added to their anxiety.

Table 2: Possession of the North German bishoprics c.1590–1650

Territory	Size (km²)	Religion		Ruler
Lower Saxony				
Bremen	5,170	P	1596–1634	Johann Friedrich of Holstein-Gottorp
		P	1634–44	Frederick III of Denmark
		P	1645–1714	Sweden
Magdeburg	5,005	P	1598–1631	Christian Wilhelm of Brandenburg
		C	1631–8	Archduke Leopold Wilhelm (Habsburg)
		P	1638–80	August of Sachsen-Weissenfels
Halberstadt	1,705	P	1616–23	Christian of Brunswick-Lüneburg
			1623–5	Vacant
		C	1627–48	Leopold Wilhelm (see Magdeburg)
Hildesheim	1,760*	C	1612–50	Ferdinand of Cologne
Schwerin	770	P	1603–24	Ulrich II of Denmark
		P	1624–33	Ulrich III of Denmark
		P	1634–48	Adolf Friedrich of Mecklenburg
Lübeck	522	P	1607–34	Johann Friedrich (see Bremen)
		P	1634–55	Johann X of Holstein-Gottorp
Ratzeburg	374	P	1610–36	August of Brunswick-Lüneburg
		C	1629–30	Bernhard von Mallinkrodt
		P	1636–48	Gustav Adolf of Mecklenburg
Westphalia				
Münster	10,500	C	1612–50	Ferdinand of Cologne
Paderborn	975	C	1618–50	Ferdinand of Cologne
Osnabrück	2,025	P	1591–1623	Philipp Sigismund of Brunswick-Lüneburg
		C	1623–5	Eitel Friedrich Count of Hohenzollern
		C	1625–61	Franz Wilhelm von Wartenberg
Verden	1,320	P	1586–1623	Philipp Sigismund (see Osnabrück)
		P	1623–9	Frederick III of Denmark (see Bremen)
		C	1630–1	Franz Wilhelm (see Osnabrück)
		P	1631–4	Johann Friedrich (see Bremen)
		P	1634–44	Frederick III of Denmark (see Bremen)
		P	1645–1714	Sweden
Minden	1,198	P	1599–1629	Christian of Brunswick-Lüneburg
		C	1629–48	Franz Wilhelm (see Osnabrück)
		P	1648–1806	Brandenburg-Prussia

Note: Bremen and Magdeburg were archbishoprics, the rest bishoprics
* includes the 'Greater Diocese' held by the Guelphs
C   Catholic
P   Protestant

Danish Motives

Christian IV of Denmark watched these developments with concern. He saw the church lands as convenient sinecures for his younger sons and a means to extend Danish influence across the great trading rivers of the Elbe and Weser. But Danish intrusion had proved unwelcome to the Guelphs and the Hanseatic cities, as well as to the Holstein-Gottorps who were Christian's vassals and rivals, especially for the control of Bremen. Christian sought better relations and greater influence in Lower Saxony, an area that had long been a Guelph preserve. A combination of factors encouraged him to consider military intervention from early 1624. Religious solidarity had little to do with this, since the time to aid the Bohemian and German Protestants had passed. However, concern that Sweden might send an army encouraged Christian to think about deploying first, and once Gustavus Adolphus became bogged down in his own war with Poland, it was safer for Christian to contemplate full-scale intervention in Germany.

This was unpopular with the Danish nobility, who feared the costs of a war waged for Christian's dynastic interests. Christian's large cash reserve meant he could ignore domestic opposition and start without additional taxes. Realizing a long conflict would require more support, he welcomed a renewed appeal on Frederick's behalf from his brother-in-law, James I. Denmark joined the negotiations in The Hague in January 1625 for an evangelical alliance. Sir Robert Anstruther, a fluent Danish speaker, arrived with the first instalment of a large British subsidy in June. By then, Christian had assembled over 20,000 men in Holstein and mobilized a fleet of thirty ships.

It has been claimed that he intended to break past Tilly and rally potential allies like Hessen-Kassel, or the restless Upper Austrian peasants.[2] This is unlikely at this point. Christian's activities remained restricted to Lower Saxony where his representatives lobbied for his election to the vacant post of Kreis colonel at the assembly in March 1625, to give him command of any troops mobilized to protect the bishoprics. He sought a legitimate framework to consolidate Danish influence and present his dynastic objectives as upholding the imperial constitution. The Lower Saxons saw through this and chose Duke Friedrich Ulrich of Brunswick-Wolfenbüttel instead. Christian forced the assembly to reconvene in May, when the earlier decision was annulled and he was

THE THIRTY YEARS WAR

duly elected. The delegates also agreed to mobilize 12,900 men and accepted Danish pay and disciplinary codes.[3] Around 7,000 soldiers actually collected at Verden near the junction of the Aller and Weser rivers. Christian's troops crossed the Elbe just west of Hamburg and moved to Nienburg on the Weser at the beginning of June. The show of force was to improve his hand in negotiations with Tilly and Ferdinand with whom he maintained contact by courier after operations began. No firm agreement had been reached at The Hague and he did not embrace the wider anti-Habsburg alliance until he had become isolated by the end of 1625. Already his actions caused consternation in Lower Saxony. The Lüneburg Guelphs condemned Friedrich Ulrich's decision to relinquish Kreis command. Duke Georg, the future grandfather of Britain's George I, resigned his Danish commission and joined the imperial army as part of a deal to save his elder brother's duchy of Celle from imperial sequestration.

The Problem of Neutrality

The crisis makes much clearer one of the war's main causes: the dispute over authority in the Empire. The Bohemian Revolt already posed the dilemma whether imperial Estates could remain neutral during conflict in the Empire. The emperor had tolerated Lower Saxon neutrality despite its breach by Duke Christian, but Danish intervention made this impossible. Ferdinand ordered the imperial Estates not to assist the Danes and issued a mandate on 7 May authorizing the Liga to counter the enemies of the Empire. A refusal to obey these instructions threatened to render the Empire ineffective through what later generations would call the 'free-rider problem'. Imperial Estates were happy to enjoy the Empire's protection, but were often reluctant to contribute to the cost of that protection, especially when problems occurred far from their own lands. Confessional tension merely added a further reason not to participate. The Protestant refusal to contribute since 1618 stopped well-short of secession, and the Lower Saxons presented their armed neutrality as upholding the public peace and thus in conformity with the emperor's wishes. But for Ferdinand, the liberty of the Empire took precedence over that of individual territories, which were not free to decide when they wanted to help.

This constitutional issue had an international dimension, since it remained unclear whether the emperor or princes were free to help allies elsewhere. Maximilian of Bavaria was particularly concerned lest Ferdinand use his current advantages to divert German resources to help Spain. For Maximilian, the Empire was a collective and any decision to involve it in external conflicts required consultation, at least with the electors whose ranks he had just joined.[4]

The modern concept of neutrality had no place either in the seventeenth-century imperial constitution or in international law that remained governed by Christian morality. This was reflected in Hugo Grotius' seminal work, *De jura belli ac pacis*, which appeared in 1625. War was about restoring justice, implying one side was right, and the other wrong. Absolute neutrality was morally indefensible, because it entailed indifference to both sides. A neutral should still favour the just cause by, for example, allowing transit for its troops, or providing war materials and even auxiliaries. These guidelines reflected the actual expectations of belligerents towards would-be neutrals. Naturally, each party considered its cause as just, demanding cooperation in return for respecting territorial integrity and refraining from forcing full participation. The situation was especially difficult for the imperial Estates as they owed allegiance to the emperor who was clearly a belligerent in the present conflict. As Tilly told the Hessians, 'It's called obedience, not neutrality. Your lord is an imperial prince whose overlord is the emperor.'[5]

Benevolent neutrality was possible for those who sympathized with one side and were sufficiently distant from the other to be safe from reprisals. Salzburg presented its refusal to join the Liga as proof of its neutrality in its dealings with Protestants during the war yet supplied soldiers and cash to Bavaria and the emperor.[6] Strasbourg favoured the other side, selling supplies and occasionally providing access across its strategic bridge. The three Hanseatic cities of Hamburg, Bremen and Lübeck enjoyed a more even neutrality, thanks partly to modern fortifications strengthened during the 1620s, but also to their ambivalence towards major Protestant powers like Denmark who seemed more threatening than the emperor to whom they made token payments to discharge their obligations. Their Catholic counterpart was the imperial city of Cologne that also enjoyed wide trading connections regardless of confession, and became a convenient venue for negotiations and financial transactions. Like Salzburg, Cologne refused to join the Liga, but paid imperial taxes and loaned money to the emperor. Ferdinand tolerated its selling supplies to the Dutch, but censured the council when transactions involved his direct enemies in the Empire.[7]

Peace Talks Fail

Ferdinand had no intention of allowing the Lower Saxons to remain neutral, but equally he did not want a new war against a powerful opponent. The imperial army was in no condition to take on the Danes, especially since Spain had withdrawn its auxiliaries at the end of 1623. The situation in Hungary remained uncertain due to continued speculation surrounding Bethlen's intentions. Ferdinand combined a show of force with conciliatory gestures, confirming the Mühlhausen guarantee on 27 July. Two days later, Tilly seized the Weser crossings of Höxter and Holzminden, baring Christian's route southwards. Maximilian cooperated because Christian's activities in Lower Saxony suggested he was organizing a new Protestant union.

Tilly had only 18,000 men, having left the rest with Anholt on the Lower Rhine in case Mansfeld attacked from the Dutch Republic. He remained west of the Weser in Westphalia, while King Christian concentrated his forces on the opposite bank at Hameln to the north. He rode round Hameln on 30 July, inspecting its defences. Allegedly drunk, he fell from his horse into a seven-metre ditch and was knocked unconscious. Though he recovered, he lapsed into a two-month depression. Exactly how serious this was remains unclear, since his injury provided the excuse to continue negotiations with both the emperor and his potential allies in The Hague. Most of the Lower Saxons took the opportunity to withdraw their contingents during these discussions, while the Danes retreated to Verden in August. Johann Georg of Saxony received Ferdinand's approval to host a peace conference in Brunswick where he tabled his now standard solution: foreign troops should withdraw in return for Ferdinand's confirmation of the 1555 Peace and the Mühlhausen guarantee. Philip IV and Isabella urged Ferdinand to settle with Christian to prevent a resumption of war in the Empire. Ferdinand was prepared to accept, provided Christian withdrew first. This seemingly petty demand was essential to maintain his authority otherwise it would appear he was open to extortion.

Christian talked peace in Brunswick while preparing for war in The Hague. He demonstrated his Protestant credentials by insisting not only that Tilly withdraw, but that the Liga dissolve itself. Britain promised £30,000 a month, to which the Dutch added £5,000 in a convention agreed on 9 December. Meanwhile, Mansfeld moved his 4,000 survivors into Cleves once Breda fell to the Spanish. He was joined by another 2,000 Britons and 4,000 German, French and Dutch recruits, while Duke Christian recruited three cavalry regiments. Together, they marched across northern Westphalia to join the Danes in October. Tilly was too weak to stop them, or to take Nienburg on the Weser. His army lost 8,000 to plague and lack of supplies, and only captured one position east of the river, at Calenberg on 3 November. The prospect of Anglo-Dutch subsidies enabled Christian IV to commission former paladins, like Margrave Georg Friedrich and the Weimar brothers, to raise more Germans, while another 8,000 Britons arrived during 1626, including Donald MacKay's Scottish regiment made famous by Robert Monro's memoirs.[8]

The long-awaited evangelical alliance was at last taking shape, raising militants' hopes for a double blow against the Habsburgs, to be launched by Christian's reinforced army in north-west Germany while Bethlen struck from the south east. Such dreams were wholly unrealistic. Bethlen's representative in The Hague failed to convince anyone that his master would actually appear: Maurice of Nassau had even joked that he doubted whether Bethlen was a real person.[9] Anglo-Dutch aid was compromised by their separate decision to attack Cadiz that September, ensuring that the promised subsidies were soon in arrears. Christian delayed ratifying The Hague convention until March 1626, only doing so because the arrival of a new imperial army under Wallenstein forced his hand.

WALLENSTEIN

Rise to Prominence

There was little about Wallenstein's early life to suggest he would become the most controversial figure of the war. From a junior branch of the extended Waldstein family and orphaned at the age of twelve, he was raised by an uncle, eventually assuming control of his father's estate on the Elbe. With just 92 dependent households, this placed him in the ranks of the minor Bohemian nobility. 'Tall of stature, slender, lean and almost perpetually melancholic', he accentuated his sombre appearance by austere, black clothing and by keeping his dark hair short and combed back. All contemporaries testified to his penetrating gaze and frosty, unsmiling expression. He could be charming and 'was very liberal and when he gave presents he very much rejoiced and indeed was a man who gave the most to him who least expected it, but his gifts were golden snares which indissolubly obliged'.[10] He seems to have been a hard man to like, alternating between icy self-control and violent outbursts that became more frequent as his health waned. He never fully recovered from malaria in 1605 and, despite drinking moderately and eating (by contemporary standards) healthily, he already suffered from gout by 1620. A decade later he was suffering heart trouble and panic attacks, nervous disorders, constipation, colic and depression, all of which no doubt encouraged his interest in astrology.

His upbringing was conventional and included a brief spell at the Calvinist Altdorf University, from which he was expelled for brawling. He entered Habsburg service during the Turkish War, converting to Catholicism to further his career. His real opportunity came when he married a rich widow in 1609 whose early death from plague left him property worth nearly 400,000 fl. He became a colonel in the Moravian Estates army in 1615, defecting four years later to the emperor for whom he had already raised two regiments. He owed his later influence not to military glory but clever integration into the post-revolt order. Rather than following the war as it moved to the Rhine after 1620, he remained in Bohemia as Liechtenstein's subordinate, assisting in confiscating rebel property and participating in the notorious mint consortium of 1622–3 that contributed to the hyperinflation of that time. He emerged as a major beneficiary of the land transfers, increasing his share by some astute sales and purchases to amass nearly 1,200km^2 in north-east Bohemia, including 9 towns and 57 villages and castles. The profits were invested in advancing his influence by loaning the emperor 1.6 million fl. between 1619 and 1623. With an empty treasury, Ferdinand repaid his creditors with honours, raising Wallenstein's estates to the duchy of Friedland in March 1624. His ties to the Habsburg elite were strengthened by his second marriage, to Isabella Katharina, younger daughter of Count Harrach, an imperial privy councillor and a member of the 'Spanish' faction around Ferdinand's trusted adviser, Eggenberg.[11]

This rapid rise to wealth and influence had already made Wallenstein controversial by 1625. Historical interest was shaped subsequently by

Schiller's drama that established the trope of a man of destiny reaching beyond accepted norms and being punished for it. Later writers have variously presented him as a military dictator, or a Czech or German national hero, thanks largely to speculation that he was ready to betray the Habsburgs to bring either Bohemian independence or peace for Germany. More recently, he has appeared as a man out of time, the last of the great mercenary captains soon made irrelevant by the growth of the modern state.[12]

Despite the publication of virtually every surviving document with any connection to him, the 'Wallenstein Problem' persists because his motives remain unclear. He was clearly driven by a thirst for status that remained unsatisfied in 1625, but rumours that he wanted to be a king or even emperor were just wild speculation. It is often forgotten that Wallenstein lacked a key element driving dynastic ambitions. His daughter was safely married to Count Rudolf Kaunitz, while his only son died in January 1628 aged barely three months. Six months later Wallenstein named his cousin Max as heir. Wallenstein's focus seems to have shifted from personal advancement to consolidating what he had achieved before his health failed: his doctors gave him only two years to live by the end of 1633. He grew defensive and frustrated at the accusation that he had risen above his station and was not worthy to mix with princes and crowned heads. The mounting criticism simply fuelled his ingrained arrogance, especially as it became obvious by the end of 1631 that Ferdinand considered him indispensable. Convinced he alone could win the war, he resented any attempt at supervision, but his self-confidence was undermined by the growing realization that he was no longer trusted by the imperial government.

The Creation of a New Army, 1625-6

Wallenstein had been promoted to major-general in June 1623 for his service against Bethlen. Although it was the most junior general's rank, his vast wealth enabled him to punch above his station, allowing him to offer that year to raise an entire army as a way of catapulting himself into the forefront of the political and military elite. He already had the backing of powerful friends in Vienna, as well as the new Spanish ambassador, the marquis de Aytona, who was likewise convinced by Wallenstein's apparent Midas touch. The fresh crisis in Lower Saxony added urgency by revealing the extent of Ferdinand's dependency on the Liga. The original balance had been reversed so that the remaining imperial units were attached as auxiliaries to Tilly's army. By forming his own field force, Ferdinand could trump Maximilian, who had begun to criticize him for not pulling his weight against the Danish threat.[13]

Negotiations were opened with Wallenstein in April 1625, which led to a contract in June authorizing the raising of 6,000 cavalry and 18,000 infantry.[14] It is often forgotten that this was not the emperor's only force. Ferdinand also sent 2,000 men from the Tirol into Italy and allowed Spain to recruit 10,000 more to reinforce the Army of Lombardy to repel the Franco-Savoyard attack, as we have seen in the previous chapter. He retained 16,000 men in Hungary and the Habsburg hereditary lands, and assigned his new general another 12,500 withdrawn from Hungary earlier that year, leaving Wallenstein to find only 11,500 new recruits to meet the contract. The official strength of the new force matched what contemporaries considered an *exercitus formatus*, or formidable field army capable of fighting a major battle. The size was deliberately chosen to match Tilly's force and place Ferdinand militarily on par with the Liga. Wallenstein informed Tilly that he sought 'conjunction', meaning cooperation on an autonomous footing. His refusal to be Tilly's subordinate undoubtedly suited his own desire for independence, but also served Ferdinand's intention of assuming the leading role in the war.

This depended on raising sufficient troops. Though Wallenstein boasted 50,000 men at the start of 1626, he mustered less than 16,000 at Aschersleben, the town south-east of Halberstadt that became his new base. Moreover, many were raw, ill-disciplined recruits. They failed to impress Aytona who regarded Ferdinand as still dependent on Maximilian.[15] The subsequent military expansion more than redressed the imbalance during 1626: Tilly mustered 35,000, of whom 20,000 were with his main army and the rest in garrisons. The imperial army meanwhile reached around 70,000 combatants, an immense escalation over the earlier phase of the war, though those under Wallenstein's immediate command rarely exceeded Tilly's own field force. The expansion was driven partly by strategic necessity, since Mansfeld's invasion of Silesia in October 1626 was to oblige Wallenstein to deploy a second force there. Growth was also part of a deliberate policy to amass an overwhelming force to compel King Christian to make peace. Wallenstein presented this plan to a meeting with his father-in-law Harrach and Eggenberg at Bruck an der Leitha on 25–26 November. Though his demand for 100,000 troops was temporarily reduced to 70,000, he secured authorization for the higher establishment through a personal visit to Vienna in May 1627.[16] Further units were authorized after 1628, partly in response to Ferdinand's expanding commitments, but it is unlikely that the total effective strength ever exceeded 110,000, including those units that remained outside Wallenstein's control (see Table 3).

Table 3: Strength of the imperial army

Date	Paper Strength			Probable Effective Total
	Infantry	Cavalry	Total	
1625	45,300	16,600	61,900	40–50,000
1626	86,100	25,000	111,100	60–70,000
1627	83,100	29,600	112,700	100,000
1628	102,900	27,300	130,200	110,000
1629	111,000	17,900	128,900	110,000
1630	129,900	21,000	150,900	95,000

Paper strength calculated from the *Kriegslisten* printed in *Documenta Bohemica Bellum Tricennale Illustrantia*, Vol. IV, pp.414–46.

Wallenstein's Powers and Subordinates

Wallenstein's position was not as exceptional as is sometimes suggested and he was far from all-powerful. The existing generals resented his rapid promotion and autonomy. His acerbic personality undoubtedly created tension, but there was an underlying structural problem beyond his control. All early modern armies lacked clear, unified command structures and even monarchs who led their troops in person, like Gustavus Adolphus, found it hard to assert authority over some of their subordinates. Talent and proven experience were only two of several factors determining appointment. Senior aristocrats often demanded command by right of their elevated birth, or because they raised regiments at their own expense, as in Spain and France. Even officers from more humble backgrounds could acquire sufficient influence to insist on their own commands. The result was to assign virtually independent commands to important officers who acted autonomously in their own areas. Fortresses were entrusted to governors who were also not required to report to the nearest field commander. What contemporaries called a 'general staff' was little more than a collective label for all officers of that rank.

The imperial army followed this pattern. Ferdinand retained exclusive control over the appointment and promotion of generals, though Wallenstein was allowed to nominate candidates from April 1628.[17] The emperor was assisted by the Court War Council, but this functioned as an administrative clearing house with limited capacity for strategic planning. The dispersal of Ferdinand's enemies encouraged fragmentation, with senior officers assigned separate commands in Hungary, Alsace, the hereditary lands and the contingents sent to Italy and the Empire. Each general reported directly to the emperor with the question of their relative seniority left deliberately vague. Wallenstein's appointment only partially centralized this by giving him control of all the forces in the Empire, including the two regiments in Alsace previously under Archduke Leopold, and the six intended to help Spain in the Netherlands. The other units in the hereditary lands and Hungary remained outside his jurisdiction, as did those sent to Milan.

Twenty years his senior, the veteran Marradas was mollified by his retention of command in the Habsburg lands and promotion to field marshal in March 1626. Caraffa had been enticed at great expense from the Spanish army to command in Hungary and was not so easily satisfied, rejoining his former comrades in 1628. Liechtenstein, Wallenstein's former superior, retired, as did Tieffenbach, though Collalto remained head of the War Council. Wallenstein was far from officially free to choose his own subordinates either. He could negotiate contracts to raise new regiments, but Ferdinand retained the final say in appointing their colonels. Recruiting patents continued to be issued by the War Council with Ferdinand's signature. Despite his denials, however, Wallenstein was clearly issuing these on his own authority by 1627 and he met little opposition to his own choice of colonels, especially after the Bruck conference where he secured the right to nominate Protestants. One of the first was Arnim, a Brandenburg Lutheran noble appointed in January 1627 having served Sweden, Poland and Mansfeld. A man of considerable ability, Arnim was already a field marshal by April 1628 and Wallenstein's second-in-command. Many Scottish, English and Irish officers also entered imperial service at this point.[18] Wallenstein also appointed French-speaking Walloons, notably Count Merode who became his principal recruiter, raising at least 74 companies by 1629 when he enlisted another 2,500 men.

The appointment of another Walloon, Gil de Haas, a barely literate stonemason from Ypres who eventually became a Bavarian general, indicates that Wallenstein did not share his contemporaries' snobbery. Nonetheless, many older officers felt the newcomers lacked experience, poking fun at colonels allegedly too young to grow beards. The rapid expansion of the imperial army after 1626 undoubtedly led to a decline in overall quality. Of the 15 regiments in imperial service at the beginning of 1625, 14 still existed after Wallenstein's dismissal in November 1630, whereas only 66 of the 103 regiments raised during his first generalship remained. Of those disbanded prior to 1631, 30 were in existence for less than two years (see Table 4). Early disbandment rarely resulted from battle casualties; instead it usually reflected a colonel's inability to find sufficient recruits to meet his contract. Impermanence inhibited good discipline and it is not surprising that Merode's name is said to provide the origins of the word 'marauder'.

The notoriety of some of Wallenstein's new appointments obscures the presence of a core of senior officers he inherited from the existing

Table 4: Regiments of the imperial army 1618–30

Date of Raising	Total Regiments Raised that Year	Those Surviving in Mid-1625	
Before 1618	–	2	
1618	10	2	
1619	18	4	
1620	11	–	
1621	17	5	
1622	5	–	
1623	5	–	
1624	3	2	
Total 1618–24	69	15 plus 3 disbanded in 1625	
		Surviving in Dec. 1630	Lasting Less than 2 Years
1625	18	11	1
1626	19	8	5
1627	21	7	12
1628	10	7	2
1629	14	14	–
1630	21	19	10
Total 1625–30	103	66	30
Total 1618–30	172		

Sources: G. Tessin, *Die Regimenter der europäischen Staaten im Ancien Régime* (Osnabrück, 1986); A. Wrede, *Geschichte der K.u.K. Wehrmacht* (5 vols., Vienna, 1898–1905).

army with whom he was obliged to work thanks to their social status or connections. They included four imperial princes: Duke Adolf of Holstein-Gottorp and three of the four Sachsen-Lauenburg dukes who were converts to Catholicism and had already raised regiments against the Bohemian rebels. Both Franz Albrecht of Lauenburg and Duke Adolf were poor commanders and lax disciplinarians, but they had to be tolerated. The rest were solid professionals, like the Breuner cousins from Lower Austria, or Moravians and Silesians who had already changed sides like Heinrich Schlick and Baron Schaffgotsch. The latter served Wallenstein loyally, but Schlick and most Bohemians remained lukewarm towards their new commander. The same was true of the many Italians who were already in imperial service, like the Colloredo brothers, had transferred from Spain, like Octavio Piccolomini and Ernesto Montecuccoli, or who had joined from the Liga army, like Matteo Gallas. Their connections to Spain and the Italian states provided alternative potential patrons, notably in the case of Piccolomini who came from a prominent Florentine family that had already provided two popes.[19] Others had impeccable aristocratic pedigrees, such as Torquato Conti, Wallenstein's erstwhile collaborator in raising his cavalry regiments in 1619, who was marquis of Quadagnola, while Collalto was a distant relative of the emperor's second wife, Eleonore of Gonzaga.

Wallenstein's inability to satisfy his subordinates' ambitions encouraged disloyalty. Francesco Grana found his career blocked by Wallenstein's distaste for his rapacious plundering. Piccolomini and Gallas suspected Wallenstein of favouring Bohemians and Germans, something that was patently untrue. Some were simply the victims of his violent outbursts. A serious rift developed with Johann Aldringen whom Wallenstein had appointed colonel and de facto chief of staff in 1625. During an argument two years later Wallenstein called him a 'pen-pusher', a remark that Aldringen, acutely conscious of his humble origins as a scribe, felt unable to forgive. Though promoted general in 1629, Aldringen found his career overtaken by more recent appointees and so cultivated alternative patrons, including Gallas who became his brother-in-law when they both married daughters of Count Arco in 1630.

Finally, the persistence of separate commands outside Wallenstein's jurisdiction left the emperor with alternative fields for patronage. The best example is one of Ernst Mansfeld's distant relations, Count Wolfgang Mansfeld, who commanded the Saxons in 1619–21 before converting to Catholicism and joining the emperor in 1622. One of the most important, if now forgotten, commanders of the middle stage of the war, he served in Italy until 1628 and so remained outside Wallenstein's influence.

War Finance

Wallenstein's grip on the army's financing was also less secure than generally believed. He is widely regarded as the perfecter, if not the inventor, of a system of military funding known as 'contributions'. Aptly dubbed a 'tax of violence' by John Lynn, this decentralized war finance, removed it from the Estates and handed it to officers who forced communities to maintain their units. The method offered the possibility for a near-bankrupt monarch to make war at his enemies' expense. However, it was not Wallenstein's intention to wage war by 'offensive logistics' as some have claimed, deliberately raising more men than necessary to deny territory to his opponent.[20] The main evidence for this assertion comes from Khevenhüller's near-contemporary account of Ferdinand's reign where he claims Wallenstein demanded over twice the authorized establishment. In fact, he only received permission to levy contributions in enemy territory, none of which had been captured in 1625. Actual military funding relied on more varied methods, of which what have been termed contributions were but one element.

The real core was credit, not extortion, heightening the importance of Wallenstein's personal relationship with the emperor. Like Spinola, Wallenstein was able to raise an entire army because he was already a wealthy man. Officers volunteered to raise new units because they knew Wallenstein could not only advance them start-up capital but, thanks to the emperor's trust, could guarantee repayment of their expenses. The muster system provided most of the money. Acting under imperial authority, Wallenstein assigned towns to accommodate soldiers while their unit assembled. Colonels were authorized to demand food and wages for full establishment numbers from the first day, even though it might take weeks to gather all the recruits. Wallenstein increased his colonels' personal allowances to 500 fl. a week (although they were reduced to 300 fl. in 1629), in contrast to their colleagues in the Liga who were permitted 402 fl. a month. Soldiers' pay remained unremarkable, at

7.5 fl. for an infantryman each month, plus bread worth another 2.5 fl.[21] Whereas other rulers still tried to pay their officers' costs directly, Wallenstein freed Ferdinand from this obligation by allowing his colonels to recoup the expense of equipping, clothing and feeding their men from the local population.

Wallenstein also relieved the indebted imperial treasury of the obligation to pay soldiers once they marched to the front. Both the Liga and imperial armies had struggled to maintain direct monthly payments to their men after 1618 and resorted to expedients already tried during the Turkish War, such as reducing pay rates and persuading men to accept rations or uniforms in lieu. Accumulating pay arrears became a major feature of the war and would partly dictate its course in the 1640s. Governments could hope to write off some of the money if men died on campaign, but the balance owed to the others exceeded any realistic hope of settlement. It became impossible to demobilize armies, because regiments refused to disband until they were paid. The usual practice was to off-load responsibility by raising loans guaranteed by the Estates who won concessions in return for amortizing additional debts. Ferdinand had already obliged the Bohemian Estates to assume 8.2 million fl. of debt in 1623.

Christian IV's problems illustrate the limits to direct state maintenance. The war cost Denmark 8.2 million riksdalers between 1625 and 1627. Ordinary revenue covered little more than a quarter of this sum, while foreign subsidies brought in around 3 million, or about half of what was promised. The Lower Saxons contributed a mere 120,000 rd., obliging Christian to borrow over 2.5 million, chiefly from his mother. This exhausted his reserves, precipitating a crisis after 1627 as the subsidies dried up, while the resumption of Swedish-Polish hostilities caused toll revenues to crash to a third of their pre-war levels.[22]

Wallenstein broke convention by insisting on full payment of both wages and rations by the local population, in contravention of imperial law. The Reichstag had ruled in 1570 that soldiers could expect accommodation on the march, but should pay for everything else at pre-arranged prices, or provide receipts. Some effort was made initially to adhere to the rules. Wallenstein's officers sent the required notification letters (*Requisitoriales*) to territories on their line of march from Bohemia in 1625 so the local authorities could make arrangements to feed and accommodate them.[23] However, this swiftly became impossible, due to the size of the new army, the rapidity of its advance and, above all, its complete inability to pay its way.

Lack of money widened the gap between the strategic necessity for speed and flexibility, and the limited capacity of the largely agrarian economy to support the army. Military regulations envisaged a daily ration of around 1kg of bread, 0.5–1kg of meat, and about 1.5 litres of wine or twice that quantity of beer. In addition, each soldier was entitled to *servis* of candles, firewood, salt and, if mounted, fodder at 3.5 litres of oats or their equivalent for his horse. This diet would be supplemented (technically at the soldier's own expense) with peas, beans and semolina eaten with the meat, plus cabbage or sauerkraut and dried fruit depending on the season, as well as butter and eggs when available. Accepting that much of the meat ration was delivered as inedible bone and gristle, the allowance was still higher in protein than an average peasant's diet and provided 3,000 calories daily.[24]

Most soldiers were obliged to share their food with their dependants. The number and composition of these 'camp followers' are two of the least studied aspects of the war. Many later commentators have seized on remarks from critics such as Wallhausen or Gronsfeld to suggest there were three to four non-combatants for every soldier. Surviving musters suggest a more common ratio of one to one, but sometimes as low as four soldiers to one non-combatant.[25] Around half of the followers were women, often legally married to the soldiers, or widows, as well as captives and prostitutes. The latter had received official protection a century before, but were now the target of punitive regulations, influenced by the new moral vigour following the Reformation and the practical efforts to restrict the size of the 'baggage' which, as Bernhard of Weimar argued, was 'the root of the disorder and cause of confusion in the army'.[26] Other women led a more independent existence as sutlers, fencing stolen goods and selling alcohol and other supplies like Mother Courage, one of Grimmelshausen's characters now better known through the later dramatization by Berthold Brecht. Eyewitnesses report women carrying children in bundles on their heads to leave their arms free for more bags.[27] Women also helped to forage and clean clothes, and provided the mainstay of the rudimentary medical service. The other followers were 'boys', generally teenagers who carried weapons and looked after the horses. Many later became soldiers, like Grimmelshausen's semi-autobiographical character Simplicissimus who became a servant and then a musketeer after his home was plundered.

Though excluded from official allowances, the numerous camp followers undoubtedly increased the actual demand on resources. A peasant family could consider itself fortunate if it had sufficient surplus after tax and rent to feed itself between each harvest. At best, a large farm might have stored the equivalent of 3,000 rations – the daily requirement of a full-strength imperial infantry regiment. Even a modest town was unlikely to contain enough food for more than a few days for a larger force. Matters worsened if the local population hid their supplies, or took them with them as they fled to the woods, marshes or nearest fortified city. Already in 1625, Mainz officials reported that villagers faced 'total ruin' as Wallenstein's regiments marched through.[28] Fear bleeds through the pages of contemporary correspondence as the authorities grasped at every rumour of troop movements in desperate attempts to take precautions.

Wallenstein began recruiting in June 1625, but did not issue his pay and ration regulations until he occupied Halberstadt that November. The 'contributions' he demanded prior to then were close to what contemporaries termed 'fire taxes' (*Brandschatzung*) due to the consequences of non-payment. These were levied on areas threatened but not actually occupied by troops. The Dutch and Spanish had already threatened raids to extort money from German communities after 1575. Wallenstein used the muster system to force such payments from the wealthy south German trading cities that agreed to pay lump sums in return for his rescinding authorization to colonels to muster new units within their territories. He used this method throughout his first generalship, extracting at least 440,000 fl. from Nuremberg alone. The cities agreed because these payments were still less than the cost and destruction that invariably followed actual occupation.

What contemporaries came to call 'contributions' were a more regular form of this initial extortion. The army would conclude a formal agreement with the authorities of a particular territory that would pay regular monthly instalments to troops who were not necessarily in occupation. In return, commanders would issue protection warrants (*Salva guardias*), exempting the population from further burdens and promising good behaviour of any soldiers left behind to safeguard payment. Wallenstein employed this method as operations extended into the minor Upper

Saxon territories after March 1626 and into Brandenburg that autumn. The ducal parts of Holstein were included after September 1627, despite an explicit imperial guarantee to the contrary, while around 12,000 men occupied Württemberg earlier in July, extending the system to south-west Germany. It was imposed on Pomerania in the Franzburg convention with its duke in November 1627 and on Mecklenburg after its occupation the following month. In this form, contributions were a device to expropriate existing territorial taxes. Brandenburg simply diverted payment from the elector to the occupying imperial forces after November 1627. Pomerania secured a notable exception to provide contributions in kind, introducing new taxes to buy grain that was collected in local magazines before distribution to the soldiers. The same method was used in the Habsburg hereditary lands, notably in Silesia where the Estates authorized the customary direct levy in June 1627 but renamed it 'Soldier Tax' and collected it weekly, rather than in the usual larger, but less frequent instalments.[29]

'Contributions' as understood in later historical literature were actually a form of billeting. Colonels were allowed to collect food at rates specified in the Halberstadt ordinance direct from the communities lodging their men. There was a considerable overlap between this and the negotiated contributions, particularly since the latter involved quotas calculated according to the regulation food and wage bill. The distinction was that negotiated contributions were intended to continue once the main force had left, whereas billeting often assumed a more improvised character, as units switched quarters. It frequently proved difficult to extract contributions once the army had left, so the soldiers took hostages to ensure compliance. Failure to pay had little to do with religious or political motivation, but followed the sheer impossibility of paying sums exceeding local resources. For example, the Franzburg convention with Pomerania specified monthly instalments of 40,000 talers intended to maintain 22,000 men, whereas the usual annual tax bill was only 90,000. By 1630, it was claimed the duchy was occupied by 7,540 cavalry and 31,500 infantry and that these had cost the eastern half alone over 6.6 million talers since their arrival.[30]

Lack of accountability made matters worse. Staff work was not as rudimentary as sometimes claimed and efforts were made to keep accounts and liaise with civil authorities. Nonetheless, colonels were allowed considerable leeway and often arrived unannounced, or with far more soldiers than expected. They routinely extorted further sums in return for maintaining discipline, even when their men subsequently ignored the regulations. Frequently, official demands were deliberately inflated by the officer sent to negotiate, who would then pocket a present from a grateful community in return for agreeing a more reasonable sum. Additional demands were imposed, especially for clothing and transport, while even the wealthiest dukes and princes were not above helping themselves to extra luxuries.[31]

Profiteering was rife, though few made large fortunes. Fritz Redlich's now classic study of the 'company economy' overemphasizes the mercantile character of mercenary recruitment.[32] Officers frequently paid for weapons and clothing, but it is clear these were also provided from state magazines and through centralized procurement. Profits, such as they were, came incrementally by accumulating bribes, plunder and other chicanery like drawing rations for non-existent soldiers. Such money was just as easily lost, either through personal folly, usually gambling, or misfortune, especially following a defeat. Captured officers generally had to pay their own ransoms until the 1640s, when prisoner exchanges became more common. Governments frequently failed to pay salaries or reimburse legitimate expenses. As we shall see, the main sources of mutinies in the last two decades of the war were unpaid officers who stirred discontent among the soldiers. Capital accumulation was rarely a personal goal and few officers had a merchant's head for business.[33] Money provided the means to further a career intended to enhance status. Real wealth still came from land, though, as possession grew more precarious after 1631, prudent profiteers like Aldringen invested cash with bankers in safer locations.

The hierarchical, corporate character of society ensured burdens were distributed unequally. Agreements like the Franzburg convention exempted nobles, princely residences, privileged towns, the clergy, university staff and other professional groups. Magistrates and urban officials were usually exempt from billeting, inclining them to be more accommodating to officers' demands, conscious of the soldiers' ability to devastate vineyards and other assets belonging to richer burghers beyond the walls. This helps explain the social tension generated by sieges where the poor were often the most determined to resist, knowing they lacked the means to buy protection if the soldiers captured their town. Resistance entailed considerable risks. Piccolomini fined the

Pomeranian town of Stargard 10,000 talers after an ensign was killed trying to enter. However, such violence was relatively rare (see Chapter 22). Towns offering armed resistance were generally assisted by regular garrisons, though their inhabitants were exposed like the soldiers to plunder and massacre if they failed to surrender before the besiegers broke in.

The decentralized character of Wallenstein's system is widely interpreted as 'privatizing' war, enabling still underdeveloped states like the Habsburg monarchy to raise large armies without concomitant expansion of their administrative and fiscal structures. Contributions and military contracting thus become temporary expedients along a linear path of modernization, employed until the state was sufficiently developed to 'renationalize' warfare.[34] This is misleading, since it distracts attention from the continued significance of regular taxation, as well as the client-patron relationship between the emperor and his officers. Even where existing fiscal structures collapsed under the strain, the army still relied on civil officials to find money and billets. Plunder could not make war pay and restricted the size of armies. It was wasteful and inefficient in the short term, as soldiers either gorged themselves, throwing away what they could not immediately consume, or failed to find the food and valuables civilians had carefully hidden. In the longer term, plunder was self-destructive as normal economic activity ceased and resources disappeared. Local chronicles are littered with accounts of garrisons crammed into a few remaining houses after the soldiers had broken the others up for firewood. Above all, soldiers were largely outsiders, without local knowledge of hiding places or an area's real wealth. Contribution and billeting demands were presented as lump sums, leaving it to local officials to work out who provided what in their community. Officials were caught between the officers' incessant demands and the inhabitants' pleas to be spared. Territorial administration undoubtedly broke down in many areas during the 1630s and it became hard to fill vacancies left by officials who had been killed or simply given up. Officials also falsified accounts and sometimes collaborated with officers in dividing up the spoils. The overall impression, however, is of a group of underpaid, poorly supported men struggling to do their best in fearful times. One Hohenlohe steward diligently kept his accounts despite his office being ransacked eight times by rival forces.[35]

The mounting burdens nevertheless corroded established relationships after 1625. If some people secured exemption, or shirked their share, the burden fell harder on the rest of the community. Good neighbourliness broke down as families denounced those suspected of falsifying tax returns. The overriding desire to minimize violence compelled authorities to abandon previous patterns of benevolence. Rulers and landlords had generally accepted reduced returns during subsistence and other crises in the sixteenth century, allowing their subjects time to recover. Such tolerance was now impossible, as military demands brooked no delay. Even comparatively small territories like the county of Hohenlohe were compelled to place their rudimentary fiscal systems on a firmer footing, and pursued collection ruthlessly to forestall the greater evil of military reprisals.[36]

Wallenstein boasted he would maintain the army without drawing on the already overstretched Habsburg treasury, but in practice he relied heavily on the monarchy's existing taxes. The treasury had already admitted the impossibility of sustaining the enlarged army in November 1626.[37] Regular Habsburg taxation nonetheless continued to provide 1.2 million fl. annually to maintain the Military Frontier, as well as supplying 4 million fl. from 1625 to 1630 to Wallenstein, who received Spanish subsidies worth 3 million in the same period.[38] The cash flowed into Wallenstein's war chest, which was also full of money extorted from cities and territories in return for exempting them from mustering and billets.

The cash was used to finance operations and bulk purchases of artillery and munitions, as well as underpin vital credit arrangements. Credit was present already in the money advanced by Wallenstein to his colonels, the Habsburg treasury and even the emperor, paying, for example, for Ferdinand's attendance at the Regensburg congress which terminated Wallenstein's first generalship in 1630. These advances totalled 6.95 million fl. by 1628, financed by Wallenstein's private fortune and loans raised by his banker, Jan de Witte, a Calvinist refugee from Antwerp who had settled in Prague and made large profits providing credit to Rudolf II. Witte offered the antidote to the cash-flow impasse threatening to choke Wallenstein's system. Taxes and contributions usually fell short and arrived late. Aschersleben was supposed to pay 106,400 fl. at the end of 1625, but delivered only 40,000 after 28 weeks, while payments from Brandenburg dried up after the first four months in 1627. Witte provided bridging loans, initially secured on specific sources of future revenue, but soon tied only to Wallenstein's personal guarantee. The intricate credit network extended to 67 cities, from London to Constantinople, operating through middlemen so that many lenders had no idea where their money was really heading. In return for a 2.5 per cent cut, Witte paid regular monthly instalments only partially recouped from remittances from Wallenstein's war chest.[39]

The system was inherently unsound. Unlike Dutch borrowing that was sustained by an expanding economy, the emperor had no means of repaying the total liability. In addition to the money claimed by Wallenstein, Ferdinand owed 912,000 fl. to Merode, Arnim and Adolf of Holstein by 1628. Meanwhile the army reached a total of over 100,000 men, the largest force yet seen in Central Europe. The growing crisis exposed the system's true foundation – the personal relationship between the emperor, his general and the officers. Though Ferdinand lacked money, he remained feudal overlord with the final say over possession of rights and properties. Confiscation of rebel property in the Habsburgs' hereditary lands had already sustained the imperial war effort before 1625. Land was sold to raise money for current expenses or distributed in lieu of pay and arrears. Ferdinand and his successor, Ferdinand III, skilfully manipulated every aspect of their prerogatives to maximize the value of such transactions. While some particularly urgent or deserving cases received land immediately, others were put on waiting lists attached to particular properties that meanwhile provided revenue to the treasury. Places on such lists became exchangeable commodities that could be traded or inherited, always subject to imperial approval. Fees were deducted each time, allowing the emperor to reduce his existing liabilities, or offset new ones. Even when an individual received sole entitlement, more money could be deducted for formal enfeoffment, or special privileges such as elevating the property's status, as with Wallenstein's duchy of Friedland.[40]

Political Repercussions

Property confiscation had already been extended to the Rhineland in the wake of Tilly's victories over the paladins, while the spread of the war to north Germany opened fresh possibilities to redistribute power to Ferdinand's supporters. Protests at the material damage accumulated as soon as Wallenstein marched from Bohemia in September 1625. The duke of Coburg complained that imperial officers behaved in his territory 'as if in a self-service inn'.[41] Such complaints were sincerely meant and have attracted most of the historical interest, but it was the political repercussions that proved really controversial because the redistribution of land and resources fundamentally shifted power in the Empire.

Following the earlier pattern, Ferdinand placed Christian IV under the imperial ban in December 1625, ordering all inhabitants of the Empire to refrain from assisting him or face similar consequences.[42] As the military situation improved, commissioners were appointed by the Reichshofrat from February 1628 to seize estates in Westphalia and Lower Saxony from officers serving in Christian's army. Land worth at least 740,000 fl. had been sequestrated by June 1630, while other property was confiscated in the royal Danish parts of Holstein and the Jutland peninsula. More seriously, the commissioners were empowered to proceed against those princes who failed to submit to Ferdinand's mandate. Finance, politics and religion intersected in the fates of Magdeburg and Halberstadt. Lying either side of the Elbe between neutral Brandenburg and the Danish army occupying the Guelph duchies, these two ecclesiastical territories secured Christian's eastern flank. Wallenstein's approach in October 1625 prompted their Lutheran administrator, Christian Wilhelm of Brandenburg, to join Christian IV, immediately providing Ferdinand with the excuse to sequestrate his territories.

These provided Wallenstein with welcome billets as winter approached, as well as a forward base linked by the Elbe to Bohemia where he organized a form of command economy in his enormous personal territory of Friedland. Certain sectors there, like iron production, supplied the army directly, but generally Wallenstein conserved Friedland's resources. Troops were also instructed to avoid this *Terra Felix*, while he spent lavishly on a new palace at its capital, Gitschin, as well as on another in Prague.[43]

Meanwhile, he secured Tilly's agreement to remain west of the Leine that winter, reserving Magdeburg and Halberstadt for imperial troops, and allowing Ferdinand to trump the Wittelsbachs in the scramble for the bishoprics. The emperor had already deferred to the Bavarians that October when he recognized Ferdinand of Cologne's cousin, Franz von Wartenberg, as the new bishop of Osnabrück.[44] The emperor had his own family to consider, and wanted Magdeburg and Halberstadt for his younger son, Leopold Wilhelm. Though not ordained until 1638, Wartenberg was already an experienced administrator and 21 years older than his Habsburg rival. Local Catholics and the pope recognized his genuine religious zeal, leading to prolonged wrangling over who should be elected. Wallenstein had little enthusiasm for the emperor's plans as these would curtail his exploitation of the bishoprics' resources. The Halberstadt cathedral chapter eventually elected Leopold Wilhelm in December 1627, but the Protestant canons in Magdeburg chose August of Sachsen-Weissenfels, Johann Georg of Saxony's second son. Magdeburg itself defied all parties, refusing to admit an imperial garrison in a stand-off lasting until May 1631.

DENMARK'S DEFEAT 1626–9

The Battle of Dessau Bridge

Christian IV's ratification of The Hague alliance in March 1626 committed Denmark irrevocably to war. His dwindling funds increased his dependency on his unreliable allies and made it harder to impose his authority on the generals who joined him. Contributions did not free armies from supply lines, despite claims to the contrary.[45] Armies got larger, but the field force remained the same as the additional troops were deployed to secure bases supplying money and food. There was also a tendency, already present in 1626, to remain in billets as long as possible to recuperate at the locals' expense. It proved difficult to amass supplies during winter to support operations beyond the zones of contribution, especially as uncertainty surrounding the enemy's intentions left it unclear where to place stockpiles. The lull in the fighting provided a chance for negotiations that were a constant feature of the entire war. The aborted Brunswick talks already reopened in May 1626 and resumed in September after that summer's campaign, continuing intermittently throughout 1627. Operations were essentially intended to secure local military advantage to lend weight to these negotiations and compel the other side to be more reasonable.

Christian was obliged to concentrate his main army of 20,000 men at Wolfenbüttel early in 1626 to intimidate the Guelphs and keep Wallenstein and Tilly divided. Wallenstein was at Halberstadt to the south-east with roughly the same number of troops, while Tilly with slightly less stood on the Weser to the west with the Harz mountains between them. Christian sent Johann Ernst of Weimar with a small detachment across the Weser to distract Tilly and try to capture Osnabrück. Duke Christian mustered at Göttingen ready to push south into Hessen where Count Philipp Reinhard of Solms had collected 4,000 peasants. Aware that Landgrave Moritz would join them if they got through, Tilly wanted to take Münden, Northeim and Göttingen to secure the frontier and protect Hessen, which continued to pay a large part of his army.

Tilly's refusal to cross the Harz mountains to join Wallenstein disheartened the imperial commander, who tendered his resignation no less than six times between February and March 1626 in protest at the imperial treasury's abject failure to provide funds. Wallenstein was also concerned at a new threat to his forward base from Mansfeld, who now had 12,000 men at Lauenburg on the Elbe ready to invade Brandenburg and turn his flank. Ferdinand had no desire to spread the war into Upper Saxony and ordered Wallenstein to remain west of the Elbe where he began operations around Goslar against Duke Christian. He was forced to turn back in mid-February when Mansfeld advanced along the right bank of the Elbe through western Brandenburg, while a small Danish corps under Fuchs followed west of the Elbe. Mansfeld announced he was coming to liberate the archbishopric of Magdeburg and began occupying Anhalt territory east of the river. Wallenstein soon chased away Fuchs, but learned that Mansfeld was threatening his outpost under Aldringen at Rosslau near Dessau, which guarded the only permanent bridge between Magdeburg and Dresden. If this fell, Mansfeld could disrupt supplies from Bohemia to the imperial army.

Mansfeld increased the pressure on Aldringen's entrenchments on the right bank from 12 April. Wallenstein fed in reinforcements, arriving himself with the main army on 24 April, bringing the defenders up to at least 14,000. Mansfeld had bitten off too much, having quarrelled with Fuchs who was still too far north to help. With only 7,000 men and 25 guns, he was too weak to take the entrenchments. He gambled everything on a final assault at 6 a.m. on 25 April, not realizing that Wallenstein had concealed troops in a wood to the east. These counter-attacked just as Mansfeld's assault was flagging. Mansfeld's cavalry fled downstream to Havelberg, abandoning the infantry who surrendered.[46]

The failure to exploit the victory is usually blamed on rivalry between

Tilly and Wallenstein and their continued logistical problems. Tilly had been obliged to detach Anholt to clear Osnabrück, while he dealt with Duke Christian in Wallenstein's absence. The duke's death on 16 June 1626 temporarily halted Danish operations in the area. Wallenstein eventually met Tilly at Duderstadt near Göttingen on 30 June and secured his agreement to invade Lower Saxony. The attack was delayed by a rebellion in Upper Austria that represented the most substantial popular outburst of unrest to date.

The Upper Austrian Rebellion 1626

In contrast to the situation in 1620, many Protestants in Upper Austria were now prepared to condone rebellion, especially when it defended their faith. Religious grievances certainly helped spark the unrest.[47] Ferdinand expected the Bavarian governor of Upper Austria, Herberstorff, himself a convert from Lutheranism, to enforce the re-Catholicization measures. Pastors and teachers were expelled in October 1624, a fine of 1 million fl. was imposed in 1625 on those accused of supporting the revolt in 1618, and all Protestants were told to convert or leave. The measures stirred opposition, especially among the province's Estates that had run a campaign to discredit Herberstorff in order to deflect local criticism of their failure in 1620. Duke Maximilian had no desire to disturb Upper Austria since he depended on its taxpayers to clear the huge war indemnity agreed in 1623 with Ferdinand. The fine was moderated to 600,000 fl. and the Bavarian garrison reduced to 5,000 men.

It is difficult to gauge exactly what the peasants wanted since their demands were written down by a former judge and a lawyer who may or may not have been reflecting their feelings. The document attacked the new 'Reformation mandate' Ferdinand obliged Herberstorff to issue on 10 October 1625 extending the deadline for conversion until Easter 1626. The principal criticism was that the authorities were placing re-Catholicization before good government and failing to address real grievances – peasant indebtedness and business failures had soared after the hyperinflation of 1622. The re-Catholicization measures also hit communal autonomy by taking schools and village funds from local hands, while many wanted to replace clerical with peasant representation on the Estates. Contemporary broadsheets drew parallels with the Peasants War, displaying images of the 1525 leaders but with the weapons and demands of 1626.[48]

The rising was planned like that in 1595. Stefan Fadinger, a wealthy farmer, conspired with his brother-in-law, the innkeeper Christoph Zeller, but the outbreak began prematurely after a brawl with Bavarian soldiers in Lembach on 17 May 1626. The rebels drew on the experience of the 1611 Passau emergency and the 1619–20 revolt, using the provincial militia system to mobilize 40,000 men from a population of only 300,000. They lacked artillery and cavalry until some burghers declared their support. Three nobles also joined, including Achaz Wiellinger who took command once Fadinger was killed, but the local Protestant elite otherwise abstained, believing the rising would fail and only harm their interests. The movement remained decentralized, with individual bands led by men who were increasingly embittered. Some were militants, like the trainee pastor simply known as 'Student' whom the authorities thought was deranged. However, popular Lutheranism expressed demands for wider liberties, as it had in 1525.

The rising began in the north-west corner of Upper Austria either side of the Danube near the Bavarian border. Herberstorff marched out of Linz to suppress it, but was ambushed by Zeller at Peuerbach where most of his men were massacred on 21 May. Herberstorff escaped to Linz but his hold on the town was undermined by widespread sympathy among its inhabitants for the rebels outside. Like so many early modern rebels, Fadinger and Zeller squandered their initial advantage by roaming the countryside gathering further support. Herberstorff opened talks on 25 May to buy time, and the peasants were prepared to pay the 1623 mortgage to redeem the province for Ferdinand, provided the emperor granted religious toleration. The truce was broken by frequent skirmishes in which Fadinger and Zeller were killed. The peasant army on the heights above Linz was further demoralized by minor reverses inflicted by small imperial and Liga columns operating from Bohemia and Bavaria.

Maximilian assembled 8,000 men, half of them recruits, in Bavaria south of the Danube. Their advance on 18 September ended the truce, but they were routed within days by the peasants in the mountains along the frontier. Maximilian summoned General Pappenheim who advanced with 4,750 men from Passau to relieve Linz on 4 November. Reinforced by the Linz garrison and a small imperial detachment, Pappenheim subdued the area south of the Danube in four hard-fought battles, killing 12,000 rebels. Resistance collapsed, enabling Herberstorff to arrest 100 alleged leaders. It proved impossible to find evidence against Upper Austrian nobles other than Wiellinger who was executed along with over twenty others. Fadinger's corpse was even exhumed so it could be hanged. Ferdinand refused to impose renewed fines and delayed the re-Catholicization measures until 1631.

Political Uncertainty

In the meantime, Christian IV had remained inactive at Wolfenbüttel, accepting the resumption of Saxon mediation in May. He faced the same difficulty that would confront Gustavus Adolphus in 1630: how to win the wider German support necessary to defeat the emperor. Christian needed Hessen's support to go south and Brandenburg's agreement to move east. Hessen refused to declare its hand without a Danish victory, while Elector Georg Wilhelm took a dim view of Mansfeld's incursions.

Calvinists held the majority on the Brandenburg privy council, led by Chancellor Pruckmann who declared 'this is a religious war'. They were blocked by the Lutheran old guard around the elector's mother and Count Adam Schwarzenberg, the only Catholic councillor. (Gustavus Adolphus told the Calvinists they 'should defenestrate the count and treat him in the Bohemian manner'.)[49] The Lutherans shared the elector's doubts about the war's alleged religious dimension, while Schwarzenberg believed the emperor would reward Brandenburg if it supported him. Wallenstein's victory at Dessau Bridge increased the pressure on Brandenburg and was quietly welcomed in Dresden, where Johann Georg gave the Imperialists permission to cross Saxony if Mansfeld moved east.

Having rebuilt his army to 10,000, and backed by 7,000 Danes under Johann Ernst of Weimar, Mansfeld unexpectedly left Havelberg on 11 July, skirting Berlin to the north to reach the Oder, where he turned south to enter Silesia nine days later having covered 250km. The Silesian militia crumbled, allowing him to overrun the province and head for Upper Hungary. This bold stroke opened a new front and renewed the possibility of Transylvanian intervention. Bethlen had just been admitted to The Hague alliance, having improved his standing by marrying Georg Wilhelm of Brandenburg's sister, Katharina, in March. Wallenstein had not expected Mansfeld to recover so quickly. Aware of the power struggle in Berlin, he hesitated to weaken the pro-imperial faction by infringing Brandenburg neutrality. After three weeks it became obvious where Mansfeld was headed, and Wallenstein set off in pursuit with 20,000 men, leaving 16,000 to protect his base and cooperate with Tilly.

The Battle of Lutter

The latter had methodically reduced the three strongholds of Münden, Northeim and Göttingen held by the Protestant forces between Lower Saxony and Hessen-Kassel. Münden was stormed in early July, losing between two- and four-fifths of its 2,500 inhabitants who were massacred as Liga troops plundered the town.[50] Tilly then brought in Harz miners to dig under the defensive ditch at Göttingen to drain the water from it. A relief force under the Rheingraf (Raugrave) Salm-Kyrburg was ambushed and scattered at Rössing on 27 July. Göttingen capitulated on 11 August 1626, having resisted for seven weeks. Christian IV hastened south to save his last garrison at Northeim, but failed to stop Aldringen joining Tilly with 4,300 Imperialists. The king retired north through Seesen on 25 August, intending to escape to Wolfenbüttel. His decision depressed Danish morale and revived Tilly's flagging spirits. The Liga army harried the Danish retreat, cutting off parties left to delay its pursuit. King Christian faced the same dilemma as his namesake had at Höchst and Stadtlohn of whether to jettison his valuable baggage. He chose not to, and the wagons soon jammed the Wolfenbüttel road where it crossed thick woods north-east of Lutter-am-Barenberge. Christian was forced to deploy early on Thursday 27 August, hoping a more substantial rearguard action would dislodge the pursuit. Tilly had no intention of giving up and sought a decisive battle.

Both armies numbered about 20,000, though the Danes had a few more cannon. Their position lay in a cleared valley surrounded by forest. The recent hot weather had dried the Neile stream on the Danish right, though the Hummecke stream to their front and left appears still to have been wet.[51] Tilly brought up his heavy guns, protected by musketeers, to bombard the Danes while the rest of his army came up around noon. His men ate lunch while the Danes waited uneasily in the rain. Anholt opened the main action early in the afternoon by crossing the Hummecke and attacking the Danish left. Christian had gone ahead to disentangle

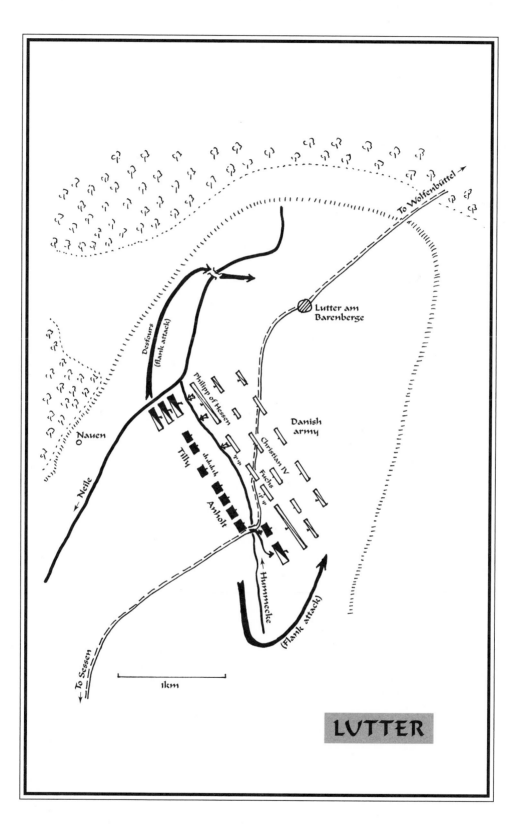

To Wolfenbüttel

Desfours (flank attack)

Lutter am Barenberge

Nauen

Neile

Phillipp of Hessen

Danish army

Tilly

Christian IV

Fuchs

Anholt

Hummecke

(Flank attack)

To Sessen

1km

LUTTER

the baggage train, without making it clear who commanded in his absence. Landgrave Moritz's younger son, Philipp, made an unauthorized counter-attack in an attempt to silence the bombardment. Meanwhile, detachments sent earlier by Tilly worked their way through the woods to turn both Danish flanks. The Danes wavered around 4 p.m., enabling Tilly's centre to cross the stream and capture their artillery. The Danish royal escort successfully charged to cover the retreat of the second and third lines, but the first was unable to disengage and had to surrender. Christian lost up to 3,000 dead, including Philipp of Hessen-Kassel, General Fuchs and other senior officers. Another 2,000 deserted, while 2,500 were captured along with all the artillery and much of the baggage, including two wagons loaded with gold. Tilly lost around 700 killed and wounded.

Christian blamed Duke Friedrich Ulrich who had withdrawn the Wolfenbüttel contingent four days earlier. The Danes burned 24 villages around Wolfenbüttel and plundered their way across Lüneburg as they retreated to Verden. The Guelphs negotiated the bloodless evacuation of Hanover and other towns, and assisted the imperial blockade of the Danes still holding Wolfenbüttel itself. The victory boosted Tilly's prestige and enabled his beloved nephew Werner to marry the daughter of the wealthy Karl Liechtenstein. The Liga army swiftly overran the archbishopric of Bremen and sent a detachment into Brandenburg to encourage Georg Wilhelm to recognize Maximilian as an elector. However, Tilly's troops were entering an area already eaten out by the Danes. Christian offered 6 talers to every deserter who rejoined his army and most of the 2,100 prisoners pressed into the Liga ranks promptly left. Weak and exhausted, Tilly's troops could not deliver the knock-out blow. Conditions deteriorated over the winter, and the Bavarian Schönburg cavalry regiment took to highway robbery to sustain itself.[52]

Mansfeld's Last Campaign

Lutter prevented Christian sending aid to Mansfeld who was now cut off in Upper Hungary. It is likely that Wallenstein deliberately delayed his pursuit until Mansfeld had gone too far to turn back. His gamble paid off, as Mansfeld was stuck in the Tatra mountains waiting for Bethlen, who was typically late. Despite the numerous exiles with his army, the Bohemian and Moravian peasants refused to follow the Upper

Austrian example and remained loyal to the emperor. Those of Upper Hungary hid their harvest before Mansfeld and Johann Ernst of Weimar arrived. Mansfeld lost faith that Bethlen would appear and decided to cut his losses and dash across Bohemia to Upper Austria where the rising was still under way. Johann Ernst, though, still trusted Bethlen and thought Mansfeld's plan too risky.

Wallenstein crossed Silesia in the second half of August and marched past his opponents to the Military Frontier where the Turks were harassing the forts. This show of force was sufficient to deter the pasha of Buda from helping Bethlen, who agreed a truce with the emperor on 11 November. Hardship, disease and desertion had reduced Mansfeld's and Johann Ernst's forces to 5,400. Having quarrelled with the duke, Mansfeld set out with a small escort intending to cross the mountains and escape to Venice. Though only 46, he was crippled by asthma, heart trouble, typhus and the advanced stages of tuberculosis. Insisting on standing up, he allegedly met his end fully armed when death caught him in a village near Sarajevo on 14 December. Johann Ernst died of plague just two weeks later.[53]

Bethlen had waited until the harvest was in before advancing to meet Mansfeld with 12,000 cavalry and a similar number of Turkish auxiliaries. The latter had already left by the time Mansfeld reached Upper Hungary and Bethlen's operations ran parallel with his talks with Ferdinand's representatives. The truce was confirmed as the Peace of Pressburg on 20 December that accepted revisions to the Treaty of Nikolsburg in Ferdinand's favour. The pasha of Buda had already suspended operations, and renewed the 1606 truce at Szöny in September 1627.

Bethlen remained untrustworthy; he offered his light cavalry to Gustavus Adolphus for his war against Poland, but died on 15 November 1629 before agreement could be reached. His erstwhile lieutenant, György Rákóczi, staged a coup in September 1630, displacing Bethlen's widow Katharina who was negotiating to accept Habsburg overlordship. Transylvania was plunged into internal strife from which Rákóczi emerged triumphant in 1636 thanks to his closer ties to the sultan and the local Calvinist clergy.[54]

Many felt that Wallenstein should have defeated Bethlen rather than negotiate with him. Wallenstein defended himself against his critics at the Bruck conference in November 1626 and his extended visit to Vienna the following April, securing a free hand for the coming campaign. His success prompted Georg Wilhelm of Brandenburg to declare for the emperor. The elector had gone east to Prussia, taking only Schwarzenberg with him. Free from his Calvinist councillors in Berlin, he signed an alliance in May 1627. Winterfeld, the Brandenburg envoy who had worked indefatigably from 1624 to 1626 to forge a Protestant alliance, was arrested three months later on trumped-up charges of treason. The alliance allowed an imperial corps under Arnim across Brandenburg to Frankfurt on the Oder to trap the remnants of Mansfeld's army holding out in the Silesian fortresses.

These had come under the command of Joachim von Mitzlaff, a Pomeranian in Danish service, who managed to rebuild the army to 13,400 and organize an effective base in the Upper Silesian mountains around Troppau and Jägerndorf.[55] Wallenstein concentrated 40,000 men at Neisse in June 1627. As his fortresses surrendered one by one, Mitzlaff headed north with 4,000 cavalry hoping to dodge past Arnim. Wallenstein sent Merode and Colonel Pechmann after him, who caught and destroyed his detachment on 3 August. Mitzlaff escaped, but numerous Bohemian exiles were captured, including Wallenstein's cousin Christoph whom he imprisoned. Wallenstein then marched north-west across Brandenburg towards Lauenburg, despatching Arnim northwards into Mecklenburg.

The mounting reverses encouraged Christian IV to resume negotiations. Ferdinand was known to be planning a conference to confirm the decisions of the Regensburg princes' congress of 1623 as the basis for a general peace. He knew that the Palatinate and its Stuart backers would have to be included and accordingly welcomed an initiative from Württemberg and Lorraine to host talks at Colmar in Alsace in July 1627. Christian urged Frederick V to accept the emperor's terms, since this would enable him to make peace without losing face. Frederick at last gave real ground, offering to renounce Bohemia, accept Maximilian as an elector, provided the title reverted to the Palatinate on his death, and to submit to imperial authority by proxy to avoid personal humiliation. Agreement was close since Ferdinand would probably have dropped his demand for reparations if Frederick had swallowed his pride and submitted in person. This was too much to ask, however, and the talks collapsed on 18 July.[56]

The 1627 Campaign

Christian was obliged to fight on, receiving some reinforcements from Britain and France. The 5,000 British and Dutch auxiliaries were posted on the lower Weser with outposts at Nienburg and Wolfenbüttel, while the main army of 15,000 held the Elbe at Lauenburg. Margrave Georg Friedrich arrived to assume command of the remaining 10,000 troops at Havelberg, covering the east. The fortresses of Glückstadt, Krempe and Pinneburg north of the Elbe defended the western approach to Holstein, while Rendsburg to the north secured the entrance to the Jutland peninsula. The weak spot lay to the south-east between neutral Hamburg and the Baltic, which was protected only by Trittau castle and the Holstein militia.

Operations started late, with Tilly not advancing from the Aller towards the Elbe until 15 July, leaving Pappenheim to besiege Wolfen-büttel and sending Anholt to take Nienburg and the other positions along the Weser, while Duke Georg of Lüneburg attacked Havelberg. Georg Friedrich abandoned Havelberg once he learned of Mitzlaff's defeat, and retreated north across Mecklenburg to Poel island off Wis-mar, where he waited five weeks for transport ships to evacuate him to Holstein. Wallenstein arrived with his army from Silesia, sending Schlick to pursue the margrave, while he pressed on through the now open Danish eastern flank. Meanwhile, Tilly outwitted Christian, feinting towards Lauenburg and then crossing the Elbe upstream at Bleckede. Monro records a heroic defence of Boitzenburg where 800 Scots alleg-edly repulsed Tilly, inflicting 2,000 casualties. Though this is accepted by some modern historians, the Danish army was demoralized and in fact offered little resistance.[57] Christian repeated his mistake at Lutter, leaving the incompetent Bohemian Count Thurn in charge of defence while he went into Holstein to organize reinforcements. Thurn quickly abandoned the Elbe and retreated north-west into Glückstadt. Belated orders were sent to General Morgan to evacuate the British troops defending the Weser before they were cut off. Morgan's men were unpaid and mutinous. He agreed with the British ambassador to ignore orders and retreat to Stade instead, from where he had a chance of escaping by sea to England.

Wallenstein joined Tilly just north of Lauenburg on 5 September and they overran Holstein in just two weeks. Thurn and the surviving 8,000

Danes fled north, leaving the remaining garrisons to their fate. Pinneburg fell on 28 September, but Wolfenbüttel and Nienburg both resisted until December, while Morgan held Stade until 5 May 1628. The besiegers were unable to enter for three days after he sailed to England, because of the rotting corpses. The Danes could resupply the Glückstadt garrison by sea, while the Elbe flooded on 17 November 1628 and destroyed the imperial siege works there. Tilly was wounded by a musket ball at Pinneburg and spent the rest of the campaign convalescing – it was possibly an excuse not to play second fiddle to Wallenstein who now assumed overall command.[58]

Confusion and mismanagement hindered further defence. Insufficient transport meant Georg Friedrich had to leave 2,000 men on Poel island. He landed with the remaining 6,000 at Heiligenhafen at the tip of a narrow peninsula on the east Holstein coast intending to join Thurn, but the latter's precipitous retreat enabled Schlick to trap the margrave. The Danes dissolved in panic as the Imperialists bombarded their camp on 26 September 1627. Only 1,000 managed to escape on their ships. Like the fortress garrisons, most of the men who surrendered had not been paid and promptly enlisted in the imperial army.[59] The fall of Rendsburg on 16 October opened the Danish peninsula to Ferdinand. The local nobles either failed to answer Christian's summons, or fled as the Imperialists approached, while the peasant militias opposed the Danish authorities. Another 3,000 cavalry got left behind as the main army was evacuated from Ålborg to the Danish islands.

Wallenstein becomes Duke of Mecklenburg

The Danish retreat left Lower Saxony at the mercy of Ferdinand and his allies. The emperor regarded Friedrich Ulrich's defection just before Lutter as opportunistic and fined him 400,000 talers, lodging a garrison in his capital at Wolfenbüttel to guarantee payment. Other lands were distributed to cope with the army's mounting pay arrears. Parts of Magdeburg and Halberstadt were assigned to Schlick and Merode, while Wallenstein had already received the Silesian duchy of Sagan in May 1627 in lieu of 150,850 fl. owed him by the emperor. Detachments under Arnim overran Mecklenburg that September after its two dukes supplied troops to Christian and refused to submit to imperial authority.[60]

Rumours of Mecklenburg's transfer spread after Wallenstein paid a rare visit to the imperial court, and were confirmed when the emperor assigned both it and the neighbouring bishopric of Schwerin to him in February 1628.[61] The arrangement mirrored those over the Upper Palatinate and Lusatia, enabling the Habsburg treasury to write off 4.75 million fl. it owed to Wallenstein, who was not enfeoffed as duke of Mecklenburg until 16 June 1629, a week after its previous rulers were placed under the imperial ban. Wallenstein's elevation as full imperial prince was unprecedented and immediately controversial. Its full impact can only be appreciated in the context of the sweeping changes in the Empire since 1621. Frederick V, the senior secular elector, had been deposed and his possessions handed to the emperor's supporters. Though the ban on his most prominent collaborators, Anhalt and Hohenlohe, had been rescinded, the Mecklenburg dukes had joined Georg Friedrich of Baden-Durlach as fugitives. Landgrave Moritz of Hessen-Kassel had been forced to abdicate and Friedrich Ulrich of Brunswick-Wolfenbüttel humiliated. The presence of Wallenstein's troops in Pomerania, Holstein and Württemberg, parts of Brandenburg, Anhalt and other territories suggested further venerable ruling houses would soon lose their possessions. Wallenstein deliberately fostered these fears, partly to deflect criticism from his own elevation, suggesting that Tilly should become duke of Calenberg, while Pappenheim could have Wolfenbüttel.[62] Coinciding as they did with the growing clamour from the ecclesiastical princes and religious orders to recover church property these developments profoundly alarmed Lutherans, as well as the surviving Calvinists.

The Mühlhausen Electoral Congress

Despite an initial enthusiasm for the restitution of church land (see Chapter 13), the Liga's leadership shared these concerns. Duke Maximilian especially opposed the expansion of Wallenstein's army, fearing it would give Ferdinand the means to embroil the Empire in the Dutch War. The integrity of the Liga army was also threatened as its officers defected to imperial service. The military balance prevailing before 1625 had been reversed, as Wallenstein now had three times as many soldiers as Tilly to whom Ferdinand sent orders without consulting Maximilian.

Complaints about the growing military burden after October 1625 frequently failed to distinguish between Liga and imperial units. By 1627 the protests were almost exclusively directed against Wallenstein – not that Tilly's men behaved any better, but because the issue had become politicized. The three spiritual electors lodged a joint protest at Wallenstein's conduct of the war on 2 February 1627 and agreed to press the concerns of the other imperial Estates at their forthcoming congress following a petition from Nuremberg.[63]

The congress had been planned to settle not just the Palatine question and the Danish war, but also the balance between the victorious Catholics. It opened on 18 October and lasted until 12 November 1627, attended in person by the Mainz and Saxon electors, while the others sent representatives. The presence of numerous princely and civic delegations gave it the appearance of a Reichstag and, as the first substantial meeting for four years, it offered an opportunity to debate and criticize Habsburg policy.[64]

Maximilian had already lent his voice to the criticism of Wallenstein in April, but was fatally compromised as the chief beneficiary of the Catholic victories. While concerned at the fate of venerable princely dynasties, he was not above ordering his archivists to investigate possible Bavarian claims to Brandenburg.[65] Moreover, he could not rock the boat until his own status was secure. Saxony had recognized the transfer of the Palatine title in 1624. Brandenburg accepted it in its treaty with the emperor in May 1627, clearing the way for the next stage to convert it from a purely personal into an hereditary title. For this, Maximilian needed Ferdinand's consent, as well as that of his fellow electors, obliging him to mute his criticism of the emperor's general.[66]

Maximilian struck just the right balance, condemning the worst abuses of Wallenstein's subordinates, while backing the emperor's political agenda. He was rewarded with recognition as hereditary elector on 12 November, despite Saxon and Brandenburg objections. Bavaria also rid itself of the costly occupation of Upper Austria by relinquishing it to Ferdinand in return for Maximilian's enfeoffment with the whole Upper and eastern half of the Lower Palatinate on 22 February 1628. The arrangement included the added promise that Ferdinand would repay Bavaria's war expenses, now set at 13 million fl., if Maximilian subsequently lost these lands. This transfer ran parallel to Wallenstein's enfeoffment with Mecklenburg, confirming the other princes' worst fears about Ferdinand's apparent disregard for their traditional liberties.

The Peace of Lübeck

Christian IV had lost his mainland possessions, but still held out on the Danish islands. The relatively mild winter of 1627–8 enabled his navy to raid imperial positions along the coast, and to retake Fehmarn island, capturing eighty boats Wallenstein had collected to ferry his army across to Copenhagen. The army was rebuilt by extending conscription to Norway and eventually reached 20,000 men, excluding the Glückstadt and Norwegian garrisons. The Danish raids encouraged peasant risings in Ditmarschen, Holstein, parts of Jutland and Nordstrand, one of the Frisian islands off western Schleswig where a third of the 9,000 inhabitants took up arms. Danish troops also intervened in Arnim's siege of Stralsund, while their warships disrupted Wallenstein's fledgling imperial navy (see pp.426–8).

Christian attempted to recover a foothold on the mainland by landing with 6,000 men at Wolgast on the Pomeranian coast east of Greifswald. Having abandoned the siege of Stralsund, Wallenstein attacked with 8,000 men on 24 August, trapping the Danes as Schlick had done the year before at Heiligenhafen. Christian's troops put up stout resistance behind a marsh, enabling their king to escape to his fleet, leaving 1,000 dead and 1,100 captured. He returned in the spring of 1629, landing with 10,000 men on the east coast of Jutland and marching south with the intention of joining Morgan, who had sortied with 4,750 British and Dutch on ships from Glückstadt to land on Nordstrand. Despite detaching troops to assist in a new war in Mantua, Wallenstein was easily able to respond and by 6 June was ready to repeat the entrapment of Wolgast against the new Danish bridgehead.

Fortunately, Christian made peace just in time, accepting the emperor's revised terms at Lübeck the day before. Pressured by his nobles, the king had reopened talks on 22 January 1629. Wallenstein was eager for peace and had advised Ferdinand to return the conquered Danish provinces without demanding compensation to win Christian as an ally against potential Swedish intervention. In view of the Mantuan crisis, Ferdinand agreed, provided Christian abandoned the Lower Saxons. Christian's agreement shattered the already battered Hague alliance. Richelieu condemned him as a coward, but to the Danes the peace appeared a gift from heaven and they readily forgot the ideal of Protestant solidarity that, anyway, had not been very prominent in their attitudes to the war.[67]

13

The Threat of European War 1628–30

A dangerous coincidence of political and military factors threatened to merge Europe's conflicts into a common struggle after 1628. The imperial advance to the Baltic alarmed Sweden, which considered allying itself with Denmark and it emboldened Poland to offer support to Ferdinand. The latter negotiated with Spain for assistance to create an imperial navy that might challenge Sweden and attack the Dutch. Denmark's defeat released imperial troops to help Spain in the Netherlands and Italy, as well as assist Poland against Sweden. France intervened in Italy, while Britain helped the Huguenots in their final rebellion. The fusion of these different struggles came to rest on seven great sieges: La Rochelle, Danzig, Stralsund, Magdeburg, Casale, Mantua and s'Hertzogenbosch. The fate of each city determined whether one or more powers would be free to intervene elsewhere. The character of La Rochelle, Stralsund and Magdeburg as Protestant strongholds sharpened the confessional edge of the conflicts. Ferdinand further heightened religious tension by demanding the return of all church land in the Edict of Restitution in 1629. The feverish pace of events appeared to confirm the arrival of the long-prophesied Armageddon.

Yet, all parties drew back from the brink. Intervention remained limited and short-lived. More significantly, it was not intended to provoke general war, but resolve separate issues and deter others from interfering. While some diplomats lobbied for new alliances, others worked hard to settle disputes and to prevent fresh hostilities. Those who race ahead to examine Swedish involvement in Germany after 1630 overlook the real chances for peace in these years and the genuine attempts to find a general solution to the Empire's problems.

THE BALTIC

The Polish War

Though they ran in parallel, each conflict had separate roots. The Baltic struggle provides a logical place to start because it overlapped with Denmark's defeat. Gustavus Adolphus was determined to conquer Livonia, a region vulnerable to attack from Sweden's bridgehead in Estonia. The Ottoman attack on southern Poland in 1620–1 provided him with an opportunity to launch the largest Swedish amphibious operation to date as 12,000 troops landed on the Livonian coast, while 4,000 more crossed from Estonia to attack Riga.[1]

The city fell in September 1621 after a five-week siege, but the invasion set a pattern that Gustavus was unable to break. Command of the sea enabled him to pick his point of attack, but once ashore, he only had a short time to achieve his objective before sickness and autumn rains made further operations impossible. The area was sparsely populated and the great distances between settlements often proved a greater hindrance than the outnumbered Poles. The Swedes had to land in force, because disease rapidly depleted their ranks, and additional men were needed to garrison captured towns. The better-mounted Poles easily evaded the Swedish cavalry whose small horses could not catch them. These conditions encouraged Gustavus to seek a truce each autumn to secure his gains over the winter while he collected reinforcements in Sweden. When the Poles refused, they often recovered much of the lost ground, raiding deep into Swedish-held territory and picking off isolated garrisons. These successes were not enough to evict the Swedes, but were usually sufficient to disrupt Gustavus's plans for the coming campaign.

Sigismund III accepted a truce in August 1622, but negotiations to convert this into peace foundered on his refusal to renounce the Swedish crown. It took a while before Gustavus believed Denmark's preparations for war were not directed against him. However, once he was convinced Christian would attack Germany, he encouraged Danish intervention to ensure his rival remained mired in the Empire's problems. Negotiations were held with Britain and the Dutch in the hope of persuading them to fund a renewed Polish war as a 'diversion'. The Dutch envoy travelled to Sweden only to discover Gustavus had already gone to Livonia in

July. When he finally found the Swedish monarch, he was treated to a lengthy harangue in Latin from Chancellor Oxenstierna outlining the evils of the Polish Vasas. British efforts failed to overcome Gustavus's distrust of the Danes and so Sweden remained outside the Hague alliance.

Gustavus's victory at Wallhof in January 1626 finally completed his conquest of Livonia and allowed him to occupy Courland to the south. He decided against pressing into sparsely populated Lithuania, switching to Polish Prussia further down the coast. This richer, more densely inhabited province was easier to reach by sea and better-able to sustain the invaders. Gustavus's prime target was Danzig, the Polish-Lithuanian Commonwealth's largest port and one of Europe's richest mercantile cities. The largely German-speaking burghers preferred their current privileged place in the Commonwealth to an accommodation with Sweden. Since Danzig was too difficult to attack directly, Gustavus concentrated on conquering the boggy, fertile Vistula delta to the east, as well as the lagoon separating the city from the Baltic in order to control trade entering or leaving the Commonwealth. Ignoring his brother-in-law Georg Wilhelm of Brandenburg's protests, he consolidated his hold by occupying the ducal Prussian port of Pillau further east.[2]

Initially distracted by Tartar raids, Sigismund III sent his best general, Hetman Koniecpolski, to reinforce the few troops in Polish Prussia, while the Hanseatic League helped their fellow-member Danzig to recruit German mercenaries. Koniecpolski's inability to defeat Gustavus at Dirschau in August 1627 signalled the beginning of a long war of attrition, as the Swedes could not take Danzig, while the Poles were unable to recover the delta.

The Baltic Design

The Swedish advance along the southern Baltic shore coincided with the Imperialists' arrival in Pomerania in November 1627. Wallenstein negotiated the duchy's occupation with Duke Bogislav XIV to find additional food for his army. However, possession of the western end of the Baltic coast offered a chance to strike at the Danish islands onto which Christian had retreated. For this, ships were needed and it seemed as if Spain would provide them. Known as Wallenstein's 'Baltic Design', this Austro-Spanish naval cooperation attracted considerable interest in

426

the nineteenth century when it was seen as a precursor to imperial Germany's naval and colonial policies.[3]

The plan actually originated in Spain as part of Olivares' bid to strangle Dutch trade through the Almirantazago licence system outlined in Chapter 11. Spain wanted the emperor to persuade the Hanseatic League to back the project. Discussions rapidly established that Wallenstein would seize and garrison the necessary ports, while Spain would provide naval experts, materials and most of the money. Talks were widened to include Sigismund III after January 1626. The Habsburgs maintained a gunboat flotilla on the Danube, but had no expertise in organizing a high seas fleet, whereas the Poles had a small coastal defence force that scored a minor victory in the Danzig lagoon against the Swedes in November 1627. The first proper sea-going Polish warship was launched in 1622 and by 1628 Sigismund had twelve ships and another fifteen fitting out.[4]

Discussions then stalled as one party lost interest, just as another warmed to the project. The location of the naval base proved an important area of disagreement. Spain originally envisaged Emden or some other North Sea port to support a blockade of the Dutch coast, whereas Ferdinand and Sigismund favoured the Baltic. Polish participation remained a low priority, because Sigismund's objective of invading Sweden to recover his crown was not only of little interest to either Habsburg branch, but appeared downright fantastical. A Baltic base posed considerable problems for Spain, not least in sending a fleet through the Danish-controlled Sound. Olivares was reluctant to extend Spanish commitments and insisted that any Baltic action be done in the emperor's name, even if Spain provided the money and materials. The chances of agreement temporarily receded as the emperor expected Olivares to provide assistance without having to help Spain in turn against the Dutch. However, by February 1628 Olivares was prepared to send 28 ships, provided Ferdinand placed the Dutch under the imperial ban. Having not paid subsidies since 1621, Spain resumed financial assistance to Ferdinand in 1626, sending 2.49 million fl. by 1629, most of which was delivered in 1628 as negotiations on the navy intensified. Gabriel de Roy, a naval and commercial expert, was sent with 200,000 talers to start buying ships and recruiting crews.

Ferdinand felt that the provision of bases in Mecklenburg and Pomerania was already sufficient and refused to declare war on the Dutch.

Attention increasingly focused on the Hanseatic League members, who were to be enticed to provide 24 ships by offering them preferential treatment under the Spanish licence scheme. Wallenstein would buy or build another 24 ships using de Roy's money. The fleet would operate in the emperor's name and Wallenstein was duly named Captain General of the Oceanic and Baltic Seas in February 1628.

Stralsund and Magdeburg

Despite their hostility toward Denmark, the Hanseatic League remained suspicious of the emperor and his motives. Any prospect of winning them over was wrecked by Wallenstein's dealings with the Hanseatic cities of Stralsund and Magdeburg. Stralsund is generally viewed in isolation as the last Protestant stronghold defying Catholic tyranny until rescued by Sweden. However, its epic siege needs to be placed in the wider context of Hanseatic diplomacy and Wallenstein's parallel blockade of Magdeburg.

The occupation of Mecklenburg gave Wallenstein control of Rostock, but he wanted another base for his fleet. Keen to deflect attention from his own residence in Stettin, Bogislav encouraged Wallenstein to use Stralsund instead. The town was part of Pomerania but with a long tradition of defying ducal authority, and Bogislav thought he might as well use imperial billeting as a way of reasserting his jurisdiction. Meanwhile, Wallenstein's forward base on the Elbe remained insecure as long as Magdeburg refused to admit an imperial garrison.

His approach was the same in both cases. He delegated authority to the general commanding the detachment in the area: Arnim at Stralsund, Wolfgang Mansfeld at Magdeburg. Both placed the cities under loose blockade and demanded heavy contributions to pressure the councils into negotiating. Neither general wanted to harm imperial prestige by using force, and both accepted Hanseatic mediation. Settlements looked likely as the city councils were dominated by rich patricians who favoured compromise. The poorer citizens opposed agreement, fearing they would suffer most if troops were admitted. Pastors stirred up opposition, especially in Magdeburg, a city with a proud tradition of defying Catholicism, playing on the meaning of the city's name as 'maiden's castle' to emphasize the purity of their cause.[5] Internal divisions were heightened by pressure from outsiders on the cities to resist. The Danes and then the Swedes encouraged the Stralsunders to hold out, while Christian Wilhelm, the dispossessed Magdeburg administrator, conspired with his supporters in the city to oppose Wolfgang Mansfeld.

Stralsund was built on a triangular island separated from the mainland by lagoons that dried to marsh in the summer and could only be crossed by five causeways. The open channel to the east provided a sheltered roadstead for shipping between the coast and Rügen, Germany's largest island. These natural defences were strengthened in the winter of 1627–8 at the insistence of the militant faction led by the radical lawyer Gosen by burning down the suburbs and recruiting 1,000 mercenaries to reinforce the 2,450-strong militia.[6] Arnim's Imperialist army mustered only 8,000 and he offered to accept 150,000 talers in return for dropping his demand to garrison the town. To add weight to his offer, he seized Dänholm island at the south-east entrance to the harbour on 14 February 1628. With imperial guns in range of the city, the council agreed to pay 80,000, handing over the first 30,000. One faction hoped Hanseatic mediation would resolve the situation without further violence, but Gosen's party vowed to fight to the death and forced the council to blockade Dänholm until it surrendered on 15 April. Reinforced by 6,000 men, Arnim attempted a night assault a month later, only to be repulsed. Efforts were renewed on 23 May and continued for ten days without success.

Stralsund's resistance proved a welcome diversion for Christian who sent 1,000 Germans and Scots to help the town, including MacKay's regiment with Monro. The failure of Ferdinand's talks with the Hanseatic League since December 1627 meant there was still no imperial navy to stop them. The loss of Dänholm reopened the harbour and the Danes sailed in on 7 June. Acceptance of foreign assistance fatally compromised the Stralsunders who were now openly associated with Ferdinand's enemies.

Danish involvement piqued Swedish interest. Gustavus had sought an accommodation with the town since 1625, appreciating its significance as the nearest German harbour to Sweden. He had welcomed Denmark's predicament, negotiating secretly with Wallenstein throughout 1627 for an alliance that would let him invade Norway. Wallenstein had acted on his own initiative and received Ferdinand's retrospective approval only in December, two weeks before Gustavus broke off the talks.

STRALSUND

RÜGEN
ISLAND

Imperial
siege
lines

BALTIC
SEA

Camp

Imperial
siege
lines

Lagoon

Harbour

Dänholm
Island

Stralsund

Imperial
siege
lines

Camp

Imperial siege lines and redoubts

Lagoon

Lagoon

Camp

Camp

Camp

1km

Wallenstein genuinely feared Swedish intervention and regarded the imperial navy plan as purely defensive. To Gustavus, however, Wallenstein's actions contradicted his good words as he appeared to be doing everything to provoke Sweden. Gustavus made an agreement with Christian to save Stralsund in April 1628. The two monarchs met in Ulvsbäck parsonage on the Halland–Scania frontier the following February. The rapprochement improved Christian's position in the Lübeck peace talks, but Danish-Swedish differences were too deep to permit a lasting alliance. Gustavus took an immediate dislike to his neighbour who drank too much and insisted on Danish pre-eminence.

The balance was already slipping in the other direction. Swedish reinforcements arrived in Stralsund harbour on 20 June 1628 but refused to land until the town signed a twenty-year pact and accepted Sir Alexander Leslie as governor. Denmark acquiesced on 27 September when it relinquished all claims to protect Stralsund. The Swedes had arrived just in time. Wallenstein appeared on 7 July, bringing the besiegers up to 25,000, and immediately began a fresh assault that lasted three days. The town was subject to an intense bombardment, one shot decapitating fourteen defenders; 'who doubts of this, he may go and see the reliques of their braines to this day, sticking to the walls'.[7]

Stralsund remained defiant, obliging Wallenstein to reopen negotiations. The council agreed to pay the remaining 50,000 talers and accept a ducal Pomeranian rather than an imperial garrison.[8] Swedish officers prevented the council from carrying out its promise and Wallenstein lifted the siege on 31 July, using the face-saving excuse that Duke Bogislav had requested his withdrawal. Stralsund had succeeded in keeping the Imperialists out, but at the cost of what would prove to be 187 years of Swedish occupation. What Wallenstein had feared now transpired. Gustavus had a German base, but it was unclear what he would do with it.

The outcome emboldened the Hanseatic League to reject the navy plan in September, refusing even to sell ships or stores, and Wallenstein was forced to use the smaller Mecklenburg port of Wismar instead. Even with de Roy's assistance, it proved difficult to recruit experienced sailors or find the forty ships Wallenstein now deemed necessary. Danish warships caught the fledgling imperial squadron off the Pomeranian coast that spring and inflicted considerable damage. Increasingly desperate, Wallenstein obtained Vienna's permission to resettle Uskok pirates in Pomerania and proposed paying a Scottish merchant to burn the Swedish fleet.

Imperial Intervention in Poland

Wallenstein also opened negotiations with Sigismund who offered his naval squadron in return for military assistance in the Vistula delta. The Poles had collected 35,000 men, but only a third of them were with Koniecpolski in the delta, as the rest had to be deployed to counter the Ottomans and other Swedish threats. Ferdinand ordered Wallenstein to agree, and Arnim was despatched from Pomerania in May 1629. The campaign was a military success, but a diplomatic failure. The Poles distrusted Arnim who had previously served Sweden and claimed that he had brought only 5,000 men. He arrived in fact with 7–8,000, though still 7,000 short of what had been promised.[9] Arnim himself was openly against the intervention, and complained the Poles failed to pay or feed his troops.

Nonetheless, he managed to dodge the Swedish outposts and cross the Vistula to join Koniecpolski on the eastern bank. Gustavus had 23,000 men, but most were blockading Danzig, leaving him only 7,000 near Marienwerder on the Vistula north of Graudenz (Grudziadz). He decided to retreat downstream to his headquarters at Marienburg, setting out early on 27 June 1628 by sending his baggage down the highway while the main force took a side road across Stuhm heath to the east. Though the Poles had wanted imperial infantry, Koniecpolski did not wait for them to catch up as he raced after the Swedes strung out on the march, attacking their rearguard at Honigfelde village. The Swedes broke after initial resistance, fleeing north to the next village of Pulkowitz where they rallied around a detachment under Colonel Hermann Wrangel. The Polish and imperial cavalry caught up, and again outflanked their opponents. An Austrian trooper seized Gustavus's belt, but the king slipped it over his head and escaped with only the loss of his hat, which was sent by Arnim as a prize to Wallenstein.

The chase continued to Neudorf where the side road rejoined the highway to cross the Bach river. Stuck at this bottleneck, some Swedes were driven into the marshes either side of the road, where they surrendered. A final counter-attack then dislodged their pursuers long enough for the rest to escape, having lost at least 1,000 men and so many horses that the remaining cavalry were mostly dismounted. Only around 3,000 Polish and imperial cavalry had been engaged in the fighting, sustaining 400 casualties. It was the type of action the Poles excelled at and Gustavus had seriously underestimated the risks in starting his retreat.

The victory did nothing to ease the tension between the allies. Arnim claimed the Poles had killed twenty of his men by mistake during the battle. As a Brandenburger, he refused to endorse Sigismund's plan to move deeper into less-devastated ducal Prussia, and he resigned in protest at the Poles' failure to supply his soldiers who were reduced to eating grass.

Sigismund's nobles pressed him to negotiate, because the Swedes still held most of the delta. It was clear to Gustavus that he could not win either. Over 35,000 of the 50,000 Swedish conscripts sent to Prussia since 1625 had died or deserted, increasing his reliance on foreign mercenaries. This helped push his war costs to over 5.3 million riksdalers.[10]

Both sides accepted Anglo-French mediation. With Denmark out of the picture and the situation in Italy deteriorating, Richelieu wanted Sweden to disengage from its Polish struggles and threaten the Empire instead. His envoy, Charnacé, brokered the Truce of Altmark on 26 September 1629 by which Sweden evacuated Courland but retained most of Livonia, and virtually all the Prussian ports except Danzig, Königsberg and Puck, which gave it annual toll revenues worth half a million riksdalers.

The surviving Imperialists left the delta immediately. Sigismund's displeasure increased when he discovered he had lost his navy, which was now trapped in Wismar. The eight Polish ships that reached Wismar in 1629 provided the core of the imperial fleet, including the *King David*, which, at 400 tonnes with 33 guns, was the most powerful.[11] The fleet grew to 25 vessels by the end of 1629, but Wallenstein was running out of money, despite levying a kind of ship-money tax on his new Mecklenburg subjects. He had also hired an Italian engineer to dig a canal from Wismar through the Schwerin lakes to the Elbe to allow his ships and merchantmen licensed by Spain to avoid the Danish Sound tolls. The project was overly ambitious, but far-sighted, pre-dating the idea of the Kiel Canal by over 260 years. De Roy resorted to privateering to maintain the fleet, despite Wallenstein's orders to avoid provoking Sweden. The Peace of Lübeck removed the Danish threat, but the Swedes simply sailed into their place to blockade Wismar. De Roy drove them off, but Wallenstein's dismissal removed the fleet's advocate. The unpaid crews deserted and the ships were laid up until the Swedes captured their rotting remains when Wismar surrendered in January 1632.[12]

THE NETHERLANDS

Spanish Bankruptcy

Spain's participation in the Baltic Design met constant criticism in Madrid and Brussels from those who considered it a waste of precious resources.[13] The capture of Breda (see Chapter 11) proved a pyrrhic victory, costing Spain more than it harmed the Dutch. Taxation doubled between 1621 and 1627, while borrowing soared 500 per cent. Though Philip IV slashed 300,000 ducats of household expenditure, it made little difference when the cost of the Dutch War jumped from 1.5 to 3.5 million ducats, while spending on the Atlantic fleet doubled to 1 million. As Spain's traditional Genoese creditors grew nervous, the crown swallowed its religious scruples and borrowed from the Portuguese Jews and *Conversos* for the first time.[14] The move fuelled Portuguese resentment of Spanish rule without preventing financial collapse in January 1627, when the government suspended interest payments and issued additional paper *juros* to cover current expenditure.

These difficulties prevented Spain exploiting the temporary disarray among the Dutch following Maurice of Nassau's death in April 1625. Opting for continuity, the States General elected his younger brother, Frederick Henry, as the new stadholder. Frederick Henry was associated with the militant Calvinist faction and, like his brother, was committed to the full reunification of both the north and south Netherlands as a Protestant republic. However, as the third of his family to lead the Dutch, he thought more dynastically, notably after the birth of his son in 1626, and sought broader support by ending the Gomarist persecution of the Arminians.[15] The arrival of French subsidies after the Treaty of Compiègne in June 1624 added further stability. Worth 1 million fl. a year, these covered 7 per cent of military expenditure, enabling the Republic to add 7,000 men to its army in March 1626. Subsequent increases raised the total to 70,000 by 1629, backed by 50,000 militiamen and a navy of 40,000 tonnes manned by over 8,500 personnel. The fleet was a third larger than in 1621, while command passed to more skilled and daring admirals like Piet Hein, and later Maarten Tromp and Michiel de Ruyter.

Hein had over thirty years' experience, including the Uskok War and the Bahia expedition of 1624. He led the second Bahia expedition of 1626, sailing up the Capivari river to flush out the Portuguese sugar fleet that was hiding there. His Atlantic cruise the following year netted 55 prizes. He was just the man to score a much-needed major victory. Previous attempts to intercept the Spanish treasure fleet had failed. Even when the Dutch managed to find the convoy in the vast Atlantic, the large Spanish galleons proved formidable opponents. Financed by the Dutch West India Company (WIC), Hein set sail with a new expedition of 31 ships, cruising for four months before spotting the Spanish off Cuba on 8 September 1628. He swiftly overpowered the nine smaller vessels, but the other six escaped to Matanzas Bay, east of Havana. The sun was setting when Hein caught up, but he decided to attack to stop them landing their precious cargo, or burning their ships. The Spanish crews abandoned their ships as the Dutch opened fire. Hein captured over 80,000kg of silver, as well as thousands of animal hides, crates of sugar and bags of costly cochineal and indigo dye. The haul was worth at least 11 million fl., and possibly 6 million more. He returned, dodging severe storms and the Dunkirkers sent to intercept him, as well as English customs officials at Falmouth who demanded a share, to arrive home to a hero's welcome. WIC shareholders received a 75 per cent dividend; ordinary sailors got 17 months' wages, while Hein was given 6,000 florins and a gold medal. He did not live long to enjoy his fortune, however, dying in a minor skirmish with Ostend privateers on 18 June 1629.

The real impact of Hein's success was psychological, wrecking Olivares' attempts to restore confidence in the Spanish economy after the 1627 bankruptcy. Fearing another attack, the *flotas* abandoned their regular sailing schedules and began leaving later, during the hurricane season. The consequences were felt in 1631 when the Vera Cruz fleet was wrecked off Yucatán with the loss of another 5 million ducats. The entire New Spain fleet went down a decade later with the equivalent of a third of the Matanzas loot. The crown confiscated a third of the private silver arriving with the Tierra Firma fleet in 1629, which further undermined confidence and encouraged widespread fraud to avoid such seizures in future. Spain entered a deep recession, worsened by the return of the plague, famine and drought. Sickness struck at the heart of the monarchy when the king himself fell seriously ill in August 1627.

Archduchess Isabella was now sixty and weary of the war. General Spinola wanted to retire before a major defeat ruined his reputation, and he feared Madrid would never repay his considerable expenses. News that Olivares had embarked on a new war over Mantua convinced him that the Spanish government had lost grip on reality. The continued struggle seemed pointless, because the earlier victories had already prompted the Dutch to suggest renewing the Truce in 1625. Since Olivares controlled Philip's correspondence, Spinola took the extraordinary step of travelling to Madrid in January 1628. He presented Olivares with a stark choice: compromise with the Dutch or send massive reinforcements. Olivares was prepared to discuss peace on the terms offered in 1621, but the most he would concede was trade with the East, not West Indies. He remained convinced Spain's position was improving and haughtily rejected Spinola's requests, scoffing that the Romans had conquered the world with 100,000 soldiers, whereas Spinola had nearly as many and could not defeat the Dutch.[16]

Spain's inability to send reinforcements to the Netherlands placed a premium on imperial assistance. The Brussels government had lobbied the Catholic Liga relentlessly for help. Anholt briefly entered the Spanish Netherlands in pursuit of Mansfeld in 1622, while Duke Christian's use of Dutch territory as a refuge after Stadtlohn added another reason to intervene. Isabella offered subsidies and reciprocal assistance. Anholt moved the small corps covering Cologne to help the Spanish at Breda in February 1625 on the excuse of executing the ban against Mansfeld who had just arrived in the Dutch camp. Anholt withdrew in June, but Mansfeld's appearance among the Dutch garrisons on the Lower Rhine alarmed Ferdinand of Cologne, who requested Spanish protection and urged an attack to evict the Dutch from Emden. Isabella sent 2,000 men, but Maximilian of Bavaria refused to allow them across the Rhine and ordered the Liga units not to cooperate to avoid inflaming the situation in the Empire. His brother endorsed this once the crisis passed as Mansfeld crossed Westphalia to join the Danes. The danger returned in 1627 when Count van den Bergh led a Spanish corps into Münster in a futile attempt to save Groenlo (Groll) from attack by Frederick Henry.[17] The

Liga leadership was now convinced the Dutch would leave them alone provided they did not assist Spain, and Elector Ferdinand worked hard to broker a truce.

The Siege of s'Hertzogenbosch

Frederick Henry's renewed offensive against the southern Dutch provinces in 1629 disturbed the situation. He wanted a major victory to consolidate his domestic position and the Matanzas loot provided the means. Having sent diversionary forces against Wesel and Lingen to the east, he struck west with 28,000 men and 118 guns to besiege s'Hertzogenbosch (Bois-le-Duc), Brabant's second city after Antwerp. The place was surrounded by a marsh and three strong outworks, and garrisoned by 4,600 regulars and 2,000 militiamen. The Dutch siege started on 1 May, and by 18 July they had taken the outworks and were only 25 metres from the main wall.

Having failed to relieve the city directly, van den Bergh crossed the Ijssel with 25,000 men on 22 July in the hope of raising the siege by threatening Amsterdam. The Peace of Lübeck had just freed imperial units and the emperor directed Count Johann VIII of Nassau-Siegen to join Bergh with 17,000 men.[18] The Imperialists seized Amersfoort on 13 August 1629, helping Bergh to advance to within 40km of Amsterdam, nearly cutting the Republic in two. Frederick Henry refused to be distracted. The Dutch citizens' militia mobilized – a largely symbolic gesture – while sailors were disembarked to help bring the land forces up to an unprecedented 128,000 men. The Imperialists were poorly disciplined and the advance ground to a halt. A Dutch raid captured the strategic Rhine crossing at Wesel on 19 August. Fierce fighting at s'Hertzogenbosch culminated in the explosion of a huge mine under the main wall on 10 September. The garrison held out for another week before surrendering after five and a half months of heroic resistance.

Nassau-Siegen's corps was recalled and retreated to Duisburg. Wallenstein was keen to bring it back, having opposed intervention from the outset. The Dutch sent 12,000 men along the Rhine, capturing most of the remaining Spanish outposts. Spain's defeat was the most serious setback between the Armada and the battle of Rocroi in 1643.[19] It certainly deflated what little optimism remained in the country and prevented reinforcements being sent to Italy, contributing to the defeat there too. Work on the unfinished Fosse Eugeniana canal was abandoned. Many of the smaller garrisons had already been withdrawn from Germany in 1628, and Spain now dismantled Pfaffenmütze and handed over Lingen and six positions in Mark and Ravensberg to the Liga in July 1630, retaining only Düsseldorf, Orsoy, Rheinberg and the enclave of Gelderland between the Rhine, Liège and Jülich. The retreat sharpened the demarcation between the war in the Empire and that in the Netherlands.

Meanwhile, Philip IV overruled Olivares and authorized Isabella to reopen talks on a truce. Frederick Henry was prepared to negotiate, especially as a growing faction around the new pensionary of Holland, Adriaen Pauw, favoured peace. Both sides remained far apart, but at least agreed to make north-west Germany neutral ground: an arrangement the emperor and electors were happy to accept in 1630.[20]

MANTUA AND LA ROCHELLE

The Mantuan Succession

As Spinola had predicted, Olivares' decision to intervene in Italy weakened Spain's resistance in Flanders. The new conflict was a dispute over the Mantuan inheritance, which comprised Mantua itself and its dependency of Monferrato. Neither was very large or rich, but both were strategically located along the river Po, either side of Spain's duchy of Milan. Emperor Ferdinand in turn despatched an army over the Alps to uphold his jurisdiction over imperial Italy. Despite the involvement of the major powers, the causes were local and dynastic like those of the earlier Jülich crisis. War could have been avoided if either of the last Mantuan dukes had produced a legitimate male heir. The Gonzaga family tried to settle the inheritance question itself. Unfortunately, the best claim was advanced by their French relation, Duke Charles, who controlled the autonomous duchies of Nevers and Rethel in north-east France.

Charles was recklessly brave, impetuous and filled with a sense of his own destiny and Catholic zeal. He served as a volunteer at the siege of Buda in 1602 and founded the aristocratic international Christian Militia in 1616 that was involved in various conspiracies, including an attempt to depose Gustavus Adolphus. Like other French aristocrats, he found it difficult to reconcile his inflated sense of his own lineage with his subordinate status as vassal of the French crown. He was not going to let the opportunity to succeed to a sovereign principality pass by and sent his son to pre-empt the other claimants. The son married the niece of the dying Duke Vincenzo on 23 December 1627 with papal blessing. Vincenzo died just three days later, but the newly-weds had their supporters declare Charles duke before informing either Spain or the emperor. Charles arrived in Mantua on 17 January and sent an envoy to Vienna requesting imperial recognition.[21]

The coup disconcerted all the major powers, none of whom was looking for a fight in Italy. War followed because Spain and Ferdinand failed to control their officials on the ground, or coordinate a response, creating a rift that Richelieu exploited. Even then, conflict could have been avoided if Charles had compromised. He was distrusted in France, where Richelieu was preoccupied with the Huguenots until October 1628. Neither Spain nor the emperor wanted to fight France, and many believed the dévots would soon oust Richelieu anyway.

Formally, matters rested with Emperor Ferdinand, whose jurisdiction over northern Italy, as part of the Empire, made him the ultimate arbiter of the succession dispute. The Habsburgs had promoted the Gonzaga family to counter French and papal influence. Ferdinand had married Vincenzo's sister, Eleonora, in 1622, six years after the death of his first wife. Eleonora disliked Charles, but did not want her homeland devastated and so promoted his cause in Vienna. It was precisely this connection that made Richelieu think twice about backing him, since it looked as if Charles would join the Habsburg clientele. Ferdinand was reluctant to recognize him immediately for fear of alienating the rest of the Gonzaga who had served loyally during the Bohemian Revolt. He wanted Charles to compensate the Gonzaga for renouncing their claims and expected him to surrender the strategic fortress of Casale in Monferrato to imperial control. Above all, he wanted to exclude everyone else from the decision so as to assert his superior, imperial jurisdiction.

The earlier struggles over Monferrato made it clear that both Spain and Savoy coveted the territory. Spanish interference was especially unwelcome since it followed long efforts to supplant imperial jurisdiction over northern Italy. Already on 26 January 1628, Córdova, Spain's governor in Milan since 1627, had received the emperor's order not to

439

send troops to Mantua or Monferrato. Two months later, Ferdinand named Johann of Nassau-Siegen as commissar to sequestrate both territories pending a final verdict.[22] Nassau reached Milan on 17 May, by which time the situation had altered dramatically.

Cordóva had repeatedly warned Madrid of the impending crisis, but had received no instructions because Olivares was busy with the Dutch War. Left to his own devices, he decided to settle Spain's long-standing tension with Savoy at Mantua's expense and signed a pact with Duke Carlo Emanuele on 25 December to partition Monferrato, with Casale going to Spain. He wrote to Spain two days later requesting permission to occupy Monferrato in the emperor's name. Opinion was divided in Madrid, especially following Spinola's arrival in February, but the government inferred from Cordóva's letter that he already held Casale and so sanctioned the action.[23] In fact, Cordóva did not move until 29 March 1628, because the Army of Lombardy was undermanned. Only 10,000 men could be collected, while Savoy fielded 5,500. They soon overran their respective halves of Monferrato, but stalled before Casale where Charles's commandant called Cordóva's bluff when he claimed to have a letter from the emperor summoning the fortress to surrender. Cordóva was obliged to send to Genoa for engineers, artillery and a large loan to begin a formal siege.

The delay allowed Charles to collect 13,500 militia and mercenaries in Casale and Mantua, while another 6,600 under General d'Huxelles were raised on his French estates. Safe behind Mantua's walls, he rejected Spanish and imperial proposals to surrender Casale in return for recognition. Key figures in France still opposed intervention and the governors of Burgundy and the Dauphiné did their best to frustrate d'Huxelles' preparations. With his men deserting, d'Huxelles made a dash across the Alps towards Casale in August, but was caught and his army dispersed by Savoyard troops.

The Siege of La Rochelle

Despite his defiance, it was obvious Charles could not last long without assistance. This could only come from France, but Richelieu was fully engaged at La Rochelle, having decided to settle the problem finally with what the pope called 'the synagogue of Satan'. Control of the islands of Oleron and Ré allowed him to blockade the Rochellais whose plight attracted considerable sympathy in England. The arrival of the French Henrietta Maria as Charles I's queen intensified criticism of royal policy in general and the duke of Buckingham in particular. Buckingham sought to save his position by swinging behind the growing Franco-phobia, and he invested £70,000 from his own pocket to fit out a naval expedition to demonstrate British resolve and deter Richelieu from besieging La Rochelle. It was a major undertaking: at a time when Britain had only 145 ships over 200 tonnes, Buckingham found 115 vessels with 4,500 sailors and 7,000 soldiers.

He landed on Ré on 21 July 1627, intending to break Richelieu's blockade by capturing the island. The 3,000 royalist infantry simply retreated into their new citadel which had just been reprovisioned. The sandy island offered few resources and it became a question of who would run out of food first. Buckingham received 70 supply ships and 1,900 Irish reinforcements in September, but his situation continued to deteriorate. The French used a moonless night to ferry more food to their garrison who displayed fresh chickens impaled on their pikes the next morning to taunt the starving besiegers. Buckingham gambled everything on an assault on 6 November, only to find his soldiers had made their ladders too short and could not get over the wall. The 2,000 survivors were evacuated two days later. Buckingham had been typically overconfident, failing to prepare a back-up plan in case his initial landing failed to take the island. His presence merely compromised the Rochel-lais, providing Richelieu with an excuse to expand his blockade to a full siege. The cardinal arrived with the king and 15,000 fresh troops to start operations in September, building a 1,500-metre dam and sinking ships to block the harbour.[24]

The Rochellais remained confident under their determined mayor, Jean Gaiton. Henri de Rohan had raised 5,000 Huguenots in the Langue-doc, while Buckingham planned another relief effort. The British fleet arrived on 15 May 1628, but its admiral lacked the resolve to attack the barrier across the harbour. Tension mounted as Europe waited to see whether Cordóva could take Casale before La Rochelle fell to Richelieu. The British returned on 18 September and shelled the barrier without effect. By then it was really too late. The besiegers had risen to over 25,000 men, while famine gripped the defenders, reducing the city's population from 27,000 to 8,000. The siege was not as smooth as Richelieu's propaganda claimed, but he overcame significant practical problems and benefited from the general consensus among the Catholic elite that it was time to finish the Huguenots. The Rochellais surrendered unconditionally on 28 October, nearly four weeks after the British had sailed away.[25]

The fall of La Rochelle transformed the international situation, yet Richelieu hesitated to intervene in Italy after the failure there three years before. Intervention would require a large army and risk war with Spain. All parties made a last effort to persuade Charles de Nevers to accept a compromise, which he rejected since it was obvious Richelieu would lose face if Casale fell. The duke did all the right things to goad the cardinal, opening negotiations with the dévots and writing to say he would be obliged to become a Spanish client unless rescued.

Richelieu gambled, deciding to march from La Rochelle to relieve Casale, and then recross the Alps before the surviving Huguenots could recover. His objective was to save Casale, not secure the duke's full inheritance. It was still risky, since the French army numbered considerably less than the 40,000 or so he felt necessary for success. The king led 9,400 infantry across the Mont Genèvre pass on 28 February 1629, through snow drifts, to the defile at Susa where 4,000 Spanish and Savoyards blocked the way behind a six-metre high barricade. An assault carried the position at 3 a.m. on 5 March, the French losing more to avalanches than enemy action.[26] Savoy made peace two days later, which was confirmed in May when Louis XIII promised to recognize Carlo Emanuele's possession of his part of Monferrato in return for France's right to garrison Casale. Discouraged by the lack of support from Madrid and Vienna, Cordóva accepted this arrangement and lifted his siege on 19 March. Three thousand French reinforced the Casale garrison, while others now held Susa to guard the route over the Alps and ensure Savoy's good behaviour.

Having achieved Richelieu's objective, Louis XIII led the bulk of the army back over the Alps to deal with the Huguenots holding out in the Languedoc. All 3,000 inhabitants of Privas were killed or expelled after the town fell on 26 May in a deliberate attempt to break resistance. It worked and the Huguenots accepted the Grace of Alais (now called Alès) on 28 June, which confirmed their religious and judicial privileges but abolished what remained of their military and political autonomy. Rohan was permitted to go into exile to Venice. Richelieu capitalized on his success, playing up the king's heroic role and presenting the Alpine campaign and subsequent suppression of the Huguenots as a magnificent triumph that thwarted the monarchy's internal and external foes.

Imperial Intervention in Italy

This was all too much for Olivares who feared the world would think the loss of silver at Matanzas had so weakened Spain that it had been forced to acquiesce in Italy. The Council of State repudiated Cordóva's action and pressed the emperor to join Spain in ejecting the French from Casale and imposing their own settlement in Mantua. The Army of Lombardy was strengthened by calling in favours from Parma and Tuscany, as well as additional Neapolitan recruits, to give 18,000 men by September 1629 when Spinola arrived to replace Cordóva.[27]

Richelieu's bargain with Savoy infuriated Duke Charles who used the opportunity of French intervention to open a second front by striking from Mantua at Cremona in the eastern Milanese. Convinced of Charles's inflexibility, Ferdinand II now believed military intervention was the only way to uphold imperial authority over his Italian vassals. Count Merode had already occupied the Valtellina with an advance party of 5,000 in April 1629. Peace with Denmark allowed Ferdinand to despatch more troops in May and 30,000 under Collalto poured through the valley over the next two months towards Mantua, while the Spanish blockaded Casale. Savoy shifted with the new military balance and rejoined Spain. Though Collalto cooperated with the Spanish forces, diplomatic relations remained strained. Madrid failed to see that its assertiveness in Italy had forced the emperor to intervene to preserve his own authority, rather than because he wished to counter France. Moreover, the diversion of Collalto over the Alps lessened the likelihood of imperial assistance against the Dutch, which still remained Spain's primary goal.

The arrival of 7,000 Venetian auxiliaries failed to stop the Imperialists overrunning the Mantuan countryside by October, confining Duke Charles and 4,000 French, Swiss and Italians to Mantua itself. The town was surrounded on all sides by lagoons formed by the river Mincio and could only be reached by long, exposed bridges from the west, north and east, or crossings to the Isola del Te to the south. Though imperial troops captured the latter, the high water table flooded their trenches. Assaults across the S. Giorgio bridge from the east were repulsed with heavy losses, while the lagoons placed the siege batteries at too great a distance to be effective. Having boasted he would take the place in two weeks, Collalto was obliged to try to starve Mantua into submission. Spinola had no luck at Casale either and both armies were forced to relax their grip as winter set in.

Imperial intervention placed Richelieu in a difficult position. He would lose face if he abandoned Charles, but the 18,000 men massed on the Savoyard frontier in October had failed to deter the Habsburgs. Another expedition over the Alps would be extremely unpopular with the pro-Spanish dévots, while the French army was only half the size considered necessary for success. Nonetheless, Louis XIII advanced in February 1630 along the road immediately south of the Susa pass, capturing Pinerolo on 31 March and taking Saluzzo. The main Savoyard army was recalled from Casale to meet the French, only to be defeated at Avigliana just west of Turin in July. This success relieved the pressure on Casale, but Richelieu remained far from his objective. Disease carried off two-thirds of the 20,000 French troops by September, obliging them to suspend operations until reinforcements crossed the mountains.

Both Casale and Mantua were subjected to renewed close siege from May. Spurred on by France, Venice sent 17,000 troops to relieve Mantua, but these were routed by Gallas and Aldringen at Villabuona. The defenders' situation deteriorated rapidly thereafter. The plague had already appeared in Lombardy during 1629. After a lull over the winter, the outbreak grew more virulent with the warmer spring weather, especially in Mantua where the population of over 30,000 was swollen with refugees. By mid-July, only 700 soldiers remained fit for duty. Aware of their weakening condition, Collalto attacked across the bridges on 16 July, supported by additional troops in boats. Charles retreated into the Porto Fortezza citadel, but capitulated two days later.

Mantua was subjected to thorough pillaging. Collalto and Aldringen purloined the duke's fine art collection, while the booty was said to total 18 million ducats, or twice the annual revenue of the kingdom of Naples. At least 10,000 inhabitants died during the siege and no more than 9,000 remained in the city afterwards. The scale of the tragedy received little public acknowledgement. Charles simply accepted it as divine will and sought asylum in Rome; most contemporaries blamed his inadequate defence or the Venetians' lacklustre relief efforts, rather than the imperial commanders or their men who did the killing.[28] With Mantua

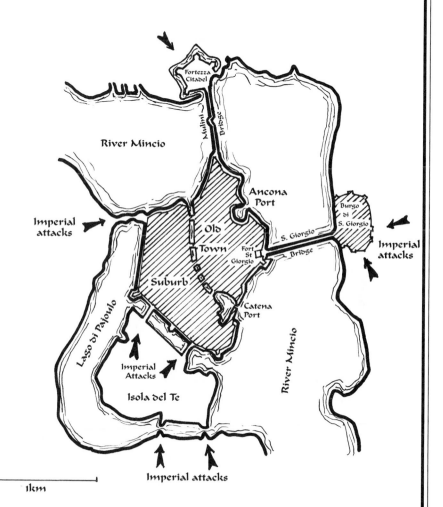

MANTVA

Fortezza
Citadel

Mulini
Bridge

River Mincio

Ancona
Port

Burgo
di
S. Giorgio

Imperial
attacks

Old
Town

S. Giorgio

Fort
St
Giorgio

Bridge

Imperial
attacks

Suburb

Catena
Port

Lago di Pajoulo

Imperial
Attacks

River Mincio

Isola del Te

Imperial attacks

1km

in imperial hands, it seemed merely a matter of time before Casale fell to Spinola.

THE EDICT OF RESTITUTION

Genesis

Imperial intervention in Italy was overtaken by events in Germany, where Ferdinand committed a grave error by issuing the Edict of Restitution in March 1629. Like much of his policy, this measure was intended to facilitate peace, but achieved the opposite. Far from capitalizing on his victory over Denmark, as his critics claimed, Ferdinand regarded the Edict as complementing the Lübeck talks to effect a general settlement of the Empire's problems. By providing the legal framework to recover ecclesiastical land, the Edict sought to restore harmony in the Empire by resurrecting what Ferdinand considered the true interpretation of the 1555 Peace of Augsburg. The goal was unrealistic and the method ill-advised. Above all, the process of restitution was impossible to detach from other measures to restore Catholicism, as well as the controversial land transfers, contributions and military demands that stirred well-founded suspicions in many Catholics as well as Protestants.

Restitution emerged from the general re-imposition of Catholic political and spiritual authority since 1620. The process became progressively controversial as it spread out from the Habsburg and Palatine lands to embrace wide swathes of Franconia and the Rhineland after 1623. The initial targets were the most vulnerable, like the Protestant Franconian knights who were obliged to expel pastors from their estates and resubmit to Bamberg and Würzburg's Catholic spiritual jurisdiction.[29] Troops were used in some cases to recover individual monasteries, but generally the former owners, or rather their heirs, petitioned the imperial courts to authorize restitution. Danish intervention temporarily disrupted this, but it resumed after the battle of Lutter and was placed firmly on the agenda in February 1627 when the bishops of Konstanz and Augsburg opened a raft of cases against Württemberg, the first major Protestant territory to be affected.

Many Catholics believed the time was ripe for decisive action to recover the millions of souls lost to heresy since the Reformation. The

446

near-unbroken run of Catholic victories since 1620 suggested that God was not only on their side, but summoning them to holy war. Events like the apparently miraculous survival of the three defenestrated officials, or the fall of La Rochelle, were interpreted as evidence of divine favour. Crucially, both Duke Maximilian's Jesuit adviser, Adam Contzen, and Ferdinand's confessor, William Lamormaini, ardently promoted this interpretation.[30] Lamormaini was the more influential, since he had the emperor's ear. Originally from Luxembourg, he joined the Jesuits aged twenty and rose rapidly at the Habsburg court, becoming rector of Vienna University in 1623 and the emperor's confessor a year later. He possessed none of Ferdinand's agreeable qualities and exceeded him in religious fundamentalism, coming close to the Protestant stereotype of the malevolent Jesuit conspirator. Forceful, wilful and austere, he was so jealous of his own status that he persuaded his superior general, Vitelleschi, to channel all Jesuit correspondence to Ferdinand through him. As calls for restitution gathered pace, Vitelleschi promised 2,500 masses a week to encourage Ferdinand to embark on what Lamormaini was proclaiming a 'glorious enterprise', oblivious to the fact that Spain's ill-fated Armada of 1588 had been called the same.

Such a heady atmosphere makes it difficult to distinguish political from religious motives, nor should we attempt to separate what contemporaries regarded as related. Nonetheless, the militants' goal of promoting Catholicism advanced only because it complemented political ambitions. Moreover, many senior clergy distanced themselves from Lamormaini's providentialism and urged greater restraint.[31] Ferdinand also hesitated and asked the Catholic electors for advice on 3 July 1627. They wanted to recover church property, not eradicate Protestantism. The elector of Mainz composed their response, which concentrated on the monasteries as these were mediate property and therefore less controversial than actual bishoprics. However, Maximilian urged the emperor to state that only adherents of the 1530 version of the Augsburg Confession could enjoy the benefits of the 1555 Peace. This would clearly exclude the Calvinists and was intended to prevent Frederick V recovering the Palatine lands and title. The electors thought Ferdinand would simply issue new guidelines to the imperial courts handling the petitions and accordingly agreed at Mühlhausen in October 1627 to let him devise a suitable text.[32]

News soon leaked from Vienna once the Reichshofrat began working on the document in January 1628. Protestant envoys requested clarification, but many accepted that restitution was not only likely, but lawful.[33] Despite some effort to consult Protestants, it is clear that Jesuit militants exercised disproportionate influence on the final text. The Reichshofrat's president, Imperial Vice-Chancellor Stralendorf, drew directly on arguments prepared by Paul Laymann, a leading theologian at the Jesuit University of Dillingen. Laymann's tract 'The way to peace' (*Pacis compositio*) concentrated on legal arguments synthesizing the extreme Catholic interpretation of 1555. The Edict was dated 6 March 1629, but was actually issued on 25 March, the day Laymann's work hit the stalls at the Frankfurt book fair.[34]

Consternation in the Empire

Whereas the electors and Protestants had expected guidance that would allow the courts to continue making decisions on a case-by-case basis, Ferdinand conceived the Edict as the definitive verdict. He felt he was responding to the calls from all parties to rule on what constituted the 'clear letter' of the 1555 Peace. This was impossible, because the strength of that document lay in its deliberate ambiguity. Ferdinand's Edict simply stated the extreme Catholic interpretation, excluding Calvinism and demanding the return of all land taken since 1552, including the bishoprics. Like the confiscations from 'notorious rebels', the Edict highlighted the controversy surrounding the imperial constitution. Though Ferdinand maintained the fiction that Mühlhausen had represented a judicial hearing, it remained highly contentious whether he possessed the power to make such a sweeping unilateral decision.

As a final verdict, the Edict was supposedly incontestable and all that remained was to implement it by recovering the archbishoprics of Magdeburg and Bremen, 13 north German bishoprics and over 500 monasteries, mainly in Lower Saxony, Württemberg and Franconia. The Reichshofrat duly appointed commissioners for each Kreis, generally selecting a local Catholic prince, assisted by Habsburg officials and army officers. Wallenstein and Tilly were already authorized on 24 March to use force if necessary.

The Edict was not a uniform attack on German Protestants, because the former church lands were unevenly distributed between them. Brandenburg and Saxony stood to lose three bishoprics apiece, but it was unclear whether these were protected by the Peace of Augsburg because their incorporation had been gradual, across the sixteenth century. The main victims were Denmark, which accepted its losses at Lübeck, and the Guelphs and others in northern Germany, as well as Württemberg where Catholics claimed fifty monasteries, representing a third of the duchy's wealth.[35]

It was not so much the scale of the potential losses as the fear that they might not be the limit that proved so alarming. Germany appeared to have returned to the dark days of Charles V's Interim. On reading a copy of the Edict, Magdeburg's mayor, Johann Dauth, remarked to his travelling companion that they were unlikely to see peace in their lifetime. The Protestant Swiss believed they would be next, thinking the imperial troops heading for Italy that summer had come to impose the Edict on them.[36]

Many Catholics were also dismayed. Predictably, Lamormaini was enthusiastic, writing to the pope that 'no Roman pontiff has received such a harvest of joys from Germany since the time of Charlemagne'. Urban's reply was carefully crafted, congratulating Ferdinand that 'heresy will have learned that the gates of hell do not prevail against the church ... and the arms of powerful Austria'.[37] This fell short of a full endorsement which Urban could not give without recognizing the validity of the 1555 Peace. The pope resented that his nuncios were excluded from supervising the restitution, as Ferdinand regarded this as a judicial, not a spiritual matter. Later, no doubt with hindsight, he declared he had never approved it.

More serious was the opposition in Spain and Vienna. Philip IV advised Ferdinand to 'find a more suitable outlet for his piety and zeal'.[38] Spain had long advocated concessions to the German Lutherans to pacify the Empire and win support for an alliance to deter France and others from assisting the Dutch. A concerted effort was made to remove Lamormaini, notably through the Capuchin Quiroga who arrived in Vienna early in 1631 as confessor to Archduke Ferdinand's wife, the Infanta Maria Anna. Ferdinand's trusted adviser Eggenberg retired to his estates, while Collalto protested that the controversy was undermining the Mantuan War. The chorus of complaint was joined by senior Habsburg clergy, like Bishop Wolfradt of Vienna and cardinals Pazmany and Dietrichstein.

Implementation

Wallenstein openly opposed the Edict, even writing to Johann Georg of Saxony to say so.[39] Imperial troops subjected Magdeburg to 28 weeks of close blockade from 29 March, but this had little to do with the Edict. The city resented the army's use of the Elbe to carry Bohemian grain, suspecting officers were using this as cover to undercut local merchants. The council appeared to lose control when the more militant burghers seized an imperial grain transport. Pastors like de Spaignart stopped short of openly defying the emperor, but their sermons contributed to the self-righteous, wholly unrealistic expectations gripping the local leadership. The councillors justified their refusal to accept a garrison by declaring that Emperor Otto had exempted their city from all military obligations 700 years ago – a claim that contradicted their parallel bid for imperial city status. Foolishly, given what was coming, they vowed 'they would rather die, than accept a garrison, and promised they would rather set fire to their houses and burn everything to ashes'.[40]

Wishing to avoid another Stralsund, Wallenstein displayed uncharacteristic patience and accepted Hanseatic mediation to defuse the situation. The city council was restructured, satisfying popular demands by replacing the co-option of councillors by direct election. Wallenstein dropped demands for a garrison and exempted the city from the Edict in return for 150,000 talers, to which the Hanseatic League contributed a further 50,000.[41] The Imperialists demolished their entrenchments, but maintained a loose cavalry cordon around the city monitoring those going in or out. Wallenstein did nothing to promote Ferdinand's project to install his younger son, Archduke Leopold Wilhelm, as archbishop. Eventually, the emperor formed a new, pliant cathedral chapter that deposed the Saxon Prince August and elected the archduke instead in May 1630.

In addition to the archbishopric of Magdeburg, imperial commissioners recovered from Protestant control the archbishopric of Bremen, the bishoprics of Verden, Halberstadt, Minden and Ratzeburg, 2 imperial abbeys and around 150 monasteries, convents and churches, including 50 in Württemberg and 30 in Wolfenbüttel. Swedish intervention halted restitution by autumn 1631, but it encountered serious difficulties long before that. The commissioners were expected to reverse local changes stretching back seventy years or more. Monasteries had often been demolished, or converted to other uses, while ecclesiastical land had been sold or built on. The original occupants were long dead, raising the question of who should receive their possessions now. The result was an unseemly scramble in which the Jesuits distinguished themselves by their rapaciousness. None of the former properties had belonged to them, but they felt uniquely entitled to them thanks to their special contribution to securing the Edict and more recent and active missionary zeal in Germany. Lamormaini's New Year gift to Ferdinand in 1630 was a list of ninety convents and houses he wanted. This demand started the 'monasteries controversy', lasting into the twentieth century as rival orders contested ownership.[42]

The orders also found themselves at odds with the bishops who had long resented monastic autonomy and wanted to incorporate the recovered property directly into their sees. Such infighting damaged Catholic prestige, as did blatant opportunism such as that of Johann of Nassau-Siegen, himself a convert only since 1613, who spread rumours that his cousins in Dietz had backed the Danes in order to establish grounds to confiscate their property. Such behaviour made it harder for those Catholics who sought amicable compromise with their neighbours.[43] Re-Catholicization frequently remained superficial. There were not enough monks, nuns and priests to look after the recovered properties. Protestant pastors were expelled and city councillors replaced, but generally with poorer, less-well qualified candidates.

The Protestant Response

Ferdinand's interpretation of the Edict as judicial rather than spiritual allowed Protestants to mount legal challenges that frustrated the objective of a clean, simple settlement. For example, Ludwig Friedrich of Württemberg had to relinquish monastic property, but petitioned the Reichskammergericht against claims to recover over a century of taxes the monasteries had paid since secularization. Ferdinand backed the duke of Württemberg's assertion of political jurisdiction over his lost monasteries, agreeing these were separated only from the Lutheran church, not the duchy. Such wrangling gave the local population a welcome excuse for disobedience as two or more prospective masters disputed lordship.

Ferdinand had badly misplayed his hand. The Edict alienated the moderate Lutherans, while fostering unrealistic expectations among militant Catholics. Having issued such an uncompromising statement, it was difficult to withdraw or modify it without weakening imperial authority. Johann Georg did his best to provide Ferdinand with an honourable way out, by stressing that the Peace of Augsburg was a treaty that could not be altered without mutual consent. Without directly attacking Ferdinand's judicial authority, the Saxon elector argued each case should be judged on its merits by the courts. He rejected appeals from Württemberg and other victims to link objections to the Edict with protests at Wallenstein's military contributions. Instead, he argued that pressure should be applied to persuade Catholics to moderate their demands and use less confrontational means to obtain them. This entailed closer cooperation with Brandenburg to present a united front. It was a difficult course to steer as Protestant militants mistook Saxon policy as a step towards a new confessional alliance, and their vocal lobbying made it harder for Johann Georg to convince Catholics of his good intentions.

Talks opened with Brandenburg in October 1629 and led to a joint summit in Annaburg in April 1630, accompanied by theological discussions to bridge Lutheran-Calvinist differences.[44] Johann Georg refused to table the issue of the Edict at the electoral congress convened by Ferdinand in July 1630, because it was too divisive. Instead, talks were pursued behind the scenes. The proposal to hold a Protestant convention in September was a device to pressure the Catholics to negotiate. Elector Anselm of Mainz was already receptive and advocated resuming Cardinal Klesl's old 'composition' programme of bilateral talks between Catholic and Protestant delegations. He seized on a Darmstadt suggestion not to challenge the Edict directly, but suspend its implementation for fifty years, leaving ecclesiastical possession as it had been in 1621. This came close to the compromise accepted in the Peace of Prague five years later and had a real chance of success. All three ecclesiastical electors were willing and even Duke Maximilian admitted in private he would accept it. The news alarmed zealots. Vitelleschi assured Lamormaini that 1,000 masses and 4,000 roseries were being offered each week to stiffen Ferdinand's resolve. Fatally, Maximilian then slammed on the brakes. He had used the issue to force Ferdinand to make concessions over Wallenstein's dismissal (see page 455 below). Once the emperor agreed, Maximilian withdrew support for the compromise. He later admitted it was a grave error and claimed he had been swayed by his Jesuit confessor to safeguard Catholic interests.[45]

Three issues stand out from the controversy surrounding restitution. First, the divisions among Catholics indicate the weakness of confessional solidarity and the primacy of politics over religion. Important Catholics opposed the Edict from its inception and not just when it became expedient to do so after Sweden's victory at Breitenfeld. Religious conviction certainly motivated the Edict's supporters who clung to its validity even after its political shortcomings became obvious, but it was the unrepresentative, hierarchical structure of imperial government that allowed this minority to put their views into practice.

Secondly, the Edict was a blunder of the first order. It did not precipitate Swedish intervention, since this had little to do with the plight of German Protestants, but it did ensure the door was wide open when Gustavus landed. The controversy wrecked any chance of extending the Peace of Lübeck into a general settlement for the Empire. Most Protestants had expected some form of restitution by 1627 and even accepted Catholics had valid claims in some cases. It is likely that most would have swallowed restitution of some mediate property and the loss of Magdeburg and Halberstadt, given their administrators' open support for the Danes. By insisting on wholesale restitution without adequate regard to individual circumstances, Ferdinand rendered the entire process untenable and increased the number of embittered German Protestants.

Thirdly, the controversy underscored the vitality of an Empire-wide political culture that continued to bridge confessional divisions. Even those who stood to benefit from the Edict doubted whether it was the proper way to recover their property. The majority favoured the traditional approach of judging each case on its merits, since this gave them the chance to validate their claims against potential rivals, as well as the current owners. Even militants recognized the strength of the constitution, basing the Edict on legal rather than spiritual arguments. Despite overwhelming military superiority, they refrained from wholesale seizure in favour of the judicial process. This also explains why the controversy perplexed the emperor: he genuinely believed he was acting within his constitutional rights. More significant still was the victims' response. Rather than rising in rebellion as the French grandees and Huguenots had done after 1614, the Empire's inhabitants lodged legal injunctions and negotiated for a compromise. Even the besieged Stralsunders considered it worthwhile to request assistance from the elector of Mainz.[46]

THE REGENSBURG ELECTORAL CONGRESS 1630

Wallenstein's Dismissal

The resilience of imperial political culture suggests we should not write off Ferdinand's attempt to settle the Empire's problems by meeting the electors in Regensburg in July–November 1630. The congress has been overshadowed by Gustavus's landing in Pomerania a few days after it opened, and the discussions in Regensburg are generally presented as governed by events beyond the Empire, marking the end of 'the German period of the war, and the beginning of the foreign period'.[47]

There is something in the charge of failure levelled at the emperor and electors who were unable to resolve the underlying constitutional and confessional problems, despite the solution offered by the parallel Mainz-Darmstadt peace initiative. The congress was nonetheless a significant demonstration of the Empire's collective purpose, attended by over 2,000 people. It opened amid widespread concern that Ferdinand had exceeded his authority. The emperor's ambitions were outlined in his demands, already circulated to the electors in April. None objected to his intention of extending Lübeck into a general settlement, but they were concerned at how he proposed achieving this. Ferdinand wanted to stabilize the Empire by removing further doubts over the Habsburg succession through the election of his eldest son, Archduke Ferdinand, as king of the Romans. The electors were not prepared to surrender this, their main leverage, while so many other issues remained unresolved.

Ferdinand's solution to the Empire's external threats was also defeated. The electors refused to sanction military assistance to Spain in the Netherlands or Italy, nor would the Catholics consent to the dissolution of the Liga and the amalgamation of its forces with Wallenstein's imperial army. Instead, the electors demanded Wallenstein's dismissal before they would consider anything. Several imperial advisers hesitated to take such a step, fearing the general would turn the army against

Vienna. Yet the seemingly all-powerful generalissimo proved surprisingly vulnerable.

Unlike Richelieu or Olivares, Wallenstein did not create a network of loyal followers at court. His reluctance to appear at important events, like Archduke Ferdinand's coronation as king of Bohemia in November 1627, alienated senior figures, notably the archduke himself who had never approved Wallenstein's generalship and considered himself a potential replacement. His distance from the court created room for misunderstanding, especially as his tendency to act on his own initiative aroused suspicions that he was exceeding his authority. He was poorly placed to counter the rumours that were deliberately fanned by Maximilian, who was being fed secret information by Capuchins at the imperial court.[48] Critically, the failure of the Baltic Design disillusioned Ambassador Aytona who swung from supporting Wallenstein to accusing him of always promising but never delivering assistance to Spain.

The criticism was already constructing the later historical image of Wallenstein as haughty, scheming and untrustworthy. A growing number of pamphlets appeared after 1625 drawing parallels with Lucius Aelius Sejanus, who had risen as adviser to the Roman Emperor Tiberius only to fall ignominiously from grace. Criticism of Wallenstein also provided a safe outlet for Protestant resentment, allowing Lutherans to cling to the hope that Ferdinand was really a benign monarch simply misled by evil advisers. Wallenstein's own vocal objections to both the Edict and the Mantuan War began to shake even Ferdinand's faith in his general. Finally, it was obvious he had lost his Midas touch. By May 1629 he was no longer able to pay the interest on de Witte's loans, forcing his banker to sell his own property and borrow at extortionate rates. Wallenstein's proposal to send troops back into Silesia to collect tax arrears indicated the threat this posed to the Habsburg monarchy.

Ferdinand agreed to dismiss his general on 13 August. He waited two weeks before sending envoys to tell Wallenstein, who had gone to Memmingen in southern Germany to be closer to the Mantuan operations. Matters initially remained unclear, because Ferdinand had not yet named a replacement and still expected Wallenstein to give advice. Wallenstein urged the emperor not to believe his critics and correctly predicted his removal would paralyse the army and prevent an effective response to the still limited Swedish intervention. Disgruntled, he then retired to his palace at Gitschin. The news plunged de Witte into despair.

With no hope of recovering his money, he drowned himself in the well of his Prague mansion on 11 September. The financial breakdown coincided with the onset of autumn when supplies grew scarce. The army's condition had already been deteriorating, from March 1630, when Wallenstein halved what officers could demand in contributions and then stopped further recruitment on Ferdinand's orders in April.

Army Reform

The question of Wallenstein's replacement was complicated by Maximilian's refusal to surrender Liga autonomy. Eventually, it was agreed on 9 November that supreme command rested with the emperor who would delegate it to Tilly, who was now named imperial lieutenant-general. The imperial and Liga armies would remain distinct, but now shared the same commander.[49] A real effort was made to address the problem of war finance. Wallenstein's system was abandoned in favour of a smaller, but more securely funded army. Imperial forces were to be reduced to 40,000, largely by disbanding the units still in Italy, while the Liga army was cut by a third to 20,000. All territories in the Empire were to pay war taxes according to the matricular system to total 96 Roman months a year, with two-thirds going to the Imperialists and the rest to the Liga. Each army was assigned specific regions for its winter quarters. Based on receipts of such taxes under Rudolf II, the emperor could expect 5.7 million fl. from the non-Habsburg parts of the Empire, assuming all territories paid their share. This would represent about a third of the previous burden. However, it was recognized that many territories would default, so Tilly was authorized to levy contributions to cover the shortfall. Elements of the old system thus persisted, and with them resentment of the imperial and Catholic presence. The arrangements also implied revising the constitution, reducing the Kreise to a framework for sustaining a permanent army under the emperor's exclusive control.

This unsatisfactory arrangement was dictated by imperial politics and had nothing to do with the Swedish threat. Tilly was the compromise candidate intended to balance imperial and Bavarian interests. His position was unenviable, since he answered to two masters with different agendas. Command remained decentralized because imperial units in Italy and the Habsburg hereditary lands remained under their own generals, as did the separate Liga corps in Westphalia that had been commanded by Anholt, but passed on his death in 1630 to Pappenheim. Pappenheim has entered history as a zealot after converting to Catholicism in 1614 and vowing six years later to suffer a wound for every year he had lived a heretic. His promise was kept at White Mountain where he was left for dead, earning the sobriquet 'Scarred Heinz' (*Schrammheinz*). His reputation suffered from his role in repressing the Upper Austrian Rebellion (in 1626) and the destruction of Magdeburg (1631). He was certainly ruthlessly ambitious, but his advocacy of bold action was intended to win the war quickly and he was free of many of the vices displayed by his contemporaries, notably his abstinence from alcohol.[50] His desire for an independent command suited Ferdinand of Cologne's security policy, but made Tilly's task more difficult.

Peace in Italy

The electors consistently opposed the Mantuan War, which appeared to be going well for Ferdinand. Casale still mounted a spirited defence, but it was obvious it could not hold out much longer. Under papal pressure, Richelieu sent his 'grey eminence', Father Joseph, and Brûlart de Leon to Regensburg in August. Alarmed by reports from Italy, the two envoys requested additional instructions from Richelieu, but received only confusing replies. Louis XIII was rumoured to be mortally ill and it was well known that the dévots were plotting to unseat the cardinal. Some see the negotiations as a missed opportunity, arguing that Ferdinand was overconfident and failed to offer satisfactory concessions to France.[51] Rumours of Italian principalities promised to Wallenstein and Collalto inaccurately reflected the emperor's aims. Ferdinand had already decided to compromise and offered generous terms to Father Joseph and Leon who accepted on 13 October. France and the emperor were to withdraw, Casale would be demilitarized, but Louis XIII could keep Susa and Pinerolo. Ferdinand would arbitrate the Mantuan dispute, promising to recognize Duke Charles provided he compensated his Gonzaga relatives and let Savoy retain part of Monferrato. Imperial jurisdiction was upheld, while all parties except Spain made modest gains.

Reinforced to 20,300 men, the French had resumed their advance in Savoy and were only a few kilometres from Casale when a dusty papal envoy, the future Cardinal Mazarin, arrived with news of the peace. The treaty appeared to snatch the fortress just as it was within Richelieu's grasp. Worse, his representatives had agreed that France would not assist the emperor's enemies. This standard expression of good faith threatened to constrict Richelieu's diplomatic options. The dévots urged ratification, eager for the long-awaited Franco-Habsburg rapprochement. To refuse seemed folly, yet acceptance would acknowledge Richelieu's defeat.

The crisis deepened with the king's illness and by 30 September he had received the Last Sacrament. It looked likely that Gaston d'Orleans would succeed his brother. The dévots and other anti-cardinalists met in Marie de Medici's Palais du Luxembourg on the afternoon of Sunday 10 November, and agreed to accept the Regensburg peace. Marie concluded the meeting by informing Richelieu she would have nothing more to do with him. Fearing for his life, he prepared to flee to Le Havre, but received an invitation to meet the king at the royal hunting lodge of Versailles. Arriving on 11 November, he found Louis fully recovered and was assured of continued royal support. It had been the 'Day of the Dupes'. The next morning, Louis signed warrants for the arrest of Richelieu's opponents. With his critics imprisoned or dispersed into exile, Richelieu could resume course and repudiated the treaty of Regensburg.

Spinola had suspended operations against Casale on 4 September in view of the Regensburg talks. Plague caught his army, killing him within the month. The failure to contain the Swedish occupation of Pomerania prompted the recall of the imperial troops to Germany, themselves also infected with the epidemic. Ferdinand was obliged to reopen talks on the Regensburg settlement, revising it as the Peace of Cherasco on 19 June 1631 without a promise from France not to aid his enemies. The Mantuan War had cost Spain 10 million escudos and there was no money left to contest the terms of the settlement. Charles de Nevers was installed as duke and promptly allowed France to station 2,400 men in Casale where they remained until 1652. Richelieu bullied Savoy into ceding Pinerolo permanently, holding this until 1696. The Peace of Cherasco still upheld imperial jurisdiction across northern Italy, but at the significant cost of souring relations with Spain.[52]

14

The Lion of the North 1630–2

SWEDISH INTERVENTION

Swedish Preparedness

Few could have predicted that Gustavus's landing at Usedom off Pomerania on 6 July 1630 would prolong the war another eighteen years. Sweden possessed the technical expertise and manpower for its invasion, but not the resources to sustain it. Gustavus was gambling his country's fortunes on the chance he could succeed where Christian of Denmark had failed and break south from his bridgehead. The 80,000 men conscripted since 1621 already represented a considerable drain on Sweden's population. There were 43,000 Swedes and Finns in the army and navy in 1630, as well as 30,000 foreign mercenaries, but no money. The 4,000 cavalry still in Prussia refused to move until they received their 16 months' pay arrears. Gustavus and Oxenstierna reckoned they needed 75,000 men to conquer the north German coast, plus another 37,000 to protect Sweden's existing possessions. They planned to attack with 46,000, but lack of transport reduced this to 13,600 who joined the 5,000 already in Stralsund. A second wave of 7,000 arrived in the summer, joining additional German recruits, but even in November the army mustered only 29,000, a third of whom were sick.[1]

This was more than Gustavus had commanded before, but whereas he previously faced the outnumbered Poles, he now confronted 50,000 imperial and Liga troops in northern Germany, with around 30,000 more to the west and south. Even without Wallenstein and in their present poor condition, they were formidable opponents. The disparity helps explain why, though concerned, the emperor and electors meeting at Regensburg were not unduly alarmed by his arrival. Gustavus was still to achieve his full fame that has clouded appreciation of the huge risk he was taking. The great run of victories from September 1631 suggests success was inevitable, and has led many military historians to conclude that the Swedish army was inherently superior. Morale was certainly high. To the Swedes and Finns, accustomed to the harsh conditions of the Polish theatre, Germany appeared a land of plenty, despite twelve years of war. The Finnish and Scottish contingents already had a fearsome reputation. Travellers' tales of strange Scandinavians had piqued interest that grew once Gustavus landed. Hamburg papers reported a contingent of ferocious Laplanders riding reindeer. The Finns were known as 'Hackapells' after their war-cry 'Hack 'em down!' They were said to possess magical powers to change the weather, or cross rivers without fords. Gustavus exploited this, always appearing accompanied by a detachment of Finnish cavalry and the equally exotic Scottish infantry. His propaganda claimed his men were inured to cold, never mutinied or ran away, survived on minimal rations and worked till they dropped.[2]

Gustavus had yet to face a 'western' opponent. His organization and tactics had been developed to fight the Poles, against whom success had been mixed. He was not an innovator but drew on existing practices, especially those of the Dutch.[3] Kirkholm (1605) and other defeats at the hands of the Poles led the Swedes to combine infantry, cavalry and artillery in close support. The famous lightweight leather artillery pieces designed to accompany the infantry were not new: they had been around since the fourteenth century. Nor were they particularly successful and they were abandoned after 1626 in favour of more durable bronze cannon mounted on light carriages weighing just over 280kg and firing a 1.5–2kg ball about 800 metres. These guns could be dragged by three men or one horse to keep pace with the infantry and increase their firepower.[4] The infantry deployed in brigades of three to four units (called squadrons) of 400 men each, mixed pike and shot, arranged in chequerboard formation for mutual support. Additional musketeers were detached to support the cavalry, sometimes also accompanied by the light cannon. Later writers stress speed and decisiveness, but in fact these tactics were defensive, developed to repel the superior Polish cavalry. The musketeer detachments were to help the cavalry disrupt an enemy attack through firepower and only then would the horsemen counter-charge. The infantry were trained by 1631 to fire by salvo, or general discharge, designed to maximize the psychological impact on the enemy prior to a counter-attack. Cavalry and infantry formations were thinned to only six ranks to increase firepower and extend their frontage to prevent their being outflanked. These tactics were largely unproven and the Swedes arrived in Germany having been routed at Stuhm, their last major engagement.

Strategy and Objectives

Hindsight also distorts assessment of Swedish strategy and aims. Gustavus's principal biographer presents Swedish expansion across Germany as a strategy that followed carefully planned stages intended to culminate in an invasion of the Habsburg hereditary lands. But the king in fact landed with a map that extended only to the Saxon frontier and when he reached that, he had his cartographers make a new one to cover the area to the south.[5]

The aims were also improvised. Certainly, Gustavus had long resolved on war and deliberately ignored chances to avoid it. Intervention in Germany had been considered in December 1627 when Oxenstierna managed to persuade the king to settle with Poland first, opening negotiations in February that concluded in the Truce of Altmark. Representatives were sent to the Lübeck conference, but were turned away since Sweden was not party to Denmark's war with the emperor. Denmark nonetheless sought to improve Swedish-imperial relations and the emperor sent envoys to Danzig in April 1630. Sweden consented to talks to alarm France into improving its alliance offer, and to demonstrate its alleged willingness to embrace peace. In fact, Oxenstierna had already spoken openly 'of the forthcoming campaign' to the English ambassador, Sir Thomas Roe, in January 1630.[6] The Council of State reluctantly agreed an offensive war in April, accepting Gustavus's claim that it was necessary to avenge the humiliation suffered by his representatives at Lübeck. The king strung the Danes and emperor along with various excuses to delay the Danzig talks before finally presenting totally unacceptable demands in June to ensure they collapsed just before his troops landed.

Gustavus expected the emperor to withdraw from northern Germany without himself evacuating Stralsund. Exactly what he wanted beyond this is a matter of conjecture, since he never presented Ferdinand with precise terms. Public statements, like his famous manifesto, were propaganda intended to justify intervention, not substantiate demands. Written by Salvius and published in German and Latin at Stralsund in June 1630, the manifesto went through 23 editions in 5 languages before the year was out. There were small but significant differences between the versions, reflecting how Sweden wished to present itself to different countries. Gustavus and Oxenstierna made contradictory statements, depending on their audience, while remaining careful not to commit themselves. Ideas were often floated in apparent jest to alarm or test the reaction of allies and enemies, such as the suggestion that Louis XIII might become emperor, while Richelieu could be pope.[7] The economic motives perceived by some later historians are hard to find. Little effort was made to integrate the German conquests into a Swedish-controlled market.[8]

Protestantism featured in domestic propaganda, but was omitted from the manifesto since intervention had to be presented as confessionally neutral so as not to alienate France. Having been disappointed in Frederick V and Christian IV, Protestant militants placed their hopes in Gustavus as their new saviour. A print issued shortly after his landing shows the king posed heroically in full armour, while his troops disembark in Pomerania. The hand of God reaches from a cloud to give him the sword of divine justice to smite Catholic tyranny. Many Catholics believed this. Abbess Juliane Ernst of the St Ursula convent in Villingen was convinced the duke of Württemberg and other Protestant princes had invited Gustavus 'for help so that they could get the monasteries back again'.[9] Gustavus did not intend this. Oxenstierna later admitted that religion was merely a pretext, while Gustavus said that if it had been the cause then he would have declared war on the pope.

The first real motive to be presented in public was 'security' (*Assecuratio*). All the threats cited in the manifesto were already receding: the imperial navy was laid up; Ferdinand had agreed to talks and was in the process of dismissing Wallenstein and reducing the army. What Gustavus wanted was to ensure the emperor was never in a position to pose a danger again. Swedish security thus lay in revising the imperial constitution to emasculate the emperor, and reversing the recent revival of Habsburg power, especially in northern Germany. The details changed with the nature and extent of Swedish involvement. Initially, Gustavus refrained from criticizing Ferdinand and did not declare war.

Instead, intervention was cloaked in the humanist argument of assistance to the repressed. This was an extremely weak position since, despite the best efforts of his envoys, Gustavus failed to persuade any Germans other than the Stralsunders to request his help.[10] His claim to the Swedish diet that a state of war existed since Arnim attacked Stralsund deliberately obscured how his envoys had bullied the city council into asking for help in the first place.

To counter Ferdinand's claim of unprovoked aggression, Gustavus championed German liberties. Swedish propaganda developed the idea that the Empire's internal balance was essential to European peace. Sweden was thus acting in Europe's best interests to restore the imperial constitution to its 'proper' state. German writers were liberally paid to articulate just what this was. The most influential was Bogislav Philipp Chemnitz, better known by his pseudonym Hippolithus a Lapide. His access to Swedish confidential papers makes his history of events after 1630 still valuable today. However, his interpretation of the constitution was deliberately partisan; the Empire was presented as an aristocracy with the emperor merely first among equals. Not surprisingly, his book was banned and symbolically burned by Ferdinand's hangman.[11]

The Swedes were far more reticent about their second objective of 'satisfaction' (*Satisfactio*), or recompense for their noble efforts. These territorial ambitions were present from the start, even if their scope changed with military fortunes. As soon as the Imperialists abandoned the siege of Stralsund, Oxenstierna renegotiated Sweden's position there into a formal protectorate. The Council of State decided in May 1630 to retain the town indefinitely. Having landed in July, Gustavus marched to Stettin and told the childless Duke Bogislav that Pomerania was his by right of conquest. This claim rested on Hugo Grotius's helpful recent book that implied that the Swedes could do as they pleased provided they treated conquered peoples humanely.[12] Gustavus told Bogislav to accept an alliance as a mark of special favour instead. The duke capitulated on 20 July, accepting Swedish command over his duchy and its maritime tolls. Article 14 of the agreement entitled Sweden to sequestrate Pomerania after the duke's death, though nominally only if the other claimants (principally Brandenburg) refused an amicable settlement. Though the Pomeranian Estates still hoped to recover their autonomy, the duchy had effectively been annexed.

The third objective was the *contentment* of the army, since it became clear that Sweden could not make peace without additional means to pay off its troops. Not anticipated in 1630, this was essentially already present in the desire to make war at Germany's expense. As one member of the diet remarked, 'it is better to tie the goat at the neighbour's gate than one's own'.[13]

Alliance with France

Gustavus had resolved on war well before he concluded his alliance with France. The alliance gave Sweden access to French influence in Germany, as well as annual subsidies of 400,000 talers. The arrangement was utilitarian. French interest in Sweden had been slight until 1629. Sweden had closer ties to Spain, still an important market for its timber and minerals, and it refused to become a party to France's war with Spain after 1635. Nonetheless, the Franco-Swedish alliance endured until the late eighteenth century and broadened the foreign cultural influence in a Sweden previously dominated by Protestant Germans and Britons.

Richelieu had pressed for the alliance against his envoy Charnacé's better judgment. Charnacé knew France would not be able to control the Swedish lion once it was let loose on Germany, but Richelieu wanted a counterweight to replace Denmark to check the Habsburgs. He needed Sweden to create a diversion, but wanted to disassociate France from the destruction this would cause. He was also concerned to safeguard Catholicism and insisted Gustavus guarantee freedom of worship in any German lands he conquered – something that was absent in the Truce of Altmark which had been followed by the suppression of Catholicism in Swedish-occupied Livonia and Prussia.

Richelieu's real interest was Bavaria, not Sweden. French assistance in arranging the Ulm Truce (1620) and support for Maximilian's new electoral title created a favourable impression in Munich. Richelieu saw Maximilian as a potential successor to Emperor Ferdinand and wanted an alliance with the Liga to neutralize southern and western Germany, and to prevent Austria assisting Spain. Maximilian's reluctance to break with the Habsburgs convinced Richelieu he had to deal with Sweden instead. He did not want to burn his bridges to Bavaria and insisted Gustavus promise not to attack Liga members. Gustavus was reluctant to have any constraints, but his failure to break out of Pomerania forced him to accept Richelieu's terms in the Treaty of Bärwalde on 23 January

1631. France would sponsor Sweden for five years, during which Gustavus would respect Richelieu's conditions and not agree peace without consulting him.[14]

Maximilian had already secured French guarantees to defend his electoral title in a treaty agreed with Richelieu's envoys during the Regensburg congress in November 1630. Richelieu reluctantly ratified this as the Treaty of Fontainebleau on 31 May 1631, even though it formally obliged France to defend Bavaria against all enemies, including Sweden, while freeing Maximilian from assisting France against the Habsburgs. Both parties recognized that the treaty was unenforceable, but regarded it as a statement of mutual good intentions.

BETWEEN THE LION AND THE EAGLE

The Leipzig Convention

Taking Stettin was easy compared to breaking out of Pomerania. The duchy was too small and poor to sustain a large army, and it proved impossible to collect sufficient troops to punch through the imperial cordon that repulsed attacks along the Oder to the east and Mecklenburg to the west throughout the rest of 1630. Success depended entirely on the German Protestant princes who were now caught between the Swedish lion and the imperial eagle. Gustavus was a largely unknown quantity. Knowledge of Sweden was slight. Rumours of its semibarbarous inhabitants appeared to be confirmed by Gustavus's harsh demands. As he told his Brandenburg brother-in-law, 'I don't want to hear about neutrality. His grace must be my friend or foe ... This is a fight between God and the Devil. If His grace is with God, he must join me, if he is for the Devil, he must fight me. There is no third way.'[15]

Yet the middle course was precisely what the majority of the Protestants wanted. Despite their horror at the Restitution Edict, most hoped Ferdinand could be persuaded to moderate his demands without recourse to violence. Saxony and Mainz had continued their talks and secured the emperor's permission for a cross-confessional 'composition congress' to meet in Frankfurt. Johann Georg meanwhile summoned the Protestants to a parallel convention in Leipzig that opened on 16 February 1631. All major territories sent representatives except Darmstadt, which backed Ferdinand, and Pomerania, which was prevented by Sweden. Despite Saxony's sponsorship of a rabidly anti-Calvinist jubilee to celebrate the Augsburg Confession the year before, Brandenburg continued to back Johann Georg. The new Brandenburg chancellor, Sigismund von Götz, told the convention 'the Swede is a foreign king who had no business in the Empire'.[16]

The ultra Lutheran Hoë von Hoënegg muted his earlier criticism of Calvinists and even hinted at the necessity of resistance. This was not a call for holy war, despite later claims to the contrary.[17] The convention's concluding manifesto on 12 April envisaged an army of 40,000 funded by diverting the payments agreed in Regensburg the previous November from the imperial army. This was not a confessional alliance. There was no reference to acting on God's higher authority. Instead, it was to 'uphold the basic laws, the imperial constitution and the German liberties of the evangelical Estates'. It was certainly not 'a stupid plan'.[18] By rallying the Protestants into a neutral block, Johann Georg increased their collective weight. Maximilian appreciated this and the Liga congress at Dinkelsbühl agreed in May to moderate implementation of the Edict, while the delegates in Frankfurt continued to discuss Darmstadt's suggestion to suspend it for fifty years.

Nonetheless, Johann Georg's legitimist line cost him much sympathy among those still burdened with imperial and Liga billeting. The Swedish landing meant the cancellation of the troop reductions agreed at Regensburg, and though its effective strength was still lower than under Wallenstein, the army remained expensive. Much depended on Ferdinand's response, but he offered little. The Swedes' unspectacular performance since their landing fostered a false confidence that was sustained by the prospect of units returning from Mantua to reinforce Tilly. Ferdinand's obstinate refusal to accept the way out offered by Johann Georg compounded the error of the Edict.

The lack of concessions convinced some they had no choice but to join Sweden. These activists comprised the usual suspects: the fugitive Mecklenburg dukes, Wilhelm and Bernhard of Weimar, Württemberg, Hessen-Kassel and Margrave Friedrich V, son of the outlawed paladin Georg Friedrich of Baden-Durlach. Hessen-Kassel was bankrupt and faced disintegration as the local knights negotiated with Ferdinand to escape its jurisdiction. The Leipzig manifesto provided a convenient cover to collect troops. Together with the Weimar brothers, Landgrave

Wilhelm V assembled 7,000 men in his fortresses of Kassel and Ziegen-hain. He stopped paying contributions to the now much-reduced Liga occupying forces and blocked supplies intended for Tilly's garrison in the archbishopric of Bremen, pushing it close to mutiny. Regent Julius Friedrich of Württemberg packed his young charges, Duke Eberhard III and his two brothers, off on a grand tour and put their mother into Urach castle for safety, while his militia began evicting imperial garrisons. Talks were opened with his Franconian neighbours who assembled 2,600 men, mainly in Nuremberg.[19]

All remained cautious, reluctant to side openly with Gustavus until he proved himself capable of defending them against imperial retribution. Moreover, most still looked to Elector Johann Georg to take a more forceful stance and compel Ferdinand to accept their demands without having to join a foreign invader.

The Siege of Magdeburg

Only Christian Wilhelm, the dispossessed administrator of Magdeburg, declared for Sweden. He slipped past imperial sentries into Magdeburg where he stormed the town hall on 27 July 1630 with a handful of supporters. The cathedral canons and the city councillors had placed their hopes in Saxony. Christian Wilhelm's arrival forced their hand and they duly agreed a Swedish alliance. To ensure they did not change their minds, Gustavus sent Colonel Falkenberg, disguised as a boatman, into the city where he took command in October. The Imperialists under Pappenheim soon chased the civic guard and militia back inside the city walls, but with only 3,000 infantry he could not begin a siege.[20]

Tilly wanted to mount an offensive to drive Gustavus into the sea, but Maximilian refused since this would require Liga units to fight the Swedes, challenging the Bärwalde treaty of January that the king published deliberately for this reason.[21] Pappenheim was sent 7,000 reinforcements to tighten the grip around Magdeburg instead. Gustavus could not afford to let the city fall, since it would deter potential allies. He planned to have 100,000 men by the beginning of 1631, but in fact mustered only 20,000 field troops, a third of whom were sick, plus 18,000 in garrisons. The shortfall could be made up only by German recruits, who would not join unless he scored a major success. A surprise Swedish offensive chased the Imperialists from Gartz and Greifenhagen, securing the lower Oder on 5 January. However, the Brandenburg garrison at Küstrin blocked his advance upstream, while Tilly dashed with 7,500 reinforcements from Halberstadt, covering 320km in ten days, to rally the demoralized imperial troops.

Thwarted, Gustavus retraced his steps, carefully avoiding Brandenburg to head west across Pomerania into Mecklenburg, where he took Demmin on 25 February. Tilly rushed after him, storming Neubrandenburg on 19 March. A third of the 750 Swedish defenders died during the assault. To sway opinion at the Leipzig convention, propagandists presented it as a massacre during a church service.[22] Realizing his troops were outnumbered, Tilly fell back to Magdeburg, raising the besiegers to 25,000. Another 5,000 were posted at the Dessau bridge, while Ferdinand of Cologne collected 7,000 reinforcements in Westphalia and Maximilian and other Liga members mustered a further 8,000 at Fulda. Peace in Italy allowed Ferdinand to recall the 24,000 men from there, who began re-crossing the Alps in May.

These numbers precluded any direct relief for Magdeburg, so Gustavus left a few men to help the Mecklenburg dukes besiege the remaining imperial garrisons in their duchy, and marched east to the Oder again with about 18,000 soldiers. He stormed Frankfurt on the Oder on 13 April, killing 1,700 of the 6,400-strong garrison as a reprisal for the alleged atrocity at Neubrandenburg. Landsberg was taken two weeks later, securing eastern Pomerania and the lower Oder for the Swedes.[23]

Tilly refused to be distracted from his siege of Magdeburg that got under way when he took the outworks on 1 May. The suburbs fell two weeks later. The defenders had only 2,500 regular troops, backed by 5,000 armed citizens of whom only 2,000 were adults. The population numbered around 25,000, already reduced by a plague outbreak five years before and the city's long-term economic decline. Many of the city councillors were lukewarm about the Swedish alliance and pressed Falkenberg to accept Tilly's repeated offers for honourable surrender. Falkenberg continued to insist that Gustavus was coming, even though he was still 90km away at Potsdam when Tilly launched his final assault at 7 a.m. on Tuesday 20 May. Pappenheim had distributed a wine ration to the besiegers to boost morale. At a pre-arranged signal, 18,000 imperial and Liga troops converged on the city from five directions.

The following events are well-documented by several gripping eye-witness accounts. These need to be treated with care. The best-known is that by Guericke, a councillor keen to shift the blame onto Falkenberg and the clergy, while exonerating his colleagues who subsequently seized power.[24] Falkenberg was taken by surprise, having expected Tilly to continue negotiations and he was still arguing with the councillors in the town hall when the Imperialists broke in around 8 a.m. Several councillors left to find their families. Defence was hindered by a shortage of ammunition, but those on the walls put up stiff resistance. Two companies of Croats rode through the low water by the river bank to sneak through a side gate on the poorly fortified Elbe front, spreading panic. The infamous fire started at this point, sparking a controversy that burned far longer and almost as brightly into the twentieth century. Some Protestant propagandists created the myth of the Magdeburg maiden who immolated herself rather than surrender, while others simply blamed the Catholic commanders. Gronsfeld, who had no axe to grind, reported that Pappenheim told him he had ordered a house set on fire to drive out some musketeers who were preventing his men entering the city. Others present similar stories and it seems certain the conflagration was an accident, especially as the whole purpose of the siege was to capture the city intact.[25] The fire spread quickly once it reached an apothecary's house used to store gunpowder, and the city was fully ablaze by 10 a.m.

Resistance collapsed on the northern front, letting Pappenheim's column in. Once they were in the city, the other sectors collapsed as well. Falkenberg died relatively early on. The inhabitants began barricading themselves in their houses as soon as they saw the defenders leave the walls. Tilly entered and ordered his men to stop plundering and extinguish the fires. Many of the troops were out of control, but enough remained under orders to save the cathedral where 1,000 people had sought shelter. The Premonstratensians also protected 600 women in their monastery which also escaped the flames, but it proved impossible to save more as the wind fanned the fires, destroying 1,700 of the city's 1,900 buildings. Even Catholic accounts admit the violence continued for several days. The monks saw six soldiers rape a twelve-year-old girl in their courtyard. Despite her death, they were too frightened to report it, until finally one of them went to Tilly, but it proved impossible to identify the perpetrators.[26]

Councillor Daniel Friese escaped by changing into old clothes so he would not be taken as a rich man worth holding for ransom. His house was nonetheless ransacked. Some soldiers were simply happy just to find a new pair of shoes. Others became violent if they could not find anything more valuable. Friese survived by staying with his family in the attic, until his maid tried to join them from her hiding place in the coal shed just as a fresh party of plunderers appeared. By this point, there was nothing visible left to take and the men began beating him until his toddler son approached a soldier and offered his pocket money. According to his eldest son, the soldier 'immediately changed and turned to us in a friendly rather than a cruel manner. He looked at us children as we stood about him and said: Aye, what fine little lads you are!' The soldier helped them escape to the imperial camp, where his own wife was greatly annoyed to find he had not brought booty instead. The family had managed to secrete a few valuables away and paid their way out of the camp three days later.[27] This was not an isolated case amid the horror, and other soldiers helped civilians, including clergy, to escape.

Around 20,000 defenders and civilians died, along with at least 300 besiegers killed during the assault in which another 1,600 were wounded. There were too many bodies to bury, so most were thrown into the river. Most died in the conflagration, or were suffocated hiding in their cellars. A census revealed only 449 inhabitants in February 1632 and a large part of the city remained rubble until 1720. The disaster became a defining event in the war and did much to shape its subsequent interpretation as a benchmark for brutality. At least 205 pamphlets describing the city's fall appeared in 1631 alone, and later massacres, including the Cromwellian atrocities at Drogheda and Wexford in 1649, were immediately compared to Magdeburg.

The End of Neutrality

Ferdinand moved against the other Protestant militants before Magdeburg fell. An imperial decree annulled the Leipzig manifesto on 14 May and ordered the signatories to disband their troops. The units returning from Italy were already in place at Lake Constance to begin enforcement. They rapidly overran Württemberg before the Franconians could arrive. Outnumbered, the Württemberg regent surrendered on 24 July, agreeing to resume contributions to an imperial garrison. The Franconians capitulated soon after as Aldringen arrived with the main force from Württemberg. Magdeburg's fall freed Tilly to turn on Hessen-Kassel, but he waited until he received imperial authorization. Landgrave Wilhelm prevaricated when summoned to disband his men, but was saved by Gustavus whose advance across the Elbe forced Tilly to turn back on 19 July. Since his refusal to disarm placed him clearly against the emperor, Wilhelm openly declared for Sweden on 27 July.

His support mattered little unless Gustavus could win over Brandenburg and Saxony whose prestige would convince others to follow. While Tilly's troops stormed Magdeburg, Gustavus's men blockaded the Brandenburgers in Küstrin and advanced on Köpeneck to force Georg Wilhelm to negotiate. As Württemberg was invaded and Hessen-Kassel threatened, Gustavus massed 26,000 men outside Berlin and trained his artillery on the electoral palace. Georg Wilhelm capitulated on 20 June, agreeing to pay regular contributions and let the Swedes occupy most of Brandenburg. Gustavus also pressed Georg Wilhelm to marry his son, Friedrich Wilhelm, to Princess Christina, but the elector hesitated, aware this was a device to usurp his claims to Pomerania.[28]

The king sent Åke Tott with 8,000 men to complete the conquest of Mecklenburg, and then concentrated 16,000 men in an entrenched camp at Werben. Tilly approached, having collected the units he had left around Magdeburg. Maximilian was unable to prevent clashes between Liga units and the Swedes and these gave Gustavus an excuse to ignore Richelieu's restrictions. Tilly got the worst of the skirmishing in the scorching heat of late July and early August, but his losses were only a fraction of the 7,000 claimed by Gustavus who was obliged to magnify the slightest successes in his relentless campaign to win allies. He still had fewer than 24,000 men in his main army, whereas Fürstenberg arrived from south Germany to bring Tilly's troops up to 35,000, while another 24,000 were on their way, in addition to the men still collecting at Cologne.

The breakthrough came when Elector Johann Georg, having waited until the last possible moment, abandoned his neutrality. Ferdinand and Maximilian had refrained from condemning Saxon military preparations that now totalled 18,000 men and instructed Tilly not to infringe Saxon territory. Even the action against Hessen-Kassel had been delayed out of consideration for Johann Georg, and Tilly's advance guard had merely plundered the border rather than attack the landgrave's troops. Throughout, imperial diplomats sought to win Saxony by offering concessions over Lusatia. Maximilian was also prepared to accept tactical concessions over the Edict and backed the Frankfurt composition congress that was still in progress.[29] Finally, Tilly was authorized to advance to the Saxon frontier and demand supplies to lend weight to diplomacy. When this failed, imperial troops invaded, disarming the electoral garrison in Merseburg on 5 September. The failure of the Protestants to pay war taxes since April had caused considerable problems. With his army swollen by reinforcements, it was imperative for Tilly to leave the devastated area around Magdeburg and enter fertile Saxony. He pushed on to Leipzig, which surrendered on 15 September. Though he had begun to burn Saxon villages, he still hoped to reach an agreement, but the elector had opted for Sweden instead on the 12th.

The decision was applauded by Protestant observers. Broadsheets that had been circulating with Gustavus's image were reissued to show the elector riding alongside him. However, the move represented a change in tactics, not policy. The elector had no enthusiasm for the king's grandiose schemes and refused to see it as a religious war. His alliance was simply intended to increase the pressure on Ferdinand to make peace on the basis of restoring the pre-war situation. Despite their willingness to talk, the Catholics had not given enough ground. Their intransigence would cost the Empire dear, because it was clear that an agreement was close. Already by mid-November, six theologians consulted by Ferdinand admitted it would be preferable to annul the Edict than risk the Empire's ruin. By then, however, it was already too late.[30] It is uncertain whether the Swedes appreciated how widely Saxon aims diverged from their own. The alliance was nonetheless crucial and they granted the elector far wider autonomy than that accorded to any other German partner.

The Battle of Breitenfeld

Gustavus crossed the Elbe at Wittenberg and moved south to join the elector at Düben, north-east of Leipzig. The 16,000 Saxons present were resplendent in new uniforms and included 1,500 of the local gentry and their retainers. They outshone the 23,000 Swedes who 'having lyen over-night on a parcell of plowd ground, were so dusty, they looked out like kitchen-servants, with their uncleanely Rags'.[31] The Swedes were 'old experimented blades', whereas the Saxons had been drilling only since April. Their commander, Arnim, joined once his own master,

Georg Wilhelm of Brandenburg, had also accepted the Swedish alliance in June. The combined force was the largest Gustavus had yet brought together and he was determined to strike the decisive blow he hoped would finally persuade the German Protestants to join him. Tilly was equally resolved to fight, finally free to pursue the offensive strategy he had advocated since the beginning of the year.[32] His masters were also determined, recognizing that only a clear victory would deter others from following Brandenburg's and Saxony's example.

The two sides converged on a relatively broad plain by the village of Breitenfeld, just north of Leipzig for what would be the second biggest battle of the war and one of the most important. Tilly had around 37,000 men with 27 guns, meaning he was both outnumbered (by over 1,000) and outgunned (by at least 29 pieces). The 7,000 Imperialists under Fürstenberg had only just arrived and were still tired, but morale was high as the men 'had an invincible courage, believing they would be victorious'.[33] Tilly drew up his troops on a slight rise running east to west along the edge of the plain. The infantry were deployed in twelve large blocks, grouped in threes with two further battalions posted on either flank to support the cavalry. Around 4,000 of the latter were on the left under Pappenheim who had the cream of the imperial cuirassiers. Fürstenberg commanded around 3,100 Liga heavy cavalry and 900 Croats on the right. Another 1,000 men had been left holding Leipzig.

The Swedes and Saxons had camped about 8km to the north and skipped breakfast to advance early on 17 September with the morning sun in their eyes. It took several hours to cross a marshy stream and arrive within cannon shot of Tilly, and it was not until about midday that the Swedish artillery began to reply to the imperial guns that had already opened up from their positions in front of the infantry. The artillery duel lasted two hours, with the deeper imperial formations sustaining heavier casualties. Gustavus deliberately kept his own army separate from the raw Saxons who were deployed in a relatively deep formation east of the Leipzig–Düben road. The Swedes formed up to the west, with General Horn commanding the cavalry immediately next to the road, then seven infantry brigades in two lines with Gustavus and the rest of the cavalry on the extreme right opposite Pappenheim.

Gustavus extended his troops further west, intending to outflank the Imperialists. Seeing this, Pappenheim charged around 2 p.m., but was repulsed by a general salvo from the 2,500 Swedish troopers who were

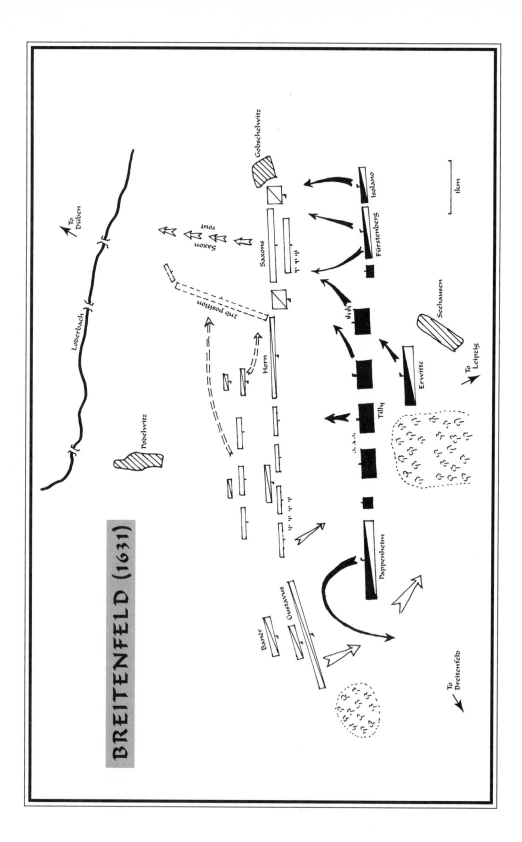

BREITENFELD (1631)

stiffened by 860 musketeers. Pappenheim's cuirassiers rode forward another seven times, closing to within pistol range and each time they got the worst of the exchange. Meanwhile, Fürstenberg bore down on the Saxons, sending Isolano's Croats to wheel round their flank. Despite being shaken by the artillery bombardment, the Saxons offered initial resistance, until the gentry levies took to their heels. Two cavalry regiments containing the elector's only experienced soldiers remained to join Horn. The rest fled, taking Johann Georg with them and losing 3,000 men, mainly in the pursuit.

By now it was becoming difficult to see what was happening as gun smoke was thickened by the dry dust stirred up by thousands of feet and hoofs. Fürstenberg was unable to rally his troopers, many of whom were pursuing the Saxons, or plundering their baggage. His rapid advance had outstripped the infantry that reached the former Saxon position only around 3.30. Horn had time to regroup along the road at right angles to the rest of the army, reinforcing his front with infantry from the second line of the centre. The imperial and Liga infantry were sent forward piecemeal as they arrived while Horn's fresh cavalry soon dispersed Fürstenberg's tired troopers. Worse, Tilly's right had to swing east to face Horn's new position, opening a gap between it and Pappenheim. After two hours of fruitless attacks, Pappenheim's men were exhausted. They were routed when hit by Gustavus's counter-attack, exposing the overstretched imperial centre. This came under attack around 5 p.m., just as Tilly's right began to collapse. The battered infantry retreated in good order to make a last stand at a wood behind their original position. Resistance collapsed at dusk once the Swedes dragged their artillery within range. Around 6,000 were taken on the field, and a further 3,000 fugitives surrendered at Leipzig the next day. Well over 7,000 lay dead, while many of those who escaped were wounded, including Tilly. Others deserted, and Tilly was able to collect only 13,000 survivors at Halberstadt a few days later. The Swedes lost 2,100 men, but more than made up for this by pressing the imperial prisoners into their army.

At last, Gustavus had achieved the spectacular victory that had eluded him since his landing. Protestant propagandists were swift to trumpet the success as a general call to arms, citing it as divine retribution for the sack of Magdeburg. Breitenfeld was the first major defeat of Catholic forces since the beginning of the war and it cemented the militants' faith in Gustavus as their saviour. Later commentators have regarded it as the inevitable outcome of an allegedly superior military system.[34] Certainly Tilly's deeper formations contributed to the Imperialists' heavier casualties, but the real failings were in the command and control of such large numbers, which created the opportunity for Gustavus's decisive counter-attack.

THE SWEDISH EMPIRE

A New Alexander

Breitenfeld transformed the image of the Swedish king. Protestant opinion lost its earlier caution and assumed a more militant tone; by the middle of the following year he was routinely presented as a new Joshua. Hero-worship spread among the devout. Sir Thomas Roe grew his beard and moustache to copy the king's style. However, many were disappointed he did not use the opportunity to negotiate peace.[35] A pagan undercurrent hinted at his real motives. As Gustavus reached southern Germany speculation mounted that he would cross the Alps and sack Rome like the Goths had done in AD 410. Sweden already made much of its Gothic heritage to present itself as an empire equal to any European monarchy. Humanist pseudo-history claimed Swedish derived from Hebrew and that the country had been founded by Noah's grandson after the Flood, making it the oldest in the world. Gustavus appeared at a tournament celebrating his coronation in 1617 dressed as a Goth. Some went further to suggest he was a new Alexander, implying that, far from restoring German liberty, he was seeking his own *Imperium Macedonicum*.

Tilly retreated rapidly westwards through Westphalia, then south across Hessen into Franconia to join his long-awaited reinforcements, giving him 40,000 men. Another 20,000 Imperialists were massing in Silesia, while a few more were still returning from Italy. Direct pursuit was no longer an option for Gustavus, while a push up the Oder into Austria was out of the question. Still unwelcome in much of Protestant Germany, the Swedes knew it would be almost impossible to operate in the hostile Habsburg lands. Gustavus decided to swing south-west instead, through Thuringia, to seize as much land as possible before

476

winter closed in. This would enable Wilhelm of Hessen-Kassel to join him, and possibly Württemberg and other south Germans too.

Opposition proved unexpectedly weak. Erfurt fell on 2 October. Würzburg was next, surrendering on 15 October. Capital of the rich bishopric of that name, Würzburg was particularly strong thanks to the Marienberg fortress perched on a steep hill across the Main from the town. The garrison's pleas for mercy were answered by cries of 'Magdeburg quarter' during the assault.[36] After a brief rest, Gustavus surged down the Main, taking Frankfurt and then crossing the Rhine at Oppenheim to capture Mainz on 23 December. Much of the Lower Palatinate right of the Rhine was conquered over the next two weeks, including Heidelberg. A second, smaller army meanwhile completed the conquest of Mecklenburg, before crossing the Elbe into the Guelph lands.

Sweden's Allies

These conquests determined the structure of Sweden's presence in Germany until the end of the war, establishing four elements: allies, the Baltic bridgehead, strategic bases and German collaborators. Allies were essential, but represented a weak link. Gustavus insisted on 'absolute direction' over his partners, but found this hard to maintain. The Saxons were the most important. Their poor performance at Breitenfeld obscures their potential. Having rallied his scattered troops, Johann Georg continued recruiting, mustering 24,000 men by 1632. These were backed by around 13,000 Brandenburgers and a few thousand cavalry raised by the 200 Bohemian and Moravian exiles who had joined Sweden since 1630. Even after deducting garrisons, this was a potent force.[37] Arnim crossed into Bohemia on 1 November 1631, entering Prague two weeks later in a move that eased Gustavus's victorious advance by compelling Ferdinand to recall 18,000 men from Tilly's army.

This display of Saxon belligerence was simply to force Ferdinand to negotiate. Since Johann Georg knew any viable peace would fall short of militant Protestant expectations, he wanted to negotiate from a position of strength. This way, concessions at Protestants' expense would appear magnanimous gestures. These intentions were concealed, but the choice of Arnim as commander had already raised Swedish suspicions. When the Bohemian exiles trashed one of Wallenstein's castles, Arnim wrote to his former chief to apologize. Contacts developed through Kinsky and other, less vindictive Bohemians and continued until Wallenstein's death.[38] All parties were careful not to commit themselves and what they did write down was often a ploy to compromise the other side. As a result, it is impossible to identify the protagonists' true motives. Some have speculated that Wallenstein was already disaffected by his dismissal and deliberately sabotaged Tilly's command by withholding grain in Mecklenburg and Friedland. While he did little to help Tilly, it seems unlikely that he was motivated by revenge.[39] Led by Count Thurn, the exiles were prepared to let him keep his estates and even make him king of Bohemia if this would help them recover their former possessions. Wallenstein played along because this offered the emperor a useful conduit to Saxony and Sweden. Sweden and France encouraged discussions of a possible Bohemian crown in 1633 to entice him to defect and gather incriminating evidence should he remain loyal. With Sweden refusing to discuss peace, Wallenstein pinned his hopes on an understanding with Saxony through Arnim and the exiles. Ferdinand knew of these discussions, even if he remained in the dark about their precise content. Agreement with Saxony had been his objective all along and it is against this background that we should see the wide powers granted to Wallenstein upon his reinstatement as imperial commander at the end of 1631 (see below, p.492).

News of Arnim's contacts leaked out as he met Wallenstein several times, while Wallenstein's former assistant, Franz Albrecht of Lauenburg, arrived in Dresden early in 1631. Gustavus was sufficiently alarmed to forbid any further mediation by German princes, but this did not stop Johann Georg's clandestine correspondence. Saxon operations continued to lend weight to the negotiations. Arnim would sit apparently idle for months, only to make a sudden aggressive move if Johann Georg's position was slipping. There was little Gustavus could do. Open criticism would shatter the façade of Protestant unity and alienate Brandenburg which, though much weaker, was his rival over Pomerania. The king had taken a considerable risk advancing to the Rhine, because this left defence of the Oder and communications to the Baltic resting on the two lukewarm electors.

By contrast, Hessen-Kassel was more committed to the Swedish cause because Ferdinand's intransigence had left Wilhelm V little choice. Ruling the largest secular principality not yet an electorate, the landgrave was ambitious and backed Gustavus's plan to revise the imperial constitution. Wilhelm proposed redistributing the three ecclesiastical electoral titles to secular princes, clearly expecting to be one of the beneficiaries. Able to field around 10,000 men, Wilhelm had some weight as an ally, having already helped to capture Mainz, and was the only one to be promised extensive territory by Gustavus. In return for ceding Marburg to Darmstadt, whose neutrality Gustavus accepted, Wilhelm was to receive most of the Westphalian church land.[40] The danger of such an arrangement was soon apparent, as the Hessians concentrated on conquering these areas rather than helping the Swedes.

Gustavus treated the Palatinate with far less consideration. Like Denmark, he viewed the Palatine cause as a way to obtain British assistance. The failure of the Ré expedition and Buckingham's subsequent assassination deepened that country's domestic crisis. The birth of the Prince of Wales – the future Charles II – lessened the dynastic imperative of backing the Winter Queen and her children, since Charles I now had his own heir. He returned to his father's policy, patching up relations with Spain in November 1630 in the hope that this would effect at least a partial Palatine restoration. His sister grew impatient, urging collaboration with Sweden: 'If this opportunity be neglected, we may be in despair of ever recovering anything, for by treaty it will never be done.'[41]

Charles engaged in a typical Stuart half-measure, antagonizing the Habsburgs by sending an expeditionary force, but providing these as auxiliaries without obliging Gustavus to commit himself to a Palatine restoration. Command was entrusted to the inexperienced marquis of Hamilton who has entered military history as Captain Luckless.[42] News that 20,000 Britons were going to land on the Weser proved a serious distraction for Tilly during 1631. In fact, Hamilton brought only 6,000 troops and disembarked at Stettin in August, moving up the Oder to watch the Imperialists in Silesia. Fearing that he might establish an autonomous Palatine presence there with the exiles, Gustavus redirected Hamilton across Saxony to support the Swedish operations in the Guelph lands. British leverage declined as Hamilton's force melted away from desertion, malnourishment and disease, leaving only 500 survivors by December.

Sweden's intervention in the Empire had been welcomed by the Dutch as reducing the likelihood of imperial assistance for Spain. However, the Republic's leaders rejected notions of religious war and only paid limited subsidies in 1631–2 to induce Gustavus to drop plans to monopolize the Baltic grain trade. They refused to back Frederick V beyond paying his expenses as he travelled to join Gustavus on the Rhine in January 1632. The elector's presence suited Gustavus by putting pressure on Duke Maximilian, who now thought Sweden would restore Frederick to his lands. However, Gustavus made restoration conditional on Britain sending another 12,000 men and paying out £25,000 a month. In return, Frederick could have his lands back, but only as fiefs of the Swedish crown. These terms would have reduced him to a 'marionette' and were duly rejected in March. Frederick left the king's entourage in disgust in September. Already ill, he died in Mainz on 30 November, further weakening the Palatine cause.[43]

The Baltic Bridgehead

Sweden's primary interest lay in consolidating its hold on the Baltic coast. Stralsund formed the irreducible core that, as a matter of prestige, Sweden refused to relinquish. Gustavus clearly intended to hold the rest of Pomerania, as well as the Mecklenburg port of Wismar that had served as the imperial naval base. Interest in Bremen and Verden arose from fear that Denmark might intervene on the emperor's behalf. The Lutheran administrator in Bremen, Johann Friedrich of Holstein, believed Ferdinand would cut a deal at his expense and declared for Sweden at the end of 1631. The archbishopric not only commanded the Weser, but its fortress of Stade dominated the lower Elbe. The situation grew urgent as Danish troops exchanged shots with the Swedes outside Bremen in spring 1632. The Swedes saw the administrator as a means to keep the Danes north of the Elbe and helped him eject the small Liga garrison and conquer Verden to the south. However, Johann Friedrich's death in 1634 and the Guelphs' subsequent defection in 1635 convinced Oxenstierna to dispense with unreliable local allies, although it was not until 1645 that Sweden conquered Bremen and Verden and added these to its list of territorial demands (see Chapter 19). Together with Pomerania, these lands linked Sweden to its armies in Germany. They were garrisoned by native Swedish and Finnish units under trusted commanders, and received the bulk of the additional conscripts sent after the mid-1630s.

Strategic Bases

The bridgehead was extended by strategic forward bases at operational centres in each region. The first and most important was Erfurt, a town that belonged to Mainz but had a long tradition of autonomy and aspirations to emancipate itself as an imperial city. Erfurt controlled the roads between Magdeburg, Saxony, Hessen and Franconia and thus secured the route from Pomerania into central Germany. Neighbouring Magdeburg also served as a base once it was captured early in 1632. However, its ruined state, together with Johann Georg's claim for his son to be administrator, lessened its utility. Würzburg secured Franconia, especially as Bamberg further up the Main was difficult to defend. Mainz became the principal base in the Rhineland and the unofficial capital of Sweden's German empire. A huge fortress, the Gustavusburg, was constructed on Darmstadt territory across the river from the city to serve as a safe refuge if the army had to retreat from southern Germany.[44] The other bases were imperial cities cajoled into joining Sweden. A garrison in Frankfurt guarded the lower Main, while Nuremberg supplemented Würzburg in Franconia. Augsburg offered a base in Swabia, but its proximity to Bavaria left it vulnerable.

Though Erfurt was held throughout the war, the others were lost by 1635. The fact that the bases were nearly all Catholic territories was an additional factor in the more provisional Swedish presence there than in the bridgehead. Catholic observance represented defiance of the occupiers and was encouraged wherever possible by militant clergy. Most priests were expelled, but consideration for France obliged Gustavus to leave a few churches in Catholic hands. The Swedes and their German appointees faced strong pressure from local Protestant minorities bent on revenge. The particularly vindictive re-Catholicization measures in Augsburg were reversed in 1632. Little effort was made to hinder local initiatives, such as Frankfurt's expulsion of the Capuchins, or the Hohenlohe counts' attempts to impose Protestantism on conquered areas.[45] Elsewhere, it proved more difficult to promote Protestantism. Mainz was wholly Catholic and the Lutheran congregation was confined to the Swedish garrison. The university collapsed after its staff and students fled. Otherwise, Catholic schools generally remained open, and many local officials kept their posts because the occupiers lacked sufficient qualified loyal Protestants to replace them.

The bases enabled Sweden to tap German resources to sustain its war effort. Gustavus had landed with only enough cash to cover one week's pay. The initial expectations to make war pay proved wildly optimistic. The full annual cost of maintaining a soldier averaged 150 talers, or three times what had been expected. Whereas 1.9 million tlr had been thought sufficient for a year's campaign, overall military expenditure already exceeded 10 million during 1631, excluding requisitioned food and other payments in kind. Sweden spent 2.3 million tlr of its own money launching the invasion, but cut back its own expenditure to 3.2 million more spread over the next three years. Prussian tolls provided another 3.7 million across 1629–35, but returns from those in Pomerania proved disappointing at 171,000 tlr, roughly equivalent to the meagre Dutch subsidy. French payments were more substantial, and enabled Sweden to raise loans in Hamburg and Amsterdam through Gustavus's resident agent, Johan Salvius. Totalling 11 million, these sources nonetheless only covered 30 per cent of the actual cost to Sweden of the German war.[46]

Seeking the rest in Germany, Gustavus copied Wallenstein's system of contributions. A major reason for Sweden's search for German allies was to divert their taxes to sustain the Swedish army. Pomerania, Mecklenburg, Brandenburg and Magdeburg all paid considerable sums, but Gustavus had unreasonable expectations of German wealth. He demanded 240,000 tlr from Augsburg in 1632, when the normal annual taxes raised no more than 50,000.[47] The Swedes always wanted large sums immediately, upsetting the delicate balance between tax and production. Communities were forced to borrow, leaving them heavily indebted. The situation was worse in the conquered areas where the Swedes showed even less restraint. Würzburg was ordered to pay 150,000 tlr in October 1631, followed by another 200,000 only nine months later. Munich paid 100,000 in cash and 40,000 in jewellery in 1632, but the Swedes wanted another 160,000 and took 42 hostages. One escaped, but four died before the rest were liberated three years later. Mainz was given only twelve days' notice to raise 80,000 in December 1631, or eighteen times its usual tax. The Swedes grudgingly accepted payment at 1,500 tlr a week, but this stopped in June when the inhabitants ran out of money. The Jewish community meanwhile paid 20,000 to save their synagogue.

As with Wallenstein's, the decentralized character of contributions provided scope for corruption and inefficiency. Colonel Baudissin was suspected of pocketing 50,000 tlr of the money collected from Thuringia in the autumn of 1631, while Gustavus's commissioner accepted 6,000 tlr from Würzburg in return for halving the original demand.[48] The situation shifted as it appeared Sweden would retain its conquests. Receipts revived when contributions were abandoned in Mainz in favour of the electorate's existing tax structure that delivered 80 per cent of what was demanded. German money not only paid the mercenaries who comprised between three-quarters and nine-tenths of the total army, but also covered 51 per cent of the 1 million riksdalers spent on the Swedish and Finnish contingent each year between 1630 and 1648.

German Collaborators

German manpower was crucial as Gustavus discovered his soldiers died as quickly in the Empire as they had in Poland. Despite their hardy reputation, 46 per cent of those who landed in July 1630 were dead within six months, mainly due to infection from unfamiliar microbes. He had lost 50,000 men by the end of 1631 when his army in Germany contained only 13,000 Swedes and Finns. The normal annual attrition rate among conscripts thereafter was one in five, with most living no more than four years after arriving in Germany.[49] Experience mattered as well as numbers. Many native officers were not up to the job. Åke Tott, a Finnish veteran with a fearsome reputation from the Prussian campaigns, proved incapable of handling the small army sent to conquer Lower Saxony. Baudissin, a Lausatian who replaced him in May 1632, proved little better.

German collaborators stepped in to raise and command troops. Unlike the Swedes, they possessed local knowledge and often their own small territories were capable of providing men and money. Würzburg's capture convinced many princes and nobles that Breitenfeld was not an isolated success and they flocked to greet the conquering hero. No one obtained the wide autonomy left to Saxony or the de facto freedom allowed Hessen-Kassel. Instead, collaborators had to surrender their forts and troops to Sweden's absolute direction and redirect their revenue to support the war.[50] They received commissions and, if they were lucky, small cash advances to recruit additional regiments. Nearly five hundred German regiments were raised for Sweden over the course of the war, with up to a hundred serving at any one time. These units formed the new regional armies. Wilhelm of Weimar was assigned to defend Erfurt, while his younger brother Bernhard held Franconia, both using their own regiments plus units supplied by Nuremberg, the Franconian knights and militia from Sachsen-Coburg. Württemberg and Baden-Durlach formed a Swabian army around their militia in May 1632. A Rhenish force was assembled by the Nassau and Wetterau counts to operate from Mainz. A more disparate army collected in Lower Saxony around units raised by the dukes of Mecklenburg and the administrator of Bremen. They were joined by Duke Georg of Lüneburg, who resigned his imperial commission, and Friedrich Ulrich of Wolfenbüttel.

None of these armies was fully reliable. At around 5,000 men each, they were too small to achieve much without additional help. Swedish units and officers were attached to them, notably in Lower Saxony and the Rhineland, but partly as minders and were themselves often vulnerable. Duke Georg pursued his own war to capture Hildesheim, while Friedrich Ulrich concentrated on trying to recover Wolfenbüttel. The Swedish units tagged along to avoid being left to face the local Liga forces alone. Overall, troop numbers doubled at the beginning of 1632, and grew by another 40,000 to reach an all-time high of 140,000 by the middle of the year. However, the royal strike force remained relatively small. Early in 1632, Gustavus had only 16,000 at Mainz, while Horn had 10,000 in Franconia.

The German units swore loyalty to Sweden, but this remained conditional on continued success. Some collaborators were already irrevocably committed to the Protestant cause, leaving them little alternative. The two commanders of the Rhenish army, Rheingraf Salm-Kyrburg and Prince Christian of Birkenfeld, were veteran paladins. Prince Kraft of Hohenlohe, named governor of Franconia in May 1632, was a former Protestant Union member, while his brother Georg Friedrich had been the Bohemian field marshal. As these examples illustrate, Sweden's collaborators came largely from the ranks of the minor princes, counts and imperial knights. They were Protestants, though many were Calvinists, a confession Sweden refused to recognize. More significantly, they belonged to the ranks of the partially disenfranchised within the imperial constitution. Like Hessen-Kassel, they hoped to profit from the anticipated changes. Count Philipp Reinhard of Solms, another paladin who had joined Sweden in 1627 after fighting with the Danes, proposed abolishing the position of emperor and converting the Empire into a *status aristocratus*.

More immediately, all expected to receive church land confiscated from their neighbours. This practice, known euphemistically as 'donations', began in 1630 to feed the Swedish war monster. Property belonging to Duke Bogislav in Pomerania was appropriated and sold to Stralsund for 100,000 tlr. Jesuits and other religious orders were targeted for punitive measures as the Swedes moved south in 1631, while those who fled automatically had their assets seized. That taken in Frankfurt alone was worth 800,000 florins.[51] Expropriation became systematic by 1633 when Kraft of Hohenlohe received the rich Ellwangen priory and Schöntal abbey, while his brother was given Count Fugger's properties and pieces of Mainz and Würzburg.

Like the beneficiaries of restitution, many discovered donations were poisoned fruits. Kraft of Hohenlohe only obtained Ellwangen after paying 18,000 tlr to Colonel Sperreuter whose troops had captured it. He discovered that Oxenstierna had already given many of the priory's assets to other officers. Vital documents had been lost and local government was in chaos. With the Catholic population uncooperative, Kraft relied on outsiders who were unable to meet the Swedes' demand for regular contributions. Having already raised three regiments for Gustavus, Kraft reckoned the deal cost him 100,000 tlr by the time the Imperialists recovered the priory in 1634. Donations likewise raised unrealistic expectations, leading inevitably to disillusionment with Swedish service. Christian Wilhelm was disappointed not to be restored to Magdeburg and Halberstadt after their capture in February 1632, and having been caught by imperial troops, he promptly converted to Catholicism. Meanwhile, the Swedish governor, Ludwig of Anhalt-Köthen, tried to incorporate both sees into his own principality but was compelled to resign in July 1635.[52]

A New Augustus?

The donations were an expedient that nonetheless revealed Gustavus's plans for the Empire. A Venetian diplomat noted that 'Gustavus' was an anagram of 'Augustus', the name of the first Roman emperor.[53] Gustavus signalled the imperial direction of his ambitions by a carefully staged triumphal entry into Frankfurt on 17 November 1631. It was not lost on contemporaries that he 'was now seated ... in the very same roome, where the Emperours at their Coronation use to be entertained. There may be a signe of good lucke in that: & perchance this may not be the last time, that he shall there be seated.'[54] Such speculation misses the point that he had no intention of leaving the existing constitution intact. Citing the right of conquest, Gustavus declared occupied areas as Swedish fiefs that were distributed to supporters on the condition they would revert to Sweden if their new rulers died without heirs. This condition was even applied to 'liberated' areas like Mecklenburg and the Lower Palatinate. Allies who escaped conquest, like the Guelphs or Hessen-Kassel, nonetheless had to accept Swedish protection superseding existing ties to the emperor. The same was written into agreements with the imperial cities, while towns like Magdeburg, Rostock and Erfurt were promised city status only if they accepted Swedish overlordship.

Allied and conquered territories were instructed early in 1632 to ignore imperial mandates and pay feudal dues to Gustavus instead. By June Gustavus was talking about converting his military alliances into a permanent *corpus politicorum*, naturally under his 'absolute direction'. This would use elements of the existing constitution. The Kreis structure already served to group allies and collaborators on a regional basis. However, the imposition of governors in Franconia and Swabia, as well as Thuringia, which was not a Kreis, suggests this element of the constitution was simply used for convenience. The governors were charged with asserting Swedish overlordship and had no intention of allowing the Kreis assemblies to hold them to account.[55]

Existing boundaries and jurisdictions were not respected. Towns and districts were taken from one territory and assigned to another according to the Swedes' own system of punishments and rewards. The Thurn und Taxis family were deprived of their imperial postal monopoly which was instead entrusted to Protestant officials to distribute Swedish propaganda.[56] Disputes would be arbitrated by the Reichskammergericht, but this was to be reorganized to exclude Catholics, who were to remain outside the new *corpus evangelicorum*. It remained unclear how this corpus would relate to the Empire. Gustavus referred to it as 'a body within a body', but it is unlikely that he would subordinate himself to the existing emperor. There was already considerable speculation after the capture of Mainz that Oxenstierna would be installed as its new elector and imperial chancellor. While the details were probably never decided, the clear direction of Sweden's German policy was to usurp imperial authority and partition the Empire, restricting Habsburg influence to its hereditary lands.[57]

Gustavus's ambitions were far from popular among his inner circle. Gabriel Oxenstierna, Axel's younger brother and the country's chief justice, urged a moderate peace based on restoring an ideal balance between the different parts of the Empire. Anything more, he argued, would alienate Sweden's friends and drag the country into endless war. Even Axel doubted the wisdom of extending the war into southern Germany, acknowledging in retrospect that it simply antagonized the emperor and prolonged the war. Opposition was greater still in Germany. Johann Georg jealously guarded his leading position in Upper Saxony, while the Guelphs resisted Swedish attempts to manipulate the Lower Saxon assembly. The presence of numerous Catholics prevented the use of Swabian institutions, but Sweden's failure in Franconia is more noteworthy since the opposition there was led by the Lutheran Margrave Christian of Bayreuth who was Kreis colonel. He refused to attach his militia to Bernhard of Weimar's regional army and forced the Swedes to make agreements with individual collaborators, rather than a comprehensive alliance through the Kreis.[58]

CALLS FOR ASSISTANCE

Catholic Panic

The rapid Swedish advance spread alarm throughout Catholic Germany. Tilly's forces were disorganized and demoralized. Breitenfeld had shattered his confidence and he avoided battle. While the Swedes rested in the relatively fresh conquered ecclesiastical territories, Tilly's troops were crammed into Bavaria and a few outposts in Westphalia. Numbers fell further with the onset of winter and the impact of plague carried by the units returning from Italy.

Catholic nobles and clergy wrestled with the dilemma of staying to protect their property or fleeing for their lives. Maria Anna Junius, a Dominican nun at the Heiligengrab convent on the outskirts of Bamberg, readily believed reports that blood flowed down the walls of neighbouring Würzburg as the Swedes massacred the garrison while – she thought – they were at prayer in the fortress chapel.[59] She recorded their approach with mounting dread, while her mother superior desperately sought advice on whether they should abandon their home. They stayed, but others fled, many travelling in secular clothing to avoid capture. Some managed to take valuables with them, like the abbess of Buchau who escaped with 27 horses and a herd of cows. Those that could went to other houses of their order in Switzerland or Austria, but these were often overwhelmed and rarely admitted yet more refugees. Constance, the Tirol and Salzburg were more welcoming. Franconians and Rhinelanders generally headed for the imperial city of Cologne, soon to be home to the electors of Mainz and Cologne, the bishops of Würzburg, Worms and Osnabrück, the duke of Pfalz-Neuburg and a host of others.

Sometimes fears proved unfounded. Junius records with some embarrassment the gentlemanly behaviour of the Swedish officers once Bamberg fell in February 1632. Many were curious about convent life and brought their wives to visit the nuns. Later, Junius and her sisters entertained Bernhard of Weimar by singing during a visit by the Swedish officers. When the Swedes departed after another occupation, the sisters gave a present to a grateful sentry who had protected the convent gate. Such civilized relations stirred resentment among the Bambergers already angry at their bishop's precipitous flight. For most people, regardless of confession, the rapid spread of the war brought disease, hardship and uncertainty.

The earlier imperial intransigence over restitution was bitterly regretted. Maximilian now joined Mainz in backing the indefatigable Landgrave Georg of Darmstadt who still lobbied for a compromise based on suspending the Edict.[60] The overtures were welcomed by Saxony's Johann Georg, but the timing was inappropriate in view of Sweden's current dominance. With the bulk of the imperial army withdrawn to Bohemia and Silesia, and many of its members occupied, the Liga felt exposed. Pope Urban was so concerned that Maximilian might make peace that he briefly resumed papal subsidies to the Liga at the end of 1631. The amounts were pretty minimal and Maximilian cast about for more substantial support, turning first to Duke Charles IV of Lorraine.[61]

Lorraine

Lorraine was formally part of the Empire, but enjoyed wide autonomy and its rulers were deeply involved in French affairs. Maximilian's wife, Elisabeth Renate, was Charles's aunt, and the family had led the militant Catholic Ligue during the French Wars of Religion. Charles repeatedly sought to join the Liga during the 1620s but was always rebuffed for fear of alienating France. It was a sign of Maximilian's desperation that he invited cooperation now. Lorraine represented a flashpoint for Franco-Habsburg relations and Charles's activities unwittingly drew these powers closer to war. His own character was partly to blame. Though he could be charming and generous, his restless scheming earned him a reputation for inconstancy. His court at Nancy became a haven for anti-Richelieu exiles, including the arch-intriguer Mme de Chevreuse. Their ranks were swelled after the Day of the Dupes by none other than the king's brother, Gaston d'Orleans.[62] His presence attracted Spanish attention since, as a royal brother, he was considered a more appropriate ally than the Huguenot rebels with whom Olivares had flirted briefly in 1625. Lorraine remained involved with the exiles once Gaston joined his mother who had fled to Brussels in June 1631. Plotting continued until the chief conspirators were defeated in 1641. The details vary, but Gaston essentially sought a greater role in France. He resented his brother's refusal to let him marry, a ploy obviously intended to prevent him siring a potential heir to the throne (Louis XIII was childless until 1638). Gaston secretly married Charles's younger sister, Marguerite de Vaudemont, in January 1632.

The duke wanted to throw off the French influence seeping across his duchy thanks to that country's protectorate over the bishoprics of Metz, Toul and Verdun. With relations already elected to the latter two, Charles wanted to neutralize the influence of the first, the principal French base in the region. At his invitation in February 1630, 2,700 Imperialists seized the Metz enclaves of Vic and Moyenvic that straddled the main road from France over the Vosges to Alsace. Coming as it did at the height of the Mantuan crisis, Richelieu mistook this for the actions of an advance guard of a full invasion force and assembled an army in Champagne immediately to the west.

In fact, Ferdinand had no intention of going further, but Olivares was prepared to fund Charles to help Gaston invade France. Intended to distract France from aiding the Dutch, this considerably raised the stakes.[63] Gaston went to Mömpelgard, a Württemberg possession between Alsace, Basel and Lorraine. Arriving in September 1631, he had collected 2,500 cavalry by May 1632, while Charles assembled 15,000 men. Unable to maintain these, and fearing their presence might prompt the French army still in Champagne to invade, Charles crossed the Rhine in October 1631 to assist Tilly. His force was decimated by fever and singularly failed to stop the Swedes capturing the Lower Palatinate. Within a month, the 7,000 or so unruly survivors were back across the Rhine.

Their temporary absence allowed the French to invade Lorraine, and the, now much reduced, imperial garrison surrendered Vic and Moyenvic at the end of December. A brief attempt to remove French influence was punished by a second invasion in May 1632, leading to the Treaty of Liverdun on 20 June. Charles surrendered key towns and bridges, enabling France to connect the conquered enclaves to the three bishoprics and thus secure a route to Alsace. With typically poor timing, Gaston invaded his homeland three days later with only 5,000 men. Though he was joined by the governor of the Languedoc, the Huguenots and grandees had learned their lesson and failed to rise in support. Gaston escaped, but the execution of the unfortunate governor provided a scapegoat and permitted a temporary royal brotherly reconciliation in October 1634.[64]

Spain

Spanish assistance proved equally problematic and ineffectual. Archduchess Isabella believed the Swedish advance would finally force the Liga to drop its opposition to assisting Spain. She offered over 3,000 men to garrison Cologne, but the city politely declined. There were around 9,000 Spanish in the Lower Palatinate when Gustavus reached the Rhine, but they were all west of the river. Only 400 arrived to reinforce Mainz and they were disgruntled Germans who entered Swedish service once the city surrendered.[65] Maximilian still distrusted Spain and refused Isabella's terms.

The emperor had sought better relations with Spain after the failures of the Baltic Design and the Mantuan War. Archduke Ferdinand had married the Spanish Infanta Maria Anna in February 1631, but it was not until a year later that the Spanish ambassador promised 24,000 men and 200,000 escudos a month to contain the Swedes. Spain temporarily increased the force in the Lower Palatinate to 18,000 and delivered subsidies and other indirect aid totalling 2.59 million fl. between 1630 and 1633. However, the February 1632 treaty was never ratified, because Ferdinand transferred Alsace, Further Austria and the Tirol as hereditary possessions to his younger brother, Leopold of Passau. This settled internal tension over the Austrian succession, but contravened the Oñate Treaty of 1617 that promised Alsace to Spain.

France

To Ferdinand's horror, Maximilian approached France as an alternative source of help. Troublesome though Lorraine was, Richelieu did not intend to punish Charles so harshly. The Swedes' unexpected arrival on the Rhine forced his hand. By landing in Pomerania, Gustavus fulfilled Richelieu's requirement of preventing the emperor assisting Spain. His subsequent rampage through Catholic Germany was another matter, changing the entire balance of power in Central Europe. Richelieu had already opened negotiations in October 1631 to convert his current understanding with Bavaria into a full alliance. His preferred option was for the Liga to declare itself neutral, establishing a buffer between the Spanish-Dutch war and the Swedish-imperial one. Failing that, he would negotiate treaties of protection with individual princes in strategic locations.

The French advance into Lorraine in December 1631 was accompanied by an open invitation to all Catholic princes for protection against both Sweden and Spain. The capture of Vic and Moyenvic improved this offer by enabling French troops to reach Alsace. Elector Sötern of Trier accepted Richelieu's offer on 23 December. A serious cleric and long-standing Liga member, he was disillusioned with Spanish infringement of his property in the Netherlands and its failure to protect him now.[66] Maximilian hesitated. He was under great pressure from Gustavus, who considered that the resistance of Liga units since March 1631 had removed his obligation to treat Bavaria as neutral. The Swede gave Maximilian two weeks to accept his conquest of church land and reduce Liga forces to 12,000 men, or face invasion.[67]

Negotiations were complicated by Richelieu's distraction with Gaston's plot and the fact that Mainz and Count Franz Hatzfeldt, bishop of Würzburg, opened their own talks with the French in Metz. Richelieu's inability to oblige Gustavus to improve his terms persuaded Maximilian that France could not tame the Swedish lion. He also hesitated to jeopardize his new lands and title by breaking with Ferdinand. By February 1632, Maximilian was working hard to repair his relations with Vienna and dropped objections to Wallenstein's reinstatement. As it became clear Maximilian would remain loyal, Ferdinand offered military aid. Meanwhile, both he and Spain promised to recover Mainz for its elector. These assurances persuaded the other ecclesiastical princes not to forsake the leaking imperial ship for the French lifeboat.

Wallenstein's Recall

With Lorraine, Spain and France unable to rescue Catholic Germany, Bavaria and the other principalities saw there was no choice but to rejoin the emperor and fight on. All realized this was only possible if Wallenstein was recalled. Many imperial soldiers had lost confidence in Tilly and resented serving under him. Ferdinand opened serious talks with his former general after the fall of Frankfurt on the Oder in April 1631. Negotiations intensified in November and ran parallel to Wallenstein's contacts with Arnim and his discussions with Christian IV for Denmark to join the emperor.[68] Ferdinand named him 'boss' (*General Capo*) for three months on 15 December, renegotiating this as the situation continued to deteriorate. Once Maximilian signalled agreement, Ferdinand formalized the arrangement at Göllersdorf, north of Vienna on 13 April 1632. The original copy is lost, probably destroyed along with other papers that might have incriminated Ferdinand after Wallenstein's murder, forcing us to reconstruct the terms from various near-contemporary printed versions.[69]

In addition to a generous salary and safeguards for his properties, Wallenstein secured unconstrained military and plenipotentiary powers *in absolutissima forma*. This was intended to end the friction with Vienna that Wallenstein believed had led to his dismissal. Ferdinand accepted it, because he believed Wallenstein was the only man who could retrieve the situation. While some claim the treaty made Wallenstein a dictator, he remained subordinate to the emperor whose agreement would be necessary for any treaty to be binding. Wallenstein could now issue recruiting patents and appoint colonels, but all senior promotions remained subject to imperial approval. He was permitted to draw on the resources of the Habsburg hereditary lands, but this was scarcely surprising given that the Imperialists had been driven out of the rest of Germany. Wallenstein's reappointment also enhanced Ferdinand's authority by ending the dual command structure conceded to Maximilian in 1630. Tilly's death on 30 April 1632 removed any potential complication over who was senior general. Maximilian assumed command of his own troops in Bavaria, advised by Aldringen, while Pappenheim at last obtained unhindered independent command over the scattered imperial and Liga garrisons in north-west Germany.

Despite his new powers, Wallenstein remained isolated. His father-in-law Count Harrach's death and Eggenberg's resignation removed his principal supporters in Vienna. Several of his earlier collaborators had left, either joining the other side like Arnim, or were incapacitated like Conti, terminally ill with tuberculosis. He relied heavily on Gallas and Aldringen, both of whom he promoted in December 1631. Other subordinates were drawn from the existing colonels, notably Bönninghausen, a minor Westphalian noble distinguished primarily by his ability to raise cavalry, and Baron Götz, a Lüneburg Lutheran who defected from the wreck of Mansfeld's army in 1626 and was made a general in 1633. Colonel Hendrik Holk left Denmark only in March 1630, but was already an imperial field marshal by December 1632. These were all men of ability and experience. Nonetheless, it is striking that Wallenstein now favoured his brother-in-law Trčka, who rose from colonel to senior general in just two years. He also promoted Christian Ilow, a smarmy minor Brandenburg noble whose gossipy, excitable manner he had previously despised, but who was now promoted and became his principal subordinate after Holk's death in September 1633.

The relatively rapid reconstruction of the imperial army after December 1631 was assisted by the presence of men left unemployed since the reductions of the previous year, as well as recruits from the Habsburg lands willing to enlist for only half the previous bounty.[70] Regiments were generally smaller than those of the 1620s, partly of necessity, but also reflecting the new tactical thinking that favoured units of 500 to 1,000 men in place of the larger tercios. The infantry now deployed in seven to ten ranks, or about half the previous depth, to maximize their firepower, reduce vulnerability to artillery fire and improve command and control. Both the Liga and imperial foot were trained to fire salvos and were accompanied by regimental guns like the Swedes. Cavalry regiments were still intended to be 1,000 strong, but often remained weaker. In battle they were grouped into squadrons of 100 to 400 men, with inexperienced troopers more likely to form the larger units, while veterans deployed in smaller numbers. Squadrons drew up in four to five ranks like the Dutch, but still a rank deeper than the Swedes. Experience remained the decisive factor in battlefield performance and the imperial cavalry that fled at Lützen (1632) and Hessisch-Oldendorf (1633) did so because they were composed of recruits, not because their organization or deployment was inferior to that of the Swedes.

ZENITH

The Expansion and Regionalization of the War

The war had now entered its most destructive phase and both sides fielded around 100,000 men each. The 1632 campaign marked the zenith of Swedish power in Germany and was the most intensive of the entire war as Gustavus sought to consolidate his empire. Five major battles were fought at Bamberg, the Lech, Steinau, Alte Veste and Lützen, in addition to numerous smaller engagements. The location of these actions indicates the greater scope of the conflict, but also its increasingly regional character, dictated by the Empire's physical and political geography. The logistical difficulties of concentrating large numbers of troops in one place combined with the dependency of Sweden and the emperor on German allies to scatter the rival armies across the Empire, establishing the strategic pattern that persisted, with some important modifications, until 1648.

At this point, each side fielded several large armies simultaneously, contributing to the frequency of major battles. As overall troop strength declined after 1635, the number of field armies fell, initially to two apiece, and then one each by 1647. Regional operations persisted because the rapid spread of hostilities in 1631–2 left each belligerent with garrisons across the Empire. These outposts, often supplemented by a few additional regiments, pursued their own struggles for regional dominance against local rivals. They survived by levying contributions in their immediate vicinity, encouraging what contemporaries termed the 'little war' of raids and sieges to obtain additional resources and capture more territory. Garrisons provided bases for the main armies should they need to operate in that region. Infantry could be drawn out as temporary reinforcements, and artillery taken from large fortresses to provide a siege train. Later, especially from 1638 as the field forces dwindled, scratch armies could be improvised from garrison infantry, new recruits and whatever regiments were still available.

The principal imperial effort concentrated on defending the emperor's hereditary possessions against Swedish and (until 1634) Saxon attacks. This remained the main theatre of imperial operations apart from a temporary recovery between 1634 and 1638 when the main army moved to the Rhine and then the Elbe. The ability of the senior imperial commander to send aid elsewhere depended on the security of Bohemia and Silesia, not least since these now provided much of the money sustaining the Imperialists. The main Liga army was reduced to Bavarian regiments defending their home and pushing into Franconia and Swabia when possible. The remaining Liga units were concentrated in West-phalia. Some were deployed west of the Rhine to guard against possible Dutch incursions, while the bulk, numbering under 10,000 men in early 1632, were scattered in positions to the east, and included the Imperialists holding out in Wolfenbüttel.

The Westphalians faced over 50,000 men raised by Gustavus's Lower Saxon and Hessian collaborators whose mutual rivalry split them into six corps with divergent agendas. Gustavus made matters worse by trying to direct operations by courier and then summoning 20,000 soldiers to join him in Franconia in the middle of the year. Pappenheim conducted a brilliant campaign, spreading rumours he was advancing with 10,000 men, rather than the 3,000 he could draw from his garri-sons. Dashing east in January, he rescued the 3,500 men holding out in Magdeburg, withdrew the best cannon, tipped the others into the Elbe, blew up the fortifications and escaped to Wolfenbüttel in the fog. Having surprised the Swedes and Hessians at Höxter in March, he repeated the coup by evacuating the Stade garrison. He then spent the summer run-ning rings around his opponents who failed to combine against his troops.[71]

The imperial units remaining in south-west Germany passed to the now autonomous Tirolean administration in Innsbruck. A few isolated garrisons contested control of Alsace against the much larger army of the Rhenish counts operating from Mainz. The remainder clung onto the strategic routes around the Black Forest. A strong garrison guarded the Rhine bridge at Breisach and held the less-defensible provincial capital of Freiburg. Other detachments garrisoned the four Forest Towns (*Waldstädte*) of Rheinfelden, Laufenburg, Säckingen and Waldshut that controlled the Upper Rhine between Basel and Lake Constance. This was the only feasible way from Alsace around the southern end of the Black Forest where the route divided. One branch ran north east to the upper reaches of the Danube around the Württemberg enclave of Tuttlingen and thence to Bavaria. This route was overlooked by the duke's impregnable castle of Hohentwiel perched on an extinct volcano 263 metres above the surrounding plain. The other branch ran east through the towns of Überlingen, Lindau and Radolfzell along the northern shore of Lake Constance to the Bregenzer Klause, the pass giving access to the Tirol and Valtellina. The area between the lake, the Danube and the Bavarian frontier was studded with walled imperial cities, notably Ravensburg, Kempten, Memmingen, Ulm and Augsburg. The emperor was rarely able to devote significant resources to defending these positions, despite a strategic importance that grew with French intervention in 1635. Defence was left largely to local militia, especially in Villingen and the imperial city of Rottweil which guarded the back door from Württemberg through the Black Forest to Breisach.

After Archduke Leopold's death in September 1632, responsibility for his Austrian and Tirol lands passed to his widow, the indomitable Princess Claudia of Tuscany, as regent for their son. Highly intelligent, she pursued her own military and diplomatic strategy, often with little help from Vienna.[72] As in Westphalia, regional defence was assisted by disunity among her opponents. Württemberg would have preferred neutrality and continued discussions with Swabian Catholics and Bavaria until May 1632, when Swedish pressure obliged Regent Julius Friedrich to sign an offensive alliance. Gustavus not only restored the monasteries lost to restitution, but promised Württemberg the Catholic secular principality of Fürstenberg as a Swedish fief. Julius Friedrich did not expect to retain additional territory, but saw temporary gains as bargaining chips to exchange for Catholic renunciation of restitution. Like the Guelphs, he pursued his own war, largely without Swedish support and only loosely in cooperation with his neighbour Baden-

Durlach across the Black Forest. Württemberg forces numbered around 6,200, but were mainly militia and lacked adequate siege artillery. They only began action after the initial Catholic panic subsided. Whereas towns had fallen like ninepins after Breitenfeld, the Catholic population soon learned that surrender would bring expropriation, persecution and extortion.

The new resolve was demonstrated by several episodes after Horn broke the truce with Bavaria by attacking the city of Bamberg on 10 February. Abandoned by the Liga regulars, the Bamberg citizens and militia held for nine hours until their ammunition ran out and they had to surrender. If stiffened by a few professionals, militia could defy even large forces. But then, despite holding the capital, the Swedes never controlled the rest of Bamberg because the two small fortified towns of Kronach and Forchheim repulsed all efforts to take them throughout the war. Though Rottweil fell to Württemberg in January 1633, Villingen likewise remained impregnable, and the Tirolean peasants repulsed Bernhard of Weimar's attempt to seize the Bregenzer Klause in July 1632.

The Battles of Bamberg and the Lech

Horn's attack on Bamberg renewed the war in earnest. Tilly drew in garrisons from the Upper Palatinate, called up 8,000 Bavarian militia, and advanced north from Nördlingen with 22,000 men to surprise Horn at the city on the evening of 9 March. There were only two Swedish regiments present, with the rest of the 12,000 men being German recruits assembled by the Bohemian exiles and Gustavus's new local collaborators. The Liga advance guard routed Horn's cavalry outposts south-east of the city. The fleeing troopers panicked the defenders behind their unfinished entrenchments in the suburb east of the river Regnitz. The Imperialists broke in at the Heiligengrab convent where Sister Junius saw how a Croat 'cut down a Swede on our field . . . splitting his head from back to front leaving an ear hanging down'.[73] The defenders were soon overwhelmed, but a fierce fight developed at the bridge giving access to the main part of the city to the west. After two of Horn's infantry regiments retook the bridge, Tilly placed two heavy guns in a beer garden to fire across the river. The first shot allegedly mortally wounded Count Solms-Laubach, a veteran of White Mountain. 'The

497

next passed through a house and through two walls of the next where a child was sleeping in its crib, doing no damage beyond depositing some dust on the infant.' The struggle continued until midnight, when the Swedish rearguard abandoned the city now that the rest of the army had escaped. Horn lost a third of his army, largely through desertion, and retreated to Schweinfurt.

Tilly was too weak to exploit his victory, while Gustavus had to act to maintain the momentum of success: already Württemberg was hesitating to sign its alliance because of Horn's defeat. The king marched from Mainz, collecting Horn and other units to enter Nuremberg where he was hailed as the avenging 'lion of midnight' two weeks later on 31 March. Within a week he had captured Donauwörth, the success marred by the indiscriminate massacre of surrendering Catholic soldiers and welcoming Protestant burghers.[74] Further reinforcements gave him 37,000 men and 72 cannon – sufficient to attack Bavaria.

Gustavus faced the dilemma confronting all invaders. The Danube cut the electorate in two, with only a few bridges at Ingolstadt, Kehlheim, the great imperial city of Regensburg, and finally at Straubing and Passau further east. He could not attack both north and south without dividing his army, and so he decided to invade the southern side since this contained the rich capital of Munich. This necessitated crossing the Lech that flowed from the Upper Bavarian mountains down the Swabian frontier to join the Danube between Donauwörth and Ingolstadt. The main bridge at Augsburg was still held by 5,000 Bavarians, while others secured the other crossing at Rain where the Lech joined the Danube. Tilly and Aldringen had entrenched 21,000 men and 20 guns on the firm ground south of Rain. The Lech divided into a series of parallel, fast-flowing streams each 60 to 80 metres wide. Heavy spring rain and melting mountain snow had swollen them to a depth of at least 4 metres, while most of the Bavarian bank consisted of semi-submerged woods or marsh. Crossing this obstacle was to be one of Gustavus's greatest achievements.

The only practical route lay five kilometres south of Rain where there was an island separated from the western bank by a deep channel, but from which it was possible to ford to the eastern side. Gustavus drew up on the open ground directly opposite Tilly's camp on 14 April and began an artillery bombardment suggesting he would try to cross here. Meanwhile, other troops moved into the woods opposite the island

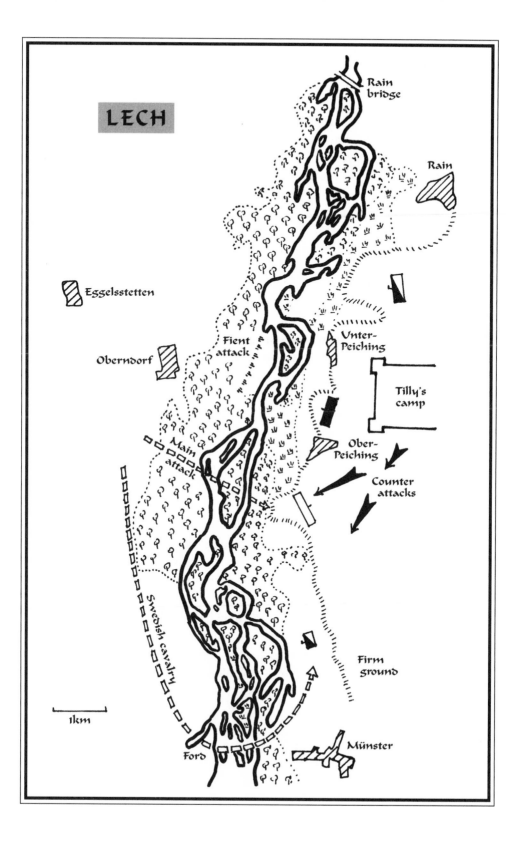

LECH

Rain
bridge

Rain

Eggelsstetten

Fient
attack

Oberndorf

Unter-
Peiching

Tilly's
camp

Main
attack

Ober-
Peiching

Counter
attacks

Swedish cavalry

Firm
ground

1km

Ford

Münster

and bridged the channel. Musketeers collected on the island the next morning. Covered by a smoke screen of burning wet straw mixed with gunpowder, 334 Finns, motivated by the promise of five months' extra pay, rowed across to the Bavarian bank. Pre-fabricated bridge sections were then floated across and secured, enabling the rest of the army to start crossing covered by the fire of additional batteries concealed in the woods on the western bank and on the island.

Tilly despatched troops as soon as he learned of the crossing and a fierce fight developed south of the Liga encampment. Unknown to Tilly, however, 2,000 elite Swedish cavalry had forded the Lech two kilometres further south and arrived as the fighting reached its climax at 4 p.m. Aldringen was temporarily blinded by a small cannonball striking a glancing blow, while Tilly's right thigh was shattered by a 3-pound ball and he lost consciousness, dying two weeks later. Command devolved to the personally brave but inexperienced Bavarian elector, who ordered a retreat. Both sides had lost about 2,000 men, but the retreat led to a further 1,000 Bavarians and imperial troops being captured. The defeat demoralized the Augsburg garrison, who accepted the honours of war and marched out ten days later.[75]

Maximilian reinforced the Ingolstadt and Regensburg garrisons and retreated north of the Danube. Gustavus lost almost as many men as at the Lech in a futile attempt to storm Ingolstadt on 3 May. He could not press on into Austria with Maximilian poised on his flank, so he devastated the southern half of the electorate in an effort to force Maximilian to make peace. Accompanied by Frederick V, Gustavus entered Munich on 17 May, staying ten days to dig up 119 cannon that had been buried on Maximilian's orders and take whatever else the Bavarians had not managed to move to the mountains. His attendance at a Catholic mass convinced no one of his tolerance. Catholic peasants waged a bitter guerrilla war against the invaders that spread into Swabia and was directed against Swedish plundering.[76] Maximilian remained defiant. Gustavus stayed around Augsburg until he had bullied Württemberg and the other Swabians to join him, and then marched north through Donauwörth to confront Wallenstein's new army.

The Battles of Steinau and Alte Veste

Wallenstein had brought the imperial army back up to about 65,000 men. He advanced from Znaim into Bohemia with nearly half that number at the end of April. Saxon resistance collapsed. The Saxons and Bohemian exiles had thoroughly alienated the Bohemians by their plundering so that even the Protestants were glad to see them re-cross the mountains in mid-June. Wallenstein decided against invading Saxony. Leaving troops to guard Bohemia and Silesia, he headed west to join Maximilian at Eger on 1 July. Both men made an effort to get along. Maximilian was careful to address Wallenstein as duke of Mecklenburg, and loaned him 300,000 fl. for provisions.

Gustavus had left Johann Georg to fight alone. He knew the elector was still negotiating with Wallenstein and feared he might defect. He headed northwards, entrenching at Nuremberg on 16 June when he learned imperial detachments were already moving to intercept him. It would have been safer to have marched north-west to Würzburg to be closer to his other armies in Lower Saxony and the Rhineland, but Gustavus could not afford to lose a prominent Protestant city like Nuremberg. Six thousand peasants were conscripted to dig a huge ditch around the city and emplace 300 cannon borrowed from the city's arsenal. The cavalry were left outside to maintain communications while Gustavus waited for his other armies to join him.

Having arrived on 17 July, Wallenstein resolved not to repeat Tilly's mistake at Werben and to starve the Swedes out rather than attacking their entrenchments. He built his own camp west of the city at Zirndorf that was 16km in circumference and entailed felling 13,000 trees and shifting the equivalent of 21,000 modern truck-loads of earth.[77] Imperial garrisons in Fürth, Forchheim and other towns commanded the roads into Nuremberg, while cavalry patrolled the countryside. Gustavus was trapped. He had 18,000 soldiers, but faced insurmountable supply problems as the city's 40,000 inhabitants had been joined by 100,000 refugees. The Imperialists burned all the mills outside the Swedish entrenchments and the defenders were soon on half rations.

The situation was initially much better in Wallenstein's camp because it received supplies from as far away as Bohemia and Austria. Things worsened with the hotter weather in August though. The concentration of 55,000 troops and around 50,000 camp followers produced at least four tonnes of human excrement daily, in addition to the waste from the 45,000 cavalry and baggage horses. The camp was swarming with rats and flies, spreading disease. Wallenstein had become a victim of his own strategy and by mid-August his army was no longer fully operational after the Swedes captured a supply convoy. He was unable to intercept a relief force of 24,000 men and 3,000 supply wagons sent by Oxenstierna to join Gustavus.

As tension mounted in Franconia, Johann Georg tried to improve his bargaining position by sending Arnim to invade Silesia. The hagiography surrounding Gustavus has overshadowed these events that involved significant numbers of troops and are very revealing about tension within Sweden's alliance. Arnim had 12,000 Saxons, plus 3,000 Brandenburgers and 7,000 Swedes. The latter were under the command of Jacob Duwall, born MacDougall in Scotland, who had served Sweden since 1607 and raised two German regiments that formed the bulk of his corps, and whose presence was to ensure Arnim remained loyal.[78] Duwall was a man of considerable energy, but like many professional officers he had become an alcoholic.

Imperial reinforcements were rushed from Bohemia to join the Silesian garrisons under the elderly Marradas, who collected 20,000 men at Steinau, an important Oder crossing between Glogau and Breslau. He entrenched on the Gallows Hill, south-east of Steinau, between it and the river, and posted cavalry on the Sand Hill west of the town to watch the approach. Musketeers occupied the Geisendorf suburb to the west and a nearby churchyard. The advance guard under the firebrand Duwall arrived at midday on 29 August, and immediately engaged the imperial cavalry. After two hours of skirmishing the Imperialists retreated into the marshy Kalterbach valley south of Steinau. Saxon artillery had now arrived on the Sand Hill and compelled the cavalry to retreat further into Marradas's camp, exposing the musketeers. Duwall's younger brother led 1,000 Swedish and Brandenburg musketeers who stormed the suburb and churchyard. The Imperialists set the town on fire to forestall further attack, virtually destroying it. Duwall wanted to press on, but Arnim refused. The two were barely on speaking terms and Duwall was convinced Arnim was still negotiating with the enemy on the Gallows Hill.

Rather than assault the camp the next day, Arnim marched south to Dieban further upstream where he built a bridge, intending to cross and

STEINAU (1632)

To Glogau

Geisendorf

Steinau

Kalterbach

Imperial cavalry 29 August 1632

Sand Hill

Church yard

Georgendorf

Gallows Hill

Marradas' camp

River Oder

Kreischau

Kalterbach

To Wohlau and Breslau

Arnim's camp 30 August to 4 September 1632

Grossendorf

Boat Bridge

Imperial attack 4 September

Dieban

To Breslau

1km

cut Marradas off from the other side. Marradas belatedly attacked Dieban, but was repulsed on 4 September and retreated, having left a small detachment at the Steinau bridge to delay pursuit. The allied losses were slight, but the Imperialists lost 6,000, mainly prisoners or men who fled during the initial engagement. The losses indicate the continued poor condition of parts of the imperial army, especially when irresolutely led. Arnim pressed on, taking Breslau and Schweidnitz where he reversed the re-Catholicization measures. The Imperialists were driven into the mountains. Arnim had conquered Silesia with fewer troops and against greater odds than Frederick II of Prussia's celebrated invasion in 1740.

Wallenstein decided to punish Saxony, and ordered Holk with 10,000 men from Forchheim to invade the Vogtland that formed the south-western tip of Johann Georg's territory. As Holk began systematic plundering to intimidate the elector, the pressure mounted on Gustavus to break out of Nuremberg. The reinforcements sent by Oxenstierna arrived on 27 August, giving him the largest army he ever commanded: 28,000 infantry, 17,000 cavalry and 175 field guns. Disease and Holk's detachment had reduced Wallenstein's force to 31,000 foot and 12,000 horse. The odds were still not in Gustavus's favour, especially considering Wallenstein was entrenched on high ground above the Rednitz river over 6km from Gustavus's camp. The river prevented attack from the east, while the more open southern and western sides were furthest from Gustavus and would be difficult to reach without exposing his flank. This left the north, held by Liga units under Aldringen, and which was the strongest, highest side. The entrenchments were covered by abatis, the seventeenth-century equivalent of First World War barbed-wire entanglements made by felling and trimming trees to leave only sharpened branches pointing towards the enemy. The ruined castle that gave the position its name (Alte Veste) provided an additional strong point.

Surprise was impossible. Gustavus's intentions were clear once he seized Fürth to cross the Rednitz on the night of 1–2 September. There is some indication that Gustavus only attacked because he thought Wallenstein was withdrawing, but this was probably put about just to excuse the debacle.[79] The king planned to pin Wallenstein with artillery fire from east of the Rednitz, while he and Wilhelm of Weimar attacked Aldringen, and Bernhard of Weimar worked his way round to hit the weaker western side. A preliminary bombardment failed to silence the

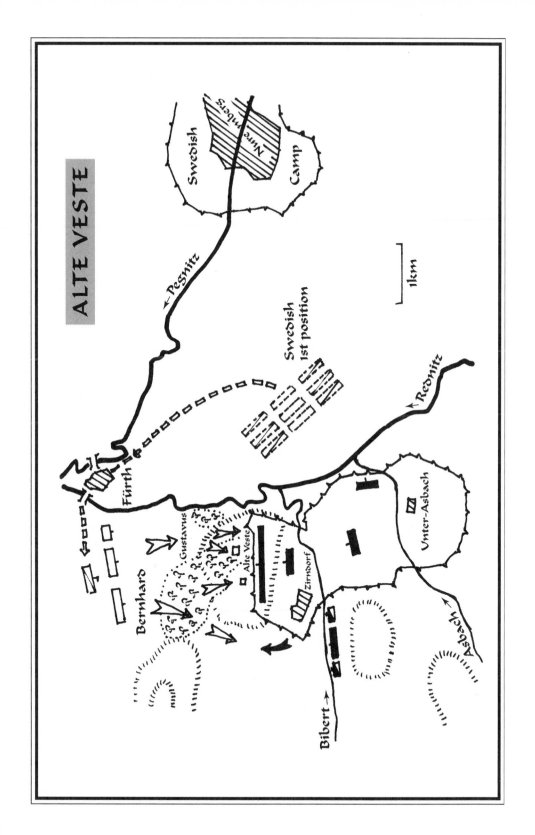

ALTE VESTE

Swedish
Camp

Nürnberg

Pegnitz

Swedish
1st position

Fürth

Rednitz

1km

Bernhard

Gustavus

Alte Veste

Zirndorf

Unter-Asbach

Bibert

Asbach

imperial artillery. Gustavus pressed on regardless, sending his infantry up the wooded northern slope early on 3 September. Thin drizzle had already made the ground slippery, and it proved impossible to bring up the regimental guns as the rain grew heavier during the day. The assault was renewed repeatedly into the night, but only gained a few imperial outworks on the western side. Gustavus gave up. He retreated covered by his cavalry, having lost at least 1,000 killed and 1,400 badly wounded. General Banér's wounds left him incapacitated for the rest of the year. Worse, demoralization prompted 11,000 men to desert. Altogether, at least 29,000 people died in Gustavus's camp during the prolonged stand-off, while animal casualties left only 4,000 of his cavalry mounted by the end.

Unable to remain in Nuremberg, Gustavus pulled out on 15 September. He waited a week at Windsheim to the west, before deciding that Wallenstein no longer posed an immediate threat and marching south, intending to winter in Swabia. Wallenstein had lost less than 1,000 men, but his army was sick. So many horses had died that 1,000 wagons of supplies were abandoned when he burned his camp on 21 September. He moved north, overrunning the rest of Franconia and into Thuringia, while Gallas marched through north-east Bohemia to reinforce Holk's raiders putting pressure on Saxony. The Imperialists occupied Meissen and despatched Croats towards Dresden with the message that Johann Georg would no longer need candles for his banquets as the Imperialists would now provide light by burning Saxony's villages.

Maximilian and Wallenstein parted ways at Coburg in mid-October. The elector agreed that Pappenheim and the Liga field force would join Wallenstein from Westphalia in return for Aldringen and fourteen imperial regiments being assigned to stiffen the Bavarians. The arrangement proved unsatisfactory, and the resulting acrimony revealed the continued tension between Maximilian and the emperor. Wallenstein complained that Pappenheim did not arrive fast enough, and indeed repeated orders had to be sent before that general finally gave up his independent role and marched to Saxony.[80] Maximilian resented Aldringen for still reporting to Wallenstein, who already recalled some of the regiments by late November. Maximilian returned south to protect Bavaria, while Wallenstein marched north-east into Saxony, ordering the plundering to stop as he now intended to winter in the electorate.

The Battle of Lützen

Gustavus realized his mistake. Wallenstein was not only threatening his principal ally, but endangering communications with the Baltic bridgehead. Against Oxenstierna's advice, he raced north, covering 650km in 17 days at the cost of 4,000 horses. En route he passed Maximilian heading in the opposite direction. The armies were only 25km apart, but unaware of each other's presence. The main Saxon army was still with Arnim in Silesia. Johann Georg had only 4,000 men, plus 2,000 Lüneburgers under Duke Georg who shadowed Pappenheim through Lower Saxony. Leipzig surrendered a second time to the Imperialists and its commandant was executed by the furious elector, who then made his widow pay the cost of the court martial.[81]

Pappenheim joined Wallenstein on 7 November, while the Saxons retreated into Torgau and Gustavus rested at Erfurt after his long march. It was now very cold. Wallenstein dispersed his troops to find food, sending Colonel Hatzfeldt with 2,500 men to watch Torgau. Pappenheim was restless, wanting to return to Westphalia where the Swedes were known to be picking off his garrisons. Sick with gout, Wallenstein lacked the energy to argue, and let him go with 5,800 men. Gallas was summoned from the Bohemian frontier to replace him, but it would be some time before he arrived.

Gustavus had moved east down the Saale, taking Naumburg on 10 November. He decided to force a battle, hoping for another Breitenfeld to restore his reputation, dented by Alte Veste. As he approached the Imperialists, he learned from peasants how weak Wallenstein was and pressed on to catch him. General Rodolfo Colloredo, commanding a detachment of 500 dragoons and Croats, blocked him at the marshy Rippach stream east of Weissenfels, delaying him for four hours on 15 November. It was now too late for battle, and Gustavus was forced to camp for the night.[82]

Wallenstein abandoned his retreat to Leipzig when he received word from Colloredo, halting at Lützen still 20km short of his destination. He had only 8,550 foot, 3,800 horse and 20 heavy guns. His right was protected by the marshy Mühlgraben stream. The Weissenfels–Leipzig highway crossed this at Lützen, a town that comprised 300 houses and an old castle surrounded by a wall. Wallenstein guessed correctly that Gustavus would not attempt another frontal assault, but would cross further south-east to outflank him. Accordingly, he drew up just north east of the town parallel to the road. Musketeers spent the night widening the ditches either side of the road, while Holk supervised deployment of the main army, lighting candles to guide units into position. Four hundred musketeers were posted in Lützen to secure the right, and thirteen guns were placed on the slight rise of Windmill Hill just north of the town. Around half the cavalry drew up behind with the rest on the left. The infantry deployed in between in two lines, with another 7 guns on their left and 420 musketeers lining the ditches in front. There were not enough cavalry to cover the gap from the left to the Flossgraben ditch that cut the highway beyond Wallenstein's position. Isolano's 600 Croats were posted as a screen across the gap with the camp followers and baggage massed in the rear holding sheets as flags to create the impression of powerful forces behind. They were supposed to wait until Pappenheim, recalled during the night, could replace them.

Johann Georg refused to send reinforcements from Torgau, but Gustavus had nearly 13,000 infantry, 6,200 cavalry and 20 heavy guns and so remained confident. His army assembled in thick fog about 3,000 metres to the west early on 16 November to hear the king's stirring address. As Wallenstein predicted, Gustavus swung east across the Mühlgraben and then north over the Flossgraben to deploy around 10 a.m. in front of him. The action began as the fog lifted around an hour later and the Swedes made a general advance towards the imperial positions. Gustavus used his customary deployment in two lines, with the cavalry on the flanks stiffened with musketeer detachments. The best infantry were in the first line, while the king commanded most of the Swedish and Finnish horse on the right and Bernhard of Weimar led the 3,000 mainly German troopers on the left.

The Croats soon scattered, prompting the decoy troops to take to their heels. Gustavus was nonetheless delayed by the musketeers hidden in the ditch. Widely cited reports that Wallenstein spent the day carried in a litter stem from Swedish propaganda. Despite pain from gout, he mounted his horse to conduct an energetic defence. Lützen was set on fire to stop the Swedes entering and turning his flank. The wind blew the smoke into his enemies' faces and, as at Breitenfeld, it quickly became impossible to see what was happening. Bernhard's men were unable to take either Lützen or Windmill Hill. The real chance lay on the other flank where Gustavus had more space to go round the end of the imperial

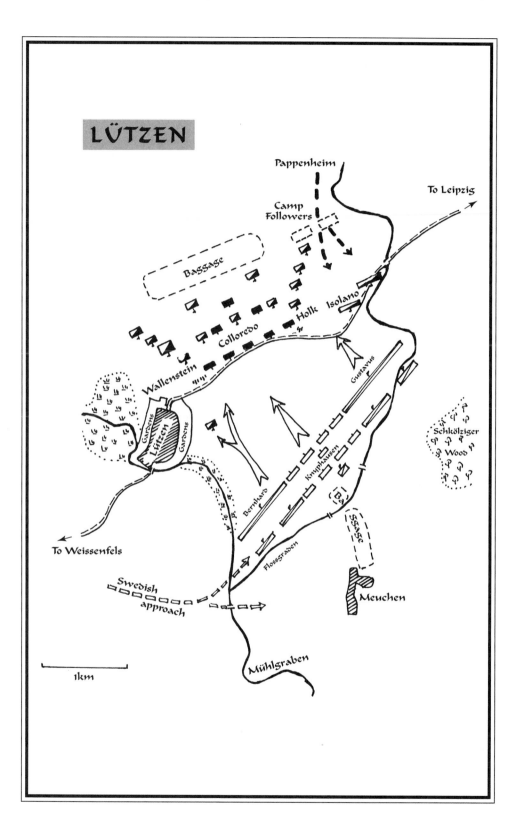

line. Wallenstein switched cavalry from his right to stem the king's advance.

Pappenheim arrived in the early afternoon with 2,300 cavalry, having ridden 35km through the night. His arrival encouraged the Croats to return and together they drove the Swedes back across the road. The veteran Swedish infantry also suffered heavy casualties and fell back, having failed to dislodge the imperial centre. Wilhelm of Weimar's bodyguard fled, panicking the Swedish baggage which also took off. Several imperial units had also broken, and both armies were losing cohesion. Pappenheim had been shot dead early in his attack; Wallenstein's order summoning him was later retrieved bloodstained from his body. The battle disintegrated into isolated attacks by individual units.

Gustavus appears to have got lost as he rode to rally his shattered infantry and was shot, probably by an imperial infantry corporal. His entourage tried to lead him to safety, but blundered into the confused cavalry mêlée still in progress amid the smoke on the right where he was shot again, by Lieutenant Moritz Falkenberg, a Catholic relation of the defender of Magdeburg, who himself was then slain by the Swedish master of horse.[83] The fatal shot burned the face of Franz Albrecht of Lauenburg who was accompanying the king as a volunteer. Under attack himself, Franz Albrecht could no longer support the king in his saddle and he fell dead to the ground. The Swedes never forgave the duke for abandoning their monarch's body, which was subsequently stabbed and stripped by looters. Rumours of the king's death added to the growing despondency in the Swedish ranks. Knyphausen, commanding the infantry, insisted Gustavus was only wounded and the royal chaplain, Jacob Fabricius, organized psalm singing to boost morale. Unaware of what had happened, Bernhard continued his fruitless attacks on Lützen.

The fighting subsided around 3 p.m. Knyphausen advised retreat, but Bernhard, now appraised of the situation, urged another assault that finally carried Windmill Hill. Firing ceased two hours later, after dark. Pappenheim's 3,000 infantry arrived an hour after that. Wallenstein was exhausted and appalled at the loss of at least 3,000 dead and wounded, including many senior officers. He decided to retreat and abandoned his artillery and another 1,160 wounded, who were left behind in Leipzig as he fell back into Bohemia. The Swedes lost 6,000 and were on the point of retreating themselves when a prisoner revealed that the Imperialists had already gone.

The disparity of the losses, magnified by Gustavus's presence among the Swedish dead, fuelled the controversy over who really won. Protestant propaganda and Gustavus's firm place on later staff college curricula have ensured that Lützen is generally hailed as 'a great Swedish victory'.[84] Wallenstein showed far superior generalship, whereas Gustavus relied on an unimaginative frontal assault with superior numbers. The Swedes were able to claim victory because Wallenstein lost his nerve and retreated, not least because he was not certain until 25 November that Gustavus was dead. Wallenstein probably regretted this mistake. He certainly vented his fury on the units that had fled in the battle, insisting on executing eleven men, but he also distributed bonuses to the wounded and richly rewarded those who distinguished themselves like Holk and Piccolomini.

Lützen's real significance lay in Gustavus's death. The Swedes continued fighting, already helping the Saxons evict the remaining Imperialists from the electorate by January. But their purpose had changed and Oxenstierna sought, albeit with little success, to extricate his country under the best possible terms.

15

Without Gustavus 1633–4

THE HEILBRONN LEAGUE

Stabilization of the Swedish Crown

The Swedish government presented their monarch's death as a national emergency, and encouraged the population to close ranks and secure a satisfactory outcome to the war. Material intended for an external audience depicted him dying for the Protestant cause and sought to perpetuate his memory as a reminder to Germans of Sweden's sacrifice on their behalf. Peace was not considered, because the government feared negotiations would be interpreted as a sign of weakness, implying Swedish power had rested on the king alone.[1]

Gustavus left a six-year-old daughter, Christina, and a constitution that made no provision for rule without a king. His widow, Maria Eleonora, was incapable of exercising power. Distraught at the news, she locked herself and her daughter in a room, blackening the windows. When her husband's embalmed body eventually reached Nyköping in August 1633 she ordered the coffin be left open so she could visit him every day. Oxenstierna managed to have the corpse interred in Ridderholm church in Stockholm ten months later, but had to post guards after she tried to dig it up. The grief suggests mental instability, but may also have been an attempt to postpone her inevitable loss of influence, as control over Christina represented Maria Eleonora's only asset. Oxenstierna finally freed Christina from her mother's gloomy apartment by banishing the queen to Gripsholm island in 1636. She fled in disguise to Denmark four years later and spent seven miserable years in Brandenburg before her daughter consented to see her again.[2]

The political vacuum was filled by ten councillors of state who assumed responsibility for the regency until Christina was declared of age in 1644. The Riksdag ratified these arrangements early in 1633 and they were confirmed by constitutional reforms drafted by Oxenstierna the following year. The largely aristocratic regents were not whole-heartedly behind Oxenstierna, but all recognized him as indispensable and he was confirmed as Sweden's high chancellor and legate in Germany in January 1633. He received wide powers, but 'where the king would have simply ordered, the chancellor must seek to persuade and convince'.[3] He remained the man on the spot, conducting policy largely on his own initiative since it took a month or more for letters to reach him from Stockholm. He maintained cordial relations with the precocious Christina who initially was in awe of him but soon began to resent his tutelage. She asserted herself after her majority, notably backing those councillors more inclined to make concessions to obtain peace. By then, however, Swedish policy was firmly established and there was little she could have done to change it and few indications that she really wanted to. Her Francophile cultural sympathies and interest in Catholicism already inclined her towards Sweden's main ally. Her poor health and reluctance to marry proved more worrying, because they left open the question of the succession and sustained Polish hopes of recovering the crown.

The Question of Command

If the home front proved relatively unproblematic, Oxenstierna faced far greater difficulties in Germany, where the first priority was to secure the army's loyalty. Swedish service remained attractive thanks to the prestige attached to Gustavus's victories, and well-qualified officers continued to join after his death, but there were few native-born generals of sufficient experience and reputation to command respect. Oxenstierna was the first to recognize he could not lead himself, since his skills as a strategist fell far below those as a statesman and he lacked the personal charisma necessary for authority on the battlefield. His preferred choice was his son-in-law, Gustav Horn, himself a councillor of state since 1625. Horn was a cautious commander, unable to assert himself over the other generals. Johan Banér, a more forceful character, had yet to prove himself and fully came to the fore only once Horn was captured in 1634. Gustavus's rising star, the artillery general Lennart Torstensson, had been captured at Alte Veste. Though released in a prisoner exchange in 1633, his health had been broken by his imprisonment in poor conditions in Ingolstadt and he remained unavailable until 1635.

Even had a suitable Swede been available, it is unlikely Oxenstierna could have imposed him on the German generals. There was never any thought of giving command to Johann Georg of Saxony, whom Oxenstierna distrusted and despised as 'an insignificant tosspot'.[4] Wilhelm of Weimar was formally next in line as Gustavus's official second-in-command, but he had left the army after Alte Veste citing ill-health to mask his disappointment at not being given conquered land. Having effectively excluded himself from the top position, he tried to recover influence by organizing his own army as Sweden's governor of Erfurt. However, he was already overshadowed by his ambitious younger brother Bernhard, who became Oxenstierna's main problem. Interpretations of Bernhard have been coloured by nineteenth-century German historians who present him as a national Protestant alternative to both the emperor and the Swedes.[5] His own courage and enthusiasm won loyalty from his men who became known as the 'Bernhardines'. He was capable of sudden, bold moves that disconcerted his opponents, but often ended in near-disaster. He also frequently changed his mind, wasting time marching in different directions to little effect. This, and his subsequent defection to France in 1635, already made him a controversial figure, but it was his political ambition that caused the greatest difficulties. As the youngest of the (originally eleven) Weimar brothers, he resented deferring to his elder siblings. Their father's arrangement of 1605 entrusting rule to them jointly left little scope for Bernhard to act as a full imperial prince. He was determined that Sweden reward him with his own principality and he insisted on being made commander.

Oxenstierna was well-aware of Bernhard's ambitions and struggled to avoid a firm commitment that would inevitably complicate his task of persuading the emperor and other princes to accept Sweden's own territorial demands. The situation was precarious, because 'ownership' of the army was unclear. German officers had raised regiments under contract with Gustavus. His death raised doubts over their continued obligations to Sweden and they were owed considerable pay arrears. There was a danger that Johann Georg would persuade the Germans that their prospects lay in joining Ferdinand in return for an amnesty and minor concessions.

The issue was debated by a special committee in Vienna that reported on 28 January 1633, condemning the restitution policies. Trauttmannsdorff, Stralendorff and Wallenstein all urged peace, but Ferdinand had not learned the lessons of the two previous years and saw the revival of the military situation as a chance to resume his hard line. Nonetheless, the death of his Swedish rival allowed Christian IV of Denmark to renew his offer to mediate, sending emissaries to Saxony and Wallenstein. Encouraged, Johann Georg still feared Swedish reprisals and so remained discreetly behind Landgrave Georg of Darmstadt who pressed on with his proposal for a temporary suspension of the Edict. Saxony briefly held direct talks with imperial representatives at Leitmeritz in March 1633, but was unable to persuade Brandenburg to abandon Sweden.[6] Ferdinand gave ground, authorizing Trauttmannsdorff in July to offer a suspension of the Edict and a revision of the normative year to 1612, thereby safeguarding the Lutheran administrators. Denmark could recover Bremen and Verden, but Magdeburg and Halberstadt would be reserved for the emperor's younger son, Archduke Leopold Wilhelm.

Oxenstierna moved swiftly to neutralize the threat. He rejected Bernhard's call to combine all armies under his command for a decisive strike against the emperor. Instead, Bernhard was sent to command in Swabia and Franconia, and Horn, who was to join Bernhard from Alsace, was assigned to keep an eye on him. Banér was kept busy with the honour of taking Gustavus's body back to Sweden. Duke Georg of Lüneburg and Landgrave Wilhelm V were left their separate commands in Lower Saxony and Westphalia respectively. The best Swedish units were withdrawn to garrison Mecklenburg and Pomerania, though Oxenstierna still hoped at this point to obtain Bremen, Verden and Mainz and left garrisons there too. A few regiments commanded by German and Bohemian exiles were assigned to assist Saxony and Brandenburg and prevent either from defecting. Command in Silesia was entrusted to Thurn. Oxenstierna knew he was a poor general, but he needed a prominent figure to counterbalance Arnim. Actual command was exercised by Duwall who refused to take orders from Duke Franz Albrecht whom Johann Georg had promoted to Saxon field marshal. Duwall's small contingent of largely German troops was Oxenstierna's insurance for the Oder should Saxony change sides.[7]

The League of Heilbronn

Having secured the army for the moment, Oxenstierna pre-empted Johann Georg's attempt to draw Sweden's German allies into a neutral party by pushing ahead with Gustavus's planned Protestant *corpus politicorum* in January 1633. It was vital to move quickly because Richelieu was considering dropping Sweden in favour of sponsoring the more easily controllable Saxony.[8] French subsidy payments had already slowed down during 1632 and stopped altogether after Gustavus's death. Richelieu sent the marquis de Feuquières to assess who would be the better partner for France. Oxenstierna opened his congress in the relatively safe Protestant imperial city of Heilbronn in March, where he received strong support from the minor counts and princes already compromised as Sweden's collaborators. By contrast, Johann Georg's rival meeting in Dresden was poorly attended. Anxious France should not fall between two stools, Feuquières renewed the Treaty of Bärwalde on 19 April. Crucially, France agreed to continue paying subsidies to Sweden, rather than to the new alliance Oxenstierna had negotiated with the German collaborators in Swabia, Franconia and the Upper Rhine. This enabled Oxenstierna to retain the commanding position in the organization that was formally constituted as the League of Heilbronn on 27 April 1633. The Germans agreed to continue fighting until Sweden secured 'proper' compensation for its efforts, while Oxenstierna promised to press the emperor to restore the Empire to its pre-war condition, which now became the official League negotiating position. They accepted Oxenstierna as League director with an absolute veto in military affairs. He was to be advised by ten councillors, three of whom were Swedes while the others were largely veteran collaborators like Count Solms-Hohensolms, or other enthusiasts like the Württemberg chancellor, Dr Löffler.

Formation of the League was a remarkable achievement given the circumstances. The organization's effectiveness depended, however, on continued military success to persuade its members to remain on board. Members promised to make regular contributions to maintain 78,000 soldiers, but the organization was not large enough to raise the money needed to pay these men properly. At best, members' contributions would raise 2.5 million tlr a year, whereas the real cost of the army was 9.8 million. Richelieu was also not happy at Sweden's autonomy and directed Feuquières to undermine Oxenstierna's authority as director. Feuquières held out the offer of switching French subsidies to the League if members accepted that country's protection. This policy was contradictory. France needed the League as a stop-gap while it marshalled the Germans into a broad cross-confessional neutral block, but it would have to destroy the organization to achieve this goal.

Oxenstierna had to win over the Lower and Upper Saxons, including Saxony and Brandenburg, for his new League to be truly effective. Feuquières came close to persuading Brandenburg's Georg Wilhelm of the League's merits at its first general congress that convened in July to September 1633. However, Brandenburg only joined a Franco-Swedish alliance on 28 October, not the League because this had agreed that Sweden could have Pomerania. Oxenstierna bullied Darmstadt into paying contributions by threatening to invade, but visits to Lower Saxony and Berlin all hit the Pomeranian rock on which the chancellor's 'whole German policy foundered'.[9]

The Swedish Mutiny

The deteriorating military situation hardly encouraged wider support. Aldringen had exploited the confusion after Lützen to clear southern Germany of Swedish garrisons at the beginning of 1633. Horn counter-attacked from Alsace with the Rhenish army, while Bernhard swept through Thuringia with the remnants of the royal army, picking up units there and in Franconia. Having crossed the Danube at Donauwörth, he joined Horn at Augsburg on 9 April, creating a total force of 42,700 men. These outnumbered the Bavarians and Imperialists in southern Germany by more than two-to-one, but any chance of using this superiority was wrecked by a mutiny on 30 April, just as the combined army entered Bavaria.

The soldiers had not been paid in full since 1631 and were owed bonuses promised after Breitenfeld and Lützen. Discipline was declining, as demonstrated by Bernhard's disorderly march through Franconia and the four-day sack of Landsberg on the Lech where 300 of the surrendering garrison were cut down, along with 154 inhabitants, including children. Many have concluded that the officers had lost control and that the subsequent destruction during the war was due to insubordination by ordinary soldiers.[10] In fact, all the major mutinies were orchestrated by senior officers who manipulated or fanned soldiers' grievances for their own ends.

The mutiny revealed how far Sweden had mortgaged its policy to the German officers. The sense of serving a great, victorious leader had checked discontent while Gustavus was alive. However, they were no longer prepared to wait, especially as news of the Heilbronn League and renewed French subsidy suggested Sweden could easily pay the 3 million tlr it owed them. This was not the case, nor was money alone the problem. Bernhard used the lull in official operations to attempt his own conquests, invading Eichstätt in May with the nominally mutinous troops.

Oxenstierna capitulated when Bernhard arrived in Heilbronn to press his demands. Gustavus had donated individual monasteries and districts, carefully reserving Swedish overlordship to expand his empire. The chancellor abandoned this political programme and assigned territories wholesale to satisfy the officers. The bishoprics of Eichstätt and Augsburg were sold to Colonel Brandenstein, along with four large lordships and an abbey, for 800,000 tlr and the promise of another 1 million over two years in lieu of the bishopric of Konstanz, yet to be captured. Brandenstein was an opportunist. A former Saxon officer, he deserted to the Swedes despite having been made a count by the emperor. As only a minor noble, it was impossible for him to pay these sums himself and it was accepted they would be delivered from contributions. To legitimize this licence to plunder, Brandenstein was appointed treasurer to the Heilbronn League. The arrangement typified the sort of expedients that now undermined Sweden's war effort since it merely transferred assets to an officer in return for money the army would have raised anyway.[11] Monasteries and districts were distributed to colonels and League war councillors. As Gustavus's illegitimate son, Colonel Gustavsson was particularly handsomely rewarded with the city of Osnabrück. Most doubted Sweden's long-term chances of holding these recently acquired lands and sold their new possessions at knock-down prices. In all, 250 donations were made in 1631–5, including 92 in Swabia. Those in Franconia alone were valued at 4.9 million tlr.

By far the most significant was the transfer in June 1633 of Bamberg and Würzburg to Bernhard as hereditary possessions with the title of duke of Franconia. He was to pay 600,000 tlr spread over four years over and above the contributions expected from his territories as League members. He had little time to enjoy his new status. Government was entrusted to his brother Ernst, who struggled against mounting local opposition and the hostility of the other Franconians. Their brother Wilhelm was compensated with the Eichsfeld in August. Horn had already received the Teutonic Order's headquarters at Mergentheim the year before and opposed the mutiny, widening the rift between himself and Bernhard.

TENSION ALONG THE RHINE

Trier and Maastricht 1632-3

Bernhard and Horn did not resume operations until July 1633, by when the wider situation had shifted decidedly against Sweden. To understand this, we need to review what had happened along the Rhine since Gustavus captured Mainz at the end of 1631. Sweden's growing difficulties removed it as a competitor to France in the Rhineland. Richelieu continued his precarious strategy of keeping Sweden embroiled in the Empire after 1631, covertly assisting the Dutch, extending protection to German Catholics and neutralizing Lorraine, all without provoking Spanish retaliation. While this continued to work into 1634, it succeeded only because Sweden remained successful in Germany while Spain suffered further reverses. These developments were viewed with deep suspicion by the Liga, which became convinced by Trier's fate of the wisdom of its decision in 1632 to reject French protection.

Elector Sötern's new alliance with France was unpopular among his cathedral canons who had let Spanish troops into Trier city and Koblenz before the French arrived in April 1632. Lieutenant-Colonel Bamberger, commandant of Sötern's fortress of Philippsburg, defected to the emperor, denying France an important bridge over the Rhine that gave access round the northern end of the Black Forest. D'Effiat and a French army allegedly 23,000-strong advanced from Lorraine to eject the Spanish from Trier in May, cooperating briefly with Swedish troops to capture the Ehrenbreitstein fortress that commanded the crossing at Koblenz. Trier and Koblenz briefly changed hands again as the French were distracted by Gaston's rising and d'Effiat's death, but the French returned and secured them in August.[12] These exchanges were significant, because they placed both French and Swedish troops in close proximity with the Spanish just as the Dutch under Frederick Henry attacked Maastricht. Again, it looked as if Europe's hostilities might fuse into general war.

Frederick Henry pinned his hopes on provoking an uprising in the southern Netherlands provinces thought to be growing restless at the continued burden of war. Count van den Bergh, who replaced Spinola as commander in Flanders in 1628, was convinced the conflict could not be won and had fled into nominally neutral Liège. While one Dutch column feinted at Antwerp, Frederick Henry advanced with 30,000 troops up the Meuse (Maas), through Liège, to attack Maastricht, the bishopric's second city, on 8 June 1632. The attack infringed the neutrality agreed with Ferdinand of Cologne, who was also bishop of Liège. The Dutch had no desire to involve themselves in the Empire's war, however; their attack was dictated by strategic reasoning, as possession of Maastricht would help cut communications between the two halves of the Spanish Netherlands. The Brussels government appealed for help. Despite the critical situation in Germany, Pappenheim took 8,000 men of the Westphalian army across the Rhine to relieve the city in return for much-needed Spanish subsidies.[13]

The siege of Maastricht drove a wedge between the two great conflicts, by obliging the Spanish to pull out of Trier and recall most of their men from the Lower Palatinate. A combined attack with Pappenheim failed to breach the Dutch siege lines on 17 August. Three days later Dutch engineers exploded mines under the walls and the surviving Spanish capitulated on 23 August. Limburg to the south-east surrendered after slight resistance on 5 September. The remaining Spanish garrisons further east on the Lower Rhine and in Westphalia were now cut off from the southern provinces.

The crisis compelled Isabella to permit the Netherlands Estates to reassemble for what would be their last meeting under Spanish rule. She already favoured peace and opened negotiations in November, while the Estates sent their own delegation as well.[14] Many hoped it would lead to a general pacification across north-western Europe. Richelieu was sufficiently alarmed to send Charnacé to stiffen Dutch resolve in January 1633. Frederick Henry meanwhile continued operations to force Isabella to improve her terms, launching another offensive along the Meuse and Lower Rhine in April 1633 with 16,000 men. These reprovisioned the Maastricht garrison and captured the Rhine crossings at Rheinberg and Orsoy, reducing the Spanish holdings to Jülich itself, Düren and a few other towns west of the river. The campaign completed the reshuffling of garrisons under way since Spain abandoned most of its German outposts in 1630 (see Chapter 13, pp.436–8). The Liga forces occupying Lingen since 1630 now abandoned it to avoid contact with the advancing Dutch. The Dutch had already evacuated their posts in the duchies of Jülich and Berg, and returned those in Mark to Brandenburg control in April 1632, allowing them to concentrate their forces in the duchy of Cleves closer to home. Swedish forces on the middle Rhine had grown to 19,000 by June 1632, but 8,000 were recalled to join Gustavus at Alte Veste the following month. Though Horn pushed into Alsace, capturing the bishop of Strasbourg's fort at Benfeld in November, he lacked the men to conquer the rest of the province. The wars remained separate because the belligerents' interests diverged and they had no intention of making new enemies.

Lorraine 1633–4

In 1633, news that Spain was sending a new army to Alsace prompted Richelieu to settle with the duke of Lorraine. Charles IV was already wriggling free of the constraints imposed on him in June 1632 and had rebuilt his army to 9,000 men by August 1633. Renewed strength improved his credentials as a potential protector for the Rhinelanders, and the Habsburg governor in Alsace had already invited him to garrison Hagenau and Saverne in December 1632. Richelieu engineered a rupture between France and Lorraine by demanding Charles accept French jurisdiction over his subsidiary duchy of Bar, and then promptly declared him a rebel in July when he predictably refused. The French then waited until he crossed into Alsace with most of his army to relieve Hagenau which was under siege by Christian von Birkenfeld's 8,000-strong Swedish Rhine army.[15] Birkenfeld caught the duke at Pfaffenhofen on 11 August, routing the Lorraine army in a battle that cost it 1,500 men.

Now that it was safe to attack, Richelieu ordered Marshal La Force to occupy Bar three days later. Reinforced to 30,000 men, La Force proceeded to overrun most of Lorraine, taking Nancy on 25 September where he captured Charles's wife Nicole as a hostage. Charles evaded French pursuit, retreating into the Franche-Comté with 1,000 followers.

His brother, Cardinal Nicolas François, initially agreed to French terms, but managed to escape Nancy disguised as a valet, while his sister Marguerite left dressed as a soldier. This provided Richelieu with the excuse to occupy the rest of Lorraine, capturing the last stronghold in August 1634. The Rhinelanders bowed to the new conditions and by January 1634 the French were admitted to Mömpelgard, Hagenau, the bishopric of Basel and the Alsatian possessions of the count of Hanau.[16]

The Battle of Hessisch-Oldendorf 1633

Sweden also lost its grip on north-west Germany where its local allies refused to join the Heilbronn League. Oxenstierna tried to reimpose Swedish control over them by extending the territorial concessions promised by Gustavus, but this only fuelled fragmentation as each concentrated on its own conquests. The Hessians under Melander broke into Westphalia, intent on capturing Münster, while Duke Georg and the Lüneburgers besieged the remaining imperial outposts of Corvey, Höxter and Hameln. Duke Friedrich Ulrich refused to cooperate altogether, hoping that negotiations with the emperor would secure a return of Wolfenbüttel. The few Swedish units under Knyphausen were too small to impose any central command.

This dispersal of Swedish and allied forces allowed the Liga regional commander, Gronsfeld, to rebuild his army around the few units left by Pappenheim when he marched to Lützen. He was reinforced by 4,000 Walloons recruited by Merode with money provided by the fugitive Catholic princes in Cologne. With these he repulsed an attempt by the Swedish Rhine army to advance downstream from Mainz at the start of 1633. By June he had assembled 10,800 infantry, 3,900 cavalry and 15 guns and marched east to relieve Hameln. In a rare show of solidarity, Melander and Knyphausen force-marched to join Duke Georg at Hessisch-Oldendorf, 20km north-west of Hameln, arriving on 7 July to give 7,000 foot, 6,000 horse and 37 guns.[17]

The battle the next day was the largest action in Westphalia during the war and, like Steinau (1632), it allows valuable insight into the relative flexibility of seventeenth-century tactics. The allies deployed at night on a 20-metre high plateau north of the town facing north-west with their left, under Knyphausen, resting on Oldendorf and the right under Melander in front of the village of Barksen, where the ground rose sharply into the Weser hills. Georg commanded the infantry and artillery in the centre, while the entire line was protected by a marshy stream. This prevented him from crossing, but equally nullified Gronsfeld's superior numbers of infantry. Gronsfeld deployed about 500 metres away with his left, under Geleen, largely screened from the enemy by two further streams and a wood projecting from the hills. He had slightly more infantry, but many were new recruits, while his cavalry was outnumbered. He proposed staying put, pinning the enemy down while Bönninghausen slipped past to relieve Hameln, which was now blockaded by a mere few hundred enemy musketeers. Merode and the other officers objected that they would be accused of cowardice and felt they would miss a chance to crush the enemy with one blow.

The action commenced at 7 a.m. with the customary cannonade, while opposing parties of musketeers contested possession of the wood. Melander's regimental guns and cavalry supported their foot, riding forward in small detachments to tip the balance against Geleen's infantry. The imperial and Liga cavalry officers, by contrast, refused to lead their units forward, arguing that they would get disordered in the trees. Geleen lost the wood and fell back, exposing the centre which was now subject to growing fire on its flank as well as Georg's guns to its front.

Knyphausen meanwhile led 900 cavalry across the stream against the imperial right. Gronsfeld charged, expecting to drive them off the plateau, but was himself repulsed, enabling more Swedes to deploy. Further attacks were also beaten off and soon Knyphausen outflanked the imperial right, which now collapsed and fled. Geleen's troopers gave way around the same time, leaving the infantry alone. They fought bravely until 2 p.m., but were surrounded and cut down. Only 4,200, mainly cavalry, escaped, while at least 6,000 were killed in the final stages and the pursuit. The allies lost around 300 men. It was one of the most complete victories of the war.

Hameln surrendered on 18 July, followed by Osnabrück in October. The latter remained the principal Swedish base in the region until 1643, because Oxenstierna refused to hand it over to Duke Georg. He also withdrew five of Knyphausen's regiments to Franconia in August, weakening the common army and frustrating Hessian and Lüneburg plans to capture more land west of the Weser. Dispirited, Knyphausen resigned on 26 February 1634, leaving the surviving Swedish units effectively leaderless.

HESSISCH-OLDENDORF

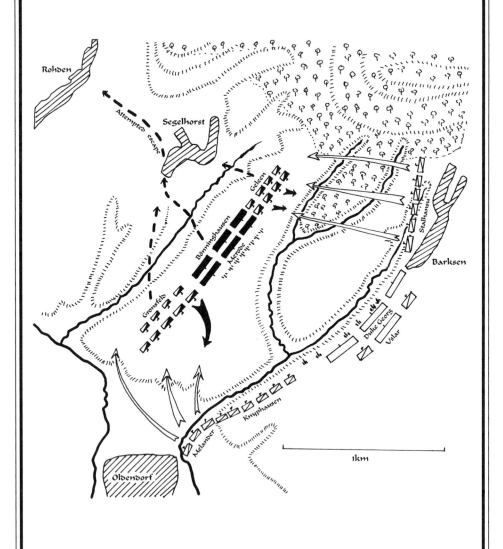

Rohden

Attempted escape

Segelhorst

Geleen

Dösninghausen

Merode

Stahansu

Barksen

Gronsfeld

Duke Georg

Velar

Knyphausen

Melander

Oldendorf

1km

Hessian Policy

The Swedish weakness unsettled the Hessians whose operations in West-phalia were intended to conquer the bishoprics and thereby establish a land bridge to the Dutch Republic. Dutch assistance had long been sought and Landgrave Wilhelm V now redoubled his efforts, hoping the Republic would prove a more reliable partner than Sweden. Oxenstierna supported Hessian diplomacy as a device to entice the Dutch to back the Heilbronn League. Melander and 1,000 Hessian and 2,600 Swedish cavalry joined Frederick Henry's army in August 1633. Like the earlier Swedish thrusts to Trier and Cologne, this threatened to merge the two wars. However, Frederick Henry was annoyed by the Hessians' late arrival and thought they had only come at all because they had eaten everything in Westphalia. He sent them and the Swedes back over the Rhine in late October. The Hessians were increasingly resented by the Dutch as rivals, especially after they captured Lippstadt in December and proceeded to take the entire line of the Lippe river, occupying posts the Dutch had just returned to Brandenburg. Additional outposts gave them most of the western half of Münster next to the Dutch frontier.[18]

Melander pursued negotiations for a Dutch alliance into 1635, coming closest to an agreement in 1634 when the Republic offered a subsidy and 3,500 auxiliaries. Their purpose was to use the Hessians to carve out a buffer along the Dutch eastern frontier to insulate the Republic from the German war. Success depended on the Hessians capturing Münster city, which was still held by the Imperialists. For this the Hessians were too weak, and the Guelphs refused to help, preferring to besiege Hildesheim and Minden instead, finally taking them in June and November 1634 respectively.

The 1633-4 campaigns established a regional balance that persisted with minor modifications until 1648. The Swedes were restricted to Osnabrück until they conquered Bremen and Verden in 1645. The Guelphs held Minden and Hoya in north-east Westphalia, as well as Hildesheim and Lower Saxony south of the Elbe. The Hessian conquests cut the Liga and imperial positions in two, isolating the remaining garrisons along the Ems valley in east Münster from the core positions in Cologne, its associated duchy of Westphalia, and Paderborn. The Imperialists had largely lost Lower Saxony, but Wolfenbüttel remained strongly garrisoned as a staging post should their main army need to cross that region. Periodic attempts to conquer the Lippe valley proved counterproductive, as it left much of the area devastated.

The failure to evict the Hessians destroyed Westphalian hopes of neutrality. Ferdinand of Cologne had deliberately rejected Archduchess Isabella's appeal for aid against Frederick Henry in 1633 so as not to alienate the Dutch. The Estates of his duchy of Westphalia and various other Catholic micro territories made a pact with the neighbouring Calvinist counties to maintain the neutrality of much of the area south of the Lippe that August. Meanwhile, the partial Dutch withdrawal in 1632 encouraged Wolfgang Wilhelm of Pfalz-Neuburg to declare Jülich and Berg neutral. The Estates of these two duchies renewed their alliance with their counterparts in Cleves and Mark to the same ends.

These promising developments were frustrated by the breakdown of the Dutch-Belgian talks following Isabella's death on 1 December 1633. Olivares had long distrusted her efforts and his interim governor, the marquis de Aytona, dissolved the southern Estates assembly and helped arrest its negotiators on suspicion of involvement with Count Bergh. Dutch policy moved in a similar direction as Frederick Henry swung behind the Gomarist war party. Though Richelieu refused to sign an open alliance, he agreed on 15 April 1634 to increase the subsidy paid to the Republic since 1630 from 1 million to 2.3 million livres in return for the Dutch suspending the talks.

Disheartened, Ferdinand of Cologne saw no option but to renew efforts to eject the Hessians. For their part, the Hessians dug in, recognizing that the conquered areas not only sustained their army but were bargaining chips should their homeland be overrun. Both sides were short of men and money and viewed Wolfgang Wilhelm of Pfalz-Neuburg's territories as the only remaining soft target. Appreciating the danger, the duke raised his army to (on paper) 7,365 to defend 52 castles and towns. This merely whetted the appetites of Ferdinand and the Hessians who hoped to incorporate his soldiers into their own forces. Ferdinand sent Bönninghausen to raid Berg, while the Hessians seized Elberfeld in November 1633, disarming the Pfalz-Neuburg garrison, forcing the men to undress and giving them pieces of their flag as clothing in a deliberate attempt to humiliate them. The emperor meanwhile backed the Estates' refusal to pay the duke's soldiers, in the hope that they would redirect their money to him instead. Unpaid and demoralized, the Pfalz-Neuburg soldiers deserted in droves, but the duke stuck to his neutrality.[19]

These events have been covered in some detail because they are generally overlooked. They demonstrate the danger posed by the Swedes' initial appearance on the Rhine, shattering the Liga-imperial dominance that had prevailed since 1622 and creating a vacuum which was increasingly filled by France. France and Spain drew closer to war, but Europe's conflicts remained distinct. Confessional solidarity proved insufficient to forge an alliance between the Dutch, Swedish and German Protestants. The latter remained disunited, pursuing their own objectives with little regard to Sweden and failing to capitalize on their numerical superiority. Relative failure fuelled rivalry and resentment of Sweden's supposed lack of support, contributing to a willingness to defect to the emperor in 1635.

SPAIN INTERVENES

Wallenstein's Secret Diplomacy

Peace was impossible as long as Swedish power in southern and central Germany remained unbroken. The task of ejecting the Swedes devolved to Wallenstein and an imperial army that totalled 72,000 men in Bohemia and Silesia, with another 30,000 scattered in garrisons across Alsace, Westphalia, Lake Constance and the Danube.[20] Wallenstein's strategy hinged on persuading Saxony and Brandenburg to abandon Sweden, thereby exposing the Baltic bridgehead and isolating Swedish bases elsewhere. What he intended to follow remains uncertain, but it seems likely he sought a genuine compromise, involving a partial reversal of the Restitution Edict and the cession of at least part of Pomerania to Sweden to enable Oxenstierna to withdraw with honour. Oxenstierna negotiated with Wallenstein, because he preferred him to the Danish mediation efforts which remained totally unacceptable. Wallenstein kept Ferdinand informed, even reporting his use of Bohemian exiles as intermediaries, and relaying some information about the terms discussed.[21]

Many opposed compromise, not least Brandenburg that stood to lose Pomerania. There is little evidence that Wallenstein would have upheld the Bohemian exiles' demands either, since he and his closest relatives were leading beneficiaries of the land transfers. His discussions with them nonetheless raised suspicions in Vienna that grew with his practice of presenting each partner with different terms. These inconsistencies became increasingly obvious as the various parties conferred and rumours leaked out. For example, the Swedes intercepted his letter to the duke of Lorraine in October 1633 which suggested that Wallenstein intended to exclude them from Germany altogether.[22]

Though he sent a few units to reinforce Aldringen in Bavaria at the beginning of 1633, he wasted the opportunity presented by the Swedish mutiny. His failure to move out of the Habsburg hereditary lands left these bearing the brunt of the financial burden. Already in January 1632 he had demanded 200,000 florins up front, followed by 100,000 fl. monthly. He received at least 1.3 million to purchase artillery and equipment. Some of the cost was recouped by a second round of confiscations following the ejection of the Saxons and exiles from Bohemia in May 1632, when property worth 3 million fl. was seized from 16 lords, 126 knights and 190 commoners.[23] The windfall was soon exhausted, while Wallenstein expected Bohemia and Silesia to feed, house and clothe his troops throughout 1633. He mollified his more distinguished critics by exempting their properties from billeting. This simply shifted the burden onto the medium and lesser landlords whose peasants then fled, initiating a vicious cycle of more demands for contributions to feed his hungry troops as agriculture ground to a halt.

Instead of moving, Wallenstein sent emissaries to Arnim and Thurn in April. The moment was opportune as the formation of the Heilbronn League caused consternation in Saxony, but without the other Protestants, Johann Georg felt too weak to abandon Sweden. Arnim urged the elector to increase the army to pursue a more independent course, but there was no money. He remained suspicious of Wallenstein whose troops outnumbered his two-to-one. Rumours of his talks nonetheless alarmed Oxenstierna who ordered Banér to stay in Pomerania to take command of the Saxon forces if necessary. Reliable officers were sent to Silesia to ensure that the small Brandenburg corps there served under Swedish, not Saxon command.

Wallenstein marched with 25,000 men and 28 new cannon (cast from melted-down Prague church bells) in mid May to join Gallas who had a similar number of troops in Upper Silesia. Heavily outnumbered, Arnim retreated northwards to Langenöls near Schweidnitz. The two armies closed to within cannon shot, but Wallenstein offered a truce on 7 June 1633, which was extended for two weeks for more talks. Wallenstein ended the truce on 2 July, and tried to surprise the 1,800 allied garrison in Schweidnitz two days later, but was repulsed and fell back to Wilkau, while Arnim entrenched nearby on virtually the same ground occupied by Frederick the Great at Bunzelwitz in 1761. On 11 August Wallenstein directed Holk with 10,000 soldiers from Eger to raid Saxony to put pressure on its elector. Holk retired after two weeks and, on Wallenstein's orders, renewed talks with Arnim who was then visiting Johann Georg. The two generals met for dinner when Holk suddenly fell ill. Fearing poison, he was assured otherwise and left in his coach to confer with his subordinates. By now it was obvious he had the plague and they refused to see him. He died by the roadside alone, his coachman having gone to fetch a priest.

Wallenstein's behaviour was by now alienating the Spanish, who had initially welcomed his reinstatement. Olivares opened unofficial contact with the general through Quiroga and a series of special envoys who from May 1632 brought subsidies that totalled 1 million fl. by the end of 1633. Spain's intentions were clear. The money was to bring the German war to a swift conclusion so Wallenstein could attack the Dutch. He was offered the title of duke of West Frisia, yet to be recaptured from the Republic, as compensation for the loss of Mecklenburg. He refused the bait, regarding Spain's problems as separate from those in the Empire.[24]

The Decision to Send Feria

Talks continued into January 1634, but from the previous February Olivares had already sought an alternative plan, resolving on substantial intervention in the Empire to reverse the deteriorating situation along the Rhine. The decision represented a significant change of course and evolved as Olivares tried to harmonize several partially contradictory objectives. One was to continue the existing policy of strengthening the emperor, but now through means other than Wallenstein. Saaveda was despatched to Munich to revive plans shelved in 1630 to elect Archduke Ferdinand as king of the Romans. This got nowhere and made it harder for Spain to win backing for Olivares' plan to reinforce the Army of Flanders by sending reinforcements along the Spanish Road, blocked since 1632.

Feria, governor of Milan, received instructions in May 1633 to collect an army to cross the Alps and reopen the Road. This expedition would fulfil another objective by escorting Philip IV's younger brother, Fernando, to replace the then ailing Isabella as governor of the Netherlands. With manpower declining throughout the Spanish monarchy, Olivares' agents paid the Tirolean government to recruit 6,000 Germans, while another 4,500 Burgundians were levied in the Franche-Comté. Once Feria joined them, he should have 4,000 cavalry and 20,000 infantry. This powerful *Ejército de Alsacia* would face down the French and restore Spanish power throughout the Rhineland.[25]

With Fernando ill, Feria set out without him at the head of 11,000 Spaniards and Italians in August 1633, making the first transit of the Valtellina for ten years.[26] Richelieu had made arrangements to prevent just such a move, paying the Rhetian free states to maintain a small force under the Huguenots' former leader Henri de Rohan since 1631. However, the cardinal proved too clever for his own good. Suspecting Rohan of plotting with the Protestant Swiss, he ordered all but one of the French-paid regiments to be disbanded at the end of 1632. News of Feria's march prompted hasty orders for Rohan to reassemble, but it was too late and the Spanish advance guard was already in the valley.

Feria's approach transformed the situation in Germany. Bernhard and Horn had resumed operations against Bavaria in July, while Wallenstein remained inexplicably inactive in Silesia. Ferdinand formally appealed to Philip IV to redirect Feria into Germany once he was over the Alps. By now, the emperor was seriously concerned about Wallenstein's inactivity, which he blamed for reverses elsewhere. War Council President Schlick was sent to find out what Wallenstein was doing and why he was so adamant in opposing Feria's march. Schlick arrived in Silesia on 22 August to discover Wallenstein had just agreed another four-week truce that was eventually extended until October. Ferdinand now broke the Göllersdorf agreement with Wallenstein, which had given him sole command of the imperial army, by placing Aldringen's imperial detachment in Bavaria directly under the command of Maximilian on 18 September. This persuaded the elector to consent to Spanish intervention and the arrangement was confirmed when Spain granted a small subsidy to Bavaria for a year.[27]

The Siege of Konstanz

Feria's approach prompted Bernhard and Horn to separate their forces. The former continued operations against Aldringen and the Bavarians under Werth, but was defeated and driven from most of the earlier gains, including Eichstätt. Horn meanwhile headed south on 18 August, intending to take Konstanz and block the exit from the Tirolean passes into south-west Germany. The (then Austrian) town of Konstanz sat on a short promontory protruding from the south side of the lake. It could only be reached by crossing the Upper Rhine downstream and marching through Swiss territory to attack it from the south.

Individual Swiss had joined the Swedes, but the Protestant cantons had consistently rebuffed approaches for an alliance, knowing this would split the Confederation. Gustavus's empire-building contradicted their republican ideals and they were antagonized by his hostility towards their Calvinist religion. Horn gambled on infringing Swiss neutrality, hoping that capturing Konstanz would persuade the Protestant cantons to join him and block the Alpine passes for good. Having left infantry and gunboats to watch the town from the northern shore, he crossed the Rhine at Stein on 7 September, arriving to bombard Konstanz the next day. He had around 10,000 men and might have broken in if he had attacked immediately, because the town had relied on Swiss neutrality and its defences only faced the lake. There were only 1,200 defenders, half of whom were militia. The bishop and clergy fled by boat to Lindau on the other side of the lake, but the local commander showed greater resolve. Gaps in the defences on the south side of the town were hastily blocked with earth, while infantry and militia were ferried over to bring the garrison to over 3,000.

Though Bernhard and others were marching to reinforce Horn, the situation grew critical with the news that Feria was across the mountains. France offered mediation, hoping to achieve Horn's objective by persuading the town to accept neutrality with a Swiss garrison. Some citizens were willing, but the authorities refused. Only Zürich connived at Horn's presence which the other Swiss felt was endangering their neutrality. In desperation, Horn launched a series of costly assaults against the town, but Feria with 9,200 men joined Aldringen and another 12,000 at Ravensburg on 29 September and pushed towards Überlingen near the lake's western end to trap the Swedes in Switzerland. Having failed to take the town with a final assault, Horn retreated on 2 October, escaping just in time.

The French claimed he had withdrawn out of courtesy to the Swiss, but no one was convinced. The episode weakened the influence of Protestant militants within the Confederation and prompted the Catholic cantons to renew the 1587 transit agreement with Spain that had expired in 1626. The Confederation also incorporated Spanish Franche-Comté within their neutrality in March 1634.[28]

Disaster

Lorraine's unexpected and sudden collapse under French invasion that September had transformed the situation on the Rhine by the time Aldringen and Feria arrived and it was now dangerous to march through Alsace with La Force's powerful army on the other side of the Vosges. Horn was already across the Rhine and joined Birkenfeld in northern Alsace, confining Feria and Aldringen to the south. Meanwhile, Bernhard doubled back with 12,000 men, surprising Werth's small Bavarian detachment and capturing Regensburg on 14 November after a mere ten-day siege. The loss of such a prestigious imperial city was a major blow to the emperor and enabled Bernhard to ravage previously untouched areas in eastern Bavaria.

Aldringen was forced to send his cavalry back to Bavaria to help Maximilian, further weakening the combined army on the Rhine. With winter drawing in and no food left, Feria and Aldringen re-crossed the Rhine, harried by Horn. Weakened by plague the Habsburg forces now disintegrated. Maximilian refused to let them into Bavaria, and Ferdinand reluctantly agreed some could winter in Lower Austria with the rest going to Salzburg. Prior Friesenegger reported 'that was a spectacle. Many companies only half strength, black and yellow faces, emaciated bodies, half covered, or hung with rags, or masked in stolen women's clothing, looking just like hunger and need. Yet the officers next to them were handsomely and magnificently dressed.'[29] The archbishop of Salzburg also refused shelter and eventually the survivors joined their comrades in Austria in January 1634, by which time Feria was already dead.

The rapid spread of the war since 1631 combined with the plague to stir widespread discontent that was an important, if understudied aspect of the war. Whereas the Westphalian civic rebellion of 1622-3 (see Chapter 10) and the Upper Austrian Rebellion of 1626 (Chapter 12) contained political and religious grievances, the new unrest was fuelled largely by resentment of the soldiers and the disruption of daily life. The movement was primarily rural and uncoordinated. Peasants ambushed foraging parties and stragglers, or resisted raids on their villages. They received assistance from the authorities in areas where the imperial military presence was slight, leaving the Swedes as the primary targets for popular fury. Catholic peasants rose against the Swedes in the Sundgau, a Habsburg possession in southern Alsace, in January 1633, while those in Westphalia were joined by local nobles and Bönning-hausen's imperial cavalry to harass the Hessians. Peasants in Upper Swabia and Bamberg assisted the official militia in raiding Swedish outposts, while the Bavarians resisted Horn and Bernhard's invasion in the summer of 1633. Swedish reprisals were swift. At least 4,000 people were killed in the Sundgau alone, while numerous villages were torched without ever entirely suppressing the guerrillas.[30]

However, the unrest also contained a strong element of protest against the authorities who were failing in their duty to preserve tranquillity. Bavarian discontent turned against the poorly behaved imperial units left by Aldringen to defend the electorate when he marched to join Feria in September 1633 and was concentrated in the area between the Isar and Inn where these were based, and not further west towards the Lech where the Swedes were operating. Protests grew to involve at least 20,000 as the plague-ridden Habsburg troops tried to enter the electorate at the end of the year. Troops confronted a large assembly at Ebersberg on 18 January and attacked when they realized the peasants were poorly armed. Around 200 were killed and the authorities were able to pros-ecute 100 alleged ringleaders. The local authorities accepted the peas-ants' argument that they were acting in self-defence. Even Maximilian was eventually persuaded to approve the relatively mild court verdicts. One was beheaded for rebellion, five executed for having murdered soldiers and eleven banished for three years, but the rest were released.[31]

Sporadic unrest in Upper Austria since 1630 deepened after 1632, but unlike in 1626 it was restricted to those suffering most from the social dislocation of the war. Fiscal pressures ended patrimonial benevolence as the authorities were no longer prepared to allow leeway for struggling families unable to pay taxes. This may explain why the Upper Austrian unrest was expressed in mystical, religious terms as its leader, Michael Aichinger called Laimbauer, claimed visions of a better future. He lived on the run, sheltered by sympathizers until he was finally cornered in the ruins of Frankenberg church by a mixed force of 1,000 mercenaries, local officials and armed Catholic civilians. Only 60 of his 300 followers were armed men, the rest were women and children. Allegedly found hiding under the skirts of two of his followers, he was cruelly executed along with six others, including his four-year-old son, on 20 June 1636.[32]

WALLENSTEIN: THE FINAL ACT

The Second Battle of Steinau

The same epidemic that swept away Holk and Feria ravaged the armies in Silesia, the effects worsened by dysentery in the imperial camp and hunger in the Saxon. Wallenstein's effective strength fell by 9,000 to 36,000, while Arnim lost nearly a third of his 25,000 men.[33] Wallenstein finally ended the truce on 2 October 1633, sending Piccolomini with a small detachment westwards through Lusatia. Piccolomini spread rumours that he was the advance guard of the main army, deceiving Arnim who marched after him. Wallenstein followed to make sure the Saxons had gone and then sent Isolano and seven Croat regiments to continue the pursuit, while he double-backed with 30,000 men north-eastwards to the Oder. He intended to capture Steinau to isolate the 6,000 Swedes and Saxons holding the Silesian fortresses further south. Thurn and Duwall mustered only 2,400 infantry in Marradas's old camp by the burned-out town, with 2,300 cavalry scattered in villages east of the river.[34]

Thurn ignored warnings from his outposts that 8,000 imperial cavalry under Schaffgotsch had crossed downstream at Köben. These swept south early on 11 October, while Wallenstein and the infantry advanced to the Sand Hill west of the town. The Swedes claimed the officers commanding the outposts deliberately ordered their troopers not to fire as Schaffgotsch's men crossed. Certainly, both colonels subsequently entered imperial service. Duwall was blind drunk and incapable of uttering a word of command. Thurn surrendered, including all the garrisons in his capitulation, which naturally increased Swedish suspicions of treachery. Wallenstein kept Thurn and Duwall with him as he summoned the fortresses to accept these terms. Glogau and Leignitz agreed, but the others refused and Duwall escaped and organized an energetic defence from Breslau until he died, probably from liver failure, in April 1634.

Georg Wilhelm of Brandenburg reinforced his garrison at Küstrin in case Wallenstein decided to advance down the Oder, but 11,000 Imperialists swept past, capturing Frankfurt and Landsberg on the War-the, before fanning out either side to overrun much of eastern Pomerania and Brandenburg. Oxenstierna sent frantic appeals to Bernhard to march from south Germany to threaten Bohemia from the Upper Palatinate. Bernhard belatedly obeyed once he had taken Regensburg. His siege had already caused great alarm in Munich and Vienna, prompting calls for Wallenstein to march to its relief. Wallenstein had left detachments to mop up the remnants of the allied forces in Silesia and was already on his way across Bohemia when Regensburg fell. He left his advance guard of 2,000 cavalry to continue over the mountains to Passau, but turned back with the main force and went into winter quarters around Pilsen.

The Plot against Wallenstein

Wallenstein's actions no longer appeared those of a rational person – people found his inactivity inexplicable. Many observers now openly attributed his behaviour to an alleged obsession with astrology. He was certainly fascinated by this branch of the magic arts that contemporaries associated as much with medicine as astronomy. He famously commissioned Kepler to prepare his horoscope in 1608 and again once he became commander in 1625. Kepler formally entered his service in 1628, while Wallenstein later consulted others, notably Gianbattista Senno from Genoa who had been Kepler's assistant. He also possessed an astrolabe and an amulet, and had asked Arnim to discover Gustavus's date of birth so he could read his horoscope. However, he was aware that the church condemned astrology as blasphemy and was careful, as in all matters, to conceal his true thoughts. His interest was already known by 1627, however, when pamphlets appeared claiming his decisions were guided by astrologers' predictions. This was a deliberate fabrication propagated by Maximilian as part of his campaign to get Wallenstein dismissed and was calculated to appeal to Ferdinand's piety.

It spread swiftly through diplomatic reports and had gained wide credence by 1633, assisting the task of those who now sought to remove him again.[35]

Whereas external pressure had been decisive in Wallenstein's first dismissal, opposition this time came from within the Habsburg monarchy where Ferdinand had viewed Wallenstein's inactivity with mounting suspicion. Maximilian worked discreetly to fan Ferdinand's doubts, but did not demand Wallenstein's dismissal until 18 December and had no direct role in events. Lamormaini and the Jesuits also opposed the general, but likewise were not instrumental in removing him. Spanish pressure was more significant. Though Quiroga admired Wallenstein and still wrote favourable reports, Oñate immediately sensed the change of mood in Vienna when he arrived in November, having accompanied Feria's army.[36] Crucially the moderate faction that favoured a compromise peace along the lines suggested by Wallenstein no longer trusted him to obtain it. Opposition became personal, not political, as moderates closed ranks with militants, all arguing that Wallenstein's behaviour was undermining imperial authority and prestige. Wallenstein's aversion to court life rebounded against him. He had not spoken to Ferdinand since 1628 and had deliberately failed to use the negotiations in nearby Göllersdorf to visit Vienna in 1632. There was now virtually no one left there to defend him. It was widely believed he had told the Bohemian exiles that Ferdinand was too dependent on clerics to make the concessions necessary for peace, and that he would arrange terms himself and use the army to force the emperor to accept them. This was tantamount to treason. Having conferred with Trauttmannsdorff and Bishop Anton Wolfradt, Gundacker Liechtenstein sent Ferdinand a formal memorandum on 11 January 1634 recommending Wallenstein's 'liquidation'.[37]

Wallenstein's alienation of the army made this feasible. He had spent most of 1633 in Silesia far from other senior officers whom he left largely to their own devices. His passivity caused concern. Inactivity damaged the army's morale and health, while offering no opportunities for the officers to distinguish themselves and gain promotion. Reluctant to approach their chief directly for fear of his notorious temper, they discussed matters among themselves, becoming increasingly conspiratorial and finally corresponding in code by August 1633. Piccolomini emerged as their leader. Despite continued promotion through Wallenstein's favour, Piccolomini sensed the emperor's mounting dissatisfaction with the general and possibly hoped to be chosen as the new imperial commander.[38] One of Piccolomini's subordinates, Fabio Diodati, penned an anonymous tract known as the *Bamberger Schrift* that summarized the army's grudges against its general.

Ferdinand sent Trauttmannsdorff to meet Wallenstein after Schlick returned from Silesia in August without a satisfactory explanation for his conduct. Trauttmannsdorff met the general in Pilsen on 28 November after he had already abandoned his march to Regensburg. Wallenstein was aware of the criticism and defended himself, for example responding to Ferdinand's fury at his release of Thurn from captivity by claiming it would be more use to have the incompetent count commanding the enemy army than in prison. He also wrote to the emperor explaining that he did not want to risk the army's health in a winter campaign, repeating this argument again at the end of December.[39]

These letters effectively sealed his fate by providing evidence of his direct disobedience of imperial orders. He appeared unaware of the consequences, not least because there were in fact good reasons for not continuing into Bavaria as it was now filling with Aldringen's and Feria's troops retreating from the Rhine. However, arriving after months of suspicious behaviour, his refusals now appeared to confirm he was planning to defect to the enemy. He compounded the situation by seeking to reassure himself of his subordinates' loyalty, summoning his colonels to Pilsen and threatening to resign. Of those present, 49 signed a declaration of personal loyalty on 12 January, known as the First Pilsner Reverse. Wallenstein directed Schaffgotsch to secure the signatures of officers still in Silesia, while General Scherffenberg was instructed to do the same in Upper Austria. Most signed because they expected that Wallenstein's resignation or dismissal would precipitate another credit collapse as in November 1630, which would ruin them personally and destroy the army's cohesion.

Piccolomini meanwhile presented his own damning critique of Wallenstein on 10 January. This carried weight in Vienna where he had been regarded as the commander's trusted subordinate and because news of the Pilsner Reverse appeared to confirm his accusations. Ferdinand met Trauttmannsdorff, Bishop Anton and Eggenberg in the latter's mansion in mid-January and agreed that Wallenstein should be taken dead or alive. Eggenberg's involvement indicates Wallenstein's complete isolation. By the time Piccolomini received word of this decision on

22 January, he had established contact with a small group of Scottish and Irish officers prepared to act as assassins. Walter Butler was colonel of a German dragoon regiment largely officered by fellow Irishmen, including Major Robert Fitzgerald and captains Walter Devereux, Dennis MacDonnell and Edmond Boorke. John Gordon, a Scot, was the exception in that he was a Calvinist, whereas the others were all Catholics. As lieutenant-colonel of Trčka's infantry regiment, he served as commandant of the Eger garrison, assisted by his friend Major Walter Leslie.[40]

It is likely that senior Habsburg officials were aware of this. With Wallenstein now considered a notorious rebel, there was no need for a formal trial. Ferdinand signed a patent on 24 January, releasing all officers from obedience to Wallenstein and instructing them to follow Gallas until a new commander was appointed. A second, harsher patent was signed on 18 February that directly accused Wallenstein of conspiracy and was essentially a death warrant. It was not publicized immediately, because all were convinced of the need for secrecy to avoid splitting the army. It was still unclear how many officers would follow Wallenstein. There were 54,000 Imperialists in Bohemia, Silesia and the eastern parts of Brandenburg and Pomerania at this point. Less than a third were scattered around Pilsen, while there were another 20,000 men under Aldringen in Austria, Ossa in the Tirol and Gronsfeld in Westphalia. Piccolomini signed the Pilsner Reverse so as not to arouse suspicions. He returned with Gallas to Pilsen on Wallenstein's orders for consultations, but managed to leave on 15 February. Copies of the emperor's first patent were distributed to loyal officers ready for publication to their units. The Upper and Lower Austrian Estates met in emergency session and agreed to vote additional funds to keep the soldiers content.

Events moved rapidly after Wallenstein's ally Scherffenberg was arrested in Vienna on 17 February. The next day, Ferdinand ordered the Prague garrison to be reinforced and Aldringen to collect loyal troops to capture Wallenstein. Other units were concentrated at Budweis and in the Upper Palatinate to stop him escaping. Wallenstein suspected nothing until Colonel Diodati left Pilsen with his regiment on the night of 17–18 February. A series of couriers were despatched to Vienna with letters refuting the rumours against him, while the remaining officers were reassembled to sign a second declaration on 20 February. Only thirty complied this time and were sent to collect their units and assemble at Prague. As soldiers began deserting the regiments still in Pilsen, Wallenstein realized he could no longer trust the army. Having spent the night packing, he left on 22 February, heading west for Eger from where he could join the Saxons or Swedes. Franz Albrecht of Lauenburg was still acting as intermediary for the secret talks with Saxony and was sent to tell Bernhard to meet Wallenstein in the Upper Palatinate.

There is no evidence that this defection had been planned. As late as 18 February, Johann Georg was still instructing Arnim to continue talks and, if the rumours were true, to dissuade Wallenstein from defecting. The second truce of August–October 1633 had convinced Oxenstierna of Wallenstein's insincerity. Arnim failed to persuade the chancellor during a five-hour meeting on 11 September that Wallenstein genuinely sought peace. The death in October of Lars Tungel, Sweden's envoy in Dresden, removed Oxenstierna's main source of news and heightened his suspicions of Saxony. He now sought Wallenstein's downfall to prevent him detaching Saxony in a separate peace, and spread rumours through the Frankfurt papers, playing on Wallenstein's known opposition to Feria's march to sow dissension in Vienna.

The Eger Bloodbath

Wallenstein abandoned most of the slow-moving infantry and artillery still with him in Pilsen, marching out with around 1,300 men and summoning Butler to join him with his 900 dragoons. Butler sent his confessor, Patrick Taaffe, to assure Piccolomini that he was still loyal and was only acting under duress. The conspirators had expected a long struggle and were encouraged by the rapidity of the army's disaffection from Wallenstein. Colonel Wangler secured the Prague garrison and units poured in from their outlying billets to declare loyalty to Ferdinand. Piccolomini set off in pursuit of Wallenstein with 2,000 cavalry, cutting off his rearguard outside Mies. Piccolomini halted there, subsequently claiming his men were too tired to go further, but probably to distance himself from the coming massacre.

Wallenstein's dwindling party reached Eger late in the afternoon on 24 February. Gordon gave him his own quarters in the Pachabel house, a fine three-storey building on the main square that had been commandeered from a Lutheran citizen living in exile. Most of the troops were obliged to camp outside the town as it was already occupied by Gordon's 1,200 infantry. Ilow, Wallenstein's trusted second-in-command, held a series of meetings the next day with Gordon, Leslie and Butler trying to persuade them to remain loyal to their chief. All three wrestled with their consciences. Professions of religious and dynastic loyalty loom large in their later statements, but clearly personal advancement was a factor. They also realized they had already gone too far: if they did not execute Wallenstein they would be implicated in his crimes. They agreed privately to separate Wallenstein from his remaining inner circle of Ilow, Trčka, Kinsky and Captain Niemann who commanded his bodyguard. They took a calculated risk of inviting all five to dinner in the castle, guessing correctly that Wallenstein would decline. The meal started after 6 p.m. with Gordon as host. Leslie excused himself to let MacDonnell and a party of Butler's dragoons into the castle. Having returned to the table, he waited until a servant entered and nodded, indicating all was ready. Six dragoons burst in crying 'Who is a good Imperialist?' Gordon, Leslie and Butler leapt to their feet shouting 'Long live Ferdinand!' Kinsky was killed in his chair, while the others were butchered after a brief but violent fight in which the table was overturned. Butler then rushed to the Pachabel house, arriving around 10 p.m. Fitzgerald secured the doors, while Devereux dashed upstairs, killing a page who got in the way. Having broken his sword, he grabbed a half-pike and burst into Wallenstein's bedroom. The general had taken off his sword, boots and coat and was about to go to bed. After a moment's hesitation, Devereux ran him through. The corpse was dragged down the stairs, bundled into a chest and taken to the castle.[41]

The assassins spent the next day assuring the loyalty of the soldiers. Leslie went to Vienna to report, while Butler, who must have had detailed knowledge of Wallenstein's plans, sent a party of dragoons to capture the unsuspecting Franz Albrecht as he rode back from seeing Bernhard. They also tried as an additional coup to kidnap Arnim by sending a forged letter sealed with Kinsky's signet ring, but rumours of the murder were already out. The Saxons had genuinely believed Wallenstein was defecting, but Bernhard suspected his appeals were yet another trick.

The situation remained confused. Unaware of what had happened, the commandant of Troppau declared for Wallenstein on 1 March, but was forced to surrender when his men accepted an imperial amnesty.

Imperial garrisons in Swabia offered little resistance as Horn exploited the situation and 3,000 enlisted in his army.[42] Bernhard only left Regensburg on 1 March when he learned of the murder and dashed north hoping to seize Eger and rally disgruntled imperial units to the allies, but it was already too late.

Rewards and Cover-up

Discontent continued nonetheless, because credit collapsed as feared, and the conspiracy split the officer corps. The prime movers were Italians, while Scots and Irish had done the deed. The victims were Bohemians, Silesians or north Germans. Melchior von Hatzfeldt regarded his appointment to the court martial to review the events as a trick by Gallas to land a German with the disagreeable task. He managed to dodge this duty, but resentment remained, especially towards the unsympathetic Piccolomini.[43] Protestant propaganda, initially hostile to Wallenstein, switched to fan tensions and destabilize the army.

The emperor moved quickly, announcing his son, Archduke Ferdinand, as the new commander on 27 April, with Gallas as second-in-command. He reassumed responsibility for appointing colonels who were now forbidden to command more than two regiments simultaneously. Some other attempts were made to improve discipline and to rationalize the artillery, but otherwise the army and its funding remained unchanged.[44] Finances and loyalty were underpinned by accelerating the confiscation of Wallenstein's properties and those of his collaborators, already authorized on 20 February, netting assets estimated at over 13 million florins.[45] Butler, Leslie and Gordon all received estates. Butler did not enjoy his for long, dying of plague in December 1634, while Gordon soon left imperial service for that of the Dutch, probably because his arrogance alienated his comrades. Leslie, by contrast, became a wealthy and influential figure without exercising further active command. The actual assassins received cash and more modest honours, but remained without significance. Devereux died five months later as a colonel. The real beneficiaries were the chief conspirators like Piccolomini, Gallas and Aldringen, who all received large estates, partly as rewards, but also to settle their pay arrears.

The contemporary press reported 24 executions.[46] In fact only the commandant of Troppau was executed, as was General Schaffgotsch despite lack of evidence. Seven others were deprived of their regiments and a few more temporarily imprisoned, including Franz Albrecht who was released in August 1635 once Saxony changed sides. A series of reports concluded by July 1634 that the two Pilsner Reverses constituted mutiny and justified assassination on the 'notorious rebel' argument. The findings were belatedly published as an official justification in October. The search for evidence continued, but little could be unearthed, beyond a confession from Rasin, one of Wallenstein's Bohemian intermediaries.

Ferdinand had no desire for a witch hunt, especially once the initial investigations confirmed that Wallenstein had acted largely alone. Like Maximilian, he was simply relieved that the danger had passed and wanted the matter buried. It is clear that potentially incriminating documents like the Göllersdorf agreement were destroyed to silence possible criticism of the emperor. Wallenstein's relations did not protest and provision was belatedly made for his widow, who was allowed to live on one of his properties. Only Eggenberg displayed any real disquiet, resigning his post as privy councillor, but his death shortly after minimized the impact of this gesture.

Wallenstein passed rapidly from current controversy to literature and drama; a play about him was performed in London as early as 1640. Interest waned around 1700, but revived with Schiller's trilogy at the end of the eighteenth century that sparked historical debate about his significance. Perhaps the real tragedy was that he was already slipping into irrelevance by the time of his murder. With the Saxons actively seeking peace, he was more a hindrance than help. The general conclusion is that he represented the last of the condottieri, or great mercenary captains who emerged in the Italian Renaissance.[47] Such figures are thought to represent a transition in historical development as expedients employed by states until governments were capable of organizing armies themselves. This is misleading. Wallenstein's failure to secure his subordinates' loyalty indicates the relative strength of the Habsburg state. The officers recognized that, ultimately, it was the emperor, not Wallenstein, who guaranteed their funding and legitimized their actions. Wallenstein might have won support if he had acted as spokesman for the officers' grievances, as Bernhard had done during the Swedish mutiny. The First Pilsner Reverse suggests this. However, the events proved very few were prepared to follow him in an act of political disloyalty.

THE TWO FERDINANDS

Renewed Spanish Intervention 1634

Wallenstein's murder cleared the way for Olivares to renew his strategy of 1633 to combine the restoration of Spanish power along the Rhine with pressure on the emperor to assist against the Dutch. He did not expect Ferdinand to declare war on the Republic, but hoped an improved position in the Empire would prompt the emperor to detach part of his army to Flanders. Matters there were pressing following Isabella's death in December 1633 and further evidence of Count van den Bergh's conspiracy. A new army was collected in Milan to escort Philip's brother Fernando to the Netherlands. This would collect the survivors of Feria's expedition who were still in Bavaria, restore the situation in southern Germany, clear the Spanish Road and provide a powerful reinforcement for Flanders. Oñate was instructed to offer more substantial subsidies to be released as soon as Ferdinand agreed to reciprocate with military assistance.[48]

Oñate met senior Bavarian and imperial advisers in Vienna in late April 1634 to make the necessary arrangements and plan the liberation of southern Germany. With Bavarian support, he persuaded the Imperialists to remain on the defensive against Saxony and direct their main effort against Bernhard and Horn. Archduke Ferdinand and Gallas advanced a month later with 25,000 men from Pilsen to join Aldringen who had 3,000 Imperialists, 7,500 Bavarians and 4,000 Spanish survivors on the Danube. Rodolfo Colloredo was left with 25,000 in Bohemia, while his brother Hieronymus had 22,000 in Silesia and along the Oder. There were about 6,000 holding Breisach and the remaining outposts around Lake Constance, while the Liga units in Westphalia totalled 15,000.[49]

These were substantial numbers and indicate the continued scale of an imperial effort capable of maintaining several large armies simultaneously. With Wallenstein gone, command was also more coherent, in contrast to the Swedes who remained disunited. Horn stayed bogged down besieging Überlingen in an effort to close the Lake Constance route to Fernando. Bernhard was still in Franconia and did not think the Imperialists would attempt anything until the Spanish arrived, giving him time to resume the fruitless attacks on Kronach and Forchheim that would secure his possession of Bamberg.

This dispersal of the two main Swedish armies exposed Regensburg, their chief prize from the previous year. Imperial and Bavarian forces besieged the city from 23 May. Lars Kaage conducted an energetic defence with his 4,000-strong garrison, but could not hold out indefinitely. Horn and Bernhard united near Augsburg on 12 July, but campaigning had reduced their combined strength to only 22,000. They pushed east into Bavaria, defeating a blocking force at Landsberg on the Lech where Aldringen was killed on 22 July. A week was wasted before they resumed their advance, by when it was already too late because Regensburg surrendered on 26 July. Kaage was recalled to Sweden in disgrace, but had done his job well, weakening the besiegers who lost 8,000 casualties and 6,000 deserters. The static character of sieges gave ample opportunity for sickness and hunger to bite, making them often more costly than battles. The imperial losses were compounded by bad news from the Habsburg hereditary lands where a combination of poor leadership and insufficient numbers prevented the exploitation of the gains following the second battle of Steinau.

Oxenstierna was determined to eliminate the threat to Pomerania and distract Johann Georg from his peace talks. Alexander Leslie retook Landsberg on the Warthe on 16 March while Hieronymus Colloredo was busy blockading Breslau far to the south. It was not until May that Banér rebuilt the wreck of Thurn's army to 14,000 men. Georg Wilhelm sent 3,000 Brandenburgers, while Arnim arrived with 14,000 Saxons. The combined army routed Hieronymus Colloredo at Liegnitz on 8 May in a hard-fought battle decided by the better-disciplined Saxon infantry. The imperial army disintegrated, losing over 5,000 troops. Colloredo was court-martialled and briefly imprisoned. By June Banér had retaken the positions along the middle Oder, including Frankfurt. He then turned west with Arnim to invade Bohemia, appearing before Prague the day Regensburg fell.

Archduke Ferdinand marched down the Danube towards Bohemia, but stopped on 2 August when news arrived that Arnim had already withdrawn, citing lack of supplies as an excuse to abandon Banér. Eleven regiments continued to reinforce Rodolfo Colloredo, while the rest of the archduke's men headed back to capture Donauwörth on 16 August. The Imperialists' crisis had passed, but it had alarmed Spain sufficiently to instruct Fernando to make a detour and assist the Imperialists in Franconia.

The 11,700 Spanish and Italians who crossed the Valtellina in July represented both the largest and last contingent to use that route. Their advance was delayed by high water at Lake Como at the entrance to the valley, but they joined the remnants of Feria's army in August to total 3,892 cavalry and 18,700 infantry.[50] Archduke Ferdinand, meanwhile, advanced a short distance north-west to besiege Nördlingen, held by only 500 men, sending cavalry to relieve Forchheim, which was still blockaded by around 4,000 troops under Cratz. The thrust into Franconia struck the heart of the Heilbronn League. Oxenstierna struggled to maintain flagging support at the League's second congress, currently meeting in Frankfurt. Nördlingen had little strategic value, but Oxenstierna could not afford to lose it and directed all available forces to its relief.

The Battle of Nördlingen

Having fallen back into Swabia to regroup, Horn and Bernhard reunited at Ulm and marched east through Aalen and Bopfingen, arriving too late to stop Archduke Ferdinand commencing his siege of Nördlingen on 18 August. Horn refused to attack across the river Eger against superior numbers. He knew the Spanish were on their way, but expected the reinforcements organized by Oxenstierna to arrive first. Having cleared the Croats screening the town on 24 August, Horn threw in 250 musketeers and promised to relieve the defenders within six days. Around 7,000 troops arrived on 28 August, but they were mainly Württemberg militia and of limited value. Bernhard and Horn heard the sounds of celebration as Fernando arrived in the enemy camp on 3 September. The meeting between the two Ferdinands was commemorated in a painting by Rubens. The two cousins got on well, but actual command was exercised by their experienced lieutenants – Gallas and Spinola's son-in-law, the marquis of Leganés. The fugitive duke of Lorraine arrived as the Bavarian commander following Aldringen's death.[51] The Spanish were already infected with the plague that had killed 4,000 since their arrival in Bavaria, but the combined army was still powerful, numbering 15,000 cavalry, 20,500 infantry and at least 52 cannon. Of these troops, 15,000 were 'Spanish', 8,500 Bavarian, 10,000 Imperialists and 2,000 Croats.

Nördlingen came under heavy bombardment and nearly fell to an assault on 4 September. Alerted by distress flares, Horn and Bernhard conferred at midnight. Horn wanted to wait for Solms who was expected within six days with 6,000 men, but Bernhard rightly believed the town would not last that long and argued that Cratz's arrival from Forchheim the next day would already give them 16,000 foot, 9,700 horse and 70 guns. They were probably unaware of the true odds and certainly only had a sketchy idea of the ground beyond the river, because the imperial Croats and dragoons prevented effective reconnaissance. They decided to march west as if retreating to Ulm, but cross the Eger upstream at Bopfingen and then head south to seize a line of hills 2km south of Nördlingen to outflank the two Ferdinands. Setting off at 5 a.m., they picked up Cratz, left their baggage at Neresheim guarded by 3,000 Württembergers and headed east across the wooded Jura hills. Horn and Bernhard had been alternating command of the advance guard so neither would feel subordinate to the other. It was Bernhard's turn to lead and he pressed on, making but slow progress along the single-track road.

He was spotted by imperial pickets around 4 p.m. Leganés and Gallas reacted immediately to secure the line of hills to their left. These ran north-west to south-east from the Eger and were separated from the Jura by the marshy Retzenbach stream. Bernhard's troops appeared by the Himmelreich hill in the west shortly after 4 p.m. and engaged the Spanish and imperial pickets, including Butler's dragoons.[52] A struggle developed as Bernhard tried to clear the hills one after another from west to east. His troops were still disgorging from the Jura and crossing the Retzenbach, but after three hours he had taken the Himmelreich, the wooded Ländle and the open, lower Lachberg in succession. The time allowed Spanish and imperial musketeers to collect on the wooded Heselberg where they continued to resist, backed by cavalry. Horn arrived after 10 p.m. to relieve Bernhard's exhausted troops and the Heselberg finally fell four hours later.

The delay proved crucial, allowing 6,600 Spanish and 1,500 Bavarian infantry to occupy the Albuch at the eastern end of the hills that was the key to the entire position, because it blocked the way around the Habsburg flank. They spent the night digging three small entrenchments for 14 cannon, while 2,800 Burgundian and Italian cavalry drew up nearby. The rest of the army deployed along another line of hills running north to Nördlingen where 2,000 infantry were left in the entrenchments to prevent a sortie.

The Habsburgs expected the enemy to cross the Himmelreich and deploy on the Herkheimerfeld plain between their position and the Eger. Bernhard and Horn had no intention of carrying out such a dangerous manoeuvre. Instead, Bernhard's tired troops would wait on the Ländle and Lachberg, while Horn's slightly fresher men attacked the Albuch from the Heselberg and the Retzenbach valley. Horn had about 4,000 cavalry and 9,400 infantry, though 3,000 of the latter were Württemberg militia. He attacked at dawn on 6 September, probably prematurely because his cavalry commander misinterpreted a reconnaissance and launched an assault up the steep south-east slope. The cavalry were repulsed, but the crack Scottish and German infantry from the first wave soon overwhelmed the Habsburg front line composed largely of Germans recruited that winter for Spanish service. The Protestants blamed the subsequent debacle on a powder wagon exploding, temporarily throwing their victorious infantry into confusion. It is more likely they were caught unprepared by a sudden counter-attack by the veteran native Spanish Idiaquez regiment that had been waiting behind the entrenchments. Within an hour, Horn's troops were back in their starting positions.

Each subsequent assault was pressed with dwindling enthusiasm, whereas the Spanish could feed fresh troops from their reserves northeast of the hill. The Spanish also knew how to deal with the feared Swedish salvo, crouching down each time the enemy prepared to fire. As soon as the bullets whistled over their heads, the Spanish sprang up and fired a volley of their own. Bernhard sent over two infantry brigades to assist and moved his own cavalry onto the plain to distract the Habsburgs and deter them from reinforcing the Albuch. The fresh infantry were soon pinned at the foot of the hill by Spanish musketry and then attacked by the Italian cavalry waiting to the north. A fierce cavalry mêlée developed as Horn sent his own horse to the rescue, while Duke Charles, typically bored of sitting idle at the other end of the line, rode over at that point and organized a counter-attack. The sound of battle carried as far as Andech, 120km away.[53]

Horn gave way around 10 a.m., exposing Bernhard's other infantry still waiting on the Lachberg. Reinforced by more Bavarians, the Spanish carried the Heselberg, scattering the last of Horn's troops who tried to

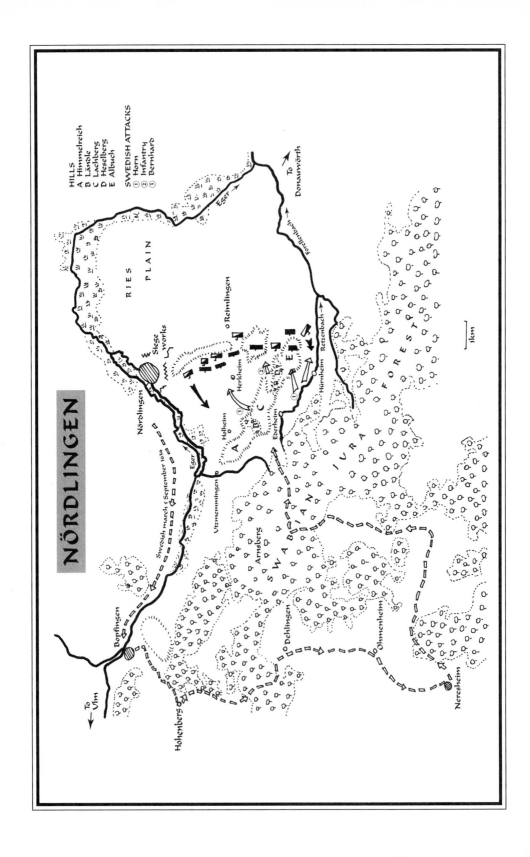

NÖRDLINGEN

HILLS
A Himmelreich
B Ländle
C Lachberg
D Heselberg
E Albuch

SWEDISH ATTACKS
① Horn
② Infantry
③ Bernhard

To Donauwörth

Forellenbach

Eger

RIES PLAIN

Reimlingen

Rettenbach

JURA FOREST

Siege works

Nördlingen

Herkheim

Hürnheim

Holheim

Eger

Utzmemmingen

A B C

D E

Eberheim

Swedish march 5 September 1634

SWABIAN JURA

Arnsberg

Dehlingen

Bopfingen

To Ulm

Hohenberg

Ohmenheim

Neresheim

1km

escape across the Retzenbach. The Croats had meanwhile worked their way along the Eger to pass the Himmelreich, turning Bernhard's flank. Even he realized the situation was hopeless and tried to extricate himself from the plain. 'The Spanish cut everyone down.'[54] Bernhard escaped only because a dragoon lent him a fresh horse. Horn was captured along with 4,000 others. The Bavarian and imperial prisoners pressed into Swedish service now rejoined their units, as did many of the men captured from the Heilbronn League regiments. Around 8,000 were killed, including 2,000 of the Württembergers who were massacred when the Croats captured the baggage left at Neresheim. Only about 14,000 men remained when Bernhard reached Heilbronn a few days later. He admitted to Oxenstierna that 'the great misfortune is so bad it could not be any worse'.[55]

Sweden Loses Southern Germany

Against this the Habsburg loss of 2,000 seemed slight and enabled them to claim a major triumph. Following a long succession of defeats, Nördlingen appeared to be vindication for Wallenstein's murder and cemented the influence of Gallas and Piccolomini by associating them with victory. As at Breitenfeld, the scale was magnified by the demoralization of the enemy army. News of the defeat reached Frankfurt on 12 September along with a flood of refugees. The remaining Heilbronn delegates fled the next day. Oxenstierna tried to improvise a new line of defence along the Main to contain the defeat to the south. No one cooperated. Johann Georg failed to launch the requested diversionary attack against Bohemia, while Duke Georg refused to move south to hold the middle section of the river. Wilhelm of Weimar abandoned Franconia and fell back with 4,000 men to his base at Erfurt, exposing the upper Main to Piccolomini and Isolano who approached with 13,000 troops from Nördlingen and north-west Bohemia. Piccolomini took Schweinfurt, while Isolano destroyed the Suhl arms workshops that had supplied most of the Swedes' small arms and munitions since 1631. Isolano and 6,000 Croats then swept down the Main in November, rampaging into the Hessian possession of Hersfeld.

The main imperial army moved west, bypassing Ulm to enter Stuttgart on 19 September. Duke Eberhard III fled to Switzerland and the last Württemberg fort surrendered in November. Only the isolated

Hohentwiel on the upper Danube held out. While the Imperialists made themselves at home, the Spanish continued westwards and the Bavarians, now under the command of Werth, captured Heidelberg on 19 November, though its castle remained defiant. Riding ahead, Werth's cavalry harried the remnants of Bernhard's army as it fled to Frankfurt. The commanders of Sweden's Rhine army refused to join him, on the ground this would spread demoralization to their own troops. Birkenfeld abandoned Heilbronn and retreated to the Kehl bridgehead opposite Strasbourg. His hopes of replacing Bernhard were dashed by Oxenstierna, who felt there was no realistic alternative to the defeated general. The death of Count Salm-Kyrburg to plague on 16 October enabled Bernhard to incorporate the former Alsatian units into his command.

Leaving Werth and Duke Charles to complete the conquest of the Lower Palatinate, Fernando continued his march down the Rhine, crossing at Cologne on 16 October to reach Brussels nineteen days later. Meanwhile, Philipp Count Mansfeld collected the Westphalians at Andernach, allegedly accompanied by a hundred coach-loads of Catholic lords and clergy eager to recover their property.[56] As Philipp marched south, it looked as if Bernhard would be crushed between his hammer and Gallas's anvil.

The situation mirrored that of 1631, only this time Protestant areas were the ones affected as government collapsed in the wake of the headlong flight of Sweden's German collaborators. Suffering was also more general because the plague hindered the harvest, causing widespread hardship. There were signs that Emperor Ferdinand had learned the lessons of 1629 as efforts were made to restrain over-zealous Catholics. He intervened to stop Bishop Hatzfeldt punishing the Franconian knights for collaborating with the Swedes and the Jesuits were refused permission to take over Württemberg's university at Tübingen. Political considerations undoubtedly influenced this, since Vienna did not want to jeopardize promising negotiations with Saxony. Archduke Ferdinand's presence was another moderating factor. However, it often proved impossible to stop officers and administrators exploiting the situation, either to enrich themselves or to find cash for the perennially underpaid imperial army.[57] Catholic government resumed relatively quickly in Würzburg despite the Swedish garrison holding out on the Marienberg and in Königshofen until January and December 1635 respectively.

Oxenstierna worked feverishly to salvage what he could of the situation, reconvening the Heilbronn League congress at Worms on 2 December. Though some members were willing to fight on, most sought a way out through Saxon mediation. Saxon and Darmstadt envoys agreed draft peace terms, known as the Pirna Note, on 24 November. Oxenstierna tried to stem desertion by publishing what he could discover of the terms, notably the suggestion of 1627 as a new normative year that would secure many of the Catholic gains.[58]

The French Take Over

His position was undermined by Richelieu who saw an opportunity to displace Sweden and convert its League into a cross-confessional neutral block. France had offered Sweden a closer alliance on 15 September 1633, but made ratification dependent on handing over Philippsburg, which had eventually been captured by Salm-Kyrburg in January 1634. Oxenstierna hesitated to relinquish the fortress since this would allow France into Germany. The remaining League militants increasingly saw France as a more desirable partner. All were aware that the sultan had suspended operations against southern Poland in 1633 in order to attack Persia. Poland made peace with Russia after a two-year struggle in June 1634, leaving it free to resume war with Sweden once the Altmark truce expired in 1635.[59] Wilhelm V of Hessen-Kassel had already opened talks with France, in parallel to his negotiations with the Dutch, and had accepted a French pension in February 1634. French troops were admitted to Philippsburg on 26 August, though the fortress nominally remained under League control with the duke of Württemberg as commandant.

The Württemberg chancellor Löffler and Palatine envoy Streiff von Lauenstein now went to Paris to negotiate behind Oxenstierna's back. The terms they accepted on behalf of the League on 1 November give a good indication of Richelieu's objectives. France would effectively assume control of the League and the League promised not to make peace without its consent. A subsidy of 500,000 livres would be paid direct to the League treasury, cutting out Sweden. Richelieu would also send 12,000 troops – who would not be Frenchmen so as to distance Louis XIII from open war with the emperor. The League would restore Catholic worship throughout its remaining conquests. Finally, it would provide appropriate 'satisfaction' for France's efforts in the form of the

Austrian parts of Alsace, Breisach, Konstanz and all the Rhine forts in between.[60]

Some of these concessions were already in French hands before the ink was dry. In the panic and confusion following Nördlingen, Swedish officials made their own arrangements. Mockel, the resident in Alsace, surrendered seventeen towns, including Colmar and Sélestat, to the French on 9 October, retaining only Benfeld. While Rohan occupied these with 5,000 men, La Force moved 19,000 to the Rhine opposite Mannheim, and another 3,000 in Nancy held down Lorraine.

The scramble for the League's assets now focused on its army at Frankfurt, which still numbered about 18,000, and the garrisons in Mainz, Speyer, Hanau and Heidelberg castle. Feuquières was prepared to kidnap Oxenstierna to prevent him moving the troops north of the Main beyond French influence. The Heilbronn delegates in Worms offered Bernhard exclusive command provided he remained in the south to protect them. Oxenstierna reluctantly conceded absolute control over the army on 12 March 1635 on the condition Bernhard remained subordinate to him as League director. The princes' representatives ratified Löffler and Streiff's treaty, but their civic colleagues and Oxenstierna refused. Feuquières withheld the promised subsidy, but had to authorize military intervention when the situation deteriorated as Philipp Count Mansfeld advanced slowly up the Rhine and Gallas tightened his siege of Heidelberg castle. La Force sent 7,000 men across the Mannheim boat bridge to help Bernhard relieve Heidelberg on 22 December. Mansfeld did not reach the Main until after the French had arrived and fell back to avoid contact.

The pressure continued to mount regardless. Imperialists disguised as peasants tricked their way into Philippsburg and overpowered its garrison of French infantry and Württemberg militia on 24 January 1635. With this threat eliminated, Werth led 3,700 men over the frozen Rhine to take Speyer on 2 February. Charles of Lorraine crossed upstream at Breisach with 9,000 Bavarians and Imperialists, occupied Mömpelgard and began reconquering Alsace. La Force had no choice but to abandon Heidelberg and re-cross the Rhine at Mannheim on 22 February. Though he recovered Alsace and Speyer, the operation drew off men assigned to another army Richelieu had intended should assist the Dutch. The winter campaign reduced La Force to only 9,000 effective combatants, obliging him to retreat to Metz to join 11,000 reinforcements assembling under Cardinal La Valette. Both were kept busy until June repelling Duke Charles's attempts to recover his duchy.[61]

The Worms congress reconvened on 17 February 1635 after four weeks' recess. The Lutheran members accepted the Pirna Note that the Calvinists still rejected. The congress broke up on 30 March without agreement, effectively dissolving the League. The Pirna Note offered Sweden nothing. Oxenstierna had already sent Hugo Grotius to Paris in February, but Richelieu refused to meet him. The chancellor swallowed his pride, bought new clothes and set out with a deliberately large retinue numbering 200 to meet the cardinal at Compiègne on 27 April. Louis XIII gave Oxenstierna a ring as a token of respect, but refused to agree anything beyond a vague treaty of friendship. By then Sweden was not France's only problem, as Richelieu and his master were in the midst of embarking on an entirely different war.

16

For the Liberty of Germany 1635–6

While Ferdinand capitalized on Nördlingen by making peace in the Empire, France and Spain moved towards war. The two developments were related, but had distinct roots. The emperor partially pacified the Empire with the Peace of Prague, brokered by Saxony, which left Sweden isolated by the middle of 1635. Before exploring this further, it is necessary to examine Franco-Spanish tension. As the next two sections indicate, France did not seek war in the Empire, but was dragged deeper into that conflict to support Sweden and prevent Ferdinand assisting Spain. The intervention worked, distracting the emperor sufficiently to enable Sweden to recover. Peace between the emperor and Sweden nonetheless remained possible into 1636, and it is important to look at the interaction between diplomacy and military operations to see why both sides squandered the opportunity. Imperial and Bavarian troops joined the Spanish in attacking France, but refrained from engaging the Dutch. Spain welcomed Ferdinand's assistance, but had envisaged it for its existing struggle in the Netherlands. Austro-Spanish military cooperation continued until 1639, but the emperor restricted his commitment and refused to allow Spanish interests to dictate policy in the Empire.

RICHELIEU RESOLVES ON WAR

Spanish Policy

There are good reasons to discount Spanish propaganda presenting themselves as innocent victims of unprovoked French aggression. Olivares had grown more hostile towards France since the Mantuan War.

He signed a new, secret pact with Gaston d'Orleans on 12 May 1634, promising 6,000 auxiliaries plus subsidies to enable him to invade France again. However, it is unlikely that he actively sought a major war with France to make himself indispensable to Philip IV.[1] The Spanish Council of State had voted against war on 13 April and the deal with Gaston was merely a repeat of the earlier arrangement in 1631-2 to keep Richelieu busy.[2]

Oñate concluded negotiations with Ferdinand in the Treaty of Ebersdorf on 31 October 1634 that was publicly directed at upholding the integrity of the Empire. Secret articles endorsed Spain's interpretation of the 1548 Burgundian Treaty that the emperor should help against the Dutch on the grounds that the Netherlands were part of the Empire. Oñate persuaded Ferdinand to accept a very wide definition of these obligations as requiring aid against any of Spain's enemies. Nonetheless, he was careful to restrict his promise to Austria, merely undertaking to do his best to persuade the other imperial Estates to join him. Moreover, it became clear the two Habsburg branches had very different ideas on how the assistance was to be provided. Olivares expected the emperor to send part of the imperial army, whereas Ferdinand simply intended to let Spain recruit more German soldiers.

Despite the potential obligation to assist against France, the arrangement remained directed against the Dutch. Fernando's army had marched to Flanders, not into France. Imperial operations at the beginning of 1635 remained restricted to ejecting the French and Bernhardines from Speyer and other imperial territory. Duke Charles's invasion of Lorraine in April and May was on his own initiative. Furthermore, the whole point of Olivares' strategy since 1633 had been to assemble enough troops in Flanders to achieve decisive superiority and compel the Dutch to accept an honourable peace. The Spanish Council of State endorsed this again on 2 February 1635 when it agreed to continue to prioritize the Dutch War.[3]

The general trend of Spanish policy nonetheless remained hostile towards France. Richelieu could not afford to let Spain defeat the Dutch any more than he could allow the emperor to crush Sweden. Both Protestant powers remained counterweights to perceived Spanish dominance. Worse, the deteriorating situation on the Upper Rhine coincided with a Spanish intervention further downstream that unwittingly challenged Richelieu directly. The failure of Feria's expedition to clear Alsace prompted Olivares to authorize the governor of Luxembourg to remove the French from Trier, thereby opening an alternative route from Germany to the Netherlands. Alarmed at Elector Sötern's plans to name Richelieu as his coadjutor, the Trier canons cooperated with the Luxembourg governor who sent 1,200 men. These surprised the French in Trier on 26 March, seizing Sötern while the canons took over the government. Another 1,500 Imperialists evicted the French from Koblenz in April, but they fled into the Ehrenbreitstein fortress and held out for a further 28 months. Olivares had nothing to do with Sötern's arrest, which was possibly organized by Fernando to precipitate what he regarded as an inevitable conflict with France and so force the Empire in general, and Austria in particular, to honour their commitments.[4]

French Belligerence

The French government grew more bellicose from December 1633, encouraged by a war party around Abel Servien who wanted Richelieu to move more decisively. The cardinal was certainly heading towards open conflict with Spain, but did not want it so quickly. War with Spain entailed openly joining the Dutch who remained divided, with a strong peace party favouring resumption of the talks suspended in April 1634. Frederick Henry circumvented the formal institutions where the peace faction held a majority and used his influence in the provinces, enhanced by French bribes, to win support to extend the war. Indirect French assistance was converted into an offensive alliance on 8 February 1635. Both parties promised to field 30,000 men and 15 ships each for a joint invasion of the Spanish Netherlands. Following invasion, the region was to be given three months to declare independence, or be partitioned between France and the Republic.[5]

The treaty had not yet been ratified when news of Sötern's arrest reached Paris on 30 March. Spain's action forced Richelieu's hand. His entire position since the Day of the Dupes rested on an assertive foreign policy and he could not afford to accept the humiliation of the arrest of the most senior foreign prince under French protection.[6] A series of hasty meetings with Louis XIII led to a decision for war on 5 April. Meanwhile, Richelieu sent a demand to Brussels for Sötern's release to win time and establish grounds for a 'just war' by displaying an ostensible willingness for peace. The arrest conveniently allowed him to present the conflict as a struggle against Spanish tyranny. The manifesto drafted by Father Joseph carefully avoided criticism of the emperor. French units were already entering the Netherlands when a herald, resplendent in his traditional costume of tabard and plumed hat, and accompanied by a trumpeter, rode into Brussels to deliver the manifesto. Fernando refused to see him, obliging him to pin it to the border post and go home.[7]

French Preparedness

After nearly forty years without a major war, France was relatively poorly prepared and only harnessed its true potential a few years into the struggle. There has been considerable debate over the size of its army, but while historians disagree on the exact total, all revise older estimates downwards. Overall strength was certainly below the 120–150,000 men widely cited for the first year of the war. The army probably numbered about 49,000 at the end of 1634, rising to a maximum of 65,000 infantry and 9,500 cavalry in 1635, and 90,000 in all the following year.[8] Most soldiers were unseasoned and their officers inexperienced. Count Guiche, later known as the duke of Gramont, recalled the events of 1635:

> ... the opening of the campaign and everything appeared difficult to the troops, and even to the officers, who had lived softly for too long; the cavalry was not used to pitching camp, and did it clumsily ... The army regarded it as a prodigy to have to pass four or five days without bread, and their attitude produced an almost general sedition.[9]

The usual financial problems helped wreck Richelieu's optimistic expectations of rapid success. Though the war began with an offensive, the French spent most of the first six years operating on their own soil. They were unable to levy contributions on their enemies, and while neutrals paid for 'protection', troops still had to be stationed to uphold this. Money was extorted from Lorraine and Alsace, but the latter was increasingly treated as a French province after 1643, entailing a degree of restraint. Units operating in Germany (and later in Catalonia) did live at the locals' expense, but France did also continue to pay substantial subsidies to the Dutch, Sweden and other allies.

Annual revenue rose significantly, from 32.5 million livres in 1610 to

57.5 million on the eve of war, reaching 79 million by 1643. Inflation accounted for some of the growth, but the rest followed a relentless race to keep pace with the burgeoning military expenditure. The latter already averaged nearly 16 million a year in the 1620s, approaching 20 million with the fighting in La Rochelle and Mantua, but rocketed to over 33 million in 1635 and exceeded 38 million after 1640. At 138 per cent, the rate of increase outstripped that of gross agricultural production which rose by only 37 per cent. The per capita tax burden more than doubled, representing the equivalent of nearly five weeks' wages, compared to less than a fortnight's wages under Henri IV.[10] As this was at a time when the average household spent most of its income on food, this caused widespread hardship, precipitating a series of major revolts into the middle of the century.

The war strained a system that worked only imperfectly even in peacetime. The monarchy always overspent, forcing it to borrow heavily. As in Spain, specific sources of revenue were mortgaged to financiers in return for loans. Revenue was not only spent before it had been collected, but large parts of the fiscal system were transferred into private hands, largely beyond government control. Only 49 per cent of expenditure under Richelieu was submitted to the royal audit office, with the remainder only presented in total. The government claimed exemption on grounds of national security, but the real reason was to hide the exorbitant rates of interest paid to financiers. A total of 700 million livres of loans (*affaires extraordinaires*) was raised between 1620 and 1644 at the cost of 172 million.[11] The formal structure of ordinary taxation 'became little more than a front behind which the financiers carried on their affairs with studied indifference towards the damage that they did to the government and contempt for the suffering of the tax-paying element of the population'.[12]

Richelieu was aware of these problems and made periodic efforts to eliminate the worst abuses. Many of the taxes alienated to financiers were clawed back in 1634 when a new military tax, called the *subsistence*, was introduced. The war frustrated reform and taxes were again mortgaged by 1642. The system had been evolving for nearly two centuries and there was considerable reluctance to challenge the vested interests of those charged with collecting and spending the money. Perhaps more fundamentally, those in charge did not feel the need. Central government was almost entirely in the hands of Richelieu's clients by 1635, removing any incentive to change existing institutions. The monarchy might lurch from one financial crisis to the next, but at least it kept moving forward. The famous centrally appointed inspectors, called *intendants*, were clearly not impartial agents of royal absolutism as once thought, yet they did ensure money reached the treasury, troops were paid and warships equipped.[13] French troops remained ill-disciplined, but they did not mutiny like Sweden's German army.

THE WAR IN THE WEST 1635–6

Habsburg Military Cooperation

The French declaration of war on Spain was extremely unwelcome to Ferdinand who had hoped to avoid conflict. The imperial envoy left Paris in August, but it was the end of December before the emperor sanctioned joint operations with Spain, and March 1636 when the French ambassador was expelled from Vienna. Neither Louis XIII nor Ferdinand declared war on the other. The emperor still hoped France and Spain would resolve their differences without prolonged conflict.[14] Military cooperation with Spain was already under way, but imperial forces restricted their participation to targets within the Empire. Fernando's army, totalling 11,540 on its arrival in Brussels, was absorbed into the Army of Flanders. The Ebersdorf Treaty envisaged Spanish subsidies to form a new army of 13,300. Ferdinand reluctantly allowed Spain to recruit around 8,000 Germans by February 1635, and transferred 5,000 Croats and Polish cavalry who had recently joined Gallas on the Rhine. Another 9,000 recruits were sent south over the St Gotthard pass in October to reinforce the Spanish Army of Lombardy operating in northern Italy. Ferdinand also allowed Spain to collect 10,781 men discharged from the Polish army in September. Having wintered in Silesia, 7,000 eventually joined Gallas in October 1636, while the rest reinforced the Spanish in Milan. This represented only indirect assistance and came at a price, since Spain paid 910,000 florins towards recruiting costs in 1635–7, compared to 1.2 million in direct subsidy to Austria over the same period.[15]

Spain withheld 540,000 fl. of the promised subsidy in 1635 to pressure Ferdinand to provide more direct assistance. Gallas was assigned 35,000 of the then 90,000 troops of the imperial army to make a diversion on the Rhine. Maximilian agreed to support this because French interference in the siege of Heidelberg in December 1634 persuaded him to reject Richelieu's renewed offer of protection. The Bavarians numbered about 18,000, while the Cologne-Westphalian forces were only around 6,000 strong. Some Bavarians helped blockade the French in the Ehrenbreit-stein, while the others cooperated with Gallas along the Upper Rhine.

Spain approached Gallas directly, offering the title of duke while also discreetly looking into his past for incriminating evidence to use if he proved difficult. He nonetheless remained loyal to the Empire, blaming his failure to invade France on operational problems. Many of these difficulties were indeed genuine. He had been obliged to send 10,000 men to help Spain clear the Valtellina that had just been blocked by Henri de Rohan's corps from Upper Alsace (see below, Chapter 18). The abject failure of that operation further discouraged the Austrians from helping their cousins. Another 6,000 were assigned to reinforce Charles of Lorraine who was essentially pursuing his own war to recover his duchy. Finally, Gallas detached 10,000 more to join Piccolomini who had wintered in Franconia and returned down the Main in June. Piccolomini's force eventually numbered 22,000, but this probably included imperial units under Mansfeld who remained east of the Rhine in support of the Westphalians.[16]

Piccolomini crossed the Rhine near Andernach and advanced west towards the Meuse. His approach greatly helped Fernando who now faced a war on two fronts, like his distant predecessor the duke of Parma in the 1580s. Units had to be detailed to garrison the towns along the southern frontier with France as well as the existing posts to the north facing the Dutch. This took nearly half of his 70,000 men, leaving him outnumbered by the Franco-Dutch field armies. The French were 4,000 short of the strength promised the Dutch because of the men diverted to help La Force in Alsace at the beginning of the year. Nonetheless, they advanced down the Meuse from Sedan and defeated a Spanish blocking force under Prince Tommaso of Savoy at Avesnes on 22 May 1635. Having joined the Dutch at Namur, the combined army turned west towards Brussels, taking Tienen (Tirlemont) on 9 June. Things then started to go wrong as they became bogged down besieging Leuven (Louvain). The French cut poor figures alongside the Dutch veterans. Supply arrangements collapsed, reducing the French to only 8,000 effec-

tives to the consternation of the Dutch. As Piccolomini advanced into
Cleves, the Spanish captured the fort of Schenkenschans commanding
the Rhine just downstream from Emmerich. These moves threatened to
strand the Dutch in Belgium, forcing them to retreat rapidly, while the
French hurried back up the Meuse. The Franco-Dutch invasion frustrated Spanish plans to recover Maastricht, but its failure nonetheless
strained relations between the two allies.

The Rhine Campaign 1635

The requirements of the new war placed a premium on manpower. The
poor showing by the French in Flanders, as well as the losses suffered
by La Force at the end of 1634, indicated the importance of seasoned
soldiers. Richelieu wanted to avoid an open breach with the emperor,
yet he needed an army to contest control of Alsace. It became imperative
to acquire Sweden's army on the Rhine, either through the Heilbronn
League, or by agreement with Bernhard of Weimar. The latter's growing
significance was not lost on Ferdinand, who sent the Scottish colonel
John Henderson to persuade the duke to defect at the end of 1634.
These efforts would continue, but always foundered on the emperor's
reluctance to grant the political and financial concessions demanded by
Sweden's German officers.[17] Ferdinand's stress on patriotic duty paled
compared to France's offer to Bernhard in April of Alsace as a French
fief in compensation for the loss of Bamberg and Würzburg, together
with a renewed promise of 12,000 men to stiffen his army. Bernhard
hesitated, wanting proof that France could deliver its commitments.

This seemed unlikely at first, because the situation remained precarious along the Upper Rhine. The operations are worth following in detail,
because they reveal how matters remained in flux, despite France's war
with Spain and the emperor's peace with most of the German Protestants
at Prague. The inability of Ferdinand's generals to neutralize Bernhard
not only pulled France deeper into the German war, but encouraged
Sweden to continue fighting.

Operations resumed on the Rhine only as news of the Prague settlement spread in June. Archduke Ferdinand arrived with reinforcements,
bringing Gallas's army back to 20,000. These were used exclusively in
support of the Prague peace by besieging the remaining Swedish outposts
along the Rhine and attempting to crush Bernhard. While the Bavarians

under Gronsfeld reduced those outposts on the right bank, Gallas besieged Mainz and Saarbrücken in the west. Having detached 6,000 men to hold these positions, Bernhard was left with only 7,500, too few to do much. Heidelberg castle surrendered to Gronsfeld on 24 July, followed by Frankfurt (21 August) and Mannheim (10 September). Richelieu directed Cardinal La Valette with 10,000 of the 26,000-strong French army in Lorraine to help Bernhard, and together they relieved Mainz in August.[18] Gallas withdrew, but the French suffered the same problems that hindered their operations in the Netherlands. Two-thirds of La Valette's army deserted as supply arrangements broke down. As it became obvious the Hessians would not cooperate, the cardinal retreated precipitously to Metz that September. Gronsfeld crossed with 6,500 Bavarian troops to join Gallas in pushing south from Saarbrücken into Lorraine. This struck clearly at French interests, but was intended to restore the situation there prior to the French invasion of 1632, not to attack France itself. Duke Charles had launched his third attempt that year to recover his duchy, striking across Alsace from Breisach at the end of June with the help of two Bavarian cavalry regiments. His second sister, Henriette of Pfalzburg, accompanied the troops in male attire and participated in the fighting.

Louis XIII was obliged to move his reserve army of 12,000 newly enlisted Swiss mercenaries to eject the duke from the west, while La Valette, La Force and Bernhard faced Gallas's invasion from the north. The two sides faced each other in fortified camps near Moyenvic between 12 October and 23 November. Both suffered terribly from the plague and malnutrition, just like Wallenstein and Arnim in 1633, or the two armies at Nuremberg the year before. The situation deteriorated more rapidly in the imperial camp where Duke Charles's arrival added to the pressure on resources, while Gallas spent days drinking. He finally gave up and retreated through Saverne in the snow, having been forced to leave his artillery behind because the soldiers had eaten the transport animals. His army lost up to 12,000 men, though French losses, including deserters, were probably at least as high.[19] Nonetheless, Gallas had prevented the French from relieving Bernhard's garrison in Mainz which remained under imperial blockade. Abandoned and reduced to eating their boots, the surviving 1,000 defenders in Mainz capitulated in January in return for safe conduct to Metz. The city's fall eliminated the last major Swedish position on the Upper Rhine.

Though his strong points in Germany had been reduced to just Hanau on the Main, held by Sir James Ramsay, Bernhard was nonetheless sufficiently reassured of French help to agree a formal alliance at St Germain-en-Laye on 27 October.[20] He transferred his army to France, dropping the pretence of serving the defunct Heilbronn League. A secret article promised him a pension, plus the Austrian part of Alsace as a French fief once this was fully secured. Richelieu intended the arrangement to continue the war in Alsace without the need for further French troops. These could then be reduced to those garrisoning Lorraine. It proved unsatisfactory to both parties. Though under French direction, Bernhard remained autonomous and his operations, like his earlier Swedish service, remained at least partly focused on securing the promised territory. France pledged an annual subsidy of 4 million livres (1.6 million talers), but this would cover only a third of the cost of the 6,000 cavalry and 12,000 infantry he was supposed to maintain, compelling him to extend operations in search of contributions. These always fell short, and he rarely mustered more than half the official establishment, with the result that France withheld part of the subsidy, compounding the problem. Moreover, Richelieu's refusal to relinquish Sweden's former Alsatian outposts raised Bernhard's suspicions that the French intended to keep the province.

The Year of Corbie

Olivares continued to prioritize the war against the Dutch in 1636, which was more popular in the Netherlands than fighting France.[21] Fernando still had nearly 70,000 men, but Frederick Henry struck first, retaking Schenkenschans and the other places lost the year before. The Dutch offensive ground to a halt as the Republic temporarily ran out of money, but it had again disrupted Spanish plans. France meanwhile directed its main effort against the Franche-Comté, remaining on the defensive against the Netherlands and launching only subsidiary attacks in Italy. The prince de Condé led 20,000 men into the Franche-Comté and besieged its capital of Dôle on 26 May. The invasion breached the neutrality guaranteed by the Swiss Confederation, but was considered essential to eliminate Duke Charles who had retreated there at the end of 1635.

Charles and the local Spanish forces were too weak to resist. Olivares pressed Ferdinand to act, but the emperor again agreed only indirect assistance. A new treaty had been concluded on 30 December 1635 whereby Spain promised monthly subsidies of 100,000 tlr until the end of the war, in return for 25,000 Germans to enter its service. Olivares held back the money and only released instalments when imperial generals did something in Spain's interests.[22] Gallas refused to budge from his entrenched camp at Drusenheim in Alsace. He was still rebuilding his army and was engaged in long and ultimately fruitless negotiations with Strasbourg to use its Rhine bridge. His failure enabled Bernhard and La Valette to hold their own in Alsace.

Continued lack of action by the imperial generals prompted Olivares to order Fernando to launch a diversionary attack from the Netherlands. Fernando and Prince Tommaso invaded Picardy with 25,000 men. At last, Piccolomini moved west from the Rhine to join Werth and seven Bavarian regiments that had wintered in Liège and together they attacked Champagne with about 12,000 troops. The rich French farmland was thoroughly stripped by the experienced plunderers.[23] The invaders brushed aside the 9,000 French under Soissons and captured the minor border forts of La Capelle and Le Câtelet after minimal resistance in July. Fernando besieged Corbie on the Somme north of Noyon on 7 August, as Werth's cavalry raided as far as Compiègne. Corbie fell on 15 August and Fernando moved south to join Werth, while another 10,000 Spanish soldiers crossed the western Pyrenees and captured St Jean de Luz.

Panic gripped the French court, Richelieu's entire policy seemingly in ruins. Refugees streamed south to Chartres and Orleans. Louis XIII summoned the militia and royal guards. Even Gaston rallied to the cause, rushing from his estates where he had been sulking since 1634 and arriving with 4,800 hastily raised reinforcements. Frederick Henry launched an attack with 13,000 Dutch against the southern Netherlands to distract the Habsburg forces, while Condé abandoned his siege of Dôle on 15 August and sent 9,000 men to join the king. Piccolomini wanted to press further on into France, but the Spanish had been surprised by their success and had no resources to exploit it. Fernando never intended capturing Paris and merely wanted to consolidate his present positions to winter in Picardie and the Champagne. He retreated as Louis and Gaston advanced from Paris. Corbie was retaken on 14 November and the situation stabilized.

The crisis did allow Gallas to advance through the Belfort Gap from Alsace into the Franche-Comté and join Duke Charles to give a total of 40,000 men. Any chance of using their numerical superiority was wrecked by the plague and autumn rains, however. The Imperialists fell back eastwards along the upper Saône to end the year at Breisach. Duke Charles attacked into his duchy, starting the *'guerre des châteaux'*, a vicious cycle of raids and counter-raids between garrisons across Lorraine.[24]

The invasion of France had been improvised and there was no real chance of forcing Louis XIII to make peace.[25] Its real impact was to oblige the French court to accept that it was now engaged in a protracted struggle. Habsburg cooperation remained ineffective, with the Austrian and Spanish branches pursuing separate objectives. Gallas's operations failed to secure Alsace and merely increased Richelieu's determination to eliminate what he saw as a threat to his possession of Lorraine.

THE PEACE OF PRAGUE 1635

Peace-making

Peace in the Empire remained Ferdinand's priority. The victory at Nördlingen at last allowed him to negotiate from the position of strength necessary to avoid concessions appearing as weakness. He adopted what Konrad Repgen has described as a three-step plan: to unite all the imperial Estates behind him; achieve military superiority; and drive foreigners from the Empire.[26] This was to be achieved through a general peace with his largely Catholic supporters and Sweden's Protestant German allies and collaborators. He was prepared to give some ground on the Restitution Edict to secure sufficiently broad agreement and isolate those unwilling to accept his terms. All forces within the Empire were to be united under imperial command to achieve the numbers and coordination necessary to defeat Sweden. The latter would also be offered peace, but only by being invited to accept the emperor's settlement.

This strategy is generally interpreted as secularizing the conflict that was now sustained (it is thought) by foreign involvement. French intervention is credited with defeating an attempt to base peace on 'imperial absolutism'.[27] The war certainly lost its superficial confessional character as Saxony, Brandenburg and the majority of Lutheran territories accepted the emperor's terms of 30 May 1635. Militants like Lamormaini largely lost their former influence on policy, which passed firmly into the hands of Trauttmannsdorff and other more pragmatic men. However, the war had never been exclusively a religious struggle and the confessional issues associated with the constitutional dispute persisted beyond 1635 because Ferdinand's terms left a dissatisfied minority who continued to stress religious grievances alongside political objectives.

The war did change character, because the emperor insisted that the original problems had been settled and the enemies were now malicious foreign crowns bent on disturbing the Empire's peace and grabbing its territory. He had to argue this because the terms obtained at Prague met many of his objectives, and he had no desire to jeopardize these gains in later negotiations. However, it was precisely these terms that France and Sweden contested. The Peace did not make Ferdinand an absolute monarch, and his intention was to restore what he regarded as the proper constitutional order.[28] It was nonetheless a monarchical solution, devised through a series of exclusive deals with the electors and presented to the other imperial Estates without further discussion. Ferdinand claimed it was impossible to hold a Reichstag, in view of growing French interference, but this conveniently reserved peace-making as an imperial prerogative. The general direction of the terms of the Prague treaty suggested a degree of imperial authority unacceptable to Sweden and France, who therefore drew closer together to break the nascent Habsburg revival. Their continued intervention was facilitated by Ferdinand's grave error of excluding some princes from the amnesty offered at Prague. This allowed the two crowns to present their intervention in the language of 'German liberty', a slogan that obscured their programme of keeping the emperor weak and the Empire open to external manipulation.

Ferdinand's advisers were concerned at his failing health, which made it imperative to prepare for the election of his eldest son as king of the Romans. With Wallenstein gone and Sweden in retreat, it was easier to hold direct talks with Saxony on the basis of the Pirna Note.[29] Ferdinand realized peace would work only if he won acceptance from his Catholic supporters as well, especially as the pope had already announced his opposition to concessions involving ecclesiastical land. It was relatively easy to keep the ecclesiastical princes informed, because they were still sheltering together in Cologne.[30] Many, especially Mainz, were prepared to give ground on the Restitution Edict, but Ferdinand wanted to go further and dissolve the Liga, both to allay Protestant fears and to assert control over war-making. Several Catholic princes were dissatisfied with the actions of Bavaria, while the Liga had seemed decidedly less attractive ever since Tilly's failure to protect them after Breitenfeld. Stadion, the Teutonic Grand Master and adviser to Archduke Ferdinand, was an influential critic who argued that the Liga represented an obstacle to the unity of command deemed essential to winning the war.[31]

Securing Bavarian approval became a key prerequisite for peace. Maximilian was won over by special concessions agreed at the Stuttgart Recess on 19 November 1634 that allowed him to retain command of the Bavarian army as a distinct corps in the new, combined *Reichsarmada*. The deal was sealed by a dynastic alliance following the death of Maximilian's first wife on 4 January 1635. The elector was still childless and needed a son to secure his gains as hereditary possessions. He married the emperor's eldest daughter, Maria Anna, on 17 July 1635 and was gratified by the birth of a son, the future Elector Ferdinand Maria, on 31 October the following year. Bavarian support rendered the elector of Cologne's continued opposition relatively unimportant.[32]

As talks progressed with Saxony, all that remained was to silence the remaining militants in Vienna and salve the emperor's conscience. Cardinal Dietrichstein convened a committee of 24 theologians on Ferdinand's orders in February. Lamormaini and the eight Jesuits were overruled by the majority who argued concessions were justifiable on the doctrine of the lesser evil.

The Terms

The Peace dissolved the Liga and all alliances, except for that between the electors who were still allowed to meet on their own initiative. The constitution was stressed as the bedrock of the Peace that appealed to all the Empire's inhabitants to 'behave truthfully, like Germans', regardless of confession.[33] An amnesty was extended to those who had taken up arms against the emperor since 1630. The two dukes of Mecklenburg were expressly pardoned and restored, but articles 31 and 57 excluded the elector Palatine and confirmed Bavarian possession of his lands and titles. A separate list agreed with Saxony excluded Württemberg, Hessen-Kassel and others who were, nonetheless, invited to make their own peace with the emperor. The Peace followed the Edict of Restitution in referring to Protestants as adherents of the Augsburg Confession, meaning Lutherans, but avoided restricting this to the 1530 text, which would have explicitly excluded Calvinists like Brandenburg from the settlement.

Those excluded from the amnesty faced full restitution according to the 1629 Edict. The others received a forty-year suspension for church lands they had appropriated between 1552 and 12 November 1627. The latter date was selected for this new normative year because it followed the Mühlhausen electoral congress that had established the legal basis for the Edict. In other words, the basic legitimacy of Ferdinand's policy was upheld, but its implementation was substantially modified. The Peace stressed that efforts to find an amicable settlement over restitution were to continue during its suspension. If these talks failed, the emperor could reimpose the Edict only after consulting a delegation of princes to be drawn equally from Catholics and Protestants. Article 11 stated that the new normative year of 1627 was to remain in force if this cross-confessional group failed to reach agreement. This amounted in practice to the Edict's permanent suspension. The emperor conceded Magdeburg to Elector Johann Georg's son for life, while a separate article granted Saxony full possession of Lusatia. Halberstadt was still reserved for Archduke Leopold Wilhelm, but safeguards were written in for the Protestant inhabitants. Ferdinand gave so much ground because his core goal of excluding Protestantism from the Habsburg hereditary lands was secured, apart from some minor concessions in Silesia to preserve face for Saxony.

Article 42 indicated that the war was to be a common effort by explicitly extending assistance from the emperor and Catholics to loyal Protestants. Signatories agreed a *conjunctis viribus*, a combined army that was to swear loyalty to the constitutional formula of 'emperor and Empire'. Article 69 obliged all imperial Estates to pay 100 Roman months in six instalments from 1 September 1635 to fund the army. Articles 70 to 75 stipulated that logistics and billeting were to adhere to imperial ordinances, in an unrealistic attempt to tame war-making.

The Peace was agreed between imperial and Saxon representatives only, with the other imperial Estates simply invited to join. To encourage

them, the emperor distributed printed copies that omitted the controversial exclusions from the amnesty. After a celebratory banquet in
Prague, Trauttmannsdorff wrote optimistically that the army could be
reduced now to concentrate on the few remaining enemies.[34]

Winning Acceptance

Saxony retained an important role as broker between the emperor and
his remaining enemies. Johann Georg was named imperial commissioner
in both Saxon Kreise to enforce the Peace and negotiate with Sweden.
Like Bavaria, he was allowed to retain his own army as a distinct corps.
Arnim was compromised by his service against the emperor after 1631
and resigned its command, eventually retiring to his estates in Brandenburg. The Swedes placed a reward on his head, capturing him in March
1637, though he did manage to escape. He was replaced as Saxon
commander in August 1635 by Baudissin who had quit Swedish service
in March 1633. The Saxons evacuated Silesia and concentrated their
25,000 men at Leipzig in July.[35] They were assisted by 7,000 Imperialists
on the lower Oder under Count Marazzino, another Italian officer who
had supported Wallenstein's assassination.

Brandenburg had already signed a truce with the emperor in February
1635 and swiftly accepted the Peace. Elector Georg Wilhelm remained
concerned at potential Swedish reprisals, especially as the Swedes still
occupied many of his towns. He eventually discharged his military
obligations by assigning three regiments to Saxon command in October,
but otherwise tried to remain neutral.[36] Sweden's Lower Saxon collaborators had also agreed a truce with the emperor in February and negotiated to accept Prague after May. Duke Georg of Lüneburg had emerged
as the dominant figure here after the childless Friedrich Ulrich of Wolfenbüttel died falling down the stairs in his palace in August 1634. Georg
bullied his relations into redistributing the family territories by May
1636, at last emerging with his own principality comprising Calenberg,
Göttingen and Hildesheim. The latter was especially problematic since
it was supposed to be restored to Ferdinand of Cologne under the Prague
terms. Georg accepted these on 10 August 1635, resigning his Swedish
command and sending a few units to cooperate briefly with the Saxons.
However, he refused to submit completely to Ferdinand who merely
offered to reappoint him an imperial general. He retained six regiments

in common with his elder brother August II, who had inherited Wolfen-büttel. Their uncooperative behaviour persuaded Ferdinand to leave the imperial garrison under Colonel Ruischenberg in Wolfenbüttel town as leverage for the return of Hildesheim. August protested that the garrison, allegedly numbering 7,000 including dependants, was an intolerable burden. The town's population had fallen from 1,200 to 160 and the entire principality had 'become almost completely desolate'.[37]

Brandenburg and the Guelphs escaped reprisals because neither the Swedes nor the emperor was sufficiently strong to force them onto their side. Their stance restricted operations to the Elbe and Oder corridors, thus offering a measure of protection for Sweden's bridgehead in Pomerania. Failure to recover Hildesheim was just one factor behind Ferdinand of Cologne's sceptical attitude towards the Peace. He was reconciled by concessions negotiated on his behalf by Maximilian in October 1635 that added a further exception to the military structure by permitting the Westphalian army to remain a distinct corps under its own generals. Its autonomy was more restricted than that enjoyed by Bavaria and Saxony, mainly because the army was smaller and depended on additional Bavarian and imperial units that were often recalled in times of crisis elsewhere. The October 1635 agreement did, however, consolidate Bavarian autonomy, especially as Maximilian managed to get rid of Duke Charles and replace him with Count Johann Götz as his new field marshal in January 1636.

The other territories also retained units under the loopholes of Articles 64 and 66 that allowed imperial Estates to keep garrisons in their own territories. Würzburg, for example, maintained around 2,000 men in 1636, though some were detached to reinforce the imperial army.[38] Nonetheless, considerable pressure was applied to Wolfgang Wilhelm of Pfalz-Neuburg, the only Catholic who refused to cooperate under the Prague system. The episode illustrates the central place of the constitution as the basis for peace. Rather than invade, the emperor prosecuted the duke through the Reichshofrat. Piccolomini still threatened force, especially as his men desperately sought warm billets at the end of 1635. Unpaid, most of the Pfalz-Neuburg troops defected to the Imperialists, leaving just 870 holding out in Düsseldorf.

The Amnesty Question

The exclusion of the more important Heilbronn members from the terms of the treaty became known as the 'amnesty question' and ultimately wrecked the Peace. Archduke Ferdinand had favoured a comprehensive amnesty for all those prepared to accept the Peace, but his father excluded the elector Palatine, Hessen-Kassel, Württemberg, Hohenlohe, many Rhenish counts and all the Bohemian exiles. Some of these were prominent Calvinists, but confession played only a modest part in this fateful decision. Johann Georg, it is true, always maintained Calvinists were not included in the Peace of Augsburg that the Prague settlement also confirmed. However, Ferdinand's targets were his inveterate enemies whose possessions had largely already been given to his allies. The elector Palatine could not be granted amnesty without contradicting arrangements with Bavaria. The Hohenlohe counts were outlawed in 1634 for their prominent place among Sweden's collaborators. All the counts were pardoned in 1635 except Georg Friedrich, whose support for Sweden broke the terms of his earlier amnesty after the Bohemian Revolt.

Württemberg's exclusion had nothing to do with religion, since it was Lutheran. Capture of its archive revealed the extent of its collaboration with Sweden since 1632 and provided an excuse to use the duchy to satisfy the clamour for rewards after Nördlingen. Bavaria wanted Heidenheim, the Tirolean Habsburgs coveted the Württemberg enclaves in their Swabian possessions, the prelates expected their monasteries back, while senior imperial officials petitioned for a share in the spoils. Seven districts were given to Schlick, Trauttmannsdorff and Bishop Wolfradt in June and July 1635, though Ferdinand resisted the other demands. He also rejected calls to exclude the imperial knights from the amnesty to allow Würzburg and others to expropriate their estates.[39]

Despite its genuine contribution towards the Peace, Darmstadt's expectation to receive all of Kassel was wholly unreasonable. Nonetheless, Ferdinand felt obliged to give it a few more Palatine districts, and territory belonging to the counts of Solms and Isenburg-Büdingen. The four counties of the Nassau-Walram line were distributed to Mainz, Schwarzenberg, Prince Lobkowitz and Duke Charles of Lorraine, while Zweibrücken was sequestrated after its capture in October 1635 on the grounds its prince, Johann Casimir, was Gustavus's brother-in-law.[40]

The decisions were understandable. The beneficiaries were the emperor's loyal supporters, many of whom had suffered at the hands of those whose lands they now obtained. Nonetheless, Ferdinand made it much harder to resolve the amnesty question by enlarging the numbers of those with a vested interest in opposing a pardon. Yet, by excluding so many, he undermined the desired character of Prague as a general peace. His son was left with the almost impossible task of resolving the issue that soon stuck on the discrepancy between the partial pardon he could offer the banished rulers and the full restoration they and their foreign backers demanded.

The Problem of Hessen-Kassel

The cases discussed so far were politically but not militarily important since the outlaws had but few troops and these were now under Bernhard's command and beyond their control. Hessen-Kassel was more dangerous, because it still possessed its own army and had entrenched across much of Westphalia. The ruling family was genuinely concerned at the exclusion of Calvinists from the Peace, but was also determined that it would not come out of the war empty-handed. At the very least it wanted the former imperial abbey of Hersfeld that had passed into its hands only in 1606. Landgrave Wilhelm V felt that Ferdinand had treated his family with unnecessary severity. He assured Oxenstierna in July 1635 that he would remain loyal to Sweden, but he despaired after Bernhard retreated over the Rhine, and the main Swedish army mutinied again (see below). Having left garrisons in Kassel and Ziegenhain, he retreated with 4,000 men under Melander to join his Westphalian outposts at the end of August.

The Imperialists massed 12,000 men from the Westphalian army and Piccolomini's forces on the Lahn ready to invade Hessen-Kassel, which forced Melander to agree a truce on Wilhelm's behalf in October. Archduke Ferdinand was keen to see an agreement and intervened, suspending operations against the Hessians occupying Fulda and offering some concessions. Ferdinand of Cologne also favoured compromise as the best way of removing the Hessian parasites infecting his Westphalian territories.[41] The prospects looked bright as Wilhelm provisionally accepted the Prague treaty on 12 November, but the emperor failed to clinch the deal, and imperial units entered the Westphalian bishoprics.

The emperor renewed contact through the bishop of Würzburg, but the landgrave no longer trusted him and only continued talks to alarm France into making a better offer.

Oxenstierna sent Alexander Leslie to assume command of the remaining Swedish units left leaderless by Knyphausen's death in January 1636. Better known in British history by his later title as the earl of Leven, Leslie was one of the many able Scottish officers in Swedish service, having joined in 1608 and fought with distinction under Gustavus.[42] He immediately revived the morale of the 3,000 or so German mercenaries still holding out in Osnabrück and other north German garrisons. Several of Duke Georg of Lüneburg's regiments defected to him in May, giving him command of the Weser and parts of Lüneburg by August. These developments emboldened Wilhelm to renounce the truce in May 1636. His decision was influenced by his wife, Amalie Elisabeth, who, as countess of Hanau, was concerned to save her home town, still defended by Ramsay's Bernhardine garrison. Along with Queen Christina, Archduchess Isabella and Claudia of the Tirol, she was one of a group of female rulers exercising considerable influence on events. Though presented as a peace-maker[43] she was in fact even more determined than her husband to obtain new territory. Hessian troops marched south-west from Hamm, joining Leslie to punch through the imperial cordon and throw supplies into Hanau.[44]

The Westphalian army used the Hessians' absence to capture most of their outposts along the Lippe, temporarily reducing the Hessians to Lippstadt, Dorsten and Coesfeld. Oxenstierna was obliged to recall Leslie eastwards in August, leaving the Hessians no choice but to retreat north from Hanau, exposing their homeland again. Ferdinand lost patience. He placed Wilhelm under the imperial ban in October and began to collect troops to sequestrate Hessen-Kassel.

APPEALS TO PATRIOTISM

The Powder Barrel Mutiny

The amnesty issue helped Oxenstierna to present the Peace as contrary to German liberty. The allies' collapse following Nördlingen caused consternation in the Swedish government. Salvius reported, 'all here are calling Peace, Peace, Peace'.[45] The chancellor was also disillusioned: 'The Polish war is *our* war; win or lose, it is our gain or loss. This German war, I don't know what it is, only that we pour our blood here for the sake of reputation, and have nought but ingratitude to expect.'[46] The Prague settlement confirmed his worst expectations: 'The emperor has achieved more in this peace than if he had won two battles of Nördlingen.' There was widespread bitterness at what was perceived as German betrayal. Swedish propagandists published documents at the Frankfurt autumn fair intended to demonstrate their German policy as altruistic. Criticism of Saxony was muted until it became obvious that Johann Georg could not be won back. Chemnitz, Sweden's leading German writer, then penned a damming personal attack, accusing the elector of dishonouring Gustavus's sacrifice. Sweden tried to steal the emperor's patriotic language. 'Regardless of whether you are Catholic or Protestant,' wrote Chemnitz, 'you are always a German whose ancestors preferred death to foreign oppression.'[47] This attempt to associate Prague with Spanish tyranny rang hollow in view of Sweden's own costly presence in the Empire. Likewise, Sweden's efforts to assume the mantle of the defeated Protestant activist party by playing up confessional issues was contradicted by the alliance with France.

In fact, Oxenstierna was looking for an honourable way out of Germany and was prepared to renounce the earlier extensive demands and settle for a few token Pomeranian ports. The situation looked desperate in 1635. The entire southern and western armies had been lost, either destroyed or transferred with Bernhard to French control. The Saxons, Brandenburgers and Lüneburgers had defected, while the Hessians were known to be negotiating to do so. Forces in north-west Germany were reduced to nine regiments numbering 3,000 men under Colonel Sperreuther and stranded in Lower Saxony, and another 4,000 under Wilhelm of Weimar at Erfurt. The main army under Banér totalled only 26,000, or 18,000 below establishment. Around 11,000 of this army garrisoned Pomerania, reducing the field force to just 15,000 in Magdeburg and Halberstadt. There were fewer than 3,000 Swedes and Finns among them. Sweden had experienced four bad harvests in a row. For a country where large proportions of taxes were still paid in kind, this was a crippling blow. Oxenstierna knew he had little to offer the army.

Peace depended on Ferdinand's willingness to offer realistic terms and on how far his patriotic rhetoric would induce Sweden's remaining German mercenaries to defect. Both issues were devolved to Johann Georg as imperial commissioner in north-east Germany. The elector was highly sensitive to Swedish criticism and excused his defection on the grounds of necessity to save the Empire from destruction by bringing about long-desired peace. He also played on widespread resentment of Swedish plundering. However, the core argument was a new appeal to patriotism deliberately couched to transcend confession and present the Empire as a common fatherland. These arguments would eventually produce the consensus facilitating the Peace of Westphalia, but they encountered serious difficulties in the short term. As long as hope remained that Sweden's German troops might defect, Johann Georg had to refrain from denouncing them as traitors and instead appeal to them to end Germany's suffering by changing sides.[48]

This hamstrung Saxon policy, obliging the elector to delay military action and giving Oxenstierna critical breathing space. News of Prague prompted the German officers of Banér's army to elect a committee to negotiate with both Sweden and Saxony. They were deeply disgruntled, in contrast to the imperial officers who were still content with the recent distribution of property confiscated following Wallenstein's murder. Those who had been paid in Swedish donations since 1632 had lost these after Nördlingen. Many were subjects of princes who had just accepted the emperor's peace. The imperial summons (*avocatoria*) to leave Swedish service issued in July gave them a face-saving excuse to abandon Sweden on the grounds of higher loyalty to the emperor. Such a move would, however, automatically forfeit the back pay Sweden owed them.[49]

Peace became a matter of haggling over the officers' demands. Oxenstierna negotiated mainly for show, carefully concealing his intention to keep at least part of Pomerania so as not to alienate the Germans. He halved his original demand for 8 million tlr to pay off the army and proposed a phased withdrawal in return for a full amnesty and restoration of the Empire to its condition in 1618. This was wholly unrealistic, but so too was Johann Georg's offer of only 1 million tlr, to be paid by Saxony and the Protestant Germans, in return for Sweden's renunciation of all territorial ambitions.

Sensing that Oxenstierna's envoys were not representing their interests, the officers sent their own delegation to meet the elector.[50] The

elector increased the pressure on 19 August by issuing an ultimatum to
Banér to leave Magdeburg. This was accompanied by another summons
to the officers that set out the Prague terms. Realizing that the Swedes had
misrepresented these, the officers seized Oxenstierna who had just arrived
in their camp having returned to Germany by sea from his meeting with
Richelieu. The result was the 'Powder Barrel Convention' extracted from
the chancellor on 21 August 1635. He agreed not to make peace without
consulting the officers and to include their 'contentment' in the Swedish
war aims. The latter was a ploy to induce them to continue fighting by
off-loading responsibility to the enemy to pay them off.

Their loyalty nonetheless remained suspect. Mitzlaff, the former
Danish officer from Pomerania we last encountered in 1627 and who
had subsequently entered Swedish service, engineered the defection of
Wilhelm of Weimar's corps on 24 August. Four regiments joined the
Saxons, while the rest were disbanded. The Swedes still held Erfurt, but
Johann Georg advanced from Leipzig eleven days later to enforce his
ultimatum. News that the elector of Brandenburg had accepted the
Prague treaty outflanked Banér, who left five regiments to hold Magde-
burg and retreated north to Stendal on 28 September. Oxenstierna took
the opportunity to slip away to the more reliable garrison in Wismar.

Johann Georg exploited the officers' renewed fury to open direct
talks with their delegation at Schönebeck on the Elbe upstream from
Magdeburg. While his troops overran Halberstadt, the elector improved
his offer to 2.5 million tlr payable direct to the generals. Not until Count
Kurz, the imperial envoy, arrived on 16 October did Johann Georg
authorize General Baudissin to use force. The elector was overconfident
and expected the German regiments to remain neutral. Joined by Brandenburg and Lüneburg units, the Saxons advanced downstream, taking
Werben the next day. Banér no longer trusted his men and tried to
escape through Dömitz to Mecklenburg. Baudissin sent 7,000 infantry
over the Elbe to the right (north) bank to cut him off, but these were
surprised and routed by a sudden counter-attack by Banér's remaining
reliable units. The Saxons lost 5,000 men and Baudissin escaped only
by swimming the Elbe. The success improved Banér's authority, but
he took no chances and continued his retreat to Malchin behind the
Pomeranian lakes. Johann Georg followed to Parchim, while Marazzino
had taken Gartz and now marched west to join him.

The Stuhmsdorf Truce

French diplomacy saved the Swedes from this desperate situation. The officers had been waiting to see what would happen when the Swedish-Polish Truce of Altmark expired that September. Sigismund III had been succeeded by his more pragmatic son, Wladyslaw IV, in 1632. After Sweden rebuffed his offer to renounce his claims to the Vasa crown in return for compensation, and had encouraged Russia to attack Smolensk that year, Wladyslaw allowed Ferdinand to recruit more cavalry and renewed Poland's alliance with the Habsburgs in 1633. Despite having to send another army to repel Tartar and Turkish incursions to the south, Wladyslaw relieved Smolensk in September 1633, forcing the tsar to make peace in May 1634 and confirm Polish possession of the lands ceded in 1618. Riding high on this victory, Wladyslaw persuaded the Sejm to agree an offensive war against Sweden once the Truce of Altmark expired.

The Baltic crisis could not have come at a worse time for Richelieu, coinciding as it did with the start of the Franco-Spanish War, the Peace of Prague and the Swedish mutiny. The emperor offered Silesia to Poland if Wladyslaw would convert his renewed alliance into a joint offensive against Sweden. Oxenstierna shipped 20,000 men to reinforce his Prussian garrison in a show of force, but recognized the impossibility of fighting two wars simultaneously. He accepted a 26-year extension to Altmark brokered by Richelieu's envoy d'Avaux in talks at Stuhmsdorf on 12 September. Sweden made major concessions. Its previous expansion in the Baltic had been incremental, seizing land by force, confirming initial occupation by truce and then converting this to full possession by further belligerence. Sweden could reasonably expect to annex Royal (Polish) Prussia in this manner. Relinquishing it at Stuhmsdorf thus represented a major retreat, disengaging from the country's primary imperial arena until now in order to concentrate on a very uncertain German war.[51]

Wladyslaw retained hopes of exploiting Sweden's difficulties and renewed his Habsburg alliance in September 1637 by marrying Ferdinand II's daughter, Cecilia Renata. However, his subjects had lost their enthusiasm for an offensive against Sweden. He soured relations with the Habsburgs by pursuing parallel talks with England and France, as well as alienating Denmark by raising the Prussian tolls. He was prepared to let Spain recruit 30,000 auxiliaries for Flanders, but the

Sejm blocked this by 1641.[52] The Stuhmsdorf truce held, containing the Thirty Years War within the Empire.

More immediately, the truce allowed Oxenstierna to move Lennart Torstensson and 9,700 men from Prussia. These troops began arriving in Pomerania in late October 1635 along with a morale-boosting delivery of new clothes for Banér's ragged army. Torstensson's units surprised Marazzino, prompting Johann Georg to fall back to protect Berlin in December, while Banér retook Werben and relieved Magdeburg in January 1636. The unpaid, hungry Saxons retreated to Halle, back virtually to where they had started the previous summer.

Why Saxony Failed

The Saxon elector had renewed negotiations in November, but the improved military situation allowed Oxenstierna to be deliberately obstructive, now demanding that any settlement be ratified by the entire Empire. The outcome was deeply disappointing. Unrest in Banér's army continued until May 1636. At least six generals and several experienced colonels defected, but the wholesale rejection of Sweden failed to materialize. For example, as a Mecklenburger, Colonel Sperreuther no longer felt bound to Sweden once his own dukes had accepted the Prague Peace. Knyphausen came out of retirement and rushed with 15,000 tlr advanced by the French ambassador to secure Sperreuther's soldiers' loyalty: only eighty horsemen followed Sperreuther to the imperial lines in December 1635.[53]

Appeals to German patriotism undoubtedly proved effective in some cases, but the choice was usually the result of a mixture of personal motives. The example of Augustus von Bismarck illustrates this. A distant ancestor of the later German chancellor, Bismarck was the son of a Brandenburg landowner and entered Swedish service in June 1631, transferring with his unit under Bernhard to the French in 1635. His brother wrote to him that their lord, the elector of Brandenburg, had accepted the Peace of Prague and summoned his subjects to leave enemy service. Arriving three days after he had been promoted, Augustus stuck the letter in his pocket, waiting to produce it much later when his regiment marched to northern Germany and he had accumulated a small fortune, enabling him to retire to a more comfortable existence as a Brandenburg fortress commandant.[54]

The hope of persuading more officers to defect seriously hampered Saxon military operations at a time when forceful action might have crushed Banér's army. The constant delay sapped morale that was already low, because many Saxons were unenthusiastic about fighting their former allies. They had little confidence in Baudissin as their new commander. Once an energetic officer, he was now an alcoholic who could out-drink even Johann Georg and once fell asleep during a battle. One officer noted in his diary after yet another minor reverse:

Early in the morning, Baudissin addressed the cavalry who were standing up to their knees in muck, telling them that they should feed their horses because he intended to attack the enemy. I daren't say what kind of swearing and uproar this caused. Tell the dog turd he should feed his wife, the whore, should we feed the muck to our horses?[55]

Serious financial problems contributed to the shambles. Johann Georg wanted to avoid calling his Estates to deny them, especially the knights, a chance to criticize his policy. No diet was called in 1618 during the controversy surrounding his decision not to support the Bohemians. Assemblies did meet in 1622 and 1628 and extended existing taxes at higher rates, but this was insufficient even to cover the costs of the modest mobilization in 1618-24. Electoral debts more than doubled to 7 million fl. by 1628 when tax collection was falling into arrears. Full military engagement after 1631 deepened the crisis. A diet had met in January 1635, but merely extended existing arrangements. The electorate plunged deeper into debt, which soared to 25.2 million fl. by 1657, despite having written off 10 million fl. worth of interest arrears the year before.[56]

The Treaty of Wismar 1636

Saxony's failure stiffened Oxenstierna's resolve. The defections had deprived Sweden of some experienced officers, but they had eased its liabilities since the pay arrears could be written off. Those who remained with Sweden were now imperial outlaws with little choice but to fight on. Oxenstierna knew it was imperative to place Sweden's alliance with France on a firmer footing. Richelieu was also anxious to improve relations. The failure of the French offensive in the summer of 1635 heightened Sweden's significance, and the cardinal sent the marquis de

St Chamont to ensure the chancellor did not make a separate peace with Ferdinand.

Oxenstierna met the envoy in Wismar in February 1636, agreeing a new treaty on 30 March that was ratified by Louis XIII on 11 May. France paid the 60,000 tlr arrears claimed by Sweden from the subsidy terminated on Gustavus's death. The money enabled Oxenstierna to recruit another four British regiments to reinforce the army. Though even higher subsidies were now promised, the chancellor refused to ratify the treaty, because it obliged him not to make peace without France. The alliance had already been announced, serving Oxenstierna's purpose of putting pressure on the emperor and confounding renewed Danish offers of mediation. France could not afford to lose even such an unreliable ally during the disastrous 'Year of Corbie' and Richelieu reluctantly released the subsidies even without ratification. Oxenstierna was finally able to return home to silence his domestic critics in July 1636, leaving Sten Bielke and Salvius to represent Sweden in the Empire.[57]

Talks continued without result, because Ferdinand remained over-confident, while Oxenstierna was convinced further fighting would win better terms. With Lower Saxony temporarily neutralized under the Guelphs, and operations in Westphalia largely suspended during talks with Hessen-Kassel, fighting remained restricted to the area between the Elbe and Oder.

The Battle of Wittstock

The lull in the Westphalian operations allowed Ferdinand to switch 10,000 Imperialists under Count Melchior Hatzfeldt from there to reinforce the Saxons. Hatzfeldt was one of several senior officers to emerge from the regiments raised by the Sachsen-Lauenburg brothers. He had served the emperor since 1620, fighting in major actions like Dessau and Breitenfeld, and had been rewarded with part of the estates confiscated from Schaffgotsch in 1634. He was comparatively well-educated and connected: his brother Franz was bishop of Bamberg and Würzburg. He was a skilled strategist, but his desire to micro-manage battles meant he often lost control of his forces once they became engaged, and he had the disagreeable tendency to blame subordinates for his own mistakes. Marginalized and dispirited, Baudissin resigned on 10 July 1636, clearing the way for Hatzfeldt to be appointed Saxon commander as well.

Sweden's German army was down to 45,000 men, mainly holding Mecklenburg and Pomerania. The Baltic froze during the winter, preventing the despatch of reinforcements from Sweden and leaving the field forces numbering only 6,000 under Leslie in Westphalia and 12,000 under Banér at Magdeburg. Banér still distrusted his army and fell back to Werben on 5 May. More forceful than Johann Georg, Hatzfeldt besieged rather than blockaded Magdeburg, capturing it on 13 July. The city's population still numbered only 2,600, but its capture secured an important Saxon war aim that had been promised in the Peace of Prague.

With plague again ravaging the area and all the grass eaten, Banér abandoned Werben on 12 August, moving west to collect Leslie who was falling back through Lower Saxony. Hatzfeldt detached Klitzing and 4,000 men to protect Brandenburg, which was still not fully committed to war against Sweden. Marrazino was summoned from the Oder to join the main imperial army now posed at Tangermünde to invade western Pomerania and Mecklenburg. Banér staked all on a battle to save the bridgehead. He marched north-east over the Elbe to meet 3,800 men detached from the Pomeranian garrisons, giving him a total of 17,000 men. He then headed eastwards, severing Hatzfeldt's communications and forcing him to recall Klitzing and collect at Wittstock just south of the Pomeranian lakes. Banér hastened to attack before Klitzing could arrive.

Both sides were fairly even in numbers, though Hatzfeldt probably had around 1,000 more men, as well as a strong position facing south along the south-eastern end of the low Schreckenberg ridge south-west of Wittstock. His left (east) was covered by the Dosse river and the wooded Fretzdorf heath. The south face of the ridge was strengthened by entrenchments and wagons that had been chained together, and was in any case difficult to approach across the wooded and marshy Natte heath. The approach from the west was blocked by the large Heiligengrab forest.

Banér took the only feasible route, crossing the Dosse early on Saturday 4 October at Fretzdorf and advancing over the heath to the Scharfenberg hill between the river and Hatzfeldt's position. He quickly appreciated the difficulties, but resolved to attack anyway, splitting his army by sending King and Stalhansk with 3,100 cavalry west across the

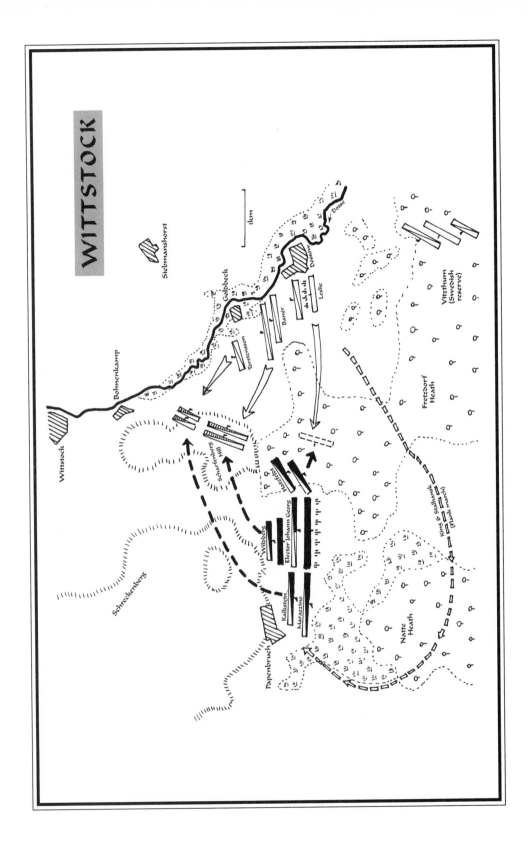

WITTSTOCK

Siebmanshorst

Dosse

Golbbeck

Banér

d. d. d. dr

Leslie

Bohnenkamp

Torstensson

Vitzthum
(Swedish
reserve)

Wittstock

Scharfenberg Hill

Fretzdorf
Heath

Hatzfeld

Wittberg

Elector Johann Georg

King & Stallhanск
(Flank march)

Schreckenberg

Kallistein

Marazzino

Natte
Heath

Papenbruch

1km

Nette heath to turn the enemy's other flank. Leslie and 5,800 men were directed north-west to pin Hatzfeldt's front, while Banér and the rest continued round the Scharfenberg to turn his left. This was an extremely risky plan, since the three parts of the army risked being defeated in detail. The terrain concealed their initial approach, but they were spotted around 2.30 p.m. and a fierce fight developed for possession of the Scharfenberg. Hatzfeldt fed men from his centre to reinforce his left and pushed the Swedes off the hill and into the Fretzdorf wood. Leslie's men were drawn in to stem the imperial advance. Rumours spread that Banér had been killed. It was not until 6.30 that King fired signal guns to indicate he was in position on the other side of the battlefield. The imperial right was taken by surprise and lost its artillery, but it was growing dark and King soon had to suspend his attack.

Banér had lost at least 3,500 casualties. It was unclear who had the advantage at nightfall, but the imperial-Saxon army was sufficiently battered and demoralized that Hatzfeldt and Johann Georg decided to retreat. Banér claimed to have taken 5,000 men during the pursuit, but this is unlikely since the Saxons and Imperialists drew off in good order. Their total loss was around 5,000 including 2,000 dead, but all their artillery and baggage was abandoned.[58]

Wittstock was one of the most important battles of the war. A Swedish defeat would have destroyed the last field army in Germany and encouraged Hessen-Kassel to convert its truce into a peace. Hatzfeldt's defeat not only prevented this but discouraged the Guelphs from bowing to the emperor. Panic gripped Berlin as the elector and his court fled to Küstrin. Hatzfeldt's Imperialists lost cohesion, plundering their way westwards to the Lower Rhine, while the Saxons went home. Banér swept south-west through Thuringia to relieve Erfurt and reopen communications with the Hessians, before turning east into Saxony and taking Torgau by February.

RENEWED EFFORTS FOR PEACE

The Cologne Congress 1636

Pope Urban VIII was genuinely horrified by the suffering, but was neither prepared to assist a Habsburg victory, nor sanction concessions to Protestants to obtain peace. He wanted to preserve his status as *padre commune*, a benevolent father chiding his Catholic children to resolve their petty squabbles to unite against the Protestant bullies. This required him to remain distant from the Habsburgs who appeared too powerful and alienated many other Catholics. His envoys helped broker peace in the Mantuan conflict (see Chapter 13 above), but he had achieved little since then, concentrating instead on enlarging the Papal States by annexing Urbino.

Richelieu's declaration of war on Spain forced him to act, however, especially because it brought renewed fighting in north Italy (detailed in Chapter 18). Cardinal Ginetti was named papal legate in August 1635, posing a dilemma for the Catholic powers. Papal mediation was unwelcome, especially for Ferdinand who had already accepted the necessity for concessions at the expense of the imperial church. Yet, the pontiff could not be rebuffed outright. Ferdinand consented to talks on 18 August, counting on the other parties to drag their feet.[59] Since the pope refused to invite Protestants, while France insisted its allies be included, Venice eventually volunteered to mediate between them and the Habsburgs. The deteriorating military situation made a congress more viable and Ginetti set out in July, eventually reaching Cologne on 22 October 1636.

Frederick V's son, Karl Ludwig, turned eighteen in January 1636, making him old enough to rule if restored. Charles I of England took the opportunity to launch his own peace initiative, spending £70,000 to despatch a lavish embassy headed by the earl of Arundel in April. Arundel made his way up the Rhine to the Habsburg lands where he was received politely, but it was obvious that both Ferdinand and Maximilian regarded the Palatine question closed. After an extended sight-seeing tour of those areas that had escaped destruction, Arundel returned home through the ravaged Main-Rhine region.[60]

Meanwhile, France consented to talks at Cologne but failed to send a representative. Ferdinand's envoy belatedly arrived in April 1637, followed by his Spanish colleague. Richelieu sent terms. He was prepared to renounce Alsace and negotiate over Lorraine, but only if Ferdinand recognized the French protectorate over Metz, Toul and Verdun and admitted the German princes to the congress. This constituted a better deal than the one the emperor eventually accepted at Westphalia eleven years later. The inclusion of the princes represented a significant development in French diplomacy, moving the imperial constitution to the centre of their public demands to legitimize their growing military involvement in the Empire and to undermine the Prague peace. This was completely unacceptable to the emperor in 1637, who still expected the military situation to improve.[61] Without the inclusion of the Protestants as full partners, the Cologne talks had no chance of success, especially as the rival Danish initiative (ongoing since 1633) offered alternative discussions in Hamburg. Though Ginetti left in October 1637, Urban persisted, entrusting the fruitless task to a series of officials, before handing it late in 1643 to Fabio Chigi who had assumed the post of nuncio in Cologne in August 1639.

The Regensburg Electoral Congress 1636–7

The papal initiative and Arundel's mission were overshadowed in the Empire by a more important meeting: that of the electors in Regensburg, which opened on 15 September 1636 and remained in session until 23 January.[62] It was the first imperial assembly since 1630 and the first after Prague. Several princes attended in person, as well as three electors, while many others sent envoys, as did Denmark, Poland, France, Spain and the papacy. Ferdinand was determined to rally support after the disappointing 1635 campaign and to consolidate the Peace of Prague by having his son elected king of the Romans. Spain saw an opportunity to push Austria to honour the Ebersdorf treaty and increase assistance against France. Oñate bankrolled the congress, paying at least 209,000 florins to Bavaria, Mainz, Cologne and Saxony, who were all going to vote for Archduke Ferdinand anyway. The money nonetheless smoothed their rejection of a Dutch call for the Empire to formally declare itself neutral in their war with Spain. Oñate was also pleased with their apparently hard stance towards France, demanding the return of Metz, Toul and Verdun. Such statements were already routine and did not indicate real enthusiasm for fighting France. In fact, the electors were inclined to accept papal mediation and it took some effort from Ferdinand to persuade them that the Empire's problems had to remain separate from the Franco-Spanish conflict.

Spain released Elector Sötern into imperial custody to avoid charges of meddling in the Empire's affairs. The Trier vote was suspended. Johann Georg and Georg Wilhelm of Brandenburg both excused themselves from attending, citing the war as an excuse. Under Swedish pressure, Georg Wilhelm insisted on discussing the progress of Saxony's talks with Oxenstierna. However, none of the electors saw an alternative to Johann Georg's proposal that the Protestant Germans should pay the Swedes to leave the Empire. Sweden could retain tolls and a Mecklenburg port until the money was delivered.

The defeat at Wittstock paradoxically strengthened Ferdinand, because the subsequent Swedish occupation of Brandenburg convinced its elector that he could not expect anything from Oxenstierna. Having fled east to Prussia, Georg Wilhelm opened negotiations for a new alliance with Ferdinand in November as the best way to prevent the emperor sacrificing Pomerania to obtain peace with Sweden. Duke Bogislav's death on 20 March 1637 added impetus to the negotiations that were concluded on 22 June. In return for financial assistance, Georg Wilhelm promised a large corps to reinforce the imperial army. His position remained weaker than either Bavaria's or Saxony's, because his army was smaller, reaching no more than 11,000 men by June 1638. Though under the command of Klitzing, who entered Brandenburg service, the corps lacked the autonomy of the Bavarians and Saxons and its soldiers had to swear loyalty to both Ferdinand and the elector.[63]

Closer cooperation with Brandenburg helped secure Ferdinand's other objectives. The electors extended the financial arrangements agreed at Prague for a further year. Archduke Ferdinand was duly elected as king of the Romans on 22 December 1636 (just in time, because his father died a month after the congress closed). His election was bought at the cost of further restrictions on his prerogatives, of which the most important was the promise to consult the electors before placing anyone else under the imperial ban.[64]

Nonetheless, another opportunity for peace had slipped by. The emperor and the Catholic electors had done nothing to make Johann Georg's task as mediator any easier. They felt the Protestants alone should pay the Swedes to leave, on the alleged grounds that they had invited them into the Empire. Johann Georg was unable to increase his offer to Oxenstierna and refused to mediate any further. Negotiations continued through other intermediaries largely for form's sake. All were to find the continued war far more expensive than the peace they might have obtained in 1635-6.

17

Habsburg High Tide 1637–40

STALEMATE

Emperor Ferdinand III

Aged just 29, the new emperor had grown up amid dynastic crisis and war. His mother was Ferdinand II's first wife, Maria Anna of Bavaria, making him nephew to Elector Maximilian. Considered a sickly child, his two elder brothers predeceased him. A regular fitness routine improved his own health, but the strain of his early involvement in politics – he was crowned king of Hungary at the age of seventeen – took its toll, leading to an early death in 1657. Two of his three wives and six of their eleven children died before him, contributing to his naturally melancholic disposition. Alongside a sincere sense of duty, he took a lively interest in contemporary culture and was one of the most artistically talented of the Habsburgs. In addition to laying out new palace gardens and augmenting the family's already substantial art collection, he was a skilled musician, composing several respectable works in the then fashionable Italian early baroque style.

Though educated by the Jesuits, he remained more moderate than his father, distinguishing more clearly between private morality and public pragmatism. He shared his father's conviction that the family fortunes depended on keeping their hereditary lands free from heresy. Catholicism remained the test for political loyalty. This goal had been achieved after White Mountain and secured at Prague in 1635, but protecting the dynasty's gains in its homeland remained at the heart of Ferdinand III's programme. He was more flexible towards the Empire where the priority was to uphold constitutional prerogatives, rather than imposing confessional goals.

The new emperor faced considerable difficulties, not least over the amnesty question. However, his presence at Nördlingen had associated him with success and he was supported by able advisers. Chief among these was Maximilian von Trauttmannsdorff, who had headed his household since 1633 and was the only man Ferdinand fully trusted. Honest, loyal and clear-sighted, he was already Austria's top diplomat, having negotiated peace with Bethlen in 1622, the Bavarian withdrawal from Upper Austria, and the Prague Peace. He emerged as the head of court and government after 1637. His position was strengthened by the appointment of his friend Kurz von Senffenau as imperial vice-chancellor to succeed Stralendorf who died in October 1637. Both favoured peace, provided Sweden offered acceptable terms.

The change in government weakened Spanish influence, but this was already on the decline after 1634. Olivares made a concerted effort to engender support for a major offensive against France, arguing that Sweden would pull out if France were defeated. The Year of Corbie augured well for a renewed combined assault and Spain requested Piccolomini's men be reinforced to 30,000 on the Meuse, as well as another imperial army to attack across the Rhine and permission to recruit 16,000 more Germans. There were some in Vienna who still favoured cooperation with Spain. Even a year later, during the planning for the 1638 campaign, Schlick proposed a drive on Paris he claimed would spark 'factions and mutinies' in France.[1] The imperial army, however, was in no condition to fulfil Spain's expectations. The main force under Gallas numbered only 16,110 men on Ferdinand III's accession.[2] As emperor, Ferdinand could no longer accompany the army because of the political damage that would follow association with a defeat. He nonetheless agreed to send 26,000 Imperialists and Bavarians under Gallas, Piccolomini and Werth from Luxembourg up the Meuse into Champagne, while Duke Charles attacked from the Franche-Comté with 12,000, half of whom were to be Spanish. This pincer movement was intended to liberate Lorraine, not invade France, and even this was aborted due to other events.

Ferdinand III did not feel obliged to do more, because Olivares was still not paying the promised subsidy in full. Bank charges eroded the value of what was sent, adding to Austrian mistrust. Philip IV was obliged to recall Oñate as a scapegoat for the deteriorating relations later in 1637.[3] Piccolomini's corps remained to support the Spanish in

Luxembourg until the end of 1639 when its commander and most of its 12,000 men were withdrawn. A smaller force remained under Baron Lamboy, a Liègois who was already an imperial colonel by 1621, but who made a poor general. The imperial corps did not help Spain against the Dutch, but instead covered the Lower Rhine against French incursions and provided limited assistance to Duke Charles.

The Rhine Campaign

Werth's Bavarians were withdrawn from Picardy in January 1637 and joined the Imperialists who had been blockading the French in the Ehrenbreitstein since August 1635. France paid for 117 wagon-loads of Dutch supplies to be escorted to the area by Melander's Hessians from Dorsten. This international relief effort failed when Werth captured the convoy. The defenders' situation was desperate. The vicomte de Bussy-Lameth, in command of the garrison, claimed to have survived by eating eighty rats, and he reduced pressure on supplies by allowing half his garrison to scramble down the walls and escape. Ramsay sent barges with more food from Hanau along the Main, but they were intercepted at Mainz. Under bombardment since 8 May 1637, the 195 survivors of the original 2,000 soldiers surrendered on 28 June in return for repatriation to France.[4] The Imperialists had tightened their grip on the electorate of Trier, containing the Hessians east of the Rhine far from French help.

The defeat, combined with Bernhard of Weimar's lacklustre performance in Alsace, prompted Richelieu to increase French involvement along the Rhine. He had withheld 1.6 million livres of Bernhard's subsidy, because the general mustered only 9,000 men. Instead of money, which might make Bernhard too independent, Richelieu sent 5,800 French troops under du Hallier instead. Having wintered on the upper Marne, Bernhard drove south-east into the Franche-Comté in May, largely because it appeared a softer target than Alsace.[5] He joined the duc de Longueville who had replaced Condé in command of the 10,000-strong Army of Burgundy and had advanced through Lorraine in March. Together they defeated Duke Charles's 6,000 soldiers on the Saône in June, and commenced a systematic conquest of the Spanish province, avoiding strong-points like Besançon in favour of reducing outlying castles.

Leaving de Longueville to complete the task, Bernhard broke into Upper Alsace at the beginning of August, drawing supplies from the garrison in Benfeld that remained loyal to Sweden. Short of money, he resolved to conquer the area beyond the Rhine to winter at the enemy's expense. The moment seemed opportune, because the main imperial army under Gallas had marched east in June to assist the Saxons, leaving only weak detachments under the incompetent Savelli and the turncoat Sperreuter. Richelieu approved the plan, hoping to relieve the burden on France while increasing pressure on the emperor. The objective would dominate French strategy in the region for the next three years.

The imperial city of Strasbourg stuck to its neutrality, denying either side use of its bridge. Bernhard tried to cross using the islands at Rheinau (Rhinau), north-east of Sélestat on 6 August. The attempt was overly optimistic, because his army was too weak. After much prompting, Maximilian agreed to release Werth with 7,000 Bavarians, available since the capture of Ehrenbreitstein. They reinforced the imperial units at Ettenheim, forcing Bernhard back over the river on 2 September. The Bernhardines were now down to 6,900 including du Hallier's men. They retreated south into the bishopric of Basel, ignoring Swiss protests. The local population fled, exacerbating an already critical supply situation, and Bernhard only survived the winter thanks to provisions forwarded by the French garrison in Mömpelgard.

Hessen-Kassel

Failure in Westphalia confirmed the experience of the Rhine campaign – that France could not pursue its objectives in the Empire solely through German surrogates. Richelieu had intended Hessen-Kassel to fulfil a similar role in north-west Germany as Bernhard was supposed to play in Alsace. With little prospect of Swedish assistance, Landgrave Wilhelm V had made an alliance with Louis XIII in the Treaty of Wesel on 21 October 1636. He agreed to Richelieu's standard terms of not to make peace without France and to respect Catholicism in conquered areas. In return, he would receive 200,000 talers a year to help maintain 10,000 troops, and the promise of diplomatic support for his objectives.[6]

Richelieu planned to recruit another 12,000 men on the Lower Rhine with French money to reinforce the Hessians who could then act as a barrier between the war in the west and Sweden's conflict with the

emperor. The man entrusted with the task was Count Rantzau, a Protestant Holsteiner who had served the Dutch, the Swedes and the emperor
before joining France in 1635. He was a favourite of the French queen
and was later rumoured to have fathered Louis XIV. He claimed to have
been wounded sixty times, and certainly lost an eye, a foot, a hand and
an ear over his career. Arriving in March 1637, he managed to find only
1,000 recruits by September.[7] Together with the failure to relieve the
Ehrenbreitstein this raised more suspicions about France's reliability as
an ally.

Ferdinand III would have preferred to negotiate with Wilhelm V, but
his father had already published the imperial ban in October 1636 and
named Landgrave Georg of Hessen-Darmstadt as imperial commissioner. Lack of troops provided an excuse for last minute talks, but
these failed to persuade Wilhelm to abandon the war. Ferdinand III
reluctantly approved an invasion in April 1637, but the bulk of the
Westphalian army under Götz and Hatzfeldt had already left in March
to reinforce Gallas, leaving only weak detachments under Geleen, Wahl
and Velen. Darmstadt had backed the emperor energetically since
Prague, raising 5,500 men, but most of these were serving with the
Imperialists in Saxony, or watching Ramsay in Hanau.[8] Wilhelm's troops
were able to escape northwards into Westphalia where they helped
their comrades recapture Vechta and Bielefeld in June. The fall of the
Ehrenbreitstein finally released enough Imperialists to invade Hessen-
Kassel in October, when 17 towns and 300 villages were torched to
intimidate the landgrave.

Hessian garrisons still held out in Kassel and Ziegenhain, while Wilhelm used his new French alliance to revive negotiations with the Dutch.
The Republic had consistently rebuffed his overtures in favour of good
relations with Cologne. However, when it renewed its own French
alliance in October 1636, it saw advantages in using the Hessians as a
buffer along its eastern frontier. Conscious of the earlier difficulties
with Count Mansfeld (see Chapter 10), the Dutch prepared the ground
thoroughly, securing agreement from Emden and the East Frisian Estates
to pay 12,000 tlr a month to maintain 2,500 Hessians. Wilhelm retreated
into East Frisia in September 1637. The arrangement was intended to
last six months, but the Hessians stayed until August 1650. Significantly,
neither Ferdinand of Cologne nor the emperor chose to challenge their
presence so as not to disturb the tacit understanding with the Republic.

Götz returned with 4,000 men through Thuringia, clearing the Hessians from Paderborn and Lemgo by November, but refrained from pursuing them into East Frisia.[9]

Wilhelm V died in Leer on 1 October leaving his young son in the charge of his widow Amalie Elisabeth. As a distant relation of the Bourbons, she expected France to support her ambitions. Richelieu made considerable efforts to retain her loyalty, sending her a diamond-studded cross and transferring her husband's pension to her son. Fears that Colonel Ramsay might hand Hanau, her homeland, over to France prompted the Imperialists to break the uneasy truce that had prevailed there since the Hessian relief in 1636. Wilhelm von Metternich, a colonel in Mainz service, stormed the place without the loss of a man on 18 February 1638, though Ramsay was mortally wounded in the fighting. Metternich was rewarded with the Bohemian estate of Königswart that became the home of his descendant, Prince Clemens, the Austrian statesman.[10]

Even before this, Amalie Elisabeth was convinced France would provide little direct help, and turned instead to the Dutch, presenting herself, like Elizabeth of Bohemia, as a poor widow. The hard-nosed burghers gave her shelter until 1639, but were not prepared to sacrifice their good relations with the elector of Cologne for her. She became an embarrassment to the Dutch as had the Winter Queen. Her troops in East Frisia and Westphalia disrupted Dutch trade and oppressed towns otherwise friendly to the Republic.

The emperor thus still hoped the Hessians might defect. Spain offered money, Schlick negotiated with Melander, while the electors of Mainz and Cologne persuaded Ferdinand to remove the bellicose Darmstadt landgrave as imperial commissioner and to recognize Amalie Elisabeth as regent during her son's minority. The emperor also renounced claims to Hersfeld and was prepared to grant de facto toleration for Calvinism, as he did for Anhalt and Brandenburg. In return, Amalie Elisabeth was merely expected to accept the loss of Marburg to Darmstadt. Duke Georg of Lüneburg and others advised her to accept this generous offer, but she used the emperor's alleged hostility to Calvinism as an excuse to reject it. She would only finally agree a truce on 3 March 1638, retaining possession of her existing garrisons as she waited for the general situation to improve.

The Palatinate's Final Throw

Ferdinand accepted this, because he wanted to concentrate Götz's small force to deal with a new threat unexpectedly posed by the Palatine exiles. The failure of the earl of Arundel's embassy in 1636 prompted a typical violent swing in Stuart policy: Charles I abandoned his nominal alliance with Spain made in 1634 and signed a new treaty with France on 27 February 1637. In return for a rather vague promise of diplomatic support over the Palatine question, Charles was prepared to declare war on the Habsburgs, provide 30 ships and let France recruit 6,000 men. Richelieu never ratified the agreement. He had no desire to compromise relations with Elector Maximilian who remained his preferred partner in the Empire. The prospect of French help was sufficient for Charles to send Sir Thomas Roe on a fool's errand to Hamburg where French, Swedish and imperial envoys were gathering under nominal Danish mediation. The Danes still resented the English for what they regarded as inadequate support during the 1620s, while the Swedes failed to understand why Charles, as a Protestant monarch and Karl Ludwig's uncle to boot, did not back the Palatinate to the hilt. Their impatience led them in July 1638 to sell arms to the Scottish malcontents whose defiance of the king led to the First Bishops' War, thus opening the British Civil Wars in 1639, and effectively removing the country as an active participant in European affairs for over a decade.[11]

Elizabeth of Bohemia had long given up hope of full restoration 'otherwise than by arms'.[12] Her son's expedition proved even more quixotic than the campaigns of the earlier paladins. Knyphausen's widow let a small party into Meppen, a town seized from the bishop of Münster and given to her husband as a Swedish donation. Alongside Karl Ludwig, the party included his younger brother Rupert and a number of English gallants dedicated to the Winter Queen, like the earl of Northampton and Lord Craven. Lying on the Münster–East Frisian frontier, Meppen offered a base to collect an army to march south and recover the Lower Palatinate. Even considering that they brought 41 barrels of English gold, the plan was far-fetched. Long negotiations failed to secure Hessian support since Amalie Elisabeth did not want to risk her truce with the emperor.[13] James King, a Scottish veteran who assumed command of the Swedes in Westphalia in 1637, did promise

594

1,000 men from his base between Minden and Nienburg, allegedly because he was thinking of retiring and wanted to please Charles I.

Karl Ludwig managed to recruit 4,000 men, including some discharged recently by the Catholics.[14] Ferdinand of Cologne feared the worst as imperial units had been withdrawn again. Command was entrusted to Hatzfeldt with instructions to raise a new army of 4,500 from men detached from the Westphalian garrisons in March. By May he was sufficiently strong to surprise Meppen, capturing twenty cannon and scattering the Palatine forces. Karl Ludwig regrouped in Cleves to the south, protected by the local Dutch garrisons, but he was left with only 1,700 men, whereas Hatzfeldt mustered 6,420 by July 1638.[15]

Karl Ludwig joined King and the Swedes at Stadtlohn on 9 September and headed north to retake Meppen. This was held too strongly by the Imperialists, while the East Frisians flooded their frontier so that the Palatines could not enter, and nor could the Hessians leave to join them. The Palatines headed east through Osnabrück, hoping to capture Lemgo as a new base nearer the Swedish posts along the Weser. Hatzfeldt's approach forced them to abandon their siege and retreat towards Minden. They assumed Hatzfeldt would be content at just relieving Lemgo and did not expect him to pursue them. However, he had 5,800 men, mainly cavalry, and dashed east to cut off their retreat at the Vlotho bridge on 17 October.

Prince Rupert and the Swedish cavalry tried to break through, but he was captured by Walter Devereux, Wallenstein's assassin, along with 1,200 others. King reached Minden with just five companions. Karl Ludwig tried to escape (rather unheroically) in his coach but it sank in the Weser, drowning the horses and driver. He survived by clutching a willow branch and hauling himself ashore. He hid in Minden for two months before he eventually returned to his Dutch exile. Hatzfeldt suffered only 79 casualties and followed up his success by capturing Vechta that November.

The defeat extinguished the last flicker of an independent Palatine cause, leaving it wholly dependent on unscrupulous foreign backers. The start of the British Civil Wars removed the most consistent of these, as well as prompting many Britons to return home. Spain refused to release the 6,000 who were serving in its Army of Flanders, but at least 30 experienced Scottish officers left Swedish service during 1639. No more than 10 Scots became Swedish officers each year after 1638, compared to the 1,900 who joined over the previous decade.[16]

The Swedish Retreat

With negotiations stalled, the Imperialists made a third attempt to drive the Swedes into the sea and, for the first time, prioritized operations against them. Gallas took the main army of 20,000 men from the Rhine to join the much reduced imperial and Saxon forces, numbering around 10,000, at Pretzsch on the Elbe between Wittenberg and Torgau in June 1637. Further Saxon units garrisoned Magdeburg and Wittenberg, isolating Banér's 14,000 men in Torgau where he had been blockaded since March. Gallas bridged the river above and below the town, ready to cross and surround the Swedes. However, Banér again evaded destruction, this time breaking out at night on 28 June having distributed 300,000 litres of wine plundered from the elector's cellars. Unlike Mansfeld and Duke Christian, Banér had no scruples about burning his baggage and mounting his infantry on the transport horses for a quick escape.

The direct route north to Pomerania was blocked by the Brandenburgers, who were now arming on behalf of the emperor. Banér headed north-east instead, through Jüterbog and Lübben to the Oder. As well as pursuing the Swedes directly, Gallas sent columns to race ahead and reach Küstrin first, trapping Banér between the river and the Polish frontier. Banér sent the officers' wives, including his own, and the remaining baggage towards the frontier as if he intended to escape that way, but double-backed westwards across the river south of Frankfurt and then dashed north on the other bank to meet Wrangel and 5,000 men at Eberswalde. His 16-day trek cost 4,000 men, but the army was still intact.

However, there were only 9,000 garrison troops in Pomerania and just 1,200 in Mecklenburg. All were unpaid and demoralized. The fortresses were in a poor condition and the garrisons had long since consumed the palisades for firewood. There was little Banér he could do to stop Gallas picking them off. Landsberg, Gartz, Demmin and others all fell to the imperial army again, reducing the Swedes to Stettin, Stralsund, Wismar, Wärnemünde, Greifswald, Anklam, Kammin and Kolberg. The costly retreat dashed the hopes raised by the battle at Wittstock the previous year.[17]

The situation forced Oxenstierna to scale down his demands. He was prepared now to make peace in return for holding some Baltic ports for fifteen years while the Germans paid 3 million tlr, part of which would be used to disband the army. All constitutional revisions were abandoned, but he still held out for an amnesty for those excluded from the Prague Peace to retain his current allies as potential checks on Habsburg power. He was even prepared to accept the detested Franz Albrecht of Lauenburg and his brothers Franz Carl and Julius Heinrich as new intermediaries. Ferdinand III sent Vice-Chancellor Kurz for direct talks in Hamburg in January 1638. Gallas was optimistic, but the Swedes now stalled, citing the emperor's refusal to negotiate over the Palatinate and Bohemian exiles.

This was simply a ruse, since Sweden was happy to abandon both in 1648 to obtain peace. The real reason was that Oxenstierna was now simply playing for time until he concluded parallel negotiations with France. With its own forces making no headway, France needed Sweden to maintain the pressure on the Empire and prevent the feared Habsburg combination. Richelieu accepted Oxenstierna's terms in the Treaty of Hamburg on 15 March 1638. The annual subsidy of 400,000 riksdalers was extended for three years and Richelieu accepted that Sweden was not a party to its war against Spain. Similar arrangements were written into the Franco-Dutch alliance that was also renewed in March, though Richelieu obliged the Republic not to make a separate peace with Spain, whereas Oxenstierna merely consented to coordinate diplomacy with France.[18]

The military situation had returned to that of summer 1630, only this time the odds were more in Sweden's favour. Banér was established in his bridgehead, with Stettin as his main base. The new French subsidies allowed Oxenstierna to deliver three ship-loads of new uniforms, as well as 14,000 conscripts and 180,000 talers in cash by July 1638. Gallas, by contrast, mustered just 15,000 and had been obliged to winter in an extended cordon across Mecklenburg and Pomerania to contain the enemy. The Saxons were busy blockading Erfurt, and though Gallas was reinforced by 8,500 Brandenburgers, these were poorly organized and ineptly led by men like Conrad von Burgsdorf who 'were little better than gangsters'.[19] The effort was nonetheless considerable for Brandenburg, and reflected the elector's determination to claim Pomerania after Duke Bogislav's death. Brandenburg's government was already more authoritarian and militarized under Count Schwarzenberg, whose reputation was unduly blackened by generations of Prussian historians glorifying the reign of Georg Wilhelm's son after 1640 as that of 'the Great Elector'.[20] The elector entrusted command to Schwarzenberg who reorganized the army in December 1638, but this alienated Klitzing who joined the Guelphs the following May, while another colonel defected with his regiment to the Swedes. Effective strength fell below 6,000 and Brandenburg operations were restricted to defending their own forts.

Meanwhile, Banér broke the imperial cordon by recapturing Gartz and then liberating Mecklenburg in October 1638. Gallas fell back across the Elbe, plundering Brandenburg and sending units into Bohemia and Silesia to ease the pressure on scarce supplies.[21] It had proved impossible to assemble the numbers needed to crack the last Swedish defences because the area between the Elbe and Oder had been devastated by the fighting since 1635. Though it was not clear at the time, the Imperialists would not get another chance.

RESOLUTION ON THE RHINE

Imperial Military Finance

Financial difficulties contributed to the failure. The Peace of Prague essentially adopted the system of military funding devised at Regensburg in 1630 to maintain a single army through regular payments from the imperial Estates. Assessed at 80 Roman months a year, these payments would produce at best 8 million florins, but even predicted returns were considerably less than this because the Swedes still held Pomerania, Mecklenburg and other areas. Failure to win over Hessen-Kassel or the Guelphs further eroded receipts. Gallas complained that the cities of Hamburg, Bremen and Lübeck were lending millions to the enemy but refused to billet his exhausted troops.[22] Those that did pay were chiefly former Liga members who now considered themselves the emperor's allies and expected to be treated accordingly, with exemption from billeting and winter quarters.

The electoral congress extended the grant by another 120 Roman months in October 1636, but the emperor had already begun assigning regions to support the separate corps of his main allies. Upper Saxon payments went directly to Johann Georg's troops, while Cologne units maintained themselves at Westphalia's expense. The Bavarian, Franconian and Swabian Kreise payments were allocated to Maximilian's army in January 1636. The practice eroded the already fragile distinction between the official war taxes and the numerous other payments demanded by individual commanders. The Franconians claimed in February 1638 that these additional costs amounted to between two and five times what they owed in Roman months, and they tried to offset them by withholding the official taxes. They also requested measures to improve army discipline, reduce pay and allow Kreis officials to supervise transit through their region.[23]

Ferdinand III responded to these complaints by approaching all the imperial Estates through the Kreis assemblies, rather than just the electors, when the 1636 grant expired in November 1638. Saxony and Brandenburg backed the call at the Upper Saxon assembly, knowing full well that the 120 Roman months it agreed would go to their own soldiers. Westphalia did the same, but the Franconians refused on the grounds that their region was already supporting a large part of the imperial army in addition to local garrisons. As a result, the emperor assigned Swabia and Bavaria to Maximilian, reserving Franconia and the Upper Rhine for his own forces on 20 November.[24]

These difficulties contributed to a slow but steady decline in the size of the imperial army from its peak under Wallenstein. The Prague arrangements envisaged 80,000 men, but the army still totalled over 100,000 including the Bavarians and Saxons. The impact of the plague, lack of funds and growing logistical problems made it impossible to sustain these numbers after 1635. By the beginning of 1638, the Habsburg War Council estimated there were 73,000 men including the Saxons, Bavarians and some auxiliaries paid by Spain, but planned to add just 10,000 recruits. The decision to switch Gallas and the main army to Saxony in 1637 seriously depleted the forces left on the Upper Rhine under Savelli. The 14 imperial cavalry regiments there had just 80 to 200 men each, while the 10 foot regiments averaged only 200 apiece, except for Colonel Reinach's unit in Breisach which was 800 strong. Numbers improved slightly in February, but the regiments all remained seriously under-strength and in a poor condition. Many of the officers were ill and the unpaid soldiers sustained themselves by plundering. Concerned for the welfare of his own units, Maximilian allowed Werth to move the Bavarians back to slightly fresher areas in Upper Swabia, Württemberg and Donauwörth. The Bavarian army remained in generally better shape and its horse and foot regiments averaged 800 to 1,000 men each between 1639 and 1645, with only a slight decline thereafter.[25]

Failure to maintain regimental strength caused considerable problems. Units had to be combined to achieve the strength required by tactical formations. More seriously, they were disproportionately expensive, because the higher-paid officers survived better than their men. Plans were drawn up in November 1638 to amalgamate the numerous under-strength regiments into fewer, but larger, more effective ones. At this point, it was reckoned there were only 29,500 men left in the two main armies, on the Upper Rhine and under Gallas.[26] The total troop number intended for 1639 was only 59,000, excluding the Bavarians and Saxons, or barely half what the imperial army had mustered five years earlier.

Partisan Leaders

The horrendous losses of the 1638 Rhine campaign were a major factor behind this decline. Bernhard of Weimar was determined to achieve the objective set the year before and establish a firm foothold for France east of the river. This time he prepared thoroughly. Since he had wintered in Mömpelgard and the bishopric of Basel, he was already close to the stretch of the Rhine along the Swiss frontier to Lake Constance. This route offered an alternative to the previous year's attempt to punch directly across the Black Forest. Though he had been joined in person by Rohan, who had escaped from the Valtellina (see Chapter 18), he still had few troops. Savelli's Imperialists held Rheinfelden with 500 men, with other garrisons in Waldshut, Freiburg and Philippsburg and Reinach's regiment in Breisach. These posts would have to be taken if the river was to be secured. He also needed a base beyond the Black Forest to tap the richer resources of Württemberg and the Danube valley.

Fortunately, Bernhard had an excellent spy network and knew how weak his opponents were. He also had the services of Colonel Erlach, a veteran of Dutch service who had been wounded at White Mountain and subsequently served Mansfeld and Sweden until 1627. Since then he had commanded the militia of his homeland, the Protestant canton of Bern. He joined Bernhard's army in September 1637, although he did not leave Bernese service until the following May. His contacts with the canton's patriciate ensured a good flow of supplies to Bernhard's army.

Erlach also opened negotiations with Major Widerhold, a Hessian who was the Württemberg militia's drill instructor and commandant of the Hohentwiel, the duchy's only fortress still holding out against the emperor. Though he has now faded from the local popular consciousness, Widerhold occupied a prominent place in Swabian patriotic folklore into the twentieth century. He exemplifies the partisan leaders who played an increasingly important role as the rapid escalation of the conflict left numerous isolated garrisons scattered across the Empire. These sustained themselves by raiding and acted as potential bases should friendly forces return to their area. The Swedes in Benfeld, Ruischenberg's Imperialists in Wolfenbüttel and Ramsay's Bernhardines in Hanau are three examples encountered already. Others included the Hessians in Lippstadt under the Huguenot refugee Baron St André and his subordinate, Jacques Mercier from Mömpelgard, known as Little Jacob, who rose through the ranks of Hungarian, Bohemian, Russian and Dutch service. Both were contemporary celebrities incorporated by Grimmelshausen into his novel. A counterpart in Habsburg service was the Swiss patrician Franz Peter König, ennobled in 1624 as von Mohr, who distinguished himself in skirmishes around Lake Constance in the early 1630s. As these background sketches indicate, such men generally came from relatively humble backgrounds and made reputations and fortunes through daring exploits. They never rose to command armies and were often difficult to control. König was dismissed after becoming embroiled in a feud with the highly disagreeable Wolfgang Rudolf von Ossa, Habsburg military commissioner for south-west Germany.

Widerhold acted nominally in the name of Duke Eberhard III of Württemberg, but pursued his own agenda. Mixing terror with benevolence, he spared the immediate vicinity of the Hohentwiel and concentrated on longer-range raids against Catholic communities, forcing 56 villages, monasteries and hamlets to provision his garrison that rose to 1,058 men and 61 guns by the end of 1638.[27] He was well-supplied with intelligence from friendly villagers who often participated in his plundering expeditions. He returned the favour on his death, leaving a large endowment for the local poor. His exploits became legendary. Once he caught the bishop of Konstanz out hunting and stole his horse and silver, and later he netted 20,000 talers by capturing the local imperial war chest in Bahlingen.

Blockaded since Nördlingen, Widerhold agreed to remain neutral after February 1636 because of renewed talks to include Württemberg in the Prague amnesty. Ferdinand III made surrender a condition for restoring Eberhard III in 1637, but Widerhold ignored ducal orders to comply and declared for Bernhard in February 1638. He remained a constant thorn in the Habsburg side, not least by raiding the Tirolean enclaves, and did not submit to ducal authority until 1650.

The Battles of Rheinfelden

The Rhine campaign of 1638 was an epic struggle that reveals the difficulties in assembling and sustaining armies. In the opening phase, Bernhard contested control of the Forest Towns route from the Rhine to the upper Danube, while the second stage saw a fierce struggle over the Austrian Breisgau that could serve as a French base and became one of Richelieu's territorial demands.

Bernhard advanced with only 6,000 men and 14 guns through Swiss territory to cross at Basel on 28 January and surprise Savelli's men at Rheinfelden. The garrison resisted, blocking his onward path and forcing Bernhard to begin a siege with his limited resources. The main works faced the town on the south bank, with two cavalry regiments posted on the other side opposite the gatehouse protecting the bridge. An infantry regiment was detached to guard the Laufenburg bridge further upstream, while four cavalry regiments secured the ferry at Beuggen, a fortified manor belonging to the Teutonic Order.[28]

Werth immediately saw the need to relieve Rheinfelden and prodded Savelli into helping him collect 2,600 infantry and 4,500 cavalry from the Breisgau outposts and rushing with only minimal ammunition and no artillery through the mountains. The Imperialists appeared early on Sunday 28 February 1638 outside Beuggen, but were blocked by Bernhard's dragoons posted behind a hedge. Unable to deploy, the Imperialists took another, more difficult road parallel to the river and headed west towards Rheinfelden. Bernhard used the four hours it took them to ferry over 600 musketeers and 8 light guns, as well as concentrating the cavalry already north of the river under Taupadel on the higher ground above the town. Taupadel charged as the Bavarian cavalry tried to deploy from the road at Karsau. The Bavarians were thrown back, but the charge left Rohan and Johann Philipp von Salm-Kyrburg, another paladin veteran, both mortally wounded, while Colonel Erlach was captured. Savelli and the imperial infantry now arrived and gained the heights. Bernhard held his position until nightfall, then slipped past the enemy to retreat eastwards along the river to Säckingen, abandoning at least three of his guns and having lost 150 men.

The absence of pursuit is unsurprising given that Savelli and Werth had just force-marched their men through the mountains in winter on low rations. Bernhard regrouped at Lauffenburg, 14km upstream, where he was joined by the rest of his army from the south bank on 2 March. He now undertook one of the risky strokes that made him famous, setting off early the next day back along the north bank to Beuggen, collecting the three cannon that the Imperialists had failed to find.[29]

He was spotted by imperial pickets around 7 a.m. Werth and Savelli hastily deployed behind a ditch that drained at right angles into the Rhine, but 'before we had got our people together, the first had already been shot dead'.[30] The Bernhardine infantry advanced in good order, firing a salvo at half range, backed by their light cannon. The cavalry on either flank then charged. The imperial infantry replied with a salvo, but were still reloading as their opponents rushed across the ditch. They broke, discouraging their cavalry who now tried to escape, some throwing off their armour to lighten the load. Werth made a stand with the best Bavarian infantry regiment until they were forced to surrender. In all, 500 were killed and 3,000 captured, including Savelli, General Enkevort and Sperreuter. The latter was one of the first to flee, fearing for his life if captured by his former employers, but was caught on Basel territory. Bernhard hated Werth who had openly denounced him as a traitor to the Empire. He enjoyed himself immensely watching Werth and Savelli blame each other for the defeat at a banquet he gave the captured officers to celebrate his victory.

Savelli's behaviour somewhat resembles Mr Toad's. He soon escaped thanks to the woman charged with bringing food to his cell. Unfortunately, the authorities were not as forgiving as the characters in Kenneth Grahame's story and she was executed along with seven other alleged accomplices. Bernhard should have celebrated instead, because Savelli was more a liability than an asset to any army, owing his command to his court connections. Enkevort, a competent officer who had risen to

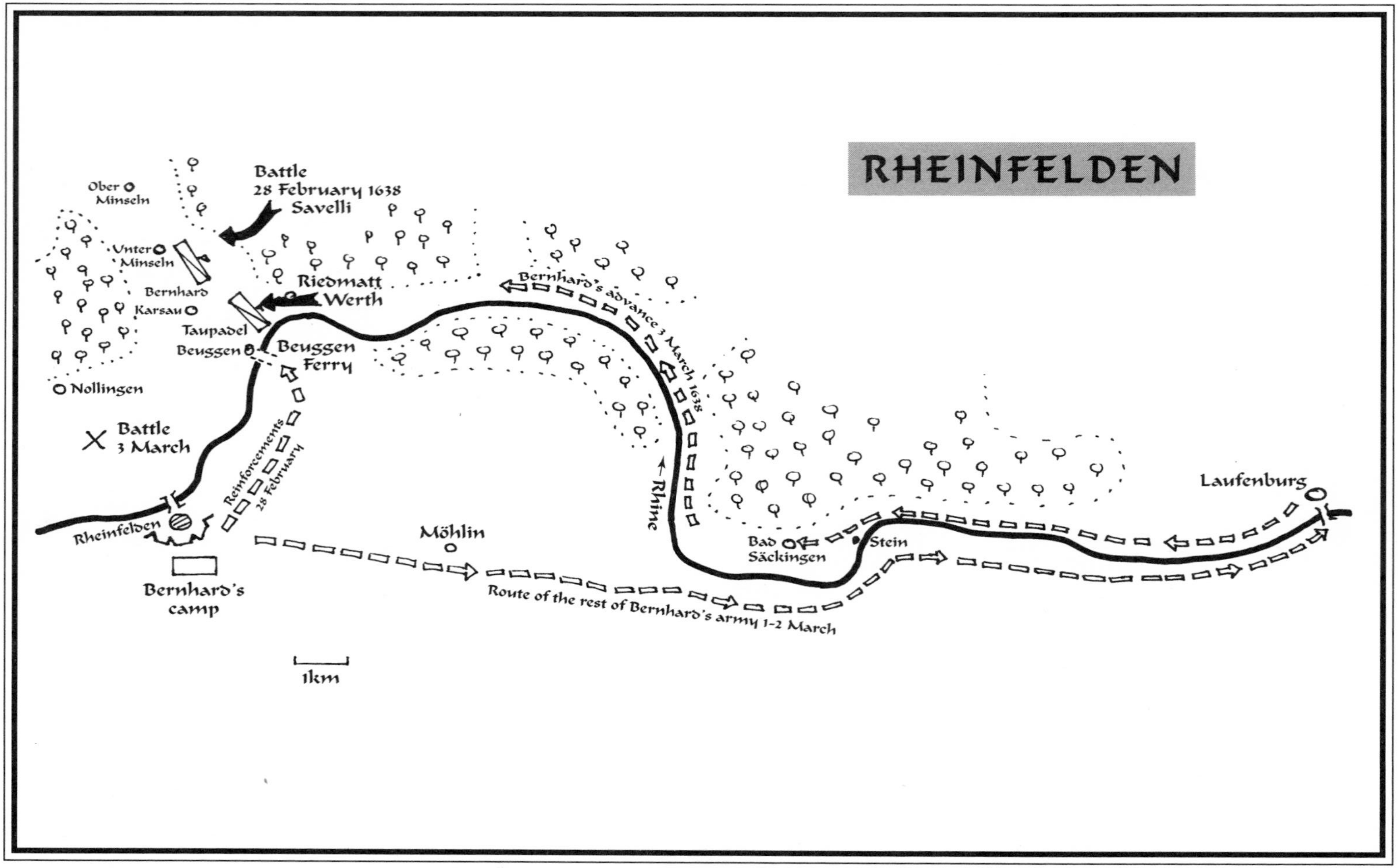

RHEINFELDEN

Laufenburg

Stein

Bad
Säckingen

← Rhine

Bernhard's advance 3 March 1638

Route of the rest of Bernhard's army 1–2 March

Möhlin

1km

Battle
28 February 1638
Savelli

Ober
Minseln

Unter
Minseln

Bernhard

Ricomatt
Werth

Karsau

Taupadel

Beussen
Ferry

Beussen

Reinforcements
28 February

Nollingen

Battle
3 March

Rheinfelden

Bernhard's
camp

his command partly thanks to a timely defection from Wallenstein in 1634, was held by the French along with Werth until they were exchanged for Swedish generals in 1641 and 1642 respectively. Sperreuter was held hostage with his wife and child on the Hohentwiel until 1641 when he was swapped for Taupadel who had been captured in the meantime. His confinement was rather less easy than that of Enkevort and Werth who attended French society events, and his family died during the bombardment of the Hohentwiel in July 1639. The loss, albeit temporary, of such officers was serious at a time when military efficiency was closely linked to the skill and reputation of commanders. Rheinfelden also frustrated the emperor's efforts to eliminate Hessen-Kassel, because Götz and the former Liga units had to be diverted from Westphalia to the Upper Rhine in April.

Rheinfelden resisted bravely for another three weeks, but was forced to surrender on 24 March. Even after pressing the imperial prisoners into service, Bernhard's force still numbered only 12,000, half of whom were cavalry. He lacked the infantry to besiege the other towns that still resisted. Whereas du Hallier's French detachment had been recalled at the end of 1637, Richelieu now sent a contingent of 4,500 infantry that was to remain with Bernhard's army. French troops regarded the Rhine like the river Styx, fearing they would never return if they ventured into Germany. The new detachment lost 2,000 deserters within a month, but Richelieu was determined that Bernhard should eliminate the threat to Alsace and sent another 1,900 infantry in July. Both detachments were led by exceptional officers who were to represent French interests in Germany until the end of the war. Guébriant, the more senior, already knew Bernhard from the 1636 campaign and volunteered to lead the reinforcements. Brave and honest, he was able to assert himself over his fractious subordinates. His equally courageous wife assisted him, even leading 400 recruits from Paris to join him for his last campaign. His early death in 1643 prevented him reaching the front rank of French generals military history has chosen to commemorate, leaving him overshadowed by Turenne who commanded the second detachment. The younger brother of the duc de Bouillon, Turenne's association with Huguenotism slowed his career and he served the Dutch instead until 1632. Despite a weak physique and a speech impediment, he distinguished himself as a courageous and skilful commander, becoming the only Frenchman Napoleon later considered a truly great general. He was soon switched after 1638 to Italy and Roussillon, but returned to assume command in Germany after Guébriant's death and remained there until 1648.[31]

The Siege of Breisach

Rather than push on along the Forest Town route, Bernhard turned against the Breisgau immediately to the north. Freiburg, the administrative centre, was difficult to defend and fell on 10 April. He then concentrated his infantry and artillery outside Breisach from 15 June, leaving Taupadel and the cavalry east of the Black Forest to deter relief efforts. Perched on a rocky hill above the Rhine, Breisach commanded a permanent bridge resting on two islands and protected by entrenchments on the western bank. Colonel Reinach was an experienced Bavarian officer who had commanded Pappenheim's infantry at Lützen and later transferred to imperial service. His garrison had been reinforced to 3,000 men with 152 cannon. The rest of the imperial campaign of 1638 became a series of increasingly desperate attempts to relieve him.

The task was entrusted to Johann Count Götz, one of the many Lutherans in the imperial army. From Lüneburg, he had served the Palatinate and then the Dutch, before joining the imperial army. He was identified with Wallenstein's 'German' faction, but survived the purge in 1634 only to be court-martialled after a poor performance in Silesia the following year. His reputation for bravery and experience ensured his appointment as Bavarian commander in 1636, despite Maximilian's normal antipathy to Protestant officers. He also enjoyed Ferdinand III's confidence and was named imperial commander on the Rhine in September 1638. Götz collected 13,500 men at Rottweil east of the Black Forest, intending to coordinate a relief effort with Charles of Lorraine, who still held out with 5,000 men in the Franche-Comté against de Longueville's 13,000 French.

Götz climbed the mountains to appear north of Breisach on 26 June. He slipped in supplies, but was too weak to attempt relief directly and crossed over into Alsace hoping that taking French positions there would force Bernhard to lift the siege. The French garrisons proved too strong, while Bernhard switched Taupadel's cavalry west of the Rhine to confront him. Thwarted, Götz retreated to Württemberg, leaving Savelli opposite Strasbourg. Having recuperated, he rejoined

Savelli to give a combined total of 15,000 men at Offenburg on 7 August.

The Battle of Wittenweier

Götz attempted to reprovision Breisach by using his entire army to escort supplies that were to be loaded onto barges at Rheinau. Bernhard realized he could never take Breisach while Götz remained in the field and decided to force a battle. He drew 11,400 men from his siege lines and headed north through Kensingen and Lahr. It was not until scouts reported his approach on Sunday 8 August that the imperial commanders realized he was no longer at Breisach. The imperial cavalry in the vanguard were driven back into the village of Friesenheim, about 4km north of Lahr. Götz reacted quickly, placing infantry and artillery on a vine-covered hill at Schuttern 2km to the west, while the rest of the army drew up behind a boundary ditch between there and Friesenheim. Bernhard sent his French infantry who cleared Friesenheim, which the Imperialists had set on fire. Götz regrouped his troops on the hill, while Bernhard moved artillery into the vineyards opposite. He soon realized that the terrain was unsuitable for the cavalry that comprised more than half his force and so broke off the action, falling back to more open ground at Mahlberg having lost around 50 men to the enemy's 120. The fighting was typical of the many relatively bloodless confrontations between the armies that go largely unrecorded, but which was to be the prelude to a more significant action.[32]

Determined to get his supply convoy through, Götz gave Savelli two-thirds of the army and sent him early the next day towards Wittenweier to reach Rheinau. Götz hoped the large Kaiserwald wood would screen this move, but Bernhard was alerted and headed north-west after morning prayers to catch Savelli as he emerged through a gap in the trees. Savelli had failed to take precautions and had moved too far ahead of the supply train that blocked the road behind. Bernhard and Guébriant arrived at the gap first, deploying the cavalry on their left, followed by the infantry in the centre and Taupadel and the rest of the cavalry coming up on the right. Savelli's cavalry were disordered by 400 musketeers and 2 guns Bernhard had posted in a wood by the Rhine. They gave way as Bernhard charged, some units fleeing, disordering their infantry and plundering the provision train. Savelli and the fugitives escaped through the defile as Götz arrived with the rearguard. However, Taupadel's cavalry on the right faced better regiments, and were thrown back by Götz who attacked Bernhard's infantry and captured their artillery. Bernhard replied using cannon abandoned by Savelli, while two veteran infantry regiments arrived from the reserve. Götz made repeated attacks with his cavalry until midnight when he retreated, having already evacuated 3,000 wounded to Offenburg. He nonetheless lost 2,000 killed, 1,700 captured, 13 cannon and over 3,000 wagons full of food and munitions. Bernhard lost 1,000 casualties, but recouped these by pressing enemy prisoners and deserters into service.

It was a serious defeat that exposed significant weaknesses in an imperial army that then disintegrated during the retreat. Regiments remained under-strength and contained too few experienced men. Only 3,000 men remained with the colours by the time Götz reached Offenburg. He was furious with Savelli whose court connections enabled him to escape a court martial, though other officers, including Werth's brother, were arrested. Götz complained that the Strasbourg burghers treated his fugitives worse than the enemy, stealing their clothes and beating them before sending them packing.[33]

Desperate Measures

Though wounded himself, Götz persisted, regrouping at Rottweil to wait for General Lamboy and 3,900 men originally intended to reinforce the Spanish in Italy but who were now directed to join him, along with others scraped from garrisons in Bohemia and Franconia. The soldiers had lost confidence in their commander, believing wrongly that he 'was not really Bavarian, but more Weimarian' and in secret negotiation with Bernhard.[34] An attempt to supply food to the Breisach garrison through the Black Forest failed, but Savelli, now posted to Philippsburg, did slip some across the river by sending Croats down the west bank to the Breisach bridgehead. Bernhard was down to 9,000 men and could no longer isolate the fortress completely. Peasants were able to enter and sell food at extortionate rates. The situation inside Breisach was nonetheless growing desperate; Reinach had already expelled the civilians and was down to 1,600 effectives. Bernhard tried to sow dissent within the garrison, sending letters he had captured in Savelli's baggage suggesting that the Habsburgs suspected the commandant of disloyalty.

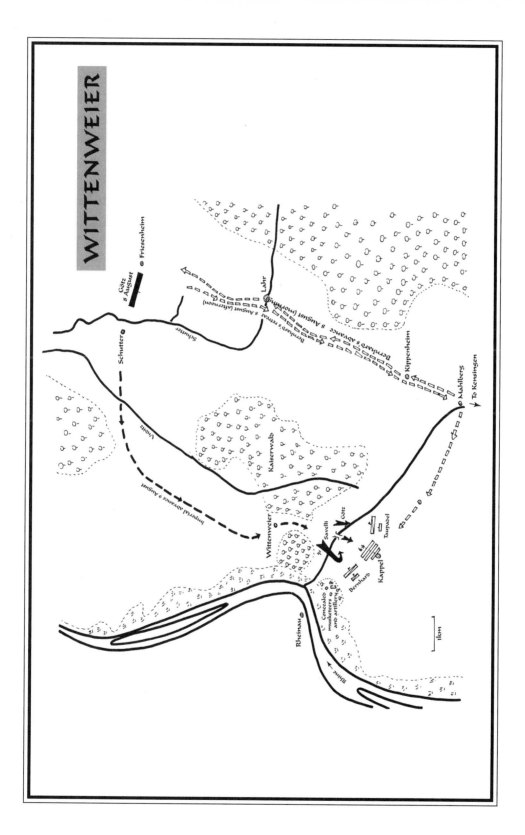

WITTENWEIER

Götz 8 August
Friesenheim
Lahr
Schutter
Schutter
Bernhard's retreat 8 August (afternoon)
Bernhard's advance 8 August (morning)
Kippenheim
Mahlberg
To Kensingen
Urolte
Schutter
Imperial advance 9 August
Kaiserwald
Wittenweier
Savelli
Götz
Taupadel
Bernhard
Kappel
Concealed musketeers and artillery
Rheinau
Rhine
1km

Duke Charles made his own, poorly timed relief effort before Götz's new army was ready, and marched from the Franche-Comté with 4,000 men into Upper Alsace without interference from the French under Longueville. Bernhard gambled correctly that Götz could not intervene, and crossed the Rhine, picking up detachments on the other side to give 4,800 men to block Charles outside Thann, south-west of Colmar, on 15 September. Bernhard's cavalry displayed superior discipline, returning to the field having broken the Lorraine horse and assisting their infantry to crush Charles's foot soldiers, who fought on for two hours before breaking.

Götz was not ready to move until a month later, when he marched with 10,000 men up the Glotter valley past Freiburg, to appear at Breisach on 22 October, only to find Bernhard safely back in his entrenchments. Having been repulsed, Götz sent 1,000 musketeers over the Rhine to clear the besiegers from the Alsatian side, but these were dispersed by Turenne. Despondent, he re-crossed the Black Forest.[35] With his army in poor shape, he relied on local militia to attack the Forest Towns in a last attempt to relieve Breisach by going round the southern end of the mountains, while Charles advanced to Thann again and Savelli sortied from Philippsburg. The three detachments collectively outnumbered Bernhard's army, but each was individually too weak to achieve anything and the operation was aborted in late November.

The local inhabitants had fled, leaving the Imperialists to subsist on thistles, snakes and a meagre bread ration. They were without shoes or stockings. Their horses were dying. The reinforcements that arrived in October lost half their strength within a month and the total number fell to 12,000, including Savelli, despite 13,000 men joining them since August.[36] Götz was arrested as a scapegoat, but despite the best efforts of Savelli's friends at court he was exonerated and resumed command in 1640.

The Fall of Breisach

The garrison had fallen to 400 men who had gone without bread for four weeks, surviving by chewing horse and cow hides. Reinach finally agreed to surrender on 19 December in return for free passage.[37] Bernhard was furious to discover that thirty of his prisoners of war had starved to death during the siege. Three of the corpses had allegedly been eaten by the survivors, attracting widespread notoriety. Stories of cannibalism had been circulating since 1629 and became more common in the mid-1630s. Though they declined after 1640, they entered folk memory and re-emerged in mid-nineteenth-century writing under the influence of other cannibal tales from the age of European colonialism. They were clearly believed at the time and were still cited as hard evidence a century later.[38]

Seventeenth-century accounts were already influenced by Classical mythology and baroque drama that used tales of mothers eating their children as motifs for absolute horror and depravity. There were numerous direct accounts of people eating dogs, mice and other less palatable animals, but those of cannibalism were always based on hearsay.[39] The tales were fabricated and certainly embroidered in propaganda, mostly written by south-west German Protestants to rally sympathy, or as a metaphor for moral breakdown caused by the war.

As a reprisal for the alleged atrocity, Bernhard deliberately humiliated Reinach's troops as they staggered out of Breisach. He was determined to claim his triumph, riding Werth's horse captured at Rheinfelden as he entered the fortress. He obliged Reinach to leave the government archive behind as he intended Breisach as a capital for his own principality. He also insisted on garrisoning it with his own men and not those of the French, who had spent 1.1 million talers on a campaign that claimed at least 24,000 lives. Pamphlets appeared celebrating Bernhard as a German Achilles who had captured the *Porta Germaniae* for Louis XIII.

In fact, Bernhard had not so much opened a door to Germany than closed one into France. Breisach was a useful bridgehead, but France needed towns on the other side of the Black Forest to open a route into Germany. Its significance was not in severing the Spanish Road, which was already cut, but in blocking imperial incursions into Alsace, giving France a real chance to hold that province permanently. France shifted from military to civil administration, no longer treating the Alsatians as foreigners.[40] It also spelled the end for Duke Charles. Thann, his last Alsatian outpost, fell early in 1639. He escaped with his mistress and 1,600 troops across the western edge of his duchy to Sierck on the Luxembourg frontier in February, leaving a few isolated garrisons in Lorraine, but exposing the Franche-Comté. The war had shifted deeper into the Empire, as Bernhard could now be reinforced to operate east of the Rhine.

PEACE FOR NORTH GERMANY?

Ferdinand III Addresses the Amnesty Question

The worsening military situation encouraged Ferdinand to tackle the amnesty problem bequeathed by his father. Renewed efforts were made to win Hessen-Kassel and the Guelphs for the Prague settlement and to use what remained of the military momentum to persuade Sweden to make peace. France and Sweden responded by tightening pressure on the Germans to remain loyal to them, or at least neutral.

The emperor's hands had been tied by his father's policies. Hildesheim had been promised to Cologne in return for its support at the 1636 Regensburg congress, while five further Württemberg districts were transferred to the Tirolean Habsburgs and the Bavarian Chancellor Richel as rewards at the beginning of 1637. Johann Georg of Saxony was concerned the amnesty exclusions were undermining the chances for peace, while Duke August of Wolfenbüttel petitioned Ferdinand III on his accession for the return of his capital.[41]

Ferdinand did his best. Georg Friedrich, the only Hohenlohe count excluded from the amnesty at Prague, was pardoned in 1637.[42] The emperor also accepted that Eberhard III was not responsible for Widerhold's behaviour and agreed to allow him back into Württemberg provided he accepted the loss of the monasteries and donated districts. Zweibrücken was included in these arrangements that were all completed by October 1638. The four Nassau-Walram counts were also pardoned in 1640, but as their lands were not restored they remained French pensioners in Metz and Strasbourg.

Wolfenbüttel proved far more difficult because it became the fulcrum of initiatives to neutralize all north-west Germany. Saxon and Brandenburg troops tried to force the Guelphs to rejoin the war in 1637 by invading from the east. Duke Georg persuaded them to leave by getting the Swedes to evacuate the town of Lüneburg that they had been occupying since April 1636.

A New Third Party

Convinced he needed to bolster his neutrality, Georg opened negotiations with Amalie Elisabeth of Hessen-Kassel after she renewed her
truce with the emperor in March 1638. Together they had 12,000
troops, offering a viable basis to uphold a common neutrality.[43] The
proposal appealed to the Hessian commander Melander, who advocated
widening it to include Cologne, Pfalz-Neuburg and Hessen-Darmstadt
to form a new third party that could achieve a general peace by forcing
the emperor to modify the Peace of Prague.

The initiative coincided with further Danish efforts to protect its
Lower Saxon interests following the renewal of the Franco-Swedish
alliance at Hamburg in March 1638. Christian IV backed Georg's plan,
writing to Banér asking for the Swedish forces to spare the Guelph
duchies.[44] This obliged Ferdinand to instruct Gallas to refrain from
demanding Lower Saxon billets, as well as send Vice-Chancellor Kurz
to discuss the proposal. Christian also intervened on Duke August's
behalf, requesting Ruischenberg to evacuate Wolfenbüttel.[45] The
imperial garrison now numbered 2,500, excluding dependants, and cost
the inhabitants 6,428 tlr a month, in addition to forage for its horses.
The soldiers were also cutting down valuable trees in the surrounding
forests for heating. The duke found their presence in his ancestral home
an affront to his dignity and said they disrupted the good government
of his duchy. Danish support proved decisive in Ferdinand's decision to
allow the duke back into the town that September, but the garrison
remained.[46]

While strategic reasons played a part in Ferdinand's decision to retain
the garrison, it was also politically impossible to relinquish Wolfenbüttel, because both Cologne and Bavaria insisted it be held as security for
the return of Hildesheim. Unfortunately, Hildesheim was occupied by
Georg, not August, who could not persuade his younger brother to
cooperate.[47] Georg pressed on with his plans, using the emperor's request
for war taxes in November as an excuse to convene the Lower Saxon
assembly to debate neutrality instead. Ferdinand condemned the move
to create a 'private defence' as contrary to the Peace of Prague and
ordered the Guelph troops to join the imperial army.[48]

The prospect of north German neutrality was initially welcomed by
Richelieu and, especially, d'Avaux who represented French interests in

Hamburg after 1637. Both saw a chance to achieve the long-desired neutral block around Bavaria. Maximilian invited the electors of Mainz, Cologne and Saxony to meet in Nuremberg in June and opened notionally secret talks with France at Einsiedeln monastery in Switzerland. Oxenstierna feared this would enable France to disengage, leaving Sweden to fight on alone. Banér, now confined to his coach by terminal illness, crossed the Elbe from Mecklenburg and invaded Lüneburg in January 1639. Though they provided supplies, the Guelphs refused to join Sweden, obliging Banér to move into Saxony two months later. The Lower Saxon assembly formally proclaimed their region neutral on 22 March, arguing it was in the public interest to exclude Sweden from the area.[49]

Banér's Offensive

Banér's advance into Saxony proved unexpectedly successful, encouraging him to push into the Habsburg hereditary lands. Though it ended in failure, the attack offered the first real proof that the high tide of imperial power since Nördlingen was ebbing. Ferdinand III appeared vulnerable at precisely the time when he needed to persuade the doubters to join him. Having collected troops at Erfurt in mid-March, Banér swept through the archbishopric of Magdeburg to enter Saxony with 18,000 men. Zwickau and Chemnitz soon fell, but he stalled before Freiberg where he hoped to capture Johann Georg's silver mine. The miners reinforced a garrison that resisted stoutly. Furious at the delay, Banér ordered an assault that cost him 500 men. The bitter cold prevented their burial as the bodies froze solid.

General Marazzino had assumed command of the Saxons in October 1638, amalgamating the weaker regiments, but even with units sent by Gallas, he mustered only 5,000 men. Having relieved Freiberg, he made the mistake of pursuing Banér to Chemnitz. Banér faced about and routed his forces, taking 1,500 prisoners on 14 April 1639. The Saxons were shattered and never recovered. Ferdinand overruled Johann Georg's indulgence and had Marazzino court-martialled. Banér pressed south-eastwards again, capturing Pirna on 3 May to give access to Bohemia. Leaving 3,000 men to hold the gorge, he surged south into a land free from war since 1634. Gallas massed 10,000 men under Hofkirchen to stop him at Melnik as he emerged from the mountains on

29 May. Against his subordinates' advice, Hofkirchen threw away his initial advantage with a premature attack, losing 1,000 casualties and 400 prisoners.[50] The Imperialist position collapsed further when the Swedish general Lilliehook advanced from Pomerania and captured more Brandenburg garrisons, while Stalhansk with another detachment pushed up the Oder, defeated Mansfeld and overran most of Silesia by the middle of the year.

The successes were largely due to the Imperialists' weakness after their costly Rhine campaign the previous year. Banér's army was too small to occupy Bohemia and he could not take Prague.[51] His men were poorly disciplined, killing 38 Bohemian exiles and wounding another 153 during their assault on Pirna. Not surprisingly, few answered his proclamation promising Bohemian freedoms. Ferdinand summoned Hatzfeldt from Westphalia and withdrew most of Geleen's Imperialists from south Germany. These combined with the remnants of Gallas's army to give 30,000 men under the emperor's younger brother, Archduke Leopold Wilhelm, at Prague by July. Without Prague, Banér could not stay in Bohemia. He switched from liberator to destroyer in October, ravaging a third of the kingdom in the worst destruction to date in the vain hope of intimidating the emperor.

Competition for the German Armies

The Guelph alliance with Hessen-Kassel was formalized by a treaty brokered by the Hessian commander Melander in April 1639. Melander worked to recruit additional members, opening negotiations with Saxony through Arnim who had escaped Swedish captivity the previous autumn and was back in Dresden. Other contacts ran through Melander's fellow members of the Fruitful Society (see above, p.263), extending his network to the Swedish, imperial and Bavarian armies.[52]

Richelieu grew concerned when Melander approached Bernhard, offering to make him commander of the third party's proposed combined army. Bernhard had around 14,000 men in April when the Hessians numbered less than 11,000, half of whom were in garrisons. Despite capturing Breisach, Bernhard had been unable to sustain his army in the devastated Breisgau. He re-crossed the Rhine that January to invade the virtually undefended Franche-Comté, scattering the peasants who tried to bar the way in the Doubs valley. Having established himself at

Pontarlier, he spent the next six months looting, burning and pillaging. He had grown disgruntled with France, wanting to be more than Richelieu's German recruiting officer, and demanded to be given Alsace, the Breisgau and the bishopric of Basel as his own principality. There was no place for such ambitions in Melander's scheme as this aimed for a compromise peace. Objecting that 'a new alliance, a third party would be a third war', Bernhard opened discussions to rejoin Sweden instead.[53]

Before these could be completed, he died on 18 July 1639, probably from the epidemic that had already ravaged the Franche-Comté that winter. Realizing he was dying, he summoned his colonels the day before and appointed Erlach, Reinhold von Rosen, Johann Bernhard Ohm and Count Wilhelm Otto von Nassau as the army's 'directors'.

There were now three substantial non-aligned armies holding the fate of western and northern Germany in their hands: the Hessians in Westphalia, the Bernhardines on the Rhine and the Guelph troops in Lower Saxony. Ferdinand had been negotiating both with Melander and, through Savelli, with Bernhard since 1637. He offered to make Melander an imperial count and appealed to his patriotism to persuade him to change sides. Coercion was impossible: Hatzfeldt had taken 7,600 men from Westphalia when he marched to Bohemia in April, reducing the Imperialists there to 9,000, including 5,500 Cologne troops under Velen. A concerted effort now began, assisted by Mainz, Darmstadt and Baden-Baden, to persuade the Bernhardine directors to defect.[54] Two emissaries were sent to offer to have Bernhard's corpse escorted to Weimar with full military honours. Joachim von Mitzlaff, who had been instrumental in suborning Wilhelm of Weimar's army in 1635, was despatched to repeat the coup.

France and Sweden countered these moves. Casualties and the Scottish exodus to fight at home in 1638 had reduced the number of qualified, reliable senior officers in Swedish service. Oxenstierna took a calculated risk in naming Königsmarck, a German, to replace King in north-west Germany, despite his poor showing at Vlotho bridge. An impoverished Brandenburg noble, Königsmarck had enlisted as a cavalry trooper in the imperial army in 1620, resigning in 1630 having only risen to ensign. His promotion in Swedish service after 1631 was rapid as his talents were soon recognized. He now commanded around 5,000 men, mainly restricted to Erfurt. These were too few to coerce the Guelphs, but they represented a potential reinforcement should they declare openly for

Sweden. He also demonstrated Swedish potency by raiding Bamberg, Würzburg and Kulmbach in August in the first incursion into Franconia since 1634.

Mitzlaff did not reach Weimar until late October 1639. His presence alarmed dukes Wilhelm and Ernst who feared Swedish reprisals, and in any case they had no influence over the Bernhardine directors. Mitzlaff returned empty-handed, only just evading 700 Swedish cavalry sent from the Zwickau and Chemnitz garrisons to capture him.[55] France meanwhile moved to prevent anyone, including the Swedes, from securing the armies. Melander's existing French pension was doubled to 18,000 livres and he was named second-in-command of Louis XIII's German troops. Another 20,000 talers were added to Amalie Elisabeth's subsidy in the Treaty of Dorsten. However, she obliged Richelieu to keep the agreement secret until Sweden ratified its treaty with France. This was to preserve her fragile truce in Westphalia that protected her garrisons.[56]

An attempt by Karl Ludwig to recruit the Bernhardines for the Palatine cause was easily thwarted by Richelieu's agents who arrested the hapless prince as he travelled incognito across France. Meanwhile, Guébriant, in charge of the French contingent in Bernhard's army, persuaded the directors to remain loyal to France in a new agreement on 9 October.[57] The troops passed fully into French service as the *Armee d'Allemagne* dedicated 'to restore and stabilize German freedom'. All its conquests were surrendered to Louis XIII, but Erlach remained governor of Breisach and the colonels retained control over the internal management of their units.

Ferdinand regarded the third army of the Guelphs as already lost. He formally enfeoffed the elector of Cologne with Hildesheim on 22 August, and authorized Hatzfeldt to enforce this in October and compel the Guelph troops to join the imperial army.[58] Piccolomini had already moved his 15,000 men from Luxembourg in September to assist. Duke Georg responded by tightening his mutual defence pact with Hessen-Kassel on 9 November, while Melander broke the Hessian truce to capture Bielefeld. The concentration of imperial forces east of the Rhine exposed the other bank. Guébriant appreciated that the Bernhardines were too weak for a renewed offensive over the Rhine, but moved north along the west bank, shadowed by the Bavarians on the other side, to occupy the lower Moselle just vacated by Piccolomini. The move was partly driven by a lack of supplies, but also to shift France's principal force closer to support the Hessians. Some of the Bernhardines crossed the Rhine at Bingen to invade the electorate of Mainz and occupy the Westerwald to the rear of the new imperial concentration.

The emperor did authorize operations to eject Guébriant, who re-crossed the Rhine on 27 December, retiring through Limburg and then south to winter at Hagenau and Breisach. However, he still preferred a diplomatic solution and postponed the invasion of the Guelph lands. Negotiations were opened with Banér, whom Ferdinand believed was authorized by Sweden to make peace.[59] There was also still hope that some of the Bernhardine officers might defect. The emperor issued an open pardon to all those willing to join him in throwing off the 'foreign yoke'.[60] Rosen remained belligerent, but the others doubted the sincerity of French claims to be fighting for *la liberté Germanique*. Colonel Ohm told a Mainz agent that if France opposed a true peace, 'the devil take anyone who picks up a sword or pistol to fight His Imperial Majesty. They [the colonels] are all tired of war.'

Cash, as usual, proved the sticking point. The officers wanted assurances from the emperor that he would meet their pay arrears. Hard-pressed, Ferdinand could not match the French who were channelling money through Frankfurt bankers to keep the colonels sweet.[61] Wider-hold also rejected Archduchess Claudia's generous offer of a full pardon, 30,000 florins and a post in the Tirolean forces. Nonetheless, Guébriant was sufficiently alarmed to ask the Bernhardine colonels to reaffirm their loyalty to France on 17 August 1640 and Richelieu continued to treat them with respect.

The War Moves North

By draining other regions of their troops, Ferdinand III managed to collect 44,000 men in Bohemia by January 1640.[62] Of these, only 12,400 were available as a field army under Archduke Leopold Wilhelm, reinforced by 4,100 under Hatzfeldt who had wintered in Franconia. Piccolomini was down to 13,000 in Westphalia, while the Saxons mustered 6,648, or only a quarter of their strength five years earlier. The Brandenburgers had effectively been knocked out. The Bavarians still totalled about 17,000 men, most of whom were on the Upper Rhine where there were perhaps 10,000 in total, including a few Imperialists.

The rest were in winter quarters around Donauwörth and Ingolstadt. As these figures suggest, it was now very difficult to launch major operations in more than one region at a time.

His enemies were in a similar position. Banér was reduced to 10,000 effectives, while the other Swedish commanders had only enough men to hold their current positions. Banér had little choice but to evacuate Bohemia in March and fall back the way he had come the previous year to join Königsmarck at Erfurt. The units left to hold Saxony were defeated at Plauen on 20 April 1640, forcing the garrison in Chemnitz to surrender while most of the others abandoned their positions.[63]

The challenge over the coming two years was for France and Sweden to establish a viable framework for military and political cooperation that had to include the Hessians and Guelphs, while Ferdinand pinned his hopes on frustrating this with one last effort to rally all Germans behind the Prague settlement. The emperor's preference for negotiation was cruelly exploited by the Guelphs and Hessians who had used the winter to gather their strength and now declared their hand in May 1640. Duke Georg did this openly by sending troops to Banér, counting on Swedish help to prevent an invasion of Hildesheim. He nominally mustered 20,000, but in fact had 6,000 at Göttingen and garrisons along the Weser, plus a field force of 4,500 under Klitzing. Amalie Elisabeth acknowledged her French alliance in March, but still promised to respect the truce in Westphalia. With French agreement, Melander moved the 4,000-strong Hessian field force east to the Eichsfeld in May to reinforce Banér. Richelieu summoned de Longueville from Italy, hoping that he possessed sufficient personal authority as a duke to master the 8,000-strong Bernhardine field army. This moved back down the Rhine to join the allied concentration.

The emperor was obliged to match these moves. He still hoped to win over the Hessians and so accepted Amalie Elisabeth's assurances. Nonetheless, Wahl, the new Cologne commander, was authorized to recover the positions her troops had seized over the last two years in breach of the truce. Hessian garrisons also became bolder, now raiding Paderborn. Piccolomini followed Melander east and joined Leopold Wilhelm at Saalfeld, south of Erfurt, on 5 May. They entrenched to block the way into Franconia. After a two-week stand-off, Banér fell back north-west into Lower Saxony, alarming the Guelphs who feared he would abandon them. Once they had promised another 5,000 men, he marched south again to Göttingen and Kassel. Leopold Wilhelm shadowed him, moving through Hersfeld to entrench again at Fritzlar in August. It was cold all year, the summer was wet and miserable and food proved hard to find.[64] Banér's second wife died and de Longueville fell ill, relinquishing command to Guébriant again. The Bavarian field army arrived from Ingolstadt, bringing Leopold Wilhelm back up to 25,000 men. After another four-week stand-off, Banér withdrew, allowing the archduke to advance north down the Weser to join Wahl's 4,000 field troops. Together, they took Höxter in October, but the men were exhausted and ill-disciplined. The weather grew windy and even colder. Leopold Wilhelm retreated south to winter at Ingolstadt. Banér left 7,000 to blockade Wolfenbüttel, while the rest of his army made themselves comfortable at the expense of the Guelphs' villagers.

Seemingly uneventful, this campaign completely shifted the war's focus to northern Germany, transplanting the 'little war' of outposts from Westphalia to the Upper Rhine instead. Under Erlach's direction, the Bernhardine garrisons operated from Breisach and the Forest Towns in conjunction with Widerhold in the Hohentwiel. The Bavarians retaliated from Philippsburg, Heidelberg and Offenburg, while the Imperialists sortied from Konstanz and Villingen. Neither side managed to spare more than 3,000 men from their fortresses, severely restricting what they could achieve. Erlach helped disrupt plans to besiege the Hohentwiel in 1640 by sending cavalry to collect the Swabian harvest. Claudia scraped together another expedition against Widerhold in 1641, but heavy snow and lack of food forced this to be abandoned in January 1642. Erlach and Widerhold scored the only success, briefly combining the following January to take Überlingen by surprise.[65]

What south Germany gained by way of respite, the north lost. Desperate attempts by the Weimar dukes failed to persuade the belligerents to respect Thuringian neutrality. The Dutch feared that the arrival of France's Army of Germany in their vicinity would merge the two wars. However, the withdrawal of Piccolomini's corps from Luxembourg at the end of 1639 reduced the imperial presence west of the Rhine to a few units under Lamboy who spent most of their time extinguishing the last of Pfalz-Neuburg authority in Jülich. The Hessians did the same in Berg on the other side of the Rhine, as well as capturing Kalkar in 1641, a move that gave them a bridgehead on the left bank of the river and established communications with the French. Kalkar was turned into a major fortress, sustained by taking hostages from surrounding communities to ensure regular contributions.

Though the Hessians refrained from provoking the Spanish in Jülich itself, Melander had already resigned at the end of 1640 in protest at Amalie Elisabeth's policies. He and his brother Jacob were rewarded the following December by Ferdinand with elevation as hereditary imperial counts 'von Holzapfel'. Melander was also made imperial field marshal in February 1641, but was both too compromised and too useful a diplomat to be given actual command. Instead, Ferdinand sent him on an ultimately fruitless mission to broker peace between Spain and the Dutch Republic until he replaced Wahl as Westphalian commander in October 1645. The emperor still controlled most of southern and central Germany, but the loss of the north meant the overall situation now hung in the balance.

18

In the Balance 1641–3

THE FRANCO-SWEDISH
ALLIANCE 1641

The Relationship of War to Diplomacy

Melander's dramatic rise from humble peasant to the senior ranks of the imperial aristocracy epitomized what appeared to be a world turned upside down. He amassed a vast fortune, allegedly totalling 1.5 million talers, and bought a lordship from his former master, Count Johann Ludwig of Nassau-Hadamar. Though often dismissed as a boorish provincial bumpkin,[1] Melander was in fact well-educated, fluent in French (and probably Italian as well), and had already received letters of nobility in 1608, making his subsequent prominence rather less remarkable.

Even Melander's experience indicates therefore the resilience of established social conventions. The same was true for the Empire's political culture. This had been strained by the conflict, but it still guided behaviour. The war is customarily portrayed as entering its most destructive and meaningless phase after 1640, as it allegedly descended into 'universal, anarchic and self-perpetuating violence'.[2] The development is often attributed to the deaths of the 'great captains' like Gustavus, Wallenstein and Bernhard, and is associated with the supposed internationalization of the war. 'The soldiers alone ruled' as junior officers acted on their own initiative to sustain their units or enrich themselves.[3]

Much of this is a myth deliberately fostered by the territorial authorities after the war to justify tighter control and surveillance of the population. Rulers wanted to persuade their subjects to continue paying high taxes to support armies in peacetime. These were considered necessary to promote princely dignity and facilitate a greater role in

European affairs. The post-war personnel, especially as they grew more numerous in the 1660s, were presented as disciplined soldiers (*Soldaten*), not the lawless soldiery (*Soldateska*) supposedly characterizing the era before 1648.[4]

There were certainly serious problems by the 1640s. The war's rapid expansion dislocated social and economic structures and disabled territorial administration. It became harder to recruit, even when bounties were offered.[5] However, armies were now smaller and more mobile than before 1635. Overall numbers fell by at least a third, and though the forces mustered for individual battles were still substantial, their composition had changed significantly. Whereas cavalry formed between a quarter and a third of field armies before 1635, over half were generally mounted thereafter. Some of the infantry now also rode horses on the march to speed movement. With some important exceptions, less time was spent on sieges in Germany – in contrast to operations in Flanders that remained dominated by protracted struggles around key towns. There is some evidence that garrison commanders surrendered more readily as massacres became less common. Officers were generally released on their word of honour, though the ordinary soldiers were usually pressed into the victor's ranks. This practice rarely worked well, and most deserted to their former masters as soon as possible. Driven by the growing shortage of seasoned soldiers, this probably explains why some believed desertion was a more serious problem than in the 1620s.[6]

The greater proportion of cavalry to infantry in armies partially offset the overall decline in numbers by enabling commanders to respond more rapidly to unexpected threats in poorly defended regions. However, it was also dictated by logistical constraints, since mounted men could forage more widely and carry supplies on their saddles. This put a premium on rural recruits since armies needed men who could both ride and look after their mounts. Animal casualties were generally high, especially as operations continued in winter when forage became scarce. Around half the cavalry were dismounted by the end of each campaign, contributing to the often slow start the following year as new mounts were procured and generals waited for the grass to grow.

The changed composition of armies does not support the standard interpretation of military development. The technologically determinist character of most military history sees change dictated by weaponry. The proportion of pikemen declined from between 33–50 per cent in

1618 to about 20 per cent or less by the 1640s. This is usually related to a supposed trend towards linear tactics where infantry units no longer fought autonomously but in long lines, with only narrow intervals between regiments.[7] The intention was to maximize firepower as had already been the case in the Dutch Orangist reforms of the 1590s. Linear tactics became the norm in European warfare from the 1670s as all armies emphasized the rapidity and volume of musketry delivered under tight supervision. The proportion of cavalry again declined to under a third by 1700. Whereas these developments were consciously promoted, those of the later Thirty Years War were not. The shortage of pikemen was considered a disadvantage since they were generally the more seasoned fighters needed for aggressive tactics. The growing reliance on musketry made infantry less use offensively. They were often posted behind fieldworks or in woods to protect them against the now more numerous cavalry.

While troop quality was uneven, there was no marked decline in the skill of either senior or junior officers. The deaths of generals military history has chosen to remember cast a shadow over those commanding in the later stages of the war. The presence of Turenne and the younger Condé in the French army, as well as the less widely celebrated Wrangel and Königsmarck in the Swedish forces, has led one writer to suggest the emperor was out-generalled.[8] However, men like Mercy, Melander, Montecuccoli and Piccolomini were at least a match for Wallenstein, Tilly and the other earlier imperial generals.

The continued effectiveness of the combatants leads to a further, more significant point. War still wreaked havoc, but it also remained firmly controlled and directed.[9] Operations continued to support political objectives as rulers sought to improve their negotiating positions. If anything, the interrelationship between warfare and diplomacy tightened as it became obvious that no one could achieve their goals solely by military means.

The Regensburg Reichstag

The absence of a decisive victory persuaded Ferdinand III to summon the first Reichstag for 27 years. Though intended to revitalize the Prague settlement, the decision departed from the 1635 political programme. His father had tried to manage imperial politics by consulting just the electors, denying the other imperial Estates a public forum to criticize his policy and impose constraints. Ferdinand III had already shown himself more flexible in his approach, but he nonetheless guarded his prerogatives. The approach to the Kreis assemblies in November 1638 brought the minor territories back into the formal political process, but was also intended to limit discussions to the emperor's agenda of more war taxes. These discussions, together with the negotiations over northern neutrality, indicated the growing desire for peace. The electors added their voices to this call, using their right of self-assembly to convene their own congress at Nuremberg in February 1640. Maximilian of Bavaria had already backed the papal peace initiative in 1636. He now indicated his willingness to invite the Kreis-convening princes to the Nuremberg congress.[10] The emperor decided to pre-empt the elector from emerging as the leader of a peace party by summoning all imperial Estates to a Reichstag where he could set the agenda. The invitation made the Nuremberg congress superfluous and it closed on 7 July. The electors' representatives reassembled with those of the other Estates in Regensburg on 13 September and remained in session until 10 October 1641.

The agenda closely resembled that of the 1636-7 electoral congress. The Empire was asked to extend the taxes agreed by some Kreis assemblies in 1638 that had now expired. All were to rally behind the emperor to defeat the two crowns of France and Sweden bent on suppressing German liberty.[11] Ferdinand made some concessions. An attack on the Hohentwiel was postponed so as not to antagonize the Protestant Swabians. The amnesty issue was addressed by an offer to widen the terms already granted to Württemberg by returning some of the monasteries, and even to extend a pardon to Hessen-Kassel and the Palatinate provided they joined the imperial war effort. It was suggested that a new, eighth electoral title might be created to persuade the elector Palatine to accept his Bavarian cousin's new status. Lastly, Ferdinand hinted he might accept 1627 as a more permanent normative year, allowing some of the Protestant administrators to keep their bishoprics indefinitely. These proposals were condemned by the papal nuncio, but were eventually accepted by the Catholic princes, including those like the electors of Mainz and Cologne that stood to lose territory.

The proposed modifications to Prague came very close to the adjustments adopted in the Peace of Westphalia. Had they been offered in 1636, or even 1637, the emperor might have achieved the united front he desired. Now it was too late, since the Guelphs and Hessians were committed to a Swedish alliance. The emperor renewed the mandate summoning Germans to renounce French and Swedish service. An imperial Recess incorporating Ferdinand's proposals was adopted thanks to the support of the electors and cities, though 31 of the 46 princely representatives voted against it. This confirmed the mandate and extended the war taxes by retrospectively sanctioning 240 Roman months across 1640–1. Compliance was poor, however, because even loyal territories wanted to deduct the cost of billets and plundering.[12]

Banér's Winter Offensive 1641

Despite its limited results, the Reichstag alarmed France and Sweden who doubted their German allies' loyalty. Despite failing health, Banér struck south from Thuringia in January 1641 to disrupt proceedings. Guébriant and Taupadel led France's Army of Germany into northern Franconia, not to conquer as a decade before, but to extort contributions. Banér was left to make the main attack, advancing rapidly through Hof and Bayreuth across 200km despite thick snow. He relied on moving as fast as any messenger to pre-empt countermeasures, and managed to reach Regensburg on 20 January. Three cavalry regiments crossed the frozen Danube downstream to approach the city unexpectedly from the south side, and surprised the imperial hunting party. Though they netted the emperor's prized falcons, he had been delayed leaving the city and avoided capture. A sudden thaw thinned the ice on the river, forcing the Swedes to beat a hasty retreat. Banér briefly bombarded the city, but had only light artillery with him and the shelling was simply a demonstration of power. Ferdinand refused to leave the city, gaining new credit for his coolness under fire.

Sensing the expedition was rebounding to his disadvantage, Banér headed north again. Guébriant refused to be drawn into operations against the Habsburg lands and retired north-west towards Lower Saxony, leaving the Swedes to retreat alone to Cham in the Upper Palatinate. Banér hoped to rest amid the forested hills, before breaking into Bohemia via Eger. The emperor responded with unexpected vigour. Archduke Leopold Wilhelm, Piccolomini and Mercy assembled 22,000 Imperialists and Bavarians on the Danube and advanced north in March. Banér hastily summoned his forces to rejoin him at Cham and was only saved by a detachment under the one-armed Erik Slang who briefly delayed the enemy at Neunburg on 19 March. The other Swedes escaped north at a punishing 20km a day along roads turned to mud by the renewed thaw, and then over the Preßnitz pass into Saxony at the beginning of April. They lost their baggage, plus over 2,000 prisoners and 4,000 sick and deserters.[13]

Renewed Swedish Mutiny

Banér died on 10 May shortly after his army had rejoined Guébriant at Halberstadt. Following Duke Georg of Lüneburg's death a month earlier, this left Sweden dangerously exposed.[14] Ruthless and forceful, Banér had been instrumental in rebuilding the army and saving Sweden's position in Germany after 1635. The consequences of his absence were immediately apparent. Under contingency plans, command devolved to three major-generals: the Swede, Count Karl Gustav Wrangel; the Finn, Avid Wittenberg; and the German, Adam von Pfuhl. Only 500 of the 16,000 soldiers were native Swedes. The situation returned to that of the 1635 'powder barrel' mutiny, as 23 of the 30 colonels established a committee under Caspar Mortaigne to press their demands.

Ferdinand seized the opportunity to offer an amnesty and worked hard to win over Pfuhl. Pfuhl's sister had been one of Queen Maria Eleonora's ladies-in-waiting and Banér's first wife. These connections and his own service record led him to expect to be named Banér's successor. Oxenstierna had no intention of choosing a German and appointed Lennart Torstensson, despite his fragile health.[15] Torstensson was still in Sweden, leaving a vacuum quickly filled by Pfuhl who sided with the colonels. They opened negotiations with August of Wolfenbüttel who had used the opportunity of his belligerent brother's death to resume talks with the emperor. Disaffection spread to the German officers in Guébriant's army as well.

As in 1635-6, peace negotiations resumed and ran in parallel with talks with the officers. France and Sweden had failed to harmonize their objectives when renewing their alliance in 1638. Richelieu wanted a universal peace that would settle all France's conflicts to his satisfaction. Oxenstierna's goals remained restricted to Germany and he considered breaking with his partner to clinch a separate peace with Ferdinand. Swedish resentment of France grew after Richelieu incorporated

Bernhard's army in 1639. Kurz and the Lauenburg dukes had been negotiating on the emperor's behalf in Hamburg since 1639. The mood at the Reichstag prompted Ferdinand to send a separate mission to Brussels to renew mediation between Spain and the Dutch. Meanwhile, the Lauenburg dukes relayed a much improved offer to Sweden, incorporating the concessions discussed in Regensburg to accommodate the Palatinate, Guelphs and Hessen-Kassel within the Peace of Prague.

Unlike his father, Ferdinand responded to Oxenstierna's desire for territory to enable Sweden to leave the war with honour. The Swedes had conquered the Altmark (western Brandenburg) and Frankfurt on the Oder in 1640. Elector Georg Wilhelm died that December and it was obvious to his ambitious successor, Friedrich Wilhelm, that Pomerania could not be obtained by force of arms. The new elector opened negotiations with Sweden under cover of an embassy to announce his succession. Count Schwarzenberg's death in March 1641, the only Catholic on the duchy's privy council, removed the principal opponent of this rapprochement. Predicting correctly that Brandenburg was about to defect, Ferdinand sought to pre-empt this. He secured Bavarian and Mainz agreement to offer all Pomerania to Sweden at the end of 1640.[16]

Unfortunately, Ferdinand's envoys failed to convince Salvius that the offer was serious. Rumours of talks nonetheless alarmed the French who had been pressing Oxenstierna to renew the 1638 alliance that was due to expire in March 1641. D'Avaux added another 80,000 riksdalers to the annual subsidy to be paid until both parties secured a satisfactory peace. Oxenstierna felt it was worth sacrificing diplomatic autonomy for this firm support and gave his assent on 30 June 1641. The two crowns were now committed to a common front, each obliged to fight until both were satisfied.

Confirmation of the French alliance improved Oxenstierna's position in his other negotiations. Brandenburg accepted a two-year ceasefire on 24 July, leaving Sweden in possession of Gardelegen, Driesen, Landsberg, Crossen and Frankfurt on the Oder, thereby securing access between Pomerania and Silesia. Friedrich Wilhelm also promised to supply 10,000 tlr and over 177 kilolitres of grain each month. He tried to forestall the inevitable imperial protests by transferring part of his army to the emperor, leaving only 2,200 men holding Berlin, Spandau, Küstrin and Peitz. Many of his officers were furious. Colonel Rochow threatened to blow up Spandau, while Colonel Goldacker took his regiment over to the Imperialists. Though Franz Albrecht of Lauenburg, now an imperial field marshal, drove Stalhansk's detachment from Silesia, Brandenburg's defection secured the approaches to Pomerania and gave Oxenstierna time to deal with the officers' mutiny.

The chancellor invited the colonels to send two representatives to Stockholm in July. Both were fêted, flattered and rewarded, while the committee's spokesman, Colonel Mortaigne, was promoted to major-general and given land in Pomerania to settle his pay arrears. Salvius found 60,000 tlr to meet the other officers' most pressing claims. The army was then reorganized by amalgamating the understrength regiments and agreeing pay arrears at 330,000 tlr to be split between the remaining units. Salvius eventually handed over 486,260 tlr, much of it raised on credit using the new French subsidies as collateral. Pfuhl was replaced by the Swede Lilliehook as interim commander until Torstensson arrived. Guébriant meanwhile persuaded his own officers to desist from their negotiations with the emperor by warning them of Saxony's fate since 1635.

The Battle of Wolfenbüttel

Clandestine contact with the emperor persisted into the autumn of 1641, but the army had already demonstrated its reliability by intervening at Wolfenbüttel. Sweden needed to secure Guelph loyalty and prove it could assist its German partners. Klitzing had blockaded Ruischenberg's imperial garrison since the autumn, but his 7,000 men were too few to take the town. Wolfenbüttel had been strengthened in the Dutch manner with earth walls covering bomb-proof stone casemates sheltering the defenders. It was surrounded by a broad, wet ditch fed by sluices from the river Oker, while a separate castle served as a citadel. Klitzing copied Pappenheim's methods from the 1627 siege, conscripting peasants to dam the Oker below the town from the middle of March 1641. Despite Ruischenberg's sorties, the dam was finished at the end of June with a strong redoubt at either end. A large entrenched camp protected the besiegers at Thiede west of the river as they waited for the water to back up and flood the town.[17]

Archduke Leopold Wilhelm and Piccolomini waited at Egeln on the Saale for the negotiations with the mutinous officers to bear fruit, before heading west in June as the situation grew critical in Wolfenbüttel.

Wahl's Bavarians were summoned from Westphalia to give 22,000 men altogether. Guébriant, Königsmarck and the remaining loyal Swedish units force-marched to the area, joining Klitzing on 28 June just two hours before the Imperialists arrived. In addition to the 7,000 Guelph troops, there were 6,000 ex-Bernhardines and 13,000 Swedes. A carriage draped in black carried Banér's body in their midst.

The large inundation from the Oker prevented any attack on the allied left (east), while their camp was too strong to be attacked frontally. Leopold Wilhelm ordered Wahl through the woods west of Fümmelse to outflank the enemy on the other side, while the Imperialists made a diversionary attack against the camp. Wahl was already in position at 9 a.m. on 29 June, opposite the Swedes on the allied right, but the Imperialists were delayed by the terrain. The Bavarians attacked without them at midday. A fierce fight developed for possession of a wood just beyond the Swedish position as Königsmarck tried to stop Wahl outflanking him. The Imperialists eventually arrived, but instead of merely feinting against the enemy front, they became drawn into the struggle for the wood. The tightly packed mass of infantry was caught in crossfire between a redoubt at the end of the camp and Königsmarck's troops in the open. The gunfire tore bits off trees, inflicting further casualties. The Bavarians pressed on, routing the crack Swedish 'Old Blue' regiment and capturing the redoubt. Their cavalry also broke through further west, but all were hurled back by a counter-attack. Guébriant and Klitzing sent their cavalry from the camp to threaten the Imperialists to the east. The struggle continued until the late afternoon when Leopold Wilhelm ordered his exhausted troops to withdraw, having lost at least 3,000 casualties.

The allies were also battered, losing around 2,000, and had no inclination to leave their entrenchments and pursue the imperial troops. Inactivity fuelled disagreements between their generals, while the imperial army opened a long and ultimately fruitless siege of Göttingen to the south. Having broken the dam on 1 October, the allies finally retreated to Sarstedt between Hanover and Hildesheim where they remained for two months awaiting the outcome of renewed talks.

These had opened at Goslar on 7 October after Duke August of Wolfenbüttel apologized to the emperor for the recent battle. Duke Georg's successor, Christian Ludwig, was a young and inexperienced youth who was no match for his uncle who had the backing of the

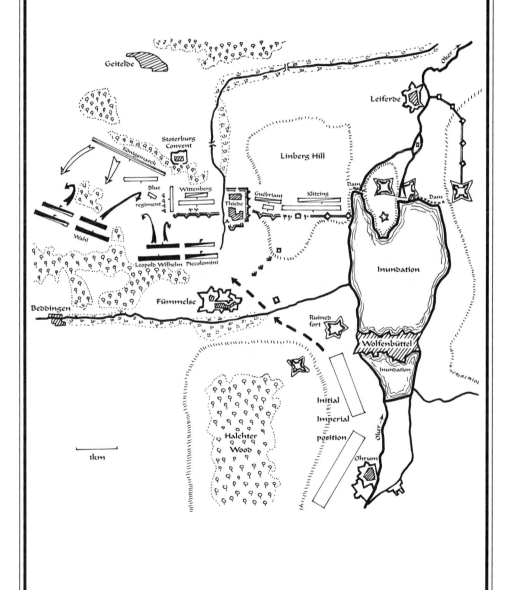

WOLFENBÜTTEL

Geitelde

Oker

Leiferde

Stoterburg
Convent

Königsmarck

Linberg Hill

Dam

Blue
regiment

Wittenberg

Thiede

Guébriant

Klitzing

Dam

Wahl

Leopold Wilhelm Piccolomini

Inundation

Fümmelse

Ruined
fort

Wolfenbüttel

Beddingen

Inundation

Initial

Imperial

position

Halchter
Wood

Oker

Ohrum

1km

third Guelph duke, Friedrich of Lüneburg. Having no direct interest in Hildesheim, August sacrificed it to recover his own capital. Wahl arranged a compromise on 16 January 1642, confirmed and extended by several later agreements. The Guelphs accepted the Peace of Prague and restored the disputed Hildesheim districts in return for the face-saving promise from Ferdinand of Cologne to respect Lutheran worship there for the next forty years. The Guelphs were formally pardoned and Ruischenberg finally evacuated Wolfenbüttel on 23 September 1643. The Treaty of Goslar represented a defeat of Guelph ambitions. They retained a few thousand garrison troops for the rest of the war, but had ceased to influence events.[18] Guelph neutrality ruptured Franco-Swedish military cooperation by removing the link of Lower Saxony. Guébriant marched west to help the Hessians, while the Swedes eventually moved east into Silesia.

Brandenburg's defection and the failure of the renewed talks with the enemy officers, however, negated the modest imperial success in Lower Saxony. With the imperial Estates growing restless, Ferdinand made another gesture towards peace. His envoy had agreed the peace preliminaries in Hamburg with France and Sweden on 25 December 1641. These settled the form but not the content of the future peace congress. France and the Catholic powers would meet in the Westphalian town of Münster. Sweden and the Protestants would gather in nearby Osnabrück. Both venues would be declared neutral, while security was guaranteed for envoys and post between them and to the home capitals. These terms signalled a radical departure from the previous imperial stance of only negotiating with Sweden to settle the war in the Empire before dealing with France. Ferdinand now reluctantly ratified the preliminary arrangements in July 1642, knowing that negotiations with France might entail a breach with Spain. He nonetheless delayed exchanging the credentials necessary for the envoys to assemble in the hope that the military situation might yet improve.[19] For the moment, matters still hung in the balance.

THE WAR IN THE EMPIRE 1642–3

The Battle of Kempen 1642

The emperor could not afford a defeat, however minor. Having declared for Sweden, the Hessians in turn needed a victory before they could resume talks with Ferdinand. They collected 7,000 men under General Kaspar Count Eberstein, a Pomeranian who joined from the Swedes in 1631 and was promoted to replace Melander. Guébriant arrived in December 1641, but he had to threaten to invade Overijssel before the Dutch finally allowed the combined army over the Rhine at Wesel on 12 January. Guébriant's 12 infantry regiments mustered only 2,000 men, while the 12 of cavalry were little better at a total of 3,500. Eberstein's force had already dropped to 4,000, half of whom were cavalry.[20]

They nonetheless posed a serious danger to the electorate of Cologne as they now began to ravage it. Lamboy's 9,000 Imperialists were recalled from assisting the Spanish and crossed the Meuse to protect Cologne, while Hatzfeldt hurried up from winter quarters in Würzburg with 7,000 reinforcements. Hatzfeldt arrived ahead of his troops on 8 January and collected boats ready for them to cross at Andernach. Guébriant and Eberstein decided to attack Lamboy before Hatzfeldt's men arrived. It was a big risk, since they had already run out of food and a defeat would leave them no choice but to run off into the Dutch Republic like Mansfeld and Duke Christian had in 1622–3. A third of Lamboy's men were either sick or inadequately armed, while he had only 6 cannon to the enemy's 23, yet Lamboy was overconfident and ignored instructions to wait for Hatzfeldt. He camped at Hüls, now a suburb of Krefeld, drawing up behind a double dry boundary ditch not far from Kempen from which the coming action took its name.

Lamboy was still eating breakfast when the enemy appeared on 17 January on the other side of the ditch. The action swung both ways until dragoons and musketeers detached by Guébriant appeared on Lamboy's flanks, having crossed either side of his position. The Imperialists collapsed, losing 2,000 dead. Lamboy and another 5,000 were captured. Only 2,000 escaped. They refused Spanish offers of food for fear they would be pressed into the Army of Flanders and eventually crossed the Rhine to join Hatzfeldt in the Wetterau.

Lamboy had wasted a valuable opportunity to crush France's Army of Germany. It had been on the point of disintegration and had not scored a major success since capturing Breisach over three years previously. A grateful Louis XIII promoted Guébriant to Marshal of France, and sent 3,600 Breton recruits by sea to Rotterdam to join him. The Dutch discharged 3,000 men into French service as an additional reinforcement. He spent the next nine months taking minor places in the electorate of Cologne, including Kempen and Neuss, as well as Düren in Jülich. His forces captured so much food that hungry Spanish and imperial soldiers deserted to them.

The imperial countermeasures indicate how difficult it was becoming to raise new armies. The emperor sent 135,000 tlr, while Hatzfeldt spent 8,000 from his own pocket and Elector Ferdinand sold his silver to provide more. As the enemy were detaining travellers and holding merchants to ransom, the city of Cologne relaxed its neutrality to provide 500 men and 6 cannon from its civic guard, while 2,000 Lorrainers arrived from Luxembourg and the Spanish put in 1,500 men to protect Aachen. Wahl arrived with 2,600 Bavarians in June, followed two months later by Werth, just released from French captivity, who appeared at the head of three imperial cavalry regiments. Werth's arrival demonstrated the significance of personality: even peasants fell on their knees when they saw the famed commander, believing he would rid them of the enemy.[21] The Imperialists now had about 15,000 men, matching their opponents, but Hatzfeldt hesitated to risk another battle, especially as he was short of horses and dependent on the Spanish for food, because he could not afford the exorbitant prices demanded by local traders.

The allies had gorged themselves on their earlier bounty and were now also hungry. Guébriant and Eberstein argued constantly, because the Frenchman refused to let the Hessians garrison the captured towns. They gave up first, retreating over the Rhine at the end of September after Guébriant had browbeaten Amalie Elisabeth into giving him 1,000 men from Eberstein's army in return for handing the captured towns to her control.[22] Guébriant marched east in a fruitless attempt to stop the Guelphs signing the Peace of Goslar. The electorate of Cologne had suffered its worst devastation, but the balance of power had been restored on the Lower Rhine.

Swedish Recovery

The Swedes remained inactive at Winsen (near Celle) after abandoning the siege of Wolfenbüttel until Torstensson finally arrived with 7,000 conscripts on 25 November 1641. He withdrew the army east of the Elbe to a position near Werben where he spent the next four months restoring discipline after the mutiny. Lamboy's defeat at Kempen robbed the emperor of any chance of exploiting this inactivity. Torstensson displayed his considerable strategic skills by sending Königsmarck and the cavalry to raid Saxony in April, drawing the imperial forces there while he marched his main force of 15,000 across Brandenburg to join Stalhansk's 5,000 men on the Oder.

Torstensson recognized that Banér's invasion of the Habsburg lands in 1639 had foundered because it relied primarily on speed and failed to capture the fortresses necessary to hold conquered territory. He opened his invasion of Silesia by storming Glogau on 4 May, then taking Jauer and Striegau as he advanced south-west to Schweidnitz. The province was weakly defended, but Franz Albrecht of Lauenburg rushed 7,000 imperial and Saxon cavalry over from Saxony to disrupt further progress. The duke was unaware that Striegau had already fallen and mistakenly believed Torstensson was heading directly south towards Breslau. He also did not know that Königsmarck had followed him from Saxony with 6,000 Swedish cavalry. Königsmarck deceived the duke by appearing and then pretending to retreat, drawing the Imperialists against the Swedish infantry posted on a hill east of Schweidnitz on 31 May. Some imperial regiments fled early on, but the others fought on for five hours before retreating. As at Kempen, defeat meant the virtual destruction of the army as units swiftly lost cohesion, leaving 1,800 dead and 2,000 prisoners. Among the former was Franz Albrecht, who had been mortally wounded by angry Swedes still convinced he was to blame for King Gustavus's death. Schweidnitz surrendered three days later, completing the Swedish victory.[23]

Torstensson left Lilliehook with half the army to finish the conquest of Upper Silesia while he took the rest through Troppau into Moravia, capturing Olmütz which surrendered quickly – allegedly because the Swedes captured the commander's wife.[24] Banér had not penetrated so far east in 1639 and the region was still relatively fresh. The Swedes captured 5,000 new uniforms, broke into monasteries, held the monks to ransom, and opened the crypts to steal rings from the corpses. They took even more from the living, including 10,000 books which they sent to quench Queen Christina's thirst for knowledge. By the time they left Olmütz in 1650, only 1,675 of the city's 30,000 inhabitants remained. The richer citizens had fled immediately, spreading panic in Vienna.

However, Brieg still resisted in Silesia, while the Imperialists collected at Brünn, to the south of Olmütz, and were joined by 2,670 Bohemian militiamen. By July 1642, Leopold Wilhelm had assembled 20,000, though many of these were recruits who wanted to go home once the cold, wet autumn set in.[25] While some blockaded Olmütz, the rest pushed passed Troppau to relieve Brieg, recovering most of Silesia by August. Torstensson's strategy now paid off, because Leopold Wilhelm was unable to recover Glogau which secured Swedish communications to Pomerania and allowed the 6,000 Swedes left to cover the Oder to join the main army. Moreover, the Imperialists' failure to recapture Olmütz gave Sweden a base deep in Habsburg territory that remained a threat until the end of the war. The Imperialists were forced westwards through Lusatia into Saxony, to the despair of its elector who saw his land becoming a battlefield again.[26]

The Second Battle of Breitenfeld

Torstensson pursued the imperial army, besieging Leipzig to force his opponent to give battle. Leopold Wilhelm duly arrived with 26,000 men, including 1,650 Saxons, and the Swedes withdrew to Breitenfeld, scene of Gustavus's great triumph eleven years earlier.[27] Piccolomini was suspicious and urged caution, but disturbing reports had arrived that Guébriant and the Hessians were marching to join Torstensson, so the archduke decided to accept battle on 2 November.[28]

The two armies camped the night before at right angles to the positions taken in 1631. The Imperialists were on the eastern side at Seehausen facing west, opposite Torstensson at Breitenfeld. Between them lay the Linkelwald where Tilly's infantry had made their final stand, with a shallow valley formed by the Ritsche stream to the south. Torstensson was significantly outnumbered by 7,000 men, but was determined to smash the emperor's only remaining substantial army.

Both armies advanced at dawn, Torstensson crossing the Ritsche to deploy in front of the Linkelwald. Leopold Wilhelm accepted

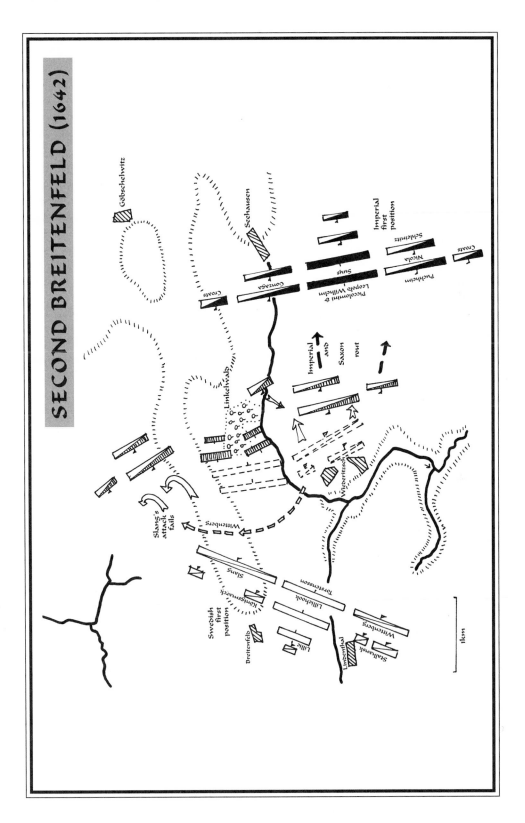

SECOND BREITENFELD (1642)

Göbschelwitz

Sehausen

Croats

Gonzaga

Croats

Suys

Piccolomini &
Leopold Wilhelm

Imperial
first
position

Schleinitz

Nicola

Puchheim

Croats

Imperial
and
Saxon
rout

Linkelwalb

Wulceritzsch

Wittenbers

Slang's
attack
fails

Slans

Königsmarck

Swedish
first
position

Breitenfels

Lillie

Lilliehook

Torstensson

Linsenthal

Stalhansk

Wittenbers

1km

Piccolomini's advice and sent sixteen cuirassier regiments north around the wood to turn the Swedish left and cut them off from the Torgau road. Torstensson shifted his army northwards to confront this and the action became general around 10 a.m. The imperial infantry were split by the wood, but nonetheless made progress against their opponents in Torstensson's centre. Like the Swedes, the Imperialists were now employing regimental guns to support their infantry. They fired chain-shot, assisting in pushing the Swedes back and capturing some of their cannon.

Wittenberg and Stalhansk on the Swedish right advanced from the Ritsche valley, out-riding their accompanying musketeers. The rapid approach worked, giving Puchheim no time to deploy the imperial cavalry properly. Several regiments in the imperial first line broke before contact, taking the Saxons in the second with them as they fled. The rest resisted stoutly, but were overwhelmed by superior numbers. Stalhansk pursued with half the Swedish horse, while Wittenberg led the rest behind Torstensson's infantry to help Slang on the left. The latter had stuck to Gustavus's tactic of advancing slowly to allow the musketeers to keep up. He was killed in the initial imperial onslaught, while his men gave way as Croats turned their flank to the north. Königsmarck rallied them and held long enough for General Wittenberg to arrive around midday. The Swedes now enjoyed local superiority and swept round their opponents' flank, driving them back towards the infantry still struggling in the centre.

Leopold Wilhelm and Piccolomini led their bodyguards in a counter-attack to enable the infantry north of the wood to escape. A Swedish dragoon levelled his pistol at the archduke, but it misfired. Nothing could be done for those who were south of the wood; they resisted for another hour or so before surrendering. It had been a hard-fought battle. The Swedes lost 4,000 killed and badly wounded, but the poor quality of some of Leopold Wilhelm's cavalry cost him the battle. In addition to 3,000 dead, the Imperialists lost nearly 5,000 prisoners, all 46 cannon and their entire field treasury and supply train.

The margin of victory was far narrower than in 1631, but the action nonetheless had important repercussions. News of the defeat spread alarm throughout Catholic Germany where the population feared a repeat of the consequences of the first battle.[29] Maximilian summoned his Bavarian militia and prepared for the worst. Leipzig predictably surrendered on 7 December, making a large payment to avoid plunder and admitting a Swedish garrison that stayed till 1650. The Swedes relieved their outpost at Chemnitz, which had been isolated since 1639, and made another unsuccessful attack on Freiberg where they lost 2,000 men in February 1643. Ferdinand hastened to reassure Johann Georg he would do all in his power to save Saxony, and the Swedes were disappointed that the elector did not immediately make peace.[30]

The Drift to Neutrality

Friedrich Wilhelm of Brandenburg was not so sanguine. Convinced the emperor would sacrifice Pomerania to the Swedes to obtain peace, the elector improved relations with Sweden by converting his ceasefire from 1641 into a truce on 9 May 1643 that was to last until a final peace settlement. Oxenstierna restored the Brandenburg countryside to electoral administration in return for the continuation of the contributions agreed in 1641. As Brandenburg appeared trustworthy by remaining neutral, Oxenstierna returned Crossen and Frankfurt on the Oder in July 1644 as well. Other negotiations with France since September 1643 extended neutrality to the elector's Westphalian possessions in return for the Hessians evacuating all their positions in Cleves except Lippstadt. The arrangement gave the elector greater autonomy, but brought little relief to his subjects who were expected to continue paying war taxes, but now to the modestly expanded Brandenburg army.[31]

Brandenburg neutrality directly contravened the 1641 imperial Recess that forbade such arrangements without the emperor's express approval. Friedrich Wilhelm excused himself by saying the military situation left him no choice. His political stature and the emperor's lack of military muscle enabled him to escape reprisals. Elsewhere, rulers avoided such open agreements, but nonetheless withdrew incrementally from the conflict. Frequently, local officials negotiated agreements for their districts with tacit approval from their masters. The Bavarian administration in Heidelberg paid regular contributions to the nearby French garrison to stop its depredations in the Lower Palatinate.[32] Such arrangements clearly represented a first step towards leaving the war. The bishop of Bamberg and Würzburg signed a formal treaty with the Swedish garrison in Erfurt on 21 March 1641 following a series of local agreements concluded by officials in the frontier districts. The bishop not only promised regular contributions in return for the release of hostages, but both parties agreed to collaborate to revive trade in the area. Johann Philipp von Schönborn confirmed the arrangement when he became bishop of Würzburg in June 1642. Bamberg and Würzburg paid a relatively modest 500 florins a month until the Peace of Westphalia. It was neutrality in all but name.[33]

The trend was not restricted to the Empire's core regions. Ever since the French invaded the Franche-Comté in 1636, the Swiss had worked to restore the neutrality of all Burgundy agreed between France and Spain in 1522. Cut off from all prospect of help following Duke Charles's defeats, the Spanish administration in Dôle agreed a local truce in April 1642 that was extended, with Madrid's permission in July 1644, to last until peace was concluded. This eased tension on the Upper Rhine, encouraging the French to restore Mömpelgard to the local Württemberg administration in 1645 in return for its promise of neutrality.[34]

These developments are important. First, they dispel the misconception of the war's later stages as generalized, unlimited destruction. Considerable efforts were being made to curb and contain violence, although these had the unfortunate consequence of channelling the fighting into areas unable to escape. Second, the drift to neutrality further reduced the resources available to the imperial war effort and discouraged the emperor's remaining supporters. Bearing the brunt of the burden with no immediate prospect of victory, they grew disillusioned with Ferdinand's leadership. The 1641 imperial Recess had again postponed the question of judicial reform, but did promise an imperial Deputation to discuss it. A Deputation was a formal committee drawn from all three categories of imperial Estate. By demanding in May 1642 that the Deputation be convened, the electors of Bavaria, Mainz and Cologne signalled their willingness to continue broad cooperation with the princes and cities, rather than return to their exclusive relationship with the emperor. Ferdinand was unable to prevent them expanding the Deputation's remit to include peace and military discipline. He met a similar response when he summoned the Kreis assemblies that summer to discuss renewing the war taxes agreed in Regensburg the year before.[35]

The 1643 Campaign

Ferdinand needed to continue operations while avoiding serious risks to begin the now inevitable peace congress from a position of strength. It was felt imperative to replace Leopold Wilhelm as the imperial army's commander. Hatzfeldt refused to take over, because he felt his advice had been ignored in the past. Ferdinand eventually appointed Gallas, ignoring the fact that he was now an alcoholic. Piccolomini felt superseded and accepted Philip IV's offer to assume command of the Army of Flanders. Wahl, now crippled, was replaced by Mercy as the Bavarian commander. The combined force remained formidable at over 70,000 troops, excluding those on the Habsburg Military Frontier. Gallas had 32,000 of these, a third of which were cavalry, while Hatzfeldt commanded 15,000 imperial and Cologne troops, including the former Wolfenbüttel garrison. The Bavarians had increased their numbers to 22,650, but the Saxons were down to a few thousand, mainly in Magdeburg and other garrisons. A few thousand other Imperialists and Tiroleans still guarded the Upper Rhine.

Having failed to bully Saxony into peace, Torstensson renewed his invasion of the Habsburg lands by attacking through Lusatia into northern Bohemia in March 1643, intending to relieve Olmütz and join potential Transylvanian support. Gallas concentrated his forces at Königgrätz to block him, sending General Krockow and 4,000 cavalry as a diversion into Pomerania. Krockow was one of the many Pomeranians who had left Swedish service in disgust at the treatment of their homeland. He was, unfortunately, over-optimistic. Though he quickly overran most of eastern Pomerania, he was too weak to attack the better fortified western half and was soon cut off as Königsmarck hastened to catch up with him with the 3,000-strong allied detachment left to occupy Saxony. Krockow rode at a punishing 50km a day to escape, reaching Breslau with only 1,200 survivors at the end of October.[36] The diversion at least prevented reinforcements reaching Torstensson, who was unable to achieve anything beyond relieving Olmütz before retiring into Silesia. The Imperialists followed, eventually retaking Schweidnitz in 1644.

After the unsuccessful attempt to prevent the Guelphs making peace, Guébriant had arrived on the Saxon frontier at the end of 1642. Torstensson persuaded the French not to enter, in the vain hope that this might induce Saxony to make peace. With only 7,000 men and no prospect of cooperation with the Swedes, Guébriant risked being cut off. He marched west again, this time down the Main valley and into Württemberg, until he was driven out by the Bavarians in January, losing 1,600 men by the time he reached Breisach. France's Army of Germany was back where it had been five years earlier. The main focus of the war moved with it, again bringing relief to north-west Germany where the Hessians were left isolated.

The military situation was simplifying in line with new French objectives following Richelieu's death and the new regime under Mazarin (see below, p.666). Rather than direct cooperation, the two crowns evolved a division of military labour. The French would strike across the Black Forest to knock out Bavaria, while the Swedes hit the Habsburg hereditary lands from their new positions in Saxony, the Oder valley and Olmütz. The Hessians would keep the Westphalians busy. It took two years before this strategy was in place, not least because the Swedes and Hessians had other objectives to achieve first, but once it was set by 1645 it determined the remainder of the war.

Things did not go well for France at first. It remained busy with its primary war against Spain and was unable to commit sufficient resources to Germany. French difficulties explain why Ferdinand was eventually prepared to open the peace congress. The arrival of his wife with a few reinforcements, as well as men drawn from his garrisons, gave Guébriant a field army of 11,000 by June. Prompted by Mazarin who needed successes to stabilize his government, Guébriant advanced via the Forest Towns to the Hohentwiel. Mercy's Bavarians moved up the Danube to block him, so he reduced his plans to consolidating his hold on the south-east slopes of the Black Forest, ready for a renewed offensive the following year. He attacked Rottweil, but again Mercy was there to relieve it in July. Guébriant gave up and retreated back over the mountains, while Mercy moved to their northern end and reoccupied Baden-Durlach and parts of Lower Alsace.[37]

The Battle of Tuttlingen

This was not what Mazarin wanted. The fall of Sierck in Lorraine in September enabled the despatch of 6,000 more reinforcements under Rantzau. Guébriant advanced again, but was mortally wounded taking Rottweil on 18 November. Command devolved to Rantzau who was despised by the ex-Bernhardine colonels. Rantzau left Taupadel holding Rottweil and went into winter quarters along the upper Danube at Tuttlingen with detachments either side at Mühlingen and Möhringen.

Hessian inactivity permitted the despatch of Hatzfeldt with six regiments from the Lower Rhine while the fugitive Duke Charles arrived from Sierck, giving Mercy around 15,000 men, roughly equivalent to Rantzau's force. Originally from Lorraine, Mercy gained valuable experience in the imperial army before transferring to Bavarian service in 1638. He was an outstanding general, skilled in handling all three arms and able to second-guess his opponents. He won agreement from the other generals for a bold march eastwards round the end of the Black Forest, and then south through Württemberg to surprise the French. Having crossed the Danube at Sigmaringen, he marched west through Messkirch to approach Tuttlingen from the south-east. The plan was well-conceived, since the more direct route through Bahlingen to the north would have exposed his flank to Taupadel's garrison in Rottweil and necessitated attacking across the Danube. The woods beyond Messkirch allowed Mercy to approach Tuttlingen unobserved by mid-afternoon on 24 November.

The Bavarian dragoons captured the French pickets, so Rantzau was caught completely unawares when the enemy burst from the trees and captured his weakly guarded artillery park in the cemetery outside the town. Other units surprised the French posted in near-by Homberg castle. Rosen rushed the ex-Bernhardine cavalry up from their billets downstream in Mühlheim. They were soon chased away by Mercy's brother Kaspar, who destroyed the French infantry Rosen had left behind. Meanwhile, Werth and 2,000 horsemen hit the French cavalry upstream at Möhringen, riding down the 500-strong Mazarin infantry regiment in the process – an action that was regretted since the unit was largely composed of Spanish prisoners of war who would have welcomed an opportunity to change sides. The French cavalry fled, abandoning the rest of their infantry who surrendered Möhringen once the captured artillery was trained against them the next day. Rantzau and the two foot regiments in Tuttlingen now also capitulated, followed by the 2,000 men in Rottweil a week later.

All the French generals and the officers' wives were taken, along with silver plate worth 100,000 tlr and a month's pay in cash. Peasants hacked down stragglers and barely 4,500 reached the French garrisons

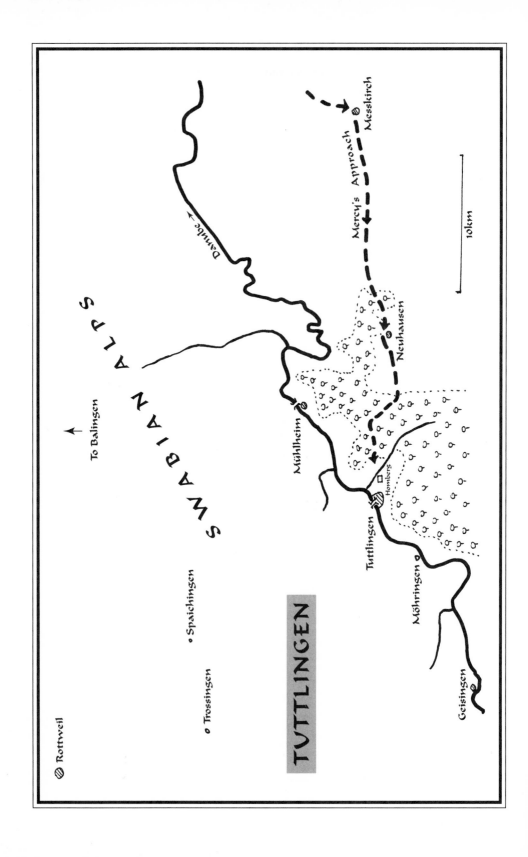

TUTTLINGEN

Rottweil

SWABIAN ALPS

To Balingen

• Spaichingen

○ Trossingen

Danube

Mühlheim

Tuttlingen

Homberg

Neuhausen

Mercy's Approach

Messkirch

Möhringen

Geisingen

10km

along the Rhine. Rosen, Taupadel and a few German officers escaped, but most of the remaining Bernhardines were lost. The French court downplayed the disaster so successfully that the battle scarcely features in most histories of the war, but it was a major setback. France had lost a veteran army and was still no further forward on the Rhine than it had been five years earlier.

SPAIN'S GROWING CRISIS 1635-43

Tuttlingen temporarily restored the balance in the Empire, but the general trend was turning against the emperor. France's ability to rebuild its Army of Germany over the winter reflected a general improvement in its position since the initial setbacks against Spain. The latter's growing internal problems in turn ended any prospect of further assistance for Ferdinand. As Spain weakened, it became harder to postpone the Westphalian congress agreed in the Hamburg Preliminaries. To understand these developments, we need to review the western wars since the mid-1630s.

These conflicts had grown considerably in scale. France had become a direct participant in the Dutch War in 1635 and the two allies continued to coordinate attacks against the Spanish Netherlands. France also began what would prove to be its own war against Spain by attacking that country's Italian possessions. A new front was opened in the Pyrenees after 1637, precipitating revolts in Catalonia and Portugal in 1640.

The War in Italy 1635-42

French intervention in Italy trespassed on the emperor's jurisdiction and disturbed the balance established by the Peace of Cherasco in 1631 (see above, Chapter 13, p. 458). In keeping with Richelieu's general strategy, the attack on Spain's possessions was not made alone, but in partnership with Italian princes. Known as the League of Rivoli, this alliance proved rather feeble. Savoy was the most potent member, fielding 12,250 professional troops in return for French backing for its royal ambitions and a promise of part of Milan. Mantua was still recovering from the earlier war and could provide only 3,000 men, while Parma sent another 4,500. The other Italian rulers remained neutral. Despite promises to his allies, Richelieu accorded Italy a low priority and it was not until October 1635 that the French army there reached 12,000 men. By then, operations had collapsed amid bickering between the French and Italian commanders.

Spain not only held its own in Lombardy but launched an amphibious counter-attack, capturing the Lérin islands off Provence in September. French attempts to recover them were repulsed in 1636–7, enabling Spain to disrupt the flow of aid to Richelieu's allies. France made a more substantial effort against Lombardy in 1636, but still started a month late and at only two-thirds of intended strength. French forces helped repel an attack on Vercelli protecting Savoy, but the distraction allowed Spain to knock out Parma and Mantua by February 1637.[38]

The fighting assumed some significance for the Empire by drawing imperial forces into the final struggle over the Valtellina. Spain's use of the pass to intervene in Germany in 1633–4 convinced Richelieu that it had to be closed, and that the only way to do this was to restore Protestant Rhetian control over the Catholic inhabitants. He sent Henri de Rohan from Alsace across Protestant Swiss territory to join 2,000 Rhetians who had been raised with French money. The combined force of about 7,400 crossed the Splügen pass waist-deep in snow on 27 March 1635 to surprise the Spanish at Chiavenna at the south end of the valley. With this taken, the other garrisons further up were trapped and soon knocked out. Thus began one of the most daring and brilliantly led campaigns of the entire war. Rohan's force was too weak to hold both ends of the valley simultaneously, so he took up position near the more vulnerable northern entrance at Bormio with detachments watching the south.

The Habsburg attempt to take the valley exposed the weakness in their military cooperation following Nördlingen. Gallas reluctantly detached 10,000 men under Fernemont and sent them to the Tirol to attack the northern end of the valley, but Cardinal Albornoz, the new Spanish governor of Milan, feared a Franco-Savoyard attack and only belatedly sent Count Serbelloni with 2,000 men to the south end. Fernemont advanced before the Spanish were ready. Rohan let him overrun the northern half of the valley, and then outflanked him using the Engadin, taking him by surprise and sending him packing by mid-July. Serbelloni had only just occupied the south entrance and quickly withdrew as Rohan turned against him. The failure of the Franco-Savoyard offensive against Milan by October 1635 emboldened the Habsburgs to take advantage of the mild autumn for another attempt. Fernemont had been reinforced to 15,000, while Serbelloni now mustered 5,000 men. Again, the Austrians moved prematurely and were defeated after heavy fighting by Rohan, whose superior understanding of mountain warfare enabled him to outflank them. The French then dashed south to rout the Spanish on 9 November.[39]

Rohan had been welcomed by the Rhetians as 'the Angel Gabriel in person', but was put in an invidious position by Richelieu's instructions not to let the Rhetians reimpose Protestantism on the valley. Spanish transit of the Valtellina in 1629–34 had brought the plague and halved the population. The 40,000 survivors struggled to feed even Rohan's small force. The Rhetians had no interest in wider French objectives and refused to support Rohan's attempted invasion of Milan in May 1636. The war's return to the Alps heightened tension within the Swiss Confederation, where the Catholics allowed Spain to send its 10,000 German recruits through the St Gotthard pass that year to reinforce the Army of Lombardy, now under Leganés, who had replaced Albornoz.

Rohan was cut off. He owed his Rhetian infantry 1 million livres in pay arrears, and many of the officers shared their government's suspicions of French intentions. Colonel Jenatsch, a former fundamentalist Protestant pastor who, for reasons unknown, had recently converted to Catholicism, led a mutiny among Rohan's troops in October 1636 and seized strategic points along the valley. The Habsburgs were taken by surprise, but swiftly accepted his offer of an alliance on 17 January 1637, agreeing to drive the French out in return for Spain settling the soldiers' pay arrears, while Austria rescinded its 1629 prohibition on Protestantism in the areas of the Ten Parish League under its jurisdiction. Rohan was obliged to withdraw his remaining French troops in April. The alliance with heretics was initially presented as a necessary evil, but by 1639 Spain abandoned its remaining scruples and formally returned the Valtellina to Rhetian control in return for guarantees the Free State would not tamper with the Catholic character of the valley and would allow Spain transit. The latter requirement was now largely worthless since French control of Alsace cut the Spanish Road. Nonetheless, the alliance secured the service of the Protestant Rhetians who comprised a seventh of Leganés' army by 1640.

The Savoyard Civil War

French failure in Italy widened the divisions at the Savoyard court following the unsatisfactory outcome of the Mantuan War. Though Savoy had acquired the northern half of Monferrato, it had been obliged to surrender Pinerolo to France, giving that country access across its territory. Lorraine's fate during the early 1630s underscored the dangers of such a position. French influence in the duchy grew following the death of Charles de Nevers in September 1637. French troops seized his part of Monferrato, including Casale, while the Venetians occupied Mantua. Tensions spilled over into war after Duke Vittorio Amedeo I's death the following month.[40]

The pro-French faction was led by Louis XIII's sister, the duke's widow Marie Christina, who acted as regent for her two young sons, the first of whom had already died by 1638. It is possible that she was jealous of her sisters, Henrietta Maria and Elisabeth who were respectively queens of England and Spain. Certainly, her own ambitions reflected those of a Savoy dynasty that already claimed royal blood based on alleged links to the kingdom of Cyprus. Richelieu manipulated these ambitions, saying that France could only recognize Savoy as a kingdom if it enlarged itself at Milan's expense. Madame Reale, as she styled herself, was opposed by her two brothers-in-law, princes Tommaso and Cardinal Maurizio, whom she excluded from the regency. Tommaso had recently returned from serving in the Army of Flanders. He had married Marie, daughter of the duc de Bouillon, associating himself closely with the anti-Richelieu faction in France. Rumours circulated that Madame Reale had poisoned her husband to stop Savoy defecting to Spain. Tommaso and Maurizio also drew on resentment in the regions against Turin's centralization. While these factors were important, the heart of the Savoyard civil war was a dynastic struggle for control of the regency.[41]

The conflict between the *madamisti* and the *principisti* seriously undermined France's position in Italy just as Richelieu wanted to withdraw forces to concentrate on the other fronts. The French rarely mustered over 10,000 men in the duchy, half of whom were needed to hold Casale and other fortresses. Leganés joined the principisti with 13,000 Spanish to capture Vercelli, Ivrea, Verue and Nice in 1638. French relations with Madame Reale deteriorated as Richelieu used her current predicament to pressure her to surrender her other garrisons to French control. Emperor Ferdinand exercised his imperial jurisdiction and declared Tommaso and Maurizio regents in March 1639 as the Spanish pushed deeper into Savoy. Tommaso entered the capital at the head of 10,500 men on 27 July, but Madame Reale escaped into the citadel with her 2,000 French guards. The remaining French forces agreed a truce lasting until October, which allowed the Spanish to extend their control over the duchy, while Tommaso blockaded his sister-in-law.

A new French army of 7,000 men arrived under the comte d'Harcourt and though it defeated the Spanish field force, it was unable to relieve the Turin citadel before winter. Leganés tried to divert Harcourt by besieging Casale early in 1640 to give Tommaso time to take the citadel. Harcourt stripped the remaining French garrisons to increase his field force and relieved Casale. Having received further reinforcements giving him 19,000 men in total, he appeared outside Turin in May. An extraordinary triple siege began. Madame Reale defended the citadel against Tommaso and 12,000 men, who were besieged in Turin by Harcourt, while Leganés and 17,000 Spanish troops surrounded Harcourt outside the city. Tommaso ran out of supplies first and broke out, allowing the French to relieve the citadel in November 1640.

The result was a stalemate. With only 8,000 effectives in the field, the French were unable to dislodge the Spanish from the captured towns, but the Catalan and Portuguese revolts at the end of the year prevented reinforcements reaching Leganés. Both Madame Reale and the princes realized that what they were fighting for was being destroyed in the process. Despite Spain holding his wife and children hostage, Tommaso opened negotiations with the French. He and his brother were accepted as co-regents in May 1642 and given large French pensions and their own palaces. Tommaso assumed command of the combined Franco-Savoyard army, which increased to 20,000 by the later 1640s. France returned Turin to Madame Reale, but kept a garrison in its citadel until 1657, securing the duchy's allegiance for the remainder of the war.

The Papacy

Pope Urban VIII was dismayed by French intervention in Italy after 1635, but was unable to respond because he relied on France to counterbalance Spain. He was also compromised by his own opportunism. Having already annexed Urbino in 1631, he used Spain's distraction to try to enlarge the Papal States by attacking the small duchy of Castro in October 1641. Modena, Venice and Tuscany all had long-standing grievances against the papacy and joined the duke of Parma, who owned Castro, in counter-attacking in August 1642. Urban's forces proved surprisingly successful in resisting the onslaught, but it was clear he had overreached himself, and he accepted a French-brokered peace, returning Castro to Parma in March 1644.

His death four months later dealt a severe blow to the French faction in Rome, already weakened by the departure of its leader, Mazarin, who was now in France. Spain was determined to recover its influence as fifty cardinals met in the blazing August heat to chose Urban's successor. Spanish troops massed in Naples to the south, while those of their Tuscan ally moved to the northern frontier of the Papal States. Malaria hit Rome and the cardinals began dying or fleeing. Urban's Barberini relations and their allies switched allegiance to Spain in return for a promise of protection, and duly elected Spain's candidate as Pope Innocent X. The papacy's new orientation was demonstrated when Innocent made Mazarin's rival, Jean de Retz, a cardinal. France's Roman clientele, like the Orsini, accepted Spanish pensions. The recovery of Spain's influence in Rome stabilized that power's presence in Italy and proved a significant factor in its ability to defeat the revolt that convulsed Naples in 1647. 'Had Urban VIII been in power there is no question but that he would have tried to claim Naples for himself or given it to France.'[42]

The Pyrenean Front

Fighting continued on the Savoyard–Milanese frontier, but Italy's strategic significance declined after 1642 as France found it easier to hit Spain directly thanks to the Catalan and Portuguese revolts. Previous attacks along the Pyrenees had stalled against Spanish defences, but the cost of repelling them contributed to the outbreak of both revolts.

There were only two viable routes over the Pyrenees. France could attack at the western end from Gascony into Spanish Navarre, but this was guarded by the fortress of Fuenterrabia. Perpignan in the earldom of Roussillon at the eastern end blocked the way into Catalonia. Attempted incursions at either end in 1636–7 were frustrated by lack of money, peasant unrest and poor coordination between military and naval commanders. Spain then sent 15,000 troops from Catalonia against the French fortress of Leucate on the Mediterranean coast north of Perpignan. The assault was unexpectedly repulsed, while a 5,000-strong detachment that had taken St Jean de Luz just across the frontier in Gascony pulled back in October 1637.[43]

This modest success encouraged Richelieu to divert additional resources for a new offensive. In place of provincial governors and local militias, the French now had Condé with a substantial army of 17,000 men to attack Fuenterrabia. The decision to concentrate on the western end of the Pyrenees was influenced by the growing importance of the Atlantic seaboard now that the French occupation of Alsace had cut the Spanish Road. A major programme of naval construction gave Spain 150 warships, and with additional vessels still on the stocks in Biscayan yards, it hoped to have 50,000 tonnes afloat for 1638. Command of a new squadron at La Coruña was entrusted to Lope de Hoces who had risen from the Dunkirk privateers. He had already convoyed 5,000 reinforcements to Flanders at the end of 1637, assisted by the Dunkirkers for the last stretch. Cruising back through the Channel, he captured 32 enemy vessels.[44]

The French attack was intended to disrupt Spanish preparations and prevent the development of the Channel route. Richelieu's protégé, Admiral Sourdis, led a fleet of 41 ships to blockade Fuenterrabia, which is on a promontory north of San Sebastian, while Condé besieged it from the landward side. Sourdis detached part of the fleet along the coast, destroying Spanish shipyards and catching Hoces at the small port of Guetaria on 22 August 1638. The Spanish lost 11 ships and 4,000 men; Hoces saved himself by swimming ashore. However, on land a Spanish relief force of 8,000 approached the French siege lines. Sourdis landed sailors to reinforce the army that Condé threw at Fuenterrabia in a desperate attempt to break in on 7 September. Repulsed, he abandoned the siege the next day and retreated into Gascony. The army's failure negated the navy's success, fuelling the endemic personal rivalries within the French high command. One general even fled to England for fear he would be made a scapegoat for the setback.

The relief of Fuenterrabia was hailed as a great success in Madrid where the mob broke into the royal wine cellar to toast Olivares as the architect of victory. Yet the year had really concluded in France's favour. The losses at Guetaria, especially among experienced officers, impaired the Spanish navy's efficiency. Perhaps more ominously, Philip IV had been obliged to recall two crack Irish regiments from Flanders to assist at Fuenterrabia. Future contingents of Irish recruits were now shipped directly to Spain, contradicting the overall Spanish aim of concentrating efforts in Flanders against the Dutch.[45]

The pattern was repeated the following year when France switched to attack Roussillon at the opposite end of the mountains. Leaving 6,000 men to protect Provence and the Languedoc, Condé struck south with 16,500, taking Opoul on the border on 10 June and then the more significant fortress of Salces, just north of Perpignan, on 19 July. Viceroy Santa Coloma mobilized 11,237 Catalan militiamen, but Condé felt he had achieved enough, especially as sickness had reduced his force to 8,000 effectives. He retired to French territory, leaving a garrison in Salces. The Spanish counter-attacked with an army of 17,000 collected under Felipe Spinola, son of the great captain. Spinola lost 2,500 in fruitless assaults as Condé returned with 24,000 men to relieve the garrison. Having been repulsed from the Spanish siege lines on 2 November, Condé's army dissolved in torrential rain, leaving just 2,500 with the colours. He retreated a second time, leaving Salces to surrender four days later.

The Salces campaign proved even more costly to Spain than the defence of Fuenterrabia. The Spanish lost 10,000 men, while only 2,146 of the Catalan militia remained by the time the town was retaken. Most of these went home over the winter, much to the disgust of Olivares who felt the province was not pulling its weight under the Union of Arms. Though Roussillon belonged to the kingdom of Catalonia, it had been saved by a largely Castilian, Irish, Walloon and Italian army.[46] Nine thousand Castilians were billeted on the southern part of the earldom, drawing protests from the Catalan authorities that their historical liberties were being infringed.

The Catalan and Portuguese Revolts

Olivares' initial response was relatively mild, but he grew impatient when the Catalans continued their protests that by April 1640 had turned into armed resistance against the troops there to defend them. The troops were merely the focus of much deeper popular discontent at years of corrupt administration. The famed liberties were mainly restricted to the aristocracy that dominated the kingdom's assembly (the *Corts*) and manipulated their privileges for their own ends. The right to bear arms, for example, was used to cloak widespread banditry as lords sponsored gangs to pursue feuds with their neighbours. 'A mafia-type regime prevailed in parts of Catalonia, sustained by violence and extortion.'[47] Under these conditions, the protesters did not see their actions as disobedience but as an attempt to draw Philip IV's attention to their plight.

Peasants armed with scythes entered Barcelona on 22 May 1640 and opened the jail. Alarmed, the viceroy cancelled the Corpus Christi procession scheduled for 7 June. Around 2,000 'reapers' (*segadors*) protested anyway, triggering four days of rioting.[48] The viceroy and a leading judge were murdered, while other officials fled or went into hiding. Madrid and the provincial authorities blamed each other for the disorder that now spread across the kingdom.

The insurrection threatened the aristocracy's privileges, but these would also be curtailed if Philip IV were to crush the revolt. The aristocrats sought another way out, opening negotiations with France, and agreeing on 29 September to open the ports to French ships and maintain the 3,000 auxiliaries despatched by Richelieu to assist them. Olivares believed he was facing a second Dutch Revolt and summoned an emergency levy of men across the loyal provinces. The marquis de los Vélez was sworn in as the new viceroy at the head of 20,000 men in southern Catalonia on 23 November. He retook Tortosa and the important port of Tarragona, which was also the seat of the archbishop of Catalonia.

Richelieu initially regarded the revolt as a welcome diversion from the crisis in Italy as the siege of Turin reached its climax. He was prepared to recognize Catalonia as an aristocratic republic that could serve as a useful buffer between France and Spain. The deteriorating situation following Los Vélez's advance forced him to despatch another 13,000 men to reinforce the rebels. The royalists reached Barcelona at the end of December. Their appearance compromised the provincial government that was accused of failing to defend the kingdom. Following the murders of five more judges, the survivors placed themselves under French protection on 23 January 1641, accepting Louis XIII as 'count of Barcelona' and effectively ceding Roussillon. Three days later, the combined Franco-Catalan army defeated Los Vélez on Montjuic hill outside the city.

The rebels had passed the point of no return, but 'acquired the burden of power without any of the fruits'.[49] Half the French effort was directed at conquering Roussillon where Spain still held Perpignan and other key fortresses. Only half the army was sent into Catalonia where fighting concentrated around Lérida (Lleida) to the west of Barcelona, the town that commanded the main road from Castile into the kingdom.

The Catalans were joined from December 1640 by the Portuguese, opening a new Iberian front to the west. The Portuguese had contributed a comparatively modest 1 million cruzados to Spain's war effort after 1619. Madrid's demand for 3 million in 1634 struck them as completely unreasonable. Tax revolts erupted in three of the kingdom's provinces during 1637 just as key parts of the Portuguese empire were lost to the Dutch as well. These problems stirred the latent resentment at the loss of independence. Olivares' suppression of the Council of Portugal in 1638 did nothing to help this. Anti-Hispanicism mixed with anti-Semitism as Lisbon Jews and Conversos were integrated into Spain's financial system after 1627 to take up the slack left by the inability of Genoese bankers to manage the burgeoning debt. Anti-Semitism encouraged popular and clerical support for the break with Spain. The yearning for independence was expressed as the Sebastian myth – that the country's last native king who 'disappeared' at the battle of Alcazarquivir (al-Qasr el-Kabir) in Morocco in 1578 would eventually return. Unlike in Bohemia or Catalonia, the presence of the native Braganza dynasty offered a powerful focus for the coming revolt.

Its trigger was the demand in June 1640 for 6,000 Portuguese troops to assist in crushing the Catalonians. Portuguese malcontents stormed the Lisbon palace of the vicereine, Margarita of Savoy, and threw her adviser, Miguel de Vasconcellos, out of the window in the Bohemian fashion on 1 December. The vicereine was bundled over the frontier and Spanish resistance collapsed. Apart from Ceuta in North Africa, the Portuguese colonial empire recognized the new regime in 1641.[50]

The ensuing conflict is known in Portuguese history as the War of Restoration (1640–68). Left largely alone, the Portuguese were able to improvise an army almost from scratch and launch an offensive into Spain in June 1641. Pope Urban received their ambassador, implying recognition, in 1642, while the English agreed an alliance that was later (1660) renewed with the marriage of Catherine of Braganza to Charles II, the match that saw Bombay and, briefly, Tangiers pass to English rule. However, fighting remained limited until the 1650s because Olivares concentrated on combating the Catalan revolt, since this provided an open door to French invasion. The Portuguese opposed Spanish rule, but they still shared a common enemy in the Dutch who continued their conquests in the Portuguese colonies.

The Fiscal-Military Burden

The revolts indicated Spain's imperial overstretch. The monarchy remained rich, but it could no longer cope with the mounting cost of war. Defence spending jumped from 7.3 million escudos in 1635 to over 13 million two years later thanks to the new struggle with France. The crown had already relied on reckless financial expedients in the 1620s, leaving few other options to meet the additional expenses. The fiscal system had reached diminishing returns by 1640. The government's growing use of copper *vellón* coins encouraged creditors to insist on payment in silver. Silver imports remained high, despite periodic losses like the capture of the silver fleet at Matanzas, with the crown receiving an average of 6 to 8 million ducats every five years between 1618 and 1648. This was not enough, so it began confiscating private silver as it landed at Seville, seizing 5 million ducats worth by 1640. Merchants responded by falsifying their manifests and other fraudulent measures, thereby hitting the normal customs levy on private silver that now also fell. Meanwhile, taxpayers paid the government in its own debased currency, causing real revenue to fall by a third. The crown simply piled on new taxes, adding imposts on sugar, paper, chocolate, fish and tobacco in Castile in 1632, while doubling the existing indirect levy known as the *millones*.[51]

Manpower demands also grew. Over 3,000 Castilians were despatched annually to Flanders between 1631 and 1639, while total recruitment in Iberia was probably three times that level.[52] The Castilian

Cortes agreed to add another 8,000 men on top of the 18,000 it was already paying in response to the Fuenterrabia crisis in 1638. Though promised as a temporary measure, the crown proposed levying another 12,000 Castilians in 1640. Though Catalonia refused to provide the 6,000 demanded in 1637, Aragon, Valencia and Majorca were now sending more cash and recruits as well. The threat to the Pyrenees had already compelled the reinstitution of the militia in 1635, adding another burden since this had to be armed and maintained at provincial expense.

Altogether, recruitment increased between six and ten times between 1620 and the 1640s, depending on the region. The army reached its greatest strength of around 200,000 men by the early 1640s, but the opening of new fronts in Iberia meant that a higher proportion was now deployed at home. From a peak of 88,280 men in January 1640, the Army of Flanders declined slowly but steadily to 65,458 by February 1647. Though this was still higher than under Philip II, it was insufficient to fight both France and the Dutch Republic.

Even these numbers could no longer be sustained. Casualty and wastage rates may have reached 20,000 a year after 1635 and it was claimed widows formed a sixth of the population of Mérida by 1646. Emigration from Spain to the New World grew after 1621 as people sought a better life; the peninsula's population probably declined by a quarter between the 1580s and 1630s, while agrarian output fell by 40 per cent. There were fewer people to carry the growing burden. Castilian taxes rose from the equivalent of less than 25 days' wages in 1621 to 42 days' by 1640. Arrears accumulated as taxpayers defaulted, owing 36 million ducats of *millones* alone by 1649. It proved harder to borrow to cover the shortfall. Expenditure through the central treasury totalled over 250 million ducats between 1621 and 1640. Of this, 30.5 million went to the civil budget; 44.2 million directly to the armed forces; and 175.8 million to bondholders and contractors for loans and interest.[53] The crown was compelled to decentralize, assigning the still-viable local sources of income directly to specific expenditures, such as fortress garrisons, losing oversight and accountability. The revolts only made this worse. By 1644 the crown was running out of assets to sell or pawn, having pledged revenue for the next four years to cover its existing liabilities.

Military service met growing resistance. Soldiers received only a third of what an agricultural labourer earned. Militia service was especially resented since it was obviously a disguised form of conscription. Only a quarter of the 11,000 Castilian militia mobilized in 1636 could be armed, while some of those serving in 1641 were given slings to hurl rocks, and even those with muskets had only four to six bullets each. Unsurprisingly, desertion was rife. Draft dodging extended to the grandees who were asked to raise their own regiments in 1632 in return for the dubious honour of calling themselves colonel. When the request was repeated in 1634, Olivares raised 1,500 men, but the others sent excuses.[54]

Resistance to recruitment and taxation was motivated by more than fear of dying or inability to pay. There was also a growing sense that royal demands were no longer reasonable. Catalans felt justified in refusing conscription not only thanks to their kingdom's traditional exemption, but because they were contributing in other ways, including sending their militia. Across society, people felt they were already doing more than they were obliged to. They did not feel responsible for the defeats, since command was reserved for the monarchy. Where the crown saw disobedience, its subjects saw ineptitude and injustice. The proliferation of special juntas created by Olivares to solve the mounting problems merely clogged an already slow administrative system, providing additional opportunities to dodge unwelcome commands.[55]

Setting aside Philip IV's personal shortcomings, which were detailed in Chapter 11, the Spanish monarchy was structurally ill-equipped to respond. Its ideal of majesty required the monarch to remain aloof to avoid association with potential failures. Olivares also had a personal interest in ensuring the king stayed out of daily affairs. To keep the monarch busy, he began expanding the royal apartments in the San Jerónimo monastery on the eastern outskirts of Madrid after 1630, creating what became the Buen Retiro palace. A cycle of twelve huge paintings was commissioned from leading artists to commemorate Spanish victories since 1621 to decorate the Hall of Realms inaugurated in 1635. The project entailed considerable risk – the paint was scarcely dry on Velázquez's masterpiece depicting the capture of Breda when the Dutch retook the city in 1637. The temporary upsurge in patriotism following the French declaration of war was squandered as the king stayed in his pleasure palace while his subjects groaned under the oppressive burden.[56]

The Colonial War

The general sense of failure was magnified by bad news from the Indies, the region that had come to symbolize Iberian wealth and power. The Portuguese held on to Goa and Mozambique, but were expelled from Japan by local opposition in 1639. A protracted struggle with the king of Kandy for control of Sri Lanka opened the island to the Dutch who joined the local campaign to eject the Portuguese after 1636. The conflict drained the resources of the *Estado da India*, undermining resistance elsewhere to the Dutch who had captured most of the Indonesian spice islands by 1641.[57]

The situation in the West Indies was equally bleak. Using the Matanzas loot, the Dutch West India Company fitted out 67 ships, with 1,170 guns and carrying 7,280 men under Admiral Hendrik Loncq. This was twice the manpower and three times the number of ships deployed to defend Portuguese Brazil. Loncq captured Olinde and Recife, the principal ports of Pernambuco in February 1630. Olivares despatched Spain's senior admiral, Antonio Oquendo, with 56 ships and 2,000 soldiers to retake the towns before the Dutch could penetrate the sugar-producing hinterland. Oquendo eventually defeated the Dutch off Abrolhos in September 1631. Battered and with no harbour in which to refit his ships, Oquendo was obliged to return to Lisbon.[58] The Dutch extended their positions, occupying the Guianan coast between the Amazon and modern Venezuela. The subsequent capture of Curaçao island in 1634 secured the local salt trade, vital to the Dutch herring industry.

A second relief effort in 1635 similarly failed to dislodge the Dutch, in stark contrast to the successful expedition a decade before. The Brazilian planters realized they would have to collaborate with the occupiers to safeguard their incomes. Portuguese control in Brazil shrank dramatically after the arrival of the energetic Prince of Nassau-Siegen as Dutch governor in January 1637. He won local support by allowing Catholic convents and monasteries to remain open, conducted the first scientific survey of the area and extended Dutch control to 1,800km of the coast by 1641 with a force of only 3,600 Europeans and 1,000 Indians. Two further Portuguese expeditions were repulsed in 1638 and 1640. Meanwhile, the Dutch capture of Elmina on Africa's Gold Coast in 1637 gave them Portugal's main slaving base. The Dutch exploited

Portugal's difficulties with Queen Njinga to take Luanda and other positions in Angola by 1641. Axim, the last Portuguese fort on the Gold Coast, fell the following year. Dutch slavers had shipped 30,000 Africans to Brazil by 1654. Dutch sugar exports to Europe between 1637 and 1644 already totalled 7.7 million florins, while other colonial produce worth 20.3 million was shipped over the same period.[59]

Spain's transatlantic trade collapsed in 1638-41. No treasure reached Seville in 1640. The Tierra Firme fleet brought only half a million ducats the following year, while the New Spain fleet sailed too late in the season and was hit by a hurricane as it left the Bahama Channel. Ten ships went down with 1.8 million ducats. The gross tonnage crossing the Atlantic by the later 1640s was nearly 60 per cent below that during the Twelve Years Truce. Silver continued to get through, but little more than 40 per cent of that produced in the New World was officially declared in Seville, while crown receipts were less than half those of the 1630s. Part of the decline was due to the increased cost of colonial defence, but much disappeared through fraud and the fact that the war forced the colonies to become more self-sufficient and develop their own trade outside the official system.

FROM BREDA TO ROCROI 1637-43

The Loss of Breda 1637

Spain's mounting problems concerned the Empire because they undermined Philip IV's war against the Dutch. A Spanish success in the Netherlands would enable Ferdinand III to withdraw his troops from Luxembourg, while a Spanish defeat would free France to reinforce its army in Germany. As the war dragged on, Ferdinand urged his cousin to at least settle with the Dutch and concentrate on the conflict with France. Spain viewed the events in the Empire with similar impatience, failing to understand why the emperor had not been able to crush Sweden after Nördlingen. Imperial commanders repeatedly promised Spain cooperation during the winter planning rounds, only to march in the opposite direction when the campaign opened to stop Swedish attacks on Saxony or Bohemia.

The effects were felt in 1637, dispelling the optimism following the

Year of Corbie. The unexpected success of the unplanned invasion of France in 1636 encouraged Olivares to switch three-sevenths of the then 65,000-strong Army of Flanders to Artois and Hainault for an invasion of Picardy. However, he refused to surrender the remaining outposts on the Lower Rhine to obtain peace with the Dutch, tying down the bulk of the other troops in garrisons. Conscious that the strike force was insufficient, he pressed Ferdinand to make diversions along the Moselle and in Alsace that, as we have seen in the previous chapter, failed to materialize.

While Spain massed in the south, in the Republic Frederick Henry staked his political capital on a major blow against the northern frontier. He was under growing pressure to negotiate. Though he managed to sideline Adriaen Pauw, the leader of the Dutch peace party, by sending him as ambassador to Paris in 1636, his support was falling away. The open French alliance after 1635 split opinion among the Gomarist militants who had been the war's principal backers, because Frederick Henry had promised Richelieu he would accept Catholicism in conquered areas. Moreover, Amsterdam merchants had no interest in liberating Antwerp, a city that might resume its former place as the region's commercial centre. Increasingly, support for the war was restricted to three groups. The southern provinces of Zeeland, Utrecht and Gelderland still felt vulnerable and wanted Frederick Henry to capture more land beyond the Rhine as a buffer. These provinces were also home to the majority of Belgian Calvinist refugees who hoped military success would enable them to return home. Finally, there were those who benefited materially from the war, notably shareholders in the West India Company, an organization that proved remarkably successful in attracting investors from across the Republic.[60] These groups were still strong in 1637, but it was significant that the Holland States implemented the first budget cut since the Twelve Years Truce, disbanding the most recently raised regiments in the winter of 1636–7.

Frederick Henry seized his chance to attack Breda on 21 July while the Spanish were still collecting troops on the southern frontier. Fernando had to march north again. Unable to break the Dutch siege, he tried to distract the stadholder by taking Venlo and Roermond. His absence enabled Cardinal de la Valette and 17,000 French to capture Landrecies and Maubeuge, forcing Fernando to retrace his steps southwards. Breda fell on 7 October, removing the last of Spain's gains from its year of victories in 1625. The defeat prompted Olivares to revert to his Dutch strategy, instructing Fernando on 17 March 1638 to make a major effort to compel the Republic to accept reasonable terms in negotiations that were now reopened. Victory was no longer expected; the aim now was to leave the war with honour.[61]

The End of Imperial Assistance 1638–9

The planned Spanish offensive in Artois was aborted when well-coordinated Franco-Dutch attacks hit both the northern and southern frontiers of the Spanish Netherlands simultaneously in May 1638. Frederick Henry and 22,000 Dutch marched on Antwerp, while Marshal Châtillon and 13,000 French thrust towards St Omer, covered by La Force and another 16,000 troops in Picardy. The Spanish were pinned, but Frederick Henry retreated after a sortie from Antwerp captured 2,500 of the besiegers at Kallo, one of the worst Dutch defeats of the war. The reverse undermined the stadholder whose increasingly regal behaviour was attracting republican criticism. Piccolomini was obliged, as usual, to wait until sufficient troops had been collected to protect Cologne, before marching west to help Prince Tommaso of Savoy relieve St Omer in July. The French took a few minor posts and recovered Le Câtelet, but Louis XIII was disappointed.

The French command was entrusted to Richelieu's relative, La Meilleraye, who marched on Hesdin with 14,000 men in 1639, covered by Châtillon and a similar number on the frontier. Feuquières and 20,000 troops were sent to pin Piccolomini in Luxembourg and prevent further imperial intervention by capturing Thionville, the town that gave access to the area between Namur and Koblenz. Spain had withheld its subsidy to compel Ferdinand to leave Piccolomini in Luxembourg.[62] After being joined by Duke Charles of Lorraine, Piccolomini appeared unexpectedly at sunrise on 7 June with 14,000 Imperialists and Spanish outside Feuquières' siege lines at Thionville. Unable to assemble from their billets, the French were routed, losing 7,000 prisoners and some of the best regiments in their army. Louis XIII's presence with the main army meant the siege of Hesdin could not be abandoned without a serious loss of prestige and it was continued until the place surrendered on 29 June. Most of Piccolomini's forces were then withdrawn from the area to confront the Swedish invasion of Bohemia, bringing the era of direct military cooperation between Spain and the emperor to an end.

The Downs

The diversion of French resources to Flanders and to the eastern end of the Pyrenees allowed Spain to collect a new armada at La Coruña tasked with breaking the blockade of Dunkirk and landing substantial reinforcements for a new offensive in 1640. It was a major undertaking, and negotiations were opened with England in February to secure naval assistance. The Spanish fleet comprised 70 warships and 30 transports, totalling 36,000 tonnes, with 6,500 sailors, 8,000 marines and 9,000 troops to reinforce the Army of Flanders. Admiral Sourdis raided the Spanish coast in June and August, but was unable to disrupt the preparations and withdrew exhausted, leaving it to the Dutch to intercept the armada when it finally sailed on 27 August.

Maarten Tromp attacked with seventeen ships as the Spanish entered the English Channel on 16 September. Oquendo was overconfident and failed to issue adequate instructions to his subordinates. He remained wedded to the traditional tactics of duels between rival ships, having won the battle off Pernambuco in 1631 by destroying the Dutch flagship. Tromp sailed in tight formation line ahead, so that each time a Spanish ship ventured to attack it was met by his combined firepower. An experienced Portuguese officer observed that 'Oquendo, [was] like a brave bull which is ferociously attacked by a pack of hounds and blindly charges those which assault him, so he with his ship full of dead, wounded and mutilated gallantly tacked upon those which were nearest him.'[63] Despite having pinned Tromp and his fleet against the French coast, Oquendo gave up around 3 p.m. because his own ship was too battered to continue. The two fleets were becalmed the next day, but Tromp was joined by another seventeen warships on 18 September and renewed the fight until he ran low on powder. With Dunkirk still blockaded, Oquendo realized there would be no safe port in which he could refit if he sailed beyond Calais, so he crossed the Channel to anchor at the Downs off Deal in Kent, believing the English would provide assistance.

Admiral Pennington appeared with thirty ships, but only to uphold English neutrality. The English did help ferry the troops and 3 million escudos in cash to Flanders by November, but apart from selling some overpriced gunpowder, did little to help the Spanish fleet. Most of the smaller ships escaped past the Dutch into Dunkirk, but Tromp had been reinforced by large armed merchantmen from the Dutch Indies companies' fleets and now had 103 warships to Oquendo's 46. Tromp entered English waters to attack on the morning of 21 October. Oquendo beached his twelve lighter ships and fought his way out with the rest. His flagship was hit 1,700 times, but made it to Mardyck. Ten of the beached ships were refloated early in November and also escaped to Flanders.

Tromp was severely criticized for his failure to capture the Spanish flagship. Oquendo refitted in Dunkirk and sailed back to Spain early the next year with 24 ships. While 1,500 troops had been intercepted, part of the mission had been completed successfully and the Army of Flanders mustered 77,000 men in December 1639, while the navy still totalled 34,131 tonnes. Despite the continued blockade, Spain managed to convoy another 4,000 recruits to Flanders from 1640 until Dunkirk fell in 1646. Nonetheless, the campaign cost at least 35 ships, over 5,000 dead and 1,800 prisoners. Losses in 1638–40 totalled 100 warships, 12 admirals and 20,000 sailors, or the equivalent of ten Trafalgars.[64]

Spain could not sustain this rate of attrition. The effort was in vain since the entire strategy was flawed. As the 1640 campaign again proved, it was impossible to mount an offensive either north or south as long as France and the Republic coordinated their attacks against both frontiers. While the Dutch were repulsed, the French captured Arras on 9 August after a two-month siege. Following the armada's defeat and the outbreak of the Catalan revolt, this was a major blow. Thousands fled to Lille as the French overran the rest of Artois. More bad news arrived in November when the French relieved Turin, but the situation worsened in December as the Portuguese rose in revolt.

The repeated setbacks altered the balance of Austro-Spanish relations. Having paid a respectable 426,000 florins to Austria in 1640, Spain was in no position to help any longer, delivering only 12,000 fl. the following year and 60,000 as a loan in 1642. Piccolomini had been recalled from Luxembourg and the emperor cancelled the Hohentwiel operation for which Spain had paid the Tirol to raise 4,000 men.[65] Spanish influence declined further as its experienced ambassador, Castañada, returned to Madrid in 1641, whereas Ferdinand was now represented in Madrid by Field Marshal Grana, a forceful character who shared the emperor's opinion that Spain was wasting its resources and squandering opportunities for peace.

Clutching at Straws

Olivares grew increasingly desperate, renewing contacts with the French malcontents who had been plotting against Richelieu since 1636. Several had fled to London where they backed Spain's fruitless efforts to persuade Charles I to join an alliance against Louis XIII. The outbreak of the British Civil Wars rendered this a lost cause. By 1640 Olivares had turned his attention to a group around Count Soissons who had fled to the sovereign duchy of Bouillon on the Netherlands frontier. Encouraged by the ambitious marquis de Cinq Mars, they believed they had the support of the French queen, Anne of Austria, and that a show of force would prompt Louis to dismiss Richelieu. Olivares regarded the conspirators as the 'sole means of salvation from shipwreck' and promised support.[66]

The malcontents in exile in England were supposed to sail with a scratch fleet to raise the Huguenots in Guyenne, but never arrived. Details of the plot had already reached Richelieu by April 1641 and he altered his campaign plan to counter it, massing 12,000 men under Châtillon in the Champagne to block Soissons in Bouillon. The plotters panicked. Frédéric-Maurice de Bouillon declared that his current capacity as French commander in Italy prevented him from joining the rebels' planned expedition. He nonetheless urged Soissons to act. General Lamboy arrived in Bouillon with 7,000 Spanish and Imperialists in June to give 9,500 troops altogether and they advanced south, defeating Châtillon at La Marfée on 9 July. Any hope of exploiting the victory was wrecked by Soissons' death, allegedly self-inflicted by raising his visor with a loaded pistol that accidentally went off.[67] The revolt collapsed, enabling Richelieu to mop up the plotters by the following June once he had gathered more evidence and was certain of Louis XIII's support. Cinq Mars was executed, while Bouillon escaped death by converting to Catholicism and surrendering his duchy. Implicated in treason again, Louis' brother Gaston fled to Savoy.

Duke Charles of Lorraine had meanwhile accepted French terms on 2 April 1641 in order to recover his duchy as a French fief. However, his failure to assist France during Soissons' invasion raised suspicions and led to his expulsion again in August. He invaded the duchy with 5,000 men from Luxembourg in April 1642, scoring a few minor successes, but lacked the means to exploit these and was back across the frontier within five months. The situation returned to that prior to April 1641, except that the duke had recaptured Sierck, La Mothe and Longwy.[68]

The intervention of Soissons and Lorraine at least frustrated any immediate exploitation of the capture of Arras by France. Richelieu then switched resources to Catalonia, while the Dutch were distracted by the return of the war to north-west Germany at the beginning of 1642. At last the Spanish were able to go onto the offensive, but rather than being intended to force the Dutch to make peace, operations were now simply to distract France from attacking Spain itself. The new governor of the Spanish Netherlands, de Melo, advanced up the Scheldt into Artois, retaking Lens (19 April) and La Basseé (11 May). The two small French armies in the area under Harcourt and Guiche failed to coordinate an effective defence. De Melo and 19,000 troops caught Guiche's 10,000 men at the abbey of Honnecourt on 26 May, killing 3,200 and capturing 3,400 along with most of the baggage and the pay chest.[69] The victory allowed de Melo to complete the recovery of northern Artois.

Changing of the Guard in Spain and France

The success did little to help Olivares who had become the scapegoat for Spain's mounting problems. His fall from grace demonstrates how the exercise of power in early modern Europe rested as much on personal relationships as policy. Olivares had alienated those around him as his 'method of government became more and more autocratic, his manner more tactless, his reactions more unreasonable'.[70] The poet Francisco de Quevedo was one of the many at the receiving end of the count-duke's ill-temper, whisked away from his lodgings one night in 1639 to become one of the 'disappeared' (*desaparecido*) after he had passed the king a satirical attack on Olivares written on a napkin.

The discontent was fanned by the queen and other court ladies, notably Margarita of Savoy who blamed Olivares for failing to support her in Portugal. Their efforts were discreetly encouraged by Ambassador Grana on Ferdinand's behalf. Philip IV sent Olivares a careful and tactful letter on 17 January 1643, presenting dismissal as a gracious response to his repeated requests to resign. Grandees rushed to Madrid to ensure the king did not change his mind and angry crowds gathered as Olivares finally left for his estates five days later.

A few of the count-duke's closest associates were arrested, but policy remained unchanged. Philip intended to govern himself. He attracted some sympathy after the deaths of his wife (1644) and son (1646), but remained an uninspiring monarch. He relied increasingly on Olivares' nephew Haro, who eventually emerged as the new prime minister after 1648. Many of Olivares' other protégés retained their posts because their experience was invaluable. The problems remained the same and they were unable to think of an alternative to the count-duke's strategy of *conservación* and *reputación*.

In France, Richelieu died on 4 December 1642, followed by Louis XIII on 14 May, leaving the crown to his son aged four and a half. Queen Anne had been largely ignored for the previous thirteen years, having been distrusted by her husband thanks to her Spanish birth. She now outmanoeuvred both Gaston and the prince de Condé to claim sole regency, distributing so many rewards to secure support that one courtier quipped that the French language had been reduced to the five words, 'the queen is so kind'.[71] The government was staffed with men more inclined to the dévot peace policy, but continuity was symbolized by Anne herself, who took up residence in the Palais Cardinal bequeathed by Richelieu to the crown and now renamed the Palais Royal. She also relied on his protégé Mazarin, who had been involved in drafting French peace objectives.

Despite their foreign births, both Anne and Mazarin identified with France and rejected inducements from Philip IV to make a quick peace. They were determined to wear their opponents down by a war of attrition until they improved their terms. Mazarin was more pragmatic than Richelieu and was willing to abandon the chimera of universal peace and the slogan of 'German Liberty' that had been considered essential to French prestige. He was also more interested in larger territorial gains since these played better to the home audience that needed to be convinced he was the best man to guide the monarchy.

The Battle of Rocroi 1643

The Flanders campaign would test the two new regimes. De Melo was ordered to repeat his success of the previous year to distract France from attacking other Spanish territory. Leaving 15,000 men to protect the northern frontier, he advanced in four columns. They converged on the small fortified town of Rocroi near the Meuse valley and besieged it from 15 May. Despite de Melo's claim that it was 'the key to Champagne',[72] Rocroi had little strategic value, but the attack assumed great political significance given Louis XIII's death the day before. The new regime in France could not afford to start with a defeat. Command of the northern army had just been entrusted to Condé's son, the duc d'Enghien, as part of Richelieu's strategy of neutralizing threats from the grandees by distributing patronage. Having removed the elder Condé as a liability, the cardinal persuaded Louis XIII to compensate the family by appointing the prince's inexperienced son to what was expected to be a secondary front. It was now too late to change these arrangements that seem wise only with hindsight. D'Enghien has entered French history as the 'Great Condé' from the title he assumed on his father's death in 1646. Fourth in line to the throne, he was prickly and self-important, but conviction in his own distinguished lineage gave him unshakeable confidence.[73]

D'Enghien was determined to prove himself in battle and overruled advice to force de Melo to lift the siege by threatening his communications with the Netherlands. Instead, France's stability was staked on an extremely risky direct attack. Rocroi could only be approached along tracks through a forest and the French army would be exposed as it emerged until it could deploy on the plain south-east of the town. D'Enghien was also slightly outnumbered, with 15,000 infantry, 6,000 cavalry and 12 guns to de Melo's 18,000 foot, 5,000 horse and 18 cannon. The Spanish army also included many of the regiments that had helped destroy Guiche the year before.

Whether by luck or design, the French timed their arrival well as they appeared late on the afternoon of 18 May and the day was too far advanced for de Melo to begin battle. He deployed on the plain opposite the French, sending urgent orders to General Beck with the fourth and last of his columns to join him. Both armies slept on the plain, but d'Enghien was alerted to his opponent's dispositions by a deserter who told him that de Melo had posted 500 musketeers on the edge of the forest. Three hundred French musketeers caught the Spanish here still fast asleep at 3 a.m. and routed them. The artillery then opened up on both sides, but visibility was still poor, giving time for the two armies to stand to. Both commanders placed their infantry in two lines in the centre with their artillery in front, flanked by two lines of cavalry on either wing.[74] The French also had a reserve of their best infantry and cavalry as a third line under Sirot behind the centre. The Spanish line stretched 2,500 metres between the eastern edge of the forest and the St Anne marsh to the west. The French would have to break through if they wanted to relieve Rocroi. The Spanish cavalry were still organized as independent squadrons, whereas the French had theirs under tighter control grouped into regiments. They copied the Swedish practice of attaching musketeers to the cavalry to increase firepower.

De Melo was happy to wait, expecting Beck's imminent arrival. Impatient, d'Enghien led the French cavalry on the right to attack around 5 a.m., soon followed by La Ferté and the horsemen on the left. La Ferté began his charge too far away and his horses were blown by the time they neared the German cavalry under Isenburg on the Spanish right. The French were routed, many fleeing into the marsh or forest. The French infantry fell back, abandoning some of their artillery. Meanwhile, d'Enghien's attack had been broken by Albuquerque's counter-charge that overran most of the supporting French musketeers. It was now that the superior French organization made a difference. The Spanish cavalry had dispersed and took too long to rally, allowing Sirot to move the reserve to block Isenburg long enough for some of the French cavalry on the left to return and help him push the German troopers from the field. D'Enghien despatched Gassion with half of his cavalry for a second attack that eventually forced Albuquerque's scattered men to retreat.

The Spanish infantry were now exposed. D'Enghien attacked their second line with the other half of his cavalry, hitting the Walloon regiments immediately on the left. He struck each regiment in turn, using weight of numbers and a combination of charges and supporting firepower from his infantry to break them. One by one, the Walloon regiments left the field, followed by the Germans further west. The French now turned on the stronger first line, hitting the Italians on its left. They repulsed the initial attack, but then left the field in good order, probably on their own initiative. The French were happy to let them leave since this isolated the five Spanish tercios. Three were broken after further hard fighting, but the other two repulsed three more attacks with a general salvo at fifty paces. It was now 10 a.m. and they were short of ammunition. The French were also exhausted and feared Beck's arrival. D'Enghien offered terms. One regiment of about 2,000 men laid down its arms in return for being allowed to march home across France. The other soldiers remained defiant, but further resistance was hopeless and they soon surrendered as prisoners of war. De Melo had escaped, dropping his marshal's baton, to join Beck on the other side of the forest. D'Enghien captured Thionville on 10 August after a long siege, and then Sierck on 2 September, eliminating the duke of Lorraine's main base. These were welcome gains, but hardly indicative of Spanish collapse.

Rocroi owes its place in military history to the French propaganda that hailed it as a major victory, as well as Condé self-promotion, since it cemented d'Enghien's reputation. This in turn ensured he influenced eighteenth- and nineteenth-century generals and found his way onto staff college syllabuses. The latter regularly cite the battle as a demonstration of the superiority of French linear tactics, combining infantry firepower with cavalry charges.[75] Victory was in fact due to superior regimental command and control. Spanish firepower successfully repulsed the French, but their key commanders were killed or wounded relatively early on, while de Melo failed to capitalize on the initial success by sending his infantry forward. Spanish losses were serious, especially because they included so many veterans and came in the humiliating form of surrender.[76] The French took 3,862 prisoners, excluding those they allowed to march home. Most of the prisoners were exchanged in July 1643 for the men taken at Honnecourt. Other Spanish casualties totalled 3,500, compared to 4,500 French killed and wounded. The French lost a further 7,000, mainly to sickness, in the rest of the campaign. The Army of Flanders remained potent, numbering 77,517 in December, compared to the Dutch establishment that had sunk to 60,000. Rocroi's real significance was the French avoidance of a defeat that might have destabilized Anne's regency and obliged the country to make peace.

France's success was not matched by their Dutch allies who were losing interest in the European war. Many in the Republic began to see the Spanish Netherlands not as a threat, but as a buffer against an aggressive, expansionist France. Spain's reception of Dutch envoys as full ambassadors signalled a willingness for peace on the basis of independence. The States of Holland forced a further reduction in the size of the army in 1641–2 and by 1643 had blocked the secret committees that had allowed Frederick Henry to manage war and diplomacy unsupervised. His own failing health contributed to the growing inclination for peace and by March 1644 only Utrecht and Zeeland still opposed a compromise with Spain. The Westphalian congress could begin at last.

19
Pressure to Negotiate 1644–5

THE WESTPHALIAN CONGRESS

The Westphalian peace congress began two years late and took a further five to complete, yet it proved to be a milestone in global relations. Its immediate achievements were mixed and fell short of contemporary expectations. The practical results were nonetheless substantial, while the ideals and methods of the peace-makers have profoundly influenced the theory and practice of international relations to the present. The emperor's decision to participate proved decisive in the congress's success. Ferdinand ratified the Hamburg Peace Preliminaries only in July 1642, followed reluctantly by Philip IV on 22 April 1643. The deteriorating military situation and the prospect of more princes declaring their neutrality persuaded the emperor finally to convene the peace congress in 1643. Johann Krane arrived in Westphalia in May and completed the formalities necessary for the delegates to assemble in the designated venues of Münster and Osnabrück. His Spanish colleague arrived in October, while the French delegation appeared only in April 1644, followed gradually by others – the Dutch not until January 1646. Most delayed sending delegates until their own circumstances improved enough to permit them to negotiate from a position of strength. Some found waiting to their disadvantage, however, and Spanish participation was dictated by a deteriorating situation and the desire to preserve a united front with Austria.

The congress had been intended to bring a *pax generalis*, but each participant understood this differently and there was no clear agreement of what constituted 'Europe' or how that continent should interact with other parts of the world. In practice, no attempt was made to tackle tensions in the Baltic and the Balkans, or to settle the British Civil Wars

– the participants in the latter were not even represented, nor were Russia, the Ottoman empire and some minor Italian states like Modena. Instead, the congress addressed the three great conflicts of Central and western Europe, with the Thirty Years War paramount. Of the 194 official participants, 178 came from the Empire. These included the emperor, the electors and another 132 imperial Estates, as well as 38 other parties like the imperial knights and the Hansa.[1] The other sixteen participants were European states like France, Sweden and Spain. Denmark and Poland were present to safeguard their German interests and did not negotiate on their respective problems with Sweden. Italian concerns were treated as subsidiary to the Franco-Spanish war, as were the Catalan and Portuguese revolts, though Spain refused to discuss these. Colonial issues were subsumed within Spanish-Dutch talks with no attempt to involve non-Europeans.

Despite these shortcomings, the congress was a ground-breaking event. Medieval church councils were the closest precedent, but this was the first truly secular international gathering. It drew on established protocol and negotiating styles, but its sheer scale and the complexity of the issues compelled innovation and dissemination of common guidelines. First and foremost, the congress eroded the medieval principle of hierarchy. The presence of so many representatives from rulers of different rank required a new, simpler form of interaction. It was agreed that all kings had the title of 'majesty' and that all royal and electoral ambassadors were to be addressed as 'excellency' and could arrive in a coach pulled by six horses. Such matters were far from trivial. They represented a major step towards the modern concept of an order based on sovereign states interacting as equals, regardless of their internal form of government, resources, or military potential. The congress established a new way to resolve international problems through negotiation among all interested parties. Attempts to resolve later European wars drew directly on this precedent, notably the congresses of Utrecht (1711–13) and Vienna (1814–15), and the method was extended in line with the changing global order at the Paris Conference of 1919 and, ultimately, with the United Nations.[2]

Negotiating Methods

Acceptance of full equality lay far in the future, however. The delegations arrived to impress as part of a deliberate strategy to demonstrate status and overawe rivals. Altogether, 235 official envoys and representatives attended, but the total number of participants was far larger, since all were accompanied by additional staff. The Swedes rolled up with an entourage numbering 165 that included its own medical personnel, cooks, a tailor and a personal shopper.[3] The two principal French envoys arrived with 319 assistants, while their chief negotiator, the duc de Longueville, had 139 bodyguards and 54 liveried servants. Even delegations from imperial cities could include seven or eight staff. Spain and France each spent over half a million talers on their representation, while that of the emperor, Sweden and the Dutch cost about a quarter of a million apiece. The total cost was around 3.2 million, which was chiefly spent on food and entertaining, rather than bribes or other costs.[4]

The presence of so many people nearly overwhelmed their hosts. The 29-man Bavarian delegation had to share 18 beds, while the Swiss representative lodged above a wool weaver's shop in a room that stank of sausage and fish oil. The congress nonetheless represented a welcome boost to local economies hard hit by the war. Buildings were renovated as delegations sought accommodation appropriate for their political ambitions. The locals were regarded mostly with disdain as provincial bumpkins, who drank beer instead of wine and ate pumpernickel bread.[5]

The proceedings attracted wide public interest, which the delegates deliberately cultivated and manipulated. At least 27 German-language papers alone reported the negotiations, which ensured news reached the furthest corners of the Empire. Key documents, like the Franco-Swedish peace proposals, swiftly appeared in print, though not always accurately. There were visual depictions too, notably engravings of Gerard ter Borch's painting of the oath ceremony sealing the Spanish-Dutch peace in May 1648.[6]

The congress broke new ground in that it dispensed with an official chair or mediator. Ironically, Fabio Chigi, the papal envoy, undermined the pontiff's pretensions to broker peace by helping to simplify protocol. There were no plenary sessions. Instead, negotiations proceeded through bilateral talks, often held in parallel with multiple partners. Talks with the Swedes were held in Osnabrück, while those with France took place in Münster. Mediation was restricted to that by Chigi and his able Venetian colleague Alvise Contarini who acted as go-betweens for France with the Habsburgs who refused formal direct talks. This enabled the emperor and Spain to maintain a common front, though Spain could negotiate directly with the Dutch because Ferdinand was not party to that conflict. Religious differences mattered little and Protestants and Catholics were present in both venues. Major powers, like the emperor, maintained envoys in both towns, while representatives met frequently for more informal talks in Lengerich, Ladbergen and other villages half-way between the two. Such meetings were essential for France and Sweden to coordinate their common front at the congress.[7] Münster remained the venue for Spanish-Dutch talks to settle their war. It also saw negotiations for peace between France and the Empire. Osnabrück assumed greater importance once the imperial Estates were admitted and became the venue where most of the Empire's problems were resolved.

The process was slowed by the need to confer with home governments, especially as the military situation kept opening new possibilities while closing others. It took eight to ten days for letters to reach Paris, longer for those to Vienna and nearly a month to arrive in Madrid. The postal service was intended to be protected. The Dutch garrison in Maastricht, cut off from the Republic and a law unto itself, caused disruption until international protests finally encouraged better behaviour from 1646. Other, more covert interception also occurred as the envoys tried to discover their opponents' intentions.[8]

The Representatives and their Objectives

The emperor had the most impressive negotiating team, though Maximilian von Trauttmannsdorff, its leading member, did not arrive until November 1645 when he became the 'dominant figure in the congress'.[9] Affairs were handled in the interim by the competent Count of Nassau-Hadamar, seconded by counts Auersperg and Lamberg who were chosen for their social status and experience in the Reichshofrat. Their non-noble assistants were men of real ability. In addition to the Westphalian Krane who helped open the congress, the other key figure was Dr Volmar, the Alsatian chancellor who had won the trust of both the emperor and Archduchess Claudia of the Tirol. Volmar was a disagreeable character who undermined colleagues to further his own career, but he was also an expert on the complex situation in Alsace and his advice proved invaluable in negotiations with France. The emperor's presence was enhanced by additional envoys representing him in his capacities as king of Bohemia and archduke of Austria, as well as a delegation for Archduke Leopold Wilhelm on behalf of his eight ecclesiastical territories.

Spain had the weakest team, represented only by junior officials until Count Peñaranda arrived in July 1645. A protégé of Olivares, his career in financial administration had scarcely prepared him for a task that was made harder by his imperfect command of French. Worse, he hated being in Münster, complaining constantly that the wet Westphalian weather was ruining his health while the negotiations kept him from his family. His friend Castel Rodrigo was soon replaced as governor of the Spanish Netherlands by Leopold Wilhelm whom Peñaranda, rightly, suspected of promoting Austrian rather than Spanish interests. If this was not bad enough, he was at odds with his principal assistant Saavedra who, as Spain's leading political thinker, resented his subordinate role. Both men were at least united in their pessimism over Spain's prospects. Saavedra believed his country was in terminal decline. His recall in the summer of 1646 isolated Peñaranda still further. However, the real problem was that none of the Spanish representatives really negotiated, instead just relaying the wishes of their government, which were often overtaken by military events by the time they arrived in the post.

Jealousies likewise divided the French and Swedish delegations. Oxenstierna was reluctant to return to Germany and had already appointed his son Johan as principal envoy in October 1641. Johan waited in Stralsund until the congress opened in 1643. In contrast to his father, he was coarse and disagreeable, determined to assert Swedish power and extract the maximum for his country's costly intervention in Germany. His presence was resented by Salvius, twenty years his senior, who had represented Sweden in the Empire since the chancellor returned to Stockholm in 1636. His long experience of imperial politics convinced him that peace could come only through compromise and he maintained a private correspondence with Queen Christina who thought the same and promoted this line in Paris through Grotius as her own envoy. The divisions in the French team were more personal than political. The two principal negotiators were both members of the administrative nobility, but d'Avaux was richer and more ostentatious, and sought to displace his colleague Abel Servien. The latter had Mazarin's full support and was determined to obtain the maximum benefit for France, whereas d'Avaux was rather more flexible, though he was also concerned not to associate France with concessions to Protestants. The duc de Longueville was sent in June 1645 to stop the bickering and act as an imposing figurehead for the delegation.

The French and Spanish instructions each included the identically phrased objective of achieving 'peace for Christendom' (*repos de la Chrestienté/reposo de la Christiandad*).[10] This was not intended in an abstract, unrealistic sense of resolving all European conflicts. Instead, both countries wanted to end all their own problems in a settlement the other could not overturn later. The French conceived this in line with their general policy to act as arbiter of Europe. Peace would bring a favourable alliance that would collectively guarantee the treaty and assist France to uphold it in future. The Spanish thought more in terms of traditional Habsburg dominance and this explains their reluctance for the emperor to make peace without them. Tragically, these aims were mutually exclusive, condemning both powers to fight on in the hope of achieving the military advantage necessary to arrange peace on their terms. Their objectives remained distinctly early modern, despite the underlying trend at the congress pointing to the future. Reputation remained paramount, since it was integral to sustaining pretensions to the pole position in a European order that was still conceived as a hierarchy. If the negotiations were to fail, both parties wanted to make sure the other took the blame. This engendered an atmosphere of mistrust and the rival delegations were quick to accuse each other of using religion as a pretext for seeking universal, hegemonic monarchy.

Spain's proposals were drawn up in June 1643 using guidelines already prepared by Olivares in 1636 for the Cologne congress. They reflected an era when Spain had been stronger, and the overall objective of restoring the pre-war status quo with France was wholly unrealistic in the aftermath of the Catalan and Portuguese revolts. At the most, Peñaranda was authorized to cede some towns the French had already captured in Artois, and possibly also the indefensible Franche-Comté. These were to be disguised as a dowry for a marriage between Philip IV's daughter Maria Theresa and the boy king Louis XIV, to preserve Spanish prestige. In return, the French were expected to withdraw from Lorraine, Italy and Catalonia. Spain really had only one card to play: a separate peace with the Dutch to concentrate on winning the war against France.

The imperial instructions from July 1643 were deliberately vague so as to preserve a united front with Bavaria and Saxony who were both sent copies. The emperor's envoys were told to continue the existing policy of seeking a compromise peace with Sweden in order to isolate France. Formally, Sweden was to be offered the same terms as presented by Saxony in the 1635 negotiations, but secretly the emperor had already authorized the sacrifice of Pomerania. No such concessions were to be granted France, because the emperor considered all matters settled by the Treaty of Regensburg that Richelieu had failed to ratify in 1630. These international issues were to be arranged first to keep them separate from the constitutional issues that Ferdinand still hoped to settle on the basis of the Peace of Prague. France and Sweden already anticipated this by publicly championing 'German liberty' and insisting the imperial Estates be admitted as full participants at the congress. They deliberately omitted their own territorial demands in both their initial proposals of 4 December 1644, and their second, more specific set on 11 June 1645, precisely not to alienate German opinion. The French made a fuss about restoring the elector of Trier, Sötern, whose arrest featured so prominently in their declaration of war in 1635. In addition, the emperor was to grant a full amnesty extending to the Bohemians and return the distribution of land and religious observance to the situation in 1618.

Serious disagreements between the two crowns obliged them to omit other issues from their joint proposals. Sweden backed the full restoration of the Palatinate and the exiles to preserve its status as champion of constitutional liberties. France continued to court Bavaria and was prepared to give the Palatine title and the Upper Palatinate to Maximilian. Each wanted the other to give ground over territory to secure a compromise with the emperor. France rejected concessions at the expense of the imperial church, while the Swedes were divided among themselves over Pomerania. Horn opposed annexation altogether, Salvius would settle for half, while Johan Oxenstierna demanded the entire duchy. More fundamentally, the two allies found it hard to reconcile their diverging priorities. Sweden needed money to satisfy its army to disengage with honour, while France had to split the emperor and Spain to cope with its problem of fighting two wars simultaneously. The proposals were not yet intended to secure peace but to present a positive public face and gauge the enemy's willingness to negotiate.

Diplomacy remained wedded to the warfare that would shape the congress over the next five years. The first round concentrated on deciding who could participate in the talks, since Spain objected to the presence of Catalan and Portuguese delegations, France refused to talk to the Lorrainers, Sweden rejected Danish pretensions to mediate, and the emperor struggled to exclude the imperial Estates. These issues were resolved by the military campaigns of 1644–5, opening the second round that discussed the dispute over the imperial constitution, and the demands for territory and compensation lodged by France and Sweden. These issues made up most of the peace settlement and were decided in a series of agreements during 1646–7. Progress was hindered by persistent anxiety, because all arrangements remained provisional and might be revoked unilaterally if one party's fortunes improved on the battlefield. The congress resembled a construction site with rival teams of argumentative builders, some periodically dismantling parts of the structure the others were still working on. The final round involved the struggle to convert these provisional agreements into a common, definitive treaty and the decision over whether any participants would be excluded from the peace during 1648.

FRANCE IN GERMANY 1644

The Freiburg Campaign

The situation appeared promising for the emperor at the beginning of 1644. Sweden's decision to attack Denmark at the end of the previous year (see below, pp.685–91) removed the threat to the Habsburg hereditary lands. The forces there were reduced to 11,000 men under the rehabilitated Field Marshal Götz, allowing Ferdinand to mass 21,500 under Gallas who marched down the Elbe to help the Danes. Buoyed by their success at Tuttlingen the previous year, Mercy's Bavarians totalled 19,640, or twice the size of France's Army of Germany despite Mazarin spending 2 million livres to rebuild it during the winter. This was the first time since 1637 that the emperor and his allies began the year with an army large enough to go on the offensive on the Upper Rhine.

General Turenne had been recalled to command in Alsace, but his forces were too weak to fulfil Mazarin's expectations of conquering land beyond the Black Forest. Mercy attacked instead, retaking Überlingen on 10 May, eliminating the last French gain from 1643. Having been repulsed from the Hohentwiel, he left 1,000 men to blockade Widerhold's garrison and crossed the Black Forest to recover the areas lost in the 1638 campaign. Turenne was forced to abandon his own advance through the Forest Towns, double back into Alsace and re-cross to save Breisach. Duke Charles broke off another of his periodic negotiations and renewed raiding into Lorraine. Mazarin was obliged to redirect d'Enghien from covering Champagne to retrieve the situation on the Rhine. Despite dashing 33km a day, d'Enghien arrived too late to save Freiburg, which had surrendered to the Bavarians after a prolonged bombardment on 29 July.

D'Enghien brought 4,000 elite French cavalry and 6,000 infantry, giving the combined force at Krozingen south-west of Freiburg 9,000 horse, 11,000 foot and 37 guns. Typically pugnacious, d'Enghien proposed an immediate attack to throw Mercy back over the mountains. Turenne pointed out the strengths of the enemy position at a council of war on 3 August. Freiburg lay near the western end of a deep valley narrowing further east in the mountains to a pass that gave access to Tuttlingen and the upper Danube. The entrance to the valley was flanked by the steep, wooded Schönberg hill on the south side, with the thick Moos Wood to the north. A stream close to the wood further restricted access, while Mercy had blocked the other side with two redoubts on the Bohl hill, part of the lower slope of the Schönberg above Ebingen village. Both were commanded by another, larger 'star redoubt' further up, while a smaller sconce represented a third barrier behind that at the St Wolfgang Chapel. These positions were held by five veteran Bavarian infantry regiments under Ruischenberg, the former Wolfenbüttel commandant. The rest of the army was further north on the other side of the stream behind a further series of entrenchments between Wendlingen and Haslach villages, with 340 men in Freiburg itself. Campaign attrition had reduced Mercy's force, but he still mustered 8,200 cavalry, 8,600 infantry and 20 guns.[11]

Turenne and Rosen proposed going north along the Rhine to cross the Black Forest through the Glotter valley at Denzingen above Freiburg, and so force Mercy to retreat by threatening his communications with Württemberg. Such a manoeuvre would become standard practice from

FREIBVRG

Freiburg

St. Peter Valley

Sternenwald

Abelhausen

Kaspar mercy

Mercy 5 August

Wohrhalbe

Schönberg

Dreisam

Eschholz

Wolverbach

Höhenlierbach

Haslach

French Artillery

D'Enghien 5 August

Turenne 5 August

Mercy 5 August

Becher Wood

Merzhausen

Damstein Pass

Günterstbal

1km

Schönberg

Turenne 3 August

Bavarian cavalry 3 August

St. Georgen

Bavarian Camp

Uffhausen

Star redoubt

Bohl Hill

St. Wolfang Chapel

Wendlingen

Mooswald

Höllenstrasse

Leutersberg

D'Enghien 3 August

Ebingen

Thalhausen

the later seventeenth century, but d'Enghien insisted on a frontal assault. He did consent to send Turenne's army through the Bannstein Pass that separated the Schönberg from the Black Forest to the east and led to a narrow valley through Merzhausen behind Mercy's main position. Turenne had a long march from Krozingen to reach the Bannstein Pass, but d'Enghien decided nonetheless to attack that day, so both assaults were scheduled for 5 p.m., leaving only three hours of daylight to achieve success. D'Enghien synchronized two watches and gave one to Turenne.

D'Enghien began on time, sending three infantry brigades from Ebingen to assault the Bohl redoubts. The French suffered horrendous casualties as they struggled under heavy fire across sharpened branches and other obstacles placed to slow their advance. The successive attacks of the first two brigades were thrown back. D'Enghien led the third forward covered by a screen of musketeers sent ahead to provide covering fire. The display of reckless bravery showed d'Enghien at his best. Allegedly, he threw his marshal's baton into the first redoubt and told his men to fetch it. His presence induced some men from the first two brigades to rejoin the attack. The tired defenders had virtually exhausted their ammunition repelling the earlier assaults and fled when some Frenchmen appeared in their rear having worked they way through the trees. D'Enghien had lost 1,200 men, or one-in-three of his force and twice what the Bavarians suffered. It was now dark and raining heavily, and the Bavarian main defences had yet to be breached.

Turenne had begun his attack three-quarters of an hour early, sending 1,000 musketeers to clear the Bannstein Pass only to discover that Mercy had anticipated them and blocked the valley with five lines of entrenchments. An outpost on top of the Schönberg had already signalled Turenne's approach, enabling Mercy to move four infantry regiments from his main army to reinforce the one already at the pass. They arrived in time to repulse Turenne's advance guard. Turenne renewed the attack, but the confined space prevented him using his numerical superiority to full effect. He broke off the action at 4 a.m. having lost 1,600 men, or four times the enemy losses. The old Bernhardine infantry, already depleted at Tuttlingen, now effectively ceased to exist. However, Mercy recognized he would be cut off if another attack got through the pass and so ordered a general withdrawal to the Schlierberg ridge further up the Freiburg valley.[12]

The rain continued throughout the next day, turning the valley floor to mud. The French occupied Merzhausen and Mercy's old camp at Uffhausen, but were too exhausted to do more, leaving the Bavarians the whole day to entrench their new position. A large redoubt was constructed at the northern end for ten cannon, with a further seven guns on the southern, higher end called the Wohnhalde. A third, smaller battery was placed on the saddle between the two peaks. The left could not be turned, because there was virtually no space between the Wohnhalde and the spur of the Black Forest leading north from the Bannstein Pass. Mercy thus massed his cavalry on his right between the Schlierberg and the Dreisam river flowing through Freiburg. The French now had no choice but to launch another frontal assault if they wanted to renew the fight.

It was a bright, sunny morning as the French moved into position on 5 August. D'Enghien ordered Turenne to make the main attack from Merzhausen against the Wohnhalde since the entire Bavarian position would have to be abandoned if this fell. Turenne's approach would be protected by the Becher Wood composed of fir trees with limited undergrowth to hinder movement. D'Enghien would make a diversionary attack against the rest of the ridge to prevent Mercy reinforcing his left. Poor staff work frustrated this plan. Both generals rode to verify a report that the Bavarians were retreating and were not on hand to stop the commander on their left beginning a frontal assault by mistake. The sound of gunfire prompted Turenne's subordinates to launch their planned attack as well. D'Enghien again dived into the fray, rallying the infantry of the Army of Germany as they were repulsed from the Wohnhalde, and leading further, equally fruitless assaults. By the afternoon he had used up most of Turenne's army to little effect, and rode north to his own force on the left that had also been repulsed in the morning. He sent the infantry forward again. The slope here was less steep, but it was still a hard climb through vineyards under the steady fire of the Bavarian battery and musketeers on the top. Three attacks were repulsed, so d'Enghien dismounted his cavalry and sent these up as well. The Bavarians were tiring, so Mercy's brother Kaspar led the cavalry round the north end of the ridge in a counter-attack to stem the French advance.

The sky was completely obscured by gun smoke when the French drew off at 5 p.m., having lost another 4,000 killed and wounded. Unsympathetically, d'Enghien is said to have exclaimed 'Bah! So many will be conceived in a night in Paris.'[13] The Bavarians lost 1,100, mostly wounded, but Kaspar was killed during his attack. There is considerable evidence that his brother's death plunged Mercy into despair.[14] He was certainly pessimistic and convinced he was outnumbered. His army was also exhausted and its horses were weak from lack of fodder.

D'Enghien had indeed been reinforced by over 5,000 men, drawn from every garrison in the vicinity. However, even he recognized the necessity of accepting his subordinates' advice and set off four days later to turn Mercy's position by marching through the Glotter valley. Mercy appreciated the danger and raced east to the St Peter's valley that intersected the Glotter at the abbey of that name. His cavalry secured the abbey that evening, and the rest of the army began arriving at dawn the next day when Rosen appeared with the old Bernhardine cavalry. The Bavarian infantry broke Rosen's charge with a well-timed volley and their cavalry chased him back up the Glotter. The Bavarians were nonetheless demoralized by having to retreat after such hard fighting. Their cavalry horses had been saddled for eight days due to the constant alarms. The entire French army arrived to support Rosen who gained the credit for Mercy's precipitous retreat to Villingen. The French plundered the abandoned baggage, burned St Peter's abbey and retired back across the Black Forest.

Freiburg was the longest and one of the toughest battles of the war. The damage done to the Bavarian army was serious enough, but what gave the action its true significance was the unexpected collapse of the imperial position on the middle Rhine. Turenne persuaded d'Enghien not to waste time retaking Freiburg, but to press northwards into the virtually undefended Lower Palatinate. The French overran Baden and the bishoprics of Speyer and Worms, and then captured Philippsburg after a three-week siege on 12 September. The latter had been in imperial hands since January 1635, but was defended by only 250 men and the hot weather had dried the marshes that protected it. Its loss was compounded by that of Mainz which surrendered without resistance five days later, because the cathedral canons wished to avoid a siege. Occupation by the Catholic French was an altogether different prospect from the earlier Protestant Swedish presence. The French installed a garrison of 500 men maintained at the citizens' expense, but left the canons to administer the electorate throughout their occupation until 1650. The city's rapid capitulation frustrated Mercy's countermeasures as his reinforcements arrived to find the French already inside Mainz. He retook Pforzheim and Mannheim in early October, razing the latter's defences to deny it as a potential French base. Gallas's defeat (see below, p. 690) prevented him doing more and he retired to winter in Franconia, Württemberg and the Lake Constance area.

Mercy's tactical victory at Freiburg had been completely overturned by the subsequent French strategic success. In Philippsburg, Speyer and Mainz, France at last had a viable route into Germany that avoided the Black Forest. The war shifted from the Rhineland into Swabia and Franconia, sealing Duke Charles's fate. The emperor, Bavaria and Spain were all too busy to help him. The French captured La Mothe in 1645, and Longwy in 1646, eliminating his last Lorraine strongholds and leaving him a fugitive in the Netherlands.

Westphalia

Cologne was also left largely to its own devices. It was clear by 1641 that peace would entail concessions to Protestant princes at the expense of the ecclesiastical territories. Though not an hereditary ruler, Ferdinand of Cologne took his responsibilities towards the imperial church seriously. The Treaty of Goslar had recovered Hildesheim and reduced his immediate enemies by neutralizing the Guelphs. The start of the Westphalian congress extended neutrality to Münster and Osnabrück, removing the latter as a Swedish base. The elector widened this by agreeing in December 1643 to pay 5,500 tlr a month to Sweden in return for their recognition of Hildesheim as neutral.

These moves isolated Hessen-Kassel. Amalie Elisabeth had no interest in wider French objectives and recalled Eberstein's troops from Guébriant's army as it returned to the Upper Rhine in 1642. She had 4,000 men poised to attack her Darmstadt rival when news arrived of France's defeat at Tuttlingen. Units then had to be redirected to East Frisia in 1644 to face down the count who was assembling his own troops to eject the Hessian garrison, leaving insufficient forces to attempt anything else that year. It was obvious the Hessians were too weak to act unilaterally.

Ferdinand of Cologne saw an opportunity to be rid of them for good, and summoned his neighbours to pool their dwindling resources and create a common army under the collective authority of the Westphalian

Kreis. This would free them from dependency on imperial units that were recalled all too often at awkward moments. The army would expel the Hessians and then uphold neutrality against all-comers. Brandenburg refused to cooperate, preferring to reinforce its own garrisons in Cleves and Mark. Wolfgang Wilhelm of Pfalz-Neuburg also objected, convinced the scheme would not work. Instead he opened negotiations with France in the summer of 1643 in the mistaken belief Mazarin would restrain the Hessians in return for his assistance in frustrating Cologne's plans. The other Westphalians did agree in June 1644 to pay their war taxes directly to the new army. Since the elector had lost confidence in Hatzfeldt's ability to stop looting, command was given to Geleen, an honest Liègois who had risen in the Catholic Liga service since 1618. Though many minor territories soon fell into arrears, the army nonetheless mustered 15,000, or only 4,000 below target. Ferdinand also had additional Liège and Cologne garrisons under Velen, replaced in 1646 by Otto Christoph von Sparr.[15]

Cologne assumed the emperor's role in assisting Spain to defend the Mosel region. The Brussels government agreed in December 1644 to pay 260,000 tlr in return for 7,000 men in the coming campaign. These were entrusted to Lamboy who had paid his own ransom to escape French captivity after Kempen. The emperor accepted these arrangements as the only way of defending the Lower Rhine. The enlarged Westphalian army was to prove its worth when war returned to the region early in 1646 (see Chapter 20).

THE BALTIC BECOMES
SWEDISH 1643-5

A New Baltic War

Early in October 1643 Torstensson received a letter dated 5 June from Oxenstierna telling him to prepare for war against Denmark. The general was reluctant to comply, fearing his recent gains in Bohemia and Silesia would be lost if he marched north. He nonetheless consolidated his garrisons by abandoning the more vulnerable posts and, having announced he was heading for Pomerania, set off on 13 November from Upper Silesia across Brandenburg.

This apparently sudden change in Swedish strategy had in fact been long planned. Oxenstierna had observed Denmark's rapid recovery since 1629. The tight fiscal management imposed by that country's aristocratic council in 1628 was an unwelcome intrusion on Christian IV's prerogative, but it swiftly mastered the war debt and, together with the 2 million riksdalers Christian inherited from his mother, restored royal solvency by 1631. New taxes enabled the army to be rebuilt around a conscript militia that was doubled in 1641 to provide 16,000 Danish and 6,500 Norwegian infantry, plus 2,000 cavalry. A defence pact with the duke of Holstein-Gottorp helped expand the regular army, which totalled 11,000 by 1642, while the navy was maintained at 20,000 tonnes with 35 major warships.

These preparations enhanced Denmark's defensive, not offensive capacity and posed no direct threat to Sweden. What concerned Oxenstierna was Christian's dogged attempts to interpose himself as mediator in the Empire's war. Pro-imperial mediation had already secured Bremen and Verden for Christian's son Frederick at the Peace of Prague. Though Danish influence declined thereafter, the emperor's difficulties allowed Christian to resume a greater role, notably in promoting north German neutrality after 1638 (discussed earlier in Chapter 17, pp.612–21). The shift of the stalled Cologne talks to Hamburg in 1641 brought negotiations within his sphere of influence. The Hamburg Peace Preliminaries were signed as Christian massed 10,000 men at Fühlsbüttel only 10km away. With the opening of the Westphalian congress it became imperative for Sweden to eliminate any chance of the king asserting himself as mediator. Oxenstierna's fears were justified, since the Danish delegation was instructed to oblige Sweden to disband its German army and to prevent it obtaining any Baltic territory, including Pomerania. Attacking Denmark would both prevent this and silence Oxenstierna's critics who were accusing him of neglecting Sweden's 'true' Baltic interests.[16]

The chancellor carefully steered his colleagues into agreeing war during a seven-day debate in the council, the first attended by the seventeen-year-old Queen Christina, at the end of May 1643. The cause was presented as national indignation at Christian IV's 2.5 per cent hike in the Sound tolls at the end of the 1630s. Danish warships had temporarily blocked the Elbe and had begun levying tolls on ships leaving the Pomeranian ports under Sweden's control. These complaints were despatched in a letter carefully phrased not to arouse Danish suspicions that Sweden planned war, but which could be cited later as justification for Oxenstierna's pre-emptive strike. The toll dispute also provided the ideal moment for such an attack, because the Dutch were also angry at the increase. Christian's ban on arms exports through the Sound in 1637, issued as part of his peace-making, further alienated influential Dutch merchants, notably Louis de Geer who controlled most of the weapons and minerals trade with the Baltic.[17] Denmark's failure to reach agreements with Poland, Russia or England increased its isolation.

Sweden was better prepared than in its last Danish war of 1611-13. Despite the continual military attrition, Sweden still mustered 90,000 soldiers, of whom 50,000 were Germans. Unlike the Danes, its troops were battle-hardened and could draw on two decades' experience of continental warfare. They also possessed what Wallenstein had lacked in the 1620s: naval superiority. Rapid construction since 1640 had increased the fleet to 35,000 tonnes by 1645, including 58 sailing warships plus galleys for coastal assaults, manned by 6,152 sailors and 3,256 marines. To be doubly sure, Oxenstierna hired de Geer to raise a mercenary fleet in the Republic, comprising 32 ships crewed by 3,000 merchant sailors under Maarten Thijsen, an experienced naval officer.[18]

Sweden's Surprise Attack

The toll issue was played up at the Riksdag that finally authorized war on 26 November. By then, Torstensson was already well on his way, reaching Havelberg on 16 December. Only now did he tell his 16,000 men their true destination. Many objected, because they had not signed up to fight outside the Empire, and questioned how war with Denmark matched Sweden's stated objective of fighting for German liberty. They were pacified by the prospect of wintering in the Jutland peninsula, a region that had been free from war since 1629. The army crossed into Holstein on 22 December without a formal declaration of war, as if they were simply seeking winter quarters.

Taken by surprise, the Danes sent a trumpeter to ask Torstensson what he was doing, while further protests were despatched to Stockholm. Oxenstierna deliberately delayed sending the formal declaration until 28 January 1644 to give Torstensson more time to exploit the Danes' confusion. The Swedes meanwhile stormed the Christianpreis fort that guarded Kiel, massacring the sixty defenders and renaming it

Christinapreis. The brutality demoralized the other garrisons in Holstein and these now surrendered, opening the way into Jutland. Duke Friedrich III of Holstein-Gottorp abandoned his defence pact and paid large contributions to Torstensson in return for neutrality.[19] Knowing what to expect after Wallenstein's campaign in the region, the rich fled into Hamburg or the Danish islands. Formal resistance collapsed, but like the Imperialists, Torstensson encountered resistance from peasant guerrillas. The Danes also still had 10,000 men in Glückstadt and the archbishopric of Bremen to the south west.

The second element of Oxenstierna's plan now ran into difficulties. General Horn had been recalled from retirement and given 10,600 conscripts to invade Scania, the Danish-held part of southern Sweden. He took Helsingborg in February 1644 and blockaded Malmö, while another, smaller force occupied the (then) Norwegian province of Jämtland. The local population were already terrified by stories of Swedish behaviour in Germany and fled. However, the governor of Scania mobilized 8,000 militia, stemmed Horn's advance and began retaliatory raids into Swedish territory. The Norwegians then blockaded Gothenburg on its landward side while a Danish squadron under Christian IV cruised outside its harbour. The Swedes were stuck until their navy asserted control of the seas.

Christian sailed south from Gothenburg with nine ships to intercept Thijsen's auxiliary fleet, catching it off Lister Deep between Sylt and Römö islands on the south-west Jutland coast on 26 May. Though heavily outnumbered, the Danish vessels were purpose-built warships mounting guns up to 36-pounders, twice as large as the biggest Dutch guns. Thijsen's fleet was battered and forced to shelter in the Deep. He ventured out again at Torstensson's insistence, only to receive another drubbing. His now mutinous crews sailed home. The defeat turned Dutch opinion against Sweden and for a time de Geer, one of the leading supporters of the alliance, feared to leave his Amsterdam mansion.

Christian left a squadron to continue the blockade of Gothenburg and sailed through the Sound to join his main force under Admiral Mundt against the proper Swedish navy in the Baltic. His opponent, Admiral Fleming, had arrived at Kiel with 41 ships and helped Torstensson capture Fehmarn as a first step to invading the Danish islands. Christian's arrival enabled the Danish fleet to attack on 11 July, catching Fleming in the Kolberger Heide, a stretch of water at the eastern exit of

Kiel Bay. Neither side attempted boarding and instead relied on long-range gunfire. Christian lost an ear and his right eye to flying splinters, but refused to break off the action that continued till nightfall. Casualties were light, but Fleming chose to retire into the bay, allowing the Danes to trap him.

Imperial Intervention

The threat to the Swedish fleet exposed the risks of Oxenstierna's policy of starting a new war without disengaging from that in the Empire first. Ferdinand III was not deceived by a renewed offer for talks that was obviously intended to dissuade him from aiding Denmark. Relations with Christian had been cordial since 1629, but Ferdinand II had done little to exploit the potential for cooperation against Sweden. His son now resolved to help Denmark even without a formal alliance.[20] Gallas advanced down the Elbe and then north into Holstein, arriving with 18,000 men in July 1644, ready to trap Torstensson in Jutland and Fleming in Kiel Bay. Contrary winds prevented the latter from escaping. The Danes landed guns and bombarded the stricken Swedish ships, one shot taking off Fleming's right leg on 4 August. General Karl Gustav Wrangel assumed the role of admiral on Torstensson's recommendation and reinvigorated the crews. The wind changed and with their lights extinguished they slipped past the Danish fleet on the night of 12 August. Gallas arrived at the edge of the bay just in time to see their sails disappear over the horizon the next day.

With Gallas distracting Torstensson, Christian ferried part of his army from the Danish islands to relieve Malmö in September and drive Horn from Scania. A Norwegian counter-attack had already recovered Jämtland in August. Oxenstierna's strategy appeared to be unravelling. His new war strained relations with France just as the Westphalian peace congress opened. A success was urgently needed and Wrangel provided it. The main Swedish fleet had been repaired and had joined Thijsen, who returned with 21 survivors of the auxiliary fleet and slipped through the Sound in August. The combined force, now 37 strong, cruised westwards along the Mecklenburg coast towards Kiel, catching Admiral Mundt off Fehmarn island on 23 October. The Danes had not expected further naval activity that year and had already laid up half their fleet for the winter. Mundt had only seventeen under-manned ships, some of which tried to escape without orders shortly after the battle began. He was killed as his flagship was boarded, while the others were set on fire. A thousand men were captured and only three ships escaped.

The disaster forced Christian to drop plans to invade Sweden and even consider pawning Iceland and Scania to raise emergency loans. The situation worsened with the destruction of the imperial army through skirmishes, hunger and desertions. Gallas had captured Kiel and Rendsburg but was then outmanoeuvred by Torstensson, who forced the Imperialists to retreat over the Elbe and then retire up the river the way they had come earlier that year. The area was completely exhausted. Torstensson was reinforced by Königsmarck's small detachment and the Hessian field force. With Gallas blind drunk, two of his disillusioned subordinates tried to escape with 4,000 cavalry but were intercepted in November. Around 3,000 survivors of the main force eventually reached Wittenberg in December. Overall losses were not as severe as often stated, but were amply sufficient to justify the soldiers' protests at their general as an 'army wrecker'.[21]

Gallas was dismissed on 24 January 1645, but the disaster was not entirely his fault. The imperial army had not operated in the region since 1638 and had to shift its base 750km from Bohemia to north-west Germany. Planning had been based on unrealistic expectations that supplies could be obtained in devastated Mecklenburg where the Swedes held the main towns. The troops were already on half rations by August, while a critical shortage of transport animals prevented fresh supplies reaching them in time.

The final blow came in January as Königsmarck and 3,000 Swedes turned north-west into the archbishopric of Bremen, while another detachment pinned down the remaining Danish units in the west Holstein marshes. Stade fell on 15 February 1645 and by March Königsmarck was master of both Bremen and Verden, capturing the principal gains of Christian's diplomacy since 1629. Danish power appeared broken. Already in 1644 the Dutch could send a merchant convoy to the Baltic paying only the old toll rates. Their navy returned in July 1645 with 300 merchantmen who now paid no dues at all.

The Peace of Brömsebro 1645

France and the Dutch Republic had agreed in January 1644 to limit Swedish gains, however, since neither wanted to see Sweden simply displace Denmark as mistress of the Baltic. Talks opened at Brömsebro on the frontier between their possessions in southern Sweden in February 1645. Christian had already abandoned his pretensions to mediate at Westphalia in August 1644. He agreed peace at Brömsebro a year later, ceding the Baltic islands of Ösel and Gotland, as well as the Norwegian provinces of Härjedalen and Jämtland. Denmark also relinquished the province of Halland on the western Swedish coast for thirty years as a bond to ensure it stuck to a new toll agreement and abandoned claims to inspect cargoes. The Hanseatic cities of Hamburg, Bremen and Lübeck had supported Sweden diplomatically throughout the war and were included in the peace. Subsequent talks obliged Denmark to stop levying tolls at Glückstadt and accept Hamburg's autonomy (though it did not renounce claims to the city until 1768).[22]

The new toll arrangements severely reduced Danish royal revenue but they enabled Christian to escape diplomatic isolation by removing the main source of friction with other countries. He was obliged to make further concessions to his nobility, but in return received new taxes. His son and successor imposed an absolutism in 1660 that lasted until the 1849 revolution, but while the monarchy recovered its domestic position, its international status was in terminal decline. Attempts to recover the country's former role ended in disaster by 1679 with the loss of its surviving possessions in southern Sweden. The Sound tolls remained until international pressure achieved their abolition in 1857.

Oxenstierna more than achieved his objectives, not only eliminating the threat of Danish mediation, but improving his bargaining position in Westphalia with renewed victories. New instructions were sent to the delegation in November 1645, expanding Sweden's 'Satisfaction' to include Bremen and Verden, as well as Pomerania and Wismar.

1645: *ANNUS HORRIBILIS*
ET MIRABILIS

The year 1645 proved to be a 'year both terrible and miraculous' for Ferdinand III.[23] A further series of defeats brought the Swedes to the gates of Vienna in the first threat to the imperial capital since 1620, only to be repulsed by tenacious Austrian resistance. All was not lost, but by the end of the year it was clear a turning point had been reached, obliging the emperor to move from form to content in the Westphalian negotiations.

The Battle of Jankau

Denmark's defeat and the destruction of Gallas's army prompted Elector Maximilian to open new talks with France. With his position crumbling, the emperor summoned his closest advisers for their candid opinion at New Year.[24] None thought victory was possible or believed in the Prague strategy of uniting the Empire to expel the foreigners. However, they were not yet prepared to relinquish the gains from 1635 and had little faith in achieving a satisfactory peace in Westphalia. They recommended renewed military effort to compel Sweden to agree more favourable terms, while remaining unrealistically hopeful that the election of Pope Innocent X in 1644 would assist a separate settlement with France.

The Austrian Estates had already been summoned and voted increased taxes and food supplies. The emperor sold part of the crown jewels and, following his example, the churches surrendered their silver, while nobles advanced loans. Ferdinand rejoined the army as part of a strategy to rally popular and divine support that culminated in his leading a religious procession in Vienna on 29 March. Here he announced his intention to build a monumental column dedicated to the Virgin like the one completed in Munich seven years earlier to commemorate White Mountain. Actual command was entrusted to Hatzfeldt who had spent most of 1644 in charge of the reserve army in Bohemia and Franconia. Maximilian was persuaded to despatch Werth with 5,000 Bavarian veterans despite the critical situation on the Upper Rhine, while Johann Georg sent 1,500 Saxon cavalry. This gave a combined field force of

11,000 cavalry, over 500 dragoons, 5,000 infantry and 26 guns that collected at Pilsen in January.[25]

The Swedes were determined to exploit the unexpected bonus of the disintegration of Gallas's army. They had 43,000 men in Germany at this point. Some were with Königsmarck completing the conquest of Bremen and Verden, while others garrisoned the Baltic bridgehead and positions in Silesia and Moravia. The main strike force under Torstensson numbered 9,000 horse, 6,500 foot and 60 cannon and was in western Saxony where it had arrived in pursuit of Gallas. Torstensson was already on the march by 19 January to deny the Imperialists time to recover. Hatzfeldt guessed correctly he was heading for Olmütz, but did not know whether he would go north or south of Prague to get there. Operations were disrupted by a February thaw that turned the roads to mud. Torstensson dodged south of Prague as it turned cold again and crossed the frozen Moldau. Hatzfeldt recovered quickly, and moved east to block him in the hills by Jankau (Jankov) on 6 March.

The imperial right was protected by steep, rising ground and thick woods. The left was more exposed, but the entire front was covered by the freezing waters of the Jankova stream and a network of ponds south of Jankau itself. Torstensson decided to feint against the enemy right, while going round their left to outflank them in a move that resembled Frederick the Great's tactics at Leuthen in 1757. The Swedes set off at 6 a.m., around ninety minutes before dawn, heading for Chapel Hill, a small rise they had to secure to get safely past the ponds. Hatzfeldt had gone to reconnoitre, leaving Count Götz vague instructions to hold the hill. For reasons that remain unclear, Götz moved the entire left wing south into the valley leading to the hill. This move was constricted by thick woods either side of his route and Hatzfeldt returned to find the soldiers struggling across the very obstacles he intended to disrupt the enemy's advance. It was too late to turn back.

The frozen ground gave the Swedes a firm footing and they were able to drag their heavy guns onto Chapel Hill, whereas the imperial artillery got stuck in the woods. Hatzfeldt moved his centre and right southwards in support as a fierce fight developed to prevent the Swedes advancing beyond the ponds. Werth and the Bavarian and Saxon cavalry overran two Swedish infantry brigades, before being compelled by artillery fire to retire. The Swedes then pushed east, gaining the high ground on the imperial flank and forcing Hatzfeldt to retire northwards. After an

JANKAU

hour of musketry, Hatzfeldt disengaged and withdrew further across his original position towards Skrysov village, where he redeployed facing south with his right on the Jankova and left on Hrin. Torstensson followed, taking up position between Jankau and Radmeritz. He had expected Hatzfeldt to continue his retreat, but noticed imperial musketeers entrenching on a small wooded hill in front of Skrysov. Hatzfeldt intended this as an outpost while he waited until nightfall to slip away. Once the Swedes had dislodged the musketeers he grew concerned and launched a counter-attack, renewing the battle around 1 p.m.

Werth, now on the left, led another successful charge, this time routing the best Swedish cavalry that had deployed opposite him at Radmeritz. However, his comrades in the centre and right were dispirited after the defeat that morning and cracked under the strain of renewed fighting. The Bavarian cavalry had dispersed to plunder, capturing the Swedish army's loot and women, including Torstensson's wife. The Swedes rallied and drove them off, rescuing the women. As the imperial horse on the right had also given way, the infantry in the centre were abandoned like the Spanish at Rocroi and their own comrades at both battles of Breitenfeld. They fought on till dark. Some escaped into the woods to the rear, but 4,500 were captured. Götz, along with several other senior officers, was killed, as were around 4,000 men, many during the pursuit. Hatzfeldt was caught because his horse was exhausted and, having been robbed, he was handed over to Torstensson.

The battle was clearly a disaster for the emperor. A muster of 36 regiments outside Prague a week later revealed that only 2,697 officers and men remained. Another 2,000 fugitives were left stranded by the rapid Swedish advance through Moravia and lived as marauders in a running conflict with local peasants. The veteran Bavarian cavalry had been virtually destroyed, while the loss of so many senior officers left the army leaderless. It is a sign of Ferdinand's desperation that he even recalled Gallas to help reorganize the army. However, comparisons with Rocroi or White Mountain are exaggerated, as the battle was not followed by military or political collapse.[26]

Torstensson claimed he lost only 600 men, but the later Swedish General Staff history puts the casualties at a more realistic 3–4,000. The victory allowed him to widen his objectives beyond merely resupplying Olmütz. He swept on through southern Moravia and over the frontier hills into Lower Austria to arrive outside Vienna with 16,000 men on

9 April. The advance renewed the possibility that Transylvania might intervene for another combined siege of the imperial capital.

Transylvania Rejoins the War

Sweden had courted the new Transylvanian prince, György I Rákóczi, since 1637, finally concluding an alliance on 16 November 1643. Rákóczi agreed to attack Upper Hungary and cooperate in Silesia in return for a subsidy and 3,000 infantry to stiffen his cavalry army. His domestic situation had become more secure and he wanted to resume Bethlen's policy of expansion. The sultan had agreed another twenty-year extension to the 1606 truce at Szöny in March 1642, but Ferdinand had delayed ratification to avoid the humiliation and expense of paying the 200,000 florins in tribute needed to confirm the agreement. Therefore the sultan felt free to give his consent to Rákóczi who crossed into Upper Hungary in February 1644. Sweden saw the attack as a useful diversion to cover the withdrawal of Torstensson's army for the invasion of Denmark.

The Transylvanian attack caused considerable alarm, delaying Gallas's departure for Holstein and disrupting Götz's operations against Olmütz. However, Rákóczi encountered unexpected resistance in Hungary where, unlike in the 1620s, most of the magnates were now Catholics loyal to the Habsburgs. He was also reluctant to risk his full force until his allies provided concrete support. This the Swedes were unable to do, as they were busy in Denmark. The campaign petered out as Rákóczi accepted Ferdinand's offer of talks, and resumed only in the wake of Jankau and the promise of French subsidies in April 1645.

Ferdinand and Leopold Wilhelm were in Prague when news of Jankau arrived. The archduke went directly to Vienna to organize its defence, while his brother hurried through the Upper Palatinate to Bavaria to reassure Maximilian that all was not lost.[27] He then rejoined the archduke in Vienna on 20 March, displaying the same calm that had rallied support during Banér's bombardment of Regensburg. The Austrian Estates summoned their militia, while 5,500 citizens and students reinforced the city's 1,500 regular soldiers. The blockade of Olmütz was abandoned and all forces regrouped south of the Danube apart from a reinforced garrison in Brünn and the men holding Prague. After long negotiations Leopold Wilhelm accepted command on 1 May when the main army totalled 15,000. Another 6,000 cavalry were by then raiding the Swedish communication lines through Bohemia and Silesia, a flying column of 4,000 was heading for the Elbe pass into Saxony, and additional units confronted the Transylvanians in Hungary.

Torstensson now faced the same problems that had defeated Count Thurn in 1619-20. First, he could not cross the Danube to attack Vienna. His Finnish pioneers were accustomed to using local boats to build their bridges, but found that the Imperialists had already secured these to the south bank. The 14,200 Transylvanians who joined him in May and July proved unreliable, demanding pay he did not have. Above all, Torstensson was concerned about how far he had come from his Pomeranian bridgehead with only Olmütz to link him to the weak detachments holding Saxony and Silesia. He decided to capture Brünn to secure Moravia for the winter while he waited for reinforcements. The fortress was held by 1,500 dragoons, Jesuit students and unwilling burghers under de Souches, a Huguenot refugee from La Rochelle who had left Swedish service after falling out with Stalhansk. Torstensson threatened to hang de Souches as a deserter unless he surrendered, but he held out between 5 May and 19 August, providing the main 'miracle' in Ferdinand's year. The Swedes and Transylvanians lost 8,000 men during the siege, mainly through a fresh outbreak of the plague.

The failure disheartened the Transylvanians, who renewed negotiations with the emperor. Ferdinand had sent the Bohemian Count Czernin and a deliberately impressive entourage of 160 to Constantinople in June 1644. Czernin arrived at a critical time. The Knights of St John had just captured a large Turkish ship in the Mediterranean. The sultan blamed the Venetians and faced a choice between fighting them or backing Rákóczi. Czernin skilfully outmanoeuvred his French and Swedish counterparts to persuade the sultan to accept the emperor's belated ratification of the Szöny extension to the truce. The Ottomans launched an amphibious assault on Crete in April 1645, beginning a war with Venice that would last until the island's fall in 1669. Rákóczi swiftly fell into line, accepting Ferdinand's offer in August of the seven Upper Hungarian counties previously ceded to Bethlen for his lifetime.[28]

The Transylvanians' withdrawal obliged Torstensson to lift his siege of Brünn, but the Peace of Brömsebro that month encouraged him to return south for a second attempt against Vienna. The Imperialists had sent 3,000 men to aid Saxony and 1,200 to help Bavaria, but still mustered around 20,000 thanks to new recruits. Torstensson was by now so ill he could barely sit two hours in the saddle. His own force was down to 10,000 men by October when he gave up and retreated across Saxony into Thuringia, where he handed over command to Admiral Wrangel on 23 December. Having briefly helped Maximilian in October, Leopold Wilhelm returned with Bavarian assistance and expelled the remaining Swedish garrisons from Bohemia by February 1646.

Jankau, though serious, was not decisive and the Habsburg monarchy displayed considerable resilience and ingenuity in repelling the combined Swedish-Transylvanian attack. What proved critical, however, was that this prevented effective aid to Bavaria and Saxony for much of the year, leading to defeats that left Ferdinand dangerously isolated.

The Battle of Herbsthausen

The capture of Philippsburg and Mainz had given France secure access over the Rhine, but the Lower Palatinate was too devastated to provide an adequate base for them inside Germany. The local truce ruled out use of the Franche-Comté to the south, heightening the importance of securing Swabian territory east of the Black Forest to sustain French forces in the Empire. News of Jankau emboldened Mazarin to believe there was a real chance of knocking Bavaria out of the war and Turenne was ordered to achieve this.[29]

Both sides spent the opening months of 1645 raiding each other across the Black Forest. Turenne was delayed by the need to rebuild his infantry shattered at Freiburg, while Mercy had detached Werth and most of the cavalry to Bohemia. Only 1,500 troopers returned in April. Turenne was able to attack first, crossing the Rhine with 11,000 men near Speyer on 26 March and advancing up the Neckar into Württemberg, which he thoroughly plundered. He then moved north-east, taking Rothenburg on the Tauber to open the way into Franconia. Mercy deliberately feigned defeatism, keeping to the south while he collected his forces. Turenne remained cautious, but was unable to sustain even his relatively small army in the Tauber valley. He moved to Mergentheim, billeting his cavalry in the surrounding villages in April.

Having received Maximilian's permission to risk battle, Mercy planned to repeat his success at Tuttlingen. Werth's arrival gave him 9,650 men and 9 guns at Feuchtwangen. He force-marched his troops

60km to approach Mergentheim from the south-east on 5 May. Turenne had been alerted by one of Rosen's patrols at 2 a.m., but there was little time to collect his troops at Herbsthausen, just south-east of the town. He knew he could not trust his largely untried infantry in the open, so posted them along the edge of a wood on a rise overlooking the main road. Most of the cavalry were massed to the left ready to charge the Bavarians as they emerged from a large wood to the south. He had only 3,000 troopers and a similar number of infantry, though not all were present at the start of the battle and another 3,000 billeted in the surrounding area never made it at all.

Werth appeared first at the head of half the Bavarian cavalry to cover the deployment of the rest of the army on the other side of the narrow valley opposite the French. Mercy used his artillery to pound the wood, increasing the casualties as the shot sent branches flying through the air, just as the Swedes had done to the Bavarians at Wolfenbüttel. None of the six French cannon had arrived. Their infantry fired an ineffective salvo at long range and fell back as the Bavarians began a general advance. Turenne charged down the valley, routing the Bavarian cavalry on the left that included the units beaten at Jankau. However, a regiment held in reserve stemmed the attack, while the few French cavalry posted on Turenne's extreme right were swept away by Werth's charge. The French army dissolved in panic, many of the infantry being trapped around Herbsthausen. Turenne cut his way through almost alone to join three fresh cavalry regiments that arrived just in time to cover the retreat. The subsequent surrender of Mergentheim and other garrisons brought the total French losses up to 4,400, compared to 600 Bavarians.[30]

The success was not on the scale of Tuttlingen, but it was sufficient to lift the despondency in Munich and Vienna after Jankau. The sequence of these actions underscores the general point about the interrelationship between war and diplomacy, as each change of military fortune raised the hopes in one party of achieving their diplomatic objectives, while hardening the determination of the other to continue resisting until the situation improved. In this case, Mercy was too weak to exploit his victory beyond securing the area south of the Main. Mazarin moved swiftly to restore French prestige before negotiations moved further in Westphalia. D'Enghien was directed to take another 7,000 reinforcements across the Rhine at Speyer, and in a new show of common resolve Sweden agreed to despatch Königsmarck from Bremen to join the

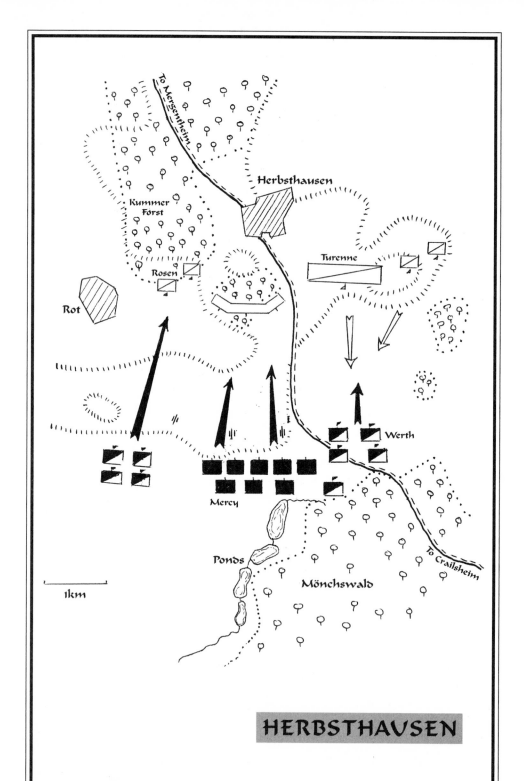

Kummer
Först

To Mergentheim

Herbsthausen

Turenne

Rosen

Rot

Werth

Mercy

Ponds

Mönchswald

To Crailsheim

1km

HERBSTHAUSEN

French. Having reinforced the garrisons in Meissen and Leipzig, Königsmarck arrived on the Main with 4,000 men. The return of the war to the Main area allowed Amalie Elisabeth to revive Hessian plans to attack Darmstadt under cover of the general war. She agreed to provide 6,000 men under their new commander, Geyso, who assembled at Hanau to invade Darmstadt in June.[31]

The Battle of Allerheim

Ferdinand of Cologne sent Geleen and 4,500 Westphalians south past the allies to join Mercy on 4 July, to give him about 16,000 men against the enemy's 23,000. Mercy then retired south to Heilbronn, blocking the way into Swabia. The allied troop concentration soon broke up. One commonly cited reason was that d'Enghien had managed to insult both Geyso and Königsmarck. However, the real cause of the latter's departure in mid-July was an order from Torstensson to knock out Saxony. The instructions, dated 10 May (Old Style), were later copied and sent to Johann Georg to put pressure on him to negotiate.[32] Given Torstensson's inability to take Brünn, there was only a limited period of time in which to intimidate Saxony before the Imperialists recovered sufficiently to send assistance. D'Enghien meanwhile resumed Turenne's earlier plan and marched east through southern Franconia heading for Bavaria. The division of military labour evolving since 1642 was now complete. Sweden would eliminate Saxony and attack the emperor while France knocked Bavaria out of the war.

Mercy deftly checked the French advance by taking up a series of near impregnable positions, obliging d'Enghien to waste time outflanking him. The game ended at Allerheim near the confluence of the Wörnitz and Eger rivers on 3 August. Though it is also known as the second battle of Nördlingen, the action was fought on the opposite side of the Eger to the events of 1634. Mercy had deployed with his back to the Wörnitz between two steep hills on which he entrenched some of his 28 cannon. The infantry, who comprised less than half his army, were positioned behind Allerheim in the centre. The cemetery, the church and a few solid houses were filled with musketeers, while others held entrenchments around the front and sides of the village. The cavalry were massed either side, with Geleen and the Imperialists on the right (north) as far as the Wenneberg, and Werth with the Bavarians on the left next to the Schloßberg hill, named after the ruined castle on the top.[33]

D'Enghien had not expected to find the enemy, but seized the opportunity for battle despite his subordinates' reservations. Königsmarck's departure had left him with 6,000 French troops, plus 5,000 more under Turenne and the 6,000 Hessians, with 27 guns. He placed most of the French infantry and 800 cavalry in the centre opposite Allerheim, while Turenne stood on the left with the Hessians and his own cavalry. The rest of the French were deployed on the right (south) under Gramont opposite the Schloßberg.

It was already 4 p.m. by the time they were ready, but d'Enghien knew from Freiburg how quickly the Bavarians could dig in and did not want to give them the night to complete their works. The French guns could not compete with the Bavarians' that were protected by earthworks, so d'Enghien ordered a frontal assault at 5 p.m. He was soon fully occupied with the fight for Allerheim, leading successive waves of infantry over the entrenchments, only to be hurled back again by fresh Bavarian units fed by Mercy from the centre. The thatched roofs of the village soon caught fire, forcing the defenders into the stone buildings. The French commander had two horses shot under him and was himself saved by his breastplate deflecting a musket ball. Mercy was not so fortunate as he entered the burning village around 6 p.m. to rally the flagging defence. He was shot in the head and died instantly. Ruischenberg assumed command and repulsed the French.

Werth meanwhile routed Gramont who thought a ditch in front of his position was impassable and allowed the Bavarians to approach within 100 metres. The French cavalry offered brief resistance before fleeing, leaving Gramont to fight on with two infantry brigades until he was forced to surrender. Werth's cavalry dispersed in pursuit and it is possible that the smoke from Allerheim obscured the battlefield. Either way, he discovered that the rest of the army was on the point of collapse only when he returned to his start position around 8 p.m. Turenne had saved the day for the French with a desperate assault on the Wenneberg that allowed the Hessians, the last fresh troops, to overrun the Bavarian artillery and hit Allerheim in the flank. Parties of Bavarian infantry were cut off in the confusion and surrendered. Werth assumed command, collected the army at the Schloßberg and retreated around 1 a.m. in good order to the Schellenberg hill above Donauwörth.

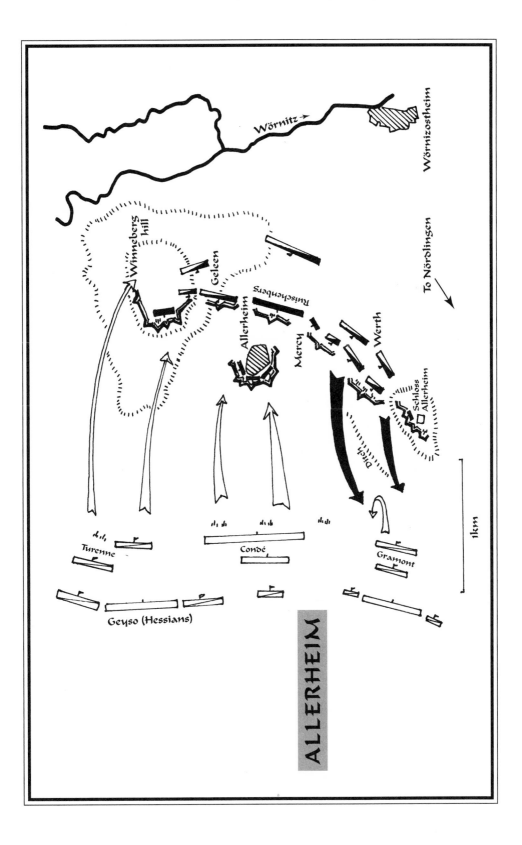

Wörnitz →

Wörnizostheim

To Nördlingen

Winneberg hill

Geleen

Allerheim

Rutschenberg

Mercy

Werth

Schloss Allerheim

Ditch

1km

Turenne

Condé

Gramont

Geyso (Hessians)

ALLERHEIM

Werth attracted considerable blame, especially from later commentators like Napoleon, for failing to exploit his initial success by sweeping round behind the French centre to smash Turenne as d'Enghien had done with the Spanish at Rocroi. Werth defended himself by pointing out the difficulties of communicating along the length of the Bavarian army that probably measured 2,500 metres. His troopers were also short of ammunition and it was getting dark by the time they reassembled. Indeed, the late hour probably proved decisive, limiting what Werth could see. His withdrawal was prudent under the circumstances, depriving the Bavarians of a chance for victory, but at least avoiding a worse defeat that would have wrecked the army.

D'Enghien had been fortunate to escape with victory, losing at least 4,000 dead and wounded. The infantry in the centre had been almost wiped out and the French court was aghast at the extent of casualties that included several senior officers. Like Freiburg, it was the Bavarian retreat that transformed the action into a strategic success, partly because at least 1,500 men were captured as Werth pulled out of Allerheim in addition to the 2,500 killed or wounded. Retreat after another hard-fought battle eroded morale. The Bavarians vented their fury on the unfortunate captive Gramont, who narrowly escaped being murdered by Mercy's servant and was grateful to be exchanged for Geleen the next month.

The Kötzschenbroda Armistice

The immediate repercussions were soon redressed. The French captured Nördlingen and Dinkelsbühl, but got stuck at Heilbronn where d'Enghien fell ill. Mazarin refused to send reinforcements to replace the casualties, leaving Turenne outnumbered as Leopold Wilhelm and 5,300 Imperialists arrived from Bohemia in early October. By December, Turenne was back in Alsace having lost all the towns captured that year.

The stabilization of southern Germany was offset by a major blow in the north-east that indicated that the new allied strategy was working. Though the French had been unable to knock out Bavaria, their campaign in Franconia prevented relief reaching Saxony, which had been left isolated after Jankau. Königsmarck had force-marched the Swedish forces up the Main and burst into the electorate early in August. Johann Georg appealed to Ferdinand, protesting that the Swedes were deliberately ravaging his land. The emperor replied on 25 August that he had just made peace with Rákóczi and help was on its way. It was too late. Before the letter arrived, the elector had already given up hope; he concluded an armistice at Kötzschenbroda on 6 September.[34]

Saxony secured a six-month ceasefire on relatively favourable terms. The Swedes accepted the electorate's neutrality, but allowed it to continue discharging its obligations to the emperor by leaving three cavalry regiments with the imperial army. In return, Saxony had to pay 11,000 talers a month to maintain the Swedish garrison in Leipzig, the only town Königsmarck insisted on retaining in the electorate. The Swedes were allowed to cross the electorate, but they also agreed to lift their blockade of the Saxon garrison in Magdeburg.

Ferdinand Gives Way

Sweden and France had not achieved a decisive military dominance, but their successes at Jankau, Allerheim and Kötzschenbroda outweighed their defeats at Herbsthausen and Brünn. Sweden's separate war with Denmark had banished the spectre of Christian IV's mediation in Westphalia. France's insistence on Portuguese and Catalonian participation at the congress was a ploy to put pressure on Spain. Spain blocked it with a counter-demand on behalf of Lorraine. Representatives from all three arrived, but their credentials were not recognized.[35] Ferdinand was unable, however, to prevent the admission of the imperial Estates. This settled the form of the congress and enabled discussions to move on to the content of the final peace.

The imperial Estates used the Deputation to demand access. Promised by the imperial Recess issued at Regensburg in 1641 (see Chapter 18, pp.624–6), the Deputation finally convened in January 1643 in Frankfurt where representatives of forty territories had been waiting since the previous September. Mainz used its arch-chancellor's prerogative to place discussions about peace as the first item on the agenda.[36] The emperor was happy to let the Estates attend the Westphalian congress as observers but wanted to preserve his prerogative by denying them negotiating rights. Sweden and France appreciated the chance to weaken the emperor by involving all the Estates in the name of German liberty. To their surprise, Württemberg returned their invitation to attend unopened. The others also hesitated to defy the emperor.

Conveniently, Amalie Elisabeth was determined to participate and assumed the role abandoned by the Palatinate as champion of the aristocratic interpretation of the constitution. The Hessian position was even more radical, because their ruler was not an elector and had less interest in the established hierarchy. Buttressing their position with the writings of Bodin and historical examples, the Hessians pressed the two crowns to support constitutional changes. Other than Marburg, all Hessian territorial demands would come at Catholic expense. The Hessians accordingly renewed the old Palatine demand for the Estates to assemble as two confessional bodies (*corpora*) rather than the customary three hierarchical colleges. Sweden and France accepted the general aim of undermining the emperor, but had no intention of supporting specific Hessian proposals if these proved inconvenient later. France was more accustomed to dealing with the electors, but soon embraced the more expansive concept of German liberty and made this the central plank of its first peace proposal in December 1644. The victories of 1644–5 expanded French and Swedish territorial demands, but they agreed in April 1645 to conceal these and instead reiterated calls for constitutional change in their second joint proposal of 11 June. Both were happy to receive Hessian advice on the imperial constitution and had welcomed Amalie Elisabeth's declaration on 30 August 1643 that all Estates should attend even without the emperor's permission.

Sweden issued a general invitation to all Protestant Estates in November, followed by a similar one to the Catholics from France in April 1644. The Hessian envoy arrived in Osnabrück in June 1644 and was soon joined by his Brunswick colleague, but the rest stayed away, fearing that acceptance was tantamount to supporting French demands. French successes like the capture of Mainz (September 1644) made it harder to ignore repeated invitations. In addition, the delegates in Frankfurt were growing concerned at the lack of progress in Westphalia. The new bishop of Würzburg, Johann Philipp von Schönborn, persuaded the Franconian Kreis assembly to back calls for participation in November 1644, and the Swabians followed suit in January. The battle of Jankau prompted Ferdinand to reassure the princes he was serious about peace, but their replies simply urged him to make concessions to obtain it.[37] Elector Maximilian sensed the changing mood and swung behind it by demanding admission for all Estates, including the imperial cities. The emperor finally accepted the Bavarian argument, recognizing that full participation in the three colleges was preferable to the Franco-Swedish option of two confessional groups, since it would allow the Catholics to exercise their majority vote. He had already released Sötern of Trier on 12 April to take the sting out of French demands that made this a precondition for peace. Ignoring growing alarm among militant Catholics who feared concessions at their church's expense, Ferdinand formally invited all imperial Estates to the congress on 29 August.[38]

Then, in the wake of Brömsebro, Kötzschenbroda and Torstensson's second attack on Vienna, Ferdinand personally drafted a set of secret instructions that were sent to Trauttmannsdorff on 16 October. At last, the imperial plenipotentiary was told to begin negotiations on the content of the peace and no longer to use excuses to delay matters in the hope the army could retrieve the situation. Operations would continue, but Ferdinand accepted the inevitability of major concessions. These were placed in a carefully arranged sequence of what the emperor believed he could sacrifice while protecting his core interests. Trauttmannsdorff was authorized to give way in stages until the enemy agreed terms.

The first step entailed giving Sweden the Baltic territory it wanted. Ferdinand had already accepted this by 1643, but now added Bremen and Verden to what could be relinquished. This was a significant step since both were ecclesiastical territories whose loss clearly contradicted the efforts at Prague in 1635 to retain the programme of Catholic restitution. Moreover, Magdeburg and Halberstadt were to be granted to Brandenburg to reconcile it to the loss of Pomerania. The second step entailed concessions at Austria's expense to appease France. These were agreed to satisfy Maximilian who was convinced it was the only way to persuade Mazarin to end the war.[39] Trauttmannsdorff was authorized to surrender Alsace, because this was what France wanted and also because it belonged to the heavily indebted Tirolean Habsburgs who might be persuaded to part with it in return for French financial compensation. Step three entailed abandoning restitution, which was already implicit in the concessions to Sweden and Brandenburg. Here, Ferdinand was prepared if necessary to return the confessional balance in the Empire to 1618, provided the gains in the Habsburg hereditary lands were preserved. The problem of the Palatinate was next, because Ferdinand hoped to avoid anything that would alienate Bavaria, his principal German ally. Trauttmannsdorff was authorized to agree that the electoral title would alternate between the two Wittelsbach branches, or, failing that, to agree to the creation of an eighth title to compensate the Palatinate. Abandoning Spain in a separate peace was the fifth and last step, to be conceded only if peace could be obtained no other way. The campaigns of the next three years would decide how far Trauttmannsdorff would have to go.

20

War or Peace 1646–8

A CRISIS OF CONFIDENCE 1646

Preliminary Agreement

The start of serious talks in Westphalia focused attention more clearly on the choice between war or peace. With the military balance shifting towards his opponents, Ferdinand struggled to retain German loyalty while his generals recovered the strength necessary for an acceptable compromise. He began 1646 with a solid success, scored not on the battlefield but by Trauttmannsdorff in the negotiations.

The imperial Estates had gratefully accepted the emperor's invitation to participate. Though the Protestants and Catholics gathered separately in the two venues, they debated in their three colleges of electors, princes and cities by exchanging written statements. France and Sweden had not wanted this, partly because it would delay matters, but they could not oppose it without contradicting their professed support for the constitution. The emperor regained the initiative as the three colleges discussed the second Franco-Swedish proposal in October 1645. It was obvious that the two crowns were trying to break the Habsburgs' grip on the imperial title. Most of the Estates felt that there was no realistic alternative to the Austrians and endorsed the emperor's interpretation of the constitution in December.

The two crowns ignored this in their third proposal, delivered on 7 January. They wanted to leave the constitutional questions open until they obtained their territorial demands and raised minor issues as a distraction. Some doubt still surrounded the rights of the imperial cities, for example, but the emperor's decision to invite them to the negotiations as well cemented their status as imperial Estates. Most other matters were settled in May when Ferdinand conceded he needed the Reichstag's consent for a formal declaration of war or peace to be binding on the entire Empire. Sweden tried to delay matters further by promoting the aspirations of Erfurt and Eger to be recognized as imperial cities. This was blatant opportunism since its negotiators singularly failed to support similar petitions from Rostock, Stralsund, Osnabrück, Münster, Magdeburg, Minden and Herford, because these crossed other Swedish objectives. Already embroiled in their own dispute with the imperial knights over status, the existing cities refused to admit any new members and all bids ended in failure. The knights also lobbied for a voice in imperial institutions. They were not without influence at that point when over eighty of them were colonels or generals in the imperial army. However, the rather too enthusiastic support by some knights for Gustavus Adolphus had left them fatally compromised and they were happy to settle for imperial confirmation of their existing status.[1]

The fate of the Palatine lands and titles posed a more serious problem. Elector Maximilian realized his own status would never be secure until he obtained international recognition to counter the influence of his Palatine rival's wide dynastic connections. The issue allowed the two crowns to press their own territorial demands in January 1646, though these were only presented orally to minimize the damage to their reputations in Germany. Maximilian swung behind Mazarin's demands for Alsace, presenting this as a defence of Catholic interests on the grounds that peace with France would allow Ferdinand to save the church lands by defeating Sweden. Trauttmannsdorff saw through this immediately, and informed Ferdinand that 'the elector of Bavaria wants to buy French favour by giving them Alsace'.[2] Maximilian persisted, supplying the French negotiators with detailed information about the complex network of jurisdiction and property rights in Alsace. His interest in further military operations was mainly to pressure France into presenting its demands in a form the emperor could accept, and on 7 April he threatened to follow the Brandenburg and Saxon examples and sign a truce unless Ferdinand relinquished Alsace. Meanwhile, Mazarin accepted Maximilian's assurances that Bavaria would do nothing provided Turenne remained west of the Rhine.

The emperor was naturally reluctant to surrender the territory, since giving up Alsace would antagonize his Spanish and Tirolean relations. Trauttmannsdorff nonetheless still had a few cards to play. Despite

Bavarian assistance, the French remained confused about Alsace and acquired a map of the province only in March 1646. By contrast, Trauttmannsdorff could draw on Dr Volmar's 26 years' experience in Alsatian administration. On Volmar's advice, he offered France sovereignty over the impressive-sounding 'Landgraviate of Upper and Lower Alsace', as well as the Sundgau. Since Elector Sötern had already conceded France the right to garrison Philippsburg on 19 July, Trauttmannsdorff included this as well. Other terms, again carefully phrased, suggested the emperor confirmed sovereignty over Metz, Toul and Verdun. The exact status of the other Alsatian territories, including Strasbourg and the ten imperial cities known as the Decapolis, was left deliberately vague. Thinking they had got what their master wanted, the French delegation of Servien and d'Avaux readily accepted Trauttmannsdorff's other conditions in a draft treaty on 13 September. France would pay 3 million livres (1.2 million talers) compensation to the Tirolean Habsburgs, as well as assume two-thirds of the debts attached to their Alsatian possessions. French demands for the Breisgau and the Forest Towns were dropped. Ferdinand withheld ratification in the hope Alsace might yet be saved on the battlefield or by Trauttmannsdorff dividing France and Sweden through a separate deal over Pomerania.[3]

The 1646 Campaign

The military situation nonetheless looked bleak. Ferdinand's inability to send assistance to Saxony convinced Johann Georg not to rejoin the war and instead to extend the Kötzschenbroda armistice. He agreed the Treaty of Eulenberg on 31 March 1646, promising to remain neutral until the end of the war. In return, the Swedes accepted a reduction in the monthly contribution to 7,000 tlr. Saxon neutrality consolidated the buffer zone protecting the Swedish bridgehead. The Swedes could easily block an attack down the Oder that would, in any case, position the imperial army too far east to help the Bavarians. Indeed, it took two small imperial armies most of 1646 to recover the Lower Austrian and Silesian towns captured by Torstensson the year before. The absence of both Saxon and Bavarian support deepened Archduke Leopold Wilhelm's pessimism and the main imperial army remained in billets around Bayreuth in Franconia until May.

The Swedes still held Olmütz as a forward base from where they could either renew their attack on Austria, or strike into Bohemia. Having knocked out Saxony, Königsmarck rejoined the main army under Wrangel that had wintered in Thuringia. Together they numbered 15,000 cavalry and 8,000 infantry with a further 17,000 conscripts on their way from Sweden. The Swedes, however, were reluctant to jeopardize their bargaining position at the congress by risking battle. After long consultations, the generals decided to attack Westphalia as a softer target than the Habsburg hereditary lands.

This decision was also influenced by the delay in renewed French operations. France not only had to rebuild its Army of Germany after the costly 1645 campaign, but did not want to rupture its tacit understanding with Maximilian. To maintain their allies' goodwill, the French delegation in Münster hired General Bönninghausen to recruit reinforcements for the Swedes. Bönninghausen had quit imperial service in 1640, believing his talents were receiving insufficient recognition. He used his former imperial credentials to dupe 2,300 men into thinking they were enlisting in the emperor's army, whereas they actually found themselves in Hessian service.[4]

Wrangel advanced westwards in April, picking up the Hessians and overrunning the weak imperial cordon along the Weser that screened Westphalia. He repeated the tactics Königsmarck had used to intimidate Saxony, demolishing houses, blowing up churches, destroying crops and cutting down fruit trees, murdering and raping those who got in the way.[5] Ferdinand of Cologne refused to be browbeaten, especially as his core territories were still defended by the recently enlarged Westphalian army. Leopold Wilhelm finally arrived from Franconia in June to join Bavarian and Westphalian troops in the Wetterau. This concentration of 40,000 men forced Mazarin to direct Turenne's 8,000 field troops across the Rhine at Wesel on 15 July to bring the allies' numbers up to 34,000. Turenne's advance into north-west Germany was a calculated risk to bolster France's allies without breaking relations with Bavaria. The French arrival accelerated Trauttmannsdorff's discussions over the surrender of Alsace.

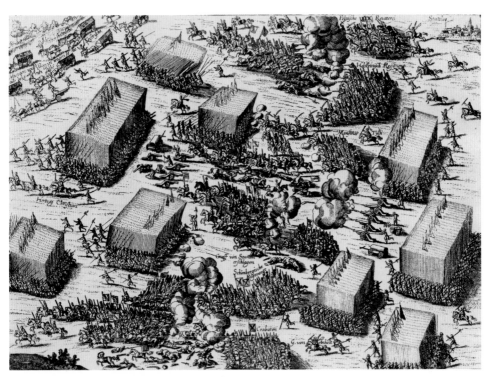

20. The Battle of Stadtlohn, 1623. Christian's army disintegrates as Tilly attacks from the right of the picture.

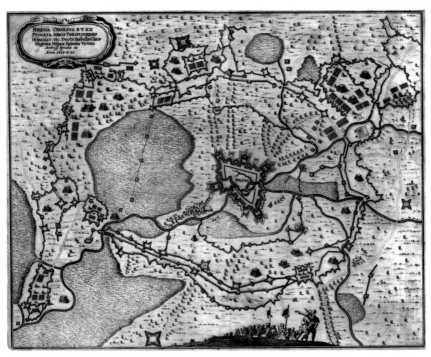

21. The Dutch town of Breda (*centre*) surrounded by Spanish entrenchments during Spinola's costly siege of 1624–5.

22. Elector Johann Georg of Saxony joins Gustavus (*foreground*) in this Protestant propaganda print of 1631.

23. Wallenstein depicted as imperial generalissimo in 1626.

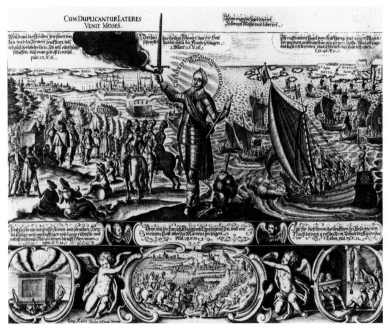

24. Gustavus receives the sword of divine justice as his troops disembark in Pomerania. Protestant print from 1630.

25. Gustavus at Lützen: the king is about to meet his death as an imperial musketeer fires the first of several fatal shots.

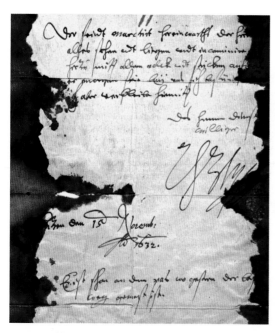

26. Wallenstein's letter stained in Pappenheim's blood (*see p. 510*).

27. Queen Christina of Sweden, aged eight.

28. The Eger Bloodbath, 1634. Captain Deveroux runs Wallenstein through with a partisan.

29. Ferdinand III, a more pragmatic and ultimately more successful emperor than his father.

30. This rather unflattering portrait of Amalia Elisabeth of Hessen-Kassel nonetheless conveys something of her steely determination.

31. Dutch boats rescuing drowning Spanish sailors at the Battle of the Downs, 1639.

32. Maximilian Count Trauttmannsdorff, chief Habsburg negotiator at the Westphalian Congress.

33. Dedication of the Marian Column in Munich, erected to commemorate White Mountain. Singers and musicians perform in the tent to the left.

34. Votive painting commissioned by the six Bavarian cavalrymen shown in the foreground as thanks for having survived the Battle of Allerheim, depicted in the distance.

35. Hans Ulrich Franck's 'Memento Mori'.

36. Peasants' revenge: a
cavalryman is waylaid in a forest.

37. Soldiers plunder a village.

38. The flag of Captain Concin's
company of Count Hardegg's
imperial infantry regiment, 1632,
showing 'Fortuna' balancing on
a ball.

39. The Swedish fireworks display celebrating the implementation of the Peace of Westphalia at the Nuremberg congress, 1650. The emperor held his own rival display.

40. Gerhard te Borch's celebrated depiction of the signing of the Peace of Münster between Spain and the Dutch Republic, 15 May 1648. The artist looks out from the left of the canvas behind the man holding a hat.

The Hessian War

The presence of both armies disturbed the fragile peace between the two Hessian dynasties. Amalie Elisabeth had twice postponed an invasion of Darmstadt – once after Tuttlingen and again in the summer of 1645 as the Hessian commander Geyso was drawn into the Allerheim campaign. Colonel St André attacked from Westphalia in September 1645 but was too weak to take Gießen or the other towns. Like Torstensson in Holstein, the Hessians maintained the fiction they were only looking for winter quarters. The ruse was exposed when they shelled Marburg in late October. The sons of the Darmstadt landgrave were studying at its university along with those of many other princes who raised a storm of protest. Darmstadt indignantly pointed to its 1631 neutrality treaty with Gustavus Adolphus, while Württemberg and Saxony offered mediation.

Amalie Elisabeth risked alienating all Protestant Germany but pressed on, rightly suspecting the two crowns would sacrifice her objectives if necessary at the peace congress. Her Estates refused support, claiming she was ruining the country. The return of Geyso's contingent from Allerheim enabled her troops to capture Marburg on 15 January, but the local officials refused to cooperate, and the university collapsed as staff and students fled. Darmstadt re-raised its army under the command of Count Ernst Albrecht von Eberstein, a Franconian relative of the former Hessen-Kassel commander.[6] The force eventually mustered around 5,000, while Landgrave Georg formally aligned himself with the emperor on 26 July 1646.

The allies received supplies from Kassel, whereas imperial logistics broke down, forcing Leopold Wilhelm to shift position. Wrangel and Turenne slipped past him at the end of August, crossing the Main and sweeping south in two columns through Württemberg and Franconia without serious opposition. Ferdinand of Cologne refused to let Geleen's 8,000 men accompany the archduke as he set off in pursuit. Geleen retired northwards to confront the perennial Hessian raiding on the Lower Rhine, leaving Darmstadt and Kassel to fight their own war unaided. By October Eberstein had recovered all the lost ground except Marburg itself, and launched a counter-invasion of Hessen-Kassel. His defeat by Geyso at Frankenberg on 20 November forced Darmstadt to accept a new truce.

Leopold Wilhelm, meanwhile, had marched eastwards through Bamberg and then south into Bavaria, crossing the Danube at Regensburg in late September. This route was a safe one, but it allowed Wrangel and Turenne to raid across the Lech and devastate western Bavaria. Only Augsburg defied them. Unlike 1632, the city did not open its gates, because its now bi-confessional council rallied the Protestant inhabitants with religious concessions. The city withstood a three-week bombardment until Leopold Wilhelm appeared on the other side of the Lech to lift the siege on 12 October.[7]

The imperial army was exhausted and unable to prevent Wrangel and Turenne from consolidating their hold over Swabia. The Swedes went into winter quarters at Isny near Lake Constance. Patrols had alerted Wrangel to the vulnerability of Bregenz at the lake's eastern end where the surrounding population had deposited their valuables. He appeared outside the pass on 4 January 1647 with 8,000 men and 24 guns. The Klause (defile) by the lake shore was the only viable route over the mountainous Bregenz forest along the Tirolean border. It was blocked by three successive fortified gates, plus a line of palisades up the hillside to the east manned by 2,200 Tirolean soldiers and militia who had spent the previous few days shivering at their posts during a heavy snowfall. They resisted stoutly until a Swedish detachment gained a mountain path and overran the palisades, turning the positions along the road. The defenders joined the civilian population that had already started fleeing that morning. The Swedes broke into Bregenz and took over 4 million florins in booty – 'more than the Swedish army had taken before'.[8]

Wrangel spent two weeks plundering the western Tirol. Unlike Horn's operations in 1633, he had no intention of forcing the Valtellina, which had lost its strategic value. Instead, he tried to consolidate his grip around Lake Constance where he organized a gunboat flotilla that captured Mainau island, another treasure trove of hidden valuables. He then blockaded the imperial city of Lindau located on another island just north of Bregenz, while Turenne besieged Überlingen.

The Ulm Truce, March 1647

The repeated failures convinced Maximilian that the emperor could no longer protect him. He despaired at the woeful condition of the imperial army and Leopold Wilhelm's defeatism. The archduke resigned at the end of December, only to be replaced by Gallas who was incapable of exercising command now and died on 25 April 1647. Maximilian was now 73, while his son was a mere boy aged 9. Anxious about his legacy, the elector pinned his hopes on a general truce to hasten a definitive peace. Wrangel felt a truce would merely allow Bavaria time to recover. The Swedish government also feared France would disengage from the Empire if Bavaria left the war, since the creation of a neutral Catholic alliance was a long-standing French objective. Under French pressure, Wrangel reluctantly consented to talks in Ulm on 8 December 1646, concluding terms with Maximilian's representatives on 14 March.

The terms were more favourable than those imposed on Brandenburg and Saxony. Bavaria was not obliged to pay contributions, but it did have to surrender its Swabian outposts in Memmingen and Überlingen to Swedish garrisons and hand Heilbronn over to the French. In return, the allies evacuated their positions in western Bavaria. Maximilian promised to remain neutral until a peace settlement. Augsburg and the Lower Palatinate were included in the arrangement on the condition Maximilian signed on behalf of his brother in Cologne, imposing upon the latter the obligation to eject the imperial garrisons from Westphalia. The Upper Palatinate was specifically excluded because Wrangel wanted access to attack Bohemia.

Sötern had already confirmed Trier's neutrality in a new treaty with France on 29 November 1645. Anselm Casimir saw no choice but to do the same for Mainz on 9 May 1647. All the electors bar Ferdinand had now left the war, many other princes were effectively neutral and Spain appeared on the point of collapse as revolt engulfed its kingdom of Naples (see pp.728-31 below).

TOWARDS CONSENSUS

The Territorial Settlement

News of Bavaria's negotiations prompted Ferdinand to renew efforts to settle with Sweden. Matters had stalled on the Pomeranian question. Sweden was not ready to risk its standing in the Empire by forcing Brandenburg to give up Pomerania. Elector Friedrich Wilhelm realized Swedish hesitation offered him little security. He was also concerned about his Pfalz-Neuburg rival in Westphalia. As he had snubbed a dynastic alliance to resolve their feud over Jülich-Cleves, the elector only had himself to blame when Wolfgang Wilhelm's son Philipp Wilhelm married the king of Poland's daughter in June 1642. Moreover, with interest arrears totalling over 1 million tlr, there was no prospect of paying the Hoefyser loan from 1616 that legitimized the Dutch presence in Cleves and Mark. As the Republic's garrisons offered more effective protection than the elector's weak forces, this lessened the already tenuous loyalty of his Westphalian subjects.

Fearing he might lose the provinces altogether, Friedrich Wilhelm resolved to acquire a more 'impressive reputation' through a programme of militarization.[9] Much trumpeted by later Prussian historians as the appropriate response, this policy was seriously misguided. It was encouraged by Johann von Norprath, a former Neuburg officer who had defected to become Brandenburg's governor in Cleves and Mark and was bent on revenge against his former master. Brandenburg forces in the region were increased to 4,100, with another 2,900 in the electorate and 1,200 more plus 6,000 militiamen in Prussia. The elector moved his court from Berlin to Cleves in 1646 to be nearer the peace congress. The increased military presence had some positive results as the Hessians evacuated some towns in Mark. Negotiations were opened to win French support, while his marriage to Stadholder Frederick Henry's eldest daughter helped minimize potential Dutch objections. Overconfident, the elector now tried to settle his dispute with Pfalz-Neuburg by invading Berg in November 1646.

The results were other than he expected. Wolfgang Wilhelm had suffered foreigners in his lands throughout his reign. He refused to be intimidated by the new arrivals who soon ran out of bread and went home. All that Friedrich Wilhelm achieved were minor revisions to the last (1629) partition treaty assigning him Pfalz-Neuburg's share of Ravensberg.

The major players had no intention of letting ambitious princes settle matters themselves. Brandenburg's rejection of the by-now very stale carrot of a Swedish dynastic marriage prompted Oxenstierna to accept Trauttmannsdorff's offer to partition Pomerania. Sweden obtained the richer, western part, including Stralsund, Stettin, Garz and the islands securing the Oder delta, on the condition these remained part of the Empire. Exposed by his failed invasion of Berg, Friedrich Wilhelm hastened to make sure he was not left out. The emperor was prepared to be generous, appreciating the utility of Brandenburg support over other issues. He rejected a Franco-Bavarian suggestion to save the church lands by compensating Brandenburg with Silesia instead. In addition to eastern Pomerania, Ferdinand agreed Brandenburg could have the bishoprics of Kammin, Halberstadt and Minden, as well as the archbishopric of Magdeburg when its current Saxon administrator died. The latter measure alienated Saxony, but since that electorate had left the war, there was little Johann Georg could do. Brandenburg accepted on 19 February 1647, acquiring considerably more land than Sweden and enlarging its total territory by well over a third (see Table 5).[10]

Table 5: The territorial settlement

Swedish Gains	Size (km²)	Brandenburg's Gains	Size (km²)
Western Pomerania	9,600	Eastern Pomerania	19,635
Archbishopric of Bremen	5,170	Archbishopric of Magdeburg	5,005
Bishopric of Verden	1,320	Bishopric of Kammin	2,365
Port of Wismar	181.5	Bishopric of Halberstadt	1,705
	16,271.5	Bishopric of Minden	1,198
			29,908

One factor behind Ferdinand's largess was the desire to bolster Brandenburg as a buffer to contain the Swedish bridgehead. Another was that the concessions were part of a remarkably favourable settlement brokered by Trauttmannsdorff. Friedrich Wilhelm dropped his earlier support for the radical Hessian constitutional programme and swung behind the other electors in asserting their collective pre-eminence over the other imperial Estates. Realizing their own status depended on preserving the Empire's hierarchical character, the electors stoutly defended the emperor's remaining prerogatives.[11] Sweden dropped its support for constitutional reform in return for the Pomeranian deal. Mazarin fell into line in April 1647 in return for Trauttmannsdorff's confirmation of the September 1646 agreement to cede Alsace. Both crowns now accepted his face-saving device of postponing discussion of the remaining constitutional issues as *negotia remissa* to be tackled by the first Reichstag after the peace.

Agreement on the Normative Year

The Pomeranian deal dealt a powerful blow to militants on both sides of the confessional divide. The redistribution of ecclesiastical land was in line with a new consensus over the thorny problem of church property. Three solutions had been employed since the mid-sixteenth century.[12] The Peace of Augsburg had used dissimulation in a deliberately ambiguous document both parties could accept without losing face. This reflected the early modern ideal of a compromise peace without clear winners or losers. This ideal guided the Westphalian discussions, where it was increasingly accepted that lasting peace depended on preserving the honour of all signatories. It was equally clear, however, that the settlement needed to remove the more problematic ambiguities from the 1555 Peace.

A second method was also present in the 1555 Peace, which both sides saw as providing guidelines for temporary co-existence until they persuaded the other to accept the exclusive validity of their interpretation of Christianity. The Edict of Restitution attempted a definitive verdict favouring the Catholic interpretation. However, imperial political culture always left room for exceptions to defuse tensions by postponing difficult decisions. The emperor had already extended de facto toleration to Calvinists from the 1560s though it was obvious their beliefs differed from those protected by the 1555 Peace. The Peace of Prague simply added further provisional arrangements by suspending the Edict for forty years. Trauttmannsdorff opened negotiations at Westphalia by offering to extend the suspension for a century.

The third approach entailed compromise on the basis of actual possession (*uti possidetis*) that had also been employed in 1555 through the use of 1552 as a 'normative year' that allowed Lutherans to retain church lands they held on that date. Later problems stemmed largely from the diverging interpretations of these arrangements. Catholics regarded it as a fixed limit, whereas Protestants refused to see it as a barrier to the further advancement of their faith through peaceful persuasion. Catholics countered with the principle of restitution, insisting peace could only be restored if Protestants redressed the wrong they had done by returning the 'stolen' property. This argument under-pinned the 1629 Restitution Edict that Catholic militants still considered valid.

The solution entailed combining restitution with the law of possession in a permanent settlement. This fourth option had already been sug-gested by moderate Lutherans in the decade before 1618. They offered to renounce their elastic interpretation of the normative year in return for Catholic acceptance of the additional land they had acquired in the meantime. This foundered on the Catholics' mistrust and the sheer scale of what they were being asked to relinquish. Nonetheless, the idea gained ground with Darmstadt and Saxon attempts to moderate the 1629 Edict by brokering cross-confessional compromise. Crucially, it shifted the debate from a clash over which interpretation was 'correct', and focused attention on the practical consequences of alternative nor-mative years. Restitution and possession ceased to represent opposing positions, since both principles would apply to each side: Protestants and Catholics would retain much of their existing land while exchanging some areas to restore the situation to the new chosen date.

The challenge was to find a mutually agreeable date. Matters were complicated by the amnesty question, since the emperor's interpretation of the war as rebellion provided the grounds to expropriate his oppon-ents' lands. From Ferdinand's perspective, there had been two wars. The first began in 1618 with the Bohemian Revolt and had been settled in 1629–30 with the Restitution Edict, the Peace of Lübeck and the unrati-fied Treaty of Regensburg with France. The second war began in 1630 with the Swedish invasion and had been partially resolved at Prague five years later. Trauttmannsdorff was instructed to begin negotiations in May 1646 on the premise that the amnesty could only go back to 1630, while the normative year should be 1627 as agreed at Prague. Only as a last resort should he offer 1618 in both cases, though Ferdinand was extremely reluctant to extend the amnesty to the Bohemian exiles since this would imply the Habsburgs had failed to defeat their revolt.

The Swedes backed the radical Protestant insistence on 1618 for both the amnesty and restitution, but France only supported the former as the latter would entail a significant reduction in church property. The deadlock was broken by the Saxon representative who, for reasons that remain unclear, suggested 1 January 1624 as the new normative date for the Empire, excluding the Habsburg monarchy where the situation could remain as agreed at Prague. The proposal encouraged both sides to produce lists of land that would have to be restored, depending on which normative year was adopted. Confessional solidarity was weakened as each group divided internally between those who stood to lose and those who could accept or even profit from the Saxon proposal. By November 1646 it was clear that three groups were emerging. The largest, composed of both Protestants and Catholics, accepted the Saxon proposal. Bavaria joined this group once Maximilian negotiated an additional exception to preserve the re-Catholicization of the Upper Palatinate that only began after 1624. Ferdinand was naturally pleased with the blanket exemption for the Habsburg monarchy, though the guarantees extended by Johann Georg to the Silesians in 1621 were to remain in place to preserve Saxon prestige. The amnesty was settled on the same basis, because the special arrangements for the Habsburg monarchy and Bavaria meant Ferdinand and Maximilian could accept a full pardon elsewhere in the Empire. This would restore the elector Palatine, but permit Maximilian to retain the title and the Upper Palatinate (see p.726 below). Many Lutherans were won over by the more favourable date that ended the emperor's attempts to place a Habsburg prince in Magdeburg and Halberstadt, and removed Catholic claims to other north German bishoprics and the Württemberg monasteries.

The emergence of this broad cross-confessional consensus marginalized the militants as two small groups of uncompromising extremists on either flank. The Catholics were led by Franz Wilhelm von Wartenberg, bishop of Osnabrück, Verden and Minden, who was entrusted with the votes of a third of the other ecclesiastical princes. He was backed by Adam Adami, Benedictine abbot of Murrhardt, who represented the Swabian prelates. Further support came from Dr Johann Leuchselsing, a bigoted magistrate from the city of Augsburg who also wielded additional votes from several Swabian counts. Their collective position was summed up by Carafa, the new Jesuit superior general, who declared 'a peace that will enslave souls is worse than any war and the ruin of souls is more to be avoided than that of bodies'.[13] The papacy had already resolved in 1641 to reject any concessions, not with the intention of preventing peace entirely, but to preserve the legitimacy of the hardline Catholic position in case the situation improved.

The death of Bishop Knöringen of Augsburg in 1646 deprived the group of an important, long-standing member. The rest were compromised by the Ulm Truce that allowed Trauttmannsdorff to claim Catholic Bavaria and Cologne had taken the weapons out of Austria's hands, forcing the Catholic emperor to grant concessions. Bavarian support for the zealots had only been tactical and Maximilian now pushed his brother Ferdinand to remove Bishop Wartenberg from the official Cologne delegation. Elector Ferdinand was careful not to associate himself openly with the concessions, but he now ignored Wartenberg and allowed the pragmatic Paderborn chancellor, Peter Buschmann, to accept the deal over the normative year.[14]

Wartenberg remained at the negotiations on his own account with Adami, but both were isolated. Many of their core supporters were disillusioned. A good example is Georg Gaisser, Benedictine abbot of St Georgen that was recovered from Württemberg in 1630. Though a beneficiary of the Edict of Restitution, he had spent most of his time in fruitless negotiations with Catholic officers to curb soldiers' indiscipline and destruction. The experience led him to reject Adami's view of the war as divine punishment for the Empire's 'sinful' toleration of heresy, instead seeing it as the product of human failings.[15] A more influential case was Johann Philipp von Schönborn, already bishop of Würzburg, who succeeded Anselm Casimir in Mainz on 19 November 1647. He recognized the need to salvage the bulk of the imperial church by making wider concessions, not only over territory, but also freedom of conscience (*Freistellung*) for recognized minorities. His representative spent more time talking to the Protestants in Osnabrück than with his fellow Catholics in Münster. With Austria, Bavaria, Mainz and Cologne backing the moderate position, others like Salzburg fell into line to avoid isolation.

Brandenburg's acceptance of the compromise by February 1647 likewise marginalized the Protestant militants who were already divided due to Saxony's dogged opposition to the inclusion of Calvinists. Johann Georg had lost credit by accepting minority rights for Catholics when he received full possession of Lusatia in the Peace of Prague. Led by

Duke Friedrich Wilhelm of Altenburg, his Ernestine relations saw a chance to reassert their leadership of the German Protestants lost with the transfer of the Saxon electoral title in 1547. Their stance combined confessional objectives with the long-standing resentment of the minor territories at their subordinate place within the constitution. Dr Lampadius, representing Brunswick-Grubenhagen, advocated imposing a *capitulatio perpetua* to fix imperial prerogatives and stop the electors bargaining new privileges from each new emperor. Together with Thumshirn, his Altenburg colleague, Lampadius proposed extending German liberty to ordinary people by granting full freedom of conscience. This was further than most Protestants were prepared to go, especially when they realized it would be difficult to deny Catholic minorities similar rights.[16] Calvinist millenarianism had encouraged many to go to war. Though diehards were still predicting the imminent end of the Habsburg monarchy ten years after the war, most had long stopped believing such nonsense. War had become part of everyday life and had lost its impact as a sudden scourge of God.[17]

The Spanish Succession

Trauttmannsdorff tried to use the growing consensus to wrap up the remaining issues in April 1647, negotiating over compensation claims lodged by Hessen-Kassel, Baden-Durlach, the Guelphs and the Bohemian exiles. Sweden and the Protestant imperial Estates had largely agreed by July. However, Sweden still needed money to 'content' its soldiers, demanding 20 million tlr, whereas the imperial Estates offered only 1.6 million. It also had to pay some regard to the exiles, many of whom were serving as officers in its army. Having previously ignored Lampadius's proposals, Sweden now championed them as another device to force the emperor to improve the money offered to its army.

The real sticking point was France's insistence that Ferdinand make peace without Spain. Spain's position had improved with a draft treaty with the Dutch in January 1647 that suspended operations along the Netherlands frontier (see below, p.734). It now saw less need to grant Mazarin's terms, obliging France to redouble its efforts to split the Habsburgs. Despite the lack of Spanish assistance since 1642, Ferdinand was now even more concerned not to alienate Spain. Philip IV's wife had died in October 1644 and he did not remarry until 1649. Since his younger brother Fernando died in 1641, while his own son followed in October 1646, his Austrian relations were currently next in line to the throne. The situation remained open until the birth of the future Charles II in 1661, who proved to be the last of the Spanish Habsburgs. Madrid appreciated that the open question of the succession gave it far better leverage over Austria than the earlier subsidies.

Philip IV accepted Archduke Leopold Wilhelm as the new governor of the Netherlands. Arriving in April 1647, he remained until July 1656, disrupting the previously good relations between Brussels and the Spanish delegation in Münster. The king also dangled his daughter Maria Theresa as a possible match for the emperor's son Ferdinand, but concealed that he had been negotiating since 1644 to end the war with France by marrying her to Louis XIV. Meanwhile, Spain spun out talks for the emperor's daughter, Maria Anna, to become Philip's new wife. With the succession to the entire Spanish empire at stake, Ferdinand did not want to offend his cousin by abandoning him through a separate peace. Bishop Wartenberg's continued objections to the religious concessions offered a convenient excuse to delay peace and give the generals more time to force France to drop its demand.[18]

Operations During the Truce

Wrangel's concern about the Ulm Truce proved well-founded. France benefited most, as the surrender of Heilbronn at last consolidated its positions east of the Black Forest. Turenne spent the rest of March 1647 eliminating some small imperial outposts not included in the terms, while Wrangel suspended his fruitless siege of Lindau and evacuated his positions in the Tirol. With Bavaria no longer a target, Wrangel headed north-east through Ravensburg and Nördlingen into Franconia, detaching Königsmarck to assist the Hessians on the Main. The importance of the Upper Palatinate's exclusion from the Truce now became clear as Wrangel arrived there to attack north-western Bohemia. He believed all previous invasions of Bohemia had failed due to insufficient manpower and preparation. He summoned the 7,000-strong corps under Wittenberg from Silesia to cross Saxony and join him at Eger, and he fattened his own troops at the Franconians' expense while he waited.

French strategic priorities had changed. Mazarin was concerned that the Spanish-Dutch truce from January would allow Leopold Wilhelm to switch troops to the southern frontier. Secret instructions were sent to Turenne to launch a diversionary attack into Luxembourg. At first his men thought they were simply heading to help the Hessians until Turenne turned left across the Rhine at Philippsburg. By the time they reached Saverne on 15 June it was obvious they were leaving the Empire. Eleven regiments under former Bernhardine officers refused to go any further. The officers voiced the usual concerns about their pay arrears, not wanting to march far from Breisach and the other towns still held by their comrades as security for payment. This time, however, the mutiny had a genuinely popular element, since the majority of the 3,000 men involved were Lower Saxons recruited during the operations there in 1640–2. Like the French who had crossed the Rhine in the opposite direction since 1637, they feared they would never return home. Anxieties were stoked by unfounded rumours that their real destination was Catalonia. Rather than trust their officers, they elected a comrade, Wilhelm Hempel, a former student from Jena University, as their leader and re-crossed both the Rhine and the Neckar rivers later in July.

General Bönninghausen now defected back to the emperor in return for a pardon and was sent to negotiate with the mutineers. Three hundred were won over to the imperial cause, but Turenne re-crossed the Rhine and surprised the rest. Around 1,660 escaped northwards in August to join Königsmarck, who had meanwhile moved to Hildesheim. It was a welcome reinforcement but the Swedish government was not entirely happy, suspecting Königsmarck might become another Duke Bernhard with his own army.[19]

In addition to depriving Sweden of French support, the Ulm Truce allowed the Imperialists to recover. With Bavaria as a neutral buffer, they could concentrate on defending the Austrian lands. Command was given to Melander who had led the Westphalians since 1645. He took over on 17 April, a week before Gallas's death. He enjoyed not only the emperor's support, but the backing of Imperial Vice-Chancellor Kurz and the confidence of the army. A concerted effort was made to improve discipline and overcome logistical difficulties. Incompetent or corrupt officers were punished and each company received a wagon loaded with hard tack packed into barrels to feed it if the regular bread supply was interrupted.[20]

The main force, only 20,000 strong, was concentrated in Bohemia to receive Wrangel's expected attack. Defence of Silesia was left to the Saxon contingent still with the imperial army under the terms of its elector's truce, backed by some Croats and imperial cavalry, while Polish troops secured Oppeln and Ratibor for the emperor. Melander waited around Pilsen, because Ferdinand hoped the 18,700 Bavarians would defect. These were summoned on 8 May to return to imperial authority. Though he assured Maximilian this call was directed only towards four recently disbanded regiments, it was clearly intended to suborn the entire army. It was a conflict between the emperor's appeal to 'German patriotism', and the soldiers' loyalty to Maximilian as their lord and territorial master.

Werth had consistently opposed the Truce, and had felt personally slighted when he was passed over in favour of Gronsfeld to replace Mercy as the Bavarian commander. He moved twelve regiments towards Passau claiming he was looking for recruits. Realizing what was happening, Maximilian placed a 10,000 tlr reward on his head, dead or alive. Bavarian officials refused to give him transport or supplies, but loyal regiments evaded their mutinous comrades rather than confront them. However, most of the mutineers were reluctant to cross over into Bohemia where food was scarce. General Gayling encouraged a counter-mutiny, reducing Werth's followers to General Sporck, 800 dragoons and two isolated garrisons in Swabia that declared for the emperor. General Sparr, Melander's replacement in Westphalia, secured several more garrisons with the cooperation of the Cologne canons who also opposed the Truce. However, local loyalty won out and the vast majority of the men remained true to Bavaria. Maximilian never forgave Werth, giving his position as cavalry commander to Gayling instead.[21]

Waiting for Werth delayed Melander's departure and he failed to reach Eger before it surrendered to Wrangel and Wittenberg on 18 July. Undaunted, he sat across the Eger valley, blocking the way into Bohemia. Ferdinand's arrival boosted morale, and Melander brought off another of his celebrated coups by surprising Wrangel's camp at Triebl on 22 August, inflicting 1,000 casualties and taking 300 prisoners for slight losses.

The End of the Truce

This minor victory greatly improved the emperor's position in negotiations with Bavaria and Cologne. Elector Ferdinand had accepted his brother's truce only with reluctance because it did not include the Hessians. He had no intention of forcing the small imperial garrisons from Westphalia and they predictably refused to go voluntarily. This provided an excuse for Königsmarck to attack once he arrived in Westphalia from Hessen-Kassel, taking Vechta in May and Wiedenbrück in June. Cologne formally renounced the Truce on 15 August, resuming operations with its army under Lamboy. The latter showed his deficiencies as a general in a bungled attack on the Hessians' position in East Frisia that was foiled when the defenders flooded the countryside. By November, he had been driven back into the Sauerland.

Bavarian support was more important if the emperor was to turn the war sufficiently to avoid peace without Spain. Ferdinand had consistently postponed the Palatine question at Westphalia to retain his hold over Bavaria. As talks opened with Maximilian in April, Ferdinand rapidly gave way, concluding a deal in August that represented the first modification to the Empire's fundamental charter since 1356. An eighth electoral title would be created for Karl Ludwig who would recover the Lower Palatinate. Maximilian would retain the more senior, former Palatine title, as well as the Upper Palatinate and 660,000 florins in compensation from the emperor for relinquishing the Lower Palatinate.[22]

As it became clear that France would not offer a better deal, Maximilian renounced the Ulm Truce in the Passau Recess on 7 September. This enhanced his military autonomy, bringing him the Bavarian, Franconian and Swabian Kreise to maintain his troops, as well as command of the imperial units in these regions. In return, Maximilian rejoined the war, but only against Sweden, trusting the tensions between the two crowns following Turenne's departure to Luxembourg would prevent the need to fight France. The return of both Cologne and Bavaria also boosted the imperial cause, briefly raising hopes of a full 'conjunction', or the arrival of Saxon and Brandenburg troops as well.

Around a third of the Bavarian army joined General Enkevort who had been harrying Swedish positions around Lake Constance since Wrangel's departure in March. From Brabant, Enkevort is another of those competent imperial officers military history has overlooked. Out of deference to Maximilian, he avoided French-garrisoned towns like Heilbronn, but retook Swedish-held Memmingen on 23 November after a two-month siege, as well as other less-significant places in Swabia and Franconia. He continued his energetic operations against the Swedes throughout 1648, building a gunboat flotilla to contest control of Lake Constance.[23]

The march of the other 12,000 Bavarians under Gronsfeld to join the Imperialists was delayed by Maximilian's fury at the presence of the former mutineers Werth and Sporck in the imperial army. Eventually, Ferdinand agreed to remove them from active command and they retired to Prague having been richly rewarded. Gronsfeld finally joined Melander in Bohemia on 15 October. Coordination remained poor, because Gronsfeld had never forgiven Melander for defeating him at Hessisch-Oldendorf in 1633, while Maximilian did not want the Bavarians to move too far west into Germany for fear of provoking France. They could neither retake Eger, nor stop Wrangel retiring along the Saxon frontier, across Thuringia and Lower Saxony to the Weser.

Melander followed slowly, eventually moving into Hessen-Kassel in November. Amalie Elisabeth had benefited greatly from the Truce. Königsmarck and Turenne helped her as they passed through on their way out of Swabia in April. With the local balance in her favour, she tried to settle with her Darmstadt rival before the congress imposed a less agreeable settlement. The same urgency had driven Brandenburg's abortive invasion of Berg six months earlier. She failed to learn from its mistake. Her troops likewise scored initial success, taking Rheinfels on 18 July and forcing Darmstadt to agree another truce. Melander's arrival then encouraged Darmstadt to retaliate. Though the Imperialists failed to take Marburg in December, their presence frustrated Amalie Elisabeth's objective.

The other princes were heartily sick of the dispute, regarding it as a private matter that was delaying the general peace. Sweden and the German Lutherans were alienated by Amalie Elisabeth's vocal championing of Calvinist rights, while even her closest supporters were shocked when she revealed the extent of her territorial demands on 25 April 1646. These were opposed by France since they would be at the expense of the imperial church. The congress gave both sides an ultimatum on 2 April 1648 to accept arbitration, which led to a settlement twelve days later. Darmstadt retained a few districts, but otherwise accepted the loss of Marburg and Rheinfels to Kassel. Kassel agreed to tolerate Lutheranism in Marburg, and both would share administration of its university. Meanwhile, France persuaded Amalie Elisabeth to renounce her territorial claims in return for 800,000 tlr, a quarter of which was to pay off her troops.

Melander's modest success had reinvigorated the imperial army which again appeared a credible force, and helped persuade Maximilian to rejoin the war. The tide was still against the emperor, however. Swedish pressure forced France to send a trumpeter to Munich at the end of 1647 to announce it no longer felt bound by the Truce. Bavaria's temporary neutrality had re-emphasized Maximilian's importance to Ferdinand, especially as nothing more could be expected from Spain.

SPAIN'S PEACE WITH THE DUTCH

The Neapolitan Revolt 1647

The convulsions of the Catalan and Portuguese revolts threw Spain onto the defensive by 1643. Thereafter, its energies were consumed fighting multiple fires. It kept these under control, but it could not extinguish any. As soon as progress was made in one theatre, resources had to be switched to deal with a new threat elsewhere. The situation in Italy quietened temporarily as the Castro War diverted the Italian princes, whose armies therefore became unavailable to either Spain or France. Spain's own Army of Lombardy had fallen from nearly 25,000 men in 1635 to 15,000 by the mid-1640s. A resurgence in raiding by the Barbary pirates on the Sicilian and Neapolitan coasts was another sign of Spain's weakness.

Mazarin launched a major expedition in 1646 against the Spanish possessions on Elba and the Tuscan coast intended to cut communications between Naples and Genoa and encourage the princes to re-enter the war. The Neapolitans were known to be restive and Mazarin thought a bold stroke would prompt a rising against their Spanish government. Prince Tommaso of Savoy presented himself as a potential candidate for the Neapolitan throne. The French Mediterranean fleet ferried him and 8,000 men to the Tuscan ports known as the Presidencies that were separated from the rest of the mainland by the malarial strip of the Maremma. Landing in April, Tommaso stalled before the fortress of Orbitello, while his soldiers died from typhus and malaria. The arrival of the Spanish fleet forced him to evacuate the survivors in June.

Despite the setback, the Neapolitans rose anyway in July 1647. Like the events in Catalonia and Portugal, the revolt had both long-term causes and immediate triggers. The economy was distorted by investments in Spanish government bonds that earned high interest when Neapolitan export markets were contracting. Investment spread throughout society, with some holding bonds worth several thousands, but many owning just one ducat's worth. The consequences were felt after 1622 when the Spanish government fell into arrears on the interest, defaulting entirely in 1642. Bonds rapidly lost value. An official devaluation in 1637 alone wiped out over 20 million ducats. The local economy was starved of capital. Small farmers were driven into debt bondage and other forms of dependency. The barons owning the countryside exploited the situation, manipulating debt as a means of social control and using the poor and landless as bandits in feuds with their neighbours. Meanwhile, food supply became a pressing concern as rural emigrants fuelled the growth of Naples to 225,000 inhabitants, making it the largest city in the Spanish empire.

Spain's viceroy was preoccupied meeting Madrid's demands for soldiers and taxes. The kingdom of Naples supplied 48,000 men and 5,500 horses in 1631–6 alone. Though its revenue rose from 4.3 million ducats (in 1616) to 5.8 million (1638), much of the effort was funded by borrowing. The debt quadrupled to 40 million ducats, consuming four-fifths of current revenue just in interest payments.[24] Expedients like the sale of offices spread corruption, especially because the government sold jurisdiction over the smaller towns to the barons. Ordinary people suffered food shortages, debt, corruption and violence, but the political situation remained confused. Local elites were split between those who represented Spain, those profiting from Spanish policies and those who were losing out. Some barons conspired with the French, but most remained aloof, generally concentrating on their own immediate advantage.

The situation worsened as winter flooding, plague and a succession of poor harvests caused famine across much of the Mediterranean in 1647. Unrest on Sicily forced the authorities there to suspend some taxes in May. News of the Palermo disturbances reached Naples on Sunday 7 July when the city was crowded for a religious festival. The situation resembled that in Barcelona seven years earlier as the violence escalated once the authorities lost control of the streets. Leadership of the revolt passed to Tommaso Aniello, a fisherman better known in Italian folklore as Masaniello, who focused popular violence against symbols of general repression. Alongside ransacking the viceroy's palace, the crowd also attacked the bandits used by the barons for their feuds. Masaniello was proclaimed 'king' by his supporters, but was unable to control the escalating cycle of ritualized murders and decapitations.

Unlike in Catalonia, the viceroy escaped death and remained in charge of government. He won over the moderates who were appalled by the violence and had Masaniello beheaded, claiming he was seeking a dictatorship. In the continuing anxiety over escalating food prices, Masaniello quickly acquired superhuman status. The government was obliged to give him a state funeral where it was claimed his head miraculously rejoined his body. He was already compared to Cromwell in the 1650s and was a source of inspiration for the overthrow of the Neapolitan monarchy in 1799. Though the viceroy now lost control of the city, he escaped to the Castel dell'Oro fortress on a spit in the bay. The Spanish fleet under Don Juan José, Philip IV's illegitimate son, landed reinforcements and shelled the city on 1 October, prompting the rebels to declare independence three weeks later.

France was caught unprepared by the revolt. The delay in offering assistance was lengthened by the distaste for aiding rebellion. Eventually, the rebels persuaded Henri de Guise to become their leader. In Rome arranging his divorce, the duke had a distant claim to the Neapolitan throne and offered a more respectable partner for the French. The French Mediterranean fleet arrived on 18 December, forcing Juan José to re-embark his troops. The rebellion then stalled. Mazarin distrusted Guise as a member of the Lorraine clan whose involvement had frustrated the earlier plans to back Prince Tommaso of Savoy. The duke was also unable to assert his authority. The Neapolitans were conscious of Catalonia's fate and were divided over the question of French intervention. Much time was lost in worthy debates over social justice and utopian reforms. Those on the mainland failed to coordinate action with the Sicilians whose own divided leadership was unable to prevent Spain reoccupying the island by July 1648. When the Spanish fleet returned and landed an army, Naples opened its gates on 6 April 1648 and handed over Guise in return for a general amnesty. The French fleet appeared on 4 June with Prince Tommaso, but it was now too late.

The revolt dealt Spain another serious blow. There was no possibility of balancing the budget, and the crown was forced to declare another bankruptcy, suspending interest payments and meeting its obligations with another bond issue. Nonetheless, the feebleness of French intervention and the revolt's ultimate collapse demonstrated Spain's continued resilience. Despite its regional significance, the revolt made little difference to the monarchy's overall position. As always, the Netherlands proved the decisive theatre.

The War against the Dutch

The Franco-Dutch alliance had been renewed on 1 March 1644, each party promising to continue fighting until both were satisfied. A coordinated effort was made to eliminate the Dunkirkers by conquering the Flemish coast. The Dutch provided naval support by blockading each position as it was besieged by a French army advancing from Artois. The fall of Gravelines breached Dunkirk's outer defences in July 1644. The French took Mardyck a year later and Courtrai in June 1646. The Spanish offered stiff resistance, retaking Mardyck in December 1645, only to lose it again the following August. Under d'Enghien, now Prince de Condé, the French went on to capture Furnes in September 1646 and finally Dunkirk in October. The effects were immediate. Whereas the Dunkirkers had sunk or captured 2,029 Dutch ships between 1627 and 1635, the numbers fell to 547 in 1642-6.[25]

Dutch land operations were rather less successful. Frederick Henry faced a difficult task, having to start each campaign north of the Rhine, whereas the French had no natural obstacle between them and the Flanders coast. Like the French, he also had to thin his forces, detaching troops along the frontier to repel possible Spanish raids. He wanted to expand the Republic's buffer to the south and east. The 1626-7 campaign had conquered land east of the Ijssel, while the capture of s'Hertzogenbosch in 1629 widened the south-eastern salient providing security for Gelderland. The conquest of Maastricht in 1632 secured an outpost further up the Meuse and helped disrupt Spanish communications between their remaining positions on the Lower Rhine and those in the rest of the Netherlands. The Breda campaign of 1637 improved the situation further west, offering protection for Utrecht. Frederick Henry's subsequent operations expanded this by taking Sas van Gent in 1644 and Hulst in 1645, giving the Republic control of the western side of the Scheldt estuary.

The 1646 campaign was intended to complete this by taking Antwerp. Sensing their ally was flagging, France increased its subsidy and promised 6,000 troops under Gramont to assist. Gramont managed to dash from France across Flanders to join Frederick Henry as he approached Antwerp. The operation nonetheless failed and the Dutch retreated. The French were angry that the Dutch fleet arrived late off Dunkirk, and Gramont thought Frederick Henry had gone insane.[26] The Dutch retorted with complaints at French ill-discipline and eventually shipped Gramont's contingent home.

News from the colonies proved equally disappointing, and the Dutch now lost the commanding position they had attained by 1644. Despite their tolerant regime in Pernambuco, many Brazilians remained loyal to Portugal and moved south to develop a rival sugar industry in Bahia. Another new colony was founded at Maranhão, north-west of Pernambuco towards the Amazon basin, and together they soon outstripped Dutch sugar production. The cost of defending its new conquests placed the West India Company under great strain and it needed a government subsidy to remain in business. Its share value had already fallen after 1629, despite its continued conquests. By 1640 the WIC's debts had reached 18 million florins and share prices crashed from 117 points to 14 by 1650. Already under pressure from investors, the directors slashed the defence budget in 1644. This coincided with the recall of Johan Maurits as governor and cleared the way for a Brazilian revolt in 1645. Neither side could put more than 1,000 men in the field. Dutch reinforcements arrived in 1646, but the rebels received assistance from Portuguese Bahia and the WIC was soon reduced to Recife and three other coastal forts.

WIC activities seriously compromised Dutch diplomacy by preventing effective cooperation with the Portuguese rebels who were natural allies in Europe, but enemies in the colonies. The Republic did agree a truce with Portugal for the East Indies in 1644 that lasted until 1652. King John of Portugal stopped helping Brazil in the hope that the Dutch would support Portuguese independence at the Westphalian negotiations. However, the Brazilians simply organized their own expedition that crossed the Atlantic in 1648 and retook Angola and Sao Tomé. Though Portugal lost most of its remaining East Indies posts to the Dutch East Indies Company (VOC) by 1663, it exploited the First Anglo-Dutch War (1652–4) to expel the WIC altogether from Brazil by 1654. The company was in terminal decline and was dissolved in 1674.

War no longer seemed profitable to the majority of the Dutch by 1645. The WIC directors dropped their earlier opposition to peace and began considering alternatives, especially as their rival VOC's trade with Asia, Spain, the Levant and Archangel was now worth 50 million fl. a year. Other sectors suffered too. Textiles and agriculture had profited from the slump in the Spanish Netherlands following France's entry into the war. Combined with the sugar boom and the slave trade, this overheated the Dutch economy, symbolized by the tulip craze in 1636–7 as speculators cashed-in on the fashionable passion for exotic flowers. The subsequent downturn made the Dutch less willing to continue paying for the war. There were signs that their famed financial system had reached its limit. Large sums were still raised in taxation, but the armed forces relied on private financiers (*soliciteurs militair*) who advanced captains money to maintain their company or crew in return for a cut when their official pay arrived. Credit depended on prompt repayment, but by January 1643 the seven provinces owed 5 million in arrears. The States General reduced the army's official establishment by 20,000 to 60,000 two months later.[27]

The reduction also acknowledged that the majority no longer shared the war party's faith in total victory. Ironically, Frederick Henry's military successes were his political undoing. The conquest of land beyond the Rhine made the Republic's southern provinces feel more secure. Calvinism had also changed, growing stronger with deeper roots and a more established church structure. Most Calvinists no longer felt like an embattled minority in their own home. Some were prepared to be more tolerant, while religious fervour found alternative outlets in a range of small groups of spiritualist dissenters.[28]

Spain's Negotiations with the Dutch and French

These considerations created a favourable climate in the Republic for Spain's renewed offer of a truce on 28 January 1646. Though obliged to consult France, the renewed alliance of 1644 allowed the Dutch to negotiate separately and the Republic now sent representatives to Münster. Talks opened in May, but led swiftly to a draft treaty effectively offering formal independence to the Republic. Backed strongly by Holland, the other provinces agreed to convert this into a permanent peace with Spain on 8 January 1647. Hostilities were suspended pending formal ratification, but a joint Spanish-Dutch commission already began marking the new frontier on the basis of what either side currently held.

Some feared the Republic would be exposed if it lost French goodwill by ratifying the peace, but most of the dwindling war party opposed the treaty for more selfish reasons. Frederick Henry's impatient son, William II, at last became stadholder on his father's death in March 1647 and wanted a chance to cement his new status by acquiring military glory. The three van Reede brothers who dominated the Utrecht States were sons of a South Netherlands refugee. Godard van Reede, who represented Utrecht at Münster, had invested heavily in the WIC and the arms trade with Sweden. He lived beyond his means and accepted a 100,000 fl. bribe from France to oppose ratification. He persuaded his colleague, Johan de Knuyt representing Zeeland, to do the same.[29] The Republic's constitution made their personal feelings significant, because the founding Union of Utrecht (1579) required unanimity between the seven provinces for treaties to take effect.

The French envoy Servien left Münster on 29 December 1646 to arrange campaign plans for the coming year. He reached The Hague on 8 January, the day that the Dutch concluded their draft peace. The moment was unfortunate for France because its own talks with Spain had stalled, having scarcely moved beyond the exchange of initial proposals over two years earlier. It had become clear that the emperor was prepared to concede France's territorial demands in the Rhineland and that the remaining obstacle to peace was Mazarin's insistence that Ferdinand agreed to neutrality in the Franco-Spanish war. Concerned that Trauttmannsdorff would agree to this, Peñaranda at last offered Spanish concessions in March 1646, but the French regarded these as derisory. Spain increased its offer to include giving Roussillon to France and an amnesty to the Catalan rebels. Mazarin was overconfident, believing another campaign would bring the cession of Artois and Catalonia as well.

French confidence waned during the summer of 1647. The truce along the northern frontier enabled Spain to switch its forces southwards to retake Armentières in June and Landrecis in July. The French commander La Gassion skilfully consolidated his hold over Artois, capturing La Bassée in July, but he was killed at Lens in October. The mutiny in the Army of Germany, meanwhile, delayed the diversionary attack against Luxembourg that had scarcely begun when Turenne was redirected back to the Empire following the end of the Ulm Truce.

The situation also deteriorated for the French in the Pyrenees. Olivares' dismissal produced a more flexible approach towards the Catalans, especially once Lérida's capture in August 1644 enabled Philip IV to offer concessions as a magnanimous gesture. Entering the city in triumph, he solemnly swore to uphold Catalan liberties. This stood in stark contrast to France as it revealed its intentions after capturing Perpignan in September 1642. French laws were introduced into Roussillon as it was treated as Louis XIII's possession. Most of the Catalan elite swung over to support Philip, whose troops repulsed an assault on Lérida in November 1646. Condé was sent to make a second attempt, but was also repulsed in June 1647. Though the French took Tortosa (July 1648), the Spanish remained entrenched in Lérida and Tarragona. The reassertion of Spanish authority in Naples was accompanied by a successful defence of Cremona against two assaults by the French and the duke of Modena, the only Italian prince to rejoin the anti-Habsburg alliance.

Chigi and Contarini, papal and Venetian mediators respectively, managed to restart Franco-Spanish talks in April 1647. It was a sign of Spain's trust in the Dutch that it let them help broker peace. Forty-three articles were agreed on 16 November, leaving just six outstanding issues, of which territorial concessions to France were the chief obstacle. Both sides remained mistrustful, especially Spain that saw a chance to contain France by ratifying its draft treaty with the Dutch. This helped convince the Dutch of Spanish sincerity and they confirmed their draft treaty as the Peace of Münster on 30 January 1648. Spain recognized Dutch independence and agreed to keep the Scheldt closed to trade. The Dutch retained their conquests south of the Rhine, including Maastricht, but without the obligation to respect Catholicism previously demanded by Spain. They also retained their overseas conquests and right to trade there.[30] These were very good terms and were ratified by six of the seven provinces on 9 March. Pressure mounted on van Reede who, in failing health, finally consented on 30 April and peace was formally sworn on 15 May 1648 in the ceremony commemorated by ter Borch's great painting. The last Spanish-Dutch fight occurred in the forests of Ternate island in July 1649 before news of the peace finally reached the East Indies.

France lost its ally at a critical stage. The ten-year-old Louis XIV was only just recovering from potentially fatal smallpox, while his younger brother remained ill. The Spanish government was convinced Mazarin would soon be toppled by French aristocrats who would offer more favourable peace terms. D'Avaux was recalled in March 1648 to satisfy criticism from the princes of the blood. Longueville, who opposed Mazarin, had already left the month before, reducing French representation to just Servien. Ratification of the Spanish-Dutch peace coincided with the end of the Neapolitan revolt. Not surprisingly, Philip IV rejected the draft peace with France on 6 May 1648 and ordered Peñaranda to negotiate an entirely new one. Peñaranda finally persuaded his master to let him leave Münster on 29 June by saying it impinged Spanish honour to leave him there now the main French representatives had gone. Negotiations were delegated to junior officials, reflecting the low priority they now received from both governments.

From Lens to the Pyrenees

France needed a success and Mazarin ordered Condé to secure it, reassigning him to the Flanders front with instructions to capture Ypres. Operations were delayed by bad weather and a shortage of fodder, but Condé took Ypres on 28 May 1648 after just two weeks. The gain was offset by the recapture of Courtrai by Leopold Wilhelm who, as governor, had replaced Piccolomini in command of the Army of Flanders. A French attack on Ostend was repulsed, while the Spanish also retook Furnes on 2 August. Even such relatively minor Spanish successes were doubly damaging, affecting both public opinion in Paris and the French position in Westphalia.

The French army was in tatters, ill-fed and demoralized. Mazarin persuaded Erlach to take 3,500 men from the Army of Germany and march from Alsace to reinforce Condé. This time the troops did not mutiny and his arrival gave Condé 16,000 troops and 18 cannon. Leopold Wilhelm had retaken Lens on 17 August and drew up his 18,000 men and 38 guns on a ridge to the west covered by a marsh. Condé deployed on the plain opposite on 19 August, tired and thirsty. It was obvious the Spanish position was too strong and he began to retreat. Part of Leopold Wilhelm's army left the ridge to pursue, breaking the French rearguard. Their success fatally persuaded the archduke to move the rest of the army forward, which led to a general engagement. Condé recovered quickly, defeating the Spanish cavalry who fled, taking Leopold Wilhelm with them and exposing the infantry as at Rocroi. The French took 5,000 prisoners, having killed 3,000 more for a loss of only 1,500.[31]

Lens was a mixed blessing. The victory boosted Mazarin's prestige and encouraged him to reject the new Spanish proposals. He used the thanksgiving service on 26 August to attempt the arrest of his two most vociferous opponents in the Parlement of Paris. The move failed and simply led to rioting, known as the Days of the Barricades. These started the *Fronde*, or struggle in France for the control of the regency government.[32] Open warfare followed when the Parlement declared Mazarin an outlaw on 8 January 1649. Though temporarily pacified in March, the country again erupted in more serious violence when Condé, regarding himself as the saviour of the monarchy, rebelled in 1650. Mazarin had thwarted all attempts to oust him by 1653, obliging Condé to flee into Spanish service.

Negotiations were to continue in Münster for form's sake until the last envoys departed in March 1649. The Franco-Spanish war lasted a further decade. The duke of Modena had already made peace with Spain in February 1649. Though he defected back to France in 1654-8, the Spanish held their own in Italy. The Fronde prevented reinforcements reaching Catalonia where the French lost support. Plague killed one in ten Catalonians between 1650 and 1654, further undermining enthusiasm for the war. Don Juan José besieged Barcelona from 1651. With no prospect of French relief, the city surrendered on 13 October 1652, accepting Juan as viceroy. Spain recovered the rest of Catalonia, as well as (briefly) Dunkirk and Gravalines in 1652, but hard fighting prevented it from fully exploiting the Fronde. Nonetheless, Marazin was obliged to accept far less satisfactory terms in the Peace of the Pyrenees in 1659 than he could have obtained in November 1647. Spain ceded only part of Artois, plus Roussillon (without the fortress of Rosas) and part of Cerdagne (Cerdanya) disguised, as Philip had hoped, as a dowry for the Infanta as wife of Louis XIV. France was obliged to restore the duke of Lorraine, while it had already surrendered Dunkirk to the Cromwellian regime that had intervened against Spain after 1655. France did not recover Dunkirk until Charles II sold it back in 1662.[33]

THE FINAL ROUND 1648

The Last Campaign

Spain's partial recovery in 1647–8 limited what France could do in the Empire, where the exact outcome of the war remained unclear. It was obvious the emperor was losing, but even a local victory could still upset the two crowns at Westphalia. They had gained ground, but still lacked a decisive preponderance and reports that they outnumbered the imperial and Bavarian forces two-to-one at the end of 1648 are exaggerated.[34]

The proportion of Swedish nationals in that country's army was now much higher, at 18,000 out of 63,000, due to mistrust of the Germans. A major effort was made to improve the cavalry as these represented 22,000 of the 37,500 field troops. The eleven German cavalry regiments that defected from Turenne were reorganized into four larger units, while 14,000 horses were rounded up across Lower Saxony as remounts. The ratio of horse to foot was now the reverse of that in 1618. Logistical reasons continued to propel this, but the Swedes also needed to be mobile to assist their negotiators in Westphalia.

Nearly a third of the garrison troops were left to secure the Baltic bridgehead, while 1,000 held Benfeld in Alsace for political reasons, as the only Swedish outpost in the province coveted by France. Others were spread across the remaining bases, while 7,500 field troops were positioned in Franconia and Thuringia, with Wittenberg and another 5,700 in Silesia and Moravia. Other detachments left only 12,500 cavalry and 6,000 infantry in the main strike force under Wrangel, with an additional 1,500 cavalry under Königsmarck as the advance guard.[35]

The Hessians, still numbering around 10,000, were fully occupied holding their existing positions. This greatly increased the significance of Turenne's return to the Upper Rhine at the end of 1647 with 4,000 horse and 5,000 foot. A further 8,000 French held Breisach and other posts in the Rhineland.

Melander's hardest task for the emperor in 1648 was to prevent a conjunction of Turenne and Wrangel, since he mustered only 10,000 Imperialists and 14,000 Bavarians. Around half his army were cavalry, and there were other imperial and Bavarian detachments in south-west Germany and Bohemia. He ended the 1647 campaign between the upper Weser and the Main, between Wrangel on the lower Weser and Turenne on the Upper Rhine. His position was not only exposed, but also in a region already exhausted by the fighting in 1645-7. He could not move against either enemy without endangering his communications with Bohemia and Bavaria. It was more important politically to confront the Swedes, so Melander planned to draw them towards Bohemia while Lamboy and the Westphalian army advanced up the Rhine to threaten Turenne's communications with France. Cologne autonomy helped frustrate this, because Elector Ferdinand refused to let Lamboy out of Westphalia. Instead, Lamboy continued his fruitless war against Geyso's Hessian outposts for the rest of the year.

French possession of the middle Rhine gave them bridges nearer the Swedish position. Turenne crossed at Mainz with 6,000 men on 15 February and marched east up the north bank of the Main while Wrangel moved south up the Weser to join him. Melander escaped their clutches by retreating south east to Nuremberg. The allied onward march was temporarily blocked by snow and disagreement between their commanders. Eventually they advanced south over the Main into Franconia, picking off minor garrisons. Melander retired slowly, while Gronsfeld positioned the Bavarians at Ingolstadt. The allies captured Donauwörth together, but then parted; the arguments over the Swedes' incorporation of Turenne's mutinous cavalry into their army the year before masked deeper political disagreements about the direction of the war. Mazarin was still reluctant to fight Bavaria and Turenne withdrew north-west to the Tauber valley to benefit from the spring grass and recuperate while the dispute was resolved.

Wrangel meanwhile marched north-east to capture imperial posts in the Upper Palatinate and relieve Eger, which had been blockaded since the autumn. His shift of focus was in line with Sweden's overall strategy of delivering a substantial blow to the Habsburg hereditary lands to force Ferdinand to make peace. However, Swedish generals also saw a renewed attack on Bohemia as their last chance to plunder that country before the inevitable peace.[36] As Wrangel was unable to break through from Eger, he won Turenne's agreement to further joint operations intended to knock out Bavaria and invade Austria along the Danube instead.

The Battle of Zusmarshausen

Melander was too weak to exploit his enemies' brief estrangement, and had received secret instructions not to risk the army. Ferdinand recognized that a victory would now bring only modest benefits at the congress, whereas a defeat could be catastrophic. Melander moved westwards to between Ulm and Augsburg to ease the supply situation and was joined reluctantly by Gronsfeld and the Bavarians. Their combined effective strength had dropped to 15,370 and around 2,000 of the 7,220 cavalry were now without horses.[37]

The allies marched south-west to Württemberg, before swinging back east to Lauingen, a French-held outpost on the Danube downstream from Ulm. They crossed on 16 May and headed south to cut Melander off from Bavaria. Already aware of their approach, Melander had withdrawn eastwards through Burgau to Zusmarshausen. Nonetheless, news that the enemy was actually across the Danube caused alarm when it reached him that evening. He rejected Gronsfeld's advice to march north to confront them, because it was unclear how many were already over the river. Instead, he continued eastwards heading for Augsburg to escape over the Lech into Bavaria. The decision placed him in a position similar to Mansfeld's at Mingolsheim or Duke Christian's at Höchst and Stadtlohn of having to retreat encumbered with baggage in the face of the enemy. He had to cover a 20km stretch through wooded hills between the Zusam and Schmutter streams to reach the Lech valley. Raimondo Montecuccoli was left with 800 musketeers and 2,000 cavalry and Croats as a rearguard, while Melander set out with the rest of the army at 4 a.m. on 17 May.

Wrangel and Turenne had a considerable numerical superiority at 14,500 cavalry and 7,500 infantry, but were hindered by the terrain from deploying this to full effect. The action developed as a running battle with Montecuccoli's rearguard as it fell back along the narrow route through the forest. The allied vanguard of three French and six Swedish cavalry regiments attacked around 7 a.m. Montecuccoli held for more than an hour, before retiring over the Zusam stream once it became clear the entire enemy army was arriving. He fell back to where the forest narrowed at Herpfenried village, intending to resist until Melander could establish another position further on at Horgau. The French cavalry worked their way along the easier southern side of the road and outflanked Montecuccoli. Melander dashed back with his bodyguard to rescue him. The rush to get going that morning had left Melander no time to put his armour on and he was hit in the chest by a pistol shot and killed shortly before midday. Imperial detachments continued to resist, but the fighting became confused as the French and Swedes pushed up the road, capturing part of the baggage.

Montecuccoli's resistance nonetheless bought time for Gronsfeld to get the bulk of the army across the Schmutter just east of Biburg and to dig in on the Sand Hill on the other side. The Bavarian entrenchments had already reached knee height by the time Montecuccoli crossed with the survivors of the rearguard at 2 p.m. Bavarian pioneers then destroyed the bridge before the allies could appear in strength. The French used six captured cannon to support an attempted crossing, but were beaten back. Their infantry were still toiling along the road, denying them the advantage of numbers. Gronsfeld was able to slip away at night to Augsburg, having lost 1,582 casualties, but only 315 prisoners and 353 wagons. Melander's objective had been achieved, but it could have been done with less cost had the baggage been sacrificed.

The allies had failed to destroy the emperor's last army and it continued to repulse probes along the Lech. Gronsfeld had learned from Tilly's experience in 1632 and remained well back from the river, ready to pounce as the enemy crossed. Wrangel wanted to win fame by repeating Gustavus's feat and began sending cavalry swimming across on 26 May. One of Gronsfeld's patrols encountered them and mistakenly reported that the entire enemy army was already across. Gronsfeld retreated to Ingolstadt, exposing southern Bavaria to the enemy as in 1632–3 and 1646. The main imperial army dissolved in the retreat, falling to only 5,000 effectives, with the Bavarians numbering not many more. Gronsfeld had been shaken by Zusmarshausen and the constant

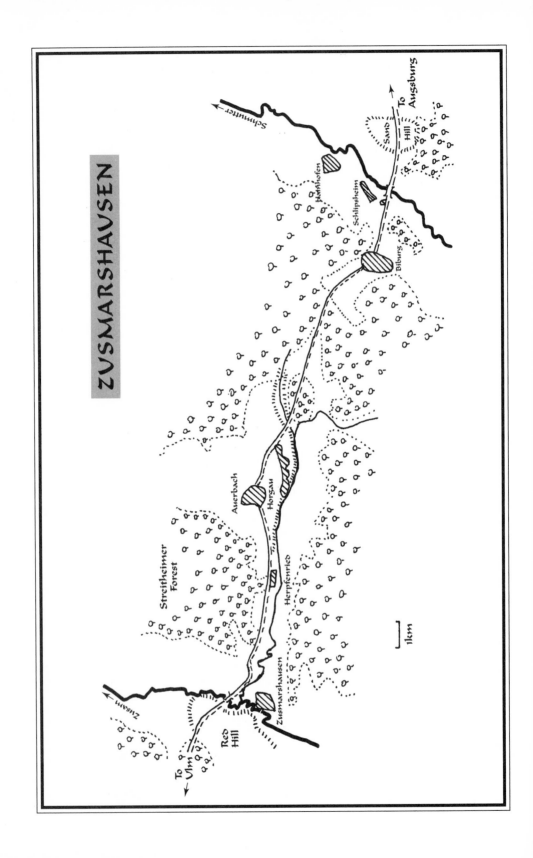

ZUSMARSHAUSEN

Schmutter

To Augsburg

Sand

Hill

Schlipsheim

Hainhofen

Biburg

Streitheimer
Forest

Auerbach

Horsau

Herpfenried

Zusam

Zusmarshausen

Red
Hill

To Ulm

1km

alarms of the previous two weeks. This final retreat cost him Maximilian's confidence and he was arrested along with two subordinates on 3 June and replaced by General Hunoldstein, who was followed in turn by Enkevort in August.

The elector vented his frustration on the army, and commandants of minor positions like Windsheim found themselves executed if they surrendered. More realistically, the crisis prompted him to drop his objections to Werth who was ordered to collect 6,000 imperial cavalry from Bohemia to reinforce the Bavarians. Ferdinand meanwhile entrusted imperial command to Piccolomini who had been without a position since resigning in the Netherlands in 1647. They were all competent officers, but it would take time to reorganize the demoralized army behind the river Isar. In the meantime, Maximilian joined 12,000 of his subjects and fled to Salzburg, where he had already placed his archive and treasury for safe keeping two years before.

Modest Recovery

Wrangel and Turenne invaded southern Bavaria with 24,000 men. Though Munich was spared, the rest of the area between the Lech and the Isar was plundered systematically to pressure Maximilian into another truce. Operations slowed as the generals waited for news from the peace conference. Wrangel then punched over the Isar at Freising. He reached the Inn in late June but found it swollen by heavy rain and strongly fortified by Hunoldstein. Piccolomini arrived with 3,100 Imperialists, followed by Werth and the cavalry on 3 August. Their arrival boosted morale, assisted by Piccolomini's gesture of distributing his own salary to the unpaid troops. The Imperialists now mustered 14,000, while the Bavarians were back to 10,000 with additional militia and garrisons along the Inn and other positions across the electorate. They were on the march by 17 July.

Wrangel and Turenne retired slowly to avoid a reverse that might disrupt the final peace negotiations. Wrangel additionally wanted to deny Queen Christina an excuse to replace him as army commander. In fact, she had already named her cousin Carl Gustav of Pfalz-Zweibrücken as commander of all Sweden's forces in the Empire on 2 June. The decision was part of her complex manoeuvres to resolve the problem of the succession without the need to marry. She recognized the difficulties she faced in persuading her subjects to accept Carl Gustav as her successor and wanted to raise his prestige by associating him with the final victory in the Empire. He had already proved himself a good subordinate under Torstensson. She now overruled objections from the Council of State and sent him with 7,150 native troops to Pomerania in late July.[38]

Despite having to send 2,000 men to redress the situation in Bohemia, Piccolomini continued his strategy of harrying the enemy. This placed Werth in his element. He learned that Wrangel, Turenne and a large entourage had gone hunting in the Dachau woods north of Munich on 6 October. Despite the allies posting 1,400 cavalry around the edge for security, no one noticed additional firing as Werth's troopers attacked, until a Swedish captain collapsed, followed by the lieutenant next to him. Werth had overrun the cordon and was in the wood. The hunters became the hunted. Twenty officers disappeared in the treacherous bogs. Wrangel found himself sinking until, so he claimed, a deer sprang over the marsh showing him the way through. He escaped, but Werth took 94 prisoners and 1,000 horses. The allies burned nearby Bavarian villages in retaliation for this unsporting behaviour.[39]

The Final Confrontation at Prague

The real action had meanwhile shifted to Bohemia. Königsmarck had set out from the Lech on 18 May through the Upper Palatinate and the Eger valley, picking up garrison troops to arrive with 3,000 men in Pilsen on 22 July. His task was to drive a rift in Austro-Bavarian relations by forcing the emperor to recall his army to protect Bohemia. Piccolomini had drained the kingdom of troops to rebuild the main army, leaving Prague weakly held. Königsmarck decided to score a coup by surprising the city that offered the last chance of a really big prize before peace prevented further plunder. He had been contacted by Ernst Ottovalsky, a Protestant lieutenant-colonel who had lost his right arm in imperial service and was disgruntled at the lack of compensation he had received.

Having given Königsmarck an address list of the rich and famous, Ottovalsky guided a party of a hundred Swedes across the battlefield of White Mountain on the night of 25 July to the western 'Little Side' of the city left of the Moldau. He led them to a place where the wall was being strengthened and the workmen had left a pile of earth. The Swedes used this as a ramp to get over the defences, overpower the guards and open one of the gates to Königsmarck and the main body of troops. The Swedes swiftly captured the entire Little Side, including the Hradschin, but Rodolfo Colloredo, the imperial commander, escaped by boat to the other side of the Moldau and the mayor rang the bells sounding the alarm. Prague had surrendered without a fight in 1620, 1631 and 1632, but this had taught its inhabitants what to expect from enemy occupation and they were now determined to resist. Students and citizens blocked the Charles Bridge, preventing the Swedes from entering the larger New Town east of the river.

Königsmarck let his troops loose for three days. They murdered two hundred inhabitants and plundered the vast treasures of Bohemia's aristocracy and clergy, including Schlick's hoard, alone worth half a million talers. Further valuable monastic libraries were shipped to Stockholm to please Christina, along with what remained of Rudolf II's art collection. Those aristocrats unfortunate enough to be caught were held to ransom. The Swedes also threatened to hold the bones of St Norbert to ransom, until they discovered these had been removed to safety. At around 7 million tlr the loot exceeded even the haul from Bregenz.

Other Swedish detachments headed for the honey pot. Wittenberg arrived on the opposite bank with 6,000 men from Silesia on 30 July, followed by Carl Gustav and 8,000 from Saxony on 4 October. However, Puchheim and 3,500 Imperialists beat them to it, racing up the Moldau to reach Prague three days before Wittenberg. The Swedes had expected an easy success and were disheartened by the tenacious resistance from the New Town. Wittenberg temporarily drew off to ravage the countryside, giving the defenders a chance to strengthen the fortifications and drill their militia. It was not until Carl Gustav arrived that the Swedes were strong enough for a regular siege and planted batteries on the north and south-eastern sides of the New Town. Further guns fired across the Moldau from the Little Side, while infantry tried to cross the Charles Bridge protected by a movable barricade. Fighting intensified on 11 October as the besiegers tried to break in before peace was signed. Colloredo persuaded the citizens to hold out. News of the peace arrived on 5 November, but the Swedes continued their assaults for another five days until the advance guard of Piccolomini's army finally arrived from Bavaria.[40] The Imperialists had followed Wrangel who had also headed for Prague in October but had stopped at Nuremberg once he heard reports of the peace. Piccolomini continued his march and by 20 November the entire imperial army had withdrawn into Bohemia. Talks were already under way with Carl Gustav to demarcate the areas both sides would occupy until demobilization could be completed.

Concluding the Peace

The fighting added urgency to the last round of negotiations in Westphalia. Under pressure from Bavaria and Mainz to settle with Sweden, Trauttmannsdorff held separate talks with representatives of the moderate Protestants and Catholics in Johan Oxenstierna's residence in Osnabrück from early March. The remaining obstacles fell away as Trauttmannsdorff extended confessional parity to the Reichskammergericht as well as the Reichshofrat when it judged religious cases, and then agreed to include the Calvinists in the peace. Saxony lodged a formal protest at the latter concession, but still cooperated with Brandenburg in persuading most other Protestants to accept the rest of the deal, while Bavaria and Mainz accomplished the same with the Catholics. Sweden finally dropped its tactical support for the exiles, and accepted Trauttmannsdorff's proposal on 12 June to postpone the remaining constitutional issues until the next Reichstag. In return, the imperial Estates promised to pay 5 million talers as 'contentment' for the Swedish army, which would remain at their expense in the Empire until the money could be raised. The level of compensation had delayed the settlement, yet the loot from Bregenz and Prague alone totalled 11 million tlr, suggesting that the Empire's aristocracy and clergy could have paid the Swedes to leave much earlier. These agreements were combined in a settlement on 6 August that was essentially the Peace of Osnabrück. Sweden remained in the field only because France had not yet agreed peace, and Carl Gustav wanted to plunder Prague.

Given that the Spanish-Dutch war had already been settled at Münster in January, only France's disputes with the Habsburgs remained unresolved. Mazarin presented the Empire with an ultimatum in June: either the imperial Estates excluded the Burgundian Kreis (i.e. Spain's territory in the Empire) from the peace, or France would continue operations east of the Rhine. After some hesitation, the Estates agreed his terms on

9 September, enabling the French and Mainz representatives to complete the Franco-imperial Peace of Münster six days later. Ferdinand was left with the choice of alienating Spain by accepting this, or fighting on without German support. At least the Estates' prior agreement allowed Ferdinand to blame them for leaving him no choice but to abandon Spain. Philip IV was disappointed and issued a formal protest on 14 October that also upheld his claims to Alsace (something which he did not renounce until 1659). Privately, however, he accepted Ferdinand's arguments.[41]

The two treaties concluded the Thirty Years War. The emperor and Empire settled their own problems and those with Sweden in the Peace of Osnabrück (*Instrumentum Pacis Osnabrugense* or IPO) that simultaneously served as a new statement of the imperial constitution applying across the Empire. The parallel Peace of Münster (*Instrumentum Pacis Monasteriense* or IPM) with France was less complete, because it excluded the Burgundian Kreis, as well as the duchy of Lorraine that remained occupied by French troops. It covered Austria's territorial concessions to France, as well as articles confirming the constitutional arrangements agreed with Sweden and the imperial Estates in the IPO. Both treaties were formally sworn on 24 October accompanied by a seventy-gun salute. Two copies of each were prepared for the ceremonies, followed by further copies over the subsequent days that were witnessed by the envoys to ensure no changes were slipped in. These were despatched to the relevant courts, while at least another 42,000 copies were printed for an eager public over the coming year.[42]

PART THREE

Aftermath

21

The Westphalian Settlement

THE INTERNATIONAL DIMENSION

Westphalia and World History

Interpretations of the peace settlement have broadly assumed one of two positions. Political scientists are generally positive, seeing the treaties as the birth of the modern international order based on sovereign states. Historians have, until recently, been largely negative, claiming 'the war solved no problem. Its effects, both immediate and indirect, were either negative or disastrous. Morally subversive, economically destructive, socially degrading, confused in its causes, devious in its course, futile in its result, it is the outstanding example in European history of meaning-less conflict.'[1]

The general conclusion of German historians was that 'the Empire in its former sense had ceased to exist'.[2] 'Germany' was supposedly no longer a nation but a loose collection of independent principalities. Austria pursued a separate existence, becoming a great power through expansion in the Balkans at the Ottomans' expense after 1683, as well as acquisition of Spain's former possessions in the Netherlands and Italy in 1700. It allegedly neglected 'German' affairs until challenged by Frederick the Great of Prussia in 1740. As with much of the received interpretation of German history, this is a distortion articulated by those favouring national unification under Prussian leadership during the 1860s. Traces of this remain today, and the most recent edition of the standard history of the Westphalian settlement describes 1648 as 'one of the years of greatest catastrophe' in German history.[3]

These problems of interpretation derive from misconceptions sur-rounding the character of both the war and the peace. The Thirty Years

War was not a general European, let alone global conflict. The dates 1618–48 make little sense as a frame for the history of countries outside Central Europe, and nor can the Empire's war be fitted into a general, global crisis.[4] Other countries certainly experienced major upheavals. The Mughal emperor Shah Jahan retired grief-stricken at his wife's death, precipitating civil war between his sons across India in 1657–8. The last Han Chinese emperor hanged himself as the Manchurians overran China in 1644. Despite the presence of some European traders, these events remained unconnected with those in the Spanish and Austrian empires. Likewise, turmoil elsewhere was not indefinite or without results. The Mughal empire did not collapse, while the new Manchurian Qing dynasty asserted China's authority over Mongolia, Tibet and Turkestan. Upheaval in Japan after 1600 was followed by relative stability under the Tokugawa shogunate and a prolonged period of international isolation from 1639 to 1858.

Spain's conflicts with the Dutch, French, Portuguese and English did see fighting in Brazil, parts of Africa, Sri Lanka and Indonesia. The period also witnessed the development of European trading companies and the growing involvement of previously minor players in overseas ventures. Foremost were the English, who established themselves in Virginia and other parts of North America's Atlantic coast by the 1620s, and then penetrated the Caribbean and established a presence in Madras in 1639. Unlike the treaties ending the War of the Spanish Succession (1701–14) or the Seven Years War (1756–63), those of Westphalia did not settle these colonial conflicts, though Spain's Treaty of Münster did end the fighting in the Dutch East Indies. Neither the Thirty Years War proper nor the associated Spanish-Dutch and Franco-Spanish wars, can match claims made for the Seven Years War for the dubious honour of being labelled the true first world war.[5] On closer inspection, even this later alleged world war mirrors the seventeenth-century experience as a conflict exported by Europeans, rather than one involving non-European states as full belligerents.

The negative assessment of Westphalia has some sense when measuring the terms against the framers' aspirations for European peace. Clearly, it did not end all European wars, or prevent new conflicts occurring soon after. The Franco-Spanish war lasted until 1659, and while the Catalans lost their independence struggle in 1652, the Portuguese eventually won theirs in 1668. The continuation of these conflicts represents real failures, since all three struggles were on the congress's agenda. However, no attempt was made to end the British Civil Wars or the Veneto-Turkish conflict that started in 1645. Baltic tensions had been checked at the Peace of Brömsebro in 1645, but erupted again with wars between Sweden, Poland and Russia after 1655, as well as three further Swedish-Danish struggles that lasted into the eighteenth century. Those who stretch the Thirty Years War to encompass all European conflicts argue that the Franco-Spanish Peace of the Pyrenees (1659) and the general Baltic settlement at Oliva (1660) mark Westphalia's real conclusion.[6] This raises the same problem encountered in explaining the origins of the Thirty Years War, since the causes, course and conclusion to these struggles were all distinct and the fact that some countries participated in more than one does not make them into a single general war.

Westphalia's significance lies not in the number of conflicts it tried to resolve, but in the methods and ideals it applied. The first article of both the IPO and IPM stated they were instruments of a 'Christian, general and permanent peace' intended to establish lasting friendship across the continent. This was more than merely a statement of good intentions. The congress offered a new charter for European relations. The sections on the imperial constitution did refer to the Empire's earlier settlements of 1552 and 1555, but otherwise the documents made no mention of other European treaties, instead offering a new framework for peace. The treaties ending other wars were regarded as extensions to Westphalia, pacifying additional parts of the continent. The Westphalian treaties continued to be invoked in major European settlements up to the Congress of Vienna in 1814–15 that ended the Napoleonic Wars. These later settlements rested on the same understanding of international law as a voluntary contract superior to all existing secular and religious law.[7]

Like many important innovations, the intentions behind this development were more modest than its effects, since the relevant articles about international law were there simply to thwart the expected papal protest. The pope was not the only one to object. Spain and Lorraine protested at their exclusion from the IPM, Saxony objected to the inclusion of the Calvinists in the IPO, Bishop Wartenberg rejected the religious concessions in general, while Mainz, Magdeburg and others raised specific points.[8] Eighteen territories failed to sign, because they were not represented at the congress. However all, including Wartenberg, accepted the general validity of the treaties. Only the pope rejected the entire settlement in his decree *Zelo domus Dei*, which he issued in August 1650 but backdated to 26 November 1648 to reaffirm his envoy Chigi's earlier verbal protests.[9]

The positive interpretation of Westphalia regards it as the birth of the modern international order based on sovereign states interacting (formally) as equals within a common secularized legal framework, regardless of size, power or internal configuration. The classic 'Westphalian state' rests on indivisible sovereignty that both excludes external agencies and does not share the exercise of internal governance with other domestic bodies. In addition, it possesses well-demarcated, non-porous borders, and a common identity and culture among its inhabitants. The latter element assumed greater significance in the nineteenth century when the ideal of each nation with its own state was propagated; a factor contributing to conflicts to expel minorities or extend frontiers to include those sharing language and culture currently under 'foreign rule'.

Handbooks of international relations and diplomatic history still routinely take 1648 to frame their discussions, but historians and most political scientists are no longer so confident in asserting the date as a turning point.[10] One reason is that the development of this new order was clearly a lengthy process, beginning well before 1648 and continuing long after. Another is that the nation state no longer appears the final destination of political development. One recent study of the European Union presents it not as a single, centralized Westphalian super-state, but as a 'neo-medieval empire', with the process of integration re-modelling the continent along lines not dissimilar to the Holy Roman Empire.[11]

These are important points that nonetheless do not detract from Westphalia's significance as a general marker for international development. Europe remained a hierarchical, fragmented international system after 1648, but was clearly moving towards a secular order based on more equal, sovereign states. By pacifying Central Europe, the peace treaties of 1648 provided sufficient stability to build a new international order on these principles.[12] This model assumed global significance through its articulation in theories of international relations and by its use by western colonial powers in their dealings with other parts of the world.

The Empire and Europe

The negative historical assessment of Westphalia is correct in the general sense that the settlement confirmed a decline in the Empire's size and international standing. This was neither as sudden nor as decisive as German historians once thought. The issue of Dutch and Swiss 'independence' illustrates this. Spain renounced rule over the Dutch in the first article of its Treaty of Münster, but the word 'sovereignty' appears only in the English translation of the original text.[13] Spain also accepted Dutch neutrality towards the Empire. The emperor recognized that the Dutch would not contribute to imperial defence in 1653, but neither he nor the Reichstag accepted that the Republic was no longer part of the Empire until 1728. The Swiss were included in both the IPO and IPM thanks to the lobbying of the Basel mayor, Johann Wettstein. Wettstein attended the congress because Basel had joined the Swiss Confederation in 1501, two years after Emperor Maximilian I had been forced to free the Swiss from their obligations to contribute to imperial defence and conflict resolution. Basel wanted a similar exemption so that it would no longer have to pay for imperial institutions; upkeep of the Reichskammergericht alone cost the city 14,239 talers in 1647. Emperor Ferdinand III granted Basel's request, but neither the Westphalian treaties nor the 1499 peace formally ended Switzerland's incorporation within the Empire.

The remaining ties appear unimportant. Neither the Dutch nor the Swiss participated as imperial Estates in imperial politics and they felt no obligation to assist the emperor, though the Dutch were generally allies of Austria after 1673. Nonetheless, the absence of clear statements indicates the lingering sense of the Empire as embodying the ideal of a single European political community. Zurich finally removed the imperial coat of arms from its town hall in 1698, while Schaffhausen considered itself part of the Empire until 1714. Savoy failed to recover Pinerolo from France or to gain electoral status, yet it also remained part of the Empire, regarding its loose association with the organization north of the Alps as useful additional security in an uncertain international situation.[14]

Both the IPO and IPM combined revisions to the imperial constitution with the international settlement and placed Sweden and France as guarantors of the new order within the Empire. The older assessment that this left the Empire at the two crowns' mercy no longer holds. Both powers were entitled to intervene only if the imperial Estates were unable to resolve a dispute amicably within three years. Intervention still depended on an invitation from the injured party. These formal rights added little to either power's ability to influence imperial affairs, which still depended on its own military potential and its diplomatic standing within the Empire.

Trier's example illustrates the rapid decline of French influence after 1648. Sötern's restoration as elector had been the chief justification for French intervention after 1635. He was reinstated but had little authority over his subjects. Dependent on French support, he agreed to support Mazarin's candidate as coadjutor in April 1649. Most of the cathedral canons rebelled, and raised a few hundred troops with Austrian and Spanish backing. Mazarin was distracted by the Fronde and conscious his interference in Trier was damaging France's reputation in Germany. Abandoned by France and now bedridden, Sötern was powerless to prevent the installation of a pro-imperial coadjutor, who succeeded him after his death in February 1652.[15]

France made use of its guarantor powers during a dispute between Mainz and the Palatinate in the early 1660s, but Louis XIV's subsequent aggression ensured no one afterwards was prepared to risk appealing for French help.[16] Philippsburg was recaptured in 1676, and though lost again to France in 1688, it was recovered permanently nine years later. Austria also regained Breisach, pushing the French presence back across the Rhine. France then used its military strength to impose its own interpretation of Westphalia in a process known as the Reunions (1679–84) that saw the annexation of Strasbourg and the other territories saved for the Empire by Volmer and Trauttmannsdorff's ambiguous terms. France also conquered the Franche-Comté in the 1670s and eventually acquired Lorraine in 1766.

France always denied these gains were part of the Empire since this would imply its king was subordinate to the emperor. It preferred to sacrifice the formal influence of constitutional rights to retain the freedom to ally with groups of princes when necessary. Gradually, France upgraded its partners, moving from an alliance of smaller principalities in 1658–68 to rely on Bavaria by the late seventeenth century, then Prussia and finally Austria after 1756. These changes reflected a shift in policy towards the emperor as France switched from using the constitution to contain a perceived Habsburg threat to upholding the existing order to preserve its major European ally.[17]

Sweden followed a similar course, but more immediately and for different reasons. Unlike France, Sweden accepted its gains as full imperial Estates, giving it representation in the Reichstag as well as the Lower and Upper Saxon assemblies. The Swedish monarch thus acted like the Danish king who was represented in imperial institutions as the duke of Holstein. Swedish authority remained curtailed by imperial law. It was granted exemption from the imperial courts equivalent to that enjoyed by the electors, but was obliged to establish its own tribunal in Wismar to uphold imperial law. In practice, this entailed leaving the existing legal systems in place and respecting the privileges of the Estates in its new territories. Taxes increased, but they were spent locally on maintaining garrisons of German professionals. No effort was made to introduce the national conscription practised in Sweden and Finland. Religious affairs also remained in local hands, with church management and theological matters handled by a German consistory.[18]

Ferdinand III was unable to prevent the incorporation of the remaining mediate church property (see below), but did thwart Swedish efforts to extend possession of the archbishopric of Bremen to include the city as well. Immediately after the conquest of the archbishopric in 1645, the emperor confirmed the city's status in return for a much needed 100,000 florins. Sweden objected belatedly in 1654, but significantly did not push matters to an open breach.[19] Whereas its representatives had posed as self-confident executors of Gustavus Adolphus's glorious legacy during the Westphalian congress, they now sought closer collaboration with the emperor to preserve Sweden's existing possessions. Their vulnerability was exposed when Brandenburg and Denmark attacked Sweden once it embroiled itself in the Northern War with Poland (1655–60). Sweden's relative decline became clearer after 1675 when it was cajoled by France into trying to invade Brandenburg during Louis XIV's Dutch War (1672–9). As a result, a combination of Brandenburg, Denmark, Münster and the Guelphs swiftly conquered all of Sweden's German possessions and it was only thanks to French intervention at the peace of 1679 that they were returned.

The Empire's protective framework already demonstrated its utility with the neutralization of north-western Germany that safeguarded Bremen and Verden during 1655–60. Sweden responded by sending a contingent to assist the emperor repel an Ottoman attack in 1664. More troops and money followed during the Great Turkish War of 1683–99 that saw the Habsburg conquest of Ottoman Hungary and Transylvania. King Charles XII's intervention in the Empire in 1705–7 was likened by the press to a return of Gustavus, not least because the Swedes overran Saxony in their efforts to conquer Poland. However, Charles's subsequent defeat in Russia (in 1709) again exposed his German possessions and led to the permanent loss of Bremen and Verden to Hanover by 1714. Sweden retained Wismar and western Pomerania, but saw the preservation of the imperial constitution as a primary safeguard and for this reason joined France to back Austria against Prussia during the Seven Years War. By now, Sweden was one of the chief supporters of the established order. In contrast to Bavaria and other south German states that joined Napoleon, Sweden's King Gustavus IV bitterly opposed the Empire's dissolution in 1806 and told his German subjects he hoped it would be restored.[20]

A CHRISTIAN PEACE

The Religious Settlement

It is a common misconception to see Westphalia as bringing peace by taking religion out of politics.[21] Though it promoted secularization in the longer term, it was not a fully secular peace. The Empire remained Holy in the sense of Christian. Toleration was extended only to include Calvinists. Other dissenters, along with Orthodox Christians, Jews and Muslims, were denied similar constitutional rights.

Westphalia formally endorsed the Peace of Augsburg, but addressed its shortcomings by modifying it within a permanent settlement. Article V, paragraph 50 of the IPO forbade any attempt to question the religious peace or derive contradictory interpretations of it. Any future difficulties were to be resolved through the process of 'amicable composition' already favoured by moderates prior to 1618. This is the reason behind the change to the constitution to allow discussion as two confessional bodies, rather than the customary three hierarchical colleges. Known as *itio in partes*, this practice was reserved for religious issues and not, as the earlier radical Protestant programme intended, for all matters.

The significance of this change was reduced by the adoption of 1 January 1624 as the new normative date, since this fixed the official faith of each territory as it had been on that day. The new arrangements significantly curtailed princely prerogatives. Rulers retained the 'right of Reformation' granted in 1555, but only as supervision of their territorial churches. They were no longer able to impose their own theological beliefs on their subjects. Any subsequent conversion was to remain a private matter. Rulers gained personal freedom of conscience but lost a key aspect of their political authority. This removed much of the controversy surrounding the ecclesiastical reservation that was formally confirmed but now became largely irrelevant because further secularization had been ruled out.

Only the Habsburgs retained the full right of Reformation in its previous form, because the IPO merely obliged them to respect the Protestant faith of the Lower Austrian nobility, the city of Breslau, and the Silesian princes and their tenants. Elsewhere, they remained free to suppress Protestant minorities, even if these had existed in 1624. In addition, Article IV, paragraph 53 expressly confirmed the confiscation of rebel property in Bohemia and Austria, and exempted Habsburg possessions from the checks imposed on the rulers of other territories. Ferdinand III and his successors were free to continue extending their authority over their subjects by promoting Catholicism and fostering a loyal aristocracy. Whereas half of Europe had been under Protestant rule in 1590, that proportion fell to a fifth a century later with the most significant Catholic gains made in the Habsburg monarchy.[22]

The constitutional changes safeguarded political equality elsewhere between the three recognized confessions and extended a wide range of personal freedoms to their adherents. Religious discrimination was banned from commercial companies, guilds, societies, hospitals, burial grounds, schools and universities and in inheritance law. Nonetheless, this stopped short of full toleration in the modern sense. Instead, three levels of religious freedom received constitutional guarantees. The new normative year associated each territory with one of the three confessions. Adherents received full rights of public worship, complete with processions, bells, church spires, feast days and the other trappings required by their particular doctrine. Those minorities with official recognition in the territory on 1 January 1624 received lesser rights of private worship, denying them, among other things, the right to summon their followers by ringing bells, or processing in public. Minorities without recognized rights in 1624 were granted reduced rights of domestic worship, allowing them to practise their faith within their own homes and to visit churches in neighbouring territories.

Toleration was thus not based on individual equal rights but on membership of a community with corporate rights. All people received legal protection, but this was less extensive for those belonging to the third category of unofficial minorities. The authorities were encouraged to display 'patient toleration' towards such groups, but their powers under the 1555 Peace to expel them were confirmed, subject to three years' notice to sell their property and leave.[23] Despite the uneven distribution of rights, they were more extensive and better secured than those in other countries, because they were embedded in a judicial system that did not depend on the arbitrary power of a centralized state. Even the famously tolerant Dutch Republic offered no legal protection for those dissenting from Calvinism.

The arrangements worked because they were a genuine compromise that brought gains for Catholics and Protestants alike. The Protestants had defeated the hated Edict of Restitution by securing 1624 as a more favourable normative year, and enhancing their political position through greater confessional parity in imperial institutions. The Calvinists finally secured full protection under imperial law, and the Catholics upheld their inflexible interpretation of the Religious Peace by obliging Protestants to renounce further claims to church land. The ecclesiastical reservation was confirmed, but now cut both ways with Catholics accepting that former church land would remain secularized even if its ruler converted from Protestantism. Though the losses entailed by 1624 were painful, that date was considerably better than those originally proposed by the Protestants, who were obliged to restore the property taken after Swedish intervention. This reconciled Catholics to the rules permitting freedom of conscience, especially as their right to expel dissenters had been confirmed.

Rather than secularizing politics, the Thirty Years War discredited the use of force to obtain confessional or political objectives within the Empire. Confessional militancy did persist after 1648, personified by Christoph Bernhard von Galen who was known as the 'cannon bishop' of Münster for his attempts to impose his authority over his largely Protestant capital city.[24] Galen had some success, but was increasingly

THE WESTPHALIAN SETTLEMENT

out of step with the more moderate Catholics represented by Schönborn of Mainz, the dominant figure in the imperial church until his death in 1673. Schönborn promoted long-standing efforts to reconcile German Christians within a national church that would finally banish the threat of secularization of the ecclesiastical territories. This programme was picked up by others, notably after the mid-eighteenth century when the Catholic church lands often embraced more progressive social reforms than their 'enlightened' Protestant neighbours. It failed, because secular Catholic rulers, including those of Austria and Bavaria, increasingly regarded the imperial church as a convenient arena for their territorial ambitions and withdrew support for its autonomous existence during the Empire's last reorganization in 1802–3.[25]

Other practical impulses encouraged moderation. The need to repopulate territories after 1648 encouraged rulers to relax insistence on confessional conformity. Already by 1662, the counts of Neuwied extended toleration to Christian sectarians by issuing their own legislation that went beyond the basic rights guaranteed by imperial law. Other minor territories extended toleration to Jews on the same basis. Moreover, many rights were open to people regardless of religion. For example, Jews could prosecute Christians in the imperial courts on the basis of property law. This complex web of legal rights combined, in some cases at least, with a more genuine spirit of toleration to offer a range of freedoms largely absent elsewhere in Europe: the Jewish inmates of the Hamburg workhouse were allowed to observe the Sabbath, for instance.[26]

The Empire's religious settlement thus offered an alternative route to the more common path towards a modern secular society provided by a centralized state. Both routes had drawbacks. Centralized states imposed official uniformity through an established church and then widened opportunities for others through limited toleration. In most cases, gradual pluralism led eventually to the disestablishment of the official church, as in the modern French Republic where the state is fully secular. The disadvantage of this approach has been the long purgatory of persecution endured by dissenting minorities whose limited freedoms came as gifts from above from a state that could revoke them, as the French monarchy chose to do with the abolition of the Huguenots' religious freedoms in 1685. The Empire took a different direction, accepting three privileged churches with equal status. This reduced official persecution and intolerance, while creating greater opportunities for mutual understanding, especially as national identity was not primarily linked to a particular creed. Its drawback lay in rooting religious freedom in a web of corporate rights, and thus in a conservative social order that saw the rule of law, not democracy, as the guarantee for stability.

The Nuremberg Execution Congress

The preceding becomes clearer when we examine how the peace treaties were implemented. Their success lay not in settling every dispute, but providing guidelines to defuse conflict peacefully. The IPO had deliberately postponed a range of contentious issues to bring the war to a conclusion. These problems were not ignored, however. One important example was the normative year, where the IPO established a basic rule but left it to the emperor and imperial Estates to work out the detailed implementation together. Likewise, the treaty specified the amount of compensation to be paid to Sweden and Hessen-Kassel, but did not provide a detailed schedule for troop withdrawal. Tight deadlines were imposed: implementation of the normative year was to be completed within two months, while the Reichstag was to convene within six to debate the postponed constitutional issues, by when demobilization was also supposed to have been completed.

All three deadlines were missed. The peace was ratified on 18 February 1649, but it was not until 1654 that the last foreign garrison was removed. The Reichstag met three years late in June 1653 and concluded with an imperial Recess in May 1654 that still left many important matters open.[27] An imperial decree entrusted implementation of the normative year to the Kreis convenors on 7 November 1648, but some cases were still pending when the Empire was dissolved in 1806. It is easy to see why many have considered the peace a failure and the Empire an empty shell after 1648. However, the unrealistic timetable reflected the widespread impatience to restore peaceful relations and prevent a resumption of hostilities. These basic objectives were achieved, even if the details took longer to finalize.

The Reichstag was delayed by Sweden's reluctance to relinquish eastern Pomerania to Brandenburg. Appreciating the advantages of Brandenburg goodwill, Ferdinand III withheld formal enfeoffment from

Queen Christina, preventing her from exercising the constitutional rights associated with her German possessions. She gave way in May 1653, surrendering eastern Pomerania in return for half its toll revenue, clearing the way for her investiture. Her representative at last travelled to Regensburg where the emperor and other delegates had been waiting with growing impatience.

The more pressing matters of troop withdrawal and the normative year had meanwhile been handled by a special Execution Congress (*Exekutionstag*) in Nuremberg to 'execute', or implement, the peace. Delays in demobilization and restoring property were eroding confidence in the settlement. Implementation of the normative year immediately hit the difficulties encountered by those charged with enforcing restitution in 1629. It proved difficult to disentangle the competing claims accumulated over decades of changing ownership.[28] Ferdinand was keen to reassert his authority by assigning the matter to the Reichshofrat, which named a Protestant and a Catholic prince as commissioners in cases where the Kreis convenors encountered local resistance. Several princes appealed directly to the court to uphold their interpretation of the normative year. Though some applicants were Protestant, many distrusted the Reichshofrat as it had only two Protestants among its fourteen judges. Moreover, referral through the court was very slow, because the commissioners had to review the evidence before making a recommendation to the judges.

The Swedes were very concerned at the delay. They regarded the restoration of Protestant property as an essential part of Gustavus's legacy, and believed that it should be completed before they withdrew their troops. However, Christina and her advisers wanted a quick withdrawal because they feared they were losing their hold over an army that threatened to act independently. There were lingering suspicions that senior officers would simply seize territory in lieu of their arrears. Such unilateral action would damage Sweden's standing, yet the army could not simply be dismissed either. Under growing pressure to act, its commander, Carl Gustav, invited his French, Hessian and Bavarian counterparts to meet him in Nuremberg to arrange a phased withdrawal (see below, p.769). As it became clear that France and Spain would not make peace, most representatives still in Westphalia moved to Nuremberg by early May 1649. While the generals discussed demobilization, the imperial Estates seized the initiative over the normative year by establishing their own bi-confessional deputation to review the outstanding cases.

Ferdinand's reaction to this challenge to his judicial authority indicates his willingness to work within the new constitutional framework. He accepted the deputation as an auxiliary to the Reichshofrat that retrospectively sanctioned its decisions. In the meantime, he was spared the difficult task of judging the appeals. The deputation was wound up in May 1651 having resolved only 31 of the 117 cases it received, handing the remainder back to the Reichshofrat. This resumed the appointment of commissioners who appeared increasingly suspect to some Protestants. Importantly, there was no return to the 'religious cases' that had undermined imperial justice in the later sixteenth century. Brandenburg did manipulate the issue at the Reichstag in 1653 in an attempt to revive the radical Protestant political programme. Ferdinand neatly deflected this challenge by issuing his own revised ordinance for the Reichshofrat before the radicals imposed one themselves.[29] The number of Protestant judges was raised to six out of eighteen, sufficient to ensure parity on bi-confessional panels dealing with individual cases, but the court stayed under the emperor's immediate jurisdiction.

Relative Success

The remaining cases over the normative year were referred to another imperial deputation that met in Frankfurt in 1655 that was soon charged with additional matters and was unable to clear the backlog. Cases were soon referred back to the Reichshofrat, or the revived Reichskammergericht after 1663. The persistence of these disputes did not detract from the overall success. Of the 313 petitions received by June 1651, around half were settled by 1654, with most of the remainder resolved within the next decade. Only 5 per cent of cases involved substantial property rights. Most concerned the exercise of fiscal privileges like tithes, or items such as religious paintings, documents, or compensation for alleged injuries.[30]

Some of the most serious cases were resolved before the Nuremberg congress opened. The duke of Württemberg recovered his monasteries, while Protestant rights were restored in bi-confessional Augsburg. The normative year was then implemented successfully in most other Swabian cases. Elsewhere, the rule was ignored or bent to suit local rulers. There was little Ferdinand could do to prevent the Swedes redistributing the remaining church land in their German possessions as additional compensation for their senior officers. Other rulers suppressed dissident minorities and recovered churches for their own faith, contrary to official protection. Osnabrück was an important example as it was regulated by a special article intended to reconcile the Catholic bishop Wartenberg and the Guelphs to the IPO. Wartenberg remained bishop on the condition Osnabrück passed to a Guelph duke on his death. It would then alternate between an elected Catholic bishop and a Protestant Guelph duke. The normative year was to apply there, as well as to the part of Hildesheim retained by the Guelphs where they had to accept fifty Catholic parishes alongside eighty Lutheran ones. Wartenberg falsified documents to 'prove' the Tridentine decrees had been implemented in Osnabrück in 1571, rather than 1625 – a deception not discovered until 1988.[31] Nonetheless, Protestants remained in the majority, while the high incidence of cross-confessional marriages suggests a measure of social harmony.

The overall impact varied. In some areas, the coexistence of two faiths in the same community hardened divisions by creating an 'invisible frontier'. The most notorious example was the city of Augsburg where guilds, taverns and even pigsties were now segregated along confessional lines. However, many territories successfully integrated dissenting minorities and even individual communities accommodated two faiths. After initial conflict in the village of Goldenstadt between Bremen and Minden, Catholics and Lutherans agreed to share the local church after 1650. Lutherans attended high mass while the Catholic organist played Lutheran hymns. Lutherans remained silent during Catholic singing, and the local Catholic authorities instructed the priest to avoid controversy.[32] It is important not to see this as progressive secularization or modern tolerance. Rather, it represented a return to the earlier pragmatism that had been eroded by confessional militancy during the war. For example, mixed marriages were already common in areas of territorial and confessional fragmentation before 1618, and they resumed as fear and hostility abated after 1648.[33]

The Düsseldorf Cow War

The key point was not the imperfect implementation of the normative year, but that violence had been discredited as a tool of repression. This became obvious when Brandenburg tried to use force to resolve the long-standing Jülich-Cleves dispute in 1651. The inheritance remained divided according to the treaty Elector Friedrich Wilhelm imposed on Duke Wolfgang Wilhelm in 1647 (see Chapter 20, p. 717). Brandenburg held Cleves, Mark and Ravensberg, leaving Jülich and Berg to Pfalz-Neuburg. The arrangement confirmed the earlier settlements of 1609 and 1614 regarding church property in all five territories. These arrangements pre-dated the normative year. Wolfgang Wilhelm argued that the normative year took precedence as imperial legislation and ordered its implementation in his two duchies in March 1651. He hoped to stabilize his authority by this move, because more parishes had been in Catholic hands in 1624 than a decade before. Friedrich Wilhelm objected to this unilateral action while the relevant Reichshofrat commission was still reviewing the evidence. He presented himself as protector of the 62,000 Protestants living in the duchies and despatched 3,800 troops into Berg in June.

The Brandenburgers killed two civilians as they advanced, before shelling one of Wolfgang Wilhelm's palaces and seizing a herd of cows belonging to his wife. The Pfalz-Neuburg envoy in Vienna coined the term 'Cow War' to belittle Brandenburg objectives and place its elector on a par with a cattle rustler. The invasion was no minor affair, however. The foreign powers had not yet completed their withdrawal and it was feared they would side with their co-religionists. Brandenburg increased its forces in the region to 7,500 by July, allegedly mobilizing 16,000 men altogether across its possessions. Outnumbered with only 3,000 men, Wolfgang Wilhelm called on Duke Charles of Lorraine who had been subsisting as a Spanish auxiliary since 1644. Charles now posed as a good Catholic, launching a counter-invasion of the duchy of Mark that was really intended to find food for his small army.

The struggle represented a very serious challenge to the Westphalian settlement, because it exemplified the tensions that caused the war in 1618. This makes the reaction to the crisis all the more significant. During the 1640s, the Dutch garrisons in Orsoy and Rheinberg regularly kidnapped priests in Jülich and Berg to pressure Wolfgang Wilhelm to tolerate Protestant worship in his duchies. Now, however, the Dutch roundly condemned Brandenburg's invasion and backed the Estates of all five territories that refused money to either side. Sweden advised Friedrich Wilhelm to back down, while Hatzfeldt arrived from Vienna and browbeat Wolfgang Wilhelm into agreeing a truce. Imperial mediation then persuaded Brandenburg to accept a new Reichshofrat commission in October and both sides withdrew their troops by the end of the year.

The distribution of church property was left on the basis of current possession in 1651 while the commission sought a definitive settlement. The fact that it did not impose the normative year should not be considered a failure. The whole purpose of that arrangement was to end violent disputes. The crisis proved the redundancy of force. Pfalz-Neuburg had failed to get its way completely, while Brandenburg's invasion left it diplomatically isolated. Even ardent Protestants realized the elector's real motive was to repeat his attempt of 1646 to conquer the entire inheritance. His submission to Ferdinand greatly enhanced the emperor's standing on the eve of the new Reichstag. Even the subsequent collapse of the new commission mattered little. Brandenburg and Pfalz-Neuburg were compelled to resolve their differences through amicable agreements in 1666 and 1672 that confirmed the distribution of territory and church property on the basis of the 1647 and 1651 arrangements.[34]

The Palatine Controversy

The general success of the religious settlement can be gauged from the disputes in the Lower Palatinate that provided the most contentious and prolonged controversy over the normative year. The Thirty Years War left the Calvinist elector Karl Ludwig with so few subjects that he was forced to build churches for the Lutheran community and even to grant limited toleration to Catholics. The electorate passed in 1685 to his Catholic Pfalz-Neuburg relation Philipp Wilhelm, son of Wolfgang Wilhelm. The new elector began a concerted campaign to promote Catholicism in defiance of the normative year. The issue assumed prominence because it concerned an electorate and occurred against a backdrop of general Protestant decline. Louis XIV revoked the Edict of Nantes in the year of Philipp Wilhelm's accession, while Protestantism in the Empire lost its patrons as 31 German princes converted to

Catholicism between 1648 and 1769. The most significant conversion was that of Elector Augustus of Saxony who embraced Catholicism in 1697 to ensure his election to the Polish throne. This coincided with the reimposition of Catholicism on parts of the Lower Palatinate with French connivance, leading to a partial re-confessionalization of imperial politics that lasted into the 1730s.[35]

The period saw a third of the 750 official complaints received by imperial institutions between 1648 and 1803 about infringements of religious rights.[36] Religion clearly still mattered, otherwise appeals along confessional lines would have lacked resonance. The root cause of the controversy was, however, political and lay in the development of Brandenburg ambitions after 1648 to join the front rank of European powers. The then elector Frederick III (King Frederick I of Prussia from 1700) saw a chance to wrest political leadership of the German Protestants from Saxony by exploiting Augustus's conversion and the threat posed by the re-Catholicization of the Palatinate. The episode draws our attention to the constitutional changes introduced at Westphalia to defuse confessional tension.

The new arrangement of *itio in partes* permitted the Protestant imperial Estates to convene as the *corpus evangelicorum* to discuss issues relating to their religious rights. This fell far short of the earlier radical Protestant proposal to split the Reichstag permanently along confessional lines. The more reduced format enabled Saxony to assume leadership of the group that was inaugurated on 21 July 1653. The Saxon decision was broadly welcomed by Lutherans and ensured the organization remained a forum to debate common concerns, rather than an alternative to the Reichstag. Saxony appreciated the danger of deadlock inherent in the *itio in partes* rights. While Protestants debated among themselves, Saxony refrained from invoking the new rights in the Reichstag itself where the Estates continued to meet in their three hierarchical colleges and take decisions by majority vote. The corpus became more problematic once Saxon leadership faltered in the wake of its elector's conversion to Catholicism in 1697. In its bid to replace Saxon leadership, Brandenburg-Prussia proved a far tougher bully than the Palatinate a century earlier, but it likewise found confession a poor vehicle for a viable alliance. Saxony repelled all efforts to displace it and generally acted as a break on confessionalized politics. The right of *itio in partes* was only used five times after 1648, beginning in 1727, and each occasion was the result of Prussian manipulation intended to derail Austrian Habsburg management of the Empire. The last, in 1780, disrupted the Reichstag for five years, but did not prevent that institution from reviving and functioning well until 1806.[37]

The elector Palatine meanwhile defused the confessional problem by granting equal rights to all three Christian churches in his lands in 1705, although bickering over minor infringements continued for another decade or so.[38] The controversy underscores how the Thirty Years War changed imperial political culture. The disputes after 1648 no longer concerned fundamental truth, but the relative weight of Protestant and Catholic territories in imperial institutions. This political aspect had been present before 1618, but was overlaid by a theological militancy lacking after 1648. Theologians no longer influenced policy. The Prussian kings Frederick I and his son, Frederick William I, embraced the Lutheran fundamentalist revival known as Pietism from the 1690s, but largely as a means of promoting useful values like obedience, thrift and duty. Frederick the Great, king of Prussia in 1740–86, was personally indifferent to religion and used it opportunistically in his rivalry with Austria, but it remained subordinate to his wider use of the existing constitution. Unlike the elector Palatine Frederick V, the Prussian Frederick sought constitutional stasis, not change, regarding the post-Westphalian framework as the best means to constrain Austrian influence.[39]

DEMOBILIZATION

Alongside its role in implementing the religious settlement, the Nuremberg Execution Congress successfully oversaw demobilization. The withdrawal of foreign garrisons made peace tangible, restoring confidence and enabling other aspects of reconstruction to commence. It was a formidable task. There were around 160,000 soldiers and probably a similar number of dependants to be evacuated or discharged (see Table 6). They were scattered across the Empire, often far from their own homes or the countries of their paymasters. The Swedes held 84 towns and castles, and had 31 garrisons in the provinces they had just received in the peace. The French occupied 56 places, while the Hessians had 27, in addition to 10 garrisons on their own territory. The

Imperialists, Bavarians and Westphalians were already concentrated on their own soil, but still held 33 posts elsewhere in total. More problematic was the presence of the Spanish in Frankenthal and the Lorrainers in seven castles between the Saar and the Rhine, because neither of these belligerents was included in the peace.

Table 6: Military strength in the Empire, October 1648

Army	Cavalry and Dragoons	Infantry	Total
Swedish	23,480	40,218	63,698
French	4,500	4,500	9,000
Hessian	2,280	8,760	11,040
	30,260	53,478	83,738
Imperial	20,300	22,000	42,300
Westphalian	3,200	9,300	12,500
Bavarian	9,435	11,128	20,563
Spanish	?	1,000	1,000+
	32,935+	43,428	76,363+

Note: The above excludes Spanish forces in the Burgundian Kreis, those in imperial Italy, as well as Austrian Habsburg troops outside the Empire in Hungary. It also excludes the 6–7,000 Lorrainers (mainly in Luxembourg), as well as the neutral Brandenburg, Guelph and Saxon forces that probably totalled around 15,000. The figures for the Westphalian army relate to February 1649 by which time some men had already been discharged. The total for October 1648 was probably around 15,000.

Sources: T. Lorentzen, *Die schwedische Armee im Dreißigjährigen Kriege und ihre Abdankung* (Leipzig, 1894), pp.184–92; P. Hoyos, 'Die kaiserliche Armee 1648–1650', in *Der Dreißigjährige Krieg* (issued by the Heeresgeschichtliches Museum, Vienna, 1976), pp.169–232; H. Salm, *Armeefinanzierung im Dreißigjährigen Krieg* (Münster, 1990), pp.154–61; B.R. Kroener, ' "Der Krieg hat ein Loch . . ." Überlegungen zum Schicksal demobilisierter Söldner nach dem Dreißigjährigen Krieg', in H. Duchhardt (ed.), *Der Westfälische Friede* (Munich, 1998), pp.599–630; C. Kapser, *Die bayerische Kriegsorganisation 1635–1648/49* (Münster, 1997), p.220.

As long as the soldiers remained, people feared the war might restart. All yearned for a 'peace dividend' after decades of onerous military burdens, yet the IPO stated that soldiers were to be maintained at local expense until the withdrawal was completed. The Swedes initially claimed their army was 125,000 strong to press as much money from Germany as possible, but they were soon obliged to provide detailed lists that revealed their actual strength was only half that. Queen Christina suspected her cousin Carl Gustav of deliberately delaying demobilization to prolong his influence. In fact, he asserted his authority over other generals like Wrangel and worked hard to accelerate matters. He got rid of the cumbersome baggage and amalgamated regiments, reducing the total number of companies from 952 to 403 at the beginning of

1649. The discharge of the 2,200 superfluous officers greatly reduced monthly maintenance costs, which were halved after January 1649 to 500,000 talers by October. Maintenance of the Swedes nonetheless cost the Empire 15 million tlr in addition to their 5 million 'satisfaction' money.[40]

Many soldiers were also disgruntled at the delay and suspected they would be cheated of their arrears and the promised rewards. Several Swedish units in southern Germany mutinied, prompting Carl Gustav to abandon the garrisons there and concentrate the troops in northern Germany where he could supervise the soldiers more closely. Sweden thereby lost its hold over the south German territories and feared these areas would not deliver their share of the satisfaction money. Carl Gustav pressed the north German Protestants even harder, deliberately obstructing implementation of the normative year to encourage payment. The process of reducing the armies also slowed as some rulers used the remaining units to reimpose their authority on recalcitrant areas. Ferdinand of Cologne sent 3,500 Westphalian troops to bring his subjects in Liège to heel in the summer of 1649.[41]

These problems concentrated minds in Nuremberg. A phased withdrawal was agreed on 21 September 1649, setting out which towns each army had to evacuate as the satisfaction money came in. A supplementary agreement on 4 March 1650 added 200,000 tlr to the Swedish satisfaction in return for accelerating their withdrawal. The congress concluded arrangements with Sweden that June, followed by France in July. The French had largely pulled back into their own territory already by the end of 1648, leaving only a few posts in south-western Germany that were abandoned in the summer of 1650.

Payments were organized through the Empire's system of assigning tax quotas to each territory. The emperor received 100 Roman months to reduce his forces, which had already been withdrawn into the Habsburg hereditary lands by early 1649 so as not to incur blame for delaying the peace. Total strength fell to 26,230 men by September 1650, but these were retained thereafter, giving Ferdinand a considerably larger peacetime standing army than his predecessors before 1618. Generals Hatzfeldt and Sparr meanwhile oversaw the disbandment of the Westphalians, completed by September 1650.[42] Another thirteen Roman months (250,000 tlr) were paid to Spain in return for its evacuation of Frankenthal in 1652 in a deal brokered by the emperor.

Sweden received 133.5 Roman months (5.2 million tlr) from seven of the ten Kreise. Burgundy was exempt, because it was excluded from the peace. The Austrian lands were assigned exclusively to the imperial army, while the Bavarian Kreis helped pay off Maximilian's army. Though Salzburg objected, the other members of the Bavarian Kreis paid a heavy levy of 125 Roman months to raise 753,303 fl. that cleared the army's arrears.[43] The electorates of Mainz and Cologne and the various Westphalian lands occupied by the Hessians were also exempted, because their payments went to disband Amalie Elisabeth's troops instead. The Hessians received the full 800,000 tlr they had been promised and evacuated their last post (Lippstadt) in 1652. The Swedes received a remarkable nine-tenths of their money by the June 1650 deadline, despite much of the money having to come from Catholic territories, and not just the Protestants as originally envisaged in the 1635 negotiations. A mere 3 per cent remained outstanding when they evacuated Vechta in 1654 which they had held as security for the final arrears.

The 18,000 native Swedes and Finns were shipped home. Only 6,000 Germans were retained by the Swedes to garrison their new possessions, while the rest were disbanded. Bavarian demobilization was the most complete, as the entire army was discharged apart from the elector's bodyguard. Saxony and Brandenburg retained only around 1,500 men each; the other princes simply kept bodyguards and a few garrison companies. Other than the emperor, no prince really had an army. Bavaria did not recruit new troops until 1657, and most territories continued to rely on reorganized militias rather than professional troops into the 1660s. German armies therefore cannot be said to have 'been left standing' after 1648.[44] It was not until the onset of French aggression after 1666 that most major princes armed themselves with new, permanent forces.

At least 130,000 men were discharged into civilian life at a time when the Dutch also reduced their establishment by around 20,000 men. The Swedes used some of the satisfaction money to transport the native soldiers home, distributing the rest to the men who were demobilized. The other armies paid their men off in a similar fashion, sometimes also giving them surplus weapons and munitions in lieu of pay arrears. Infantry privates in Swedish service received 6 tlr each, 10 tlr less than their comrades in the cavalry. These were decent amounts, but hardly sufficient to retire on. Both the IPO and IPM forbade the transfer of soldiers into armies of countries still at war, except for that of Venice which received special dispensation because it was fighting the infidel Ottomans. A large proportion of the Bavarian, Dutch and probably other soldiers entered Venetian service. Contrary to the prohibition, France recruited around 8,000 Dutch and Germans at the end of 1648, but reduced the numbers of foreigners in its service after 1655. The remaining Bernhardine officers lost their special status with the incorporation of the Army of Germany into the other French forces. French commanders distrusted Germans for their Protestantism and their reputation for mutiny. Some men enlisted for the brief Cow War of 1651, but both Pfalz-Neuburg and Brandenburg drastically reduced their armies once this finished. Some of those discharged then joined the Lorraine army. A recent modern estimate placed the total entering service outside the Empire at no more than 30,000.[45]

Once those numbers still in imperial and Swedish service are deducted, this suggests about 80,000 former soldiers remained to be absorbed into civil society around 1650. There was widespread fear they would not be able to adjust. The immediate post-war years were disturbed by marauding bands that included many former soldiers, but also other displaced persons. Many soldiers found new employment as watchmen hired by villages and small towns for their own security. Much of the fear proved unfounded and the reduction in the numbers of watchmen in the early 1650s suggests a fairly swift return to relative tranquillity.[46] Soldiers, especially those with skills or families, were generally welcomed by most territorial governments keen to repopulate the countryside and bring abandoned land under cultivation.

THE IMPERIAL RECOVERY

Habsburg Power

The relatively swift demobilization was just one factor promoting an impressive recovery of the emperor's influence. As with other aspects of the settlement, this did not represent a return to the past. The war had changed perceptions of the imperial office in ways that only gradually became clear. Ferdinand II's programme to increase his authority had been defeated outside the Habsburg lands. Many leading thinkers believed that real power in the Empire was shifting to the electors and more important princes, eroding both the emperor's authority and the autonomy of the weaker imperial Estates. Later historians accepted their verdict too readily, presenting the Empire after 1648 as a loose federation of independent states. This federalist tendency persisted as a current in imperial politics, but never fully asserted itself until Emperor Francis II dissolved the Empire in August 1806 under pressure from Napoleonic France.[47]

Far from turning his back on the Empire to concentrate on Austrian interests, Ferdinand III made a concerted effort to rebuild Habsburg influence. He and his two immediate successors pursued a much more intensive imperial policy than Rudolf II had before the war. Rudolf attempted to rule by cultivating an aura of lofty majesty that merely isolated him from the Empire. Ferdinand II sought to impose his will unilaterally, consulting only the electors and denying the lesser imperial Estates a chance to share responsibility. His son accepted the new political conditions, turning them to his advantage to govern by consent, not coercion. He realized that active involvement in imperial institutions allowed him to shape their development. The postponement of the outstanding constitutional questions as *negotia remissa* by the IPO left large aspects of executive authority undefined. The emperor retained the initiative in many areas. To be effective, he had to win the confidence of the imperial Estates by carefully cultivating influential figures, presenting Habsburg interests as common concerns, and avoiding rash or controversial actions.

This direction was signalled at the 1653–4 Reichstag, the last meeting before that of 1663 that remained in permanent session as the 'eternal diet'. Despite concluding a Recess of 200 articles in 1654, the Reichstag left open key areas of security policy and judicial reform. These omissions did not hinder the functioning of the existing arrangements. Far more significant was the confirmation of the framework for taking decisions in the Empire. The 1654 Recess reprinted the entire IPO and IPM, along with the two concluding Nuremberg recesses of 1650. Its Article 6 declared these as permanent fundamental laws, stabilizing the Empire as a mixed monarchy where power was exercised in unequal shares by the emperor and imperial Estates. The lack of precision in certain areas left room for further modification in response to circumstances, as well as preserving the remaining imperial prerogatives by leaving them undefined and hence unlimited.

Ferdinand was thus able to accept curbs on other aspects of his authority. Most notably, he agreed that all future elevations in status among the imperial Estates depended on the electors' and princes' agreement. In return, the Reichstag accepted his creation of nine new princes to reward loyal supporters from the war, including Nassau-Hadamar and Piccolomini. Only ten further elevations were approved over the next century. Meanwhile, the remaining counts were integrated into the Reichstag by granting them collective votes in the college of princes. These changes confirmed the Empire as a hierarchy of imperial Estates under the emperor's authority but not his direct control. He would have to rule by persuasion, not formal power.

The emperor had already impressed the Estates by attending the Reichstag with a 3,000-strong entourage and spending 46,000 fl. on opera and other festivities to demonstrate his continued wealth despite the war. He also took more practical steps to alleviate the pressing problem of Duke Charles of Lorraine, who had invaded the bishopric of Liège. He persuaded the Reichstag to raise 300,000 tlr to pay the Lorrainers to evacuate their seven castles in the Rhineland. He then cooperated with Spain, for whom the duke had become an embarrassment, to arrest him in February 1654. France and Spain agreed that Liège, as part of the Westphalian Kreis, was henceforth to be treated as neutral in their war. The remaining Lorraine troops were incorporated into the Spanish army.[48] The arrangement completed the demobilization process and preserved peace along the Empire's western frontier.

Spanish cooperation was a sign of the changing balance between the two branches of the Habsburg dynasty that had been under way since the early 1640s. In contrast to Ferdinand II's reign, it was now Austria that assisted Spain. Ferdinand III circumvented the restrictions imposed by the IPM to discharge 4,000 troops directly into the Spanish army by 1651. (Plans four years later to send another 12,700 over the Alps to Milan were thwarted when the men refused to go.) Austria continued to help Spain for the rest of the seventeenth century. In return, Spain transferred its feudal jurisdiction over parts of Italy to the emperor, strengthening the bonds of that region to the Empire and providing a basis for the eventual incorporation of Spain's Italian possessions into the Austrian monarchy after 1700.[49]

Ferdinand's cultivation of good relations in the Empire was rewarded by the election of his son, Ferdinand IV, as king of the Romans during the Reichstag in 1654. This triumph confirmed the defeat of the French-backed plans to prevent the election of consecutive emperors from the same dynasty. Ferdinand also thwarted efforts to impose a set of further, permanent restrictions on imperial prerogatives (the *capitulatio perpetua*). This element of the radical Protestant programme from the 1640s remained on the agenda into the eighteenth century but never became law, because the electors backed the emperor in vetoing it.[50]

Ferdinand IV's early death on 9 July 1654, just two months after the Reichstag closed, temporarily threatened the imperial recovery. A new successor had not been approved before Ferdinand III died on 2 April 1657, creating an interregnum that lasted fifteen months. Ferdinand III's second son was eventually elected as Emperor Leopold I thanks to strong Bavarian support.[51] Leopold continued his father's policies with considerable success. The length of his reign (to 1705) contributed to the consolidation of imperial authority. It is a measure of his achievement that he secured the Empire's backing, albeit with some reluctance, for Austria's claim to the Spanish succession opened by the death of the last Habsburg king there in 1700. In contrast to the early 1600s when the Habsburg monarchy lurched towards disaster thanks to a surfeit of quarrelling brothers, Emperor Charles VI's death in 1740 without a son exposed it to a new succession crisis. Prussia's seizure of Silesia in December 1740 began an open contest for influence, fundamentally altering the political balance within Central Europe. Austria was thrown increasingly onto its own resources as the other territories tried to avoid being crushed between it and Prussia. Nonetheless, the imperial title remained significant to the Habsburgs' international prestige and they only relinquished it with great reluctance after their defeat by Napoleon.[52]

Territorial Sovereignty

The IPO codified existing territorial jurisdictions, rather than granting significant new rights. Though collectively labelled 'territorial sovereignty' (*Landeshoheit*), these jurisdictions did not make the territories independent states, because such rights remained firmly associated with the status of imperial Estate. Those who exercised them remained part of the Empire that both legitimized their authority and protected their status and possessions.[53] The war's main impact was not to loosen the bonds between the Empire and its component territories, but to strengthen the authority of the latter over their subjects. The IPO clearly associated territorial sovereignty with the electors, princes and magistrates of the imperial cities, eliminating all chance of intermediary bodies within the territories claiming such rights themselves. Prior to 1618, provincial Estates like those in Austria and Bohemia maintained militias and sent envoys to foreign powers. Such actions were now clearly illegal under the imperial constitution.

The full implications of this change only emerged slowly. Imperial politics remained a matter of interpretation defined by practice, rather than abstraction. Territorial rulers remained bound by imperial law that took precedence over their own legislation. A good example is their right to make alliances with foreign powers that has often been cited as evidence for their supposed 'independence'. All alliances remained subject to the restriction that they were not to be directed against the emperor or Empire.[54] Alliance rights were not new, and princes like the elector Palatine already signed treaties with foreign powers before 1618. In fact, the IPO tightened the restrictions by displacing confession and 'German freedom' as legitimate bases for such alliances. All future treaties were to be directed at sustaining the constitution, not promoting particular interests. This stipulation was largely respected after 1648, as the war had proved the redundancy of confession as a viable basis for alliances, and underscored the danger of foreign entanglements generally. Sweden's manipulation of the elastic concept of 'German freedom' made this slogan less attractive than the security offered by the current constitution.

Ambitious princes still used alliances to advance their own dynastic interests. Major powers like France, the Dutch Republic and, later, Britain paid subsidies in return for troops supplied by the princes. Such arrangements were roundly condemned in the nineteenth century as 'blood money' and a waste of 'German' effort that could have been put to a more 'national' purpose. They were expedients used by the princes to win political support to improve their status in a rapidly changing international order. Very few resulted in the soldiers being used against the Empire, and most princes ensured clauses were added that permitted them to supply their contingent to the imperial army, even if this was being sent against their new ally.[55]

Far from leaving the Empire an empty shell, the Westphalian settlement thus injected new life into its constitution and strengthened its political culture. Stabilization of the Empire contributed to European peace by removing a source of tension from the heart of the continent. The spectre of Catholic Habsburg hegemony had been banished, not least because Spain had been bled dry by its own prolonged conflicts. The Empire remained a hierarchical political order, but its internal balance had shifted significantly. The line between imperial Estates and other authorities was more sharply drawn, reducing the number claiming to act beyond local affairs. However, those now recognized as imperial Estates participated more equally in collective decisions through the Empire's representative institutions. The emperor no longer decided policy in consultation with an exclusive group of electors, but with all Estates, especially once the Reichstag remained in session after 1663. Though cumbersome, this mechanism was still capable of reaching collective decisions, enabling the Empire to defend itself successfully against French and Ottoman attacks between 1664 and 1714. The role of confession in imperial politics declined significantly, and the Empire's subsequent problems lay in the emergence of Austria and Prussia as separate great powers that outgrew its collective framework.

22

The Human and Material Cost

AN ALL-DESTRUCTIVE FURY?

The Myth of Absolute Destruction

The sense of the Thirty Years War's destructiveness remains deeply embedded in the popular consciousness. The extent to which this reflects how contemporaries perceived it is the subject of the last chapter. What follows here concentrates on measuring the loss of life, economic dislocation, political disruption and impact on German culture. Perception and reality remain nonetheless entwined, even if they are teased apart for analytical convenience. Contemporary texts and images do convey a sense of all-pervasive violence and unremitting destruction. The war in the Empire had already become a benchmark for atrocity elsewhere in Europe before 1648. British readers were informed by publications like Dr Vincent's illustrated *The Lamentations of Germany* (published in 1638), showing murder, mutilation and mayhem in graphic detail. All parties in the subsequent British Civil Wars struggled to avoid their conflict descending into the depravity they believed afflicted Germany.[1]

The emphasis on violence receded in accounts published during the later seventeenth and early eighteenth centuries that concentrated on personalities and constitutional and confessional issues.[2] This changed with the publication of Schiller's history of the war (1791–3) and his Wallenstein drama trilogy (1797–9), as well as the rediscovery and popularization of Grimmelshausen's near-contemporary novel *Simplicissimus*. Schiller and the others engaged in this literary revival were representatives of the German Romantic movement, fascinated with death, destruction and the loss of identity. They wrote at a time of renewed upheaval following the French Revolution and the Napoleonic

779

Wars. They witnessed the Empire's final destruction and the controversy surrounding what kind of German state should replace it. The era after 1815 was generally repressive, restricting public discussion of politics and nationhood. Literature and history offered alternative arenas to express opinion on current issues. Above all, the Romantics were interested in human emotions and the search for supposedly authentic experience through personal testimonies and folklore. The most influential expressions of this were the popular accounts compiled by Gustav Freytag in his multi-volume *Pictures from the German Past*.[3] In contrast to his academic colleagues Freytag paid little attention to high politics in favour of stories from everyday experience.

Three elements emerged from this Romantic interest that shaped both academic and popular writing on the war. The first is the sense of unlimited, indiscriminate and pointless violence that supposedly broke all bounds. We have already encountered aspects of this in the debate on the character of the war's later stages in Chapters 17 and 18. In addition to the tales of cannibalism associated with the siege of Breisach, the most prominent motifs were rape, mutilation and torture, and images of a beautiful land left desolate and despoiled. The second element was a belief that these horrors were largely inflicted on innocent Germans by a merciless enemy. This could assume confessional form, as with Protestant stories of the Catholic 'rape' of Magdeburg. More commonly, various 'foreign' perpetrators were identified: Croats, Cossacks, Swedes, Finns, Scots, Irish, Hungarians, Transylvanians and, less often, French and Spaniards. The third element fitted the war into a typology of national redemption: a new, stronger German nation (later also 'race') would arise from the ashes. The tales of horror thus offered not just titillation, but hope that suffering and humiliation would eventually be rewarded. The power of this aspect lay in its roots in the Christian tradition that already influenced seventeenth-century perceptions of the war.

Some historians started to question this Gothic atrocity narrative around 1900. The military historian Robert Hoeniger sparked controversy by arguing the German population declined by only an eighth, not the three-quarters claimed by Freytag.[4] Played out against the backdrop of renewed destruction during the First World War, this debate divided opinion into what have become known as the 'Disastrous War' and 'Early Decline' schools. Whereas the former propagated the received wisdom of Germany as innocent victim, the latter countered by arguing the Thirty Years War merely accelerated existing problems stemming from overpopulation and a reorientation of Europe's economy towards the Atlantic seaboard in the late sixteenth century. This argument was pushed to its logical extreme following the further devastation of the Second World War by Sigfrid Henry Steinberg writing in the United States. Steinberg claimed the Empire experienced some slackening of growth and redistribution of inhabitants and economic activity, but overall both the economy and population increased. Though he cited very little evidence, his interpretation rapidly gained acceptance, because it appeared more reasonable than the excesses of the Gothic all-destructive fury.[5]

General Trends

A major reason for this debate is that the war's impact varied across time and space, producing seemingly contradictory evidence. Western Westphalia and parts of the Lower Rhine had already suffered from Spanish and Dutch raids from the 1580s onwards, as well as the operations associated with the Cologne War (1584–7) and the two Jülich crises. The rest of the Empire last saw major conflict in 1546–52 with the Schmalkaldic War and the Princes' Revolt. The Habsburg Brothers' Quarrel involved relatively little fighting, and while the Long Turkish War (1593–1606) represented a considerable financial burden, actual operations were restricted to Hungary and Transylvania. The absence of serious violence for several generations no doubt magnified the sense of horror when war arrived after 1618.

Even then, the fighting varied in intensity and scope. It was concentrated after 1618 along the Danube, Upper Hungary and the passes into southern Bohemia and Moravia. It shifted to central Bohemia between Pilsen and Prague with the imperial-Liga invasion of July 1620, while fighting continued in Upper Hungary and parts of Moravia and Silesia into 1622. All the horrors traditionally associated with the war's last phase were already present: brutality, plunder, murder of civilians, plague. These regions then largely escaped serious conflict for up to a decade, though the aftershocks were still felt, notably in the Upper Austrian Rebellion of 1626. Other pressures also continued with war taxation and the population displacement brought by re-Catholicization.

The main focus of the fighting meanwhile shifted to Alsace, the middle Rhine and lower Main valleys that saw the principal operations of 1621–3. Parts of Lower Saxony and Westphalia were also affected by the beginning of 1622 as Duke Christian of Halberstadt attacked Paderborn and moved south to join Count Mansfeld, before both were driven into East Frisia. This phase was one of relatively rapid movement that minimized damage, because armies did not stay in one place for long. Transit routes certainly suffered from looting and physical destruction, but areas a short distance either side of the road generally escaped. The war's primary impact was still indirect as territories raised taxes to pay for the rapid establishment of comparatively large armies. The combined strength of all the forces operating in the Empire between 1618 and 1626 probably averaged 80–100,000 men. Such numbers had not been seen for seventy years. Charles V had mustered 56,000 men against the 50,000 Protestants in the summer of 1546 at the height of the Schmalkaldic War.[6] Whereas that conflict was over within a year, the militarization after 1618 had to be sustained under worsening economic and ecological conditions. Crop failures in 1621–2 caused food prices to double the following year, exacerbated by hyperinflation, and transformed a subsistence crisis into an economic one that persisted into 1626.

Frederick V of the Palatinate had been comprehensively defeated by 1623, freeing the south from further direct conflict for eight years. Danish intervention after 1625 was concentrated in Lower Saxony. Areas to the west, south and east were occupied by Liga and imperial troops to contain the Danes. Hessen-Kassel and much of Westphalia were subjected to a prolonged Liga presence that proved costly financially, rather than in terms of human life. By contrast, the arrival of Wallenstein's imperial army on the middle Elbe in the autumn of 1625 was disastrous. The Imperialists brought the plague, killing up to 40 per cent of the urban population in the archbishopric of Magdeburg and bishopric of Halberstadt, returning the population size to that of 1562.[7] Operations spilled over into parts of Thuringia and Upper Saxony along the Elbe valley during 1626, while Mansfeld's dash south-east brought the war back to Silesia and Upper Hungary that autumn. Wallenstein's steady increase of the imperial army helped push the total number of combatants up to around 160,000 by 1629, or double that of only five years previously. The larger army establishment required the extension of the billeting system across much of the Empire, replacing indirect maintenance through taxation with direct occupation. This brought the war back to southern Germany ahead of the Swedish invasion as imperial units moved into Württemberg and some other territories to extend Wallenstein's contributions and to enforce the Edict of Restitution.

The Swedish landing in June 1630 did not immediately alter this pattern. Active operations resumed after a year's lull, but remained contained in Pomerania and Mecklenburg. Imperial and Liga units were withdrawn from other parts of Germany, either to confront the Swedes or to join the siege of Mantua. The impact of rising troop numbers was initially cushioned by better harvests in many areas during 1630 and 1631. The full effects were delayed until the Swedish exploitation of their victory at Breitenfeld rapidly spread the war into all parts of Germany by 1632. Total troop numbers reached an unprecedented 250,000 thanks to the new regional armies formed in Westphalia, Lower Saxony, the Upper Rhine and Swabia, as well as the main forces campaigning in Bavaria, Franconia and electoral Saxony.

Sweden's determination to make war pay extended billeting and con-fiscations into new areas, and plunged many territories into crisis. The remaining stocks of grain, wine and other essentials were sold in a desperate attempt to satisfy mounting military demands. Production declined as seed corn was consumed and vital assets like tools or mills were destroyed. The extensive operations and rapid reversals of fortune fostered a climate of uncertainty. Refugees had tended to return rela-tively quickly after troops had left areas during the 1620s but they now stayed away, leaving large areas deserted. Major transit routes like the Elbe, Rhine and Main valleys were especially severely affected. The earl of Arundel's party, travelling along the Main in May 1636,

came to a wretched little village called Neukirchen, which we found quite unin-habited yet with one house on fire. Here, since it was now late, we were obliged to stay all night, for the nearest town was four miles away; but we spent that night walking up and down with carbines in our hands, and listening fearfully to the sound of shots in the woods around us . . . Early next morning, His Excellency went to inspect the church and found it had been plundered and that the pictures and the altar had been desecrated. In the churchyard we saw a dead body, scraped out of the grave, while outside the churchyard we found another dead body . . .[8]

The depopulation was hastened by the plague that returned to southern Germany after 1631 and spread to the north by 1636. Arundel's party 'hurried from this unhappy place and learnt later that the villagers had fled on account of the plague and had set that particular house on fire in order to prevent travellers from catching the infection'. Since the plague hit the young as well as the old and sick the hardest, it eliminated what demographic recovery there had been in areas like Magdeburg since the earlier outbreak in 1625–6. However, it could also bring some element of relief. Villages along the Bavarian-Swabian border suffered constant marauding from both sides during 1632–4, but the soldiers stayed clear once the plague struck and the inhabitants displayed straw crosses, a recognized warning sign.[9]

Rising unrest indicated the partial breakdown of government in many areas. Peasant guerrillas appeared in parts of Westphalia, Alsace, Swabia and the Lake Constance regions after 1631. As we have seen, they often opposed both sides with equal vehemence (Chapter 15, pp.532–4). People lost confidence in the established authorities' ability to protect them. Unrest ranged from rural conspiracies and petitions in Hohenlohe in 1631–2, and renewed unrest in Upper Austria after 1632, to the large revolt in Bavaria in 1633–4.[10] The two years following the battle of Nördlingen produced the most severe impact. The rapidity of Sweden's collapse across southern Germany proved catastrophic for the Protestant territories there. The total value of damage and military exactions in Württemberg during the war was estimated at 58.7 million florins, of which three-quarters occurred in the four years following Nördlingen. The duchy's population plummeted by between 23 and 69 per cent, depending on the district, during the same period. The mid-1630s also proved the worst for the lower Meuse region, because of the fighting around Maastricht. French intervention in the Rhineland, followed by the imperial attempts to clear Alsace and recover Lorraine, intensified destruction and spread plague to these areas as well.[11]

The rapid escalation and spread of the war between 1631 and 1636 affected more than human life and activities. The shift of population, changes in land use and spread of unfamiliar microbes destabilized the eco-system. There was an explosion in the rodent population during 1636 that lasted several years and exacerbated the food shortage. Wolves roamed south-western Bavaria during 1638, returning in the early 1640s, while packs of wild pigs destroyed crops in 1639. Other animals disappeared as they became alternative sources of food. A Bavarian soldier marching along the Lower Rhine in February 1636 recorded there 'was neither cat nor dog', while there are numerous accounts of urban populations consuming both types of animal during the hunger years of the 1630s.[12]

French intervention actually lessened rather than intensified the over-all impact, because imperial and Bavarian forces initially moved west of the Rhine, either to assist the Spanish in Picardy or to campaign in Lorraine and the Franche-Comté. While these areas suffered, much of southern Germany experienced some respite, boosted by a better harvest in 1638. Meanwhile, the Swedes were on the defensive and confined to the middle Elbe, Saxony and Brandenburg until 1639. Overall troop numbers declined following the collapse of the Heilbronn League and the dispersal of many of Sweden's German auxiliaries. The Bavarian army remained roughly constant, but the imperial army contracted considerably after 1636, as did the Saxons two years later. These reductions were involuntary, forced upon all belligerents by the diffi-culties of recruiting and sustaining troops in the wake of plague deaths, economic decline and widespread devastation. The latter was now con-centrated along the Upper Rhine and middle Elbe that saw the worst fighting between 1637 and 1639.

These shifts in theatres allowed some regions to recover after 1636. Much of the Habsburg monarchy was spared fighting during the later 1630s, while the prolonged negotiations with the Hessians and Guelphs restricted operations in Westphalia, the lower Main valley and Lower Saxony. The burden of war in these three regions was now largely static as communities sustained garrisons in their immediate vicinity. The same was true of Mecklenburg and Pomerania after the failure of Gallas's campaigns there by 1639. Sweden's garrisons nonetheless remained a heavy burden and prevented demographic recovery on the Baltic coast until forces there were reduced after 1648. North-west Germany experi-enced renewed fighting after the collapse of peace negotiations there in 1640. The former Bernhardine army arrived to support the Swedes and Guelphs, while the emperor and Bavaria sent reinforcements to Westphalia. However, the overall reduction in troop numbers meant these movements drained other areas of soldiers, notably south-west Germany where fighting was restricted to raiding until 1644. Alsace and the Franche-Comté were also spared active operations from this point. The pockets of relative tranquillity were expanded as Brandenburg,

Hildesheim and the Guelph duchies left the war after 1642, while other areas paid contributions in return for garrison evacuation or a suspension of raiding. Such neutrality did not remove all the problems associated with the conflict, but it at least prevented a return of the frightful conditions prevailing in the mid-1630s.

Areas still exposed to active operations thus suffered disproportionately during the final years of the war. The Elbe valley saw renewed destruction during Sweden's invasion of Denmark in 1644–5. Though Sweden forced Saxony into neutrality in August 1645, it lacked the forces to do the same in Westphalia. Fighting there after 1646 returned to the relatively static war of raiding between imperial and Hessian outposts. Instead, the main effort moved southwards again, with heavy fighting along the Upper Rhine and into Franconia during this period, as well as in Moravia and Lower Austria after an absence of over twenty years. The final phase was fought mainly along the Danube, returning the conflict to its area of origin.

THE DEMOGRAPHIC IMPACT

Overall Losses

The preceding discussion has already indicated some of the problems hindering any assessment of the war's human and material cost. There was no uniform method of gathering population statistics even in the regions where this was carried out. Comparison of data across 1618–48 provides a very imperfect guide to actual losses, especially as the war only reached many areas after 1631, by which point the population had probably grown since the Defenestration of Prague. Demographers are obliged to extrapolate from other sources, such as lists of taxpayers or numbers of houses. There is no agreement on the 'average' size of households to use as a multiplier in these calculations. Lists of burned-out or abandoned houses are no real guide to actual population decline, because survivors either huddled together in the remaining buildings, or went elsewhere. Many modern estimates are distorted by estimating population only within later German borders (themselves hardly fixed historically) and thereby excluding areas that were previously part of the Empire like Lorraine, or Bohemia.

Steinberg asserted population rose by at least a million to between 16 and 18 million by 1650, largely by selective use of data drawn from areas experiencing a net gain. The only comprehensive survey remains that by Günther Franz who concluded that urban areas declined by a third, while the population in the countryside fell by 40 per cent. Most other accounts broadly agree by putting the overall loss at a third. Franz's work remains problematic, not least given his membership of the Nazi Party who manipulated interpretations of the Thirty Years War for their own propaganda. Whilst no one still supports Steinberg's claims, some modern estimates reduce the total decline to between 15 and 20 per cent.[13]

Even a 15 per cent decline would make the Thirty Years War the most destructive conflict in European history. By comparison the Soviet Union, which suffered the heaviest casualties of the Second World War, lost less than 12 per cent of its population. Both twentieth-century world wars were of course briefer, with the casualties each year correspondingly higher. Nonetheless, around 20 million of those lost during the First World War were due to the influenza outbreak at its end. A significant proportion of the casualties of the Second were killed in deliberate genocide, a feature mercifully absent from the Thirty Years War that was also waged with much less-potent weaponry (see Table 7). Total deaths in the Empire may have reached 8 million, given the relatively high number of military casualties and the fact that the true extent of civilian losses is often masked by the presence of wartime births recorded in overall population totals.[14]

Table 7: Comparative total deaths in major conflicts

Conflict	Deaths (millions, incl. from disease)	% of Pre-war Population
1618–48	5	20.0 (Empire only)
1914–18	27	5.5 (Europe only)
1939–45	33.8	6.0 (Europe only)

Overall totals of course obscure wide regional variations. The most comprehensive figures cover the Habsburg monarchy (see Table 8). The overall decline was relatively modest, but this was thanks to some growth in areas that largely escaped violence, whereas regions like Lower Austria or Bohemia that suffered repeated invasion saw a significant drop. More local data indicates further variations within this broad pattern. For instance, losses around Prague and the parts of the Elbe valley that experienced the worst fighting in Bohemia reached at least 50 per cent.[15]

Table 8: Population change in the Habsburg monarchy 1600–50

Region	1600	1650	Change (%)
Austrian Lands			
Lower Austria	600,000	450,000	−25
Upper Austria	300,000	250,000	−17
Styria	460,000	540,000	+17
Carinthia	180,000	200,000	+11
Krain	290,000	340,000	+17
Görz and Gradisca	130,000	150,000	+15
	1,960,000	1,930,000	−2
Further Austria			
Tirol	390,000	440,000	+13
Voralberg	40,000	45,000	+13
	430,000	485,000	+13
Bohemian Lands			
Bohemia	1,400,000	1,000,000	−29
Moravia	650,000	450,000	−31
Silesia	900,000	700,000	−22
	2,950,000	2,150,000	−27
Hungarian Lands			
Royal Hungary	1,800,000	1,900,000	+6
Total	7,140,000	6,465,000	−10

Source: Adapted from T. Winkelbauer, *Ständefreiheit und Fürstenmacht* (2 vols., Vienna, 2003), I, p.14.

Variations in other parts of the Empire could be even more extreme. As in the Habsburg monarchy, the overall decline was offset by net gains in fortunate areas like Hamburg, as well as below-average losses suffered in parts of Westphalia, Alsace and the Guelph duchies. Some territories suffered heavily early on, but then largely escaped further destruction – Holstein is a good example of this, where the severe losses of the mid-1620s had been made good by 1648. By contrast, areas along transit routes or under prolonged occupation suffered well above average losses. Some towns in the bishopric of Halberstadt lost between seven- and nine-tenths of their inhabitants. The population in Halberstadt itself fell from around 13,000 at the time of Wallenstein's arrival in 1625 to under 2,500 by 1648. Brandenburg suffered in the decade after 1627, reducing the urban population from 113,500 to 34,000, while the number of rural inhabitants declined from 300,000 to 75,000, leaving around half the villages empty. The area next to the Elbe known as the Altmark was the worst hit, whereas the Oder region escaped serious action from the mid-1640s and had already recovered by the time government surveys were conducted in 1652. Fairly reliable data from Württemberg indicate the population fell by 57 per cent between 1634 and 1655, largely as a result of the prolonged imperial occupation, followed by intensified raiding and the major operations of the mid-1640s. Again, these figures alone do not give a complete picture. The population fell by three-quarters in the immediate aftermath of Nördlingen that also brought plague in its wake. It then recovered to around 30 per cent of the earlier level by 1645, reviving further by the time the census was conducted in 1655. At 60 per cent, Lorraine's losses were roughly similar, again mainly falling during the 1630s. The Franche-Comté was ravaged between 1636 and 1639, but recovered thanks to its neutrality after 1644, which reduced the overall decline by 1648 to 48 per cent.[16]

Though not as severe, several other regions suffered considerable losses. The Bavarian population declined by 30 to 50 per cent depending on the estimate, with the 1630s being the worst decade. Much of Franconia lost 30 to 40 per cent of its population. The latest estimate for Pomerania suggests its population declined from 160,000 in 1630 to 96,000 by 1648, a fall of 40 per cent compared to the 50–66 per cent claimed by Franz. Nonetheless, based on pre- and post-war trends, Pomerania's population would have grown without the war by 25,000. If these missing births are factored in, at least another 3 million need to be added to the overall impact on the Empire's population.[17]

Causes of Mortality

The causes of mortality are as controversial as its scale. Accounts of battles and notorious massacres convey a false impression of violent death. Contemporary diaries are indeed full of stories of rape and murder, most of which rest on hearsay. Half the 72 eyewitness accounts analysed by Geoffrey Mortimer note the killing of named individuals, and one in five report personal assaults by soldiers, yet very few say these resulted in serious injury.[18] Official papers rarely record rape, due to the difficulties of prosecuting such cases: only five rapists were convicted in Munich during the first half of the seventeenth century and three in Frankfurt between 1562 and 1695. The actual incidence was far higher and was probably one of the most common forms of serious interpersonal violence during the war.

Death records are more comprehensive. The Saxon town of Naumburg had 8,900 inhabitants in 1618, falling to 4,320 by 1645, yet only 18 citizens were listed as killed by soldiers, despite the place being sacked by the Swedes who plundered it for a week in 1635. Only 5 of the 699 deaths recorded in the Westphalian parish of Elspe were directly related to military violence, and though 241 people died in the Hohenlohe town of Ingelfingen during 1634, just 7 of these fell during its capture after the battle of Nördlingen, compared to the 163 who died of plague that year.[19]

Soldiers predominate among the victims of violence. Modern estimates place the total military casualties from combat at 450,000, calculated by aggregating the known losses from battles and sieges. Of these, 80,000 fell in French, Bernhardine and Hessian service, while the Imperialists lost 120,000 and the rest are accounted for by the Swedes, Danes and other German armies, including the Bavarian. Another 2–300,000 French were killed or wounded in the struggle against Spain from 1635 to 1659, making that country's total combat loss significantly above the 280,000 casualties suffered in two further wars between 1672 and 1697.[20]

Survival rates for the wounded are difficult to calculate, because what few data exist for hospital returns rarely distinguish the causes of admission. Most men were hospitalized through sickness, rather than injury. Conditions fell far below modern standards of hygiene and care, but some effort was made to ensure good food and attention. Only 10 out of 71 wounded imperial soldiers admitted to a hospital in August 1645 failed to return to their regiment, while 42 died out of 143 hospitalized in November 1646.[21]

Disease proved more potent than muskets, swords and cannon. On average, one in ten soldiers was sick, even if most generally recovered. Logistical failure or epidemics increased this proportion significantly. A form of typhus known as 'Hungarian fever' (*morbus Hungaricus*) killed 14,000 Liga soldiers during the 1620 campaign, compared to only 200 shot or hacked to death at White Mountain.[22] However, Liga losses at

White Mountain were exceptionally light and armies that were routed, like their Bohemian opponents, suffered far greater casualties, especially if they were pursued. It is likely that three men died of disease for every one killed in action, suggesting that up to 1.8 million soldiers died during the war. This figure is plausible when compared with the evidence culled from Swedish and Finnish parish registers and military archives. Around 150,000 Swedish and Finnish conscripts died in 1621–48, including 40,000 in the Prussian and Livonian campaigns in 1621–9, with the rest in Germany. Given that conscripts generally composed less than a fifth of the army in Germany, it is likely that at least another 400,000 Germans, Britons and others died from all causes in Swedish service.[23]

Though violence caused relatively few deaths among civilians, fear of it helped drive people from their homes. Flight and emigration were major factors behind the losses recorded in the areas of the greatest population decline, accounting for 60 per cent of that in Waldeck and 80 per cent in the area belonging to the abbey of Ottobeuren near Memmingen.[24] Immigration offset or at least slowed population decline in many areas. For example, Munich's population fell from 22,000 (in 1618) to 14,000 (1651), largely due to plague in 1633–4 and 1649–50, but at least 7,000 people settled in the city over the same period. They were rural artisans fleeing hardship and danger, mostly from other parts of Bavaria, with a fifth from neighbouring Franconia and Swabia. Augsburg experienced a broadly similar pattern as its population fell from 45,000 in 1618 to 16,400 by 1635 following Swedish occupation and the imperialist siege. It then revived to 20,000 by the end of the war thanks partly to immigration. Migration helped double the population of Nancy, the only town in Lorraine to experience growth, and also contributed to Hamburg's net gain during the war.[25]

Migration meant change in more than just numbers. The Empire's Jewish population became more fractured as it dispersed to new areas and its members engaged in more diverse forms of economic activity.[26] Not all arrivals were welcome. Migrants often lacked prior association with their new community. They were generally poorer than those who had died or left, other than exceptional cases like the Catholic elite sheltering in Cologne after 1631. Many migrants did not want to stay but were simply waiting until it was safe to return home. Others arrived with occupying forces, heightening the sense of an alien population whose numbers could nonetheless be considerable in towns of strategic importance: in January 1647 Überlingen contained only 650 taxpaying citizens, compared to 652 peasant refugees, 592 'foreign' women with 909 children, as well as a garrison of 239 soldiers with 61 wives and 72 children.[27]

Flight could increase mortality due to the cramped, unhygienic conditions that bred disease in the places of apparent refuge. Migrants generally arrived malnourished and exhausted after their journey. At least 104 refugees died on the streets of plague-ridden Landsberg during the Swedish invasion of Bavaria in the 1630s, while refugees accounted for a third of deaths in the Hohenlohe town of Kirchberg in the aftermath of Nördlingen.[28] Most towns were small and poorly fortified. Overcrowding quickly caused serious food shortages, while strategic concerns often made towns military targets. The decade after 1625 saw many people fleeing urban areas for the countryside that could be safer and offered more food. Urban flight appears to have declined thereafter as the more mobile warfare made the countryside in its turn increasingly unsafe. Rural communities were particularly hard hit, because they were generally smaller and quickly lost their viability if too many people moved away. This helps explain the rural depopulation that became pronounced by the 1640s as people abandoned farms and hamlets to congregate in larger villages and towns. Location nonetheless often proved decisive, since many smaller isolated communities could potentially escape both plague and military depredations.

The pattern of civilian deaths confirms the general picture of military casualties, indicating that disease was the main killer. The first major plague epidemic occurred in 1622–3, followed by more serious outbreaks around 1625 and 1634, with the timing varying by a year or two depending on the region. A fourth, generally less fatal epidemic struck between 1646 and 1650. Bubonic plague was responsible for most of the mortality in the 1630s. Another major killer was typhus (*Fleckenfieber*), an infection spread by lice on clothing. Plague generally hit communities once every ten to twenty years during the sixteenth century. The frequency and scale of the outbreaks after 1618 suggests a pandemic where the infection ebbed but never completely disappeared due to increased mobility and malnutrition.[29]

Areas hit in the first outbreak suffered fewer deaths in the second, though the impact remained proportionally high given the intervening population decline. For example, Naumburg recorded 1,642 plague deaths in 1625, or eight times the pre-war annual average mortality. Another 799 died the following year, but the peaks in the second outbreak reached only 702 (1633) and 741 (1636). The small town of Kroppenstadt, east of Halberstadt, likewise recorded peaks of 695 (1626) and 226 (1636), in contrast to an average of 50 deaths each year before the war. It is clear that the plague was the biggest single factor in overall mortality: 44 per cent of the deaths in Elspe parish in 1622–49 fell in its plague year (1636–7).[30] It was so significant, because infection generally proved fatal. Around 80 per cent of men and 70 per cent of women admitted to the Viennese plague hospital never recovered. Children suffered disproportionately, accounting for a third of victims in Magdeburg and Halberstadt in 1625.[31] Plague also left communities vulnerable to other diseases, especially if military operations also disrupted the food supply. Mortality remained high in Naumburg after the 1633–6 outbreak because of Banér's operations in its vicinity. The town recorded 411 deaths in 1639, mainly to malnutrition, followed by a further 1,109 across 1641–3 largely due to dysentery.

Though undoubtedly high, these figures need to be placed into their contemporary context, where high mortality was the norm. Augsburg recorded 38,000 plague victims in eight years in the first half of the sixteenth century, followed by 20,000 in seven years between 1550 and 1600, compared to the 34,000 lost during the nine years of epidemics in 1600–50. London lost a fifth of its population in each of its outbreaks in 1595, 1603 and 1625, and had only eleven years without high mortality rates between 1625 and 1646. It is thus very likely that many of the people who died in the Empire between 1618 and 1648 would have had their lives cut short even without the war. The 1622 epidemic reached Augsburg not through soldiers but commerce with Amsterdam, for instance. The initial impact was magnified by adverse economic and climatic conditions. The year 1619 saw the first of a series of cold, wet summers contributing to a succession of poor harvests until 1628. The 1622–3 epidemic coincided with hyperinflation that eroded purchasing power and left many malnourished.

However, troop movements clearly made things much worse. The 1620 Bohemian campaign already saw high mortality from typhus which was then carried by Mansfeld's army as it fled westwards to the Lower Palatinate. The army's arrival in the autumn of 1621 spread panic as 20,000 civilians fled to Alsace, contributing to 4,000 deaths in overcrowded Strasbourg. Mansfeld's men continued to spread typhus as they marched north into the Netherlands and then East Frisia, and he eventually succumbed to the disease himself in 1626. Plague also killed other prominent political and military leaders, including Elector Frederick V, Bernhard of Weimar, Governor Feria and General Holk.

The first epidemic flared again in Alsace during 1624–5 and spread through Metz into France, probably with refugees, where its impact was again magnified by malnutrition. The bad harvest of 1627 led to the first serious food shortages in France since the 1590s and the impact deepened with another poor harvest in 1629. The war clearly made a difference. Paris and the north largely escaped the epidemic that spread to the south with the troop movements during the last Huguenot rising. In all, the plague epidemic killed between 1.5 and 2 million of France's population of 17–20 million.[32]

The second, more lethal epidemic followed Wallenstein's northwards march and the spread of operations across northern Germany during 1625–6. The relative decline in German plague deaths in 1630–1 despite the renewed troop movements is probably due to the better weather and harvests of these years. By contrast, northern Italy suffered its worst outbreak that, again, was clearly exacerbated by the operations around Mantua and Casale. The population of the duchy of Milan fell by a third to 800,000, while that of Mantua was halved. As in Germany, the impact of these losses was magnified by the relative absence of serious fighting in Italy for a century.

Southern Germany was re-infected by imperial and then Spanish troops marching north over the Alps in 1631. The epidemic spread eastwards with the Swedish invasion of Bavaria in 1632–3, eventually reaching Salzburg by December 1635, probably having been brought by refugees. It also swept westwards to the Rhine in the wake of Sweden's collapse after Nördlingen. Mortality in that town was already two and a half to three times above its pre-war average in 1629–33, but jumped to over seven times in the year of the siege and battle as the plague arrived with the Spanish reinforcements. Its reappearance in Augsburg also coincided with that city's blockade during the winter of 1634–5. The fourth outbreak in Augsburg followed the Franco-Swedish siege of September 1646. Behind these statistics lie innumerable personal tragedies. Only one of the cobbler Hans Heberle's ten children outlived him. Two of them died, along with Hans' own parents and four siblings, in the 1634–5 epidemic.[33]

The post-war demographic recovery flowed from a rising birth rate and a fall in mortality. Württemberg's population grew about 0.5 per cent annually prior to the war, but the rate shot up to 1.8 per cent in the two decades after 1648. Travellers reported Germany as a land of children: nearly half of Württembergers were under the age of fifteen during the 1660s.[34] Unfortunately many of these became the recruits for the prolonged wars after 1672 that retarded and in some areas reversed the recovery. Most sources agree that the 1618 population levels were generally not reached again until 1710–20. Again, there were variations. The duchy of Berg experienced a 20 per cent decline in total population in 1618–48, but had recovered by 1680, whereas neighbouring Jülich did not make good its 28 per cent loss until 1720. Economic decline retarded recovery in some areas. Stralsund did not recover its 1627 population until 1816, while the pre-war Nuremberg birth rate was not matched until 1850.[35]

THE ECONOMIC IMPACT

The 'Kipper and Wipper' Hyperinflation

The more recent work on German economic history suggests that the Empire was neither flourishing nor in decline on the eve of the war. Some sectors were booming, while others contracted. The earlier population growth had levelled off, and land use had intensified, but a significant number of people were underemployed. Business failures, rising prices and growing numbers of beggars contributed to a widespread perception of worsening times. Most people felt life had been better in their parents' day. Less than 7 per cent of households in Augsburg in 1618 were recorded as relatively wealthy in the city's tax books, compared to over 48 per cent listed as penniless.[36]

The sense of growing hardship was greatly magnified after 1621 by what is popularly regarded as the western world's first financial crisis.[37] This period of hyperinflation became known as the Kipper and Wipper era, probably from the words for clipping coins and swinging the money-changer's scales. The episode demonstrates the Empire's strengths and weaknesses during its wider political crisis, as well as indicating the difficulties governments encountered in financing warfare. It brought widespread misery and made it harder for people to cope with the resumption and intensification of the conflict from 1625.

Inflation followed the ill-judged manipulation of the Empire's monetary system that relied on a combination of nominal units of account and actual coins used in daily transactions. The former were the silver taler used primarily in the north and the southern gold or silver florin. These were indeed minted as actual coins, but most people used small change (*Schneidemünzen*) that included a growing copper content. Mint rights were an imperial prerogative that had long been devolved to princes and imperial cities that issued their own coinage. Regulation was provided by the 1559 Imperial Currency Ordinance that related coins to each other according to their precious metal content measure using the Cologne silver mark (about 233g). Adjustments in exchange rates were negotiated at regional currency conventions charged with upholding the 1559 rules that threatened death to those who infringed them.

Enforcement proved difficult as more territories established their own mints. The number operating in Lower Saxony alone rose from six in 1566 to thirty by 1617. Territorial fragmentation undoubtedly added to the complexity, but what followed cannot be blamed entirely on the imperial constitution. The 1559 ordinance reflected the wider early modern ideal of a static order. It left little room for fluctuations in the supply of copper and precious metals, or changes in demand due to economic and demographic growth. Interruptions in the supply of New World bullion were offset by growing use of copper in Spain and the Dutch Republic, fuelled by Japanese imports and, above all, greatly increased Swedish output. The difficulty of distinguishing between metal as a commodity and a means of exchange added to the general problem. The cost of silver rose above the nominal value of the coins it was used to make, encouraging mint operators to debase their production by adding more copper to the mix.

Debasement had been relatively rare until governments encountered problems in paying for the war after 1618. Underdeveloped credit facilities made borrowing difficult, whereas debasement appeared a deceptively simply solution, especially as the inflationary risks were poorly understood. The Bohemian rebels already resorted to it in 1619, as did a number of other territories, some merely seeking easy profits. The

Habsburgs continued the practice after they recovered control of the Bohemian mint and silver mines in 1620. However, debasement only fully got under way in January 1622 when Emperor Ferdinand II entrusted the mint to a private consortium largely composed of his own officials, including the governor of Bohemia, Karl Liechtenstein. Whereas one silver mark had produced 19 florins of change in 1618, the consortium diluted it to mint coins with a total face value of 79 fl. and later even 110 fl., issuing a nominal 29.6 million fl. in bad coin in return for paying the Habsburg treasury 6 million. The operators' profits have been put as high as 9 million, but were more likely only 1.3 million. Their real return came from using debased coin to buy the confiscated rebel properties that the emperor released for sale in September 1622. Using bad coin for good deals soon became widespread. Municipal debt repayment in the imperial city of Überlingen jumped from a pre-war annual average of 1,900 fl. to 8,000 fl. as its astute treasurer paid its creditors in debased coin.[38]

The scale of the mint consortium's activities has attracted considerable attention, but it played a relatively small role in the overall crisis. The worst period of inflation began in March 1621 and was already dissipating as the Prague operation got under way. The presence in the consortium of Jacob Bassevi, head of Prague's Jewish community, fuelled the virulently anti-Semitic Protestant critique of debasement, but some of the worst offenders were based in Lutheran north Germany, as well as parts of Franconia, Alsace and Calvinist Hessen-Kassel. Illegal 'hedge mints' (*Heckenmünzen*) sprouted in minor provincial towns, sometimes with covert backing from neighbouring rulers hoping to profit at others' expense.

The consequences rapidly became obvious. The Leipzig city council ruined municipal finances by speculating on the copper market. Good coins disappeared from circulation, while taxes were paid with debased currency. The real value of civic revenue fell by nearly 30 per cent in Naumburg.[39] Prices soared as traders demanded sackfuls of bad coins for staple commodities: the cost of a loaf of bread jumped 700 per cent in Franconia between 1619 and 1622. Those on fixed incomes suffered, like theology student Martin Bötzinger whose 30 fl. annual grant became worth only three pairs of boots.[40] Serious rioting spread from 1621, with that in Magdeburg leaving 16 dead and 200 injured.

The Saxon response is typical of the action taken by the larger territories. The elector agreed a joint commission with his Estates in March 1622 to close illegal mints and recall coins so that they could be reissued with the full silver content.[41] Such measures were implemented at regional level through the Kreis structure in Lower Saxony, Bavaria and Franconia, while elsewhere, neighbouring territories also co-operated. Ferdinand II refused to renew his consortium's contract when it expired in January 1623 and ordered an 87 per cent devaluation of its coinage that December.

On the surface, the Empire made a remarkable recovery as monetary probity was restored by the end of 1623. Illegal mints were closed and the Kreise resumed their currency regulation meetings. Revenue also recovered in areas unaffected by military operations. This relative success demonstrates the resilience of the imperial constitution, as well as the continued ability of Protestants and Catholics to use formal institutions to resolve common problems. Official currency regulation only encountered serious difficulties with the disruption caused by the Swedish invasion, but the constitutional framework remained the preferred means to tackle a resurgence of debasement in the 1630s fuelled by spiralling military expenditure.[42]

More serious problems lurked behind the formal return to probity. The Kipper and Wipper inflation combined with the poor harvest of 1621–2 to wipe out most of the gains from the previous two decades of relative stability in the countryside. The previously wealthier sections of rural society sold assets and exported the remaining agricultural surpluses to cover their losses. Though only temporary, inflation frustrated the customary response to subsistence crises: lenders refused to extend new loans unless repaid in good coin that became hard to find. Territorial governments were forced to extend credit to their own subjects by, for instance, allowing taxes to fall into arrears. The continuation of the war left no room for any respite, leaving many vulnerable precisely when military exactions increased after 1625.[43]

Trade and Industry

There seems little evidence to support the nineteenth-century lament that the failure of Wallenstein's Baltic Design and the loss of Pomerania to Sweden denied Germany a chance to become a colonial power until the 1880s.[44] Bremen and Hamburg, the two largest ports, remained free from foreign occupation and retained access to the North Sea. Other ports also remained available, despite the presence of foreigners, such as Emden that became the base for Brandenburg's attempt to break into the slave trade after 1680. Lübeck and Rostock were still free to trade in the Baltic. Germans formed the majority of personnel serving the Dutch East India Company and were a significant element in Portugal's presence in India.[45] The real reason for the late participation of Germans in colonial ventures, especially at state level, was the lack of incentive. Central Europeans long benefited from a pattern of trade that only gradually reoriented westwards to the Atlantic. Denied access to much of this earlier pattern thanks to their location on Europe's western periphery, the Portuguese and Spanish struck out across the oceans seeking what at the time seemed a very risky and unprofitable alternative.

The war made a more direct impact in other areas of trade, but, like the affects on population, there were considerable variations in experience. Towns generally fared better than the countryside, though as Prague's example illustrates their concentration of wealth often made them tempting military targets. A few were completely destroyed, like Magdeburg's two suburbs that were razed during its siege of 1630–1. Rather more were damaged severely through repeated attacks. These included Magdeburg itself, as well as Bamberg, Chemnitz, Pirna and Marburg. Most others suffered at least some damage but this did not always inhibit growth – as indicated by the rising populations of Vienna, Nancy and Frankfurt am Main. Much depended on individual circumstances, especially location and whether the town possessed dependent villages. Hamburg's surrounding territory suffered greatly, in contrast to the city itself where the number of inhabitants grew by 50 per cent. Damage around Magdeburg was even greater, because the city was subjected to repeated sieges and blockades. Around half the houses in its immediate vicinity were destroyed, compared to 15 to 35 per cent across the rest of the archbishopric. Likewise, a quarter of Rothenburg's 100 dependent villages had been abandoned by the 1640s. Towns that closed their gates to soldiers displaced the burden on to the countryside. Raiders often devastated the surrounding area to intimidate towns, or to put pressure on territorial rulers.[46]

Less immediately visible but just as fundamental were the changes among the inhabitants in the trade centres. City councils favoured citizens (who elected them) over the disenfranchised rural subjects and immigrants. Trades serving essential needs generally fared better. The numbers of bakers and brewers, for instance, experienced lesser declines than musicians, builders, textile workers and those in service industries. Metal workers also fared better thanks to their involvement in the arms industry. Individuals clearly made money, but there were relatively few war profiteers. Most producers tried to remain on good terms with all parties, not just for profit but to avoid reprisals. Manufacturers in Aachen, a centre of arms production, made good returns until the 1630s when rival armies began seizing weapons without payment. The Swedes failed to pay for large shipments of weapons from Suhl in Thuringia.[47] Such behaviour affected other sectors too. Naumburg's municipal brewery closed in 1639 because soldiers had stopped paying: a serious blow in a town famed for its beer. However, the relatively small scale, decentralized character of seventeenth-century industry enabled it to recover relatively quickly provided markets remained for the goods. The Imperialists destroyed most of the plant in the Suhl arms workshops in October 1634, but production soon resumed once the workers returned.

Fear and uncertainty contributed to the disruption of trade, especially as travelling became unsafe. Often, this merely accentuated existing trends. Established centres frequently benefited from the decline of lesser regional rivals. Leipzig, for instance, profited at Naumburg's expense. Major financial centres like Hamburg and Frankfurt also remained prosperous. Occupation was not invariably disastrous. Wesel did suffer when it was captured by the Spanish in 1614, but it recovered rapidly after 1629 once it was garrisoned by the Dutch with whom it had previously traded.

The fighting disrupted economic cooperation between territories in the Empire. Schemes to improve navigation along rivers were abandoned, and the failure to maintain defences caused flooding along the Lower Rhine. Ambitious plans such as Wallenstein's canal to link the Baltic and North Sea came to nothing. Fear that soldiers would simply steal things led to a disregard for vital resources. Forestry laws were broken in Württemberg after 1634 as communes sold off protected oak trees for cash and plundered woods, especially during harsh winters. However, the human impact of these actions remained restricted compared to that of the twentieth century, and the ecology recovered quickly after the war.[48]

Though the war's impact was overwhelmingly negative, it did not prevent economic development entirely. The archbishop of Salzburg began a major drainage project in 1625 and stepped this up at the height of the crisis in southern Germany in 1632, laying the foundation stone for a new suburb on the reclaimed land. The project was completed in 1644 using Dutch, and hence probably Protestant, engineers. Similarly, the abbey of Ottobeuren developed textile weaving after 1625, training new apprentices even if their certificates could be registered only after the war.[49]

Agriculture

The physical character and location of activity influenced how the rural world fared during the war. Livestock was especially vulnerable because it could be rounded up and driven away by soldiers. A survey in the abbey of Ottobeuren found only 133 horses and 181 cattle in 1636, compared to 2,094 and 6,607 respectively 16 years earlier. The loss of draught animals was particularly serious, because it affected food production. Peasants around Bamberg were left to pull their own ploughs after the Swedes stole their horses and oxen in 1633.[50]

The overall impact mirrored that for urban areas and settlement patterns generally. Larger farms usually fared better, because they already had greater resources and more fertile land. Following the Swedish depredations in Bavaria in the 1630s, one district recorded 58 per cent of cottages burned down or abandoned, 69 per cent of medium farms, but only 37 per cent of the larger ones.[51] However, recent research no longer sustains the older belief that the war promoted the consolidation of farms into large manorial estates east of the river Elbe. The domain economy had already developed in this area in the sixteenth century, though it was by no means all-pervasive. Some landlords did enlarge their estates by incorporating abandoned land. However, there was no wholesale bargain with rulers at the peasantry's expense. Depopulation increased the labour value of the survivors. Peasants were often able to negotiate better conditions such as hereditary leases from landlords who, rather than being the princes' natural allies, were often ground between an increasingly assertive territorial state and adverse economic conditions. Some lords did impose greater obligations on their peasants to perform labour service, notably in Bohemia, but this was far from universal and does not justify the old label of 'second serfdom'.[52]

Land prices fell due to the destruction of assets like barns or vineyards, as well as rural depopulation. Around a third of the Empire's cultivated land had been abandoned by 1648 and in some areas the proportion was nearer a half. Even areas still being worked often had to be sold by hard-pressed owners. Überlingen sold its principal rural territory in 1649 to raise its share of the Swedish satisfaction money. The market was quickly flooded. A farm in Franconia that cost 500 fl. in 1614 could be bought for 37 fl. in 1648. The scarcity of capital made it hard even for those willing to buy. In this case, the purchaser lacked even 37 fl. and raised the money by taking on a partner he bought out five years later.[53]

The Credit Crunch

Growing indebtedness was already common before the war and is one area where the 'Early Decline' interpretation of the economic impact of the war rests on firmer ground. The bishopric of Bamberg's debt hovered at around 800,000 fl. between 1554 and the late sixteenth century, despite paying off 470,000 fl., because the bishop contracted new liabilities in the meantime. The fighting during the Princes' Revolt of 1552 quintupled Nuremberg's debt to 4.3 million fl., of which only 300,000 was paid off by 1618. The Kipper and Wipper inflation caused serious problems, pushing Bamberg's liabilities to 1.2 million fl., and those of Nuremberg to 5.7 million. Against these increases, those caused by the rest of the war seem relatively modest. Nuremberg's debt rose to 6 million, but Bamberg reduced its liabilities to 831,802 fl. by 1653. As with all statistics from the war, these figures need careful interpretation. Debts were potentially much higher, because most territories and communities defaulted on their interest payments. Überlingen's debt more than doubled to 280,000 fl., but was nearly three and a half times the pre-war level if the 163,553 fl. of interest arrears were also included.[54]

Rising indebtedness was not solely due to the cost of the war. Count Eitel Friedrich of Hohenzollern-Hechingen accumulated over 610,000 fl. of debts in twenty years of mismanagement and absence from his territory as an imperial general. Other rulers continued to spend lavishly despite widespread hardship among their subjects. The supposedly thrifty Friedrich Wilhelm of Brandenburg bought tapestries, jewellery and silverware worth 29,200 talers at the height of the Swedish occupation of his electorate in 1641–5. Together with the pre-war record of poor financial management, this suggests many territories would have run into difficulties even without the war. The conflict certainly made matters worse through military burdens and the shrinking tax base. Revenue from Count Eitel Friedrich's small Swabian territory declined from a respectable 30–40,000 fl. a year in 1623 to only 4,000 fl. two decades later. The value of taxable assets in the Lower Palatinate crashed from 18.8 million to 3.8 million fl., while annual revenue fell from 441,508 fl. to 76,977 fl. between 1618 and 1648. Though this was an extreme case, the number of taxpayers fell faster than the overall population decline almost everywhere, reflecting widespread impoverishment.[55]

Imperial institutions played an important part in easing these problems after 1648. Rulers, Estates and communities borrowed from individuals, religious foundations and (less often) rich bankers. Money was also raised by selling annuities. German debt, like that in Naples, was thus spread among a relatively broad cross-section of society, including many who depended on regular interest payments for their income. For example, Protestant refugees fleeing the Habsburg lands in the 1620s had to sell their property before leaving and invested the proceeds in annuities issued by the cities of Regensburg, Ulm and Nuremberg. By 1633 only Regensburg was still paying interest. Because of the risk of debt defaulters, imperial law traditionally favoured creditors over debtors. However, the war made repayment difficult and debtors faced ruin if creditors sequestrated their assets. The Pomeranian Estates had already taken steps to protect debtors in 1628, followed by numerous other territories. Debt was still considered something to be avoided. Governments refused to allow debtors to write off their liabilities. They made some allowance through short-term moratoria, but rejected arguments that the exceptional circumstances of the war overrode obligations to repay loans.

Debt levels soared as interest arrears compounded the original liabilities. The smaller territorial governments feared the courts might sequestrate their possessions as the only way to recover what they owed. The matter was raised by the imperial city of Esslingen at the 1640–1 Reichstag, which was unable to resolve it due to other pressing problems. Emperor Ferdinand III nonetheless instructed the Reichshofrat to pay more attention to debtors' interests in cases lodged by their creditors.

However, the Reichskammergericht continued to issue injunctions against debtors, arguing that lenders' interests had to be protected to avoid a collapse in financial confidence. The issue was taken up again by the Imperial Deputation in Frankfurt after 1643 and then at the Westphalian congress, where it was postponed along with the rest of judicial reform to the next Reichstag. Article IV of the IPO merely annulled debts resulting from military extortion, obliging creditors to prove the legality of their claims within two years through the courts.

The issue prompted intense debate across the Empire. Both imperial supreme courts submitted detailed opinions to the Reichstag as it convened in 1653, while the Bohemian and Austrian exiles lodged petitions, fearing the loss of their properties would now be followed by that of their annuities. The Reichstag issued a landmark ruling in its final Recess of 1654. This was of considerable general significance since it signalled the Empire's collective superiority over territorial autonomy: the relevant passages of the Recess were passed despite Brandenburg and Bavarian objections that a general ruling infringed their princely jurisdictions guaranteed by the IPO. It confirmed the illegality of military exactions, issued a three-year moratorium on capital repayments in valid debts and allowed debtors to set their own level of payment for the following seven years. In addition, it wrote off a quarter of the interest arrears up to 1654 and delayed repayment of the remainder until after 1664. The Palatinate received a special exemption from all interest payments for a decade and was allowed to pay only 2.5 per cent (half the official rate) for the following ten years.

Like the normative-year rule, actual implementation varied considerably. Many territories expanded the capital repayment moratorium to their own advantage. Saxony wrote off nearly 600,000 tlr on the grounds it had been contracted in debased coin, as well as unilaterally repudiating 10 million tlr of interest arrears in 1656, writing off the remainder five years later. Brandenburg, Bamberg, the Palatinate and others repudiated around a fifth of their debts, while Württemberg wrote off all its communes' interest arrears and those of private individuals. The duchy's Estates had already written off half their own debt of 4 million fl. Private creditors were generally lucky to receive a third of their original capital.

Nonetheless, the Reichstag upheld the overall integrity of the capital market by stopping well short of using the war to justify complete repudiation. It was a conservative arrangement that confirmed the prevailing attitude to debts. Old obligations remained valid and could be passed down the generations through inheritance. Subsequent difficulties like the mid-eighteenth-century wars further delayed repayment. Debts persisted well beyond the Empire, because the successor states were obliged to assume their predecessors' liabilities. The Westphalian town of Werl finally cleared its debt from the Thirty Years War in 1897. The 5 per cent ceiling on interest rates fixed in 1654 remained the norm in much of Germany until 1867. The success of the ruling was assisted by local pragmatism. Rulers and landlords generally tried to avoid foreclosures because eviction hit production and rents. Tenants' wartime debts were renegotiated into the 1670s to ease pressure on them and allow agrarian production to revive.[56]

Level of Recovery

Territorial revenues rose relatively rapidly immediately after the war. Whereas the bishopric of Hildesheim raised only 7,670 tlr across 1643–5, annual revenue was more than three times that figure by the 1651–2 financial year.[57] Much of this was due to the peace dividend following demobilization. Money previously diverted as contributions to occupying garrisons now flowed back into territorial treasuries. Such figures are thus a poor guide to actual economic recovery.

Beyond debt and currency regulation, imperial institutions made little effort to coordinate the recovery. The IPO and IPM abolished all wartime tolls except those of Sweden, the emperor and the electors. Like the debt arrangements, this asserted the collective good over territorial autonomy. Rulers were forbidden to disrupt trade, impose new tolls or raise pre-war ones without express permission from the emperor. The Nuremberg Execution Congress entrusted enforcement to the Kreise. Some minor territories did gain exemption by following the rules and appealing to the emperor. Bremen was allowed to retain its Weser toll first imposed in 1623. The Franconian Kreis had some success in abolishing illegal tolls and, along with Swabia and some other regions, in coordinating economic activities among its members into the eighteenth century. However, many rulers placed short-term gain in revenue over the longer-term advantages of free trade, and new excise taxes were soon imposed in most territories.[58] The constitution did not necessarily hinder growth. A far more significant constraint was the reluctance to shed traditional customs and inflexible business practices. For example, the reluctance of most towns to modify criteria for citizenship deterred the migrants needed to repopulate them.

Commerce recovered relatively quickly along the major routes, though much of the evidence comes from toll receipts that provide only a proximate indication of the true volume of activity. The Lobith toll on the Rhine and that at Lenzen on the Elbe, both of which were controlled and administered by Brandenburg, plummeted during the war but recovered their former levels within a decade of the peace. Land tolls levied on goods crossing the electorate displayed a similar revival.[59] Recovery was nonetheless uneven. Some sectors revived faster than others. The construction industry that had been one of the hardest hit during the conflict prospered with reconstruction and the revival of municipal finances that allowed communities to tackle a backlog of repairs on their public buildings.

It proved relatively easy to take over abandoned farms, but harder to resume agriculture. Animal husbandry recovered fastest, provided there was money to restock the farms. However, it took fifteen to twenty years to bring wasteland back under cultivation, because the soil had often deteriorated through lack of fertilization or had become overgrown. Labour and capital shortages further slowed recovery, but the worst effects had been overcome by the 1660s. Grain production returned to pre-war levels around 1670, well ahead of the demographic recovery, assisting other economic activity by keeping food prices low.

Capital- and time-intensive activities were the hardest to revive. A major wartime casualty was the Empire's wine industry. Vineyards were expensive and time-consuming to develop, yet very vulnerable to soldiers who uprooted or burned them during sieges or raids. The area of vineyards owned by the Überlingen burghers contracted by nearly two-thirds during the war; wine-makers were obliged to mortgage their homes to Swiss banks to rebuild the industry after 1648, but the area used for viticulture was still only half what it had been in 1618 when the city lost its autonomy in 1802. Überlingen's fate was far from unique and the damage to what had been the mainstay of the local economy helps explain the stagnation of many south-west German towns. The picture was rarely completely black, however. Contraction of the wine industry, for example, proved a boon to the region's brewers whose recovery was speeded by the relatively rapid revival of grain production.

THE CRISIS OF THE TERRITORIAL STATE

War and State-building

While war is usually regarded as retarding economic activity, historians and political scientists widely see it as promoting political development through the need to coordinate human action.[60] A recent influential summary of the Thirty Years War presents it as Europe's 'state-building war', forging new states like the Dutch Republic, or enabling old ones to regain their independence, like Portugal. The war is interpreted as a consequence of the imperfect level of state development around 1600. Executive authority, in the sense of the ability to take binding decisions, was not fully monopolized by a recognized, legitimate central government. Other 'deficits' included the challenge of alternative claims on inhabitants' loyalties, such as those of the rival Christian confessions, each purporting to be 'universal'.[61]

The Empire is usually interpreted in line with the earlier, negative assessment of its constitution. At best, it emerges as 'partially-modernised', stuck in the early modern stage of European development, failing to make the transition to a centralized, sovereign state.[62] Political dynamism is generally believed to have shifted to the larger principalities like Brandenburg and Bavaria that consolidated their external autonomy and imposed greater authority within their own borders. These developments have customarily been labelled 'absolutism', which has been used to define the entire period between 1648 into the nineteenth century.[63] The territorial Estates lost their ability to constrain princely power. Many reasons have been advanced for this, but indebtedness was clearly prominent among them. Unable to maintain their status from traditional sources of income, nobles either had to accept alternative employment as the state's servants or relinquish political power in return for confirmation of their social and economic privileges.[64] This trend was already present prior to 1618, but it was accelerated by the war. Several examples have been noted in the course of this book, especially the Habsburgs' success in reshaping the social basis of their monarchy through patronage and the expulsion of opponents.

The war also helped change political behaviour. Dire threats like foreign invasion fostered acceptance of 'necessity' as an argument to legitimize change. If established patterns and methods no longer proved adequate, rulers could impose new ones in the interests of the 'common good', the early modern equivalent of modern arguments like 'national security'. Necessity was the mother of absolutism. Monarchs and princes claimed unfettered powers on the grounds that a single ruler deriving authority directly from God could stand above subjects' petty squabbles and see their true interests. Such a ruler, born and raised in the appropriate environment, alone understood the 'mysteries of state', whereas subjects pursued selfish individual or sectional interests.[65]

Absolutism's emergence is generally fitted into a longer-term process of taming violence, in which the Thirty Years War again played a prominent part. Much of the state-building literature draws on the German sociologist Max Weber's influential definition of a state as the monopoly of legitimate violence. 'Violence' in this sense is a translation of the German term *Gewalt* and can be related to other aspects of power. The centralized state embodied power (*Gewalt*), authority (*Potestas*) and strength (*Vis*), enabling it to triumph over violence (*Violentia*). We have already encountered aspects of this in the discussion of the alleged lawlessness of the war's last phase, allegations that were rooted in post-war efforts by territorial governments to monopolize armed force and present their peacetime armies as superior to the undisciplined soldiery employed before.[66]

These developments wrought changes throughout society. Authority was more centralized but still remained hierarchical. Male heads of household possessed the authority to discipline other family members and servants, but only within limits set by the state's overarching power resting on moral and secular norms. Actual violence was de-legitimized and forced from public life. Heads of household might still be abusive, but only provided this went unnoticed by their neighbours or the local authorities. Public violence was reserved for the state, but much of this was also tamed. Executions were ritualized and gradually removed from public view into prison yards, or abolished altogether in many places after the later eighteenth century. In the meantime, the use and toleration of violence (in the sense of what was considered acceptable) varied between social groups, but was also subject to tighter state supervision.

This interpretation is broadly helpful provided state development is regarded as largely unintended. European rulers were rarely conscious state 'builders', at least prior to the later eighteenth century. Rather than being planned according to some abstract ideal of what a state should be, political change was driven by rulers' desires to achieve other, largely dynastic goals. A second important caveat is that state development did not follow a smooth linear path of progressive modernization.

War and State Destruction

A third qualification is to note war's destruction of political institutions, as well as human life and material objects. There are good grounds for seeing the Thirty Years War as the crisis of the Empire's territorial states. This should not be misconstrued as a return to the once-fashionable 'general crisis' theory that presented seventeenth-century wars and revolts as 'crises of authority'.[67] Clearly there were challenges from below against attempts to impose greater authority from above. The Bohemian Revolt loosely fits this pattern. But there was no generalized danger of Estates-led risings, still less of popular revolt prior to 1618. The real challenge to the established order emerged only once the war began.

The war disturbed dynastic continuity and traditions, and undermined fundamental pillars of established authority. Significant areas of land were redistributed in the wake of major victories: in 1620, 1629, 1631 and 1634. Entire territories changed hands, like the Palatinate, Mecklenburg, Bamberg, Würzburg and Mainz. Districts were removed from one territory and assigned to another. Numerous lordships, abbeys and manors were confiscated and redistributed. Some of the Empire's oldest and most distinguished families found themselves branded as outlaws. Others lost heirs killed in battle. The new owners included men like Wallenstein whose rapid rise to prominence broke social conventions. These changes were profoundly unsettling. They severed associations between land, inhabitants and rulers hallowed by lineage and custom, replacing them with an order seemingly based on brute force. Speculation, however unfounded, that Wallenstein might crown himself king of Bohemia or even emperor indicates a general anxiety at the loss of stability. Nothing seemed sacred, while authority passed to those who often lacked the roots or status to make it legitimate in the eyes of their subjects.

The latter felt betrayed and abandoned by those who were supposed to protect them. Sister Junius recorded how, when the bishop of Bamberg fled as the Swedes approached, 'the wicked people shouted as he drove out: "He's getting out again now and leaving us in the lurch; may this and that [i.e. the devil's hangman and other terms of abuse] take you; may you fall and break every bone in your body."' Likewise, the Lutheran pastors regarded the flight of Regent Anna Maria of Hohenlohe-Langenburg after Nördlingen as a sin.[68]

The departure of rulers and their officials also curtailed effective government. Local officials and community leaders were among soldiers' favourite targets as hostages to ensure contributions were paid. Even when they were left alone, billeting disrupted their activities and brought officers whose military authority and demands competed with those of civil government. This posed a serious challenge if the soldiers remained in prolonged occupation. The Swedish commandant in Olmütz told its councillors that 'he was master in the town and could do what he liked'.[69] Temporary transit could also bring chaos and make it dangerous to leave safe areas to attend to pressing problems. The breakdown of justice was felt especially keenly since the population regarded this as one of their rulers' primary tasks. Military requisitioning and plunder were experienced as robbery, yet the courts seemed powerless to prevent it. People feared to answer court summonses to assist in the apprehension of criminals because they feared that those caught would be drafted into the army and return as soldiers to take reprisals. The organized church structure suffered too. By the end of the war only 64 of Bamberg's 110 parishes still had a priest, while the ratio of clergy to parishioners in the Habsburg Sundgau in Alsace fell from 1:345 to 1:1,177.[70]

The war also disrupted the functioning of the Estates. The bailiff, mayor and council of Lauffen apologized for not attending the Württemberg diet, on the grounds their homes were full of soldiers and two French cavalry regiments were roaming the surrounding countryside.[71] The growth of military taxation eroded the Estates' role, since the burdens were often imposed without consultation. Many territorial rulers continued these taxes after 1648, citing the necessity argument that the prevailing international uncertainty, or the need to assist the emperor against the Turks, made this unavoidable. As taxes became permanent, diets were no longer summoned, denying Estates their chance to extend their privileges or air grievances. However, their decline was far from universal and some emerged stronger by 1648. Estates acquired new functions because of the war, especially in areas where the prince and his officials had fled, or were unable to exercise effective rule.

The New Order

Though in crisis, territorial rule did not collapse. It survived because there was no alternative. The army was unable to assume its functions, and commanders preferred to use the existing civil administration to collect money and supplies. The Imperialists received cash and services worth 284,600 fl. from public funds from the Franconian town of Kitzingen in nine years after they recaptured it in September 1634, compared to only 144,000 fl. directly from private individuals.[72] Where rulers were deposed, the conquerors rarely altered existing institutions and generally confirmed officials in their posts. Bavarian practice in the Palatinate and Upper Austria, as well as Sweden's conquest of Mainz and the Franconian bishoprics, indicates that even confessional differences did not mean the automatic expulsion of incumbent personnel (see Chapters 10 and 14).

Administrators adapted. New, simpler forms of taxation were introduced during the 1630s, because there were insufficient numbers of staff or information to take account of personal circumstances. The new levies were generally flat-rate poll taxes or excises on staples that naturally hit the poor hardest. Officials in Gotha, for instance, assumed control of tax administration from the Estates as part of a new effort to coordinate security after 1640. They mediated between soldiers and civilians, securing exemptions from military exactions in return for regular contributions. Evacuation measures were instituted should these safeguards fail to prevent soldiers returning. People and property would be moved to fortified towns in each district. The militia was revived in 1641 to assist this. Tax burdens were redistributed to compensate those communities close to transit routes that were suffering the most.[73]

This more active and innovative role would continue during post-war reconstruction and help change the ideal of the state from guardian of the established order to promoter of the common good. One example is how the high incidence of plague drove secular officials to interfere in more aspects of daily life, often in the face of popular and clerical opposition. Pope Urban VIII excommunicated Florentine public health officials after they banned religious assemblies and processions to help combat infection. German officials also encountered protests as they prevented grieving relatives from holding funerals and instead disposed of corpses with quick, nocturnal burials.[74] People insisted on returning to what they considered 'proper' customs and behaviour as soon as the crisis passed, but it proved impossible to reverse the process of secular rationalization inherent in state development. With a more effective claim on resources, the state alone seemed capable of coordinating activity. Even the hard-pressed duke of Pfalz-Neuburg managed to distribute 1,200 oxen and 17,000 tlr worth of wine and corn to help his subjects recover from the plague and Swedish occupation in 1635.

The war also weakened the ability of local elites to manage affairs without official assistance. Tenant farmers, millers, clergy and innkeepers all saw their wealth diminished or destroyed. Their prestige suffered from their inability to protect those in their community who had depended on them. They looked to the district and central authorities for help and protection. For example, they collaborated with officials to preserve patterns of inheritance that left the best land in their hands. In return, they helped enforce territorial legislation, public order and tax collection. Post-war princely government was built on these foundations.

CULTURAL IMPACT

Cultural Destruction

Interpretations of the war's cultural impact have followed those for its other consequences.[75] Both Czech and German nationalists believed the conflict destroyed vibrant, pre-war cultures and led to alien domination. In the former case, this came in the form of 'German' Habsburg rule. In the latter, it followed the slavish copying of foreign styles and a rejection of everything later considered authentically German. Frederick the Great, a nationalist hero despite his disdain for German literature, wrote that after the war 'the land was devastated, the fields lay barren, the cities were almost deserted . . . how could someone in Vienna or Mannheim compose sonnets or epigrams?'[76]

Alongside this cultural equivalent of the 'Disastrous War' school, there is also an interpretation suggesting earlier decline. The war supposedly exacerbated an existing trend inherent in the confessional polarization to further fragment the earlier, cosmopolitan humanism, destroying its values of moderation, tolerance and intellectual exchange. Already before the war, rulers founded their own universities to promote their chosen faith and to train administrators and clergy for their territory. 'A series of outstanding thinkers, left isolated, turned inwards, attempting to preserve in themselves a unitary grasp of the world, to recreate in an individual intellect the totality of human wisdom.'[77] This introspective project failed, leaving only what absolutist rulers considered useful to instil thrift in their subjects and to promote dynastic grandeur with new baroque palaces.

Neither approach is helped by the tendency among many art and literary historians to judge the vibrancy of a culture by criteria of originality and innovation. The Empire appears in decline after 1600 when measured against the 'heights' achieved by painters like Albrecht Dürer or Lucas Cranach, the innovation of Johann Gutenberg's printing press, and a series of outstanding humanist scholars in the late fifteenth and early sixteenth centuries. Those working in the first half of the seventeenth century allegedly only produced derivative works. There were no 'national' cultural centres, equivalent to Rome, London or Paris to attract talent and develop new styles.[78]

The war certainly disrupted artistic activity and destroyed or removed cultural artefacts. Queen Christina's plundering of Catholic libraries has already been noted. Libraries represented expensive cultural assets and priceless repositories of knowledge. All governments struggled with a shortage of expertise and qualified personnel. Sweden had just a single university (Uppsala) and could send only theology graduates to serve as army secretaries, because there were no others with sufficient skills. Universities and libraries were thus strategic targets. Marburg University was at the centre of the dispute between the rival Hessian dynasties. Maximilian of Bavaria coveted the famed *Bibliotheca Palatina* in Heidelberg that held an astonishing (for the time) 8,800 books and manuscripts, including ancient Greek texts and a large collection of Protestant theology. The pope wanted this to gain insight into the mind of the enemy. Concerned not to lose papal goodwill, Maximilian reluctantly sent the library to Rome in February 1623 where it remained until 1815. The contents of monastic libraries in Mainz were despatched to Sweden within weeks of the electorate's capture. Others were deliberately sought out later by Swedish generals eager to win favour by sending them to

Christina. Libraries were also depleted by sale as universities, schools and monasteries compensated for falling incomes by selling valuable works. Once lost, they were difficult to replace, especially as the war also caused the decline of the Frankfurt book fair. Würzburg University did not reopen until 1636, two years after its liberation from the Swedes, because it had to wait until the bishop could replace the 5,000 books stolen from its library.[79]

Protestant schools and universities declined when the Restitution Edict removed church property previously used to sustain them. Calvinist institutions suffered the most. Heidelberg University was captured early in the war. By 1622 more than half the staff had gone, mostly fleeing with the students to Switzerland or the Dutch Republic. The remainder were dismissed in 1626, except for one who converted to Catholicism. The conversion of intellectuals was highly prized by the authorities, keen to demonstrate the supposed superiority of their own creed. The conversion of Christoph Besold, a professor at Württemberg's Lutheran university at Tübingen, was trumpeted as a Catholic triumph.

The fate of German universities does support part of the generally negative assessment of the cultural impact. Whereas many had been centres of European importance, they became increasingly parochial as foreign students stopped enrolling and failed to return once the war ended. The number of aristocratic students also declined disproportionately due to the attraction of military careers as an alternative to studying. The disruption and, in several cases, collapse of universities worsened the skills shortage and adversely affected territorial administration.

Creativity and Innovation

Other activities suffered too. Numerous artists fled abroad. Less money was left for patronage, while measures like the Restitution Edict and the Swedish donations removed assets previously used to sustain theatre, and especially music. Heinrich Schütz, one of the century's greatest composers, despaired in 1637, believing there was no longer a future for Lutheran church music. Reduced resources obliged him to innovate, however. He pushed creative boundaries by composing works for smaller groups of musicians and singers.[80]

Poetry was another area of creativity that has been underestimated because it was an art form that lost favour in Central Europe soon after the war. Lutherans predominated, though they included men like Martin Opitz who was named imperial poet laureate. Other leading poets were Pastor Johann Rist, Daniel von Czepko, Johann Moscherosch and the Silesians Andreas Gryphius and Friedrich Baron Logau. Their work was a direct response to the war that they struggled to comprehend, comment on and suggest ways to overcome the violence. Some caution is required when drawing wider conclusions from their large body of work. Much was introspective and most open to diverging interpretation. Nonetheless, they did produce a distinctly national, poetic culture. Moscherosch and Logau ridiculed the imitation of foreign styles and fashions. Opitz, who fled to Holland in 1620, published his *Prosodia Germanica* four years later in a conscious attempt to free German poetry from confessional strife and make it the equal of classical Latin and Greek verse.

Their efforts flowed into the cultural politics of the largely Protestant literary societies that began in the decade before the war and continued beyond the peace. Opitz and Rist both belonged to the Fruitful Society associated with Christian of Anhalt's efforts to rally Calvinists and Lutherans within the Protestant Union. Rist also belonged to the *Pegnesischer Blumenorden* (Flower Order of the Pegnitz River), based in Nuremberg, and founded the *Sprachgesellschaft des Elbschwanenordens* (Linguistic Society of the Order of the Elbian Swan). Rist and his contemporaries did not reject foreign influence on modern nationalistic grounds. Its presence was a symptom, not a cause of Germany's greater sin. Far from being innocent victims of foreign aggression, Germans had brought misfortune upon themselves by failing to live in harmony as true Christians.

Rist developed this theme in various works after 1630, notably his 572-verse – baroque poetry applauded epic scale – 'Peace Trumpet' (*Frieden-Posaune*, 1646), his 'Germany longing for Peace' (*Das Friedewünschende Teutschland*, 1647) and the post-war music drama 'Germany Jubilating Peace' (*Das Friedejauchzende Teutschland*, 1653). In the latter work, 'Mars' as god of war makes 'Ratio Status' (reasons of state) his supreme privy councillor to help him undermine the tranquillity of 'Germany'. 'Peace' puts 'Mars' in chains, but warns 'Germany' that he will be released if she does not behave.[81] The story was thus closely in tune with the official message propagated by the territorial church and state that inhabitants should shun sin and lead obedient lives to prevent God sending another war to scourge their homeland.

Critical Voices?

This example raises the thorny question of whether artists criticized war in more general terms. Most historians have concluded that poetry, literature and painting raised only moral and theological objections to war in line with Rist's drama. One example is the interpretation of a cycle of engravings produced by Hans Ulrich Franck entitled *Memento Mori*. The last image shows the rotting corpse of a cavalryman with a gallows on one side and a still-intact church on the other. It seems a warning to repent before it is too late.[82] This has been rejected as a neo-conservative interpretation that denies that early modern Europeans were able to empathize with the suffering of others and use art as a mirror and a tool of political consciousness. Paintings, these modern critics claim, were explicit denunciations of war as a crime against the innocent. Far from demonstrating faith in divine punishment, artists suggested that people could not rely on God's saving grace and instead should confront the problems of this world through practical solutions.[83]

This critical interpretation cites the famous cycle of engravings entitled *The Miseries of War* (1633) produced by Jacques Callot from Lorraine. Many of these show soldiers attacking villages, plundering, murdering and raping. One, however, depicts marauders being strung up from a tree. It has been suggested the cycle thus illustrates both the problem and a potential solution in tighter discipline, not prayer and penance.[84]

The problem is that Callot also produced panoramic engravings and other more propagandist images, such as a large picture illustrating how Spinola captured Breda in 1625. Dutch artists alone produced several million paintings in the sixteenth and seventeenth centuries, of which perhaps 10 per cent survive. When placed alongside engravings and other images, the number from the war years is truly vast. It is impossible to fit these into simple categories, especially as the majority are by artists who are only now being studied. Even less is known about the market for such images. It is clear that many artists produced critical works as personal attempts to come to terms with what they had witnessed or heard, rather than as acts of political commentary. Valentin Wagner, for instance, constantly drew sleeping figures that have been interpreted as a personal attempt to escape the horrors of war. Rudolf Meyer's etchings of soldiers massacring civilians were drawn in the early 1630s but not published until twenty years later.[85]

Such scenes of violence were common, but need to be placed in their context. Meyer, Callot and Franck were among many artists producing cycles of engravings showing all aspects of military life. Variously entitled *Kriegstheater* (Theatre of War) or *Soldatenleben* (Soldier's Life), these prints showed cavalry skirmishes, raids, camps, men drilling, gambling or fighting in drunken brawls. Numerous small-scale paintings also used such themes. Depictions of war and violence thus belong to the general contemporary world of genre painting. The scenes of rowdy or violent soldiers are not dissimilar to other cycles showing rustic life, with inebriated peasants fighting or eating to excess. Franck and others also depicted the peasants' revenge, showing soldiers being set upon and murdered by villagers.

Though also not free from controversy, princely commissions and other propaganda paintings are rather easier to interpret. The patron is generally depicted mounted in the foreground on an elevation painted into the pseudo-realistic landscape. The middle distance displays a panoramic view of their victorious battle or siege under a suitably dramatic sky. Corpses, usually lying near the hoofs of the general's horse, function less as victims of war than to evoke the classical image of the victor trampling his foe underfoot. The Netherlands painter Pieter Snayers also produced images of soldiers looting, but made his name with a cycle of 21 vast battle paintings commissioned by Piccolomini to commemorate his career.

Snayers' prodigious output also included a painting of the battle of White Mountain that later hung in the bedroom used by successive Bavarian electors. Maximilian had already donated his personal standard carried in the battle, along with twenty banners taken from the enemy, to a church dedicated in Rome as thanks for the victory. The building was decorated with a specially commissioned series of paintings with scenes from the action, while a monumental column was later erected in Munich and dedicated to the Virgin. The connection with thanksgiving extended to more humble commissions, especially from Catholics. An adjutant and six trumpeters from the von Salis Bavarian cavalry regiment had a votive painting made around 1651 showing them kneeling before the Madonna in thanks for surviving the battle of Allerheim six years earlier.[86]

Celebrations of war can been found in other art forms, though they are now less well known than the apparently more critical works. Wolfgang

Helmhard von Hohberg wrote a verse epic *Der Habspurgische Ottobert* (1664), set in the sixth century but clearly addressed to the seventeenth-century Habsburgs. This offered conventional praise for the dynasty's heroism in fighting a just war. Conflict was presented as part of the human condition, while peace appeared impermanent. Hohberg had served in the imperial army in 1632–41, rising to captain, and was eventually elevated as baron. His experience was thus different to the fugitive baroque poets for whom the war often brought dislocation and disrupted careers.[87]

Hohberg illustrates how soldiers were not just destroyers, but could be creators and facilitators. Piccolomini and Archduke Leopold Wilhelm were famous patrons, especially of painters. Philip IV's Buen Retiro palace is another example with its Hall of Realms decorated with vast battle paintings. Officers formed a major proportion of the Fruitful Society members, including General Lohausen who spent his captivity after the battle of Lutter translating foreign literature into German. General Horn also studied while a prisoner and participated in Jesuit theatre. Colonel von dem Werder, a German in Swedish service, translated books, while General Gronsfeld was a well-educated and published author.

Grimmelshausen

A soldier also produced the most famous work about the war. Johann Jacob Christoffel von Grimmelshausen was born around 1621 in Gelnhausen, north-east of Frankfurt. His Lutheran father died while he was still young. His mother remarried and sent him to be raised by his grandfather who was a baker and innkeeper. Johann was still attending Latin school when the Swedes plundered Gelnhausen whose inhabitants fled to the surrounding woods. Johann was later taken to nearby Hanau to escape the aftermath of Nördlingen. While playing on the ice outside the fortress he was kidnapped by Croats and taken to Hersfeld. He was captured by the Hessians soon after, and later witnessed the Saxon siege of Magdeburg and the battle of Wittstock as a stable boy in the imperial army. He was a soldier by 1637 and participated in Götz's fruitless attempts to relieve Breisach. His colonel discovered that he could read and write and made him regimental clerk in 1639. Johann saw out the rest of the war in that capacity in the imperial garrison of Offenburg on the Upper Rhine. He converted to Catholicism while in imperial service and married Catharina Henninger, the daughter of an NCO in the same regiment. After the war he became a steward on his former colonel's estates. Grimmelshausen's family claimed aristocratic ancestry and he assumed the 'von' as his fortunes prospered in the 1650s when he enjoyed a comfortable life, acquiring some land, running two taverns and eventually becoming mayor of Renchen, a small town belonging to the bishop of Strasbourg. He ended his days as he began, amid foreign invasion, in this case the French attack on Alsace led initially by Turenne, in August 1676.

Grimmelshausen's life is worth recounting just as an example of how it was still possible to prosper despite the war. What made him truly significant, however, was the astonishing literary output that began only in the last decade of his life. His first work was his greatest success. *The Adventurous Simplicissimus* was issued in five parts in 1668, followed by a sixth a year later. Another four works appeared using common characters and themes, notably *The Life of the Arch-Cheat and Renegade Courage* (1670) made famous as the play *Mother Courage* by Berthold Brecht, written in 1938 and premiered in Zurich in 1941.[88]

Much of *Simplicissimus* is clearly autobiographical. The central character's rustic childhood is abruptly terminated once his family's farm is plundered. Forced to live in the woods, he is adopted as a fool by Ramsay, the Swedish commandant of Hanau. He is captured by Croats and witnesses the battle of Wittstock. Here the stories diverge, as Simplicissimus rises through the ranks as a daring partisan in the war between outposts in Westphalia, followed by various adventures in France, Switzerland and the Rhineland.

The novel can be read as disillusionment with, and even criticism of, religion and the established order. The key scene (Book 1, chapter 4) certainly lends itself to this. It describes in graphic detail how the soldiers systematically plunder the hero's farm and torture its inhabitants, made all the more effective by recounting it through Simplicissimus's childlike perspective. Not surprisingly, it is the most quoted section of the book, occasionally surfacing in general accounts that use it uncritically as 'eyewitness' testimony. The common interpretation is as an expression of doubt in divine justice: how can God allow such cruelty? It seems that Grimmelshausen despaired of religion providing peace and prosperity. The novel ends with Simpicissimus leaving society altogether and living as a hermit on a desert island.[89]

Such apparent despair sits ill with what we know of the author's comfortable later life. More importantly, there are relatively few descriptions of violence, beyond the famous farm scene. By contrast, soldiers and military life often appear in a positive light. The characters are modelled on real figures, or openly depict them, such as the Hessian partisan Little Jacob.[90] Grimmelshausen also defends General Götz against criticism over the Breisach campaign. Much of the social critique reads like the grumblings of the neglected foot soldier against his superiors. A widely quoted passage about military oppression (Book 1, chapter 15) is followed by a lament on the difficulties of getting promoted from the ranks. There is much that is conventional and conservative. Simplicissimus, like Grimmelshausen, turns out to have been of noble birth, a common wish-fulfilment motif. Like his creation, the author also had his eye on the main chance. He wanted a best-seller and packed his story full of eclectic information, travelogue, middle-brow Bible references and classical allusions, alongside rustic folk tales and superstition. The presence of the latter belies the novel's complexity and its author's erudition. His account of Wittstock reads like first-hand experience, yet it is based on Sir Philip Sidney's 1590 novel *Arcadia*. Large parts are plagiarized from other picaresque novels and courtly romances, while the hermit conclusion echoes contemporary interest in castaways and exploration.

Conclusions

The problems of interpretation underscore the wider difficulty of generalizing about the war's impact. First, there were wide variations across time and space for its impact on culture, like that for other aspects of life. The war did not immediately halt cultural production across the Empire. Salzburg University opened in 1622. The elector of Mainz built a new riverside palace in his capital after 1626. Such ventures represented the continuation of existing plans associated with the Catholic revival. They redoubled after the war with a flowering of baroque architecture across southern and western Germany.

Some activities continued regardless. Europe's first opera performance outside Italy was staged in Salzburg in 1614. The subsequent decline of music there stemmed largely from personal taste, as the new archbishop after 1619, Paris Count Lodron, favoured the theatre instead: the university theatre staged at least a hundred productions during the war. Lodron also promoted the construction of the new cathedral, begun in 1613 to replace the earlier one that burned down in 1598. The building was essentially finished by 1622 and decorated in 1623–35, all despite the war. On a more modest scale, schooling continued in Naumburg despite cutbacks in other areas of municipal expenditure. Teachers were still appointed and study grants awarded. Drama and music were also introduced into the school, reflecting a second general point about continued innovation and creativity. The rector of Naumburg's main school wrote sixteen plays in 1642–6, a prodigious output even in good times, but more remarkable still considering these were the inhabitants' worst years.[91]

Other trends that can be classed as cultural were accelerated by the war, including the use of tobacco that entered the Empire in the 1580s and was spread by troop movements after 1618. Print culture also boomed (see the following chapter). Smoking would probably have spread anyway, and it is important not to let the war obscure the influence of other factors. European culture was already changing rapidly under the impact of world exploration, trade and scientific discoveries, all of which helped free minds from the deadening grip of theology. The conflict furthered this by demonstrating the futility of religious fundamentalism, but this came at a very high price. While creativity and ingenuity still flourished, much was needlessly destroyed. The human cost becomes clearest when we examine the psychological impact of the war in the final chapter.

23

Experiencing War

THE NATURE OF EXPERIENCE

Personal Testimony

What the war was like for those living through it is one of the most interesting, yet difficult questions. Any answer faces considerable problems in identifying and interpreting the evidence. For post-structuralists and other theorists, these difficulties invalidate the entire concept of experience as an analytical category. This has not prevented it transforming how the war and other early modern conflicts have been studied since the 1990s.[1] Recent work overcomes some of the problems by distinguishing between two forms of experience. The first, *Erlebnis*, is the fleeting experience an individual feels through the constant succession of lived events. This subjective dimension cannot be studied with any real precision for the past. The second, *Erfahrung*, is the accumulative knowledge an individual acquires from his or her transient experience, involving a process of selection and reflection on life. Experience in this sense can be studied, because such reflections have been committed to paper and preserved.

The approach is still not without its problems. The most important is the relationship of individual to wider, collective experience. This is not just a matter of how 'typical' an individual's experience might have been. It is also a matter of how individuals perceive and record events, since these are filtered through what they already know and think life is like. These problems become clearer when we examine the first-hand personal testimonies that survive in a variety of forms. Letters are the most immediate, since they were generally written closest in time to actual events. Correspondence among princes, generals and other members of the elite has long been staple fare for historians, but letters from humbler folk are only now being used, partly because far fewer of them still exist.[2] Next in terms of immediacy are the household record books that contain an eclectic mix of personal statements, prayers and family data. Diaries and chronicles also survive, usually compiled by an individual, but sometimes added to by a relation and continued as a family record. Diary keeping became more common with the spread of printed calendars around 1600, as these encouraged a more chrono-logical sense of time. Hans Heberle, a bonded shoemaker from a village near Ulm, began his in 1618 when he was twenty and kept it until 1672, just five years before his death. The most retrospective form of testimony is the autobiography. These are rather variable for the early seventeenth century. They range from sparse personal details prepared as a basis for a funeral oration, to more extensive recollections. A catalogue published a decade ago lists 240 diaries, chronicles and autobiographies by 226 men and 9 women from the war years that have already been published. The total number is probably far greater as new material is still being discovered.[3]

Like diaries, autobiographies were influenced by the European tra-dition of recording events as a chronicle. Seventeenth-century authors generally strove for a detached, impersonal style, placing themselves in what they regarded as their wider context. They generally lack reflection on events, descriptions of emotions or psychological insights that can be found in some sixteenth-century works and which become more common with those written after the 1770s. There were many motives for writing. Some were purely personal, perhaps as a way of coming to terms with difficult events. Others were compiled for the edification of family, friends or a community. The latter was the case with diaries kept by nuns, who form the majority of the few female writers whose works still survive.[4]

The often mundane character of many of these texts led to their general neglect until the early 1990s in favour of more dramatic, fictional accounts like Grimmelshausen's novel, or seemingly more 'reliable' official records. While there is a risk of myopia in the current fashion for 'micro history', recent work has done much to dispel the earlier concern over the reliability of personal testimony. Such sources are useful not so much as an accurate portrayal of events but for how the war was perceived and remembered. Identifying what authors chose to record or omit tells us much about what they considered important or traumatic. The reoccurrence of stock motifs and passages copied from other texts or pasted from newspapers allows us to trace the flow of ideas and information.[5]

The War as Media Event

The outbreak of the war coincided with new developments in European print culture that were greatly accelerated by the subsequent thirst for news from the Empire. Information still circulated by word of mouth spread by travellers and refugees, as well as hand-written through networks of correspondents maintained by governments, companies, merchants and, frequently, senior military and church figures. These networks were greatly assisted by the development of regular postal systems, of which the most important was the imperial postal service operated as a monopoly by the Thurn und Taxis family after 1490. The service maintained regular routes with riders, and later post coaches, intersecting at major centres like Frankfurt am Main. Relays of horses enabled it to deliver a letter across 100km within 24 hours. The Thurn und Taxis were richly rewarded, acquiring the status of hereditary nobility in 1515, becoming barons (in 1608), then counts (1624) and ultimately imperial princes (1695).

Their service facilitated the spread of regular newspapers by providing the distribution needed to make printed news commercially viable. Papers began in Strasbourg and Antwerp in 1605 and had been started in at least five other cities by 1618. The Defenestration of Prague on 23 May 1618 was already reported in the Frankfurt paper in June. The war's spread fuelled a rapid expansion with six new titles appearing in 1619 alone, followed by another seventeen over the 1620s and twelve more after Sweden's intervention. Several folded, or appeared only irregularly, but around thirty weekly papers were running in 1648 with a total distribution of 15,000 copies, compared to only a hundred a week before 1618. Total readership was up to twenty times the distribution figure, because papers were circulated among friends or read aloud to illiterate neighbours. The Empire led the way. There was no French equivalent until 1631, while most other countries had to wait until the later seventeenth century.[6]

There are substantial differences between these publications and their modern equivalents. Early seventeenth-century papers avoided explicit comment and did not see their mission as shaping opinion. The first editorial appeared in a German paper in 1687. Much, if not all, of the text was filled by printing official pronouncements, treaties, documents and letters. The rest concentrated on diplomatic, military and political events, virtually ignoring local news or 'human interest' stories, except for papers like the Viennese *Ordentliche Postzeitung* based in court residence cities that relayed information about the ruling dynasty. There was a considerable overlap with the related genre of the newsletter like the famous *Theatrum Europaeum*, begun by the Strasbourg publisher Johann Philipp Abelin in 1633 and continued for a century. This was a high-quality record of events that printed many documents verbatim and included exceptional engravings produced by the Merian family from Frankfurt. The first volume covered the war from the Defenestration, while subsequent ones appeared with less of a time lag.[7]

The sober tone did not reflect a belief in neutral objective journalism. Truth was not regarded as something standing above or between different viewpoints, but as directly related to singular, definitive legal and confessional concepts. This raises the question of whether print media and other forms of communicating news reflected or shaped opinion. The most overtly polemic form was the pamphlet that emerged around 1490 in Europe's first 'media revolution' following the invention of printing. Pamphlets focused on single issues and clearly sought to both comment and influence. Along with broadsheets combining images with (often) rhymed texts, they were a major feature of the Reformation, cleverly exploited by Luther and allowing him to become the world's first best-selling author.[8]

The first imperial censorship law was passed in 1521, the year of the ban on Luther's writings. The legislation was revised six times by 1570, establishing a censorship committee based in the postal centre of Frankfurt that issued verdicts to be enforced by the relevant territorial authorities. Territorial fragmentation inhibited effective enforcement, but printing required large, heavy equipment. It was fairly easy to punish printers for producing offensive material, encouraging an element of self-censorship as publishers refused to accept dangerous works. The result was a varied media landscape. Publications in cities like Hamburg or Wolfenbüttel generally refrained from extremist views, because these venues wished to remain on good terms with everyone. Those in cities more firmly associated with one of the belligerents were more partisan. A good example is the Viennese *Ordentliche Postzeitung* where war reporting accounted for 55 per cent of articles, followed by material on the court that composed another third. Nearly two-thirds of articles were decidedly in favour of the emperor's cause, with a quarter directly hostile to the enemy.[9]

The authorities quickly appreciated the power of the press. The Antwerp publisher Abraham Verhoeven persuaded Archduke Albert to grant him a licence for a regular paper in 1620 by saying the government would enhance its reputation by publicizing details of its victories.[10] However, the official attitude remained ambivalent. There was no desire for transparency, or freedom of information. Public affairs were considered beyond the comprehension of ordinary mortals, reserved as 'mysteries of state' for those whose elevated birth supposedly endowed them with superior understanding. Representative institutions might challenge monarchical or princely secrecy but they rarely wished to share the knowledge they obtained with the wider population. Yet there was also a sense of a public that encompassed the living and those still to be born. Rulers craved the social capital attached to reputation. They wanted to project their acts as conforming to idealized virtues, such as justice, prudence and clemency, not merely to assist current objectives, but to leave a glorious legacy for posterity. These considerations shaped how policy was presented, as we have seen with the Bohemian Confederates' *Apologia*, Gustavus's manifesto and Richelieu's declaration of war.

Major events like the sack of Magdeburg forced papers to provide explanations that inevitably entailed taking sides. Some, like those operating from the safety of Zurich, were able to be openly partisan. However, papers were commercial ventures, as were most pamphlets except those with government subsidy. They also faced practical and technical difficulties, relying on deliberate 'leaks', official documents, travellers and unpaid informants for their information, since none maintained its own journalists. In the absence of copyright laws much of the material was simply lifted from other publications. Printers typeset texts as news came in with little thought to layout, sometimes inadvertently including contradictory or blatantly false reports. Few rulers wanted to tarnish their reputations by appearing openly tyrannical and it remained possible to print dissenting views. Around 5 per cent of the *Ordentliche*

Postzeitung's war reporting was hostile to the emperor, while another 7 per cent actually favoured the enemy.

The same applied to pamphlets that more closely employed stylistic devices to foster sympathy with the author's views, and were more likely to include sensationalist reporting and graphic descriptions of violence. Protestant commentaries on the Valtellina massacre of 1620 generally labelled it a 'bloodbath', while Catholics referred to 'the extirpation of heresy'. Yet, neither side saw the violence as senseless. The real question was how to judge the participants according to the rival versions of legality. This opened the door to self-criticism. For example, Catholics were concerned whether the perpetrators had sinned by using religion as an excuse to seize Protestant property.[11] Confessionally motivated propaganda sought to rally opinion on the basis of faith and to undermine and isolate opponents. It undoubtedly convinced many that the conflict was a religious war. Yet the general trend was secular. The various armies appeared not as Protestants or Catholics, but as Swedes, Bohemians, Bavarians or Imperialists. News about the Muslim sultan appeared alongside reports of the activities of Christian rulers. The prominence given to generals and other personalities further suggested the essentially human, not divine, character of events.

MILITARY—CIVIL RELATIONS

The Military Community

Soldiers existed as a distinct group united by their oath upon enlistment to obey the 'articles of war', or military code setting out death and other dire punishments for misdemeanours. The sworn oath lay at the heart of early modern society as the basis of all forms of association. Subjects paid homage to lords and princes on their accession. Citizens and craftsmen swore to uphold civic and guild charters. The ceremony symbolized the reciprocity of rights and duties. The associational element of military life was being eroded by the stress on hierarchy, obedience and discipline. However, official regulation remained only one factor, alongside custom and personal honour, to determine behaviour.

Interpretations of soldiers in the Thirty Years War have been coloured by the pejorative connotations of the term 'mercenary'. Most military history written in the nineteenth and twentieth centuries rests on the assumption that volunteers or conscripts serving their country in a permanent, professional army were inherently superior soldiers. The recent stress on religious war suggests that faith would have provided motivation and cohesion during the Thirty Years War, yet traditional military historians have concluded that soldiers lacked ideals and simply served whoever paid the most.[12] The standard interpretation stresses institutional deficits, such as the lack of permanent regiments, and the apparent absence of national or political loyalty. Early seventeenth-century military institutions are measured against their successors and found wanting. The problems inherent in such comparisons become clear when they are reversed. For example, the Revolutionary and Napoleonic Wars are often hailed as the birth of modern armies based on motivated 'citizens-in-arms', but they were also protracted and destructive, and displayed many of the characteristics found during the Thirty Years War, including high desertion rates.

An earlier survey concluded there was insufficient evidence to generalize about the soldiers who fought in the Thirty Years War.[13] Nearly 25 years on, the situation remains one of the most under-researched aspects of the conflict, but enough work has appeared to offer some general insight. There is no compelling evidence to suggest that criminals were disproportionately represented within the ranks. Bavaria stopped condemning men to the Venetian galleys when the war broke out and instead sentenced them to serve as 'matrosses' (*Handlanger*), or gunners' assistants, to help position the artillery. No more than 200 men entered the Bavarian army this way between 1635 and 1648.[14] Most soldiers either volunteered or were conscripted through the territorial militia in the Empire, or through the draft in Denmark, Sweden and Finland. Both compulsory systems targeted men from similar backgrounds: young, unmarried, who could be spared from the civilian economy. Official rules were ignored if manpower was short. Nonetheless, most new recruits were single men in their early twenties. By contrast, four out of five of those transferring from one army to another came with a wife and often a family in tow. They were welcomed nonetheless, since their prior experience was greatly valued by officers, despite the logistical problems of their dependants swelling the numbers of camp followers.

Former textile and building workers formed the largest group taken directly from civilian life. These trades were among those most easily disrupted by the war. They were also urban and there is considerable evidence that a disproportionate number of recruits came from towns, though many of them may well have been rural refugees.[15] Rural recruits were largely farm labourers rather than peasants with their own land. Students, former public officials and other educated men formed a tiny minority, though they predominate among those who left personal accounts. The Swedish, and to a lesser extent the Danish, armies were unusual in that they were recruited primarily in Germany and contained relatively few natives. Around a fifth of the French army was foreign, largely Swiss (a quarter of the foreigners), then Irish, German, Alsatian and Italian in that order. The Swiss and Irish were raised as separate regiments by military contractors, but the others usually enlisted because French units were serving in the area. The same applies to the Bavarian army. Units raised in Cologne had a higher proportion of non-Germans, thanks to the proximity to the Netherlands and other good recruiting grounds. Though the elector's own subjects were a minority in the Bavarian army, only one or two out of every ten 'Bavarian' soldiers came from outside the Empire. The foreign element often included prisoners pressed into service after a victory or capture of a town. This practice became common after 1620. The Bavarians pressed 1,494 men taken at Nördlingen in 1634 to make up for the casualties suffered by their infantry, while 2,487 French prisoners were incorporated after Herbsthausen in 1645.[16] Captured officers were released on parole, or ransomed. Prisoner exchange cartels were already used in the 1620s and became more common in the 1640s, but generally only officers were involved.[17]

The impressment of prisoners diluted confessional uniformity. Military codes had followed the general trend of imperial legislation during the sixteenth century in using deliberately ambiguous terms to enable men of all confessions to swear a generic Christian oath of loyalty. Confession assumed greater importance after 1618. Militants felt only true believers could win with God's blessing. Dissenters were suspect. Wartenberg blamed the defeat at Breitenfeld in 1631 on the presence of Protestant officers in the imperial army. Maximilian preferred Catholics to command his Bavarians, and in 1629 Bishop Ehrenberg of Würzburg insisted the unit guarding his capital be composed only of Catholics.[18]

Such insistence reflected a desire not matched in reality. The Lisowski

Cossack cavalry were led by Polish Catholics who declared they were fighting for their religion, yet the majority of the troopers were Orthodox Cossacks and Ukrainians. The Orthodox church in Kiev also opposed Protestantism and the men simply transferred their local anti-Protestantism to Germany, tending to treat all those who could not recite the Ave Maria as enemies. The fact that, while they also served France, Cossacks were not found in Protestant armies does suggest an element of religious allegiance.[19]

However, confession was only one factor influencing the choice of service. Protestant Scots served in the Polish and imperial armies. Though far more joined the Danish and Swedish forces, these countries were also easier to reach from Scotland. Leading Scots Catholics recruited for Protestant powers, while some Scots Calvinists entered French service. The latter choice may well have been prompted by dynasticism, given King Charles I's French marriage. Loyalty to the Stuarts was also a factor for those entering Danish, Swedish and Palatine service, all of which could be reconciled with the British monarchy's political objectives.[20] Professionalism was another factor, and it especially attracted men to armies with established reputations, like the Dutch and, later, Swedes. Career security and the hope for better prospects encouraged frequent transfers between armies. Eight Polish regiments led by Scottish and Irish officers entered imperial service after the extension of the Swedish-Polish truce in 1635. Many men converted to the faith of their employer, though not always immediately. There are examples of this happening the other way round too, as in the case of the Englishman Sydenham Poyntz who became a Catholic after joining the Protestant Saxon army. Adherence to the 'wrong' religion was not a barrier to promotion, though it did not help. Melander rose in imperial service despite remaining a Calvinist. To an extent, the imperial army stood above confession as it was politically expedient to include Lutherans as well as Catholics. Wallenstein placed ability above confession and promoted several Protestants to senior positions. Far less attention was in any case paid to the religion of ordinary soldiers who made up the bulk of personnel.

Melander's case and other examples, like the peasant and later Bavarian general Jan van Werth, indicate it was possible to rise from humble origins to the highest ranks. Many junior officers were commoners but nobles did predominate from the rank of captain upwards.[21] While some officers were educated men, very few had formal military training. Most learned by experience, serving as a non-commissioned volunteer before joining or raising a company. This placed a premium on personal reputation and connections, and especially on knowing respected men who could write a letter of introduction or secure an offer of appointment. Augustus von Bismarck transferred from the Alt-Rheingraf cavalry regiment to the Schmidtberg infantry regiment within the Bernhardine army when he failed to get advancement. He chose Schmidtberg because he already knew some of its officers, who became godparents to his children after the war.[22] The lack of formal education should not be equated with the absence of skill or knowledge. Command of even a relatively small unit required a host of practical skills in personnel management, logistics, accountancy, negotiation and an understanding of topography and the rural economy.

Officers' higher status and responsibilities undoubtedly set them apart from the mass of ordinary soldiers, but all were part of a wider military community that also included camp followers and civilian dependants. All travelled together and shared a common fate in the success or failure of operations that determined not only whether they would eat or sleep comfortably, but could also mean life or death.

High alcohol consumption was another obvious characteristic. Alcohol was an important part of soldiers' daily diet, though beer was much weaker than it is today. It deadened the gnawing hunger that came from rarely having enough to eat. Though excessive drinking was condemned as immoral, the authorities derived a significant income from alcohol levies, while German monks were already famed for their beer- and wine-making. Attempts to restrict brewing were often motivated not by morals but the desire to conserve scarce grain and wood stocks. A soldier's official daily allowance was one measure (1.4 litres) of wine, or two of beer. Soldiers billeted in Augsburg drank one or more measures of wine or beer with a meal, and continued with further drinking in the evening that proved particularly dangerous when combined with the fashion for smoking. Officers ate and drank more, consuming finer wines and, together with their wives, shots of brandy or vermouth in the morning. Officers also held lengthy and costly banquets lasting up to a week. Gallas and Franz Albrecht of Lauenburg emptied sixteen barrels of wine during negotiations in July 1633, while Banér regularly spent the entire day drinking and had his artillery fire 400 shots to accompany one bout. Like the characters in Dumas' *Three Musketeers*, officers considered prompt payment beneath them, frequently leaving bills of up to 1,500 fl., equivalent to half the value of a tavern, behind them.[23]

Plunder

Contemporary art and literature suggest military–civil relations were generally antagonistic. The most common image is that of soldiers plundering villages and torturing peasants, followed by depictions of the latter taking their revenge on marauders. The frequency of these motifs suggests the war was perceived as a violent intrusion into settled existence. It also fits the official presentation from Protestant and Catholic pulpits of the conflict as the scourge of God to punish a sinful people. The perpetrators in tales of violence are overwhelmingly exotic foreigners like Croats, Cossacks, Finns or Swedes.

Detailed analysis of plundering suggests a more complex relationship. A good example is the Hessian raid on Hilden, a village with 700 inhabitants in the duchy of Berg. Advancing from Hamm, the Hessians reached the outskirts of Hilden on 2 August 1648, seizing 17 horses and 54 cows from the meadows belonging to 16 peasants. Livestock was a favourite target, because it could be driven away quickly and either slaughtered for immediate consumption, or sold. An anonymous soldier records how his 'boy' (servant) took a horse and 'a fine cow' at Durlach in 1634, selling the latter for 11 fl. at Wimpfen nearby. There are also many cases of soldiers harvesting crops for their own use, which required more time and effort than cattle rustling.[24] The Hessians also broke into seventeen homes, all on Hilden's western side where they arrived, taking bread, butter, meat, rye and other food, as well as portable utensils like tin plates, kettles, harness, clothing and bed linen that were either useful or could be sold for modest profit. They ripped open bedding, scattering the feathers, both to steal the linen and to look for hidden valuables. The search for valuables could result in further damage, especially to beds that were usually worth a quarter to a third of the household inventory. Cupboards and chests were also broken open. Furniture, however, was mainly at risk from more prolonged occupation when it was burned as firewood. Raiders rarely stayed long enough to do more damage, unless they set the place on fire. Their haste increased the risk of violence. Torture to reveal hiding places is another stock image from the war. It appears frequently as hearsay. Pastor Martin Bötzinger is one of the few to record being compelled to swallow the infamous 'Swedish draught, filled with manure, that loosened almost all my teeth'.[25] But unlike the 26 families who suffered in Hilden, Bötzinger was a community leader with 300 tlr in cash to hide. The Hilden experience was more common, where the worst that occurred was a beating for those who got in the way or were caught by soldiers frustrated at not finding anything more valuable. The highest single loss was 112 tlr suffered by a farmer, largely through the theft of nine cows. The total loss for the village was 1,178 tlr.

There is little to suggest that plundering became worse or more systematic later in the conflict. Recruits and newly raised units might need to learn how to work together to seal off a community and seize its assets, but it did not take a generation to perfect techniques that were already widespread in the Netherlands and Hungary before 1618. Plundering only worked thanks to the civilian market for stolen goods. Civilians could also participate directly. Servants helped rob masters, sometimes willingly. People settled scores, betraying their neighbours' hoarded treasure, or diverting robbery from their own door by telling soldiers of allegedly better booty elsewhere. Civilians joined raiding parties, behaving as badly as soldiers. They plundered corpses after battles, often finding looted treasure on the bodies that they then sold on. War eroded neighbourliness, and those still with money could benefit at the expense of the less fortunate. The Augustine nuns of Mariastein near Eichstätt were able to restock their convent after Nördlingen with utensils and other items 'people pleadingly gave up or sold for next to nothing or for a bit of bread'.[26]

Negotiation

The civilian interest in the military could extend beyond pure materialism. Travelling from his home town of Leipzig with his father who was taking up a post in Magdeburg, Friedrich Friese recalled how they passed through the city's checkpoints on a cold night in 1628. While his sisters shivered, 'we saw musketeers with burning match, that we had otherwise never seen . . . the smell of match struck us as most wondrous'.[27] Likewise, Sister Junius's diary records considerable military detail, including her opinion on tactics and commanders. This suggests a familiarity with, and even positive appreciation of, some aspects of the military. Certainly, the abstract definition of the enemy in official propaganda soon broke down with actual encounters, as opposing troops could behave well while nominally friendly forces murdered and tortured.

Military–civil relations were not necessarily asymmetrical.[28] The soldiers' advantages combined the coercive 'stick' of an armed body with the 'carrot' of their officers' promise to reduce burdens in return for cooperation. Civilians, however, generally possessed superior numbers, assets and resources, plus local knowledge and the threat of flight. Armies might harvest crops, but they could not grow their own food and a march through a depopulated, barren area spelled disaster, as Gallas's operations proved in 1644.

Violence cannot be explained entirely by reference to material factors, as some have claimed.[29] There were robberies without violence, but also violence without material gain. Soldiers occupied an ambiguous place in society as servants of the authorities who engaged in activities breaching the most basic Christian commandments. The inflation of the later sixteenth century eroded their pay well before 1618 and they were generally despised. Several historians have argued that violence was a means of demonstrating individual or collective superiority in the face of such hostility.[30] Even activities that included elements of material gain could have additional psychological motives. Breaking into a town or house to plunder disrupted the tranquil world of the honest burgher. Wanton destruction struck at what others held dear. The theft of clothing humiliated the victims. Soldiers made public figures wear fools' caps or walk barefoot.[31] Captive women included those from a more elevated social status, who could be forced to cook, clean or do other menial chores. Some have explained rape in this context, especially as the act was sometimes committed in public to dishonour the husband who was forced to watch.[32] Nonetheless soldiers were not totally detached from society but came from much the same backgrounds as those civilians they attacked. Their behaviour was influenced by wider social norms to which they often conformed, even when not supervised by their officers.

Violence tended to be a consequence of the breakdown of negotiation. This might explain the frequent reference to foreign perpetrators since they could not make their demands understood to the local population. Negotiation relied on information. Communities exchanged news about troop movements to prepare themselves. The appearance of troops was rarely met by open defiance. Instead, community leaders would bargain with officers on the edge of their settlement. As we have seen in the analysis of the contributions system in Chapter 12, officers needed civilian cooperation and were prepared to reduce their demands to obtain it. Relations became easier as people talked, but could break down if soldiers were in a hurry, such as during a retreat. The only time Sister Junius's convent was seriously threatened was during the Swedish retreat after Nördlingen when the soldiers ignored the orders to spare those who had paid the army for protection. The nuns were saved by a captain who had visited them before and who turfed out the plunderers.[33]

Flight

Flight was another civilian option, but one fraught with risk. Approaching soldiers forced people to confront what really mattered. Most remained rooted until the last minute through fear of leaving their home or business unattended, an absence of alternative livelihood or connections elsewhere, or through a sense of duty and family responsibility. Martin Bötzinger only left Heldburg in Franconia, where he was a teacher, when his father-in-law was murdered in 1632. He became a pastor in Poppenhausen, but was forced to leave two years later after the war and plague left only nine inhabitants.

Geography was another factor affecting decisions. Mecklenburg had few strong towns, so its population took to the woods, marshes or lakes. Large, active cities were more attractive, but became overcrowded. Strasbourg sheltered 30,000 extra people in March 1636, doubling its population. Confession and language also influenced destination as refugees headed for places where they would both feel more at home and be welcomed. Social status and connections gave some an entrée. Merchants went where they already had business contacts, while clergy headed for houses of the same religious order. Towns were more prepared to accept rich people than the poor. Leipzig responded to the flood of refugees after the sack of Magdeburg by tightening its residence requirements in 1631. The city was almost overwhelmed with those fleeing the plague in 1639 when the 16,000 inhabitants were supporting 2,268 on civic welfare. Five hundred wagon-loads of refugees descended on Hanover's 6,000 inhabitants when the Imperialists entered the area in September 1635. Many of these people could not support themselves: children composed 40 per cent of those receiving welfare in Hamburg in 1633 and half of them were refugees who had fled Magdeburg two years earlier. Nonetheless, Leipzig relaxed its two-year residency requirement when richer refugees applied for citizenship.[34]

The better-off often had good reasons to stay put. Their connections to local elites offered some protection. People like pastors, university staff and officials also had salaries to lose. Nobles found it difficult to leave their properties unsupervised. Christoph von Bismarck, the landowner in the Brandenburg village of Briest (population 140), suffered from his proximity to the important Elbe crossing of Werben. Each time troops appeared after 1626 he sent his wife and family to Stendal, but this provided no protection from the plague that killed three of his children in as many days in September 1636. A fourth died a few weeks later, as well as a nephew and a niece. Troop movements prevented him from burying them in the family grave until two months later, while the proper funeral service was held only in March 1637. The family's frequent absences exposed their estate to robbers. The nuns of the Cistercian convent of Oberschönenfeld near Augsburg made a similarly unpleasant discovery when they returned in 1635 after sheltering for three years in the Tirol. The Swedes had given their house to Colonel Schlammersdorf who had stripped it of its contents and discovered the treasures they had left walled up.[35] Thus, the poor were often more mobile than the rich. Many were already used to travelling, such as journeymen, or had experience of setting up in a new town already. Most craftsmen's tools were relatively portable. Cobbler Hans Heberle fled 28 times from his village to nearby Ulm alone, as well as making other escapes to different towns or into the woods during the war.

Where people could not flee themselves, they tried to protect the next generation. Children were sent to relations or to schools in safer areas. The Catholic church did not benefit from this trend. The late sixteenth-century revival in the number of novices stalled or fell as families clearly hesitated to send children to institutions with an uncertain future.[36]

Resistance

The poor performance of militiamen in formal battles obscures the strength of popular resistance to soldiers. It was nonetheless a feature from the outbreak of the war. Official attitudes were ambivalent. There was general distrust of popular action, yet the authorities also expected people to participate in official defence measures. These represented a continuation of the pre-war territorial defence structures based on a notional universal obligation to serve, with only a select portion of the population undergoing actual training. Familiarity with weapons was widespread. For instance, every Hohenlohe peasant knew how to handle a gun and many owned one. Aware of the potential for popular resistance, the Imperialists occupying the principality after Nördlingen ordered all firearms to be handed over.[37] Militias and armed volunteers often put up stiff resistance when defending their homes, as in Magdeburg (1631), and the Bregenz pass (1647). Both these examples ended in failure, but armed citizens and militia formed the bulk of those successfully defending Vienna, Villingen, Kronach, Forchheim, Konstanz and Prague.

The authorities also expected ordinary people to resist marauders. Duke Wolfgang Wilhelm of Pfalz-Neuburg offered a 10 tlr reward for each dead marauder presented to his officials. Such action often needed no prompting; though the Bohemian Confederates stood down their militia in 1619, both sides encountered peasant guerrillas. Other examples include the resistance of the Westphalian towns (1622–3), the Upper Austrian Rebellion (1626), and the widespread insurgency as the war spread after 1631. Official structures could provide a basis for this, as in the Upper Austrians' use of the militia system against the Bavarian occupiers. Resistance could also be spontaneous. Neighbours responded when two cavalrymen set upon a married couple in the Westphalian village of Leitmar in July 1622, soon overpowering the soldiers and beating them to death so brutally that their faces were left unrecognizable.[38]

Soldiers certainly feared reprisals as peasants murdered stragglers and patrols. Monro reports the Bavarians' response to the Swedish invasion in 1632,

where the Boores [peasants] on the march cruelly used our Souldiers (that went aside to plunder) in cutting off their noses and eares, hands and feete, pulling out their eyes, with sundry other cruelties which they used, being justly repayed by the Souldiers, in burning of many Dorpes [villages] on the march, leaving also the Boores dead, where they were found.

An anonymous Imperialist recorded during the 1642 campaign in Westphalia:

I had a bit to drink in the evening and fell behind my regiment in the morning because of a hangover. Three peasants hiding in the hedge beat me up thoroughly and took my coat, satchel, everything. By divine intervention they suddenly ran off as if being chased even though no one was behind them. Thus beaten up, without coat or bag, I rejoined my regiment and was laughed at.[39]

Contemporaries often noted the involvement of women in resistance. Sister Junius records with approval tales of women at Höchstadt (in March 1633) and Kronach (March 1634) who threw boiling water and stones down at the Swedes. While Höchstadt ended in a massacre of the inhabitants, Kronach held out 'and the Swedes told us themselves that this hurt more than any shooting or hacking'. She further noted with pride how the nuns stopped marauders entering their convent and ends her diary with praise of having withstood horror and preserved virginity, 'and the enemy themselves expressed amazement that we, as women, remained living in this exposed spot in such dangerous times'. Male writers also noted the resistance of such 'Viragoes' that reflects the contemporary fascination with the concept of Amazons fed by stories from the New World.[40]

It has been suggested that resistance was an act of final desperation of those with nothing left to lose but their lives.[41] However it often seems to have begun well before that stage had been reached, generally once communities had had a taste of military demands, but had not yet lost everything. They fought to preserve their lifestyle and community. Hans Heberle recounts how the village of Weidenstetten near Ulm drove off bands of Bernhardine troops for two days during the summer of 1634, while sheltering their livestock in the churchyard and their belongings in the church. The soldiers retaliated by setting the houses on fire. 'Once that happened, each one of us went to look after his own property, and common defence collapsed.'[42] As we have seen in the discussion of material damage in the previous chapter, soldiers deliberately targeted exposed assets like vineyards to pressure communities into cooperating.

These examples illustrate that resistance had very little to do with the official exhortation to confessional or dynastic loyalty. It was also a form of negotiation, a means to persuade soldiers to go away or moderate their demands. It did not necessarily end in death, though it was more likely to than flight or collaboration. Just as civilians joined raiding parties, soldiers could assist local resistance. Jürgen Ackermann, a former captain, helped defend Kroppenstadt where he had retired as a farmer. The inhabitants successfully repulsed two weak imperial regiments who were demanding quarters. On another occasion he helped neighbours recover a cow stolen by Swedish troops.[43]

PERCEPTIONS

The War as Defining Event

As contemporaries struggled to understand what was happening they confronted a question central to early modern life: the relative roles of God and people in shaping events. Their responses are revealed through their personal testimonies that indicate how they saw the war shaping their lives. Diary and chronicle entries tend to be fullest when the war directly affected the writer, whereas the text reverts to the more familiar, routine entries as the conflict moved away. Some record months of anxiety as the writers followed events elsewhere with mounting dread as the enemy approached. Others seem to have deliberately omitted the war, or reduced it to a small part of another story as possibly too traumatic to confront in writing.

The war generally assumed a prominent place in second-hand accounts of experience. It looms large in funeral sermons as an explanation for life events, appearing as a direct cause of death, for the advancement or postponement of marriage, moving house, and the loss of relatives. It was also used as a general metaphor for difficult times, and a means of demonstrating the deceased as a good Christian, giving charitably to refugees, or enduring hardship with fortitude. The war thus provided people with a ready explanation of events and a means of linking their own lives to wider developments. The same is true for Jewish memoirs. War and plague constantly intervene in those of Rabbi Reutlingen, influencing his decisions to move and take up different employment. Ascher Levy planned his memoirs in two sections, with the first covering his own life and family and the second dealing with their war experiences, yet he was unable to keep the conflict out of his initial narrative.[44]

War, and its accompanying horrors of plague and famine, encouraged a sense of living in what one contemporary called an 'iron century' of exceptional hardship. The Silesian poet Gryphius wrote of the pointlessness of human existence. The human body was just a 'house of grim pain' and an 'arena of bitter fear filled with keen sorrow'.[45] There was a general sense of waste, decline and abandonment, symbolized by grass growing in the streets of empty communities, derelict farms and untilled fields. Many felt society was collapsing, pointing to a rise in prostitution, loose morals, heavy drinking and children swearing in the street. However, such observations generally come from clergy and officials charged with post-war reconstruction and need to be treated with caution.[46]

Many have noted an apparent lack of emotion among soldiers towards death, even of their own relations. It has also been suggested that the close-quarters fighting denied participants the ability to distance themselves from conflict the way people today can do merely by observing war on the TV news.[47] Certainly seventeenth-century combat would have made a profound impact on those participating in it, involving stabbing, hacking, clubbing and hitting the enemy directly. Even distance weapons like muskets had a relatively short range so that it was possible to see their terrible effects, at least until smoke and dust obscured the view. Many memoirs are indeed full of stock references to 'divine punishment', or laconic lists of the fallen. But others express regret at the loss of comrades. Much of Monro's writing implies resentment at civilian ingratitude at the soldiers' sacrifices. Augustus von Bismarck was clearly an adventurer, pleased that his service had given him an opportunity to see Italy, but he was also conscious of war's dangers and how few of his comrades had survived.[48]

Fear

A few expressed what many must have felt in recording their fear of combat. 'At my first coming before the towne,' records Thomas Raymond, an Englishman in the Dutch army in 1633, my courage began somewhat to faile me, and, being younge and never being on such an employment, wrought the more upon me. I remember I had a aurange tauny feather in my capp, and at first I thought that every great gun that was discharge[d] towards our quarters had been aymed at it, the Spaniards not enduring that colour. But within a few dayes I tooke my selfe to be a very gallant fellow, and had noe more dread of danger than if I have been in a fayre.[49]

Fear and apprehension were all-pervasive and fed by sensationalist reports and rumour. Sister Junius records being almost paralysed by fear after the fall of Würzburg in 1631 and was greatly relieved when she realized the Swedes would not harm them and would let the nuns stay in their convent. She still could not sleep for 'great fear and anxiety' while the soldiers helped themselves to vegetables from the convent garden. Familiarity reduced the fear and Junius was much less anxious when the Swedes returned in 1632 as she knew more what to expect.[50]

Territorial fragmentation heightened uncertainty by placing people of different confessions in close proximity. The Protestant inhabitants of Weikersheim in Franconia believed neighbouring Catholic villagers were preparing ladders to storm their town in 1619. However, the situation was not clear cut, and there are also examples where practical co-existence continued despite the violence.

Fear nonetheless proved debilitating, reducing the quality of life. The early modern world was already a dangerous place. Half the population failed to live beyond their fifteenth year, mainly due to malnutrition and disease but also because of accidents. Adult life was also not without risk. Even in peacetime, most people carried a knife or club if they went out after dark or any distance from home. The war heightened these everyday anxieties. People were afraid to travel, send messages or goods in case they were robbed. The increased uncertainty violated the familiar. Routine activities like going to church or synagogue might become dangerous, or even impossible. Sister Junius notes how the bells no longer rang out at the times of Catholic services but at a different hour to summon the Protestants during the Swedish occupation of Bamberg.

Witchcraft

The wider social and environmental problems of the later sixteenth century encouraged millennial and apocalyptical beliefs. The deteriorating conditions tipped the balance between those who saw difficulties as a test of faith and those who sought more immediate scapegoats. The result was a revival and intensification of witchcraft accusations that peaked during the war. The distinct early modern concept of witchcraft originated in the 1480s when existing notions of evil black magic were transformed into an inverted form of Christianity. Whereas earlier practitioners of magic were thought to act alone using powers acquired through ancient learning or experimentation, witchcraft was a supposedly collective activity involving a pact with the devil.[51]

The belief waned from the 1520s, but revived after 1600. The first witch ordinance in the electorate of Cologne was issued in 1607, followed by a revised and more extensive one in 1629. That appeared during the peak of accusations that followed the Kipper and Wipper hyperinflation. All three confessions participated, but the Catholic ecclesiastical territories suffered particularly severely. Over three hundred people were executed in Ellwangen around 1611, with fifty more dying in Würzburg in 1616–17. Bamberg was swept by three escalating waves of prosecutions (1612–13, 1616–19, 1626–30) that probably claimed a thousand victims. A similar number perished in the duchy of Westphalia in 1628–31.

Some were the outcome of popular fear, such as cases brought by the inhabitants of the lordship of Wildenberg that resulted in two hundred executions between 1590 and 1653.[52] Most were promoted by local officials, especially in Bamberg where prosecutions were instigated by the suffragan bishop Friedrich Förner, whose accession triggered the initial wave in 1612. In all cases, prosecutions were facilitated by the Empire's wider constitutional crisis that inhibited the Reichskammergericht's supervision of territorial justice. Special witch courts were established outside the existing judiciary, circumventing the normal controls on the use of torture. Since witchcraft was allegedly a communal activity, those accused were tortured to reveal the other members of their coven, rapidly multiplying the numbers of suspects. Victims were not only executed but had their possessions confiscated, adding a material incentive for witch-hunters to continue their work. Förner and his accomplices seized property worth over half a million florins in Bamberg.

Förner's activities did meet strong local opposition. Around three-quarters of victims were women, several of them were well-connected. Sister Junius's father, Johannes, the Bamberg mayor, was executed and she was probably sent to the convent for safety, and the Bamberg chancellor, Georg Haan, was executed along with his family after opposing the witch trials. These executions were in defiance of Reichskammergericht mandates to end prosecutions. Förner continued, claiming the victims had already confessed. A special Malefactors' Hall (*Malefizhaus*) was built, complete with chapel and torture chambers. Finally, the Reichshofrat intervened, issuing six further mandates and numerous letters of protection for those accused. The Bamberg representative was also pressed on the matter at the 1630 Regensburg electoral congress and the bishop was sent a dire warning to desist and ordered to suspend property confiscation, even if the accused had been found guilty. Supervision was entrusted to another, fortunately still surviving local opponent of the trials who halted further prosecutions. Förner had meanwhile moved his operation to the smaller and less public town of Zeil. The last ten prisoners were found by Swedish troops in November 1631 and released on the condition they swore never to speak of their experiences.[53] The dissipation of the 'witch craze' around 1631 is certainly no coincidence. The war's violent intrusion burst the bubble and gave local officials more pressing concerns. It was one of the war's very few positive effects. Despite the destruction of other assets by soldiers, local inhabitants themselves demolished the hated Malefactors' Hall in 1634.

Normality

Fear fills the pages of personal testimonies, but it is clear that there were long stretches where, for most people, conflict was either distant, or at least bearable. The sheer length of the war made it an everyday element in the lives of millions. These lives were full of events that had little or no connection to strife. Some diaries barely mention the war or any traumatic experience that might explain its omission. Zacharias von Quetz, tutor to the hereditary prince of Bayreuth from 1622 to 1632, recounts life at a court apparently little disrupted by fighting. He was able to take a holiday to Italy, including a gondola ride in Venice and a visit to Mantua to marvel at the duke's art and scientific treasures, all in 1629 – the year of the Mantuan crisis.[54]

Others record attempts to continue life despite the conflict. The Swedish occupation of Bamberg did not stop Junius and her sisters from organizing a nativity scene, complete with crib and four peasant children in their best clothes as Mary, Joseph (with false beard) and two angels. Jesuits brought local children to the convent to sing carols, 'but today also did not pass without horror' as a raid by the Forchheim garrison (i.e. Catholics) spread panic.[55]

Personal misfortune could be due to other, mundane causes. Stephan Behaim from a rich Nuremberg family enjoyed an expensive education at the Latin school and Altdorf University, followed by a stint as trainee at the Reichskammergericht. He squandered this opportunity, wasting his guardian's money on riotous living until his allowance was cut off. He joined the Swedish army in 1632, but failed to advance and eventually died in Brazil having entered the Dutch West India Company's service in the hope of better prospects. His relation Hans Jakob also wasted his education at Altdorf, which was cut short because his father could no longer afford to indulge him. He decided to 'hazard' his life as a soldier, but had no patience for its hard realities. He later became a lieutenant in the French army, but still expected his father to subsidize a life of wine, women and song that was cut short by a Spanish bullet at the siege of Mardyck.[56]

Soldiers' lives were filled with long periods of inactivity, followed by bursts of hectic, often exhausting action. One Imperialist recorded marching for seven weeks without a break during the summer of 1629, then resting two days before moving on to halt for twenty weeks at Lauterbach in Hessen over the winter. He spent the entire winter to May 1631 also in billets. Over the following years, his time in winter quarters ranged up to five months, but just three months of the 1641 campaign saw him involved in eight sieges. In all, he tramped 25,000km from 1625 to 1649. His experience was one of extremes. 'On Good Friday [1628] we had bread and meat enough, but on holy Easter Sunday we couldn't get even a mouthful of bread', while in Baden during 1627, 'we lay in quarters, guzzling and boozing. It was wonderful.' Occasionally, soldiers could even afford to be choosy. When his regiment reached untouched northern Germany in 1629 'we didn't want to eat beef any more; we had to have goose, duck or chicken'.[57]

Fortuna

Sudden changes of fortune became a defining characteristic of the conflict. It engendered a sense of impermanence and the unpredictability of events. Despite the official stress on patience and fortitude, many people clearly lived for the moment, grabbing what opportunities they could. Food reserves and hoarded treasure were at risk from plunderers. As a mobile community without a permanent home, soldiers found it difficult to deposit any riches they might have. General Götz ordered his army to leave its valuables behind in Offenburg when it marched to relieve Breisach. Major von Hagenbach debated with his friend Captain Augustin Fritsch what they should do. Fritsch advised 'where the head stays, the rest remains as well', and they both took their accumulated booty with them, only to lose it in the rout at Wittenweier. Fritsch's loss totalled 5,000 tlr in cash, a sack of silver cutlery, some tapestries, six horses, two servants and a wagon – more than sufficient for a modest man to retire on.[58]

The precariousness and capriciousness of life were embodied in literature and art as Fortuna, a naked woman balancing on a ball and holding a sail. She was an ambivalent figure, associated both with good luck and sin. Similar attributes were derived from astrology. Jupiter and Venus symbolized good luck, whereas Saturn and Mars were considered 'bad' planets, held responsible for the comet of 1618 that had been widely regarded as an ill-omen (and confirmed by what followed). Soldiers were frequently referred to as 'Mars' children'. The term 'soldier of fortune' had connotations of boldness and enterprise, but was primarily associated with greed and thus condemned for placing greater value on earthly success than on true Christian spirituality.

COMMEMORATION

Peace Celebrations

The literary and artistic critique of fortune chimed with the broader interpretation of the war as divine punishment. This was expressed in sermons and proclamations throughout the conflict and was re-emphasized during the official celebrations of the peace. The Westphalian congress raised expectations of peace. Daniel von Campen, a district official in Brunswick, built the new village of Friedenswunsch (Desire for Peace) in 1646 on the edge of the former settlement of Ildehausen that had been burned to the ground by the Imperialists twenty years earlier.[59] Many were not convinced the peace would last after 1648. The Swedes scheduled public celebrations in the areas they occupied for New Year 1649, but most communities waited until 1650 when demobilization and the return of refugees raised confidence.

Festivities were held in over 200 locations across Europe, 180 of them in the Empire, underscoring the Central European character of the war, especially as the Spanish-Dutch Peace of Münster was celebrated in only Brussels, Antwerp and six Dutch towns. These celebrations provide a valuable insight into how the survivors regarded the war and tried to come to terms with their experience. By examining how these events were transformed into annual commemorative ceremonies, we can trace the passage of the conflict into collective memory.

The celebration of peace resembled that of victory in being instigated and organized by the authorities. The events followed a common format, starting with the tolling of the church bells to summon the inhabitants. Those of the city of Cologne rang for an hour to celebrate the major imperial victories. The population then gathered for a service of thanksgiving, generally processing through their town beforehand. Having withstood the Swedes throughout 1633, the Forchheim garrison celebrated the enemy's evacuation of the surrounding area by firing all their cannon and playing trumpets and kettledrums.[60] Martial noise was an integral part of the peace celebrations too.

Peace celebrations were relatively muted in Catholic areas, suggesting that many regarded the war as a defeat. Militants especially felt they had been cheated of victory, having beaten the Protestants both by 1629 and again by 1634, only to be forced to concede their demands by foreign invasion. Bishop Wartenberg stayed away from the relatively low-key festivities accompanying the signing ceremony in Münster in October 1648. Nonetheless, Catholics generally welcomed the peace, and major Catholic rulers had much to celebrate. Bavaria celebrated with a Te Deum in the principal church, a special mass and a procession through Munich led by the Jesuits accompanied by the obligatory gun salutes. Similar events are recorded for Cologne, Salzburg, Vienna, Prague and other Habsburg towns. Those in Prague were especially important as they took place in the city where the war had started. The inhabitants' heroic resistance against the Swedish siege of 1648 was swiftly woven into a myth of Catholic and dynastic loyalty to smother the earlier stigma of rebellion. St Barbara, the patron saint of Catholic artillerymen, was popularly believed to have saved the St Henry Church by catching a Swedish grenade during the bombardment. The grateful emperor richly rewarded the city councillors, who were ennobled along with students who had helped to block the Charles Bridge and save the New Town. The city received a new charter in 1649 giving it a privileged place in the Bohemian diet.[61]

Catholic celebrations centred on the mass which was traditionally used for thanksgiving. The Protestants' rejection of the mass obliged them to stage their events somewhat differently. They drew on the Reformation jubilees of 1617 and 1630, as well as the days of prayer and penance that had been observed since 1532 during imperial campaigns against the Turks and which were revived after 1618. Unlike with the Reformation jubilees, however, electoral Saxony did not provide coordination across Lutheran Germany, leaving it open to other territories to organize their own events. Nonetheless, these proved very similar and the Saxons used both jubilees as templates for their own ceremonies, even recycling some of the earlier sermons.

Celebration focused attention on the relative role of God and people in the war. Dynasticism assumed a more prominent place than in the Reformation jubilees. The Saxon celebrations in 1650 were held on the electress's name day, not the anniversary of the peace treaties. Peace was presented as a gift from both God and the authorities. Congregations were asked to pray for the welfare of the dynasty and of the Protestant imperial Estates in general as the guarantors of tranquillity. Members of the Fruitful Society contributed to the events in Coburg and Weimar that contrasted the horrors of war with *Concordia*, the baroque ideal of mutual understanding that at least contained the potential to reach across confessional boundaries. Numerous broadsheets appeared across the Empire presenting it as a common, imperial peace: the female figure of Germania was shown marrying 'Peace'.[62]

The theological content followed the pattern established in the days of prayer and penance that had also been used in times of natural disaster. Celebrations took place over one or two days, beginning with prayers and sermons to set the appropriate tone and to inculcate the official interpretation of the war as divine punishment. War, like flood and fire, was thus not 'natural', but a product of divine will. Catholic sermons delivered a similar message, and had also used regular days of prayer to ward off evil during the conflict.[63] Lutherans added a second element – the conflict as a test of faith, equating enemy occupation with the Babylonian Captivity of the Israelites. Pastors also drew on the Book of Revelation, arguing that God had entrusted his sword to the evil-minded to wreak punishment, but could sheath it again if the population displayed true faith. The length of the war was used to argue how easy it was to stray from the proper path. The population were encouraged to redouble their efforts to lead morally upright, thrifty and productive lives to retain divine favour. The emphasis on future good behaviour was reflected in the prominent place given to school children in the Protestant processions. Peace was to be celebrated as a God-given chance for Lutherans to prove themselves worthy of His grace and to show the misguided Catholics the true path to salvation by their good example. Though distinctly Lutheran, the emphasis on sin also lessened the confessional polemic. The war became a product of the population's own failings, not the aggression of their Catholic neighbours. Such a message not only suited the need for harmony within the Empire, but fitted the social-disciplining agenda of post-war reconstruction. Confessional antagonism was being sublimated by obedience to the authorities. Rulers were able to dodge responsibility for the war, while appearing instrumental in mitigating its worst effects and assisting in hastening the peace.

The stress on penitence and sobriety sat uneasily with the more secular elements of the festivities like feasting, drinking and lavish public displays, including the first recorded use of fireworks in Hamburg's celebrations of 1650. Concussion from the 370-gun salute during Nuremberg's ceremony caused 3,000 fl. worth of damage to the city walls. The discrepancy was not lost on poets, novelists and broadsheet writers who parodied the excessive praise of peace and unrealistic expectations of a post-war paradise.

The presence of such satire casts doubt on claims that religion helped people cope with the conflict, and helped avoid widespread protest or the collapse of the social order.[64] Many people certainly put their faith in God. Four-year-old Johanna Petersen admonished her elder sister for not thanking God that they had not been spotted escaping their manor house during a raid.[65] Such evidence requires caution: Petersen was later prominent in Lutheran Pietism, and clearly was very devout.

A more representative example is the bewilderment felt by the inhabitants of Rottweil during the French siege of November 1643.[66] An all-night prayer vigil was held to seek divine assistance to save the city. Many people thought they saw the statue of the Madonna change colour and move her eyes heavenwards. Even those who later confessed to seeing nothing still believed the miracle happened, attributing an apparent failure to notice it to their poor eyesight, or to their having been at the back of the church. Yet, the event did not stiffen the defenders' resolve and the city surrendered a week later. Later, especially in centenary celebrations staged by the Jesuits, the church tried to link the miracle to the imperial victory of Tuttlingen and Rottweil's subsequent recapture. Those who were in the church were far less certain. For some, it reinforced their conviction that Catholicism was the sole, true faith. Others were terrified, interpreting the statue's apparent loss of colour as a foreboding of death. Some Lutherans in the city also believed the statue had moved, despite their own church's condemnation of such beliefs.

At its height in the 1630s, the war clearly threatened the established order. A decade later the situation was not as bad in many areas, dampening any protest. The war nonetheless left people traumatized. Though patchy, there is evidence of what today would be called post-traumatic stress disorder. Survivors experienced flashbacks, nightmares, mood swings and other psychological problems.[67] The widespread yearning for stability undoubtedly encouraged acceptance of the official disciplinary agenda after 1648.

Commemoration

The protracted peace implementation helped transform one-off celebration into annual commemoration. Many areas already marked the signing of the peace with thanksgiving services at the end of 1648. Additional events followed in 1649 with the ratification of the treaty and the start of the troop withdrawals, while the conclusion of the Nuremberg congress in 1650 prompted further, generally more elaborate festivities. Saxony chose not to repeat these, concentrating instead on renewed Reformation anniversaries: the centenary of the Peace of Augsburg in

1656, and the 110th anniversary of Luther's Ninety-Five Theses in 1667. Other Lutheran territories chose to incorporate these with commemoration of Westphalia. Elsewhere, commemoration also continued by combining it with other events; in Hohenlohe, the Westphalian anniversary was moved to combine with the harvest festival.

This transition to annual commemoration had multiple causes. One was the territorial state's continuing agenda of discipline and obedience, for which commemoration was well-suited. Another was the desire to reinforce communal solidarity. The latter was especially marked in bi-confessional Augsburg where the Protestant citizens celebrated each 8 August – a date with no connection to the peace but which had been the day in 1629 when the Lutheran pastors had been expelled under the Restitution Edict. Their festivities carefully avoided any reference to the Catholics, as if their city were entirely Lutheran.

Commemoration kept the war in popular consciousness. It peaked in the centenary year of 1748 that also saw the Peace of Aix-la-Chapelle that concluded the eight-year struggle of the War of the Austrian Succession. Leutkirch, for instance, staged two weeks of celebrations that included the usual sermons, processions and fireworks, but also an examination for school children to test their knowledge of the Westphalian settlement. Participants received a commemorative coin. The Hamburg festivities were graced by a cantata specially composed by Telemann. Interest waned thereafter, but Coburg continued to mark the anniversary until 1843, while 8 August is still a public holiday in Augsburg.

What was being commemorated also changed over time. The Peace of Westphalia became woven into the Protestant narrative of German history. The IPO and IPM were still fundamental charters of the Empire at their centenary. A century later the Empire had gone and the peace was celebrated as completing the Reformation by securing Protestant political rights. Festivities assumed an increasingly folkloric character. Augsburg children no longer processed dressed as the emperor, electors and imperial eagles, but disguised as 'Swedish' soldiers. Far more than religion, the passage of time overcame the trauma of the conflict and allowed it to pass into history.

Most of Europe has had the good fortune of almost a lifetime of peace since 1945, spared the horrors of foreign invasion, violence and destruction. The succession of European conflicts through the seventeenth into the twentieth century sustained an oral folk tradition from the Thirty Years War that has now faded. In contrast to the historicization of the war through commemorative pageantry, folk tales 'pre-remembered' incidents from the war for future use.[68] Stories of atrocities and harm to civilians offered advice on possible responses should these circumstances reoccur. The basic tales could be transposed to other communities and times. Stories involving the Swedes or Croats from the Thirty Years War became mixed with Russian Cossacks from the Napoleonic period or even soldiers from the home country. These tales persisted in parts of Europe into the later twentieth century. Though they are now largely silent, the voices from the seventeenth century still speak to us from the innumerable texts and images we are fortunate to possess. They offer a warning of the dangers of entrusting power to those who feel summoned by God to war, or feel that their sense of justice and order is the only one valid.

Abbreviations

AHVN	*Annalen des Historischen Verein für den Niederrhein*
APW	*Acta Pacis Westphalicae* (gen. ed. K. Repgen, 36 vols., Münster, 1961–)
ARG	*Archiv für Reformationsgeschichte*
BA	*Briefe und Akten zur Geschichte des Dreißigjährigen Krieges*, New Series (issued by the Historische Kommission der Bayerischen Akademie der Wissenschaften, 8 vols., Munich, 1906–97)
BDLG	*Blätter für deutsche Landesgeschichte*
CEH	*Central European History*
Doc. Bo.	*Documenta Bohemica Bellum Tricennale Illustrantia* (M. Kouril et al. eds., 7 vols., Prague, 1971–81)
EHQ	*European History Quarterly*
EHR	*English Historical Review*
FBPG	*Forschungen zur Brandenburg-Preußischen Geschichte*
GH	*German History*
HHStA	Haus-, Hof- und Staatsarchiv Vienna
HJ	*Historical Journal*
HJb	*Historisches Jahrbuch*
HZ	*Historische Zeitschrift*
IHR	*International History Review*
IPM	Instrumentum Pacis Monasteriense (Peace of Münster)
IPO	Instrumentum Pacis Osnabrugense (Peace of Osnabrück)
JMH	*Journal of Modern History*
KA	*Kriegsakten*
MEA	*Mainzer Erzkanzler Archiv Vienna*
MIÖG	*Mitteilungen des Instituts für Österreichische Geschichtsforschung*
MÖSA	*Mitteilungen des Österreichischen Staatsarchivs*
NASG	*Neues Archiv für Sächsische Geschichte*
NTSR	*Neues Teutsches Staatsrecht* (J.J. Moser, 20 vols. in 36 parts, Frankfurt and Leipzig, 1767–82)
P&P	*Past and Present*
TE	*Theatrum Europaeum oder Außführliche vnd Wahrhafftige Beschreibung aller und jeder denkwürdiger Geschichten* (M. Merian ed., vols. I–IV, Frankfurt am Main, 1633–52), available online at www.digbib. bibliothek.uni-augsburg.de/1/index.html
VOC	Verenigde Oostindische Compagnie (Dutch East India Company)
VSWG	*Vierteljahreshefte für Sozial und Wirtschaftsgeschichte*
WIC	Westindische Compagnie (Dutch West India Company)
WVJHLG	*Württembergische Vierteljahreshefte für Landesgeschichte*
WZ	*Westfälische Zeitschrift*

ZBLG	*Zeitschrift für Bayerische Landesgeschichte*
ZGO	*Zeitschrift für die Geschichte des Oberrheins*
ZHF	*Zeitschrift für Historische Forschung*
ZNRG	*Zeitschrift für Neuere Rechtsgeschichte*
ZPGLK	*Zeitschrift für Preußische Geschichte und Landeskunde*
ZSRG GA	*Zeitschrift der Savigny Stiftung für Rechtsgeschichte Germanistische Abteilung*
ZSRG KA	*Zeitschrift der Savigny Stiftung für Rechtsgeschichte Kanonistische Abteilung*

Notes

Introduction

1. Slavata's account is available in English in R. Schwarz, *The Imperial Privy Council in the Seventeenth Century* (Cambridge, Mass., 1943), pp.344–7. See also H. Sturmberger, *Aufstand in Böhmen. Der Beginn des Dreißigjährigen Krieges* (Munich, 1959), pp.7–14.
2. K. Cramer, *The Thirty Years War and German Memory in the Nineteenth Century* (Lincoln, Nebr., 2007), pp.9, 146–7.
3. K. Repgen, *Dreißigjähriger Krieg und Westfälischer Friede* (Paderborn, 1998), pp.112–52; D. Moldenhauer, 'Die Darstellung des Dreißigjährigen Krieges zwischen "Aufklärungshistorie" und "Historismus"', in M. Knauer and S. Tode (eds.), *Der Krieg vor den Toren* (Hamburg, 2000), pp.389–418.
4. The work is most accessible in English in the version edited by G. Schulz-Behrend (Rochester and Woodbridge, 1993).
5. D.M. Hopkin, *Soldier and Peasant in French Popular Culture 1766–1870* (Woodbridge, 2003), pp.240–50; J. Canning, H. Lehman and J. Winter (eds.), *Power, Violence and Mass Death in Pre-modern and Modern Times* (Aldershot, 2004), pp.199–200.
6. A. Buchner and V. Buchner, *Bayern im Dreißigjährigen Krieg* (Dachau, 2002), p.7.
7. The concept was introduced in a series of articles in *Past and Present* that were brought together in T. Aston (ed.), *Crisis in Europe, 1560–1660* (London, 1965). Later articles were collected in G. Parker and L.M. Smith (eds.), *The General Crisis of the Seventeenth Century* (London, 1997). See also T.K. Rabb, *The Struggle for Stability in Early Modern Europe* (New York, 1975).
8. For more extended analysis of this and the other interpretations, see P.H. Wilson, 'The causes of the Thirty Years War', *EHR*, 123 (2008), 554–86.
9. For example, S.R. Gardiner, *The Thirty Years War 1618–1648* (London, 1889).
10. H. Schilling, *Konfessionalisierung und Staatsinteressen 1559–1660* (Paderborn, 2007), pp.415, 417.
11. G. Parker (ed.), *The Thirty Years War* (London, 1984), quote from p.xvi. See also D. Maland, *Europe at War 1600–1650* (London, 1980); P. Kennedy, *The Rise and Fall of Great Powers* (London, 1988); M.P. Gutmann, 'The origins of the Thirty Years War', *Journal of Interdisciplinary History*, 18 (1988), 749–70. The origins of the international war school can be found in the work of S.H. Steinberg that first appeared as an article in 1947 and was reworked as *The Thirty Years War and the Conflict for European Hegemony 1600–1660* (London, 1966). Nicola Sutherland takes it to its logical extreme by subsuming the Thirty Years War within three centuries of Franco-Habsburg rivalry: 'The origins of the Thirty Years War and the structure of European politics', *EHR*, 107 (1992), 587–625. The most recent German interpretation sees the war as growing out of the Empire to become a general European conflict: C. Kampmann, *Europa und das Reich im Dreißigjährigen Krieg* (Stuttgart, 2008).

12. Repgen, *Dreißigjähriger Krieg*, pp.27–8, 62–87; G. Mortimer, 'Did contemporaries recognise a "Thirty Years War"?' *EHR*, 116 (2001), 124–36.

13. Further elaboration in P.H. Wilson, 'On the role of religion in the Thirty Years War', *IHR*, 30 (2008), 473–514. See also the useful discussion in E. Labouvie, 'Konfessionalisierung in der Praxis – oder: War der Dreißigjährige Krieg ein Konfessionskrieg?' in *Konfession, Krieg und Katastrophe. Magdeburgs Geschick im Dreißigjährigen Krieg* (issued by the Verein für Kirchengeschichte der Kirchenprovinz Sachsen, Magdeburg, 2006), pp.69–92.

Trouble in the Heart of Christendom

1. T.C.W. Blanning's remark comes from his entertaining and illuminating discussion of German history at the 'Culture of Power' conference, Peterhouse College, Cambridge, September 2005. Moser's major work, *Neues Teutsches Staatsrecht* (20 vols. in 36 parts, Frankfurt and Leipzig, 1767–82) can still be read with profit as it is a mine of detail. For more modern discussions, see H. Neuhaus, *Das Reich in der frühen Neuzeit* (Munich, 1997); P.H. Wilson, *The Holy Roman Empire 1495–1806* (Basingstoke, 1999).

2. M. Merian, *Topographia Germaniae* (14 vols., Frankfurt am Main, 1643–75; reprint Brunswick, 2005).

3. Imperial Italy included the entire region north of the Papal States that lay across the centre of the peninsula, except for the Venetian Republic in the north east. The duchy of Savoy was the exception in that it retained formal representation in imperial institutions, even though its rulers no longer exercised their rights.

4. Colour reproduction in D. Hohrath, G. Weig and M. Wettengel (eds.), *Das Ende reichsstädtischer Freiheit 1802* (Ulm, 2002), p.139. For the depiction of the Empire through symbol and metaphor see R.A. Müller (ed.), *Bilder des Reiches* (Sigmaringen, 1997).

5. Good introductions include R. Bireley, *The Refashioning of Catholicism 1450–1700* (Basingstoke, 1999); D.L. Luebke (ed.), *The Counter Reformation* (Oxford, 1999); R. Po-Chia Hsia, *The World of Catholic Renewal 1540–1770* (Cambridge, 1998); A. Pettegree (ed.), *The Reformation World* (London, 2002); C.S. Dixon, *The Reformation in Germany* (Oxford, 2002); G. Murdock, *Beyond Calvin. The intellectual, political and cultural world of Europe's reformed churches* (Basingstoke, 2004).

6. L. Riccardi, 'An outline of Vatican diplomacy in the early modern age', in D. Frigo (ed.), *Politics and Diplomacy in Early Modern Italy* (Cambridge, 2000), pp.95–108; K. Jaitner, 'The popes and the struggle for power during the sixteenth and seventeenth centuries', in K. Bussmann and H. Schilling (eds.), *1648: War and Peace in Europe* (3 vols., Münster, 1998), I, pp.61–7. For the papacy generally, see A.D. Wright, *The Early Modern Papacy from the Council of Trent to the French Revolution 1564–1789* (Harlow, 2000).

7. J. O'Malley, 'The Society of Jesus', in R. Po-Chia Hsia (ed.), *A Companion to the Reformation World* (Oxford, 2004), pp.223–36; R. Bireley, *The Jesuits and the Thirty Years War* (Cambridge, 2003); G. Heiss, 'Princes, Jesuits and the origins of the Counter Reformation in the Habsburg lands', in R.J.W. Evans and T.V. Thomas (eds.), *Crown, Church and Estates* (Basingstoke, 1991), pp.92–109.

8. Jesuit influence on south German universities is explored by A. Schindling, 'Die katholische Bildungsreform zwischen Humanismus und Barock', and T. Kurrus, 'Die Jesuiten in Freiburg und den Vorlanden', both in H. Maier and V. Press (eds.), *Vorderösterreich in der frühen Neuzeit* (Sigmaringen, 1989), pp.137–76 and 189–98 respectively. The development of German universities can be accessed through the excellent case study by M. Asche, *Von der reichen hansischen Bürgeruniversität zur armen mecklenburgischen Landeshochschule. Das regionale und soziale Besucherprofil der Universitäten Rostock und Bützow in der frühen Neuzeit (1500–1800)* (Stuttgart, 2000).

9. See the works of M.R. Forster, *The Counter Reformation in the Villages: Religion and reform in the Bishopric of Speyer 1560–1720* (Ithaca and London, 1992), and his *Catholic Renewal in the Age of the Baroque. Religious identity in south west Germany* (New York, 2001).

10. P. Blickle, *The Revolution of 1525* (Baltimore, 1985); J. Witte, Jr., *Law and Protestantism. The legal teachings of the Lutheran Reformation* (Cambridge, 2002).

11. M. Schaab, 'Territorialstaat und Kirchengut in Südwestdeutschland bis zum Dreißigjährigen Krieg', and R. Postel, 'Kirchlicher und weltlicher Fiskus in norddeutschen Städten am Beginn der Neuzeit', both in H. Kellenbenz and R. Prodi (eds.), *Fiskus, Kirche und Staat im Konfessionellen Zeitalter* (Berlin, 1994), pp.71–90 and 165–85 respectively; R. Po-Chia Hsia, *Social Discipline in the Reformation. Central Europe 1550–1750* (London, 1989).

12. M. Heckel, 'Die Religionsprozesse des Reichskammergerichts im konfessionell gespaltenen Reichskirchenrecht', *ZSRG KA*, 77 (1991), 283–350; H. Rabe, *Reichsbund und Interim. Die Verfassungs- und Religionspolitik Karls V. und der Reichstag von Augsburg 1547/1548* (Cologne, 1971); V. Press, *Das Alte Reich* (Berlin, 1997), pp.67–127; T.A. Brady, 'Phases and strategies of the Schmalkaldic League', *ARG*, 74 (1983), 162–81. The League's development and policies can be followed in more detail in Brady's book, *Protestant Politics. Jacob Sturm (1489–1553) and the German Reformation* (Atlantic Highlands, 1995).

13. R. Kolb, 'Dynamics of party conflict in the Saxon late Reformation: Gnesio-Luthers vs Philippists', *JMH*, 49 (1977), 1289–305.

14. Examples in D. Breuer, 'Raumbildung in der deutschen Literaturgeschichte der frühen Neuzeit als Folge der Konfessionalisierung', *Zeitschrift für deutsche Philologie*, 117 supplement (1998), 180–91; U. Lotz-Heumann and M. Pohlig, 'Confessionalization and literature in the Empire, 1555–1700', *CEH*, 40 (2007), 35–61; P.C. Hartmann, *Kulturgeschichte des Heiligen Römischen Reiches 1648 bis 1806* (Vienna, 2001). However, as these examples show, the confessional differences only became pronounced after the war.

15. B. Roeck, *Eine Stadt in Krieg und Frieden. Studien zur Geschichte der Reichsstadt Augsburg zwischen Kalenderstreit und Parität* (2 vols., Göttingen, 1989); B.A. Tlusty, *Bacchus and Civic Order. The culture of drink in early modern Germany* (Charlottesville, 2001). See also for coexistence between Lutherans and Calvinists in East Frisia N. Grochowina, *Indifferenz und Dissens in der Grafschaft Ostfriesland im 16. und 17. Jahrhundert* (Frankfurt am Main, 2003). Another useful study, focusing on Upper Hessen, is D. Mayes, *Communal Christianity. The life and death of a peasant vision in early modern Germany* (Boston, 2004).

16. Martin Opitz in 1625 and Andreas Gryphius in 1627. For the following see also H. Peterse, 'Irenics and tolerance in the sixteenth and seventeenth centuries', in Bussmann and Schilling (eds.), *1648: War and Peace*, I, pp.265–71; H. Gabel, 'Glaube – Individuum – Reichsrecht. Toleranzdenken im Reich von Augsburg bis Münster', in H. Lademacher and S. Groenveld (eds.), *Krieg und Kultur. Die Rezeption von Krieg und Frieden in der Niederländischen Republik und im Deutschen Reich 1568–1648* (Münster, 1998), pp.157–77.

17. K. Brandi (ed.), *Der Augsburger Religionsfriede vom 25. September 1555. Kritische Ausgabe des Textes mit den Entwürfen und der königlichen Deklaration* (Göttingen, 1927) provides a modern edition of the text. The full imperial Recess appears in J.J. Schmauss and H.C. von Senckenberg (eds.), *Neue und vollständige Sammlung der Reichsabschiede* (4 vols., Frankfurt am Main, 1747), III, pp.14–43, with the new Reichskammergericht regulations printed on pp.43–136. A. Gotthard, *Der Augsburger Religionsfrieden* (Münster, 2004) provides a thorough, if rather critical, overview of the Peace and subsequent controversy, that should be read in conjunction with the extended review by M. Heckel, 'Politischer Friede und geistliche Freiheit im Ringen um die Wahrheit zur Historiographie der Augsburger Religionsfrieden von 1555', *HZ*, 282 (2006), 394–425. See also G. May, 'Zum "ius emigrandi" am Beginn des konfessionellen Zeitalters', *Archiv für Katholische Kirchenrecht*, 155 (1986), 92–125.

18. G. Parker (ed.), *The Thirty Years War* (London, 1987), p.18.

19. W. Ziegler, 'Die Hochstifte des Reiches im konfessionllen Zeitalter 1520–1618', *Römische Quartalsschrift*, 87 (1992), 252–81. For the following, see also M. Heckel, 'Autonomia und Pacis Compositio', *ZSRG KA*, 45 (1959), 141–248.

20. A.P. Luttenberger, *Kurfürsten, Kaiser und Reich. Politische Führung und Friedens-sicherung unter Ferdinand I. und Maximilian II.* (Mainz, 1994); M. Lanzinner, *Friedens-sicherung und politische Einheit des Reiches unter Maximilian II. (1564–1576)* (Göttingen, 1993); J. Arndt, 'Die kaiserlichen Friedensvermittlungen im spanisch-niederländischen Krieg 1568–1609', *Rheinische Vierteljahrsblätter*, 62 (1998), 161–83; P.S. Fichtner, *Emperor Maximilian II* (New Haven, 2001). Further discussion in Chapter 7.
21. For the following: M. Heckel, 'Staat und Kirche nach den Lehren der evangelischen Juristen Deutschlands in der ersten Hälfte des 17. Jahrhunderts', *ZSRG KA*, 42 (1956), 117–247, 43 (1957), 202–308; R.R. Benert, 'Lutheran resistance theory and the imperial constitution', *Il pensiero politico*, 6 (1973), 17–36; W. Schulze, 'Estates and the problem of resistance in theory and practice in the sixteenth and seventeenth centuries', in Evans and Thomas (eds.), *Crown, Church and Estates*, pp.158–75; R. von Friedeburg, *Self-defence and Religious Strife in Early Modern Europe. England and Germany, 1530–1680* (Aldershot, 2002); K. Repgen, 'Kriegslegitimationen in Alteuropa', *HZ*, 241 (1985), 27–49.

Casa d'Austria

1. A. Kohler, *Ferdinand I. 1503–1564* (Munich, 2003), pp.177–84, 297–303, 311; P. Rauscher, *Zwischen Ständen und Gläubigern. Die kaiserlichen Finanzen unter Ferdinand I. und Maximilian II. (1556–1576)* (Munich, 2004).
2. Those seeking general introductions should consult J. Bérenger, *A History of the Habsburg Empire 1273–1700* (London, 1994), and C. Ingrao, *The Habsburg Monarchy 1618–1815* (Cambridge, 2000). There are two excellent detailed studies for this period: R.J.W. Evans, *The Making of the Habsburg Monarchy 1550–1700* (Oxford, 1977); T. Winkelbauer, *Ständefreiheit und Fürstenmacht. Länder und Untertanen des Hauses Habsburg im konfes-sionellen Zeitalter (Österreichische Geschichte 1522–1699)* (2 vols., Vienna, 2003). For Austria's enclaves in western Germany see H. Maier and V. Press (eds.), *Vorderösterreich in der frühen Neuzeit* (Sigmaringen, 1989).
3. See the three pieces by J. Pánek, 'Das Ständewesen und die Gesellschaft in den Böhmischen Länden in der Zeit vor der Schlacht auf dem Weissen Berg (1526–1620)', *Historica. Les sciences historiques en Tchécoslovaquie*, 20 (1985), 73–120; 'Das politische System des böhmischen Staates im ersten Jahrhundert der habsburgischen Herrschaft (1526–1620)', *MIÖG*, 97 (1989), 53–82; 'Der böhmische Staat und das Reich in der frühen Neuzeit', in V. Press (ed.), *Alternativen zur Reichsverfassung in der frühen Neuzeit?* (Munich, 1995), pp.169–78, and J. Bahlcke, 'Das Herzogtum Schlesien im politischen System der böhmischen Krone', *Zeitschrift für Ostmitteleuropa-Forschung*, 44 (1995), 27–55.
4. L. Kontler, *A History of Hungary* (Basingstoke, 2002); E. Pamlényi (ed.), *A History of Hungary* (London, 1975). The remaining 31 counties comprising Habsburg Hungary encompassed over 92,000km² with over 1.2 million inhabitants. Another three Slovenian counties were associated with the separate kingdom of Croatia in the south west, collec-tively comprising 25,000km² with 300,000 subjects.
5. For the best introduction to the Estates of the Habsburg provinces and German territories, see the collection of essays edited by R.J.W. Evans and T.V. Thomas, *Crown, Church and Estates* (New York, 1990).
6. R. Schwarz, *The Imperial Privy Council in the Seventeenth Century* (Cambridge, Mass., 1943), p.280.
7. Adam von Puchheim quoted by K. MacHardy, *War, Religion and Court Patronage in Habsburg Austria. The social and cultural dimensions of political interaction, 1521–1622* (Basingstoke, 2003), p.51. For the nobles' local power see also T. Winkelbauer, 'Sozial-disziplinierung und Konfessionalisierung durch Grundherren in den österreichischen und böhmischen Ländern im 16. und 17. Jahrhundert', *ZHF*, 19 (1992), 317–39.
8. For the spread of Protestantism in the Habsburg lands, see K. Benda, 'Hungary in turmoil, 1580–1620', *European Studies Review*, 8 (1978), 281–304; D.P. Daniel, 'Calvinism in

Hungary: the theological and ecclesiastical transition to the Reformed faith', in A. Pettegree (ed.), *Calvinism in Europe 1540–1620* (Cambridge, 1996), pp.205–30, and his 'Ecumenicity or orthodoxy: the dilemma of the Protestants in the lands of the Austrian Habsburgs', *Church History*, 49 (1980), 387–400; K. Maag (ed.), *The Reformation in Eastern and Central Europe* (Aldershot, 1997); J.E. Patrouch, *A Negotiated Settlement. The Counter-Reformation in Upper Austria under the Habsburgs* (Boston, 2000); R. Pörtner, *The Counter-Reformation in Central Europe. Styria 1580–1630* (Oxford, 2001); Z.V. David, *Finding the Middle Way. The Utraquists' liberal challenge to Rome and Luther* (Washington, DC and Baltimore, 2003).

9. O. Pickl, 'Fiskus, Kirche und Staat in Innerösterreich im Zeitalter der Reformation und Gegenreformation', in H. Kellenbenz and P. Prodi (eds.), *Fiskus, Kirche und Staat im konfessionellen Zeitalter* (Berlin, 1994), pp.91–110, at p.97.

10. Though focusing on Brandenburg, W.W. Hagen's book is central to understanding these processes: *Ordinary Prussians. Brandenburg Junkers and villagers 1500–1840* (Cambridge, 2002). For the situation in Austria, see H. Rebel, *Peasant Classes. The bureaucratization of property and family relations under early Habsburgs absolutism, 1511–1636* (Princeton, 1983), and T. Winkelbauer, 'Krise der Aristokratie? Zum Strukturwandel des Adels in den böhmischen und niederösterreichischen Ländern im 16. und 17. Jahrhundert', *MIÖG*, 100 (1992), 328–53.

11. Though the politics of his reign remain under-researched, there is an excellent account of his personality and intellectual interests: R.J.W. Evans, *Rudolf II and His World* (2nd edn, London, 1997). His role as art patron is covered by H. Trevor Roper, *Princes and Artists. Patronage at four Habsburg courts 1517–1633* (London, 1976), pp.79–115, and P. Marshall, *The Theatre of the World. Alchemy, astrology and magic in Renaissance Prague* (London, 2006). There are also useful short biographies of Rudolf and the other emperors in A. Schindling and W. Ziegler (eds.), *Die Kaiser der Neuzeit 1519–1918* (Munich, 1990). For the following, see also H. Louthan, *The Quest for Compromise. Peacemaking in Counter-Reformation Vienna* (Cambridge, 1997).

12. H.C.E. Midlefort, *Mad Princes of Renaissance Germany* (Charlottesville, Va., 1994).

13. This is the conclusion of H. Angermeier, 'Politik, Religion und Reich bei Kardinal Melchior Khlesl', *ZSRG GA*, 110 (1993), 249–330; J. Rainer, 'Kardinal Melchior Klesl (1552–1630). Vom "Generalreformator" zum "Ausgleichspolitiker" ', *Römische Quartalschrift*, 59 (1964), 14–35.

14. There were a further 1,000 smaller houses outside the walls and another 2,700 homes and cottages in the surrounding area. See A. Weigl (ed.), *Wien im Dreißigjährigen Krieg* (Vienna, 2001).

15. Viscount Doncaster to Sir Robert Naunton, 30 May 1619, in S.R. Gardiner (ed.), *Letters and Other Documents Illustrating the Relations Between England and Germany at the Commencement of the Thirty Years War* (London, 1868; reprint New York, 1968), p.103. J. Franzl, *Ferdinand II: Kaiser im Zwiespalt der Zeit* (Graz, 1978) provides an overview. Ferdinand's character and policies are covered in detail from a Catholic perspective by R. Bireley, *Religion and Politics in the Age of the Counterreformation. Emperor Ferdinand II, William Lamormaini, S.J., and the formation of imperial policy* (Chapel Hill, 1981), and his 'Confessional absolutism in the Habsburg lands in the seventeenth century', in C. Ingrao (ed.), *State and Society in Early Modern Austria* (W. Lafayette, Ind., 1994), pp.36–53. See also G. Franz, 'Glaube und Recht im politischen Denken Kaiser Ferdinands II.', *ARG*, 49 (1958), 258–69; P.K. Monod, *The Power of Kings. Monarchy and religion in Europe 1589–1715* (New Haven, 1999), pp.81–93; K. Repgen (ed.), *Das Herrscherbild im 17. Jahrhundert* (Münster, 1991); A. Wandruszska, 'Zum "Absolutismus" Ferdinands II.', *Mitteilungen des Oberösterreichischen Landesarchivs*, 14 (1984), 261–8; H. Sturmberger, *Land ob der Enns und Österreich* (Linz, 1979), pp.154–87. Carafa's account from 1628 is quoted at length in F. von Hurter, *Friedensbestrebungen Kaiser Ferdinands II.* (Vienna, 1860), pp.212ff.

16. Pörtner, *Counter-Reformation in Central Europe*, p.95.

17. The protest of the Styrian Estates, published in English translation in 1620 as 'Two very lamentable relations', reprinted in C. A Macartney (ed.), *The Habsburg and Hohenzollern Dynasties in the Seventeenth and Eighteenth Centuries* (London, 1970), pp.13–22.
18. This was Charlemagne's crown that was stored in Nuremberg between imperial coronations. Rudolf's predecessors all had 'private crowns' they wore on other ceremonial occasions, but the monarchy's indebtedness had led to these having been melted down. Rudolf's crown from 1602 survived the vicissitudes of the Thirty Years War and subsequent financial crises to become the Austrian state crown when a separate hereditary imperial title was adopted in 1804. See G.J. Kugler, *Die Reichskrone* (Vienna, 1968).

The Turkish War and its Consequences

1. The literature on the Ottomans is now very rich, but tends to concentrate on the period before 1600 or after 1650. For good introductions and further detail see P.F. Sugar, *Southeastern Europe under Ottoman Rule 1354–1804* (Seattle and London, 1977); B. Jelavich, *History of the Balkans* (Cambridge, 1983); S. Faroqhi, *The Ottoman Empire and the World Around It* (London, 2004); C.V. Findley, *The Turks in World History* (Oxford, 2005); D. Goffman, *The Ottoman Empire and Early Modern Europe* (Cambridge, 2002).
2. A. Höfert, *Den Feind beschreiben: 'Türkengefahr' und europäisches Wissen über das Osmanische Reich 1450–1600* (Frankfurt, 2003); A. Çirakman, *From 'terror of the world' to the 'sick man of Europe'. European images of Ottoman empire and society from the sixteenth century to the nineteenth* (New York and Frankfurt, 2002); M. Grothaus, 'Zum Türkenbild in der Kultur der Habsburgermonarchie zwischen dem 16. und 18. Jahrhundert', in A. Tietze (ed.), *Habsburgisch-osmanische Beziehungen* (Vienna, 1985), pp.67–89.
3. For the internal problems of the 1620s see G. Piterberg, *An Ottoman Tragedy. History and historiography at play* (Berkeley, 2003). For the army and Ottoman ways of war see R. Murphey, *Ottoman Warfare 1500–1700* (London, 1999); G. Agoston, 'Ottoman warfare in Europe 1453–1826', in J. Black (ed.), *European Warfare 1453–1815* (London, 1999), pp.118–44; V. Aksan, 'Ottoman war and warfare 1453–1812', in J. Black (ed.), *War in the Early Modern World 1450–1815* (London, 1999), pp.147–76; J. Grant, 'Rethinking the Ottoman "decline". Military technology diffusion in the Ottoman empire, fifteenth to eighteenth centuries', *Journal of World History*, 10 (1999), 179–201.
4. M. Arens, *Habsburg und Siebenbürgen 1600–1605* (Cologne, 2001); G. Murdock, *Calvinism on the Frontier 1600–1660. International Calvinism and the Reformed Church in Hungary and Transylvania* (Oxford, 2000).
5. P. Broucek, 'Logistische Fragen der Türkenkriege des 16. und 17. Jahrhunderts', *Vorträge zur Militärgeschichte*, 7 (1986), 35–60. See also L. Mákkai, 'Economic landscapes: historical Hungary from the fourteenth to the seventeenth century', in A. Maczak et al. (eds.), *East-Central Europe in Transition* (Cambridge, 1985), pp.24–35.
6. O. Regele, 'Zur Militärgeschichte Vorderösterreichs', in F. Metz (ed.), *Vorderösterreich* (2nd edn, Freiburg, 1967), pp.123–37; P. Broucek, 'Der Krieg und die Habsburgermonarchie', in A. Weigl (ed.), *Wien im Dreißigjährigen Krieg* (Vienna, 2001), pp.106–54; A. Veltzé, 'Die Wiener Stadtguardia', *MIÖG*, supplement 6 (1901), 530–46. New outworks were completed 1624–37.
7. G. Dávid and P. Fodor (eds.), *Ottomans, Hungarians and Habsburgs in Central Europe* (Leiden, 2000); G. Pálffy, 'Türkenabwehr, Grenzsoldatentum und die Militarisierung der Gesellschaft in Ungarn in der Frühen Neuzeit', *HJb*, 123 (2003), 111–48; C.W. Bracewell, *The Uskoks of Senj. Piracy, banditry and holy war in the sixteenth-century Adriatic* (Ithaca, 1992); E. Heischmann, *Die Anfänge des stehenden Heeres in Österreich* (Vienna, 1925); G. Agoston, 'Habsburgs and Ottomans: Defense, military change and shifts in power', *Turkish Studies Association Bulletin*, 22 (1998), 126–41.
8. W. Schulze, *Reich und Türkengefahr im späten 16. Jahrhundert* (Munich, 1978); W.

Steglich, 'Die Reichstürkenhilfe in der Zeit Karls V.', *Militärgeschichtliche Mitteilungen*, 11 (1972), 7–55.

9. For the Italians, see G. Hanlon, *The Twilight of a Military Tradition. Italian aristocrats and European conflicts 1560–1800* (London, 1998). Mansfeld's distant cousin, Wolfgang Count Mansfeld, also served in the imperial army against the Turks and later commanded the Saxon forces during the Bohemian Revolt, before rising to imperial field marshal.

10. The principal contributions to this debate are reprinted in C.J. Rogers (ed.), *The Military Revolution Debate* (Boulder, 1995). See also G. Parker, *The Military Revolution: Military Innovation and the Rise of the West 1500–1800* (Cambridge, 1988); J. Black, *A Military Revolution? Military change and European society 1550–1800* (Basingstoke, 1991).

11. B.S. Hall, *Gunpowder, Technology and Tactics. Weapons and warfare in Renaissance Europe* (Baltimore, 1997). For discussions of weaponry and tactics that pay more attention to Central Europe, see C. Beaufort-Spontin, *Harnisch und Waffe Europas. Die militärische Ausrüstung im 17. Jahrhundert* (Munich, 1982); E. Wagner, *European Weapons and Warfare 1618–1648* (London, 1979); H. Schwarz, *Gefechtsformen der Infanterie in Europa durch 800 Jahren* (Munich, 1977); G. Ortenburg, *Waffe und Waffengebrauch im Zeitalter der Landsknechte* (Munich, 1984). Siege warfare will be discussed in Chapter 5.

12. A. Wasilkowska, *Husaria. The winged horsemen* (Warsaw, 1998); R. Brzesinski and A. McBride, *Polish Armies 1596–1696* (2 vols., London, 1987–8).

13. H. Lahrkamp, 'Kölnisches Kriegsvolk in der ersten Hälfte des Dreißigjährigen Krieges', *AHVN*, 161 (1959), 114–45, at pp.124–31; E. von Frauenholz, *Das Heerwesen in der Zeit des Dreißigjährigen Krieges* (2 vols., Munich, 1938–9), I, pp.29–34.

14. J. Niederkorn, *Die europäischen Mächte und der 'Lange Türkenkrieg' Kaiser Rudolfs II. (1593–1606)* (Vienna, 1993); J. Müller, 'Der Anteil der Schwäbischen Kreistruppen an dem Türkenkrieg Kaiser Rudolfs II. von 1595 bis 1597', *Zeitschrift des Historischen Vereins für Schwaben und Neuburg*, 28 (1901), 155–262, with useful detail on the extent and cost of the imperial mobilization. See also T. Szalontay, 'The art of war during the Ottoman-Habsburg long war 1593–1606 according to narrative sources' (University of Toronto PhD, 2004); J.F. Pichler, 'Captain John Smith in the light of Styrian sources', *Virginia Magazine*, 65 (1957), 332–54.

15. C.F. Finkel, 'French mercenaries in the Habsburg-Ottoman war of 1593–1606: the desertion of the Papa garrison to the Ottomans in 1600', *Bulletin of the School of Oriental and African Studies*, 55 (1992), 451–71.

16. L. Toifl and H. Leitgrab, *Ostösterreich im Bocskay-Aufstand 1605* (Vienna, 1990).

17. R.R. Heinisch, 'Habsburg, die Pforte und der Böhmische Aufstand (1618–1620)', *Südost Forschungen*, 33 (1974), 125–65, at pp.143–51; H. Valentinitsch, 'Die Steiermark, Ungarn und die Osmanen, 1606–1662', *Zeitschrift des Historischen Vereines für Steiermark*, 45 (1974), 93–128; G. Wagner, 'Österreich und die Osmanen im Dreißigjährigen Krieg', *Mitteilungen des Oberösterreichischen Landesarchivs*, 14 (1984), 325–95. Transylvanian intervention is covered more fully in Chapter 9.

18. I. Hiller, 'Feind im Frieden. Die Rolle des Osmanischen Reiches in der europäischen Politik zur Zeit des Westfälischen Friedens', in H. Duchhardt (ed.), *Der Westfälische Frieden* (Munich, 1998), pp.395–404, and his 'Ungarn als Grenzland des christlichen Europa im 16. und 17. Jahrhundert', in R.G. Asch et al. (eds.), *Frieden und Krieg in der Frühen Neuzeit* (Munich, 2001), pp.561–76.

19. 69% of these were Hungarians, 16% Croatians and 15% Germans: T. Winkelbauer, *Ständefreiheit und Fürstenmacht* (2 vols., Vienna, 2003), I, p.442. For the Croat regiments, see F. Konze, *Die Stärke, Zusammensetzung und Verteilung der Wallensteinischen Armee während des Jahres 1633* (Bonn, 1906).

20. J.W. Stoye, *The Siege of Vienna* (London, 1964); T.M. Barker, *Double Eagle and Crescent: Vienna's Second Turkish Siege and its Historical Setting* (Albany, 1967); E. Eickhoff, *Venedig, Wien und die Osmanen. Umbruch in Südosteuropa 1645–1700* (Munich, 1973).

21. The Tirolean branch had died out in 1595, with its lands reverting to the main line. H. Noflatscher, 'Deutschmeister und Regent der Vorlande. Maximilian von Österreich (1558–1618)', in H. Maier and V. Press (eds.), *Vorderösterreich in der frühen Neuzeit* (Sigmaringen, 1989), pp.93–130. For the Brothers' Quarrel, see also H. Sturmberger, *Land ob der Enns und Österreich* (Linz, 1979), pp.32–75.

22. B. Rill, *Kaiser Matthias. Bruderzwist und Glaubenskampf* (Graz, 1999).

23. K. Vocelka, 'Matthias contra Rudolf. Zur politischen Propaganda in der Zeit des Bruderzwistes', *ZHF*, 10 (1983), 341–51.

24. H. Sturmberger, *Georg Erasmus Tschernembl. Religion, Libertät und Widerstand* (Linz, 1953); A. Strohmeyer, *Konfessionskonflikt und Herrschaftsordnung. Das Widerstandsrecht bei den österreichischen Ständen (1550–1650)* (Mainz, 2006).

25. *BA*, 1st series, vol. II, p. 221.

26. Rill, *Kaiser Matthias*, p.156.

27. J. Bahlcke, 'Theatrum Bohemicum. Reformpläne, Verfassungsideen und Bedrohungsperzeptionen am Vorabend des Dreißigjährigen Krieges', in W. Schulze (ed.), *Friedliche Intentionen –Kriegerische Effekte* (St Katharinen, 2002), pp.1–20.

28. H. Eberstaller, 'Zur Finanzpolitik der oberösterreichischen Stände im Jahre 1608', *Mitteilungen des oberösterreichischen Landesarchivs*, 8 (1964), 443–51.

Pax Hispanica

1. C. R. Boxer, *The Portuguese Seaborne Empire 1415–1825* (London, 1969); M. Newitt, *A History of Portuguese Overseas Expansion, 1400–1668* (London, 2005); D. Birmingham, *Trade and Empire in the Atlantic 1400–1600* (London, 2000); J. Lockhart and S.B. Schwartz, *Early Latin America. A history of colonial Spanish America and Brazil* (Cambridge, 1983).

2. For an introduction see H. Kamen, *Golden Age Spain* (2nd edn, Basingstoke, 2005). Good detailed studies include J. Lynch, *Spain under the Habsburgs* (2 vols., Oxford, 1981); J.H. Elliott, *Imperial Spain 1469–1716* (London, 1963); J.H. Elliott, *The Old World and the New 1492–1650* (London, 1972); H. Thomas, *Rivers of Gold. The rise of the Spanish empire* (London, 2003); J.H. Parry, *The Spanish Seaborne Empire* (London, 1966); H. Kamen, *Spain's Road to Empire. The making of a world power 1492–1763* (London, 2003); P. Bakewell, *A History of Latin America. Empires and sequels 1450–1930* (Oxford, 1997); B. Loveman, *Chile. The legacy of Hispanic capitalism* (3rd edn, Oxford, 2001); D. Rock, *Argentina 1516–1987* (Berkeley, 1987). For the debate on the demographic decline see J.J. Vidal, 'The population of the Spanish monarchy during the baroque period', in E. Martínez Ruiz and M. de P. Pi Corrales (eds.), *Spain and Sweden in the Baroque Era (1600–1660)* (Madrid, 2000), pp.443–69.

3. P.J. Bakewell, *Silver Mining and Society in Colonial Mexico, Zacatecas 1546–1700* (Cambridge, 1971).

4. G. Parker, *Spain and the Netherlands 1559–1659* (London, 1979), p.188. For the significance of silver imports, see S.J. Stein and B.H. Stein, *Silver, Trade and War. Spain and America in the making of early modern Europe* (Baltimore, 2000); M. Drelichman, 'American silver and the decline of Spain', *Journal of Economic History*, 65 (2005), 532–5. For the following, see also A. Calabria, *The Cost of Empire. The finances of the Kingdom of Naples in the time of Spanish rule* (Cambridge, 1991); R. Mackay, *The Limits of Royal Authority. Resistance and obedience in seventeenth-century Castile* (Cambridge, 1999).

5. David Goodman, *Spanish Naval Power 1589–1665. Reconstruction and defeat* (Cambridge, 1997).

6. R. Quatrefages, 'The military system of the Spanish Habsburgs', in R.B. Martinez and T.M. Barker (eds.), *Armed Forces and Society in Spanish Past and Present* (Boulder, 1988), pp.1–50; I.A.A. Thompson, *War and Government in Habsburg Spain 1560–1620* (London, 1976).

7. For an example, see M. de Andrada Castel Blanco, *To Defend Your Empire and the Faith. Advice on a global strategy offered c.1590 to Philip II* (translated by P.E.H. Hair, Liverpool, 1990). For the historical discussion, see J.H. Elliott, 'Self-perception and decline in early seventeenth-century Spain', *P&P*, 76 (1977), 41–61; R.A. Stradling, 'Seventeenth-century Spain: decline or survival?' *European Studies Review*, 9 (1979), 157–94, and his *Europe and the Decline of Spain. A study of the Spanish system 1580–1720* (London, 1981).

8. A. Feros, *Kingship and Favouritism in the Spain of Philip III 1598–1621* (Cambridge, 2000), pp.12–31.

9. G. Parker, *The Grand Strategy of Philip II* (New Haven, 1999).

10. T.J. Dandelet, *Spanish Rome 1500–1700* (New Haven, 2001). Spanish Catholicism is analysed by H. Rawlings, *Church, Religion and Society in Early Modern Spain* (Basingstoke, 2002).

11. A. Pagden, *Lords of all the World. Ideologies of empire in Spain, Britain and France c.1500–c.1800* (New Haven, 1995); E.Straub, *Pax und Imperium. Spaniens Kampf um seine Friedensordnung in Europa zwischen 1617 und 1635* (Paderborn, 1980); M. Tanner, *The Last Descendant of Aeneas. The Hapsburgs and the mythic image of the emperor* (New Haven, 1993).

12. For more detail see F. Edelmayer, *Söldner und Pensionäre. Das Netzwerk Philipps II. im Heiligen Römischen Reich* (Munich, 2002).

13. A. Sommer-Mathis, 'Ein *pícaro* und spanisches Theater am Wiener Hof zur Zeit des Dreißigjährigen Krieges', in A. Weigl (ed.), *Wien im Dreißigjährigen Krieg* (Vienna, 2001), pp.655–94; M. Golobeva, *The Glorification of Emperor Leopold I in Image, Spectacle and Text* (Mainz, 2000). For the following, see also M.S. Sanchez, *The Empress, the Queen, and the Nun. Women and power at the court of Philip III of Spain* (Baltimore, 1998), pp.118–21, 177–8.

14. J. Lynch, *The Hispanic World in Crisis and Change 1598–1700* (Oxford, 1992), p.19. Philip II's claim is quoted in R.T. Davies, *The Golden Century of Spain 1501–1621* (New York, 1937), p.230. Another writer is even more damning: 'If no one really understood his character, it was mostly because there was precious little to understand': C.H. Carter, *The Secret Diplomacy of the Habsburgs, 1598–1625* (New York, 1964), p.67.

15. R.A. Stradling, *Philip IV and the Government of Spain 1621–1665* (Cambridge, 1988), p.8. For the following see P. Williams, *The Great Favourite. The duke of Lerma and the court and government of Philip III of Spain, 1598–1621* (Manchester, 2006), and the contributions to L.W.B. Brockliss and J.H. Elliott (eds.), *The World of the Favourite* (New Haven, 1999).

16. The figure of 100,000 executions is still cited today by some historians, but the actual number was around 1,000 out of 8,950 charged by the Council of Troubles by 1572: J.I. Israel, 'The Dutch-Spanish War and the Holy Roman Empire (1568–1648)', in K. Bussmann and H. Schilling (eds.), *1648: War and Peace in Europe* (3 vols., Münster, 1998), I, pp.111–21, at p.112. See also H. Kamen, *The Duke of Alba* (New Haven, 2004). For the Revolt, see G. Darby (ed.), *Origins and Development of the Dutch Revolt* (London, 2001); A. Duke, *Reform and Revolt in the Low Countries* (London, 2003); and the excellent general history by J.I. Israel, *The Dutch Republic. Its rise, greatness and fall 1477–1806* (Oxford, 1995). The role of the Orange family is covered by K.W. Swart, *William of Orange and the Revolt of the Netherlands 1572–84* (Aldershot, 2003), and H.H. Rowen, *The Princes of Orange* (Cambridge, 1988).

17. H.G. Koenigsberger, *Monarchies, States Generals and Parliaments in the Netherlands in the Fifteenth and Sixteenth Centuries* (Cambridge, 2001); H.F.K. van Nierop, *The Nobility of Holland from Knights to Regents 1500–1650* (Cambridge, 1993).

18. G. Parker, 'Mutiny and discontent in the Spanish Army of Flanders 1572–1607', *P&P*, 58 (1973), 38–52.

19. C. Duffy, *Siege Warfare. The fortress in the early modern world 1494–1660* (London, 1979). Geoffrey Parker's version of the 'military revolution' thesis argues that the new

style of fortification was responsible for the growth of armies, but it seems more likely that this stemmed from political ambition and the relative ability to raise more men, particularly as population growth led to widespread underemployment by 1600. On this issue, see M.S. Kingra, 'The *trace italienne* and the military revolution during the Eighty Years War 1567–1648', *Journal of Military History*, 57 (1993), 431–46.

20. For the following see G. Parker, *The Army of Flanders and the Spanish Road 1567–1659* (Cambridge, 1972); J. Albi de la Cuesta, *De Pavía a Rocroi. Los tercios de infantería española en los siglos xvi y xvii* (Madrid, 1999); R.A. Stradling, *The Spanish Monarchy and Irish Mercenaries: The Wild Geese in Spain 1618–68* (Blackrock, 1994); D. Worthington, *Scots in the Habsburg Service 1618–1648* (Leiden, 2003) and the sources cited in n.6 above.

21. B. Rill, *Tilly. Feldherr für Kaiser und Reich* (Munich, 1984) offers an accessible biography of this important figure. There is more detail in M. Kaiser, *Politik und Kriegführung. Maximilian von Bayern, Tilly und die Katholische Liga im Dreißigjährigen Krieg* (Münster, 1999), esp. pp.16–31. The operations around Cologne and Strasbourg are covered in Chapter 7. For the following, see also H. Lahrkamp, *Jan von Werth* (2nd edn, Cologne, 1988); M. Kaiser, 'Die Karriere des Kriegsunternehmers Jan von Werth', *Geschichte in Köln*, 49 (2002), 131–70, and the relevant entries in the *Allgemeine Deutscher Biographie*. Spanish professionalism is discussed by F.G. de León, ' "Doctors of the military discipline": Technical expertise and the paradigm of the Spanish soldier in the early modern period', *Sixteenth Century Journal*, 27 (1996), 61–85.

22. M. van Geldern, *The Political Thought of the Dutch Revolt 1555–1590* (Cambridge, 1992). For the following, see also S. Groenveld, 'Princes and regents. The relations between the princes of Orange and the Dutch aristocrats and the making of Dutch foreign policy in theory and practice during the seventeenth century', in R.G. Asch et al. (eds.), *Frieden und Krieg in der frühen Neuzeit* (Munich, 2001), pp.181–92; and the two good general introductions of M. Prak, *The Dutch Republic in the Seventeenth Century* (Cambridge, 2005), and the similarly titled book by J. Price (Basingstoke, 1998).

23. H. Pirenne, *Histoire de Belgique* (7 vols., Brussels, 1900–32), III, p.428. For the following, see C. R. Boxer, *The Dutch Seaborne Empire 1600–1800* (London, 1965); J. De Woude Vries, *The First Modern Economy. Success, failure and perseverance of the Dutch Republic* (Cambridge, 1997).

24. Parker, *Spain and the Netherlands*, pp.195–6; P. Kriedte, *Peasants, Landlords and Merchant Capitalists. Europe and the world economy 1500–1800* (Leamington Spa, 1983), p.41. The Baltic trade was worth 12.5 million fl. in 1636, or over 40% of the European goods arriving in Amsterdam that year: Prak, *Dutch Republic*, p.97. See generally J.I. Israel, *Dutch Primacy in World Trade 1585–1740* (Oxford, 1989).

25. See C. Lesger, *The Rise of the Amsterdam Market and Information Exchange* (Aldershot, 2006); M. de Jong, 'Dutch public finance during the Eighty Years War', in M. van der Hoeven (ed.), *Exercise of Arms. Warfare in the Netherlands, 1568–1648* (Leiden, 1997), pp.133–52, and the two works by M.C. 't Hart, *The Making of a Bourgeois State. War, politics and finance during the Dutch Revolt* (Manchester, 1993), and 'The United Provinces, 1579–1806', in R. Bonney (ed.), *The Rise of the Fiscal State in Europe* (Oxford, 1999), pp.309–26. Credit was further eased by the provincial treasuries that shouldered a far larger share of the debt than the central budget.

26. H. Vogel, 'Arms production and exports in the Dutch Republic, 1600–1650', in Hoeven (ed.), *Exercise of Arms*, pp.197–210; P.W. Klein, 'The Trip family in the 17th century. A study of the behaviour of the entrepreneur on the Dutch staple market', *Acta Historiae Neerlandica*, 1 (1966), 187–211; J. Zunckel, *Rüstungsgeschäfte im Dreißigjährigen Krieg* (Berlin, 1997). For Geer, see R. Schulte, 'Rüstung, Zins und Frommigkeit. Niederländische Calvinisten als Finanziers des Dreißigjährigen Krieges', *Bohemia*, 35 (1994), 45–62.

27. The fleet totalled around 20,000 tonnes in 1600. Further details in J.R. Bruijn, *The Dutch Navy of the Seventeenth and Eighteenth Centuries* (Columbia, 1990); A.P. van Vliet, 'Foundation, organisation and effects of the Dutch navy (1568–1648)', in Hoeven

(ed.), *Exercise of Arms*, pp.153–72; V. Enthoven, 'From sea-beggars to admiralty. The Dutch navy after Lepanto', *Armi del Sovrano* (2001), http://www.assostoria.it.

28. Maurice was formally only count of Nassau-Dillenburg, since he only inherited the title of prince of Orange on his elder brother's death. Maurice's mother was Anna of Saxony who left her husband and was later jailed for an adulterous relationship with Jan Rubens, the future father of the painter Paul Rubens. He was entrusted to his Dillenburg relations to be raised and grew up rather withdrawn and taciturn.

29. The Dutch reforms are discussed by B.H. Nickle, 'The military reforms of Prince Maurice of Orange' (University of Delaware PhD, 1975), with their influence further explored by H. Ehlert, 'Ursprünge des modernen Militärwesens. Die nassau-oranischen Heeresreformen', *Militärgeschichtliche Mitteilungen*, 38 (1985), 27–56; W. Reinhard, 'Humanismus und Militärismus', in F.J. Worstbrock (ed.), *Krieg und Frieden im Horizont des Renaissancehumanismus* (Weinheim, 1985), pp.185–204; and O. van Nijmwegen, 'The Dutch army and the military revolutions (1588–1688)', *Militär und Gesellschaft in der Frühen Neuzeit*, 10 (2006), 55–73. For the Dutch army, see H.L. Zwitser, *'De militie van den staat'. Het Leger van de Republiek der Verenigde Nederlanden* (Amsterdam, 1991). Operations are covered in great detail by F.G.J. Ten Raa et al., *Het staatsche Leger 1568–1795* (8 vols., The Hague, 1911–59).

30. For Lipius see G. Oestreich, *Neostoicism and the Early Modern State* (Cambridge, 1982). The emphasis on discipline and rationality is explored further by H. Eichberg, 'Geometrie als barocke Verhaltensnorm', *ZHF*, 4 (1977), 17–50, and the two articles by H. Kleinschmidt, 'The military and dancing', *Ethnologia europaea*, 25 (1995), 157–76, and 'Mechanismus und Biologismus im Militärwesen des 17. und 18. Jahrhunderts', in D. Hohrath and K. Gerteis (eds.), *Die Kriegskunst im Lichte der Vernunft* (vol. I, Hamburg, 1999), pp.51–73.

31. Gheyn's work is available in a new English edition as *The Renaissance Drill Book* (London, 2003). Wallhausen's texts have also been reprinted as *Kriegskunst zu Fuß* (Oppenheim, 1615; reprinted Graz, 1971), *Kriegskunst zu Pferdt* (Frankfurt am Main, 1616; reprinted Graz, 1971), and *Ritterkunst* (Frankfurt am Main, 1616; reprinted Graz, 1969). For another example of the dissemination of Dutch ideas, see H. Hexham, *The Principles of the art militarie Practised in the Warres of the United Netherlands* (London, 1637).

32. Johann's instructions are printed in E. von Frauenholz (ed.), *Das Heerwesen in der Zeit des Dreißigjährigen Krieges* (2 vols., Munich, 1938–9), II, pp.47–76. See also W. Hahlweg, *Die Heeresreform der Oranier. Das Kriegsbuch des Grafen Johann (VII.) von Nassau-Siegen* (Wiesbaden, 1973). Frauenholz's work contains numerous other documents relating to their adoption in other territories: the Palatinate (1588), Celle (1598), Württemberg (1599), Pfalz-Neuburg (1599), Hessen-Kassel (1600), Anhalt (1600), Prussia (1602), Brandenburg (1604), Baden-Durlach (1604), Wolfenbüttel (1605) and Saxony (1613). Further discussion in W. Schulze, 'Die deutschen Landesdefensionen im 16. und 17. Jahrhundert', in J. Kunisch (ed.), *Staatsverfassung und Heeresverfassung* (Berlin, 1986), pp.129–49; G. Thies, *Territorialstaat und Landesverteidigung. Das Landesdefensionswerk in Hessen-Kassel unter Landgraf Moritz (1592–1627)* (Darmstadt, 1973); H. Schnitter, *Volk und Landesdefension* (Berlin, 1977).

33. D. Götschmann, 'Das Jus Armorum. Ausformung und politische Bedeutung der reichsständischen Militärhoheit bis zur ihrer definitiven Anerkennung im Westfälischen Frieden', *BDLG*, 129 (1993), 257–76.

34. Overall numbers could be impressive. The Lower Palatine militia mustered 12,000 in 1600, with a further 16,000 in the Upper Palatinate. Wolfenbüttel mobilized 16,000 infantry and 1,600 cavalry in 1605, while the Pfalz-Neuburg militia totalled 10,000 and those in Baden-Durlach and Württemberg around 5,000 and 4,500 respectively. For the Saxon militia, see L. Bachenschwanz, *Geschichte und gegenwärtiger Zustand der Kursächsischen Armee* (Dresden, 1802), and R. Naumann, *Das Kursächsische Defensionswerk (1613 bis 1709)* (Leipzig, 1916). The older literature on the other territories is

summarized by G. Papke, *Von der Miliz zum stehenden Heer* (Munich, 1983), pp.66–100.

35. Strictly speaking, it was Spain that first moved in this direction, by occupying Rheinberg in 1589 at the end of the Cologne War (see Chapter 7). However, this was not followed by Dutch retaliatory measures, unlike the Spanish reaction to Maurice's campaign. The town changed hands so many times that it became known as 'the whore of war'.

36. These events are covered from a local perspective in I. Sönnert, 'Die Herrlichkeit Lembeck während des Spanisch-Niederländischen und des Dreißigjährigen Kriege', in T. Sodmann (ed.), *1568–1648* (Vreden, 2002), pp.139–69, esp. pp.140–5. The other chapters in this volume offer a good insight into the effect of the war on the Dutch–German border.

37. The best account of the battle in English is P. Lenders, 'Nieuwport 2nd July 1600', *The Arquebusier*, 24 (2000), nr.3 pp.2–14, nr.4 pp.36–44.

38. Althusius's work is available in a fine modern translation edited by F.S. Carney (Indianapolis, 1995). For the situation in East Frisia, see J. Foken, *Im Schatten der Niederlande. Die politisch-konfessionellen Beziehungen zwischen Ostfriesland und dem niederländischen Raum vom späten mittelalter bis zum 18. Jahrhundert* (Münster, 2006), pp.281–374. B. Kappelhoff, *Absolutistisches Regiment oder Ständeherrschaft?* (Hildesheim, 1982) mainly covers the early eighteenth century, but offers detailed background. The Emden Calvinists have been examined by A. Pettegree, *Emden and the Dutch Revolt. Exiles and the development of Reformed Protestantism* (Oxford, 1992); H. Schilling, *Civic Calvinism in Northwestern Germany and the Netherlands* (Kirkville, Mich., 1991), and 'Sündenzucht und frühneuzeitliche Sozialdisziplinierung. Die Calvinistische, presbyteriale Kirchenzucht in Emden vom 16. bis 19. Jahrhundert', in G. Schmidt (ed.), *Stände und Gesellschaft im alten Reich* (Stuttgart, 1989), pp.265–302.

39. V.W. Lunsford, *Piracy and Privateering in the Golden Age Netherlands* (Basingstoke, 2005). The Dunkirkers are considered at greater length in Chapter 11.

40. These difficulties are abundantly clear from D. Howarth's gripping account from the Spanish perspective: *The Voyage of the Armada. The Spanish story* (Guildford, Conn., 2001, first published 1981).

41. R.A. Stradling, *The Armada of Flanders. Spanish maritime policy and European war, 1568–1668* (Cambridge, 1992), p.241 slightly modifying the figures given in Parker's seminal *Army of Flanders*. For the Spanish Road, see also G. Parker, *Empire, War and Faith in Early Modern Europe* (London, 2003), pp.127–42 and C. Paoletti, 'L'Italia e il cammino di Fiandra', *Armi del Sovrano* (2001), http://www.assostoria.it.

42. The wars are well covered in three modern accounts: M.P. Holt, *The French Wars of Religion 1562–1629* (Cambridge, 1995); R.J. Knecht, *The French Civil Wars 1562–1598* (Harlow, 2000); P. Roberts, *The French Wars of Religion* (London, 1999).

43. For the efforts to control mercenary recruitment, see M. Lanzinner, 'Friedenssicherung und Zentralisierung der Reichsgewalt. Ein Reformversuch auf dem Reichstag zu Speyer 1570', *ZHF*, 12 (1985), 287–310; L. Eppenstein, 'Beiträge zur Geschichte des auswärtigen Kriegsdienstes der Deutschen in der zweiten Hälfte des 16. Jahrhunderts', *FBPG*, 32 (1920), 283–367. For the following, see also M. Harsgor, 'Die Spieße unter der Lilienblume. Deutsche Söldner im Dienste Frankreichs (14.–16. Jh.)', *Tel Aviver Jahrbuch für deutsche Geschichte*, 16 (1987), 48–81; P. de Vallière, *Treue und Ehre. Geschichte der Schweizer im fremden Diensten* (Neuenburg, 1912), pp.210–12.

44. Savoyard policy is covered by G. Symcox, 'From commune to capital. The transformation of Turin, sixteenth to eighteenth centuries', and R. Oresko, 'The House of Savoy in search for a royal crown in the seventeenth century', both in R. Oresko et al. (eds.), *Royal and Republican Sovereignty in Early Modern Europe* (Cambridge, 1997), pp.242–69, and 272–350 respectively; T. Osborne, *Dynasty and Diplomacy in the Court of Savoy. Political culture and the Thirty Years War* (Cambridge, 2002).

45. A.E. Imhoff, *Der Friede von Vervins 1598* (Aarau, 1966).

46. F. Gallati, 'Eidgenössische Politik zur Zeit des Dreißigjährigen Krieges', *Jahrbuch für schweizerische Geschichte*, 43 (1918), 1–149, and 44 (1919), 1–257. For the following see A. Wendland, *Der Nutzen der Pässe und die Gefährdung der Seelen. Spanien, Mailand*

und der Kampf ums Veltlin 1620–1641 (Zürich, 1995); R.C. Head, *Early Modern Democracy in the Grisons. Social order and political language in a Swiss mountain canton, 1470–1620* (Cambridge, 1995).

47. C. Kampmann, *Arbiter und Friedensstiftung: Die Auseinandersetzung um den politischen Schiedsrichter im Europa der Frühen Neuzeit* (Paderborn, 2001).

48. The young Louis XIII of France married Philip III's sister, Anne of Austria, while Louis' favourite sister, Elisabeth, married the future Philip IV. Here I follow Feros, *Kingship and Favouritism* against Parker's pupil, P.C. Allen, *Philip III and the Pax Hispanica, 1598–1621* (New Haven, 2000), who tries to sustain the 'International War School' argument that peace-making was simply a tactical expedient.

49. C.H. Carter, 'Belgian "autonomy" under the Archdukes, 1598–1621', *JMH*, 36 (1964), 245–59; W. Thomas and L. Duerloo (eds.), *Albert and Isabella* (Brussels, 1998); H. de Schlepper and G. Parker, 'The formation of government policy in the Catholic Netherlands under "the Archdukes", 1596–1621', *EHR*, 91 (1976), 241–54; M. Dlugaiczyk, ' "Pax Armata": Amazonen als Sinnbilder für Tugend und Laster – Krieg und Frieden. Ein Blick in die Niederlände', in K. Garber et al. (eds.), *Erfahrung und Deutung von Krieg und Frieden* (Munich, 2001), pp.539–67.

50. As does Allen, *Philip III and the Pax Hispanica*, p.236.

51. For an account by one of these soldiers, see H.T. Gräf (ed.), *Söldnerleben am Vorabend des Dreißigjährigen Krieges* (Marburg, 2000).

Dominium Maris Baltici

1. D. Kirby, *Northern Europe in the Early Modern Period. The Baltic world 1492–1772* (Harlow, 1990) offers a useful general introduction. Finland, while still considered distinct, was not a kingdom and was governed as part of Sweden at this period. For Denmark, see K.J.V. Jespersen, *A History of Denmark* (Basingstoke, 2004). International links are covered by S. Murdoch, *Britain, Denmark-Norway and the House of Stuart, 1603–1660* (East Linton, 2003).

2. R.I. Frost, *The Northern Wars 1558–1721* (Harlow, 2000); S.P. Oakley, *War and Peace in the Baltic, 1560–1790* (London, 1992); J. Lisk, *The Struggle for Supremacy in the Baltic 1600–1725* (London, 1967).

3. L. Jespersen, 'The *Machtstaat* in seventeenth-century Denmark', and O. Rian, 'State and society in seventeenth-century Norway', both in *Scandinavian Journal of History*, 10 (1985), 271–304 and 337–63 respectively; J.H. Hein, 'The "Danish War" and Denmark's further role in the conflict', in K. Bussmann and H. Schilling (eds.), *1648: War and Peace in Europe* (3 vols., Münster, 1998), I, pp.103–10.

4. E.L. Petersen, 'From domain state to tax state', *Scandinavian Economic History Review*, 23 (1975), 116–48, and his 'Defence, war and finance. Christian IV and the Council of the Realm 1596–1629', *Scandinavian Journal of History*, 7 (1982), 277–313; K. Krüger, 'Die Staatsfinanzen Dänemarks und Schwedens im 16. Jahrhundert', in H. Kellenbenz and P. Prodi (eds.), *Fiskus, Kirche und Staat im konfessionellen Zeitalter* (Berlin, 1994), pp.187–207.

5. In all, 400,000 individual transits through the Sound were registered between 1497 and 1660. See W.S. Unger, 'Trade through the Sound in the seventeenth and the eighteenth centuries', *Economic History Review*, 2nd series, 12 (1959), 206–21. The king received 100,000 rd. directly from the tolls in 1608, while the remainder represented 22% of crown income (637,900 rd.) through the treasury.

6. J. Lavery, *Germany's Northern Challenge. The Holy Roman Empire and the Scandinavian struggle for the Baltic, 1563–1576* (Boston and Leiden, 2002), p.22.

7. J. Glete, *Navies and Nations. Warships, navies and state building in Europe and America 1500–1860* (2 vols., Stockholm, 1993), I, pp.130–5.

8. P.D. Lockhart, *Frederick II and the Protestant Cause: Denmark's role in the Wars of Religion* (Leiden, 2002), and his *Denmark in the Thirty Years War 1618–1648. King*

Christian IV and the decline of the Oldenburg state (Selinsgrove, 1996). See also the useful discussion in M. Bregnsbo, 'Denmark and the Westphalian Peace', in H. Duchhardt (ed.), *Der Westfälische Friede* (Munich, 1988), pp.361–92.

9. R. Postel, 'Hamburg at the time of the peace of Westphalia', in Bussmann and Schilling (eds.), *1648: War and Peace*, I, pp.337–43; G. Schmidt, 'Hansa, Hanseaten und Reich in der Frühen Neuzeit', in I. Richefort and B. Schmidt (eds.), *Les relations entre la France et les villes Hanséatiques de Hambourg, Brême et Lübeck* (Brussels, 2006), pp.229–59.

10. P.D. Lockhart, *Sweden in the Seventeenth Century* (Basingstoke, 2004) provides a good introduction. See also J. Lindegren, 'The Swedish "military state", 1560–1720', *Scandinavian Journal of History*, 10 (1985), 305–36.

11. A.V. Berkis, *The Reign of Duke James in Courland 1638–1682* (Lincoln, Nebr., 1960).

12. M. Roberts, *Gustavus Adolphus* (2 vols., London, 1953–8), I, pp.60–72.

13. Michael Roberts' two-volume biography remains the standard account in English. Nils Ahnlund's older Swedish history from 1932 still offers many insights and is available in a good English translation as *Gustavus Adolphus the Great* (New York, 1999). The positive Protestant tradition has been continued by Günter Barudio in *Gustav Adolf der Große. Eine politische Biographie* (Frankfurt am Main, 1982). The king's contemporary image is dealt with at greater length in Chapter 14.

14. Quoted in Ahnlund, *Gustavus Adolphus*, p.207.

15. Quoted in Ahnlund, *Gustavus Adolphus*, p.97n. Balanced discussion is given in J.P. Findeisen, *Axel Oxenstierna. Architekt der schwedischen Großmacht-Ära und Sieger des Dreißigjährigen Krieges* (Gernsbach, 2007).

16. K. Glamman, 'European trade 1500–1750', in C.M. Cipolla (ed.), *The Fontana Economic History of Europe. The sixteenth and seventeenth centuries* (London, 1974), pp.427–526, at pp.491–8. For the following, see also K.R. Böhme, 'Schwedische Finanzbürokratie und Kriegführung 1611 bis 1721', in G. Rystad (ed.), *Europe and Scandinavia* (Lund, 1983), pp.51–8; J. Lindegren, 'Men, money and means', in P. Contamine (ed.), *War and Competition between States* (Oxford, 2000), pp.129–62.

17. J. Glete, 'Bridge and bulwark. The Swedish navy and the Baltic, 1500–1809', in G. Rystad (ed.), *The Baltic in Power Politics* (Vol. I, Stockholm, 1994), pp.9–59; and his 'Amphibious warfare: the Baltic 1550–1700', in D.J.B. Trim and M.C. Fissel (eds.), *Amphibious Warfare 1000–1700* (Leiden, 2006), pp.123–47.

18. The extensive Swedish literature is summarized in M. Busch, *Absolutismus und Heeresreform. Schwedens Militär am Ende des 17. Jahrhunderts* (Bochum, 2000). The Swedish codes are printed in E. von Frauenholz (ed.), *Das Heerwesen in der Zeit des Dreißigjährigen Krieges* (2 vols., Munich, 1938–9), I, pp.355–424. For the local impact, see N.E. Villstrand, 'Adaptation or protestation: local communities facing the conscription of infantry for the Swedish armed forces, 1630–1679', in L. Jespersen (ed.), *A Revolution from Above? The power state of 16th and 17th century Scandinavia* (Odense, 2000), pp.249–314.

19. T.N. Dupuy, *Military Life of Gustavus Adolphus* (New York, 1969). Quotations from pp.xi and 55.

20. B.H. Liddell Hart, *Great Captains Unveiled* (Edinburgh, 1927), p.77. See ibid. pp.149–52.

21. R.F. Weigley, *The Age of Battles. The quest for decisive warfare from Breitenfeld to Waterloo* (London, 1993), pp.3–36.

22. For the debate on the Prussian system, as well as its links to Danish and Swedish conscription, see P.H. Wilson, 'Social militarisation in eighteenth century Germany', *GH*, 18 (2000), 1–39.

23. M. Roberts, *The Swedish Imperial Experience 1560–1718* (Cambridge, 1979) sums up the debate from the perspective of the 'old school'. Ahnlund and Barudio also fall into this camp. The most prominent representative of the 'new school' was Artur Attman, whose opinions are best accessed in English summary through his *Swedish Aspirations and the Russian Market during the Seventeenth Century* (Göteborg, 1985). Further discussion of

NOTES TO PP. 189-201

this issue can be found in S. Troebst, 'Debating the mercantile background to early modern Swedish empire-building: Michael Roberts versus Artur Attmann', *EHQ*, 24 (1994), 485–510. See also S. Lundkvist, 'Die schwedischen Kriegs- und Friedensziele 1632–1648', in K. Repgen (ed.), *Krieg und Frieden* (Munich, 1988), pp.219–40. The statistics cited in this paragraph come from Krüger, 'Die Staatsfinanzen Dänemarks und Schwedens', p.189.

24. E. Ringmar, *Identity, Interest and Action. A cultural explanation of Sweden's intervention in the Thirty Years War* (Cambridge, 1996). For the following, see also K.R. Böhme, 'Building a Baltic empire. Aspects of Swedish expansion 1560–1660', in Rystad (ed.), *The Baltic in Power Politics*, I, pp.177–220; K. Zernack, 'Schweden als europäische Großmacht der frühen Neuzeit', *HZ*, 232 (1981), 327–57; J. Glete, 'Empire building with limited resources', in E. Martínez and M. de P. Pi Corrales (eds.), *Spain and Sweden in the Baroque Era* (Madrid, 2000), pp.307–36.

25. Quoted in Ahnlund, *Gustavus Adolphus*, p.88. See ibid. pp.74–86 and Roberts, *Gustavus Adolphus* I, pp.174–81 for the marriage negotiations.

26. R. Butterworth (ed.), *The Polish-Lithuanian Monarchy in European Context c.1500–1795* (Basingstoke, 2001); D. Stone, *The Polish-Lithuanian State, 1386–1795* (Seattle, 2001); N. Davies, *God's Playground. A history of Poland* (2 vols., Oxford, 1981); K. Friedrich, *The Other Prussia. Royal Prussia, Poland and liberty 1569–1772* (Cambridge, 2000). The principal Polish source for this period is H. Wisner, *Zygmunt III Waza* (Warsaw, 1991).

27. M.G. Müller, 'Later Reformation and Protestant confessionalization in the major towns of Royal Prussia', in K. Maag (ed.), *The Reformation in Eastern and Central Europe* (Aldershot, 1997), pp.192–210.

28. R.I. Frost, *After the Deluge. Poland-Lithuania and the Second Northern War 1655–1660* (Cambridge, 1993). For the Commonwealth's armed forces, see the works cited in Chapter 4 n.12, and R.I. Frost, 'Scottish soldiers, Poland-Lithuania and the Thirty Years War', in S. Murdoch (ed.), *Scotland and the Thirty Years War 1618–1648* (Leiden, 2001), pp.191–213.

29. Frost, *Northern Wars*, pp.63–7. Frost calculates that 82% of the Swedish army died in the battle.

30. Michael Roberts terms the attempt to monopolize Russian trade the 'pursuit of a shadow': *Gustavus Adolphus* I, pp.45–6. See also H. Ellersieck, 'The Swedish Russian frontier in the seventeenth century', *Journal of Baltic Studies*, 5 (1975), 188–97.

31. Sigismund married Anna, sister of Archduke Ferdinand, in 1592. After her death in 1598, he took Ferdinand's other sister, Constantia, as his second wife in 1605, while his eldest son and eventual successor, Wladyslaw, married Ferdinand's daughter Cecilia Renate in 1637.

From Rudolf to Matthias

1. F. Göttmann, 'Zur Entstehung des Landsberger Bundes im Kontext der Reichs-, Verfassungs- und regionalen Territorialpolitik des 16. Jahrhunderts', *ZHF*, 19 (1992), 415–44.

2. E. Schubert, 'Staat, Fiskus und Konfession in den Mainbistümern zwischen Augsburger Religionsfrieden und Dreißigjährigen Krieg', in H. Kellenbenz and P. Prodi (eds.), *Fiskus, Kirche und Staat im konfessionellen Zeitalter* (Berlin, 1994), pp.111–40. For the following see also K.E. Demandt, *Geschichte des Landes Hessen* (Kassel, 1980), pp.342–6; J. Kist, *Fürst- und Erzbistum Bamberg* (3rd edn, Bamberg, 1962), pp.88–99.

3. M. Spindler (ed.), *Handbuch der bayerischen Geschichte* (2nd edn, 2 vols., Munich, 1988); S. Riezler, *Geschichte Baierns* (Vols. 3–6, Gotha, 1899–1903).

4. Echoes of this view can be found today, for example in A. Gotthard, ' "Politice seint wir bäpstisch". Kursachsen und der deutsche Protestantismus im frühen 17. Jahrhundert', *ZHF*, 20 (1993), 275–319. For recent reappraisals, see F. Müller, *Kursachsen und der Böhmische Aufstand 1618–1622* (Münster, 1997); D.M. Phelps, 'Reich, religion and dynasty: the formation of Saxon policy 1555–1619' (University of London PhD, 2005).

5. P. Sutter-Fichtner, *Protestantism and Primogeniture in Early Modern Germany* (New Haven, 1989).

6. Joachim Friedrich's two half-brothers, Christian and Joachim Ernst, received Kulmbach (Bayreuth) and Ansbach respectively, while his son Johann Georg was given the Silesian duchy of Jägerndorf that had been acquired by Ansbach in 1523.

7. The Rheinfels branch died out in 1583 and was shared between the other three. As senior line, Hessen-Kassel possessed 6,100km² with 160,000 inhabitants, while Darmstadt had 1,300km² and 50,000 inhabitants and Marburg the remaining quarter. For the following, see H.T. Graf, *Konfession und internationales System. Die Außenpolitik Hessen-Kassels im konfessionellen Zeitalter* (Marburg, 1993); H. Weber, *Der Hessenkrieg* (Gießen, 1935), pp.11-19.

8. B. Nischan, *Prince, People and Confession: the Second Reformation in Brandenburg* (Philadelphia, 1994).

9. V. Press, *Calvinismus und Territorialstaat. Regierung und Zentralbehörden der Kurpfalz 1559-1619* (Stuttgart, 1970), and his 'Die Reichsritterschaft im Kraichgau zwischen Reich und Territorium, 1500-1623', *ZGO*, 122 (1974), 35-98 that illustrates how the elector Palatine sought to extend his jurisdiction over the neighbouring imperial knights.

10. C. Tacke, 'Das Eindringen Hessen-Kassels in die Westfälischen Stifter', in K. Malettke (ed.), *Frankreich und Hessen-Kassel* (Marburg, 1999), pp.175-87, esp. pp.178-80; Graf, *Konfession und internationales System*, pp.135-44.

11. W. Ziegler, 'Die Hochstifte des Reiches im konfessionellen Zeitalter 1520-1618', *Römische Quartalsschrift*, 87 (1992), 252-81, at 262-3. Guelph policy is covered by H. Lietzmann, *Herzog Heinrich Julius zu Braunschweig und Lüneburg (1564-1613)* (Brunswick, 1993).

12. H.G. Aschoff, 'Das Hochstift Hildesheim und der Westfälische Frieden', *Die Diozese Hildesheim in Vergangenheit und Gegenwart*, 66 (1998), 229-69; H.J. Adamski, *Der Welfische Schutz über die Stadt Hildesheim* (Hildesheim, 1939).

13. A. Gotthard, '"Macht hab ehr, einen bischof abzusezen". Neue Überlegungen zum Kölner Krieg', *ZSRG KA*, 113 (1996), 270-325; Graf, *Konfession und internationales System*, pp.131-5; Phelps, 'Reich, religion and dynasty', pp.72-9. For the events see M. Ritter, *Deutsche Geschichte im Zeitalter der Gegenreformation und des Dreißigjährigen Krieges (1555-1648)* (3 vols., Stuttgart, 1889-1908), I, pp.573-646.

14. Rudolf had proposed Cardinal Andreas, son of Ferdinand of the Tirol by his first wife Philippine Welser from the great banking dynasty. However, her status as a commoner deprived Andreas of the necessary aristocratic pedigree to qualify in the highly exclusive Cologne chapter. The Tirol pulled out of the Landsberg Alliance in disgust at Rudolf's mishandling of the election.

15. G. Aders, *Bonn als Festung* (Bonn, 1973), pp.26-9.

16. P. Sauer, *Herzog Friedrich I von Württemberg 1557-1608* (Munich, 2003), pp.239-44.

17. P.D. Lockhart, *Frederick II and the Protestant Cause: Denmark's role in the Wars of Religion* (Leiden, 2002), pp.242-72.

18. A. Gotthard, '1591 – Zäsur der sächsischen und der deutschen Geschichte', *NASG*, 71 (2000), 275-84, at 276-8. This is disputed by Phelps, 'Reich, religion and dynasty', pp.88-94. For Christian I, see T. Nicklas, 'Christian I. und Christian II.1591-1611', in F.L. Kroll (ed.), *Die Herrscher Sachsens* (Munich, 2004), pp.126-36.

19. Gotthard, '"Politice seint wir bäpstisch"'.

20. Press, *Calvinismus und Territorialstaat*, p.504. For the following, see V. Press, 'Fürst Christian I. von Anhalt-Bernberg', in K. Ackermann (ed.), *Staat und Verwaltung in Bayern* (Munich, 2003), pp.193-216.

21. R. Bonney, *The King's Debts. Finance and politics in France 1589-1661* (Oxford, 1981), p.273.

22. V. Press, 'Die Grundlagen der kurpfälizischen Herrschaft in der Oberpfalz 1499-1621', *Verhandlungen der historischen Vereins für Oberpfalz und Regensburg*, 117 (1977), 31-67.

23. H. Duchhardt, 'Der Kampf um die Parität im Kammerrichteramt zwischen Augsburger Religionsfrieden und Dreißigjährigen Krieg', *ARG*, 69 (1978), 201–18. For the following, see also M. Heckel, 'Die Religionsprozesse des Reichskammergerichts im konfessionall gespaltenen Reichskirchenrecht', *ZSRG KA*, 77 (1991), 283–350, and B. Ruthmann, *Die Religionsprozesse am Reichskammergericht 1555–1648* (Cologne, 1996).

24. Phelps, 'Reich, religion and dynasty', pp.97–8.

25. D. Albrecht, *Maximilian I. von Bayern 1573–1651* (Munich, 1998); A. Edel, 'Politik und Macht bei Herzog Maximilian von Bayern. Die Jahre vor dem Ausbruch des Dreißigjährigen Krieges', in W. Schulze (ed.), *Friedliche Intentionen – Kriegerische Effekte* (St Katharinen, 2002), pp.107–39.

26. E. Ortlieb and G. Polster, 'Die Prozeßfrequenz am Reichshofrat (1519–1806)', *ZNRG*, 26 (2004), 189–216; S. Ehrenpreis, 'Die Tätigkeit des Reichshofrats um 1600 in der protestantischen Kritik', in W. Sellert (ed.), *Reichshofrat und Reichskammergericht* (Cologne, 1999), pp.27–46, and his *Kaiserliche Gerichtsbarkeit und Konfessionskonflikt. Der Reichshofrat unter Rudolf II. (1576–1612)* (Göttingen, 2006). Protestants formed a tenth of the judges, but the court assumed an increasingly Catholic interpretation of religious issues after 1580.

27. For example, C.V. Wedgwood, *The Thirty Years War* (London, 1957 edn.), p.48. The Donauwörth incident is covered from a variety of perspectives by Albrecht, *Maximilian*, pp.395–418; T. Hölz, *Krummstab und Schwert. Die Liga und die geistlichen Reichsstände Schwabens 1609–1635* (Leinfelden-Echterdingen, 2001), pp.137–40; R. Breitling, 'Der Streit um Donauwörth 1605/1611', *ZBLG*, 2 (1929), 275–98; C.S. Dixon, 'Urban order and religious coexistence in the German imperial city: Augsburg and Donauwörth, 1548–1608', *CEH*, 40 (2007), 1–33.

28. M. Ritter, 'Der Ursprung des Restitutionsediktes', in H.U. Rudolf (ed.), *Der Dreißigjährige Krieg* (Darmstadt, 1977), pp.137–74, at pp.149–51. See Chapter 13. The Augsburg settlement had last been formally confirmed in the 1566 imperial Recess.

29. The alliance is reproduced in T. von Moerner (ed.), *Kurbrandenburgsiche Staatsverträge von 1601–1700* (Berlin, 1867), pp.36–40. See the discussions in A. Gotthard, 'Protestantische "Union" und katholische "Liga" – subsidiäre Strukturelemente oder Alternativentwürfe?', in V. Press (ed.), *Alternativen zur Reichsverfassung in der frühen Neuzeit?* (Munich, 1995), pp.81–112; H. Gürsching, *Die Unionspolitik der Reichsstadt Nürnberg vor dem Dreißigjährigen Kriege (1608–1618)* (Munich, 1932); G. Horstkemper, 'Die protestantische Union und der Ausbruch des Dreißigjährigen Krieges', in Schulze (ed.), *Friedliche Intentionen*, pp.21–51.

30. F. Neuer-Landfried, *Die katholische Liga. Gründung, Neugründung und Organisation eines Sonderbundes 1608 bis 1620* (Kallmünz, 1968), with the founding document printed on pp.222–9. See also Albrecht, *Maximilian*, pp.408–17; Hölz, *Krummstab und Schwert*, pp.143–60.

31. G. Parker (ed.), *The Thirty Years War* (London, 1984), p.24. S.H. Steinberg, *The Thirty Years War and the Conflict for European Hegemony 1600–1660* (London, 1966) claims the war started in 1609. Others also see the crisis as a 'prelude' to inevitable general conflict: H. Ollmann-Kösling, *Der Erbfolgestreit um Jülich-Kleve (1609–1614). Ein Vorspiel zum Dreißigjährigen Krieg* (Regensburg, 1996). The most recent discussion of this crisis is A.D. Anderson, *On the Verge of War. International relations and the Jülich-Kleve succession crises (1609–1614)* (Boston, 1999). See also R.A. Mostert, 'Der jülich-klevische Regiments- und Erbfolgestreit – ein "Vorspiel zum Dreißigjährigen Krieg"?', in S. Ehrenpreis (ed.), *Der Dreißigjährige Krieg in Herzogtum Berg und seinen Nachbarregionen* (Neustadt an der Aisch, 2002), pp.26–64.

32. H. Smolinsky, 'Formen und Motive konfessionaller Koexistenz in den Niederlanden und am Niederrhein', in K. Garber et al. (eds.), *Erfahrung und Deutung von Krieg und Frieden* (Munich, 2001), pp.287–300. Half the Berg Protestants were Calvinists by 1609.

33. For Johann Wilhelm's illness and its repercussions, see H.C.E. Midlefort, *Mad Princes of Renaissance Germany* (Charlottesville, Va., 1994), pp.98–124.

34. Brandenburg initially only had 180 men in May 1609, but increased them to 770 cavalry, 3,000 infantry and 21 guns, while Pfalz-Neuburg contributed 600 horse and 2,000 foot. Brandenburg raised another 1,000 cavalry and 650 infantry on its home soil by August 1610, but these were disbanded because of the fall of Jülich. For the operations, see C. Jany, *Geschichte der preußischen Armee vom 15. Jahrhundert bis 1914* (4 vols., Berlin, 1928–9), I, pp.31–3; O. Bezzel, *Geschichte des kurpfälzischen Heeres von seinem Angfängen bis zur Vereinigung von Kurpfalz und Kurbayern 1777* (2 vols., Munich, 1925–8), I, p.133.

35. This was twice what he was required to provide in assistance to the Union. The French army totalled 6,300 infantry, 3,650 cavalry and 4,000 garrison troops at the beginning of 1610. The king levied another 30,000 infantry and 8,000 cavalry, but not all of these were actually raised: B.R. Kroener, 'Die Entwicklung der Truppenstärken in den französischen Armeen zwischen 1635 und 1661', in K. Repgen (ed.), *Forschungen und Quellen zur Geschichte des Dreißigjährigen Krieges* (Münster, 1981), pp.163–220, at p.166 n.13. Henri IV's relations with the Protestant German princes are covered by F. Beiderbeck, 'Heinrich IV. von Frankreich und die Protestantischen Reichsstände', *Francia*, 23 (1996), 1–32; 25 (1998), 1–25.

36. J.I. Israel, *The Dutch Republic. Its rise, greatness and fall 1477–1806* (Oxford, 1995), pp.406–7. Maurice's force included two French Huguenot regiments and 4,000 English infantry. Châtre's French army comprised 5,000 French and 3,000 Swiss infantry, plus 1,000 to 1,200 cavalry.

37. The three princes agreed 900 cavalry and 4,200 infantry, of which Württemberg was to provide half, with the rest coming from Baden and the Palatinate. In practice, Württemberg sent only 600 infantry, while the Palatinate provided 1,000 militia and a few mercenaries. Leopold's forces rose meanwhile to 4,000 infantry and 500 cavalry by the summer. L.I. von Stadlinger, *Geschichte des württembergischen Kriegswesens* (Stuttgart, 1856), p.273.

38. This force was separate from the troops assembled on the members' territories, and consisted of 2,000 cavalry, 6,500 infantry and 463 artillerymen, mainly from the Palatinate and Hessen-Kassel: Bezzel, *Geschichte des kurpfälzischen Heeres*, I, pp.54–6.

39. P. Steuer, 'Der vorderösterreichische Rappenkrieg (1612–1614)', *ZGO*, 128 (1980), 119–65; Bonney, *The King's Debts*, pp.65–9. Spanish subsidies to Leopold probably totalled no more than 100,000 fl.

On the Brink?

1. B. Rill, *Kaiser Matthias. Bruderzwist und Glaubenskampf* (Graz, 1999), pp.191–6.

2. V. Press, *Calvinismus und Territorialstaat. Regierung und Zentralbehörden der Kurpfalz 1559–1619* (Stuttgart, 1970), pp.498–500. Johann did issue a decree annulling some of Rudolf's more controversial verdicts, including the mandate against Aachen city council, but his status as regent robbed this of its legitimacy.

3. See the sources cited in Chapter 3 n.13, and J. Müller, 'Die Vermittlungspolitik Klesls von 1613 bis 1616 im Lichte des gleichzeitig zwischen Klesl und Zacharias Geizkofler geführten Briefwechsels', *MIÖG*, supplement 5 (1896/1903), 609–90.

4. S. Ehrenpreis, 'Die Rolle des Kaiserhofes in der Reichsverfassungskrise und im europäischen Mächtesystem vor dem Dreißigjährigen Krieg', in W. Schulze (ed.), *Friedliche Intentionen – Kriegerische Effekte* (St Katharinen, 2002), pp.71–106.

5. For important revisions to this view, see F. Müller, *Kursachsen und der Böhmische Aufstand 1618–1622* (Münster, 1997), pp.40–65; A. Gotthard, 'Johann Georg I. 1611–1656', in F.L. Kroll (ed.), *Die Herrscher Sachsens* (Munich, 2004), pp.137–47.

6. B.C. Pursell, *The Winter King. Frederick V of the Palatinate and the coming of the Thirty Years War* (Aldershot, 2003) presents a sympathetic, if somewhat rosy view of the elector, rather overstressing his concern for the Empire's established constitution. See also P. Bilhöfer, *Nicht gegen Ehre und Gewissen: Friedrich V, Kurfürst von der Pfalz – der Winterkönig von Böhmen (1596–1632)* (Mannheim, 2000).

7. The marriage is described by C. Oman, *Elizabeth of Bohemia* (London, 1964), pp.52–117. For James's policy, see S.L. Adams, 'Spain or the Netherlands. The dilemmas of early Stuart foreign policy', in H. Tomlinson (ed.), *Before the English Civil War* (London, 1983), pp.79–101.

8. P. Sauer, *Herzog Friedrich I von Württemberg 1557–1608* (Munich, 2003), pp.181–4; H.W. O'Kelly, 'War and politics in early seventeenth-century Germany: the tournaments of the Protestant Union', in Centro Studi Storici Narni (eds.), *La civilta del torneo (sec.xii–xviii)* (Rome, 1990), pp.231–45. The bride was Barbara Sophia. For the Union leadership's attempts to present themselves as good patriots, see A. Schmidt, *Vaterlandsliebe und Religionskonflikt. Politische Diskurse im Alten Reich (1555–1648)* (Leiden, 2007), pp.328–50.

9. F.H. Schubert, 'Die pfälzische Exilregierung im Dreißigjährigen Krieg', *ZGO*, 102 (1954), 575–680, esp. 610.

10. D. Albrecht, *Maximilian I. von Bayern 1573–1651* (Munich, 1998), pp.452–65; E. Stahl, *Wolf Dietrich von Salzburg. Weltmann auf dem Bischofsthron* (Munich, 1987). Maximilian justified armed intervention because Raitenau had seized the priory of Berchtesgaden during a long-running dispute over the salt trade.

11. Ferdinand had already become coadjutor in Cologne in 1595, as well as prior of Berchtesgaden. He was subsequently elected bishop of Paderborn as well in 1618. See J.F. Foerster, *Kurfürst Ferdinand von Köln. Die Politik seiner Stifter in den Jahren 1634–1650* (Münster, 1979).

12. The alliance was initially with Würzburg, Bamberg and Eichstätt, and was joined by the bishops of Passau and Regensburg, as well as the duke of Pfalz-Neuburg after his conversion to Catholicism. They reaffirmed their 'neighbourly assurance' on 27 May 1617, but this was little more than an agreement to correspond about issues of mutual concern.

13. A.D. Anderson, *On the Verge of War. International relations and the Jülich-Kleve succession crises (1609–1614)* (Boston, 1999), pp.133–63. Dutch involvement is covered by H. Gabel, 'Sicherheit und Konfession. Aspekte niederländischer Politik gegenüber Jülich-Berg vor und während des Dreißigjährigen Krieges', in S. Ehrenpreis (ed.), *Der Dreißigjährigen Krieg in Herzogtum Berg und seinen Nachbarregionen* (Neustadt an der Aisch, 2002), pp.132–79. There is a useful biographical sketch of Wolfgang Wilhelm by B. Fries-Kurze, 'Pfalzgraf Wolfgang Wilhelm von Neuburg', *Lebensbilder aus dem bayerischen Schwaben*, 8 (1961), 198–227. The political reasons for his conversion are stressed by E.O. Mader, 'Füstenkonversionen zum Katholismus im Mitteleuropa im 17. Jahrhundert', *ZHF*, 33 (2007), 373–410.

14. Brandenburg raised 694 cavalry and 3,164 infantry: C. Jany, *Geschichte der preußischen Armee vom 15. Jahrhundert bis 1914* (4 vols., Berlin, 1928–9), I, pp.43–5. The Hoefyser loan was never repaid, and was eventually written off by the Republic in 1685 in return for a political alliance when the electorate was much more powerful. Wolfgang Wilhelm increased his forces to 7–800 horse and 4–5,000 foot by the time the Spanish arrived.

15. For the details, see B. Ruthmann, 'Das richterliche Personal am Reichskammergericht und seine politischen Verbindungen um 1600', in W. Sellert (ed.), *Reichshofrat und Reichskammergericht* (Cologne, 1999), pp.1–26, at pp.19–22.

16. H. Valentinitsch, 'Ferdinand II., die innerösterreichischen Länder und die Gradiskaner-krieg 1615–1618', in P. Urban and B. Sutter (eds.), *Johannes Kepler 1571–1971* (Graz, 1975), pp.497–539. For the causes, see G.E. Rothenberg, 'Venice and the Uskoks of Senj 1537–1618', *JMH*, 33 (1961), 148–56. The Venetian military effort is analysed by M.E. Mallett and J.R. Hale, *The Military Organisation of a Renaissance State. Venice 1400–1617* (Cambridge, 1984), esp. pp.241–7.

17. G. Parker (ed.), *The Thirty Years War* (London, 1984), pp.38–43.

18. The Neapolitan fleet consisted of 18 ships, 38 galleys and 2,000 crew. The viceroy also had 12,000 regular troops on land.

19. M.S. Sanchez, 'A house divided: Spain, Austria and the Bohemian and Hungarian

successions', *Sixteenth-Century Journal*, 25 (1994), 887–903; H. Ernst, *Madrid und Wien 1632–1637* (Münster, 1991), p.14.

20. Albrecht, *Maximilian*, pp.476–503.

21. Printed in G. Lorenz (ed.), *Quellen zur Vorgeschichte und zu den Angfängen des Dreißigjährigen Krieges* (Darmstadt, 1991), pp.186–209, and discussed in W.E. Heydendorff, 'Vorderösterreich im Dreißigjährigen Krieg', *MÖSA*, 12 (1959), 74–142, at 113–15, and P. Brightwell, 'Spain, Bohemia and Europe 1619–21', *European Studies Review*, 12 (1982), 371–99, at 364–5.

22. A. van Schelven, 'Der Generalstab des politischen Calvinismus in Zentraleuropa zu Beginn des Dreißigjährigen Krieges', *ARG*, 36 (1939), 117–41. For the following, see H. Hotson, *Johann Heinrich Alsted, 1588–1638* (Oxford, 2000); R. M. Kingdon, 'International Calvinism and the Thirty Years War', and W. Schmidt-Biggermann, 'The Apocalypse and millenarianism in the Thirty Years War', both in K. Bussmann and H. Schilling (eds.), *1648: War and Peace in Europe* (3 vols., Münster, 1998), I, pp.229–35 and 259–63 respectively.

23. J.R. Christianson, 'Tyge Brahe's German treatise on the comet of 1577', *Isis*, 70 (1979), 110–40.

24. K. Manger (ed.), *Die Fruchtbringer – eine teutschherzige Gesellschaft* (Heidelberg, 2001); R.J.W. Evans, 'Learned societies in Germany in the seventeenth century', *European Studies Review*, 7 (1979), 129–51.

25. H.D. Hertrampf, 'Hoë von Hoënegg – sächsischer Oberhofprediger 1613–1645', *Beiträge zur Kirchengeschichte Deutschlands*, 7 (1970), 129–48.

26. J. Burkhardt, 'Die kriegstreibende Rolle historischer Jubiläen im Dreißigjährigen Krieg und im Ersten Weltkrieg', in Burkhardt (ed.), *Krieg und Frieden in der historischen Gedächtniskultur* (Munich, 2000), pp.91–102. F. Kleinehagenbrock, *Die Grafschaft Hohenlohe im Dreißigjährigen Krieg* (Stuttgart, 2003), pp.284–7 indicates the Saxon influence on the celebrations in Hohenlohe.

27. Quoted by C. Kohlmann, ' "Von unsern Widersachern den Baptisten vil erlitten und ussgestanden". Kriegs- und Krisenerfahrungen von Lutherischen Pfarrern und Gläubigen im Amt Hornberg des Herzogtums Württemberg während des Dreißigjährigen Krieges und nach dem Westfälischen Frieden', in M. Asche and A. Schindling (eds.), *Das Strafgericht Gottes* (Münster, 2002), pp.123–211, at p.151.

The Bohemian Revolt

1. G. Schramm, 'Armed conflicts in east Central Europe', in R.J.W. Evans and T.V. Thomas (eds.), *Crown, Church and Estates* (London, 1991), pp.176–95, at p.189. See also J. Bahlcke, 'Theatrum Bohemicum. Reformpläne, Verfassungsideen und Bedrohungsperzeptionen am Vorabend des Dreißigjährigen Krieges', in W. Schulze (ed.), *Friedliche Intentionen – Kriegerische Effekte* (St Katharinen, 2002), pp.1–20, at pp.15–18.

2. Printed in G. Lorenz (ed.), *Quellen zur Vorgeschichte und zu den Angfängen des Dreißigjährigen Krieges* (Darmstadt, 1991), pp.237–50. A. Gotthard stresses confessional motives, yet the text avoids the language of religious martyrdom in favour of legalistic and constitutional arguments: 'Eine feste Burg ist vnser vnnd der Böhmen Gott. Der Böhmische Aufstand 1618/19 in der Wahrnehmung des evangelischen Deutschland', in F. Brendle and A. Schindling (eds.), *Religionskriege im Alten Reich und in Alteuropa* (Münster, 2006), pp.135–62.

3. Apologia, Lorenz (ed.), *Quellen zur Vorgeschichte*, p.249.

4. F. Schiller, *Geschichte des Dreißigjährigen Krieges* (DTV edn, Munich, 1966), p.60. The other two Regents in the room were Adam von Sternberg, the senior castellan, and Diepold von Lobkowitz, the grand prior of the Knights of Malta.

5. Slavata's account in R. Schwarz, *The Imperial Privy Council in the Seventeenth Century* (Cambridge, Mass., 1943), pp.344–7, at p.345.

6. J. Krebs, 'Graf Georg Friedrich von Hohenlohe und die Schlacht am Weißen Berge bei Prag', *Forschungen zur Deutschen Geschichte*, 19 (1879), 475–95.

7. H. Angermeier, 'Politik, Religion und Reich bei Kardinal Melchior Khlesl', *ZSRG GA*, 110 (1993), 249–330, at 301. Klesl's memorandum of 18 June 1618 recommending force is printed in Lorenz (ed.), *Quellen zur Vorgeschichte*, pp.253–6.

8. Quoted in B. Rill, *Kaiser Matthias* (Graz, 1999), p.308. Detail in J. Rainer, 'Der Prozeß gegen Kardinal Klesl', *Römische Historische Mitteilung*, 5 (1961), 35–163.

9. P. Broucek, 'Feldmarschall Bucquoy als Armeekommandant 1618–1620', in *Der Dreißigjährige Krieg* (issued by the Heeresgeschichtliches Museum, Vienna, 1976), pp.25–57; J. Polisensky, *War and Society in Europe 1618–1648* (Cambridge, 1978), pp.79–80.

10. K. MacHardy, *War, Religion and Court Patronage in Habsburg Austria. The social and cultural dimensions of political interaction, 1521–1622* (Basingstoke, 2003), pp.108–16.

11. P. Brightwell, 'The Spanish origins of the Thirty Years War', *European Studies Review*, 9 (1979), 409–31; E. Straub, *Pax und Imperium. Spaniens Kampf um seine Friedensordnung in Europa zwischen 1617 und 1635* (Paderborn, 1980), pp.131–7; R.A. Stradling, *Philip IV and the Government of Spain 1621–1665* (Cambridge, 1988), pp.9–11; P. Williams, *The Great Favourite. The duke of Lerma and the court and government of Philip III of Spain, 1598–1621* (Manchester, 2006), pp.231–6.

12. F. Müller, *Kursachsen und der Böhmische Aufstand 1618–1622* (Münster, 1997), pp.149–57; D.M. Phelps, 'Reich, religion and dynasty: the formation of Saxon policy 1555–1619' (University of London PhD, 2005), pp.214–64.

13. H. Gürsching, *Die Unionspolitik der Reichsstadt Nürnberg vor dem Dreißigjährigen Kriege (1608–1618)* (Munich, 1932), pp.76–85. Udenheim was rebuilt as Philippsburg 1623–32, see K.H. Jutz and J.M. Fieser, *Geschichte der Stadt und ehemaligen Reichsfestung Philippsburg* (Philippsburg, 1966), and the similarly titled work by H. Nopp (Speyer, 1881).

14. HHStA, KA 138, 16 August 1618.

15. J.G. Weiß, 'Die Vorgeschichte des böhmischen Abenteuers Friedrichs V. von der Pfalz', *ZGO*, 92 (1940), 383–492, at 408–11; M. Rüde, *England und Kurpfalz im werdenden Mächteeuropa (1608–1632)* (Stuttgart, 2007), pp.165–77.

16. G. Mann, *Wallenstein* (Frankfurt am Main, 1983), pp.139–42; H. Diwald, *Wallenstein* (Munich, 1969), pp.113–23.

17. J. Polisensky, *The Thirty Years War* (London, 1971), p.121.

18. A. Stögmann, 'Staat, Kirche und Bürgerschaft', in A. Weigl (ed.), *Wien im Dreißigjährigen Krieg* (Vienna, 2001), pp.482–564, at pp.531–3. For the following, see also K. Völker, 'Die "Sturmpetition" der evangelischen Stände in der Wiener Hofburg am 5. Juni 1619', *Jahrbuch der Gesellschaft für die Geschichte des Protestantismus in Österreich*, 57 (1936), 3–50; H. Kretschmer, *Sturmpetition und Blockade Wiens im Jahre 1619* (Vienna, 1978).

19. HHStA, KA 138, which also contains details of envoys sent to key princes and to Denmark.

20. A. Gotthard, 'Der deutsche Konfessionskrieg seit 1619', *HJb*, 122 (2002), 141–72, at 164–6.

21. Doncaster's report in S.R. Gardiner (ed.), *Letters and Other Documents Illustrating the Relations between England and Germany at the Commencement of the Thirty Years War* (London, 1868), pp.188–202, at p.199. For the election, see also B.C. Pursell, *The Winter King* (Aldershot, 2003), pp.66–75; Weiß, 'Vorgeschichte', pp.430–55.

22. Text of the Confederation in Lorenz (ed.), *Quellen zur Vorgeschichte*, pp.332–58. J. Bahlcke, 'Die Böhmische Krone zwischen staatsrechtlicher Integrität, monarchischer Union und Ständischen Föderalismus', in T. Fröschl (ed.), *Föderationsmodelle und Unionsstrukturen* (Munich, 1994), pp.83–103, at pp. 97–102 offers a more positive interpretation opposed to the older view represented by H. Sturmberger, *Aufstand in Böhmen* (Munich, 1959), pp.47–53.

23. T. Winkelbauer, *Ständefreiheit und Fürstenmacht. (Österreichische Geschichte 1522–1699)* (2 vols., Vienna, 2003), I, pp.62–3.

24. F. Müller, *Kursachsen*, pp.260–8; Phelps, 'Reich, religion and dynasty', pp.249–62.

25. M. Glettler, 'Überlegungen zur historiographischen Neubewertung Bethlen Gabors', *Ungarn Jahrbuch*, 9 (1978), 237–55.

26. R. Kleinman, 'Charles Emanuel I of Savoy and the Bohemian election of 1619', *European Studies Review*, 5 (1975), 3–29. For the election, see A. Gindely, *History of the Thirty Years War* (2 vols., New York, 1892), I, pp.148–50.

27. P. Wolf, 'Eisen aus der Oberpfalz, Zinn aus Böhmen und die goldene böhmische Krone', in P. Wolf et al. (eds.), *Der Winterkönig* (Augsburg, 2003), pp.65–74. For the decision, see also Pursell, *The Winter King*, pp.65–86.

28. Frederick's declaration of 7 November 1619 is printed in Lorenz (ed.), *Quellen zur Vorgeschichte*, pp.409–18.

29. There are good descriptions of the journey and ceremonies in C. Oman, *Elizabeth of Bohemia* (London, 1964), pp.178–98.

30. Quoted by Gotthard, 'Eine feste Burg ist vnser vnnd der Böhmen Gott', p.160. See also A. Gotthard, *Konfession und Staatsräson. Die Außenpolitik Württembergs unter Herzog Johann Friedrich (1608–1628)* (Stuttgart, 1992), pp.271–301; G. Horstkemper, 'Die protestantische Union und der Ausbruch des Dreißigjährigen Krieges', in Schulze (ed.), *Friedliche Intentionen*, pp.21–51, at pp.46–7.

31. E. McCabe, 'England's foreign policy in 1619. Lord Doncaster's embassy to the princes of Germany', *MIÖG*, 58 (1950), 457–77, at 460. See also C.H. Carter, *The Secret Diplomacy of the Habsburgs 1598–1625* (New York, 1964), pp.118–30.

32. Grey's regiment reached Bohemia in August 1620. See J. Polisensky, *Tragic Triangle. The Netherlands, Spain and Bohemia, 1617–1621* (Prague, 1991), and his 'A note on Scottish soldiers in the Bohemian War 1619–1622', in S. Murdoch (ed.), *Scotland and the Thirty Years War 1618–1648* (Leiden, 2001). British Catholics also sent money to help Spain recruit: A.J. Loomie, 'Gondomar's selection of English officers in 1622', *EHR*, 88 (1973), pp.574–81.

33. C.V. Wedgwood, *The Thirty Years War* (London, 1957 edn), p.141.

34. Pursell, *The Winter King*, pp.4–5, 95–100 presents a rather too rosy picture of Frederick's tolerance. See also J. Pánek, 'Friedrich V. von der Pfalz als König von Böhmen', in Wolf et al. (eds.), *Der Winterkönig*, pp.101–6.

35. T. Winkelbauer, 'Nervus belli Bohemici. Die finanziellen Hintergründe des Scheiterns des Ständeaufstands der Jahre 1618 bis 1620', *Folia Historica Bohemica*, 18 (1997), 173–223; S. Riezler (ed.), 'Kriegstagebücher aus dem ligistischen Hauptquartier 1620', *Abhandlungen des Phil.-Hist. Klasse der Bayerischen Akademie der Wissenschaften*, 23 (1906), 77–210, at 210; O. Chaline, *La Bataille de la Montagne Blanche* (Paris, 1999), esp. pp.100–2; O. Bezzel, *Geschichte des kurpfälzischen Heeres von seinem Angfängen bis zur Vereinigung von Kurpfalz und Kurbayern 1777* (2 vols., Munich, 1925–8), I, appendix 2.

36. J. Tiege et al., *Na Bile Hora* (Prague, 1921), pp.54–5.

37. Detailed breakdown in K. Oberleitner, 'Beiträge zur Geschichte des Dreißigjährigen Krieges mit besonderer Berücksichtigung des österreichischen Finanz- und Kriegswesens ... vom Jahre 1618–1634', *Archiv für österreichische Geschichte*, 19 (1858), 1–48, at 8–9. See also P. Broucek, *Kampf um Landeshoheit und Herrschaft im Osten Österreichs 1618 bis 1621* (Vienna, 1992); S. Reisner, 'Die Kämpfe vor Wien in Oktober 1619 im Spiegel zeitgenössischer Quellen', in Weigl (ed.), *Wien*, pp.446–81.

38. R. Frost, *The Northern Wars 1558–1721* (Harlow, 2000), pp.96, 102.

39. H. Wisner, *Wladyslaw IV* (Warsaw, 1995), p.32. My thanks to Kacper Rekawek for assistance with this and the other Polish literature.

40. P. Jasienica, *Rzeczpospolita obojga Narodowa* Vol. II (Warsaw, 1986). See also H. Wisner, 'Die Adelsrepublik und der Dreißigjährige Krieg', in H. Duchhardt (ed.), *Der Westfälische Friede* (Munich, 1998), pp.405–12.

41. J. Besala, *Stanislaw Zolkiewski* (Warsaw, 1988), p.349; H. Wisner, *Lisowczycy* (Warsaw, 1995).

42. G. Gajecky and A. Baran, *The Cossacks in the Thirty Years War*, Vol. I (Rome, 1969), pp.32–7.
43. Ibid., pp.40–52; Broucek, *Kampf um Landeshoheit*, pp.28–35.
44. R.R. Heinisch, 'Habsburg, die Pforte und der Böhmische Aufstand (1618–1620)', *Südost Forschungen*, 33 (1974), 125–65, and 34 (1975), 79–124; Gindely, *Thirty Years War*, I, pp.208–11.
45. Oberleitner, 'Beiträge', pp.1–12; Winkelbauer, 'Nervus belli Bohemici', pp.185, 196.
46. T. Hölz, *Krummstab und Schwert. Die Liga und die geistlichen Reichsstände Schwabens 1609–1635* (Leinfelden-Echterdingen, 2001), pp.372–91; D. Albrecht, *Maximilian I. von Bayern* (Munich, 1998), pp.491–7.
47. A. Gotthard, 'Protestantische "Union" und Katholische "Liga"', in V. Press (ed.), *Alternativen zur Reichsverfassung in der Frühen Neuzeit?* (Munich, 1995), pp.81–112, at p.104. It is clear that Bavaria, not Spain as sometimes claimed, held the initiative in these negotiations: A. Edel, 'Auf dem Weg in den Krieg. Zur Vorgeschichte der Intervention Herzog Maximilians I. von Bayern in Österreich und Böhmen 1620', *ZBLG*, 65 (2002), 157–253.
48. Treaty printed in *BA*, I, pp.242–7.
49. M. Kaiser, 'Ständebund und Verfahrensordnung. Das Beispiel der Katholischen Liga (1619–1631)', in B. Stollberg-Rillinger (ed.), *Vormoderne politische Verfahren* (Berlin, 2001), pp.331–415; Albrecht, *Maximilian*, pp.495–8, 502–11; R.R. Heinisch, *Paris Graf Lodron. Reichsfürst und Erzbischof von Salzburg* (Vienna, 1991).
50. M. Kaiser, 'Maximilian I. von Bayern und der Krieg', *ZBLG*, 65 (2002), 69–99. For a detailed analysis of Maximilian's objectives and relationship to Tilly, see the same author's *Politik und Kriegführung. Maximilian von Bayern, Tilly und die Katholische Liga im Dreißigjährigen Krieg* (Munich, 1999).
51. D. Albrecht, 'Zur Finanzierung des Dreißigjährigen Krieges: Die Subsidien der Kurie für Kaiser und Liga 1618–1635', *ZBLG*, 19 (1956), 534–67; G. Immler, 'Finanzielle Beziehungen zwischen Kirche und Staat in Bayern zur Zeit des Dreißigjährigen Krieges', in H. Kellenbenz and P. Prodi (eds.), *Fiskus, Kirche und Staat im konfessionellen Zeitalter* (Berlin, 1994), pp.141–63.
52. Albrecht, *Maximilian*, pp.511–14; Straub, *Pax und Imperium*, pp.137–62; P. Brightwell, 'Spain and Bohemia: the decision to intervene, 1619', *European Studies Review*, 12 (1982), 117–41, and his 'Spain, Bohemia and Europe, 1619–21', in the same publication, 371–99.
53. 27,000 in Italy, 16,000 in Iberia, North Africa and the Atlantic outposts, and 15,000 in Flanders. Additional recruitment doubled the latter force during 1619.
54. See the sources in n.52, with additional data from G. Parker, *The Army of Flanders and the Spanish Road 1567–1659* (Cambridge, 1979), p.272.
55. The Mühlhausen declaration of 20 March 1620 is printed in Lorenz (ed.), *Quellen zur Vorgeschichte*, pp.451–3. See also T. Nicklas, *Macht oder Recht. Frühneuzeitliche Politik im obersächsischen Reichskreis* (Stuttgart, 2002), pp.198–215; F. Müller, *Kursachsen*, pp.338–49; Albrecht, *Maximilian*, pp.516–17.
56. Numbers from Bezzel, *Geschichte des kurpfälzischen Heeres* I, pp.59–60; Gindely, *Thirty Years War*, I, pp.225–8. For the following, see R. Bireley, *The Jesuits and the Thirty Years War* (Cambridge, 2003), pp.47, 50–6; D. Albrecht, *Die Auswärtige Politik Maximilians von Bayern 1618–1635* (Göttingen, 1962), pp.44–7.
57. C.R. Markham, *The Fighting Veres* (London, 1888), pp.394–420. For the following, see also H.G.R. Reade, *Sidelights on the Thirty Years War* (3 vols., London, 1924), I, pp.323–45.
58. F. Müller, *Kursachsen*, pp.389–406.
59. Riezler (ed.), 'Kriegstagebücher', pp.84, 109.
60. Ferdinand to Johann Georg, 5 December 1619, in E. von Frauenholz (ed.), *Das Heerwesen in der Zeit des Dreißigjährigen Krieg* (2 vols., Munich, 1938–9), I, pp.105–6. For Cossack atrocities see Gajecky and Baran, *Cossacks*, p.40.

61. Riezler (ed.), 'Kriegstagebücher', pp.90–4, 144.
62. T. Johnson, ' "Victora a deo missa?" Living saints on the battlefields of the Central European Counter Reformation', in J. Beyer et al. (eds.), *Confessional Sanctity (c.1500–c.1800)* (Mainz, 2006), pp.319–35; O. Chaline, 'Religion und Kriegserfahrung. Die Schlacht am Weissen Berge 1620', in Brendle and Schindling (eds.), *Religionskriege*, pp.511–18.
63. B. Rill, *Tilly. Feldherr für Kaiser und Reich* (Munich, 1984), p.90.
64. Chaline, *Bataille*; J. Krebs, *Die Schlacht am Weißen Berge bei Prag* (Breslau, 1879); M. Junkelmann, 'Das alles entscheidende Debakel: Die Schlacht am Weißen Berg', in Wolf et al. (eds.), *Der Winterkönig*, pp.12–26.
65. Berlin newspaper report dated 30 November 1620, in H. Jessen (ed.), *Der Dreißigjährige Krieg in Augenzeugenberichten* (Düsseldorf, 1963), pp.93–4. The panic is described in Sir Edward Conway's report in A. Gindely (ed.), *Die Berichte über die Schlacht auf dem Weissen Berge bei Prag* (Vienna, 1877), pp.156–63.
66. These are printed in Gindely (ed.), *Berichte*, pp.118–45.
67. Winkelbauer, 'Nervus belli Bohemici', pp.215–16. See also Gindely, *Thirty Years War*, I, pp.129, 237.
68. V. Urbánek, 'The idea of state and nation in the writings of Bohemian exiles after 1620', in L. Eriksonas and L. Müller (eds.), *Statehood before and beyond Ethnicity* (Brussels, 2005), pp.67–84.
69. I. Auerbach, 'The Bohemian opposition, Poland-Lithuania and the outbreak of the Thirty Years War', in Evans and Thomas (eds.), *Crown, Church and Estates*, pp.196–225, esp. pp.197–200; J. Burkhardt, *Der Dreißigjährige Krieg* (Frankfurt am Main, 1992), pp.81–2.
70. P. Mat'a, 'The making of state power and reflections on the state in Bohemia and Moravia between the Estates' rebellion and Enlightenment reforms', in H. Manikowska and J. Pánek (eds.), *Political Culture in Central Europe* (Prague, 2005), pp.349–67, at pp.353–8.
71. Z.V. David, *Finding the Middle Way. The Utraquists' liberal challenge to Rome and Luther* (Washington, DC, 2003), pp.302–48.
72. There has been a great deal of recent interest in early modern courts. For good guides to the debates and further references, see J. Duindam, *Vienna and Versailles. The courts of Europe's dynastic rivals, 1550–1780* (Cambridge, 2003), and J. Adamson (ed.), *The Princely Courts of Europe 1500–1750* (London, 1999).
73. MacHardy, *War, Religion and Court Patronage*, esp. pp.188–98; T. Winkelbauer, 'Krise der Aristokratie? Zum Strukturwandel des Adels in den böhmischen und niederösterreichischen Ländern im 16. u. 17. Jh.', *MIÖG*, 100 (1992), 328–53; P. Mat'a, 'Der Adel aus dem böhmischen Ländern am Kaiserhof 1620–1740', in V. Buzek and P. Král (eds.), *Slechta v habsburské monarchii a císarsky avur (1526–1740)* (Budweis, 2003), pp.191–233.
74. A point well made by Burkhardt, *Der Dreißigjährige Krieg*, pp.85–7.

Ferdinand Triumphant

1. Father H. Fitz-Simon, *Diary of the Bohemian War of 1620* (Dublin, 1881), p.103.
2. F. Maier, *Die bayerische Unterpfalz im Dreißigjährigen Krieg* (New York, 1990), p.18.
3. See G. Lorenz (ed.), *Quellen zur Vorgeschichte und zu den Angfängen des Dreißigjährigen Krieges* (Darmstadt, 1991), pp.513–19; A. Gindely, *The Thirty Years War* (2 vols., New York, 1892), I, pp.301–3.
4. J. Gorst-Williams, *Elizabeth the Winter Queen* (London, 1977), p.157. See also N. Mout, 'Der Winter König im Exil. Friedrich V. von der Pfalz und die niederländischen Generalstaaten 1621–1632', *ZHF*, 15 (1988), 257–72.
5. V. Press, *Calvinismus und Territorialstaat* (Stuttgart, 1970), pp.493–4; F.H. Schubert, 'Die pfälzische Exilregierung im Dreißigjährigen Krieg', *ZGO*, 102 (1954), 575–680; M.

Hroch and I. Bartecek, 'Die böhmische Frage im Dreißigjährigen Krieg', in H. Duchhardt (ed.), *Der Westfälische Friede* (Munich, 1998), pp.447–60.

6. C. Oman, *Elizabeth of Bohemia* (London, 1964), pp.236–40, 255; M. Rüde, *England und Kurpfalz im werdenden Mächteeuropa (1608–1632)* (Stuttgart, 2007), pp.226–43. For Anglo-Palatine relations, see E. Weiss, *Die Unterstützung Friedrichs V. von der Pfalz durch Jakob I. und Karl I. von England im Dreißigjährigen Krieg (1618–1632)* (Stuttgart, 1966), pp.31–124.

7. A. Gotthard, *Konfession und Staatsräson. Die Außenpolitik Württembergs unter Herzog Johann Friedrich (1608–1628)* (Stuttgart, 1992), pp.350–434; T. Hölz, *Krummstab und Schwert. Die Liga und die geistlichen Reichsstände Schwabens 1609–1635* (Leinfelden-Echterdingen, 2001), pp.408–30. For the following, see Gindely, *Thirty Years War*, I, pp.306–9; R. Zaller, ' "Interests of state". James I and the Palatinate', *Albion*, 6 (1974), 144–75, at 153–72.

8. M. de Jong, 'Dutch public finance during the Eighty Years War: the case of the province of Zeeland, 1585–1621', in M. van der Hoeven (ed.), *The Exercise of Arms. Warfare in the Netherlands, 1568–1648* (Leiden, 1997), pp.133–52, at pp.139–40; J.I. Israel, *The Dutch Republic* (Oxford, 1995), pp.410–49.

9. A. Duke, *Reformation and Revolt in the Low Countries* (London, 2003), p.234.

10. H.H. Rowen, *The Princes of Orange* (Cambridge, 1988), pp.45–6.

11. J.I. Israel, *The Dutch Republic and the Hispanic World 1606–1661* (Oxford, 1982), pp.76–81 and the same author's *Dutch Republic*, pp.450–74. Mijles, in whose house Frederick initially stayed, was Oldenbarnevelt's son-in-law.

12. Quoted in J.H. Elliott, *The Count-Duke of Olivares* (New Haven, 1986), p.58. See also C.H. Carter, *The Secret Diplomacy of the Habsburgs 1598–1625* (New York, 1964), pp.213–32; J.I. Israel, *Conflicts of Empires. Spain, the Low Countries and the struggle for world supremacy 1583–1715* (London, 1997), pp.35–9.

13. Quoted in B.C. Pursell, *The Winter King* (Aldershot, 2003), p.129. See also S. Murdoch, *Britain, Denmark-Norway and the House of Stuart, 1603–1660* (East Linton, 2003), pp.22–48, 58–61. Swedish offers are covered by M. Roberts, *Gustavus Adolphus* (2 vols., London, 1953–8), I, pp.220–40. For Sweden's war with Poland from 1621 see Chapter 13.

14. Paradoxically, this helped Frederick, because Christian loaned James I the £100,000 used to pay the British volunteers defending the Palatinate in return for his help in containing Dutch protests at Danish bullying of the Hansa. Denmark also loaned a further 1 million talers to the German princes who eventually declared for Frederick in 1622. For this and Segeberg, see P.D. Lockhart, *Denmark in the Thirty Years War 1618–1648* (Selinsgrove, 1996), pp.87–93.

15. Weiss, *Unterstützung*, pp.117–23. Recruitment methods and impact are analysed by S.J. Stearns, 'Conscription and English society in the 1620s', *Journal of British Studies*, 11 (1972), 1–24, while money transfers are explained in A.V. Judges, 'Philip Burlamachi. A financier of the Thirty Years War', *Economica*, 6 (1926), 285–300.

16. P. Broucek, *Kampf um Landeshoheit und Herrschaft im Osten Österreichs 1618 bis 1621* (Vienna, 1992), p.50.

17. For the contemporary evaluation of Bucquoy's death, see V. Malvezzi, *Historia de los primeros años del reinado de Felipe IV* (London, 1968), pp.37–40.

18. Gindely, *Thirty Years War*, I, pp.324–31; J. Polišenský, *The Thirty Years War* (London, 1971), pp.150–4.

19. F. Redlich, *The German Military Enterpriser and his Workforce* (2 vols., Wiesbaden, 1964–5), I, esp. pp.211–15. Mansfeld lacks an adequate biography. Older studies include A. de Villermont, *Ernest de Mansfeldt* (Brussels, 1866), and the entry in *Allgemeine Deutsche Biographie*, 20 (1884), 222–32.

20. Negotiations with Mansfeld in J. Staber, 'Die Eroberung der Oberpfalz im Jahre 1621', *Verhandlungen des Historischen Veriens für Oberpfalz und Regensburg*, 104 (1964), 165–221, at 190–4, 196–207.

21. For Mansfeld's troops and resources see O. Bezzel, *Geschichte des kurpfälzischen Heeres* (2 vols., Munich, 1925–8), I, pp.61–81.

22. G. Thies, *Territorialstaat und Landesverteidigung. Das Landesdefensionswerk in Hessen-Kassel unter Landgraf Moritz (1592–1627)* (Darmstadt, 1973), esp. p.167. The older literature on the Hessian army is summarized by D. Wright, 'The development of the army of Hesse-Cassel during the Thirty Years War', *Arquebusier*, 29, no.1 (2005), 2–15.

23. H.T. Gräf, 'Der Generalaudienzierer Wolfgang Günther und Landgraf Moritz von Hessen-Kassel', in M. Kaiser and A. Pečar (eds.), *Der zweite Mann im Staat* (Berlin, 2003), pp.59–76. Useful detail is in F.L. Carsten, *Princes and Parliaments* (Oxford, 1959), pp.175–8. For the following see also, G. Schmidt, *Der Wetterauer Grafenverein* (Marburg, 1989); C. Cramer, 'Territoriale Entwicklung', in B. Martin and R. Wetekam (eds.), *Waldeckische Landeskunde* (Korbach, 1971), pp.214–20.

24. L.J. von Stadlinger, *Geschichte des württembergischen Kriegswesens* (Stuttgart, 1856), pp.275–81.

25. H. Wertheim, *Der Tolle Halberstädter. Herzog Christian von Braunschweig im Pfälzischen Krieg, 1621–1622* (2 vols., Berlin, 1929); J.O. Opel, *Der niedersächsisch-dänische Krieg* (3 vols., Halle and Magdeburg, 1872–94), vol. I.

26. F. Müller, *Kursachsen und der Böhmische Aufstand 1618–1622* (Münster, 1997), pp.171–3; A. Klinger, *Der Gothaer Fürstenstaat* (Husum, 2002), p.57.

27. M. Ventzke, 'Zwischen Kaisertreue und Interessenpolitik. Sachsen-Altenburg zu Beginn des 17. Jahrhunderts', *NASG*, 69 (1998), 64–72.

28. K. Obser, 'Der Feldzug des Jahres 1622 am Oberrhein nach den Denkwürdigkeiten des Freiherrn Ulysses v. Salis-Marschlins', *ZGO*, 7 (1892), 38–68, at 47; G. Gajecky and A. Baran, *The Cossacks in the Thirty Years War*, Vol. I (Rome, 1969), pp.65–77.

29. H. Gabel, 'Sicherheit und Konfession. Aspekte niederländischer Politik gegenüber Jülich-Berg vor und während des Dreißigjährigen Krieges', in S. Ehrenpreis (ed.), *Der Dreißigjährige Krieg im Herzogtum Berg und seinen Nachbarregionen* (Neustadt an der Aisch, 2002), pp.132–79, at pp.154–6; M. Kaiser, 'Überleben im Krieg – Leben mit dem Krieg', in ibid., pp.181–233, at pp.195–7.

30. T. von Moerner (ed.), *Kurbrandenburgische Staatsverträge von 1601–1700* (Berlin, 1867), nos.40, 44. For the following, see also Israel, *Conflicts of Empires*, pp.23–39.

31. M. Kaiser, *Politik und Kriegführung* (Munich, 1999), pp.239–40; H. Lahrkamp, 'Kölnisches Kriegsvolk in der ersten Hälfte des Dreißigjährigen Krieges', *AHVN*, 161 (1959), 114–45.

32. The campaign can be followed in detail in the notes of a senior Bavarian official edited by Staber, 'Eroberung der Oberpfalz'.

33. The notion that Mansfeld deliberately lured Tilly into a trap stems from Protestant propaganda, e.g. Anon., *A true relation of all such battles as have been fought in the Palatinate, since the king's arrival there, until this present the 24 of May* (London, 1622), pp.1–10. See Obser, 'Feldzug', pp.57–8.

34. K. Frhr. von Reitzenstein, 'Der Feldzug des Jahres 1622 am Oberrhein', *ZGO*, 21 (1906), 271–95.

35. Contemporary account in K. Lohmann (ed.), *Die Zerstörung Magdeburgs* (Berlin, 1913), p.241.

36. Obser, 'Feldzug', p.53.

37. Maier, *Unterpfalz*, pp.36–7, 70–96.

38. H.G.R. Reade, *Sidelights on the Thirty Years War* (3 vols., London, 1924), II, pp.59–79.

39. W. Brunink, *Der Graf von Mansfeld in Ostfriesland (1622–1624)* (Aurich, 1957), pp.62–84. This work offers the best coverage of Mansfeld's occupation.

40. Pursell, *Winter King*, pp.201–10.

41. O. Schuster and F.A. Francke, *Geschichte der sächsische Armee* (3 vols., Leipzig, 1883), I, pp.22–4; T. Nicklas, *Macht oder Recht. Frühezeitliche Politik im obersächsischen Reichskreis* (Stuttgart, 2002), pp.216–19.

42. H.E. Flieger, *Die Schlacht bei Stadtlohn am 6. August 1623* (Aachen, 1998); U. Söbbing, *Die Schlacht im Lohner Bruch bei Stadtlohn* (Stadtlohn, 1998); Major Gescher, 'Die Schlacht bei Stadtlohn am 5. und 6. August 1623', *Vestische Zeitschrift*, 1 (1891), 102–11.

43. Kaiser, *Politik und Kriegführung*, pp.205–7.

44. E. Berger, ' "Zwischen Pestilenz und Krieg" – Kriegsalltag und Friedenssehnsucht in der Region des heutigen Kreises Steinfurt', *Westfalen*, 75 (1997), 63–72; J. Barnekamp, ' "Sie hausen uebell, schlagen die Leuth und schatzen über die Maßen". Velen und Ramsdorf 1580–1650', in T. Sodermann (ed.), *1568–1648* (Vreden, 2002), pp.29–63.

45. W. Keim, 'Landgraf Wilhelm V. von Hessen-Kassel vom Regierungsantritt 1627 bis zum Abschluss des Bündnisses mit Gustav Adolf 1631', *Hessisches Jahrbuch für Landesgeschichte*, 12 (1962), 130–210, at 133–85.

46. R. Bireley, *Religion and Politics in the Age of the Counter Reformation* (Chapel Hill, 1981), pp.28–9.

47. W. Eberhard, 'The political system and the intellectual traditions of the Bohemian Ständestaat from the thirteenth to the sixteenth century', in R.J.W. Evans and T.V. Thomas (eds.), *Crown, Church and Estates* (Basingstoke, 1991), pp.23–47, at p.23.

48. D. Uhlir, *Cerny den a Bilé Hore 8. Listopad 1620* (Brno, 1998). See also V.S. Mamatey, 'The battle of White Mountain as myth in Czech history', *East European Quarterly*, 15 (1981), 335–45.

49. G. Wagner, 'Pläne und Versuche der Erhebung Österreichs zum Königreich', in Wagner (ed.), *Österreich von der Staatsidee zum Nationalbewußtsein* (Vienna, 1982), pp.394–432.

50. T. Winkelbauer, *Ständefreiheit und Fürstenmacht* (2 vols., Vienna, 2003), I, pp.74–8, 207–13; H.W. Bergerhausen, 'Die "Verneuerte Landesordnung" in Böhmen 1627', *HZ*, 272 (2001), 327–51.

51. More grisly detail in Gindely, *Thirty Years War*, I, pp.273–8.

52. Polišenský, *Thirty Years War*, p.144. More balanced assessment in T. Knoz, 'Die Konfiskationen nach 1620 in (erb)länder-übergreifender Perspektive', in P. Mat'a and T. Winkelbauer (eds.), *Die Habsburgermonarchie 1620 bis 1740* (Stuttgart, 2006), pp.99–130; R.J.W. Evans, *The Making of the Habsburg Monarchy 1550–1700* (Oxford, 1977), pp.201–9.

53. J. Weber, 'Der große Krieg und die frühe Zeitung', *Jahrbuch für Kommunikationsgeschichte*, 1 (1999), 23–61, at 27.

54. Lorenz (ed.), *Quellen zur Vorgeschichte*, pp.513–19. For this and the following, see E. Straub, *Pax und Imperium* (Paderborn, 1980), pp.174–96; R. Bireley, *The Jesuits and the Thirty Years War* (Cambridge, 2003), pp.56–61; D. Albrecht, *Maximilian I. von Bayern* (Munich, 1998), pp.548–9, and his *Die auswärtige Politik Maximilians von Bayern 1618–1635* (Göttingen, 1962), pp.50–77.

55. Maier, *Unterpfalz*, pp.143–54; K.H. Frohnweiler, 'Die Friedenspolitik Landgraf Georgs II. von Hessen-Darmstadt in den Jahren 1630–1635', *Archiv für hessische Geschichte und Altertumskunde*, new series 29 (1964), 1–185, at 171–2.

56. Müller, *Kursachsen*, pp.435–45, 460–1.

57. Tilly declined two subsequent offers to be made a prince. For the elevations, see T. Klein, 'Die Erhebungen in den weltlichen Reichsfürstentums 1550–1806', *BDLG*, 122 (1986), 137–92, at 148–55; *NTSR*, III, pp.37–44.

58. For the following see T. Johnson, *Magistrates, Madonnas and Miracles. The Counter Reformation in the Upper Palatinate* (Aldershot, 2009); Maier, *Unterpfalz*, pp.130–42, 160–204; M. Forster, *Catholic Germany from the Reformation to the Enlightenment* (Basingstoke, 2007), pp.85–93; R. Pörtner, *The Counter-Reformation in Central Europe* (Oxford, 2001), pp.108–261.

59. A. Rank, *Sulzbach im Zeichen der Gegenreformation (1627–1649). Verlauf und Fazit einer beschwerlichen Jesuitenmission* (Amberg, 2003).

60. R. Schlögl, 'Absolutismus im 17. Jahrhundert – Bayerischer Adel zwischen Disziplinierung und Intergration', *ZHF*, 15 (1988), 151–86.

61. A. Stögmann, 'Staat, Kirche und Bürgerschaft', in A. Weigl (ed.), *Wien im Dreißigjährigen*

Krieg (Vienna, 2001), pp.482–564, at p.536. I have used the estimates for emigrants given in Winkelbauer, *Ständefreiheit und Fürstenmacht*, II, pp.27–8, 51, 182.

62. A. Coreth, *Pietas Austriaca. Österreichische Frömmigkeit im Barock* (Vienna, 1982).

63. Only 50,000 of the 4.3 million Bohemians and Moravians came forward in 1781 to claim the new freedom of Protestant worship.

64. W. Wäntig, 'Kursächsische Exulantenaufnahme im 17. Jahrhundert', *NASG*, 74/75 (2004), 133–74.

Olivares and Richelieu

1. Quoted in J.H. Elliott, *The Count-Duke of Olivares* (New Haven, 1986), p.42.

2. J.H. Elliott, 'Staying in power: the Count-Duke of Olivares', in J.H. Elliott and L.W.B. Brockliss (eds.), *The World of the Favorite* (New Haven, 1999), pp.112–22, at p.118. Further comparison in the same author's *Richelieu and Olivares* (Cambridge, 1984).

3. D. Goodman, *Spanish Naval Power, 1589-1665* (Cambridge, 1997), pp.9–19; R.A. Stradling, *The Armada of Flanders. Spanish maritime policy and European war, 1568–1668* (Cambridge, 1992), pp.16–32, 46–57.

4. G. Redworth, *The Prince and the Infanta* (New Haven, 2003); T. Cogswell, *The Blessed Revolution. English politics and the coming of war 1621–24* (Cambridge, 1989); A. Samson (ed.), *The Spanish Match. Prince Charles' journey to Madrid 1623* (Aldershot, 2006); J. Alcala Zamora, *España, Flandes y el mar de Norte (1618–1639)* (Barcelona, 1975), pp.216–28. See also R. Lockyer, *Buckingham: the life and political career of George Villiers, first duke of Buckingham* (London, 1981).

5. R.B. Manning, *An Apprenticeship in Arms. The origins of the British army 1585–1702* (Oxford, 2006), pp.105–7; B.C. Pursell, *The Winter King* (Aldershot, 2003), pp.222–8.

6. H.G.R. Reade, *Sidelights on the Thirty Years War* (3 vols., London, 1924), II, pp.406–18, 430–42.

7. P. Sigmond and W. Kloek, *Sea Battles and Naval Heroes in the 17th-century Dutch Republic* (Amsterdam, 2007). For the following see also A. James, *Navy and Government in Early Modern France 1572–1661* (Woodbridge, 2004), and the sources in n.3 and ch.5 n.27 above.

8. The ship was raised in 1961 and preserved as a museum: A. Franzen, *The Warship* Vasa (Stockholm, 1960).

9. R. Baetens, 'The organization and effects of Flemish privateering in the seventeenth century', *Acta Historiae Neerlandica*, 9 (1976), 48–75. See also A. Thrush, 'In pursuit of the frigate, 1603–40', *Historical Research*, 64 (1981), 29–45; R.A. Stradling, 'The Spanish Dunkirkers 1621–48', *Tijdschrift voor Geschiedenis*, 93 (1980), 541–58; J.I. Israel, *Dutch Primacy in World Trade 1585–1740* (Oxford, 1989), pp.134–56.

10. S.B. Schwartz, 'The Voyage of the Vassals', *American Historical Review*, 96 (1991), 735–62.

11. J. Glete, *Navies and Nations. Warships, navies and state building in Europe and America 1500–1860* (2 vols., Stockholm, 1993), I, p.130. See R. Harding, *The Evolution of the Sailing Navy, 1509–1815* (Basingstoke, 1995), pp.31–57; K.R. Andrews, *Ships, Money and Politics. Seafaring and naval enterprise in the reign of Charles I* (Cambridge, 1991); N.A.M. Rodger, *The Safeguard of the Sea* (London, 1997), pp.347–410.

12. J. Lynch, *The Hispanic World in Crisis and Change 1598-1700* (Oxford, 1992), pp.133–4. In contrast, see Elliott, *Olivares*, pp.245–77.

13. E. Solano Camón, 'The eastern kingdoms in the military organization of the Spanish monarchy', in E. Martínez and M. de P. Pi Corrales (eds.), *Spain and Sweden* (Madrid, 2000), pp.383–403.

14. M.A.S. Hume, *The Court of Philip IV. Spain in decadence* (London, 1907), pp.156–7, repeated in G. Parker, *The Military Revolution* (Cambridge, 1988), p.45, and J. Burkhardt, *Der Dreißigjährige Krieg* (Frankfurt am Main, 1992), pp.214–15. Half a million were said to be militia, and the rest regulars. Compare with the more realistic estimates in J.

Glete, *War and the State in Early Modern Europe. Spain, the Dutch Republic and Sweden as fiscal-military states, 1500–1660* (London, 2002), pp.33–7.

15. E. Straub, *Pax und Imperium* (Paderborn, 1980), p.289; J.I. Israel, *The Dutch Republic and the Hispanic World, 1606–1661* (Oxford, 1982), pp.217–23, and his *Conflicts of Empires* (London, 1997), pp.45–62.

16. J.I. Israel, 'The politics of international trade rivalry during the Thirty Years War', *IHR* (1986), 517–49, at 517–18.

17. M. Greengrass, *France in the Age of Henri IV* (London, 1984), pp.201–4. For more detail see R. Bonney, *The King's Debts. Finance and politics in France 1589–1661* (Oxford, 1981); Y.M. Bercé, *The Birth of Absolutism. A history of France 1598–1661* (Basingstoke, 1996).

18. A.L. Moote, *Louis XIII the Just* (Berkeley, 1989).

19. G. Dethan, *Gaston d'Orleans. Conspirateur et prince charmant* (Paris, 1959).

20. C. Kampmann, *Arbiter und Friedensstiftung* (Paderborn, 2001), pp.140–68.

21. J.A. Clarke, *Huguenot Warrior: the life and times of Henri de Rohan, 1579–1638* (The Hague, 1966).

22. J.M. Constant, 'Die französischen *Dévots* und der Frieden mit Spanien. Die Opposition gegen Richelieu 1628–1643', in R.G. Asch (ed.), *Frieden und Krieg* (Munich, 2001), pp.193–206.

23. D.P. O'Connell, *Richelieu* (London, 1968) is one of the better biographies. For his early career, see J. Bergin, *The Rise of Richelieu* (New Haven, 1991).

24. Richelieu's memoirs are available in English as *The Political Testament of Cardinal Richelieu* (Madison, Wisc., 1961). For an attempt to calculate his fortune, see J. Bergin, *Cardinal Richelieu. Power and the pursuit of wealth* (New Haven, 1985).

25. Quoted in P. Sonnino, 'From d'Avaux to *dévot*: politics and religion in the Thirty Years War', *History*, 87 (2002), 192–203, at 192. For the contemporary controversy over Richelieu's foreign policy see W.F. Church, *Richelieu and Reason of State* (Princeton, 1972).

26. D. Parker, *La Rochelle and the French Monarchy* (London, 1980); J.F. Bosher, 'The political and religious origins of La Rochelle's primacy in trade with New France, 1627–1685', *French History*, 7 (1993), 286–312.

27. R. Desquesnes et al., *Les fortifications du litteral–La Charente Maritime* (Chauray, 1993).

28. Straub, *Pax und Imperium*, pp.44–88; P. Schmidt, *Spanisches Universalmonarchie oder 'teutsche Libertät'* (Stuttgart, 2001).

29. S. Externbrink, 'Kleinstaaten im Bündnissystem Richelieus: Hessen-Kassel und Mantua 1635–1642', in K. Malettke (ed.), *Frankreich und Hessen-Kassel* (Marburg, 1999), pp.135–57; H. Weber, *Frankreich und das Reich im 16. und 17. Jahrhundert* (Göttingen, 1968), pp.36–52; K. Malettke, 'France's imperial policy during the Thirty Years War and the Peace of Westphalia', in K. Bussmann and H. Schilling (eds.), *1648: War and Peace in Europe* (3 vols., Münster, 1998), I, pp.177–85.

30. W.H. Stein, *Protection royale. Eine Untersuchung zu den Protektionsverhältnissen im Elsass zur Zeit Richelieus 1622–1643* (Münster, 1978), esp. pp.6–10, 52–133.

31. It had been a Rhetian regiment that saved Mansfeld from complete defeat at Mingols- heim. For the following see A. Wendland, *Der Nutzen der Pässe und die Gefährdung der Seelen. Spanien, Mailand und der Kampf ums Veltlin 1620–1641* (Zürich, 1995). The contemporary Spanish perspective can be found in V. Malvezzi, *Historia de los primeros años del reinado de Felipe IV* (London, 1968), pp.17–18, 46–51, 84–5, 161–4. See also Chapter 5.

32. Some Protestants had been planning to massacre the Catholics. See Reade, *Sidelights*, II, pp.12–36.

33. See T. Osborne, *Dynasty and Diplomacy in the Court of Savoy* (Cambridge, 2002), pp.33–4; Reade, *Sidelights*, II, pp.418–20, 446–65.

34. R. Rodenas Vilar, *La politica Europea de España durante la Guerra de Treinta Años*

(1624–1630) (Madrid, 1967), pp.18–37, 67–9; O'Connell, *Richelieu*, pp.77–96. The Austrians allowed the areas seized in 1622 to rejoin the Rhetian free states in 1629 on the condition they remained Catholic.

Denmark's War against the Emperor

1. There was a sixth Westphalian bishopric, Liège, along with eight important imperial abbeys that lay mainly on or beyond the Rhine and consequently outside the area of the coming operations. By contrast, the secular duchy of Westphalia that belonged to the electorate of Cologne and so, despite its name, was part of the electoral Rhenish Kreis, was east of the river and vulnerable.

2. W. Guthrie, *Battles of the Thirty Years War* (Westport, 2002), p.119.

3. J.C. Lünig, *Corpus juris militaris des Heiligen Römischen Reiches* (Leipzig, 1723), pp.663–9. See P.D. Lockhart, *Denmark in the Thirty Years War, 1618–1648* (Selinsgrove, 1996), pp.108–41. Lockhart's work remains the best analysis of Christian's German policy.

4. M. Kaiser, *Politik und Kriegführung* (Munich, 1999), pp.205–35.

5. Quoted in K. Hauer, 'Frankreich und die Frage der reichsständischen Neutralität', in K. Malettke (ed.), *Frankreich und Hessen-Kassel* (Marburg, 1999), pp.91–110, at p.93.

6. R.R. Heinisch, 'Die Neutralitätspolitik Erzbischof Paris Lodrons und ihre Vorläufer', *Mitteilungen der Gesellschaft für Salzburger Landeskunde*, 110/111 (1970), 255–76.

7. For example, see the receipt from the elector of Mainz for the loan of 37,000 tlr to re-equip imperial troops, 19 Aug. 1634, HHStA, MEA Militaria 11, as well as the emperor's warning not to supply the Bernhardine garrison in Hanau, HHStA, KA 91 (neu) 1 Oct. 1636. Further discussion in H.W. Bergerhausen, 'Die Stadt Köln im Dreißigjährigen Krieg', in S. Ehrenpreis (ed.), *Der Dreißigjährigen Krieg im Herzogtum Berg* (Neustadt an der Aisch, 2002), pp.101–312; C. Bartz, *Köln im Dreißigjährigen Krieg* (Frankfurt am Main, 2005), pp.141–273.

8. R. Monro, *Monro, his expedition with the worthy Scots regiment called Mac-Keys* (London, 1637, reprinted Westport, 1999); E.A. Beller, 'The military expedition of Sir Charles Morgan to Germany 1627–9', *EHR*, 43 (1928), 528–39; K. Obser, 'Markgraf Georg Friedrich von Baden und das Projekt einer Diversion am Oberrhein 1623–1627', *ZGO*, 5 (1890), 212–42.

9. N. Mout, 'Der Winter König im Exil', *ZHF*, 15 (1988), 257–72, at 266.

10. Quotes from a contemporary French pamphlet printed in A.E.J. Hollaender, 'Some English documents on the end of Wallenstein', *Bulletin of the John Rylands Library Manchester*, 40 (1957–8), 359–90, at 388–9.

11. Further marriages reinforced this. Wallenstein's favourite cousin, Max, had already married Harrach's elder daughter in 1622. Harrach himself had married Eggenberg's daughter and his son, Ernst Adalbert, soon to be cardinal, was in charge of the re-Catholicization measures in Bohemia (see Chapter 10). Harrach and Liechtenstein were also members of the mint consortium.

12. The latter interpretation is presented by F.H. Schubert, 'Wallenstein und der Staat des 17. Jahrhunderts', *Geschichte in Wissenschaft und Unterricht*, 16 (1965), 597–611. The most recent, and balanced, biography revives the emphasis on peace without the nationalist overtones: J. Polišenský and J. Kollmann, *Wallenstein. Feldherr des Dreißigjährigen Krieges* (Cologne, 1997).

13. Kaiser, *Politik und Kriegführung*, pp.256–8.

14. Appointment and instructions printed in H. Hallwich, 'Wallensteins erste Berufung zum Generalat', *Zeitschrift für allgemeine Geschichte, Kultur, Literatur und Kunstgeschichte*, 1 (1884), 108–34. See also M. Ritter, 'Das Kontributionssystem Wallensteins', *HZ*, 90 (1903), 193–249.

15. E. Straub, *Pax und Imperium* (Paderborn, 1980), pp.247–8.

16. P. Suvanto, *Wallenstein und seine Anhänger am Weiner Hof zur Zeit des zweiten Generalats 1631–1634* (Helsinki, 1963), pp.32–41.

17. F. Konze, *Die Stärke, Zusammensetzung und Verteilung der Wallensteinischen Armee während des Jahres 1633* (Bonn, 1906), pp.10–12, 17, 22–3.

18. G. Irmer, *Hans Georg von Arnim* (Leipzig, 1894); D. Worthington, *Scots in Habsburg Service, 1618–1648* (Leiden, 2004), pp.145–76; R.D. Fitzsimon, 'Irish swordsmen in the imperial service in the 30 Years War', *Irish Sword*, 9 (1969–70), 22–31. More detail available on the Scotland, Scandinavia and Northern Europe database at http://www. st-andrews.ac.uk/history/ssne.

19. T.M. Barker, *The Military Intellectual and Battle. Raimondo Montecuccoli and the Thirty Years War* (Albany, NY, 1975); G. Schreiber, *Raimondo Montecuccoli* (Graz, 2000); H. Büchler, *Von Pappenheim zu Piccolomini* (Sigmaringen, 1994).

20. As suggested by S. Adams, 'Tactics or politics? "The military revolution" and the Hapsburg hegemony, 1525–1648', in J.A. Lynn (ed.), *Tools of War* (Urbana, 1990), pp.28–52. Further discussion in J. Lynn, 'How war fed war: the tax of violence and contributions during the *Grand Siècle*', *JMH*, 65 (1993), 286–310; F. Redlich, 'Contributions in the Thirty Years War', *Economic History Review*, 2nd series, 12 (1959), 247–54; V. Loewe, *Die Organisation und Verwaltung der Wallensteinischen Heeren* (Leipzig, 1894).

21. Ordinances printed in J. Heilmann, *Das Kriegswesen der Kaiserlichen und Schweden zur Zeit des Dreißigjährigen Krieges* (Leipzig, 1850), pp.169–74; E. von Frauenholz (ed.), *Das Heerwesen in der Zeit des Dreißigjährigen Krieges* (2 vols., Munich, 1938), vol. I.

22. K. Krüger, 'Dänische und schwedische Kriegsfinanzierung im Dreißigjährigen Krieg bis 1635', in K. Repgen (ed.), *Krieg und Politik 1618–1648* (Munich, 1988), pp.275–98, at p.280.

23. E.g. the request to the elector of Mainz for transit through the Eichsfeld, 27 Sept.1625, HHStA, MEA Militaria 8.

24. J. Pohl, *'Die Profiantirung der keyserlichen Armaden ahnbelangendt'. Studien zur Versorgung der kaiserlichen Armee 1634/35* (Kiel, 1991), pp.63–9.

25. Gronsfeld estimated the combined Bavarian-imperial army of 40,000 had 140,000 camp followers in 1648: Heilmann, *Kriegswesen*, p.199. For example musters see H.H. Weber, *Der Hessenkrieg* (Gießen, 1935), pp.59–60, 78; J. Krebs, 'Zur Beurteilung Holks und Aldringen', *Historische Vierteljahrsschrift*, 3 (1900), 321–78, at 346; P. Engerisser, *Von Kronach nach Nördlingen. Der Dreißigjährige Krieg in Franken, Schwaben und der Oberpfalz 1631–1635* (Weißenstadt, 2004), pp.513–14.

26. Quoted in G. Droysen, *Bernhard von Weimar* (2 vols., Leipzig, 1885), II, p.45. For a frank admission of taking a female captive, see J. Peters (ed.), *Ein Söldnerleben im Dreißigjährigen Krieg* (Berlin, 1993), p.59. Further discussion, P.H. Wilson, 'German women and war 1500–1800', *War in History*, 3 (1996), 127–60.

27. S. Riezler (ed.), 'Kriegstagebücher aus dem ligistischen Hauptquartier 1620', *Abhandlungen des Phil.-Hist. Klasse der Bayerischen Akademie der Wissenschaften*, 23 (1906), 77–210, at 171.

28. HHStA, MEA Militaria 8, 19 Dec. 1625.

29. H.G. Ufflacker, 'Das Land Anhalt und die kaiserliche Kriegsführung 1625–1631', *Sachsen und Anhalt*, 9 (1933), 95–108; G. Knüppel, *Das Heerwesen des Fürstentums Schleswig-Holstein-Gottorf, 1600–1715* (Neumünster, 1972), pp.100–6; T. Rudel, 'Die Lage Pommerns vom Beginn des Dreißigjährigen Krieges bis zum Eintreffen Gustav Adolf (1620–1630)', *Baltische Studien*, 40 (1890), 68–133; H. Branig, 'Die Besetzung Pommerns durch Wallenstein während des Dreißigjährigen Krieges', *Baltische Studien*, 64 (1978), 31–40; H. Conrad and G. Teske (eds.), *Sterbezeiten. Der Dreißigjährige Krieg im Herzogtum Westfalen* (Münster, 2000), pp.37–42, 280–6.

30. M. Spahn, 'Auswärtige Politik und innere Lage des Herzogtums Pommern von 1627–30', *HJb*, 19 (1898), 57–88, at 63, 65–6. Figures for the western half were unavailable due to the fighting around Stralsund after 1628.

31. Examples in A. Ritter, 'Der Einfluß des Dreißigjährigen Krieges auf die Stadt Naumburg a.d. Saale', *Thüringisch-Sächsische Zeitschrift für Geschichte und Kunst*, 15 (1926), 1–96,

at 65–72; L. Radler, *Das Schweidnitzer Land im Dreißigjährigen Krieg* (Lübeck, 1986), pp.25–47.

32. F. Redlich, *The German Military Enterprizer and His Workforce* (2 vols., Wiesbaden, 1964–5).

33. See the excellent case study of a Bavarian general by S. Haberer, *Ott Heinrich Fugger (1592–1644). Biographische Analyse typologischer Handlungsfelder in der Epoche des Dreißigjährigen Krieges* (Augsburg, 2004).

34. J. Kunisch, 'Wallenstein als Kriegsunternehmer. Auf dem Weg zum absolutistischen Steuerstaat', in U. Schultz (ed.), *Mit dem Zehnten fing es an. Eine Kulturgeschichte der Steuer* (Munich, 1986), pp.153–61; G. Papke, *Von der Miliz zum stehenden Heer* (Munich, 1983), pp.140–50; M. Hüther, 'Der Dreißigjährige Krieg als fiskalisches Problem', *Scripta Mercaturae*, 21 (1987), 52–81.

35. F. Kleinehagenbrock, *Die Grafschaft Hohenlohe im Dreißigjährigen Krieg* (Stuttgart, 2003), pp.107–216, esp. p.184.

36. T. Robisheaux, *Rural Society and the Search for Order in Early Modern Germany* (Cambridge, 1989), pp.108–20. Examples of denunciations in Conrad and Teske (eds.), *Sterbezeiten*, pp.291–2.

37. Treasury report printed in G. Lorenz (ed.), *Quellen zur Geschichte Wallensteins* (Darmstadt, 1987), pp.111–14.

38. K. Oberleitner, 'Beiträge zur Geschichte des Dreißigjährigen Krieges', *Archiv für österreichische Geschichte*, 19 (1858), 1–48, at 18–19.

39. A. Ernstberger, *Hans de Witte, Finanzmann Wallensteins* (Wiesbaden, 1954), pp.160–267.

40. Further example in J. Krebs, *Aus dem Leben des kaiserlichen Feldmarschalls Grafen Melchior von Hatzfeldt 1632–1636* (Breslau, 1926), pp.95–6.

41. Quoted by T. Nicklas, *Macht oder Recht* (Stuttgart, 2002), p.226.

42. HHStA, MEA Militaria 8, 20 Dec. 1625. For the following see C. Kampmann, *Reichsrebellion und kaiserliche Acht* (Münster, 1992), pp.79–98.

43. G. Mann, *Wallenstein* (Frankfurt am Main, 1983), pp.237–86.

44. The Wartenberg line stemmed from the marriage of Duke Ferdinand of Bavaria (1550–1608) to the commoner Maria Pettenbeck (1574–1614).

45. M. van Creveld, *Supplying War* (Cambridge, 1977), pp.5–18.

46. The battle is poorly documented, but the details are summarized in H. Diwald, *Wallenstein* (Munich, 1969), pp.343–5. Mansfeld lost about 5,000 men including the prisoners. For operations generally see J.O. Opel, *Der niedersächisch-dänische Krieg* (3 vols., Halle and Magdeburg, 1872–94), vols. I and II.

47. G. Heiligsetzer, *Der oberösterreichische Bauernkrieg 1626* (Vienna, 1985); T. Winkelbauer, *Ständefreiheit und Fürstenmacht* (2 vols., Vienna, 2003), I, pp.68–71; H. Rebel, *Peasant Classes. The bureaucratization of property and family relations under early Habsburg absolutism, 1511–1636* (Princeton, 1983), pp.230–70; D. Albrecht, *Maximilian I. von Bayern* (Munich, 1998), pp.582–90.

48. Reproduced in J.R. Paas (ed.), *The German Political Broadsheet 1600–1700* (7 vols., Wiesbaden, 1985–98), IV, pp.250–2.

49. Quotes from U. Kober, 'Der Favorit als "Factotum". Graf Adam von Schwarzenberg', in M. Kaiser and A. Pečar (eds.), *Der zweite Mann im Staat* (Berlin, 2003), pp.231–52, at pp.236, 245.

50. Useful material available on http://muenden.kossert.net.

51. The exact battle site remains disputed, but the position south-west of Lutter seems the most likely. For the battle see D. Schäfer, 'Die Schlacht bei Lutter am Barenberge', *Neue Heidelberger Jahrbücher*, 10 (1900), 1–37; K.J.V. Jespersen, 'Slaget ved Lutter am Barenberg 1626', *Krigshistorisk Tidsskrift*, 9 (1973), 80–9; Guthrie, *Battles*, pp.128–45.

52. H. Weigel, 'Franken im Dreißigjährigen Krieg', *ZBLG*, 5 (1932), 1–50, at 18.

53. More detail on the campaign in J.V. Polišenský, *The Thirty Years War* (London, 1971), pp.114–21; Polišenský and Kollmann, *Wallenstein*, pp.117–27.

54. G. Murdock, *Calvinism on the Frontier 1600–1660* (Oxford, 2000), pp.36–44.

55. Lockhart, *Denmark*, p.154. His charge that Mitzlaff was 'greedy and incompetent' seems unfair. He proved an effective organizer, even if his subsequent career entailed betrayal.

56. B.C. Pursell, *The Winter King* (Aldershot, 2003), pp.257–9; A. Gindely, *The Thirty Years War* (2 vols., New York, 1892), I, p.425.

57. Monro, *Expedition*, pp.21–2, repeated in S. Murdoch, 'Scotsmen on the Danish-Norwegian frontier *c.*1580–1680', in A. Mackillop and S. Murdoch (eds.), *Military Governors and Imperial Frontiers c.1600–1800* (Leiden, 2003), pp.1–28, at p.14.

58. Polišenský and Kollmann, *Wallenstein*, p.137. For the sieges see F.C. Rode, *Kriegsgeschichte Schleswig-Holsteins* (Neumünster, 1935), pp.18–19; H. Eichberg, *Festung, Zentralmacht und Sozialgeometrie. Kriegsingenieurwesen des 17. Jahrhunderts in den Herzogtümern Bremen und Verden* (Cologne, 1989), pp.498–500.

59. Graphic account of the rout at Heiligenhafen in Monro, *Expedition*, pp.28–39. For an account of one of those enlisting in the imperial army, see J. Ackermann, *Jürgen Ackermann, Kapitän beim Regiment Alt-Pappenheim 1631* (Halberstadt, 1895), pp.12–13.

60. H. Schmidt, 'Die Stadt Hannover im Dreißigjährigen Kriege 1626–1648', *Niedersächsisches Jahrbuch*, 3 (1926), 94–135, at 96–108; F. Watson, *Wallenstein. Soldier under Saturn* (London, 1938), p.245. Schlick received the Magdeburg dependency of Querfurt, while Blankenburg and Regenstein under Halberstadt jurisdiction were given to Merode.

61. Kampmann, *Reichsrebellion*, pp.90–8. Schwerin was confiscated from its Danish administrator, Prince Ulrich.

62. See Kaiser, *Politik und Kriegführung*, pp.26–30. Tilly refused the offer, though he did accept the fine levied on Wolfenbüttel in lieu of his arrears. Pappenheim, by contrast, was rapacious and lodged a claim for 1 million fl. worth of land around Magdeburg.

63. The electors' protest is printed in Lorenz (ed.), *Quellen zur Geschichte Wallensteins*, pp.121–3. The response to Nuremberg from the elector of Mainz, 20 April 1627, is in HHStA, MEA Militaria 8.

64. K. Breuer, *Der Kurfürstentag zu Mühlhausen* (Bonn, 1904); R. Bireley, *Religion and Politics in the Age of the Counterreformation* (Chapel Hill, 1981), pp.46–56. Minutes printed in Lorenz (ed.), *Quellen zur Geschichte Wallensteins*, pp.141–4.

65. M. Kaiser, 'Bayerns Griff nach Brandenburg', *FBPG*, new series 5 (1995), 1–29.

66. Albrecht, *Maximilian*, pp.679–83; Kaiser, *Politik und Kriegführung*, pp.256–77; Gindely, *Thirty Years War*, I, pp.426–36.

67. E. Wilmanns, *Der Lübecker Friede* (Bonn, 1904); G. Lind, 'Interpreting a lost war: Danish experiences 1625 to 1629', in F. Brendle and A. Schilling (eds.), *Religionskriege im alten Reich* (Münster, 2006), pp.487–510. Paul Lockhart terms the peace 'the greatest diplomatic coup in Danish history', *Denmark*, p.205.

The Threat of European War

1. M. Roberts, *Gustavus Adolphus* (2 vols., London, 1953–8), I, pp.201–20, 245–6.

2. K.R. Böhme, *Die schwedische Besetzung des Weichseldeltas 1626–1636* (Würzburg, 1963).

3. K. Cramer, *The Thirty Years War and German Memory in the Nineteenth Century* (Lincoln, Nebr., 2007), pp.46–50. For the project, see O. Schmitz, *Die maritime Politik der Habsburger in de Jahren 1626–1628* (Bonn, 1903); A.E. Sokol, *Das habsburgische Admiralitätswerk des 16. und 17. Jahrhundert* (Vienna, 1976).

4. A. Makowski, 'Polish naval force in the Baltic in the first half of the 17th century', *Armi del Sovrano* 2001, http://www.assostoria.it/prod01.htm (accessed 28 Sept. 2005). Correspondence between Sigismund and Wallenstein in *Doc. Bo.* IV, nos.222, 226–7. For Austro-Spanish negotiations, see E. Straub, *Pax und Imperium* (Paderborn, 1980), pp.218–51, 288–314; J. Alcala Zamora, *España, Flandes y el mar de Norte (1618–1639)* (Barcelona, 1975), pp.236–42, 267–82; R. Rodenas Vilar, *La politica Europea de España durante la Guerra de Treinta Años (1624–1630)* (Madrid, 1967), pp.113–47.

5. H. Mack, 'Die Hanse und die Belagerung Stralsunds im Jahre 1628', *Hansische Geschichtsblätter*, 20 (1892), 123–58. For factionalism in the city see E. Neubauer, 'Johann Schneidewind, magdeburgischer Stadtkommandant und schwedischer Oberst', *Geschichtsblätter für Stadt und Land Magdeburg*, 27 (1892), 257–323. Magdeburg told the Hanseatic League it paid 133,000 tlr of contributions to Wallenstein in 1627 to buy off the demand to admit a garrison, but in fact spent the money on strengthening its defences.

6. This represented a significant popular mobilization, given that the town's population was less than 15,000. For the siege see G. Mann, *Wallenstein* (Frankfurt am Main, 1983), pp.457–77; F. Watson, *Wallenstein* (London, 1938), pp.258–69.

7. R. Monro, *Monro, his expedition with the worthy Scots regiment called Mac-Keys* (London, 1637, reprinted Westport, 1999), p.789. For Sweden's take-over, see H. Langer, *Stralsund 1600–1630* (Weimar, 1970), pp.242–6.

8. Treaty of 11 July 1628 printed in G. Lorenz (ed.), *Quellen zur Geschichte Wallensteins* (Darmstadt, 1987), pp.188–91. The same volume contains details of the other negotiations and Wallenstein's correspondence over the Baltic Design.

9. The units are listed in *Doc. Bo.* IV, no.295. Wallenstein claimed he had sent 15,000: ibid., IV, pp.325–6.

10. E.L. Petersen, 'Defence, war and finance. Christian IV and the Council of Realm 1596–1629', *Scandinavian Journal of History*, 7 (1982), 277–313, at 311. For the following, see J.K. Fedorowicz, *England's Baltic Trade in the Early Seventeenth Century* (Cambridge, 1980), pp.193–201.

11. R.I. Frost, 'Poland-Lithuania in the Thirty Years War', in K. Bussmann and H. Schilling (eds.), *1648: War and Peace in Europe* (3 vols., Münster, 1998), I, pp.197–205, at pp.200–1.

12. The 14 surviving ships are listed in R.C. Anderson, *Naval Wars in the Baltic 1522–1850* (London, 1969), p.44. The *King David* had already been driven into Lübeck in 1630 and interned.

13. R.A. Stradling, *The Armada of Flanders* (Cambridge, 1992), pp.60–5, 76–7.

14. J.C. Boyajian, *Portuguese Bankers at the Court of Spain, 1626–1650* (New Brunswick, 1983).

15. H.H. Rowan, *The Princes of Orange* (Cambridge, 1988), pp.56–76.

16. J.H. Elliott, *The Count-Duke of Olivares* (New Haven, 1986), pp.346–58; Straub, *Pax und Imperium*, pp.316–411.

17. Rodenas Vilar, *La politica Europea*, pp.73–83; M. Kaiser, *Politik und Kriegführung* (Münster, 1999), pp.210–35; H. Terhalle, 'Der Achtzigjährige Krieg zwischen dem König von Spanien und den Niederlanden in sienen Auswirkungen auf des Westmünsterland', in T. Sodmann (ed.), *1568–1648* (Vreden, 2002), pp.171–229, at pp.194–204. See also Chapter 12.

18. This is the total given by Wallenstein in his letter to Ferdinand, 10 October 1629, *Doc. Bo.* IV, nos.325–6. The force included units already stationed in Westphalia.

19. J.I. Israel, 'The Dutch-Spanish War and the Holy Roman Empire (1568–1648)', in Bussmann and Schilling (eds.), *1648: War and Peace*, I, pp.111–21, at p.119.

20. J.I. Israel, *The Dutch Republic and the Hispanic World, 1606–1661* (Oxford, 1982), pp.223–49, and his *The Dutch Republic* (Oxford, 1995), pp.508–19; A. Waddington, *La République des Provinces-Unies, la France et les Pays-Bas Espagnoles de 1630 a 1650* (2 vols., Paris, 1895), I, pp.137–45.

21. For the Mantuan succession see T. Osborne, *Dynasty and Diplomacy in the Court of Savoy* (Cambridge, 2002), pp.29–33, 144–9; D. Parrott, 'The Mantuan succession, 1627–31', *EHR*, 117 (1997), 20–65, and his 'A *prince souverain* and the French crown: Charles de Nevers 1580–1637', in R. Oresko et al. (eds.), *Royal and Republican Sovereignty* (Cambridge, 1997), pp.149–87.

22. H. Ernst, *Madrid und Wien 1632–1637. Politik und Finanzen in den Beziehungen zwischen Philipp IV. und Ferdinand II* (Münster, 1991), pp.36–8; Straub, *Pax und*

Imperium, pp.327–61; B. Schneider, *Der Mantuanische Erbfolgestreit* (Bonn, 1905), pp.8–39. For the course of the war see H.G.R. Reade, *Sidelights on the Thirty Years War* (3 vols., London, 1924), III, pp.169–350; T.F. Arnold, 'Fortifications and the military revolution: the Gonzaga experience, 1530–1630', in C.J. Rogers (ed.), *The Military Revolution Debate* (Boulder, 1995), pp.201–26.

23. Elliott, *Olivares*, pp.337–44; R.A. Stradling, *Spain's Struggle for Europe 1598–1668* (London, 1994), pp.53–7, 72; Rodenas Vilar, *La politica Europea*, pp.149–235.

24. S.J. Stearns, 'A problem of logistics in the early 17th century: the siege of Ré', *Military Affairs*, 42 (1978), 121–6; Reade, *Sidelights*, III, pp.42–151; M.C. Fissel, *English Warfare 1511–1642* (London, 2001), pp.261–9; R.B. Manning, *An Apprenticeship in Arms. The origins of the British army 1585–1702* (Oxford, 2006), pp.115–23.

25. For the royalist siege effort, see D. Parrott, *Richelieu's Army. War, government and society in France, 1624–1642* (Cambridge, 2001), pp.54, 88–91, 194; D.P. O'Connell, *Richelieu* (London, 1968), pp.160–82.

26. A.L. Moote, *Louis XIII* (Berkeley, 1989), p.202.

27. Straub, *Pax und Imperium*, pp.362–9.

28. S. Externbrink, 'Die Rezeption des "Sacco di Montova" im 17. Jahrhundert', in M. Meumann and D. Niefanger (eds.), *Ein Schauplatz herber Angst* (Göttingen, 1997), pp.205–22.

29. J. Kist, *Fürst- und Erzbistum Bamberg* (Bamberg, 1962), pp.100–2. For other examples, see H. Conrad and G. Teske (eds.), *Sterbezeiten. Der Dreißigjährige Krieg im Herzogtum Westfalen* (Münster, 2000), pp.377–81; M. Ritter, 'Der Ursprung des Restitutionsediktes', *HZ*, 76 (1896), 62–102.

30. R. Bireley, *Maximilian I. von Bayern, Adam Contzen SJ und die Gegenreformation in Deutschland 1624–1635* (Göttingen, 1975); A. Posch, 'Zur Tätigkeit und Beurteilung Lamormains', *MIÖG*, 63 (1955), 375–90.

31. K. Repgen, *Dreißigjähriger Krieg und Westfälischer Friede* (Paderborn, 1998), pp.344–52.

32. M. Frisch, *Das Restitutionsedikt Kaiser Ferdinands II. von 6. März 1629* (Tübingen, 1993), pp.77–93; H. Urban, *Das Restitutionsedikt* (Munich, 1968), pp.177–99; D. Albrecht, *Maximilian I. von Bayern* (Munich, 1998), pp.699–708; R. Bireley, *Religion and Politics in the Age of the Counterreformation* (Chapel Hill, 1981), pp.44–60.

33. A. Gotthard, ' "Politice seint wir bäptisch". Kursachsen und der deutsche Protestantismus im frühen 17. Jahrhundert', *ZHF*, 20 (1993), 275–319, at 310–12.

34. R. Bireley, 'The origins of the "Pacis compositio" (1629)', *Archivum historicum societatis Jesu*, 152 (1973), 106–27.

35. S. Zizelmann, *Um Land und Konfession. Die Außen- und Reichspolitik Württembergs (1628–1638)* (Frankfurt am Main, 2002), pp.30–42.

36. Friedrich Friese's account in K. Lohmann (ed.), *Die Zerstörung Magdeburgs* (Berlin, 1913), p.189; F. Gallati, 'Eidgenössische Politik zur Zeit des Dreißigjährigen Krieges', *Jahrbuch für schweizerische Geschichte*, 43 (1918), 1–149, at 16–54.

37. Quotes from R. Bireley, *The Jesuits and the Thirty Years War* (Cambridge, 2003), pp.91–3 and his *Religion and Politics*, pp.83–4.

38. Quoted in Bireley, *Jesuits*, p.125.

39. Mann, *Wallenstein*, pp.631–2, 635–9; H. Diwald, *Wallenstein* (Munich, 1969), pp.421–3.

40. As reported by the Bremen mediator quoted in H. Holstein, 'Zur Geschichte der Belagerung Magdeburgs durch Wallenstein im Jahre 1629', *Zeitschrift für Preußische Geschichte*, 13 (1876), 593–620, at 609. For the role of the pastors see J. Finucane, ' "To remain unaltered in the courage you have inherited from your ancestors": Magdeburg under siege 1547–1631' (Trinity College Dublin, PhD, 2008); H. Schultze, 'Domprediger Bake und die Magdeburger Pfafferschaft im Dreißigjährigen Krieg', *Konfession, Krieg und Katastrophe* (issued by the Verein f. Kirchengesch. Der Kirchenprovinz Sachsen, Magdeburg, 2006), pp.25–42.

41. Agreement of 13 October 1629 in Lorenz (ed.), *Quellen zur Geschichte Wallensteins*, pp.209–10.
42. W. Seibrich, *Gegenreformation als Restauration. Die restaurativen Bemühungen der alten Orden im deutschen Reich um 1580 bis 1648* (Münster, 1991), pp.340–77.
43. Good example in G. Menk, 'Restitution vor dem Restitutionsedikt', *Jahrbuch für Westdeutsche Landesgeschichte*, 5 (1979), 103–30. For the following see also Zizelmann, *Um Land und Konfession*, pp.112–13, 131–6; C. Kohlmann, 'Kriegs- und Krisenerfahrungen von Lutherischen Pfarrern und Gläubigen im amt Hornberg des Herzogtums Württemberg während des Dreißigjährigen Krieges und nach dem Westfälischen Frieden', in M. Asche and A. Schindling (eds.), *Das Strafgericht Gottes* (Münster, 2002), pp.123–211, at pp.160–7.
44. B. Nischan, 'Reformed irenicism and the Leipzig colloquy of 1631', *CEH*, 9 (1976), 3–26.
45. D. Albrecht, *Die auswärtige Politik Maximilians von Bayern 1618–1635* (Göttingen, 1962), pp.379–81; Albrecht, *Maximilian*, pp.761–7; Bireley, *Religion and Politics*, pp.123–7.
46. Stralsund to Mainz, 30 June 1629, HHStA, MEZ Militaria 8.
47. C.V. Wedgwood, *The Thirty Years War* (London, 1957 edn), pp.231–6, at p.236. Similar perspective in G. Parker (ed.), *The Thirty Years War* (London, 1987), pp.111–13. See also O. Heyne, *Der Kurfürstentag zu Regensburg* (Berlin, 1866); Albrecht, *Maximilian*, pp.733–59.
48. See Albrecht, *Maximilian*, pp.676–7, 685; P. Suvanto, *Wallenstein und seine Anhänger am Wiener Hof zur Zeit des zweiten Generalats 1631–1634* (Helsinki, 1963), pp.57–63. For the following, see also C. Kampmann, 'Zweiter Mann im Staat oder Staat im Staat? Zur Stellung Wallensteins in der Administration Kaiser Ferdinands II.', in M. Kaiser and A. Pecar (eds.), *Der zweite Mann im Staat* (Berlin, 2003), pp.295–315.
49. See Kaiser, *Politik und Kriegführung*, pp.279–302. Parker (ed.), *Thirty Years War*, p.112 is incorrect in claiming the armies were merged.
50. B. Stadler, *Pappenheim und die Zeit des Dreißigjährigen Krieges* (Winterthur, 1991); M. Kaiser, 'Pappenheim als empirischer Theoretiker des Krieges', in H. Neuhaus and B. Stollberg-Rillinger (eds.), *Menschen und Strukturen in der Geschichte Alteuropas* (Berlin, 2002), pp.201–27.
51. Parker (ed.), *Thirty Years War*, p.124. See also Albrecht, *Maximilian*, pp.746–50 and the useful accounts by D.P. O'Connell, 'A cause célèbre in the history of treaty making. The refusal to ratify the peace treaty of Regensburg in 1630', *British Yearbook of International Law*, 42 (1967), 71–90; Osborne, *Dynasty and Diplomacy*, pp.167–71.
52. Ernst, *Madrid und Wien*, p.41; Bireley, *Religion and Politics*, pp.163–6.

The Lion of the North

1. There were another 13,000 garrison troops in the Pomeranian towns. J. Glete, *War and the State in Early Modern Europe. Spain, the Dutch Republic and Sweden as fiscal-military states, 1500–1660* (London, 2002), pp.34–5, 179–80; T. Lorentzen, *Die schwedische Armee im Dreißigjährigen Kriege und ihre Abdankung* (Leipzig, 1894), pp.8–12; L. Erickson, 'The Swedish army and navy during the Thirty Years War', in K. Bussmann and H. Schilling (eds.), *1648: War and Peace in Europe* (3 vols., Münster, 1998), I, pp.301–7. The latter summarizes the Swedish literature and is a good source for the size of the army throughout the war.
2. H. Ruffer and K. Zickermann, 'German reactions to the Scots in the Holy Roman Empire during the Thirty Years War', in S. Murdoch (ed.), *Scotland and the Thirty Years War* (Leiden, 2001), pp.271–93; D.H. Pleiss, 'Finnen und Lappen in Stift und Stadt Osnabrück 1633–1643', *Osnabrücker Mitteilungen*, 93 (1990), 41–94, at 46–9, and his 'Finnische Musketiere in fränkischen Garnisonen 1631–1634', *Mainfränkishes Jahrbuch*, 44 (1992), 1–52, at 6–7.

3. William Guthrie is right to strike a note of caution in his assessment of Swedish tactics: *Battles of the Thirty Years War* (Westport, 2002), p.14.

4. J. Heilmann, *Das Kriegswesen der Kaiserlichen und Schweden zur Zeit des Dreißig-jährigen Krieges* (Leipzig, 1850), pp.64–7, 286–8.

5. M. Roberts, *Essays in Swedish History* (London, 1967), pp.72–4. For cartography see B. Gäfvert, 'Maps and war: the Swedish experience during the Thirty Years War', in Bussmann and Schilling (eds.), *1648: War and Peace*, I, pp.309–17.

6. M. Roberts, *Gustavus Adolphus* (2 vols., London, 1953–8), II, p.409. See also E. Ringmar, *Identity, Interest and Action. A cultural explanation of Sweden's intervention in the Thirty Years War* (Cambridge, 1996), pp.113–18; J.P. Findeisen, *Axel Oxenstierna* (Gernsbach, 2007), pp.141–50; S.S. Goetze, *Die Politik des schwedischen Reichskanzlers Axel Oxenstierna gegenüber Kaiser und Reich* (Kiel, 1971), pp.53–9.

7. Findeisen, *Oxenstierna*, p.198. The English version of the manifesto is printed in G. Symcox (ed.), *War, Diplomacy, and Imperialism, 1618–1763* (New York, 1974), pp.102–13.

8. For these attempts see A. Rieck, *Frankfurt am Main unter schwedischer Besatzung 1631–1635* (Frankfurt am Main, 2005), pp.265–73.

9. Quote from J. Ernst, 'Ein gleichzeitiger Bericht über das württembergische Kriegsvolk vor der österreichischen Stadt Villingen vom Jahre 1631 bis 1633', *WVJHLG*, 1 (1878), 129–37, at 130. See also P. Piirimäe, 'Just war in theory and practice. The legitimation of Swedish intervention in the Thirty Years War', *Historical Journal*, 45 (2002), 499–523.

10. Swedish efforts to secure invitations included subsidizing anti-imperial newspapers and bribing pastors to make inflammatory sermons: D. Böttcher, 'Propaganda und öffentliche Meinung im protestantischen Deutschland 1628–36', in H.U. Rudolf (ed.), *Der Dreißigjährigen Krieg* (Darmstadt, 1977), pp.325–67, at pp.327–31; Roberts, *Gustavus Adolphus*, II, pp.432–4.

11. Goetze, *Politik*, pp.240–57; M. Stolleis, *Geschichte des öffentlichen Rechts in Deutschland*, Vol. I (Munich, 1988), pp.203–7.

12. M. Meumann, 'Die schwedische Herrschaft in den Stiftern Magdeburg und Halberstadt', in M. Kaiser and J. Rogge (eds.), *Die besetzte res publica* (Berlin, 2005), pp.241–69, at pp.264–7.

13. Quoted in Ringmar, *Identity*, p.130.

14. C. Hallendorff (ed.), *Sverges traktater med främmande Magter*, Vol. V, part 1 (Stockholm, 1902), pp.438–42. For the negotiations, see D.P. O'Connell, *Richelieu* (London, 1968), pp.250–7; C.T. Burckhardt, *Richelieu and his Age* (3 vols., London, 1970–1), II, pp.364–8; D. Albrecht, *Maximilian I. von Bayern* (Munich, 1998), pp.647–61, 719–30.

15. Quoted in H. Jessen (ed.), *Der Dreißigjährige Krieg in Augenzeugenberichten* (Düsseldorf, 1963), p.242. For similar threats, see C. Deinert, *Die schwedische Epoche in Franken 1631–5* (Würzburg, 1966), pp.83–90.

16. Quoted in B. Nischan, 'Brandenburg's Reformed Räte and the Leipzig Manifesto of 1631', *Journal of Religious History*, 10 (1979), 365–80, at 375. For a list of the territories attending the convention see W. Watts, *The Swedish Intelligencer* (3 vols., London, 1633–4), I, p.19a.

17. T. Kaufmann, 'The Lutheran sermon during the war and at the time of the peace agreement', in Bussmann and Schilling (eds.), *1648: War and Peace*, I, pp.245–50, at p.248.

18. Guthrie, *Battles*, p.2. For the following see M. Kaiser, *Politik und Kriegführung* (Münster, 1999), pp.362–72.

19. W. Keim, 'Landgraf Wilhelm V. von Hessen-Kassel vom Regierungsantritt 1627 bis zum Abschluss des Bündnisses mit Gustav Adolf 1631', *Hessisches Jahrbuch für Landesgeschichte*, 13 (1963), 141–222, at 146–204; T. Schott, 'Württemberg und Gustav Adolf, 1631 und 1632', *WVJHLG*, new series 4 (1895), 343–402, at 349–51.

20. K. Lohmann (ed.), *Die Zerstörung Magdeburgs* (Berlin, 1913), pp.48–63.

21. Kaiser, *Politik und Kriegführung*, pp.313–15, 328–33. This work provides the best

treatment of the military and diplomatic events of 1631. For Swedish operations, see also *Sveriges Krig 1611–1632* (compiled by the Swedish General Staff, Stockholm, 1936–9), vols. V and VI.

22. R. Monro, *Monro, his expedition with the worthy Scots regiment called Mac-Keys* (Westport, 1999), pp.148–51. The Swedes killed most of the 300 sick Imperialists left in the town when Tilly retreated.

23. Monro, *Expedition*, pp.159–69; Watts, *Swedish Intelligencer*, I, pp.51a–54a.

24. In addition to the accounts (including Guericke's) printed in Lohmann (ed.), *Zerstörung*, see also those in E. Neubauer (ed.), *Magdeburgs Zerstörung 1631* (Magdeburg, 1931); J. Ackermann, *Jürgen Ackermann, Kapitän beim Regiment Alt-Pappenheim 1631* (Halberstadt, 1895).

25. H. Lahrkamp, 'Die Kriegserinnerung des Grafen Gronsfeld (1598–1662)', *Zeitschrift des Aachener Geschichtsvereins*, 71 (1959), 77–104, at 93. Zacharias Bandhauer who, as superintendent of the Catholic monastery was inside the city, says Pappenheim had ordered the house set on fire to create a smokescreen for his men crossing the wall, while Captain Ackermann of Pappenheim's regiment says two houses were set on fire to encourage burghers still resisting to leave the walls to fight the flames.

26. Bandhauer in Lohmann (ed.), *Zerstörung*, pp.170–1.

27. Friedrich Friese's account in ibid., pp.197–213. For the violence and its reception see M. Schilling, 'Der Zerstörung Magdeburgs in der zeitgenössichen Literatur und Publizistik', in his *Konfession, Krieg und Katastrophe* (Magdeburg, 2006), pp.93–111; H. Medik, 'Historical event and contemporary experience: the capture and destruction of Magdeburg', *History Workshop Journal*, 52 (2001), 23–48; M. Kaiser, ' "Excidium Magdeburgense". Beobachtungen zur Wahrnehmung von Gewalt im Dreißigjährigen Krieg', in M. Meumann and D. Niefanger (eds.), *Ein Schauplatz herbe Angst* (Göttingen, 1997), pp.43–64, and his 'Die "Magdeburgische Hochzeit" 1631', in E. Labouvie (ed.), *Leben in der Stadt. Eine Kultur- und Geschlechtergeschichte Magdeburgs* (Cologne, 2004), pp.196–213. See also the contributions to H. Pühle (ed.), *Ganz verheeret! Magdeburg und der Dreißigjährige Krieg* (Magdeburg, 1998).

28. J. Kreztschmar, 'Die Allianz-Verhandlungen Gustav Adolfs mit Kurbrandenburg in Mai und Juni 1631', *FBPG*, 17 (1904), 341–82; V. Buckley, *Christina Queen of Sweden* (London, 2004), pp.51–3. Georg Wilhelm retained Küstrin and 3,000 men under Colonel Burgsdorf.

29. Kaiser, *Politik und Kriegführung*, pp.388–96; S. Zizelmann, *Um Land und Konfession* (Frankfurt am Main, 2002), pp.126–31; Albrecht, *Maximilian*, pp.768–90.

30. M. Frisch, *Das Restitutionsedikt* (Tübingen, 1993), pp.166–8.

31. Monro, *Expedition*, p.189.

32. Guthrie, *Battles*, p.23 repeats the old story that Tilly was reluctant, but was forced into battle by Pappenheim who was convinced the Saxons were rabble and the Swedes weak. However, Tilly's eagerness is clear from his correspondence with Maximilian. See Kaiser, *Politik und Kriegführung*, pp.447–54. For useful contemporary accounts of the battle, see Monro, *Expedition*, pp.190–8; T.M. Barker, *The Military Intellectual and Battle* (Albany, NY, 1975), pp.174–81; W. Watts, *The Swedish Discipline* (London, 1632), unpaginated.

33. Ackermann, *Ackermann*, p.18.

34. G. Parker, *The Military Revolution* (Cambridge, 1988), p.23.

35. E.A. Beller, 'The mission of Sir Thomas Roe to the conference at Hamburg 1638-40', *EHR*, 41 (1926), 61–77, at 61; J.R. Paas, 'The changing image of Gustavus Adolphus on German broadsheets, 1630–3', *Journal of the Warburg and Courtauld Institutes*, 59 (1996), 205–44; Böttcher, 'Propaganda', pp.345–56. For the following, see Ringmar, *Identity*, pp.156–64.

36. See P. Engerisser, *Von Kronach nach Nördlingen* (Weißenstadt, 2004), pp.22–5. Contemporary accounts from the Swedish side confirm the massacre: Monro, *Expedition*, pp.207–9; Watts, *Swedish Intelligencer*, II, pp.13a–16a.

37. O. Schuster and F.A. Francke, *Geschichte der sächsische Armee* (3 vols., Leipzig, 1885),

I, pp.25–46; C. Jany, *Geschichte der preußischen Armee vom 15. Jahrhundert bis 1914* (4 vols., Berlin, 1928–9; reprinted Osnabrück, 1967), I, pp.67–73.

38. Much of the surviving documentation is printed in G. Irmer (ed.), *Die Verhandlungen Schwedens und seiner Verbündeten mit Wallenstein und dem Kaiser* (3 vols., Stuttgart, 1888–91).

39. As argued by A. Ernstberger, 'Wallensteins Heeressabotage und die Breitenfelder Schlacht', *HZ*, 142 (1930), 41–72; J. Pekař, *Wallenstein 1630–1634* (Berlin, 1937), pp.77–180; F. Watson, *Wallenstein* (London, 1938), pp.321–2, 327–9.

40. The proposed redistribution of the electoral titles can be found in the correspondence of Wilhelm V to Gustavus, 5 March 1632, Irmer (ed.), *Verhandlungen*, I, pp.124–33. Gustavus promised the following: Münster, Paderborn, Höxter, Corvey, Fulda, the Mainz enclave of Eichsfeld and parts of electoral Cologne. See C. Tacke, 'Die Eindringen Hessen-Kassels in die Westfälische Stifter', in K. Malettke (ed.), *Frankreich und Hessen-Kassel* (Marburg, 1999), pp.175–87.

41. Elizabeth to Charles I, 17 October 1631, in L.M. Baker (ed.), *The Letters of Elizabeth Queen of Bohemia* (London, 1963), pp.81–2. See also K. Sharpe, *The Personal Rule of Charles I* (London, 1992), pp.70–97.

42. H.L. Rubenstein, *Captain Luckless. James, First Duke of Hamilton 1606–1649* (Edinburgh, 1975); E. Weiss, *Die Unterstützung Friedrichs V. von der Pfalz durch Jakob I. und Karl I. von England im Dreißigjährigen Krieg (1618–1632)* (Stuttgart, 1966), pp.108–16.

43. Quote from Goetze, *Politik*, pp.78, 219–20.

44. H.D. Müller, *Der schwedische Staat in Mainz 1631–1636* (Mainz, 1979), pp.155–66; F.P. Kahlenberg, *Kurmainzische Verteidigungseinrichtungen und Baugeschichte der Festung Mainz* (Mainz, 1963), pp.104–16.

45. Sweden's religious policy is covered from a Protestant perspective by Deinert, *Franken*, pp.112–28, 146–50, and from a Catholic one by R. Weber, *Würzburg und Bamberg im Dreißigjährigen Krieg* (Würzburg, 1979), pp.64–81. Further examples in F. Kleinehagenbrock, *Die Grafschaft Hohenlohe im Dreißigjährigen Krieg* (Stuttgart, 2003), pp.47–52, 271; Rieck, *Frankfurt*, pp.204–15; B.J. Hock, *Kitzingen im Dreißigjährigen Krieg* (Tübingen, 1981), pp.59–87; B. Roeck, *Als wollt die Welt schier brechen. Eine Stadt im Zeitalter des Dreißigjährigen Krieges* (Munich, 1991), pp.244–62; Müller, *Mainz*, pp.167–83.

46. K. Krüger, 'Dänische und schwedische Kriegsfinanzierung', in K. Repgen (ed.), *Krieg und Politik* (Munich, 1988); S. Lundkvist, 'Schwedische Kriegsfinanzierung 1630–1635', in Rudolf (ed.), *Der Dreißigjährige Krieg*, pp.298–323.

47. Roeck, *Als wollt die Welt*, pp.256–7. Further examples in Findeisen, *Oxenstierna*, pp.213–14, 223; Lorentzen, *Armee*, pp.23–4. For the following, see Müller, *Mainz*, pp.132–4, 153–6; W. Dobras, 'Die kurfürstliche Stadt bis zum Ende des Dreißigjährigen Krieges (1642–1648)', in F. Dumont and F. Schütz (eds.), *Mainz. Die Geschichte eine Stadt* (Mainz, 1998), pp.227–63, at pp.259–61.

48. Monro, *Expedition*, pp.206–7; W. Kopp, *Würzburger Wehr* (Würzburg, 1979), p.43.

49. J. Lindegren, 'The politics of expansion in seventeenth-century Sweden', in E. Martínez and M. de P. Pi Corrales (eds.), *Spain and Sweden* (Madrid, 2000), pp.169–94.

50. Details of the agreements in G. Droysen, 'Die niedersächsischen Kreisstände während des schwedisch-deutschen Krieges 1631 und 1632', *ZPGLK*, 8 (1871), 362–83, at 366–77; Findeisen, *Oxenstierna*, pp.166–7, 180–1.

51. Rieck, *Frankfurt*, pp.229–52; H. Langer, *Stralsund 1600–1630* (Weimar, 1970), pp.250–1.

52. K. Schumm, 'Die Hohenlohische Herrschaft über Ellwangen 1633/34', *Ellwanger Jahrbuch*, 17 (1956), 102–35.

53. Roman inscriptions used 'v' for 'u'. For the following see H. Duchhardt, *Protestantisches Kaisertum und Altes Reich* (Wiesbaden, 1977), pp.151–62; Goetze, *Politik*, pp.77–88; Roberts, *Essays*, pp.85–105.

54. Watts, *Swedish Intelligencer*, II, p.24b.

NOTES TO PP. 486–97

55. E. Böhme, *Das Fränkische Reichsgrafenkollegium im 16. und 17. Jahrhundert* (Stuttgart, 1989), pp.263–7; F. Magen, 'Die Reichskreise in der Epoche des Dreißigjährigen Krieges', *ZHF*, 9 (1982), 408–60.
56. Rieck, *Frankfurt*, pp.280–3; Müller, *Mainz*, pp.150–2.
57. Günter Barudio's attempt to exonerate the king on the basis of his public statements and present him as a champion of liberty is unconvincing given the imperial character of his actions: *Gustav Adolf der Grosse* (Frankfurt am Main, 1982), pp.492–502.
58. E. Sticht, *Markgraf Christian von Brandenburg-Kulmbach und der Dreißigjährige Krieg in Ostfranken 1618–1635* (Kulmbach, 1965).
59. M.A. Junius, 'Bamberg im Schweden-Kriege', *Bericht des Historischen Vereins zu Bamberg*, 52 (1890), 1–168, at 18. For further evidence of mounting panic, see M. Friesenegger, *Tagebuch aus dem 30jährigen Krieg* (Munich, 2007), pp.14–17; N. Schindler, 'Krieg und Frieden und die "Ordnung der Geschlechter". Das Tagebuch der Maria Magdalena Haidenbucherin (1609–1650)', in K. Garber (ed.), *Erfahrung und Deutung von Krieg und Frieden* (Munich, 2001), pp.393–452; R. Henggeler, 'Die Flüchtlingshilfe der schweizerischen Benediktinerklöster zur Zeit des Dreißigjährigen Krieges', *Studien und Mitteilungen für die Geschichte des Benediktinerordens und seiner Zweige*, 62 (1950), 196–221.
60. Albrecht, *Maximilian*, pp.790–2; Müller, *Mainz*, pp.48–50; K.H. Frohnweiler, 'Die Friedenspolitik Landgraf Georgs II. von Hessen-Darmstadt in den Jahren 1630–1635', *Archiv für hessische Geschichte und Altertumskunde*, new series 29 (1964), 1–185, at 30–88.
61. Urban sent 223,000 fl. to the Liga and 570,000 fl. to the emperor. All payments stopped after Nördlingen (1634) and the papacy provided no further aid during the war.
62. R. Babel, *Zwischen Habsburg und Bourbon. Außenpolitik und europäische Stellung Herzog Karls IV. von Lothringen und Bar vom Regierungsantritt bis zum Exil (1624–1634)* (Sigmaringen, 1989); P. Martin, *Une guerre de Trente Ans en Lorraine 1631–1661* (Metz, 2002); G. Dethan, *Gaston d'Orléans* (Paris, 1959), pp.83–106; M. Prawdin, *Marie de Rohan Duchesse de Chevreuse* (London, 1971).
63. J.H. Elliott, *The Count-Duke of Olivares* (New Haven, 1986), pp.379–81, 434, 473–4.
64. O'Connell, *Richelieu*, pp.244–9; Burckhardt, *Richelieu*, II, pp.76–90.
65. Not the 2,000 men claimed by Monro: see Müller, *Mainz*, pp.44, 52. For negotiations with Spain, see C. Bartz, *Köln im Dreißigjährigen Krieg. Die Politik des Rates der Stadt (1618–1635)* (Frankfurt am Main, 2005), pp.73–7, 148–9, 161–2; H. Ernst, *Madrid und Wien 1632–1637* (Münster, 1991), pp.18–54.
66. H. Weber, *Frankreich, Kurtrier, der Rhein und das Reich* (Bonn, 1969). For the following, see Weber, *Würzburg*, pp.98–120; Müller, *Mainz*, pp.75–8; D. Albrecht, *Die auswärtige Politik Maximilians von Bayern 1618–1635* (Göttingen, 1962), pp.320–43.
67. The truce was agreed on 20 January 1632. Text in Watts, *Swedish Intelligencer*, II, pp.39a–41b.
68. More detail in J. Polišenský and J. Kollmann, *Wallenstein* (Cologne, 1997), pp.226–38; P. Suvanto, *Wallenstein und seine Anhänger am Wiener Hof zur Zeit des zweiten Generalats 1631–1634* (Helsinki, 1963), pp.97–107, 123–37.
69. See Suvanto, *Anhänger*, pp.138–62. Probable text in G. Lorenz (ed.), *Quellen zur Geschichte Wallensteins* (Darmstadt, 1987), pp.228–39.
70. See J. Krebs, *Aus dem Leben des kaiserlichen Feldmarschalls Grafen Melchior von Hatzfeldt 1632–1636* (Breslau, 1926), pp.3–13.
71. H. Lahrkamp, 'Lothar Dietrich Frhr. von Bönninghausen', *WZ*, 108 (1958), 239–366, at 259–67; G. Droysen, 'Das Aufreten Pappenheims in Norddeutschland nach der Schlacht bei Breitenfeld', *ZPGLK*, 8 (1871), 401–28, 601–22.
72. There is some information in M. Schennach, 'Das Verhältnis zwischen Tiroler Landbevölkerung und Militär von 1600 bis 1650', in S. Kroll and K. Krüger (eds.), *Militär und ländliche Gesellschaft* (Hamburg, 2000), pp.41–78.
73. This and the following quotation from Junius, 'Bamberg', pp.56, 60–1. More detail in

894

Engerisser, *Von Kronach*, pp.46–50; W. Reichenau (ed.), *Schlachtfelder zwischen Alpen und Main* (Munich, 1938), pp.39–42.

74. See Monro, *Expedition*, p.244.

75. For the battle see Watts, *Swedish Intelligencer*, II, pp.79a–84a; Reichenau, *Schlachtfelder*, pp.44–9; Engerisser, *Von Kronach*, pp.57–60.

76. Contemporary accounts of the plundering and peasant reprisals in Monro, *Expedition*, pp.254–6; Friesenegger, *Tagebuch*, pp.17–28.

77. H. Mahr, 'Strategie und Logistik bei Wallensteins Blockade der Reichsstadt Nürnberg im Sommer 1632', *Fürther Heimatblätter*, new series 50 (2000), 29–53, at 35.

78. Duwall is frequently, but inaccurately, identified as either Irish or French. For the following see F. Taeglichbeck, *Das Treffen bei Steinau an der Oder am 11 Oktober 1633* (Breslau, 1889), pp.2–30; H. Schubert, *Urkundliche Geschichte der Stadt Steinau an der Oder* (Breslau, 1885), pp.62–4, 153–4. I would like to thank Ralph Morrison for finding a copy of Schubert's book in Breslau library.

79. Suggested by the Protestant Monro, *Expedition*, p.278. A good account of the battle is in Engerisser, *Von Kronach*, pp.108–16.

80. See G. Droysen, 'Der Krieg in Norddeutschland von 1632', *ZPGLK*, 9 (1872), 245–55, 289–312, 376–400, at 391–7; Albrecht, *Maximilian*, pp.838–40.

81. O. Rudert, 'Der Verat von Leipzig', *NASG*, 35 (1914), 68–87.

82. For an excellent, illustrated account of the coming battle see R. Brzezinski, *Lützen 1632* (Oxford, 2001). The older literature is reviewed by J. Seidler, 'Khevenhüllers Bericht über die Schlacht bei Lützen 1632', in Rudolf (ed.), *Der Dreißigjährige Krieg*, pp.33–50. Useful eyewitness accounts include, for the Swedes, Colonel Johann Dalbier's letter in the National Archives, London, SP81/39 part 2, fol.250–3. For the Imperialists, see Wallenstein's and Holk's reports in Lorenz (ed.), *Quellen zur Geschichte Wallensteins*, pp.251–6, and the account by the Bavarian officer Augustin Fritsch, in Lohmann (ed.), *Zestörung*, pp.254–6.

83. H. Ritter von Srbik, 'Zur Schlacht von Lützen und zu Gustav Adolfs Tod', *MIÖG*, 41 (1926), 231–56 who discounts the old story that it was Major Pier Martelini who fired the fatal shot.

84. T.N. Dupuy, *The Military Life of Gustavus Adolphus* (New York, 1969), p.147.

Without Gustavus

1. For the propaganda and its reception, see J. Holm, 'King Gustav Adolf's death: the birth of early modern nationalism in Sweden', in L. Eriksonas and L. Müller (eds.), *Statehood Before and Beyond Ethnicity* (Brussels, 2005), pp.109–30; L.L Ping, *Gustav Freitag and the Prussian Gospel* (Bern, 2006), pp.262–76; J. Paul, 'Gustaf Adolf in der deutschen Geschichtsschreibung', *Historische Vierteljahresschrift*, 25 (1931), 415–29. For the reluctance to negotiate, see W. Struck, *Johann Georg und Oxenstierna* (Stralsund, 1899), pp.18–50.

2. V. Buckley, *Christina Queen of Sweden* (London, 2004), pp.39–64.

3. M. Roberts, 'Oxenstierna in Germany 1633–1636', *Scandia*, 48 (1982), 61–105, at 72.

4. Quoted in ibid., p.75.

5. The line advanced by G. Droysen, *Bernhard von Weimar* (2 vols., Leipzig, 1885).

6. More detail in P.D. Lockhart, *Denmark in the Thirty Years War, 1618–1648* (Selinsgrove, 1996), pp.214–43; K.H. Frohnweiler, 'Die Friedenspolitik Landgraf Georgs II. von Hessen-Darmstadt', *Archiv für hessische Geschichte und Altertumskunde*, new series 29 (1964), 1–185, at 92–113; Struck, *Johann Georg*, pp.63–72.

7. P. Suvanto, *Die deutsche Politik Oxenstiernas und Wallenstein* (Helsinki, 1979), pp.86–90.

8. J. Öhman, *Der Kampf um den Frieden. Schweden und der Kaiser im Dreißigjährigen Krieg* (Vienna, 2005), pp.51–4. For the following, J. Kretzschmar, *Der Heilbronner Bund 1632–1635* (3 vols., Lübeck, 1922); H. Langer, 'Der Heilbronner Bund (1633–35)', in V. Press (ed.), *Alternativen zur Reichsverfassung in der Frühen Neuzeit* (Munich, 1995), pp.113–22.

9. Roberts, 'Oxenstierna', p.82; E. Schieche, 'Schweden und Norddeutschland 1634', *BDLG*, 97 (1961), 99–132.

10. C.V. Wedgwood, *The Thirty Years War* (London, 1957 edn), p.363. For the Landsberg massacre, see A. Buchner and V. Buchner, *Bayern im Dreißigjährigen Krieg* (Dachau, 2002), pp.154–61. See also M.A. Junius, 'Bamberg im Schweden-Kriege', *Bericht des Historischen Vereins zu Bamberg*, 52 (1890), 1–168, at 107–22.

11. C. Deinert, *Die schwedische Epoche in Franken 1631–5* (Würzburg, 1966), pp.139–62.

12. H. Weber, *Frankreich, Kurtrier, der Rhein und das Reich* (Bonn, 1969), pp.225–30.

13. Pappenheim was supposed to bring 24,000 in return for 80,000 escudos a month. For Bergh's conspiracy, see A. Waddington, *La République des Provinces-Unies, la France et les Pays-Bas Espagnoles de 1630 a 1650* (2 vols., Paris, 1895), I, pp.145–80.

14. See ibid., I, pp.181–231; J.H. Elliott, *The Count-Duke of Olivares* (New Haven, 1986), pp.468–73; J.I. Israel, *The Dutch Republic* (Oxford, 1995), pp.516–23 for the negotiations into 1634.

15. Birkenfeld replaced Horn who joined Bernhard in Franconia. He is known in contemporary English accounts as the Palsgrave after his title Pfalzgraf. For the invasion of Lorraine, see R. Babel, *Zwischen Habsburg und Bourbon* (Sigmaringen, 1989), pp.158–87; P. Martin, *Une guerre de Trente Ans en Lorraine 1631–1661* (Metz, 2002), pp.64–84.

16. W.H. Stein, *Protection royale. Eine Untersuchung zu den Protektionsverhältnissen im Elsass zur Zeit Richelieus 1622–1643* (Münster, 1978), pp.160–235.

17. H. Lahrkamp, 'Lothar Dietrich Frhr. von Bönningenhausen', *WZ*, 108 (1958), 239–366, at 278–85; F. Kölling, *Die Schlacht bei Hess. Oldendorf am 28.6.1633* (Rinteln, 1959).

18. L. van Tongerloo, 'Beziehungen zwischen Hessen Kassel und den Vereinigten Niederlanden während des Dreißigjährigen Krieges', *Hessisches Jahrbuch für Landesgeschichte*, 14 (1964), 199–270, at 220–3. See also H. Salm, *Armeefinanzierung im Dreißigjährigen Krieg. Der Niederrheinisch-Westfälische Reichskreis 1635–1650* (Münster, 1990), esp. maps 1–5.

19. M. Kaiser, 'Die vereinbarte Okkupation. Generalstaatische Besatzungen in brandenburgischen Festungen am Niederrhein', in M. Meumann and J. Rogge (eds.), *Die besetzte res publica* (Berlin, 2006), pp.271–314; J.F. Foerster, *Kurfürst Ferdinand von Köln. Die Politik seiner Stifter in den Jahren 1634–1650* (Münster, 1979), pp.188–91; H. Fahrmbacher, 'Vorgeschichte und Anfänge der Kurpfalzischen Armee in Jülich-Berg 1609–1685', *Zeitschrift des Bergischen Geschichtsvereins*, 42 (1909), 35–94, at 40; B. Fries-Kurze, 'Pfalzgraf Wolfgang Wilhelm von Neuburg', *Lebensbilder aus dem bayrischen Schwaben*, 8 (1961), 198–227, at 209–18.

20. F. Konze, *Die Stärke, Zusammensetzung und Verteilung der Wallensteinischen Armee während des Jahres 1633* (Bonn, 1906), pp.42–6.

21. See A. Gaedeke, 'Zur Politik Wallensteins und Kursachsens in den Jahren 1630–34', *NASG*, 10 (1889), 32–42, at 34. Useful chronology of the negotiations in G. Wagner, *Wallenstein der böhmische Condottiere* (Vienna, 1958), pp.133–46.

22. Suvanto, *Politik*, pp.159–60.

23. J.V. Polišenský, *The Thirty Years War* (London, 1971), p.193. For the following, see J. Krebs, *Aus dem Leben des kaiserlichen Feldmarschalls Grafen Melchior von Hatzfeldt 1632–1636* (Breslau, 1926), pp.38–40, 55.

24. H. Ernst, *Madrid und Wien 1632–1637* (Münster, 1991), pp.52–71; G. Mecenseffy, 'Habsburger im 17. Jahrhundert. Die Beziehungen der Höfe von Wien und Madrid während des Dreißigjährigen Krieges', *Archiv für österreichische Geschichte*, 121 (1955), 1–91, at 24–6.

25. Elliott, *Olivares*, pp.459–65; Ernst, *Madrid und Wien*, pp.47–50; K. Jacob, *Von Lützen nach Nördlingen* (Strasbourg, 1904), pp.51–66.

26. The most recent contingent of 11,000 men from Italy along the Spanish Road marched in 1631 across the St Gotthard. For the following, see J.A. Clarke, *Huguenot Warrior: The Life and Times of Henri de Rohan, 1579–1638* (The Hague, 1966), pp.187–95.

27. Ernst, *Madrid und Wien*, pp.76–7; D. Albrecht, *Maximilian I. von Bayern* (Munich, 1998), pp.849–54. Aldringen was unhappy at the arrangement, but eventually accepted.

28. For the siege see F. Gallati, 'Zur Belagerung von Konstanz im Jahre 1633', *Zeitschrift für schweizerische Geschichte*, 2 (1922), 234–43; K. Beyerle, *Konstanz im Dreißigjährigen Krieg* (Heidelberg, 1900). For its repercussions, see F. Gallati, 'Eidgenssische Politik zur Zeit des Dreißigjährigen Krieges', *Jahrbuch für schweizerische Geschichte*, 44 (1919), 1–257, at 58–107.

29. M. Friesenegger, *Tagebuch aus dem 30jährigen Krieg* (Munich, 2007), p.37. See also R.R. Heinisch, *Paris Graf Lodron. Reichsfürst und Erzbischof von Salzburg* (Vienna, 1991), pp.218–23.

30. W.E. Heydendorff, 'Vorderösterreich im Dreißigjährigen Krieg', *MÖSA*, 12 (1959), 74–142, at 134–7; C. Tacke, 'Die Eindringen Hessen-Kassels in die Westfälische Stifter', in K. Malettke (ed.), *Frankreich und Hessen-Kassel* (Marburg, 1999), pp.175–87, at pp.183–4.

31. Albrecht, *Maximilian*, pp.860–4. Contemporary account in Friesenegger, *Tagebuch*, pp.35–45.

32. The execution was witnessed by the earl of Arundel and the artist Wenzel Hollar: F.C. Springell (ed.), *Connoisseur and Diplomat. The Earl of Arundel's embassy to Germany in 1636* (London, 1965), p.65. More information in H. Rebel, *Peasant Classes* (Princeton, 1983), pp.270–84.

33. L. Radler, *Das Schweidnitzer Land im Dreißigjährigen Krieg* (Lübeck, 1986), pp.64–7; B.Z. Urlanis, *Bilanz der Kriege* (Berlin, 1965), p.232.

34. Most secondary accounts accept Wallenstein's greatly inflated figures for Thurn's force. See his report in Radler, *Schweidnitzer Land*, pp.336–8 and the other documents printed in F. Taeglichbeck, *Das Treffen bei Steinau* (Breslau, 1889), pp.76–114.

35. A. Geiger, *Wallensteins Astrologie* (Graz, 1983).

36. Ernst, *Madrid und Wien*, pp.72–9; Albrecht, *Maximilian*, pp.868–76. The plot has been unravelled by H. Ritter von Srbik, *Wallensteins Ende* (2nd edn, Salzburg, 1952); Suvanto, *Politik*, esp. pp.104ff.; C. Kampmann, *Reichsrebellion und kaiserlichen Acht* (Münster, 1992), pp.106ff.

37. Printed in G. Lorenz (ed.), *Quellen zur Geschichte Wallensteins* (Darmstadt, 1987), pp.364–71. This also reprints other key documents in the coming drama.

38. T.M. Barker, 'Generalleutnant Ottavio Fürst Piccolomini', *Österreichische Osthefte*, 22 (1980), 322–69 presents a favourable interpretation of his motives.

39. *Doc. Bo.*, V, nos.222–3.

40. C. von Pogrell, 'The German heirs and successors of Colonel Walter Butler', *Butler Journal. The Journal of the Butler Society*, 3 (1991), pp.304–16; H. Bücheler, *Von Pappenheim zu Piccolomini* (Sigmaringen, 1994), pp.61–80; J.M. Bulloch, 'A Scoto-Austrian. John Gordon, the assassinator of Wallenstein', *Transactions of the Banffshire Field Club* (1916–17), 20–9; D. Worthington, *Scots in Habsburg Service, 1618–1648* (Leiden, 2004), esp. pp.152, 177–8, 298–9.

41. There are many contemporary accounts of the bloodbath, all with slight variations. For examples, see A.E.J. Hollaender, 'Some English documents on the end of Wallenstein', *Bulletin of the John Rylands Library Manchester*, 40 (1957–8), 359–90; G. Irmer (ed.), *Die Verhandlungen Schwedens und seiner Verbündeten mit Wallenstein und dem Kaiser* (3 vols., Stuttgart, 1888–91), III, pp.286–96.

42. Jacob, *Von Lützen*, pp.176–8.

43. Krebs, *Hatzfeldt*, pp.62–7.

44. Useful overview in C. Tepperberg, 'Das kaiserliche Heer nach dem Prager Frieden 1635–1650', *Der Schwed ist im Land!* (Exhibition catalogue, Horn, 1995), pp.113–39.

45. *Doc. Bo.*, I, no.154.

46. *TE*, III, p.283. The reaction to the murder is discussed by A. Ernstberger, 'Für und wider Wallenstein', *HJb*, 74 (1955), 265–81; Srbik, *Wallensteins Ende*, pp.199–271.

47. This is the subtitle of Georg Wagner's biography. The standard interpretation is

summarized by F.H. Schubert, 'Wallenstein und der Staat des 17. Jahrhunderts', *Geschichte in Wissenschaft und Unterricht*, 16 (1965), 597–611. See also C. Tilly, *Capital, Coercion and European States, AD 990–1992* (Oxford, 1992), pp.80–1.

48. Ernst, *Madrid und Wien*, pp.80–92.

49. J. Pohl, 'Die Profiantirung der Keyserlichen Armaden ahnbelangendt'. *Studien zur Versorgung der kaiserlichen Armee 1634/35* (Kiel, 1991), p.26; W.P. Guthrie, *Battles of the Thirty Years War* (Westport, 2002), pp.262, 282–4.

50. Jacob, *Von Lützen*, appendix pp.98, 109. Jacob provides good coverage of the coming battle from a perspective favourable to Horn. The less-convincing pro-Bernhard view is presented by E. Leo, *Die Schlacht bei Nördlingen im Jahre 1634* (Halle, 1899). More detail in the excellent P. Hrnčiřik, *Spanier auf dem Albuch. Ein Beitrag zur Geschichte der Schlacht bei Nördlingen im Jahre 1634* (Aachen, 2007), and P. Engerisser, *Von Kronach nach Nördlingen* (Weißenstadt, 2004), pp.320–46.

51. Maximilian was unenthusiastic, but appointed Duke Charles under pressure from Archduke Ferdinand.

52. S. Poyntz, *The Relation of Sydnam Poyntz 1624–1636* (London, 1908), pp.109–10.

53. Friesenegger, *Tagebuch*, p.54.

54. According to an imperial soldier, see J. Peters (ed.), *Ein Söldnerleben im Dreißigjährigen Krieg* (Berlin, 1993), p.62.

55. Quoted in G. Rystad, *Kriegsnachrichten und Propaganda während des Dreißigjährigen Krieges* (Lund, 1960), pp.180–1. This book provides detailed coverage of the public reception of the battle.

56. Droysen, *Bernhard*, II, p.46.

57. Examples in F. Kleinehagenbrock, *Die Grafschaft Hohenlohe im Dreißigjährigen Krieg* (Stuttgart, 2003), pp.186–204, 224–5; S. Zizelmann, *Um Land und Konfession* (Frankfurt am Main, 2002), pp.270–333.

58. Kretzschmar, *Heilbronner Bund*, III, pp.20–62.

59. For the Russo-Polish war see B. Porshnev, *Muscovy and Sweden in the Thirty Years War, 1630–5* (Cambridge, 1996).

60. S. Goetze, *Die Politik des schwedischen Reichskanzlers Axel Oxenstierna gegenüber Kaiser und Reich* (Kiel, 1971), pp.138–41; Droysen, *Bernhard*, II, pp.11–20, 53–5.

61. Rohan had been redirected to the Valtellina: see Chapter 18.

For the Liberty of Germany

1. As argued by R.A. Stradling, *Spain's Struggle for Europe 1598–1668* (London, 1994), pp.96–107, 114–17, 281. For the negotiations with Gaston, see H. Ernst, *Madrid und Wien 1632–1637* (Münster, 1991), pp.83–4.

2. J.H. Elliott, *The Count-Duke of Olivares* (New Haven, 1986), pp.472–4.

3. J.I. Israel, *Conflicts of Empires* (London, 1997), p.69.

4. Ernst, *Madrid und Wien*, pp.126–33.

5. For the intended distribution of the spoils, see the map in J. Alcala Zamora, *España, Flandes y el mar de Norte (1618–1639)* (Barcelona, 1975), pp.360–1. Franco-Dutch negotiations in A. Waddington, *La République des Provinces-Unies, la France et les Pays-Bas Espagnoles de 1630 a 1650* (2 vols., Paris, 1895), I, pp.242–60; J.I. Israel, *The Dutch Republic* (Oxford, 1995), pp.525–7.

6. D. Parrott, 'The causes of the Franco-Spanish War of 1635–59', in J. Black (ed.), *The Origins of War in Early Modern Europe* (Edinburgh, 1987), pp.72–111, at pp.85–8.

7. It was belatedly published in suitably revised form in the *Mercure de France*: D.P. O'Connell, *Richelieu* (London, 1968), pp.308–11; H. Weber, 'Vom verdeckten zum offenen Krieg: Richelieus Kriegsgründe und Kriegsziele 1634–35', in K. Repgen (ed.), *Krieg und Politik 1618–1648* (Munich, 1988), pp.203–18, and his 'Zur Legitimation der französischen Kriegserklärung 1635', *HJb*, 108 (1988), 90–113.

8. D. Parrott, *Richelieu's Army. War, government and society in France 1624–1642* (Cam-

bridge, 2001), esp. pp.190–9. Somewhat higher figures in J.A. Lynn, *Giant of the Grand Siècle. The French army 1610–1715* (Cambridge, 1997). Further useful information in B.R. Kroener, 'Die Entwicklung der Truppenstärken in den Französischen Armeen zwischen 1635 und 1661', in K. Repgen (ed.), *Forschungen und Quellen zur Geschichte des Dreißigjährigen Krieges* (Münster, 1981), pp.163–220.

9. Quoted in W.H. Lewis, *Assault on Olympus. The rise of the House of Gramont between 1604 and 1678* (London, 1958), p.35.

10. Calculated from data in R. Bonney, *The King's Debts. Finance and politics in France 1589–1661* (Oxford, 1981), p.173, and P. Kriedte, *Peasants, Landlords and Merchant Capitalists* (Leamington Spa, 1983), p.93.

11. R. Bonney, 'Louis XIII, Richelieu and the royal finances', in J. Bergin and L. Brockliss (eds.), *Richelieu and his Age* (Oxford, 1992), pp.99–133, at p.110.

12. J. Dent, *Crisis in Finance. Crown, financiers and society in seventeenth-century France* (Newton Abbot, 1973), p.32. The annual cost of servicing the debt, paying *rentes* (interest on government bonds, like the Spanish *juros*), and the salaries of the numerous venal office holders climbed to 45.8 million by 1639/40.

13. O.A. Ranum, *Richelieu and the Councillors of Louis XIII* (Oxford, 1963); R. Bonney, *Political Change in France under Richelieu and Mazarin 1624–1661* (Oxford, 1978), pp.263–83; D.C. Baxter, *Servants of the Sword. French intendants of the army, 1630–1670* (Urbana, 1976); B.R. Kroener, *Les Routes et les étapes. Die Versorgung der französischen Armeen in Nordostfrankreich (1635–1661)* (Münster, 1980).

14. K. Malettke, 'France's imperial policy during the Thirty Years War', in K. Bussmann and H. Schilling (eds.), *1648: War and Peace in Europe* (3 vols., Münster, 1998), I, pp.177–85, at pp.182–3.

15. Ernst, *Madrid und Wien*, pp.111–20, 166–8, 180–4, 217–19; P. Hrnčiřik, *Spanier auf dem Albuch* (Aachen, 2007), pp.60–73. Spain also paid 280,000 fl. to Bavaria in 1634–7.

16. J. Krebs, *Aus dem Leben des kaiserlichen Feldmarschalls Grafen Melchior von Hatzfeldt 1632–1636* (Breslau, 1926), p.89 puts Piccolomini at only 8,000 and this seems a likely total for the force operating west of the river.

17. Henderson had a colourful career: possibly already having survived capture in Zanzibar, he served both Denmark and Sweden before entering imperial service in 1634. For the negotiations see *Doc. Bo.* V, no.334; D. Worthington, *Scots in Habsburg Service, 1618–1648* (Leiden, 2004), pp.155, 159, 171–2; G. Droysen, *Bernhard von Weimar* (2 vols., Leipzig, 1885), II, pp.58–62.

18. More detail on these operations in vicomte de Noailles, *Épisodes de la Guerre de Trente Ans. Le Cardinal de la Valette* (Paris, 1906), pp.132–88; H.D. Müller, *Der schwedische Staat in Mainz 1631–1636* (Mainz, 1979), pp.220–34; A. Börckel, *Geschichte von Mainz als Festung und Garnison* (Mainz, 1913), pp.52–9; Krebs, *Hatzfeldt*, pp.89–97; Droysen, *Bernhard*, II, pp.118–96.

19. There is a graphic contemporary account of the conditions in the imperial camp in J. Peters (ed.), *Ein Söldnerleben im Dreißigjährigen Krieg* (Berlin, 1993), pp.63–70.

20. English translation in G. Symcox (ed.), *War, Diplomacy, and Imperialism, 1618–1763* (New York, 1974), pp.117–21.

21. There seems little evidence to support the claim by R.A. Stradling that Spain agreed an all-or-nothing grand attack on France. Further discussion by J.I Israel, *The Dutch Republic and the Hispanic World, 1606–1661* (Oxford, 1982), pp.250–62; also in his *Dutch Republic*, pp.528–30, and his *Conflicts of Empires*, pp.73–9.

22. Ernst, *Madrid und Wien*, pp.192–231. Spain paid 2.4 million fl. in 1636–9, or half of what had been promised, and a third of that went directly on men recruited into its army.

23. See the account by an anonymous participant in Peters (ed.), *Söldnerleben*, pp.73–5. More detail in Parrott, *Richelieu's Army*, pp.119–23, 196–7; O'Connell, *Richelieu*, pp.348–51.

24. P. Martin, *Une guerre de Trente Ans en Lorraine 1631–1661* (Metz, 2002), pp.131–3.

25. As claimed by G. Parker (ed.), *The Thirty Years War* (London, 1987), p.152.

26. K. Repgen, 'Ferdinand III. (1637–57)', in A. Schindling and W. Ziegler (eds.), *Die Kaiser der Neuzeit 1519–1918* (Munich, 1990), pp.142–67, at p.157.

27. Examples of this approach include Parker (ed.), *Thirty Years War*, p.143; R. Bireley, 'The Peace of Prague (1635) and the Counter Reformation in Germany', *JMH*, 48 (1976), supplement 31–70, at 56–60; G. Barudio, *Der Teutsche Krieg 1618–1648* (Frankfurt am Main, 1998), pp.388–91.

28. A. Wandruska, 'Zum "Absolutismus" Ferdinands', *Mitteilungen des Oberösterreich-ischen Landesarchivs*, 14 (1984), 261–8; H. Haan, 'Kaiser Ferdinand II. und das Problem des Reichsabsolutismus', *HZ*, 207 (1968), 297–345.

29. The negotiations can be followed in K.H. Frohnweiler, 'Die Friedenspolitik Landgraf Georgs II. von Hessen-Darmstadt', *Archiv für hessische Geschichte und Altertumskunde*, new series 29 (1964), 1–185, at 120–62; M. Kaiser, 'Der Prager Frieden von 1635', *ZHF*, 28 (2001), 277–97; A. Gindely, *The Thirty Years War* (2 vols., New York, 1892), II, pp.204–31.

30. K. Bierther, 'Zur Edition von Quellen zum Prager Frieden', in Repgen (ed.), *Forschungen und Quellen*, pp.1–30.

31. A. Kraus, 'Zur Vorgeschichte des Friedens von Prag 1635', in H. Dickerhof (ed.), *Festgabe Heinz Hurten* (Frankfurt am Main, 1988), pp.265–99, at pp.269–70; R.G. Asch, 'The *ius foederis* re-examined: the Peace of Westphalia and the constitution of the Holy Roman Empire', in R. Lesaffer (ed.), *Peace Treaties and International Law in European History* (Cambridge, 2004), pp.319–37, at pp.327–9.

32. D. Albrecht, *Maximilian I. von Bayern* (Munich, 1998), pp.909–38; C. Kapser, *Die bayerische Kriegsorganisation in der zweiten Hälfte des Dreißigjährigen Krieges 1635–1648/49* (Münster, 1997), pp.10–29.

33. Article 92. Text in J.J. Schmauss and H.C. von Senckenberg (eds.), *Neue und vollständige Sammlung der Reichsabschiede* (4 vols., Frankfurt am Main, 1747), III, pp.534–48. Further discussion in A. Wandruska, *Reichspatriotismus und Reichspolitik zur Zeit des Prager Friedens von 1635* (Graz, 1955).

34. Trauttmannsdorff to Piccolomini, 30 May 1635, *Doc. Bo.*, VI, no.28.

35. Paper strength was 35,100, as listed in C. Vitzthum von Eckstädt, 'Der Feldzug der sächsischen Armee durch die Mark Brandenburg im Jahre 1635 und 1636', *Märkische Forschungen*, 16 (1881), 303–86, at 309–11.

36. Treaty of 6 October 1635 in T. von Moerner (ed.), *Kurbrandenburgische Staatsverträge von 1601–1700* (Berlin, 1867), pp.123–4.

37. August II to Emperor Ferdinand II, 10 September 1636, HHStA, KA 101 (neu).

38. E. Hagen, 'Die fürstlich würzburgische Hausinfanterie von ihren Anfängen bis zum Beginne des Siebenjährigen Krieges 1636–1756', *Darstellungen der Bayerischen Kriegs- und Heeresgeschichte*, 19 (1910), 69–203, at 71–3.

39. S. Zizelmann, *Um Land und Konfession* (Frankfurt am Main, 2002), pp.289–331.

40. K.E. Demandt, *Geschichte des Landes Hessen* (Kassel, 1980), pp.415–20, 428–9.

41. The negotiations are covered by J.F. Foerster, *Kurfürst Ferdinand von Köln* (Münster, 1979), pp.125–40; H. Lahrkamp, 'Lothar Dietrich Frhr. von Bönninghausen', *WZ*, 108 (1958), 239–366, at 315–18; H. Conrad and G. Teske (eds.), *Sterbezeiten. Der Dreißig-jährige Krieg im Herzogtum Westfalen* (Münster, 2000), pp.18–19, 145–63.

42. Knyphausen had come out of retirement in December 1635 to resume the post he had resigned in February 1634. Col. Sperreuther commanded between these dates. For Leslie, see C.S. Terry, *The Life and Campaigns of Alexander Leslie, First Earl of Leven* (London, 1899).

43. H. Wunder, 'Frauen in der Friedenspolitik', in K. Garber et al. (eds.), *Erfahrung und Deutung von Krieg und Frieden* (Munich, 2001), pp.495–506.

44. Details of the operation in HHStA, KA 91 (neu).

45. Quoted in J. Öhman, *Der Kampf um den Frieden. Schweden und der Kaiser im Dreißigjährigen Krieg* (Vienna, 2005), p.67.

46. Oxenstierna to Banér, 28 October 1634, quoted in M. Roberts, 'Oxenstierna in Germany

1633–1636', *Scandia*, 48 (1982), 61–105, at 79. The following quotation comes from Öhman, *Kampf*, p.68.

47. Cited in A. Schmidt, *Vaterlandsliebe und Religionskonflikt. Politische Diskurse im alten Reich (1555–1648)* (Leiden, 2007), p.362.

48. Ibid., pp.358–415.

49. For the mutiny see B. von Chemnitz, *Königlich Schwedischer in Teutschland geführter Krieg* (2 vols., Stettin 1648, Stockholm, 1653), II, pp.731–848; S. Goetze, *Die Politik des schwedischen Reichskanzlers Axel Oxenstierna gegenüber Kaiser und Reich* (Kiel, 1971), pp.164–88; Öhman, *Kampf*, pp.71–5.

50. Vitzthum, 'Feldzug', pp.307–8.

51. J.K. Fedorowicz, *England's Baltic Trade in the Early Seventeenth Century* (Cambridge, 1980), pp.201–34; Goetze, *Politik*, pp.179–81.

52. C.E. Hill, *The Danish Sound Dues and the Command of the Baltic* (Durham, NC, 1926), pp.108–9; Stradling, *Spain's Struggle*, pp.261–2.

53. T. Lorentzen, *Die schwedische Armee im Dreißigjährigen Kriege und ihre Abdankung* (Leipzig, 1894), pp.65–6; Krebs, *Hatzfeldt*, pp.239–40.

54. A. von Bismarck, 'Die Memoiren des Junkers Augustus von Bismarck', *Jahresberichte des Altmarkischen Vereins für Vaterländische Geschichte*, 23 (1890), 90–105.

55. Vitzthum, 'Feldzug', p.340, entry for 9 December 1635.

56. J. Falcke, 'Die Steuerverhandlungen des Kurfürsten Johann Georgs I. mit den Landständen während des Dreißigjährigen Krieges', *Archiv für sächsische Geschichte*, new series 1 (1875), 268–348; F. Kaphahn, 'Die Zusammenbruch der deutschen Kreditwirtschaft im XVII. Jahrhundert und der Dreißigjährige Krieg', *Deutsche Geschichtsblätter*, 13 (1912), 139–62, at 147.

57. H. Kellenbenz, 'Hamburg und die französisch-schwedische Zusammenarbeit im 30 jährigen Krieg', *Zeitschrift der Vereins für Hamburgische Geschichte*, 49/50 (1964), 83–107; Öhman, *Kampf*, pp.77–88; Goetze, *Politik*, pp.198–201.

58. There is a good account in Krebs, *Hatzfeldt*, pp.145–55, 245–55, that can be supplemented by the material in W.P. Guthrie, *The Later Thirty Years War* (Westport, 2003), pp.48–58.

59. *Doc. Bo.*, VI, no.79. Ginetti's instructions can be found in K. Repgen, *Dreißigjähriger Krieg und Westfälischer Friede* (Paderborn, 1998), pp.425–57. Papal policy is covered by K. Repgen, *Die römische Kurie und der Westfälische Friede* (2 vols., Tübingen, 1962).

60. F.C. Springell (ed.), *Connoisseur and Diplomat. The Earl of Arundel's embassy to Germany in 1636* (London, 1965).

61. R. Weber, *Würzburg und Bamberg im Dreißigjährigen Krieg* (Würzburg, 1979), pp.324–39.

62. H. Haan, *Der Regensburger Kurfürstentag von 1636/1637* (Münster, 1964); Weber, *Würzburg und Bamberg*, pp.313–24; Albrecht, *Maximilian*, pp.952–61; Ernst, *Madrid und Wien*, pp.232–44, 276.

63. Recruitment began in March 1637, but never reached the intended 17,700 infantry and 6,050 cavalry and dragoons: C. Jany, *Geschichte der preußischen Armee vom 15. Jahrhundert bis 1914* (4 vols., Berlin, 1928–9), I, pp.81–8; J. Schultze, *Die Mark Brandenburg* (5 vols., Berlin, 1961), IV, pp.261–80.

64. More detail in F. Hartung, 'Die Wahlkapitulationen der deutschen Kaiser und Könige', *HZ*, 107 (1911), 306–44, at 333–5.

Habsburg High Tide

1. E. von Frauenholz (ed.), 'Zur Geschichte des Dreißigjährigen Krieges', *ZBLG*, 253–71, at 254–5. This source provides useful data on the strength of the imperial army.

2. *Doc. Bo.*, VI, no.380. Of these, 3,935 were sick. W.P. Guthrie gives the slightly higher total of 11,000 cavalry and 8,400 infantry, also for January 1637: *The Later Thirty Years War* (Westport, 2003), p.94. For the following see *Doc. Bo.*, VI, nos.402ff.

3. H. Ernst, *Madrid und Wien 1632–1637* (Münster, 1991), pp.231, 259–73; G. Mecenseffy, 'Habsburger im 17. Jahrhundert', *Archiv für österreichische Geschichte*, 121 (1955), 1–91, at 49–50.

4. H. Lahrkamp, *Jan von Werth* (2nd edn, Cologne, 1988), pp.69–77.

5. His operations can be followed in his official campaign diary, E. Leupold (ed.), 'Journal der Armee des Herzogs Bernhard von Sachsen-Weimar aus den Jahren 1637 und 1638', *Basler Zeitschrift für Geschichte und Altertumskunde*, 11 (1912), 253–361, at 270–95. See also G. Droysen, *Bernhard von Weimar* (2 vols., Leipzig, 1885), II, pp.281–335; Lahrkamp, *Werth*, pp.80–7.

6. M. Hollenbeck, 'Die hessisch-kaiserlichen Verhandlungen über die Annahme des Prager Friedens', and J. Ulbert, 'Französische Subsidienzahlungen an Hessen-Kassel während des Dreißigjährigen Krieges', both in K. Malettke (ed.), *Frankreich und Hessen-Kassel* (Marburg, 1999), pp.111–22 and pp.159–74 respectively.

7. D. Parrott, *Richelieu's Army. War, government and society in France 1624–1642* (Cambridge, 2001), pp.300–2; H. Lahrkamp, 'Lothar Dietrich Frhr. von Bönninghausen', *WZ*, 108 (1958), 239–366, at 323–4.

8. Anon., *Abriß der Großherzogliche-Hessischen Kriegs- und Truppengeschichte 1567–1888* (2nd edn, Darmstadt, 1889), pp.8–10; F. Beck, *Geschichte der alten Hessen-Darmstädtischen Reiterregimenter (1609–1790)* (Darmstadt, 1910), pp.6–12.

9. L. van Tongerloo, 'Beziehungen zwischen Hessen Kassel und den Vereinigten Niederlanden während des Dreißigjährigen Krieges', *Hessisches Jahrbuch für Landesgeschichte*, 14 (1964), 199–270, at 225–34; J. Foken, *Im Schatten der Niederlande. Die politisch-konfessionellen Beziehungen zwischen Ostfriesland und dem niederländischen Raum vom späten Mittelalter bis zum 18. Jahrhundert* (Münster, 2006), pp.396–400; J.F. Foerster, *Kurfürst Ferdinand von Köln. Die Politik seiner Stifter in den Jahren 1634–1650* (Münster, 1979), pp.140–4. The Hessians still held Dorsten, Dortmund, Lippstadt and Coesfeld.

10. Report of the capture dated 24 February 1638 in HHStA, KA 94 (neu), fol.105–10.

11. E.A. Beller, 'The mission of Sir Thomas Roe to the conference at Hamburg 1638–40', *EHR*, 41 (1926), 61–77; S. Murdoch, *Britain, Denmark-Norway and the House of Stuart, 1603–1660* (East Linton, 2003), pp.78–89.

12. Elizabeth to Archbishop Laud, 1 June 1636, in L.M. Baker (ed.), *The Letters of Elizabeth Queen of Bohemia* (London, 1963), pp.92–3.

13. The Imperialists nonetheless intercepted a letter dated 11 September 1638 from Melander indicating he had offered assistance: HHStA, KA 94 (neu), fol.134–5.

14. The Imperial War Council complained on 2 September 1638 that the Palatines had recruited 300 men discharged by the city of Cologne: ibid., KA 94 (neu).

15. Strengths from H. Salm, *Armeefinanzierung im Dreißigjährigen Krieg. Der Niederrheinisch-Westfälische Reichskreis 1635–1650* (Münster, 1990), pp.54–5; Foerster, *Kurfürst Ferdinand*, pp.157–8. See also the articles by H. Peter and K. Großmann on Vlotho in *Ravensburger Blätter für Geschichte, Volks- und Heimatkunde*, 38 (1938), 73–86.

16. M.E. Ailes, *Military Migration and State-formation. The British military community in seventeenth-century Sweden* (Lincoln, Nebr., 2002), pp.15–16.

17. More detail of Banér's escape in P. Englund, *Die Verwüstung Deutschlands* (Stuttgart, 1998), pp.163–8. In addition to the north-east German towns listed, the Swedes also still held Erfurt, Benfeld, Osnabrück and a few positions along the Weser.

18. J. Öhman, *Der Kampf um den Frieden. Schweden und der Kaiser im Dreißigjährigen Krieg* (Vienna, 2005), pp.107–24.

19. F. Redlich, *The German Military Enterprizer and his Workforce* (2 vols., Wiesbaden, 1964–5), I, p.203.

20. Wolfgang Neugebauer stresses that Hohenzollern absolutism began under Georg Wilhelm and Schwarzenberg to meet the war emergency: *Zentralprovinz im Absolutismus. Brandenburg im 17. und 18. Jahrhundert* (Berlin, 2001), esp. pp.54–9. More detail of the military effort in C. Jany, *Geschichte der preußischen Armee vom 15. Jahrhundert bis 1914* (4 vols., Berlin, 1928–9), I, pp.89–92.

21. Contemporary account of the plundering in C. von Bismarck, 'Das Tagebuch des Christophs von Bismarck aus den Jahren 1635–1640', *Thüringisch-Sächsische Zeitschrift für Geschichte und Kunst*, 5 (1915), 67–98, at 81–8.

22. War Council to the Reichshofrat, 4 May 1638, HHStA, KA 94 (neu), fol.66–9.

23. R. Weber, *Würzburg und Bamberg im Dreißigjährigen Krieg* (Würzburg, 1979), pp.252–67, 321.

24. Foerster, *Kurfürst Ferdinand*, pp.164–7; T. Nicklas, *Macht oder Recht* (Stuttgart, 2002), pp.235–7; Weber, *Würzburg und Bamberg*, pp.268–86.

25. W.E. Heydendorff, 'Vorderösterreich im Dreißigjährigen Krieg', *MÖSA*, 12 (1959), 74–142, at 124–7. Bavarian strengths calculated from data in C. Kapser, *Die bayerische Kriegsorganisation in der zweiten Hälfte des Dreißigjährigen Krieges 1635–1648/49* (Münster, 1997), pp.223–49, and F. Weber, 'Gliederung und Einsatz des bayerischen Heeres im Dreißigjährigen Krieg', in H. Glaser (ed.), *Um Glauben und Reich*, Vol. II/I (Munich, 1980), pp.400–7. See also n.1 above.

26. HHStA, KA 94 (neu), fol.255–60. These calculations include the Saxons, but exclude the Bavarians and Westphalians, as well as the Habsburg Military Frontier.

27. L.J. von Stadlinger, *Geschichte des württembergischen Kriegswesens* (Stuttgart, 1856), pp.302–7; K. von Martens, *Geschichte von Hohentwiel* (Stuttgart, 1857).

28. Correspondence between the Habsburgs and Swiss over Bernhard's incursion in HHStA, KA 94 (neu). Details of the battle in Leupold (ed.), 'Journal', pp.298–308; Droysen, *Bernhard*, II, pp.336–46; Lahrkamp, *Werth*, pp.92–8.

29. C.V. Wedgwood, *The Thirty Years War* (London, 1957 edn), pp.368–70 incorrectly has Bernhard march along the south bank.

30. Anonymous eyewitness account, J. Peters (ed.), *Ein Söldnerleben im Dreißigjährigen Krieg* (Berlin, 1993), p.81.

31. Vicomte de Noailles, *Episodes de la Guerre de Trente Ans. La vie de Guébriant 1602–1643* (Paris, 1913); Anon., *Marshal Turenne* (London, 1907); M. Weygand, *Turenne, Marshal of France* (London, 1930).

32. Contemporary accounts in K. Lohmann (ed.), *Die Zerstörung Magdeburgs* (Berlin, 1913), pp.271–4; Leupold (ed.), 'Journal', pp.349–53. More detail in Droysen, *Bernhard*, II, pp.426–40; J. Heilmann, *Das Kriegswesen der Kaiserlichen und Schweden zur Zeit des Dreißigjährigen Krieges* (Leipzig, 1850), pp.72–3, 92–3.

33. Götz to Gallas, 7 October 1638, HHStA, KA 94 (neu), fol.152–3.

34. Anonymous diary, Peters (ed.), *Söldnerleben*, p.83. For the following see Leupold (ed.), 'Journal', pp.344–5; L.H. von Wetzer, 'Der Feldzug am Ober-Rhein 1638 und die Belagerung von Breisach', *Mittheilungen des K.K. Kriegsarchivs*, new series 3 (1889), 1–154, at 57–64.

35. Unsigned report dated 28 October 1638, HHStA, KA 94 (neu), fol.164–5.

36. Details from HHStA, KA 94 (neu), fol.259–60.

37. Copy of the terms in ibid., fol.316–17.

38. For example by Wedgwood, *Thirty Years War*, pp.364–5.

39. Further discussion of this point in G.P. Sreenivasan, *The Peasants of Ottobeuren, 1487–1726* (Cambridge, 2004), pp.281–3; F. Julien, 'Angebliche Menschenfresserei im Dreißigjährigen Kriege', *Mitteilungen des Historischen Vereins der Pfalz*, 45 (1927), 37–92; D. Fulda, 'Gewalt gegen Gott und die Natur', in M. Meumann and D. Niefanger (eds.), *Ein Schauplatz herber Angst* (Göttingen, 1997), pp.240–69.

40. W.H. Stein, *Protection royale. Eine Untersuchung zu den Protektionsverhältnissen im Elsass zur Zeit Richelieus 1622–1643* (Münster, 1978), pp.486–533.

41. August to Ferdinand III, 4 April 1637, HHStA, KA 101 (neu), and Ferdinand's letter of reassurance to Johann Georg, dated 28 August 1638 in HHStA, KA 94 (neu).

42. His letter of thanks, 1 January 1638, HHStA, KA (neu), fol.3–4. For the following, see S. Zizelmann, *Um Land und Konfession* (Frankfurt am Main, 2002), pp.332–69.

43. L. von Sichart, *Geschichte der Königlich-Hannoverschen Armee* (5 vols., Hanover, 1866–98), I, pp.104–6.

44. Christian IV to Banér, 19 October 1638, HHStA, KA 94 (neu), fol.157–8.
45. Christian IV to Ferdinand III, 13 July 1638, HHStA, KA 101 (neu).
46. Ferdinand's decision on 19 September followed Reichshofrat advice dated 26 August: ibid.
47. See the correspondence of Maximilian, Ferdinand of Cologne and the advice of the Reichshofrat October–December 1638, in ibid.
48. Imperial order, 17 November 1638, HHStA, KA 94 (neu), fol.216–19.
49. K. Hauer, 'Frankreich und die reichsständischen Neutralität', in Malettke (ed.), *Frankreich und Hessen-Kassel*, pp.91–110, at pp.94–9.
50. G. Schrieber, *Raimondo Montecuccoli* (Graz, 2000), pp.41–2; Guthrie, *The Later Thirty Years War*, pp.69–70.
51. Banér wrote to Richelieu that he had 15,400 infantry, 15,000 cavalry and 80 guns in June: Parrott, *Richelieu's Army*, pp.61, 66. Even with reinforcements, it is unlikely his effective strength was over 26,000.
52. F. Geisthardt, 'Peter Melander Graf zu Holzapfel 1589–1648', *Nassauische Lebensbilder*, 4 (1950), 36–53, at 44–5; T. Lorentzen, *Die schwedische Armee im Dreißigjährigen Kriege und ihre Abdankung* (Leipzig, 1894), pp.97–9; Droysen, *Bernhard*, II, pp.539–54.
53. Quoted in Droysen, *Bernhard*, II, p.547.
54. HHStA, MEA Militaria 11, esp. Darmstadt to Mainz 17 December 1639. Efforts were also made to persuade Strasbourg to permit use of its bridge.
55. Mitzlaff's report dated 24 November 1639, ibid.
56. G. Engelbert, 'Der Hessenkrieg am Niederrhein', *AHVN*, 161 (1959), 65–113, at 66–7.
57. English translation in G. Symcox (ed.), *War, Diplomacy, and Imperialism, 1618–1763* (New York, 1974), pp.121–5.
58. T. Klingebiel, *Ein Stand für sich? Lokale Amsträger in der Frühen Neuzeit* (Hanover, 2002), pp.141–50; Foerster, *Kurfürst Ferdinand*, pp.161–71.
59. These negotiations can be followed in HHStA, KA 101 (neu), fol.1–196.
60. 5 December 1639, HHStA, MEA Militaria 11. The following quotation comes from a report of discussions through an unnamed intermediary with Colonel Ohm in Strasbourg dated 3 March 1640 in ibid.
61. Johann Jacob Vinther to the elector of Mainz, 28 January 1640, ibid. See also Parrott, *Richelieu's Army*, pp.139–44.
62. *Doc. Bo.*, VI, no.963. The following is drawn from O. Schuster and F.A. Francke, *Geschichte der sächsische Armee* (3 vols., Leipzig, 1885), I, p.71; Kapser, *Kriegsorganisation*, pp.224–5.
63. *TE*, IV, p.364.
64. Peters (ed.), *Söldnerleben*, pp.91–6.
65. W.E. Heydendorff, 'Vorderösterreich im Dreißigjährigen Krieg' [part 2], *MÖSA*, 13 (1960), 107–94, at 132–83.

In the Balance

1. For example, A. Kraus, *Maximilian I. Bayerns Großer Kurfürst* (Graz, 1990), p.298. More sympathetic treatment in E. Höfer, *Das Ende des Dreißigjährigen Krieges* (Cologne, 1998), pp.44–53.
2. M. Howard, *War in European History* (Oxford, 1976), p.37.
3. According to C.V. Wedgwood, *The Thirty Years War* (London, 1957 edn), pp.373–6, 383, quote from p.362. Similar comments in S.R. Gardiner, *The Thirty Years War 1618–1648* (London, 1889), pp.183–4; T. Lorentzen, *Die schwedische Armee im Dreißigjährigen Kriege und ihre Abdankung* (Leipzig, 1894), pp.76–7.
4. B.R. Kroener, 'Soldat oder Soldateska? Programmatischer Aufriß einer Sozialgeschichte militärischer Unterschichten in der ersten Hälfte des 17. Jahrhunderts', in M. Messerschmidt et al. (eds.), *Militärgeschichte. Probleme, Thesen, Wege* (Stuttgart, 1982), pp.100–23.
5. Good example in T. Helfferich, 'A levy in Liège for Marazin's army: Practical and strategic

difficulties in raising and supporting troops in the Thirty Years War', *Journal of Early Modern History*, 11 (2007), 475–500.

6. The problem of desertion is covered by M. Kaiser, 'Ausreißer und Meuterer im Dreißigjährigen Krieg', in U. Bröckling and M. Sikora (eds.), *Armeen und ihre Deserteure* (Göttingen, 1998), pp.49–71, and 'Die Lebenswelt der Söldner und das Phänomen der Desertion im Dreißigjährigen Krieg', *Osnabrücker Mitteilungen*, 103 (1998), 105–24.

7. The most recent example of these arguments is W.P. Guthrie, *The Later Thirty Years War* (Westport, 2003), pp.122, 221.

8. Ibid., p.233.

9. D. Croxton, 'A territorial imperative? The military revolution, strategy and peacemaking in the Thirty Years War', *War in History*, 5 (1998), 253–79, at 278. See also his ' "The prosperity of arms is never continued". Military intelligence, surprise and diplomacy in 1640s Germany', *Journal of Military History*, 64 (2000), 981–1003.

10. D. Albrecht, *Maximilian I. von Bayern* (Munich, 1998), pp.962–78; R. Weber, *Würzburg und Bamberg im Dreißigjährigen Krieg* (Würzburg, 1979), pp.340–68. For the following see also K. Bierther, *Der Regensburger Reichstag von 1640/41* (Kallmunz, 1971); R. Bireley, *The Jesuits and the Thirty Years War* (Cambridge, 2003), pp.215–20.

11. As Ferdinand III expressed it to Elector Anselm of Mainz, 26 March 1640, HHStA, MEA Militaria 11.

12. The Recess is printed in J. J. Schmauss and H. C. von Senckenberg (eds.) *Neue und vollständige Sammlung der Reichsabschiede* (4 vols., Frankfurt am Main, 1747), III, pp.548–74. The mandate, dated 1 October 1640, is in HHStA, MEA Militaria 11.

13. P. Englund, *Die Verwüstung Deutschlands* (Stuttgart, 1998), pp.243–52.

14. Banér's death may well have been due to excessive drinking and eating rotten meat, but it is unlikely to have been the result of the infamous Hildesheim banquet the previous November where Georg also fell ill and two of the guests died.

15. J. Öhman, *Der Kampf um den Frieden. Schweden und der Kaiser im Dreißigjährigen Krieg* (Vienna, 2005), pp.154–62; Lorentzen, *Armee*, pp.93–104; Englund, *Verwüstung*, pp.269–70.

16. L. Hüttl, *Friedrich Wilhelm von Brandenburg, der Große Kurfürst, 1620–1688* (Munich, 1981), pp.76–87; Öhman, *Kampf*, pp.119–53.

17. O. Elster, *Geschichte der stehenden Truppen im Herzogthum Braunschweig-Wolfenbüttel* (2 vols., Leipzig, 1899–1901), I, pp.63–73. For the following, see also Englund, *Verwüstung*, pp.266–8.

18. H.G. Aschoff, 'Das Hochstift Hildesheim und der Westfälische Frieden', *Die Diozese Hildesheim in Vergangenheit und Gegenwart*, 66 (1998), 229–69, at 239–52. Klitzing entered Spanish service.

19. K. Ruppert, *Die kaiserliche Politik auf dem Westfälischen Friedenskongress (1643–8)* (Münster, 1979), pp.2–25; Bierther, *Regensburger Reichstag*, pp.185–95, 249–50; Öhman, *Kampf*, pp.175–81.

20. For this and the following, J.F. Foerster, *Kurfürst Ferdinand von Köln* (Münster, 1979), pp.198–203; G. Engelbert, 'Der Hessenkrieg am Niederrhein', *AHVN*, 161 (1959), 65–113, and 162 (1960), 35–96; D. Parrott, *Richelieu's Army. War, government and society in France 1624–1642* (Cambridge, 2001), p.219.

21. H. Lahrkamp, *Jan von Werth* (2nd edn, Cologne, 1962), pp.119–20.

22. Hatzfeldt to Archduke Leopold Wilhelm, 12 October 1642, HHStA, KA 110 (neu), fol.37–40.

23. L. Radler, *Das Schweidnitzer Land im Dreißigjährigen Krieg* (Lübeck, 1986), pp.24, 74–7; Englund, *Verwüstung*, pp.274–5.

24. B. Dudik (ed.), 'Tagebuch des feindlichen Einfalls der Schweden in das Markgrafthum Mähren während ihres Aufenthaltes in der Stadt Olmütz 1642–1650', *Archiv für österreichische Geschichte*, 65 (1884), 309–485, at 312–18, 410–16.

25. Leopold Wilhelm to Ferdinand III, 6 October 1642, HHStA, KA 110 (neu), fol.24–9. Most of the militia also soon deserted: *Doc. Bo.*, VI, no.1364.

26. Johann Georg to Leopold Wilhelm, 14 October 1642, HHStA, KA 110 (neu), fol.153–4.

27. Torstensson's account, 3 November 1642 (copy), in ibid., fol.153–4. See ibid. for two accounts by imperial soldiers (fol.155–7, 261–3). Useful coverage in Guthrie, *Later Thirty Years War*, pp.110–22, 146–7.

28. Hatzfeldt reported the allies' alleged approach to Johann Georg on 15 October 1642, HHStA, KA 110 (neu), fol.61–4.

29. M. Friesenegger, *Tagebuch aus dem 30jährigen Krieg* (Munich, 2007), p.75.

30. Ferdinand III to Johann Georg, 8 November 1642, HHStA, KA 110 (neu), fol.174–5.

31. Hüttl, *Friedrich Wilhelm*, pp.89–99, 110–13.

32. The arrangement lasted from March 1646 to January 1648: F. Maier, *Die bayerische Unterpfalz im Dreißigjährigen Krieg* (New York, 1990), pp.408–9. Other examples in H. Conrad and G. Teske (eds.), *Sterbezeiten. Der Dreißigjährige Krieg im Herzogtum Westfalen* (Münster, 2000), pp.40–2; M. Wohlhage, 'Aachen im Dreißigjährigen Kriege', *Zeitschrift des Aachener Geschichtsvereins*, 33 (1911), 1–64, at 25–37.

33. Weber, *Bamberg und Würzburg*, pp.287–8, 296; B.J. Hock, *Kitzingen im Dreißigjährigen Krieg* (Tübingen, 1981), pp.117–18, 121, 125–9.

34. W.H. Stein, *Protection royale. Eine Untersuchung zu den Protektionsverhältnissen im Elsass zur Zeit Richelieus 1622–1643* (Münster, 1978), pp.24–5, 510–23.

35. Weber, *Bamberg und Würzburg*, pp.293–4, 298–301, 359–84; F. Magen, 'Die Reichskreise in der Epoche des Dreißigjährigen Krieges', *ZHF*, 9 (1982), 408–60, at 452–3.

36. More detail in Englund, *Verwüstung*, pp.292–313.

37. For this and the following, see F. des Robert, 'La Bataille de Tuttlingen', *Mémoires de l'Académie de Stanislaus Leszinski*, 5th series, 12 (1894), 370–443; G. Hebert, 'Franz von Mercy, kurbayerischer Feldmarschall im Dreißigjährigen Krieg', *ZBLG*, 69 (2006), 555–94, at 581–3; Lahrkamp, *Werth*, 131–8. Eyewitness accounts in J. Peters (ed.), *Ein Söldnerleben im Dreißigjährigen Krieg* (Berlin, 1993), pp.109–11; *TE*, V, p.191.

38. The fighting in Italy is poorly covered in English. There is a useful overview in G. Hanlon, *The Twilight of a Military Tradition. Italian aristocrats and European conflicts, 1560–1800* (London, 1998), pp.122–34, 281–2. See also vicomte de Noailles, *Épisodes de la Guerre de Trente Ans. Le Cardinal de la Valette* (Paris, 1906), pp.375–541; Parrott, *Richelieu's Army*, pp.116–18, 139–45, 193–5, 200–13.

39. For this and the following, see A. Wendland, *Der Nutzen der Pässe und die Gefährdung der Seelen. Spanien, Mailand und der Kampf ums Veltlin 1620–1641* (Zürich, 1995), pp.152–354; J.A. Clarke, *Huguenot Warrior: The Life and Times of Henri de Rohan, 1579–1638* (The Hague, 1966), pp.199–203; H. Ernst, *Madrid und Wien 1632–1637* (Münster, 1991), pp.166–8.

40. The duke died at another of the era's poisonous banquets that also (allegedly) claimed the life of the French commander and guest of honour, Marshal Crequi, while a third of the guests fell ill. For the events in Savoy see T. Osborne, *Dynasty and Diplomacy in the Court of Savoy* (Cambridge, 2002), pp.43, 238–40, 258–66; M.D. Pollak, *Turin 1564–1680. Urban design, military culture and the creation of an absolutist capital* (Chicago, 1991), pp.108–48.

41. As argued by G. Quazza, 'Guerra civili in Piemonte, 1637–1642', *Bollettino Storico. Bibliografico Subalpino*, 57 (1959), 281–321; 58 (1960), 5–63.

42. T.J. Dandelet, *Spanish Rome 1500–1700* (New Haven, 2001), pp.188–204, quote from p.204; F.J. Baumgartner, *A History of Papal Elections* (Basingstoke, 2003), pp.153–4. The Castro War is covered by Hanlon, *Twilight*, pp.132–9.

43. Coverage of operations along the Pyrenees in Parrott, *Richelieu's Army*, pp.71–5, 126–36, 146–53, 202, 208, 216–17; E.H. Jenkins, *A History of the French Navy* (London, 1979), pp.23–6; R.C. Anderson, 'Naval wars in the Mediterranean', *The Mariner's Mirror*, 55 (1969), 435–51; J. Alcala Zamora, *España, Flandes y el mar de Norte (1618–1639)* (Barcelona, 1975), pp.399–400.

44. R.A. Stradling, *The Armada of Flanders. Spanish maritime policy and European war,*

1568–1668 (Cambridge, 1992), pp.99–105. Spain sent 28,436 men to Flanders by sea in 1631–40, compared to 22,892 by land.

45. R.A. Stradling, *The Spanish Monarchy and Irish Mercenaries: The Wild Geese in Spain 1618–68* (Blackrock, 1994), pp.26–7.

46. L.R. Corteguerra, *For the Common Good. Popular politics in Barcelona, 1580–1640* (Ithaca, 2002), pp.149–51; J. Albi de la Cuesta, *De Pavía a Rocroi. Los tercios de infantería española en los siglos xvi y xvii* (Madrid, 1999), pp.272–3.

47. J. Lynch, *The Hispanic World in Crisis and Change 1598–1700* (Oxford, 1992), p.72.

48. J.H. Elliott, *The Revolt of the Catalans* (Cambridge, 1963), pp.446–51; Corteguerra, *Common Good*, pp.156–81. The 'Song of the Segadors' is the Catalan anthem.

49. Lynch, *Hispanic World*, p.146.

50. R.A. Stradling, *Philip IV and the Government of Spain, 1621–1665* (Cambridge, 1988), pp.181–5.

51. Lynch, *Hispanic World*, pp.119–30.

52. G. Parker, *Spain and the Netherlands 1559–1659* (London, 1979), p.186. Further material from I.A.A. Thompson, 'Domestic resource mobilisation and the Downing thesis', and E. Solano Camón, 'The eastern kingdoms in the military organization of the Spanish monarchy', in E. Martínez and M. de P. Pi Corrales (eds.), *Spain and Sweden* (Madrid, 2000), pp.281–306 and 383–403 respectively; I.A.A. Thompson, 'The impact of war and peace on government and society in seventeenth-century Spain', in R.G. Asch et al. (eds.), *Frieden und Krieg in der Frühen Neuzeit* (Munich, 2001), pp.161–79; R. Mackay, *The Limits of Royal Authority. Resistance and obedience in seventeenth-century Castile* (Cambridge, 1999), pp.46–59.

53. Ernst, *Madrid und Wien*, pp.262–3.

54. L. White, 'The experience of Spain's early modern soldiers: combat, welfare and violence', *War in History*, 9 (2002), 1–38; F.G. de Leon, 'Aristocratic draft-dodgers in 17th century Spain', *History Today*, 46 (July 1996), 14–21.

55. Mackay, *Limits*, pp.1–3, 25–42, 132–72; Corteguerra, *Common Good*, pp.141–53.

56. J. Brown and J.H. Elliott, *A Palace for a King. The Buen Retiro and the court of Philip IV* (New Haven, 1980); A. Úbeda de los Cobos (ed.), *Paintings for the Planet King. Philip IV and the Buen Retiro Palace* (London, 2005).

57. M. Newitt, *A History of Portuguese Overseas Expansion 1400–1668* (London, 2005), pp.226–33; C.R. Boxer, *The Portuguese Seabourne Empire 1415–1825* (London, 1969), pp.106–27.

58. C.R. Boxer, 'The action between Pater and Oquendo, 12 Sept. 1631', *The Mariner's Mirror*, 45 (1959), 179–99.

59. J.K. Thornton, *Warfare in Atlantic Africa 1500–1800* (London, 1999), pp.100–4; W. Frijhoff and M. Spies, *1650: Hard-won Unity* (Basingstoke, 2003), pp.42, 111–12.

60. J.I. Israel, *The Dutch Republic* (Oxford, 1995), pp.527–32, and his *Dutch Primacy in World Trade 1585–1740* (Oxford, 1989), pp.187–96.

61. A. Waddington, *La République des Provinces-Unies, la France et les Pays-Bas Espagnoles de 1630 a 1650* (2 vols., Paris, 1895), I, pp.291–301, 344–61; Noailles, *Cardinal de la Valette*, pp.316–74.

62. G. Mecenseffy, 'Habsburger im 17. Jahrhundert', *Archiv für österreichische Geschichte*, 121 (1955), 1–91, at 51–2. For Piccolomini's discussions in Brussels see *Doc. Bo.*, VI, nos.724, 756, 781.

63. Dom Francisco Manuel de Mello's account printed in C.R. Boxer (ed.), *The Journal of Maarten Harpetzoon Tromp* (Cambridge, 1930), p.211. See also Alcala Zamora, *España*, pp.89, 411–57.

64. Stradling, *Armada of Flanders*, p.107.

65. Ernst, *Madrid und Wien*, p.279. Another 745,000 fl. was paid for German recruits in 1641–2. See also Mecenseffy, 'Habsburger', pp.64–76. For the Hohentwiel see p.625 above and the correspondence of the Innsbruck government August–November 1640 in HHStA, KA 101 (neu).

66. J.H. Elliott, *The Count-Duke of Olivares* (New Haven, 1986), p.614. See also D.P. O'Connell, *Richelieu* (London, 1968), pp.410–28.

67. According to the widely repeated tale: E. Le Roy Ladurie, *The Ancien Régime. A history of France, 1610–1774* (Oxford, 1996), p.53. For Lamboy's involvement see *Doc. Bo.*, VI, no.1209.

68. P. Martin, *Une guerre de Trente Ans en Lorraine 1631–1661* (Metz, 2002), pp.146–51, 273–8.

69. Parrott, *Richelieu's Army*, pp.147–50, 157–8, 217–18; Albi, *De Pavía a Rocroi*, pp.227–9. Useful account of the battle with excellent maps can be found at http://www.geocities.com/aow1617/honnecourt2.html (accessed 15 May 2008).

70. Stradling, *Philip IV*, pp.76–80, 119, quote from p.77. More useful information in Elliott, *Olivares*, pp.640–51, and the analysis of Spanish government in M. Rohrschneider, *Der gescheiterte Frieden von Münster. Spaniens Ringen mit Frankreich auf dem Westfälischen Friedenskongress (1643–1649)* (Münster, 2007), pp.92–132.

71. W.H. Lewis, *Assault on Olympus. The rise of the House of Gramont* (London, 1958), p.54. For the following, see G. Treasure, *Mazarin. The crisis of absolutism in France* (London, 1995), pp.56–67.

72. De Melo, 15 May 1643, HHStA, MEA Militaria 11.

73. Though rather hagiographic, E. Godley, *The Great Condé. A life of Louis II de Bourbon prince de Condé* (London, 1915) remains useful. For the battle, see also Albi, *De Pavía a Rocroi*, pp.40–63, and the very useful summary by P.A. Picouet, 'The battle of Rocroi', *Arquebusier*, 31 no.1 (2008), 2–20.

74. The Spanish infantry were not deployed in three lines as widely reported in most secondary accounts.

75. Guthrie, *Later Thirty Years War*, p.180; R.F. Weigley, *The Age of Battles* (London, 1993), pp.40–2.

76. For the impact of the losses see Count von Nassau-Hadamar to Elector Anselm of Mainz, 31 May 1643, HHStA, Militaria 11.

Pressure to Negotiate

1. F. Dickmann, *Der Westfälische Friede* (7th edn, Münster, 1998) remains the standard work on the congress. There is a useful overview of the issues in K. Repgen, 'Die Hauptprobleme der Westfälischen Friedensverhandlungen von 1648 und ihre Lösungen', *ZBLG*, 62 (1999), 399–438. H. Langer, 'Friedensvorstellungen der Städtegesandten auf dem Westfälischen Friedenskongreß (1644–1648)', *Zeitschrift für Geschichtswissenschaft*, 35 (1987), 1060–72 includes a list of the representatives from the imperial cities.

2. H. Duchhardt, 'Zur "Verortung" des Westfälischen Friedens in der Geschichte der internationalen Beziehungen in der Vormoderne', in K. Malettke (ed.), *Frankreich und Hessen-Kassel* (Marburg, 1999), pp.11–18. For protocol at the congress see A. Stiglic, 'Hierarchy of ceremony and status on the European diplomatic stage', in K. Bussmann and H. Schilling (eds.), *1648: War and Peace in Europe* (3 vols., Münster, 1998), I, pp.391–6.

3. G. Lorenz, 'Schweden und die französischen Hilfsgelder von 1638 bis 1649', in K. Repgen (ed.), *Forschungen und Quellen zur Geschichte des Dreißigjährigen Krieges* (Münster, 1981), pp.145–8.

4. F. Bosbach, *Die Kosten des Westfälischen Friedenskongresses* (Münster, 1984); G. Buchstab, 'Die Kosten des Städterats Osnabrücks auf dem Westfälischen Friedenskongress', in Repgen (ed.), *Forschungen*, pp.221–5.

5. H. Conrad and G. Teske (eds.), *Sterbezeiten. Der Dreißigjährige Krieg im Herzogtum Westfalen* (Münster, 2000), pp.76–87.

6. K. Repgen, *Dreißigjähriger Krieg und Westfälischer Friede* (Paderborn, 1998), pp.723–65; A. M. Kettering, *Gerard ter Borch and the Treaty of Münster* (The Hague, 1998).

7. K. Repgen, 'Friedensvermittlung und Friedensvermittler beim Westfälischen Frieden',

and G. Teske, 'Verhandlungen zum Westfälischen Frieden außerhalb der Kongreßstädte Münster und Osnabrück', both in *WZ*, 147 (1997), 37–61 and 63–92 respectively.

8. W. Fleitmann, 'Postverbindungen für den Westfälischen Friedenskongreß 1643 bis 1648', *Archiv für Deutsche Postgeschichte*, 1 (1972), 3–48; D. Croxton, *Peacemaking in Early Modern Europe. Cardinal Mazarin and the Congress of Westphalia, 1643–1648* (Selinsgrove, 1999), pp.43–8.

9. G. Schmidt, *Geschichte des alten Reiches. Staat und Nation in der Frühen Neuzeit 1495–1806* (Munich, 1999), p.179. More detail in H. Wagner, 'Die kaiserlichen Diplomaten auf dem Westfälischen Friedenskongreß', in E. Zöllner (ed.), *Diplomatie und Außenpolitik Österreichs* (Vienna, 1977), pp.59–73. For the other delegations, see M. Rohrschneider, *Der gescheiterte Frieden von Münster* (Münster, 2007); J. Öhman, *Der Kampf um den Frieden. Schweden und der Kaiser im Dreißigjährigen Krieg* (Vienna, 2005), pp.168–74, 206; A. Tischer, *Französische Diplomatie und Diplomaten auf dem Westfälischen Friedenskongress* (Münster, 1999); P. Sonnino, 'Prelude to the Fronde. The French delegation at the Peace of Westphalia', in H. Duchhardt (ed.), *Der Westfälische Friede* (Munich, 1998), pp.217–33, and his 'From d'Avaux to *dévot*: Politics and religion in the Thirty Years War', *History*, 87 (2002), 192–203.

10. The instructions and a considerable quantity of other important documentation have been published under the general editorship of Konrad Repgen as *Acta Pacis Wesphalicae* (*APW*).

11. Strengths from H. Salm, *Armeefinanzierung im Dreißigjährigen Krieg* (Münster, 1990), pp.34–8, 43; J. Heilmann, *Kriegsgeschichte von Bayern, Franken und Schwaben von 1506–1651* (2 vols., Munich, 1868), II, pp.897, 925, 955. For the campaign and battle, see H.H. Schaufler, *Die Schlacht bei Freiburg im Breisgau* (Freiburg, 1997 edn); R. Schott, 'Die Kämpfe vor Freiburg im Breisgau, die Eroberung von Philippsburg und die Belagerung mehrerer Städte am Rhein im Jahre 1644', *Militärgeschichtliche Mitteilungen*, 24 (1978), 9–22.

12. This ridge appears in many accounts as the Loretto after the chapel built on it later to commemorate the dead.

13. F. Schiller, *Geschichte des Dreißigjährigen Krieges* (Munich, 1966 edn), pp.351–2.

14. H. Lahrkamp, *Jan von Werth* (2nd edn, Cologne, 1962), p.147.

15. J.F. Foerster, *Kurfürst Ferdinand von Köln* (Münster, 1979), pp.196–271; Salm, *Armeefinanzierung*, pp.37, 83–9, 94–6.

16. G. Lorenz, 'Die Dänische Friedensvermittlung beim Westfälischen Friedenskongress', in Repgen (ed.), *Forschungen*, pp.31–61; S. Tode, 'Das Hamburger Umland im Dreißigjährigen Krieg', in M. Knauer and S. Tode (eds.), *Der Krieg vor den Toren* (Hamburg, 2000), pp.145–80, at pp.169–76; J.P. Findeisen, *Axel Oxenstierna* (Gernsbach, 2007), pp.387–94; Öhman, *Kampf*, pp.185–90.

17. C.E. Hill, *The Danish Sound Dues and the Command of the Baltic* (Durham, NC, 1926), pp.114–34.

18. Sweden refunded only a third of de Geer's 1.4 million fl. expenses: G. Edmundson, 'Louis de Geer', *EHR*, 6 (1891), 685–712. For the operations, see R.C. Anderson, *Naval Wars in the Baltic 1522–1850* (London, 1969), pp.47–58; K.R. Böhme, 'Lennart Torstensson und Helmut Wrangel in Schleswig-Holstein und Jutland 1643–1645', *Zeitschrift der Gesellschaft für Schleswig-Holsteinische Geschichte*, 90 (1965), 41–82; P. Englund, *Die Verwüstung Deutschlands* (Stuttgart, 1998), pp.358–402.

19. G. Knüppel, *Das Heerwesen des Fürstentums Schleswig-Holstein-Gottorf, 1600–1715* (Neumünster, 1972), pp.115–37.

20. K. Ruppert, *Die kaiserliche Politik auf dem Westfälischen Friedenskongress (1643–8)* (Münster, 1979), pp.48–50.

21. G. Parker (ed.), *The Thirty Years War* (London, 1984), p.175 gives the usual total of only 1,000 survivors from the original 18,000. In fact, the cavalry lost 4,133 men, or 35%, while the infantry were reduced by 5,000, or half their initial total: Salm, *Armeefinanzierung*, p.43. Gallas's personal responsibility is confirmed by his biographer: R.

Rebitsch, *Matthias Gallas (1588–1647). Generalleutnant des Kaisers zur Zeit des Dreißigjährigen Krieges* (Münster, 2008), pp.251–98.

22. M. Bregnsbo, 'Denmark and the Westphalian Peace', in Duchhardt (ed.), *Der Westfälische Friede*, pp.361–7; P.D. Lockhart, *Denmark in the Thirty Years War, 1618–1648* (Selinsgrove, 1996), pp.265–9.

23. As stated in his instructions to Trauttmannsdorff, 16 October 1645, *APW*, series I, *Instruktionen*, Vol. I (ed. H. Wagner, Münster, 1962), pp.440–52.

24. Their memoranda are printed in Ruppert, *Kaiserliche Politik*, pp.372–400. For the following, see T. Winkelbauer, 'Finanznot und Friedenssehnsucht. Der Kaiserhof im Jahre 1645', *MÖSA*, supplement 3 (1997), 1–15.

25. Swedish General Staff, *Slaget vid Jankow 1645–1945* (Stockholm, 1945). Further useful material in W.P. Guthrie, *The Later Thirty Years War* (Westport, 2003), pp.132–41.

26. As claimed by Englund, *Verwüstung*, pp.428–9.

27. Letters were sent to other key princes: HHStA, KA 121 (neu). For the military counter-measures see P. Broucek, *Der schwedische Feldzug nach Niederösterreich 1645/46* (Vienna, 1967), his 'Erzherzog Leopold Wilhelm und der Oberbefehl über das kaiserliche Heer im Jahre 1645', *Schriften des Heeresgeschichtlichen Museum Wien*, 4 (1967), 7–38, and his 'Louis Raduit de Souches, kaiserlicher Feldmarschall', *Jahrbuch der Heraldisch-Genealogischen Gesellschaft Der Adler*, 8 (1971/73), 123–36.

28. The emperor recovered six of them on Rákóczi's death in 1648: G. Wagner, 'Österreich und die Osmanen im Dreißigjährigen Krieg', *Mitteilungen des oberösterreichischen Landesarchiv*, 14 (1984), 325–92.

29. French planning in Croxton, *Peacemaking*, pp.136, 142, 152. Details of the campaign in S. Niklaus, 'Der Frühjahrsfeldzug 1645 in Suddeutschland (Schlacht bei Herbsthausen)', *Württembergisch Franken*, 60 (1976), 121–80.

30. A list of prisoners taken on the field, including Rosen, is attached to Mercy's report to Maximilian, 6 May 1645, HHStA, KA 121 (neu).

31. H.H. Weber, *Der Hessenkrieg* (Gießen, 1935), pp.46–50. Eberstein had been killed in a skirmish in East Frisia in 1644.

32. They are enclosed with Johann Georg's letter to the emperor, dated 7 August 1645 (Old Style), HHStA, KA 121 (neu).

33. K. Scheible, 'Die Schlacht von Allerheim 3. August 1645', *Rieser Kulturtage*, 4 (1983), 229–72; G. Greindl, 'Franz von Mercy in der Schlacht bei Allerheim', in A. Schmid and K. Ackermann (eds.), *Staat und Verwaltung in Bayern* (Munich, 2003), pp.241–57; G. Hebert, 'Franz von Mercy, kurbayerischer Feldmarschall im Dreißigjährigen Krieg', *ZBLG*, 69 (2006), 555–94, at 587–92; Lahrkamp, *Werth*, pp.156–60.

34. Correspondence in HHStA, KA 121 (neu), especially Johann Georg to Ferdinand on 26 August setting out his reasons for accepting the truce. For the negotiations with Sweden see *Der Waffenstillstand zu Kötzschenbroda zwischen Sachsen und Schweden* (issued by the Amt für Bildung und Kultur Stadt Radebeul, 1995); K.G. Helbig, 'Die sächsisch-schwedischen Verhandlungen zu Kötzschenbroda und Eilenburg 1645 und 1646', *Archiv für sächsische Geschichte*, 5 (1867), 264–88.

35. F. Sánchez-Marcos, 'The future of Catalonia. A *subjet brûlent* at the Münster negoti-ations', and P. Cardim, ' "Portuguese rebels" at Münster', both in Duchhardt (ed.), *Der Westfälische Friede*, pp.273–91 and 293–333.

36. R. von Kietzell, 'Der Frankfurter Deputationstag von 1642–1645', *Nassauische Annalen*, 83 (1972), 99–119; K. Malettke, 'Scheffers Gesandschaft in Osnabrück', in Duchhardt (ed.), *Der Westfälische Friede*, pp.501–22.

37. For example, the responses of Saxony (12 May) and Mainz (29 May) in HHStA, KA 121 (neu). Details on the changed mood among the Catholics in S. Schraut, *Das Haus Schönborn* (Paderborn, 2005), pp.121–5; D. Albrecht, *Maxmilian I. von Bayern* (Munich, 1998), pp.1004–7.

38. Examples of the militants' alarm include petitions lodged by a lawyer hired by the

Swabian prelates who feared the emperor would return their monasteries to Württemberg: HHStA, KA 121 (neu) 10, 26 and 29 May 1645.

39. G. Immler, *Kurfürst Maximilian I. und der Westfälische Friedenskongreß. Die bayerische auswärtige Politik von 1644 bis zum Ulmer Waffenstillstand* (Münster, 1992), pp.62–213.

War or Peace

1. G. Scheel, 'Die Stellung der Reichsstände zur Römischen Königswahl seit den Westfälischen Friedensverhandlungen', in R. Dietrich and G. Oestreich (eds.), *Forschungen zur Staat und Verfassung* (Berlin, 1958), pp.113–32; H.B. Spies, 'Lübeck, die Hanse und der Westfälische Frieden', *Hansische Geschichtsblätter*, 100 (1982), 110–24; R. Postel, 'Hansische Politik auf dem Westfälischen Friedenskongreß', U. Weiß, 'Die Erfurt-Frage auf dem Westfälischen Friedenskongreß', and R. Endres, 'Die Friedensziele der Reichsritterschaft', all in H. Duchhardt (ed.), *Der Westfälische Friede* (Munich, 1998), pp.523–78.

2. G. Mecenseffy, 'Habsburger im 17. Jahrhundert', *Archiv für österreichische Geschichte*, 121 (1955), 1–91, at 83. See also D. Albrecht, *Maximilian I. von Bayern* (Munich, 1998), pp.979–1020; D. Croxton, *Peacemaking in Early Modern Europe* (Selinsgrove, 1999), pp.161–74.

3. K. Ruppert, *Die kaiserliche Politik auf dem Westfälischen Friedenskongress (1643–8)* (Münster, 1979), pp.186–99; K. Repgen, *Dreißigjähriger Krieg und Westfälischer Friede* (Paderborn, 1998), pp.643–76, and his 'Die kaiserlich-französischen Satisfaktionsartikeln vom 13. September 1646', in Duchhardt (ed.), *Der Westfälische Friede*, pp.175–203.

4. H. Lahrkamp, 'Lothar Dietrich Frhr. von Bönninghausen', *WZ*, 108 (1958), 239–366, at 337–47.

5. H. Conrad and G. Teske (eds.), *Sterbezeiten. Der Dreißigjährige Krieg im Herzogtum Westfalen* (Münster, 2000), pp.21–2, 49–50, 226–34.

6. H.H. Weber, *Der Hessenkrieg* (Gießen, 1935), pp.42–150; K. Beck, *Der hessische Bruderzwist zwischen Hessen-Kassel und Hessen-Darmstadt in den Verhandlungen zum Westfälischen Frieden von 1644 bis 1648* (Frankfurt am Main, 1978). Estates opposition is covered by R. von Friedeburg, 'Why did seventeenth-century Estates address the jurisdictions of their princes as fatherlands?', in R.C. Head and D. Christiansen (eds.), *Orthodoxies and Heterodoxies in Early Modern German Culture* (Leiden, 2007), pp.69–94.

7. B. Roeck, *Als wollt die Welt schier brechen* (Munich, 1991), pp.309–12.

8. According to one participant: D. Pleiss, 'Das Kriegsfahrtenbuch des schwedischen Offiziers William Forbes', *Stader Jahrbuch*, 85 (1995), 133–53, at 146. Detailed coverage of the battle in P. Broucek, *Die Eroberung von Bregenz am 4 Jänner 1647* (Vienna, 1981).

9. Details in L. Hüttl, *Friedrich Wilhelm von Brandenburg, der Große Kurfürst, 1620–1688* (Munich, 1981), pp.99–135; P. Kiehm, 'Anfänge des stehenden Heeres in Brandenburg 1640–1655 unter Kurfürst Friedrich Wilhelm', *Militärgeschichte*, 24 (1985), 515–20.

10. S. Lundkvist, 'Die schwedischen Friedenskonzeptionen und ihre Umsetzung in Osnabrück', P. Baumgart, 'Kurbrandenburgs Kongreßdiplomatie und ihre Ergebnisse', and H. Langer, 'Die pommerschen Landstände und der Westfälische Friedenskongreß', all in Duchhardt (ed.), *Der Westfälische Friede*, pp.349–59, 469–99; E. Bauer, 'Johann Graf zu Sayn-Wittgenstein, Kriegsteilnehmer auf hessischer und schwedischer Seite und Hauptgesandter des Kurfürsten von Brandenburg', in G. Teske (ed.), *Dreißigjähriger Krieg und Westfälischer Friede* (Münster, 2000), pp.45–54.

11. A. Gotthard, 'Der "Grosse Kurfürst" und das Kurkolleg', *FBPG*, new series 6 (1996), 1–54, at 3–12.

12. R.P. Fuchs, *Ein 'Medium' zum Frieden. Normaljahre und die Beendigung des Dreißigjährigen Krieges* (Munich, forthcoming).

13. Quoted in R. Bireley, *The Jesuits and the Thirty Years War* (Cambridge, 2003), p.238. More detail on the militants in G. Schmid, 'Konfessionspolitik und Staatsräson bei den

Verhandlungen des Westfälischen Friedenskongresses über die Gravamina Ecclesiastica', *ARG*, 44 (1953), 203–23.

14. Albrecht, *Maximilian*, pp.1031–48; J.F. Foerster, *Kurfürst Ferdinand von Köln* (Münster, 1979), pp.306–63.

15. C. Schultz, 'Strafgericht Gottes oder menschlichen Versagen? Die Tagebücher des Benediktinerabtes Georg Gaisser als Quelle für die Kriegserfahrung von Ordensleuten im Dreißigjährigen Krieg', in M. Asche and A. Schindling (eds.), *Das Strafgericht Gottes* (Münster, 2002), pp.219–90. For the following, see G. Mentz, *Johann Philipp von Schönborn, Kurfürst von Mainz, Bischof von Würzburg und Worms 1605–1673* (2 vols., Jena, 1896–99), II, pp.60–5, 90–1; F. Jürgensmeier, 'Johann Philipp von Schönborn', *Fränkische Lebensbilder*, 6 (1975), 161–84; R.R. Heinisch, *Paris Graf Lodron. Reichsfürst und Erzbischof von Salzburg* (Vienna, 1991), pp.281–95.

16. J. Vötsch, *Kursachsen, das Reich und der mitteldeutsche Raum zu Beginn des 18. Jahrhunderts* (Frankfurt am Main, 2003), pp.23–4, 49–52; G. Kleinheyer, *Die kaiserlichen Wahlkapitulationen* (Karlsruhe, 1968), pp.78–86; R.G. Asch, ' "Denn es sind ja die Deutschen [...] ein frey Volk". Die Glaubensfreiheit als Problem der Westfälischen Friedensverhandlungen', *WZ*, (1998), 113–37, at 123–9; A. Klinger, *Der Gothauer Fürstenstaat* (Husum, 2002), pp.59–61.

17. M. Meumann, 'The experience of violence and the expectation of the end of the world in seventeenth-century Europe', in J. Canning et al. (eds.), *Power, Violence and Mass Death in Pre-modern and Modern Times* (Aldershot, 2004), pp.141–59.

18. Meceseffy, 'Habsburger', pp.78–90; M. Rohrschneider, *Der gescheiterte Frieden von Münster* (Münster, 2007), pp.133–6, 451–2; R.A. Stradling, *Philip IV* (Cambridge, 1988), pp.239–43.

19. T. Lorentzen, *Die schwedische Armee im Dreißigjährigen Kriege und ihre Abdankung* (Leipzig, 1894), p.119; Lahrkamp, 'Bönninghausen', pp.351–2.

20. E. Höfer, *Das Ende des Dreißigjährigen Krieges* (Cologne, 1998), pp.59–64; H. Lahrkamp, *Jan von Werth* (2nd edn, Cologne, 1988), pp.186–7.

21. Lahrkamp, *Werth*, pp.167–84; Albrecht, *Maximilian*, pp.1068–77; F. Göse, *Der erste brandenburg-preußische Generalfeldmarschall Otto Christoph Freiherr von Sparr 1605–1668* (Berlin, 2006), pp.50–3.

22. J. Steiner, *Die pfälzische Kurwürde während des Dreißigjährigen Krieges* (Speyer, 1985), pp.152–88; J. Arndt, 'Die Ergebnisse der Friedensverhandlungen in Münster und Osnabrück für die rheinischen Territorien', in S. Ehrenpreis (ed.), *Der Dreißigjährige Krieg im Herzogtum Berg und in seinen Nachbarregionen* (Neustadt an der Aisch, 2002), pp.299–327.

23. Höfer, *Ende*, pp.108–21; Lahrkamp, 'Bönninghausen', pp.354–7.

24. A. Calabria, *The Cost of Empire. The finances of the kingdom of Naples in the time of Spanish rule* (Cambridge, 1991); R. Villari, *The Revolt of Naples* (Cambridge, 1993).

25. J.R. Bruijn, *The Dutch Navy of the Seventeenth and Eighteenth Centuries* (Columbia, SC, 1990), pp.26–7; R.A. Stradling, *The Armada of Flanders* (Cambridge, 1992), pp.118–40.

26. W.H. Lewis, *Assault on Olympus. The rise of the House of Gramont* (London, 1958), pp.83–4; E. Godley, *The Great Condé* (London, 1915), pp.154–74.

27. J.I. Israel, *Dutch Primacy in World Trade 1585–1740* (Oxford, 1989), pp.168–70; A. Goldgar, *Tulipmania: Money, Honor and Knowledge in the Dutch Golden Age* (Chicago, 2007); O. van Nimwegen, 'The Dutch army and the military revolutions (1588–1688)', *Militär und Gesellschaft in der Frühen Neuzeit*, 10 (2006), 55–73, at 61–2.

28. W. Frijhoff and M. Spies, *1650. Hard-won Unity* (Basingstoke, 2003), pp.349–427.

29. H.H. Rowan, *The Princes of Orange* (Cambridge, 1988), pp.77–94; S. Groenveld, 'Princes and regents. The relations between the princes of Orange and Dutch aristocrats and the making of Dutch foreign policy', in R.G. Asch et al. (eds.), *Frieden und Krieg in der Frühen Neuzeit* (Munich, 2001), pp.181–92; D.E.A. Faber and R.E. Bruin, 'Utrecht's

opposition to the Münster peace process', in K. Bussmann and H. Schilling (eds.), *1648: War and Peace in Europe* (3 vols., Münster, 1998), I, pp.413–22.

30. Text of the treaty in G. Dethlefs (ed.), *Der Frieden von Münster* (Münster, 1998). For the negotiations with France, see Rohrschneider, *Frieden von Münster*, pp.373–406.

31. Useful account in Godley, *Condé*, pp.216–26; Lewis, *Gramont*, pp.91–3.

32. G. Treasure, *Mazarin* (London, 1995), pp.125–7; J.H. Shennan, *The Parlement of Paris* (2nd edn, Stroud, 1998), pp.255–77; A.L. Moote, *The Revolt of the Judges. The Parlement of Paris and the Fronde* (Princeton, 1971).

33. L. Bely, 'The peace treaties of Westphalia and the French domestic crisis', in Duchhardt (ed.), *Der Westfälische Friede*, pp. 235–52.

34. G. Parker (ed.), *The Thirty Years War* (London, 1984), p.191. The more likely totals are given in the table in Chapter 21, p.770.

35. Swedish dispositions are detailed in W.P. Guthrie, *The Later Thirty Years War* (Westport, 2003), pp.257–60.

36. Höfer, *Ende*, pp.172–3.

37. For the battle see ibid., pp.179–95; W. Reichenau (ed.), *Schlachtfelder zwischen Alpen und Main* (Munich, 1938), pp.83–91.

38. V. Buckley, *Christina, Queen of Sweden* (London, 2005), pp.98–104; P. Englund, *Die Verwüstung Deutschlands* (Stuttgart, 1998), pp.482–4.

39. Reichenau (ed.), *Schlachtfelder*, pp.92–3.

40. Z. Hojda, 'The battle of Prague in 1648 and the end of the Thirty Years War', in Bussmann and Schilling (eds.), *1648: War and Peace*, I, pp.403–11; Englund, *Verwüstung*, pp.515–20.

41. Rohrschneider, *Frieden von Münster*, pp.436–51.

42. F.J. Jakobi, 'Zur Entsehungs- und Überlieferungsgeschichte der Vertragsexemplare des Westfälischen Friedens', in J. Kunisch (ed.), *Neue Studien zur frühneuzeitlichen Reichsgeschichte* (Berlin, 1997), pp.207–21. For the original texts and various translations see http://www.pax-westphalica.de.

The Westphalian Settlement

1. C.V. Wedgwood, *The Thirty Years War* (London, 1957 edn), p.460.

2. J.G. Droysen, *Geschichte der preussischen Politik* (5 parts in 14 vols., Leipzig, 1855–86), part 3, I, p.339. For critical appraisals of this interpretation see R. Southard, *Droysen and the Prussian School of History* (Lexington, Ky, 1995); P.M. Hahn, *Friedrich der Große und die deutsche Nation. Geschichte als politisches Argument* (Stuttgart, 2007).

3. F. Dickmann, *Der Westfälische Friede* (7th edn, Münster, 1998), p.494.

4. As suggested by D.H. Fischer, *The Great Wave. Price revolutions and the rhythm of history* (Oxford, 1996). See also G. Parker, *Europe in Crisis 1598–1648* (London, 1979). For counter-arguments see J. Osterhammel, 'Krieg und Frieden an den Grenzen Europas und darüber hinaus', and H. Schmidt-Glintzer, 'Europa aus chinesischer Sicht in der Frühen Neuzeit', both in R.G. Asch et al. (eds.), *Frieden und Krieg in der Frühen Neuzeit* (Munich, 2001), pp.443–65 and 527–42, respectively.

5. For example, T. Pocock, *Battle for Empire. The very first world war 1756–63* (London, 1998). Similar claims have been advanced for the period 1792–1815.

6. Examples of this approach include P. Kennedy, *The Rise and Fall of Great Powers* (London, 1988); S.H. Steinberg, *The Thirty Years War and the Conflict for European Hegemony 1600–1660* (London, 1966). Nicola Sutherland takes it to its logical extreme by subsuming the Thirty Years War within three centuries of Franco-Habsburg rivalry: 'The origins of the Thirty Years War and the structure of European politics', *EHR*, 107 (1992), 587–625.

7. IPO Article XVII, paragraph 3; IPM Article CXIII. See H. Steiger, 'Concrete peace and general order: the legal meaning of the treaties of 24 October 1648', in K. Bussmann and H. Schilling (eds.), *1648: War and Peace in Europe* (3 vols., Münster, 1998), I, pp.437–45.

8. See *NTSR*, I, 401-3.
9. K. Repgen, *Dreißigjähriger Krieg und Westfälischer Friede* (Paderborn, 1998), pp.539-61, 597-642.
10. Examples include D. McKay and H.M. Scott, *The Rise of the Great Powers 1648-1815* (Harlow, 1983); J. Black, *European International Relations 1648-1815* (Basingstoke, 2002); E. Luard, *The Balance of Power. The system of international relations 1648-1815* (Basingstoke, 1992). A notable exception is M.S. Anderson, *The Rise of Modern Diplomacy 1450-1919* (London, 1993) that does not even list the Peace of Westphalia in its index.
11. J. Zielonka, *Europe as Empire. The nature of the enlarged European Union* (Oxford, 2006).
12. R. Lesaffer (ed.), *Peace Treaties and International Law in European History* (Cambridge, 2004).
13. C. Jenkinson (ed.), *A Collection of all the Treaties of Peace and Commerce between Great Britain and Other Powers* (3 vols., London, 1785), I, pp.10-44, at p.12. Further discussion in D. Croxton, 'The Peace of Westphalia of 1648 and the origins of sovereignty', *IHR*, 21 (1999), 569-91; N. Mout, 'Die Niederlande und das Reich im 16. Jahrhundert', in V. Press (ed.), *Alternativen zur Reichsverfassung in der Frühen Neuzeit?* (Munich, 1995), pp.143-68, at pp.145-6; P. Stadler, 'Der Westfälische Friede und die Eidgenossenschaft', in H. Duchhardt (ed.), *Der Westfälische Friede* (Munich, 1998), pp.369-91.
14. R. Oresko and D. Parrott, 'Reichsitalien and the Thirty Years War', in Bussmann and Schilling (eds.), *1648: War and Peace*, I, pp.141-60.
15. K. Abmeier, *Der Trierer Kurfürst Philipp Christoph von Sötern und der Westfälische Friede* (Münster, 1986), pp.203-57.
16. W. Dotzauer, 'Der pfälzische Wildfangstreit', *Jahrbuch zur Geschichte von Stadt und Landkreis Kaiserslautern*, 12/13 (1974/5), 235-47. For growing hostility towards France, see M. Wrede, *Das Reich und seine Feinde* (Mainz, 2004), pp.324-545.
17. H. Schmidt, 'Frankreich und das Reich 1648-1715', in W.D. Gruner and K.J. Müller (eds.), *Über Frankreich nach Europa* (Hamburg, 1996), pp.119-53; S. Externbrink, *Friedrich der Große, Maria Theresia und das Alte Reich* (Berlin, 2006); E. Buddruss, *Die Französische Deutschlandpolitik 1756-1789* (Mainz, 1995).
18. W. Buchholz, 'Schwedish-Pommern als Territorium des deutschen Reiches 1648-1806', *ZNRG*, 12 (1990), 14-33; B.C. Fiedler, 'Schwedish oder Deutsch? Die Herzogtümer Bremen und Verden in der Schwedenzeit (1645-1712)', *Niedersächsisches Jahrbuch für Landesgeschichte*, 67 (1995), 43-57; K.R. Böhme, 'Die Krone Schweden als Reichsstand 1648 bis 1720', in H. Duchhardt (ed.), *Europas Mitte* (Bonn, 1988), pp.33-9.
19. H. Langer, 'Swedische Friedenskonzeptionen und praktische Friede im Jahrzehnt nach dem Dreißigjährigen Krieg', in H. Duchhardt (ed.), *Zwischenstaatliche Friedenswahrung in Mittelalter und Frühen Neuzeit* (Cologne, 1991), pp.131-51.
20. Proclamation dated 22 August 1806, HHStA, Titel und Wappen Karton 3, folder marked 'Korrespondenz mit den Gesandschaften'.
21. A leading example of this interpretation is H. Schilling, 'War and peace at the emergence of modernity', in Bussmann and Schilling (eds.), *1648: War and Peace*, I, pp.13-22, at p.20. Similar arguments are in his 'Der Westfälische Friede und das neuzeitliche Profil Europas', in Duchhardt (ed.), *Der Westfälische Friede*, pp.1-32.
22. D. MacCulloch, *Reformation. Europe's house divided 1490-1700* (London, 2003), pp.669-70.
23. There is a good overview in J. Whaley, 'A tolerant society? Religious toleration in the Holy Roman Empire, 1648-1806', in O.P. Grell and R. Porter (eds.), *Toleration in Enlightenment Europe* (Cambridge, 2000), pp.175-95. A positive assessment of the rights is provided by G. Schmidt, 'Die "deutsche Freiheit" und der Westfälische Friede', in Asch et al. (eds.), *Frieden und Krieg*, pp.323-47. More detail on the provisions in G. May, 'Die Entstehung der hauptsächlichen Bestimmungen über das ius emigrandi', *ZSRG KA*, 74 (1988), 436-94; R.G. Asch, 'Das Problem des religiösen Pluralismus im Zeitalter der "Konfessionalisierung"', *BDLG*, 134 (1998), 1-32.

24. W. Kohl, *Christoph Bernhard von Galen* (Münster, 1964).
25. Overview of these developments in P.H. Wilson, *Reich to Revolution: German History 1558–1806* (Basingstoke, 2004), pp.198–207.
26. A. Gotzmann and S. Wendehorst (eds.), *Juden im Recht. Neue Zugänge zur Rechtsgeschichte der Juden im Alten Reich* (Berlin, 2007).
27. A. Müller, *Der Regensburger Reichstag von 1653/54* (Frankfurt am Main, 1992).
28. Example in R.P. Fuchs, 'Zeit und Ereignis im Krieg. Überlegungen zu den Aussagen Steinfurter Zeugen in einer Befragung zum Normaljahr 1624', in T. Sodmann (ed.), *1568–1648* (Vreden, 2002), pp.65–76. Further discussion in R.P. Fuchs, *Ein 'Medium' zum Frieden. Normaljahre und die Beendigung des Dreißigjährigen Krieges* (Munich, forthcoming).
29. W. Sellert (ed.), *Die Ordnungen des Reichshofrates 1550–1766* (2 vols., Cologne, 1980–90).
30. M. Schnettger, *Der Reichsdeputationstag 1655–1663* (Münster, 1996). Analysis of cases in J. Luh, *Unheiliges Römisches Reich. Der konfessionelle Gegensatz 1648 bis 1806* (Potsdam, 1995), pp.17–21.
31. H. Molitor, 'Der Kampf um die konfessionellen Besitzstände im Fürstbistum Osnabrück nach 1648', *Osnabrücker Mitteilungen*, 93 (1988), 69–75.
32. E. François, *Die unsichtbare Grenze. Protestanten und Katholiken in Augsburg 1648–1806* (Sigmaringen, 1991). For Goldenstadt and numerous other examples see Whaley, 'A tolerant society?', pp.180–1; F. Jürgensmeier, 'Bikonfessionalität in geistlichen Territorien', in K. Garber et al. (eds.), *Erfahrung und Deutung von Krieg und Frieden* (Munich, 2001), pp.261–85.
33. D. Freist, 'One body, two confessions: mixed marriages in Germany', in U. Rublack (ed.), *Gender in Early Modern German History* (Cambridge, 2002), pp.275–304; C. Kohlmann, 'Kriegs- und Krisenerfahrungen von Lutherischen Pfarrern und Gläubigen in Amt Hornberg', in M. Asche and A. Schindling (eds.), *Das Strafgericht Gottes* (Münster, 2002), pp.123–211, at pp.177–82.
34. L. Hüttl, *Friedrich Wilhelm von Brandenburg, der Große Kurfürst, 1620–1688* (Munich, 1981), pp.177–84; E. Opgenoorth, *Friedrich Wilhelm, der Große Kurfürst von Brandenburg* (2 vols., Göttingen, 1971–8), I, pp. 216–22.
35. M. Schaab, 'Die Widerherstellung des Katholizismus in der Kurpfalz im 17. und 18. Jahrhundert', *ZGO*, 114 (1966), 147–205; G. Haug-Moritz, 'Kaisertum und Parität'. Reichspolitik und Konfession nach dem Westfälischen Frieden', *ZHF*, 19 (1992), 445–82; D. Stievermann, 'Politik und Konfession im 18. Jahrhundert', *ZHF*, 18 (1991), 177–99.
36. Luh, *Unheiliges Römisches Reich*, pp.27–54.
37. G. Haug-Moritz, 'Corpus Evangelicorum und deutscher Dualismus', in Press (ed.), *Alternativen zur Reichsverfassung*, pp.189–207; K. Härter, *Reichstag und Revolution 1789–1806* (Göttingen, 1992).
38. As a result, the Palatine population became one of the most mixed of the Empire comprising, by 1795, 40% Calvinists, 30% Catholics, 20% Lutherans, 10% other minorities including Jews.
39. R.L. Gawthrop, *Pietism and the Making of Eighteenth-century Prussia* (Cambridge, 1993); P.H. Wilson, 'Prussia's relations with the Holy Roman Empire, 1740–86', *HJ*, 51 (2008), 337–71.
40. T. Lorentzen, *Die schwedische Armee im Dreißigjährigen Kriege und ihre Abdankung* (Leipzig, 1894), pp.184–92. Full coverage in A. Oschmann, *Der Nürnberger Exekutionstag 1649–1650* (Münster, 1991).
41. F. Göse, *Der erste brandenburg-preußische Generalfeldmarschall Otto Christoph Freiherr von Sparr 1605–1668* (Berlin, 2006), pp.57–9.
42. P. Hoyos, 'Die kaiserliche Armee 1648–1650', in *Der Dreißigjährige Krieg* (issued by the Heeresgeschichtliches Museum, Vienna, 1976), pp.169–232; H. Salm, *Armeefinanzierung im Dreißigjährigen Krieg* (Münster, 1990), pp.154–61.
43. D. Albrecht, *Maximilian I. von Bayern* (Munich, 1998), pp.1087–90; R.R. Heinisch,

Paris Graf Lodron (Vienna, 1991), pp.289–302. Whilst each territory's share of a Roman month was fixed, total receipts depended on how many territories were contributing; hence the discrepancy between the different amounts received.

44. As argued by J. Burkhardt, *Der Dreißigjährige Krieg* (Frankfurt am Main, 1992), pp.213–24. For the remilitarization of the German territories in the 1660s and 1670s, see P.H. Wilson, *German Armies: War and German Politics 1648–1806* (London, 1998), pp.26–67.

45. B.R. Kroener, ' "Der Krieg hat ein Loch . . ." Überlegungen zum Schicksal demobilisierter Söldner nach dem Dreißigjährigen Krieg', in Duchhardt (ed.), *Der Westfälische Friede*, pp.599–630.

46. A. Klinger, *Der Gothauer Fürstenstaat* (Husum, 2002), p.121.

47. Good overview of the contemporary debate in P. Schröder, 'The constitution of the Holy Roman Empire after 1648: Samuel Pufendorf's assessment in his *Monzambano*', *HJ*, 42 (1999), 961–83. Subsequent interpretations are discussed in P.H. Wilson, 'Still a monstrosity? Some reflections on early modern German statehood', *HJ*, 49 (2006), 565–76.

48. More detail in B. Erdmannsdorffer, *Deutsche Geschichte vom Westfälischen Frieden bis zum Regierungsantritt Friedrichs des Großen 1648–1740* (2 vols., Leipzig, 1932), I, pp.176–8.

49. H. Valentinitsch, *Die Meuterei der kaiserlichen Söldner in Kärnten und Steiermark 1656* (Vienna, 1975); K.O. Frhr. von Aretin, *Das Reich. Friedensordnung und europäisches Gleichgewicht 1648–1806* (Stuttgart, 1986), pp.76–166, 241–54; C. Storrs, 'Imperial authority and the levy of contributions in "Reichsitalien" in the Nine Years War', in M. Schnettger and M. Verga (eds.), *L'impero e l'Italia nella prima età moderna* (Bologna, 2006), pp.241–73.

50. G. Kleinheyer, *Die kaiserlichen Wahlkapitulationen* (Karlsruhe, 1968), pp.86–100; H.M. Empel, 'De eligendo regis vivente imperatore. Die Regelung in der Beständigen Wahlkapitulation und ihre Interpretation in der Staatsrechtsliteratur des 18. Jahrhunderts', *ZNRG*, 16 (1994), 11–24.

51. A.C. Bangert, 'Elector Ferdinand Maria of Bavaria and the imperial interregnum of 1657–58' (University of the West of England PhD, 2006).

52. P.H. Wilson, 'Bolstering the prestige of the Habsburgs: the end of the Holy Roman Empire in 1806', *IHR*, 28 (2006), 709–36. Good coverage of Austria's relations with the Empire in W. Brauneder and L. Höbelt (eds.), *Sacrum Imperium. Das Reich und Österreich 996–1806* (Vienna, 1996); V. Press, 'Österreichische Großmachtbildung und Reichsverfassung. Zur kaiserlichen Stellung nach 1648', *MIÖG*, 98 (1990), 131–54.

53. On the fundamental nature of the IPO for the imperial constitution, see G. Schmidt, 'Der Westfälische Friede – eine neue Ordnung für das alte Reich?', *Der Staat*, supplement 10 (1993), 45–72; J. Burkhardt, 'Das größte Friedenswerk der Neuzeit', *Geschichte in Wissenschaft und Unterricht*, 49 (1998), 592–612.

54. E.W. Böckenförde, 'Der Westfälische Friede und das Bündnisrecht der Reichsstände', *Der Staat*, 8 (1969), 449–78.

55. P.H. Wilson, 'The German "soldier trade" of the seventeenth and eighteenth centuries. A reassessment', *IHR*, 18 (1996), 757–92.

The Human and Material Cost

1. B. Donagan, 'Atrocity, war crime and treason in the English Civil War', *American Historical Review*, 99 (1994), 1137–66; I. Roy, ' "England turned Germany?" The aftermath of the Civil War in its European context', *Transactions of the Royal Historical Society*, 5th series, 28 (1978), 127–44.

2. K. Repgen, *Dreißigjähriger Krieg und Westfälischer Friede* (Paderborn, 1998), pp.112–52.

3. *Bilder aus der deutschen Vergangenheit* (5 vols., Leipzig, 1859–67), Vol. IV. Further discussion in L.L. Ping, *Gustav Freytag and the Prussian Gospel. Novels, literature and*

history (Bern, 2006), esp. pp.235–64; K. Cramer, *The Thirty Years War and German Memory in the Nineteenth Century* (Lincoln, Nebr., 2007), pp.141–216; W. Maierhofer, *Hexen – Huren – Heldenweiber. Bilder des Weiblichen in Erzähltexten über den Dreißigjährigen Krieg* (Cologne, 2005).

4. R. Hoeniger, 'Der Dreißigjährige Krieg und die deutsche Kultur', *Preußische Jahrbücher*, 138 (1909), 403–50, and his 'Die Armeen des Dreißigjährigen Krieges', *Beiheft zum Militärwochenblatt* (1914), 300–23. An example of Hoeniger's critics is G. Mehring, 'Wirtschaftliche Schäden durch den Dreißigjährigen Krieg im Herzogtum Württemberg', *WVJHLG*, 30 (1921), 58–89.

5. First developed in an article in 1947, Steinberg's views made their greatest impact through his short book *The Thirty Years War and the Conflict for European Hegemony 1600–1660* (London, 1966). His interpretation is endorsed by H.U. Wehler, in his influential general history of Germany: *Deutsche Gesellschaftsgeschichte*, Vol. I (Munich, 1987), p.54. Other important contributions to the debate included F. Lütge, 'Die wirtschaftliche Lage in Deutschland vor Ausbruch des Dreißigjährigen Krieges', *Jahrbuch für Nationalökonomie und Statistik*, 170 (1958), 43–99; T.K. Rabb, 'The effects of the Thirty Years War on the German economy', *JMH*, 34 (1962), 40–51; R. Ergang, *The Myth of the All-destructive Fury of the Thirty Years War* (Pocono Pines, Pa., 1956).

6. Troop strengths for 1546 from A. Schüz, *Der Donaufeldzug Karls V. im Jahre 1546* (Tübingen, 1930), pp.89–94.

7. L. Miehe, 'Der große Krieg und die kleinen Leute. Die sozialen Folgen des Dreißigjährigen Krieges', in *Konfession, Krieg und Katastrophe* (issued by the Verein für Kirchengeschichte der Kirchenprovinz Sachsen, Madgeburg, 2006), pp.43–54.

8. F.C. Springell (ed.), *Connoisseur and Diplomat. The Earl of Arundel's embassy to Germany in 1636* (London, 1965), p.60.

9. M. Friesenegger, *Tagebuch aus dem 30jährigen Krieg* (Munich, 2007), p.55.

10. T. Robisheaux, *Rural Society and the Search for Order in Early Modern Germany* (Cambridge, 1989), pp.217–21.

11. W. von Hippel, 'Bevölkerung und Wirtschaft im Zeitalter des Dreißigjährigen Krieges', *ZHF*, 5 (1978), 413–448; M.P. Gutmann, *War and Rural Life in the Early Modern Low Countries* (Princeton, 1980), pp.88, 152.

12. Examples in Friesenegger, *Tagebuch*, pp.60, 66, 69, 74–5, 79; H. Conrad and G. Teske (eds.), *Sterbezeiten. Der Dreißigjährige Krieg im Herzogtum Westfalen* (Münster, 2000), p.31. Quote from J. Peters (ed.), *Ein Söldnerleben im Dreißigjährigen Krieg* (Berlin, 1993), p.70.

13. G. Franz, *Der Dreißigjährige Krieg und das deutsche Volk* (4th edn, Darmstadt, 1979, first published Jena, 1940); C. Dipper, *Deutsche Geschichte 1648–1789* (Frankfurt am Main, 1991), pp.43–4; V. Press, *Kriege und Krisen. Deutschland 1600–1715* (Munich, 1991), pp.269–71. For the lower estimates and a critique of Franz's methodology, see J. Thiebault, 'The demography of the Thirty Years War revisited', *GH*, 15 (1997), 1–21.

14. The total of 8 million is given in M. Clodfelter, *Warfare and Armed Conflicts. A statistical reference to casualty and other figures 1500–2000* (Jefferson, NC, 2001), p.5.

15. M. Cerman, 'Bohemia after the Thirty Years War: some theses on population structure, marriage and family', *Journal of Family History*, 19 (1994), 149–75.

16. L. Miehe, 'Zerstörungen durch den Dreißigjährigen Krieg in westelbischen Städten des Erzbistums Magdeburg und des Hochstiftes Halberstadt', *Jahrbuch für Wirtschaftsgeschichte*, 4 (1990), 31–47; L. Hüttl, *Friedrich Wilhelm von Brandenburg, der Große Kurfürst, 1620–1688* (Munich, 1981), pp.70–1; P. Martin, *Une guerre de Trente Ans en Lorraine 1631–1661* (Metz, 2002), pp.225–31.

17. B. Roeck, 'Bayern und der Dreißigjährige Krieg. Demographische, wirtschaftliche und Soziale Auswirkungen am Beispiel Münchens', *Geschichte und Gesellschaft*, 17 (1991), 434–58; F. Kleinehagenbrock, *Die Grafschaft Hohenlohe im Dreißigjährigen Krieg* (Stuttgart, 2003), pp.90–1; J. Lindegren, 'Men, money and means', in P. Contamine (ed.), *War and Competition between States* (Oxford, 2000), pp.129–62, at p.158.

18. G. Mortimer, *Eyewitness Accounts of the Thirty Years War* (Basingstoke, 2002), p.171.
19. A. Ritter, 'Der Einfluß des Dreißigjährigen Krieges auf die Stadt Naumburg an der Saale', *Thüringisch-Sächsische Zeitschrift für Geschichte und Kunst*, 15 (1926), 1–96, at 41–7; Conrad and Teske (eds.), *Sterbezeiten*, pp.57–60; Kleinehagenbrock, *Hohenlohe*, p.79.
20. B.Z. Urlanis, *Bilanz der Kriege* (Berlin, 1965), pp.43–4. Franz, *Dreißigjähriger Krieg*, p.5 n.2 estimated the total deaths in the Empire by weapons at 325–338,000. In this case, he seems to have under- rather than overestimated.
21. Peters (ed.), *Söldnerleben*, pp.117, 122.
22. S. Riezler (ed.), 'Kriegstagebücher aus dem ligistischen Hauptquartier 1620', *Abhandlungen des Phil.-Hist. Klasse der Bayerischen Akademie der Wissenschaften*, 23 (1906), 77–210, at 84, 104. See ibid., pp.86–9 for standards of medical care. Sick rates from data in J. Pohl, *'Die Profiantirung der Keyserlichen Armaden ahnbelangendt'. Studien zur Versorgung der kaiserlichen Armee 1634/35* (Kiel, 1991), p.39.
23. The ratio of 3:1 is proposed by Clodfelter, *Warfare and Armed Conflicts*, p.6. Scandinavian data summarized in Lindegren, 'Men, money and materials'.
24. C. Cramer, 'Territoriale Entwicklung', in B. Martin and R. Wetekam (eds.), *Waldeckische Landeskunde* (Korbach, 1971), pp.171–262, at pp.223–4; G.P. Sreenivasan, *The Peasants of Ottobeuren 1487–1726* (Cambridge, 2004), pp.287–9.
25. B. Roeck, *Eine Stadt in Krieg und Frieden* (Göttingen, 1989), p.880.
26. R. Liberles, 'On the threshold of modernity: 1618–1780', in M.A. Kaplan (ed.), *Jewish Daily Life in Germany 1618–1945* (Oxford, 2005), pp.9–92, at pp.54–6.
27. J. Möllenberg, 'Überlingen im Dreißigjährigen Krieg', *Schriften des Vereins für die Geschichte des Bodensees und seiner Umgebung*, 74 (1956), 25–67, at 46.
28. A. Buchner and V. Buchner, *Bayern im Dreißigjährigen Krieg* (Dachau, 2002), p.212; Kleinehagenbrock, *Hohenlohe*, p.78.
29. E.A. Eckert, *The Structure of Plagues and Pestilences in Early Modern Europe: Central Europe 1560–1640* (Basel, 1996), esp. pp.132–54; R.J.C. Concanon, 'The third enemy: the role of epidemics in the Thirty Years War', *Journal of World History*, 10 (1967), 500–11.
30. Kroppenstadt mortality from R. Volkholz's notes to *Jürgen Ackermann, Kapitän beim Regiment Alt-Pappenheim 1631* (Halberstadt, 1895), p.37. Other examples underlining the significance of epidemics in Roeck, *Eine Stadt*, pp.630–53; A. Rieck, *Frankfurt am Main unter schwedischer Besatzung 1631–1635* (Frankfurt am Main, 2005), pp.200–1.
31. A. Weigl, 'Residenz, Bastion und Konsumptionsstadt', in Weigl (ed.), *Wien im Dreißigjährigen Krieg* (Vienna, 2001), pp.31–105, at p.67; L. Miehe, 'Die Bevölkerungsentwicklung in Städten des Erzstiftes Magdeburg und des Hochstiftes Halberstadt während des Dreißigjährigen Krieges', *Jahrbuch für Wirtschaftsgeschichte*, 4 (1987), 95–117, at 100.
32. Y.M. Bercé, *The Birth of Absolutism. A history of France 1598–1661* (Basingstoke, 1996), pp.112–16. Eyewitness account of the spread of the Alsatian outbreak in A. Levy, *Die Memoiren des Ascher Levy aus Reichshofen im Elsaß (1598–1635)* (Berlin, 1913), pp.23–4.
33. C.R. Friedrichs, *Urban Society in an Age of War: Nördlingen, 1580–1720* (Princeton, 1979), pp.35–53; H. Heberle, *Hans Heberles 'Zeytregister' (1618–1672)* (ed. G. Zillhardt, Ulm, 1975).
34. Hippel, 'Bevölkerung und Wirtschaft', pp.417, 446.
35. H. Musall and A. Scheuerbrandt, 'Die Kriege im Zeitalter Ludwigs XIV und ihre Auswirkungen auf die Siedlungs-, Bevölkerungs- und Wirtschaftstruktur der Oberrheinlande', in *Hans Graul Festschrift* (Heidelberg, 1974), pp.357–78; H. Dahm, 'Verluste der jülichbergischen Landmiliz im Dreißigjährigen Krieg', *Düsseldorfer Jahrbuch*, 45 (1951), 280–8; M. Vasold, 'Die deutschen Bevölkerungsverluste während des Dreißigjährigen Krieges', *ZBLG*, 56 (1993), 147–60.
36. B. Roeck, *Als wollt die Welt schier brechen* (Munich, 1991), pp.62–3, 95.
37. *Guardian*, Wednesday 19 September 2007, commenting on the current banking crisis.

More detailed analysis in C.P. Kindelberger, 'The economic crisis of 1619 to 1623', *Journal of Economic History*, 51 (1991), 149–75; H.J. Gerhard, 'Ein schöner Garten ohne Zaum. Die währungspolitische Situation des Deutschen Reiches um 1600', *VSWG*, 81 (1994), 156–77; J.O. Opel, 'Deutsche Finanznoth beim Beginn des Dreißigjährigen Krieges', *HZ*, 16 (1886), 213–68.

38. T. Winkelbauer, *Ständefreiheit und Fürstenmacht* (2 vols., Vienna, 2003), I, pp.483–4; Möllenberg, 'Überlingen', pp.55–6.

39. E. Kroker, *Die finanzielle Zusammenbruch der Stadt Leipzig im Dreißigjährigen Krieg* (Leipzig, 1923); Ritter, 'Naumburg', pp.22–5.

40. B.J. Hock, *Kitzingen im Dreißigjährigen Krieg* (Tübingen, 1981), pp.48–9; M. Bötzinger, *Leben und Leiden während des Dreißigjährigen Krieges* (Bad Langensalza, 2001), p.51. Further examples in Levy, *Memoiren*, pp.22–3.

41. J. Falke, 'Die Steuerverhandlungen des Kurfürsten Johann Georgs I. mit den Landständen während des Dreißigjährigen Krieges', *Archiv für sächsische Geschichte*, new series 1 (1875), 268–348, at 278–87; P. Ilisch, 'Money and coinage during the Thirty Years War', in K. Bussmann and H. Schilling (eds.), *1648: War and Peace in Europe* (3 vols., Münster, 1998), I, pp.345–51.

42. For example, see the cooperation through the Franconian Kreis: R. Weber, *Würzburg und Bamberg im Dreißigjährigen Krieg* (Würzburg, 1979), pp.246–51, 258, 262–3.

43. Robisheaux, *Rural Society and the Search for Order*, pp.205–8.

44. This interpretation is still advanced, e.g. H. Schilling, *Höfe und Allianzen. Deutschland 1648–1763* (Berlin, 1989), pp.61–70.

45. R. van Gelder, *Das ostindische Abenteuer. Deutsche in Diensten der Vereinigten Ostindischen Kompanie der Niederlande 1600–1800* (Hamburg, 2004); P. Malekandathil, *The Germans, the Portuguese and India* (Hamburg, 1999).

46. S. Tode, 'Das Hamburger Umland im Dreißigjährigen Krieg', in M. Knauer and S. Tode (eds.), *Der Krieg vor den Toren* (Hamburg, 2000), pp.145–80; Miehe, 'Zerstörungen', p.37.

47. M. Wohlhage, 'Aachen im Dreißigjährigen Kriege', *Zeitschrift des Aachener Geschichtsvereins*, 33 (1911), 1–64, at 11; H. Langer, 'Army finances, production and commerce', in Bussmann and Schilling (eds.), *1648: War and Peace*, I, pp.293–9.

48. P. Warde, *Ecology, Economy and State Formation in Early Modern Germany* (Cambridge, 2006), pp.246–7.

49. R.R. Heinisch, *Paris Graf Lodron* (Vienna, 1991), pp.209–13; Sreenivasan, *Ottobeuren*, pp.333–4.

50. Ibid., p.287; M.A. Junius, 'Bamberg im Schweden-Kriege', *Bericht des Historischen Vereins zu Bamberg*, 52 (1890), 1–168, at 135–9, 153.

51. Buchner and Buchner, *Bayern im Dreißigjährigen Krieg*, p.79.

52. There is now an extensive literature on this topic. Important recent contributions include M. Cerman and H. Zeitlhofer (eds.), *Soziale Strukturen in Böhmen. Ein regionale Vergleich von Wirtschaft und Gesellschaften in Grundherrschaften, 16.–19. Jahrhundert* (Vienna, 2002); W.W. Hagen, *Ordinary Prussians. Brandenburg Junkers and villagers, 1500–1840* (Cambridge, 2002).

53. Möllenberg, 'Überlingen', pp.35, 63; G. Rechter, 'Der Obere Zenngrund im Zeitalter des Dreißigjährigen Krieges', *Jahrbuch für fränkische Landesforschung*, 38 (1978), 83–122.

54. Möllenberg, 'Überlingen', pp.58, 61. More detail for this and the following in C. Hattenhauer, *Schuldenregulierung nach dem Westfälischen Frieden* (Frankfurt am Main, 1998).

55. E. Ortlieb, *Im Auftrag des Kaisers. Die kaiserlichen Kommissionen des Reichshofrats und die Regelung von Konflikten im alten Reich (1637–1657)* (Cologne, 2001), pp.212–18; D. McKay, *The Great Elector* (Harlow, 2001), p.71; V. Sellin, *Die Finanzpolitik Karl Ludwigs von der Pfalz* (Stuttgart, 1978), pp.77–8.

56. F. Blaich, 'Die Bedeutung der Reichstage auf dem Gebiet der öffentlichen Finanzen im Spannungsfeld zwischen Kaiser, Territorialstaaten und Reichsstädten (1493–1670)', in A.

de Maddalena and H. Kellenbenz (eds.), *Finanzen und Staatsräson in Italien und Deutschland* (Berlin, 1992), pp.79–111; Conrad and Teske (eds.), *Sterbezeiten*, pp.38, 199–204; Sreenivasan, *Ottobeuren*, pp.297–305.

57. T. Klingelbiel, *Ein Stand für sich? Lokale Amtsträger in der Frühen Neuzeit* (Hanover, 2002), p.246.

58. Repgen, *Dreißigjähriger Krieg und Westfälischer Friede*, pp.677–94; J.A. Vann, *The Swabian Kreis. Institutional growth in the Holy Roman Empire 1648–1715* (Brussels, 1975), pp.207–48.

59. K. Breysig, 'Der brandenburgischen Staatshaushalt in der zweiten Hälfte des siebzehnten Jahrhunderts', *Jahrbuch für Gesetzgebung, Verwaltung und Volkswirtschaft im Deutschen Reich*, 16 (1892), 1–42, 117–94, at 28–34.

60. Important examples include C. Tilly, *Capital, Coercion and European States AD 990–1992* (Oxford, 1992); T. Ertman, *Birth of the Leviathan* (Cambridge, 1997); R.D. Porter, *War and the Rise of the State* (New York, 1994).

61. These arguments have been advanced by Johannes Burkhardt whose ideas are more accessible in English in his 'The Thirty Years War', in R. Po-Chia Hsia (ed.), *A Companion to the Reformation World* (Oxford, 2004), pp.272–90.

62. H. Schilling, *Konfessionalisierung und Staatsinteressen 1559–1660* (Paderborn, 2007), pp.352–3.

63. J. Kunisch, *Absolutismus* (Göttingen, 1986); R. Vierhaus, *Germany in the Age of Absolutism* (Cambridge, 1988). For the debate on these developments, see P.H. Wilson, *Absolutism in Central Europe* (London, 2000).

64. R.G. Asch, 'Estates and princes after 1648: the consequences of the Thirty Years War', *GH*, 6 (1988), 113–32; V. Press, 'Soziale Folgen des Dreißigjährigen Krieges', in W. Schulze (ed.), *Ständische Gesellschaft und soziale Mobilität* (Munich, 1988), pp.239–68; R. Schlögl, 'Absolutismus im 17. Jahrhundert', *ZHF*, 15 (1988), 151–86.

65. M. Behnen, 'Der gerechte und der notwendige Krieg. "Necessitas" und "utilitas reipublicae" in der Kriegstheorie des 16. und 17. Jahrhunderts', in J. Kunisch (ed.), *Staatsverfassung und Heeresverfassung* (Berlin, 1986), pp.42–106.

66. See Chapter 18, p.622. Further discussion of this point in R. Pröve, 'Gewalt und Herrschaft in der Frühen Neuzeit', *Zeitschrift für Geschichtswissenschaft*, 47 (1999), 792–806.

67. Further discussion of this approach by S. Ogilvie, 'Germany and the seventeenth-century crisis', *HJ*, 35 (1992), 417–41.

68. Junius, 'Bamberg', p.27; Kleinehagenbrock, *Hohenlohe*, p.275.

69. B. Dudik (ed.), 'Tagebuch des feindlichen Einfalls der Schweden in das Markgrafthum Mähren während ihres Aufenthaltes in der Stadt Olmütz 1642–1650', *Archiv für österreichische Geschichte*, 65 (1884), 309–485, at 360.

70. Good insight into the breakdown of justice in U. Ludwig, 'Strafverfolgung und Gnadenpraxis in Kursachsens unter dem Eindruck des Dreißigjährigen Krieges', *Militär und Gesellschaft in der Frühen Neuzeit*, 10 (2006), 200–19. Data on the clergy from J. Kist, *Fürst- und Erzbistum Bamberg* (Bamberg, 1962), p.106; W.E. Heydendorff, 'Vorderösterreich im Dreißigjährigen Krieg', *MÖSA*, 12 (1959), 74–142, at 139.

71. 6 October 1638, HHStA, KA 94 (neu), fol.152–3.

72. Hock, *Kitzingen*, pp.172–3.

73. A. Klinger, *Der Gothauer Fürstenstaat* (Husum, 2002), pp.116–25.

74. S.C. Pils, 'Stadt, Pest und Obrigkeit', in Weigl (ed.), *Wien*, pp.353–78; Kleinehagenbrock, *Hohenlohe*, pp.92–101.

75. There is still no satisfactory cultural history of the war. Some of the 'high' art aspects are covered in vols. II and III of Bussmann and Schilling (eds.), *1648: War and Peace*. Though offering wider coverage, the only self-proclaimed cultural history of the war suffers from its origins in state-controlled East German Marxism: H. Langer, *The Thirty Years War* (Poole, 1980, first published Leipzig, 1978).

76. Frederick's tract about German literature, written in 1780, in G.B. Volz (ed.), *Die Werke*

Friedrichs des Großen (10 vols., Berlin, 1912–14; reprint Braunschweig, 2006), VIII, pp.74–99, at pp.77–8.

77. R.J.W. Evans, 'Learned societies in Germany in the seventeenth century', *European Studies Review*, 7 (1977), 129–51, at 142. See also his 'Culture and anarchy in the Empire 1540–1680', *CEH*, 18 (1985), 14–30.

78. T.D. Kaufmann, *Court, Cloister and City. The art and culture of Central Europe, 1450–1800* (Chicago, 1995).

79. H.O. Keunecke, 'Maximilian von Bayern und die Entführung der Bibliotheca Palatina nach Rom', *Archiv für Geschichte des Buchwesens*, 19 (1978), 1401–46; S. Häcker, 'Universität und Krieg. Die Auswirkungen des Dreißigjährigen Krieges auf die Universitäten Heidelberg, Tübingen und Freiburg', *Militär und Gesellschaft in der Frühen Neuzeit*, 11 (2007), 163–73; Weber, *Würzburg und Bamberg*, pp.476–9.

80. D.R. Moser, 'Friedensfeiern – Friedensfeste', in K. Garber (ed.), *Erfahrung und Deutung von Krieg und Frieden* (Munich, 2001), pp.1133–53. Examples of artists fleeing in A. Tacke, 'Der Künstler über sich im Dreißigjährigen Krieg', in ibid., pp.999–1041.

81. M. Brecht, 'Protestant peace initiative: Johann Rist's call to penance', in Bussmann and Schilling (eds.), *1648: War and Peace*, I, pp.251–7; M. Bassler, 'Zur Sprache der Gewalt in der Lyrik des deutschen Barock', in M. Meumann and D. Niefanger (eds.), *Ein Schauplatz herber Angst* (Göttingen, 1997), pp.125–44.

82. M. Knauer, *'Bedenke das Ende'. Zur Funktion der Todesmahnung in druckgraphischen Bildfolgen des Dreißigjährigen Krieges* (Tübingen, 1997).

83. D. Kunzle, *From Criminal to Courtier. The soldier in Netherlandish art 1550–1672* (Leiden, 2002); B. Roeck, 'The atrocities of war in early modern art', in J. Canning et al. (eds.), *Power, Violence and Mass Death* (Aldershot, 2004), pp.129–40.

84. Further discussion of the Callot cycle in P. Paret, *Imagined Battles. Reflections of war in European art* (Chapel Hill, 1997), pp.31–45.

85. H. Meise et al. (eds.), *Valentin Wagner (um 1610–1655). Ein Zeichner im Dreißigjährigen Krieg* (Darmstadt, 2003).

86. Reproduced in H. Glaser (ed.), *Um Glauben und Reich* (2 vols., Munich, 1980), II, part II, pp.466–7. Several of Snayers' impressive paintings now hang in the Heeresgeschichtliches Museum in Vienna. The depictions of White Mountain are reproduced in O. Chaline, *La Bataille de la Montagne Blanche* (Paris, 1999).

87. E. Rohmer, 'Den Krieg als ein "anderer Vergil" sehen', in Garber (ed.), *Erfahrung und Deutung*, pp.1043–61.

88. An English translation of *Simplicissimus* appeared in 1912. The best version is *The Adventures of Simplicius Simplicissimus* (ed. G. Schulz-Behrend, Rochester, NY, 1993) that lists some of the vast literary criticism of his output.

89. These readings are proposed by A. Merzhäuser, 'Über die Schwelle geführt. Anmerkungen zur Gewaltdarstellung in Grimmelshausens Simplicissimus', in Meumann and Niefanger (eds.), *Ein Schauplatz*, pp.65–82; W. Kühlmann, 'Grimmelshausens Simplicius Simplicissimus und der Dreißigjährige Krieg', in F. Brendle and A. Schindling (eds.), *Religionskriege im alten Reich und in Alteuropa* (Munich, 2006), pp.163–75.

90. M. Kaiser, 'Der Jäger von Soest. Historische Anmerkungen zur Darstellung des Militärs bei Grimmelshausen', in P. Heßelmann (ed.), *Grimmelshausen und Simplicissimus in Westfalen* (Bern, 2006), pp.93–118.

91. Heinisch, *Lodron*, pp.106–19, 152–70; Ritter, 'Naumburg', pp.81–3, 93.

Experiencing War

1. Post-structuralist critique presented in J.W. Scott, 'The evidence of experience', *Critical Inquiry*, 17 (1991), 773–97. Useful overview of the methodological debate in J. Nowosadtko, 'Erfahrung als Methode und als Gegenstand wissenschaftlicher Erkenntnis', in N. Buschmann and H. Carl (eds.), *Erfahrungsgeschichtliche Perspektiven von der Französischen Revolution bis zum Zweiten Weltkrieg* (Paderborn, 2001),

pp.27–50; P. Munch (ed.), *'Erfahrung' als Kategorie der Frühneuzeitsgeschichte* (Munich, 2001).

2. An important collection that has been worked on is that of the Behaim family from Nuremberg: S. Ozment (ed.), *Three Behaim Boys. Growing up in early modern Germany* (New Haven, 1990); A. Ernstberger, *Abenteurer des Dreißigjährigen Krieges* (Erlangen, 1963). Further discussion of personal testimony and the problems of interpretation in B. von Krusenstjern, 'Was sind Selbstzeugnisse?', *Historische Anthropologie*, 2 (1994), 462–71; W. Schulze (ed.), *Ego-Dokumente. Annährung an den Menschen in der Geschichte* (Berlin, 1996).

3. B. von Krusenstjern (ed.), *Selbstzeugnisse der Zeit des Dreißigjährigen Krieges* (Berlin, 1997). Four previously unpublished accounts are available at http://ub.uni-erfurt.de/mdsz/index.htm.

4. There is an excellent discussion of these in C. Woodford, *Nuns as Historians in Early Modern Germany* (Oxford, 2002).

5. J. Thiebault, 'The rhetoric of death and destruction in the Thirty Years War', *Journal of Social History*, 27 (1993), 271–90. Further discussion in G. Mortimer, *Eyewitness Accounts of the Thirty Years War 1618–48* (Basingstoke, 2002).

6. W. Behringer, *Im Zeichen des Merkur. Reichspost und Kommunikationsrevolution in der Frühen Neuzeit* (Göttingen, 2003); J. Weber, 'Strasbourg, 1605: the origins of the newspaper in Europe', *GH*, 24 (2006), 387–412; N. Peeters, 'News, international politics and diplomatic strategies', in J.W. Koopmans (ed.), *News and Politics in Early Modern Europe* (Leuven, 2005), pp.97–113.

7. The *Theatrum Europaeum* available online at http://www.digbib.bibliothek.uni-augsburg.de/1/index.html/.

8. R.W. Scribner, *For the Sake of the Simple Folk. Popular propaganda for the German Reformation* (2nd edn, Oxford, 1994).

9. C. Oggolder, 'Druck des Krieges', and S. Reisner, 'Die Kämpfe vor Wien in Oktober 1619 im Spiegel zeitgenössischer Quellen', both in A. Weigl (ed.), *Wien im Dreißigjährigen Krieg* (Vienna, 2001), pp.409–81.

10. P. Arblaster, 'Private profit, public utility and secrets of state in the seventeenth-century Habsburg Netherlands', in Koopmans (ed.), *News and Politics*, pp.79–95.

11. A. Wendland, 'Gewalt in Glaubensdingen. Der Veltliner Mord (1620)', in M. Meumann and D. Niefanger (eds.), *Ein Schauplatz herber Angst* (Göttingen, 1997), pp.223–39.

12. The standard view is summarized by E. von Frauenholz, *Das Heerwesen in der Zeit des Dreißigjährigen Krieges* (2 vols., Munich, 1938–9), I, pp.3–28.

13. G. Parker (ed.), *The Thirty Years War* (London, 1987), p.191. Important work published since then includes C. Kapser, *Die bayerische Kriegsorganisation in der zweiten Hälfte des Dreißigjährigen Krieges 1635–1648/49* (Münster, 1997); P. Burschel, *Söldner im Nordwestdeutschland des 16. und 17. Jahrhunderts* (Göttingen, 1994); B.R. Kroener, 'Conditions de vie et l'origine sociale du personnel militaire au cours de la Guerre de Trente Ans', *Francia*, 15 (1987), 321–50.

14. Kapser, *Kriegsorganisation*, p.73.

15. 52% of French soldiers came from towns, far higher than the urban proportion in the total population: R. Chaboche, 'Les soldats français de la Guerre de Trente Ans', *Revue d'histoire moderne et contemporaine*, 20 (1973), 10–24.

16. K. Jacob, *Von Lützen nach Nördlingen* (Strasbourg, 1904), appendix p.108; Kapser, *Kriegsorganisation*, p.64 n.34.

17. P.H. Wilson, 'Prisoners in early modern European warfare', in S. Scheipers (ed.), *Prisoners in War* (Oxford, forthcoming).

18. M. Kaiser, *Politik und Kriegführung* (Munich, 1999), pp.89–90, and his 'Cuius exercitus, eius religio? Konfession und Heerwesen im Zeitalter des Dreißigjährigen Krieges', *ARG*, 91 (2000), 316–53; W. Kopp, *Würzburger Wehr* (Würzburg, 1979), p.41; D. Horsbroch, 'Wish you were here? Scottish reactions to "postcards" to home from the

"Germane warres"', in S. Murdoch (ed.), *Scotland and the Thirty Years War* (Leiden, 2001), pp.245–69.

19. G. Gajecky and A. Baran, *The Cossacks in the Thirty Years War*, Vol. I (Rome, 1969), pp.89–91.

20. R.I. Frost, 'Scottish soldiers, Poland-Lithuania and the Thirty Years War', in Murdoch (ed.), *Scotland*, pp.191–213.

21. M. Kaiser, '"Ist er vom Adel? Ja. Id satis videtur" Adlige Standesqualität und militärische Leistung als Karrierfaktoren in der Epoche des Dreißigjährigen Krieges', in F. Bosbach et al. (eds.), *Geburt oder Leistung?* (Munich, 2003), pp.73–90, and his 'Die Karriere des Kriegsunternehmers Jan von Werth', *Geschichte in Köln*, 49 (2002), 131–70.

22. A. von Bismarck, 'Die Memoiren des Junkers Augustus von Bismarck', *Jahresberichte des Altmarkischen Vereins für Vaterländische Geschichte*, 23 (1890), 90–105.

23. B.A. Tlusty, *Bacchus and Civic Order. The culture of drink in early modern Germany* (Charlottesville, Va., 2001), pp.172–3, 208–10; E. Zöllner, 'Der Lebensbericht des Bayreuther Prinzenerziehers Zacharias von Quetz', *Jahrbuch für fränkische Landesforschung*, 15 (155), 201–21, at 212, 214.

24. J. Peters (ed.), *Ein Söldnerleben im Dreißigjährigen Krieg* (Berlin, 1993), pp.62–2, 100. Details of the Hilden raid from U. Unger, 'Der Dreißigjährige Krieg in Hilden', in S. Ehrenpreis (ed.), *Der Dreißigjährige Krieg im Herzogtum Berg und seinen Nachbarregionen* (Neustadt an der Aisch, 2002), pp.275–97. See also F. Redlich, *De praeda militari. Looting and booty 1500–1800* (Wiesbaden, 1956).

25. M. Bötzinger, *Leben und Leiden während des Dreißigjährigen Krieges* (Bad Langensalza, 2001), p.354.

26. Quoted in Mortimer, *Eyewitness Accounts*, pp.109–10. Further examples in H. Conrad and G. Teske (eds.), *Sterbezeiten. Der Dreißigjährige Krieg im Herzogtum Westfalen* (Münster, 2000), pp.48–54.

27. K. Lohmann (ed.), *Die Zerstörung Magdeburgs* (Berlin, 1913), pp.186–7.

28. A.V. Hartmann, 'Identities and mentalities in the Thirty Years War', in A.V. Hartmann and B. Heuser (eds.), *War, Peace and World Orders in European History* (London, 2001), pp.174–84; J. Burkhardt, 'Ist noch ein Ort, dahin der Krieg nicht kommen sey? Katastrophenerfahrung und Kriegsstrategien auf dem deutschen Kriegsschauplatz', in H. Ladermacher and S. Groenveld (eds.), *Krieg und Kultur* (Münster, 1998), pp.3–19; M. Kaiser, 'Inmitten des Kriegstheaters: Die Bevölkerung als militärischer Faktor und Kriegsteilnehmer im Dreißigjährigen Krieg', in B.R. Kroener and R. Pröve (eds.), *Krieg und Frieden. Militär und Gesellschaft in der Frühen Neuzeit* (Paderborn, 1996), pp.281–305, and his 'Die Söldner und die Bevölkerung. Überlegungen zu Konstituierung und Überwindung eines lebensweltlichen Antagonismus', in K. Krüger and S. Kroll (eds.), *Militär und ländliche Gesellschaft in der Frühen Neuzeit* (Münster, 2000), pp.79–120.

29. M.P. Gutmann, *War and Rural Life in the Early Modern Low Countries* (Princeton, 1980), p.163.

30. R.G. Asch, '"Wo der soldat hinkömbt, da ist alles sein": Military violence and atrocities in the Thirty Years War', *GH*, 13 (2000), 291–309; M. Kaiser, 'Die "Magdeburgische Hochzeit" 1631', in E. Labouvie (ed.), *Leben in der Stadt. Eine Kultur- und Geschlechtergeschichte Magdeburgs* (Cologne, 2004), pp.196–213, at pp.205–8; Burschel, *Söldner*, pp.27–33.

31. Bötzinger, *Leben und Leiden*, p.363.

32. J.C. Thiebault, 'Landfrauen, Soldaten und Vergewältigungen während des Dreißigjährigen Krieges', *Werkstatt Geschichte*, 19 (1998), 25–39, at 35–6; Kaiser, '"Magdeburgische Hochzeit"', pp.206–8. Examples in Conrad and Teske (eds.), *Sterbezeiten*, pp.308–10; F. Kleinehagenbrock, *Die Grafschaft Hohenlohe im Dreißigjährigen Krieg* (Stuttgart, 2003), pp.124–6.

33. M.A. Junius, 'Bamberg im Schweden-Kriege', *Bericht des Historischen Vereins zu Bamberg*, 53 (1891), 169–230, at 213–22.

34. B. Hoffmann, 'Krieges noth und grosse theuerung. Strategien von Frauen in Leipzig

1631–1650', in K. Garber et al. (eds.), *Erfahrung und Deutung von Krieg und Frieden* (Munich, 2001), pp.369–92; F. Hatje, 'Auf die Suche nach den Flüchtlingen und Exulanten des Dreißigjährigen Krieges', in M. Knauer and S. Tode (eds.), *Der Krieg vor den Toren* (Hamburg, 2000), pp.181–211.

35. C. von Bismarck, 'Das Tagebuch des Christoph von Bismarck aus den Jahren 1625–1640', *Thüringisch-sächsische Zeitschrift für Geschichte und Kunst*, 5 (1915), 67–98, at 74–6; Woodford, *Nuns*, pp.145, 165–70.

36. N. Schindler, 'Krieg und Frieden und die "Ordnung der Geschlechter" ', in Garber et al. (eds.), *Erfahrung und Deutung*, pp.393–452, at pp.444–5.

37. Kleinehagenbrock, *Hohenlohe*, pp.128–9.

38. Conrad and Teske (eds.), *Sterbezeiten*, pp.51–3.

39. Quotes from R. Monro, *Monro, his expedition with the worthy Scots regiment called Mac-Keys* (Westport, 1999), p.252; Peters (ed.), *Söldnerleben*, p.103.

40. Quotes from Junius, 'Bamberg', pp.178, 213, 221–2; W. Watts, *The Swedish Intelligencer* (3 vols., London, 1633–4), II, p.95a. The latter source also refers to women repulsing the Swedes with boiling water, in this case from Biberach in 1632.

41. O. Ulbricht, 'The experience of violence during the Thirty Years War: a look at the civilian victims', in J. Canning et al. (eds.), *Power, Violence and Mass Death* (Aldershot, 2004), pp.97–127, at p.108.

42. H. Heberle, *Hans Heberles 'Zeytregister' (1618–1672)* (Ulm, 1975), pp.148–53.

43. J. Ackermann, *Jürgen Ackermann, Kapitän beim Regiment Alt-Pappenheim 1631* (Halberstadt, 1895), pp.41–3.

44. P. Bloch, 'Ein vielbegehrter Rabbiner des Rheingaues, Juda Mehler Reutlingen', in *Festschrift zum siebzigsten Geburtstage Martin Philippsons* (Leipzig, 1916), pp.14–34; A. Levy, *Die Memoiren des Ascher Levy aus Reichshofen im Elsaß (1598–1635)* (Berlin, 1913).

45. J.N. de Parival, *Abrégé de l'Histoire de ce siècle de fer* (Leiden, 1653). Discussion of Gryphius in M. Meumann, 'The experience of violence and the expectations of the end of the world in seventeenth-century Europe', in Canning et al. (eds.), *Power, Violence and Mass Death*, pp.141–53.

46. Examples in E. Dössler, 'Kleve-Mark am Ende des Dreißigjährigen Krieges', *Düsseldorfer Jahrbuch*, 47 (1955), 254–96.

47. R. Pröve, 'Violentia und Potestas. Perzeptionsprobleme von Gewalt in Söldnertagebüchern des 17. Jahrhunderts', and S. Externbrink, 'Die Rezeption des "Sacco di Montova" im 17. Jahrhundert', in Meumann and Niefanger (eds.), *Schauplatz*, pp.24–42 and 205–22 respectively.

48. Bismarck, 'Memoiren', pp.97–100.

49. G. Davies (ed.), *Autobiography of Thomas Raymond* (London, 1917), p.38.

50. Junius, 'Bamberg', pp.15–37.

51. The literature on this topic is vast. Important studies for the Empire include H.C.E. Midelfort, *Witchhunting in Southwestern Germany 1562–1684* (Stanford, 1972); W. Behringer, *Witchcraft Persecutions in Bavaria* (Cambridge, 1997). For the general climate of fear, see A. Cunningham and O.P. Grell, *The Four Horsemen of the Apocalypse. Religion, war, famine and death in Reformation Europe* (Cambridge, 2000).

52. S. Ehrenpreis, 'Der Dreißigjährigen Krieg als Krise der Landesherrschaft', in Ehrenpreis (ed.), *Der Dreißigjährige Krieg im Herzogtum Berg*, pp.66–101, at pp.91–2.

53. Junius, 'Bamberg', pp.13–14; B. Gehm, *Die Hexenverfolgung im Hochstift Bamberg und das Eingreifen des Reichshofrates zu ihre Beendigung* (Hildesheim, 2000). A parallel, equally grim case in the bishopric of Eichstätt was also instigated by the Catholic clergy against opponents in the local political and social elite: J.B. Durrant, *Witchcraft, Gender and Society in Early Modern Germany* (Leiden, 2007).

54. Zöllner, 'Lebensbericht', pp.205–10.

55. Junius, 'Bamberg', pp.169–70.

56. Ozment (ed.), *Three Behaim Boys*, pp.161–284; Ernstberger, *Abenteurer*.

57. Quotes from Peters (ed.), *Söldnerleben*, pp.42–3.

58. Lohmann (ed.), *Zerstörung*, p.271.

59. M. Merian, *Topographia Germaniae* (14 vols., Frankfurt am Main, 1643–75; reprinted Brunswick, 2005), volume on Braunschweig-Lüneburg, p.84.

60. C. Bartz, *Köln im Dreißigjährigen Krieg* (Frankfurt am Main, 2005), pp.225–6, 272; Junius, 'Bamberg', pp.161–2. For the peace celebrations see C. Gantet, *La paix de Westphalie (1648). Une histoire sociale, XVIIe–XVIIIe siècles* (Paris, 2001).

61. D.R. Moser, 'Friedensfeiern – Friedensfeste', in Garber et al. (eds.), *Erfahrung und Deutung*, pp.1133–53; R.R. Heinisch, *Paris Graf Lodron* (Vienna, 1991), p.301; Z. Hojda, 'The battle of Prague in 1648 and the end of the Thirty Years War', in K. Bussmann and H. Schilling (eds.), *1648: War and Peace in Europe* (3 vols., Münster, 1998), I, pp.403–11, at pp.409–11.

62. J. Burkhardt, 'Reichskriege in der frühneuzeitlichen Bildpublizistik', in R.A. Müller (ed.), *Bilder des Reiches* (Sigmaringen, 1997), pp.51–95, at pp.72–80. For the Saxon celebrations, see B. Roeck, 'Die Feier des Friedens', and K. Keller, 'Das "eigentliche wahre und große Friedensfest . . . im ganzen Sachsenlande". Kursachsen von 1648 bis 1650', both in H. Duchhardt (ed.), *Der Westfälische Friede* (Munich, 1998), pp.633–77. For other territories, see D. Schröder, 'Friedensfeste in Hamburg 1629–1650', in Knauer and Tode (eds.), *Der Krieg vor den Toren*, pp.335–46; A. Klinger, *Der Gothauer Fürstenstaat* (Husum, 2002), pp.326–30; Kleinehagenbrock, *Hohenlohe*, pp.276–309.

63. M. Friesenegger, *Tagebuch aus dem 30jährigen Krieg* (Munich, 2007), pp.11, 14–16. The similarity in response to war and natural disaster is clear from the discussion in M. Jakubowski-Tiessen and H. Lehmann (eds.), *Um Himmels Willen: Religion in Katastrophenzeiten* (Göttingen, 2003).

64. B. Roeck, 'Der Dreißigjährige Krieg und die Menschen im Reich. Überlegungen zu den Formen psychischer Krisenbewältigung in der ersten Hälfte des 17. Jahrhunderts', in Kroener and Pröve (eds.), *Krieg und Frieden*, pp.265–79.

65. J.E. Petersen, *The life of Lady Johanna Eleonora Petersen, written by herself* (Chicago, 2005), p.64.

66. A. Holzem, 'Maria im Krieg – Das Beispiel Rottweil 1618–1648', in F. Brendl and A. Schindling (eds.), *Religionskriege im Alten Reich und in Alteuropa* (Münster, 2006), pp.191–216.

67. G.P. Sreenivasan, *The Peasants of Ottobeuren 1487–1726* (Cambridge, 2004), p.286; Ulbricht, 'The experience of violence', pp.121–4.

68. D. Hopkin, *Soldier and Peasant in French Popular Culture 1766–1870* (Woodbridge, 2003), esp. pp.240–2.

Index

Royalty, secular electors and Italian princes appear in order of their first names, while all other individuals are indexed by their family name. Monarchs with similar first names are ranked in the contemporary order of their kingdoms.

Oxenstierna, Axel
    Gustavsson – *cont.*
  and France 553, 576,
    479–80, 597, 614
  and German princes
    516–23, 525, 628, 639
  possible imperial
    chancellor 487
  influence 181, 461, 507,
    512–13
  peace-making 527–8,
    573–8, 597, 675
  relations 487, 513, 675
  meets Richelieu 553, 576
  directs war 459, 502, 504,
    513–15, 544–5,
    549–51, 573
Oxenstierna, Gabriel
    Gustavsson
    (1587–1640), chief
    justice 487
Oxenstierna, Johan Axelsson
    (1612–57), diplomat
    675, 677, 746

Pacification of Bruck (1578)
    59, 68, 71, 82
Paderborn, bishopric
  attacked 329, 332, 619,
    782
  diplomatic representation
    721
  operations in 525, 593
  plundered 333
  rulers 206, 386, 873
  size 386
painting 139, 365, 545, 657,
    673, 816–18
  disputes over 764
'paladins'
  backing for 325, 327,
    364–5
  characteristics 204,
    328–30, 594
  defeat 331–46, 407
  motives 325–30
  re-employment 391, 466,
    484–5, 606
Palatinate, electorate
  alliances 111, 202–3,
    212–16, 224–6, 228–9,
    235
  and Bohemia 216, 269,
    277, 284–5

in Cologne War 208–9,
    212
  court 215–16, 247–8,
    261, 263
  and Danes 212, 320–1,
    387, 418
  economy 284, 327
  finances 215, 238,
    803–4
  fortifications 143, 327
  intervenes in France 156,
    215–16
  government 215–16, 226,
    248–9, 285, 315–16
  and Habsburgs 109, 202,
    248, 282
  imperial heritage 202,
    247, 284
  influence 254–5
  inheritance dispute
    (1503–5) 200, 202
  attempts to liberate 365,
    385, 479, 594–5, 617
  political programme 213,
    216–19, 224, 229, 244,
    247, 250, 282
  population 18, 216
  possessions 18, 216
  regencies 209, 212–13,
    252
  religion 36, 38, 153, 199,
    212–13, 767–9, 915
  Swedes in 477, 479–80,
    486, 490
  see also Palatine question
Palatinate, army
  militia 144, 236, 277,
    300, 327, 865, 872
  size 208, 327
  see also Mansfeld
Palatinate, Lower
  Bavarian conquest 339,
    355–6, 550
  transfer to Bavaria 422
  Bavarian government 639,
    811, 813–14
  defence 300, 314, 316,
    327, 793
  Spanish in 299, 315, 331,
    333, 490–1
  see also Frankenthal
Palatinate, Upper
  transfer to Bavaria 355–6,
    358, 421–2, 726

Bavarian rule 358–60,
    639, 720
  defence 224, 285, 327
  invasion (1620) 220,
    332–3
  operations in 535, 626–7,
    739–40, 744
  revolt (1592) 213, 216
Palatine question 340,
    354–6, 447, 567–8,
    571, 586, 625, 628,
    677, 707–8, 710, 720,
    726
Palermo 730
Palsgrave *see* Birkenfeld
Panama 118–19, 122
papacy
  and Bavaria 207, 296–7,
    355, 488, 625, 813
  promotes Catholicism 27,
    357–8
  elections 650
  and emperor 27, 84, 99,
    207, 275–6, 395
  and Empire 45–6, 109,
    208–9, 409, 449, 566
  and France 156, 161,
    376–7, 379, 382–3
  international role 27–8,
    125, 156, 161, 584
  and Jesuits 31
  and Mantua 439, 457,
    584
  mediation 162, 166,
    584–6, 625, 735
  nepotism 296
  and Poland 196
  prerogatives 264
  and Spain 27–8, 125,
    156, 161, 650
  territorial ambitions 125,
    584, 650
  opposes Westphalian
    peace 721, 753–4
Pappenheim, Gottfried
    Heinrich count
    (1594–1632), general
  at Breitenfeld 473–5
  early career 457
  greed 421, 887
  Liga command 457, 493,
    495, 506, 520, 629
  at Lützen 507–10, 522,
    606